THE PSYCHOLOGY OF STEREOTYPING

DISTINGUISHED CONTRIBUTIONS IN PSYCHOLOGY
A Guilford Series

Edited by

KURT W. FISCHER　　E. TORY HIGGINS　　MARCIA JOHNSON　　WALTER MISCHEL
Harvard University　　Columbia University　　Yale University　　Columbia University

The Psychology of Stereotyping
David J. Schneider

The Construction of the Self: A Developmental Perspective
Susan Harter

Interpersonal Perception: A Social Relations Analysis
David A. Kenny

THE PSYCHOLOGY
OF STEREOTYPING

David J. Schneider

THE GUILFORD PRESS
New York   London

© 2004 The Guilford Press
A Division of Guilford Publications, Inc.
72 Spring Street, New York, NY 10012
www.guilford.com

Printed in the United States of America

This book is printed on acid-free paper.

Last digit is print number: 9 8 7 6 5 4 3 2 1

Library of Congress Cataloging-in-Publication Data

Schneider, David J., 1940–
    The psychology of stereotyping / by David J. Schneider.
      p. cm.–(Distinguished contributions in psychology)
    Includes bibliographical references and index.
      ISBN 1-57230-929-6 (alk. paper)
    1. Stereotype (Psychology) I. Title. II. Series.
    BF323.S63S36 2004
    303.3′ 85—dc21

                                                        2003008819

To Al Hastorf, mentor and friend

About the Author

David J. Schneider, PhD, graduated from Wabash College in 1962 with majors in psychology and philosophy, and earned a doctoral degree in psychology from Stanford University in 1966. He has taught at Amherst College, Stanford University, Brandeis University, the University of Texas at San Antonio, and Indiana University. In 1989 Dr. Schneider joined the Department of Psychology at Rice University, where he served as Chair of the Department from 1990 to 1996 and remains today as Professor of Psychology and Cognitive Sciences. Dr. Schneider teaches courses in social psychology and stereotyping, as well as introductory psychology, history of psychology, the psychology of beliefs, and psychology and law. He was founding editor of the journal *Social Cognition* and has written several books, including *Person Perception* (1979, Addison-Wesley), *Social Psychology* (1976, Addison-Wesley), and *Introduction to Social Psychology* (1988, Harcourt Brace).

Preface

This book has taken a long time to get from my desk to yours. I began work on the manuscript about 15 years ago, and both I and the publisher had assumed I would produce a tidy manuscript in a couple of years. Well, as I discovered, there is nothing tidy about the area of stereotyping.

There were times during this process when I had the distinct sense that people were producing relevant research papers faster than I could read them. As I put the final touches on this book, I have a working bibliography of well over 10,000 books, chapters, and papers, and I am sure I could generate another 5,000 or so by looking in more obscure places and by broadening my definition of stereotypes even slightly. I have not cited most of those materials, and it has been frustrating to have to cut out many, especially older, references.

This book documents major changes that have taken place in the ways we think about stereotypes and affiliated notions such as prejudice and discrimination. People who were studying stereotypes, say, 40 or 50 years ago were often wrong in the ways they thought about the area, but the older papers were forged in a quite different intellectual and political milieu than my own and may well have been as legitimate for their time as our present perspectives are for ours. Moreover, as someone who takes very seriously the history of psychology, I am well aware that what seems clear to me and my generation will seem naive, even wrong, 40 or 50 years from now.

But here it is. My family will be happy it is done, and my students can quit asking, "Is your book done yet?" (My colleagues quit asking a decade ago.) It has been the most intellectually rewarding effort of my life, but whether it is the best others will have to judge. My hope, of course, is that the book will be useful not only to my fellow scholars in both stereotyping and broader areas but also to students and even brave lay folks. Most of what most people (including a good many social scientists) think about stereotypes is at best slightly askew, and at worst simply wrong. In saying this I do not speak from a position of intellectual certainty or arrogance. I am not a bit sure that we know enough yet to know what's right, but we do know what's wrong. It is my hope that a book that summarizes what we do know will carry our lessons outward and onward. I can only hope that reading this will prove as useful and stimulating to others as it has been to me in writing it.

I want to thank many people. Various undergraduate and graduate classes and students have read earlier versions of the manuscript and have ever so gently pointed out errors and places of unclarity. Several undergraduate students at Rice University, almost all now in graduate school in social psychology or fellow professionals (Elizabeth Bartmess, Robert Bartsch, Ryan Brown, Camille Buckner, Lynn Clark, Riki Conrey, Amy Dixon, Kim Lawson, Jenny Morales, Keith Rozendahl, and Melissa Williams), did major undergraduate honors or senior projects with me on stereotype issues and encouraged me to think more clearly about the area. Working with them has been a pure joy. My graduate students over this time, most particularly Beth Haley, Judy Solecki, and Annette Towler, were not afraid to argue with me and stimulated my thinking in various ways. My psychology (Dan Osherson) and philosophy (Dick Grandy and Eric Margolis) colleagues in an ongoing faculty seminar on concepts helped introduce me to the rich literatures on categorization, perhaps the topic of my next book. Chuck Stangor and Monica Biernat read the entire manuscript and provided extensive and extremely helpful criticisms. Editor-in-Chief Seymour Weingarten at The Guilford Press, a friend as well as editor, was patient in waiting for this manuscript and accepted my continual apologies and excuses with a certain degree of equanimity. My wife, Doris, has maintained her usual calm demeanor in the face of excessive grumpiness and has been remarkably supportive and loving. And my daughters, Kristen and Caitlin, and their children, Alyssa, Taylor, and Zachary, continually remind me that getting a handle on stereotyping and its effects on the world is important, even vital. Finally, this book is dedicated to Al Hastorf, who over 40 years has evolved from being a mentor to a friend. He continues to be a model of personal kindness, scholarly thoughtfulness, scientific excitement, and intellectual facilitation for me and for his many other colleagues as well as undergraduate and graduate students. I have deep intellectual obligations to many former teachers and colleagues, but without Al this book never would have been written.

Contents

CHAPTER 1

Introduction

A DIALOGUE

Stereotypes wear the black hats in social science. Although the term in its modern guise has been around almost as long as social science itself, and thousands of papers have been devoted to elucidating one or another of its many facets, during this entire period almost no one has had anything good to say about stereotypes. Everyone from talk show hosts to pop psychology gurus deride them. Many of us feel we are the victims of stereotypes held by others, and we deplore racists and sexists, who seem to use more than their share of these filthy things. Stereotypes are the common colds of social interaction—ubiquitous, infectious, irritating, and hard to get rid of. And yet that kind of universal judgment always makes me a little nervous. Is there nothing good we might say about stereotypes?

When people tell me that stereotypes are bad and evil things, I sometimes ask them to conduct a thought experiment. "Imagine," I say, "that you could redesign the human mental apparatus so that no one would ever hold a stereotype again. What would that entail? How might one proceed with this redesign project?" This thought experiment forces people to think about what stereotypes really are. After all, we have to know what we are dealing with before we can eliminate it. Let's imagine the following dialogue, in which OP is an Obnoxious Psychologist and RP is a Random Person. We come in toward the beginning of the dialogue, and OP is asking RP what is objectionable about stereotypes.

OP: Perhaps you would like to tell me what you are getting rid of before you do it.

RP: You mean what I think stereotypes are?

OP: That will work for starters.

RP: Well, they're unfair statements we make about individuals because they belong to a particular group.

OP: And what is the basis of these unfair statements?

RP: People seem to assume that just because a person is black or gay, there are a whole lot of other things he or she might be.

OP: Let's stick with one group for the moment—say, male homosexuals. So you are saying that people tend to assume that because a person is a gay male, he has several traits he shares with other gays.

RP: Exactly.

OP: That kind of statement seems to me quite complex. Can you help me analyze it?

RP: It seems simple enough to me, but I'll go along with you.

OP: Perhaps I'm just a little simple-minded, but please humor me. A person making such a statement must assume that gays are all alike, at least with regard to some characteristics.

RP: That's right.

OP: So our perceiver thinks that all gay males like opera and cats and are effeminate.

RP: Something like that.

OP: But it is surely true that many gays love neither opera or cats and are not effeminate in any meaningful sense.

RP: Certainly that is true, OP.

OP: And surely most of the people who would stereotype gays realize that far from all fit the stereotype.

RP: Well, I know some people who think that all gay men are effeminate.

OP: Really? I guess I don't normally run into such extreme stereotyping. Would you say that most people who stereotype gays think that way?

RP: Not everyone.

OP: Most are not that extreme?

RP: Yeah, I would have to concede that most people don't think that *all* gays are effeminate.

OP: But that makes a mockery of your earlier statement that stereotypes are applied to everyone.

RP: Well, I didn't mean literally everyone. Just most.

OP: Suppose I could prove to you that most people realize that gay men are not generally effeminate, that only a minority are. Would you still see that as part of the stereotype?

RP: It seems a bit awkward, doesn't it?

OP: It seems that way to me. What can it mean, then, for a person to hold a stereotype that gay men are effeminate?

RP: It must mean that when they meet a gay man they have never met before, they will just assume he is effeminate.

OP: I think you're on to something here. So even if most gay men are not effeminate, and even though our perceiver (let's call her Janice) knows this, she still tends to see individual gay men in this way.

RP: That's it. That's the problem.

OP: So, as I gather from what you are saying, the problem isn't that Janice has a faulty generalization, but that she misapplies it. Even though she understands that most gay men are not effeminate, she still tends to assume that a random gay man is effeminate.

RP: That's certainly part of it. But there are other times when people really are wrong. They assume that most people in a group have some feature, and in point of fact they don't.

OP: So there may be some people who assume that most gay men are effeminate, when in fact only a small minority are.

RP: That's what I meant to say.

OP: So now we have two problems. The first is that people may have incorrect generalizations about other groups, and the second is that they may use some generalizations to make incorrect judgments about individuals.

RP: Yes.

OP: Well, let's save the issue of incorrect generalizations for the moment, and discuss the issue of whether generalizations are correctly or incorrectly applied. Do you think that bears are dangerous?

RP: Of course.

OP: So you'd be afraid of one if you met it in the wild.

RP: Of course.

OP: But, statistically, your chance of getting attacked by a bear you meet in the wilderness must be pretty small.

RP: I'll have to take your word for that. What's your point? I thought we were discussing gay men.

OP: My point is that you have a stereotype that bears are dangerous, and you act on the basis of that stereotype even though it probably fits only a minority of actual bears. And yet you complain that people act on the basis of generalizations about gay men that are probably no more or less true.

RP: I see what you mean. (*Pause*) Now that I think about it, I think the reason I am afraid of bears is that bears are generally more dangerous than other animals.

OP: Now that's fairly interesting. So what you seem to be saying is that since bears are more dangerous, say on average, than pussy cats, armadillos, and goldfish, you think it is sensible to be more afraid of them? You are playing the creature laws of averages.

RP: I think that's what I meant.

OP: So stereotypes are really comparisons we make between groups? When a person says that gay men are effeminate, she is not saying that all gay men fit this description, but only that a higher percentage of gay men than straight men fit?

RP: Yes, that seems reasonable.

OP: It does seem reasonable. But I get a little nervous when things seem reasonable. Let's push ahead with a counterexample. Suppose someone said that gay men are smarter than average. Would that count as a stereotype?

RP: Well, I suppose in some sense. But it doesn't seem quite the same.

OP: Why not?

RP: Well, it really doesn't hurt anyone to say they're smart. I don't think gays would be offended if people said they were smart, even if they weren't any smarter than anyone else.

OP: So if we think about eliminating stereotypes, are you prepared to eliminate the positive ones as well as the negative ones?

RP: Well, frankly, I'm not terribly concerned about the positive ones. So I guess I would focus on the negative ones. Those are the ones I'd want to get rid of.

OP: Have you given any thought to how you might do this? That is, how could you design a mind that filtered out negative stereotypes about gays, but not positive *ones?*

RP: This is a thought experiment after all. I'll just design the mind that way.

OP: Don't be cute. That's my job. Let's consider the following. Imagine two groups of people who both believe that gay men are, by and large, kind and caring. Now, the members of Group A—say, university students—think that, if true, such a generalization is positive and cool. So according to your rule, we would not have to redesign the stereotype maker of these students. But the members of Group B—say, a bunch of oil rig workers—think that kind and compassionate men are not real men. For them, this is a negative stereotype; they just don't like wussy men. So according to your strategy, we want to get rid of this generalization for Group B, and we have to redesign their stereotype maker. I wonder if you could speculate with me as to how that might be done. Presumably when we redesign our mental apparatus, we are talking about fundamental changes, the kind that one is born with.

RP: You're not going to get me this time; I see where you're leading. How could we do this for one group of people and not another?

OP: You're catching on. But it's more complex even than that. We could presumably apply our redesign engineering to some people and not others at birth or at time of conception, but I doubt that we'd be able to know ahead of time who will be oil rig workers and the like. In other words, we don't know who needs the revised stereotype maker at birth.

RP: Well, since this is a thought experiment, perhaps we could make the changes later in life, after we've had a chance to see how they turn out.

OP: So you're proposing a kind of mental machinery recall program?

RP: Something like that.

OP: But surely there would be problems with that as well. For example, how are you going to decide which generalizations you want to get rid of? Surely it will be hard at a basic level to distinguish between positive and negative generalizations. And the reasons for that are pretty clear, and we don't need to get into details about neurons and the like. What we consider to be positive and negative varies from person to person, culture to culture, situation to situation. For example, beliefs that gay men are artistic would be seen as positive in the context of a fund-raiser for an arts organization, but not in the context of a discussion of how to prepare a new construction site or plan the takeover of a major corporation.

RP: You made your point. Let's do get on with things.

OP: To be sure. I guess what you want to do at this point is design a mental apparatus that will not distinguish between positive and negative generalizations. I think we agree that this is difficult to do.

RP: Yes, I agree. Let's move on here.

OP: Getting a little impatient, are we? Okay. Well, we seem to agree that stereotypes are generalizations about groups—both positive and negative.

RP: That's right.

OP: And so we want to get rid of generalizations about groups?

RP: That would seem to follow, OP.

OP: Well, let's think about that. Clearly you are uncomfortable with generalizations such as that gay men are effeminate, love opera, and the like.

RP: Certainly I am.

OP: Well, let's think about a few other generalizations about people—stereotypes, if you will. How do you feel about saying that men who have been in prison are likely to be violent in the future? Would you want to make sure that people never formed that generalization?

RP: I guess I'm supposed to say yes.

OP: That would be helpful. I'm not trying to lead you astray here. You did say that you wanted to get rid of generalizations about people, and I've given you another example.

RP: And I've admitted, just to make you happy, that I would want to get rid of the stereotype about male ex-prisoners.

OP: And so—having got rid of that stereotype, that generalization—you would be perfectly happy to have dinner with such a person, walk with him through dark alleys, and generally treat him like one of your gang. In other words, you wouldn't be afraid of him in any way.

RP: Of course I would be afraid of him.

OP: But on what basis?

RP: Well, people who do time are violent.

OP: Sounds like a generalization to me.

RP: But the generalization about male ex-prisoners is true, and the one about gay men isn't.

OP: But it turns out that most male ex-prisoners never commit violent crimes, so this generalization probably doesn't apply to anything like all men who have been in prison; yet you insist on using it. It sounds just as irrational as using generalizations about gay men. I'm not persuaded that there's a difference here.

RP: Then I guess I'm irrational.

OP: Surely no more than most people. But rather than be so critical of ourselves, let's sneak up on this issue from another angle. How do you feel about the generalization that ripe, red apples taste good?

RP: That seems fine.

OP: Now what about a generalization that Honda makes reliable and good cars?

RP: Well, I'm not sure about that. I had a Honda several years ago that was a dog, and I have several friends who really won't drive Hondas because they think they're bad cars.

OP: So you wouldn't buy another Honda?

RP: That's right. Cars are expensive, and I wouldn't want to take a chance. Does that make me irrational too?

OP: Maybe; maybe not. Let's see where our argument goes. Suppose—just for the sake of argument—that I could prove to you that Hondas are terrific cars, based on consumer surveys, engineering reports, and the like. Would you then be tempted to buy a Honda?

RP: Probably not.

OP: I suspect most people would say the same thing. Most people who felt the way you do and had a miserable experience probably wouldn't take a chance, either. But I'm less interested in whether you're a rational consumer than in the status of your generalization. I'm claiming that your generalization about Hondas is faulty, and yet you insist on using it. But I thought you had earlier agreed that incorrect and faulty generalizations should be screened out.

RP: But you're talking about cars, and I was talking about people.

OP: Do you think there's a difference?

RP: It's obvious there is.

OP: Are you sure that there is a difference in terms of how the mental apparatus treats data? It strikes me as self-evident that we form generalizations and think about cars, dogs, and people in about the same ways. I do understand that gay men are neither dogs nor Hondas, but I can't seem to come up with a good reason for why generalizations about these categories differ much in terms of how we get them. Can you?

RP: Perhaps if I had more time.

OP: Yes, the world would clearly be a better place if we just had more time to think. But we do need to move on. So humor me just for a moment, and let's assume that the differences are more apparent than real. It just seems to me that your modified mental apparatus is going to have trouble distinguishing between generalizations about people and anything else. I know of no evidence that the present mental apparatus does this, and it's hard for me to imagine that we could build it in a way to do so. Generally, cognitive systems are not sensitive to stimulus properties in this way. A generalization is a generalization. So if I read you correctly, you want to abolish the capacity to generalize about everything.

RP: Of course not. I've already said, if you'd only listen, that I only want to abolish incorrect generalizations.

OP: So what makes a generalization incorrect?

RP: Obviously when there are substantial cases that do not fit.

OP: And how substantial? For example, if I say that ripe, red apples taste good, there are clearly some exceptions.

RP: Of course.

OP: And many exceptions should there be before you say it's a faulty generalization? Over 50%?

RP: That seems sensible.

OP: Any generalization that doesn't capture at least 50% of known cases is faulty and basically incorrect?

RP: That's what I'm claiming.

OP: Well, let's play with that a bit. Let's return to my example of you and a bear in the woods. You agreed that, statistically, most bear–people encounters result in no harm to either party unless you count a little anxiety. Do you still want to give up your generalization that bears are dangerous?

RP: No. I would still be afraid of a bear I met in the woods.

OP: But you might have to give up that generalization if you impose the truth criterion. In fact, I think I could prove to you that many of the generalizations we use about animals, things, and groups of people fit fewer than 50% of the individuals in that group, and yet we continue to use these generalizations. You have already indicated that you'd avoid ex-prisoners, even though most are not violent; that you'd be afraid of bears, even though most would not harm you, that you wouldn't buy a Honda, even though a majority are perfectly fine cars. Perhaps you are not so irrational after all. Sometimes generalizations can be very useful even if they are generally not true. Even if the generalization, or stereotype, that bears are dangerous is generally not true, I think we would not want to create a mental apparatus that was unresponsive to such potentially important if low-probability events. So I will continue to base my behavior on the statistically erroneous stereotype that bears are dangerous. And I will make no apologies for that. Wouldn't you agree?

RP: I suppose. Do I have a choice?

OP: You always have a choice. The problem seems to be that every time we find a potentially bad feature of stereotypes, we find that we can't get rid of just that feature. We either have to take the bad with the good, or not generalize about the world around us.

RP: That seems to be where we are. I find that discouraging. In fact, I'm now depressed, and I want to end this.

OP: Well, please don't jump off any bridges on this account. Perhaps as we work our way forward, we will find some answers. We are sure to find that the answers will not be quite as simple as we would hope, and we may have to reformulate our questions in the process. Let's see if we can get out of this intellectual swamp that we have created for ourselves.

RP: That *you* have created for us.

OP: Perhaps.

SOME BACKGROUND

Our Reactions to Stereotypes

Among other things, this dialogue reveals how difficult it is to have a clear sense of what stereotypes are. As OP consistently reminds us, it is not so clear how stereotypes differ from ordinary generalizations, and it is also not clear that they can or even should be avoided. To give up our capacity to form stereotypes, we would probably have to give up our capacity to generalize, and that is a trade none of us should be willing to make. The ability to generalize is a central, primitive, hard-wired cognitive activity (Schneider, 1992).

I raise this issue of our evaluation of stereotypes informally here, because one of the many reasons why we have had trouble coming to intellectual grips with these villains of the social world is that we have spent valuable time and energy condemning rather than in trying to understand (see Brown, 1965, for a related argument). Because we have reacted so negatively to stereotypes, we have also tended to ignore some of the important questions about their nature and use. Yes, often stereotypes are negative, untrue, and unfair. But as we will see, sometimes they are none of these things. Sometimes they are even useful (although we tend to give them different names in such circumstances), and they may even be essential. So assumptions about whether stereotypes are good or bad do not seem to buy us much. There are times for moral outrage, and there are times when we need the courage to bully our way ahead toward our goal of understanding.

The History of Stereotypes

The word "stereotype" itself comes from the conjunction of two Greek words: *stereos*, meaning "solid," and *typos*, meaning "the mark of a blow," or more generally "a model." Stereotypes thus ought to refer to solid models, and indeed the initial meaning of the term in English referred to a metal plate used to print pages. As Miller (1982) points out, such a term is likely to give rise to at least two connotations: rigidity and duplication or sameness. When applied to people, then, stereotypes are rigid, and they stamp all to whom they apply to with the same characteristics. It should be noted that the actual term was used as early as 1824 (Gordon, 1962; Rudmin, 1989) to refer to formalized behavior, and by the early part of the 20th century it was regularly used to refer to rigid, repetitive, often rhythmic behavior patterns (Schroeder, 1970). But the most familiar use of the term refers to characteristics that we apply to others on the basis of their national, ethnic, or gender groups.

Early Conceptions and Studies

LIPPMANN'S PERSPECTIVE

In that sense, the term was first used by the distinguished journalist Walter Lippmann in his book *Public Opinion* (1922). This was not a passing reference, either; he devoted a substantial portion of his book to a discussion of the concept. Lippmann viewed stereotypes as general cognitive structures, and he used the term to account for errors and biases in our conceptions of the world.

Lippmann also struck a modern theme by noting that such knowledge structures are useful:

> There is economy in this. For the attempt to see all things freshly and in detail, rather than as types and generalities, is exhausting, and among busy affairs practically out of the question. . . . But modern life is hurried and multifarious, above all physical distance separates men who are often in vital contact with each other, such as employer and employee, official and voter. There is neither time nor opportunity for intimate acquaintance. Instead we notice a trait which marks a well known type, and fill in the rest of the picture by means of the stereotypes we carry about in our heads. (pp. 88–89)

These pictures in our heads are not inevitably based on experiences. Indeed, Lippmann saw them as being driven by personality processes, functioning as rationalizations to maintain social standing. He also, however, made it perfectly clear that stereotypes are not, for that reason, inevitably false. Perhaps the most remarkable features of Lippmann's treatment are the ways in which he anticipated much of what we now take to be the modern perspective on the topic, despite his lack of training in social science and psychology.[1]

KATZ AND BRALY'S STUDIES

Actually, most of Lippmann's discussion dealt with various errors of thinking and was not specifically concerned with traits ascribed to groups of people. However, most of the first empirical studies did concern such trait attributions particularly to ethnic groups,[2] while still preserving Lippmann's notions of error. The studies of Katz and Braly (1933, 1935) are most famous. They asked Princeton University students to check traits they thought described 10 racial and ethnic groups. Those traits with considerable consensus of endorsement for a particular group were seen as stereotypic of that group. So, for example, 78% of subjects thought that Germans were scientific-minded, 84% thought that Negroes (in the terminology of that time) were superstitious, and 54% thought that Turks were cruel. In the second study (Katz & Braly, 1935), the rank order of preferences for the 10 groups (a crude prejudice measure) rated was identical to the rankings in terms of the average desirability of the traits ascribed to the groups. This began a long tradition of seeing stereotypes and prejudice as closely linked.

The 1930s were years of major interest in measurement of attitudes as a bridge between culture and individual behavior. Katz and Braly saw prejudice or attitudes toward groups as really attitudes toward labels or race names, and these attitudes in turn were thought to reflect culturally derived stereotypes or images about people representing those groups. Thus, as cultural products, stereotypes helped to explain the effects of culture on prejudice and discrimination. For the next 20 years or so, most studies on stereotypes continued the same basic focus. Although various definitions of stereotypes were offered, the working definition was in terms of traits ascribed to various racial and ethnic groups. Naturally social scientists trying to understand discrimination looked for the negative features of stereotypes. So stereotypes, which were assumed to be largely reflections of the culture rather than of individual experiences with people from these groups, promoted a negative evaluation (prejudice), which in turn justified discrimination.

More Modern Conceptions

PERSONALITY AND PREJUDICE

With the publication of *The Authoritarian Personality* (Adorno, Frenkel-Brunswik, Levinson, & Sanford, 1950), stereotypes began to be considered manifestations of a general prejudiced attitude. Stereotypes were still thought to predict discriminatory behavior, but their source tended to be seen as localized more in personality dynamics rather than in the larger culture. Stereotypes were viewed less as pictures in people's heads than as traits assigned to overly simplified categories, and while everyone sometimes employs such categories, their use was considered especially likely among people with prejudiced personalities.

This research effort had begun in the early 1940s as an attempt to understand the roots of anti-Semitism in the context of Nazi Germany. The research soon showed that those respondents who were prejudiced against Jews also had deep-seated prejudices against other groups. Thus anti-Semitism was only one part of a more general "ethnocentrism"–prejudice against those from other groups. Ethnocentric individuals in turn showed a more general set of attitudes that came to be called the "authoritarian personality."[3] Authoritarians turned out, not surprisingly, to have antidemocratic tendencies and to look a lot like Nazis. They liked clear authority structures, had an almost mystical allegiance to conservative values ("the good old days"), and were rigidly opposed to behaviors that upset their own strong sense of what was good and proper. In the definition of such a personality syndrome, stereotypes were considered reflections of deep-seated hatreds and prejudices.

The authoritarian personality research team was most impressed with the extent to which stereotypes were used to discriminate self from outgroups by making such groups homogeneous and negative. Stereotypes were rigidly held by such people as a protection against having to think about individual differences among members of hated outgroups. Stereotypes were also thought to protect against threat from negative tendencies that the prejudiced person was trying to repress. That is, the content of stereotypes came from a projection of negative characteristics to others; thus the content of stereotypes must inevitably be negative. Stereotypes tended to drive experience, rather than the reverse. Finally, in this research, stereotyping was likely to be a general process and not restricted to particular groups. Because a prejudiced person was struggling with any number of unresolved conflicts and with a host of repressed but active "dirty" tendencies, the choice of a particular target group for projection was basically irrelevant, although the authors did recognize that Western cultural history made some groups "better" targets than others.

The Authoritarian Personality was one of the most influential books in modern psychology. It deeply affected how social scientists thought about prejudice and stereotyping, as well as attitude and personality. Although the authors of that work did not believe that only authoritarians could be prejudiced, in practice the bright but narrow spotlight of social science was thrown on such wicked folks. This work also fostered a general agreement that stereotypes represented major pathologies of social cognition: They were fundamentally incorrect and derogatory generalizations about groups of people; they were not based on experience (or at least were profound corruptions of that experience); and they were relatively impervious to empirical disconfirmation.

ALLPORT'S CONTRIBUTION

In 1954 Gordon Allport published what remains the seminal book on prejudice, *The Nature of Prejudice*. Allport's background made him ideally suited to this task. He had a clear sense of the extent to which attitudes and values could serve multiple functions for the individual, and he taught at Harvard University where, in the Department of Social Relations, he rubbed shoulders with sociologists and anthropologists (so that the idea of looking at individual behavior in a cultural milieu came naturally to him). In addition, Allport's former student and then colleague, Jerome Bruner, was at that time one of the major forces in the "new look" in perception—an approach that favored examination of the role of values, attitudes, and social factors in basic perception and cognition. This work would later become an important stimulus for the cognitive revolution, and so it is no accident that in 1954 Allport featured the cognitive underpinnings of stereotypes.

Allport's book is perhaps most famous for having introduced the notion of the "prejudiced personality," a watered-down version of the authoritarian personality. However, he actually devoted more of his book to discussions of various cognitive factors involved in prejudice and stereotyping. In particular, he noted that it is a part of our basic cognitive natures to place things and people in categories, which are the cognitive buckets into which we pour various traits, physical features, expectations, and values—the stuff of stereotypes.

Allport recognized both that categorization and the use of categories are inevitable in our daily commerce with complex worlds, and also that inevitably errors will result. Although we all categorize other people and use stereotypes to some extent, prejudiced people think about their categories differently than do relatively unprejudiced people. In particular, the unprejudiced person is more likely to use what Allport called "differentiated categories," those that allow for exceptions and individual variation.

Changing Conceptions: Process and Content

THE DEAD END OF CLASSIC RESEARCH

Important as the classic Katz–Braly, authoritarian personality, and Allport conceptions were, by the late 1960s they had ceased to generate exciting research. The literature from this period is littered with reports of stereotypes of Group A by Group B, debates over fairly minute issues, and little attention to larger problems. By the early 1970s, it appeared that the study of stereotypes had run out of steam. Brigham's (1971a) classic review covered about 100 studies (limited to ethnic stereotypes), and his general tone about what had been learned was somewhat pessimistic. He suggested that many issues, even basic definitional ones, remained unresolved. For example, some authors felt that stereotypes refer to incorrect generalizations about groups, while others suggested that stereotypes have the same cognitive status as any generalization. Some saw stereotypes as due to faulty reasoning, while others viewed them as due to faulty experience, if fault was to be found at all. Most theorists described stereotypes as generally negative, but there was disagreement about whether that was a defining property. One gets the feeling from the Brigham review that stereotypes had become a sterile field of study, with little to show for all the heated argument by way of empirical generalizations. Brigham pointed the way to a more modern conception by recognizing that stereotypes had been narrowly defined, involved more than trait assignments to groups, and were not necessarily rogue cognitive constructs.

THE SOCIAL COGNITION PERSPECTIVE

In the past few decades, stereotype research has taken on new life, and there have been two major changes in the cast of the research. First, emphasis has shifted from studying the *content* of stereotypes through trait ascriptions to studying the cognitive *processes* involved in stereotyping (Hamilton, Stroessner, & Driscoll, 1994). Stereotyping (process) has replaced stereotypes (content). Second, there have been changes in examining which groups are specific targets of stereotyping.

The 1970s were years of extraordinary development in cognitive psychology, and during the 1980s this perspective was applied rigorously to the study of how we perceive, remember, and think about people and social events. Cognitive psychology generally, and social cognition more particularly, emphasized the role of abstract knowledge structures (called variously "schemas," "prototypes," "theories," etc.) in processing information about others. Stereotypes seemed closely related to these other types of constructs (Schneider, Hastorf, & Ellsworth, 1979) and could easily be construed as general theories or cognitive structures in their own right. Although there were early suggestions (e.g., Allport, 1954; Fishman, 1956; Gordon, 1962; Vinacke, 1957) that stereotypes could profitably be considered as closely related to other products of normal cognitive activity, and a few studies during the 1960s and 1970s had a clear cognitive focus, the real beginnings of the cognitive approach to stereotyping can be dated from the publication of a book edited by David Hamilton (1981a) containing a number of classic papers.[4]

Advantages of the Social Cognition Approach. The social cognition perspective has come to dominate social psychology generally, as well as the study of stereotypes (Hamilton & Sherman, 1994; Jones, 1982; Schneider, 1996; Stangor & Lange, 1994; Stephan, 1985, 1989). There are advantages to this approach. When stereotypes are seen as a normal part of the cognition family, most of the classic issues such as truthfulness, bias, and rigidity are cast in more tractable forms. Within the social cognition tradition, stereotypes are simply generalizations, and there are at least two advantages to construing stereotypes this way. First, we can "piggyback" our analyses on the existing research from cognitive psychology. Modern cognitive psychology also has produced many insights into the ways our generalization help us process information; stereotypes benefit from being seen in that light.

Second, when we stress the continuities between the ordinary processes involved in generalizations and those involved in stereotyping, we tend not to dismiss stereotypes as products of corrupt minds and diseased culture. We open the range of possible approaches when we analyze instead of condemning.

Problems with the Social Cognition Approach. Heavy reliance on the social cognition approach is not cost-free, however (Schneider, 1996). The social cognition perspective does not place much emphasis on the content of stereotypes. For example, although the content of Janice's stereotypes about gay males and Hispanics may be radically different, they will help her navigate the social world in about the same ways. It matters less what Janice thinks about gay or Hispanic people than how she arrived at her stereotypes and how she uses them. Her thought process are also seen as relatively context-free. It doesn't much matter whether she is thinking about gays at a gay bar or at the local health club. To be sure, the *content* of her thoughts may be affected by her location, but her *ways* of thinking should not be all that much different.

None of these biases is necessarily bad, but we need to recognize that there are losses as well as gains. On the negative side, the social cognition perspective does not easily nurture questions about whether stereotypes are true or false, positive or negative, acquired from individual experience or cultural tuition, shared or individual. Thus these classic issues in the study of stereotypes have been relatively ignored for the past couple of decades.

THE NEW LOOK IN CONTENT

Another factor that rejuvenated the study of stereotyping was the dramatic increase of interest in gender differences and in discrimination against women during the 1970s and 1980s. In part this mirrored an increasing cultural interest in sexism; concern with gender stereotypes has been a relatively late development (Eberhardt & Fiske, 1996).

Ethnicity and Race. Traditionally, most studies of stereotyping focused on race, nationality, and ethnic groups. The areas of race relations, discrimination, and the like have always provided a meeting ground for various social scientists. It has been obvious for many decades that in a culture so permeated by a history of racism, one could not understand relations among races solely in terms of one academic discipline. However, the tendency during the early days of social science was to assume that the most basic problem was prejudice. To be sure, understanding prejudice required studying the cultural milieu in which it arose, and this in turn required understanding the economic, social, and political forces that supported such negative attitudes. But there was general (although far from complete) agreement that the psychology of prejudice was key.

That assumption, largely implicit, changed during the turbulent decades of the 1960s and 1970s. It became clear that social pressures were often more important predictors of discrimination than overt prejudice (Harding, Proshansky, Kutner, & Chein, 1969). Political activists, for their part, were unhappy with the slow progress that had been made in reducing prejudice, and sometimes expressed the view that social scientists knew little or nothing about the arts of such change. They found that the quickest and most effective way to get the sorts of changes they wanted was through direct political, legal, and economic pressure. Legislative bodies, courts, and the streets rather than educational institutions became the laboratories of race relations during this period, and court rulings, economic boycotts, and threats of violence rather than prejudice reduction became the weapons of choice in fighting racism. These strategies were effective in the short run, regardless of other negative consequences or questions about long-term effectiveness. In this context, *psychological* approaches to racism and discrimination were shunted aside as being too slow at best and ineffective at worst.

Gender. At about this same time, people began to mount effective political, economic, and social programs for change in the status of women. Many female social scientists had been interested for decades in what we now think of as women's issues. But there were relatively few women in prestigious academic positions, and women's issues were usually seen as peripheral to "real" social science. However, during the 1970s as more women began academic careers, a larger base of support began to accumulate for the study of women's issues, gender roles, family, and the like, even among those female social scientists whose main research interests lay in other directions.[5] Thus there was a natural core of interest in gender stereotyping as well as discrimination against women.

To summarize, then, from the 1970s and 1980s onward, there has been renewed interest in stereotyping. This has resulted not only from the rise of social cognition within social psychology, but also from the larger numbers of people who have become interested in larger issues of discrimination—in this case, gender as opposed to race discrimination.

SOME CLASSIC ISSUES

There have been well over 5,000 empirical studies of stereotypes, broadly defined, in the past 70 or so years. In this long history, the same basic issues keep cropping up. Some of these, I argue, are best left aside, but others get restated from time to time precisely because in one form or another they remain important.

Definition

In trying to make sense of the disagreements, no issue could be more important than that of definition. What exactly is a "stereotype"? Before we get to the meat of the issue, it may be worthwhile pausing for a moment to think about why definitional issues are so important.

The Purpose of Definition

DEFINITIONS PARTITION

Definitions do a lot of the heavy lifting in science, and they do so in two ways. First, they draw boundaries by including some exemplars and excluding others. They partition a particular domain into things that count and others that do not. Thus, if we were to define stereotypes as beliefs about African Americans, we would include a host of attitudes and values about this group but would exclude similar sorts of beliefs about Hispanics and professors, to name two other groups. In cultures where African Americans were not prominent, there could be no stereotypes at all by this definition. There might be circumstances in which that were appropriate, but most social scientists would, I suspect, think that the universe of beliefs about blacks is not so tightly knit and separate as to require severance from nominally similar beliefs about other groups, such as Hispanics. Put another way, most of us believe that studying beliefs about both groups illuminates both areas to their mutual gain; therefore, this particular partitioning of beliefs is overly restrictive for the general study of stereotyping. That is not to suggest that beliefs about African Americans and Hispanics are so similar as to be interchangeable, but the point here is that stereotypes are more than beliefs about a particular group.

We could, of course, define the notion of "stereotype" more broadly. For example, we might define stereotypes as beliefs about people or even as beliefs about any category, so that we have stereotypes about cars, trees, butterflies, and professors. That definition is probably too broad because it makes us consider too many disparate things, and it rides roughshod over potentially important differences in the ways we think about Hondas and gay males.

Definitions, then, ought to make us include the right number and kinds of instances. What the "right" number and kinds are, of course, reflect choices. Definitions are not epistemologically neutral; they divide the world the way someone wants it divided. Normally in science, we try to use definitions to organize the world into scientifically useful categories—those that illuminate and make our science more efficient. At the same time, definitions have theoretical, political and ethical consequences.

DEFINITIONS ENCAPSULATE THEORIES

Definitions partition, but they also pack in a fair amount of theoretical baggage (often in sneaky or unplanned ways). Definitions are ways that theorists try to sell their ways of looking at a domain. *Caveat emptor.* Definitions obviously constrain us in terms of what exemplars they allow. So a definition making error a central component would not allow us to consider generalizations that are basically accurate. That might or might not be a problem. If one feels that error is an essential quality of stereotypes—in other words, that inaccurate generalizations differ in kind from accurate ones—one might well want to partition the domain in just that way. If, on the other hand, one is committed to a theory that inaccurate and accurate generalizations are more similar than different, one would not want to stress this difference as a part of the definition.

DEFINITIONS AS A FOCUS ON FEATURES

Obviously, then, definitions draw our attention to some features and indirectly shunt attention away from others. That is neither good nor bad per se. It is not right or wrong. It is not correct or incorrect. Such evaluative terms do not properly qualify definitions. There is no such thing as a right or wrong definition—one that is true or false. Rather, the term "definition" is more properly qualified by adjectives such as "useful" or "not useful," "viable" or "not viable," "accepted" or "not accepted."

There are typically many features associated with a given category, but in definitions of the category some features are essential and others are merely interesting corollaries of the category. For instance, if we were interested in defining gender, we would regard various genetic features and perhaps those sexual and secondary sexual characteristics that result from such genetic differences as essential. There may, in practice, be other features distinguishing males from females (e.g., height, strength, and style of dress) that we consider derivative or nonessential.

Similarly, when we try to define stereotypes, we should focus on the essential features—on those that are fundamental to the partitioning of the domain. Other features may be less essential; they are "along for the ride," so to speak, although explaining their whys and wherefores may be theoretically interesting and practically important. Obviously, theorists may disagree as to which features are essential and which merely corollary. Earlier theorists tended to assume that stereotypes must be inaccurate, so for them inaccuracy and error were essential features. For most modern theorists error is not an essential feature, so their definitions tend not to include this feature as defining. This does not mean that error is an irrelevant feature for modern theorists; in fact, most would probably assume that many, perhaps most, stereotypes are inaccurate in important ways. But not including this feature in the definition leaves the accuracy question quite open to debate, and also encourages us to focus on the similarities between accurate and inaccurate generalizations about groups of people. That's what we want to do these days.

Some Definitions

In due course I offer a definition, but before doing so I review several earlier definitions and then discuss some of the features that have been highlighted by such definitions. Just so that the reader can get some idea of the range of definitions, I list several classic ones here:

> "a fixed impression which conforms very little to the facts it pretends to represent and results from our defining first and observing second" (Katz & Braly, 1935, p. 181).
> "A stereotype is a stimulus which arouses standardized preconceptions which are influential in determining one's response to the stimulus" (Edwards, 1940, pp. 357–358).
> "Whether favorable or unfavorable, a stereotype is an exaggerated belief associated with a category. Its function is to justify (rationalize) our conduct in relation to that category" (Allport, 1954, p. 187).
> "a collection of trait-names upon which a large percentage of people agree as appropriate for describing some class of individuals" (Vinacke, 1957, p. 230).
> "Stereotyping has three characteristics: the categorization of persons, a consensus on attributed traits, and a discrepancy between attributed traits and actual traits" (Secord & Backman, 1964, p. 66).
> "a belief that is simple, inadequately grounded, or at least partially inaccurate, and held with considerable assurance by many people" (Harding et al., 1969, p. 4).
> "An ethnic stereotype is a generalization made about an ethnic group concerning a trait attribution, which is considered to be unjustified by an observer" (Brigham, 1971a, p. 29).
> "A stereotype refers to those folk beliefs about the attributes characterizing a social category on which there is substantial agreement" (Mackie, 1973, p. 435).
> "A structured set of beliefs about the personal attributes of a group of people" (Ashmore & Del Boca, 1979, p. 222).
> "those generalizations about a class of people that distinguish that class from others" (McCauley, Stitt, & Segal, 1980, p. 197).
> "sets of traits attributed to social groups" (Stephan, 1985, p. 600).

"a collection of associations that link a target group to a set of descriptive characteristics" (Gaertner & Dovidio, 1986, p. 81).

"highly organized social categories that have properties of cognitive schemata"
(Andersen, Klatzky, & Murray, 1990, p. 192).

"a positive or negative set of beliefs held by an individual about the characteristics of a group of people. It varies in its accuracy, the extent to which it captures the degree to which the stereotyped group members possess these
traits, and the extent to which the set of beliefs is shared by others" (Jones,
1997, p. 170).

It is readily apparent that there is no real consensus on what stereotypes are. It
is, however, also fairly clear what the dimensions of disagreement are, and to these I
now turn.

Features of Stereotypes

The definitions above seem to disagree on at least three things. The most obvious is
whether stereotypes are generally inaccurate. The second is whether stereotypes are
bad not only in their consequences, but in the reasoning processes that gave them
birth. Third, there are questions about whether stereotypes are shared among people
or whether an individual's beliefs, perhaps shared by no one else, can constitute a
stereotype.

Are Stereotypes Inaccurate?

DATA AND SPECULATION

Whether stereotypes are accurate is a reasonable question, and one that is extremely
difficult to answer. Many of the definitions above stress inaccuracy as an essential
feature of stereotypes. I take up the accuracy issue in greater detail later in this book
(Chapter 9), but for now I simply suggest that although most theorists have assumed
that stereotypes are inaccurate, there is little direct, hard, empirical support for this
assumption (Judd & Park, 1993; Mackie, 1973; McCauley, 1995). On the one hand, it
is not hard to show that many beliefs about groups are in error. For example, LaPiere
(1936) found that Armenian workers in Southern California were stereotyped as dishonest, deceitful, and troublemakers, despite the fact that such workers were less
likely to appeal for welfare and had generally better records before the law than the
average worker. Schoenfeld (1942) found that people had personality stereotypes of
people based on their first names, and it seems unlikely that first names account for
much in the way of actual personality traits.

THE KERNEL-OF-TRUTH HYPOTHESIS

On the other hand, some theorists have maintained what has come to be known as
the "kernel-of-truth hypothesis." This suggests that many (although not necessarily
all) stereotypes are based on some empirical reality, although they may exaggerate
the extent to which a particular group can be characterized in a certain way. There
are some demonstrations that stereotypes of groups match the features that these

groups claim for themselves, and that for at least some groups stereotypes match actual measured personality traits (Abate & Berrien, 1967; Campbell, 1967; Judd &
Park, 1993; Swim, 1994).

Even if the kernel-of-truth notion is correct, it is likely that many (probably most)
stereotypes are exaggerated generalizations, in the sense that groups are seen as having more of some feature that would be justified by empirical data. However, just to
complicate matters, there are even demonstrations (e.g., McCauley & Stitt, 1978) that
some stereotypic beliefs are not exaggerated enough—that groups are seen as less extreme on some characteristics than would be justified by data.

It is not hard to figure out why so many social scientists have assumed that stereotypes are inaccurate. As I have suggested, it is easy to find evidence that at least some
stereotypes are untrue or based on little or no evidence. Another suspicious fact is that
when reporting stereotypes, most people focus on negative traits, and it seems unlikely
that most groups are characterized mainly by such negative features. And, of course,
the social scientists who did early research on stereotypes were, by and large, committed to eliminating discrimination and improving race relations; quite apart from their
having a vested interest in believing that negative stereotypes of people were false, such
social scientists were likely to have had quite different experiences with members of minority groups than the average subject in their experiments had had.

THE WAYS OF INACCURACY

One major problem with all this is that many theorists have not been precise as to
what they think accuracy is. I discuss the accuracy issue extensively in Chapter 9, but
for now let me mention just three ways in which our stereotypes might be inaccurate.

The crudest form of inaccuracy, and one that seems to be the most prototypic, is
just seeing a group as being wrongly placed on some dimension. We might, for example, see professors as conservative when they are in fact liberal.

Second, we may make errors about groups by perceiving too much or too little
group homogeneity for a given trait. Perceived homogeneity is important, because it
affects how confidently we predict whether a person fits the group stereotype (see
Chapters 3 and 7). Obviously, if all or nearly all members of a group are highly intelligent, we can be confident that any given member will be intelligent. On the other
hand, if a given group is highly variable, we will be less confident about whether a
given individual fits the stereotype.

This leads to a related form of inaccuracy occurring not at the group level, but
when we apply group stereotypes to individuals. In many respects, the logic of going
from the general to the particular is even more perilous than forming generalizations
from particular instances. We all know that even excellent restaurants sometimes
serve bad food, friendly dogs can bite, and kind-looking professors can be gruff.
Thus even when our generalizations are basically accurate, they can still lead to mistakes when applied to concrete individuals.

THE STATUS OF OUR GENERALIZATIONS

It is obvious that we all have and use thousands of generalizations about groups of
people, not to mention animals, plants, and the objects around us. Many, perhaps
even most, of these generalizations are quite accurate *qua* generalizations (although
of course they tolerate exceptions), and many others are probably basically correct al-

though exaggerated. Do we then partition the domain of such generalizations such that the correct ones are not counted as stereotypes? Is that wise? Although it is possible that accurate generalizations differ from inaccurate ones in some fundamental way, this is not obviously the case, and so we should be wary of making inaccuracy a defining feature of stereotypes. I do not.

Are Stereotypes Bad?

When one reads the literature on stereotypes, one cannot avoid the conclusion that stereotypes are generalizations gone rotten. Several commentators (Brigham, 1971a; Gardner, 1973) have noted that if stereotypes are nothing more than generalizations, the term loses all meaning. Somehow stereotypes ought to be worse than most generalizations; they come with a slap to the face. I have begun this chapter with a challenge of sorts: If stereotypes are so bad, what is so bad about them? What makes them so different from ordinary generalizations? We have already seen that because inaccuracy remains an open issue, we probably do not want to define stereotypes as merely inaccurate generalizations about groups of people. Is there something else?

STEREOTYPES HAVE NEGATIVE CONTENT

One possibility is that stereotypes are bad because they emphasize the negative rather than the positive features of groups. Our interest in stereotypes obviously is fueled by the negative features that seem to support prejudice and can do real damage to members of stereotyped groups.

However, as the opening dialogue makes clear, the evaluative nature of the content of stereotypes can hardly be a defining feature. I might have a stereotype that college students tend to work hard. Is that a good or a bad thing? I think of it largely as positive, but one could imagine others (friends who want to party) who might see that as a negative feature. Karlins, Coffman, and Walters (1969) reported that 48% of their Princeton University sample described Jews as ambitious. Good or bad? Well, ambition is generally good, but one suspects that this ambition has a rather aggressive and grasping cast as part of the traditional Jewish stereotype.

We should avoid being overly precious. Obviously, almost no one has a good word to say on behalf of traits such as laziness or stupidity—but the fact is that many traits can be seen as positive in some situations and negative in others, as good by one group and bad by another, as worthy when embedded among other positive traits and as a bit sinister when part of a more negative constellation. The more important point is this: There is no a priori reason to assume that positive and negative generalizations are fundamentally different except in their consequences. Approaches such as the authoritarian personality research did emphasize that negative generalizations stem from psychological defenses in a way that positive ones do not, but on balance it seems too limiting to see that as the essential difference between all positive and all negative generalizations for all people. The evaluative nature of beliefs about others, therefore, ought not to be a defining feature of stereotypes.

STEREOTYPES ARE BASED ON FAULTY REASONING

Another reason commonly given for why stereotypes are bad is that they result from faulty reasoning processes. Certainly we are entitled to a strong suspicion that the generalizations about Hispanics formed by an overt racist differ from those formed by a community organizer not only in how positive they are, but in how they came to be. One possibility, for example, would be that the community organizer forms correct generalizations on the basis of direct and extensive contact with individuals, whereas the racist harbors incorrect ones based on hearsay and corrupt experiences driven by his or her emotions and prejudices. This certainly is what the early stereotype researchers had in mind.

From Lippmann onward, various students of the concept have noted that stereotypes are usually based on insufficient information—that they are rogue generalizations. Two further, often implicit, assumptions have often tagged along. The first is that somehow people are letting their cultures think for them; instead of forming their own generalizations from experience, they are using cultural ready-to-wear generalizations. The second is that since stereotypes are often used aggressively by prejudiced people, stereotypes must be driven by prejudice. This in turn means that stereotypes were more results of wishes and desires than of "objective" experience. In any case, it has been alleged that stereotypes are generalizations that are not derived from rational or otherwise "good" cognitive processes.

Letting Cultures Do Our Thinking. In hindsight, neither of these assumptions need be true. It is quite possible for us to form our own stereotypes without help from the culture, although we often receive various cultural boosts. Even so, we would hardly want to disallow the use of generalizations that are provided at second hand rather than based on individual experience. I have it only on hearsay that cobras are dangerous, but I would be ill advised to test this myself. Obviously, parents and our educational systems try to teach people useful (and, we can hope, largely correct) generalizations to guide their lives—generalizations that we do not expect will have to be reconfirmed throughout life.

Though we all get irritated at others (and occasionally at ourselves) for letting what turn out to be stupid and unsubstantiated generalizations guide behavior, the fact that we do not always verify our generalizations about people makes such generalizations no different from many others that we routinely use. In other words, we may be irrational by this criterion (although not by my lights), but that putative irrationality is not limited to our stereotypes of people.

Experiences. One problem with the idea that individual experience is superior to culture is that it is not clear what "good" and "bad" data for generalizations are. How many bad experiences do I have to have with a particular breed of dog before I am justified in concluding such dogs are mean? How many experiences do I need to have with a particular ethnic group to conclude that its members are smart or lazy? And suppose my own experiences have been highly parochial. Imagine, if you will, that I have been attacked by five collie dogs in the last year, and I have concluded that collies are mean and vicious. In general, five attacks seems sufficient justification for this particular stereotype. But now suppose we discover by reading a *Consumer's Guide to Dogs* that collies are even-tempered and kind, so that I happen to have been the victim of a chance distribution of naughty collie behavior. This would indicate that my own generalization is generally incorrect, but it hardly follows that it is bad in the sense of having been arrived at in some peculiarly biased way. I did the best I could do with the evidence before me.

Moreover, our own experiences with most groups are a bit like viewing a yard through a picket fence. We can see only parts at a time. For example, a store owner in a Hispanic part of town may have daily hassles with his or her Hispanic customers in terms of shoplifting and the like. This store owner's experiences certainly justify the generalization that Hispanics tend to commit lots of crimes, although for the larger city they may or may not be more crime-prone than others. The person who observes students primarily at the library will form different generalizations about them than someone who sees them primarily at bars on Saturday night will. The irony is that some students of stereotypes complain because people use hearsay or culturally provided generalizations without using their own individual experiences. Others complain because people rely too heavily on their own biased experiences. Unfortunately, we don't get to dictate the kinds of experiences people have.

Prejudiced Thinking. It has also been asserted that the cognitive processes underlying generalizing are corrupted in highly prejudiced individuals. Although we can gain a great deal by studying the cognitive processes of extremely prejudiced people—those whose thought processes seem to have lost the gyroscope of reality—we lose perspective by concentrating on these crabbed and rotten kinds. The stereotypes that the Archie Bunkers of the world hold need not be taken as prototypic. To do so is to pack too much into a working conception of stereotypes.

STEREOTYPES ARE RIGID

The very term "stereotype" etymologically refers to a kind of rigidity, and we ignore word origins at our peril. Fishman (1956) and others have declared that stereotypes are rigid and resistant to change. Some are. We all know racists whose favorable contacts with individual members of minority groups leave their stereotypes unfazed. Indeed, I have a stereotype or two of my own that I would be loath to give up in the face of mere evidence. And yet most of us have stereotypes that do change, albeit slowly, and that don't seem to be that rigid. So we ought not to include rigidity as an essential characteristic, although we should try to remember that a few people have many rigid stereotypes and many have a few.

STEREOTYPES DO NOT ENCOURAGE THINKING ABOUT INDIVIDUALS

Others have argued that although stereotypes may be generalizations, they are applied too freely and indiscriminately; they do not allow for exceptions. It is unclear what we ought to make of this claim. I have several bad experiences with collies, form a stereotypes that they are mean, and then assume that every collie I meet is vicious. That hardly seems the height of openness to new experiences, but it is the stuff of everyday generalization. Generalizations are like that. They are useful precisely because they free us from having to think about each new individual member of whatever category. And because no good deed (or cognitive achievement) goes unpunished, it is also the stuff of everyday experience that using generalizations in this way will lead to errors in our judgments. Obviously, some errors are more important than others. I may think that red apples are likely to taste good and may be disappointed at the occasional sour one, but my disappointment is personal and basically irrelevant to the rest of the world. My generalization about collies may keep me from having a perfectly nice collie as a pet, but again it is hard to claim cosmic importance for this error. However, when I fail to hire a hard-working black man because I believe that black men are lazy, the error has more important consequences for the man I have rejected, and may have legal consequences for me as well. But consequences aside, it seems clear that stereotypes do not fundamentally differ from other generalizations in terms of their tendency toward overgeneralization, and therefore let's strike this as an essential part of our definition of stereotypes.

WHY ARE STEREOTYPES BAD?

The point is that many stereotypes share at least one of the problems described above, but so do most generalizations. Therefore, it doesn't seem useful to make fault a part of the definition of stereotypes (see Ashmore & Del Boca, 1981, for related arguments). Why then do we dislike stereotypes so much? I think the answer has more to do with the politics of interpersonal behavior than with the ways our minds work. It is probably not overly cynical to suggest that stereotypes are simply generalizations that somebody doesn't like (Brigham, 1971a). It is not hard to understand why professors would object to being seen as lazy, lawyers as greedy, and computer programmers as nerdy. Well, then, what about the stereotype that Asian Americans are smart and hard-working? Why would anyone object to these positive characterizations? One reason might be that, as a generalization, it allows for no variation; seeming to shout that *all* Asian Americans are smart might offend Asian Americans who treasure their diversity. Furthermore, saying that someone is smart may be an indirect way of saying that this person isn't sociable or athletic. So even positive generalizations can impose straightjackets.

Of course, animals and plants we see as dangerous have their good points and deliver occasional pleasant surprises as well. However, there is one big difference between the world of things and people: Lawyers object when they are seen as greedy, whereas cobras and bears rarely complain that they are maligned. In a sense, then, my generalization about lawyers becomes a stereotype only when a lawyer (or a lawyer-friendly person) chooses to object. This is not a trivial fact, as it weaves its way through the fabric of everyday life and politics. However, the central point is that generalizations about bears and professors share many of the same cognitive features, and often the main ways in which they differ depend on how they play themselves out in our social worlds.

Are Stereotypes Shared or Individual?

Before 1970 or so, most social scientists who studied stereotypes assumed them to be generalizations shared with other members of a particular culture, and that assumption found its way into several of the classic definitions. This was an easy assumption to make. After all, in the days before television and when segregation along race, ethnic, gender, religious, and class lines was more pronounced than it is now, most of what most people knew about other groups came from hearsay and limited exposure to stereotyped portrayals on radio and in the movies. In the 1930s it would have been comparatively rare for a white person in the United States to know an individual black person at all well, so white stereotypes of blacks had to be based primarily on culturally transmitted information rather than detailed individual experiences. Men and women used to lead more segregated lives than they do now, and even members of different religious groups tended to have limited contact.[6] Thus the fact that the stereotypes that most people reported in these early studies matched culturally prescribed views should come as no surprise. Moreover, to investigators searching for the culprit for stereotypes, it seemed obvious that culture is the answer. Presumably children are taught stereotypes by their parents, schools, and churches; such stereotypes are reinforced by culturally created social realities and by limited contact with individuals from other groups.

Even today the content of many stereotypes is shared among people, and many of the stereotypes we most care about do seem to have at least a partial cultural basis (Stangor & Schaller, 1996). This is not trivial, because stereotypes that are shared by large numbers of people do seem to have a legitimacy and a reality that more individual stereotypes probably lack (Gardner, Kirby, & Finlay, 1973). Nonetheless, this raises an important issue: Are stereotypes shared because of cultural tuition, because of common experiences, or for some other reason? The older tradition tended to treat people as passive products of their culture, and did not invite speculation about individual cognitive processes. My own bias is to see the cognitive underpinnings of stereotypes as fundamental, and then to ask why stereotypes are often shared.

There is a middle ground of sorts. Social identity theory (Tajfel, 1981a) and self-categorization theory (Turner, Oakes, Haslam, & McGarty, 1994) both emphasize the importance of social interactions in the development, use, and maintenance of stereotypes (Augoustinos & Walker, 1998). Culture doesn't force itself upon us, but rather provides templates that help us organize our social experiences in ways that facilitate effective interpersonal behavior. The real action is in the give and take of our everyday interactions with others. Culture may provide stereotypes for us to deploy strategically, provide motives for us to explain some group differences, or channel our social experiences in ways that encourage certain stereotypes. Thus within this approach culture is a player, and an important one, in the development of stereotypes, but its role is often indirect and hard to document.

The truth is that we cannot separate the roles of culture and individual experiences in forming stereotypes or any other product of our thought systems (Schneider, 1996; Spears, Oakes, Ellemers, & Haslam, 1997; Stangor & Jost, 1997). Cultures provide categories for our cognitive activity. It is no accident that Americans are more likely to classify people on the basis of race, gender, or occupation than on the basis of religion or hair color. U.S. culture provides lessons on important ways that categories differ. This is not necessarily bad; after all, we expect children to be taught the differences between playing in the street and playing on a playground, and we want to be told which foods are healthy and which not. By the same token, we also learn important lessons about what differences are relatively unimportant. Those of us raised in U.S. culture, for example, make little of the differences between those with blond and those with dark hair (although there are clear stereotypes based on hair color—see Chapter 13). When we meet people, we tend to classify them in terms of their occupation or parental status, and not in terms of whether they grew up on a farm; matters could, of course, be different in different settings or different cultures. Furthermore, the products of our cognitive activities have social and cultural consequences that channel our thinking.

The point is this: Although it is appropriate to focus on cognitive activities somewhat apart from cultural contexts, we also lose important perspectives and insights by ignoring the social dimension, as the social cognition perspective traditionally has. In the latter chapters of this book (especially Chapters 9–14), I address some of the traditional social and cultural issues, and take up once again the question of why so many stereotypes seem to be widely shared.

A Return to Definitions

What, if anything, does this have to say about the core question of definitions? What do we need to include in our definition of stereotypes? As we have seen, a good many features have been claimed as essential to stereotypes, but my "take" is that they are generally not. Let me again be clear about what this means. I have argued that many of the traditional features of stereotypes are corollary rather than essential or defining. We should not define stereotypes in terms of their target group, their accuracy or inaccuracy, or whether they have or have not been produced by the larger culture. Such things may be true of some or most stereotypes, but to define stereotypes in terms of these features softens our focus on the more central features.

Essential Features of Stereotypes

What then are the essential qualities of stereotypes? The most basic definition I can offer, the one with the fewest constraining assumptions, is that *stereotypes are qualities perceived to be associated with particular groups or categories of people.* This definition captures at least the essential qualities that stereotypes must have, in the sense that everyone would agree on this much. Note that the definition does not place limitations on what these features might be; they could be traits, expected behaviors, physical features, roles, attitudes, beliefs, or almost any other qualities. It also is not restrictive about the types of categories that might be considered as gist for the stereotype mill. In fact, it is important to note (see Chapter 4 for further discussion) that there is no principled distinction between categories and features. Although it seems natural to think that helpfulness is a feature of the teacher category, we could just as easily say that being a teacher ("teacherness," if you will) is associated with the category of helpful people. The distinction between categories and features has more to do with cultural definitions of what a category is and with what we see as important in a given situation than with any special psychological requirements.

This definition has a "vanilla," even gutless, quality in its refusal to take stands on many of the traditional issues that have animated the stereotype literature. As I have argued, this is probably all to the good. On the other hand, it does embody one strong assumption—namely, that stereotypes involve associations between categories and qualities—and this focuses our attention on the mental representation of stereotypes in terms of memory structures (Stangor & Lange, 1994; Stephan, 1989).

Associations

THE ADVANTAGE OF ASSOCIATIONS

The main advantage of association metaphors is that cognitive psychology offers a wide range of formal models of associative networks and other modes of representation (see Carlston & Smith, 1996; Smith, 1996) on which we can draw. I should be clear that I am using "association" in the loosest possible sense here, and this does not represent a commitment to associative network models as the way stereotype information is represented. All I claim here is that feature–category relationships vary in strength and can be measured as such. A secondary advantage is that the strength of associations is typically reasonably easy to conceptualize and measure, so that a number of measurement strategies can be used.

STRENGTH OF ASSOCIATION

All modern conceptions of stereotypes recognize that features are differentially associated with categories. For example, intelligence is probably more closely tied to the category of professor than to that of bus driver, and intelligence is more closely related to the professor category than is the propensity to drive an old car. There are many ways we might conceptualize strength in this context. We might mean that professors, on average, have more of the trait than bus drivers. Alternatively, we might mean that intelligence more readily comes to mind in thinking about professors than about bus drivers. Strength could signify that a higher percentage of professors than bus drivers are above some threshold of intelligence. In this book, I tend to use probabilities as the measure of choice. Thus, when I say that intelligence is more closely associated with professors than bus drivers, I mean that people will judge that professors are more likely to be intelligent than bus drivers. However, that is not a principled decision, but one of convenience. It is usually easier to discuss strength in this domain in terms of probabilities, and it is also an idea that has great intuitive appeal.

GENERALIZATION AND DIFFERENTIATION

One of the problems with thinking about stereotypes in terms of probabilities of a group's having certain features is that these probabilities can be quite high without differentiating one group from another. Consider your generalizations about college professors, Jews, career women, homeless people, persons with AIDS, or baseball players. As you think about what features one of these groups (say, homeless people), does it occur to you to say that homeless people have hearts, are taller than 4 feet, have some body hair, have five toes on each foot, and had two biological parents? Do you think of homeless people as physically dirty, as behaviorally disturbed, as badly clothed? Those features fit my stereotype of homeless persons, and yet far fewer homeless people are physically dirty at any given time than have five toes on each foot. So why do you not list toes as a part of your stereotype? Well, you answer, because nearly everyone has five toes on each foot. So being physically dirty and exhibiting behavior problems seem to differentiate domicile-disadvantaged individuals from domicile-advantaged individuals in ways that toes do not. To be sure, this is somewhat misleading, because there are a good many other things that distinguish these two generalizations. Having behavioral problems may be seen as more central to the sociology and psychology of homelessness than toe count; more to the point, one may build a "picture in our heads" about homeless persons based on their behavior and physical state, but not on the basis of common human features. Nonetheless, the point remains that physical state, even though less strongly associated with homelessness, is more discriminating than number of toes.

Several psychologists (e.g., Campbell, 1967; McCauley et al., 1980; Tajfel, 1981a) have made such differentiation central to the conception of stereotypes. Perhaps not every feature contained in a stereotype is good at differentiating the group from others, but a large number seem to be (e.g., Diehl & Jonas, 1991; Ford & Stangor, 1992), and generally people are fairly sensitive to differences between groups (e.g., Krueger, 1992). Moreover, informally it seems that when people make public statements about their stereotypes, they usually intend to make a statement about some differentiating feature of a group. So to say that homeless people are dirty is really to say that homeless people are more dirty than the average person (or "nice" people), and to say that lawyers are greedy is implicitly to compare them with doctors and professors.

One important reason why features are associated with groups is that such features help discriminate one group from another. It is a close call as to whether differentiation is important enough to become part of our definition of stereotypes. On balance, however, I think that including it muddies some waters from which we expect clarity. Let's stay on target and keep it simple.

Stereotypes as Theories

Having pleaded for simplicity, I must somewhat guiltily argue for another important feature. Although many, perhaps most, stereotype researchers are comfortable with heavy reliance on fairly passive associative network models without additional complication, I am not. To be sure, a perceiver who finds that members of a particular group probabilistically behave in a particular way or have a particular appearance will probably come to form associations between those features and the group category, whether or not he or she feels inclined to do so. Associations sometimes just happen. But often we have theories about why groups tend to exhibit certain features—a fact that has received increasing attention in this area (e.g., Anderson & Sedikides, 1991; Furnham, 1988; Martin & Parker, 1995; McGarty, Yzerbyt, & Spears, 2002; Murphy, 1993b; Murphy & Medin, 1985; Wittenbrink, Gist, & Hilton, 1997; Wittenbrink, Hilton, & Gist, 1998; Wittenbrink, Park, & Judd, 1998; Yzerbyt, Corneille, & Estrada, 2001; Yzerbyt, Rocher, & Schadron, 1997). Is there anyone who does not have an explanation, correct or not, for why African American males dominate many sports in the United States? Do we not have a range of theories, some matters of political contention, for whatever differences we observe between males and females? Does anyone assume that homosexuality, mental illness, or artistic accomplishment simply shows up unannounced one day?

Although people's theories about their stereotypes constitute an important theme throughout this book, on balance it seems wiser not to incorporate this feature into the present definition. For one thing, there may be some associations that do not call upon theoretical knowledge or that incorporate theories only as a justification for empirically derived associations. Furthermore, understanding lay theories about groups and their features may help us understand why people associate particular features with particular groups, but usually this will not affect how we measure stereotypes or how they affect behavior.

PREJUDICE AND DISCRIMINATION

This book focuses on stereotypes, but we must consider their relationships to the feelings we have about other people and our behavior toward them. There are two related reasons why this is important. First, stereotypes are inherently private. Although my stereotypes owe a lot to my social and cultural milieus, in the final analysis I own them and you do not. Moreover, I may have less control than I would wish over their expression, but I generally enjoy the conceit that I can choose whether you or anyone else knows what my beliefs are. The bottom line is that my beliefs are of no concern to you unless and until I display them in some way. I'm tempted to say that beliefs harm no one unless openly expressed, but they may create mischief for the people who hold them (Wheeler, Jarvis, & Petty, 2001). That is not a moral point, but a simple matter of pragmatics. It then follows that, interesting as stereotypes may be, their importance rests on how and when they are translated into behaviors. From this perspective, trying to study stereotypes without discussing their relationships to prejudice and behavior is a bit like packing for a long journey, boarding the plane, and flying to our destination, only to find ourselves in an endless circling pattern over our destination. Unfortunately, social psychologists have not devoted much or nearly enough attention to discrimination compared to stereotypes (Fiske, 2000b).

"Prejudice" refers to the feelings we have about others, and "discrimination" to our behavior. Nonetheless, trying to define prejudice and discrimination is a bit like trying to define pornography: It is hard, but people know it when they see it—or at least they think they do. Unfortunately, just as people debate whether the nudes in *Playboy* or *Playgirl* are porno, so people can (and do) argue about whether a hiring policy emphasizing certain qualifications that effectively exclude disproportional numbers of African Americans is or is not "real" discrimination. Often our political dialogue and even our legal reasoning are guided by "I know it when I see it," and in some contexts this may work. However, as social scientists, we cannot afford to be so imprecise. If we cannot be clear about what the constructs we deal with are, how can we expect informed debate about issues that need debating?

Prejudice

The word "prejudice" comes from the Latin *praejudicium*, which means "a prelimi-nary hearing or presumption" and is closely related to *praejudico*, meaning "to pre-judge." The modern English word has preserved much of that meaning. In popular use, the word "prejudice" also has the connotation of a negative judgment, although we also often say that someone is prejudiced in favor of something or someone. In such cases we often have to explicitly mark it as such in contrast to the unmarked word "prejudice," which almost always connotes negativity. *Prejudice can then be de-fined as the set of affective reactions we have toward people as a function of their category memberships.*

Although almost no one has anything good to say on behalf of prejudice, it, like stereotyping, results from perfectly normal cognitive tendencies. Prejudging is as normal and almost as much a part of our basic (and, I daresay, primitive) mental tool-box as is categorization. Every day in countless ways, I must decide whether to ap-proach or avoid certain people, situations, and things. I have neither time nor incli-nation to read every book, watch every TV program, join every organization that wants my time and money, climb every mountain, conquer every continent, or sail every sea. It's not going to happen. I, like you, tend to watch TV programs that have appealed to me in the past, and to favor books by authors whose past books I have liked.

Obviously, judgments based on past experience or what we have read or heard are often quite fallible. Our prejudgments, our prejudices—positive and negative—inevitably limit our experiences and deny us important information. I see a Sylvester

Stallone movie, and on the basis of that experience decide I never want to see another. In making this judgment, I may be closed-minded, snobbish, priggish, or stupid—indeed, prejudiced—but then aren't we all sometimes? But, at the same time, our
prejudgments allow us to meander through life more efficiently and live to ripe old
ages, given that they help us avoid dangerous encounters with naughty people,
beasts, substances, and situations. We are willing to pay the price of somewhat impoverished experiences for safety and mental calm. We actually have little choice in
the matter, evolution having decided for us that this is a bargain (Keith, 1931;
Kurzban & Leary, 2001).

   There are, of course, important differences between prejudices against people
and other forms of prejudgment. Pragmatically, people complain about our judgments of and behaviors toward them, but things do not. This keeps us on our mental
toes when we judge others. Probably the most important differences theoretically are
that prejudices against people tend to be embedded more deeply into our mental
matrices and are also more likely to receive some cultural support. Some prejudices
are superficial and socially inconsequential; my prejudices against Stallone movies
have shallow resonances in my mental life and are not apparently widely supported
in U.S. culture. On the other hand, some prejudices (say, against eating dog meat for
Westerners) reek of culture. Moreover, my prejudices—pro and con—about Asians,
Hispanics, males, and females may or may not find ready support in my culture, but
they are certainly more tightly integrated into my belief structure than my prejudices
about Mexican and Thai food (both entirely positive).

Discrimination

By this point, no one will be surprised to learn that the kinds of discrimination we
decry are firmly rooted in rather ordinary cognitive and behavioral processes. The
word "discrimination" springs from the Latin *discrimino*, meaning "to divide or separate." And whatever else discrimination involves, it is based on division of people
into categories. Discrimination has a range of meanings in everyday life, some of
which are positive. So we can speak of a discriminating art collector or wine enthusi-
ast. To be sure, there is a slight hint of snobbery in such usage—as if the discriminating person is dividing the world in highly refined ways not readily available to the
rest of us—but still, in many contexts, it is good to be able to divide intelligently.

   However, most of the time when we use the term "discrimination," we have in
mind the use of category information in making judgments and behavioral choices
about people. Even that, however, is much too broad. I doubt that most people
would call my university's failure to admit people with SAT scores of 350 (verbal) and
375 (math) and barely passing high school grades discrimination, even if those people are members of disadvantaged ethnic or racial groups. Most universities and colleges discriminate on the basis of test scores and high school grades; some businesses
may hire people with certain kinds and amounts of education, plus what they take to
be relevant skills. My failures to invite homeless people to meals and a sleepover in
my guest room would not be seen as discrimination by most people, nor would my
limiting my friends to well-educated people. Obviously, all of us use category information all the time to include or exclude people—and no one gives it a second
thought, let alone labeling it as discrimination. Something more is needed, and that
something more is a sense that the use of category information is *unjustified* in some

sense. Unfortunately, what seems unjustified to one person may not to another, and so we have continuing debates. Still, to get on with things for the time being, *let's define discrimination as the unjustified use of category information to make judgments about other people.*

In the United States at the moment, both liberals and conservatives agree that members of most racial and ethnic groups should not be excluded from most organizations and jobs. They are on their way to being able to say the same for gender. However, discrimination against homosexuals and criminals is still routinely practiced and widely approved. Then there are grey areas, such as disability status. Present law requires that organizations provide reasonable accommodations for those with physical and mental disabilities to be able to perform jobs or get an education. However, it is far from clear that the majority of employers or other Americans support the idea that disability should be a protected category in this way. Other cases that do not at present constitute legal discrimination could present tangled issues for the future. Should a transsexual male be allowed to dress in female clothes and use women's restrooms, even if it makes the other employees uncomfortable? Should a devoutly religious Christian woman be allowed to decorate her desk with religious icons and to place religious tracts on the desks of coworkers, even though both practices offend many Jewish and Muslim (and, for that matter, Christian) coworkers? Where do we draw the line on Christmas decorations?

These questions do not have easy answers. For every case in which we can get a fairly good consensus for the existence of discrimination, the same principles applied to other cases will not seem as clear. For the time being, then, let us stick with our definition of discrimination as unjustified use of category information in making decisions about others, with the understanding that what appears justified to one person may not seem so to another.

Relationships among Components

Roughly speaking, "stereotypes" are category-based beliefs we have about people; "prejudice" is a set of affective reactions or attitudes; and "discrimination" refers to behavioral tendencies. Beliefs, affect, and behavioral tendencies do not easily separate themselves in our everyday lives, and they do not do so in our research endeavors. However, while it may seem natural to think of these three as part of the same package, they are clearly distinct. Beliefs may give rise to affect, but there are cool as well as red-hot beliefs. Our affective reactions to things may stir our passions and dictate our behavior, but not always. Sometimes our behaviors seem inexplicable, performed without any relevant or at least understandable preceding cognition or emotion.

There is a well-honed model for how these components are related (e.g., Ajzen & Fishbein, 2000)—that is, the standard model of attitudes. According to this model, we have beliefs about objects. Each of these beliefs is associated with one or more goals or desires; if we believe that the attitude object facilitates achieving our goals, we will feel positively toward it, and (obviously) we will feel negatively if the object hinders goal achievement. Some beliefs generate strong affective reactions, others relatively weak ones. The affect and beliefs in their turn give rise to behavioral tendencies, the exact nature of which is determined by the appropriateness of various behaviors to achieve the goals. Under certain circumstances, the behavioral tendencies will be activated in actual behavior. Obviously, social norms, laws, and considerations of expediency will affect the whether, when, and how of this translation. The standard model thus implies a strong causal or at least temporal sequence from beliefs to affect to behavioral tendencies to behavior.

This model is a useful way to think about such matters. Consider this example: Donna believes that gay males seduce young boys into their lifestyle. Because that belief is antagonistic to her moral values, she has a strong negative emotional reaction to gays. This leads her to avoid the one or two gay males she knows about, to insist that her church condemn homosexuality, and (when she can) to vote against pro-gay politicians. That sort of scenario is common enough.

Still, matters are surely more complex. It isn't hard to talk to Donna about her attitudes toward homosexuals; she's willing to admit that she has a strong negative prejudice toward them and is proud that she discriminates against them. As we discuss her beliefs, we soon find that Donna doesn't actually have any hard evidence that gay men seduce boys—but she's heard stories, thank you very much, and that's all she needs. We begin to get the feeling that maybe Donna's prejudices are driving her beliefs, rather than the reverse way it's supposed to be. We soon discover that a number of Donna's beliefs in this area are strongly held but weakly supported by actual evidence. That our stereotypes are often rationalizations for our prejudices has long been recognized (Allport, 1954; Hoffman & Hurst, 1990; Jost & Banaji, 1994; Katz & Braly, 1935; Rutland & Brown, 2001; Vinacke, 1949).

Thus we cannot blithely assume that the standard attitude model is correct all or even most of the time (Dovidio, Brigham, Johnson, & Gaertner, 1996; Mackie & Smith, 1998). Our emotions and passions can affect our beliefs as much as the reverse. Some behavior is carefully thought out, designed to further specific goals. Other actions are mindless, and affect is in the driver's seat. Sometimes behavior affects attitudes; practice makes perfect, and continuing to perform particular behaviors may lead us to like them more. Not only are there multiple "feedback loops" among beliefs, affect, and behavior, but each can arise independently of the others. Culture and classical conditioning can create positive or negative affect in the complete absence of relevant beliefs, sometimes even contradicting them. For example, I, along with most Americans, happen to have a mild aversion to snakes, despite having caught many of them as a boy and despite beliefs about them that are almost entirely positive. People may honestly believe that whites and blacks are equal in all the ways that count, and still have mild to strong distaste when interacting with someone of the other race. Behavior can result almost entirely from various social and situational pressures without having been dictated by affect or beliefs. There is no one simple equation linking stereotypes, prejudice, and discrimination, but it is still vitally important that we examine their relationships (see Chapter 8).

PLAN OF THIS BOOK

The concept of stereotypes has been around for well over half a century, and during much of that period it has been a topic of lively research interest. Despite the radical change in the 1970s in how stereotypes were viewed, some of this older research is still instructive and is covered selectively. There are five substantive parts to this book. After this chapter and another devoted to measurement of stereotypes, the next four chapters (Chapters 3–6) are devoted to various cognitive perspectives on stereotypes and stereotyping. Chapters 7–8 examine the role of stereotypes in intergroup conflict, prejudice, and discrimination. Chapters 9 and 10 discuss where stereotypes come from and how they might be changed. Chapters 11–14 explore the content of various stereotypes.

Chapters 3–6: Social Cognition

As indicated earlier, the social cognition perspective is largely responsible for rejuvenating the study of stereotyping and has dominated the area for more than two decades. At various points in the evolution of social cognition, stereotypes have been seen as analogous to several different constructs that have held center stage. Stereotypes have been viewed as products of categorization, schemas, implicit personality theories, and hypotheses to be tested. These tend to be overlapping constructs, and probably no theorist (least of all I) would claim that any single metaphor explains everything of importance about stereotypes. Indeed, one implicit theme of the present book is that stereotypes are not any one thing; rather, they are best seen as complex products of several different mental activities.

As such, each of these metaphors can illuminate part of the larger picture, and it would be fairest to consider these metaphors as foci of investigation rather than as mutually exclusive approaches. Each of these metaphors emphasizes certain features of stereotypes not emphasized by the others. For example, implicit personality theory approaches tend to focus on the structure—the interrelationships of the components—of stereotypes. Schema models focus more on memory representations of stereotypes. Categorization models alert us to the fact that when people are categorized as one thing rather than another, we tend to emphasize similarities to others in the group and to exacerbate differences between categories. Models that see stereotypes as hypotheses draw our attention to the provisional nature of most stereotypes and suggest how this might affect how we interact with and gain new information about people.

Chapters 7–8: Ingroups, Outgroups, Prejudice, and Discrimination

Stereotypes both result from and affect our behavior toward others. As I have indicated in the preceding section, the relationships between stereotypes and behavior are not simple. Chapter 7 discusses the role of group membership in stereotyping and prejudice. Common experience suggests that stereotypes are especially likely to flourish when members of one group think about those from another, often competing, group. Not only do we think about ingroups and outgroups differently, but group categorization gives rise to stereotypes. Chapter 8 discusses the many relationships of stereotypes and stereotyping to prejudice and discrimination, further expanding our consideration of the role of experiential and cultural factors and their interactions.

Chapters 9–10: Evolution and Change

Stereotypes do not arise mysteriously; nor, once they show up, do they stay fixed in culture and individual minds. Chapter 9 explicitly considers stereotype development.

Stereotypes are obviously based to some extent on individual experiences, and so accuracy issues are discussed fully in this chapter. The cultural and social contexts of stereotype development are also considered. Chapter 10 takes up considerations of stereotype change, and again focuses both on stereotype change as a fundamental cognitive issue of belief change and on various cultural factors that may encourage or inhibit change. I argue that we cannot understand stereotype change merely in terms of decontextualized cognitive processes; our stereotypes are too much embedded in the larger cultural milieu for this to work.

Chapters 11–14: Content of Stereotypes

For all its advantages, the social cognition perspective does not speak gracefully to such questions as why stereotypes include some traits but not others, and why some groups are victimized more by stereotypes than others are. As I have argued elsewhere (Schneider, 1991), the social cognition approach generally makes a strong assumption that the content of our cognitive systems is basically irrelevant to how information is processed. There are clearly ways in which this is true, and the assumption has proved to be a powerful tool in allowing us to understand our cognitions about people.

If content is basically irrelevant, then it should make little difference whether we study stereotypes of women, football players, or homeless people. As a matter of fact, much of the recent research on stereotyping has been fueled by interest in gender studies. Thus a large percentage of recent research has concerned stereotypes of women (and, less often, men). Another large category of studies has dealt with stereotypes of ethnic groups, especially blacks. However, there have been relatively fewer investigations (especially recently) of stereotypes of various occupations, car ownership, choices about how to spend one's leisure time, or style of dress. We know relatively little about stereotypes of criminals, people with AIDS, and homeless persons, despite the fact that such stereotypes do exist and undoubtedly interfere with our abilities to solve the problems faced by such people.

Our social categories differ in a great many ways, some of which are likely to be important than others. For example, some categories (such as race, age, and gender) give us plenty of visual help in determining category membership, whereas it is less easy to tell whether someone is lesbian or straight, depressed or not, a Jew or a Catholic. Some social groups have associated roles and norms that dictate behaviors and appearances, whereas others do not. Some groups are easy to join, whereas membership in other groups is assigned at birth. And so it goes. Does any of this make any difference to how stereotypes are used to judge others? Traditionally, these questions have not been salient, and I hope to provide some preliminary answers in Chapters 11–13.

We have also tended, over the years, to ignore issues about the nature of features that are part of stereotypes. Obviously, such features differ from group to group. Common stereotypes suggest that Germans are efficient, Hispanic Americans are family-oriented, and Asian Americans are smart. Apart from the positive or negative qualities of stereotypic traits, there are other linguistic ways in which such features differ. Somehow cleverness seems to differ fundamentally from intelligence, restlessness is not quite the same as anxiety, and shyness seems to have different connotations from those of introversion. Furthermore, some traits may be easy to acquire, and others hard to lose, in the face of behavioral evidence. Chapter 14 explores how specific types of traits get attributed to groups and how those features may vary.

Notes

1. To fans of the great psychologist-philosopher William James, it will come as no surprise to learn that while an undergraduate at Harvard, Lippmann was deeply influenced by James. Although James never wrote about stereotyping, his intellectual fingerprints (not to mention his lively style) are immediately evident in the passage just quoted. It is also no accident that Gordon Allport—whose Harvard lineage from James was also clear, if more indirect—picked up many of these same themes in his famous book on prejudice (to be discussed in a few pages).
2. The very first studies were done on occupational stereotypes (Rice, 1926; Litterer, 1933; Gahagan, 1933). People were asked to judge the occupations of pictures of men from magazines and newspapers. There was some consensus (often erroneous) about which occupations went with which pictures, and the authors interpreted this as evidence of stereotypes of the appearance of people in various occupations. There is also an extensive early literature on judgments of intelligence and success from photographs (e.g., Anderson, 1921; Gaskill, Fenton, & Porter, 1927; Landis & Phelps, 1928; Pintner, 1918). Rice (1928) devoted a chapter in his book on politics to the influence of stereotypes on political attitudes, although his account added nothing to Lippmann's. Despite the fact that this research on occupations and intelligence predates the Katz–Braly research, it was the latter that set the tone for most subsequent research in this area.
3. The television character Archie Bunker was a clear exemplification of the authoritarian personality syndrome—and not by accident.
4. It could be argued with considerable justice (and force) that important work by Henri Tajfel and his students in England emphasized the cognitive underpinnings of stereotyping throughout the 1960s and 1970s. The fact of the matter is, however, that Tajfel's work became dominant in England and influential in the United States only after the social cognition revolution of the late 1970s. However, the Hamilton book provided a useful synthesis and some new theoretical perspectives at just the right historical point.
5. And it should also be said that many male social scientists were active as direct participants or as strong supporters from the sidelines.
6. We sometimes forget all this. I grew up in a rural area outside Indianapolis in the 1950s. Until I went to college, I had never met a Jew (and then only one), and had never exchanged more than a few hundred words (total) with African Americans. I did not meet any Asian Americans until I went to graduate school, and I doubt that I even knew that Mexican Americans existed except as people who came by periodically to pick crops. I knew no Catholics well, other than a cousin who had married into that faith and confirmed various stereotypes by having a dozen or so children. I doubt that I knew there were such people as homosexuals; certainty lesbians were off my radar screen. I knew few adult women who worked outside the home, and all of them were either teachers, bookkeepers, or secretaries. There were only four TV channels, and they featured such "enlightened" programs as I Love Lucy and Amos 'n' Andy. My experiences (or lack thereof) were certainly parochial but hardly unique. And some people claim that those were the good old days, when life was simple and pure.

CHAPTER 2

Methods

Measurement issues have loomed large in the history of stereotype research, as in many other areas of psychology. In a scientific context, one cannot study something one cannot measure, and new measurement devices allow us to ask new questions and encourage new ways of looking at familiar problems. There is inevitably an intimate relationship between definition and measurement, and between both and theory. For example, those who believe that stereotypes are inaccurate will build this into their measurement. Those who believe that stereotypes are collective will try to discover the extent to which trait ascriptions are shared by a number of people. Therefore, measurement is hardly theoretically neutral and packs conceptual baggage. This chapter discusses the major strategies for measuring stereotypes and stereotyping.

DIRECT MEASURES

Free Responses

The easiest way to assess the content of stereotypes is simply to ask people what traits or features they associate with a given group, and such "free-response" methods make a certain amount of theoretical sense. If stereotypes consist of features associated with categories, then we can make use of a time-honored method of studying associations; strong associations will be given early and without much thought. So if a person readily mentions "violent" when asked to describe an African American, or "lazy" when asked what he or she thinks about professors, we may fairly assume that these traits are strongly associated with their groups. Free-response methodologies have been extensively used to study stereotypes and prejudice (e.g., Allen, 1996; Deaux, Winton, Crowley, & Lewis, 1985; Devine & Baker, 1991; Eagly & Mladinic, 1989; Esses, Haddock, & Zanna, 1994; Esses & Maio, 2002; Haddock & Zanna, 1998b; Jackson, Lewandowski, Ingram, & Hodge, 1997; Monteith & Spicer, 2000; Niemann, Jennings, Rozelle, Baxter, & Sullivan, 1994).

Free responses are not ideal measures. For one thing, such methods may not pick up essential content of stereotypes. For example, in a recent study using college students, most of the negative content concerning African Americans involved perceptions that they get more than they deserve and deny individual responsibility, rather than negative qualities per se (Monteith & Spicer, 2000). Sometimes we have associations that are quite strong and explicit, but that do not get reported for one reason or another. I happen to have a well-defined view that apples are harvested in the fall, but I doubt that it would occur to me to mention this if I were asked to describe apples. Similarly, a person may be quite sure that professors are smarter than average, yet may never think of that particular attribute when asked to describe professors. One might argue, of course, that the reason our perceiver does not readily mention the putative intelligence of professors is because this feature is not, for the perceiver, strongly associated with professors and hence not part of his or her stereotype. At least some of the content of our stereotypes is largely implicit and not readily available to our consciousness (Greenwald & Banaji, 1995). Many of us are not even aware of some of the associations we have, and yet these associations may guide our behavior. For instance, Sheila may not even be aware that she associates black males with violence (let alone report it on a questionnaire) until she meets a black male on a deserted street late at night.

Even if we assume that such measures are valid, however, there are several reasons why they have not been used more often. The first is the pragmatic difficulty of scoring and coding such responses. It would not be uncommon for each perceiver to generate 10 or more features per group, and if one had 100 perceivers generating responses for 5 groups, there would be 5,000 separate pieces of data to deal with. Unless the investigator is merely interested in getting a general impression of the content of a stereotype, something must be done to quantify the data and "massage" them for subsequent analysis. The usual procedure is simply to count how many or what proportion of perceivers use the same terms. This requires making time-consuming and sometimes difficult decisions. If one subject says that Asian Americans are "short" and another that they are "small," are they describing the same feature? What about two responses for blacks of "aggressive" and "violent"? What about "family-oriented" and "loves family" as descriptions of Hispanics? "Artistic" and "loves opera" for gay males? The issue is not merely one of word choice, but of whether the actual features cover the same range of events and behaviors. Probably almost all small people would be described as short and vice versa, so little is lost by combining these two descriptions as one. But "aggressive" and "violent" do not necessarily refer to the same behaviors. For instance, a violent woman hits and stabs, but an aggressive one yells and demands. So it might be best to keep these terms separate, because we are not sure whether a person who describes blacks as aggressive means "aggressive" in its more violent connotation or not.

A related problem is whether to eliminate low-frequency responses. If an individual says that professors like to play golf, this is probably idiosyncratic enough to be dropped. But what does one do with the person who says that gay males "flutter like birds in flight"? It is highly unlikely that another subject, even in a large sample, will say anything like this; yet, whether or not one endorses this description, it has an evocative quality that one might want to preserve in the data set.

Another practical problem is that such measures do not lend themselves easily to measures of intensity of association of features for individual perceivers. If we discover, as Niemann and colleagues (1994) did, that 188 of 259 subjects described Asian American males as intelligent or that 105 of 259 described African American males as athletic, we have some sense that these traits are collectively a part of their respective stereotypes. However, we probably are on thin ice in making assertions about whether this really represents strong associations for individual subjects. Does the fact that more people mention intelligence as a trait describing Asian American men than any other trait mean that this is the strongest feature in most (or even any) individuals' stereotypes? Perhaps, perhaps not.

Despite a range of theoretical and practical problems, free-response measures are important parts of our general arsenal. As we shall see, there are problems with all measures, and free responses do have their uses—especially in light of shortcomings in other methodologies.

Attribute Checking: The Katz–Braly Method

Some, but far from all, of the problems associated with free-response measures can be overcome by giving subjects a list of traits to check or rate. Such techniques save the time involved in coding free responses, and they lend themselves more easily to quantitative analysis. It is therefore no accident that such methods have been widely used.

The Basic Procedure

Chapter 1 has discussed the justly famous Katz and Braly (1933) studies. One legacy of these studies was the explicit linkage of prejudice and stereotypes; another was the suggestion that stereotypes are cultural products. But the most important legacy of all was the impact on measurement. Although it is not quite accurate to say that the Katz–Braly methodology dominated subsequent stereotype research, it is fair to say that it served as a model for at least a strong plurality of subsequent studies.

Not surprisingly for a pioneering study, Katz and Braly (1933) measured stereotypes in the most obvious and basic way. They gave subjects a list of 84 traits, and asked subjects to

> select those which seem to you typical of _____. Write as many of these words in the following space as you think are necessary to characterize these people adequately. If you do not find appropriate words on page one for all the typical _____ characteristics, you may add those which you think necessary for an adequate description. (p. 282)

Ten groups were rated in this way: Germans, Italians, Negroes, Irish, English, Jews, Americans, Chinese, Japanese, and Turks. After subjects performed this trait selection task for each of the 10 groups, they were asked to select the five traits "that seem to you the most typical of the race in question" (p. 282). Data were presented for the percentage of subjects who had checked each trait as one of the five most typical traits for each group. For some groups, there was strikingly high agreement on some traits. For example, 84% of the subjects thought Negroes were superstitious, 78% thought Germans were scientific-minded, and 79% thought Jews were shrewd. By contrast, there was less consensus for the Chinese stereotype; the most stereotypic trait was being superstitious, with only 35% of the subjects assigning that trait to the Chinese.

Uniformity

Given their interest in the cultural origins of stereotypes, Katz and Braly were also concerned to provide an index of how much people agreed on the characteristics that made up the stereotype. If each of 100 subjects checked five traits, there would be 500 "votes," and the authors simply calculated how many traits would be needed to capture 50% (250) of these votes. If the subjects had shown perfect agreement (i.e., each had chosen the same five traits), it would have taken two and a half traits to capture 250 votes (100 subjects picked Trait A, 100 picked Trait B, 100 picked Trait C, etc.). By contrast if the "votes" had been distributed perfectly randomly such that there was no consensus, it would take 42 traits to account for 250 votes. The actual index calculated for the 10 groups ranged from 4.6 for Negroes and 5.0 for Germans, to 12.0 for Chinese and 15.9 for Turks. Thus some groups seemed to have more consensually definite stereotypes than others, but there was at least some consensus for all of the groups.

On the other hand, for those who are committed to the notion that stereotypes must have some consensual representation, this is worth noting: Such uniformity does not imply that a majority of people endorse particular traits as being part of a stereotype. Given the 10 groups rated by Katz and Braly's subjects, only seven total traits were endorsed by over half of the subjects. These were "sportsmanlike" for English (53%); "superstitious" (84%) and "lazy" (75%) for Negroes; "shrewd" for Jews (79%); "artistic" for Italians (53%); and "scientific-minded" (78%) and "industrious" (65%) for Germans. In a subsequent repeat of this study by Gilbert (1951), only the two German traits were endorsed by a majority of subjects, and in a further version by Karlins, Coffman, and Walters (1969) five traits had at least 50% consensus: "materialistic" for Americans (67%), "loyal to family ties" for Chinese (50%), "conservative" for English (53%), "industrious" for Germans (59%), and "industrious" for Japanese (57%). A consensus need not mean a majority, of course. Still, in a glass half-full, half-empty situation, I might be inclined to stress the lack of consensual agreement on the stereotypes. In fairness to advocates of the consensus point of view, the percentage of traits selected was not the percentage of subjects who checked the traits, but the percentage who checked the trait as one of the 5 traits most representative of the group. Consensus would surely be higher if we counted the percentage of subjects who checked the trait in the initial phase, but those data were not presented by Katz and Braly.

Limitations

Some immediate points need to be made about such a procedure. First, it is simple; indeed, it is hard to imagine a way of getting stereotype information that is less taxing to subjects, or that deviates less from the common sense that stereotypes are traits "attached to" groups. It is probably less intrusive even than free responses, because subjects do not even have to think up their own associations. However, this very simplicity may hide problems.

WHAT ARE SUBJECTS REPORTING?

One criticism of the Katz–Braly procedure is that it is quite reactive (Ehrlich & Rinehart, 1965). Subjects are virtually forced to generate stereotypes even if they do not hold them strongly. Imagine, for instance, that Louise does not have any particular views about the Turks or the Irish. Now she faces a piece of paper and must check some traits to go with these groups. She could, of course, grumble and resist doing the task, as several of Eysenck and Crown's (1948) and Gilbert's (1951) subjects did. But if we can assume that she wants to be a "good" subject, she will want to generate something—and, having no useful stereotype of her own to draw on, she might be tempted to rely on hearsay or knowledge about what others think. Thus the traits she reports for Turks are not those she personally believes "go with" Turks, but those that seem culturally right. Obviously, if a large number of subjects do this sort of thing, data suggesting uniformity and agreement among subjects is an artifact of subjects' reporting what they think the cultural stereotype is (even if they are in error). It is probably not productive to think deeply about the epistemology of using consensus measures of consensus estimates as a worthy measure of stereotypes.

Devine and Elliot (1995) have presented data suggesting that, at least for African American stereotypes, there is considerable divergence between what college students endorse as personal beliefs and those they think represent widely held cultural stereotypes; this was particularly true for those low in prejudice. For example, low-prejudice people thought that traits such as being unreliable, lazy, athletic, rhythmic, low in intelligence, poor, criminal, hostile, uneducated, and sexually perverse were part of the cultural stereotype. However, when they were asked for their own beliefs about whether such traits described blacks, these same traits were checked by only 18% of the low-prejudice subjects but 55% of the high-prejudice subjects. The traits ascribed by the low-prejudice subjects as most characteristic were being musical, athletic, sensitive, loyal to family, artistic, honest, intelligent, kind, sportsmanlike, and straightforward. We might question whether the low-prejudice subjects were reporting their real beliefs as opposed to what they think they should believe, and whether college students have clear insight into what most Americans believe about blacks, but these data still suggest that such checklist measures may assess what people think stereotypes are rather than their own beliefs.

CHOICE OF STIMULI

One important way in which the Katz–Braly method differs from free-response procedures is that in the former, the investigator chooses the stimuli that will be used. Obviously, with this technique, one can only find stereotypes for the stimuli chosen. We would be likely to find no interesting stereotypes of racial groups if we asked subjects to check whether traits such as "happy," "sometimes sick," or "has a father" were used. In practice, of course, investigators are not so stupid as to employ a random selection of traits. Through either pretesting or their own a priori judgments about what traits are part of the general stereotype of the groups in question, traits are generally used that are likely to show differences. However, the point still remains that important aspects of the stereotype might be missed simply because subjects were not asked to make judgments about these features.

This is especially important when comparisons are made over time. The Katz–

Braly study was originally done at Princeton in the early 1930s, and it was repeated with the same trait checklist on Princeton students in the early 1950s (Gilbert, 1951), and in the middle 1960s (Karlins et al., 1969). In some respects, the stereotypes diminished over time. However, as Devine and Elliot (1995) have pointed out, the fact that later Princeton samples showed less consensus on the traits selected for various groups may say more about changes in the content of stereotypes than about a lowering of tendencies to stereotype. For example, traits such as "violent" and "athletic" (which are important parts of the contemporary stereotype of blacks) did not appear as part of the Katz–Braly list.

Ehrlich and Rinehart (1965) compared the Katz–Braly checklist format with a free-response format in which subjects were asked to provide their own "words, adjectives, or traits" to describe the target group. They found that there was much less consensus in the free-response than in the checklist format, and that there was relatively little overlap between the traits most frequently checked and those provided in free responses. However, it is not entirely clear what one should make of these results. One possibility is, of course, that the checklist format forces people to invent stereotypes on the spot for the purposes of filling out the questionnaire; in that case, such measurement would probably overestimate the extent of stereotyping in the general population, and the stereotypes would have little reality beyond the occasion of measurement. But there are other, equally plausible explanations for the discrepant results. Subjects in the free-response format conditions may have been unable to think of all the traits they ordinarily use for a particular group; we ought not to assume that people have well-articulated stereotypes ready for spewing out to inquisitive experimenters. Furthermore, the fact of little overlap between the measurement conditions may say more about the Katz–Braly traits and the changing of stereotypes over time than about measurement. It is also worth pointing out that the Ehrlich–Rinehart subjects provided a good many physical descriptions (e.g., "dark-skinned," "small") and sociological phrases (e.g., "oppressed," "poor") in their free responses that were not present in the Katz–Braly list.

ARE SUCH STEREOTYPES IMPORTANT TO SUBJECTS?

At a more basic level, the Katz–Braly method does not allow us to determine how important these stereotypes are to individuals or whether they are spontaneously used in everyday life. It is quite possible, for example, that a person may believe that Turks are cruel (as did the original Katz–Braly subjects), but may never think of accessing that trait when confronting a Turk for the first time. Katz and Braly assumed that the traits their subjects reported were accessible and part of active stereotypes, but when we stop and think about it, we all have traits that we can ascribe to groups but rarely access. If you asked me whether bananas were good sources of potassium, I would readily agree—but it hardly follows that when I eat a banana, I have deep thoughts about potassium levels.

CONSENSUS VERSUS INDIVIDUAL STEREOTYPES

Another problem with the Katz–Braly procedure is that it severely limits opportunities for sensitive analysis, particularly of stereotypes held by individuals. Their measure of stereotyping is inherently based on consensus within a group. To know that

Joe or Maria thinks that Jews are mercenary, shrewd, clannish, happy, and intelligent counts for nothing at the Joe-and-Maria level, because those traits are part of a stereotype only if others agree with them. Joe may fervently believe that Jews are greedy and athletic, but if others don't agree with him, then he doesn't have a stereotype according to the Katz–Braly method—despite the fact these beliefs may well guide his attitudes and behaviors toward Jews. Katz and Braly were simply not interested in Joe or Maria, except as a contributor of five votes to each stereotype; they regarded stereotypes as, like attitudes and prejudice, internal representations of cultural beliefs. This view does not, as we will see, preclude concern with individual differences; for example, one could easily imagine that Joe has learned his cultural lessons about what Jews "are like" better than has Maria, and simply count the number of consensually defined stereotype traits he endorses (e.g., Eysenck & Crown, 1948). Nonetheless, this procedure does not provide for an easily quantified measure of such differences.

We should also be wary of assuming that consensus is an important aspect of stereotypes. It is, after all, something of an empirical question as to which type of stereotype is most important. In one study, Stangor, Sullivan, and Ford (1991) found that measures of individual stereotypes predicted prejudice better than did consensus measures of stereotypes (see Chapter 8 for further discussion). However, it is easy to imagine situations where the consensual nature of stereotypes might be more predictive than individual measures. The possibility of assessing consensus ought to remain a live option, but we need to use measures that are less constrained by the assumption that beliefs are only stereotypes if others agree.

Attribute Rating

Some of the limitations of the Katz–Braly method can easily be finessed through slightly more sophisticated measurement. For example, although asking subjects to select traits from a list is simple enough for subjects, it is not that much more difficult for them to actually rate the extent to which each trait applies to each group. Various measures have built on this procedure.

Scale Ratings

Perhaps the most commonly used measure of stereotypes is a simple rating of the extent to which a group "processes" a particular feature. So, for example, we might ask, "How likely is it that women are assertive?" Alternatively, we could ask how typical assertiveness is of women. There are several advantages of such measures. The most important is that they provide a number that can be easily analyzed statistically and used in a number of comparisons. Pragmatically, such judgments are easy for research participants to make. Theoretically, such measures seem to probe fairly directly the associations between groups and features that are the hallmarks of stereotypes.

Yet there are familiar problems. For one thing, such measures do not readily discriminate stereotypic from universal ascriptions. I would rate it more likely that males have five toes on each foot than that they are assertive, even though the latter is certainly more a part of my gender stereotype. A more important problem, perhaps, is that we cannot be exactly sure how people are making these judgments. Possibly subjects use some sort of salience criterion—what most easily springs to mind—as a rough guide to likelihood. Could they be rating the assertiveness of the average or prototypic male? They might use a sort of exemplar availability heuristic: If they can easily think of several assertive males, they rate males as being likely to be assertive. Or perhaps they are making an implicit probability judgment: "I think 60% of males are assertive, and therefore I will rate males as 5 points assertive on a 7-point scale." In that case, why not ask directly what percentage of males are assertive? There is no reason to believe that these possibilities are at odds with one another or would produce quite different results. Still, it is mildly discomforting to realize that we use a measure with a lack of sophisticated knowledge about what it means.

The Stereotype Differential Extension

Although there is a whole family of such methods that differ in many small and probably unimportant ways, I focus here on the stereotype differential technique (Gardner, 1973), which requires subjects to rate groups on various semantic differential or trait-type scales. For example, subjects might be asked to rate Jews on the scale "shrewd—not shrewd" or "clannish—not clannish." Then the mean rating across subjects is calculated for each scale for each group. Those ratings that depart from the midpoint of the scale (4) to a statistically significant degree (via a t-test) are assumed to be part of the stereotype, and as a matter of convenience some arbitrary number (typically 10) of traits that have the highest polarizations (in terms of their t-values) are used to define the stereotype.

The stereotype differential can be thought of as simply an elaboration of the Katz–Braly technique: Traits that are extreme and have the broadest consensus (as measured by the t-test)[1] are defined as part of the stereotype. Not surprisingly, the two techniques tend to identify the same stereotype traits for a given group. For example, one group of Filipino students rated nine different nationalities on 110 traits, and another group used the Katz–Braly method; the 10 most stereotypic traits were calculated using both procedures. There was 80% agreement between methods for Americans, 70% for Russians, and so forth, with an overall mean across the nine groups of 47% (Gardner, Kirby, Gorospe, & Villamin, 1972).

It is also easy to derive an individual-difference measure from this stereotype differential measure once the cultural (or at least consensual) stereotype has been identified. Given the 10 or so traits that have been assigned to the stereotype by consensus, the individual's stereotype score might be the mean of his or her ratings on those stereotypic traits. Because this method defines stereotypes in terms of consensus, individuals who subscribe more strongly to the cultural stereotype have stronger stereotypes.

Brigham's Individual-Difference Measure

It makes a certain amount of sense to assume that stereotypes are cultural products and thus ought to be defined in terms of consensus. However, other researchers have been reluctant to make this assumption and have developed measures of stereotypes, defined in terms of individual endorsements. Often generalizations are measured in terms of percentage estimates. So people may rate the percentage of people in a group who have a particular trait. Presumably the person who thinks that 80% of all Japanese are industrious has a stronger group–trait association than one who says that only 40% of Japanese are industrious. But there are also problems with the view. As a counterexample, I happen to believe that 100% of all professors have hearts and that only 60% are politically liberal. Does that mean that "heartness" is more strongly associated with my stereotype than political orientation? That seems quite odd, especially when you consider that I would never mention the heart feature if asked to describe professors; nor, I suspect, does it play any real role in my behavior toward my colleagues, despite my occasional charges of their heartlessness.

UNJUSTIFIED GENERALIZATION

Brigham (1971a) suggested that stereotypes are generalizations, but that they can be distinguished from other generalizations in part on the basis of how justified they seem to an observer. For Brigham, the falseness of the generalization rather than its extremity per se is crucial. After all, 100% of Jews have eyes, but we would normally not count this extreme generalization as a part of the Jewish stereotype. If one were to hear someone say that all Jews are wealthy, that 80% of blacks are lazy, that 95% of professors are politically liberal, or that 90% of all newspapers are out to get conservative political candidates, one does not need to do empirical research to know that these generalizations are likely to be false and therefore stereotypes by this criterion.

High Percentages. Thus Brigham argued that an individual's stereotypes consist of any traits he or she rates as belonging to a high percentage (Brigham informally suggested 80%) of a given group, on the assumption that few if any groups have such uniformity and that this judgment must thereby be false. Another possibility is that a stereotype can be identified when a person ascribes more of some trait to one group than to another group, even though the two groups are putatively similar. For example, since there is no reason to believe that women are more or less smart than men, a person who says that men are smarter would, by this definition, be reporting a stereotype.

The Out-of-Range Criterion. There are indirect ways of "sneaking up" on the accuracy issue. For example, Brigham (1973) used whether a given ascription was outside the limits subjects had judged as permissible as a criterion. For each trait, subjects were asked not only to indicate the percentage of people in a group who possessed the trait, but also the minimum and maximum percentages they would consider reasonable or justifiable for someone else to have indicated. Consider this example: Janice might say that 60% of professors are liberal, but that ratings as low as 40% or as high as 70% would be reasonable. Thus, if the average maximum reasonable percentage across people for this trait was 70%, Sejal (who has indicated that 75% of professors are liberal) would be said to have a stereotype. In any case, stereotypes are still defined in terms of extremity of rating, although a different criterion of extremity is used.

Such extremity–falseness measures not only emphasize inaccuracy, but they focus on individual as opposed to consensual indices. Note how far this measure departs from measures built on the notion of consensus. Whereas the Katz and Braly method requires that stereotype traits be part of a general "picture," the Brigham measure requires that the trait *deviate* from this generally held idea.

It would actually be hard to convert this measure to a consensus measure, since most people would presumably give judgments that fall within the range of reasonable bounds. However, such a measure does facilitate the identification of individual differences among perceivers in the extent to which they have stereotypes. It is easy to imagine a racist who is willing to assert that all or almost all blacks are lazy, superstitious, and so forth, and whose judgments would be outside culturally defined reasonable boundaries. It is also easy to imagine a person whose judgments are so governed by the culture that all his or her judgments about other groups are moderate and well within reasonable bounds. It is also not clear how we would treat a person whose estimates are too low. Imagine a woman who says that only 1% of black males have criminal records, or that only 5% of women are assertive. She may feel justified in her stereotype, yet her judgments are surely inaccurate and outside reasonable boundaries.

PROBLEMS WITH EXTREMITY AND INACCURACY MEASURES

One problem with Brigham-type measures that rely on extremity is that they are too restrictive. I suspect that for most white Americans, crime-proneness, drug use, and being on welfare are part of the stereotype about black Americans. Clearly, however, the majority of blacks are not criminals, do not use drugs, and are not on welfare. Imagine that the percentage of blacks who actively use drugs is 2%, and that we ask a man who holds a stereotype of blacks as drug users what percentage of blacks he estimates use drugs. Suppose he indicates 30%. Now given the underlying logic of the Brigham emphasis on overgeneralization or falseness, this would surely count as a stereotype. However, it would not count as a part of a stereotype if people agreed that a range of 10%–40% would be reasonable, even though the consensual range itself is inaccurate.

The problem is not limited to examples with relatively low percentage estimates. Take the case of stereotypes presumably held by Germans about Jews during the 1930s. Suppose Horst said that 75% of Jews were materialistic, that on average Germans reported that 85% of Jews were materialistic, and that an appropriate range would have been 80%–95%. Accordingly, Horst would not have had a stereotype that Jews were materialistic; using the out-of-range criterion, we might even argue that he saw them as stereotypically nonmaterialistic. This doesn't make sense. Similarly, according to these criteria, an American male in 1890 who said that women were illogical would not have had a stereotype, because most of his countrymen would have agreed with him. We could, of course, retreat to the high ground and simply say that, regardless of public opinion, these stereotypes were inaccurate then as now.

However, it is not always clear that inaccuracy works well as a criterion of stereotypic traits. Suppose Micah reports that he thinks a lot of black women have illegitimate babies. I ask him to tell me what percentage of black children was born last year to single mothers. He thinks for a bit and announces 40% as his best estimate (and looks a little guilty for having said this). Now, in fact, the correct estimate is over 60%, so Micah has actually underestimated the prevalence of this stereotypic feature. According to any reasonable criterion of overgeneralization or inaccuracy, we cannot count this as a part of his black stereotype. Yet I think common sense suggests otherwise. Is common sense wrong? Or is there a way that we can include this as a part of a stereotype? Clearly, one thing that might count is that Micah assumes (correctly, as it turns out) that a larger percentage of black children than white children are born to single mothers. Thus this feature, for better or worse, discriminates blacks from whites in his mind.

Stereotypes as Differentiating Features

DISCRIMINATING FEATURES

McCauley and Stitt (1978) have argued that stereotypes ought to be defined in terms of discriminating features. They have, along with Brigham, argued that consensus on stereotypes is relatively unimportant, or at least is not a defining feature. Unlike Brigham, however, they are less concerned with accuracy than with whether perceivers see traits as differentiating one group from another. In other words, stereotypes are implicit comparative judgments. So Amanda, who claims that only 30% of professors are lazy, would be counted as having a stereotype of professors, provided she is willing to assert that professors are lazier than lawyers. There could be many ways to quantify this, but the easiest is to take a ratio of percentage of professors who are seen to be lazy, compared to the percentage of lawyers who are.[2] So if she persisted in her claim that 30% of professors are lazy but that only 15% of lawyers were lazy, the resultant ratio of 2.00 would indicate a laziness stereotype for professors relative to lawyers. McCauley and Stitt make it clear that ratios less than 1.00 also count as stereotypic. For example, if a perceiver says that 30% of blacks are athletic and only 10% of whites are, then we can say either that blacks are perceived as athletic or that whites are viewed as unathletic; in other words, ratios of 3.00 and 0.33 are both evidence of stereotypes. In practice, one can simply invert ratios lower than 1.00 to make sure that stereotype scores are all greater than 1.00. One interesting implication of this approach is that stereotypes may be changed either by lowering the perceived percentage of people in the target group or by raising the perceived percentage in the comparison group (Karasawa, 1998).

Consensus Measures. If ratios are averaged over subjects, a group or consensus measure could be achieved through normal statistical tests of whether a given mean ratio for the entire sample or group differs from 1.00. Individual measures of stereotyping could then be achieved in any number of ways. For example, we might count the number of traits each individual has endorsed that have ratios significantly different from 1.00. Or we could simply average the ratios (presumably inverted for ratios less than 1.00) across all traits for each subject. For those who insist that a stereotype must reflect some cultural consensus, we could get the mean judgment for each person for all traits that have high ratios for a given group. This would also have the advantage of allowing us to see whether the individual's ratio is higher or lower than the consensus. So, for example, let us suppose we are investigating stereotypes of lawyers, and for all our participants we find that of 25 traits rated, 12 have ratios that are significantly greater than 1. We then define those 12 traits as the stereotype of lawyers. Now we can find the ratio for any given subject for those 12 traits. Peter's mean ratio for those 12 traits is 1.50, and Tang's is 1.10. Thus Peter's stereotype of lawyers is stronger than Tang's.

Accuracy. Ratio measures have the distinct advantage that for some features one can directly compare stereotype ratios with ratios based on the actual distribution of characteristics in the population, so as to get a measure of accuracy. This is extremely difficult with trait ascription measures, because it is often hard to know how much of a trait an individual (let alone a group) possesses. What sense does it make to ask whether a person's rating of professors as 6.0 smart on a 7-point scale is accurate? Ratio measures do not have this problem. For example, Martin's (1987) subjects reported that about twice as many males as females were dominant (1.98 ratio), and this compared with a ratio of 1.58 of males to females who actually checked "dominant" as characteristic of them. This is a case where subjects actually exaggerated a real difference. Other studies have found "underexaggeration." For example, McCauley and Stitt (1978) found that college students believed blacks to be about twice as likely as Americans in general to be on welfare, but that the 1975 U.S. Census statistics showed the real ratio to be 4.6. Here subjects clearly minimized rather than exaggerated a real difference. In either case, for certain sorts of data, such measures allow us to readily determine the accuracy of stereotypes.

PROBLEMS WITH DIFFERENTIAL MEASURES

A case can be made that such differential ascription measures capture the essence of stereotypes better than most others. Unfortunately (and this may be getting repetitive), there are problems with such measures.

Do High Ratios Indicate Stereotypes? Not always. For example, I happen to believe (correctly) that women are much more likely than men to develop breast cancer, yet this association is hardly a major, or even a minor, part of my gender stereotype. This is part of a more general problem to which I have alluded from time to time: However we measure associations between groups and various features, there are some that are not part of the active stereotype, at least most of the time.

The Nature of Comparisons. People do make comparative judgments all the time, but it may not always be clear what kinds of comparisons are being made and how formally people do this. Suppose Darlene says that professors are liberal, and by this she means that they are more liberal than the average person (or some relevant comparison group). Is it likely that she has actually done a calculation of any sort to arrive at this judgment? Although this is not impossible, I suspect that most of us do not find ourselves performing this sort of ciphering much, if at all. In fairness, it may be sufficient that such judgments are reasonably well ordered and calibrated, such that Darlene has some fairly articulated notion that professors are more liberal than average and bankers more conservative. The judgments she produces when a psychologist asks her for exact numbers may then simply be attempts to quantify these fairly informal kinds of judgments.

A related, more empirical issue is whether comparisons really add much to the predictive power of judgments. A given perceiver thinks that 70% of professors are liberal and that 10% of bankers are. Given that the percentage of people in general who are judged to be liberal is presumably the same (say, 30%) for both judgments, what do we gain by turning the 70% into a ratio of 2.33 and 10% into a ratio of 0.33? In fact, empirical studies have shown that simple percentage judgments are generally highly correlated with ratio measures (e.g., Stephan et al., 1993), and that ratio measures provide little predictive power over and above simple percentage trait judgments for groups (Krueger, 1996b).

Comparison Groups. There is a related can of worms: What should be the comparison group? If Juanita compares professors to lawyers, professors may seem stereotypically lazy, but if she compares professors to unemployed laborers (for whom she estimates 75% are lazy), then professors are stereotypically unlazy. Conversely, the 15% of lawyers who are lazy might compare favorably with professors but unfavorably with doctors (say, 5%). Does this mean that all stereotypes are relative? We will see in later chapters that there are good reasons for accepting this idea, much as it complicates both theory and measurement.

In practice, McCauley and Stitt (1978) performed an end run around this issue by making the comparison group "people in general" or "Americans in general." However, my hunch is that when people make comparative judgments, they often have better-defined groups in mind. So when a male blue-collar worker asserts that those guys in management are "lazy SOBs," he may basically mean that a smaller percentage of managers than of his companions on the loading dock work hard. He may be willing to agree that both groups work harder than professors or actors. Furthermore, it is not clear what to make of judgments about percentages of people in general who have traits. Does it make sense to ask a person—say, a college student who has rarely left home, let alone traveled throughout the world—to estimate what perception of "people in general" have particular traits? If we make the comparison group more familiar (say, Americans, or Texans, or fellow students at the university), we may have contextualized the stereotype in strange ways. It is unclear whether a student who thinks that conservative Christians on his or her campus are more narrow-minded than the average student also thinks that conservative Christians are generally more narrow-minded than other Americans, let alone people in general.

In some cases, of course, these issues do not arise. When one assesses stereotypes of black Americans, the obvious and perhaps only meaningful comparison group (for whites, at least) would be white Americans. Similarly, the comparison group for blue-collar workers might be white-collar workers, and for people living in poverty the relevant comparison group might be middle-class or upper-class people. For males, the only relevant comparison is women. It will be obvious to some readers (but it still bears pointing out) that in situations where there are only two groups involved (e.g., blacks and whites, men and women), logically (but not necessarily empirically in people's judgments) the ratios of one group to the other and of each group to people in general provide the same information. For example, suppose a subject says that 50% of blacks are lazy, and that 25% of whites are. This leads to a black–white ratio of 2.0 for this trait. One could, of course also get data on the percentage of people in general who are lazy. A subject who knows something about the percentages of whites (roughly 80%) and blacks (roughly 12%) in the United States, and who has the ability to do quick calculations, might estimate that 0.26 of the population of blacks and whites in general is lazy. Thus the lazy ratio of blacks to people in general is 1.92 and for whites to people in general is 0.96. However, the ratio of blacks to whites is still 2.0. This is important, because subjects may not be (indeed, probably are not) precise in these sorts of calculations.

Reverse Stereotypes

Normally, we think of documenting stereotypes by having people indicate how strongly features are associated with a particular group. However, if these associations are strong, then people also ought to have a sense of what groups go with a particular trait or constellation of traits. A technique pioneered by Centers (1951) did exactly that. Subjects were presented with the Katz–Braly traits and asked which group was characterized by them. Given that the Katz–Braly subjects thought that Negroes were superstitious, would subjects think that superstitious people were likely to be Negroes? The data suggested that they were, and that in fact the traits were quite diagnostic of group membership. In a more recent version, Gardner, Kirby, and Finlay (1973) found that traits consensually assigned to groups were quite diagnostic of group membership. In conceptually similar research, Hassin and Trope (2000) found not only that people have some consensus on traits that "go with" particular photographs, but that they also tend to agree on what photos fit particular traits.

As I argue in Chapter 3, group–feature and feature–group relationships are often highly asymmetrical. The probability that an Asian male is good at math is generally not the same as the probability that someone good at math is an Asian male. Therefore, these techniques of reverse stereotyping must be used with caution. But when used judiciously, they can act as a kind of validation of existing stereotypes.

Matched-Stimuli Techniques

Another way of assessing stereotypes on various adjectives is to have subjects rate stimuli that are identical except for the category of the stimulus person. This technique is not always thought of as a way to measure stereotypes, because it is used so frequently in studies involving evaluation or evaluatively tinged discrimination. For example, in an often-cited study by Goldberg (1968), subjects were asked to rate identical essays ostensibly written by a man or a woman, and the evaluations were higher in some cases for the male. As another example, research (Bodenhausen, 1988; Bodenhausen & Lichtenstein, 1987) has shown that the same criminal case is evaluated differently when the defendant's ethnicity changes. Although such studies are normally designed to get at explicit bias and discrimination, they also provide a means to examine trait attributions as a function of group membership.

The advantage of using this strategy is that subjects may respond fairly naturally, without consciously reflecting that they are being tested for their stereotypes. Typically, each person reads only a single description, and variables such as age and gender are natural parts of that description. So the person who reads the male description may provide male-biased ratings without realizing that he or she is doing so. On the other hand, much of this advantage is lost with other designations. Whereas gender may seem a natural part of a description, other group designations (such as sexual preference, history of mental illness, and weight) are more striking, and people may deliberately respond to them despite our best efforts at semicamouflage. In that case, there may be no real advantage in having them rate a group designation plus description as opposed to a mere group designation, because the latter is so salient. Another problem is that group designation is likely to interact with the description itself. Male–female differences found in the context of a description of a business luncheon may be quite different from gender differences in the context of a family outing.

Evaluative Measures

Stereotypes are usually defined as beliefs, and in the division of labor we customarily use, this means that they must be devoid of affect. However, it is obvious that beliefs of all sorts have affective and emotional consequences. A belief that small children are messy and germ-ridden would not normally encourage someone to approach and play with such a creature, but the belief that professors are kind and considerate would, under appropriate circumstances, encourage cosier behavior.

Generally, the goal of such evaluative measurement is to get some general evaluation of particular groups by individuals or groups of subjects. Perhaps the easiest, but crudest, measure is simply to count the number of positive and negative traits that a person checks for each group (Eysenck & Crown, 1948). A more refined measure was used by Eagly and Mladinic (1989). They asked people to generate traits that they thought described women, men, Republicans, and Democrats. For each trait so generated, respondents were asked to indicate what percentage of people in that group fit the trait, and this was taken as a measure of the strength of association between the group and the feature. They also indicated how positive or negative each trait was. The evaluative index was calculated as the sum of the percentage measure times the evaluative measure across all traits. Thus a person who thought that a large percentage of Republicans were conservative, and that being conservative was a positive feature, would have a more positive stereotype about that group than someone who felt that fewer Republicans were conservative or that being conservative was negative. This same kind of index was created for traits provided by the experimenter. Both indices predicted independently derived attitudes toward the groups. That is, subjects whose stereotypes were relatively positive toward women also had favorable attitudes toward women. Similar measures used by Haddock, Zanna, and Esses (1993, 1994b) have shown that the affective nature of stereotypes is important in predicting prejudice and in accounting for various mood effects on use of stereotypes (see Chapter 4).

Variability

Usually when we think of stereotypes, we think in terms of judgments about a group of people (e.g., this group is more or less intelligent or wealthy than that group). In that sense, stereotypes refer to central tendencies or means of a group for some feature. However, we also recognize that some groups are more variable than others. For example, I have a stereotype that professional football linemen are large, and while I recognize that they are not all exactly the same size, I also am quite aware that they are more alike in size than a group of businessmen. I believe that psychology professors are less variable with regard to intelligence, but more variable with regard to physical size, than college swimmers. People do have notions about both central tendencies and variability of groups on various properties (Ford & Stangor, 1992).

This turns out to be an important aspect of stereotyping. As we shall see in Chapters 3 and 7, when we think a group is homogeneous, we are more likely to infer group properties from single individuals and more likely to see group members as fitting our stereotypes of the group. Thus our sense of group homogeneity plays a large role in the extent to which we are able to judge individuals apart from their groups.

Chapter 7 considers measures of variability in some detail. However, for present purposes, we may note that several such measures have been used. We have already examined one—namely, percentage measures. Obviously, a person who says that 40% of a group is intelligent is ascribing less homogeneity than someone who says that 80% of the group has that feature. Another direct measure is simply to ask subjects how similar people in a group are (e.g., Park & Rothbart, 1982). More complicated measures ask subjects to assign ranges, so that they indicate where the highest and lowest members of the group fall (Simon & Brown, 1987). Alternatively, we can ask people to generate a distribution across a trait scale (e.g., Judd & Park, 1988; Linville, Fischer, & Salovey, 1989; in other words, they might be asked what percentage of a group of professors is very intelligent, moderately intelligent, moderately unintelligent, and so on. As it turns out (see Chapter 7), these measures are related, albeit far from perfectly. In the meantime, while we continue to focus on stereotypes in terms of the central tendencies of groups for features, we should remember that at times perceived variability of the group is also important.

Comparison of Measures

There have been surprisingly few attempts to compare different ways of measuring stereotypes. One reason is that in the absence of definite criteria for what stereotypes ought to be, such comparisons seem a rather odd exercise: Better in what sense? One strategy has been to see which measures of stereotypes best correlate with other variables that a theory identifies as important predictors.

PREDICTIONS OF PREJUDICE

Perhaps the most widely used external measure has been prejudice, since almost all relevant theories suggest that stereotypes drive prejudice to some extent. So, for example, Brigham (1973) showed that out-of-range percentage estimates for traits predicted prejudice against blacks for undereducated respondents, and several studies (e.g., Haddock, Zanna, & Esses, 1994a; Stangor et al., 1991) showed that free-response measures predicted prejudice reasonably well.

So we know that individual stereotype measures predict prejudice, but that still doesn't tell us which stereotype measures are the best predictors. Several studies have tried to determine this. Eagly and Steffen (1988) reported that trait measures and percentage measures predicted similarly. A study by Gardner, Lalonde, Nero, and Young (1988) did compare different measurements of stereotypes of French Canadians. Basically, the stereotype differential measure correlated moderately highly (.63) with the diagnostic ratio, and neither of these measures correlated significantly with the Brigham unjustified-generalization measure. In a subsequent factor analysis involving these measures and various attitude and knowledge scales related to French Canadians, four factors emerged. The first factor represented knowledge about French Canadians, and none of the stereotype measures loaded substantially on this factor. A second factor was defined by attitudes toward French Canadians and the diagnostic ratio suggesting that those who were inclined to see French Canadians as different from people in general predicted more negative attitudes toward them. A third factor was interpreted as a social desirability factor, and both unjustified generalizations and diagnostic ratio measures loaded moderately highly on this factor.[3] Finally, a fourth factor was defined by the unjustified-generalization and stereotype differential measures and was defined as a consensual stereotype factor. Thus, in this study, prejudice was best predicted by a diagnostic ratio measure.

Biernat and Crandall (1994) obtained several stereotype measures from University of Michigan students toward three groups: students in a residential college, football players, and sorority women. These stereotypes were measured at both the beginning and the end of the freshman year. One measure of stereotypes was a simple set of trait ratings, and another was a modified diagnostic ratio (actually the difference between percentages of students in the group that had the trait minus students in general that had the trait). Subjects were also given scores based on how far their trait ratings differed from the consensus of all subjects. The students were asked how much they liked members of these groups and how much contact they had with them. The trait ratings and diagnostic ratio measures correlated reasonably highly with one another, but the trait ratings predicted liking measures (a crude measure of prejudice) better than the modified diagnostic ratio measure did. The departure-from-consensus measure did not predict liking or contact well.

TYPICALITY RATINGS

Another strategy in evaluating the adequacy of stereotype measures is to privilege one measure of stereotyping and then to see which other measures best predict it. Krueger (1996b) took a measure of typicality of the trait for the group as his standard measure and then investigated the predictive power of various percentage measures. In this study, samples of American and Italian students rated Americans, Italians, Germans, and English. Generally, the trait typicality ratings were well predicted by percentage trait attributions ($r = .68$), and the simple trait percentage measure outperformed various kinds of diagnostic measures (e.g., percentage of group members with the trait compared to percentage of the world population with the trait). For example, when Americans rated Italians, the mean correlation (across subjects) of trait percentages with typicality was .76, and the correlation of the ratio with typicality was .41. However, this latter correlation was reduced to essentially 0 when the general trait percentage measure was partialed out. Similar results have been found with assessment of gender stereotypes by Italian and American students: simple percentage measures predict typicality better than does a diagnostic ratio (Krueger, Hasman, Acevedo, & Villano, 2003). It might be noted, however, that typicality ratings are not the gold standard of stereotype measures and may, in any event, simply be another way of asking what percentage of a group has a particular feature.

SUMMARY

The best that can be said for this research is that no measure of stereotyping has consistently been found to outperform others in predictive power. This should not be surprising. As I have tried to emphasize, each of the measures of stereotyping emphasizes certain assumptions and theories about stereotypes. Stereotypes are not a single thing with a Platonic essence waiting to be molested by some pure and elegant new method. They are many things. Consider apples. Their color may be crucial to an interior decorator who wants to create an attractive display for a table, their size to a mother who believes her children should eat one with lunch, their taste to cooks, their genetic makeup to apple growers, and their chemical composition to those who have to worry about when to harvest them. An apple is thus many things (linked together in complex ways, to be sure), and it makes little sense to talk about apples as if one of these perspectives has some privileged status. Sometime an apple is not an apple is not an apple.

Similarly, we need not imagine that stereotypes have some central, essential quality. We define them and measure them as suits our particular research goals. A social psychologist who is interested in the effects of the mass media on stereotypes may well want to employ a measure that emphasizes the consensual nature of stereotypes. In predicting prejudice measures that focus on individual differences in stereotypes would be most appropriate. Another social scientist may be interested in the extent to which stereotypes help to differentiate one's self from undesirable groups, and for this scientist measures that emphasize differentiating traits may be more appropriate. Therefore it is unlikely that any one measure is the best to use in all circumstances. That does not mean we have to be agnostic about the effectiveness of the various measures; nor do we have carte blanche to measure stereotypes in any old way. The investigator who measured them in terms of the number of times a group's name appeared in a given newspaper in 1987 would be met by derision from his professional colleagues and would probably discover that his putative measure of stereotyping predicts nothing of any real interest. We need more research on the interrelationships among measures of stereotypes in order to gain a clearer understanding of the complex nature of stereotypes, but in so doing we are not likely to discover that one measure is best for all research projects.

Strength of Stereotypes

There is one important question about stereotypes that cannot easily be answered by any of the measurement strategies we have been considering: How can we measure how strong the stereotype of a given group is? That may seem a strange issue at this point; after all, isn't that what we've been discussing for several pages? Actually, it isn't. We have been considering how closely features are tied to traits, which is not the same thing at all. Knowing that Adi thinks that males are assertive doesn't tell us anything about whether she has a stronger stereotype of males or females, or of males or lawyers.

This question is important for a number of comparison issues. We may, for example, want to know whether people have stronger stereotypes of lawyers than of doctors. Or perhaps we want to know whether males have stronger stereotypes of females than females do. Maybe we are concerned with whether stereotypes of Hispanics are stronger or weaker now than 20 years ago. We can, of course, potentially answer each of those questions for individual features, but not for the stereotype as a whole. It will not do just to assume that groups with a good many features strongly attached to them have strong stereotypes. For one thing, the success of that technique depends heavily on our having a complete (or nearly so) list of all the relevant stereotype traits—hard to get. And we have to find a way to "weed out" the strong nuisance associations (e.g., women have 10 fingers). Furthermore, it is not clear whether the stereotype of a group with few but strongly attached features has a stronger stereotype than one with more but less securely associated ones.

Another way to think about strength of stereotypes is in terms of the glue that holds them together. Intuitively, a stereotype in which the various features are interrelated in complex ways, and for which there are strong theoretical justifications for group–feature and feature–feature relationships, is stronger than one in which feature–group relationships are merely associations with no special rhyme or reason. Furthermore, we might expect such stereotypes to differ in how they relate to experience and cultural explanations. We might also examine how easy it is to change stereotype features as a whole. I should imagine that devout racists, in the face of evidence inconsistent with their stereotypes, may waver for a feature or two but still strongly resist any sort of general change.

INDIRECT MEASURES

Problems with Direct Measures

There are several problems with the direct measures of stereotypes we have been discussing. One is that most measurement techniques are reactive, in the sense that they may "put ideas into people's heads" that weren't there before. The second is that people may be reluctant to report their stereotypes because they think they will be criticized, so that direct measures may actually capture more what people think they ought to believe than what they actually do.

Reactive Measures

Should we be concerned that direct measures of stereotypes force or encourage people to think about groups in ways that they normally would not do? As is the case with the other measurement issues we have considered, there are deeper theoretical issues at work here. Stereotypes, like attitudes and values, surely operate at various levels of articulateness, stability, complexity, and ease of use. There is a continuum; at one end people have clear and present knowledge of their stereotypes ("Every time I think about professors, I think how liberal they are"), and at the other there is much less definiteness ("Now that you mention it, I guess I do think that professors are generally liberal, but that really never comes to mind much when I think about professors"). It is not clear a priori that the stereotype features that spring to mind easily are more important than those that have to be prodded on stage before making an appearance. Indeed, the latter may be more practically important if they produce unconscious discrimination.

BELIEFS AND ATTITUDES ARE NOT FIXED

One of the lessons of the past 20 years in attitude research (Abelson, 1988; Fazio, 1995; Schneider, 1988) is that many attitudes are labile. A person can be pro- or antichoice on the abortion issue, depending on how the question is phrased and what other attitudes and recent behaviors are made salient. Similarly, one might imagine that recent experiences or reading, a conversation with a racist or an equality activist, and the salience of various norms might all be expected to have some impact on how people decide whether they think blacks are less or more hard-working than whites.

Because stereotypes like most attitudes and beliefs are not firmly fixed, and because many people have quite diverse and often conflicting views about groups of people, stereotypes are sensitive to conditions of measurement. This does not mean that stereotypes are somehow "unreal" or unimportant. It does not mean that our stereotypes, any more than other products of our cognitive activity, change radically or arbitrarily. It just means that different aspects of the stereotype are likely to be considered at different times.

Consider, for example, Professor Adams, who believes that her students are basically hard-working. Does that mean that she thinks all students work hard all the time? Probably not. Are there times when she is reminded that many students can't seem to get assignments done on time? Probably. Does she see her students partying and having a good time on weekends? Perhaps. If so, might she recall that "back in the good old days" when she was a student, she and her friends were far too busy reading in the library on weekends to have time for partying? It seems more than remotely possible. When she has had a bad deadline day, greeted by scores of students asking for extensions on a paper assignment, might she just for this one day remind herself of all the evidence she has that students are party animals and lazy as hell? It seems reasonable. And under the circumstances we might be forgiven for not accusing her of hypocrisy and facile attitudes if a week later, when she is having a wonderful day, she reports that her students are really quite diligent, all things considered. For many of our attitudes, we can, depending on circumstances, dredge up support for and against almost any side of the issue. We do know that stereotypes, as least as measured by perceivers' free-choice responses, are fairly unreliable over time (Berninger & DeSoto, 1985). As one might guess, there is abundant evidence that stereotypes are affected by various kinds of contexts—the nature of comparison groups, social and situational circumstances, and the context in which the group is considered.

SITUATIONS

Just as Professor Adams has different altitudes toward and stereotypes of her students, depending on a host of situational factors, so our stereotypes of most groups can be affected by any number of situational factors. Most obviously, stereotypes of outgroups that are in conflict with our own groups tend to become more negative, as many studies of group conflict show (e.g., Bar-Tal & Labin, 2000). As we shall see throughout this book, stereotypes sometimes reflect our momentary attitudes.

COMPARISON GROUPS

Obviously, some measures of stereotypes (such as the differentiating-features approach) depend heavily on what the comparison group is. Lawyers may be seen as quite sleazy compared to doctors, but as paragons of virtue when the comparison group is politicians. But even when such overt comparisons are not made, trait ascriptions to groups may be affected by the nature of implicit comparisons. Diab (1963a) had his Arab/Muslim undergraduate subjects (at American University in

Lebanon) rate Americans, English, Germans, French, and Russians along with two other groups (Algerians and Egyptians) or eight other groups (Turks, Negroes, Chinese, Italians, Japanese, Jews, Lebanese, and Irish). Stereotypes were somewhat different in the two conditions. For example, Americans were seen as rich (62%), democratic (50%), scientific (18%), fun-loving (16%), sportsmanlike (12%), and superficial (12%) in the conditions where they were rated with six other groups, and as superficial (42%), rich (36%), selfish (22%), mercantile (12%), pretentious (12%), and aggressive (10%) when they were rated with 12 other groups. Several other studies (e.g., Diab, 1963b; Haslam, Turner, Oakes, McGarty, & Hayes, 1992; Hopkins & Murdoch, 1999; Hopkins, Regan, & Abell, 1997) have also shown that stereotypes change as a function of the other groups being rated.

MEASUREMENT CONDITIONS

Stereotypes, like attitudes, are affected by instructions given to subjects, the type of measuring scale, and the like. For example, Brigham (1972, p. 67) showed that patterns of trait endorsements for the Katz–Braly groups by white subjects was similar for typical Katz–Braly instructions ("words . . . which seem to you to be typical"), personal endorsement instructions ("traits . . . which from your knowledge . . . are typical"), and facilitative instructions (which stressed the fact that groups do differ). However, instructions that emphasized reporting traits that "people in our society, as a whole, often consider typical" produced quite different patterns—ones that were more uniform, and for Negroes less favorable. As reported earlier, Devine and Elliot (1995) also found little overlap between subjects' reports of cultural stereotypes and their own personal beliefs about blacks.

DOMAIN-SPECIFIC STEREOTYPES

It is obvious, when we think about it, that each of us has different kinds of contacts with people in different sorts of situations. It may not be very surprising to find out that college professors and probation officers have different stereotypes of people in the 18- to 22-year age range. Surely, too, professors at an Ivy League school have different stereotypes of students than professors at a community college or trade school have.

However, these differences can produce a fair amount of mischief. For example, people may not recognize the extent to which their stereotypes are affected by the kinds of contacts they have, and many of our stereotypes may really be stereotypes about something else. For example, Eagly and Steffen (1984) argue that the reason general stereotypes of women emphasize their nurturing and caretaking qualities is that most people are more likely to encounter women in roles (mother and homemaker, nurse, elementary teacher) that emphasize such behavior. Bayton, McAlister, and Hamer (1956), Feldman (1972), and others have argued that what we take to be a white stereotype of blacks is heavily confounded with a stereotype of working-class people. Indeed, stereotypes of black businessmen are quite different from stereotypes of blacks in general or blacks on welfare (Devine & Baker, 1991).

Hagendoorn and Kleinpenning (1991; Kleinpenning & Hagendoorn, 1991) have studied what they call "domain-specific stereotypes" of various minority groups in Holland by Dutch school children. They have found clear evidence that such stereo-

Reaction Time Measures

DIRECT ASSOCIATION MEASURES

Often reaction time or latency measures have been used for such purposes. Subjects are asked to perform some task, and the speed with which they perform it is measured. To interpret this type of measure, we must assume that when pieces of information are associated in memory, a task that involves inferring one from the other will be performed more rapidly than when the items are not so closely associated. So if we asked people for their associations to the word "dog," most people would respond more quickly with their first association (say, "cat") than with a less salient associate such as "protection." Most Americans, if asked whether various people had been President of the United States, could answer more quickly to Reagan than to Fillmore. Similarly, a person who believes that Jews are clannish should be quick to answer a question about their clannishness.

Thus one fairly straightforward measure of whether a trait is associated with a group is simply to ask subjects to answer whether the group generally has that trait, and to measure latency of answering rather than the content of the answer itself. Several studies (e.g., Brewer, Dull, & Lui, 1981; Lalonde & Gardner, 1989; Macrae, Bodenhausen, Milne, & Jetten, 1994) showed that stimuli consistent with the stereotype of a given group are processed more rapidly or effectively than inconsistent stimuli.

LEXICAL DECISION MEASURES

Gaertner and McLaughlin (1983) made use of a related cognitive task to get at stereotypes indirectly. In a lexical decision task, subjects are asked to look at a pair of letter strings (e.g., CAST–MARK or PERSON–NBGT) and to decide whether both are words. A reliable finding is that when the stimuli are both actually words, subjects can answer "yes" faster when the two words are associated (DOG–CAT) than when they are not (DOG–FAT). Thus the latency of responding "yes" to word pairs is a reliable, if indirect, measure of associative strength. Now if associations exist between blacks and stereotype traits such as "lazy," it ought to follow that subjects could judge that BLACK–LAZY are both words more quickly than BLACK–AMBITIOUS or WHITE–LAZY.

The Gaertner and McLaughlin experiment employed several combinations of various kinds of words and nonsense letter strings, but the important comparisons for our purposes were between cases where BLACK and WHITE were presented with positive, non-black-stereotype traits (AMBITIOUS, CLEAN, SMART) or with negative, stereotypic traits (LAZY, WELFARE, STUPID). In the most direct test of the hypothesis, responses to the BLACK–negative stereotype trait pairs were no faster than responses to the WHITE–negative stereotype trait pairs. Thus there was no evidence from this measure that these white subjects believed that blacks had more negative stereotypic traits than did whites. However, for the positive traits, subjects were much quicker to make a "yes" judgment when the words were preceded by WHITE than by BLACK. Following the logic laid out earlier, we would thus have to conclude that subjects had more positive stereotypes of whites than blacks, but not more negative stereotypes of blacks than whites. However, there was a closer association between BLACK and negative traits than between BLACK and positive traits, whereas WHITE was much more

closely associated with positive than with negative traits. These results were replicated with the use of WHITE and NEGRO.

However, before we make too much of this finding, we must discuss the not altogether consistent findings of a conceptually similar study. Dovidio, Evans, and Tyler
(1986) employed a slightly different lexical decision task with a more carefully controlled list of traits. The logic here is that when a category is primed, subjects can
more quickly recognize that a prototypic instance is part of the category. Subjects
were given the words "black" and "white" as primes, and then a brief time later were
asked whether a given trait could ever be true of the group in question. Obviously,
the answer to that question is bound to be "yes" for almost any trait. Other types of
questions were included that required "no" answers, so the subjects were not answering "yes" to every question; however, in this study, only responses of "yes" were considered important to the hypotheses. Subjects were asked the question for both black
and white positive and negative stereotype traits. The results (see Table 2.1) showed
that subjects responded most quickly when the prime and the stereotype trait were
stereotypically congruent. That is, the "black" prime facilitated responses to black
stereotype traits and the "white" prime to white stereotype traits. This was true for
both positive and negative traits. Thus the Dovidio and colleagues results suggest
that black stereotypes do include negative material as well as the absence of positive
material. It is, however, worth pointing out that the black negative traits used in this
research ("lazy" and "imitative") were both less negative and more stereotypic on average than the similar traits used by Gaertner and McLaughlin.

Other results using this procedure have been even more complex. Using white
subjects, Wittenbrink, Judd, and Park (1997) found that "black" and "white" primes
facilitated stereotype-consistent terms, especially negative black and positive white
terms. However, Judd, Park, Ryan, Brauer, and Kraus (1995), using the Gaertner and
McLaughlin (1983) procedure, found that both white and black subjects responded
more quickly to positive than to negative traits, but that this was more true for black
targets. Thus these priming studies have not produced perfectly consistent results,
but there is strong evidence that at least for some subjects, category names do affect
how rapidly people can access category-related terms.

TABLE 2.1. Mean Latencies for "White" and "Black" Primes and White and Black Stereotypic Traits

Trait type	"White" prime	"Black" prime
White		
Positive	**777**	918
Negative	**949**	994
Black		
Positive	888	**820**
Negative	1,118	**954**

Note. Smaller latencies indicate larger associations, and ste-
reotype-congruent latencies are given in **bold**. From Dovidio,
Evans, and Tyler (1986). Copyright 1986 by Academic Press.
Reprinted by permission.

AFFECTIVE PRIMING

The "bona fide pipeline" technique pioneered by Russ Fazio and his students makes use of affective priming and is an indirect measure of prejudice rather than stereotypes. In affective priming, presentation of an emotionally charged stimulus facilitates evaluative judgments of similarly valanced stimuli, and inhibits judgments of stimuli that are evaluated in the opposite way. For instance, seeing a picture of a pretty sunset would facilitate judgments that words such as "happy" and "kind" are positive, and retard judgments that words such as "evil" and "kill" are negative. Fazio, Jackson, Dunton, and Williams (1995) used pictures of white and black faces as primes; they found that for white subjects, white faces facilitated judgments that positive adjectives were positive, and black faces facilitated judgments that negative adjectives were negative. For black subjects, the exact reverse occurred: Black faces facilitated responses to positive words, and white faces facilitated responses to negative stimuli. This suggests that for white subjects black faces are associated with negative emotion (since they facilitate judgments of negative words). This measure has subsequently been used to assess individual differences among people in their tendencies to associate black with negative stimuli (e.g., Fazio & Dunton, 1997; Fazio & Hilden, 2001).

COGNITIVE INTERFERENCE MEASURES

An even more indirect way to measure stereotype–feature associations makes use of Stroop-type tasks. In this situation, subjects are asked to perform a task in which other aspects of the stimuli interfere with efficient processing. Typically, subjects are asked to read a list of written color words that are printed in different colors, as quickly as they can; for example, subjects might be asked to read RED printed in blue ink and then GREEN printed in yellow ink. Inevitably, subjects have more difficulty (as judged by speed) when the names and colors are different than when the same or all color names are printed in traditional black ink. Presumably this occurs because the color of the ink automatically primes associations that interfere with the correct written name. Similarly, when people are asked to name the color of the ink, the names of colors interferes. That logic can be extended to a situation in which words have stereotype associations. Locke, MacLeod, and Walker (1994) asked subjects to give the color of the ink for words that were associated with stereotypes. They predicted that when subjects had been primed with the name of a stereotyped group, associations to the meaning of the stereotype words should interfere with color naming. That result was found, but only for subjects who had a relevant stereotype and who were also highly prejudiced—a result that makes perfect sense in view of the assumption that for such people stereotype associations should be especially strong.

THE IMPLICIT ASSOCIATION TEST

Recently Greenwald, McGhee, and Schwartz (1998) have suggested a rather complex but interesting measure, called the "implicit association test" (IAT). The basic argument is that when people have to map two sets of associations onto a common response, they will do so much more rapidly when the two sets are consistent with one another. For example, imagine that people have to respond to insect names (negative stimuli) with one response (say, pressing the N key on a computer keyboard) and to flower names (positive) with another (pressing P). Then they are asked to respond to weapons (also negative) with N and to names of movie stars (also positive) with P. Both tasks are fairly simple and can be done quickly. Note that in both cases subjects respond to negative categories (insects and weapons) with N and to positive categories (flowers and movie stars) with P. It should therefore come as no surprise that intermingling these two tasks (e.g., flowers on some trials and movie stars on others) imposes no reaction time penalty—positive things go to P and negative ones to N. But now suppose that subjects have to respond to both insects and flowers with P and to both weapons and movie stars with N. In this case, the natural association between positive categories is violated, and people should take far longer to respond to a mixture of categories. This decrement can serve as a measure of the extent to which insects and weapons are negative relative to flowers and movie stars.

By a similar logic, if it is assumed that most white subjects have negative associations to blacks and more positive ones to whites, making the same response to black names or faces and negative features or white names and positive features should take a shorter amount of time than when black names and positive features or white names and negative features map onto the same response. This is exactly what was found, and this measure was essentially unrelated to various measures of more explicit attitudes toward blacks (Greenwald et al., 1998). The IAT has since been used extensively to measure not only racial but age- and gender-related attitudes and stereotypes (Greenwald et al., 2002), and similar measures have been developed to measure attitudes toward single groups (Nosek & Banaji, 2001).

Although this measure seems complex, it is actually quite easy to administer (given access to reaction time apparatus) and has even been made available on an Internet site (Nosek, Banaji, & Greenwald, 2002a), so that people can test their own implicit stereotypes. The IAT is widely used in research these days, although questions have been raised about what it actually measures (see Chapter 8 for a discussion).

Memory Measures

EXPLICIT MEMORY MEASURES

Most of the measures we have been discussing are based on the premise that exposure to a category or activation of a stereotype will prime a set of preexisting associations between that category and various features, making them easier to access and report. Stereotype priming should affect not only speed of accessing information, but what people can remember. As one example, Perdue and Gurtman (1990) found that after rating the applicability of adjectives for young and old people, subjects recalled more of the negative words for the old and positive words for the young. Chapter 4 examines research suggesting that when stereotypes are salient, people are more prone to recall information that is associated with the stereotype. Such direct memory measures are generally used for other purposes, but they can be taken as measures of the existence of stereotypes.

IMPLICIT MEMORY MEASURES

Direct memory measures rely on people's abilities to report what they can remember, but implicit memory measures rely on the fact that some aspects of memory may not be fully available to our consciousness (see Greenwald & Banaji, 1995). To get at such "hidden" memories, investigators often use what have come to be called implicit memory measures.

One commonly used implicit memory measure is a word completion task. A person who cannot consciously recall that he or she has recently seen the word "polite" may still be more inclined to fill in the blanks for P_ L I _ _ with "polite" rather than some alternative such as "police." If stereotypes are salient or primed, they can affect such responses. For example, a study by Gilbert and Hixon (1991) showed that under certain conditions after exposure to an Asian woman, people were more likely to fill in the blanks with an Asian stereotype term (such as "polite") than with a non-stereotype term (such as "police").

Another implicit measure used by Banaji and Greenwald (1995) made use of results in a previous study by Jacoby, Kelly, Brown, and Jasechko (1989). In the Jacoby and colleagues study, subjects were given names of famous and nonfamous people, and then a day later were asked to judge whether previously presented or new names were famous. Obviously, both previously presented famous and new famous names were rated as famous. However, the old nonfamous names were also rated as more famous than new nonfamous names; for example, the name Harold Jones (non-famous) would be seen as more famous if it had been seen in the first session than if it had not been. This suggests that subjects were using a sense of familiarity with the name to judge its famousness. Banaji and Greenwald repeated this basic paradigm, but also varied the gender of the names. They reasoned that since gender stereotypes include the likelihood that males are likely to have achieved more than females, male names would be more sensitive to previous exposure than female names. Their results showed that subjects had a lower threshold for judging the fame of male than female names, thus supporting the idea that people assume that males are more likely to be famous than females.

The Use of Implicit Measures

There are many other indirect measures of stereotypes that make use of work in cognitive psychology, but the present discussion should provide a sense of what is available. One of the reasons cognitive psychology has made such remarkable advances in recent years has been the development of sophisticated measures. Many of these have been imported into social cognition and into the study of stereotyping more particularly. It is therefore important to be clear about what these measures are and are not.

A Better Mousetrap?

Implicit measures are certainly in vogue these days, and with good reason. They eliminate many of the potential problems with more direct measures; they are based on the successes of cognitive psychology; they are new; and they are, well, kinda sexy.

Should we then abandon the old for the new? Probably not, and for at least two reasons.

In the first instance, the kinds of implicit cognitive measures we have been describing are a bit cumbersome to use, and often require testing subjects individually in computer labs. This is inefficient if one simply wants to know what kinds of stereotypes people have. A more important problem is that although some investigators report respectable correlations between various implicit and explicit measures, usually correlations are positive but fairly low (see Chapter 8 for an extended discussion). So, we reflexively ask, which type of measure is the more valid? This is, at the present stage of our development, almost certainly the wrong question to ask. As we shall see (especially in Chapter 8), it is highly likely that implicit and explicit attitudes are developed somewhat independently, flow in somewhat different cognitive streams, and predict different aspects of behavior in different circumstances (Brauer, Wasel, & Niedenthal, 2000; Wilson, Lindsey, & Schooler, 2000).

This does not mean that the two streams never interact or act in concert. Chapter 1 has suggested a theme that will be important throughout this book: Stereotypes (and prejudice) are no single thing. Stereotypes are complex, and it would seem reasonable that different facets would be picked up by different ways of measuring. Thus the proper question is not which type of measure is most valid, but which is most useful for predicting behavior in which types of situations.

External Validity of Implicit Measures

Such measures also do not have much real-life validity, and that bothers some people. After all, when I am making judgments about others based on my stereotypes, how rapidly I make these judgments is ordinarily not of much concern. Who cares whether it takes 1,000 or 1,200 milliseconds? It is hard to imagine a situation in which differences of this magnitude make any practical difference. However, if such criticisms are taken to be fatal, they miss the point. When we use reaction time and other cognitive measures, we are usually not trying to say anything about how stereotypes are used in the real world; rather, we are trying to explore how they function as a part of our cognitive systems. Indirect cognitive measures are signs, symptoms, signals, or probes into the ways our minds work. An analogy may make this clear. If you have a car problem, you may be quite grateful if the mechanic has a theory about the ways engines work and uses a test of mechanical properties of the engine before he disassembles the engine to see what the problem is. Similarly, your physician may perform sophisticated (and often highly indirect) tests of your internal workings before she cuts you open to see what's wrong. Minds, of course, do not have hoods that open, nor can they be cut open; we must often rely on indirect "symptoms" of its inner workings.

Many cognitive operations are simply not available for conscious report, and as we have seen, the products of cognitive activity are often nonconsciously biased or deliberately misreported. Thus we often have very little choice in how we approach the measure of stereotypes and stereotyping. As we have begun to ask more sophisticated, better, and more important questions about stereotyping, we have moved beyond the point at which conscious reports can *always* tell us what we want to know.

None of this means that any type of measure is necessarily any better than any other. There will continue to be many situations in which direct measure of stereotypes is the weapon of choice. But, increasingly, we will be relying on the more indirect cognitive measures. In so doing, we can be reasonably assured that most such measures have passed the tests of time, and that when used carefully and cautiously, they can tell us a fair amount about how cognitive systems work as people process stereotype information.

Notes

1. This may not be obvious to statistically naive individuals. The denominator of the t-test is a function of the variance of the ratings, and this variance is low when there is consensus on the traits, thus yielding a higher t-value. The numerator is the difference between the scale value of the item and the midpoint of the scale, and thus represents extremity.
2. Some (e.g., Biernat, 1990) have argued that difference measures rather than ratios are better. In practice, difference and ratio measures are likely to produce comparable results.
3. It may seem strange that those who were high in socially desirable responding would actually have been more prone to endorse stereotypes, given that stereotypes are usually thought of as socially undesirable. However, in this study the traits were mostly positive, so those inclined to respond in a socially desirable way also endorsed positive traits for French Canadians.

CHAPTER 3

Categories and Categorization

Surely the most basic cognitive process involved in stereotyping is categorization—or at least that's the common claim (Allport, 1954; Brewer, 1988; Fiske & Neuberg, 1990; Hamilton, 1979; Jones, 1982; Samuels, 1973; Smith, 1990; Tajfel, 1969; Taylor, 1981; Vinacke, 1957). Categorization itself is ubiquitous. Our whole language of nouns (as well as adjectives and adverbs) is built around the fact that we group animals, plants, things, events, and people into categories. Those who argue that people have limited cognitive resources with which to tame a complex environment suggest that categories are helpful in simplifying the world (e.g., Hamilton & Trolier, 1986; Taylor, 1981). To say that an animal is a dog is to encourage its dog qualities, to shellac its Rover individuality—a necessary process in a world with too many unique Rovers. However, others (e.g., Medin, 1988; Oakes & Turner, 1990) have argued that the essential cognitive problems we humans face is not too much but rather too little information, and that categories help us infer information not directly given by our senses. We know that Rover can bite and bark, even if we do not catch her in the act. Both perspectives are helpful. We group things into categories because we expect that the things within a given category will be similar in some ways and different in others from things alien to the category. This gives us predictive control over the environment, a leg up in deciding on appropriate behavior (Anderson, 1991; Ross & Murphy, 1996).

Before stereotyping can take place, an individual must be seen as a member of one or more categories to which stereotypes may apply. In that sense, categorization is a necessary condition for stereotyping to occur. But it may not be a sufficient condition. I can imagine seeing a person as Asian American or as a banker without necessarily deriving any cognitive consequences from that categorization. However, it remains an open question whether categorizations and the accompanying inferences them can be divorced so easily. Why would we develop categories unless we used generalizations about them efficiently and quickly (Schneider, 1992)?

Having said that, I should note that those who operate from a Gibsonian perspective (e.g., Zebrowitz, 1996) do not think that such categorization is always necessary. Also, as we shall see later in this chapter, exemplar models of categorization do not require explicit categorization before judgments are made about individuals. A person who looks menacing does not need to be categorized as criminal or even as dangerous to elicit unpleasant associations. Indeed, physical features can lead to stereotypic inferences without overt categorization (Blair, Judd, Sadler, & Jenkins, 2002). In addition, Richard Nisbett and his colleagues (e.g., Nisbett, Peng, Choi, & Norenzayan, 2001) argue that categorization on the basis of object features is more common among Westerners than among East Asians, who tend to categorize on the basis of functional relationships.

THE NATURE OF CATEGORIES

Theories about Categories

The emphasis placed on categorization by modern stereotype researchers has been stimulated by cognitive psychologists' focus on categories and categorization (e.g., Anderson, 1991; Komatsu, 1992; Medin, 1989; Smith & Medin, 1981). Debates among cognitive psychologists about the nature of categories have, in turn, echoed debates in the fields of philosophy and linguistics that have gone on for centuries.

The Classic View

CRITERIA.

Classically, categories were assumed to be collections of examples that share certain important defining attributes. So cups may be considered objects that have handles, are round, capable of holding liquids, and so on. These defining features or attributes are both necessary and collectively sufficient. As a result, all objects that have the defining features count as members of the category, and no nonmembers have all the defining features. There are no gradations of category membership; an object is either in or out. Certainly some concepts fit the classic model quite well. For example, a square is a figure of four equal sides and four equal angles. All figures we call squares fit this definition, and all nonsquares are excluded. That's just the way squares are. Similarly, a touchdown in football or a strike in baseball has a clear set of necessary and sufficient conditions, complex as they may be. Some imposed definitions, particularly legal ones, also count. For example, suicide may be defined as the intentional taking of one's own life.

PROBLEMS

Unfortunately, most of the categories we use in everyday life do not fit the classical view all that well. One problem is that some objects fitting the definition of a category are not generally considered part of it (e.g., certain bowls fit the definition of cups given above), and many perfectly fine examples (e.g., cups for drinking Chinese tea) do not fulfill all the criteria for membership (e.g., handles).

Also, we all recognize that some things are better (more typical) examples of a category than others, even though the classic view does not allow for such distinctions (Medin, 1989). Irish setters would probably be seen as better examples of dogs than chihuahuas, although both breeds possess the essential doggy genes. Even well-defined categories such as odd numbers show typicality effects; 3 is judged as a "better" odd number than 23 (Armstrong, Gleitman, & Gleitman, 1983).

Finally, even if there are good defining features for a category, we often do not use them in our everyday categorizations. We do not perform a chromosome assay every time we want to distinguish cats from dogs or men from women. Although the essential defining features of gender are bound up with those little X's and Y's, we usually prefer to use readily visible cues to categorize people by gender, despite the fact that these cues are imperfectly correlated with biological gender.

Categories as Defined by Probabilistic Features

If there are no clear necessary and sufficient features that define most categories, perhaps features have probabilistic relationships to categories. When you wonder whether the animal before you is a cat, you probably examine features such as size, tail conformation, disposition of face, and fur type, even though none of these features is a perfect cue for "catness." Size is moderately diagnostic, but many animals are about the same size as cats without ever being confused with them. Most cats have tails that stick straight up most of the time, although some do not, and other animals we would not call cats have this same feature.

FAMILY RESEMBLANCE: PROTOTYPES

In a now classic research program, Rosch (1978) developed the idea that most category boundaries are essentially fuzzy; it is hard to know at what point a cup becomes a bowl, for example. Yet, at the same time, we all have the sense that some cups and bowls are such good examples of their categories that such confusions will not occur. Rosch argued that within a particular category, there are members that seem prototypic of the entire category. So collies or Irish setters are "better" examples of dogs than are Great Danes, and a cardinal is a more representative bird than a penguin.

Rosch built on the philosophical work of Wittgenstein (1953), who argued that exemplars of categories are similar on several attributes, but that no exemplar shares all attributes with every other. In a human family, one son may have his mother's red hair and blue eyes, his father's slender build, and his grandfather's artistic bent. A daughter may resemble her mother in the shape of her body, but may have her father's brown hair and her aunt's sharp wit. At a family reunion we might note that this extended family seems to have lots of red-haired artists in it, but we also note that the daughter who is neither red-haired nor an artist still shares many features in common with other family members. Similarly, although there may be no features that all cups or all dogs must have, there are family resemblances among the exemplars.

Consider the group of cups listed in Table 3.1. When one looks at all this array of cups and their individual features, the majority are small, are round, are made of china, and have handles; all have at least two of these prototypic features, and yet none of the five cups has all of the prototypic features. In this example, Cups A and E are more prototypic because they have more of these features (three of the four) than the others; in other words, they share the most attributes with other exemplars. Collies are "better dogs" (cognitively) than Great Danes, because their size is closer

TABLE 3.1. Features of Hypothetical Cups

	Composition	Shape	Size	Handles
Cup A	China	Round	Small	None
Cup B	Wood	Round	Large	Handles
Cup C	Wood	Round	Small	None
Cup D	China	Square	Large	Handles
Cup E	China	Square	Small	Handles

to the average dog and they have the long hair common to most dogs but lacked by less prototypic breeds. So prototypes lie at the center of the category rather than at the fuzzy perimeter; in some inexact (or at least, usually unspecified) sense, the prototypic dog is an average dog.

How are prototypes represented mentally? Many prototype theories assume that there is an actual "abstract prototype" representation. This prototypic representation of a category needs to be close to the center of the category, but it may or may not be an actual member of the category. In the cup example above, the prototypic cup is made of china, has handles, is small, and is round; yet no one cup in this sample actually has all those features, so the prototype is purely an abstraction in this case. The dog prototype may be a particular dog one knows, but it may also be an abstract dog that one has mentally knitted together from doggy features that are considered important. Alternatively, according to a "featural view," we simply determine which features are central to the category (those that many members of the category share), and each new and potential category member is evaluated on each of these relevant dimensions.

TYPICALITY EFFECTS

Prototype views emphasize the fact that some members of categories are better exemplars than others. Whether an exemplar is typical or atypical of its category turns out to have a large impact on the ways we treat those exemplars (Komatsu, 1992). Typical exemplars are identified faster and more reliably than less typical, are easier to acquire as category members, and come to mind more readily when people think about categories (Barsalou, 1987). When we think about categories, we retrieve typical instances before atypical ones, and it is also easier to retrieve information associated with the more typical instances (Rothbart, Sriram, & Davis-Stitt, 1996); we are more likely to infer category attributes from typical than from atypical instances (Rothbart & Lewis, 1988). Generally, it is easier to process information about people who are typical of their categories (Cantor & Mischel, 1979b; Livingston & Brewer, 2002).

Obviously, when we deal with the traditional stereotype categories of race, gender, age, occupation, and sexual preference, we surely have prototypes for those categories and may use such prototypes to categorize new people, to judge whether they fit the category well, and on that basis to infer other characteristics about them. A man may be judged to be gay if he fits our prototype of the typical gay male, and to the extent that he fits well, we may be inclined to assume that he has the various features that are part of our homosexual stereotype.

PROBLEMS WITH THE PROTOTYPE VIEW

Although the prototype view is a clear conceptual advance over the classic model, it too has some major shortcomings. For one thing, relevant prototypes change from situation to situation (Roth & Shoben, 1983). A prototypic car would have different features in the context of a stock car race versus a family trip. The graded structure of a category—what exemplars are seen as more typical—is fairly unreliable across contexts and sometimes even within the same individual over time (Barsalou, 1989). Moreover, ratings of which exemplars are the most prototypic of a category are not highly correlated across individuals (Beck, McCauley, Segal, & Hershey, 1988). Another indignity for prototype theory is that although typicality ratings and similarity to other members of a category are correlated for naive people, they often are not for scientific and folk experts (Bailenson, Shum, Atran, Medin, & Coley, 2002; López, Atran, Coley, Medin, & Smith, 1997).

The Exemplar Approach

The Rosch prototype approach emphasizes the importance of specific features; an object or person becomes prototypic to the extent that it has more of the features (or more of the important features) commonly found in the category. The prototype is an abstract representation, an ideal of sorts. This does not, of course, rule out the possibility that a single existing exemplar may be so close to the average that it becomes the prototype.

More recently, there have been suggestions that our cognitive representations are concrete rather than abstract (Hintzman, 1986; Jacoby & Brooks, 1984; Kahneman & Miller, 1986; Smith & Zárate, 1992). One thinks about cups in terms of concrete memory representations of a cup. Interestingly enough, the early stereotype researchers probably had something like this view in mind; for example, Lippmann (1922) discussed stereotypes as "pictures in our heads," implying a concreteness of representation.

This perspective then would suggest, for example, that Jewishness is defined less by a listing of more or less probable characteristics associated with the category than by reference to a particular Jew. Although prototype models also allow a particular, concrete prototype (which may be an actual person or thing) to represent the entire category, the exemplar view does not require that the exemplar for a category be the instance that best represents the category in some statistical sense; it may be representative because it is vivid or salient. In other words, a relevant exemplar need not be the prototype.

Most exemplar models stress that every instance of a category is stored separately, such that there is no average, abstract memory representation of the category. So when asked to think about dogs, one does not generally have a list of defining features of dogs available (the classic view); nor does one have a mental image of some average dog (prototype) or a list of features that are empirically linked to most dogs. Rather, one has available memory traces of many dogs that one has encountered. If one encounters five dogs in a given day, one will store each in terms of its tail length and the like. Indeed, in some extreme versions, each encounter with the same dog would be seen as a separate exemplar (Hintzman, 1986). Such models do not require that every feature of every exemplar be attended to, stored, or retrieved. Obviously when I encounter a dog, I may not attend to all the dog's attributes; the memories of those I do notice may decay over time; and I will probably only be able to retrieve a subset of all the attributes still stored in memory at any given time. Still other models (e.g., Smith & Zárate, 1992) allow for storage of abstract and inferred information with each exemplar. So when I think about Michael Jordan, I can recall not only specific behaviors I have observed him perform, but also previous inferences about his personality (e.g., self-confident) and assumptions about his lifestyle (e.g., the type of car he probably owns).

CATEGORIZATION

According to the exemplar view, categorization of new instances should take place in the following way: The perceiver compares the present stimulus with memories of past instances on the basis of various dimensions. When the new stimulus matches a past exemplar (or group of them) closely enough, the new stimulus may be classified as a member of whatever category the exemplar represents. For example, when I am trying to decide whether the man I have just encountered in the deep stacks of the university library is a librarian, a student, a fellow professor, or a custodian, I may explicitly compare him to exemplars of each category and put him in the category containing the exemplars that are most similar to him. Thus categorization is heavily dependent on judgments of similarity, which often prove both practically and theoretically problematic.

SIMILARITY

What attributes are used to judge similarity? The man before me in the library is neatly dressed like most librarians I know, and he is not wearing a custodian's uniform, which seems to exclude his being about to fix or clean something. On the other hand, he is rather muscular and male, like most custodians and unlike most of our librarians. His smile reminds me of a shy student I just talked to, but he is older than most students; the stack of books he is carrying seems more professor- or student-like than librarian-like. His gait reminds me of several colleagues, but his build is decidedly nonprofessorial. Which of the many ways he resembles a great many other people do I use as basis for my judgment? Smith and Zárate (1992) argue that we will inevitably pay more attention to some attributes than to others. This attention can be affected by goals (perhaps I am looking for a muscular person to fix something in my library study), personal relevance (I am especially attuned to style of dress), past experiences (I have found that smiles are indicative of helpfulness), and/ or frequency and recency of exposure (I have been talking to students all afternoon). Some cues, such as uniforms and age, may simply capture a lot of attention. So these and other factors may lead me to attend selectively to attributes of the man before me, and thus to categorize him in particular ways.

ADVANTAGES OF THE EXEMPLAR VIEW

One advantage of this exemplar approach is that it captures at least one aspect of common experiences—namely, that when we are trying to classify or judge an unfamiliar object, we may run through various exemplars of categories. However, the validity of this model does not rest on our awareness. Indeed there is abundant evidence that we may be unaware of the effects of using exemplars to judge other people (Macrae, Bodenhausen, Milne, Castelli, et al., 1998; Smith & Zárate, 1992).

Second, exemplar models allow for the influence of context in a way that prototype theories do not. When one establishes a prototype of a dog, one is, by the very nature of the abstraction process, searching for common elements and leaving out such variant features as whether the dog bites and under what circumstances. Exemplar views, on the other hand, easily accommodate such contextual information (Rover did not bite on Occasion 1, but did bite when provoked on Occasion 2; Spot did not bite on Occasions 1 through 3,450; etc.).

According to the exemplar view, categories are inherently fluid, because different exemplars may come to mind in different circumstances. Research by Sia, Lord, Blessum, Ratcliff, and Lepper (1997) has shown that when people are asked for exemplars of social categories at different times, they repeat the same exemplar only about 60% of the time. The particular exemplar that pops into mind may result from many cognitive factors, but recent exposure is certainly an important one. If I have several salient experiences with conservative professors, the exemplars of professors I draw on may be conservative, and hence my stereotype be fairly conservative. Obviously, there are implications for stereotype change. In what we might term the "Cosby effect" (after the successful black American TV actor), we might expect that exposure to successful and mainstream black families might change the stereotype of black Americans. However, as we shall see in Chapter 10, experience with exemplars does not always generalize to the category as a whole and may generalize in unexpected ways. One reason is that exemplars who disconfirm the stereotype may be seen as atypical and thus as not a sufficient basis for generalization to the category at large (Rothbart, 1996; Rothbart & John, 1985).

How much of our thinking goes on in this way is an open question, but a plausible case could be made that much of it does. A person may be seen as a homosexual because he or she is "just like" (usually in some unspecified way) another person who is known to be gay. A black man is "just like" a particular unemployed or professional black man, perhaps one known only from television, and is judged to be unemployed or professional accordingly. Predictions of behavior are often based on similarity between a person and another person known to have performed the behavior (Read, 1987), and attitudes toward categories can be affected by manipulating which exemplars people use for the category (Sia et al., 1997). Research by Susan Andersen and her colleagues (Andersen & Baum, 1994; Andersen & Cole, 1990; Andersen, Glassman, Chen, & Cole, 1995; Chen, Andersen, & Hinkley, 1999) suggests that our feelings and beliefs about significant others may form the basis of our affective reaction to strangers as well as our impressions of them and memory for their behavior. Exposure to exemplars facilitates judgments about related targets (Karylowski, Konarzewski, & Motes, 2000; Zárate & Sanders, 1999). Thus several lines of research suggest that important or salient others may serve as models for our perceptions of others.

One of the most intriguing and depressing possibilities is that people are classified as similar to exemplars of categories on the basis of superficial cues such as physical appearance, which have no diagnostic validity. For example, a person who looks like the prototypic TV criminal may be stereotyped as being one. Hollywood actors sometimes complain about typecasting, which may result from a particular type of appearance. Lewicki (1985) provides some suggestive experimental evidence. Subjects interacted with a person who behaved quite kindly. Subsequently they met two people, one of whom was superficially similar (e.g., both wore glasses) to the previous kind person, and were asked to rate the two new people on kindness. They rated the one who was superficially similar to the kind person as kinder. Now, obviously, some putatively superficial similarities may actually be important; it is possible, for example, that tough-looking males are actually more likely to be criminals than softer-appearing types. But research by Lewicki and others (e.g., Gilovich, 1981) shows that variables that cannot by any reasonable account be associated with a particular trait may lead to a nonconscious inference about that trait.

DISADVANTAGES OF EXEMPLAR VIEWS

Exemplar views of categorization and related areas constitute, in part, a backlash against the earlier dominance of cognitive models that emphasized the storage limitations of human cognitive systems and assumed that people must act as cognitive misers to process information efficiently. Fortunately, the human mind is not a computer and does not have the same limitations of operating and storage memory that affect all computers (Schneider, 1991).

Nonetheless, the main theoretical problem with exemplar models is that they must assume an enormous amount of storage of concrete information and calculations involving that information. At the extreme, every time we encounter a new person or object—something we do thousands, perhaps millions, of times a day—we must perform a very complex act. We must draw on a set of relevant exemplars (itself a complex act); make similarity judgments along many different dimensions; and then calculate whether this new thing is a dog or a cat, a librarian or a student, a friend or a foe. Does it seem reasonable to suppose that every time I see a female I must categorize her as female, based on such a complex process? It might seem on commonsense grounds that after the 10 millionth time I make this sort of categorization, I may find a less cumbersome way to perform it. A well-regulated mental apparatus may be cognitively ambidextrous—the equivalent of a switch hitter—in its ability to use both exemplar and more abstract information in its deliberations.

EXEMPLARS AND PROTOTYPES

Clearly, we do use both exemplar- and prototype-based categories (Medin, Altom, & Murphy, 1984; Smith, 1990). Zárate, Sanders, and Garza (2000) have proposed a functional association of exemplars with the right cortical hemisphere and prototypes with the left, each type of processing working essentially in parallel. This makes a certain amount of sense. A memory system that relied solely on individual experiences and did not allow us to store information about the features of general categories would leave us at the mercy of each new experience. We would bob around on rough cognitive seas. On the other hand, a memory system that only dealt with the abstract and general would be the equivalent of a cognitive bureaucracy—unresponsive to special cases and to individual experiences, unwilling and unable to change.

As it turns out, people store information both about groups and about the individuals composing those groups (Judd & Park, 1988; Park & Rothbart, 1982). Prototype representations tend to be favored when perceivers are trying to learn about categories (Wattenmaker, 1991), but exemplars should be favored when we focus on individuals (especially ingroup members) rather than on groups, or have no strong prior stereotype (Smith, 1990; Smith & Zárate, 1990). We are also more likely to use prototype representations for groups when we perceive the group to be high in entitativity (see below)—that is, to be a psychologically meaningful group from which we expect some consistency (Brewer & Harasty, 1996).

It is also probable that with increasing exposure to people in given groups, we will tend to use more abstract representations. Certainly, when we make judgments about the self (a presumably well-known person), we rely more on stored trait knowledge than on behavioral exemplars for judgments of typicality (Klein & Loftus, 1993). We also favor more abstract knowledge for people we know well and behavioral exemplars for people we know less well (Park, 1986; Sherman & Klein, 1994). More to the point, perhaps, stereotypes of groups we do not know well are based more on individual people as exemplars, whereas stereotypes of better-known groups are based on more abstract knowledge (Sherman, 1996). Additional debate about this issue occurs in Chapter 7, which discusses how ingroups and outgroups are represented cognitively.

Categories as Theories

The classic, prototype, and exemplar models differ in many respects, but they all assume that decisions about categories and categorization fundamentally depend in one way or another on similarity judgments. Although the models do not exactly assume that we humans are passive cognizers carried helplessly down a stream of stimulus information toward the safe shores of tractable categories, they also do not much emphasize the active role we often seem to play in our categorization efforts. To be sure, much of our categorization activity is implicit and nonconscious, but at times we mix it up with our categories actively indeed. We are quite good at slicing and dicing the same information in different ways. When we consider any movie we have seen, for example, we can easily categorize all the characters in terms of gender, race, relative height, and perhaps good person–bad person—artfully playing with various dimensions of similarity.

In recent years, there has been a general recognition that a full understanding of concepts and categories requires giving all of us—even racists—credit for making use of our theoretical knowledge (Murphy & Medin, 1985; Wittenbrink, Hilton, & Gist, 1998). Furthermore, even when we are mentally passive and being swept along by salient similarities, theories are always waiting in the background to provide a theoretical basis for our judgments if need be and to provide instant flexibility if we wish to use alternative categorizations. Many of our categories, especially those most central to stereotyping, are more than lists of features and stored exemplars that generate similarity relationships; we need to understand the glue that holds our categories together.

PROBLEMS WITH SIMILARITY

One reason to emphasize theory models is that there are major problems with similarity-based models, stemming from the fact that judgments of similarity between two or more things are usually based on multiple features (Medin, Goldstone, &

Gentner, 1993). If, for example, I say that Sylvester Stallone is more like Arnold Schwarzenegger than like Woody Allen, there are likely to be several features I use (body build, height, weight, types of moves they appear in, whether they employ weapons in their movie roles, whether they are likely to drive fast cars, etc.). This seems reasonable enough. What is the problem?

Feature Salience. One problem is that there are far more features that we might have used for comparison; in fact, the number of such features is infinite. For example, the first two movie stars surely both weigh over 180 pounds, whereas I doubt that Woody Allen does. They also are both similar in that they weight over 180.1 pounds, over 180.09 pounds, over 180.009 pounds, and so forth. And the problem is not limited to using finer and finer gradations. We might find that the first two are closer in age, have birthdays in the same month, live on streets that begin with the same first letter (or have the same number of letters), and owned dogs as children. Obviously, this seems silly, but on the basis of what principle do we exclude these other potentially charming facts of lives?

In judging Sly as more similar to Arnie than to Woody, we are clearly privileging some features over others. There are bound to be other features on which Sly and Woody are more similar. For example, both were born in the United States; both grew up on the East Coast; neither has been a professional body builder; neither has been married to a close relative of a U.S. President; and so forth. Obviously if we used these criteria, Sly and Woody would be seen as more similar. Well, you say, body build and types of movies are more important than where these people were born. Again, common sense would support your point of view, but we still have the right to ask what criteria you use to judge that some features are more important than others.

Similarity Is Not Always Important for Category Membership. There are now abundant data suggesting that at least some categories are not formed on the basis of perceptual similarity. Suppose I ask you, in a somewhat protective frame of mind, to walk through your home and pick out all the objects that could be used to kill you. As you pick out various vases, bottles, knives, perhaps guns, T-shirts, shoes, pesticides, drain cleaners, medications, and the like, you will be forming a coherent and meaningful category, but you are not using any simple similarity rule. There are lots of different ways to kill, and so many different objects that could be used for any given method. In forming this category, you are likely to draw on a fairly sophisticated knowledge base about how people can be killed and what objects work best for each way. For such "ad hoc categories" (e.g., murder weapons), similarity can not and does not predict category membership well, although ideals in achieving goals does (Barsalou, 1983).

More generally for many categories, there is now evidence that ratings of category membership, typicality, and similarity to a category are far from perfectly correlated (Bailenson et al., 2002; Rips & Collins, 1993). In a series of experiments, Rips (1989) has shown that similarity is not always a good predictor of category membership. In one set of experiments subjects were asked whether an object that was 3 inches in diameter was more likely to be a pizza or a quarter, and they readily chose the pizza, even though they saw it as more similar to the quarter. Rips argues that while the size of quarters is fixed (by law, in this case), that of the pizza is not. Thus subjects make use of knowledge and theories about the homogeneity of categories. In other experiments, changes in surface features of many objects did not change the category of the object but did affect its similarity ratings. For example, a bird that acquires insect qualities as a function of an accident is still a bird, even though it might be judged to be more similar to the insect. One can "drive a wedge" (to use Rips's phrase) between judgments of similarity and category membership, and this suggests that similarity cannot be the only criterion for category membership.

THEORIES AND CATEGORY RELATIONSHIPS

Even in making judgments about the similarity of two or more people, we must use a theory of sorts to decide what features are important and how strongly to weight them in a given decisional framework. When we group things together to form categories, we have implicated a theory about not only what similarities are important but why. Such theories help us in at least two different ways. First, theories provide a way of understanding category coherence (Murphy & Medin, 1985; Quine, 1977)—a sense of how the various features associated with the category hang together. Second, they tell us what features are important for the category and why.

Categories as Theoretically Coherent. The theories you have about the features that are important in determining categories do additional work for you: Such theories can also indicate how features relate to one another. Not only will you know that body build, height, weight, and types of movies made are important ways that Hollywood divides actors, and that these features predict your enjoyment of movies, but you will also have a clear sense of how these features are related to one another. Body build is an important criterion for how convincing an actor can be in playing certain sorts of roles, for example. Furthermore, this theoretical knowledge you have about category coherence allows you to understand how categories are related to one another. You understand how action movie stars fit into the action movie category, and how this relates to other kinds of movies and movie actors. In addition, for most of the categories you use, you have quite detailed knowledge about superordinate and subordinate relationships among categories. You know that movie stars and stage actors are both actors, and that actors as well as athletes, opera stars, and rock musicians are all entertainers, and you know why. Knowledge about feature relationships is helpful in learning and using categories, especially when you have a sense of the theoretical and causal reasons for these relationships (Anderson & Fincham, 1996; Murphy & Allopenna, 1994; Spalding & Murphy, 1996; Wisniewski, 1995).

Theories and Inferences. Obviously stereotypes are important, in part, because of the inferences we draw about others based on their category memberships. Many of these inferences are rather passively derived from relatively simple memories. For example, it is quite probable that for many people, features such as being politically liberal, smart, and impractical are stored directly with the category of college professors. However, other features, also characteristic of professors, are unlikely to be stored in this way: using computer programs to analyze data, advising political candidates on political polling, working with minority high school students during the summers, or visiting libraries in Europe. You might have people list features of college professors for hours and never find a single person listing all these features. Yet, if I told you that I have a friend who has just spent the summer working in the British Library, you will probably immediately infer that this friend is likely to be a professor. Professorship explains the behavior, at least at a superficial level. And that explanation is not likely to be based merely on attaching facts about libraries and the like to some professor node in memory.

People who know that professors do research (a highly typical feature) also know that sometimes research materials may be more readily available in British sources. This is not much of a theory, to be sure, but even elementary theories about categories do help us explain seemingly random bits and pieces of behavior, as well as those more centrally attached to categories. Clearly, not all our category knowledge is garbed in deep theoretical dress; many features are there just because they're there. Still, theories are important ways of giving coherence to our categories and their features.

Types of Categories

Up to this point, we have assumed that all categories are alike, at least in terms of how they are developed and used by people. However, this is surely a naive assumption. It seems unlikely, for example, that the fairly precisely defined concepts used by mathematicians work quite the same way as biological concepts, which in turn may differ from the use of legal concepts and those ad hoc categories that we find very useful in our everyday lives. Moreover, it is not clear how social categories fit into all this. Do we use gender or occupational categories in the same ways that we use categories of animals, furniture, games, and cars?

Social versus Nonsocial Categories

Much of the classic work on categories and categorization has been and continues to be conducted with nonsocial and often highly artificial categories. There is nothing inherently wrong with this strategy, and it has the decided advantage of giving investigators a great deal of control over experimental materials. Some (e.g., Brewer, 1988; Feldman, 1988) have explicitly assumed that there are no fundamental differences between social and nonsocial categories, but others (e.g., Lingle, Altom, & Medin, 1984; Medin, 1988; Ostrom, 1984; Wilder, 1986) have not been so sure. There are several obvious differences.

SOCIAL STIMULI ARE MORE COMPLEX

Perhaps the most important difference is that social stimuli tend to be more complex than nonsocial stimuli (Cantor & Mischel, 1979a; Dahlgren, 1986). It is an open question whether a picture of a human face or body is actually more complex visually than a picture of an apple, a tree, or a house. Intuitively it seems so. In addition, humans are more often active—an added bit of complexity, just to keep us on our toes. It makes relatively little difference whether we observe an apple tree blowing in the breeze or see it in its most static manifestation. But a static photograph of a person and a videotape of that person doing even the simplest behavior are likely to be seen quite differently. Speaking adds even more complexity.

PEOPLE AND THEIR BEHAVIORS READILY FIT MORE CATEGORIES

Because people are more complex than most stimuli, it is also likely that we have more ways of readily classifying people than objects. How many ways can we think of a chair? To be sure, we could easily list a dozen or so things that this chair is—a piece of furniture; something inherited from a grandfather; a big, ugly, and largely blue kind of thing. But we quickly exhaust the obvious categories. With social stimuli, we are less likely to run out of cognitive steam so quickly. The same behavior can easily be seen as rude, aggressive, hostile, immature, assertive, selfish, insensitive, harassing—the list goes on. We routinely classify people in terms of age, race, gender, occupation, marital and parental status, personality traits, abilities, possessions, hobbies, and physical appearance.

HUMAN CATEGORIES ARE NOT CLEANLY HIERARCHICAL

People, unlike objects, do not fit themselves as nicely into ready-made category hierarchies (Lingle et al., 1984). We have ready-made biological classifications that capture the family dog at some level, and chairs, cars, and computers also are easily thought of in terms of object hierarchies. For example, a computer is a type of office equipment, which is a type of equipment, and so on. People, on the other hand, rarely fit so neatly into hierarchies. To be sure, secretaries have their place in the organization hierarchy, and parents may be graded according to gender and whether they are also grandparents. But often it is not clear which people categories are subordinate to which (Trafimow & Radhakrishnan, 1995). A female lawyer is both a lawyer who happens to be female and a female who happens to be a lawyer. It is probable that socially significant categories are not related hierarchically, but rather easily combine into combinations (Brewer, 1988; Medin, Lynch, & Solomon, 2000). So, rather than worrying about whether females are types of lawyers or the reverse, we naturally combine these into what are called "compound categories" (discussed later in this chapter).

SOCIAL CATEGORIES ARE MORE OPAQUE

Most of the categories we deal with in everyday life are based on readily perceptible cues. When we look at a tree, basically what we see is what we get. Obviously, there are many important features of trees (having to do with sap flow, photosynthesis, use of nutrients, etc.) that we cannot readily observe, but generally most of what we need to know about trees in our normal encounters we get directly, without complex inferences. This tends to make classification fairly easy. With people, things tend to be different. Of course, some features that lead to social categorization (gender, attractiveness) are readily apparent, but many social categories (history of mental illness, parental status) are not so easily judged. In addition, many of the features we care most about, such as attitudes, motives, and traits, are not the least bit obvious at first (or even second) glance; important features for social categories must usually be inferred. This in turn may make the detection of feature relationships for social categories especially difficult (Holland, Holyoak, Nisbett, & Thagard, 1986). Another way of putting this is that features of social categories tend to be more abstract than for object categories (Wattenmaker, 1995) and are much more subject to interpretation and multiple meanings, which are useful in resolving inconsistencies among features.

SOCIAL CATEGORIES ARE MORE VALUE-LADEN

Obviously, we care about some categories more than others. On average, we probably have stronger emotional feelings about social than about nonsocial categories (Tajfel & Forgas, 1981). I mention two possible consequences. First, we may be inclined to use our feelings as an aid to categorization. It may, for example, be easier to group murderers and thieves together as a disliked category than lawnmowers and hedge trimmers, which are fairly neutral. Second, we may make sharper distinctions within affect-laden categories. For example, I am sometimes struck by the tendency of those who value physical appearance to divide the world neatly into ugly and beautiful individuals. Or those who care about money seem to operate with categories of people who have lots of it and those who have less than lots—serious money and less than serious money.

SOCIAL GROUPS OFTEN FORM THE BASIS OF CATEGORIES

Categories and social groups are not the same (Hamilton, Sherman, & Lickel, 1998), although there is a loose relationship between social categories and groups. Many groups are readily used as categories. On my campus, the faculty, students, and staff are groups (having their own organizations, norms and the like) and also categories. On many campuses, fraternities and sororities or other student organizations are likewise both. On the other hand, not all groups function as categories. The Rice University Board of Governors forms a fairly tight-knit group when it meets, but I would be hard pressed to consider the board members a category, since they seem to share few attributes other than wealth. I could, of course, think of Houston Astros fans as a category when I wish to mount a relevant advertising campaign, and the Rice University Board of Governors as a category when I see its members as a type of group that facilitates or hinders my goals.

To look at it from the other direction, many highly relevant social categories do not lead to a sense of "groupiness." Gender is a relevant social category, but I generally do not think of males or females as groups. Race, disability status, and age, to name but three other kinds of categories, also do not usually form the basis of groups. However, they may. It is common in many organizations and universities for women, blacks, and persons with physical disabilities to form support groups or groups designed to lobby for specific category-related goals, and many groups are restricted to people above or below a certain age.

Entitativity. Obviously, just as categories are not all alike, groups also vary a great deal in their features. In an important paper, Donald Campbell (1958) argued that some groups seem to be entities, whereas others are looser and less "groupy." Campbell pointed to the Gestalt psychology principles of proximity, similarity of group members, and common fate (group members experience common outcomes) as key components of groupiness, and he also pointed to goodness of form (corresponding to group organization), and resistance to intrusion (which can refer to the permeability of groups).

In recent years, there has been a great deal of interest in the psychological aspects of perceived groups (e.g., Brewer & Harasty, 1996; Hamilton & Sherman, 1996; Hamilton, Sherman, & Castelli, 2002; Hamilton et al., 1998). Perceived groupiness is usually called "entitativity" (i.e., the condition of being entity-like)—a mouthful, perhaps, but an accurate term for all that. What constitutes an entitative group? An extensive study by Lickel and colleagues (2000) attempted to answer this question. Subjects rated a number of types of groups, ranging from members of a family to people at a bus stop, on the extent to which they saw these groups as being groups (their measure of entitativity) as well as on several other scales. Not surprisingly, families were rated high and people at a bus stop as low on entitativity. The best predictor of perceived entitativity was the extent to which members interact with one another, but measures of the importance of the group for individual members, whether group members have common goals, and whether group members are similar to one another also predicted entitativity. Rating profiles produced five distinct types of groups. "Intimacy groups" (e.g., families) have high entitativity and levels of interaction, are small, are of long duration, and have low permeability (members' ability to enter or leave the group). "Task groups" (e.g., members of a jury) are less entitative, have high levels of interaction, are small, and are of moderate duration and permeability. "Social categories" (e.g., race) are even lower on entitativity, tend to be large, and have moderate duration and low permeability. "Weak social relationships" (e.g., people who work in the same building) tend to be low in entitativity, large, and highly permeable. Finally, "transitory groups" (e.g., people waiting for a bus) are very low in entitativity, have low levels of interaction, and are short-lived and highly permeable.

There are several implications of entitativity, which are explored in subsequent chapters (see especially Chapters 4, 5, 7, and 10). Generally, information about entitative groups is processed more with an eye to developing a consistent impression in a more integrated fashion, much as we process information about individuals we care about (Hamilton, Sherman, & Maddox, 1999). This means that we perceivers are more likely to form dispositional inferences about entitative groups (Rogier & Yzerbyt, 1999; Yzerbyt, Rogier, & Fiske, 1998), perform causal analyses on observed behavior, explain the behavior of groups in ways they do for individuals (O'Laughlin & Malle, 2002), try to integrate the information more, assign more responsibility to members of entitative groups for misdeeds (Lickel, Schmader, & Hamilton, 2003), and try to resolve inconsistencies (Welbourne, 1999). We are also likely to make more comparisons among members of entitative groups (Pickett, 2001), and to see the groups as more homogeneous (Dasgupta, Banaji, & Abelson, 1999) and the people within them as less distinguishable (Sherman, Castelli, & Hamilton, 2002).

Entitativity is not a fixed property of groups. For example, the African American students on my campus are not a particularly cohesive or entitative group; they are more a category than a group. However, at certain times (e.g., planning for Black History Week or protesting some act of discrimination), they may become very tight-knit indeed. The important question for us to answer is whether people are more likely to stereotype this group when they are in their entitative phase, and I'm speculating that they are. Some research (Schneider, Haley, & Towler, 2002) suggests that people think they have more powerful stereotypes of entitative groups, and other research (Lickel, Hamilton, & Sherman, 2001) suggests that we hold members of entitative groups more responsible for the misdeeds of one of its members. The latter suggests that entitative groups have more inductive potential (as discussed later in this chapter), and evidence does suggest that people are more willing to infer trait information about other group members from one member in entitative groups (Crawford, Sherman, & Hamilton, 2002). There is also some suggestion that entitative groups are seen as more threatening (Dasgupta et al., 1999), which can sometimes be more important than the psychological benefits of belonging to cozy groups.

Social Categories Divide the World into Ingroups and Outgroups. When categories apply to existing groups, there is a tendency to parse them into ingroups and outgroups. Although I am unlikely to think of myself as belonging or not belonging to the category of trees, or triangles, or mammals, I am keenly aware that I am a male and not a female, an American and not an Albanian, a professor and not a lawyer. As we will see (Chapter 7), this distinction between ingroup and outgroup is a powerful source of emotion and affect, but it also affects the ways we process information about people and their categories.

Physical Groupings Are Often Important for Social Categories. People have intentions and preferences, and they often move about on that basis. We are not surprised to discover that social categories also form the basis of physical groupings. People of similar occupations, political and moral persuasions, race, ethnic groupings, gender, and so forth are probably more often found together than one might expect by chance. Although this may also be true of nonsocial categories (particularly, we may expect, natural categories—"Birds of a feather flock together"), we probably do not have such extensive expectations of physical groupings in those cases.

If all this is true, there are important implications. For example, we may assume that social categories are likely to be accompanied by a cultural overlay and to be the focus for some degree of social influence. Chinese Americans are not merely a group of people with vaguely similar physical features whom we often see together; we assume that they share a common culture and set of attitudes by virtue of their frequent close contact, socialization, and social pressure. By contrast, it is unlikely that chairs or computers acquire more common features when they move from their solitary state to a collective one. A given chair is pretty much the same chair alone in my study and in the furniture store surrounded by its cousins.

Groups Change. As Wilder (1986) has pointed out, social groups (which form the basis of many social categories) can and sometimes do change themselves, just as individual people do. A literary reading group or scientific society may evolve into a group of people bound together more by friendship and social needs than by intellectual needs. In some cities, unions of police officers have become less concerned with pay and working conditions than with affirmative action issues, and because the basis of membership has changed somewhat, members have thereby become more conservative.

DOES THIS MATTER?

Are these differences psychologically important? Are we safe in generalizing the abundant research on nonsocial categories to those categories that form the basis of stereotypes? The fact of the matter is that we haven't got a clue. Despite occasional studies (Wattenmaker, 1995) in which social and nonsocial categories have been compared, there has been little systematic research on the topic. We do know that many results from the basic cognitive literatures seem to apply to social categories fairly effortlessly, but that is not the same as knowing that they always or even usually do.

Compound Categories

Everyone, everywhere, can be categorized in multiple ways. Sometimes we can deal with these categories independently (Crisp, Hewstone, & Cairns, 2001; Pittinsky, Shih, & Ambady, 2000), but often we may categorize people in terms of two or more categories simultaneously. Many of the categories we use in everyday life are compound in the sense that they operate at the intersection of two or more primary categories. For example, "pet dog" is a combination of the categories of "pet" and "dog." "Black female lawyer" is a combination of three more primary categories. It is easy to imagine an endless supply of such compound categories, but there are two basic questions we must answer about all examples. The first is what determines whether something is a member of a compound category, and the second is what determines the features associated with compounds.

COMPOUND CATEGORY TYPICALITY

What determines whether a given individual will become a member of a compound category? Not all dogs, or all pets, are pet dogs. Isn't the answer that pet dogs are in the set defined as the intersection between the two more primary sets? Generally, yes—at least for what are called "predicating combinations," which are those in which the combination of A and B can be expressed as a B that is A. For example, a pet fish is a fish that is a pet (or, alternatively, a pet that is a fish); nonpredicating combinations cannot be so expressed. So a mantle clock is not a clock that is a mantle, and a career woman is not a woman who is a career.[1] With predicating combinations, an exemplar that belongs to the combination also belongs to both constituents, so that a pet fish is both a fish and a pet. With nonpredicating combinations, the first term designates a subset of the second.

Even for predicating combinations, however, it is usually not enough merely to know whether something is formally a member of one of more categories. Given the centrality of typicality effects in categorization, it is more important to ask whether something is seen as more or less typical of various categories. And the typicality structure of compound categories is not easily predicted (Cohen & Murphy, 1984). Most examples work quite well. A golden retriever is a good exemplar of both a pet and a dog, and so naturally is a particularly "good" pet dog. But others do not. Canaries are better examples of pet birds than of birds or pets. Anita Hill is probably seen as a more prototypic black female lawyer than she is of any of the constituent categories. Because typicality is so important in our use of categories, it is important to understand typicality judgments with compound categories but unfortunately, we know almost nothing about typicality for social compound categories.

ATTRIBUTES OF COMPOUND CATEGORIES

Of greater interest to stereotyping is how we determine the features of compound categories. Think about the black female lawyer. She surely has some features of each primary category. We would expect that she has the secondary sexual features of her gender, that she has a law degree and has passed the bar exam, and that her skin is dark. But she may also lack some of the other characteristic features of each category. We would not be surprised to discover that she is not as feminine in appearance and manner as most women, that she is less materialistic than most lawyers, and that she does not share the poverty associated with the black stereotype. So one problem is that features in the primary categories do not necessarily show up in the compound; this is referred to as "inheritance failure." The opposite problem is that wholly new features may arise for this compound category that are given low weights for various primary categories; these are called "emergent properties." We might, for example, readily assume that this black female lawyer is active in fighting for the rights of poor women—a feature that does not seem to be particularly closely associated with any of the more primary categories.

Attribute Inheritance. Consider attribute inheritance. Does a gay male athlete inherit most of his stereotypic attributes from his sexual preference or from his athletic prowess? Whereas the stereotype of a black woman is that she is poor, that of a lawyer is of wealth; so is the black female lawyer poor or rich? In this case, the inheritance is almost certainly from the lawyer category. On the other hand, if one is asked about political attitudes, one imagines that the black female lawyer is more likely to inherit perceived liberalism from a stereotype of black females than from the more conservative cast of lawyer stereotypes.

Hampton (1987) found that the importance of an attribute for a compound was predicted quite well by the importance of the attributes for each constituent. If an attribute was important for one or both of the constituents, it tended to be judged as important for the conjunction, although there were several instances of inheritance failure and emergent properties. Hampton was further interested in dominance effects. As with the judgments of whether exemplars were typical, attribute ratings showed similar sorts of dominance effects. That is, attributes of weapons tended to be more important in the tool–weapon compound than were attributes of tools, and sports dominated games in similar fashion. Again, there was no perfect way to predict which category dominated, but there was some suggestion that the constituent category with the more important attributes dominated.

I and my students (Rozendal, 1995) have been investigating inheritance rules with stereotypes, and thus far it seems that there are few rules determining which primary category dominates. In the paradigm we use, subjects are asked to rate both component and compound categories on the same traits. We then simply correlate the compound category with each component across traits. This allows us to determine whether the profile (across traits) of the compound matches one component more than the other. In many cases we find clear dominance patterns. For example, a female electrical engineering major is judged to be closer to the electrical engineer ($r = .96$) than the female ($r = .41$). A homeless college-educated person is perceived to be like homeless people in general ($r = .86$) and unlike college-educated people in general ($r = -.38$). A homosexual athlete is viewed as more homosexual ($r = .72$) than athlete ($r = -.32$). On the other hand, there are some combinations without clear dominance patterns. An electrical engineering major who is an athlete is judged to be like both ($r = .69$, $r = .65$). An atheist physics major is seen to be as much like an atheist ($r = .79$) as like a typical physics major ($r = .74$).

There are a few hints in the data that may lead to a predictive model of inheritance. The first is that highly salient, perhaps deviant, categories (e.g., homosexual persons and individuals with mental illness) almost always dominate other categories. A second is that those categories that have the strongest stereotypes tend to dominate. Strongly stereotyped categories also tend to be numerically small (and perhaps perceptually more homogeneous), so it is unclear whether group size or strength of the stereotype is more important. Third, stereotypes for categories in which people choose membership (e.g., occupation, car ownership) are stronger than stereotypes for nonchosen categories (age, gender, race) and seem to dominate.

Emergent Traits. A second tradition has been to look for what we might call emergent traits. Intuitively, some features of compound categories are not strongly represented in either component. For example, I imagine that a college-educated homeless man spends much of his day in the public library—a feature I do not associate with either homeless or college-educated people generally. Two methods have been used to seek such emergent qualities. The first is to ask people to list features or traits that come to mind with the various categories. Kunda, Miller, and Claire (1990) had subjects list traits for various compound categories and their constituents. A feature was counted as emergent if several subjects listed it for the compound but no one listed it for the constituents. Several emergent qualities were found. For example, a Harvard-educated carpenter was seen as nonconformist, easygoing, and nonmaterialistic. A blind lawyer was seen as determined and confident. A feminist bank teller was seen as hypocritical and unmarried. Another strategy has been to have subjects rate all the categories on rating scales and count as emergent traits any traits associated with a compound category that get more extreme trait ratings than either component receives. Using this criterion, Hastie, Schroeder, and Weber (1990) found that 28% of their traits ratings for compound categories were emergent. Rozendal (1995) also found substantial emergence with this criterion.

There are many ways to explain the attribute results just discussed. Parallel-distributed-processing models can simulate emergent properties by making assumptions about combinations of traits associated with categories (Smith & DeCoster, 1998). Another possibility is to use basic-linear-prediction models—that is, to assume that one can predict whatever one needs to know about compounds on the basis of various attributes of the constituents (Hampton, 1987). Hampton (1987) argues that a weighted-average model, with two important exceptions, can handle these data. One exception is that any attribute that is necessary for either constituent is important for the compound. So "has feathers" is a necessary attribute of birds, does not generally characterize pets, but is important for pet birds. Second, any attribute that is impossible for one constituent is also impossible for the compound. "Migrates" is judged as highly unlikely or impossible for pets, yet is fairly characteristic of birds. As expected, "migrates" is seen as highly unlikely for pet birds.[2]

Some compound categories are so familiar that we may have ready-made feature lists for them. This might explain why pet fish as a category seems to be so poorly related to its constituents. Most of us know about pets and about fish, but have independent knowledge about pet fish. However, such rule-based inferences do not always work. We can form various kinds of compound categories seemingly at will (e.g., a college-educated homeless person, a Porsche-driving psychology professor, a socialist stockbroker), and it is difficult to formulate general rules for how we understand them, precisely because they have such little feature overlap. Emergent properties are probably more common for categories with relatively little feature overlap (Hampton, 1997), and we probably rely on theory-driven explanations for the combination (Murphy, 1990, 1993a). When subjects are asked to judge a college-educated homeless person, they probably know few, if any, exemplars. And they probably cannot rely on simply forming the union of the two constituents, because there are so many incompatible attributes. Rather, it seems more likely that the subjects would take a deep cognitive breath and begin to invent a theory, explanation, or scenario about how and why a college graduate could become homeless.

IMPLICATIONS

People are never presented to us "wearing" single categories. For instance, the person before me is male, black, a student, a psychology major, tall, articulate, and an athlete. In some cases, we simply have to decide which categories are the most important; in this context, which of the categories do I use? This chapter considers issues of multiple categories in due course. But sometimes we do the compounding. Do we then have to figure out which attributes to take from each primary category, and if so, does the compound stereotype have unique qualities? In other words, is my stereotype of black athletes notably different from those of blacks and athletes, in ways that count? Do we reserve special cognitive space for compound categories? Do we actually have a category of black athletes that we regularly use?

There are suggestions that when people are classified in multiple ways (often called "criss-cross classification"), bias that would normally be shown toward members of one category are lessened (see reviews by Crisp & Hewstone, 1999a; Migdal, Hewstone, & Mullen, 1998; Mullen, Migdal, & Hewstone, 2001; Urban & Miller, 1998). On the bases of these data, we might argue that primary category membership becomes less salient when two or more categories are relevant.

Issues of compound categories also inform this chapter's subsequent discussion of subtyping. As we will see, several people have argued that many global categories (females, males, lawyers, African Americans, Hispanic Americans) are too broad and carry little information. Most of us recognize that there are lots of different kinds of males and females, lawyers, African Americans, and Hispanic Americans. So it has been argued that we have richer stereotypes for subtypes, such as "African American on welfare," "housewife," or "corporate lawyer." However, these subtypes are, in effect, compound categories, and it becomes an important question how well their features can be predicted from the features of the more primary categories.

Features and Categories

Some categories (e.g., squares) have relatively impoverished feature lists, whereas for others (e.g., computers, males, and physicians) a listing of attributes might take hours. Furthermore, for any given category, not all features are created equal. When I think about college professors as a category, I have the sense that possessing a PhD is more closely associated with the category than driving an old car. I assume that grey hair is more characteristic of people in their 60s than forgetfulness. To some extent, the fact that some features are stronger parts of stereotypes than others may simply reflect reality, or at least our experiences with exemplars. Another possibility is that people have theories about why some features are more important than

others: Some features form an essential core of the category, while others are peripheral.

Psychological Essentialism

One of the powerful legacies that we have inherited from the ancient Greeks and
from medieval scholasticism is an emphasis on essence. Medieval scholars were inclined to suggest that every object or person has an "essence"—a set of features that
not only provides the definition of that thing, but also defines its purpose in the
larger plan created by God. So the essence of wheat would be its ability to make
bread and feed people, and the essence of cows would be to provide milk and power
for plowing fields. The fact that wheat has a yellowish color is not a part of the essence of wheat; it is an accidental property. Obviously, most modern psychologists
reject this notion of essences—in particular, the teleological part, which stems from a
religious perspective.

NATURAL KINDS

But some categories do seem to have a clear essence. Various philosophers (Putnam,
1970/1975; Quine, 1977; Schwartz, 1979, 1980) argue that some categories have a reality anchored in physical and biological laws. So the category of dogs is more natural than the category of, say, tables or pets. Dogs exist and will continue to produce
new dogs without human intervention, and regardless of whether we humans see
them as more similar to wolves or to cats. The category of pets is another story. I
might conceivably even treat my dog, cat, goldfish, and bird all alike—feeding them at
the same time every day, taking them for walks, petting and talking to them, so that
for all intents and purposes there are no distinctions in terms of my behavior to be
made among the dog, cat, bird, and fish that I own. Still, when push comes to shove,
my dog will breed with other dogs and not with the bird; my cat will eat the goldfish,
if given the chance; but the fish will not salivate over the sight of the cat. Thus the
category of dog or cat seems to reflect more than a "group by definition."

Although various other types of categories have been proposed (see Medin et
al., 2000), the usual contrast for "natural kinds" is "artifactual categories"—things that
are created intentionally for some purpose (Bloom, 1996). Take the category of
clocks. Such objects cannot be defined in terms of appearances (consider digital vs.
analog, or wall clock vs. Big Ben) or even in terms of use (one can tell time via the
sun, as people did for centuries, but we do not usually think of the sun as a clock).
Clocks are things that someone created to tell time, so the essence they have is one
defined by human intention and cultural understandings. Whereas we look for some
thing (DNA or molecular structure) for the essence of natural kinds, the essence of
artifactual categories lies in the ephemeral world of intentions. Having said that, I
should note that many kinds of artifacts (e.g., computers, manufactured medications)
seem to have an underlying essence over and above their intended uses, so that the
distinction between natural kinds and artifactual categories is not hard and fast.

Natural kinds have fairly clear defining features that may be hidden from view
(molecular structures, genetic codes), and these features give rise to observable attributes that are related in understandable ways. That is the core idea. I know how to
tell a dog from a cat, and I assume that these differences are not arbitrary, but are in

fact linked to DNA through the mysteries of biological development. It is not necessary that I personally know what that essence is, or even that anyone does; we often operate with what are called "essence placeholders," or assumptions that someone at some time will figure it out. Sometimes we even make technical mistakes. For example, we call both pines and maples "trees," even though they are biologically quite different (maples are actually biologically closer to roses than to pine trees), and when I garden I sharply distinguish between weeds and flowers—a distinction of no biological validity. Furthermore, people sometimes make peculiar judgments about what we might think of as essential features. For example, Malt (1994) had subjects rate the percentage of H_2O in various liquids, some of which we would call water and some not. In this task people rated saliva (normally not thought of as water) as having a higher percentage of H_2O than dishwater.

Such errors aside, natural kinds are ultimately subject to scientific inquiry in ways that other types of categories are not. It makes perfect sense to take a rock to a geologist or a strange animal to a biologist and ask what it is, but it seems silly to take a table to a physical scientist and ask what it is. Understanding the molecular structure of a particular table somehow misses the point of "tableness," which is more a matter for furniture designers, interior decorators, and perhaps anthropologists.

Do we think of categories of people as having an essence? Reflexively, the answer is a loud "Of course not." But think about it a little. When people talk about the criminal personality, aren't they really referencing a personality constellation that "makes" (perhaps somewhat metaphorically) a criminal a criminal, in much the same way that kitty genes make purrs and whiskers? Don't we assume that the training lawyers receive is an essence of sorts that dictates how they view laws and contracts differently from the rest of us? Isn't there an essence, composed of raging hormones and rampant peer pressure, to being a typical teenager? To be sure, DNA and molecular structure are different from legal training and personality types, but the question is whether we succumb to essentialist thinking even when we should be cautious. People do seem to be sensitive to the possible existence of hidden but basic features of all sorts of categories, and this has led Medin and Ortony (1989) to the notion of "psychological essentialism"—the idea that people act as if categories have essences, even if they do not.

EVIDENCE FOR PSYCHOLOGICAL ESSENTIALISM

The notion of psychological essentialism is highly controversial with critics (e.g., Rips, 2001; Stevens, 2000) and defenders (e.g., Ahn et al., 2001; Gelman & Hirschfeld, 1999) in full and fine fettle. And in fairness, essentialist thinking is hard to pin down. People tend to deny that they use it, at least for most people categories, and the concept is hard to get a mental grip on. The best evidence we have comes from developmental studies. Generally from an early age, children seem to have a sense that biological kinds have an essence (see Gelman, 2003, for a review). For example, children as young as age 4 have a strong intuition that removing the "insides" of an animal changes its identity more than does changing its physical appearance (Gelman & Wellman, 1991). Children as young as age 3 understand that animal movement has an internal cause, whereas mechanical movement does not (Gelman & Gottfried, 1996). Essentialism promotes drawing inferences from single exemplars of biological kinds to other instances; by age 4, children understand that if a blackbird feeds its young with mashed-up food, a flamingo (another bird) is more likely to do the same than a bat (a nonbird), even though the latter looks more like a blackbird than the former (Gelman & Markman, 1986). Children see biology as more important than socialization for both racial and gender identity. So a boy raised by all women will still be a boy, and a black child raised by whites will still be black (see Chapter 9 for further discussion).

There are three major points to be made in this regard. First, it is likely that people are born with essence-attuned "antennae," although language is also an important cause of essentialist thinking in children (Gelman, 2000, 2003). Second, whether learned or innate, the tendency to see essences for natural kinds is powerful; may well persist into adulthood; and may be extended to categories of people based on race, gender, and ethnicity. Third, however, I emphatically emphasize that such tendencies (assuming they exist) can be overridden by later experience, scientific thinking, and the like. Childhood essentialism need not grow into an adult form, although it may well do so.

ADVANTAGES OF ESSENTIALISM

Whether or not the tendency to seek and declare essences for categories is a primitive and natural tendency, assumptions that categories have essential qualities do a fair amount of cognitive work for us. Psychological essentialism has at least five cognitive advantages.

Explanations for Features. First, a belief that categories have an essence not only allows us to assume that superficial (and often identifying) qualities are the way they are because of some underlying essence, but also gives us licence to invoke causal explanations for many observed features. Essentialism involves theories, although not all theories about people are based on essentialism. Kitty genes produce kitty appearances, and diamonds glitter because of underlying physical properties. Essentialism sometimes licenses more elaborate explanations. For example, most adults could discourse extensively on the human stomach and why it is inside the body in the position it is in, and so forth. Perhaps in similar fashion, we think we know why a criminal commits crimes.

Categories as Causes. Obviously, categories can be causes only when we take "cause" in its loosest and most informal sense, captured by the term "because." Yet it seems sensible just at that level. We might, for example, think that *because* an animal is a dog it will bark, or that a piece of jewelry sparkles *because* it is a diamond. Do we use human categories as quasi-explanations in the same ways?

Categories are more likely to be seen as causes to the extent that they are seen as natural kinds and have an essence. It makes perfect sense to say that fish swim because they are fish; by this we seem to mean, as a kind of shorthand, that some sort of fish essence (presumably bound up with DNA) creates the proper body configuration, muscular arrangement, and propensity to move these muscles in particular ways. It makes little sense, however, to say that an object is flat because it's a table, or that a car runs because it's a car. By contrast, we may say that a woman is caring because she's a doctor, or that a man is quiet because he's Japanese American. There are certainly times when such statements are used informally and perhaps cause some mischief (e.g., "He's obsessed with sex because he's a guy").

If we think about the examples above, these explanations make the most sense when implicit or explicit comparisons are involved. Dogs bark, but cats do not, and a caring female physician is implicitly compared with females in other occupations (such as attorneys). And when we make these kinds of comparisons, we often explain differences in terms of a particular category. Typically, we assume that the behavior associated with one category is more or less normal (the default category), whereas the difference is due to the other, mutable category. So in Western society we think of people as men until told otherwise (so we mark women but not men, as when we say a person is a "female doctor" but rarely a "male doctor"); whites are a default category for people; people with doctoral degrees are the default category among professors; and a female is assumed to be straight unless we are explicitly told that she is lesbian.

Miller, Taylor, and Buck (1991) have suggested that the behavior of people in mutable categories may require more explanation. In their study they showed that when men and women differ in voting patterns, people tend to focus on why women vote the ways they do, even though it makes as much sense to focus on the features of men that lead them to be different from women. So in that sense what men do does not require much explanation, but people who are different (in this case, women) do. Miller and colleagues also showed that this tendency is reversed when the task is a female-oriented one. So whereas "male" may be more immutable than "female" in many, perhaps most, circumstances, this is not inevitable.

Hegarty and Pratto (2001a) have shown the same sorts of effects for homosexuality. When people were told that there were differences between gay and straight men, they were more likely to use the gay than straight category in their explanations. People could, however, focus on straight males when told to do so, or when for a particular kind of behavior gay males were in the majority. Moreover, the types of explanations offered for the behaviors differed for the two categories. Explanations for behavior performed by gays tended to be more dispositional and essentialist (in this case, childhood experiences), especially for stereotype-consistent behavior, whereas the same behavior performed by straights was seen as more situationally caused. Subjects were also asked to imagine that gays and straights became indistinguishable in their behaviors, and they thought gays were more likely to change than straights, suggesting that characteristics associated with gay males are seen as more mutable.

The situations people are in may also affect explanations for their behaviors. Grier and McGill (2000) had subjects read about blacks and whites in typical or atypical activities. Generally people mentioned race more often in scenarios that were atypical. Just as "solos" (to be discussed later) often receive undue attention, people may want to explain the behavior of people who are not usually seen in a given situation in terms of their cateogry membership. Category explanations are also especially prominent when groups are in conflict (Oakes, Turner, & Haslam, 1991). According to self-categorization theory and the fit × accessibility notion (again, to be discussed later), when social categorization fits the stereotypic behavior of group members or differentiates the behavior of one group from another, then the category itself functions as a kind of explanation for the behavior.

Obviously, few people believe that race or gender per se causes behavior, but theories about categories do suggest ways that features or background causes may have caused the behavior. In such cases, we are inclined to think that people did what they did because of their gender or race. For instance, a black man is perceived as being hostile to a store clerk because he is black (see Chapter 4 for a personal example), and a male is seen as being insensitive to the needs of his spouse because "that's the way men are."

Preservation of Identity. Third, the assumption of essence allows us to deal with developmental changes and with preservation of identity despite superficial changes. So even small children understand that acorns have the potential to become trees, despite the fact that acorns and oak trees look nothing alike (Gelman, Coley, & Gottfried, 1994; Gelman & Wellman, 1991). On the other hand, a cat that loses its tail in an accident is still a cat, although perhaps not a contented one.

This may seem a long way from stereotyping, but consider that we all make these sorts of identity-preserving statements all the time. My personality is expected to mature and change appearances, but not its fundamental essence. We are not surprised to see physicians show concern for others in a variety of ways and in a variety of circumstances. In explaining the behavior of people, we often look to personality continuities from childhood to the present.

Correlated Features. Fourth, a belief in essential features helps us to understand the correlations among features of categories, and to use such correlations to predict the unobserved. I can be relatively certain that an animal with sharp teeth eats meat, and that one with long teeth is more likely to bite than one without, because I understand the evolutionary significance of teeth. Biting is not a random correlate of being long in the tooth. Natural kinds typically have a rich internal structure provided by the underlying genetic and molecular codes. Not only does being in a particular category require that certain features be present and often within a limited range of values, but there are abundant correlations among features. Fast animals have longer legs; smarter animals tend to walk upright; and, on average, tall trees have deeper roots. Another way to put this is that once the essential features of categories are fixed, they dictate (or in some cases allow) varying degrees of correlation among less essential features. Generally, for other types of categories, we do not expect such strong feature correlation. A square must have four equal sides and four equal angles, but there are essentially no limitations on other features (size, color, breadth of lines, etc.). Squares don't have correlated features other than for sides and angles. Even for artifactual categories such as tables, it is unlikely that we expect much by way of correlations among such features as color, size, number of legs, and material composition.

Inductive Potential. Fifth (and perhaps most importantly), to the extent that categories have an essence, they are likely to have inductive potential. The issue is whether we have the cognitive license to generalize from one (or a few) known category exemplars to other category members, or from subtypes to more superordinate categories. Obviously, when category members share a common essence, they are likely to be similar with regard to several superficial features presumably caused by the essence. If we were to discover tomorrow that a particular animal has a particular biological feature—say, HHY hormone—we would be inclined to assume that all similar animals also have the HHY hormone. Most of us would have no problem with the person who encountered one mean-spirited Doberman pinscher and decided on that basis not to buy one for his family. But do I as a professor have the same "right" to assume that if one football player cheats in my class, then most (or even that many) will? I will have more to say about this important issue in a later section of this chapter, but for now I merely emphasize that categories with presumed essences readily encourage such inductive inferences.

DO SOCIAL CATEGORIES HAVE AN ESSENCE?

We should also be clear that our informal, everyday assumption of essence is a working assumption at best and a crutch at worst. Even scientists cannot be sure how most features of natural-kind categories are caused by relevant genetic codes. Barking is surely related somehow to doggy genes, but no one knows how; furthermore, some dogs do not bark at all, and others bark infrequently. Even biological taxonomies and issues of how various animal types should be classified are subject to furious debate among biologists (Dupré, 1981). Moreover, our assumptions of essentialism can create massive amounts of mischief when we deal with important person categories (Rothbart & Taylor, 1992; Yzerbyt, Rocher, & Schadron, 1997). When we claim that people commit crimes because of a criminal personality, we run the danger of falling into an essentialist trap where we let our assumptions about categories do our work for us.

Nonetheless, the cautions of social scientists notwithstanding, we all (including we social psychologists) may be prone to essentialist thinking about groups when we are not being careful. There has been little or no research devoted to the extent to which this happens, but we should at least consider the possibility that informal essentialism infects some of our thinking about important stereotype magnet categories, such as race and gender.[3]

Groups and social categories may, of course, differ in the extent to which they attract essentialist thinking. Haslam, Rothschild, and Ernst (2000) had people rate a number of groups on several dimensions related to essentialism, and they found two basic factors. The first, which they called "naturalness," was related to ratings of the naturalness of the group, the immutability of group membership, and whether certain features are necessary for group membership. Race, gender, age, and physical disability groups scored high on this dimension, and groups based on physical appearance, intelligence, interests, and occupations scored low. The second group, which they called "entitativity" (see above), was made up of ratings of whether group members are similar to one another, whether category membership is informative, and whether group membership excludes people from other groups. Political, religious, sexual orientation, and physical disability groups scored high on this dimension, and appearance, geographical region, and physique groups tended to score low. However, while this research suggests that entitative groups are not necessarily seen in essentialist terms, a study of ours (Schneider et al., 2002) suggests otherwise. We used over 100 categories and groups rated on 34 rating scales. As expected, members of entitative groups were seen as more similar to one another; members were expected to like one another and to spend time together; and they were viewed as more likely to have common goals. However, ratings that were designed to capture essentialist thinking (e.g., groups are more natural, more exclusive, and more stable over time, and have necessary features for membership) were also highly correlated with the measures of entitativity.

It would be surprising if entitativity and essentialism were not somewhat related. Yzerbyt, Corneille, and Estrada (2001) have suggested that the two mutually support one another, but that "entitativity" refers more to the observable features of groups and "essentialism" more to how we process information about the groups. The important issue for our purposes is whether any differences between them affect how we process information about groups and their members, and especially whether we are more likely to stereotype on the basis of entitativity or essentialism. In a study by Haslam, Rothschild, and Ernst (2002), blacks and women were rated high on the essentialism factor and gay men lower; however, for entitativity, gay males were rated higher than blacks and women. Essentialist beliefs did not correlate with prejudice against any category, but entitativity beliefs did predict anti-gay prejudice.

Essentialism is likely to have complex relationships with prejudice. Studies on views of stigmatized groups show that people who believe that obese people (Crandall et al., 2001) and gay people (Hegarty & Pratto, 2001b; Whitley, 1990) have a choice as to their condition tend to be more prejudiced against them. Martin and Parker (1995) found that people who believed gender differences to be biological tended to have stronger gender stereotypes, and Levy, Stroessner, and Dweck (1998) showed that people who believed traits to be relatively stable were more likely to stereotype ethnic and occupational groups. Those findings would suggest that perceptions of choice and mutability would be positively related to prejudice, and for gay men they are (Haslam et al., 2002).

The Relationship of Features to Categories

THREE TYPES OF FEATURES

The discussion of essentialism highlights but does not answer important questions about category–feature relationships. Obviously, some features are more closely linked to categories than others, and some of these relationships feed off essentialist assumptions. Genital features are almost perfectly correlated with biological sex, styles of dress fairly much so, height less so, and traits such as assertiveness even less. Moreover, the feature–category relationships are typically asymmetrical. The probability of a professor's being female is much higher than the probability of a female's being a professor.

With that in mind, let's distinguish three types of features. "Essential features" are those that are absolutely essential for category membership (e.g., certain genes). In the case of gender, for example, essential features include whether the person has an XY or an XX pattern of chromosomes and relative levels of certain hormones. "Identifying features" are those we use to identify category members. In the case of gender, they include body confirmation, hair distribution, voice tone, and certain styles of dress. Finally, "ascribed features" are those that are associated with a category, but not in any integral way. So women are seen as less aggressive and as interpersonally warmer than men. Dogs exist mostly as pets, but this is a relatively accidental feature of the dog category and so counts as an ascribed feature, unlike the tendency to bark, which is an identifying feature.

MEMBERSHIP AND FEATURE DIAGNOSTICITY

One way to think about the differences among types of features is in terms of probabilities. There are two relevant probabilities that have not been well distinguished in the stereotype literature. One is the extent to which a feature predicts a category, or "membership diagnosticity"; this is the probability of a category, given the feature [$p(C/F)$]. The other is whether the category predicts the features, or "feature diagnosticity"; this is the probability of the feature, given the category [$p(F/C)$]. Membership (feature-to-category) diagnosticity is crucial for the millions of judgments we make daily about what people and things fit into what categories. Feature (category-to-feature) diagnosticity is also important, because one of the main reasons we categorize is to allow predictions of unseen and sometimes unobservable features.

Probabilities and Diagnosticity. Does the distinction between feature and membership diagnosticity help us in assessing the importance or kinds of features for categories? Although not all categories have essential features, for those that do, the essential features must be present if something is a member of a category. In such cases, both the membership and feature probabilities must be high (usually virtually 1.00). However, that does not tell the entire story. Many features of gender and race have high feature diagnosticity but are not diagnostic of category membership. For example, all females have hearts (feature diagnosticity), but not all people who have hearts are female (membership diagnosticity). Similarly, membership diagnosticity can be nearly perfect, but feature diagnosticity may still be quite low; people who nurse babies are female, but far from all females are nursing at any given time. Deaux and Kite (1985) have argued that the features distinguishing a category from a contrast category are especially useful as identifying features. Hearts won't do the job for femaleness, but possession of a uterus works.

For gender, certain genetically determined characteristics fit. However, for the category of race, there may be no essential features by this criterion. The probability of dark skin, given that someone is African American, is high but far from perfect; the probability that someone who has dark skin is African American is even lower. There are also few distinguishing and perhaps no defining genetic differences between races (Hirschfeld, 1996).

By definition, identifying features are those that allow us to identify a category from a feature; therefore, $p(C/F)$ or membership diagnosticity is high. Identifying features differ from essential ones in that feature diagnosticity does not have to be high. Ascribed features, on the other hand, are those for which feature diagnosticity is high and for which membership diagnosticity may or may not be high. "High" in this context must be understood in a relative sense; Playing football (an identifying feature) is almost perfectly diagnostic of being a male; body build is less diagnostic, but is still used for identification. It is also possible that a feature can be both identifying and ascribed. A person who wears a dress is almost certainly a female, so it is a good identifying cue. It is also a reasonably good ascribed feature, even though the probability of a woman's wearing a dress is lower than the probability of a dress wearer's being a woman.

Dealing with features in this way has the advantage of providing a reasonably good criterion for differentiating types of features, although it remains to be seen whether it does much for us empirically. There is also the significant disadvantage

TABLE 3.2. Types of Feature–Category Relationships

Type of feature	Type of diagnosticity	
	Membership, or $p(C/F)$	Feature, or $p(F/C)$
Essential	˜1.00	˜1.00
Identifying	Relatively high	Undetermined
Ascribed	Undetermined	Relatively high

that the types are not perfectly distinct. For example, all essential features are also identifying and ascribed by this probability definition. Regardless of whether one agrees with the particular logic just employed, the distinction among these types of features makes a certain amount of intuitive sense. Certainly, in everyday life, we do distinguish between those features that must be present for a category and those that are merely along for the empirical ride. For gender, most of us know that hormonal differences (essential) are not the same as clothing styles (identifying), which in turn are not the same as propensities to taking care of household tasks (ascribed). However, a strong case could be made that our intuitions about such differences pack a lot more baggage than a discussion in terms of probabilities would imply. For example, people may have theories about how different features relate to categories, and these may be more important than a mere statement of probabilities.

The Importance of Asymmetry. I want to reiterate that category diagnosticity and feature diagnosticity are generally not the same, mostly because of differential base rates of features and categories. For example, the probability that someone who is wearing a satin pants suit is also a female (membership diagnosticity) is very high, but the probability that a given female will be thus decked out (feature diagnosticity) is very low. Alternatively, feature diagnosticity can be higher than membership diagnosticity. The probability of a Rice University professor's having a doctoral degree is very high, but the possession of a PhD will not help much in determining whether someone teaches at Rice.

Despite the fact that these two probabilities are conceptually and usually empirically quite distinct, there is good reason to believe that people often confuse them (Bar-Hillel, 1984; Dawes, Mirels, Gold, & Donahue, 1993; Wyer, 1977) and sometimes substitute one for the other. For example, Eddy (1982) suggests that physicians often confuse the probability of breast cancer, given a positive mammogram, with the probability of a positive mammogram, given breast cancer. Since the latter probability is much higher, many women are subjected to painful, potentially dangerous, and often needless biopsies and surgeries.

Igor Gavanski and his colleagues (Gavanski & Hui, 1992; Sherman, McMullen, & Gavanski, 1992) have suggested that one reason for this is that some sample spaces are more naturally represented in memory than others. For example, if we are trying to deal with the relationships between nurturing children and gender, it is probably easier to think of women and then decide what proportion are nurturing than it is to think about nurturing people and calculate the percentage of women. This is because femaleness is a well-established and easily accessed category, whereas the category of nurturing people is not. Thus, in a bind, people might use the feature diagnosticity to stand for membership diagnosticity. When the appropriate sample space is made accessible (Hanita, Gavanski, & Fazio, 1997) or subjects find it useful (McMullen, Fazio, & Gavanski, 1997), performance on probability tasks improves.

It is not inevitable that we have better representations of groups than of features. Consider the relationship of crime proneness to race. On my local television stations, which dote on crime stories, I would estimate that at least 50% of all crime suspects shown are black. In this case, it is much easier for me to estimate the percentage of serious criminals who are black than of the percentage of blacks who are serious criminals, because the former space is much better defined. To the extent that I substitute the former for the latter, I will probably dramatically overestimate the percentage of black men who commit crimes. In this case, using the wrong probability estimates has the potential to create a fair amount of civic mischief. In addition, sometimes I may not even know the group membership of an individual, leading me to use my stereotypes (feature diagnosticity) to infer group membership (see below).

Another problem, which I discuss in Chapter 4, is that there is no principled distinction between categories (or groups) and features. Although it seems natural to think of being intelligent as a feature of the category of physicians, we might also think of being a physician as a feature of the category of smart people. Certainly it is easier to imagine nouns (e.g., "physicians") as indicating categories and adjectives (e.g., "smart") as indicating features, but the fact remains that the status of the two can be reversed. And in that case, defining and ascribed features flip as well.

THEORIES, ESSENTIALISM, AND THE CAUSAL STRUCTURE OF CATEGORIES

Why are some features more closely associated with categories than others? One obvious reason is that some features actually are more often found with some categories than others, and that people merely track these empirical probabilities reasonably closely. I discuss other possibilities throughout the remainder of this book.

But there is an immediately relevant and intriguing possibility, based on notions of essentialism developed by Woo-kyoung Ahn and colleagues (e.g., Ahn, 1998, 1999; Ahn, Kim, Lassaline, & Dennis, 2000). Ahn argues that essentialism provides a theory about which features "cause" other features, and that causal features are more central to the category than effect features. So, for example, DNA produces human genital differences, which determine roles in reproduction, which may in turn affect child-rearing roles. In this example, DNA differences would be more central to gender categories than genital differences, which in turn would be more fundamental than reproductive roles. This model works well for natural kinds. What about artifactual categories? Given that the essence of a table is roughly to be a platform for things, it would follow that this intention causes tables to have a flat surface at least some distance from the ground, and that these features in turn cause tables to have legs. However, these linkages are probably weaker than those for natural kinds, in the sense that exceptions would be more readily granted. Not all tables are perfectly flat, rest off the ground, or have legs.

CUES FOR CATEGORIES

It has been generally assumed (often implicitly and unreflectively) that while categorization itself may provide important (perhaps essential) cognitive underpinnings for stereotyping, the act of categorization itself is essentially unproblematic. But when we get down to the heart of the matter, exactly how do we distinguish males from females, professors from students? Stereotype researchers usually give category information to their research participants directly and have mostly worked with gender and race, which provide highly salient and redundant bases for categorization. To be sure, even with less salient categories, group identification is often not mysterious. A person simply says that she is a career woman, Jewish, or epileptic. Or one sees her sitting behind a desk in a professor's office or notices the laboratory coat usually worn by a doctor in a hospital setting. In such cases, group identification seems to be a trivial exercise.

However, the perceiver must actually make an inference about group designation, based on what I have called membership or feature-to-category cues. The cues we use for gender, such as hair length, body confirmation, and voice tone, may be quite diagnostic (and still there will be the occasional error, often either amusing or embarrassing, or both)—but the fact remains that we must still infer gender. Moreover, cues for other categories are less than ideal. For example, appearance is a weak cue at best for Jewishness, and although first and last names may have Jewish or African American connotations, we dare not use such cues indiscriminately.

Unknown Category Membership. In addition, cues for a great many status conditions—such as history of certain physical illnesses, being terminally ill, homosexuality, divorce, ethnic identity, religious background, or prison history—may not only be less than perfectly obvious, but deliberately hidden (Goffman, 1963; Jones et al., 1984). Thus there will be situations in which perceiver and target need to play an information game: "Is she Jewish?," "Is she as crazy as she acts?" Ironically, when we do not have good identification cues, we may use feature diagnosticity information and stereotype traits themselves to identify people as members of such groups (Jones et al., 1984). Not having valid ways to identify gay males, Buck may well imagine that effeminate behavior or interests can be used to pick out such folks. Likewise, talking to oneself in public may be used to identity someone as mentally ill, even though it is likely that the probability of a mentally ill person's talking to him- or herself (feature diagnosticity) is much higher than category diagnosticity, and the latter may not even be an especially good way to identify persons with mental illness.

Drawing Category Boundaries. With continuous categories (Stangor & Lange, 1994), there are potentially important issues of where we draw category boundaries. As I see the students in my class spread out before me, I am aware of constant variation. There are various shades of hair color; how yellow does the hair have to be before I call it blond? How old are people when they become middle-aged or elderly? A student confides in me that he has had an on-again/off-again homosexual relationship with his roommate, but that he thinks he is basically heterosexual. Do I see him as gay? One way to think about this is in terms of category breadth. If we use broad enough criteria for category membership, the categories themselves tend to disappear; if everyone who has ever had a strange thought gets classified as mentally ill, then we are all mentally ill, and the category has no meaning.

A number of factors presumably affect the use of broad and few versus narrow and many categories. People who are high in need for structure tend to use broad categories, for example (Neuberg & Newsom, 1993). Mood also affects categorization behavior: People who are in a good mood tend to use broader categories and to rate marginal members of categories as more prototypic (Isen & Daubman, 1984; Isen, Niedenthal, & Cantor, 1992), especially when focusing on similarities among group members (Murray, Sujan, Hirt, & Sujan, 1990). It has also been suggested that people tend to use broader and more inclusive categories for disliked groups and outgroups (Tajfel & Forgas, 1981).

How Much Information Do We Need? A related issue concerns how much information we need to place someone in a category. For example, usually I am willing to use voice pitch as a perfectly diagnostic cue for gender, and I only require a cue or two to make gender assignments. On the other hand, I am much less willing to use voice tone as a cue for homosexuality, and I generally require more diagnostic information before designating someone as a gay male or lesbian. However, a woman who hates homosexuals probably has a nervous finger on her homosexuality trigger, such that anyone who seems even remotely gay or lesbian will be included in the category (see below). Not only is her category of homosexuality broad, but she requires relatively little diagnostic information before she invokes it. As described in Chapter 7, one body of literature shows that when people are asked to pick out pictures of Jews, anti-Semitic subjects see more pictures as being Jewish than do less prejudiced subjects. Whereas those of us with less affective involvement might not readily classify people on that basis (and, to the extent that we do, demand several diagnostic bits of information before we make the judgment), prejudiced persons are more likely to use any available cue, weak or strong, to make their judgment.

A related finding is that people are more careful about categorizing people into their ingroups than in categorizing people into groups to which they do not belong (Capozza, Dazzi, & Minto, 1996; Leyens & Yzerbyt, 1992; Yzerbyt, Leyens, & Bellour, 1995). People who identify strongly with their groups show this effect more (Castano, Yzerbyt, Bourguignon, & Seron, 2002), which further supports the idea that this ingroup overexclusion effect results from desires to protect oneself from undesirable fellow category travelers.

We know relatively little about how people make judgments about category membership for humans. As I have indicated, this is partially because social psychologists have tended to use categories such as race and gender, for which group membership is fairly obvious. However, many important potential categories for people will remain hidden from view, so to speak, and many others may remain uncertain. At present, we know little about what consequences this might have for stereotyping.

CATEGORIZATION OF PEOPLE: WHICH CATEGORIES ARE USED?

We have a large number of salient person categories, and generally people can be categorized in more ways than objects can be. One major problem we have is deciding why we place people and their behavior in one category as opposed to another. Why do we think of this person as a mother rather than as a wife, or as a woman rather than a Jew, or as a rabbi and not a mother? Three general answers have been provided as to why we use some categories and not others. The first is that some categories are so fundamental that they have pride of place. The second is that category use is affected by category salience, or what is usually called "accessibility." And the third is that some categories are cognitively more basic.

Primary Categories

Brewer (1988), among others, has argued that age and gender are especially likely to be primary categories, and I add race to that list. Several studies using free descriptions (Hurtig & Pichevin, 1990), sorting of photographs (Brewer & Lui, 1989), recall of information about photographs (Gardner, MacIntyre, & Lalonde, 1995), release from proactive inhibition (Mills & Tyrrell, 1983), recall clustering (Bem, 1981), category verification (Stroessner, 1996; Zárate & Sandoval, 1995; Zárate & Smith, 1990), and memory confusion paradigms (Stangor, Lynch, Duan, & Glass, 1992; Taylor, Fiske, Etcoff, & Ruderman, 1978) suggest that gender, age, and race are readily used for classification.

Several things make these categories special. First, race, age, and gender cues are perceptually salient. Second, both essential and identifying features tend to have at least some biological involvement for these categories. Third, age, gender, and skin color may have evolutionary significance, as our ancestors needed to distinguish people on the basis of accumulated wisdom, reproductive potential, and likelihood of belonging to the same group. Fourth, these categories form the basis of dominance hierarchies in many cultures (Sidanius & Pratto, 1999; see also Chapter 8). Fifth, such categories are among the first social categories that children learn. They distinguish between males and females (Leinbach & Fagot, 1993), among various ages (Brooks & Lewis, 1976; Pope Edwards, 1984), and among different races (Hirschfeld, 1988, 1993) early in life (certainly within the first 2 years) and with no obvious tutoring. Sixth, such categories are important culturally; age and gender are important categories in all cultures. Some of these possibilities are surely more important than others, and undoubtedly they are related in complex ways we do not fully understand. But we do not have to sort out the various chickens and eggs to recognize that age, race, and gender are privileged categories.

Such categories lead to fairly automatic categorization, and there are several potential consequences of this. First, we use primary categories immediately and without necessarily engaging in conscious thought. It is likely that such immediate classification takes priority over other, less salient forms. Second, such primary categories are based on immediately perceptible appearance cues. Ordinarily one does not have to do elaborate analysis to determine that someone is old or young, male or female, African American or Asian American. Third, such categorization is hard if not impossible to inhibit. Can you enter an interaction with another person and not notice whether the person is a he or a she? Fourth, such primary categories become immediately attached to the person in memory. It would seem quite strange if I could not remember whether someone I had just met was male or female, old or young.

No one would argue that race, gender, and age are the only ways of categorizing people, or that these putatively primary categories cannot be abandoned for other categories. It is easy to imagine cultures in which these categories are more incidental than they are in ours, and we are not doomed to see people as nothing more than male or female, Asian or Hispanic. It may matter less to me that the person I am talking with is female than whether she is competent or incompetent, a physician or a derelict, a colleague or a student. However, while other types of categories have an optional quality, primary categories do not. We must fill in the "slots" for gender, race, and age, but we have more discretion for occupation, parental status, and the like.

Category Accessibility

The notion that some categories are used fairly automatically is a controversial one, but even if this idea turns out to be correct, there are times when other categories will be used. Some categories are used because they are salient in a given situation. Sometimes we may use one category rather than another because of our goals in the situation. Or we may use some categories so often that they become almost habitual.

Cue Salience

In this section I am focusing on category salience rather than features, but feature salience may also affect the use of categories. If a cue is sufficiently salient, and if the cue has high category diagnosticity, then categorization is likely to follow. Cues may be salient for many reasons. Consider an extreme example: A man suddenly begins screaming that the Martians are out to get him. The salience of this behavior, which is probably perceived to be a good cue for mental illness, would surely lead directly to a judgment that the man is seriously deranged. So when cues are extreme or unexpected, they will become powerful stimuli for categorization.

Cue salience may also be affected by familiarity. Experiments by Macrae, Mitchell, and Pendry (2002) suggest that familiar gender-linked names not only facilitate gender categories but also gender stereotyping. In other words, whereas names such as Jennifer or Michael readily lead to gender categorization, names such as Glenda or Isaac are less efficient in that regard. One would imagine that names such as José and Maria would more likely lead to categorization in terms of Hispanic ethnicity than names such as Matthew or Catherine.

What about appearances? Faces that are more Afrocentric lead to more rapid classification as African American (Blair et al., 2002) and are judged more stereotypically. Moreover, there are stable individual differences in the extent to which people rely on skin color and physical attractiveness in their judgments, presumably partially based on differential categorization (Eberhardt, Dasgupta, & Banaszynski, 2003; Livingston, 2001).

In everyday life cue salience is likely to fluctuate, depending on various contextual cues. We categorize people, things, and events, in part, to emphasize similarities with other category members and to differentiate them from members of other categories (Rosch, 1978). Thus it is obvious that features that seem to differentiate people will often serve as the basis of categorization (Campbell, 1967). John Turner (e.g., Turner, 1991; Oakes & Turner, 1990) has proposed a principle of what he calls "metacontrast." Dimensions that emphasize differences between categories of people, relative to within-category differences, will be highly salient. For example, when people describe groups, they tend to mention features that differentiate groups more, as well as features that are less variable within a given group (Ford & Stangor, 1992); traits that differentiate groups more perceptually are also more readily used to stereotype groups (Diehl & Jonas, 1991). Stangor and Lange (1994) have speculated that we may be more inclined to use categories that are clearly differentiated, especially those for which there are only two salient ways to categorize. Thus we should be more likely to use gender (male vs. female) than age, which is a continuous dimension. This idea deserves more empirical attention.

In a room with a standard array of hair colors, there would be no real reason to categorize on that basis; hair color is muted perceptually. On the other hand, in a room of people who have either red or blond hair, one might be more tempted to divide the people up accordingly. A group of only relatively young and relatively old people invites being broken up into the old-timers and the youngsters, and a group with several blacks and whites (and no Asians) might seem naturally divided into blacks and whites. It is likely that weight status, visible handicap, and extreme height are used to categorize people, just because people in those categories seem to "stand out" perceptually, and of course are also culturally salient. Research (Van Rijswijk & Ellemers, 2002) does confirm that the salience of categories can be affected by the comparative context in just the ways I have suggested.

Numerical Minority Status

There has been a great deal of speculation that people who are in a numerical minority within a group will be especially apt to be perceived in terms of the category that makes them members of this minority. This is not a trivial hypothesis. Since women and members of racial minorities often find themselves in groups where they also constitute distinct numerical minorities ("tokens"), it can be important to know whether this is likely to make gender or race unduly salient as a basis for categorization and consequently for stereotyping.

In an often-cited paper, Rosabeth Kanter (1977b) argued that token women are likely to play special roles in groups. Tokens are highly visible, and the category memberships that lead to their token status become highly salient even when they are not relevant to the group. Kanter also argued that tokens are more likely to be stereotyped than are people in a less token status. Although there is abundant impressionistic evidence (e.g., Floge & Merrill, 1986; Kanter, 1977a; Wolman & Frank, 1975) that "solos" are treated differently than those in a stronger numerical position, actual empirical data in support of Kanter's notions presents a somewhat mixed picture.

There is evidence that both adults and children in a race or gender numerical minority are more likely to describe themselves in terms of race or gender (Dutton, Singer, & Devlin, 1998; McGuire, McGuire, Child, & Fujioka, 1978). Research on whether minority status creates salience in descriptions of others is mixed; some studies report that it does (Pichevin & Hurtig, 1996), and others report less consistent evidence (Oakes, Turner, & Haslam, 1991; Swan & Wyer, 1997).

Token women in groups do feel more pressure to conform to their assigned roles (Spangler, Gordon, & Pipkin, 1978). Tokens are more likely to fear being stereotyped (Cohen & Swim, 1995), to feel they have been stereotyped (Fuegen & Biernat, 2002), and to feel more visible and "on stage" (Ott, 1989), in part because they are in fact perceptually prominent in groups (Floge & Merrill, 1986; Taylor, 1981). Black students in predominantly white universities have chronic feelings of distinctiveness, and solo status in classes and social situations makes them especially aware of their racial membership (Pollak & Niemann, 1998). In actual job situations, tokens are likely to feel isolated and victimized by a nonsupportive environment (Yoder & Berendsen, 2001). Women are evaluated more negatively when in a numerical minority (Heilman, 1980; Ott, 1989; Yoder, Adams, & Prince, 1983) and perform less well academically in male-dominated departments (Alexander & Thoits, 1985). Being a token in a group can cause cognitive deficits (Inzlicht & Ben-Zeev, 2000; Lord & Saenz, 1985; Saenz, 1994; Sekaquaptewa & Thompson, 2003), in part because tokens are distracted by the thought that they are being scrutinized by others (Lord, Saenz, & Godfrey, 1987; Saenz & Lord, 1989). However, there are also recent, well-conducted studies showing that solo males and females do not show performance decrements and are not evaluated negatively (Fuegen & Biernat, 2002).

So it can be tough being a token, but there is little hard evidence that tokens are actually *stereotyped* more by others than are nontokens. One relevant finding is that minority people in groups are somewhat more likely to be rated extremely on personality traits (Taylor et al., 1978). This is a justly classic study in the stereotyping area. It is often cited as support for the idea that solo status affects stereotyping. However, the results did not clearly show this. The study did not show that members of numerical minorities were more likely to be categorized in terms of gender. It did show that for 7 of 20 trait ratings (creating a stronger impression; having a strong personality; and being assertive, confident, less warm, less pleasant, and more negative), the relative number of men and women in the group affected trait ratings, but these results did not affect genders differentially. For example, although men were generally rated as more assertive (a male stereotypic trait) when there were fewer males in the group, females were also rated as more assertive as their numbers decreased. One might argue that males, but not females, are more stereotyped as their numbers decrease; however, but a more parsimonious description would be that numerical minorities are seen as more assertive or generally more masculine. Interestingly, when both males and females are solos they also describe themselves and others in more masculine terms (Swan & Wyer, 1997). Oakes and Turner (1986) found more gender stereotyping of males when they were in the minority, but they also found increased stereotyping of males when the males greatly outnumbered females (five males and one female). There was no evidence of effects of minority status on the stereotyping of females. Thus the evidence that solo status increases stereotyping is at best mixed and certainly inconsistent.

There is no doubt that being in a minority in a group, and especially being the only person of a kind, does have effects on the ways people are perceived and categorized. However, the effects are neither as strong nor as consistent as most casual summaries of this literature suggest. Furthermore, such effects may be found largely for less powerful groups in nontraditional and more prestigious occupations (Yoder, 1991). In occupational settings, it is also important to disentangle gender and the gender "appropriateness" of the job (Yoder, 1994). But generally, women suffer from token status more than men (Yoder, 2002), and in some contexts men may even be advantaged by being in a small minority (Sekaquaptewa & Thompson, 2002; Williams, 1992).

Goals

The world can be carved up in different ways, depending on one's goals and intentions. I can easily divide the students before me in a class into males and females, attractive and unattractive, fat and thin, attentive and unattentive, blonds and brunettes. The same person can be the mother of a friend, a physician, and a widow. In any given situation, of course, different people may have different goals and thereby parse the world differently. In one interesting demonstration, Medin, Lynch, Coley, and Atran (1997) asked landscapers, park maintenance workers, and scientific experts to categorize several types of trees. The scientists used categories close to established scientific taxonomy, but the landscapers, as one might expect, tended to group trees on the basis of their ornamental features (e.g., weed trees, trees desirable along streets, flowering trees), and maintenance workers (who clean up tree litter) tended to use categories based on morphological features (e.g., those that have nuts, those that have fruits). Different strokes for different folks.

Stangor and colleagues (1992) have argued that perceivers often use the categories that they think have the highest "payoff" in terms of information needed in a given situation. They found that subjects in their studies more readily categorized by gender than by race, and they interpreted this to mean that their subjects felt that knowing gender gave them more information about a person. However, information yield is surely not a static quality. A man who meets several people at a party will presumably categorize them differently, depending on whether he is looking for a romantic partner or a job lead. Stangor and colleagues showed that subjects used dress style as a basis for categorization when they were trying to pick someone who would be a good media representative for a group, but not when clothing was less relevant. Other types of goals may also affect categorization as well. Pendry and Macrae (1996) have suggested that being accountable to others and wanting to be accurate lead perceivers to pay attention to individuating features and to categorize more finely. In particular, subjects who were more accountable were more likely to classify a woman as a businesswoman, whereas those who were not were more inclined to use the superordinate category of women.

We categorize, in part, to explain. Odd, infrequent, and unexplained events or people may lead us to a mad search for some appropriate category that will help us understand. The classic example used by Murphy and Medin (1985) is of a man at a party who jumps, fully clothed, into a swimming pool. It is likely that we will immediately classify him as drunk, despite the fact that jumping into pools is a low-probability behavior for drunk people and is presumably not a salient part of the stereotype of drunken partygoers. Similarly, when we observe a woman acting strangely, we may be highly prone to interpret her behavior as mentally ill, and a man's asking for change late at night on a dark street will surely invoke the "scary person" category.

Priming

Another body of literature suggests that people use categories that they have used frequently or recently (Bargh, 1996). One popular research strategy pioneered by Higgins, Rholes, and Jones (1977) has subjects work on a task designed to increase category accessibility. For example, the subjects might unscramble sentences that generally produce sentences related to hostility. The subjects are then asked to read an ambiguous passage where some of the material could be interpreted in terms of the primed category (Higgins, 1996). Whereas most of this research has primed traits or features (see Chapter 4 for a fuller discussion), there are also demonstrations (Blanz, 1999; van Twuyver & van Knippenberg, 1995) that priming social categories also increases their use. Some categories may be used by individuals so often that they become chronically accessible. Several studies show that there are reliable individual differences in the use of certain categories (Higgins, King, & Mavin, 1982), and that such chronically accessible categories function much like primed ones (Bargh, Lombardi, & Tota, 1986; Bargh & Thein, 1985).

Attitude Accessibility

Russ Fazio (1995) has argued that some attitudes are more accessible than others in the sense that they come to mind more quickly when we see a relevant object, and, furthermore, that accessible attitudes can direct attention. Consider, for example, a woman who has a strongly negative attitude toward homosexuals. Intuitively she should be attentive to cues for homosexuality and as a consequence should be prone to categorize people on the basis of sexual preference. People direct more attention to objects for which they have accessible attitudes than to objects with less accessible attitudes (Roskos-Ewoldsen & Fazio, 1992).

In research by Smith, Fazio, and Cejka (1996), attitude accessibility was used to predict categorization of stimuli that could be classified in several ways. In one study, for example, triads of words were used, one a target stimulus and the other two representing alternative ways of categorizing the target (e.g., "Pete Rose—baseball player, gambler"). Subjects were given the category words and were asked either to judge either whether they liked or disliked the category (say, "gambler"—thus making their attitudes more accessible), or whether the category (say, "baseball player") was animate or inanimate (control). Subsequently they were given the target word as a cue for recall of the category. So "Pete Rose" could help them recall either "gambler" or "baseball player," both of which terms they had previously seen. In this task, the categories for which attitudes were accessible (e.g., gambler) were more often recalled. In a variant of the category verification task used by Zárate and Smith (1990), subjects were asked to judge whether the target (e.g., Pete Rose) fit a category that had an accessible attitude (e.g., gambler) or one for which the attitude was less accessible (e.g., baseball player). They were faster at this task when the category had an accessible attitude. If we extrapolate, a person who has a highly accessible hatred of lawyers but a weakly accessible attitude toward females would be more likely to categorize a female lawyer as a lawyer than as a female. Or a person who had a highly positive attitude toward Hispanics and a weakly accessible attitude toward college professors should be inclined to see a Hispanic professor as Hispanic.

In a study more directly relevant to stereotyping, Fazio and Dunton (1997) asked subjects to rate the similarity of pictures varying in race, gender, and occupation. Those subjects for whom attitudes toward blacks were highly accessible (either positive or negative) weighed race in their judgments more than those with less accessible attitudes. Subjects with accessible attitudes also made more rapid similarity judgments, again suggesting that the salience of race allowed them to judge similarity more quickly. Other studies have shown that people who are more racially prejudiced (Stangor et al., 1992; Zárate & Smith, 1990) are more inclined to pay attention to racial categories.

Accessibility × Fit

In Bruner's important 1957 paper on perceptual readiness, he argued that the categories we use are a joint function of the categories' accessibility and of their fit to what is being categorized. That model has been considerably elaborated in terms of self-categorization theory by Penelope Oakes (1987) and subsequently by Mathias Blanz (1999). People who operate from this tradition argue that stereotypes exist not as simplification devices in a complex world, but as ways of codifying social realities. In this model, accessibility incorporates most of what has been discussed in this section. "Comparative fit" refers to whether a particular categorization incorporates the most salient differences among the people one is considering. More formally, "fit" refers to whether the proposed categorization maximizes a ratio of between-group to within-group variability—what Turner has called "metacontrast" (see above). Categories that are correlated with salient features will be used. In gazing upon a large early morning class, I may be quite aware that some students look attentive while others are sleeping, and place them into categories of interested and noninterested students; in a class where the majority of clever questions come from students sitting in the front of the room, I might use fanny location as my cue for interest or intelligence. "Normative fit" is also important. This refers to whether the categories successfully differentiate features in ways that we expect on the basis of cultural understandings and existing stereotypes.

The advantage of this kind of model is that it emphasizes the obvious interplays between what perceivers bring to the task and the various situational, social, and cultural factors that also play a role in the ways we categorize others. Category salience is thus not static; it changes constantly, depending on a host of perceiver and external variables. Research supports the idea that categorization does require both that a category be salient and also be a reasonable fit for observed differences among people (Blanz, 1999; Blanz & Aufderheide, 1999).

Basic Categories

Another factor that affects all forms of categorization has to do with level of generality. Most things exist in a hierarchy of categories. So a given animal can be seen as an animal, a mammal, a carnivore, a canine, a dog, a Pomeranian, and finally as Fifi. When we see the beast, why do we call it a dog rather than a mammal or an animal?

The Nature of Basic Categories

The answer provided by Rosch (1978) was that some categories are more basic than others. Generally, basic categories are found at some intermediate level of generality and are defined by their tendencies to maximize intercategory similarities and intracategory differences. Such basic categories have a richer set of associative links among properties, and they are also more likely to be used, especially in conversation and writing. So we are inclined to talk about tables and not end tables or pieces of furniture, dogs instead of collies or canines, and computers as opposed to Dell

PCs or computing devices. Rosch, Mervis, Gray, Johnson, and Boyes-Braem (1976) have argued that basic categories are the most informative, in the sense that they best facilitate inferences about features of category members (Corter & Gluck, 1992). So we might see someone as a black male rather than as a person or a male, because this designation tells us more about him in the sense of differentiating him from others. Of course, knowing that he is 6 feet 7 inches tall, has a Harvard MBA, and works for a particular firm in Indianapolis differentiates him from everyone, but at significant loss of information about his similarities to others. So at the basic level, we will have maximum information about both differences and similarities.

It is also likely that level of categorization affects inductive potential. Coley, Medin, and Atran (1997) gave traditional Mayans and U.S. college students novel features (e.g., "possesses a particular protein") for an animal or plant exemplar, and asked whether they thought members of categories would also have the same feature. So a participant might have been asked, "If all rainbow trout have Protein A, how likely is it that all trout have Protein A?" or "If all trout have Protein A, how likely is it that all fish have Protein A?" or "If all fish have Protein A, how likely is it that all animals have Protein A?" For the U.S. college sample, they found that generalization to generic kinds (trout, for this example) were stronger than for other levels. In other words, for these natural kinds generalizations from specific kinds to generic kinds were easy (e.g., rainbow trout to trout), but the students were much more cautious in generalizing from more general levels.

Two points need to be stressed about this research. First, in this study "induction magnets" were not generally basic categories. According to the Roschian analysis, fish should be a basic category; however, trout (a level below fish) turned out to be the most informative, according to this measure. Second, it is not perfectly clear whether this research says anything about non-natural-kind hierarchies. More to the point, we do not know whether human type categories also show these kinds of effects. If I discover something about Rice University professors of psychology, am I willing to generalize to Rice professors generally, or to psychology professors generally? If I know something about Rice professors, am I comfortable generalizing to all professors? Or from professors to all teachers or all people with higher degrees? Lest this seem an esoteric problem, keep in mind that most students actually know relatively little about professors in their own universities and less about professors outside. So if they find out that I favor gun control, do they assume that all psychology professors do? If a sample of psychology professors at this university clearly favor gun control, does that mean all professors do? This example reveals another important point stressed earlier—namely, that social kinds fit into multiple hierarchies. Does the level above Rice psychology professors consist of Rice professors or psychology professors? This is not a trivial issue for induction tasks of the sort just discussed.

Situational Determinants

Although Rosch (1978) argued that whether a category is basic is more or less a stable feature of certain hierarchies, she also recognized that what categories are basic depends heavily on context. To a person who works in a dog kennel, "Go groom the dog" is likely to elicit confusion, whereas "Go groom the Pomeranian" is likely to narrow the confusion somewhat. Similarly, categorizing someone in a small law firm as the new lawyer is likely to differentiate her from all the other lawyers, but in a large firm one might need to think of her as the new, short female with the degree from Virginia. Thus basic categories do not necessarily stay fixed across situations and goals.

Are There Basic Categories for Stereotypes?

Rosch (1978) argued that the basic level not only differentiates better, but forms the basis of a richer set of associations. This would seem to suggest that stereotyping would be stronger at the basic level of categorization. This makes sense, but a set of related but interlocked questions must be distinguished before we can be sure whether this notion is correct.

Do basic categories exist for people as they do for objects? Susan Andersen and Roberta Klatzky have investigated this issue with several trait hierarchies. In an initial set of studies (Andersen & Klatzky, 1987), they developed a set of general trait labels (e.g., "extrovert") and associated subordinate stereotype labels (e.g., "class clown," "politician"). They found that there were more nonredundant attributes listed for the stereotypes, and that these attributes were linked more closely to the stereotypes than to the more general traits. In a follow-up study by Andersen, Klatzky, and Murray (1990), subjects were asked to indicate whether a person with the trait or with the stereotype designation would be more likely to perform a mundane behavior (e.g., closing a door) or experience some state (e.g., hearing a voice). This task was performed more rapidly for the stereotypes, indicating that behaviors are more closely attached to the more basic stereotypes than to the superordinate traits. Further confirming this interpretation were data indicating that subjects could remember the stereotype label better than the more general trait label when given the behavior or state as a cue.[4]

ARE SUBTYPES BASIC CATEGORIES?

This research suggests that for at least some hierarchies of social categories there may be a basic level, but what about the categories most often associated with stereotypes? Consider gender. Although it is undeniably true that males and females are perceived to differ in some ways, there may be more informative levels of categorization. Wouldn't we learn more about a person by knowing that she is a housewife in Iowa rather than a female, or learn more about a male by knowing that he is also a father or a construction worker?

Studies on gender, racial categories, body types, physically attractive females, and older people find meaningful subtypes (see Chapters 11–13). There is no doubt that we use these subtypes as a basis of stereotypes. Who, in U.S. culture, could not distinguish the stereotype of a businessman from that of an athlete, or that of a middle-class housewife from that of a welfare mother?

However, the fact that people can distinguish subtypes does not mean that they are more basic in the Roschian sense. The work by Andersen and her colleagues hints at this, but we still need more direct evidence. Unfortunately, the evidence is not as clear as we might like. Evidence for the greater richness of subtypes comes from research by Brewer, Dull, and Lui (1981), who found that consensus on trait assignment was higher for pictures of older people who fell into meaningful subtypes (e.g., the grandmother type). However, in a study by Deaux, Winton, Crowley, and Lewis (1985), subjects did not provide more attributes for mothers, sexy women, or businesswomen than for women in general; this could be interpreted as showing that these subordinate and presumably more basic levels did not carry more information about people. So the evidence on whether we privilege some subcategories of humans as basic is mixed at best.

DOES THE PART STAND FOR THE WHOLE?

Even if we cannot be certain whether subtypes are more basic than more global person categories, it is possible that our stereotypes of the larger categories are more strongly affected by stereotypes of some subtypes of that category. For example, Eagly and Steffen (1984) have shown that traditional stereotypes of women as being more communal and less agentic than men were found only for target women who were not in the workforce; women working full time were, if anything, seen as more agentic than males. This would suggest that what pass for traditional stereotypes of women are really stereotypes of women who occupy traditional roles. Other studies (e.g., Deaux & Lewis, 1984; Riedle, 1991) have also supported the idea that stereotypes of women are determined in large part by assumptions that people make about the roles they occupy.

Is the same true for race? Devine and Baker (1991) asked subjects to generate characteristics that were associated with blacks in general, as well as various subtypes: streetwise blacks, ghetto blacks, welfare blacks, black athletes, black businessmen, "Oreo cookies," militant blacks, and "Uncle Toms." Generally subjects generated similar attributes for blacks, streetwise blacks, ghetto blacks, and welfare blacks. The attributes generated for black athletes and for black businessmen were more positive than for the other designations, although different from one another. This study seems to suggest that (with a couple of exceptions) white subjects do not have well-differentiated views of black subtypes, and that they tend to think about the larger category of blacks in terms of particular types—say, the ghetto and welfare types.

Charles Lord and his colleagues have also been interested in whether people tend to think about larger categories of people in terms of specific subtypes. Subjects described homosexuals (Lord, Lepper, & Mackie, 1984), former mental patients and drug abusers (Ramsey, Lord, Wallace, & Pugh, 1994), and murderers who receive the death penalty (Lord, Desforges, Fein, Pugh, & Lepper, 1994) in ways that fit a subtype only of the category. Furthermore, when asked to interact with a member of the category, their attitudes predicted their behavior only when the projected interaction partner fit their prototype for the category. For example, those subjects who thought that former mental patients were similar to the prototypic person with schizophrenia were less likely to want to interact with a former mental patient when he was described as having symptoms of schizophrenia than when described as having symptoms of some other mental illness. However, typicality is a less important mediator of attitudes and behavior for those more familiar with the category (Lord, Desforges, Ramsey, Trezza, & Lepper, 1991). Sia and colleagues (1997) also showed that when people changed their exemplars, their attitudes changed in a direction consistent with the evaluation of the new exemplar. This research, then, also supports the idea that stereotypes about larger groups may reflect ideas about only a minority of the people in that category. This important point is discussed again in Chapter 10 (in connection with stereotype change) and Chapter 8 (in regard to the implications of stereotypes for behavior).

SUBTYPING AND EXCEPTIONS

I have just suggested that stereotypes for some subtypes may affect stereotypes of the larger category. But some subtypes are radically different from their parent categories. Sometimes when we think of subtypes of categories, we tend to isolate disconfirming information within one or at least relatively few subtypes. So, for example, a man who insists on traditional gender stereotypes can easily form a subtype of the businesswoman, and this category may act as a repository for disconfirming information, such as the assertiveness and competence of some women. So, rather than the perceiver's having to admit that women are highly variable with regard to these traits, he can simply assume that only businesswomen are assertive and competent; this might allow him to maintain his more general stereotype of women as fragile and incompetent. On the other hand, to the extent that he has many distinct subtypes that are relatively salient, he may be led to think of women in general (when, indeed, he does think in such broad terms) as highly diverse. In effect, he says, "Well, there are many kinds of women. Some are assertive, some not; some are competent, some not. I'm not sure I can offer you any real stereotypes of women in general."

Often a distinction is made between "subtypes" (the repository of exceptions) and "subgroups" (well-articulated subordinate groups). The use of subgroups is related to perceptions of increased diversity in the larger group (Park, Ryan, & Judd, 1992). When people are instructed to group individuals according to their consistencies and inconsistencies with their general stereotypes, stereotyping of the general group is increased; however, when they are instructed to group on the basis of similarities and dissimilarities without regard to the larger group, stereotyping is reduced and the larger group is seen as more diverse (Maurer, Park, & Rothbart, 1995).

THE EFFECTS OF CATEGORIZATION

Inferences

Our categories are more than groupings based on superficial similarities. When we call something a cat, we are doing more than telling ourselves that this beast is similar to other cat-like animals encountered in the past. As I have emphasized throughout this chapter, categorization is one of the most basic cognitive activities, because it allows us to know more than we can immediately see or hear. Categorization leads to two distinct kinds of inferences. First, we infer something about individuals based on the ways we have categorized them. Second, we make judgments about categories based on individuals.[5]

Inferences about Individuals

Obviously, categorization affects what traits and other attributes are inferred about a person. Imagine that you have just met a woman at a party. Think about the different notions you entertain about her, depending on whether you initially categorize her as a minister, a mother, or a baseball fan. Our categories are useful to us precisely because they do provide this extra intellectual baggage. Although we often stress stereotypes about groups, for the most part our major practical concern is with group stereotypes applied to individual members of those groups. Thus this issue of direct inferences from categories to individuals is a central concern throughout the remainder of this book.

Inferences about Categories

Suppose I meet a native of Albania for the first time and find him to be charming and sophisticated. Do I now assume that Albanian men in general are similarly charming? Do I assume that Albanians, both men and women, generally have this characteristic? Why not Muslims generally (if this man is in fact Muslim)? Obviously, since I cannot meet all Albanian men, Albanians, or Muslims, there is a point at which I must judge categories on the basis of limited experiences with exemplars. This is a dangerous business, obviously.

Category induction has not been studied much by stereotype researchers. One reason is surely that the logic of induction is complex, but perhaps a more salient reason is that adults who have absorbed cultural wisdom about categories are beyond the induction stage. Is it likely, for example, that I need to pay close attention to a woman before me to infer things about women, professors, short people, red-haired people, smart people, or any combination of these? Obviously, I already have a pretty clear sense (or think I do) about what people in those categories are like. In other words, although inductive processes may be useful for stereotype formation, they are not ordinarily used for most of the stereotypes we already have.

But there are good reasons for being concerned with person-to-group induction. First, although we have clear ideas about many categories, we do encounter new ones all the time. Actually, I have never met an Albanian (charming and sophisticated or otherwise), and I have yet to meet a student from the University of North Dakota, a psychologist who specializes in the treatment of adult attention-deficit/hyperactivity disorder, a major drug dealer, or the chief executive officer of a Fortune 500 company. Of course, I can invent (and perhaps use) stereotypes of such categories cobbled together from bits and pieces of secondhand information; still, my first encounters with people from these categories may be revelatory.[6] And, of course, induction may be an important part of how children and young adults develop stereotypes. Second, we may not know as much as we think we do about groups or categories we think we know quite well. For example, I know next to nothing about the musical tastes of my students or what books they read for pleasure. When a student tells me that she likes a particular band or writer, I find myself inclined to believe that her tastes are widely shared by other students. For their part, students tend to think that my political beliefs are more commonly held by my colleagues than they probably are. Third, induction may well be quite important in how we change our well-developed stereotypes of categories. As we shall see in Chapter 10, one strategy for changing such stereotypes is to expose people to disconfirming exemplars, hoping that the perceiver will now infer new features for the group and change the old ones she has.

Although I cannot present a complete analysis of induction here (for some recent models, see Holland et al., 1986; Osherson, Smith, Wilkie, Lopez, & Shafir, 1990; Rips, 2001; Shipley, 1993; Sloman, 1993), a few points are in order. First, some categories seem to be more privileged targets for induction than others. For example, as I have already discussed in an earlier section, both children and adults are generally more willing to generalize from instances for natural categories than for other types (Carey, 1985; Gelman & Medin, 1993; Keil, 1989). Second, we are more likely to generalize from typical instances of a category (Rips, 1975. Third, instances or subcategories that are more diverse typically lead to stronger inferences about superordinate categories (Heit & Hahn, 2001; Osherson et al., 1990). For example, people are more willing to assume that mammals in general have a feature if they know that lions and bats both have it than if they know that lions and tigers do. By extension if I were to discover that a diverse lot of Albanians (tall and short, Muslim and Christian, male and female, etc.) are all polite, I am more likely to assume that Albanians in general are than if I have merely met a few Muslim males. Fourth, although many of these rules apply generally, experts in a domain are more likely to use domain-specific knowledge in their inductive exercises (López et al., 1997; Proffitt, Coley, & Medin, 2000). For example, inferences that a disease affecting one species might also affect another are often more dependent (for experts) on whether the two species are found close together or share an ecological niche than on formal taxonomic relationships based on physical similarities.

Fifth, some features for some categories are more likely to be generalized than others. We would expect that two 1998 Honda Accords with similar engines will get similar gas mileage, but not that they will have the same color. Similarly if I meet one likeable African American member of a jazz group, I would probably be more willing to conclude that jazz players are likeable than that jazz players are all African American. There are many reasons why we generalize some features more than others, but an important one is that we assume some features to be more variable within a category than others. I now turn to a discussion of category homogeneity.

Differentiation and Homogeneity

Categories are ways of dividing the world. When we place something in a category, we implicitly assume that it has at least something in common with other exemplars of that category, and that it differs in at least some ways from things in other categories. To think of a person as a female is to assume that she is like other females in important ways and unlike males in others. We would not use the category label otherwise. We do not generally categorize people in terms of how straight their teeth are, because we have no reason to believe that people with straight teeth have much in common besides their dental bills, or that they differ in any important way from people with crooked teeth. In our society gender makes a difference; teeth usually do not.

Tajfel's Model

Henri Tajfel (1959) has argued that the act of classification itself encourages us to see items within a category as more similar and to see items from different categories as more different, especially when the categories have emotional or affective value. Intergroup differentiation and intragroup similarity are related cognitively. To the extent that people see members of a category as more similar, they may tend to "pull in" the instances at the category boundaries, producing both greater intracategory similarity and a greater differentiation at the category boundaries (Campbell, 1956). Conversely, if intracategory differentiation is increased and the exemplars at the boundaries are pushed away from the category mean, this may tend to make category boundaries fuzzy. One way to think about this is in terms of traditional contrast and assimilation effects. To the extent that there is within-category assimilation, there will tend to be heightened intercategory contrast.

An influential experiment by Tajfel and Wilkes (1963) illustrates the general point. Subjects were shown eight lines several times and asked to give the length of each. The lines increased in length by 5% from the shortest (16.2 centimeters) to the longest (22.8 centimeters). For some subjects the lines were classified such that the four shortest lines were all labeled A and the longest B, and for other subjects the lines were not labeled. When the lines were classified, subjects overestimated the difference between lines 4 and 5 (the longest line in the short category and the shortest in the long category); this may be taken as evidence for the proposition that intercategory differences were enhanced.[7] However, there was no evidence of increased intracategory similarity. That is, there was no reduction in perceived differences among the four A lines and four B lines.

Intercategory Differentiation

THE KRUEGER–ROTHBART RESEARCH

Categories are useful precisely because they emphasize similarities among exemplars within the category and differences among exemplars from different categories. There is abundant evidence that categorization increases differentiation between categories (Krueger, 1992; Krueger & Rothbart, 1990; Krueger, Rothbart, & Sriram, 1989).

A study by Krueger and Clement (1994) using natural stimuli can illustrate the general approach. These investigators asked subjects to estimate high and low temperatures for days throughout the year. Generally (at least in New England, where this study was done), there are fairly even increases in temperatures from day to day during the first part of the year and even decreases during the latter part. Krueger and Clement asked subjects to estimate temperatures for dates that differed by 8 days; in some cases these dates both fell within a given month, and in other cases they crossed a month boundary (e.g., July 26 and August 3). Subjects' estimates were actually fairly accurate, but the question Krueger and Clement raised was whether they would tend to overestimate differences between months relative to those within months. In fact, 85% of the subjects perceived greater differences between rather than within months, even though the between-month changes were not actually higher than the within-month changes. This suggests that the subjects wanted to emphasize the differences between months, as we all tend to do in our everyday lives.

SHIFTING STANDARDS

Monica Biernat and her colleagues (Biernat, Manis, & Nelson, 1991; Biernat & Thompson, 2002; Biernat, Vescio & Manis, 1998) argue that between-category contrast effects are more robust for what we might call objective judgments, whereas such effects tend to disappear or reverse for more subjective scales. As one example, consider judgments of height. In one study (Biernat et al., 1991), subjects were shown pictures of males and females matched for height; for every picture of a male of a given height, there was a picture of a female of the same height, although subjects were not informed of this equality. They were then asked to estimate the height of the people in the photos—either in terms of feet and inches (an objective scale), or on "subjective scales" of very short to very tall compared to the average person or very short to very tall compared to the average male/female. When the judgments were objective (feet and inches), the males were judged as taller than the females, showing within-category assimilation and between-category contrast effects; such effects are exactly what one would expect if stereotypes play a role. With the more subjective scales, these effects were essentially eliminated. Similar effects have been shown for judgments of weight and income for males and females (Biernat et al., 1991), for judgments of athletic performance by males and females (Biernat & Vescio, 2002), for judgments of male and female leadership abilities in a military setting (Biernat, Crandall, Young, Kobrynowicz, & Halpin, 1998), for judgments of competence and verbal ability for males and females, and for verbal and athletic ability for blacks and whites (Biernat & Manis, 1994).

In a way these results are counterintuitive, since we usually imagine that stereotypes are somehow subjective and therefore should show up more strongly on subjective scales. Why does this occur? Biernat argues that the use of subjective scales promotes shifting standards. Consider an example. Suppose you hold the view that Asian American students are generally better at math and science than are European American students. If you were asked to estimate the Graduate Record Examination scores (relatively objective) of matched Asian American and European American students, you might be inclined to exaggerate the true difference between them. However, if you were asked to judge how smart or mathematically inclined each student was (a more subjective rating), you would be likely to judge them as more similar, because you would in effect be judging each against the standard of his or her own race. The European American student might be seen as a math whiz relative to his or her racial group, but the Asian American student might be seen as merely average for his or her group. Thus for objective ratings you would create the equivalent of within-race assimilation and between-race contrast, whereas for more subjective ratings the reverse would hold. Similarly, the same aggressive act performed by a male and a female might be seen as more aggressive for the female because, compared to the behavior of other females, it is relatively more aggressive. This is discussed further in Chapter 4.

A related phenomenon is that the same traits applied to different groups may suggest quite different behaviors or amount of behavior (Kobrynowicz & Biernat, 1997). For example, fathers and mothers who claim to perform the same general classes of behaviors (e.g., nurturing) are rated as equally good parents—a subjective rating. However, when more objective ratings are requested (e.g., the number of such behaviors typically performed or the amount of time parents spend performing them), mothers are perceived to do more. In other words, fathers have to perform fewer nurturing behaviors than women to be seen as equally good at it. Similarly, although Asian American and European American students may be rated as equally good in math (subjective), people still think that the Asian Americans have higher ability scores.

The rule of thumb, then, is that stereotypic thinking (i.e., judging a person to be consistent with stereotypic expectations) operates most strongly with more objective measures. However, stereotypes can operate in many, and sometimes mysterious, ways. Consider the oft-made claims that affirmative action programs simply result in a lowering of standards for minority candidates: Since we expect members of minority groups to perform less well, we accept lower performance as minimally acceptable from them (or so some assume). On the other hand, members of minority groups often claim that they are held to higher standards on the job—that their performance has to be much better just for them to be seen as displaying the same competence as nonminority people. At one level these claims seem to be contradictory, but Biernat and Kobrynowicz (1997) argue that this is because we are talking about two different kinds of judgments. The shifting-standards model predicts that lower-status people should be held to lower minimum standards (on objective measures). However, status characteristics theory (Foschi & Foddy, 1988) suggests that stereotypic thinking leads us to require more consistent information about abilities from lower-status people than from higher-status people to see them as having the same abilities. If we expect white non-Hispanic men to excel at certain tasks, we require relatively little evidence of competent performance before we conclude that they have the requisite ability. However, if we expect Hispanic females to lack these same abilities, we would want more evidence to decide that they have the ability. In experiments involving race and gender, Biernat and Kobrynowicz showed that for objective scales subjects set lower minimum standards for women and blacks, but required more information about ability before concluding they were competent.

Intracategory Homogeneity

Recall that Tajfel (1959) suggested both that intercategory differentiation should be enhanced and that intracategory differentiation should be reduced by the simple act of categorization. We have just seen that the first part of this prediction has been generally supported. However, Tajfel and Wilkes (1963) found little evidence in support of the proposition that intracategory similarity following categorization should be increased.[8] This effect has sometimes been hard to demonstrate, although there are several studies showing increased intracategory similarity after categorization (e.g., Doise, Deschamps, & Meyer, 1978; McGarty & Penny, 1988; McGarty & Turner, 1992), especially on dimensions relevant to the categorization (Corneille & Judd, 1999).

This has been nicely demonstrated in a set of studies by Rothbart, Davis-Stitt, and Hill (1997). In these studies subjects rated the similarity of individuals that differed by some constant amount, but sometimes these individuals were in the same category and sometimes not. As expected, they were judged as more similar when they were in the same category. In one experiment subjects evaluated job candidates who had scores along a scale running from 500 to 1,000. The scale was divided into categories of "ideal," "acceptable," "marginal," and "reject." As one example, one candidate had a score of 840; in one condition the boundary between ideal and acceptable was set at 880 (so she would be classified as acceptable), and in another condition this same boundary was set at 820 (so she would be classified as ideal). When her score placed her in the ideal category, she was seen as more similar to the other ideal candidates and less similar to other acceptable candidates than when her score placed her in the acceptable category. Note that the similarity was objectively the same, but that perceptions of similarity were affected by categorization.

COMPETING PROCESSES

One reason why it has been relatively difficult to demonstrate intracategory homogeneity is that two opposing processes may be at work. On the one hand, the act of categorization may tend to emphasize similarities among category members, as Campbell (1956), Tajfel (1959), and others have suggested, and as Rothbart and colleagues (1997) found. On the other hand, sometimes when stimuli are judged in relationship to a category, contrast effects are observed (Eiser, 1990). I may, for example, judge the performance of a man who is a marginal member of a professional basketball team as quite poor when I compare him with other members of the team, even though he is better than 99% of all male basketball players. Obviously, such within-category contrast effects would tend to work against the intracategory similarity effects just mentioned.

Manis and his colleagues have argued for just such a mechanism. An initial set of studies dealt with intracategory judgments. In a study by Manis and Paskowitz (1984), subjects were asked to read a series of either handwriting samples or definitions of words produced by patients in a hospital. The stimuli either clearly indicated severe psychopathology (e.g., "cushion—to sleep on a pillow of God's sheep," "diamond—a piece of glass made from roses") or seemed normal. After reading several of the normal or pathological handwriting samples or definitions, they were then asked to judge how pathological a moderate stimulus from a patient at the same hospital was. Subjects who had read the extremely pathological samples rated the moderate handwriting or definition as more normal than did the subjects who had been reading normal stimuli. In other words, the moderate stimulus was displaced away from the extreme stimuli subjects had been reading.

Note that within-category contrast effects can produce lessened intercategory differentiation. For example, Manis, Paskowitz, and Cotler (1986) showed that when subjects read psychopathic definitions from patients at a psychiatric facility and normal definitions from patients at a general hospital, they thought that moderately normal definitions from the general hospital were more pathological than equivalent definitions from the psychiatric hospital. Thus, at least at the boundaries, statements produced by the disturbed population were seen as less disturbed than statements produced by the normal sample. Manis and colleagues argued that intracategory contrast of the sort demonstrated by Manis and Paskowitz (1984) produced lessened category differentiation. However, additional research by Eiser, Martijn, and van Schie (1991) suggests that the lessening of category differentiation may have more to do with uncertainty of the subjects about standards of judgment than with intracategory contrast. Nonetheless, the Manis and colleagues suggestion has intuitive appeal; surely there are times when we see a person as quite different from people in his or her own category, and consequently we might also see the person as more similar to people in a contrasting category.

MOOD EFFECTS

Mood can affect perceptions of group variability (Stroessner & Mackie, 1993). Particularly when people are in a good mood, they tend to process information somewhat cavalierly. For example, Stroessner and Mackie (1992) showed that whereas people in a neutral mood correctly perceived that a highly variable group was more variable than a less variable group, subjects who were in positive or negative moods did not distinguish the two groups, suggesting that they were insensitive to variability information. Queller, Mackie, and Stroessner (1996) found that people in a good mood perceived more consistent and less inconsistent information within a group than did neutral-mood subjects. Good-mood subjects also perceived groups to be more homogeneous. However, when good-mood subjects were forced to consider evidence of diversity, they perceived the groups as diverse just as the neutral-mood subjects did.

MEMORY

Another large body of literature, on memory confusions, supports the idea that categorization increases perceptions of group homogeneity. When you see a number of people from different categories performing many behaviors, the behaviors may be remembered as having been performed by someone of a particular category or by a particular individual (Ostrom, Pryor, & Simpson, 1981). You may recall that a particularly telling quotation comes from Shakespeare but not remember which play, or may recollect that a brilliant political commentary came from a newspaper columnist but not recall which one. Alternatively, you may recall that the commentary was authored by a particular person but not recall whether it was in a newspaper, magazine, or book of essays.

Shelly Taylor (1981) and her colleagues argued that if categorization increases or makes salient perceptions of similarities among members of groups, it should be harder to distinguish among their behaviors.[9] In one experiment by Taylor and colleagues (1978), subjects viewed a videotape of a discussion involving both whites and blacks. Since race is salient, the investigators reasoned that comments made by individuals would be readily differentiated by race. Subjects did show good accuracy in remembering whether a particular comment was made by a black or a white discussant. However, discrimination within categories was relatively poor; subjects tended to remember that a comment was made by a black person but not by which one.

Such race effects have been replicated by Biernat and Vescio (1993) and Hewstone, Hantzi, and Johnston (1991), among others. Similar effects have been shown for gender (e.g., Arcuri, 1982; Branscombe, Deaux, & Lerner, 1985; Lorenzi-Cioldi, 1993; Miller, 1986; Taylor & Falcone, 1982; van Knippenberg, van Twuyver, & Pepels, 1994). Intracategory errors also occur for categories such as physical attractiveness, especially for those who have strong stereotypes about physical attractiveness (Miller, 1988); homosexuality, especially for those who are most homophobic (Walker & Antaki, 1986); expressed attitudes (Biernat & Vescio, 1993); social relationships (A. P. Fiske, Haslam, & Fiske, 1991); married couples (Sedikides, Olsen, & Reis, 1993); and academic status (Arcuri, 1982). Even dress style can be a basis for memory confusions when such categories are relevant to perceivers (Brewer, Weber, & Carini, 1995; Stangor et al., 1992).

Judgments of Groups Based on Individuals

Perceived group homogeneity is important, because it affects how easily we generalize about a group from single instances. Suppose you are in a supermarket in the process of buying grapes. You look around, determine that no one is watching, and eat a grape from what you suspect is a tasty bunch. Despite your guilt, the grape is delicious. Would you now be inclined to buy a pound or two, based on this single grape? Having performed that very experiment, I know that I would be. Now you go back the next week, and grapes are still available at an attractive price. Would you now be inclined to buy a bunch without additional taste tests? Surely this is less likely. We assume that there is relatively little variability between grapes within a given bunch, but we understand that grapes vary a good deal among various shipments, days, and the like.

In a classic experimental demonstration by Nisbett, Krantz, Jepson, and Kunda (1983), subjects were told that they had come to a little-known island, and then were asked a series of questions about what they would be willing to conclude based on single experiences. Subjects were, for example, quite willing to conclude that if a sample of some chemical element found on the island conducted electricity, other samples would also. They were less eager to generalize that a blue-colored bird meant that all birds were similarly colored, and reluctant to conclude that a single obese native meant that all natives would be similarly figured. One of the reasons we feel more confident about generalizing about physical objects than about people is that we assume that people are more variable with regard to most traits than are things. I hit a key on my computer keyboard, and a particular character appears on the screen. I am immediately convinced that this key press produced the character and that it always will, as long as conditions stay the same. Computers are built to produce reliable results of key pokes. On the other hand, we understand that because human behavior is highly variable, one person's response to a poke need not be the same as another's. People are delightfully variable, and computers comfortably reliable.[10] Obviously, to the extent that we see a category as having essentialist features, we will be see the category members as less variable on those features.

In a study more closely related to stereotyping, Park and Hastie (1987) found that for traits and goals consistent with the positive impressions formed of groups, people who thought that a group was highly variable were less willing to generalize than those who had been exposed to a less variable group. For inferences of atypical traits and goals, however, those with the variable groups generalized more. In other words, if a group was fairly homogeneous with regard to positive traits, people were relatively willing to infer that the group was generally honest if a single member was honest, and relatively unwilling to generalize about hostility.

Judgments of Individuals Based on Groups

GROUP ATTRIBUTION ERRORS

Perceived homogeneity also affects inferences about typical members of groups based on the group's collective behavior. You may, for example, think that a large majority of Republicans are pro-life on the abortion issue because a pro-life declaration has been a part of the Republican Party platform in most recent elections, especially if you think Republicans are a fairly homogeneous group. We may well assume that the majority of blacks favor policies promulgated by the National Association for the Advancement of Colored People, that most professors agree with the policies of the American Association of University Professors, and that most U.S. Catholics support the Catholic Church's position on birth control. Just as we sometimes overascribe dispositions to individuals based on a sample of behavior, so we may also overgeneralize about groups based on group decisions.

Scott Allison and his colleagues (e.g., Allison, Mackie, & Messick, 1996) have investigated the group attribution error. In one set of studies (Allison & Messick, 1985), subjects were asked to estimate the attitude of a typical city citizen on a political issue based on information about various kinds of group decisions. As expected, when the city had supported a policy by a 92% majority, subjects strongly inferred that the typical citizen supported the policy. However, they also made strong attributions (although not as strong) to the typical citizen even when the decision had been made by a 54% majority, or had been made by a city manager or city agency without any vote.

An even more striking demonstration occurred in experiments where the outcome of a vote affected attributes to group members, even when the vote was the same. For example, Allison and Messick (1985) told subjects that 57% of citizens voted for a proposition, and that either 50% or 65% was needed for passage. Despite the fact that the vote was the same, subjects inferred individual attitudes more when the proposition passed (57% voted yes and 50% were needed) than when it did not pass (57% voted yes, but 65% were needed).

The natural tendency is to assume that a group decision represents the attitudes of group members. However, sometimes we need both to take into account the degree of support within the group and to adjust our notions for contextual information, such as the criterion used to decide whether a vote is successful. As is typical for other sorts of attribution decisions (see Chapter 14), sometimes people fail to use their knowledge to correct their judgments, and this correction should especially suffer when people are cognitively overloaded. Indeed, in this paradigm the tendency to assume that a winning vote reflects stronger group opinions than a losing vote is stronger when subjects are mentally overloaded than when they are not (Allison, Beggan, Midgley, & Wallace, 1995). People are also less likely to infer individual attitudes from the group when they are encouraged to process information thoughtfully (McHoskey & Miller, 1994), when the issues are personally relevant to them (Allison, Worth, & King, 1990; Worth, Allison, & Messick, 1987), or when they agree with the issue (Mackie, Ahn, Asuncion, & Allison, 2001).

Most of the research on group attributions has been done with attitudes, but similar effects occur with traits. For example, Mackie, Allison, Worth, and Asuncion (1992b) gave subjects information about a group trying to win a college bowl competition. The group solved 70% of the problems it got, and it needed to solve either 65% or 75% to qualify. The group that succeeded was seen as smarter than the group that failed, despite identical performance. Interestingly, this effect occurred whether or not the college bowl team members were described as African American or Asian American. This general result was also found in another study by Mackie, Allison, Worth, and Asuncion (1992a). In this case, groups that failed were seen as less smart than groups that succeeded, and this was true whether the groups were janitors or college professors. Interestingly enough, these attributions generalized to the larger groups; subjects who read about a group of professors that failed rated college professors in general as less bright than those who read that the professors had succeeded despite identical performance.

INFERENCES ABOUT INDIVIDUALS

There is little direct evidence for the intuitively appealing notion that people are more likely to infer the attributes of an individual from group membership when that group is seen as relatively homogeneous. Available data tend to support these conjectures. One line of research (Ryan, Judd, & Park, 1996) showed that subjects who assumed that groups in general were extreme on a given trait also assumed that individuals were more extreme; furthermore, those subjects who also assumed that the group was relatively homogeneous were more confident of their judgments. Members of homogeneous groups are perceived to be more extreme on stereotype-relevant traits than are members of more heterogeneous groups (Park & Hastie, 1987). Other research shows that disconfirming exemplars are less likely to cause changes in the general stereotype for heterogeneous than for homogeneous groups (Hewstone, Johnston, & Aird, 1992).

Just to make life a little more complicated and interesting, we probably ought to take into account the extent to which group homogeneity extends across attributes—what Kashima and Kashima (1993) have termed "general variability." Most groups are presumably more heterogeneous with regard to some qualities than to others. A group of football players may, for example, be less variable in its strength and size than in intellectual abilities or introversion. Since we assume that some groups are homogeneous with regard to several important features, are we also likely to assume that they are equally homogeneous with regard to others? Indeed, the extent to which attributes are seen to be correlated may itself be an important aspect of stereotypes (Quattrone, 1986). Members of the NRA are presumably fairly homogeneous with regard to gun control. Even though gun control is a relatively conservative political position as we define those things in the United States, I still recognize that the NRA members probably have more diverse views on welfare reform, and more diverse positions still on how capital gains should be taxed. I may still, however, overestimate the homogeneity of the NRA on all these more peripheral issues. Whether we take account of the different kinds of diversity that groups display strikes me as a vitally important issue. For example, do we assume more homogeneity among NRA members on peripherally related issues when their homogeneity on the core issue is made salient? A proper investigation of this issue would require a better understanding of how people perceive attributes as being related than we presently have.

The lesson is this: To the extent that a group is seen as relatively heterogeneous, we will, all things being equal, be less likely to assume that observed behaviors and features of individuals are characteristic of the group as a whole than when we have reason to believe that the group is more variable or heterogeneous. Furthermore, we are more likely to infer individual attributes from the group for groups we assume to be more homogeneous. There are important and not well-investigated issues concerned with whether perceived heterogeneity is a general or specific quality.

SUMMARY

Categorization is one of the most basic and important, yet complex, of all the things our minds do. There are at least four basic ways that we categorize people, events, and things. The classic view that categories have necessary, defining features is limited to relatively few categories (e.g., square). Many of our categories are based on similarity judgments. The prototype view suggests that we assign things to appropriate categories when they are similar enough to important other category members on important features. The exemplar view suggests that we use concrete exemplars of a category as standards to judge category membership. While similarity is often important for our judgments of category membership, our theories about relationships of features to categories may also play a role. For example, ad hoc categories may be based less on similarity than on whether prospective members fulfill some goal (e.g., things to take on a picnic, murder weapons).

Much of the empirical work on categorization has been done with objects and specially prepared stimuli. There may be important differences between social and object categories that may affect stereotyping. One important difference is that social categories often combine into compounds where a person is seen as a member of two or more categories simultaneously as opposed to hierarchies. So a career woman is a type of female but is probably more easily seen as a combination of the categories "female" and "businessperson."

Another unresolved issue is whether people assume that social categories have an essence as do many natural kinds. Certain biological and physical categories (natural kinds) seem to have an essence in terms of DNA or molecular structure, which causes other features that we regard as typical of the category. The assumption that categories have an essence aids our thinking about category members in a variety of ways. In particular, it gives us "permission" to assume that category members are alike on important features, so that we are willing to infer that if one member has a feature the others are likely to as well.

Features are associated with all categories, and placing something in a category aids our inferences that it has the features of that category. Category–feature relationships may be represented in various ways, but commonly as probabilities. In thinking about category–feature relationships as probabilities, it is important not to confuse the probabilities that people in a category have a particular feature (feature diagnosticity) with the probability that someone with a particular feature is a member of that category (category diagnosticity).

People can be categorized in multiple (and in an uncountably high) number of ways, so it is important to determine why some categories seem to be favored over others. There is some evidence that gender, race, and age categories have a certain primacy in that they are almost always used, if only unconsciously. Over and above that categorization seems to reflect which categories are accessible at a given time, and such accessibility reflects such factors as salience of certain cues, whether certain categories are way underrepresented in a particular situation, the importance of momentary goals, and the accessibility of certain attitudes associated with categories. One important question for which we do not yet have definitive answers is whether subcategories (e.g., businesswoman or father) are more basic than superordinate categories (e.g., gender) in the sense of having richer stereotypes on which we can more readily draw.

Categories affect inferences we draw about people in those categories. In addition, there is good evidence that the act of categorization increases perceptions that category members are more similar and that they differ more from people in contrasting categories. This has potentially important implications for the ways we perceive individuals as members of categories, and how willing we are to infer features of other categories on members we do not know.

Notes

1. However, we can easily make most nonpredicating social combinations into predicating ones in ways that make psychological sense. In this example, we simply restate the constituent categories as females and career people.
2. As Hampton recognized the necessity and impossibility conditions can easily be accommodated in a non-linear prediction rule that weights extreme importance ratings for either constituent more strongly on the assumption that necessity means that an attribute is highly likely and impossibility that it is highly unlikely.
3. A further problem is that although the essentialism of natural-kind categories is tied to physical and biological realities, promoting more than a gentle shove in the direction of genetic essence for such groups, some social groups have an essence because of cultural values and what we might call "deep socialization." People who actively and militantly resist genetic explanations for group differences (and hence feel "in the clear" on essentialist thinking) may implicitly tolerate or even endorse socialization as a powerful cause of group differences and behave like essentialist thinkers, despite their best intentions.
4. Although the use of stereotype and trait labels may be somewhat confusing in this context, since we normally think that traits are nested under stereotypes and not the other way around, the "take-home" point is that levels of subordinate categories are more informative than more superordinate ones.
5. One is tempted to refer to the former as "deductive" and the latter as "inductive" inference, based on common and informal usage that deduction goes from the general to the particular and induction from individual cases to the general category. However, this is not the way these terms are used by philosophers and logicians. Formally, deduction involves rigorous demonstration, while induction is seen as an expansion of knowledge under uncertainty. In that latter sense, induction covers both judgments about individuals based on categories and the reverse. I will, however, consistently use the term "induction" to refer to inferences about group features from individuals.
6. I well remember meeting my first major Wall Street lawyer (actually the managing partner in a major firm), who turned out to be much smarter, socially responsible, and politically thoughtful than I had believed possible.
7. Tajfel and Wilkes (1963) emphasized increased differentiation at the boundaries—an effect that has been demonstrated many times (e.g., Crisp & Hewstone, 1999b)—but a better test would have been to show that differences between all pairs of A and B items were, on average, exaggerated. There are two reasons why the latter measure is to be preferred. First, it is rare in everyday life to find two categories with nonoverlapping memberships on some dimension. For example, men may be stronger on average than women, but we expect to find some women who are stronger than some men. In this case the Tajfel–Wilkes measure cannot be used, because there are no distinct boundaries between the categories. Second, we are normally more interested in exaggerations of mean differences between groups than in differences between individuals at the edges of the distribution. Subse-

quent research (see Krueger, 1992) has in fact shown that categorization does lead items in one category to become more different from items in the other on average.

8. This should not be confused with the well-known outgroup homogeneity effect, in which members of other groups are seen as more homogeneous than members of one's own group. This is well documented (see Chapter 7), but it apparently results from cognitive and motivational factors other than the postulated intracategory homogeneity effect discussed here.

9. Related is the Jewish name phenomenon: "I can't remember her name—Goldberg? Goldstein?—but I know it was Jewish."

10. There may be exceptions involving especially diagnostic behaviors. Intuitively, an unexpected and vicious attack by a person on a bystander would give rise quickly to attributions of a violent disposition, and might even be seen to generalize to members of other groups to which this violent chap belongs (e.g., persons with mental illness). This is despite the fact that aggressiveness as a behavior is highly variable within a given individual, across individuals, and across groups.

CHAPTER 4

Schema Theories

THE NATURE OF SCHEMAS

We categorize people, and then use those categories to draw inferences about them. Our minds are busy, so sometimes this is a passive and mindless sort of thing. But other times it is active and thoughtful. In addition to category-based knowledge, we often have more immediately observed information about people's behaviors, traits, and appearance (which also have to be labeled and interpreted), and so we also have to integrate all this preexisting and incoming information. Since the time of the ancient Greeks, most philosophers and psychologists have agreed that we often process information in a "top-down" fashion—that what we "know" dictates what we "see" every bit as much as the reverse. What we call "experience" is always a function of both prior theories held in memory and present input from our sensory apparatus. There are no naked experiences. Those that involve other people are especially likely to be cognitively adorned, just because behavior must be interpreted in terms of contextual factors and inferred intentions.

In modern cognitive psychology, the notion of schemas has been used to represent the prior-knowledge part of the equation. "Schemas" may loosely be defined as theories we have about categories, and they function as frameworks for understanding what we see and hear. Some of these theories may be quite impoverished—I do not, for example, have any sort of elaborate theory about earthworms—but for important categories (say, occupations or gender), I have extensive knowledge that is bound together by quite complex theoretical ideas. A student who observes a professor giving a lecture will have schemas for the professor role, for the lecturing process, and for various other categories (male, Hispanic, young) that this particular professor fits. Thus stereotypes can be thought of, among other things, as schemas.

The Importance of Prior Knowledge

It is not obvious that we need an elaborate psychological construct, such as that of the schema, to help us understand how people construe their worlds. For example, my cat, which screams at the back door to be let in, seems to have an exceptional fear of being hit by the screen door as it opens. And so when she hears someone approaching the door, she retreats down a couple of steps, makes exactly one full turn, and waits for the screen door to open before she darts in. Now it is quite possible that this animal has a well-developed theory about the indignities of being hit by doors and the necessity to ward off such evils with retreats and turns. But it seems more likely (given other evidence) that she has no more than a couple dozen functioning cortical cells, that her behavior is entirely a matter of conditioning and may not be represented cognitively at all. At least some, perhaps much, of human thought and behavior may also be due to conditioning and other forms of passive learning. I need have no theory about anything to be afraid of a large man in a dark alleyway.

Dictionaries versus Encyclopedias

Some models construe this past knowledge as bits of information attached to cognitive nodes, and such association models in which features are linked to categories have been popular, especially in the stereotype area (Stangor & Lange, 1994); my definition of stereotypes (Chapter 1) incorporates this assumption. Certainly we do have such knowledge representation. So just as I know that dogs have tails, bark, and have fur, and that cars have transmissions, engines, doors, and seats, I could believe that professors are politically liberal and smart. This might be called the "dictionary view" of knowledge: Knowledge of a thing consists of several features that are more or less true of the object in question. The dictionary view does not require sophisticated knowledge about the concepts under question; dictionary entries may be passively acquired, mechanically stored, and unreflectively used. If stereotypes are *nothing more than* relationships between traits and groups, then we need not assume much about the theories of the people holding them.

However, everyday observation suggests that this is a crude and limiting view, because often the theoretical basis of our knowledge seems crucial. For example, like almost any adult in Western society, I can discuss the relationships among the physical features of a car; I have some sense of why doors are where they are, where the engine is and why, and how the transmission affects speed. All of this affects my driving behavior and reactions to problems in fundamental ways. In other words, knowledge about a car is more like an encyclopedia entry, with notions about how the various parts of the knowledge base are interrelated and how each, in turn, is related to other things through a series of what we might call "hyperlinks." Accessing information about engines and how they work might put me in the frame of mind to turn to a related "entry" on power, gasoline, or the importance of oxygen in combustion. Chapter 3 has argued that many (probably most) concepts, and certainly most concepts that are foundations for stereotypes, enfold a great deal of theoretical knowledge. We know what features are important for various categories, why they are important, and how they are related. Of course, it remains to be seen whether we gain any leverage on our understanding of stereotypes by assuming that they are theories of sorts about groups of people.

This is not an either–or situation. It has long been recognized (e.g., Sloman, 1996; Smith & DeCoster, 2002) that there are at least two forms of reasoning. One is based on associations and is usually quick and fairly automatic. The other is rule-based or theory-based and takes some cognitive effort. There is evidence that both forms of reasoning occur in the use of stereotypes (e.g., Smith & DeCoster, 2002). For example, whereas some inferences surely take time (e.g., inferring someone's intelligence from the way he or she is dressed), others seem fairly automatic, at least in the sense of not being conscious (e.g., inferring that the person standing at the head of a classroom is a professor). Although this chapter focuses on theory-based processing, we need to remember that some forms of stereotype inference do not even require categorization, let alone high-level inferences. For example, prototypic African American faces cue negative evaluations (Livingston & Brewer, 2002) and stereotypes (Blair, Judd, Sadler, & Jenkins, 2002), independently of whether a person categorizes a face as African American. Also, affective/emotional reactions to features associated with salient categories may kick in quickly, well before even implicit categorization has probably taken place (Stapel, Koomen, & Ruys, 2002).

Functions of Schemas

Our theories or knowledge structures—our schemas—aid in the recognition, interpretation, and labeling of stimuli; affect memory for information; provide default values for missing information; and generally lead to efficient processing of schema-related material (Fiske & Taylor, 1991). People with well-developed theories or schemas about some domain are, in effect, experts about that domain. My knowledge about cars is extremely limited (although not as limited as that of small children). I can identity some major parts of the engine, and can recognize the difference between tires and exhaust systems. Indeed, I could probably write pages and pages of information about what I know about cars, even though I lack (by a large amount) the knowledge to discourse intelligently about the inner workings of engines or to repair them. My mechanic, who is an expert about such matters, has a much more developed theory about all this and could certainly offer a more cogent (and probably more concise) statement about the workings of cars.

Traditionally, psychologists have assumed that all this cognitive work of attention, labeling, memory reduction, and inference drawing reduces the amount of information that is we need to ponder. There is no doubt that schemas do help us process information and, in that sense, make our interactions with the world more efficient. So, for example, activating a schema when one is forming impressions of people uses fewer cognitive resources than forming impressions without such weapons (Macrae, Milne, & Bodenhausen, 1994), and having an available schema or stereotype generally facilitates processing stereotype-relevant information quickly (Kawakami, Young, & Dovidio, 2002).

However, schemas are also important because they enrich our understanding of the world (Oakes & Turner, 1990), in that they allow us to infer features that we cannot immediately perceive. Behavior that might seem incomprehensible "in the raw" may make perfect sense in the context of a relevant schema. For example, we might not understand the behavior of a man who rushes out of an important business meeting until we know that he has just received a call that one of his children has been injured at school. Perhaps even more to the point, our schemas allow us to go beyond the information given (Bruner, 1957). Once I know that a computer is using Windows 2000 as an operating system, I can predict how the computer will respond to a wide range of keyboard commands and mouse clicks.

It is true that many predictions from schema models can be made more easily from less aggressively theory-driven accounts (e.g., Alba & Hasher, 1983), and that schema models are often bloated, vague, and "underspecified" (Carlston & Smith, 1996). However, such theories have historically suggested hypotheses and lines of research not easily derived from other models, and even though schema models are not parsimonious, they do account for a wide range of phenomena. In particular, they provide a safe haven for the kinds of theoretical reasoning that I claim often (but not inevitably) accompany stereotypes.

SCHEMAS AND STAGES OF INFORMATION PROCESSING

The schema notion has generally been paired with the additional idea that we process information about others in a series of somewhat discrete but overlapping stages. I consider four here: (1) attention, (2) labeling and interpretation, (3) memory, and (4) inferences.

Suppose, at a crowded party, I introduce you to a person named Scott, a man I've been telling you has a lot in common with you. I now move away to "let you two get acquainted." So now you're stuck with Scott, and so you look him over physically and metaphorically. What do you pay attention to? Surely a lot depends on the schemas you try out. If you're thinking of Scott as a potential romantic partner, you might immediately notice that he is tall, is fairly attractive, and has a nice baritone voice. If you are the type of person who prefers intellectuals to more social types, you may particularly notice that his tie is unfashionable, his shoes are unshined, and he is wearing thick glasses—cues for intellectual interests in your schema of intellectuals. As you continue to talk with Scott, you may ask him some questions or try to steer the conversation in a revealing direction. And the categories you employ may change. At first, you may have categorized Scott as a bit of an intellectual because of his appearance, but then you find out that he is a lawyer—a category of people you do not associate with intellectualism, or even much like. Why did I introduce you to a lawyer, for heaven's sake? And how can a lawyer dress as he does? But then you discover that he works for a local poverty agency, helping abused women with legal problems, and you begin to think of him as a "liberal" or a "compassionate guy." Somewhere along the line, Scott may reveal that he lives in a fashionable part of town, and you now have to figure out how a low-paid lawyer can live there. You infer that he has inherited money, and you begin to test whether he fits your schema of a "guilty liberal." At times during the conversation you may wonder whether he is gay or straight, romantically involved with someone or unattached, a sports fan or a lover of classical music. The point is that you will pay attention to different aspects of his behavior, depending on which of your schemas holds center stage at any given moment.

So we would expect your attention to be directed by your prior knowledge. Ultimately as your attention, driven by various schemas, yields knowledge about Scott, you will label him—will place him in one, probably several, categories. Scott, you decide, is a "yuppie type" despite his job, or a "Harvard type," or even a "sensitive male type." Your interpretations of his behavior will also be affected by these decisions. His extended comments about the present administration in Washington may be labeled quite differently, depending on whether you think he is a guilty liberal or is trying to impress you. His sloppy dress will mean something different if you find that he has just come from work where he must "dress down," or is simply indifferent to his appearance.

Your memory for Scott and his behavior will surely be affected by how you label him—by what schemas you use to understand his behavior. It would be easy to imagine that when, a few months later, you try to remember Scott, you would remember some features but not others. If you have decided that he is a guilty liberal, you may recall his political views, but not his comments about his musical tastes or how nicely he smiled. On the other hand, if you were thinking of him as a friend or romantic partner, you might well recall his smiles and dress better than his intricate political theories.

Finally, we would expect that your knowledge about the type of person Scott is will affect what you infer about him. You may easily imagine that he was not in a fraternity in college, but that he was active in liberal to radical political organizations. You may suspect that he majored in political science or sociology, and then be surprised that he was a physics major. Why would a physics major go to law school and work for a poverty organization?

Obviously, although we have been discussing schemas, most of what we have been saying about Scott really applies to stereotypes. In your attempts to get a handle on Scott, you are clearly drawing on your stereotypes about lawyers, people who live in certain areas, liberals, and folks who dress in a particular way. Your stereotypes allow you to infer all manner of things about Scott you never observe, but they can also lead to errors. Some are merely amusing, such as your inference that Scott was a sociology major in college, but other errors can be embarrassing and sometimes harmful. If you assume that Scott must be neurotic because he is a guilty liberal, you may reject him before you have a chance to discover that you could be good friends. Let us now review the major functions of schemas in information processing.

Attention

Attention and Identification

Schemas have major effects on attentional processes, although the effects are complex. When you enter a room for the first time, you probably direct your attention to information that will allow you to discover what kind of a room it is; you focus on information that will allow you to discriminate bedrooms from living rooms. In this case, it will not do you much good to glance at the ceiling or the floor; bedrooms and living rooms usually have about the same requirements in those areas. You may instead examine the room for evidence of mirrors, certain types of furniture, and the like. Similarly, style of dress is more useful than hair color for discriminating lawyers from custodians. Sometimes information that is especially relevant to our interests, goals, or active schemas seems to leap out at us perceptually. In one experimental demonstration, Macrae, Stangor, and Milne (1994) primed stereotypes by having subjects list traits relevant to the stereotype. Then the subjects were asked to recognize perceptually degraded words that were related or unrelated to the stereotype, and those who had the stereotypes primed found it easier to recognize the stereotype-relevant information.

Attention to Inconsistencies

Once you have securely identified that which you perceive, you can shift your attention from these diagnostic features to whatever features seem strange or inconsistent. For example, I would imagine that finding a toilet in the middle of what otherwise seems to be a normal living room might attract and hold your attention for some time; you might even be inclined to ask your host a guarded question or two about the appliance. In a health care professional's office, you may find yourself sneaking glances at the blunt and ugly fingers of a surgeon or the misshapen teeth of a dentist. Similarly, when you meet Scott, you pay particular attention to (or sought out) information that will help you resolve what you think are inconsistencies between his profession (lawyer) and attire (scruffy).

In a study on attention to social features, White and Carlston (1983) asked subjects to watch a videotape of two people who sat at opposite ends of a library table engaged in separate conversations. The audio part of the tape was rigged in such a way that subjects heard one of the conversations more loudly and clearly than the other, but some subjects could shift the focus of attention from one conversation to the other by changing their relative loudness. Subjects were given trait information about one of the actors (kind or honest), and initially subjects spent more of their time monitoring the behavior of the person for whom they had a personality expectation, presumably to confirm their expectations. During the first several minutes, this target person performed behaviors that neither confirmed nor disconfirmed the expected trait. Consequently, over time the preference for monitoring the person for whom they had an expectation gradually decreased, and subjects spent relatively more of their time listening to the person for whom they had no prior trait information. However, at one point, the target person began to perform a behavior that was inconsistent with the kind or honest expectation, and at this point subjects' attention to that person markedly increased. What seems to have happened is that subjects selectively monitored the person for whom they had an expectation to see whether his or her behavior confirmed it. When the behavior turned out to be relatively uninformative, they "lost interest" and began to shift attention to other matters. However, when the person began to perform in unexpected ways, they once again gave much more of their attention to this person.

Several other studies also show that people attend especially to information inconsistent with their expectations and schemas (e.g., Hilton, Klein, & von Hippel, 1991; Stern, Marrs, Millar, & Cole, 1984). The implication is that when people have a stereotype about a group, they will be inclined to monitor the behavior of group members to see whether their behavior fits the stereotype. If it does, then attention may be given to other matters. If the process stops here (as it often does), the perceiver will only know that the target belongs to a category or two and perhaps has some relevant traits. However, if the perceiver is motivated to process information about the target more carefully, she may be struck by stereotype-inconsistent information that is likely to capture an undue amount of attention. When interaction is limited and basically stops after such encounters, superficial behaviors may lead to stereotype confirmation. On the other hand, when the person does perform a behavior inconsistent with the stereotype, additional attention and processing will be given to that behavior. How this inconsistent information is handled is an important theme for the rest of this chapter.

What Captures Attention?

Up to this point, I have been arguing that attention to detail is controlled by one's schemas. At different points in information processing, schema-consistent or schema-inconsistent information will receive priority in processing. However, attention may also be affected by certain features of stimuli themselves, as well as by one's own motives.

CONTRAST

One of the most obvious factors that affects attention is the intensity of stimuli or their difference from the background. Regardless of what schemas are active for you at any given moment, you are likely to pay more attention to the woman in the bright green dress than to her companion dressed in a muted brown. Or you may even stare at the man in the corner who is waving his hands wildly. Stimuli that stand out from their surroundings usually capture the most attention (McArthur & Ginsberg, 1981). The woman's bright green dress would surely attract less attention if the other women in the room were also wearing bright and lively colors. The man waving his arms would not warrant an initial glance in a room of heavy gesticulators. Being different is a magnet for attention from others. For example, as we have seen in Chapter 3, people in a solo status think they are under constant scrutiny, and often they are.

Another kind of novelty rests on departures from general norms. White Americans who travel to areas of the world where white skin and relative tallness are quite uncommon often report that natives, especially children, scrutinize them carefully.[1] Those who are physically different (e.g., those with visible disabilities) often complain that other people stare at them.[2] A study by Langer, Fiske, Taylor, and Chanowitz (1976) confirmed that when subjects' thought their staring could not be detected, they did look more at a picture of a woman in a leg brace; females (but not males) stared more at a picture of a pregnant woman. Although such attentiveness is often perceived to be rude, it may often be motivated by nothing more than curiosity about a relatively unfamiliar stimulus.

SITUATIONAL CIRCUMSTANCE

In everyday life, surely one of the more important reasons we pay attention to some things and not others is their relative availability to our sensory apparatus. We usually pay more attention to people who are physically close rather than distant, because it is easier to monitor them. People sitting across from us are more salient than those sitting to our sides (Fiske, Kenny, & Taylor, 1982 ; Taylor, Crocker, Fiske, Sprinzen, & Winkler, 1979; Taylor & Fiske, 1975).

MOTIVES AND GOALS

It is an obviously true but nonetheless important point that our attention is often controlled by our goals and motives (Erber & Fiske, 1984; Neuberg & Fiske, 1987; Ruscher & Fiske, 1990). A student visiting a professor to plead for additional points on an exam surely pays close attention to how much the professor smiles or grunts as he or she rereads the exam. It is the curse of people who are waiting for decisions about promotions within an organization that every smile, frown, and minute bit of bodily behavior of superiors is captured and interpreted for any sign of how the decision will go.

Consequences of Attention

The effects of attention are often obvious: Unless attention is paid to some stimulus, information about it is not available for further processing. You will never form an impression of the woman across the room, let alone think about her in stereotypic terms, unless you first observe her behavior.

ATTENTION AND ATTRIBUTIONAL PROCESSING

However, there are effects of differential attention even when enough attention is paid to several people to remember them. Imagine that you meet two people at a party, and that for some reason you pay far more attention to Hank than to Sara. How might we expect that extra attention to affect your perceptions of them? One speculation is that people to whom we give more attention are often seen as causally more active and powerful in a given situation. As known for some time (e.g., Schneider, Hastorf, & Ellsworth, 1979), we see people as responsible for their behavior, in the sense that we assume that their intentions, attitudes, motives, and abilities to cause their behavior. Several studies find that people to whom we attend are seen as particularly prominent or casually active (Fiske et al., 1982; McArthur & Post, 1977; Taylor et al., 1979).

ATTENTION AND INHIBITION

When we attend to one thing, processing of information about unattended objects may not be merely suspended but actively inhibited (Houghton & Tipper, 1994). Macrae, Bodenhausen, and Milne (1995) asked people to watch a videotape of a Chinese woman. When race was primed, subjects had better access to racial stereotype information, but access to gender information was inhibited. The reverse was true when gender was primed. In a study by Dijksterhuis and van Knippenberg (1996), when a category label was primed, subjects had greater access to stereotype-consistent and less access to stereotype-inconsistent information than people for whom the category was not primed.

Labeling and Interpretation

Attentional mechanisms provide a gate that allows certain information to be processed further, but they do not guarantee that further processing will take place. Most of the time, the newly arrived environmental information must be labeled and interpreted. Most human behavior is ambiguous; it takes on its meaning from the context in which it occurs and the inferences we make about the intentions underlying it.

Evaluation of New Information

Our fast-paced senses provide us with new information at an alarming rate, and we make conscious and unconscious choices about which is useful and accurate. That's what our schemas do for us. People with strong schemas or theoretical commitments evaluate evidence supporting their schemas more favorably than they do inconsistent information (e.g., Koehler, 1993; Lord, Ross, & Lepper, 1979; Miller, McHoskey, Bane, & Dowd, 1993; Munro & Ditto, 1997), and they see sources who disagree with them as biased (Giner-Sorolla & Chaiken, 1994; Vallone, Ross, & Lepper, 1985).

Dacher Keltner and Robert Robinson have argued that we humans view the world from a perspective of naive realism: We assume that we are in touch with an external reality, and that our cognitions, beliefs, attitudes, and other cognitive states reflect this reality. Therefore, because we assume that our beliefs are anchored in reality, it must follow that those who disagree are out of touch with reality and thereby biased. As a consequence, we tend to see those who disagree with us as holding extreme positions (e.g., Keltner & Robinson, 1997; Robinson & Keltner, 1996; Robinson, Keltner, Ward, & Ross, 1995)—a perception that makes our own position more reasonable than our opponents'. In some cases we even see people who agree with us as more extreme than our own perspective, which further reinforces the notion that our own views are moderate and well considered.

Interpretation of Ambiguous Behavior

We all need rather constant reminding that little about behavior, at least at the level most of us are interested in, is objective. You might describe the gross motor movements—the blinks, facial flicks and flacks, arm and finger movements, and postures—fairly objectively, in the sense that another person or an artist could reproduce them. However, such a catalogue would be time-consuming, and most of the time would be perfectly useless. Gross bodily movements can mean various things. For example, smiles can be signs of pleasure or of happiness (which are not, at least in Western culture, quite the same thing), of derision and hostility, or of sociability. And just to make things even more complicated, there are multiple ways of displaying and indicating almost any emotion or thought. One can be hostile by withdrawing from a situation or by approaching a hated other; through hitting, stabbing, or shooting; by making various kinds of well-recognized hand gestures; through an infinite array of words; or by creating a murderous look. There are relatively few direct, unambiguous correspondences between behaviors and the specific meanings of those behaviors.

If stereotypes are essentially schemas, then we ought to find that they influence the interpretation of behavior. A classic experiment by Duncan (1976) makes this case for race. He had white subjects watch a videotape of an encounter between two men, which turned increasingly hostile until one shoved the other. Duncan varied the race of the two men, such that black and white men shoved both blacks and whites. Subjects labeled the shoving by black stimulus persons as more violent than similar behavior of white stimulus persons (see Table 4.1). They also attributed the behavior of the black shover more to dispositional forces than the behavior of the white shover. Although stereotypic beliefs were not assessed in this study, it is reasonable to expect that white subjects had beliefs that blacks are more violent than whites—beliefs that, in turn, directed their interpretations of the behavior. Other

TABLE 4.1. Percentage of Research Participants Who Coded the Ambiguous Behavior

	Black shoves black	Black shoves white	White shoves black	White shoves white
Playing around	0	3	25	19
Dramatizes	6	6	38	44
Aggressive behavior	25	16	25	24
Violent behavior	69	75	13	12

Note. From Duncan (1976). Copyright 1976 by the American Psychological Association. Reprinted by permission.

studies also show that the behavior of black males is interpreted as more hostile than that of whites even by black subjects (Sagar & Schofield, 1980).

Another salient stereotype about African American males is superior athletic ability. Stone, Perry, and Darley (1997) had subjects listen to a tape recording of part of a college basketball game, and they were asked to evaluate the performance of a player who was identified as either black or white. Although subjects' memories for actual objective performance (e.g., rebounds) were not affected by the race manipulation, the player described as "black" was perceived to have more basketball ability and to be a better team player. The player described as "white," by contrast, was seen to have more "court smarts" and "hustle." In a related study, people saw athletic success for blacks as due to natural ability and for whites as due to hard work and better access to coaching and facilities (Johnson, Hallinan, & Westerfield, 1999).

A study by Darley and Gross (1983) makes a similar point about the importance of schemas for socioeconomic status. Subjects saw a videotape of a young girl, Hanna, performing various kinds of intellectual problems; her performance was inconsistent, neither strikingly good or poor. When Hanna was described as "lower class," subjects saw her as having performed less well on an achievement test than when she was identified as "middle class." This study is especially interesting, because when subjects simply were given socioeconomic information about Hanna without seeing her behavior, their inferences showed no effects of this information. Perhaps in that kind of situation, subjects guarded against showing their biases. In any event, whatever stereotypes the subjects had about socioeconomic status seemed to serve primarily as filters used to interpret Hanna's ambiguous behavior. When behavior is less ambiguous, stereotype expectancies play less of a role (Kameda, 1985).

GENDER BIASES

Surely gender also affects how we interpret behavior. A widely cited study by Phillip Goldberg (1968) initiated a controversial area of research for perceptions of male and female competence. Goldberg gave his female subjects scholarly articles to read and evaluate. Some subjects saw that the articles had been authored by a woman, and others saw that they had been written by a man. Some articles were evaluated more highly by these female students when they were supposedly written by male rather than female authors. Because this study seems to be such a clear demonstration of bias against females in evaluation of their work—a topic of much contemporary concern—it has spawned a whole body of research.

It is important to be clear as to what the original Goldberg paper did and did not show, since it has been widely miscited. Goldberg gave the subjects six essays supposedly authored by male or female scholars in various areas. For three of the essays, there were significant differences: The students thought essays written on law, city planning and linguistics were better when "authored" by a male, but for essays in the fields of dietetics, education, and art history there were no significant differences. Two of the three areas where significant differences were found are traditionally male areas (law and city planning), and two of the fields where there were no differences are traditionally female (dietetics and education). Subjects seemed to be taking additional information—namely, the gender linkage of the field—into account in making their decisions.

A related body of research was pioneered by Pheterson, Kiesler, and Goldberg (1971). They had female subjects evaluate paintings supposedly executed by male or female artists. They also gave subjects information about whether the paintings had won a prize. This study showed a clear gender bias for ratings of the competence of the artist, with the male being seen as more competent than the female, but only when the paintings had not won a prize; this effect washed out when the paintings were seen to be prize-winning. Many studies (e.g., Heilman, Martell, & Simon, 1988) find that gender stereotypes about competence in particular domains can be overridden by data on actual performance or ability. (I return to this topic later in this chapter.)

Several dozen studies have looked at variations on the Goldberg and Pheterson and colleagues paradigms, and the results in this area are surprisingly inconsistent. In a review of the existing published literature, Swim, Borgida, Maruyama, and Myers (1989) found that overall there are gender biases in such research, but that the effects are quite small and basically trivial. This does not mean that gender is not important in work-related performance. Even small biases can have large commutative effects (Martell, Lane, & Emrich, 1996). For example, small biases against a group of people at each stage of job advancement can add up to considerable reductions in their representation at higher levels.

EXPLANATIONS AND ATTRIBUTIONS

Such studies then suggest that at least with ambiguous behavior, our schemas have an impact on the ways we interpret and label that behavior. The exact mechanism for this has never been adequately spelled out, but the simplest possibility is what we might call "straight-line prejudice." For many, this represents the prototype of prejudice and discrimination (see Chapter 8). For example, if someone has a strong stereotype that females are intellectually incompetent, he might deliberately or even unconsciously rate their work as less accomplished. But stereotypes often do their dirty work less directly.

Jussim, Nelson, Manis, and Soffin (1995) argue that labels and the expectancies based on them may arouse affect or emotion, which in turn may affect ratings without additional cognitive mediation. For instance, white subjects may simply like white people more than black people, and this greater liking may lead them to label white behavior in more positive terms. In several experiments these authors had subjects rate the word definitions provided by individuals identified as "rock musicians" or "child abusers," and as expected, the same definitions provided by the former were viewed as more creative and less pathological than those associated with the latter. However, whereas liking for the two groups did mediate the effects of labels on ratings, beliefs about the creativity and likely pathology of the two groups did not. This suggests that affect or prejudice, rather than stereotypic beliefs, may have been largely responsible for the different evaluations of the stimuli. Though the role of affect in interpretation may be important, it cannot be the total explanation for schema labeling effects, since they are often quite specific to stereotype-relevant information.

Another strong possibility discussed throughout this chapter is that when a schema is primed, it may affect how behavior is interpreted. We may require less or less strong evidence to judge a behavior in line with a schema (Biernat & Kobrynowicz, 1997). So we may not require extreme behavior or many instances to label behavior as violent when we expect to see violent behavior.

Third, our schemas may simply encourage us to pay attention to some features of behavior and ignore others. If I believe that women are likely to be incompetent at mechanical tasks, I may focus on how much more slowly a woman works on repairing a car than a man does, and ignore the fact that she manages to be less messy and is less likely to make mistakes than her male counterpart. As a result, I may see her as less competent than the man, even though in some ways she is more so.

Fourth, we may see stereotype-consistent behavior as more dispositionally caused (Kulik, 1983). Wittenbrink, Gist, and Hilton (1997) suggest that some people have theories about members of stereotyped groups that allow them to interpret behavior in a stereotypic way. Specifically, they have argued that high- and low-prejudice people have different causal theories about the behavior of black Americans, which may affect their interpretations of the behavior. In their research subjects read about a fight between a white and a black man, which resulted in injury. The high-prejudice subjects saw the black man as having more causal responsibility than the white, both when he was the victim and when he was the assaulter. Those low in prejudice, on the other hand, saw the white as more responsible. Similarly, in the previously described study by Duncan (1976), where white subjects watched a black or white male shove another male who was either black or white, subjects attributed the black shover's behavior to internal characteristics more than to external; the reverse tended to be true when the shover was white. In a field study by Phillips and Dipboye (1989), interviewers who had a preexisting positive evaluation of an applicant rated a good interview performance as more internally caused than they rated a poor performance.

Kay Deaux and her colleagues (Deaux, 1984; Deaux & Emswiller, 1974) have suggested that we attribute the outcomes of male and female performance differently. Specifically, we are inclined to see males as succeeding because of high ability and failing because of low motivation, and females succeeding because of effort and failing because of low ability. It may not be immediately obvious why this is a problem. Although we prize hard work, underlying motivations are likely to ebb and flow, so that we may not be able to depend on motivation as much as ability. A review of the extensive research literature on this topic (Swim & Sanna, 1996) suggests that for traditionally masculine tasks, success is attributed to ability for males and to effort for females, and males are more likely to be seen as failing for low effort or bad luck. However, these effects have been quite modest in size.

As I have suggested in Chapter 3, sometimes categories act as causes of a sort. I

once found myself shopping at a Boston department store a couple of evenings before Christmas. The store was crowded, the clerks were busy and hassled, and the
customers seemed tired and cranky. I joined a line of several people to pay for my
purchases, and as the clerk disposed of the customers in front of me, it became clear
that she was not your prototypic helpful salesperson. She growled at people and generally communicated that her job was to ring up sales and not to answer questions.
The man in front of me happened to be a black physician (one tends to discover people's occupations in long lines), and he had seemed pleasant enough in the course of
our rather impersonal conversation. When it became his turn, the clerk sighed
deeply as it became clear that this customer would be the troublesome sort who had
questions. He posed his questions; she told him that he should ask someone on the
floor; and he replied that he had not been able to find a clerk to help him, and that
he would appreciate her help. She became more agitated, but he remained surprisingly calm for a minute or two. Finally, he told her that he was busy, that he expected
her to answer his questions, and that if she couldn't he wanted to speak to the floor
manager. All this was said in what I perceived to be a cool and nonaggressive way. In
her turn, she began to tell him that he was being rude and inconsiderate—not only to
her, but to the 10 or so people waiting in line behind him. He replied (quite reasonably, I felt) that if she had tried to answer his questions when he first asked, he would
have been out of her hair long ago. She responded that she didn't ever want him in
her hair, and asked whether he wanted to buy his merchandise or not. At this point
his voice did get angry, and he told her that he wanted to speak to the floor manager.
In due course, this person arrived and led our physician friend away so that they
could discuss his complaints in a quieter place (and away from the other customers).
She cleared her register, and as I handed her my items she said (and I'm quoting her
nearly exactly), "Damned aggressive niggers. They're so touchy and pushy. They just
want everyone to do everything they want." I asked the woman no questions and fled
with my purchases as quickly as possible.[3]

   What interested me the most about this whole thing was her subsequent interpretation of his reaction as due in part to his race. I'm not sure how she would have
responded to me had I behaved the same way. She might have said, "Some customers
are just so hostile," or she might have blamed it on the stresses of the season. But she
would not have accused me of behaving as I might have because of my race, hair
color, height, or age. She went beyond a mistaken dispositional attribution about the
customer's being hostile; she assumed that he was hostile to her as a white person *because* of his race.

Priming

The interpretation of ambiguous behavior can be affected by priming relevant categories. You may have noticed, for example, that when you leave a violent movie, you
are "primed" to see the world in terms of its violent content. In an initial and influential experimental demonstration, Higgins, Rholes, and Jones (1977) exposed subjects
to positive trait words ("adventurous," "self-confident," "independent," "persistent")
or similar words with negative connotations ("reckless," "conceited," "aloof," "stubborn"). Then in an ostensibly unrelated study, subjects read a brief essay about Donald, depicting ambiguous behaviors related to the trait adjectives. When they had
previously been exposed to the positive traits, subjects saw Donald's behavior in

much more positive terms. There are now dozens of demonstrations of exactly this kind of priming effect (Higgins, 1996). Interpretations of ambiguous material can be affected by primes people have recently been exposed to, even when they are unaware of the primes.

FACTORS THAT AFFECT PRIMING

But the effects of priming are often complex. In the first place, most of the early studies produced assimilation-type effects—when the prime exerts a cognitive "pull" on the target stimulus, and the stimulus gets interpreted as close in meaning to the primes. However, sometimes contrast effects occur—when the exemplar is displaced away from the prime, or when priming retards processing of related stimuli (Glaser & Banaji, 1999). Social and cognitive psychologists have devoted considerable energy in recent years to searching for factors that favor assimilation versus contrast (Ford & Thompson, 2000; Higgins, 1996).

One traditional argument is that assimilation effects are more likely when prime and target are close together and contrast effects as they are more distant, and by and large this is true (Herr, 1986; Herr, Sherman, & Fazio, 1983; Manis, Nelson, & Shedler, 1988). One way to look at this is that assimilation is most likely when the prime and the target overlap in meaning or evaluation. If the stimulus is ambiguous enough to require interpretation in terms of the prime (Stapel & Schwarz, 1998), or if the primed categories are sufficiently broad so as to include the stimulus (Stapel & Koomen, 2000) assimilation will occur. More specifically, Schwarz and Bless (1992) argue that assimilation will occur only if the prime is part of the larger target category. So if people are primed with "Richard Nixon," they might judge that the larger category of politicians (which includes Nixon) is less trustworthy. However, a "Richard Nixon" prime might lead people to judge Bill Clinton as more trustworthy, since Nixon is not part of the Clinton category. Similarly, examples of African American success produce more negative stereotypes of Mexican Americans—a contrast effect across groups (Ho, Sanbonmatsu, & Akimoto, 2002).

However, when the prime and target do not overlap, the prime is more likely to be seen as a standard for comparison, and if it is sufficiently distinct will lead to contrast. For example, distinct trait or person primes typically have a more narrow range of interpretative possibilities than category primes, and thus present themselves as more salient standards of comparison rather than as a basis for interpretation (Stapel & Koomen, 1997). Thus concrete exemplars should usually lead to contrast effects unless the concrete prime is very close to the stimulus (Dijksterhuis, Spears, & Lépinasse, 2001; Wänke, Bless, & Igou, 2001).

Using the prime as a standard of comparison requires a conscious comparison, and this cannot occur when the person is unaware of the prime. Therefore, when people are relatively unaware of primes, assimilation usually results. But when a person is aware of the prime and able to process the information thoughtfully (Lombardi, Higgins, & Bargh, 1987; Newman & Uleman, 1990), the prime is often seen as a standard for comparison leading to contrast. When a comparison is salient, people may be aware of its "pull" and often attempt to correct for what they imagine to be the biases it produces (Lepore & Brown, 2002; Wegener & Petty, 1997). This requires cognitive effort and will not occur unless a person has the ability and motivation to explicitly compare the prime and the stimulus to be judged (Martin, 1986;

Martin & Achee, 1992). As would be expected from this perspective, primed categories produce contrast when people have full use of their cognitive capacities, but assimilation results with high cognitive loads (Ford & Kruglanski, 1995; Newman, Duff, Hedberg, & Blitzstein, 1996). Motivational factors, such as a desire to be accurate (Sedikides, 1990; Stapel, Koomen, & Zeelenberg, 1998; Thompson, Roman, Moskowitz, Chaiken, & Bargh, 1994), also reduce assimilation.

PRIMING AND STEREOTYPES

Despite its importance in modern cognitive psychology and social cognition, such research may seem esoteric and remote from stereotyping. This is not true. In everyday life, categories central to stereotyping (such as race and gender) are frequently primed through the mass media, humor, and conversation. These primes are likely to be somewhat subtle and, because they are relatively nonconscious, may give rise to assimilative processing. For example, Dovidio, Evans, and Tyler (1986) have shown that priming of race categories can facilitate the availability of race-related terms; this finding is particularly strong for prejudiced subjects (Wittenbrink, Judd, & Park, 1997) and for those who think egalitarian values are not especially important (Moskowitz, Salomon, & Taylor, 2000). Gender stereotypes can also be primed through presentation of commonly encountered gender-related words such as "nurse," "father," and "salesman" (Banaji & Hardin, 1996).

Such primes not only may affect the availability of stereotype-related information, but may also affect prejudicial attitudes and interpretation of behavior directly. For example, following O. J. Simpson's trial for the murder of his ex-wife, people who felt he should have been found guilty became more negative in their attitudes toward African Americans (Nier, Mottola, & Gaertner, 2000). In another demonstration of racial priming, Wittenbrink and Henly (1996) primed racial stereotypes by asking subjects questions designed to elicit high or low estimates of black stereotypic behaviors. Those subjects who were high in prejudice were more likely to see a black defendant as guilty in a mock trial when their stereotypes had been so primed. Priming effects may also occur through judging the behavior of a category member. So when whites see a negative behavior by one black male, or even hear about a crime committed by a black person, this may lead to increased stereotyping of blacks as well as increased ingroup favoritism for whites (Henderson-King & Nisbett, 1996). When people infer traits from behaviors for individual black men, stereotypic trait judgments for other black men are facilitated (Stewart, Doan, Gingrich, & Smith, 1998).

Recently social psychologists have investigated one of the most important ways such priming effects may manifest themselves. Each year police officers shoot and often kill many people they believe are about to shoot at them. Most often they correctly perceive that the victim has a gun and is about to shoot, although tragically they sometimes mistake the behavior of the victim and shoot an unarmed person. Many people, and not just African Americans, believe that the police have particularly itchy trigger fingers when the other person is black. Although such decisions are obviously complex, there are at least two major components—identification of a gun and the decision to fire. Regarding the recognition component, whites primed with black faces misidentified pictures of tools as guns more rapidly than when primed with white faces (Payne, 2001). These effects seemed to be automatic, and were increased in another study when race was made even more salient through instructions to avoid using race in the decision (Payne, Lambert, & Jacoby, 2002). Decisions to fire at a person holding an object that might be a gun were investigated by Correll, Park, Judd, and Wittenbrink (2002). They found that people "correctly" shot at an armed black more quickly than at an armed white and "correctly" avoided shooting an unarmed white more quickly. Also, when research participants were under time pressure, they mistakenly shot an unarmed black more often than an unarmed white. Again, the effects appeared to be fairly automatic; interestingly, they were found for both white and black subjects, and were not predicted by personal stereotypes that blacks are violent.

In our everyday interactions, priming may result from slurs or humor. Greenberg and Pyszczynski (1985) found that subjects who overheard an ethnic slur (presumably priming a racial category) interpreted the poor performance of a black target more negatively, and an ethnic slur directed at an attorney lowered his general ratings (Kirkland, Greenberg, & Pyszczynski, 1987). Further research by Simon and Greenberg (1996) showed that ethnic labels affected evaluations only for subjects who had negative attitudes toward blacks; those with more ambivalent attitudes responded to ethnic slurs by evaluating the black target more positively.

What about ethnic humor? Harmless enough, isn't it? Ford (1997) found that after watching race-stereotypic humor, white subjects rated a black defendant as more guilty than they did after watching nonstereotypic humor. So ethnic humor is not so harmless, apparently. However, effects for other categories may be different. In several studies (Olson, Maio, & Hobden, 1999), jokes about men and lawyers had essentially no effects on stereotypic thinking, although another study (Maio, Olson, & Bush, 1997) found that people who recited humor about disadvantaged groups in Canada increased negative stereotyping. Ford (2000) argues that humor often leads to a noncritical approach to stereotype-related material, and that when people are noncritical in this way, exposure to sexist humor leads to greater tolerance of sexism (especially for those high in hostile sexism).

There are also demonstrations that priming can affect stereotypic processing of information. For example, when traditional gender stereotypes are primed, subjects are more willing to interpret the behavior of women in terms of those stereotypes (Hansen & Hansen, 1988). Men who have a strong schema for gender respond to sexual arousal by emphasizing the sexual characteristics of women they meet (McKenzie-Mohr & Zanna, 1990). Violent rap music (which is associated with black Americans) increases dispositional judgments for black persons' violent behavior, but has no effect on similar behavior by white persons (Johnson, Trawalter, & Dovidio, 2000). Rap music that is derogatory of women produces more negative evaluations of black women by white subjects (Gan, Zillmann, & Mitrook, 1997). In a striking demonstration of priming traditional sexual stereotypes, Rudman and Borgida (1995) had subjects watch actual television advertisements that were either sexist or nonsexist. Following this, they rated a female job applicant whom they interviewed. Subjects primed with the sexist humor asked more sexist questions during the interview, recalled more information about the applicat's physical features and clothing, and behaved in a more sexualized way during the interview (at least as rated by the applicant). However, the primed subjects were also more willing to hire the applicant—but not because of her qualifications, because they rated her lower on competence but higher on friendliness.

PRIMING AND BEHAVIOR

Most of these studies involve the effects of priming on perceptions and evaluations of others, but under some conditions priming can also affect perceivers' own behavior. Dijksterhuis and Bargh (2001) argue that there is an automatic perception–behavior link: Merely observing behavior increases the likelihood of performing that behavior. Certainly there is evidence that observing the motor behavior of others leads to nonconscious imitation, and that when one participant mimics the behavior of the other, the interaction goes more smoothly (Chartrand & Bargh, 1999; Chartrand & Bargh, 1999).

There are several demonstrations that priming of stereotype categories can lead to stereotype-consistent behavior. In a clever study, Becca Levy (1996) primed elderly subjects with either "senility" or "wisdom"—two contrasting aspects of the stereotype of the old. Those who were primed with the term "wisdom" actually had better memory scores than those who were primed with "senility," and the former also rated the ambiguous behavior of an older woman more positively. Elderly people primed with negative stereotypes associated with old age were less likely to endorse the use of life-prolonging medical treatments in hypothetical situations than those primed with relatively more positive stereotypes (B. Levy, Ashman, & Dror, 2000).

Such effects are not restricted to those who are stereotyped. For example, when college-age students are primed with elderly stereotypes, they perform less well on a memory test, but only if they report frequent contact with elderly persons; such contact creates a stronger association between the elderly category and stereotypic memory impairment (Dijksterhuis, Aarts, Bargh, & van Knippenberg, 2000). In a conceptually related study, Dijksterhuis and van Knippenberg (1998) showed that when subjects were primed with the role "professor" or the trait "intelligent," they performed better on a general knowledge test but performed worse when primed with "soccer hooligan" or "stupid," and whites primed with a black stereotype performed less well on a standardized test (Wheeler, Jarvis, & Petty, 2001).

Bargh, Chen, and Burrows (1996) showed priming effects for several different, more overt behaviors. Subjects primed with "rudeness" were more likely to interrupt an experimenter than those with no prime or who were primed with "politeness"; a black face primed hostile behavior more than a white face did; and when college-age students were primed with age stereotypes, they walked more slowly. Earlier I have suggested that exemplars more often lead to contrast than do trait primes in interpretative tasks, and the same appears to be true for performance measures. In another study, subjects primed with professor stereotypes performed better on a knowledge test than those primed with supermodel stereotypes, but those primed with extreme exemplars ("Albert Einstein" and "Claudia Schiffer") showed contrast effects (Dijksterhuis et al., 1998).

Stereotype Threat

The Levy research cited above suggests that people who are victims of stereotypes may behave consistently with those stereotypes. Claude Steele (1997) has pointed to a related phenomenon he calls "stereotype threat." When members of stereotyped groups are aware of negative stereotypes about them, they may fear that others will apply these negative qualities to them. These thoughts may be anxiety-provoking and lead to lower performance on a variety of tasks. Although stereotype threat is similar in some ways to assimilative priming, the two have generally been discussed in quite different ways (see Wheeler & Petty, 2001, for an extended discussion). One obvious difference is that whereas stereotype threat focuses on decrements in performance, priming can facilitate as well as hinder performance. Also, while priming is usually discussed as a fairly automatic process that directly affects behavior, stereotype threat relies on more complex intervening mechanisms. For stereotype threat to do its dirty work, people from stigmatized groups have to be identified with the area of performance and to see performance as linked to the group (Schmader, 2002). The stereotype that white men can't jump is unlikely to affect my jumping prowess, because I couldn't care less about this stereotype. By the time they get to high school, some minority students may have decided that school is more or less irrelevant to their lives, and young women may have abandoned math and science; the stereotype threat notion does not apply to these students, but only to those who still care about performing well. Finally, it is probable that stereotype threat does not affect performance on extremely easy or impossibly difficult tasks, but mainly on those where abilities are stretched to their outer limits.

Steele (1997) points to the fact that although standardized tests predict black and white performance approximately equally well, black students at every level of intellectual ability and preparation tend to perform less well. Perhaps this is a result of the performance anxiety they experience because of stereotype threat. Confirmation for this hypothesis was found in a number of studies by Steele and Aronson (1995). Black and white students, matched in ability, were asked to take difficult intellectual tests (mostly subsets of the Graduate Record Examination). When a test was presented as a diagnostic test of intellectual ability, black students performed worse than whites, although the two groups performed equally well when the test did not have these diagnostic overtones. The black students tended to be aware of black stereotypes when they thought they were being tested on intellectual abilities, and presumably this led to stereotype threat. Moreover, the effects were stronger for black students when they were identified by race, suggesting that stereotype threat is stronger when race is salient. Hispanics, especially females, also show stereotype threat (Gonzales, Blanton, & Williams, 2002); so do people of lower socioeconomic status, who stereotypically perform less well on intellectual tasks (Croizet & Claire, 1998).

What about gender? Davies, Spencer, Quinn, and Gerhardstein (2002) primed gender stereotypes by showing men and women sexist commercials. Those women for whom math performance was self-relevant underperformed on a math test and indicated less interest in vocations involving math skills. The women also underperformed (relative to performance predicted from ability tests) in math and science courses, arguably because of threat from the stereotype that women are not clever in these areas. Similar effects were found in another study for women taking math courses (Spencer, Steele, & Quinn, 1999). Although women and men performed equally well on moderately difficult math tests, the men outperformed the women on tests of greater difficulty. This difference was preserved when a test was described as one that typically produced gender differences; more importantly, it was eliminated when subjects were told that a test was gender-neutral, thus presumably reducing stereotype threat to the women. Whereas women seem most vulnerable to stereotype threat when a test is described as one that measures math weakness, men show declines in performance when the test is described as one that measures exceptional math abilities (Brown & Josephs, 1999). Females are more vulnerable to stereotype threat about their math abilities when they are in the presence of men, presumably because this makes the math deficit stereotype more salient (Inzlicht & Ben-Zeev, 2000). However, women do not experience stereotype threat decrements on math tests when in the presence of a female experimenter who is competent in math (Marx & Roman, 2002) or when they have been reminded of female competence in other areas (McIntyre, Paulson, & Lord, 2003). Of course, math and general intellectual performance are not the only features linked to gender. Stereotypically, women are not only relatively poor at math, but also at negotiating (and other forms of assertive behavior); true to form, women are less effective at negotiating when they think performance reflects abilities or is tied to masculine traits (Kray, Thompson, & Galinsky, 2001) but perform better when success is linked to feminine traits (Kray, Galinsky, & Thompson, 2002). When female traits are linked to negotiation ineffectiveness, men outperform women, but women fare better than men when male traits are seen as diagnostic of negotiation failure.

Are white males subject to stereotype threat? Aronson aned colleagues (1999) found that white male college students who had high math abilities (mean scores above 700 on the math SAT) performed less well on a difficult math test when they were told that Asian American students typically outperformed European Americans on such tests. However, in a second study, this effect was found only for those high-scoring students who said that math ability was important to their self-concept—confirming the idea that identification with the threatened area is an essential part of the psychological mix for the activation of stereotype threat. White males performed less well on a golf task when performance was said to be diagnostic of natural athletic ability, whereas black males performed less well when the same task was framed as a test of sports intelligence (Stone, Lynch, Sjomeling, & Darley, 1999). Males who are told they are poorer at affective tasks actually do perform worse (Leyens, Desert, Croizet, & Darcis, 2000).

STEREOTYPE BOOST

Sometimes activating a positive stereotype can improve performance. In a clever study using Asian American women and math tests, Shih, Pittinsky, and Ambady (2000) found that activating gender identity led to worse performance, presumably because the women were threatened by the stereotype that women are not good at math. However, when their ethnic identity was more salient, they performed better, presumably "living up" to the stereotype that Asians are gifted at math. Nevertheless, stereotype priming does not work when the primes are blatant (Shih, Ambady, Richeson, Fujita, & Gray, 2002), and other research (Cheryan & Bodenhausen, 2000) has suggested that when Asian identity is manipulated in a more public way, stereotype threat rather than boost effects are obtained.

UNDERLYING MECHANISMS

This idea of stereotype threat is an important one. It is one thing to suggest, as I have done earlier, that knowledge of others' stereotypes can sometimes lead to attempts to disconfirm the stereotype. It is quite another to assume that such efforts will necessarily be successful, or that the person has the intellectual and personal resources to do the job. Indeed, stereotype threat seems to undermine whatever confidence people bring to tasks (Stangor, Carr, & Kiang, 1998). Stereotype threat creates added burdens that may make it difficult, even impossible, to disconfirm the stereotype-based hypotheses others have.

It is not yet clear why stereotype threat occurs. Attempts to tie stereotype threat directly to anxiety have not been notably successful. Some studies find that measured anxiety partially mediates the effect (Osborne, 2001), and other studies (Blascovich, Spencer, Quinn, & Steele, 2001) find that physiological indicators of stress accompany perceived stereotype threat. General arousal may be a factor (O'Brien & Crandall, 2003). Intrusive thoughts about performance may be the culprit, as Cheryan and Bodenhausen (2000) found that stereotype threat lowered concentration. Yet another possibility is that stereotype threat may interfere with abilities to formulate and use problem-solving strategies (Quinn & Spencer, 2001). It is also possible that feeling "under the gun" directly reduces motivation to do well. In fact, there are a great many explanations involving motivation, anxiety, and cognitive processes, but to date there is little supporting evidence favoring any one of them (Steele, Spencer, & Aronson, 2002; Wheeler & Petty, 2001). Of course, many of these factors may need to be present, acting in concert, or some factors may be more important in some situations than others.

Memory

Schemas Aid Encoding

We often find ourselves using our schemas to process information as it comes to us. But many of the most important judgments we make in everyday life are based on our memories. Schemas affect both encoding into and retrieval from memory. Many of us have the experience of not really understanding what we are reading or hearing when we are exposed to new material in an unfamiliar area, but finding it much clearer once we get the "big picture." Generally, we comprehend and remember relevant material better when a relevant schema is salient (Anderson & Pichert, 1978; Dooling & Lachman, 1971). Several studies (e.g., Anderson & Pichert, 1978; Stillwell & Baumeister, 1997) have shown that the perspective that one takes in reading material may also affect what one remembers; a real estate agent and a potential burglar would surely remember different things about a house they had just cased out. A perceiver who thinks about a woman in terms of her job qualifications will remember different things about her than one who is interested primarily in her homemaking skills or potential as a sexual partner. Or a perceiver who thinks of an Asian woman as female may remember lower SAT math scores than if the perceiver thinks of her as Asian (Pittinsky, Shih, & Ambady, 2000).

Memory Errors

There is little doubt that relevant schemas facilitate understanding and encoding of new information in ways that aid later memory. But there is more to memory than simply how much we can dredge up, and this more is highly relevant to stereotyping. One straightforward prediction from schema models is that relevant schemas should facilitate retrieval of schema-relevant material more than schema-irrelevant or inconsistent material. Our schemas do not like being molested by inconsistent data, and they preserve themselves from being invalidated. A second important prediction is that sometimes our memories play us false, and we misremember what we have seen or heard; our schemas and stereotypes sometimes create false or biased memories that support their validity.

Thus a clear prediction from schema theories is that errors in memory should support the schema. In particular, people are inclined to remember, falsely, that schema-relevant material has been presented when it has not been (e.g., Lenton, Blair, & Hastie, 2001; Sherman & Bessenoff, 1999). For example, people who have strong gender stereotypes are biased to report having seen gender-consistent information about people (Stangor, 1988), and children will often misremember the gender of actors in scenes in involving gender-incongruent activities (e.g., Signorella & Liben, 1984). More formally, subjects show a relative inability to discriminate presented from nonpresented material that is relevant to a general knowledge structure or stereotype (Graesser, Woll, Kowalski, & Smith, 1980; Lui & Brewer, 1983; Rothbart, Evans, & Fulero, 1979; Woll & Graesser, 1982). Thus, when our stereotypes are activated, we sometimes have trouble remembering which of many possible stereotypic behaviors the person did or did not perform. During my annual physical last year, did my physician take my blood pressure and my temperature? Ask me how much coffee I drink a day? Tell me I need to lose some weight? Surely some of these things, but I really can't remember which ones for sure.

Reconstructive Memory?

Most theorists have assumed that knowledge structures play their greatest role at the time of encoding of new information—at a time when incoming information can be clarified by schemas or when schemas can facilitate links to other information. However, Bartlett (1932) and others have argued that memory is essentially reconstructive, and that schemas play their largest role at the time of retrieval. Extreme versions of this theory (which are surely false) suggest that we store relatively little information about details of people and events, but instead reconstruct such details when we need them during recall. So, for example, when we see a professor behaving in stereotypically professor-like ways (driving an old Volvo and taking liberal political positions), we need not record those individual facts. Rather, we could simply record that this person is a typical professor and then "retrieve" the stereotype-consistent behaviors at some later point by simply knowing that the person is like most other professors.

One interesting implication of this perspective for reconstructive memory is that it should make no difference whether stereotypes are instantiated before the incoming information or afterwards. If the main function of schemas is to act as a retrieval framework or pattern for reinterpretation, introducing a schema after presentation of relevant information should be at least as effective as presenting it before, if not more so. Suppose you observe Harry Jones attending a rally of some liberal group. You momentarily store away that fact. Subsequently you learn that he is a professor. Because you think that professors are politically liberal, this piece of information should be a good retrieval cue when you are trying to recall information about him, despite the fact that you learned it after seeing the behavior. There is some support for the reconstructive memory perspective. For example, there have been a few reports that presentation of group information after behavior affects memory for behaviors (e.g., Cohen, 1981; van Knippenberg & Dijksterhuis, 1996), but they are not common.

Clearly, the reconstructive-memory approach predicts not only that imposing a schema after the fact will aid memory, but that it should also produce errors—in particular, remembering events or behaviors that are consistent with the schema but did not actually occur. This has been demonstrated in studies showing that what subjects do with information affects subsequent recall. For example, Higgins and McCann (1984) had subjects communicate information about a person to others who were known to have a particular bias for or against the person. As expected, the subjects tended to tailor their messages to their audience. Subsequent measures of recall for the information showed that subjects distorted it to be consistent with their communication.

Ross (1989) argues that in our memories for our own lives, we often reconstruct the past to be consistent with the present. For instance, when people change their attitudes toward a persuasive communication, they recall past behaviors to be more consistent with the new attitudes (Ross, McFarland, & Fletcher, 1981). In another example, Conway and Ross (1984) had subjects participate in a study skills program. Although their actual grades did not improve, they recalled the evaluations of their preclass performance as being worse than they were, thus supporting their sense that they had improved. In a demonstration more relevant to stereotyping, Hirt (1990) and Hirt, Erickson, and McDonald (1993) investigated whether the same results would occur when subjects perceived others. They found that when subjects expected a student's performance to improve, they recalled the student's earlier performance as worse than it had been, and when they expected decline, they tended to see the earlier performance as having been higher than it had been (or than a no-expectancy control group recalled it).

Remembering Schema-Consistent versus Schema-Inconsistent Information

Most schema models strongly suggest that there should be strong preferences for schema-consistent material in memory. Suppose you know that Janice is a professor of psychology. Clearly, this should help you remember that Janice spends part of her day in her lab and has a good knowledge of statistics. It is, however, not likely to help you remember whether she lives in a brick house or grew up in Iowa. But what about finding out that she enjoys stock car races or that she spends her free time reading trashy romance novels? Is schema-inconsistent material totally lost in the dense undergrowth of our minds?

Work on this question was stimulated by classic experiments reported by Hastie and Kumar (1979). They found that schema-relevant information that was both consistent and inconsistent with the schema was remembered better than information that was irrelevant to the schema; more strikingly, the inconsistent information was actually remembered better than the consistent. People also tend to have especially good memories for information that is inconsistent with behavioral scripts (Bower, Black, & Turner, 1979), for faces (Light, Kayra-Stuart, & Hollander, 1979) and visual scenes (Friedman, 1979; Pezdek, Whetstone, Reynolds, Askari, & Dougherty, 1989). Such results are not always found (e.g., Stangor, 1988; Stangor & Ruble, 1989b; van

Knippenberg & van Knippenberg, 1994), but there is little doubt of the existence of a memory preference for inconsistent rather than consistent information under at least some circumstances (Fyock & Stangor, 1994; Rojahn & Pettigrew, 1992; Stangor & McMillan, 1992).

THEORETICAL IMPLICATIONS

This preference for incongruent material has important theoretical and practical implications. At the level of theory, simple schema models cannot easily account for the results,[4] because they emphasize the idea that elements of a schema help one remember information that fits well with the schema. Hastie (1980) and Srull (1981) have argued that such inconsistency effects are better understood within an associative-network model of memory. During encoding, incongruent information receives additional processing as people try to figure out what it means, and this leads to its being linked to other items of information. Congruent information slides in without effort and therefore does not get as readily linked to other items of information. Thus, during recall, the inconsistent items will have more links with other items that can serve as additional retrieval cues, although such retrieval cues are less relevant for recognition (see Figure 4.1).

In support of this model, evidence suggests that preferences for the incongruent information are enhanced when a person has an explicit set to try to organize or explain the incoming information rather than to remember it (e.g., Garcia-Marques & Hamilton, 1996; Srull, 1981). Interestingly, people who are highly prejudiced are especially prone to process stereotype-inconsistent information thoroughly and to be threatened by it (Förster, Higgins, & Strack, 2000). We know that people spend more time processing inconsistent information (Stern et al., 1984), which is what would be expected if people are trying to understand the incongruent information and linking it to other schema-relevant information. Memory preferences for inconsistent information seem most robust when memory is measured with recall (which takes advantage of the associations among items) rather than recognition (which does not). Also, given assumptions about more links between incongruent and other items, recall of a congruent item is more likely to be followed by recall of an incongruent item than of another congruent one (Hamilton, Driscoll, & Worth, 1989; Srull, 1981); this would be expected if incongruent items have more links to congruent items than do congruent items.

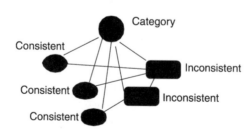

FIGURE 4.1. Memory model for representation of schema-consistent and schema-inconsistent features.

Since the memory preference for incongruent items depends to some extent on the extra processing such items receive, it follows that when people are unable or unwilling to give extra processing time to such items, memory preferences for inconsistent information should be reduced or reversed (Dijksterhuis & van Knippenberg, 1995; Garcia-Marques, Hamilton, & Maddox, 2002; Macrae, Hewstone, & Griffiths, 1993; Pendry & Macrae, 1999; Stangor & Duan, 1991). Jeff Sherman and his colleagues (Sherman, Lee, Bessenoff, & Frost, 1998; Sherman, Macrae, & Bodenhausen, 2000) have argued for a complex relationship between cognitive resources and differential processing. The basic argument is that when stereotypes are primed, people need to pay little attention to consistent information and will use valuable resources for attention to and perceptual encoding of inconsistent items. However, the conceptual meanings of consistent items require few resources and are still encoded. Inconsistent items, on the other hand, require processing capacity before their meanings can be extracted, and so they tend to get lost in the shuffle when resources are low.

PRACTICAL IMPLICATIONS

Theoretical disputes have largely driven research in this area, but there are also practical implications. If in processing information about members of stereotyped groups, people tend to remember a disproportionate amount of information that disconfirms the stereotype, then it would seem to follow that stereotypes would soon dissolve under the weight of such disconfirmations. Yet common experience suggests that this is rare. How is it possible for inconsistent information both to have an advantage in memory and yet to have less impact on our impressions of others? One possible reason is that over time, the discrepant information is forgotten more rapidly than the consistent (Graesser et al., 1980). Because the amount of explicit disconfirming information may often be much smaller than the amount of ambiguous or clearly confirmatory information, the disconfirming evidence may lose some of its salience over time (Rothbart, 1981). Or perhaps after all the extra processing the discrepant information receives, it is absorbed into the general schema in a way that alters its meaning or makes it less salient.

Not only can inconsistent information sometimes be reinterpreted to fit the existing schema or stereotype, but it may be seen as less dispositional and more subject to situational forces (Vonk, 1994). One vivid example (see Schneider, 1988, for a fuller account) of this interpretative magic was revealed when a student tried to convince me that Hispanics were actually quite lazy. His evidence was that Mexican American workers on his father's farm took frequent work breaks, but when I asked him whether they actually picked as many crops as the white non-Mexican workers, he admitted that they did—but only because they were being carefully monitored by the field foreman. Apparently even hard work can be seen as a sign of laziness.

Interestingly, in a serial reproduction paradigm (where one person hears the story, relays it to a second person, etc.), people who hear the original narrative recall more inconsistent information, as expected. However, by the third person in the chain this advantage has washed out, and by the fifth the story emphasizes consistent material (Kashima, 2000). There could be many reasons for this, but one likely one is that as the story gets condensed, the inconsistent information gets "cut loose" from the main threads, and is thereby easily forgotten. Since much of the information we get about others comes in the form of secondhand accounts and even stories, this may suggest that consensus stereotypes emphasize consistent information, even if individually held ones do not always.

Another possibility is that the person displaying the discrepant information is treated as an exception to the stereotype, which allows the stereotype to be free from cognitive molestation (Weber & Crocker, 1983). It is also important to note that memory preferences for inconsistent information occur only when people are allowed to process information fairly thoroughly, and in everyday life we may usually have neither the inclination nor cognitive resources to think about every behavior of every person we meet. Thus real-world processing conditions may favor consistent information (Hilton & von Hippel, 1996). Finally, inconsistency effects tend to be strongest for information about individuals and weak or reversed for information about groups (e.g., Stern et al., 1984), so that stereotypes as features associated with groups may be less vulnerable to this sort of problem. Also, we tend to focus more on consistencies for outgroups and inconsistencies for ingroups (Koomen & Dijker, 1997), presumably because we are more inclined to focus on the ways outgroup members are similar (see Chapter 7).

Remembering discrepant information is the way we have of individuating our experiences. When you meet a physician who seems pretty much like most of the other physicians you have met, you really don't have to remember much about him.[5] Theoretically, all you need to remember is that Dr. Fox is a typical doctor, and your schema will generate inferences about him later if you need them. Obviously, if all you ever remembered was how each doctor was like most other doctors, over time you would not be able to remember how Dr. Fox was different from Dr. Wolf. And this sort of thing happens. What was your first-grade teacher like? You may find that most of what you can remember (or at least infer) about her (and she was female, wasn't she?) is heavily driven by an vague set of memories you have for elementary school teachers in general. But just as clearly, you often do remember individual people you have known, and often the most salient features about them are what sets them apart. I can still recall my first-grade teacher, and what I most remember about her was that she was younger, more lenient, and more harried than my other elementary school teachers—features that I imagine have some important causal links to one another.

Salience Effects

I have suggested that inconsistent behaviors may "stand out" and receive extra processing that makes them highly accessible in memory. Behaviors may also be given priority in memory processing because they are extreme, vivid, or culturally deviant. Rothbart, Fulero, Jensen, Howard, and Birrell (1978) have investigated one clear stereotyping consequence of this greater accessibility. If behaviors are remembered by group rather than by individual, and if certain groups perform behaviors that are highly memorable, then it follows that the entire group will tend to be seen as likely to perform these salient behaviors—especially given the previously discussed tendency (Chapter 3) to assume that members of groups are similar to one another. One way that behaviors become memorable is by being highly deviant statistically or normatively. In their experiments, Rothbart and his colleagues presented subjects with information about height or crimes by individuals. Although the average height or crime propensity was equal for the two groups, members of one group had more very tall people or people who committed more serious crimes. When subjects were subsequently asked for judgments about the groups, the group with more tall members was judged as taller, and the group with members who committed more serious crimes was judged as having committed more crimes. Thus, through group identification of events, the entire group tends to be ascribed the behaviors of a few deviant individuals.

Misanthropic Memory

We have been looking at memory for what might be called "raw" behaviors or features of standard people or groups. Yet in our everyday lives we often encounter information about people whose group memberships have affective significance for us, and often this information comes accompanied by explanations of one kind or another. Oscar Ybarra (Ybarra, 1999; Ybarra & Stephan, 1996) has pointed to an important bias in memory—namely, that we tend to recall negative behaviors that have dispositional explanations, and positive behaviors that seem more situationally caused. He has termed this "misanthropic memory," because the net result is that we tend to see the negative behaviors of others as a fundamental part of personality and permanent, whereas more positive behaviors are regarded as fleeting. In other words, we hold people responsible for their bad behaviors and don't give them credit for their good ones.

Ybarra argues that this effect may occur because it helps to make people feel good about themselves by casting others in a bad light and, by comparison, themselves in a more favorable one. In support of that idea, Ybarra (1999) found that when people did not have the motivation (because their self-esteem had been raised) or ability to use this form of indirect self-enhancement, the misanthropic-memory effect was erased. Furthermore, such effects occur for memory for group behaviors; in particular, misanthropic memory occurs for outgroups but not for ingroups (Ybarra, Stephan, & Schaberg, 2000).

Inferences

Heretofore we have discussed the effects of schemas and stereotypes on attention, labeling, and memory, but perhaps the most obvious features of schemas is that they facilitate the inferences we make about people and objects related to the schema (Taylor & Crocker, 1981). Surely you are quite certain that the people you meet at a party have functioning hearts? And where is your direct evidence for this belief? Are you sure that the library you are about to enter for the first time will have bookshelves? Does the driver of the car that just passed you have a driver's license? Is the professor you have just met liberal? Does your obviously gay waiter have AIDS? Obviously, some of these inferences have a stronger rationale than others. You are certain that the people at the party have hearts, because you have a large store of biological and medical knowledge at your disposal; you have a theory about what humans are like. On the other hand, the belief that a gay waiter has AIDS can be based only on probabilistic reasoning that may be flawed in any number of ways. Still, when the going gets rough or we are not being especially reflective, we infer attributes from categories, whether or not these inferences are firmly justified. Our stereotypes may be crutches, but (like all generalizations) they are useful when we need them, precisely because they give us more than is before our eyes. The question is this: When do we use stereotypes, and when do we use other information?

STEREOTYPES AND INDIVIDUATING INFORMATION

Although schema theories emphasize the importance of prior expectancies and information for the processing of new information, not even the most enthusiastic schema theorist would insist that the incoming information itself has no role to play. The person who has a stereotype that professors are politically liberal would still, in most cases, take note of the fact that this particular professor voted for a conservative Republican. Similarly, the person who believes that blacks are lazy might label a wide range of ambiguous behaviors performed by black coworkers as lazy, but would probably not manage to make the work of Jones, a notoriously hard worker, fit the stereotype.

The Importance of Behavior

Still, while we would agree in principle that our perceptions, memories, and inferences are joint products of our preexisting knowledge and incoming data, in practice most stereotype researchers have focused their research attention mostly on the schema end of the business. This view was challenged quite strikingly in the early 1980s in a series of papers by Anne Locksley and her colleagues.

Locksley's Challenge

The initial set of experiments by Locksley, Borgida, Brekke, and Hepburn (1980) seemed to suggest that stereotypes have a role to play in inferences about others only when there is no other behavioral information available. In an initial study, subjects were told that a male, a female, or someone not identified by gender had performed either assertive or passive behaviors across three different situations. On ratings of assertiveness, the gender label had no effect, whereas the actual behavior did. That is, subjects were no more likely to see a male than a female as assertive, but were willing to say that a person who had been assertive was more assertive than a person who had been passive. In a second study, the diagnosticity of the behavioral information was varied; some of the behaviors strongly implied assertiveness, whereas other behaviors did not. Again, when the behavioral information was diagnostic for the rating (as it was in the first study), gender label played no role (see Table 4.2). However, subjects did infer that the male stimulus person was more assertive than the female when the behavioral information could not be used to judge assertiveness or when no behavioral information was presented. In another study, subjects were inclined to use gender when behavioral information was mixed so that the target performed equal numbers of assertive and passive behaviors (Locksley, Hepburn, & Ortiz, 1982). These studies seem to suggest that subjects prefer to infer traits from behaviors and will use gender only as a last resort, if they have no good behavioral information to go on.

On the face of it, this seems a striking set of results that might have broad implications for the use of stereotypes. They would, for example, suggest that stereotypes

TABLE 4.2. Attributions of Assertiveness

Behavioral information	Sex of target	
	Male	Female
Gender only	49.44	46.59
Gender + Nondiagnostic	48.73	44.05
Gender + Diagnostic	67.62	67.30

Note. From Locksley, Borgida, Brekke, and Hepburn (1980, Experiment 2). Copyright 1980 by the American Psychological Association. Reprinted by permission.

play a role in our perceptions of others only in those fairly rare cases where we have no additional information about them. So a racist may think that Hispanics are lazy, but may be willing to give up that belief at the first hint of hard work by José. At their most damaging, then, stereotypes would be nothing worse than initial "soft" hypotheses that could easily be overcome by "hard" data. Indeed, several studies using a variety of research methods have now shown that stereotypic inferences are severely reduced or eliminated when additional individuating information is present (e.g., Dipboye & Wiley, 1978; Eagly & Steffen, 1984; Glick, Zion, & Nelson, 1988; Jussim, Nelson, et al., 1995; Macrae, Shepherd, & Milne, 1992; Mettrick & Cowan, 1996; Weisz & Jones, 1993).

Is Locksley Correct?

Obviously, there are important theoretical issues afoot here. There are also important legal implications for how we think about discrimination (Borgida, Rudman, & Manteufel, 1995), because if stereotypes are such soft and fragile things, why subject them to the prodding of the rather more blunt and hard-nosed legal system? A lot depends on what Locksley and her colleagues wanted to claim for these data. If all they meant to say was that sometimes individuating data (such as behaviors or traits) take precedence over expectations, it would be difficult to find anyone who would disagree. If, on the other hand, they were suggesting that individuating data always or even usually take precedence over schema information and stereotypes, then they were plainly wrong—and wrong in ways that do not require elaborate experimental demonstrations. If our schemas, our expectations, our stereotypes are merely cognitive feathers that get blown away by the winds of empirical data, it is hard to imagine that they would have been taken as seriously for so long by so many social scientists and the people who have been victimized by them. The very concept of "stereotype" was invented to label a common element of our experience—namely, that our expectations, attitudes, prejudices, stereotypes, and theories bias us even in the presence of valid disconfirming behavioral data.

SOMETIMES STEREOTYPES MATTER

And lest there be those who are not convinced by argument, there are abundant data supporting the idea that category (stereotype) information often does have some weight in decisions we make about others, even in the presence of individuating behavioral evidence. For example, studies on gender (e.g., Deaux & Lewis, 1984; Dipboye, Arvey, & Terpstra, 1977; Dipboye, Fromkin, & Wiback, 1975; Jackson & Cash, 1985; Swim, 1993) show that gender remains a predictor of evaluations and job suitability ratings, even when there is information present about qualifications of the individuals. Likewise, labels and behavioral or trait data both contribute to evaluations of targets when these factors are present: minority ethnicity/race (Bodenhausen, 1988; Bodenhausen & Wyer, 1985; Gordon, 1990; Macrae & Shepherd, 1989a, 1989b), homosexuality (Laner & Laner, 1979; Millham & Weinberger, 1977; Storms, 1978), mental retardation (Skowronski, Carlston, & Isham, 1993), older age (Vrugt & Schabracq, 1996), varying physical attractiveness (Budesheim & DePaola, 1994), criminality and alcoholism (Hannah & Midlarsky, 1987), and mental illness (Link & Cullen, 1983). So sometimes individual attributes are more important than stereotypes; sometimes it is the reverse; and sometimes they interact in all manner of ways. These findings are not, perhaps, a big surprise.

One might be tempted to perform a meta-analysis of such studies to see whether stereotypes or behavior are, on average, more important. However, it is hard to offer strong generalizations about the relative power of group designation and behavioral qualifications, because so much depends on how powerful or salient each factor is. Few companies would want to hire totally unqualified males over highly qualified females, so qualifications probably are determinative when strong. On the other hand, there are bound to be situations where race and gender are powerful factors. Generally, I imagine, it takes stronger evidence to convince a sexist male (with his strong stereotype) than a nonsexist male that females really can do complex mathematics well.

Another reason why it is hard to say whether stereotypes or behaviors are more important is that they may differentially affect different sorts of inferences or decisions. Kunda and Thagard (1996) argue that for trait ratings, behavioral information tends to dominate stereotypes when the behaviors are at least minimally informative, because the link between traits and behaviors is stronger than the link between stereotypes and traits. However, for more complex judgments such as job suitability, predictions of future behaviors, or attributional judgments, stereotypes often dominate because of close ties between the fairly abstract stereotype and these more abstract types of judgments, which are less likely to be affected by particular behaviors.

WHEN STEREOTYPES ARE USED

The issue is, of course—and should have seen as such from the outset—not which kind of information is more important, but what kinds of circumstances favor one type of information over the other. Before discussing that, however, let us consider some possible relationships between stereotypes and behavior.

The Default Perspective. The default perspective (Bodenhausen & Wyer, 1985) is close to that of Locksley and her colleagues. Stereotypes act as assumptions we make about others in the absence of more useful information, but they will be abandoned at the first hint that a person violates those assumptions. As we have just seen, this model may work best for trait judgments, but in its general form this position seems untenable.

The Heuristic Perspective. The heuristic position suggests that stereotypes act like any means of simplifying a complex world: They are shortcut rules, easy to use, that owe their existence to the fact that they work at least part of the time. These heuristic rules will be used until unambiguously inconsistent information shows up. In other words, rather than being dropped at the first hint of incoming data, heuristic stereotypes must be actively disconfirmed. This is close to the traditional view of stereotypes as abstract knowledge structures that actively resist change.

Stereotypes and Behavior as Conceptually Equivalent. There are at least three other possible ways that traits and stereotypes could be related. Kunda and Thagard (1996), among others, completely abolish the category–feature distinction. In this view, the stereotype does not have a privileged status in controlling the processing of information; behavioral and category information have the same status. Thus knowing that a person is a college professor may or may not be useful in certain situations, but has no inherent advantage over knowing that the person is smart, is tall, and drives a Mazda. Not only does this provide for a certain simplicity of argument and economy of explanation for results, but it also surgically removes an important but under-explored problem about the relationships between features and categories (see Chapter 3). To be sure, it seems natural to think of features as associated with culturally or biologically salient categories. For instance, most dogs have tails, nearly all professors are well educated, and many cab drivers are rude. But there is no principled reason why we could not reverse this: "Dogness" is often a feature of animals with tails, well-educated people (category) are often professorial (feature), and rude people often include cab drivers.

   Although I am sympathetic to the Kunda–Thagard argument about abolishing the category–attribute distinction (and have stressed this in Chapters 1 and 3), I also think it important to distinguish between categories as types of information and categories as schemas that may affect attention, labeling, memory, and inferences. For cognitive or cultural reasons, some categories have a rich feature set and a long cultural history of being used as the basis of stereotypes. People define themselves as members of social categories but typically not of trait categories, and social categories are typically used to distinguish between groups, whereas feature or trait categories are typically used to distinguish individuals (Bodenhausen, Macrae, & Sherman, 1999). Others (e.g., Brewer & Harasty Feinstein, 1999) have argued for a principled distinction along these and other lines. Once all that is said, however, it is not inevitable that this distinction is always important, and in the case we are discussing now—drawing inferences about individuals—it may make more sense to see the distinction as more implicit than active.

Stereotypes and Behaviors Interact. Another possibility for the ways stereotypes and behaviors may be related is that stereotypes change the meanings of behaviors. One of the tangles we are about to enter (to be discussed later) is that behaviors themselves may change their meanings or be evaluated differently as a function of whether a stereotype is salient. Just as roles and situations affect the ways we construe behaviors, so can stereotypes.

Behaviors May Trigger Stereotypes. Just as stereotypes may affect the meaning of behaviors, sometimes behaviors can affect stereotypes. It is easy to assume that stereotypes sit waiting like ugly trolls to capture and molest unsuspecting behaviors. After all, stereotypes are a fairly stable part of the mental apparatus we carry around with us, and behaviors happen before our eyes. Yet, as indicated in the earlier discussion of priming, stereotypes are neither stable nor always available. If they're trolls, they sometimes take a vacation. Suppose I talk to my professional black neighbor. During our conversation his race is not especially salient to me, and never once do I remotely entertain the thought that he is stupid, violent, or whatever other black stereotypes are in the air.

One way in which this happens is that behaviors may key only parts of a given stereotype or stimulate particular subtypes. For instance, it is a part of Sarah's stereotype that Mexican Americans are violent and family-oriented. When she observes a large extended Mexican American family having a holiday picnic at the park, it is surely more likely that the family-oriented part of the stereotypes will be more salient that the violent part, and the latter may even be inhibited. Alternatively, we might argue that Sarah has stereotypes of two distinct subtypes of Mexican Americans, and that family behavior makes one salient and watching a young Mexican American male looking mean and angry makes the other more salient.

Many of our stereotypes are not salient for particular people, and sometimes they are held in abeyance while we check a person out. In that case, it is possible that one (or a very few) stereotypic behaviors may themselves make the stereotype salient. I've learned never to assume that my professorial colleagues are politically liberal, not religious, or the owners of old cars. Some are, but there are lots of exceptions. However, these stereotypes are loaded and ready to fire should an appropriate trigger be displayed. So if a new colleague announces that he supports a liberal political candidate, I may be all too ready to assume that he also drives an old car, shops at a health food store, does not regularly attend church, and has a large library at home. To be sure, many of these features are themselves related (liberals may well drive older, or at least cheaper, cars than conservatives). But a colleague and I have argued (Schneider & Blankmeyer, 1983) that certain stereotypes may produce even closer relationships among relevant features (see Chapter 5 for further discussion), so that a triggering behavior not only may make a given stereotype more salient, but may lead more readily to stereotypic inferences.

When Are Stereotypes Potent?

STEREOTYPE STRENGTH

Stereotypes are not any one thing, never sleeping, always alert and potent. They doze and awaken. So a given stereotype will be relatively strong under some circumstances and at some times but not others. I have suggested in Chapter 1 that little attention has been given to measuring the actual strength of stereotypes; this is certainly a relevant concern when we want to compare a given person's stereotypes of various groups. But this lacuna in our understanding haunts us here as well. In thinking about stereotype strength, it is sometimes important to distinguish between whether a stereotype is activated (i.e., salient) and whether it is applied to an individual or a group (Macrae & Bodenhausen, 2000). It is certainly possible for the first to occur without the second, although I suspect that in everyday life the two are so closely linked that they may be inseparable.

RELATIVE STRENGTH AND STEREOTYPE FUNCTIONS

As previously discussed, schemas put their best foot forward when they help us understand ambiguous information and so stereotypes are likely to be favored if behavioral or individuating information is ambiguous (Hodson, Dovidio, & Gaertner, 2002). When a person needs to make a quick decision or is mentally overloaded, stereotypes should be especially pertinent. Several studies (e.g., Gordon & Anderson, 1995; Hadjimarcou & Hu, 1999; Macrae et al., 1993; Martell, 1991; Pendry, 1998; Pendry & Macrae, 1999; Pratto & Bargh, 1991; van Knippenberg, Dijksterhuis, & Vermeulen, 1999) have shown that when subjects are cognitively busy or have to make quick decisions, they tend to reply more on initial expectations and stereotypes than on actual behavior in making their judgments. On the other hand, when cognitive resources are available and people are motivated to form accurate impressions because of uncertainty, stereotype use is diminished (Weary, Jacobson, Edwards, & Tobin, 2001).

Bodenhausen (1990) argues that stereotypes should be used more when people are not at peak mental efficiency and thereby inclined to use cognitive shortcuts. This was found to be true when "night" people were asked to judge race-stereotypic crimes during the day, or when "day" people did the task at night. People use stereotypes more when they have been deprived of control on a previous task (Ric, 1997). People who are aroused also tend to rely more on stereotypes (Paulhus, Martin, & Murphy, 1992)—an example of the well-known fact that arousal tends to restrict attention and encourage reliance on salient cues. The net result, then, is that stereotypes are probably more important than behavioral data when people are rushed, busy, hassled, or simply lazy. One interesting and somewhat paradoxical implication is that the use of stereotypes may be encouraged by having a rich array of individuating information, because so much information leads to cognitive overload (Brewer, 1996).

CATEGORY FIT

Self-categorization theory (see Chapter 3), dual-process theory (see below), and the continuum model (again, see below) all argue that at least under some circumstances, when people seem to fit a stereotype category well, they will be so categorized and relevant stereotypes will be readily applied. It is certainly pertinent to raise the question of how close the fit is before such nonreflective categorization takes place, but it is a reasonable hypothesis that people who look like or act like prototypic members of categories will fall victim to stereotypes associated with those categories.

MOTIVATIONAL AND EMOTIONAL FACTORS

Although stereotype research has tended to downplay the importance of motivation, obviously there will be times when we want to use stereotypes and other times when we will want to inhibit stereotypes. Ziva Kunda (e.g., Klein & Kunda, 1992; Kunda & Sinclair, 1999) argues that often the ways we process information about others are affected by our desires to develop and maintain a particular impression of a target. In such cases, we will deploy our stereotypes or inhibit them in ways that help support the desired impression. The ex-husband's new wife is good-looking, and therefore must be unintelligent and superficial. The daughter of an old friend is wearing multiple nose rings, and we have to inhibit our largely negative stereotype about people who would do that.

In one demonstration, Sinclair and Kunda (2000) found that although students who received a high grade evaluated a female professor slightly more positively than a male professor, when they had received a low grade they evaluated the female professor more negatively. A quite reasonable interpretation of these results is that when people's egos are on the line, they may use gender (in this case) stereotypes to excuse the outcomes they get. There are actually several demonstrations of recruiting stereotypes to serve motivational needs (see Chapter 8).

It is commonly assumed and amply demonstrated that stereotypes of outgroups are especially strong when there is threat from the outgroup (see Chapters 7 and 8). As one example, although activation of black stereotypes for whites tends to dissipate over time, they tend to be maintained when there is a disagreement between a white and a black person (Kunda, Davies, Adams, & Spencer, 2002). Stereotypes of the enemy are particularly strong during wars and economic conflicts. A related idea is that some people adopt strong stereotypes of some groups as a kind of defense mechanism; this was the idea behind the research on the authoritarian personality (see Chapters 1 and 8).

Over and above ego involvement, appearance or obvious group membership cues will give rise to strong feelings of initial liking or disliking in many cases. One possibility is that it is easier to form and use stereotypes of groups that have traits departing from normal expectations and that are perceived to have high homogeneity (Dijksterhuis & van Knippenberg, 1999). For most of us, seeing a skinhead male with a swastika on his shirt will not only give rise to immediate feelings of loathing, but will "give us permission" to activate our stereotypes of such people, to assume they have a wide range of stereotypic features associated with the category, and to interpret this man's behavior in stereotype-consistent ways. By contrast, there are circumstances when we want to be sure that our judgments are not based on our stereotypes. In some cases these motives stem from deeply held personal beliefs about equality and the importance of individuals (see Chapter 8 for further discussion), but in other cases we may be aware of normative pressures from others that can affect what information we deploy in our judgments. The social judgeability model of Yzerbyt, Leyens, and Schadron (1992) suggests that we use information about people in judging them only when we think such use is cognitively, morally, or normatively justified; clearly, there are many circumstances when we think that using stereotype information is not thus justified.

Importance of Behavior

I have been discussing factors affecting stereotype strength, but obviously, behavioral information can seem relatively strong or weak as well. Surely seeing a priest beating a cat to death would overwhelm whatever warm and kind stereotypes you have about the clergy. Extreme behaviors stand out and are probably weighted especially highly in judgments about others. In Chapter 3, I have discussed the important work of Monica Biernat and her colleagues on shifting standards (see Biernat, Vescio, & Manis, 1998). The basic argument is that a behavior or feature that would be normal for a person from one category may seem quite extreme for someone in another category. A person who is 6 feet tall would be seen as more or less average if a male, but quite tall if a female.

One way to approach this is to think about how informative or diagnostic various kinds of information are likely to be. According to Rasinski, Crocker, and Hastie (1985), Locksley and her colleagues assumed that assertive behaviors would be equally diagnostic for males and females. Is this true? Suppose that females are inhibited from being assertive, and males are encouraged to be so. Now according to standard attributional principles of information gain (Jones & McGillis, 1976), if we observe an assertive behavior performed by a male, we have not learned very much about his unique assertiveness; he is about like all males, just what we expected on the basis of our stereotype. By contrast, the assertive female is perceived to be very assertive indeed; after all, look at all the cultural conditioning she had to overcome to perform this behavior. As Biernat, Manis, and Nelson (1991) have argued, the same assertive behavior may be seen as more extreme when it is compared to a female rather than to a male standard.

Think about perceptions of assertiveness as an equation, with gender and behavioral information contributing according to their values. Maleness would lead subjects to believe that a person would be assertive (high score for gender), whereas the assertive behavior by the male would add relatively little to the final judgment because he is behaving as expected (low score for behavior). For a female, however, gender information would predict low assertiveness (low value), but this would be compensated for by the powerful behavioral information with its high evaluation. Lo and behold, subjects would see the two as equally assertive, but this is hardly a surprise. The subjects would have two pieces of information about two people, and in each case one piece would strongly lead them to believe that the person is assertive. The larger point is that, contrary to the message of Locksley and her colleagues, gender is hardly irrelevant in this analysis. It is relevant in the first instance because it would lead subjects to make direct inferences for the male, and it is relevant in the second instance because it would lead them to interpret the female's behavior as especially assertive.

RELATIVE DIAGNOSTICITY

The more general point has been made by Krueger and Rothbart (1988). They have argued the reasonable case that category information and behavioral information may have independent diagnostic values, and that these may vary from situation to situation, perceiver to perceiver, and judgment to judgment. In the Locksley case, gender may not have been highly diagnostic, because people do not expect that males and females differ all that much in assertiveness. By contrast, the behavioral information may have been seen as quite diagnostic, especially for females. Thus Locksley and her colleagues studied a case where the behavioral information was more diagnostic than the category information. However, one could easily imagine situations in which the opposite would be true. For example, one would generally be better off using stereotypes based on body type to judge whether a man might make a good football lineman than in whether he can effectively growl, as such folks are prone to do during games.

Krueger and Rothbart (1988) used information for which category was demon-

stratively diagnostic—namely, aggressiveness—under the assumption that actual aggressive behavior, as opposed to that which is merely assertive (as in the Locksley
studies), is more highly correlated with gender. They also manipulated category
diagnosticity. Subjects were told either that a male or female had performed the
behavior, or that a housewife or construction worker had, on the assumption that
subjects would assume there would be greater differences in aggressive behavior between a housewife and a construction worker than between a male and a female (so
that occupations would be even more diagnostic of aggression than gender). They
also used behavioral information that had been rated to be highly or less highly diagnostic of aggressiveness. The results showed that both sources of information had effects in proportion to their diagnosticity. That is, diagnostic behavioral information
affected ratings of aggressiveness, and so did the category information (especially in
the housewife vs. construction worker contrast).

In subsequent experiments, Krueger and Rothbart (1988) showed that the category effect could be washed out when the behavior was consistent in aggressiveness
over situations and hence indicated an aggressive disposition. That is, when subjects
were told that a person was consistently aggressive, they tended to let that information rather than gender affect their judgments. Thus a single bit of behavior will not
necessarily have precedence over category information, but will if and when behavior
gives evidence of a strong disposition. This seems sensible enough. Suppose you are
predicting whether I can hit a free throw in basketball, and you have two sources of
information. You know that I am or am not a member of a major basketball team,
and you know whether I have just hit a previous free throw. Now given that I might
have been lucky in my previous attempt, it might well be quite rational for you to
make your prediction on the basis of whether I am a regular player or not. However,
if you now are told that although I am not a regular player, I just hit the last 10 free
throws I attempted, you would probably be wise to pay attention to my past behavior.
Note that this does not represent any sort of proposition about either sort of information's being more important than the other. Rather, it recognizes that both have
their value as predictors, and that a rational person would pay attention to which is
the more important.

Although I have focused on perceived diagnosticity of information, salience
plays an analogous role. Intuitively, a vivid portrayal of one person beating up another (say, via videotape, with lots of blood and appropriate sounds) is going to be
given more weight than a brief description such as "beat up someone in a parking
lot." Similarly, category membership might be made more salient through appearance cues or frequent reminders. Beckett and Park (1995) argued that gender may
not have been especially salient for subjects in the original Locksley research, since
gender information was conveyed verbally rather than pictorially. So they conceptually replicated the studies by giving people information about a male or female who
was differentially assertive across several situations. With a mere verbal description
of the target as male or female, gender played little role in predictions of assertiveness in future situations; this replicated the Locksley research. However, when research participants also saw a picture of the person (thus presumably making gender
more salient), they did predict that the male would be more assertive than the female, although gender was still less important as a predictor than actual behavior.

Finally, the ambiguity or ease of using information may play a role. For example,
Nelson, Biernat, and Manis (1990) asked subjects to judge the heights of men and
women. Not surprisingly, men were perceived to be taller than women even when ac-

tual height was statistically controlled for. However, gender stereotypes about height played a larger role when the men and women were seated than when standing, because appearance data are more ambiguous in that case.

THE ROLE OF NONDIAGNOSTIC INFORMATION

Often the diagnosticity of category or behavioral information is readily apparent, but sometimes people may misjudge these matters. People who drive old cars are properly outraged when they are stopped in "nice" neighborhoods by police who seem to feel that old cars are diagnostic of bad intentions and a thieving disposition.[6] Many people are unnecessarily frightened of people who talk aloud to themselves in public, because they assume that such people may be dangerous and they give the behavior a higher diagnostic value than they should.

Several experiments have shown that people sometimes use nondiagnostic information in a way that reduces the effects of category information (DeDreu, Yzerbyt, & Leyens, 1995; Denhaerinck, Leyens, & Yzerbyt, 1989; Nisbett, Zukier, & Lemley, 1981). In a series of experiments, Hilton and Fein (1989) examined the role of pseudodiagnostic information in such tasks. "Pseudodiagnostic information" is information that may generally be relevant for a wide variety of judgments but is not relevant for the judgment at hand. For example, intelligence or grade point average (GPA) may be a useful bit of information to know about someone for many tasks, but it probably does not predict how helpful someone would be in most situations. In one of Hilton and Fein's studies, subjects were asked to judge the assertiveness of males and females with clearly diagnostic behavioral information (telling a seedy character to go away), clearly undiagnostic (and irrelevant) information (finding money in a phone booth), or pseudodiagnostic information (having a high GPA). Subjects saw males as being more assertive than females when the behavioral information was clearly irrelevant, but when diagnostic or pseudodiagnostic information was used, males and females were seen as equally assertive.

One reason why pseudodiagnostic information may dilute stereotype-based inferences is that it reminds people that they are judging an individual and that they should not use stereotype information as a part of their judgment. According to the social judgeability model of Yzerbyt, Leyens, and Schadron (1992), such norms play a large role in the hows and whens of information use. Irrelevant information does not trigger such norms because it does not sufficiently individuate a person.

Such results do not dispute the general point I have been making. People are generally not dopes. Sometimes they use stereotypes based on category membership to make judgments about people, and sometimes they rely more heavily on behavioral and other individuating information. The relative importance of each is highly dependent on perceived diagnosticity. Obviously, this does not mean that people are always accurate in judging diagnosticity. They may not be dopes, but they are not unbiased computers either.

STEREOTYPES AFFECT DIAGNOSTICITY AND INTERPRETATIONS OF BEHAVIOR

Up to now, we have considered behaviors and stereotypes as more or less independent contributors to impressions of people. However, the two may also interact. Suppose you read, as did the Krueger–Rothbart subjects, that a housewife or a construction worker hit someone. What kinds of mental images do you form? Perhaps when you think about the housewife's hitting, you imagine her spanking a naughty child, but when you imagine the construction worker hitting someone, images of fists and bloody noses come to mind. We certainly do imagine different types of people exhibiting traits and achieving goals in different ways (Kunda, Sinclair, & Griffin, 1997; Slusher & Anderson, 1987).

Not only do we imagine different behaviors for the same trait, depending on the actor; the same behavior can lead to different trait inferences for different actors. Dunning and Sherman (1997) used a memory paradigm to investigate people's tacit inferences when they read about behavior. For example, if you are told that the head of a computer company needed to terminate a few employees, you would probably assume that metaphorical but not actual heads would roll as people were fired. However, if you were told that the head of a drug cartel decided to terminate a few employees, you would be more likely to imagine red blood than pink slips. Dunning and Sherman presented subjects with ambiguous sentences and then tested recognition memory. Subjects were quite good at recognizing the sentences they had actually read, but they also recognized more sentences they had not read that were consistent with the stereotypes. Given the example above, subjects who read that the head of a computer company terminated employees would be more likely to think they had read that the head of the computer company fired employees than that he had killed them. Those who had read that the head of a drug cartel had terminated employees would be more likely to recognize (falsely) a sentence that he killed the employees than one where he fired them.

To return to the example of the construction worker and the housewife, one possible reason why subjects thought that the construction worker who hit was more aggressive than the housewife was that they imagined the construction worker actually behaving more aggressively. Kunda and Sherman-Williams (1993) showed that stereotypes affected judgments when such behavioral information was ambiguous (as in the example just given), but when the behavior was specified more directly so subjects could not imagine different kinds of aggressive behaviors, gender no longer played a role in judgments.

Stereotypes and diagnostic information may also interact in evaluative judgments. According to category-based expectancy theory (Jackson, Sullivan, & Hodge, 1993; Jussim, Coleman, & Lerch, 1987), behavior that violates group-based expectancies will be evaluated extremely in the direction of the behavior. If we have high expectations, we are especially negative when a person does poorly, and if our expectations are negative, we especially value positive performance. So if we expect Asian Americans to be polite, we will evaluate a cussing, angry Asian American especially negatively (more negatively than a European American performing the same behavior), and we would evaluate an award-winning African American scientist more favorably than equally competent European American colleagues. Well-behaved African Americans are a "credit to their race," and brutish European Americans are just "white trash." There is now considerable evidence in favor of this notion (Bettencourt, Dill, Greathouse, Charlton, & Mulholland, 1997; Coleman, Jussim, & Kelly, 1995; Jackson et al., 1993; Jussim, Fleming, Coleman, & Kohberger, 1996; Kernahan, Bartholow, & Bettencourt, 2000). There are important practical implications of this idea in admission, hiring, and promotion decisions, but I bring up expectancy violation theory in this context because it is another illustration of the proposition that behaviors change their meaning, depending on who performs them. That is, behaviors and stereotypes interact.

Processing Concerns

In general, as it has become clear that there is no general answer to the question of whether schemas and stereotypes are more or less important than behavioral information, attention has shifted to the ways both are used in processing information about people. Some authors have focused on cognitive factors, whereas others have been more interested in motivational effects. Three prominent models have attempted to explain how our stereotypes and individuating information contribute to our impressions of individuals.

Sequential-Processing Approaches

Marilyn Brewer (1988) and Susan Fiske and her colleagues (Fiske & Neuberg, 1990; Fiske & Pavelchak, 1986) have proposed similar models of how we process information about others. Both models suggest that in forming impressions of others, we go through a clearly defined yet complexly interrelated set of processes. Despite many common elements, however, the models also differ in important ways.

BREWER'S DUAL-PROCESS MODEL

Marilyn Brewer's dual-process model (Brewer, 1988; Brewer & Harasty Feinstein, 1999) is based on the idea that there are two different routes to forming impressions. In what is called "category-based processing," we respond to people primarily in terms of whatever categories we place them in; in "personalization processing," we are more responsive to individual features.

Categorization. In an initial, automatic stage, the person is identified by assessing age, gender, and race. This initial identification does not lead to stereotypes. Such categorization is frequently (perhaps always) automatic, at least for some categories (Chapter 3). At this initial stage, the perceiver also categorizes the person as relevant or irrelevant to present goals. The vast majority of people whom we encounter most days are not, of course, particularly relevant, and in that case we pay them no more heed and so do not process additional information about them (Rodin, 1987).

If a person is relevant or at least captures our attention, we may then try to place him or her in additional categories. Brewer suggests that we often use subtypes of larger categories or compound categories (see Chapter 3). For example, rather than classifying a woman as an Asian and then further as a student, I will immediately place her in the compound category of "Asian student." Brewer also speculates that most of our most salient categories are represented mentally in terms of images rather than semantic propositions. Thus I will make an immediate identification of this woman before me as an Asian student because she resembles other Asians.

Individuation. If my target person seems to fit the category well, and her features seem to match the stereotype associated with that category, then she will be seen in those stereotyped ways. If, however, she does not match an available category, processing will continue through various subtypes until a match is found; if this does not work, other major category families will be tried. Sometimes, however, although a person is successfully categorized, behavior or other attributes do not match the features associated with that category well. In that case, the target may be "individuated," by which Brewer means that the person is seen as a member of the category but as one whose features do not match well. The target will thus be seen as a special case. So as the perceiver continues to try to find an appropriate category for the mysterious target, eventually the target will be seen as either a good exemplar of a general category, an exemplar of a subcategory, or a member of some category with individual and somewhat peculiar features.

Personalization. There is an alternative route to forming impressions, however. A perceiver who is highly motivated to "get to know" another may engage in what Brewer calls "personalization processing." This does not occur automatically or relatively mindlessly; the perceiver has to be committed to this form of processing. Personalization also makes use of categories, but in a different sort of way. In the example above, I may see Mai Ling as a good representative of my category of Asian student, but she will be seen primarily as just that and no more unless she is individuated—in which case she is still an Asian student but one who is clearly identified as not fitting that category perfectly, perhaps because she is boisterous (see the left-hand side of Figure 4.2). On the other hand, as I personalize Mai Ling (assuming I have made the commitment to undertake the extensive processing required), I will also see her in terms of several categories, but those categories will be subordinate to her (see the right-hand side of Figure 4.2). I see her as female, Asian (in this case, Chinese), a graduate student in geology, a person with a good sense of humor, and someone who is unattractive and obese. These will be attributes of Mai Ling, rather than her being representative of each of these categories. Not only is the representation "flipped" (in the sense of categories nested under the person rather than the reverse), but the form of the representation is also likely to be semantic and propositional rather than pictoliteral. Category-based processing is close to what has been called "intergroup processing," and personalization processing to what is often called "interpersonal processing" (Brewer, 1998). In the former case, one responds to another (typically an outgroup member) primarily in terms of category membership. In

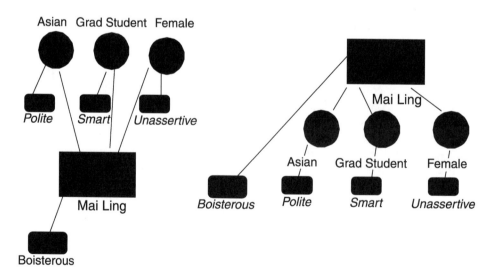

FIGURE 4.2. How individuation and personalization modes might be represented.

the latter, these categorizations are less relevant. (See Chapters 7 and 10, and further discussion below.)

FISKE AND NEUBERG'S CONTINUUM MODEL

Susan Fiske and her students (Fiske, Lin, & Neuberg, 1999; Fiske & Neuberg, 1990) have argued that a continuum of processes is used in forming impressions of individuals. At one end is "category-based processing"; impressions are formed almost entirely on the basis of stereotypes about groups to which the person belongs. At the opposite end is "attribute-oriented processing" or "piecemeal processing," where the impression is based largely on combining behavioral and other individuating information that people display. Fiske and Neuberg (1990) argue that when we meet a person for the first time, we try to fit that person into one of our ready-made categories. If these behaviors are consistent with inferences we might draw from the category itself, then we are likely to form a category-based impression. If, on the other hand, the person displays some attributes that violate our expectancies about how a person of this sort ought to behave, then we will move to a more sophisticated form of analysis. We may reinterpret the behaviors so that they fit the stereotype. For example, a person who thinks that women are careless drivers can still interpret the driving of a woman who is carefully edging into traffic on the freeway as "much too cautious and likely to cause an accident." We might attribute inconsistent behavior to luck or other external factors. Sometimes we make use of various subtypes. The articulate black president of the local PTA may come to be seen as an exemplar of a black businesswoman rather than as a black person in general for a perceiver who thinks that blacks are not intelligent. If cognitive devices such as these fail, we may simply have to push all our stereotypes aside, deal with a person who violates all our expectancies as a separate case, and form an impression without benefit of our stereotypes. The net result is that to the extent we individuate, we are more likely to pay attention to inconsistent information.

Motivational Factors. This kind of information-processing model can often seem to imply an automatic or machine-like series of steps that the perceiver goes through. However, Fiske and Neuberg (1990) argue that a perceiver has a certain amount of control over attention and interpretation, through motivational factors that may enter in at various stages. For example, you might have some reason to want to form an accurate impression of a target person. If you are going to hire Alice for a crucial job, you might pay close attention to her behavior and other attributes, which would generally push you closer to the attribute-oriented processing end of the continuum. It is also likely that as you pay closer attention to Alice's attributes, you will discover more ways that she is not like your stereotype of people like her. This too would force you to consider her even more carefully, and encourage you even further to continue attribute-oriented processing. However, here as elsewhere, a perceiver may confront a classic ability–motivation distinction: All the best intentions will not produce results without requisite ability. Even people who want to individuate do not do so when they do not have the cognitive resources, because they are too busy (Biesanz, Neuberg, Smith, Asher, & Judice, 2001; Pendry & Macrae, 1994).

There is evidence for the existence of these two kinds of processes. Fiske, Neuberg, Beattie, and Milberg (1987) had subjects form impressions of a target based on labels and attributes. When the attributes were not salient, subjects used labels to form impressions; when there was no label, impressions were formed on the basis of attributes. More interestingly, when labels and attributes were inconsistent, impressions were more attribute-based than when they were consistent. Pavelchak (1989) had subjects evaluate people who were defined by several traits. When subjects were asked to guess the person's academic major and to assess how typical the person was of that major (conditions that should encourage category-based processing), final evaluations of the target were better predicted by the subjects' evaluation of the major than by their evaluations of the individual traits. In another condition, subjects did not overtly categorize the targets, and here the final evaluation was predicted by evaluations of the defining attributes, so categorical information was less important.

Fiske and von Hendy (1992) argue that norms can affect whether people are motivated to individuate. In one study subjects were told that they were particularly good at individuation or category-based judgment. As predicted, subjects who generally pay attention to internal cues paid more attention to inconsistent information when they thought they were good individuators than when they thought they were good at category-based judgment. By contrast, those who pay attention to situational cues were more likely to individuate when norms suggested they should.

Dependency. According to Fiske, outcome dependency is one important motivator of attribute-based processing. When we are dependent on others, we should be motivated to predict their behavior accurately, because we may need to control it. Neuberg and Fiske (1987) had subjects interact with a supposed former mental patient diagnosed as having schizophrenia. When their outcomes were dependent on him, their impressions were less affected by stereotypes of schizophrenia than when they were not so dependent. Erber and Fiske (1984) had subjects work together on a task, and some of the subjects thought that the teams that worked together best might win a prize. In this condition, where the subjects' outcomes were partially dependent on their knowledge of their partners, they were much more likely to attend to the partners' attributes that were inconsistent with previous expectations. Under some conditions, people also are more likely to individuate those with whom they expect to compete (Ruscher & Fiske, 1990; Sanitioso, Freud, & Lee, 1996). It makes sense that one would want as much diagnostic information as possible about a competitor; however, but when one is competing as part of a team, opponents are individuated less than fellow team members, because knowledge about teammates is important for success (Ruscher, Fiske, Miki, & van Manen, 1991). On the other hand, noncompetitive groups that are consensus oriented tend to focus on stereotype-consistent information (Ruscher, Hammer, & Hammer, 1996).

Power. Power is in many respects the opposite of dependency, and Fiske (1993) has extended these arguments to say that generally people who are powerful will be more likely to stereotype those with less power than the reverse. So bosses will tend to see their secretaries in stereotypic ways, whereas secretaries are likely to have a much more differentiated view of their bosses. Fiske argues that those with less power are more dependent and must pay close attention to get an accurate fix on powerful persons' ways of thinking, whereas the more powerful persons often need only to know that less powerful people will behave according to their assigned roles and duties. Furthermore, whereas powerless people may have only one or two people in a given situation who can affect them (thus allowing them to devote more attention to each), more powerful persons may have several subordinates who need monitoring (leaving less cognitive capacity for individuation). On the other hand, while less powerful people may be highly motivated to individuate the more powerful, they may also be more anxious, which may reduce their cognitive capacity and ability to do the extra work involved (Fiske & Morling, 1996; Fiske, Morling, & Stevens, 1996). In general, however, according to the Fiske analysis, powerful people should pay less attention to individuating information; when they do attend to such information, they should pay closer attention to stereotype-consistent than to inconsistent information (Goodwin, Gubin, Fiske, & Yzerbyt, 2000). They may also pay particular attention to negative information about subordinates as a way of justifying their superior status (Rodríguez-Bailón, Moya, & Yzerbyt, 2000).

This analysis of power makes a certain amount of sense, and as we will see, power often does play an important role in stereotyping and prejudice. However, such effects of power are far from inevitable. As a faculty member, I often do treat my students as an undifferentiated blob of sorts—particularly in large classes, or when I prepare lectures and exams, or when I am cross about some student behavior I don't like. But at other times I am struck by what seems to me to be clear evidence that I have a much better sense of how my students differ than they seem to have of how faculty members differ (except on highly relevant features, such as teaching style). Surely there are circumstances in which norms associated with particular power positions or other circumstances lead more powerful persons to be especially attentive to the individual characteristics of their subordinates (Overbeck & Park, 2001).

Accuracy. Goals to be accurate, often increased by our desire not to be embarrassed by our inaccurate judgments, can also lead to less reliance on category-based stereotypes (Nelson, Acker, & Manis, 1996; Neuberg, 1989; Neuberg & Fiske, 1987; Ruscher & Duval, 1998). Arie Kruglanski's (1989a; Kruglanski & Webster, 1996) theory of "lay epistemology" stresses the role of accuracy demands in perceiving others. He argues that people generate hypotheses from their theories and then test these hypotheses more or less systematically. A hypothesis will be accepted as correct if a person cannot easily generate alternative explanations. The motivation to generate these alternative hypotheses is a function of (1) the need for structure, (2) the fear of invalidity, and (3) the need for specific conclusions. Need for structure can be increased by various factors, but is thought to be especially sensitive to time pressure and the need to reach a decision quickly. Therefore, people who are under such time pressures may fail to generate alternative explanations and may accept their provisional hypotheses unreflectively. Fear of invalidity is based on the social costs of making mistakes. People who are afraid of such errors will try to consider as much evidence as reflectively as possible. Finally, some people may have a vested interest in one or another hypotheses. For example, prejudiced people may want to believe that Hispanics are lazy, and hence may be relatively unwilling to entertain alternative explanations of behavior that seems to be lazy.

In one experimental test, Kruglanski and Freund (1983) manipulated time pressure and the possibility of public exposure for errors, and asked Israeli teachers to read an essay ostensibly written by a member of a high-status (Ashkenazi Jews) or low-status (Sephardic Jews) ethnic group. As expected the teachers generally rated the essay more favorably when it was supposedly authored by the higher-status student. However, this tendency was especially pronounced when they were under time pressure and when their fear of exposure for having made a mistake was low. These data then suggest that people may make decisions based on their stereotypes (initial hypotheses), as opposed to behavioral information, when they must make quick decisions and when there are relatively few social costs to doing do.

Self-Categorization. Although not a part of the formal Fiske model, one's own standing relevant to the target often plays a major role in processing concerns. Self-categorization theory (see Chapter 3) argues that when we see others in terms of outgroups (groups to which we do not belong), there is a tendency both to see members of that group as different from our own and to see them as a more homogenized bundle. By contrast, when we are perceiving fellow ingroup members (where personal and not group identity is more salient), or when we interact with others just as people without regard to their group memberships, then stereotypes should not play a major role in perceptions. Thus, when self–other relationships are categorized in terms of groups, perceptions should be less individualized than when the relationships are more interpersonal and not group-based (Reynolds & Oakes, 2000).

COMPARISONS OF MODELS

Both Brewer and Fiske and colleagues assume that the perceiver begins by trying to fit a new person into an existing category, and if this is successful, the target will be seen largely in stereotypic terms. Both assume that even if the person does not readily fit an existing category, alternative ways to create a fit are often used (subtyping, reinterpretation of behavior, etc.). Both agree that when a person is sufficiently motivated, either by a lack of fit with readily available categories or because of some extraneous motivation, fairly effortful processing can be used to see the target as something other than a member of a stereotyped category.

Beyond these important agreements, there are also some salient disagreements (see Fiske, 1988; Fiske & Neuberg, 1989). First, whereas Fiske and colleagues argue explicitly that people first try to use category-based stereotype information and individualize only if that fails, Brewer assumes that such a process occurs only if an initial decision is made to use category-based processing rather than personalization. Second, the continuum model argues that there is no warrant for assuming different forms of representation of people and categories at different stages of processing, whereas Brewer thinks that information is represented differently. The Fiske and colleagues model also tends to assume that both motivational factors and degree of fit are important at each stage of processing, whereas Brewer's dual-process model tends to use different processing rules at each stage. Although both models recognize an important role for motivationally dictated control over processing, the continuum model emphasizes this far more.

Parallel-Processing Accounts

Both the Brewer and Fiske and colleagues models assume that we form impressions of others via a series of quite distinct processes. Obviously such models allow some backtracking and feedback, so that if a good fit is not obtained at some level we may back up a step or two. Still, we do one thing at a time, much like most computers.

More recent emphasis on parallel processing, both in the computer world and in cognitive psychology, allow for the possibility that what appear to be separate steps can actually be performed at the same time. Read and Miller (1993) and Kunda and Thagard (1996) have proposed parallel-processing models for how we form impressions; I rely here on the Kunda–Thagard version. Although the details of the model are somewhat complex, the outline is clear. In this model, stereotypes, traits, and behaviors (as well as other information) are all represented as nodes with varying degrees of connection. So a node representing college professors may have direct links to traits (such as being helpful, lazy, absent-minded, intelligent, arrogant, and liberal) as well as links to classes of behavior (such as giving lectures) and particular behaviors (such as "talked with a graduate student on Friday"). Other links are indirect. Keeping regular office hours may be linked positively to being helpful but negatively to being lazy. Keeping office hours may also be linked to additional traits that are not part of the professor stereotype, such as being responsible and friendly. Being responsible, for its part, may be linked to additional behaviors such as "helps son with homework," which in turn may be linked to information such as "helps daughter with science fair project," which in turn may be linked to other traits, behaviors, and categories (e.g., being a father). Depending on the strength of the links and which nodes are activated by various contingencies, one can travel fairly far along these paths or not.

Within the Kunda and Thagard (1996) model, traits, categories, and behaviors have essentially equal status: One can move from traits to behaviors or from behaviors to categories with equal facility (assuming the links are equally strong). Thus there is no a priori reason to believe that predictions of behavior should be stronger if they are based on group labels, traits, or concrete behaviors. Note also that the various links are traversed in parallel fashion; the perceiver does not have to wait for a given behavior to be linked to one trait and then another. For example, an assertive behavior may *simultaneously* lead to nodes representing assertiveness, rudeness, gender, and the given situation. The model also allows for links both to facilitate and inhibit activation. So they may be strengthened or weakened as a result of other information being considered, since each node is capable of receiving input from several other nodes at the same time. As a result, stereotypes are not seen as primarily associations between categories and features, but rather as dynamic patterns of features and behaviors that may change from time to time and situation to situation, depending on which links are activated most strongly.

In this model, the meaning of traits and behaviors is very much the product of what associations are activated, and expectations about behaviors are a product of other information such as traits. So, for example, if I ask you to imagine a young janitor and an older professor playing computer games, you would probably imagine quite different games being played. You might assume that the janitor would be playing solitaire or perhaps Duke Nukem, whereas the professor would be playing some intricate role-playing game or perhaps one involving sophisticated logic. Now let us suppose further that your stereotype of professors includes a link to the node "intelligent," whereas your stereotype of janitors does not. If you observe both the professor and the janitor playing solitaire, your ratings of their respective intelligence might not be much affected. In this case playing solitaire is not especially diagnostic of intelligence, since nearly everyone, smart or stupid, can and does play the occasional round of this game (computer-based or otherwise). In other words, you might rate the professor as more intelligent than the janitor, because links between the two person types and intelligent are stronger than the links between the behavior and the trait. This case, where stereotypes are more important than individuating information, is diagrammed in the top half of Figure 4.3.

Now consider the alternative possibility. You observe both the professor and the janitor playing an intricate game that involves simulating the growth and development of Western civilization. In this case the behavior is highly diagnostic of intelligence, and the links between the behavior and intelligence are likely to be stronger than the links between professors or janitors and intelligence. This then would represent a case where individuating information seems to swamp stereotypes. This is diagrammed in the bottom half of Figure 4.3.

Finally, stereotypes sometimes help us interpret ambiguous behavior. Imagine that you observe a visitor to campus asking directions first of a person who seems to be a janitor, and then of a person who appears to be a professor; in both cases, the target shrugs his shoulders and walks away without giving directions. In the case of the janitor, you might have links to traits such as "unintelligent," "unfamiliar with campus," or "does not speak English well," as well as potential links to traits such as "lazy" and "unhelpful." For the professor, these first links will not be present (and indeed will probably be reversed), so that they cannot explain the behavior. On the other hand, if your stereotype of professors includes links to traits such as "head in the clouds," these will provide reasonable ways to interpret the behavior. So the same behavior may be interpreted as due to stupidity or lack of knowledge on the part of the janitor and as rudeness on the part of the professor.

One major advantage of this type of model is that it erases what turns out to be a problematic distinction between category and individuating/behavioral information.

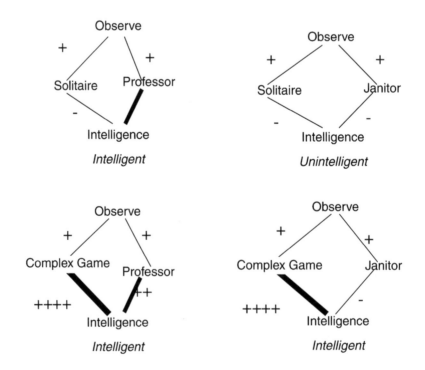

FIGURE 4.3. Various models of representing behavioral and group information.

It also obviates the need for debate about different sorts of processes, their sequencing, and different modes of representing information. In that sense the model is simpler than the sequential models of Brewer and of Fiske and colleagues. What has been left out, however, may be fairly important. There is little room for the sorts of motivational factors we have been discussing. Furthermore, since much of this processing is assumed to take place outside of awareness, it is unclear to what extent people can exert control over how they consider information about others. Finally, this model does not readily allow for different forms of representation of groups and individuals or for the effects of emotion on processing information about others. To these two areas I now turn.

Online versus Memory-Based Processing

The distinctions between sequential/serial processing and parallel processing discussed above really refer mostly to how our mental apparatus deals with information once it has been encountered. However, there is a closely related issue of how we deal with information that we get *seriatim*. One of the classic issues in person perception research has been whether we respond differently to information we acquire early as opposed to late about a person (Schneider et al., 1979). Obviously, since we can never find out everything we know about others simultaneously, we take in relevant information a little at a time. The impressions we have formed of even close friends or family members have been built up over time.

THE HASTIE–PARK ANALYSIS

An influential paper by Hastie and Park (1986) dealt with just this issue. They attempted to resolve a paradox of sorts. It would seem reasonable that if I recall mostly positive things about a person I have just met, I would have a positive impression of that person. Yet often it seems that memories and evaluations are not closely related. Hastie and Park argued that there are two ways of approaching information as it comes in. In what they called "online processing," one considers each piece of information and uses it to update a developing impression. Thus the impression is constantly being revised. In such online processing, one would normally expect that information encountered first would be most important in contributing to the overall impression, and such primacy effects are frequently found. However, when a perceiver is asked to recall information about the person, information that occurs later (recency) might dominate. In the case of online processing, it is hard to predict what relationship (if any) will be found between memory and judgment.

The second mode of processing is "memory-based processing." In this case, the perceiver does not actively integrate each new piece of information into an overall impression. Indeed, the perceiver may not even have a goal of forming an impression at all. In that case, when an impression is called for there is none to be had, and it must be formed on the spot from what can be remembered about the target. Thus there will be a close relationship between what is remembered and the final impression.

IMPRESSIONS OF GROUPS AND INDIVIDUALS

Hamilton and Sherman (1996; Hamilton, Sherman, & Maddox, 1999) have used this distinction to argue that groups and individuals will be perceived in different sorts of ways. They argue that when we perceive people, we generally assume that each individual has a core consistency to his or her personality. Thus, to the extent that we care about the target, we strive to develop an organized, consistent impression. This in turn biases us toward processing information about a person in an online fashion. When we process information about individuals online, we would expect to see primacy effects in impressions, spontaneous inferences about personality based on behavior, and explicit attempts to deal with inconsistent information (often resulting in better memory for the inconsistent information).

For instance, I meet Jane for the first time and immediately notice that she is stylishly dressed. Because I assume that she has consciously chosen to dress in a particular way, I immediately decide that she is a person who cares about appearances. Perhaps she is superficial, but I'll withhold judgment on that for now. Next I hear her make a comment about a lengthy lunch she has just had with "the ladies" at a local expensive restaurant. This piece of information confirms my suspicion that she cares about appearances, and it tilts me toward the further inference that she is superficial, concerned only with impressing people. But then I hear her make an intelligent remark about a local art show, and I begin to wonder. Perhaps she is not so superficial after all. I hear her ask what I take to be a medically sophisticated and sincere question about the illness of a mutual friend, and I'm now beginning to get the sense that there may be more to her than I thought. And so it goes. Each new piece of information is given a larger meaning in terms of dispositions and motives, and I try to make each new piece of information fit into my developing impression. I expect Jane to be all of a piece, and I'm working to make her so. Individuals can, of course, vary in their perceived consistency. Interestingly we have a variety of trait attributions for those who are inconsistent. Sometimes we see them as moody, insincere, or hypocritical. In extreme cases, unpredictability may lead to perceptions of mental illness (see Chapter 12).

However, we do not normally expect that groups will have the same degree of unity and coherence as individuals. If I observe a group of well-dressed women talking about their lunches and artistic tastes, I may or may not note basic agreements. But even if they are all praising the same artist, I do not necessarily assume that they are doing so as members of a group. I would expect Jane to be consistent from moment to moment and from conversation to conversation in her liking for a particular artist, and if she is not I am likely to try to figure out why she is being so inconsistent. However, when I observe a group of women who express differing opinions, I am not the least bit surprised, because I have no reason to believe that they should agree. Because we do not have the sense that groups have a coherent "personality," we are not as likely to process information about them online. Thus our impressions of groups are more likely to be memory-based. On the other hand, when group members perform similar behaviors, we may even think of the group as having intentions (Bloom & Veres, 1999).

ENTITATIVITY

Chapter 3 has discussed "entitativity," the idea that we expect some groups to have more unity than others. Whereas a group of women talking about art may have relatively little in common, members of a family, a religious cult, or a fraternity may often seem to be more tightly knit and to share more common features. Hamilton and

Sherman (1996) suggest that for groups with high entitativity, we expect a fair amount of consistency among members and are likely to use online processing. Groups that are not perceived to be distinct and coherent entities will be approached in a memory-based manner.

Several implications of this model have been tested. Keep in mind that the main difference between perceptions of groups and individuals is the natural tendency to use memory-based processing for groups and online for individuals. However, McConnell, Sherman, and Hamilton (1994b) have shown that when perceivers approach both groups and individuals with a goal to form an impression, information about both should be processed in an online manner. Conversely, goals that direct attention away from impression formation should lead to memory-based processing for both. McConnell, Sherman, and Hamilton (1997) directly manipulated expectations of entitativity for both groups and individuals. Subjects were given information about an individual or a group, and were told that the individual was either consistent or not and that the group members were either highly similar or not. As expected, when the group or individual was high in entitativity, information was processed in an online manner, but processing tended to be memory-based when entitativity was low. Thus, while we might generally process information about groups in a memory-based way and about individuals in an online fashion, these natural tendencies can be overcome either by changing motivation or by altering assumptions about the relative entitativity about groups and individuals. Because people generally think that individuals are more "of a whole" than groups, they make more extreme trait judgments about individuals and work harder to reconcile inconsistencies in their impressions of them (Susskind, Mauer, Thakkar, Hamilton, & Sherman, 1999).

Brewer and Harasty (1996) have argued that the perceived entitativity of groups may also be stronger for outgroups than for ingroups (see Chapter 7), and that even ingroups may be seen as having strong entity properties when social identity is crucial (see also Mullen, 1991). Perceptions of group entitativity may also be increased by a variety of goals and other motives (Brewer & Harasty, 1996). For example, during freshman orientation every fall semester, I am struck by how easy it is to divide the world of students into freshmen and upperclassmen, and to think of the former as being a distinct group with their own needs and burgeoning culture.

If we assume that category-based processing should be largely memory-based, whereas more individuated processing should be more online, perceived entitativity should also affect how much attention we give to the two kinds of information. For example, our perceptions of groups may be largely based on stereotype information, whereas perceptions of individuals from those groups may have a fighting chance to be more individuated. Mullen (1991) has argued that we can represent groups in terms of prototypes or exemplars, and it is reasonable to believe that groups high in perceived entitativity are largely seen in terms of prototypes (Brewer & Harasty, 1996).

Another implication is that groups high in entitativity should also be high in inductive potential (see Chapter 3). That is, just as we assume that one or two instances of behavior on the part of an individual give us the cognitive right to assume that similar behaviors will appear in the future, so groups that are high in entitativity will also encourage us to assume that we can generalize the behavior of one person in the groups to others. In a related argument, Hilton and von Hippel (1990) have shown that for groups high in entitativity, individuals who are moderately discrepant from the group mean are assimilated to the group stereotype, whereas for less homogeneous groups such individuals are contrasted with the stereotype. This is, of course, the very essence of stereotyping—so it is important to get a better grasp on how we perceive groups to differ in this regard.

Affect and Mood

Cognitive psychology generally, and social cognition in particular, have traditionally avoided discussion of mood and affect in information-processing accounts. However, with more recent attention to the topic, there is now abundant evidence to suggest that how we feel affects how we think (as well as the reverse). This is likely to be especially important in stereotyping, because stereotypes themselves are affectively laden and have complex connections to prejudice and discrimination, which are likewise affectively driven processes. An obvious prediction is that our moods should affect the particular content of our stereotypes, but affect, mood, and emotion also influence the ways we process information (for reviews, see Forgas, 1995; Wyer, Clore, & Isbell, 1999).

THE EFFECTS OF MOOD ON STEREOTYPE CONTENT

Perhaps the most obvious and common-sensical prediction is that negative moods should promote stereotyping, especially of groups that are negatively evaluated. Certainly there are abundant data suggesting that people in a good mood are more generous in their evaluations of people and things than those in a bad mood (Bower, 1991; Forgas & Moylan, 1991). Such mood-congruent effects have been reported in the stereotype area as well. For example, Esses and Zanna (1995) had subjects list attributes of several ethnic groups after a positive mood, a negative mood, or no mood was induced; following this, they rated the positiveness of the features they had listed. For those groups that were the most negatively evaluated (native Indians, Pakistanis, and Arabs), people in a negative mood tended to rate the features they had listed more negatively, and other experiments suggested that the mood affected how the features were rated more than what features were actually listed. Haddock, Zanna, and Esses (1994b) also found that subjects in a positive mood had more positive stereotypes and more positive emotional associations to stereotyped groups than those in a negative mood.

There are two major ways to explain such effects. One of the earliest ideas in the affect–cognition literature was that affect becomes associatively linked to other content in our memories and hence can serve as a retrieval cue for affectively congruent material (e.g., Bower, 1981). During encoding, mood may also affect what information we pay attention to and what information gets encoded.

Schwarz, Clore, and their colleagues (Clore & Parrott, 1991; Schwarz, 1990; Schwarz & Bless, 1991; Schwarz & Clore, 1988) have proposed an alterative view. They argue that moods are used as information when we are making judgments, and that we often misattribute our moods to the stimulus being judged. For instance, a woman in a bad mood might rate a group more negatively than a person who is in a good mood, because she implicitly assumes that the groups themselves are causing her affective state. On the other hand, if mood is attributed to a judgment-relevant state, there is no need for further (mis)attribution, and mood should not affect stimulus ratings (Schwarz & Clore, 1988). Mood-inducing events may also serve as standards of reference and, if extreme enough, may lead to contrast effects. Abele and Gendolla (1999) have shown that after positive or negative moods have been induced, important aspects of life (presumably extremely affective) are judged as more positive after negative moods, moods, with the reverse for positive moods (contrast). Less important (and extreme) aspects of life show assimilation to mood.

MOOD AND PROCESSING INFORMATION

Moods and affect also influence how we process information about others. I have noted earlier in this chapter that stereotypes often act as heuristics, and that they will be most often used when we are not motivated to process information about another person systematically. Mood may affect our tendencies to process information systematically or heuristically.

Moods Affect the Use of Stereotypes. Bodenhausen and his colleagues have manipulated mood and then asked subjects to judge either a cheating or an assault infraction where the offender is stereotypically linked to the infraction (e.g., a Hispanic defendant for an assault case and an athlete for cheating). Whereas subjects in a sad or neutral mood do not rate the stereotypic defendant as more guilty, those in a happy mood do (Bodenhausen, Kramer, & Süsser, 1994). Subjects who are angry (Bodenhausen & Kramer, 1990; Bodenhausen, Sheppard, & Kramer, 1994), anxious (Wilder, 1993b; Wilder & Shapiro, 1989a, 1989b) or stressed (Keinan, Friedland, & Even-Haim, 2000) also make more stereotypic judgments. Other studies (e.g., Krauth-Gruber & Ric, 2000; Park & Banaji, 2000) also show that people in a good mood are especially prone to use stereotypic thinking. Thus people who are happy or angry (but not sad) seem more likely to use their stereotypes as heuristic devices.

Why Affect Influences Heuristic Thinking. There may be many reasons for this. One possibility is that when our moods are good, we are generally inclined to slack off a little, to be just a little lazy. It is as if we reason, "Well, my mood is fine; hard work can't improve it and might lead to frustration—let's not rock the boat." Such a model would explain why happy people use stereotypes more than sad people do, but not why anger also seems to produce stereotypic thinking.

Another account (Schwarz, 1990; Schwarz & Clore, 1983) is based on the idea that moods provide information. Good moods suggest that the world is fine and needs no special cognitive work, whereas sad moods may act as a cue that all is not right with our cognitive worlds and we need to restore understanding and closure. Thus good moods may encourage heuristic thinking, whereas sad moods may lead to an active search for information about why the world seems so negative (Bless, Schwarz, & Kemmelmeier, 1996). However, anger and anxiety tend to be more intense emotions than sadness, and may create difficulties in processing information because related thoughts are so intrusive. This would explain why angry and anxious people, like those who are happy, are more likely to use their stereotypes as aids in processing information.

Affect and Processing Information about Groups. Affect has effects other than simple use or nonuse of stereotypes. For example, people in good moods tend to use broader and more inclusive categories (Isen & Daubman, 1984). People in good moods also tend to pay less attention to information about how variable groups are than those in neutral moods (Stroessner & Mackie, 1992), and tend to discriminate more between ingroups and outgroups as well (Abele, Gendolla, & Petzold, 1998). People in a good mood tend to favor the ingroup over an outgroup more than people are sad or in a neutral mood, provided the relevance of the group is low, but sad subjects discriminate more when group relevance is high (Forgas & Fiedler, 1996). There are several other demonstrations that people in a good mood process information about others in a less complex way (Bless, Clore, et al., 1996; Edwards & Weary, 1993; Martin, Ward, Achee, & Wyer,1993; Seta, Hayes, & Seta, 1994).

Finally, Lambert, Khan, Lickel, and Fricke (1997) have shown that people who are sad tend to correct for their negative but not their positive stereotypes. People who were in a happy mood and who disliked sororities had more favorable impressions of sorority nonmembers on negative traits than did those in a neutral mood. However, those in a sad mood who disliked sororities actually judged sorority members more positively on negative traits. Lambert and his colleagues argue that because people in a sad mood are motivated to be more thoughtful in their processing, they think their stereotypes are inappropriate bases for judgments and hence try to correct (in this case, they overcorrect). One could argue that such results only say something about mood congruency effects, since sad moods affected only ratings of negative traits, but the argument is more general. In another experiment, subjects rated women who were attractive (and for whom they had positive stereotypes). When judging them for a job in which attractiveness was said to be relevant, sad subjects were more willing than the neutral-mood subjects to hire an attractive candidate, but when attractiveness was said to be irrelevant to the job, sad subjects were less likely than neutral-mood subjects to hire her. Again, this suggests that people in a sad mood are more likely to process information thoughtfully than those in neutral or happy moods.

Conclusions: Stereotypes and Individuating Information

There is no simple answer to the questions of whether stereotypes or behavioral and other individuating information is more important in our perceptions of others. Fortunately, our mental apparatus is constructed so that there can be no simple answer. Imagine how awful it would be if we were always prisoners of our stereotypes, or inevitably had to form new generalizations and expectancies with each new experience. Some of our stereotypes are strongly entrenched and will resist interference from individuating data. But most are not that impervious to data, and even with those that are, we have the capacity to mentally override stereotypes and to consider people as individuals.

SUMMARY

All our experiences are joint products of incoming perceptual information and knowledge. Stereotypes can be thought of as schemas—preexisting theories and frameworks that help us understand our raw experiences. In particular, schemas help us label and interpret information, affect what we remember, and help us go beyond immediately presented data to infer additional features and other information.

Active schemas direct attention to certain features as an aid to recognition and labeling, and once something is labeled we are often especially attentive to features or objects that seem to be inconsistent with the schema in an effort to comprehend it. Because most human behavior is inherently ambiguous, our schemas help us evaluate and interpret it. More particularly, stereotypes aid our attempts to explain the behavior of others. It follows that when certain categories are primed, behavior will tend to be interpreted in terms of stereotypes associated with that category. Category and trait priming can also affect behavior, and one important effect of priming particular stereotypes occurs with stereotype threat where members of stigmatized groups tend to perform less well when stereotypes about their inferiority are salient.

We do not remember most of the information we perceive, and our schemas favor recall of information that is consistent with the schema. But because information that is inconsistent with the schema often receives special attention, it may also be remembered quite well. This means that we are prone to recall both stereotype consistent and inconsistent information, although over time the latter probably has diminished impact in our thinking about individual people.

While our stereotypes are important in the ways we think about others, they are not necessarily more important than information about individuals. There is no simple answer as to which is more important. Even strong stereotypes can be overridden by even stronger information about individuals, and which is more important is determined by the relative diagnosticity of stereotype or individuating information. This is determined by a host of motivational and cognitive factors as well as the nature of the situation and the judgment task at hand. However, it is important to note that stereotypes can affect the interpretation and thereby diagnosticity of behavior and behavior can favor activation of some stereotypes over others.

Brewer's (1988) dual process model and Fiske and Neuberg's (1990) continuum model both argue that when we meet people for the first time categorization and stereotype deployment can occur through a series of stages, but that we are also able to see people as more than, and in some instances different from, their category memberships. Kunda and Thagard (1996) have processed a model that is less based on distinct stages and that does not make a distinction between category and behavioral or feature information.

Recent attention has been given to differences in the ways we process information about groups and individuals. One important difference is that generally we expect individuals to have a greater consistency, although groups also vary in how consistent they are seen to be. Groups high in "groupiness" are called entitative and are perceived to be consistent.

Finally, recently there has also been considerable attention given to the roles of affect and emotion in thinking about others. Generally, mood and emotion affect not only the salience of stereotype content (positive moods generally leading to more positive stereotypes), but also how we process information. In particular, people in good moods tend to rely on stereotypes more than those who are sad.

Material in this chapter speaks to the heart of problems with stereotyping. Stereotypes are not brute-force instruments; their effects are more subtle, more ubiquitous, and more pernicious than we usually imagine. They affect what we know about other people and social categories.

Notes

1. One of my daughters spent some time in a fairly remote area of China. Although she was quite tolerant of such unaccustomed attention, she did report that she had an almost irresistible urge to scream "Boo!" at small Chinese children who examined her intently and at close range on trains and buses.

2. One of my students recently complained that people stared at her because she was wearing lots of earrings, nose rings, and other facial hardware. It seems to me (perhaps somewhat naively) that the purpose of such adornments is to attract attention, although presumably not from stodgy adults.

3. Although this incident happened over 20 years ago, I wrote down a detailed description of it within an hour, precisely because it seemed to be such an interesting demonstration of something. The example has finally found a useful home. Nowadays I would be more inclined to have confronted the woman about her racist comments, even though it would probably not have affected her stereotypes. But I was tired, in a hurry, and frankly a bit scared about what I had just witnessed.

4. However, schema models with more sophisticated and complex assumptions (e.g., Babey, Queller, & Klein, 1998; Graesser, Woll, Kowalski, & Smith, 1980; Woll & Graesser, 1982) can explain such results. Generally, this class of models assumes that whereas processing of congruent information is schematic, the incongruent information gets special processing and has a "tag" associated with it that sets it apart as not a part of the schema.

5. For a while, I tended to wear light tan socks on days when I taught. Sometime later I encountered a student whom I recognized as having been in one of my large classes. After we had done the usual introductory things, he told me that he didn't remember my name or even what class he had taken with me, but he did recall that I was the guy who never wore socks to class. I would have preferred to have been individuated in a somewhat more profound way.

6. This happened to me once. An initial sense of outrage quickly was rather quickly replaced by some degree of amusement—but then, since my middle-class bona fides are clearly in order, I have the luxury of being amused.

CHAPTER 5

Stereotype Structure
and Implicit Personality Theories

In Chapter 4, I have discussed the ways stereotypes help us process information about others, and some of the resulting biases. In the present chapter, I try (somewhat gingerly, to be sure) to look inside the engine of stereotypes—to examine their structure. There are many ways to approach this, but one way is to use a time-honored idea from person perception: implicit personality theories.

THE NATURE OF IMPLICIT PERSONALITY THEORIES

The term "implicit personality theory" was coined by Bruner and Taguiri (1954) to refer to a network of perceived relationships among traits and other person information, such as roles, behaviors, and values. There is abundant evidence (Rosenberg & Sedlak, 1972; Schneider, 1973) that people readily infer that certain traits "go together." For example, the average person probably thinks that kind people are warm, that stupidity implies ignorance, that hostile people are unhappy, that short people are insecure, and that financially successful people are happy. Thus there is nothing necessarily elaborate about implicit personality theories. They are simply networks of perceived relationships among features within a given domain.

Implicit Personality Theories and Stereotypes

At first glance it may seem that networks of trait relationships have little to do with stereotypes, but slightly broadening the conception of implicit personality theories makes it clear that stereotypes can actually be seen quite easily in this framework. Several authors (e.g., Ashmore, 1981; Ashmore & Del Boca, 1979; Jones, 1977; Schneider, Hastorf, & Ellsworth, 1979) have argued that stereotypes are similar to implicit personality theories, but the specific similarities have not always been spelled out carefully.

There are three basic ways we might construe stereotypes within this framework. Keep in mind that implicit personality theories are relationships among stimuli. These stimuli are usually construed as traits, but we could also broaden stimuli to include groups.

- The first and most obvious way to use this metaphor is to consider race, gender, and other group designations as stimuli that are correlated with other features. Keep in mind that there is no principled way in which categories and features differ (see Chapter 3). So just as people may see professors as likely to be smart, they may also see smart people as likely to be professorial.
- Second, group designations may be thought of as moderator variables that change trait relationships. In other words, trait relationships are different for different groups. For example, perceivers may think that clannish Jews are mercenary, whereas they may believe that the more clannish Hispanics are, the *less* mercenary they are.
- Third, we might think of groups themselves as stimuli that are more or less related. Surely most us have conceptions that some groups are more similar than others. For example, most non-Asian Americans probably think that Japanese and Chinese Americans are closer than are Americans of Hispanic and Russian descent.

We will, in due course, consider each of those uses of the implicit personality theory stereotype. But before we turn to that, we should review the actual status of implicit personality theory research, hypotheses, and methods.

Origins of the Theories

Implicit personality theories are networks of perceived relationships among features, and a basic question is where people come up with such relationships. Why, for example, should someone (anyone) assume that warm people are kind, that rich people are happy, or that ugly people are likely to be homosexual? One obvious answer is that at least some relationships are accurately perceived. Or maybe these perceptions of relationships are based more on cultural lessons and cognitive processes than on experiences.

Realism

Often perceived relationships match actual relationships fairly accurately (Borkenau & Ostendorf, 1987; Lay & Jackson, 1969). Perceivers may assume that kind people are warm because kind people actually are warm. There can be little doubt that in broad outline, what we might call the "realist" position has some validity. Although the social world has more than its share of oddities, it would be a strange world indeed if people's assumptions about the interrelationships of most characteristics were strongly at variance with reality.

INDIVIDUAL MECHANISMS

The question is how people obtain, represent, and retrieve correlation information. One possibility is that they keep more or less accurate running tallies on such covariations. As I experience the social world in all its glory, I simply count the number of times warmth appears with kindness, warmth with unkindness, and so forth. However, it would seem perverse if I had to advance a numerical counter for the warmth–kindness relationship every time I encountered a warm and kind person. At the least, such a model implies modes of processing information that lack, shall we say, epic efficiency. Since people can literally report thousands of such relationships when called upon, massive amounts of storage would be required for all the required information.

Another possibility is that such relationships are generated "on the fly." When subjects are asked about the relationship between warmth and kindness, they simply think about their experiences, imagine kind people they have known, and then estimate how many of them were also warm.

CULTURAL WISDOM

It is also possible that individual experiences are the wrong place to look. It might be argued that cultures manage to emphasize relationships among certain important features and traits that more or less match reality. So in this culture people may think that warm people are kind, because over time most people have found this to be so. Therefore, as an individual perceiver I believe in the kindness–warmth relationship and am therefore accurate—not because of my own experiences, but because I have learned my cultural lessons.

Most social psychologists feel uncomfortable with arguments of this sort, in part because such arguments place so much of the emphasis on cultural rather than individual processes, and in part because they are virtually impossible to confirm empirically (let alone study experimentally). Particularly in the area of stereotyping, where it has been historically important to assume that cultural beliefs are the culprits in incorrect judgments about others, it is easy to assume that culture is the enemy of accuracy rather than one of its mainstays. Certainly we could parade a long, long list of obvious beliefs that survived for many generations despite having been wrong (e.g., the belief that women are generally too stupid to be educated in colleges). Yet it does not follow that cultures are inevitably wrong about such matters, or even that specific cultures were wrong at specific points in time. If we can imagine for a moment the situation of women in 1900, I suspect it would have been much harder then than now to find a great number of women who were both willing and able to succeed in college. Obviously we now recognize that this was because women were denied opportunities for intellectual growth, and because people in that day and age were not looking for intellectual women. Quite apart from those women who had learned to submerge their intellectual talents, there were those who were gifted but explicitly denied opportunities for higher education by parental pressure, lack of funds, and admissions policies at many colleges and universities. Cultural beliefs may be superficial and limited, but they can still be true just at the level of what one can observe.

Idealism

The opposite kind of position is often called the "idealist" position. "Idealist" in this sense has its basic philosophical meaning—namely, that truth is represented in *ideas* (not *ideals*, as the word might lead one to believe). In the present case, this would mean that perceived relationships are partially or mostly a function of people's beliefs rather than anything based on individual experience. Our perceptions of how well traits are related may reflect our beliefs, based on values or other beliefs, about how much things should be related (e.g., liberals should be kind and conservatives egocentric, or liberals should be illogical and conservatives analytical), or even the linguistic nature of the traits (e.g., "happy" and "intelligent" are both positive traits, so they should be related). Before discussing these various sources of perceptions, we need to consider some problems with the position that perceived relationships are based on some reality.

ARE PEOPLE ACCURATE IN CORRELATION ESTIMATES?

There are, in fact, some major problems with the realist position. In the first place, even if we concede for the moment the basic accuracy of most assessments of trait relationships, it is highly likely that perceived relationships do not match the actual magnitude of relationships exactly. If perceptions are fairly inaccurate, obviously this would undercut the realist position. For example, it might well be that 60% of warm people may also be kind, but perceivers may assume that all or nearly all (say, 90%) of warm people are kind. It is exactly this sort of exaggeration that leads us to distrust stereotypes.

There is a large body of empirical work on whether people can accurately judge covariations, or the extent to which variables "go together." Typically, subjects are given information about whether members of one of two classes do or do not possess a given feature. So they might be given several pieces of information of this sort: "John is a safe driver," "Melissa is an unsafe driver." After the presentation of several such pieces of information, subjects judge whether males or females are the better drivers. Thus they are being asked to judge whether gender and driving covary, or whether there is a correlation between the two variables. We can express such information in terms of a contingency table—in this case, one expressing the relationship between driving ability and gender. An example is given in Table 5.1.

This type of research is important, because in everyday life we often get information in just this way—several pieces of information about individual members of groups arrive *seriatim*. Can we turn such data into reasonably valid estimates of how groups differ? If we begin with the example of good and poor driving by males and females, an observer would first have to code driving behavior as good or poor, and of course errors may be made at this point. Then the person would have to construct a mental contingency table like the one given in Table 5.1, and of course there is also plenty of room for error, as our observer (let's call her Joanne) might forget many of the behaviors she has observed. When she has to make a judgment, she must either retrieve the contingency table or mentally construct one on the spot from retrieved

TABLE 5.1. Numbers of Males and Females Observed to Be Good and Poor Drivers: A Hypothetical Example

	Good driving	Poor driving
Males	228	68
Females	163	36

instances. Then assuming that all has gone well, Joanne would need to actually attempt to calculate whether men or women are the better drivers. It may not be obvious to everyone that these differences represent a correlation, but they do. There are several ways of turning such a contingency table into a correlation, but the most common is the phi coefficient. However the data are calculated, there will be no correlation unless the percentage of good (or bad) drivers differs for the two groups. To say that two groups differ on a trait is simply another way of saying that the trait and group designation are correlated.

If we use the example in Table 5.1, it is not perfectly easy to determine whether men or women are the better drivers just from a quick inspection of the table. In fact, women are slightly better in this example, because a slightly higher percentage of females (163 of 199, or 82%) than of males (228 of 296, or 77%) have been observed to be good drivers. Thus, to generate the proper outcome, one needs to focus on all four of the cells, but people often do not do this. So if I asked Joanne who are better drivers, she might focus only on the "good driving" column and, reasoning that there are more men than women good drivers, conclude that men are the better drivers. On the other hand, if I asked her whether men or women are worse drivers, she might focus on the "bad driving" column and conclude that men are the worse drivers.

There is abundant evidence that most people are usually not terribly accurate at tracking empirical covariations and relationships (Alloy & Tabachnik, 1984; Crocker, 1981). When the data are presented in a straightforward way, and people do not have strong expectations about what should go with what, they are often reasonably accurate. However, real life is usually not cooperative in presenting data so neatly packaged to unbiased saints. It is not uncommon to find that people's judgments are sensitive both to their expectations and to empirical covariation (Alloy & Tabachnik, 1984). For example, Berman and Kenny (1976) presented traits that were paired together various numbers of times. Subjects' estimates of trait co-occurrences did reflect actual co-occurrences, but subjects also thought that traits pairs such as "persistent–industrious," which are semantically related, had been paired more times than they had.

SUPPORT FOR THE IDEALIST POSITION

Much of the support for the idealist position is indirect and stems from the ready demonstrations that people are often not accurate in assessing how information is related in everyday life. Several studies provide more direct support for the position that assessments of covariation and relationship are based more on the failures of human cognitive systems than on accurate mappings of real covariations. Anthropologists Roy D'Andrade and Richard Shweder (D'Andrade, 1965; Shweder, 1977, 1982) have most forcefully argued the proportion that implicit personality theories are artifacts of the interplay between cognitive systems and cultural factors. The "systematic-distortion hypothesis" suggests that when people try to assess the relationships among traits from memory, their assessments will reflect linguistic similarities and cultural notions about what traits ought to go with what traits.

The most likely culprit in all this is language. It has long been known (Schneider, 1973) that perceptions of trait relationships are often similar to the similarity of trait meanings. As long ago as the 1920s, psychologists (e.g., Thorndike, 1920) had discovered that people who are liked are rated more positively on a number of traits. More generally, what has come to be known as the "halo effect" refers to the tendency for positive traits to be seen as more closely related than they should (see Nisbett & Wilson, 1977, for a more recent demonstration). Furthermore, dimensions of perceived trait relationships often show a marked evaluative nature (Rosenberg, Nelson, & Vivekananthan, 1968). Thus it might be argued that when people report that intelligent people are happy, what they are really saying is that both traits are positive and that positive traits should go together. Judgments of trait relatedness may, then, be nothing more than judgments about how linguistically similar two trait terms are.

Shweder and D'Andrade (1980) reported a study that seems to make this case. As they watched a 30-minute videotape of the interactions among four members of a family, observers rated the behaviors of the people on 11 categories, and from these ratings a behavioral matrix was calculated of relationships among all categories. This "actual behavior matrix" was taken as the best estimate of the actual relationships among the categories. Another group of subjects watched the same tape, and only after the tape was over rated each of the people on the 11 categories. The matrix of relationships was based on memory and was called the "rated behavior matrix." Finally, another group of subjects rated the similarities of meaning among the 11 categories, and this matrix was called the "conceptual similarity matrix." Now if the realist position were correct, there should be high correspondence between the rated behavior matrix and the actual behavior matrix, but in fact these matrices were not highly related. However, the relationships between the conceptual similarity matrix (based on linguistic similarity) and the rated behavior matrix (the one done from memory) was quite high. In other words, subjects' judgments of the similarities among categories more closely matched linguistic similarities than the best estimate of actual similarities. Other studies (e.g., Gara & Rosenberg, 1981) have also shown that perceptions of trait relationships are influenced by the linguistic meaning of the trait words.

A RESOLUTION

Social scientists may have learned by this point that framing issues in terms of the absolute correctness or falsity of opposing positions almost always turns out to generate controversy that ultimately sheds more heat than light. It seems highly likely that most judgments about relationships among traits and other characteristics are mixtures of reality (or at least experience) and various linguistic and other culturally driven cognitive processes. One can find abundant data in support of either position, and common experience suggests that sometimes people are accurate in such matters, other times not, and in either case for any number of reasons.

Representation

Most subjects in experiments are perfectly adept at answering questions of this sort: "How likely is it that happy people are kind?" Indeed, given enough time and patience, such subjects can report on how closely they see thousands of trait pairs as related. But how is this possible? It is unlikely that people have abundant, readily retrievable, individual trait relationships stored in memory, given the magnitude of the storage involved. For example, the interrelations of 100 traits would require nearly 5,000 pieces of information. It seems highly improbable that human mental systems find enough use for such information to allocate that much storage space to it. Most experts have assumed that people derive such relationships as needed from more abstract structures. For example, "happy" and "warm" may seem to be related because they are similar on more basic dimensions; in this case, they are both evaluatively positive. So rather than assuming that people actually have the happy–warm relationship stored and ready to use, we usually assume that people can calculate this relationship from more basic information—say, about how similar in meaning the traits are. Much of the research on implicit personality theories deals with representation and interpretation of these structures. Two general types of structural representations have been used: dimensions and clusters. The logic of both is quite straightforward.

Dimensions

THE LOGIC

The logic of dimensional representation rests on several reasonable assumptions. First, we assume that we can represent trait relationships as normal Euclidian distances; closely related traits lie closer to one another than less closely related traits. Second, in any Euclidian space, distances between any two points can always be represented in terms of orthogonal underlying dimensions. Our old friend the Pythagorean theorem tells us that the distance (represented as a hypotenuse) is the square root of the sum of the squares of the other two sides (which are the underlying dimensions). We will represent the distance between the two points as the hypotenuse and the other two sides as projections on dimensions. Thus, in some sense, each distance can be decomposed into positions on two underlying dimensions.[1] Distances can also be calculated from nonorthogonal dimensions, but the ciphering is more complex. Obviously, if we only have a single distance to worry about, it would be inefficient to use two pieces of information (i.e., the dimensional distances) to represent this single similarity. However, if we add a few traits, the economies become more salient. For example, if we have 20 traits we would have 190 individual distances to worry about, but only 40 pieces of dimensional information (if the distances can be plotted uniquely in two dimensions). Thus the dimensional representation becomes an attractive way to conceptualize the ways people store information more abstractly.

SIMILARITIES AS DISTANCES

Dimensional structures are most often sought through multidimensional scaling (MDS). MDS begins with a matrix of distances among features and asks how many dimensions are needed to represent these distances within desired limits of accuracy. So two traits such as "warm" and "kind," which intuitively are close, would be represented at only a small distance, whereas two traits such as "warm" and "hostile" would have a larger distance between them. Such distances can be generated in various ways. The most direct is to ask subjects how similar the two traits are. Or in the case of traits, subjects might be asked how likely a person who possessed one trait would be to possess a second, with high likelihood ratings being represented as small distances. The distances could also be generated indirectly. For example, the correlations between trait ratings across a number of stimulus persons might be obtained. An even more common procedure is to ask subjects to sort the traits into piles that go together according to some criterion. From such sorts, one can construe distances based on the number of times across subjects each trait appears in the same pile.

INTERPRETATIONS OF DIMENSIONS

From a matrix of similarities, MDS programs estimate the projections of each stimulus on 1 through n dimensions. Once we have established the basic dimensions, we usually want to determine what these dimensions "mean." In some cases the dimensions produced by MDS will be immediately interpretable. For example, if the positive and negative traits lie at opposite ends of some dimension, it is a fair guess that the dimension is evaluative. But rarely are the dimensions so clear. For this reason, researchers generally get independent ratings of each of the stimuli on external scales and interpret dimensions on the basis of which ratings are most highly correlated with the dimensions.

This approach can be illustrated by the work of Ashmore (1981; Ashmore & Tumia, 1980; Del Boca & Ashmore, 1980) and associates. Matrices of perceived trait relationships were submitted to both MDS and clustering. As mentioned earlier in the chapter, external dimensions can be fitted to the multidimensional space. Several external scales were found to fit a two-dimensional space rather well (Ashmore & Tumia, 1980). Several social desirability scales were virtually orthogonal to scales representing potency ("hard–soft") and masculinity–femininity. These latter two scales were close together (about 17 degrees apart), so that traits that were rated as "hard" were also seen as masculine, whereas "soft" traits were also seen as feminine. Since these scales were basically unrelated to social desirability, subjects seemed to feel that neither masculinity or femininity was better in a social sense. However, a third set of scales representing intellectual desirability fell between the social desirability and masculinity vectors, so that the masculinity of traits was correlated with their perceived intellectual goodness.

Dimensional representation of similarities among stimuli is mathematically tractable and seems perfectly natural. Nonetheless, it is important to remind ourselves that we need to make assumptions about what these dimensions mean. Although nothing in the MDS technique requires that subjects generate trait distances by comparison along the component dimensions, we do usually assume that the underlying dimensions have meaning for the subjects and that they have played at least some cognitive role in generating the distance estimates. We also implicitly assume that dimensional representation is a natural way for people to think about their worlds. Are there alternatives?

Clusters

I have argued that it is implausible that most individual trait relationships are stored as such, and that a dimensional structure is one way people might have of making similarity judgments when asked for them. But there are other ways of representing structure. One of the most plausible is hierarchical clusters. Suppose people have in mind that certain traits simply go together as large clusters. So "warm," "kind," "generous," and "empathetic" might be seen as a kind of "altruistic" cluster, while "unstylish," "smart," "wears glasses," and "socially unskilled" might be seen as going together as a kind of "nerd" cluster. Furthermore, clusters might be joined together to form larger-scale units. The "warm–kind–generous–empathetic" cluster (which I have, for convenience, termed "altruistic") might be related to another cluster composed of "happy–outgoing–humorous" (say, "popular"). The larger cluster composed of all seven traits might be termed "social orientation" or "socially skilled."

Although people can think dimensionally, clusters may be a more natural way to represent trait relationships (Anderson & Sedikides, 1991; Sedikides & Anderson, 1994). For one things, clusters of traits map nicely onto both exemplar and prototype representations of categories. More generally, when we think about types of people, we usually imagine that they have several traits that somehow go together in an integral way. Sedikides and Anderson (1994) have shown that people tend to assume causal relationships among traits within a cluster, at least to a larger extent than between closely related traits that are not within the same cluster. This would suggest an integrity to clusters that is not captured well by dimensional analysis.

In a clustering analysis of gender trait data (reported in Ashmore, 1981), gender was used to discriminate among trait clusters. In this study gender was most discriminating when there were 30 clusters, whereas social desirability was more important when there were only three clusters. This suggests that people have a highly complex view of gender. Some of the 30 clusters were clearly male and some were clearly female, but there were several clusters that had both masculine and feminine traits. What was even more interesting was that male and female perceivers differed considerably in the clusters they had. Males seemed to divide female traits into two general categories—"soft and passive" on the one hand, and "socially outgoing" on the other. The clusters for female perceivers were labeled "weak," "cautious," "nurturant," and "thoughtful–quiet." In another clustering study, male perceivers had at least four clusters of female traits, and Ashmore labeled these "girlfriend," "neurotic," "nurturant," and "outgoing." The corresponding clusters for females were labeled "nervous Nellie" and "upper-class young woman."

A couple of points are worth making about this. First, the fact that different types of subjects organized the traits into clusters differently suggests that such techniques may be powerful means of uncovering individual differences in the structure of stereotypes. Second, this research alerts us to the important point that there may be multiple stereotype groups nested within more global ones. If indeed men do see women as divided into "girlfriend" and "nurturant" (perhaps motherly) categories, it would be reasonable that they may see additional subtypes within each of these. At this point, the work in this chapter based on implicit personality theories joins forces with that discussed in Chapter 3 on the basis of categorization and the extent to which categories have important subtypes.

If trait information is represented in terms of such clusters, similarity judgments could easily be generated by people asking themselves "how many clusters away" traits are from one another. So "warm" would be seen as close to "kind" because they are in the same low-level cluster—somewhat distant from "happy," which is a cluster away, and more distant from "smart," which is several clusters away.

ARE STEREOTYPES LIKE IMPLICIT PERSONALITY THEORIES?

Earlier I have suggested at least three ways that stereotypes can be seen as implicit personality theories. First, traits may be seen as related to groups. Second, groups may act as moderator variables that change the nature of trait relationships for different groups. Third, groups themselves may be seen as more or less closely related.

Groups as Traits

The first approach of seeing a group as a kind of trait related to other traits has been used often. Several writers (e.g., Dovidio, Evans, & Tyler, 1986; Gaertner & McLaughlin, 1983) explicitly define stereotypes in terms of group–feature correlations. Certainly it makes intuitive sense to see the traits ascribed to a group as representing a kind of correlation between features and the group. Such an approach also fits well the common definition of stereotypes as perceived associations between features and a category or group; correlations are one powerful way of expressing associations.

The basic argument underlying this approach is that people perceive relationships between traits and group membership, which can be expressed as correlations. So gender is perceived to be correlated with tendency to commit acts of physical aggression, with nurturing, and with making money. Or when someone says that blacks are athletic, they are really stating a correlation between race and athletic ability. The only requirement is that the trait under consideration has to be seen as discriminating between two groups, and as we have seen earlier (Chapters 1 and 3), stereotypic traits are those that generally discriminate the stereotyped group from others. Thus, if we say that Jews are clannish, we are really saying that they are more clannish than Gentiles. A person who asserts that a small percentage of Jews are clannish (say, 30%) would still hold a stereotype that Jews are clannish if he or she believed that only 10% of non-Jews had this trait. However, even traits that are highly characteristic of people in a given group will not be correlated with group membership unless there are contrasting groups with less or more of the trait. Jews have two eyes, but number of eyes is not correlated with Jewishness precisely because almost everyone has two eyes.[2] Differential assignment of traits to groups, usually expressed as probabilities, can easily be converted into correlations.

One problem with this, as with all differential feature assignment methods, is that the nature of the correlation depends on the groups being compared. Usually when one makes a statement that a group "has" a trait, people are asserting that people in the group are more likely to display the trait than people in general. But sometimes specific comparisons are used as well. So the person who thinks that 30% of Jews and 10% of Gentiles are clannish may also think that 50% of Hispanic Americans are. Obviously this plays havoc with the correlational approach, but again it is usually not a problem so long as groups are compared to natural contrasts (e.g., males vs. females, gays vs. straights) or to people generally.

Unconfounding Variables

One of the valuable advantages of thinking of stereotypes in correlational terms is that it automatically alerts statistically savvy people to the possibility of confounding variables. Anyone who works long with correlations comes to understand that two variables may be correlated for a variety of reasons. One possibility is that one variable causes the other, or, for that matter, each causes the other. But a second (and more common) is that both variables are affected by some third (and often unmeasured) variable. "Correlation is not cause"—or so professors often tell their students. Of course, statisticians have developed a number of methods, such as multiple regression and factor analysis, precisely to try to bring some order to this chaos. The issue before us is whether most people recognize these complexities, and if so what they do about it.

Obviously, correlations between groups and traits may have many causes. Indeed, almost all correlations between groups and traits are probably caused by some intermediary variable. If, in fact, Hispanics are more family-oriented than white non-Hispanics, lawyers are more greedy than professors, or women are more nurturant than men, we might look to the role of culture as the intermediate cause. For the most part, group memberships do not directly cause particular features. Speaking Spanish and having a Hispanic surname do not generally cause most features directly, although people may often behave as if group membership is a cause (see Chapters 3 and 4).

RACE AND SOCIOECONOMIC STATUS

Race produces more than its share of such confounded variables. For example, given that blacks are overrepresented among working-class and unemployed individuals, it has been argued that stereotypes of blacks are, in reality, stereotypes of lower-socioeconomic-status people (Bayton, McAlister, & Hamer, 1956). Feldman (1972; Feldman & Hilterman, 1975) explored the extent to which race and occupational designations implied occupational and racial stereotype traits. A first step was to establish a list of traits that distinguished between occupational groups (professional vs. working class) and race (black vs. white). So traits such as "athletic," "musical," "thrifty," and "self-satisfied" discriminated between whites and blacks, and traits such as "persistent," "coarse," "independent," and "intelligent" were differentially associated with occupational group. Subjects were given stimulus persons with varying combinations of race, occupation, and father's occupation, and asked to rate each on the occupation and race stereotype traits. Surprisingly, occupation designation was a far more important predictor than was race. For example, race of the stimulus person accounted for about 1% of the variance on race stereotype traits, and even less of the variance for ratings of the occupational traits. On the other hand, manipulated occupation accounted for about 5% of the variance on race stereotype traits and about 50% of the variance on occupation trait ratings. This means that on a race trait such as "self-satisfied," knowing that a person was black or white had less impact than knowing whether the person was professional or working class, and this difference was even greater for an occupational trait such as "persistent."

More recently, Devine and Baker (1991) had their white subjects rate black persons as well as various subtypes of blacks (e.g., black athletes, black businessmen, ghetto blacks, welfare blacks). The ratings of black businessmen seemed to have more in common with businessmen in general than with blacks in general. However, the ratings of blacks in general were fairly similar to ratings of welfare blacks, streetwise blacks, and ghetto blacks (and these latter three groups were not well differentiated). This again suggests that when subjects rate blacks in general, they may implicitly be rating an image of lower-socioeconomic-status blacks. There is some suggestion that when blacks are seen as middle-class, their race becomes less important as a factor in their ratings. This is, of course, an example of something discussed in Chapter 3: Subtypes of categories may seem prototypic and come to dominate the stereotype of the larger category.

This does not prove that the stereotype of blacks is really a stereotype of working class/unemployed people, but it certainly is consistent with the idea that to the extent that perceivers have a prototype of blacks as working class or unemployed, the occupational group rather than the race will dictate stereotypes. This may have important consequences in everyday life. For example, Kennelly (1999) argues that employers use a stereotype of black single mothers as a framework for evaluating black female employees and consequently think that such workers are poorly prepared and unreliable.

GENDER AND STATUS

What about gender? Men and women may not differ in socioeconomic status, but they do differ in the kinds of roles they occupy and jobs they perform. In an important and influential theory of gender, Alice Eagly (e.g., Eagly, 1987; Eagly & Wood, 1982; Eagly & Steffen, 1984) has suggested that stereotypes of women are actually stereotypes of women in particular occupations or social roles. Eagly and Steffen (1984) argued that women are seen as less agentic and more communal than men because they more often occupy roles (e.g., homemaker, nurse, and elementary school teacher) that foster communal and nurturant behaviors and inhibit more take-charge, agentic behaviors. In their study they asked subjects to rate men and women in various roles. As expected, women were perceived as more communal than men, but only if they occupied a low-status position or no information was given about status. When women were seen as occupying a high-status position, they were perceived similarly to men occupying the same positions.

In a conceptually similar study, Eagly and Wood (1982) showed that when subjects did not know what kinds of jobs people had, they inferred that women would have lower-status jobs than men and would be more compliant because of that lower status. However, when women were identified as having higher status, they were not seen as more compliant than the men. In other words, compliance proneness was seen to be more a matter of job status than of gender, but because women more often have lower-status jobs, perceivers may fail to take that into account and see women as having the "traits" of their position. Thus the putative correlation between gender and communal traits may turn out to be caused partially or wholly by assumptions about the kinds of roles women occupy.

However, other research presents a less sanguine picture of such matters. Schein (1973) showed that ratings by male managers at insurance companies of successful middle managers and of men were highly correlated, whereas ratings of successful middle managers and women were not. Female managers, on the other hand, saw females and successful managers as more closely related than did male managers (Schein, 1975). A more contemporary version of this study by Heilman, Block, Martell, and Simon (1989) found that men were rated as closer to successful managers (.68) than were women (–.24). The fact that the latter correlation was negative, albeit not strongly so, suggests that women were rated very low on the traits characterizing successful managers. Following the lead of Eagly and her students, one might argue that such results occurred because the raters were implicitly assuming that the women they were rating had low-status jobs that did not require managerial skills. Therefore, Heilman and colleagues also had their subjects rate male managers, successful male managers, female managers, and successful female managers. Obviously, specifying that the females were successful managers raised the correlation between ratings of successful managers and females. However, even when the females were depicted as successful managers, the correlation with successful managers in general (.94) was a bit (and statistically significantly) lower than the correlation between successful managers and successful male managers (.99). This study thus represents a sort of glass half-empty, half-full situation. On the one hand, the most strik-ing result confirmed the ideas of Eagly and her students: When women were considered in a higher-status role, much of the difference between ratings of men and women disappeared. On the other hand, it never completely disappeared even when the women were depicted as successful.

CAN PEOPLE UNCONFOUND VARIABLES?

Although evidence strongly suggests that stereotypes of blacks and women are really stereotypes about people who occupy the kinds of roles and positions they often oc-cupy, the real question is whether people know about and correct for it. The average man with a cultural stereotype at the ready about women as being kind and nurturant may well realize that women in high-level jobs do not act that way. He may even be willing, if pressed, to say that women as well as men often behave the ways they do because of various role and social pressures. The most important question, however, is whether he can easily put those observations together and unconfound the effects of role and gender on trait ascriptions. Does he understand that jobs and roles may have far more to do with stereotypic traits than actual gender?

Earlier I have suggested that people are not inevitably good at estimating covariations from contingency tables, and now I am asking whether they can perform an even more complex task—one that involves what we might call a "double-contin-gency table." Can they understand that one set of relations is based on another? Con-sider a concrete example from Schaller and O'Brien (1992). Subjects read about whether individuals in Group A or Group B had solved or not solved anagrams that were either hard (seven letters) or relatively easy (five letters). It turns out that Group B actually solved more anagrams than Group A. However, Group A had also at-tempted more of the more difficult seven-letter anagrams. In fact had subjects taken that into account they would have seen that Group A had actually, on a percentage basis, been more successful at both types of anagrams. Table 5.2 shows the relevant numbers.

As is clear from the table, the seemingly worse overall performance of Group A members was due entirely to their having attempted more difficult problems. If sub-jects were able to correct the correlation between group and performance for diffi-culty of problems, they should have seen that Group A was actually the better-performing group. Yet, on average, subjects reported that Group B was superior, suggesting insufficient correction.

However, that does not mean that people can never perform such double-contingency tasks correctly. In a second study, Schaller and O'Brien (1992) asked some subjects to think about how hard each of the problems was as they received in-

TABLE 5.2. Distribution of Stimulus Information

	Five-letter anagrams		Seven-letter anagrams		All anagrams	
	Success	Failure	Success	Failure	Success	Failure
Group A	5	0	5	15	10	15
Group B	15	5	0	5	15	10

Note. From Schaller and O'Brien (1992). Copyright 1992 by Sage Publications. Re-printed by permission.

formation about performance on that problem. In that condition, subjects correctly reported that Group A actually performed better. Subjects also made more accurate judgments when they had more time to consider each new piece of information. Furthermore, giving subjects instruction on the logic of covariation improves abilities in this area (Schaller, Asp, Rosell, & Heim, 1996).

People are also better at these tasks when the "disadvantaged group" is one to which they belong. Schaller (1992) had men and women subjects make leadership judgments about men and women who were described as good or poor leaders in different situations. Generally, both males and females were better leaders when they held executive positions and worse leaders when they were office workers. In fact, 75% of the executives were described as good leaders and only 25% of the office workers were, so there was a strong correlation between role and leadership ability. In this experiment 75% of the women were described as office workers and 75% of the males were portrayed as executives, so there was also a strong correlation between gender and role. This meant, of course, that the women (who were more likely to be in the nonleadership, office worker role) were less good leaders overall than the men. However, this correlation between leadership and gender was entirely explained by the correlations between role and leadership and between gender and role. In fact, within each role, equal percentages of males and females were good leaders. In this study both male and female subjects overestimated males' leadership ability relative to females', but the male subjects did this to a much greater extent. In other words, the women seemed to be better at adjusting for the "disadvantage" that the women stimulus persons experienced. In another experiment subjects were given the data from the anagram task shown in Table 5.2, but this time they were "assigned" to Group A or Group B. Those subjects who were assigned to the "disadvantaged" group (A in Table 5.2) were much better at discovering that Group A actually performed better.

This series of studies rather nicely shows that people do have trouble untangling the various correlated roles, groups, and behaviors that occur in everyday life, although some conditions do improve performance (Schaller, 1994). However, one problem in everyday life is that other people do not listen to such victims of multiple contingencies. For example, many whites have trouble understanding why blacks seem to be so much more hostile to police than whites. When blacks point out that they have more often (proportionally) been the victims of police brutality and rude behavior, and that these provocations account in part for their behavior, many whites reject this reasoning as self-serving. The argument here is not that every such claim is correct, or that groups are necessarily the best judge of the causes of their behavior— only that there may be occasions when groups' greater self-interest may make them more accurate observers of contingencies, and that we ought, at the very least, not to brush aside such complaints as merely self-serving and biased.

Illusory Correlation

EARLY RESEARCH BY CHAPMAN

The most prominent use of the idea that stereotypes can be considered correlations between categories and features has been a series of studies pioneered by David Hamilton, which were based on earlier research by Loren and Jean Chapman. Chapman and Chapman (1967, 1969) were concerned with why clinical psychologists used invalid signs on projective tests to infer various kinds of symptoms and clinical conditions but did not use other more diagnostic cues. For example, although the Draw-a-Person Test has generally been found to lack any empirical validity as a diagnostic test, it was being used widely by diagnosticians because they felt it was valid. So clinicians reported that paranoid patients would draw pictures with large eyes and men concerned about their manliness would draw pictures of muscular men, despite the fact that these types of drawings were empirically uncorrelated with the symptoms given. Chapman and Chapman (1967) suggested that the reason clinicians used such signs was that they just seemed to go with symptoms in some "common-sense" way. If that were correct, then college students, naive to the arts of clinical diagnosis, would also see these same correlations between signs and symptoms. This was found. The Chapmans were suggesting that clinical psychologists, like the rest of us, think things that "should" go together actually do so. We might call this a "schema-based illusory correlation."

In a subsequent set of studies, Chapman (1967) developed another basis of illusory correlation. In these studies he paired common words from two lists, such that every word from the first list appeared equally often with each word from the second list. He then asked subjects how often each pair of words had appeared together. Although every word on the first list was paired an equal number of times with every word on the second list, subjects saw some pairings as more common than others; there was a perceived, but illusory, correlation among these pairs. Words that had an associative relationship ("eggs–bacon") were seen as having appeared together more than they had, and this result was similar to the one in the clinical study described above. There was, however, another result that was more unexpected: Words that were unusual or distinctive (in this study, by being longer) also led to such illusory correlations. That is, words that were distinctive were seen as having been paired more often than they had. This is an example of a "distinctiveness-based illusory correlation."

THE HAMILTON–GIFFORD EXTENSION TO STEREOTYPING

Hamilton and Gifford (1976) extrapolated this latter result to stereotyping. They reasoned that the victims of stereotyping (1) are often infrequently encountered by perceivers, and (2) are often seen to possess relatively negative traits, which are usually less frequent and hence distinctive. Even if distinctive (say, negative) behaviors or traits were equally common among black and white people, a white perceiver who sees far more whites than blacks in a given day might form an illusory correlation between black and negative traits (because both are relatively infrequent and hence distinctive) by remembering or judging that they went together more often than they had. Having created this illusory correlation, the perceiver would then have some cognitive justification for evaluating blacks more negatively.

Hamilton and Gifford (1976) wanted to avoid using actual group designations in their experiments, because of potential confounds with existing stereotypes. So subjects were simply told that they would read (via slide presentation) a series of behaviors exhibited by members of two groups, Group A and Group B. They were further told that Group B had fewer members than Group A, so that they would see fewer behaviors from members of Group B; thus Group B was relatively distinctive because it was smaller. In reality, they saw 26 behaviors for A and 13 for B. For Group A 18 of the behaviors were positive and 8 were negative, and for Group B 9 behaviors were positive and 4 negative. Note that the proportion (approximately 70%) of positive to total behaviors was equivalent for the two groups, so that there was actually no correlation between group membership and kinds of behaviors. Note also that negative behaviors had been made distinctive by virtue of the fact that they were relatively infrequent in this study. Following the presentation of all 39 behaviors, the subjects were asked to perform three tasks. They rated the members of Groups A and B on a series of traits, so that the investigators could easily calculate an index of how positively the two groups were viewed (an evaluation task). Subjects were also given a list of the 39 behaviors and asked whether the behavior had been performed by a person from Group A or from Group B (a recognition measure). Finally, they were told that they had seen 26 behaviors for Group A and 13 for Group B, and they were asked how many of these behaviors had been undesirable (frequency estimation).

Both the frequency estimation and the recognition measures were used to assess illusory correlation. The data are given in Table 5.3. As the data in this table show clearly, the subjects did remember too many negative (distinctive by virtue of numerical infrequency) behaviors as having been paired with the numerically smaller Group B. The frequency judgments showed the same pattern. For example, whereas the subjects had seen only 4 negative behaviors performed by Group B, they indicated on the recognition test that 6.21 negative behaviors had been performed by B, and they estimated that B had performed 5.73 negative behaviors of the 9 they had seen. Not surprisingly, therefore, on trait judgments Group B was seen as more negative than Group A.

Hamilton and Gifford (1976) were naturally most interested in how negative traits get attached to minority groups, and they reasoned, quite appropriately, that negative traits are usually encountered less frequently than positive. But the basis of the effect is shared infrequency/distinctiveness and is not essentially due to types of groups or traits. Just to be sure, Hamilton and Gifford repeated the experiment, with the positive traits being the less frequent. The results were comparable with those of

TABLE 5.3. Traits Presented and Rated for Groups A and B

	Group A	Group B
Desirable		
Presented	18	9
Recognized	17.52	9.48
Estimated	17.09	7.27
Undesirable		
Presented	9	4
Recognized	5.79	6.21
Estimated	8.91	5.73
Evaluation		
Desirable traits	6.91	6.15
Undesirable traits	4.39	5.31

Note. From Hamilton and Gifford (1976). Copyright 1976 by Academic Press. Reprinted by permission.

the first study, in the sense that it was now the *positive* traits that tended to be seen as more characteristic of the smaller (minority) group.

So although the effect can be obtained with positive as well as with negative traits, Mullen and Johnson (1990) found in their review of several illusory-correlation studies that the effects are stronger when the infrequent, distinctive traits are also negative rather than non-negative. It is probable that negative stimuli are inherently more distinctive than positive ones—more so than one might predict from infrequency alone (Skowronski & Carlston, 1989).

GENERALIZABILITY OF THE EFFECT

Although in dealing with stereotypes we are most concerned with feature–category correlations, distinctiveness-based illusory correlations also occur with other stimuli. For example, subjects can develop illusory correlations between distinctive behaviors and the contexts in which they occur, seeing more negative behaviors in relatively rare contexts than is justified (McConnell, Liebold, & Sherman, 1997). Illusory correlations have also been found between objects and amount of information presented about them (Sanbonmatsu, Shavitt, & Sherman, 1991), and with altitudes of town citizens and size of towns (Spears, van der Pligt, & Eiser, 1985, 1986).

There is another more circumscribed but also important question of generality: Do these evaluative effects go beyond the behaviors that are presented? If I decide that lawyers perform more than their share of greedy behaviors, do I also assume that they are likely to have additional negative traits? In other words, do the illusory-correlation effects generalize across feature domains. Acorn, Hamilton, and Sherman (1988) addressed this issue. They used behaviors that varied along one dimension (e.g., social desirability), created the usual illusory-correlation conditions, and then measured whether the minority groups was evaluated lower on the manipulated dimension as well as on a different dimension (e.g., intellectual desirability). Groups that were seen as socially undesirable were also seen as intellectually undesirable, even though no information had been presented about intellectual qualifications. Similarly, groups that were seen as too immature were also seen as introverted, although introverted groups were not seen as more immature, so generalization across domains is apparently not universal. In everyday life there are bound to be real restraints on generalization across linguistic domains, but even if these effects occur in limited ways, they are still important.

One important qualification of the illusory-correlation effect is that it works for groups, but does not work as well for individuals (McConnell, Sherman, & Hamilton, 1994b; Sanbonmatsu, Sherman, & Hamilton, 1987). Hamilton and Sherman (1996) argue that this results from differences in how information is processed; in particular, information about individuals is more likely to be processed online and information about groups to be based on memory, because individuals are assumed to be more consistent (see Chapter 4). On average, individuals are thought (with considerable justice) to form more unitary and coherent entities than groups. But there are individuals who are inconsistent and variable, and there are groups (e.g., families, cults, and fraternities/sororities) that we expect will have a high degree of entitativity. McConnell, Sherman, and Hamilton (1997) manipulated perceived entitativity for both groups and individuals. As expected, illusory correlations were higher for groups than for individuals, but the effects were also much higher for both groups and individuals perceived to be less consistent (low entitativity).

DISTINCTIVENESS OF TRAITS AND GROUPS

Although the majority of research done within this paradigm has used frequency of behavior and size of groups as means of inducing shared distinctiveness, there is nothing sacred about this. Indeed, in everyday life there may be many other, more important ways that stimuli become salient and distinctive. For example, extreme behaviors would presumably be more distinctive than moderate ones, and hence might be ready candidates for illusory-correlation effects. Indeed, illusory-correlation effects are stronger with more extreme behaviors (Sanbonmatsu, Shavitt, & Gibson, 1994) and with more extreme, emotionally laden stimuli (Johnson, Mullen, Carlson, & Southwick, 2001). Groups might also be made more or less distinctive. We might, for example, expect that people with bright red hair would be remembered as performing more extreme (or otherwise distinctive) behaviors than those with run-of-the-mill brown hair, even if both groups had performed equal percentages of extreme behaviors. Manipulating the distinctiveness of groups via instructions to pay close attention to the group also produces the effect (Sanbonmatsu et al., 1987, 1994). In addition, when information is reported about a third Group C—which presumably makes the minority Group B less distinctive—the illusory-correlation effect is reduced but not eliminated (Sherman, Hamilton, & Roskos-Ewoldsen, 1989).

Stimuli or groups that are relevant to the self ought to be especially distinctive. Several studies have shown that illusory-correlation effects are strongest for attitudes consistent with one's own (Berndsen, Spears, & van der Pligt, 1996; Spears et al., 1985, 1986). More generally, illusory-correlation effects are enhanced when people have a vested interest in the features. Schaller and Maass (1989) were interested in whether people would be more likely to form illusory correlations when their own group was one of the groups. They found that group members saw a lower percentage of negative behaviors associated with the ingroup than with an outgroup. Moreover, illusory correlations are stronger when one's ingroup is the majority group than when it is the minority group (Haslam, McGarty, Oakes, & Turner, 1993).

WHY DO THESE EFFECTS OCCUR?

Illusory-correlation effects, though not dramatically strong, are quite robust and appear with a range of stimuli. As is inevitably the case in such situations, several theoretical perspectives have been brought to bear in explaining the phenomenon.

The Original Distinctiveness Account. As I have emphasized up to this point, Hamilton and his colleagues have assumed that the effect is produced by the relative distinctiveness of both groups and features. More particularly, they argue that the effect is produced by memory biases, and that these biases take place at time of initial encoding (e.g., Hamilton, 1981b; Hamilton & Sherman, 1989). Presumably, when the distinctive stimuli appear, they are given extra attention and additional processing that makes them readily available for retrieval. So when people try to remember behaviors and to recall which behavior went with which group, they will find it easiest to remember the distinctive behaviors attached to the distinctive groups. In support, Stroessner, Hamilton, and Mackie (1992) showed that in the usual illusory-correlation conditions, subjects paid more attention to the distinctive behaviors of the minority group; Johnson and Mullen (1994) and McConnell, Sherman, and Hamilton (1994a) found that subjects were faster in assigning comparatively rare behaviors to smaller groups.

If people generally pay more attention to the distinctive behaviors associated with the distinctive group, we might expect to find that recall would also be better for such behaviors. Hamilton, Dugan, and Trolier (1985) found that subjects recalled a larger proportion of distinctive stimuli paired with the smaller group than with any other combination of groups and stimuli. Mullen and Johnson (1990) also concluded from their review that the relative size of the "double-distinctive" cell predicts the size of the illusory-correlation effect, as one would predict if that cell is especially salient. On the other hand, there are demonstrations (e.g., Meiser & Hewstone, 2001) of illusory correlations being produced that are unmediated by differential memories for distinctive stimuli.

Retrieval Biases. The distinctive-stimuli account assumes that biased encoding is the culprit, but it is often difficult to distinguish encoding from retrieval. Others have argued that memory loss after encoding is the real culprit (Klauer & Meiser, 2000; Meiser & Hewstone, 2001; Smith, 1991). Fiedler (1991, 1996) argues that the effect can be understood in terms of well-known psychometric properties of the situation. One way to look at the situation confronting subjects is that they are trying to learn that Group A has approximately twice as many positive as negative behaviors, and that Group B has this same ratio. However, there are more opportunities for subjects to learn the ratio for Group A (26 behaviors, in the Hamilton & Gifford [1976] research) than for Group B (13 behaviors). When judgments are unreliable estimates of the true proportions, one should expect the judgments to regress toward the mean; that is, subjects should estimate more negative terms and fewer positive terms. Since reliability of judgment should be lower in the minority condition (because there are fewer opportunities to learn the true proportions of positive and negative items), it follows that such regression to the mean effects should be stronger for the minority (small-group) condition. This has been found (Fiedler & Armbruster, 1994; Fiedler, Russer, & Gramm, 1993).

Also supporting the emphasis on retrieval, illusory-correlation effects can be obtained even when behaviors are not assigned explicitly to groups (McGarty, Haslam, Turner, & Oakes, 1993)—a condition that is necessary for distinctiveness-based memory accounts. Indeed, simply presenting subjects with the information that Group A is larger than Group B, and that there are more desirable than undesirable behaviors, is sufficient to produce illusory correlations when subjects estimate what behaviors went with what groups.

Self-Categorization Theory. Another class of counterexplanations rests on the self-categorization theory assumption that when people read evaluative statements about two groups, they assume that the groups are different and attempt to process the information in ways that accentuate these differences (McGarty & de la Haye, 1997; McGarty et al., 1993). In particular, they assume that one of the groups must be "better" than the other. The most reasonable hypothesis subjects in these experiments might entertain is that the most frequent behaviors should go with the most frequent group, and so the larger group should be seen as the more positive (assuming that positive items are more frequent, as they are in most studies). Looked at one way, the actual Hamilton and Gifford (1976) items seem to support that idea; after all, there are 22 pieces of information consistent with it (18 positive items for A and 4 negative items for B) and only 17 pieces of information that are inconsistent (8 negative items for A and 9 positive items for B). One prediction from this model is that the illusory-correlation effect will not appear when subjects are not especially motivated to construe the groups differently. In support of this reasoning, Haslam, McGarty, and Brown (1996) found that when the groups were labeled as left-handed and right-handed people (two groups most of us assume do not differ in important ways), no illusory-correlation effects were found. Further support comes from a study by Berndsen, Spears, McGarty, and van der Pligt (1998), who found that illusory correlation was reduced when the two ostensible groups were both highly variable in the evaluative behaviors, presumably because group differentiation became more difficult.

The Bottom Line. At present, we do not have a definitive account of why illusory-correlation effects occur. Each of the major explanations predicts effects not predicted by the others, and there are data inconsistent with each. It is perhaps worth pointing out that these models are not generally mutually exclusive. So, for example, in a given situation illusory correlations can be produced by both biased encoding and retrieval. Our needs to discriminate between groups may lead to assumptions about which group possesses the most positive behaviors, but memory biases can still support or add to the effect. And it may be that in the laboratory as well as the outside world, different theories account for the effect in different situations or with different kinds of stimuli.

SCHEMA-BASED ILLUSORY CORRELATIONS

Like the field at large, I have emphasized distinctiveness-based illusory correlations here, because such effects are not especially intuitive. However, the Chapmans' original notion of illusory correlation was devised to explain those common situations where people assume that stimuli they expect to be correlated are in fact more highly correlated than experience would justify.

There are several demonstrations of such effects (Anderson, 1995; Berman & Kenny, 1976; Hamilton & Rose, 1980; Kim & Baron, 1988; Madey & Ondrus, 1999; Meehan & Janik, 1990; Plessner, Freytag, & Fiedler, 2000; Slusher & Anderson, 1987; Trolier & Hamilton, 1986). Just to give one example, Hamilton and Rose (1980) paired traits and group labels, and found that subjects thought that stereotypic traits had been paired more often with the relevant group than had been the case. That is, although the pair "salesman–talkative" might not have appeared more often than "salesman–wealthy," subjects saw the first as more common, because talkativeness is a part of the salesman stereotype whereas being wealthy is not. This research indicates that even when people are exposed to information suggesting that their stereotypes may be incorrect, they may still misperceive associations where none are present.

Although Fiedler's (2000) BIAS model can account for both schema-based and distinctiveness-based illusory correlations within the same framework, most think that somewhat different processes underlie the two types. Garcia-Marques and Hamilton (1996) argue that schema-consistent traits are attached more strongly to groups than are schema-inconsistent traits, but that the inconsistent information is also more strongly linked to other items of information (see Chapter 4 for a fuller argument). When people try to estimate frequency of consistent and inconsistent items, they will find it easier to access consistent information (because of the stronger links to the group), and because such information is more available, it will also be seen as more frequent. That would explain schema-based illusory correlations. On the other hand, distinctiveness-based illusory correlations are based on recall of information, and here the inconsistent information has an advantage because it can be accessed both via the group node and via other features or traits. Thus, in making memory-based judgments, people will access more distinctive information.

Groups as Moderator Variables

There is no doubt that people see relationships among stereotype components. For example, Deaux and Lewis (1984) studied the relationships between gender labels and among various gender-linked features. Not surprisingly, they found that males and females possessed different traits, physical features, and occupations. What was more interesting was that there were substantial relationships among the features. So, for example, a person who exhibited male traits was also seen to be more likely to occupy a masculine occupation, to occupy male roles, and to have masculine physical features. A person who was in a feminine occupation was seen to be more likely to have female traits, to have female physical features, and to occupy traditional female roles. There are two potentially important implications of these results. First, it is likely that these relationships are held together by theories about gender, although it is possible that they are based merely on empirical observation. Second, people seem to be willing and able to "move about" freely within their stereotypes. For instance, if I know that a male looks masculine, then I am less likely to infer that he is homosexual or to be in a traditionally female occupation. This is the power of implicit personality theories: They allow us to infer many stereotype features from the few we observe.

Of course, many of these relationships are likely to be "stereotype-free" in the sense that they exist independently of a given group or stereotype. For example, it is likely that we think kind people are also warm, whether they are black or white, male or female, professors or physicians, Texans or Hoosiers. However, it is also possible that some perceived trait relationships change from group to group.

"Moderator variables" are variables that change the pattern of correlations or relationships among other variables. It is possible that perceived trait relationships may differ for different groups, so that group designation operates as a kind of moderator variable. Perhaps white subjects may assume that musical ability implies athletic ability for blacks but not for whites. Perhaps for many a Jew's wealth implies clannishness but a Hispanic's wealth does not. Professors who are lazy may be seen as hostile, but these two traits may be seen as negatively related for other groups, such as attorneys or business executives. I am suggesting that stereotypes about groups are not merely lists of traits associated with those groups, but specific relationships among those traits that may vary by group.

Evidence for Moderation

Koltuv (1962) demonstrated that trait relationships could be affected by type of stimulus person. Specifically, she found that correlations among traits were lower when people rated people they knew well than when they rated people they knew less well. This does not, of course, say anything directly about stereotypes, but it does at least raise the possibility that trait relations may vary by group.

The data for stereotypes are mixed. Secord and Berscheid (1963) found that there was a slight tendency for black stereotype traits to be more closely related for a black stimulus person than for an undesignated (and presumably white) stimulus person, but this result was not strong. However, Veness (1969) reported that correlations among traits differed for different occupational groups, and Hanno and Jones (1973) found that the MDS results of trait co-occurrences were different for family doctors and lawyers.

In the most explicit test of this idea, a colleague and I (Schneider & Blankmeyer, 1983) used a priming task to get subjects to think about introversion or extroversion. They then were asked to judge how closely various traits implied other traits. As expected, when introversion was primed, introverted traits were seen as more closely related than when introversion was not primed, and when extroversion was primed, extroverted traits were seen as more closely related. In a second experiment similar effects were found using a less obtrusive priming task and priming of maturity and immaturity, with closer relationships found for immature behaviors when immaturity was primed (and *mutatis mutandis* for maturity). In related work, Linville, Fischer, and Yoon (1996) showed that people assumed stronger relationships among features for outgroups than for ingroups.

There may be many reasons for this kind of effect. Thinking about trait relationships within a given context may produce a biased sampling of exemplars. For example, because "athletic" and "musical" are both part of the black stereotype, it may be easier for subjects to think of people who have both traits when imagining blacks—at least those that fit the prototype. It is also possible that trait terms change meanings within different stereotypes. So for a white stimulus person "musical" and "athletic" may have connotations of playing the cello and soccer, whereas for blacks the images may be more akin to singing rap songs and playing football. How many cello-playing soccer players have you seen? How many football players doing rap performances?

Stereotype Triggering

One implication is that stereotypic behaviors may trigger stereotypic traits only when the stereotype itself has been primed. Liking opera and the singing of Judy Garland and Barbra Streisand are all part of the gay stereotype, but are not generally related otherwise, to the best of my knowledge. So seeing a random person enjoying an opera performance might not trigger an inference that the person also likes the singing of Judy Garland or Barbra Streisand unless the gay male stereotype is active.

When stereotypes are active, a metaphorical stereotype gun may be cocked, waiting for a relevant stereotype behavior to fire inferences of other stereotype traits. Members of stigmatized groups often do report that they feel they have to be especially careful in exhibiting stereotypic behaviors, lest other related behaviors be inferred. One black professional of my acquaintance worries a little about ordering barbecue when he eats in the presence of whites; he has a slight fear that they might infer that he also is lazy and will break into a rap song. Another has said somewhat jokingly that when he buys a watermelon at the grocery, he is suspicious that white customers expect that he might start tap-dancing. Because none of these features are a part of the white stereotype, whites do not have to worry about such inferences. Professional women may fear discussing their home life and children, because others may too readily infer nurturing qualities and a lack of business-related agentic ones. The culprit is that caring for children may be more closely associated with nurturing for women than for men.

Perceived Relations among Groups

Finally, within an implicit personality theory paradigm, groups as well as traits may be seen as more or less similar to one another. As noted earlier, most non-Asian Americans would presumably see Chinese and Japanese Americans as far more similar than those of Hispanic and Russian descent, despite the strong protests of the former two groups (which actually do have different cultures in many ways).

Such perceived similarities might reflect nothing more than geographical similarities or skin color, but might also well reveal some basic dimensions of perceiving people in other groups. For example, a perceiver who clearly sees a black female professional as closer to a white male professional than to a working-class black female is indirectly saying that occupational group is more important than either gender or race. A person who sees professors as similar to physicians and dissimilar to plumbers is surely weighting education more heavily than income.

Few studies have used perceived group similarities to probe the importance of features, but there have been some. Funk, Horowitz, Lipshitz, and Young (1976) obtained similarity judgments for various nationalities and ethnic groups, and found that these similarities could be represented in a two-dimensional space. Within that space there were three basic clusters: white (Italian, Irish, Jewish, Polish, Anglo, and German), "colored" (black, Puerto Rican, Indian, Mexican), and Asian (Japanese, Chinese). Several rating scales were placed through this space. For example, a dimension of activism placed dark-skinned people at one end, with Asian at the other end and whites in the middle. The whites were seen as intelligent, as contrasted with Asians and dark-skinned people. In a larger study, Jones and Ashmore (1973) found that they needed three dimensions to represent similarities among national and ethnic groups. Again, several dimensions fit the space nicely. Dominant versus subordinate and Communist versus non-Communist were essentially orthogonal to one another, with a dimension of Western versus non-Western culture falling in between.

Why is this important? The most obvious reason is that people may use these presumed similarities to transfer stereotypes across groups. Thus, most Westerners tend to see Asian cultures as being quite similar, despite real, dramatic dissimilarities, and when they learn something about someone from, say, China, may tend to assume that people from Japan, Cambodia, or Korea also have the same features. As I write this, it seems fairly clear that most Americans assume that most Middle Eastern countries are highly similar, and conclude (perhaps incorrectly) that foreign policy initiatives in one Middle Eastern country are likely to be equally effective (or ineffective) in others. At a minimum, then, assumptions that groups are similar can lead to erroneous stereotype transfer, creating interpersonal and international mischief.

SUMMARY

Chapter 3 emphasized category–feature relations, and Chapter 4 dealt with how theories about categories affect processing of new information. This chapter deals with feature relationships by building on the classic idea of implicit personality theories. When we recognize that there is no principled distinction between features and categories, we can also consider category–feature as analogous to feature–category associations. Most of the research in this tradition has assumed that stereotypes were a kind of glue that holds features and categories together. For example, the idea of illusory correlation assumes that distinctive groups (by virtue of their numerical smallness or cultural salience) will tend to attract and hold onto distinctive features (often those that are negative or infrequent or both). This then creates an artificially high perceived association between the distinctive category (e.g., racial minorities) and distinctive (e.g., negative) features.

One advantage of construing stereotypes as feature–category correlations is that it invites analysis in terms of third (or more) variables that may artificially produce the category–feature relationship. For example, people may realize but not actively consider that their stereotypes of members of minority groups may be produced associations of the roles with both features and the groups. So stereotypes of minority groups may draw on and even be produced by stereotypes of working class, and stereotypes of females as being nurturing, kind, and unassertive may say more about the roles women typically occupy than about gender as such. Unfortunately, most people are not notably skilled at untangling these factors.

Another way we may make use of implicit personality theory ideas in stereotyping is to examine the extent to which feature relationships may be different for different groups. The salience of stereotypes may make perceptions of certain feature relationships stronger so people would be more willing to infer one or more stereotype traits from presence of another.

Finally, we may also consider social categories and groups themselves to be more or less closely related. To the extent that we see one group as close to another, we may be encouraged to transfer stereotype traits from one to the other.

Notes

1. The mathematics of the extension to three or more dimensions is quite straightforward, so we are not limited to having only two dimensions. However, the practicalities of visual representation on a two-dimensional page make two-dimensional discussions appealing.

2. People in stereotyped groups often place great emphasis on traits that are not correlated with their membership, as a way of reminding others that a great many traits are actually more characteristic of them (if less discriminating). Recall Shylock's speech from *The Merchant of Venice*: "I am a Jew. Hath not a Jew eyes? Hath not a Jew hands, organs, dimensions, senses, affections, passions; fed with the same food, hurt with the same weapons, subject to the same diseases, heal'd by the same means, warm'd and cool'd by the same winter and summer, as a Christian is? If you prick us, do we not bleed? If you tickle us, do we not laugh? If you poison us, do we not die? And if you wrong us, shall we not revenge?" (Shakespeare, ca. 1596/1974, p. 268).

CHAPTER 6

Stereotypes as Hypotheses

Most of the research and analyses I have presented thus far concern features associated with groups. That is natural; after all, whatever else they may be, stereotypes are features associated with groups. However, in our everyday lives we are arguably less prone to evaluate groups than individuals. Moreover, we reserve our strongest moral hoots and howls when we think a stereotype has been unfairly applied to a particular person. Thus it is important to focus on some of the ways stereotypes affect our perceptions of individuals.

STEREOTYPES AS PROBABILITIES

One of the most striking facts about stereotypes is that they are rarely applied universally. Let's stick with a simple generalization, one that is not likely to arouse any passions or defensiveness. Suppose you believe (as I do) that red apples taste good. Put somewhat more formally, you have a generalization (or stereotype) that red apples taste good. Now let's put you to the test. How far are you prepared to take this generalization? Will you assert that all red apples taste good? Surely not, unless your experiences have been better than mine. What, then, do you mean by a statement that red apples taste good? That 70% taste good? That more than half do? Probably something like this, but, after all, who cares? No one has to suffer from your mistakes about apples but you, and if you make a bad decision based on your generalization, it is a matter between you and your grocer.

Of course, we are all imprecise in this and other ways, and we get away with it because it usually does not make much difference. To the extent that I care about what you think about red apples, I will understand that when you say red apples taste good you are not recommending every one, and I will tolerate the occasional mistake produced by your advice. However, things get somewhat trickier when we deal with stereotypes about people, where such tolerance is not as tolerated.

Some Implications of Stereotypes as Probabilities

When we apply our generalizations, our stereotypes, to individual people, we are often cognitively on our guard. To some extent, this reflects hard-learned lessons about the ways that generalizations work, but in part it reflects the social fact that generalizations applied to people often bite back. For most of us, knowledge that we have treated another person unfairly, or the interpersonal hostility that may accompany our publicly announced stereotypes, makes us cautious. Not always, to be sure, but still most of us are aware that stereotypes are only probabilistically true and do not apply to everyone. What are the implications of this?

Stereotypes Are Rarely Universally True

Most of us, even those who are intensely prejudiced, rarely if ever make generalizations about people (or red apples) that are meant to apply to 100% of cases, even when our language belies our intentions (Mann, 1967). For example, in a large national sample where respondents were allowed to indicate how many members of groups had stereotypic traits on a 9-point scale ranging from "none" to "all," fewer than 20% used one of the top 3 scale points (near the "all" end) to describe blacks as lazy, and fewer than 5% used the bottom 3 scale points (near the "none" end) for rating blacks as intelligent (Jackman & Senter, 1980). I have had conversations with highly racist individuals (including at least one Ku Klux Klan member) who readily admitted that not all blacks are stupid and lazy. As one such person proudly put it to me, "Of course, not all niggers are stupid. But it's the exception that proves the rule." And when people begin a statement by saying "Some of my best fiends are . . . ," they often mean to claim that there are important exceptions to the stereotypes they have just announced. Whether they honor those exceptions is another question.

Stereotypes May Apply Only to Minorities of Groups

A second point is that often our stereotypes are true of a relatively small number of the people in a group. My stereotype is that professors drive old and *déclassé* cars, but as I look around the faculty parking lot at my university, I see that there are plenty of fancy machines around. And I am convinced that undergraduates drive expensive cars, even though a cursory examination of their parking lot would reveal a preponderance of the very clunkers I assume my colleagues are driving. Yes, I too think Germans are scientific, even though it must surely be the case that even by the most liberal criteria of what it means to be scientific, only a minority of Germans fit. Stereotypes do cognitive work for us, even when they apply to a minority of people in a group.

Stereotypic Traits Seem to Differentiate Groups

Third, we may seem to use traits to characterize a group primarily when such traits seem to differentiate that group from others. We say that Germans are scientific because they seem (perhaps not accurately) to be more scientific than the citizens of most countries. As I have emphasized before (see Chapters 1–3), we usually do not ascribe traits to groups when they have about the same percentage of that trait as other people do. We don't usually say that females possess livers, although well over 99% of all living females do. We might, however, make much of the fact that females get breast cancer, and even call it a female disease, even though only 10% or so of all females will ever contract that disease, just because this rate is much higher than that for men.

Stereotypes May Function as Hypotheses

There is a fourth implication that is largely implicit. If our stereotypes are probabilistic in nature, it surely follows that at least sometimes we will be cautious about applying group stereotypes to individual members of those groups. You may think that Germans are scientific, but because you are also aware that this only applies to relatively few individual Germans, you will surely be unwilling to approach every German you meet with questions about quantum mechanics.

But let's not be naive; surely these probabilities ought to count for something when we meet individuals. The person who thinks that men are (probabilistically) aggressive and assertive may well approach men in a different way than a person who holds a different stereotype. But exactly how do these stereotypes come into play? One possibility (and the topic of this chapter) is that stereotypes operate as provisional hypotheses about others. When we meet someone from a relevant group, we tend to assume that it is somewhat probable that the person has some or all of the traits belonging to the stereotype for that group. Subsequent information is used to confirm or disconfirm the accuracy of this provisional hypothesis in this context. Actually, the term "hypothesis" is somewhat misleading, since it suggests that perceivers will inevitably seek to test well-formulated predictions. However, hypotheses are rarely formulated explicitly and are often tested in informal and biased ways, using whatever data are at hand. Perhaps "expectations" would be the better term, but "hypothesis" has the advantage of referring us to bodies of literature that are relevant to stereotyping.

The Bayesian Approach

In recent years there has been considerable interest in how people test hypotheses about others. Within cognitive psychology, research on hypothesis testing has been dominated by attempts to show that people do or do not select and utilize information optimally according to some external criterion. The usual criterion is one or another version of Bayes's theorem of probability, and this requires thinking of expectancies as subjective probabilities—a fairly common move (Olson, Roese, & Zanna, 1996). The theorem itself is not controversial, although the claim that it should serve as a normative model for human reasoning is.

The Essential Bayesian Model

Essential to Bayesian statistics are the notions of (1) "prior probability" (or "baseline probability") of some event, (2) a "diagnostic ratio" (sometimes also called a "likelihood ratio") for new information, and (3) a probability of the event in light of new information. You begin with some hypothesis or hunch about how likely it is that some event will happen or that a particular person will have a trait; this is the prior probability. When you receive new information that is relevant to the hypothesis, the prior probabilities are changed according to how diagnostic new information is. This new information is expressed as the diagnostic ratio. Your new estimate reflects not only your prior estimate, but the new information you have received. So you may begin every baseball season with the firm belief that the Boston Red Sox will finally in your lifetime (and probably that of your parents and grandparents as well) win the World Series, but progressively revise that estimate downward as the season goes on and the Sox do their thing.

BASELINE PROBABILITIES

Bayes's formula states that this conditional postevidence probability is equal to the prior or baseline probability multiplied by the diagnostic ratio. Let us concretely suppose that Jon tries to estimate the probability that a person, Ruth, has a trait (T). The trait might be "kind," "hostile," or "intelligent"; the model doesn't care, but we'll stick with "kind." Before even meeting Ruth, Jon will have some baseline probability estimate reflecting how likely it is that Ruth is kind. But Jon has never met Ruth; how can he know how kind she is? In such a case (which is actually quite common), his best guess about how kind Ruth is will be how kind people in general are. That is, since he knows nothing about Ruth, he may as well assume that she is like everyone else. Admittedly, he knows something about her—namely, that she is female. We could easily get around that problem by assuming that Jon doesn't even know the name or gender of this person he is going to meet. We could also get around the problem by just assuming that Jon's prior probabilities are for how kind women in general are (a gender stereotype), rather than people in general. Nothing fundamental would change in the subsequent discussion by making either assumption, although the terms would change somewhat.

So in this case Jon's assumption about Ruth is that she is as kind as the average person. Call this prior probability the probability of the trait, or $p(T)$. If he assumes that 40% of people in general are kind, $p(\text{KIND}) = .4$. Now he discovers that Ruth is a member of some group G (say, she is a professor), and the issue is whether this new evidence about group membership ought to change his estimates of the probability that Ruth is kind. This new, posterior probability is $p(T/G)$—that is, the probability that Ruth has the trait, given that she is a member of the group. So is the probability of Ruth's being kind, given that she is a professor, [$p(\text{KIND/PROFESSOR})$] higher or lower than $p(\text{KIND})$? In other words, does he see Ruth as more or less likely to be kind than the average person, once he discovers that she is a professor?

THE DIAGNOSTIC RATIO

The question, then, is how this information about group membership should affect Jon's judgment about Ruth. Logically, he should feel it more likely if the trait is associated with the group. That is, if professors are overwhelmingly kind, shouldn't he assume that Ruth will be so as well? Probably, but life gets just a little tricky at this point. Let's follow out the example. Jon may note that almost every time he meets someone who is kind, that person turns out to be a professor. We could more formally represent this as the conditional probability that a person is a professor, given that the person is kind, or $p(G/T)$. But this is not enough. Suppose Jon is himself a professor and during the course of his day he meets almost all professors; then it is trivially true that every time he finds kindness, he will also find that the person is a professor. On the other hand, if professors are comparatively rare in his life, the fact that every time he finds kindness it resides in a professor would be impressive evidence of association. In other words, is $p(\text{PROFESSOR}/\text{KIND})$ higher than $p(\text{PROFESSOR})$? Formally, then, the diagnostic ratio is $p(G/T)/p(G)$. Another way of viewing this ratio is in terms of increased confidence in encountering a group member $[p(G)]$. If $p(G/T)$—that is, the probability of a person's being a professor, given that he or she is kind—is greater than $p(G)$, or the probability of a random person's being a professor, the trait helps identify a group member. The probability of meeting a professor is .5, but the probability of meeting a professor at a meeting of kind people is .8. So kindness is diagnostic of being a professor.

Remember that we are trying to determine the probability of the trait, given the group $[p(T/G)]$, and I have said that a good beginning is the baseline probability of the trait itself $[(p(T)]$. We begin with the general hypothesis that Ruth is as likely as the average person to be kind, but we need to change that hypothesis in view of the additional information that she is a professor. The required "correction" is the diagnostic ratio. The full Bayes formula is as follows:[1]

$$p(T/G) = p(T) \times \frac{p(G/T)}{p(G)}$$

Suppose the diagnostic ratio is 1.00. This would mean that $p(G/T) = p(G)$; in other words, the probability of a kind person's being a professor is exactly the same as the probability of a random person's being a professor. So kindness tells Jon nothing about whether a person is a professor. Because the diagnostic ratio is 1.00, the probability that Ruth, a professor, is kind $[p(T/G)]$ is exactly the same as the probability of a randomly chosen person's being kind. In other words, the original hypothesis $[p(T)]$ is not revised, and $p(T/G) = p(T)$. On the other hand, when kindness helps Jon determine that a person is a professor (the diagnostic ratio is greater than 1), the probability that a professor possesses the trait is greater than average. When professors are kinder than average, then Jon should also assume that Ruth (who is a professor) is kinder than average. However, when the diagnostic ratio is less than 1, the probability that a member of the group has the trait is lower than average, and Jon should assume that Ruth is actually less kind than average.

JUDGING GROUP MEMBERSHIP

A bit of algebraic manipulation suggests another version of the Bayes equation:

$$p(G/T) = p(G) \times \frac{p(T/G)}{p(T)}$$

This version is useful in predicting group membership from other features. Sam may, for example, feel that 5% of the people he encounters are Jewish $[p(G)]$, but he may feel more confident that the person before him is Jewish if the person has some physical characteristic associated with Jewishness. Suppose, for example, that the person has a "Jewish nose" (whatever that may be), which Sam thinks is more common in Jewish than in non-Jewish people (say, 40% of Jews have this type of nose and only 10% of non-Jews do). The p (NOSE/JEWISH) is higher than the p (NOSE/NON-JEWISH), and this diagnostic ratio (4.00) should raise the probability of seeing this person as Jewish. Note, however, that this does not give Sam license to assume that the person is certainly Jewish. In the example just given, the original base rate of 5% should be raised to only 20%. Thus Sam (assuming he is rational) is now more certain, but far from completely certain, that the person before him is Jewish. Other cues for Jewishness, such as a typical Jewish name (e.g., Goldberg), may have quite high diagnostic ratios, whereas other names (e.g., Miller) that can be Jewish have low diagnostic ratios because they are also common names among non-Jews.

One problem in this kind of situation is that people tend to assume larger diagnostic ratios than they should, often because they ignore the fact that most traits also exist in comparison populations. If, in fact, only Jews have Jewish noses, then it is trivially true that a person with this feature should be seen as Jewish. But if this type of feature is also shared by non-Jews (as it most certainly is, assuming we know precisely what a Jewish nose is), then such evidence can never provide definitive evidence of group membership.

QUESTIONS ABOUT ACTUAL PROBABILITIES

Suppose another perceiver, Marcia, says that 60% of professors are lazy. Is this a stereotype? The Bayes theorem alerts us to a common-sense analysis. Surely we would not want to say that she has a stereotype of professors as lazy when they are exactly like everyone else with regard to laziness. In other words, if 60% of all people are lazy, then professors are like everyone else in this respect, and it makes little sense to call this a stereotype even though Marcia thinks that more than half of professors are lazy. On the other hand, if she were to assert that most people are not lazy (say, that only 30% are), she would really be asserting that professors (60% of whom are lazy) are twice as likely to be lazy as the average person. Then we can assume she has a stereotype that professors are lazy. But these ratios are exactly the diagnostic ratios that we have been discussing.

There is another advantage of thinking about such matters in terms of diagnostic ratios. Normally we think of stereotypes as traits possessed by a large percentage of a group. We would generally not think that a trait was stereotypic of a group if only 25% or so of the group had the trait. Yet we can easily find examples that violate this common-sense understanding. People tend to think of scientists as creative, but probably much fewer than half ever publish work that is creative in any real sense. Gay men are seen as carriers of AIDS, despite the fact that far fewer than half of gay males have AIDS or are HIV-positive (HIV+). But, of course, that is no problem for the approach suggested here. We often assign relatively low-probability events to groups because the base rate probability in the larger population is even lower. So while it is true that most gay men do not have AIDS, it is also true that at present gay men are more at risk than non-gay men for this disease.

Obviously, $p(T/G)$ is a direct measure of stereotypes, but McCauley, Stitt, and Segal (1980) have advocated the diagnostic ratio $p(T/G)/p(T)$ as a better measure of stereotyping. The $p(T/G)$ simply refers to the probability of a person's having a trait, given that he or she is a member of a group. The diagnostic ratio simply suggests that such figures must be "corrected" by the base rate of such probabilities in the general population (or some relevant comparison group).

Evaluation of the Bayesian Approach

The actual Bayes theorem is a direct derivation of laws of probability, and its logical status is not in doubt. As a psychological formulation, the theorem is not a theory so much as it is a baseline of rationality against which errors in reasoning may be assessed. However, we need not enter into the vexed question of whether we are generally capable of reasoning correctly to appreciate the advantages of using the Bayesian approach.

One major advantage of this type of model is that it forces us to be quite clear about the nature of the hypothesis under consideration; it grants the gift of precision. It will not do to claim that a certain group of people is "lazy" or "happy" without being clear what that means in terms of percentages. Many of the hypotheses we use in everyday life, though quite serviceable in their way, are also vague and ultimately untestable. The classic example is the putative psychic who claims that in the next year a famous politician will suffer reversals in private life. Since we are not quite clear how broadly "politician" is defined or what constitutes "reversals," it is hard to know what would count as telling evidence. Of course, Bayesian models are not unique in their requirements that we be precise, but they still force us to consider probabilities.

ERRORS

A long line of research makes it clear that people are often irrational decision makers and hypothesis testers by the criteria set up in a Bayesian model (Fischhoff & Beyth-Marom, 1983). An advantage of using this formal model, however, is that we have a clear idea of where to look for errors. Let's consider a common stereotype—namely, that AIDS is a gay disease. Bruce asserts that 60% of gay males are HIV+, or $p(T/G)$ = .6. This is surely wrong, perhaps dramatically so. Where did Bruce go wrong? He might have made an error in the diagnostic ratio by misconstruing either the numerator or denominator, or he might have misestimated the prior probabilities. Let us suppose that the true probabilities run something like the following: The probability of a male's being HIV+ is .005; the probability of a young male's being gay is .05; and the probability that someone who is HIV+ is gay is .60. These are perfectly reasonable estimates, at least for the United States at the moment. Churning those numbers through the familiar equation gives the "true" probability of a gay male's being HIV+ as .06. Bruce's estimate is 10 times more than this.

He could have gone wrong by assuming that being HIV+ is more common than it is—in other words, by assuming that the $p(T)$ was .05 instead of .005. After all, there's been a lot of media publicity about AIDS in recent years. Or he may have assumed that the proportion of HIV+ people who are both HIV+ and gay [$p(G/T)$] was higher than it is. Bruce may not have seen as many news stories about people who inject drugs and become HIV+. Or he may have underestimated the percentage of gay males in the relevant population, so that his $p(G)$ was .01 instead of .05. And he may even get the diagnostic ratio wrong if he fails to take into account the probability of a male's being gay, so that he ends up assuming that $p(T/G)$ is the same as $p(G/T)$, which is exactly what Bruce seems to have done (see Chapter 3 for discussion of this confusion). Obviously, these are not mutually exclusive errors, and they might all contribute to Bruce's striking error.

FAILURES TO CONSIDER BASE RATES

One common bias is the failure to consider base rate information [$p(T)$] sufficiently or to erroneously estimate it. In the example just given, Bruce may make a fundamental error if he overestimates the extent of HIV infection, the base rate. Conversely, if he simply ignores the base rate he will judge solely on the basis of the diagnostic ratio, which might also cause havoc with his judgments.

Failures to consider base rates may create two kinds of mischief. When we are trying to determine whether someone is a member of a group [$p(G/T)$], the failure to utilize information about the base rate of the group in question means that we use our diagnostic ratios (our stereotypes) to make our determination. Thus, even though effeminate behavior may be more common among gay than straight men (say, for the sake of argument, that gay men are eight times more likely to display such behavior), the fact that the base rate of gay men is probably in the vicinity of 5% (see Chapter 12) means that only 40% of effeminate men are gay. Thus, given these numbers, this commonly used cue for male homosexuality would result in errors 60% of the time, even though the stereotype is highly accurate (or so I have assumed for the sake of this argument).

Second, when we are trying to estimate a stereotype, failure to consider the base rate of the trait means that the diagnosticity of the trait for group membership will be overemphasized. What often happens in stereotype judgments is that people fail to emphasize both base rates: the probability of the trait and the probability of the group. The result is that stereotypes, or [$p(T/G)$], are equated with $p(G/T)$. So although approximately 50% of U.S. murders are committed by blacks [$p(G/T)$], this is not the same by any stretch of the imagination as the probability that a black person will commit a murder [$p(T/G)$], mostly because the probability of murder [$p(T)$] is extremely low.

Although there are many other demonstrations of failures to use base rate information appropriately (Bar-Hillel & Fischhoff, 1981; Borgida & Brekke, 1981; Kleiter et al., 1997), people do not inevitably ignore such information, and it is often used quite appropriately when it is relevant and diagnostic (Koehler, 1996). Still, existing research suggests that proper utilization of base rate information does not always come easily to people, and it almost always causes real cognitive and social mischief when it is underutilized.

ISSUES OF ACCURACY

In addition to helping us localize errors, one nice feature of the Bayesian approach is that it facilitates answering questions about the accuracy of stereotypes. In a further interesting extension of the Bayesian approach, McCauley and Stitt (1978) tried to determine how valid certain stereotypes were. In this case, data were obtained on the empirical likelihoods that black Americans and all Americans had certain characteristics (e.g., had completed high school, were on welfare). Subjects did see these characteristics as differentiating black and white Americans; for example, they saw blacks as twice as likely to be on welfare as Americans in general. The interesting thing was that the actual ratios were consistently underestimated. Given the 1975 statistical data used, black Americans were actually 4.6 times more likely to be on welfare, compared with subjects' estimates of about 2.0.

On the other hand, such underestimation is not always observed. For example, Martin (1987) found that male and female subjects tended to overestimate gender differences in personality trait ascriptions. For example, although males were 1.58 times more likely than females to describe themselves as dominant, subjects estimated that males would be 1.98 times more likely to see themselves as dominant. Although males were only slightly less likely than females to rate themselves as understanding (a male–female ratio of .95), the perceived diagnostic ratio was .68. In this study subjects tended to underestimate the trait ascriptions of both males and females, but they tended to be more accurate on stereotype-consistent judgments. So although 96% of females and 89% of males said they were understanding, subjects' estimates were 67% and 52%, so that they underestimated females' ascription of understanding by 29% but males' ascription of understanding by 37%.

Are Stereotypes Probabilities?

Throughout this chapter (and much of the book), I implicitly assume that stereotypes are probabilities that members of a group have certain features. Useful as it may be, this assumption has problems. The most major is that people may not represent stereotypes in this way at all. If I believe that men are stronger than women, I may not be making any precise statement that certain percentages of men are stronger than the average woman; all I may be saying is that men are, on average, stronger. I might be saying that most men can lift a certain weight and most women cannot, or that, on average, men can do 10 pushups and women only 5. Judgments of average magnitudes of features are not necessarily closely related to judgments about probabilities of feature possession.

Second, using probabilities in this way may give us a false sense of exactitude and only postpones a definitional problem. What does it mean to say that someone is strong? There is no gold standard for what this trait means. If I define "strong" as the ability to do one pushup, then probably over 80% of both men and women will be strong, but if I define it as being able to do 100 pushups, then perhaps only 2% of men and 1% of women will qualify. Matters may be even worse with traits such as "lazy" or "kind," which have no objective referents and which may be (see Chapter 4) defined differently for different people and different comparisons.

Third, probabilities substantially less than 1 do not help us much when we confront a concrete individual. In everyday life we more frequently judge individuals than groups, and though group memberships may alter our subjective probability that a person has a particular feature, it does not tell us for sure. Saying that 65% of men can do more pushups than the average woman is not only not easily translated into a judgment about a particular man and woman, but actually seems confusing and may not be the way people think about such matters at all.

There is a related point. As I have stated before, sometimes relatively low-probability features may be a part of our stereotypes, and such low probabilities may give us little or no leverage on judging individuals. For instance, about 10% of smokers die of lung cancer—a figure approximately 20 times higher than for nonsmokers. As an ex-smoker, this fact gives me little information about whether I will get lung cancer, although it should (and does) motivate me to get frequent X-rays of relevant body parts. But the fact of the matter is that dying of lung cancer is a strong part of my stereotype of smokers, even though it helps little in making accurate predictions about individual smokers.

THE NATURE OF HYPOTHESIS TESTING

The Nature of Hypotheses

This section explicitly evaluates the idea that stereotypes may be construed as hypotheses to be tested. We are generally aware that people and objects in everyday life do not always have all the features that are associated with their relevant categories. Therefore, when we approach an individual exemplar, we often assign category-appropriate features to that exemplar in a provisional manner. Subsequently we may confirm or disconfirm that assignment, much as if we had tested an explicit hypothesis.

Two Kinds of Hypotheses

There are actually two sorts of hypotheses that must be considered. The first is the obvious one studied by most stereotype researchers. Given that a person is a member of Group X, this person is likely—or differentially likely—to possess Characteristic A. In effect, the perceiver is asking the question, "Does this member of X have Trait A?"

But another sort of hypothesis is equally important: Given that a person has Trait A, how likely is this person to be a member of Group X? This issue of inferring group membership from traits of behaviors does not come up with some groups. For example, we rarely have a question as to whether a person is male or female, black or white, old or young. On the other hand, we sometimes have questions as to whether someone is lesbian or straight, Hispanic or non-Hispanic, Jew or non-Jew. Is this person likely to be an ex-mental patient, a killer, a flim-flam artist? And let us not be too cavalier about gender, race and age groups. There are light-skinned African Americans, dark-skinned European Americans, apparently ageless people (or at least ones with good plastic surgeons), and androgynous people of both genders—all of whom make immediate classification difficult.

I have already discussed some aspects of testing hypotheses about group membership in the earlier discussion of cue use in categorization. This section mostly deals with the more traditional kinds of hypotheses or questions—namely, of trait ascription, given group membership.

The Origin of Hypotheses

Hypotheses about what another person is like can come from various sources. Jones and McGillis (1976) distinguish two types of expectancies we may have about another person. "Target-based expectancies" are related only to the individual target, and they are based on previous encounters or hearsay. So, regardless of your gender or skin color, I may think you are especially intelligent and hard-working because I have observed your academic work or because other people have told me about you. More interesting for present purposes are what Jones and McGillis have called "category-based expectancies." These are stereotype-based expectancies, those based on assumptions about what people in a particular group tend to be like. So even though I may not know you or have heard anything about you, I still may think you are hard-working because I observe that you are Asian American and I believe that Asian Americans are hard-working.

Keep in mind a fundamental lesson of this book and recent research on stereotyping. It does not follow that these category-based expectancies are wrong, any more than it follows that our individual experiences (target-based expectancies) are correct. We may "misread" individuals or hear biased information about them, just as we may allow the media or our friends to offer us generalizations about groups that are at best overgeneralizations, and at worst simply untrue. The ideas we have about individuals are generalizations (across situations)—stereotypes, if you will—just as are our thoughts about groups (generalizations across people). A few years ago people were obsessed with how a nice man such as O. J. Simpson could possibly have murdered his ex-wife. Those who find that puzzling should consider that our generalizations about people have exceptions, much as do our generalizations about groups; nice people are not always nice.

Translating Probabilities into Hypotheses

For the remainder of this chapter, let us assume that we treat our generalizations and stereotypes as something akin to provisional hypotheses, and that instead of applying them absolutely, we test them from time to time. Clearly, this happens. I have a stereotype that Doberman pinschers are mean and liable to bite. This does not mean that I avoid all such dogs, or that I refuse to pet one after being assured by its owner that it is well behaved. Avoiding the exceptions would be somewhat irrational, as would be approaching any dog I regard as likely to attack me. Presumably the best solution would be to be wary of such dogs until I know they are safe, and then to treat them as friendly.

Stereotypes as Diagnostic Information

Let us concretely suppose that a male member of an admissions committee for psychology graduate school (Professor X) has the notion that men make better graduate students than women. If he were brave enough (and stupid enough, given the current legal climate) to articulate his views, he would (we can only hope) not be prepared to argue that all women are terrible graduate students and that all men are great. At most, he would be willing to argue that men, on average, are more successful than women, and that gender is as diagnostic as Graduate Record Examination (GRE) math scores in this regard. Therefore, when he reads a folder from a female applicant, he is predisposed to assume that she will not be a good candidate. However, just as he sometimes is willing to admit students with lower than ideal GRE scores, provided they have good letters of recommendation and high-quality research experience, he extends the same courtesy to female applicants. In short, he is perfectly prepared to have his stereotype disconfirmed for individual cases.

Here is a second case. I am interested in hiring someone as an undergraduate research assistant, and I believe that having performed well in my social psychology course is diagnostic of success in the tasks I am ready to assign to the hapless assistant. Naturally, I am prepared to believe that some people who have made A's will not be successful in my job and that some who have made B's and C's can learn what they need on the job just fine, but I begin the interviews positively predisposed toward those who have made A's.

Although we may have different moral feelings about my stereotype of people who make good grades and the arguably less accurate stereotype of Professor X, the logic of using these stereotypes as hypotheses is the same. In both these cases the stereotypes may or may not be correct, and in each case the person (Professor X or I) is using information that he thinks is diagnostic. We cannot and should not ignore the fact that most of us have very different feelings about the use of racial and gender category information than about information such as previous experience and various abilities. There are perfectly good moral, social, and psychological reasons for preferring that we not rely heavily on the former kinds of categories, even if they are diagnostic, in making important decisions. However, the point that I am making here is about the logic of hypothesis testing and not the ethics of it. We all use information we think is diagnostic.

So what's the problem? We go through life testing our little hypotheses, and we discover that some turn out to be more or less correct and some false in individual instances. Is there any ultimate harm in holding a false hypothesis, given that it is likely to be disconfirmed? Won't Professor X discover, in time, that females are just as good graduate students as males? Still, common sense suggests that there are dangers in holding false hypotheses, and in this case common sense is largely correct.

The Problem of Confirmation Bias

Common sense and research agree that the danger in having false hypotheses is that we will end up believing them to be true. More formally, we seem to have a predisposition to confirm our hypotheses (Crocker, 1981; Crott, Gisel, & Hoffman, 1998; Klayman & Ha, 1987; Leyens, Dardenne, Yzerbyt, Scaillet, & Snyder, 1999). This bias shows up in all sorts of ways. It is easiest to approach this in terms of some thought experiments. Suppose you think that a particular friend has a disease she is reluctant to discuss. How might you find out? You probably don't want to ask her directly, because the question would be invasive and rude. So you might test more indirectly. Wouldn't you look for signs of illness rather than signs of her being well? In fact, it seems almost bizarre to imagine looking for evidence that she is well, given that you want to know whether she is sick.

Consider some other examples. If you believe that people born under the sign of Leo are likely to be assertive, would you look for Leos who are assertive or those who are not? Surely the former. If I tell you that I am thinking of a number between 1 and 20,000, and you get to ask questions about the range, you would probably first ask something like "Is the number between 10,000 and 20,000?" Why would you be happier if I answered yes than if I answered no, even though logically the two answers provide equivalent information?

Our desires to confirm rather than disconfirm our hypotheses may reflect our tendency to believe information we get (Gilbert, 1991). It may also reflect an internalization of social norms against questioning and negativity. Questioning what something means or what someone intended almost always implies that normal interpretations are not good enough. Here is yet another thought experiment: Would you rather hang out with someone who constantly questions the validity of your statements and accepted realities, or someone who seems to go with the interpretative flow? I suspect that most intellectuals would have a soft spot for the former, but if so I also feel confident that they would soon tire of Mr. or Ms. Take-Nothing-for-Granted, if perhaps a bit more slowly than nonintellectual types.

TYPES OF BIAS

It is important to distinguish the several ways in which this confirmation bias works.[2] There are several possibilities. In the first place, our hypotheses may influence the kinds of information we seek, leading us to seek information that confirms rather than disconfirms our hypotheses. Second, even if we have information that disconfirms our hypothesis, we may ignore or forget it. Third, in an effort to preserve our hypotheses, we may distort information that is inconsistent with them through various processes of reinterpretation and "explaining away." In addition to these cognitive biases, there may be a social bias at work. We may, through our behavior, actually create conditions that make our hypotheses true. For example, in talking to a person we imagine to be hostile, we may make this person hostile through our own behavior.

Consider some examples of how people may show such a confirmatory bias. Professor X, who believes that women are less suited than men to graduate study, may begin his hypothesis confirmation strategy by searching past records and discovering that, in fact, the males admitted have generally gotten through the program more rapidly; given that these data confirm his expectation, he may not be enthusiastic about thinking about why women have done less well (perhaps because they have had to suffer through Professor X's sexist behavior in his classes). He may interview prospective students by phone and ask different questions of male and female applicants. For example, he may ask males about their research experiences and why they like psychology, and ask females about any low grades they have received or what other career plans they may have considered. He may examine information consistent with his expectations less critically and be more likely to look for additional information when the information he is getting isn't what he wants or expects.

Second, even after assembling the necessary information, he may conveniently forget some of the disconfirming information. His colleagues may need to remind him, when he mentions all the females who have dropped out of the program, that there have also been males who have dropped out and females who have succeeded. When he remembers his conversations with prospective students, he may forget that the young woman he interviewed is about to complete an honors project, and instead focus on the fact that she is a varsity cheerleader.

Finally, he may reinterpret some of the information he can remember. Ms. A, who graduated from the program 2 years ago and now teaches at a major university, was a classic overachiever (or so he says), and the males who dropped out were perfectly good students who had family problems they couldn't overcome. Through all of these processes, Professor X is likely to go through another admissions season with his hypothesis that women are less good graduate school material than males intact, even strengthened.

IS CONFIRMATORY HYPOTHESIS TESTING BAD?

Generally, whether one should try to confirm or disconfirm formal hypotheses is subject to many more or less formal logical factors, and there may also be perfectly reasonable social and motivational factors that tilt the balance one way or the other. Furthermore, most hypotheses we test in everyday life are probabilistic. We understand that just as black clouds in the sky usually but not always produce rain, so people from particular categories are only more or less likely to succeed at particular tasks. This means that our hypotheses are often not precise and feedback as to whether the hypothesis has been confirmed is often vague and confusing.

Another issue is that in everyday life there are often differential costs associated with hypothesis confirmation and disconfirmation, which make it easier to seek confirmatory or disconfirmatory evidence. Consider my trying to hire a research assistant. Recall that I have the hypothesis that students who have made A's in my social psychology course have learned a lot of relevant information and hence will make good research assistants. I only hire those who make A's in this course. Suppose, for the sake of argument, that the real reason for the successes I observe is that people who are willing to work hard in boring courses do well at the drudgery required of research assistants, so the real hypothesis is actually broader than the one I test. In any event, I "test" my (as it turns out, too restrictive) hypothesis that people who do well in my classes make good research assistants, and year after year I receive confirmation for my ideas: They all work out well. What costs are associated with my holding this true but limited, and therefore incorrect, hypothesis? The main problem would seem to be that I will not hire some people who would probably do very well because they excel at other boring courses but have not yet stumbled into mine, or people who do well at boring courses but accidentally got a low grade in my version. "Sorry," I say, "I only hire people who do well in my courses, and you haven't." Does the possibility that I have made this error bother me? Not in the least. From a purely "bottom-line" point of view, I have no incentive to widen my nets to test more broadly and thereby possibly disconfirm my hypothesis, and I have only slight guilt that I may be unfair to some students. I *am* unfair to some people, to be sure, but then life is sometimes like that. There are more important guilt trips I want to take.

A related problem in many situations is that the costs of not picking the right person are less than the costs of picking the wrong one. The personnel director who hires undistinguished (although competent enough) candidates for jobs will receive lots less flack than the one who takes chances, hires a few superior people, and also hires some duds. Hence, such directors will likely be far more concerned with avoiding failures than with maximizing success. In both of these cases, people would do better to look for confirming evidence than to try to disconfirm their hypotheses.

Hypotheses may be derived from or at least attached to major values, attitudes, and belief systems, and such structural rootedness may make it virtually inconceivable that a hypothesis could be wrong. We may even, on occasion, create other beliefs that help to justify a belief we want to be true (Klein & Kunda, 1992). In some cases there may be moral, legal, or political reasons for preferring that a hypothesis be right or wrong. So there are many social, cultural, and economic (not to mention moral) reasons for our not always testing hypotheses in the best ways.

ASKING QUESTIONS

Although there is a rich literature on hypothesis testing in purely cognitive tasks, for the present let us concentrate on research in which hypotheses are directly linked to social interactions. The work of Mark Snyder and Bill Swann has dominated this approach. The general paradigm has been to provide subjects with a personality hypothesis to test about another person. For example, subjects might choose what questions they would ask to test the hypothesis that a person is extroverted.

The Snyder–Swann Paradigm. In the original paper in this line of research (Snyder & Swann, 1978a), subjects were told that their task was to determine whether someone was an extrovert. Subjects were then given a list of 26 questions from which they were to pick 12 to ask. These questions were designed as extroverted (in the sense that they were likely to elicit an extroverted answer), introverted, or neutral questions. Examples of the extroverted questions were "What would you do if you wanted to liven things up at a party?" and "In what situations are you most talkative?" Examples of introverted questions were "What factors make it hard for you to really open up to people?" and "What things do you dislike about loud parties?" An example of a neutral question was "What are your career goals?" The result? Subjects asked a preponderance of questions that were consistent with the hypothesis they had been asked to test.

Snyder and Swann also examined what happened when the target people (who were naive to the purposes of the study) were actually allowed to answer the questions. Their answers were recorded and independent judges who knew nothing about the nature of the study coded them for whether they provided extroverted or introverted answers. As expected, the interviewees who had been asked extroverted questions gave more extroverted answers than those of the interviewees who had been asked introverted questions. Thus, by entertaining a hypothesis that the person they were interviewing was extroverted, subjects had produced answers that confirmed their hypotheses.

These kinds of results are remarkably robust (Snyder, 1981). The effect is stronger when people have stronger initial beliefs in the hypothesis (Swann & Giuliano, 1987), but it is not strongly reduced by desires to be accurate (Snyder & Swann, 1978b) or by pointing out the dangers of confirmatory bias (Snyder, Campbell, & Preston, 1982). One factor that seems to reduce the tendency to ask such confirmatory questions is instructing subjects explicitly to consider the opposite of their hypothesis. Lord, Lepper, and Preston (1984) asked subjects to test the hypothesis that a person was extroverted, but gave them a profile of an introvert to use as a "template" for judging extroversion after telling them that introverts are the opposite of extroverts. In that condition, subjects did show a greatly diminished bias to ask extrovert-confirming questions.

Criticisms. However, we must be careful about what we may conclude from such studies. Although the research does demonstrate one kind of confirmation bias, critics have argued that there are severe limitations on how far we can generalize these results. The fundamental problem lies with the kinds of questions that Snyder and Swann forced their subjects to ask. These questions asked have been criticized as both ecologically invalid and undiagnostic (Bassok & Trope, 1983–1984; Trope & Bassok, 1983; Van Avermaet, 1988). The questions are ecologically invalid in the sense that they are not the sorts of questions one normally asks to gain information about another. If I wanted to know whether you are introverted, I would probably ask you directly. Or perhaps I would ask some more neutral questions, such as "Do you like loud parties?" Such a question is neutral because it does not force one kind of answer; you could give either an introverted or an extroverted answer. I doubt that it would occur to me to ask how you enliven parties. In several job-related interview studies, there is mixed support at best for the kinds of confirmatory bias found in studies like Snyder and Swann's (Dipboye, 1992). Several studies (e.g., Macan & Dipboye, 1988; Trope & Bassok, 1983; Trope, Bassok, & Alon, 1984; Trope & Mackie, 1987) have shown that when allowed to generate their own questions, people tend to ask those that do not force particular answers.

The Snyder–Swann questions are undiagnostic because only one kind of answer is possible for each kind of question, so answers cannot discriminate among introverts and extroverts. Suppose you are asked what you do to enliven a party (one of the extroverted questions). Now unless you are prepared to be rude and tell the questioner that you hate parties, you will probably try to answer. The problem is that almost any reasonable answer you give will provide evidence that you are an extrovert, and that will be true no matter whether you are an introvert or an extrovert. Placed in Bayesian terms, the probability of an extroverted answer to such a biased extroverted question is the same whether you are an introvert or an extrovert. The problem is that in this case, the diagnostic ratio is exactly 1.00.

We should be clear that not all hypothesis-confirming questions are unfair and undiagnostic (Trope & Liberman, 1996). Diagnosticity has little to do with whether a question is more likely to yield yes or no answers, or whether the answers are likely to confirm or disconfirm the hypothesis. Questions are diagnostic to the extent that probabilities of a yes answer differ for the hypothesized versus the alternative hypothesized state. Suppose that for some strange reason, you want to test the hypothesis that a person behind a screen is a female as opposed to a male. The question "Have you worn a dress in the last year?" is a hypothesis-confirming question (in the sense that a yes answer will confirm it), but it is also quite diagnostic because almost all females will answer yes and almost all males no. However, asking the question "Can you drive a car?" is a confirmatory question for femaleness (most females will answer yes) but not a diagnostic one, because almost all males as well as most females will give the same answer. It is the latter type of question that is most similar to the Snyder–Swann questions. Diagnostic kinds of questions in the Snyder–Swann scenario for testing whether someone is an extrovert would be "Do you like to go to loud parties?" as opposed to the undiagnostic "What do you do to enliven parties?"

In addition, the hypotheses we test are often more specific than the alternatives, and in this case asking confirmatory questions is often a good strategy (Trope & Liberman, 1996). If you want to know whether a woman is a lawyer, asking whether she likes to argue (a feature associated with this category) will be helpful. If she answers yes, you have supporting evidence for your hypothesis that she is a lawyer, and if she answers no, you have tended to disconfirm the hypothesis; either answer is helpful. On the other hand, asking whether she is nurturant (a feature not associated with lawyers) provides some information if she answers yes (she is probably not a lawyer), but little information if she says no (she may be a lawyer, but she may also be a business executive or a stockbroker—other occupations that are not associated with nurturance).

Several investigators have tried to show that people are not immune to the charms of diagnostic information. When subjects are given questions that vary in diagnosticity, they show a clear preference for asking diagnostic questions, with a (sometimes small) residual tendency toward confirmation seeking (Devine, Hirt, & Gehrke, 1990; Trope & Bassok, 1982, 1983; Kruglanski & Mayseless, 1988; Skov & Sherman, 1986).

Furthermore, when people are asked to generate their own questions, the questions they ask are generally sensitive to contextual cues that affect diagnosticity. So, for example, in an experiment by Trope and Mackie (1987), subjects testing the hypothesis that a person was a professor formulated different questions when the alternative was a research scientist rather than a school teacher. In the former case, one might ask, "Do you grade papers?" because professors are more likely to do this than are research scientists. Such a question would not help in discriminating a professor from a teacher. For discriminating professors from school teachers, a question such as "Do you regularly read papers in scholarly journals?" would be more helpful. Note that both of these questions are confirmatory in the sense that a yes answer confirms the hypothesis that the person is a professor, and that they are differentially diagnostic for different comparisons.

What can we conclude? People have at least two cognitive impulses. The first is that they would rather confirm than disconfirm their hypotheses. The second is that they would like to find out the "truth" by seeking diagnostic information. Having said that, however, I must add that Snyder and Swann have alerted us to a major issue: People may not always be aware of the fact that some of their probes are unfair and undiagnostic. It is easy to imagine any of us asking questions that seem more diagnostic than they are. Asking a criminal, "Do you sometimes wish you had more money than you could legally earn?" seems reasonable enough but is not likely to tell us much about criminal proclivities, because most of us, criminal or noncriminal, would tend to answer this question yes. Put another way, diagnostic questions are those that discriminate the target from people in comparison groups or people in general. Remember base rates.

The Content of Questions. It is now well established (see Chapter 14) that different sorts of verbs imply different kinds of causality. For example, "James likes Marilyn" leads most people to assume that Marilyn is likeable rather than that James is a liking sort of guy, whereas "James helps Marilyn" leads most people to assume that James's helpful dispositions are more important than Marilyn's needy qualities. Gün Semin and his colleagues have extended this to the kinds of questions people ask and what we infer from the answers they produce. The problem is that some questions and their resultant answers may place the causal spotlight on the target rather than other people or the situation.

In a rape scenario, subjects asked questions that tended to focus causality on the person they thought was responsible (Semin & De Poot, 1997a). When they thought the rape victim was an untrustworthy witness, their questions tended to imply victim causality ("Did you dance with Peter that evening?"), whereas when they trusted the victim they tended to pick questions that implied the guilt of the male ("Did Peter dance with you that evening?"). The kinds of questions that people are asked tend to produce answers that confirm the causality implicit in the question. For example, when asked to think about occasions when they liked someone, subjects tended to produce narratives and explanations that implied the object of the liking was responsible, and when asked to think about occasions when they helped someone, the responses implied that the helper was responsible (Semin & De Poot, 1997b; Semin, Rubini, & Fiedler, 1995). Rubini and Kruglanski (1997) have further shown that subjects who are high in need for closure tend to use more abstract language in their questions (e.g., "Why is your favorite music appealing to you?" vs. "Why do you listen to your favorite music?"), which in turn tends to produce answers that implicate the person being questioned as the cause of the behavior. Not only are such effects likely to be important, but often both perceivers and targets will be unaware of the resultant biases.

Cutting Off the Information Supply. Our expectations can also dictate how much information we seek about others. If I talk to a woman I have just met about her children, I am unlikely to discover that she is a well-read expert on the Civil War. Unfortunately, information from others (especially in everyday interactions) does not come packaged in such a way that the most important or diagnostic material comes first, so biases can occur when we do not seek enough information. Imagine that you have a strong stereotype that women are especially likely to have skills and motives suiting them to a particular job. You are interviewing a female candidate. How much confirming evidence would you seek? Might you not be inclined to ask a question or two pertaining to each feature you care about, and then, as long as the information seems on target in terms of your stereotypic expectations, to move on quickly to the next set of questions? Basically the candidate's answers are satisfactory, and you make a mental note that she seems to fit the bill. The next candidate you interview is a male, and despite your desires to be fair, you have stereotype-based reservations about his feature set and how it fits the job. Might you not be inclined to seek more information from him, to follow up on his seemingly satisfactory answers with additional questions? You may genuinely not want to be biased to produce a negative outcome, but you sure want to be sure that you have the measure of this fellow? Trope and Thompson (1997) showed that people did tend to ask fewer questions of stereotyped than nonstereotyped targets, and that the questions they asked of stereotyped targets were more biased. Hattrup and Ford (1995) also found that people sought fewer items of individuating information about a target who was labeled in terms of a stereotypic category.

Stereotypes are, of course, not evaluation-neutral. We tend to seek more information about people for whom we have positive expectancies (Ybarra, Schaberg, & Keiper, 1999). Furthermore, we tend to avoid people for whom we have negative expectancies. The net result is that often we are able to get more information about those we like. Unfortunately, it may take more positive information to overcome a negative expectancy than negative information to overcome a positive one (Biernat & Kobrynowicz, 1997). So we need more information to disconfirm a negative stereotype, but are less likely to seek it or be in position to get it.

There is nothing essentially wrong about differential information seeking. In many contexts this is quite rational or at least efficient. How much information should I need to confirm my hypothesis that this particular Doberman pinscher is mean as compared to disconfirming it? Don't we require stronger proof that a well-established scientific hypothesis is wrong rather than right? This makes sense. To the extent that we strongly believe our hypotheses, whether based on conventional stereotypes or not, they should have the honor accorded to the tried and true. The opposite strategy, of constantly trying to disconfirm sensible hypotheses, would produce the occasional unconventional truth at the huge expense of countless hours of quixotic mental tilting at windmills.

Self-Confirming Prophecies

We have been focusing on cognitive biases associated with hypothesis testing, and we have more or less ignored the fact that most of the information we get about others comes from our interactions with them. Does this introduce additional complexities? Unfortunately, it does. The problem is that our hypotheses about a target person may also affect our behavior, leading the target to behave in ways that confirm the hypothesis. In other words, while we think we are observing "freely" performed behavior, in effect our own expectations have affected the target's behavior. When Jane suspects that Dan is hostile, she may well behave in hostile ways, which tend to produce hostile behavior from him. Such effects are termed "self-confirming prophecies" or "self-fulfilling prophecies," and they have been the subject of much research and speculation (Darley & Fazio, 1980; Dipboye, 1982; Hamilton, Sherman, & Ruvolo, 1990; Jones, 1977; Jussim, 1986; Jussim, Eccles, & Madon, 1996; Jussim & Fleming, 1996; Miller & Turnbull, 1986; Neuberg, 1996; Snyder, 1984).

TEACHER EXPECTANCIES

Although self-fulfilling prophecies have been recognized for centuries, the first major discussion in the social sciences was by the sociologist Robert Merton (1948, 1957): "The self-fulfilling prophecy is, in the beginning, a *false* definition of the situation evoking a new behavior which makes the originally false conception come true" (Merton, 1957, p. 423; emphasis in original).

Within psychology, the major stimulus was path-breaking work by Rosenthal and Jacobson (1968), which showed that teacher expectancies could affect student performance. Rosenthal and Jacobson gave a test of intellectual ability to elementary school students, and their teachers were told that this test measured the possibility that a student would "bloom" academically (in other words, spurt ahead in his or her achievement in the next year). Teachers were told that some of their children (about 29%, on average) were potential bloomers; this designation was random. The academic performance and intellectual abilities of these children and controls (who were not designated as bloomers) was subsequently measured. As expected, the students who were designated as bloomers did increase both their intellectual abilities and grades more than the controls, although these effects were mostly found for children in the lower grades. The effects, while not large, were fairly consistent. Although this work has been controversial (see Elashoff & Snow, 1971), it has been replicated in broad terms (e.g., Jussim, 1989; Meichenbaum, Bowers, & Ross, 1969; Zanna, Sheras, Cooper, & Shaw, 1975). Moreover, research done with actual classroom teacher expectancies based on socioeconomic status, race, and gender show small but consistent effects on student performance even when ability and prior performance are controlled for (Jussim, 1989; Jussim & Eccles, 1992; Madon, Jussim, & Eccles, 1997). Such effects have also been reliably found in work and organizational settings (McNatt, 2000). For obvious ethical reasons, experimental research has focused on positive expectations, the so-called "Pygmalion effect." However, in nonexperimental settings the reverse "Golem effect" (Babad, Inbar, & Rosenthal, 1982) can also occur, in which negative expectations create lower performance (see also Davidson & Eden, 2000).

SOME ADDITIONAL EXAMPLES

There are several classic experimental demonstrations of self-fulfilling prophecies outside the explicit teaching situation; I focus here on three. Snyder, Tanke, and Berscheid (1977) were interested in the fact that physically attractive people seem to have superior social skills (see Chapter 13), and wondered whether this could be produced through self-fulfilling prophecies. One could easily imagine that people expect handsome and beautiful individuals to excel at social tasks, and treat them in such a way that they come to do so. In this experiment, male subjects interacted with female subjects by using a phone hookup. The males were given photos of the females (which were actually of other women); some of these photos led the men to think they were interacting with an attractive partner, and the other half were led to believe that their partner was unattractive. The interactions between the men and women were recorded, and the tapes were submitted to naive judges who knew nothing of the manipulations. They judged that the females whose partners thought they were attractive were more friendly and socially skilled in the interview than those whose partners thought they were unattractive. There was no mystery as to how this occurred. The males who thought they had an attractive partner were friendlier to their partners. In particular their behavior was rated by independent raters as being more sociable, interesting, outgoing, humorous, and so forth. On the assumption that this sort of thing goes on over the course of a lifetime, it would not be hard to understand how attractive persons become socially skilled: Others "make" them so.

Self-fulfilling prophecies also work with gender and race. Skrypnek and Snyder (1982) found that men who thought they were interacting with men (regardless of the actual gender of the partner) produced behavior in their partners that was more masculine than did those who were interacting with partners they thought were women. In that regard, I reiterate a point made often throughout this book: Much of what we take to be the femininity of women and the masculinity of men is controlled to a large extent by social context, norms, and (in this case) the expectancies of interaction partners (Deaux & Major, 1987; see Chapter 11).

Word, Zanna, and Cooper (1974) demonstrated self-fulfilling prophecy effects for race. In an initial study, white subjects interviewed black and white confederates of the experimenter who had been instructed to behave in a standard way to all interviewers. Several nonverbal behaviors were measured, and a general index of "immediacy" (a sort of friendliness measure made up of variables such as how close the interviewer sat to the interviewee, eye contact, etc.) showed that the white interviewers were less friendly to the blacks than to the whites. In a second study, real subjects were interviewed by interviewers who were trained to behave in the immediate or nonimmediate behavioral styles found in the previous study. Independent judges rated the performance of the interviewees, and rated the performance of those inter-viewed in the more immediate style as better than the performance of those inter-viewed in the less friendly style. Although this study only shows that such effects can occur in similar situations in the real world, and not that they routinely do, the re-sults certainly give one pause. Imagine a black woman who shows up for a job inter-view and is treated in a cool and distant way. She may be quite nervous to begin with because of fears of discrimination and racism (or just because she, like most people, is nervous in an interview situation), and she might well respond to the cool treat-ment with stilted behavior that does not produce a good impression. Her white coun-terpart, who is treated more warmly, quickly relaxes and makes a good impression. The result is that the white candidate is hired for what seems to be the most legiti-mate of reasons; she did, after all, make a much better impression in the interview.

This is the sort of thing of which great social mischief is made. Members of mi-nority groups may enter a wide range of social situations involving members of the majority culture as hesitant and unconfident, and they may be greeted in a less than welcoming way. Alternatively, they may be greeted with exaggerated expressions of welcome and warmth, which are quickly perceived as fraudulent and which may pro-duce the same end result of making the minority perceivers feel uncomfortable and unwanted. The members of white majorities may not be aware that they are behaving coolly (or too effusively), and they may deny (and do so with great passion) that they treat whites and members of minority groups differently. For their part, minority tar-gets may only have a vague sense that they are not welcome, but may not be able to identify the particular cues they are picking up in the situation. Thus, because so much of what goes on in the interaction cannot easily be articulated, misunderstand-ings can easily arise.

THE STEPS IN SELF-CONFIRMING PROPHECIES

Self-confirming prophecies don't just happen, and there are several steps in the whole process of how they develop. As Darley and Fazio (1980) have argued, the fol-lowing must occur. First, the perceiver must have some initial hypothesis about the target. Second, the perceiver must behave toward the target in a way that is guided by this hypothesis or expectation. Third, this perceiver behavior must be noticed and in-terpreted by the target, which, fourth, affects the target's behavior. Fifth, the perceiver must note and interpret this target behavior. Although this normally com-pletes the sequence, it may also sometimes be useful to add a sixth step—namely, the target person's interpreting his or her own behavior toward the perceiver. Let us con-sider each of these stages in turn.

Generating the Hypothesis. We have already discussed the various ways that perceiver hypotheses may arise. Obviously, they may come from past experience with the tar-get, from hearsay about the target, or from category-based expectancies. It is the third case that is most relevant to stereotypes, because often the expectancies we have about people are based on their group memberships. Although a certain amount of distaste attends such expectancies, especially negative ones that spring from racial and gender categories, in fact we use them all the time. I expect that my students will be polite (indeed, more polite than the average person) when in my of-fice, and I can safely assume that they will be willing to talk about the classes they are taking if we run out of other topics of conversation. I feel safe in talking about upcoming contests with members of our athletic teams, and I'm probably more likely to initiate conversation about sports with male than with female students.

Directing Behavior. Expectancies do not direct behavior in any straightforward way. One major reason is that expectancies interact with goals in various ways. One important distinction is between those behaviors that terminate interactions with targets and those that continue such interactions (Darley & Fazio, 1980). Often our negative expectancies lead us to avoid targets, whereas we tend to seek contact with those for whom we have more positive expectancies. Usually I try to avoid people I think will be hostile, angry, or depressed—a tendency Newcomb (1947) called "autistic distortion." People who choose to terminate an interaction with a stigmatized other tend to form more negative impressions of that person than do people who choose to continue, in part because such impressions justify the decision (Ruscher & Hammer, 1996).

Suppose Jason has come to believe that his boss is a hostile sort of guy. Although he can't avoid his boss on the job, he might well deflect overtures from the boss for social encounters—he never "has the time" to go for a drink or to lunch with his boss—and in this circumstance Jason denies himself the opportunity to discover that the boss is really a nice person who reacts to job pressures in an unfortunate way. Obviously, this is a vicious cycle. Lack of knowledge about people leads to anxiety-based avoidance, which reinforces ignorance and does not allay anxiety. White people, especially those who want to avoid interracial conflict, do avoid contact with black people (Plant & Devine, 2003; Towles-Schwen & Fazio, 2003). Such avoidance behavior is not always due to hatred, hostility, or prejudice, as that term is usually understood. Sometimes it just reflects discomfort or uncertainty about how to behave. This is why people with terminal illness or those who have suffered family tragedies find that others tend to avoid them. In interview situations, interviewers spend less time with persons who have physical disabilities (Kleck, Ono, & Hastorf, 1966) and sit less close to those they think have epilepsy (Kleck et al., 1968). In public places, people avoid sitting near those with facial scars (Houston & Bull, 1994) and stand further away from them (Rumsey, Bull, & Gahagan, 1982). College students speak less with people they think are depressed (Elliott, MacNair, Herrick, Yoder, & Byrne, 1991) and behave more negatively toward a person they think is being seen in the counseling center for problems (Sibicky & Dovidio, 1986).

However, even in cases where beliefs do not lead to avoidance, translating of expectancies into behavior is not a simple matter. Behavior is not always consistent with expectations. For example, sometimes we are aware of our expectancies, and we bend over backwards to try to avoid acting on them. It is not a trivial matter to correct cognitively (and behaviorally) for what Wilson and Brekke (1994) have called "mental contamination." Teachers who know that they do not like black students may try to compensate for this prejudice cognitively and then behaviorally by paying more attention to their black students or trying to act in a friendlier way to them. Such correction strategies take cognitive resources, as well as some acting and self-presentational skills.

The perceiver's beliefs and values undoubtedly play a major role in the expectation-to-behavior link. Perceivers who value equality and fair play may bend over backwards (but not inevitably successfully) to conceal their expectations from the target.

Perceivers also have beliefs that may affect how their expectations translate into behavior. For example, the coach who thinks that John is a talented but lazy basketball player may think that yelling at John will motivate him, whereas a different coach might have the sense that John needs to be handled with kid gloves—that his laziness stems from a lack of confidence that would be destroyed by excessive negative feedback. Swann and Snyder (1980) showed that undergraduates role-playing teaching spent more time with those "pupils" they believed to have high ability when they had a theory that teachers should direct student behavior. However, those "teachers" who had the theory that students with high ability should be allowed to develop their skills on their own spent less time with the "high-ability pupils." Both theories have validity in different circumstances, but in this study those "teachers" with the intrinsic theory did their "students" a disservice by paying less attention to them, because the ones expected to do well actually performed less well than the ones they expected to perform poorly.

Motives of the perceiver and target can also affect confirmation processes. Neuberg (1996) has argued that perceivers have goals concerning both what information they hope to acquire about the target and how they want the target to perceive them—a self-presentational goal.[3] Sometimes perceivers are highly motivated to gain an accurate impression of the target, and we might then expect that they would also try, as best they can, to avoid biasing what the target says or does. Neuberg (1989) found that perceivers without experiment-induced goals treated targets for whom they had negative expectancies in negative ways that produced negative impressions, but those with a strong motivation to be accurate did not. On the other hand, when perceivers have a goal to make the target like them, they actually produce behavior that disconfirms their negative expectancy (Neuberg, Judice, Virdin, & Carrillo, 1993).

Mark Snyder (1992) has argued that people can enter interactions with many different goals, but among the most important are the desire to facilitate a smooth interaction and the desire to form a clear impression of the other person. Generally, when perceivers are motivated to explain targets and predict their behavior, they are more likely to get confirming behavior for their hypotheses than when they are primarily motivated to produce a smooth interaction (Copeland & Snyder, 1995; Snyder & Haugen, 1994). Presumably the need to form a stable impression of the target leads perceivers to be somewhat more directive in their interaction styles. When facing such a directive perceiver, targets who are motivated to have a smooth interaction produce behavior that is more hypothesis-confirming than those who are motivated to form impressions of the perceiver, presumably because the former are more motivated to be accommodating (Snyder & Haugen, 1995). Power is often an important mediator of many scenes from everyday life. A perceiver who is more powerful than a target not only may rely more on his or her expectations, but may have greater abilities to direct the target to conform to them (Claire & Fiske, 1998; Copeland, 1994).

There has been a considerable body of research on how expectancies are communicated to targets, and much of this work has come from studies on teacher expectancy effects. One advantage of working in this domain is that either real or simulated teaching is a natural activity that lends itself well to behavioral analysis. A review by Harris and Rosenthal (1985) has identified several variables that mediate the effects. When people are given positive expectancies about targets (typically real or simulated students for most of these studies), they both praise more and criticize the students less, initiate more contacts, ask more questions, create a warmer climate, present more and more difficult material, accept more of the students' ideas, maintain more eye contact, and ignore the students less. Moreover, many (but not all) of these types of variables have been shown to actually affect student achievement—a necessary condition for self-fulfilling prophecy effects. Such effects are not restricted to teachers. For example, elementary school children who thought that their partners were likely to show symptoms of an attention disorder were less friendly and talked to them less often (Harris, Milich, Corbitt, Hoover, & Brady, 1992; Harris, Milich, Johnston, & Hoover, 1990).

The Response of the Target. Let's imagine an interaction between a black woman named Tanya and a white perceiver named Peter. From Tanya's perspective, she has seen Peter behave in a way she interprets as hostile.[4] Tanya may ignore Peter's behavior, but she is also more than likely to do some attributional work in trying to figure out why he is so hostile. She basically has four attributional choices. First, she may assume that the behavior reflected Peter's dispositions (i.e., Peter was hostile because he is a hostile person). Second, Tanya may assume that Peter, the perceiver, was reacting to various situational forces, and may further realize that she was a part of this situation; that is, Peter's hostile behavior may be attributed in part to Tanya herself. However, common observation suggests that this sort of attribution is part of a psychologist's fantasy; people are not good at seeing themselves as part of the mental outlook of another. Third, Tanya may assume that Peter was responding to one of a number of more or less transitory situational forces (e.g., he had just arrived from a bad day at the office). Finally, most interestingly and most importantly for present purposes, Tanya may form a person–situation interaction attribution. It is not that the Peter is a generally hostile person or that Tanya in particular has induced this hostility. He has behaved this way because of the kind of a person Tanya is. He is hostile toward blacks (women, aggressive women, etc.). Although this class of attributions has not been much discussed in the literature, it is surely a common and important class in everyday life, especially in the area of stereotyping. Bigots are not generally accused of being generally hateful, but rather hateful toward a particular category of person—and, in a more refined analysis, a particular kind of person acting in particular ways (e.g., a minority woman asserting her legal rights). So Tanya comes to feel that Peter dislikes black women rather than to assume that he is dispositionally hostile. Victims of stereotyping and prejudice do sometimes, of course, make dispositional attributions to such people. We may, for example, assume that racists have deep-seated personality problems or are generally hateful and grumpy, but the fact remains that the fundamental attribution we make is likely to be a person–perceiver interaction of a person who hates particular categories of people. In any case, whatever her attribution, Tanya's reaction will be heavily influenced by what she sees as the causes of Peter's nasty behavior.

The translation of these interpretations and perceptions of the perceiver's behavior into responses by the target is tricky and often unpredictable. Certainly the most obvious kind of response is one in kind. Tanya assumes that Peter is being hostile because he's a bigot; she hates bigots; and so she feels justified in giving Peter a metaphorical finger salute. But not all behaviors are so isomorphic. For example, one perfectly legitimate response to hostility is withdrawal rather than return hostility. Alternatively, Tanya might even be super-nice to hostile Peter, either because she wants to capture the moral high ground or because she has discovered that it leads to more effective outcomes.[5] It generally makes most sense to assume that targets will try to disconfirm negative expectancies by the perceiver. But they may not always care to do so, know how to disconfirm the expectancy, or have the ability to pull it off.

Targets are not passive statues in all this, and a great deal depends on their motives. For one thing, they may favor perceivers who share their self-views—a process Swann (1996) calls "self-verification." Such self-verification motives may also play a role in how perceiver expectancies produce their effects (Madon, Smith, et al., 2001). Of course, even when targets do not select the people who perceive and evaluate them, they may present themselves in a way that confirms perceiver expectancies. Such confirmatory behavior may make interactions less stressful or lead to being hired or promoted in a job situation. Zanna and Pack (1975) asked female subjects to describe themselves to a male partner who was either attractive and desirable (e.g., no girlfriend) or less attractive and desirable, and this partner indicated that his ideal woman either fit the traditional female stereotype or was closer to the feminist ideal. When the partner was attractive, the women described themselves in line with his ideals (e.g., more traditional when he valued the traditional woman), but when he was unattractive, their self-presentations were little affected by his values. In a corresponding study von Baeyer, Sherk, and Zanna (1981) showed that female job applicants dressed more traditionally when their interviewer was known to value the "traditional" woman. Male subjects also alter their self-presentations to match their assumptions about what females want to hear when the females are desirable (Morier & Seroy, 1994). Both men and women dress in certain ways to make themselves attractive to others, people selectively present themselves in job interviews and at parties, and they do all this in a way that they think will win them approval of a desirable audience or people who have power over their lives. Thus it should come as no surprise to anyone, especially social psychologists, that we all sometimes behave in ways that confirm the expectations of others.

Obviously, we may want to confirm others' expectations of us on occasion, but there are bound to be other times when targets are highly motivated to disconfirm an expectancy (Bond, 1972; Hilton & Darley, 1985; Ickes, Patterson, Rajecki, & Tanford, 1982; Judice & Neuberg, 1998). For example, when I advise freshmen during orientation week, I expect them to be nervous about interacting with a professor, and I work hard to make sure that they leave our interaction feeling more relaxed and sure of themselves. Coaches have been known to employ "reverse psychology" by telling certain players that they are clearly not up to the coaches' standards and probably can never be. Obviously, some players wilt under this expectation, while others work hard trying to prove their stuff. The point is that targets do not automatically respond to their interpretations of perceiver behavior with congruent behavior of their own. As one demonstration, Zebrowitz, Andreoletti, Collins, Lee, and Blumenthal (1998) found that baby-faced (young-looking) teenage boys had higher academic performance than their more mature-faced peers, arguably as a reaction to the stereotype that young-looking people are intellectually weak. All was not positive, however, because baby-faced boys of low socioeconomic status were more likely than their peers to have delinquent careers—a possible reaction to the stereotype that such boys are warm and nurturant.

Interpreting Target Behavior. In one sense, once the target has responded with behavior (say, hostile behavior), the cycle is complete. But it is useful to consider the final step, which is how the perceiver interprets the target's behavior. After all, the target may not respond in kind. The perceiver makes an insulting comment, and the target responds with coolness or with sarcasm. This could be seen as hostility, as "cheek," or as a lack of politeness. For the hypothesis to be fully confirmed in the mind of the perceiver, the target must exhibit behavior that the perceiver interprets to be consistent with the hypothesis. Obviously, much of what I have said earlier about the importance of interpretation applies here.

THE POWER OF SELF-FULFILLING PROPHECIES

Self-fulfilling prophecies do exist, and each of us can probably think of many instructive examples we have witnessed or been a part of. Nonetheless, we must be cautious in assuming that such effects are ubiquitous. There is plenty of room for the sequence to get sidetracked. Relevant expectancies may be weak or ambivalent and may not be translated into behavior effectively. Relevant behaviors may be misinterpreted. The target may decide not to respond to the perceiver's behavior in a congruent way.

There is another, more tricky issue involved. Self-fulfilling prophecies, by definition, depend on the creation of congruent behaviors based on *false* expectations and hypotheses. That is, the perceiver who incorrectly assumes that the target is hostile or lazy may create confirming behaviors through his or her behavior. However, if the target really is hostile or lazy, then an interaction sequence that results in the target's behaving in a hostile or lazy manner is really not surprising and may have little or nothing to do with the expectancies of the perceiver. In other words, although accurate expectancies may have their own roles to play in social interactions, they cannot, by definition, lead to self-confirming prophecies.

In everyday life, it is usually hard to separate the effects of accurate expectations from those that are less rooted in reality. However, there is an arena where more or less satisfactory tests exist; this is the arena of intellectual and academic ability, both of which can be measured precisely if not necessarily objectively. There are reasonably high correlations between teachers' academic expectations for their students and the students' actual performance (Jussim, 1991). There are, however, two reasons (not mutually exclusive) why that may occur. First, teachers may have expectations that are totally unrelated to student abilities; these expectancies may be based on various cues (race, socioeconomic status, appearance, etc.) and may then affect performance. In other words, students may tend to live up to or work down to their teachers' expectations, and hence the correlation between expectation and performance is an example of a stereotype-caused self-fulfilling prophecy. Another possibility is that student performance is affected by a host of background factors (such as native intelligence or parental encouragement), and since teachers are neither stupid nor unobservant, their expectancies may reflect those same variables. Commonly, for example, a teacher who knows that a student has done well in the previous year's work will expect that student to continue to do well, and that expectation will normally be quite accurate. In this case, both future performance and teacher expectancies are based on the same background information. The teacher's expectancies are then partially or wholly valid, and hence any correlation between teacher expectancies and future student performance reflects reality. This has been diagrammed in

Figure 6.1, adapted from Jussim (1991). The usual self-fulfilling prophecy diagram is represented by Paths B and C. That is, background information leads to expectancies, which in turn give rise to target behavior. Path A, from background information to the target's behavior, represents the accuracy path. The question is whether the indirect paths, B and C can be explained through A. In a careful analysis of several studies, Jussim concludes that often they can be. In fact, once one takes account of the accuracy component, there is sometimes little left to be explained by self-fulfilling prophecies.

Several studies by Lee Jussim and his colleagues (Jussim, 1989; Jussim & Eccles, 1992, 1995; Madon et al., 1997, 1998; Smith et al., 1998) have examined the relative contributions of accuracy and stereotypic expectations to student performance. Although the results are quite complex, several conclusions may be drawn (see Jussim, Eccles, & Madon, 1996, for the most extensive summary). First, teachers do have expectations for their students, but these expectations are quite accurate in the sense that they reflect judgments of students' past behavior, abilities, and effort (see also Trouilloud, Sarrazin, Martinek, & Guillet, 2002). After these accuracy effects are partialed out, stereotypic expectations based on gender, race, and socioeconomic status have small effects. However, teacher expectations do have effects on some students. These effects are strongest for girls, African Americans, and children from lower-socioeconomic-status backgrounds. Although the reasons for this are not entirely clear, perhaps the greater power of teacher expectancies for such children results from the lower self-confidence that the children may bring to the school environment or from stereotype threat. Interestingly, although expectancy effects on student performance are fairly small, they tend to be persistent. In one study, teacher expectations in 7th grade (corrected for accuracy) continued to predict student achievement through the 12th grade, although the effects dissipated somewhat over time (A. E. Smith, Jussim, & Eccles, 1999).

Jussim's research does not suggest that self-confirming prophecies are never important, and they may well be for some domains under certain circumstances. Job interviews (Dipboye, 1982, 1985, 1992) provide especially fertile grounds for such effects to manifest themselves. I suspect that those people who are easily stereotyped by virtue of their physical appearance not only have the burden of direct stereotyping, but also are more likely to be victims of such self-confirming prophecies. For ex-

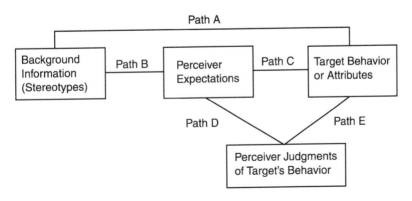

FIGURE 6.1. Conceptual paths in demonstrating teacher expectancy effects. From Jussim (1991). Copyright 1991 by the American Psychological Association. Adapted by permission.

ample, in one study (Miller, Rothblum, Barbour, Brand, & Felicio, 1990), obese women were rated as having lower social skills and as being less likeable by people who did not see them and did not know their weight status. It is obviously possible that obese women are born with lesser social skills, but a far more probable explanation is that they are not given the opportunities to develop social skills because of lessened opportunities for satisfactory social interactions. Another possibility is that obese women may attribute their bad experiences to their weight and do not use their social skills in an effective way (Miller, Rothblum, Felicio, & Brand, 1995).

Some traits and dispositions may be more prone to self-confirming prophecy effects than others. For instance, traits such as hostility (Snyder & Swann, 1978a) may produce stronger effects than behaviors that are more affected by abilities, such as math performance. In that regard, it is instructive to note that whereas teachers generally are quite accurate in their assessments of math ability among boys and girls (correctly perceiving little difference), they tend to overestimate the amount of effort for girls relative to boys (Madon et al., 1998).

Jussim is almost certainly correct that social scientists have overemphasized inaccuracies produced by self-confirming prophecies, but the latter do occur and can be important when they do. Theoretically, self-fulfilling prophecies are important in part because they speak to the important kernel-of-truth controversy (see Chapters 1 and 9). Most people who hold stereotypes feel they have adequate evidence to support them (at least as broad generalizations), and the work on self-confirming prophecies suggests they may well be correct (at least in the limited sense that they help create that reality). Thus, from this perspective, the flaws in stereotypes are not so much cognitive as behavioral. More precisely, they may lie in the failure to recognize how much one's own behavior affects the behavior of others—a point made over 50 years ago by Robert Merton (1948).

Testing Hypotheses about Group Membership

As mentioned earlier, one of the most important types of hypotheses that we entertain and test on a day-to-day basis concerns group membership. We have been somewhat deflected from the importance of this by the focus of prior stereotyping research on race and gender—two forms of categorization that normally do not produce problems. However, there are many forms of classification that do not have such readily apparent cues.

The Diagnosticity of Cues

Often we are perfectly aware that we are searching for cues to group membership. I live close to an area of Houston that has a large gay and lesbian population, and when visiting bars and restaurants in that area, people will sometimes wonder aloud whether their waiter is gay. I have friends who may or may not be Jewish, and I sometimes ask myself whether or not they are. Such wonderings often seem tinged with a bit of prejudice. "Why do you care whether he's gay or not?" is a question sometimes asked in this context, and there may even be little voices in our heads that ask similar questions. But the answer is not hard to find. If group categories mean anything at all, then they must indicate that members of those group have at least some traits in common, some shared experiences, or (at a minimum), some characteristics that

tend to distinguish them from others. At one level, it is no more threatening to wonder whether someone is Jewish than to ask whether a particular car is a Ford or a
Chevy. Unfortunately, sometimes often such questions are preludes to unjustified or
prejudiced responses.

It is also worth noting (as I have done in Chapter 3) that we categorize people
continually and that we do so on the basis of relevant cues. When I walk in my neighborhood late at night, I might rightfully be concerned with whether that man approaching me is likely to be a person who wants to do me harm. When I enter an unfamiliar office, I want to distinguish receptionists from the people whose offices are
being guarded, just as when I enter a restaurant, I need to know who serves and who
is served. Indeed, these often petty acts of categorization are so frequent and done so
automatically (or at least nonconsciously) that we can easily forget how important
they are. This does not mean, however, that such acts are inconsequential. They are
not. Given the importance of categorization cues (what in Chapter 3 I have called
"identifying cues"), it is striking how little research has been done to ferret them out.
A good head start suggests that stereotypic (or ascribed) cues are used as highly diagnostic (Diehl & Jonas, 1991), even though there is in principle a distinction (see
Chapter 3) between identifying cues [high p(category/feature)] and ascribed cues
[high p(feature/category)].

Recognition Research

RECOGNITION OF JEWS

Much of the research in this area deals with the issue of whether people can recognize Jews from physical appearance cues—admittedly a topic of more relevance a half-
century ago than now. In the first experimental study in this area, Allport and
Kramer (1946) gave subjects a series of pictures of Jewish and non-Jewish individuals
and asked them to indicate which were Jewish. The most interesting finding was that
the subjects who were anti-Semitic were more accurate in this task than the less prejudiced subjects. Lindzey and Rogolsky (1950) replicated this basic effect, and they suggested that prejudiced individuals probably feel threatened by the objects of their
prejudice and hence are likely to be particularly vigilant for cues that identify such
people.

However, before we grant bigots the virtues of accuracy, we need to consider an
important confounding variable. In particular, prejudiced subjects also identified
more pictures as Jewish (Lindzey & Rogolsky, 1950), and as Elliott and Wittenberg
(1955) pointed out, this "response bias" might easily have accounted for the results.
A crude example should make clear how this might happen. Suppose Mary, a research subject, sees an array of 50 Jewish and 50 non-Jewish faces. If she guesses randomly that half the faces she sees are Jewish, she will, on average, correctly identify
50% of the Jewish faces as Jewish. At the other extreme, if she guesses that all the
faces are Jewish, she will be correct in her identification of Jewish faces 100% of the
time! Obviously, she will also be 100% incorrect in identifying non-Jewish faces, but
that is not the variable being measured. Naturally, most subjects do not show such an
extreme bias, but "overguessing" Jewish faces is still likely to produce greater "accuracy" for identification of such faces.

In general, there is a fairly robust finding that prejudiced people do overidentify

Jewish faces, and that this accounts in large part for their greater accuracy (e.g., Himmelfarb, 1966; Scodel & Austrin, 1957). One probable cause for this has been labeled the "ingroup overexclusion effect" (Leyens & Yzerbyt, 1992). Having negative members of one's own group is threatening, and so one wants to have abundant positive information before deciding to include them. As a result of a high criterion for inclusion into the ingroup, the outgroup will necessarily be "oversubscribed," and people will make more errors in not including legitimate members of the ingroup (Capozza, Dazzi, & Minto, 1996; Yzerbyt, Leyens, & Bellour, 1995).

Such overexclusion effects are important in other areas. Consider the following possibility. Jim, an airport security guard, is convinced that all terrorists are Arab-appearing; he stops every person he thinks might be an Arab and finds that some percentage of them (say, 0.1%) are actually carrying items that could become weapons. His superiors, satisfied that he has averted several airline hijackings, shower him with awards and promotions. Yes, Jim has accurately identified potential terrorists, so what's the problem? Aside from violating the dignity of many people because of their appearance, he may also have failed to detect terrorists who do not appear to be Arabs. He may not worry about all the false positives (harmless Arabs), but we should worry about the false negatives (terrorists he doesn't catch). Police use of racial profiling is often justified in terms of the same logic: "Look how successful it is in catching bad guys!" It is worth remembering that all this represents another example of failures to incorporate base rate information in our calculations (see the discussion earlier in this chapter).

OTHER GROUPS

I have picked the Jewish example because there is a fair amount of relevant research, and because the results are instructive. In everyday life, we work at identifying whether people are members of other groups as well. For example, whites who are racially prejudiced may be especially motivated to classify people whose facial cues are not clear indicators of their race (Blascovich, Wyer, Swart, & Kibler, 1997). Other questions may also arise. Is that woman who has a masculine walk lesbian?[6] Is the man trying the neighbor's back door a criminal or a workman? Though many of us provide abundant cues for our category memberships (indeed, may emphasize them though dress and emblems), many category memberships are deliberately hidden or not advertised. It is not only gay males who remain in the closet. So do most violence-prone men and other people with hidden agendas. Generally there has been little research addressed to how we identify such people, but such questions are theoretically important and often practically significant.

SUMMARY

Stereotypes are not passively acquired and they do not sit around waiting for work. Obviously, they actively guide the ways we interpret and remember the behavior of others (see Chapter 4), but they also affect our behavior toward others and thus indirectly also affect the kinds of information we gain about them.

Most people, most of the time, recognize that most stereotype features are far from universally true of members of stereotyped groups. Thus, we often understand that features are only probabilistically attached to particular groups. So we enter our interactions with others having suspicions, hunches, or hypotheses that they will have certain features. Sometimes we test those hypotheses quite directly, but most of the time their effects are more indirect. Whether or not we are directly testing a hypothesis about other people, our stereotypes will affect what we find out about them.

Stereotypes would not cause the kinds of social mischief and hurt they do if these hypotheses were held in check until unambiguously confirmed for a particular individual. Unfortunately, research on hypothesis testing suggests that people generally do not test them optimally. More importantly, we generally prefer our hypotheses to be confirmed rather than disconfirmed, and we sometimes test them in ways that favor the former outcome. More insidiously, however, our stereotypes may lead us to behave in certain ways toward others that affect their behavior. In particular, we may create self-confirming prophecies—situations in which our hypotheses affect our behavior that lead others to behave in ways that confirm the hypotheses.

Biased hypothesis testing is one of the reasons that we are prone to believe our stereotypes are accurate, and this perceived accuracy not only has direct implications for discrimination and other behaviors toward others but may also reinforce our tendencies to confirm existing stereotypes.

Notes

1. There is another, more elaborate version comparing the odds of two different groups having a trait. Although the "odds" version is generally more useful for research purposes, it need not be spelled out here.
2. Indeed, Klayman (Klayman, 1995; Klayman & Ha, 1987) prefers to use the term "positive hypothesis testing" to refer to the preference for seeking information we expect, whereas "confirmation bias" should refer to the more general tendency to hold on to a current hypothesis. This linguistic distinction makes sense, but the use of "confirmation bias" to refer to seeking confirming evidence is now firmly entrenched.
3. One striking example occurs when attorneys question potential jurors during what is called *voir dire*. An attorney is trying to determine whether a juror will be sympathetic to the attorney's side of the case, but also trying to convey an impression that he or she personally is competent, friendly, and nice. It is not always easy to pull this off, especially when the questions imply that the juror might be biased or unfair. *Voir dire* is tricky business and fascinating to behold when done by a pro.
4. It is an irony of sorts that in discussing interracial interactions, most social psychologists (who are white) tend to discuss the interaction from the standpoint of how the white's behavior affects the black. Whites are participants and blacks objects in most renditions (Shelton, 2000). This perspective not only reflects the attempts of whites to understand their own behavior, but implicitly takes the position that blacks are victims of white behavior. Novelist Ralph Ellison has commented that social scientists tend to view blacks as "nothing more than reactions to oppression" (quoted in Jones et al., 1984, p. 180). I have no particular moral or political point to stress, but there is an important psychological point: We neglect to consider the obvious fact that the black person also enters the interaction with expectations about the white person, which contribute to the resulting mischief. Furthermore, when whites interact with members of minority groups, they may be quite aware of "metastereotypes"—minority group stereotypes of whites (Vorauer, Hunter, Main, & Roy, 2000)—which may in turn affect the quality of interracial interaction (Vorauer, Main, & O'Connell, 1998).

5. People in low-power situations often discover that this is an effective tactic. A sales clerk who is extremely nice to an obnoxious customer may get the sale after all, and a member of a minority group may find that responding to the hostility of bigots is effective not only in the pragmatic sense of making the interaction more pleasant, but also in helping to disconfirm stereotypes. Sometimes relatively powerless people also wish to make the moral point that they are unwilling to stoop to the same kinds of hostile behavior that more powerful persons engage in nonreflectively. Of course, as millions of patient members of such groups have discovered, there are "downsides" to this strategy; one potential negative consequence is the perception by more powerful people that members of less privileged groups are weak.

6. As I wrote the first draft of this chapter, my local newspaper ("Falwell thinks," 1999) reported evangelist Jerry Falwell's warning to parents that Tinky Winky, one of the Teletubbies, is probably homosexual because he carries a purse (which the inventors say is a magic bag), is purple (the gay pride color), and has a triangle-shaped antenna (a triangle being the gay pride symbol). Talk about your diagnostic cues!

CHAPTER 7

Ingroups and Outgroups

THE IMPORTANCE OF GROUPS

The Social Dimension

Up to this point, I have emphasized purely cognitive approaches to stereotypes and stereotyping. I need make no apology for this emphasis—after all, whatever else they may be, stereotypes are products of our cognitive activity. But it is time to recognize an insistent reality: Stereotypes are also social products. There are three important points to make in this regard.

Obviously, stereotypes are products of cultures, but this vague statement leaves open issues of what the relationship of culture and stereotypes is. Social scientists have generally assumed that our culture serves up the content of our stereotypes, and that we as individuals digest cultural lessons whole. But cultures also dictate, to some extent, what social categories and groups are recipients of these stereotypes. It is surely no accident that Americans are more likely to stereotype African Americans than German Americans, or that the French have stronger stereotypes of Algerians than of the Dutch. We stereotype redheads and blonds, but not those with brown hair. Americans have stronger age-related stereotypes than most countries, but tend to mute those based on religion, whereas in other countries it is the reverse. The impact of cultural, social, and historical forces on stereotyping is discussed in Chapter 9.

Some of our stereotypes are fiercely held and accompanied by strong feelings, whereas others seem devoid of emotion. I happen to think that basset hounds are ugly and stupid, but I would not be prepared to enter into long and passionate debate with a basset hound owner about my stereotype. However, my stereotypes about Texas and Houston have a warmer emotional temperature, and stereotypes about my university and profession seem downright hot.

It is unlikely that this affect is produced purely through cognitive mechanisms, and we need to account for the affect or emotion that accompanies some stereotypes but not others. More importantly, since this affect is a sibling if not quite a twin of prejudice, we need to consider the whens and whys of how our stereotypes create and support prejudice. This is done in some detail in Chapter 8.

Third, stereotypes often seem to be integrally related to our group memberships and with conflict between groups. We seem to have stronger and more negative stereotypes about groups to which we do not belong than to those to which we do. This is the topic of the present chapter.

Ethnocentrism

"Ethnocentrism" is a tendency to favor one's own group and to derogate other groups. Such derogation has been a constant feature of recorded history. The Old Testament is filled with references to the Hebrews as chosen people, and other groups usually do not get such great reviews. The ancient Greeks used the word "barbarian" to refer to those who did not speak the Greek language, and even within Greece itself there were fierce rivalries between city-states. The present ethnic and religious wars in the former Yugoslavia, and conflicts in the Middle East and Northern Ireland, have histories that go back centuries; Asian and African societies have their own violent legacies. It is probably no exaggeration to suggest that derogation of outgroups is one of the most fundamental and universal features of all societies and cultures.

In extreme cases, hostility toward outgroups can result in fighting and death, but there are more subtle and pervasive effects. For example, even the connotations of words reflect this ingroup favoritism. A series of experiments by Perdue, Dovidio, Gurtman, and Tyler (1990) showed that nonsense syllables associated with words such as "we," "our," and "us" were rated as more positive than syllables associated with the words "they," "them," and "their." Presentation of ingroup words also increased the speed of judging how positive traits were, and outgroup words facilitated ratings of negative words. This facilitation suggests again that ingroup words have a strong positive valence and that outgroup words are negative.

Is Outgroup Derogation Natural?

SUMNER'S VIEW

William Graham Sumner (1907), a pioneer American sociologist as well as a popular and influential teacher at Yale University, viewed the derogation of outgroups as natural. He was also a cheerleader for social Darwinism in the form enunciated by Herbert Spencer. Spencer (1892–1893) had argued that human behavior is governed by a "code of amity" (positive feelings and behaviors toward those in one's own group) and a "code of enmity" (negative reactions to others not in this group). Sumner, in his turn, invented the terminology of "ingroup" (which he also called the "we-group") and "outgroup" ("other-group"); he thought that hostility toward the outgroup fosters loyalty to the ingroup as well as adherence to the folkways (norms) of that group. In other words, conflict with other groups not only naturally heightens negative feelings toward the outgroup, but strengthens ingroup loyalties and feelings as well. Sumner also coined the term "ethnocentrism" to describe the tendency to measure the appropriateness of behavior in terms of one's own cultural standards, and to derogate the behavior and artifacts of other groups precisely because they are not those of the ingroup.

Although Sumner's strong suit was never well-developed, logically derived theory, the whole tenor of his argument suggests that such tendencies are largely innate or otherwise dictated by laws of nature. Sumner felt that attachment to groups is necessary for human survival and that division into competing groups is a natural part of social life. He was of a generation, influenced by the then-new theory of evolution, which saw such tendencies as closely linked to basic biological processes (then construed as instincts). Furthermore, it came easily to such people to argue in functionalist terms; in this case, they viewed adherence to one's own group as generally functional for group and individual survival.

SOCIOBIOLOGY AND EVOLUTION

Biologically based arguments about social behavior faded from center stage by the 1930s because they became bloated and vacuous. They also lent themselves easily to various forms of racism, and consequently they are still held in low esteem by contemporary social scientists. And yet, when something is as seemingly ubiquitous as ingroup favoritism, one might at least entertain the idea of some sort of biological basis.

In recent years, sociobiologists and evolutionary psychologists (see Buss, 1999) have accepted that challenge. There are a variety of arguments to be made, but the basic line is that within almost any animal species, genetic predispositions that favor closely related individuals and engender hostility to those not as closely related can serve useful functions for individual and species survival. Aggression toward conspecifics is virtually universal among higher species (certainly mammals). However, among the millions of species on earth, only humans and chimpanzees form groups to commit violence against their own kind (Wrangman & Peterson, 1996). Intergroup competition and aggression help select for physical and mental abilities, and intragroup altruism helps to keep relatives alive long enough to breed and to preserve whatever genes there are for altruism at the group level (Melotti, 1987). The winners in wars and other forms of conflict often gain considerable prestige and reputation, which protect them from future attack by others. Perhaps more to the point, collections of males (and most physical aggression, especially the collective type, is committed by males) may fight for access to women in other groups, allowing them to spread their genes more widely (Buss, 1999).

However, such functionalist arguments do not prove genetic involvement. Ethnocentrism itself is probably a complex set of reactions—cognitive, behavioral, and affective—and may have limited commonalities with ethnocentric behaviors of various animals. There is little hard evidence at present of a major genetic component to ethnocentrism in humans. Nonetheless, important and interesting work continues in evolutionary psychology approaches to social behavior, and we would be well advised to keep an open mind about the various possibilities of biological mechanisms in this area.

PSYCHOANALYTIC MODELS

Freud (1930) argued that the natural antagonism of people toward one another must be submerged when one joins a group, and that such reductions of ingroup hostility must be bought by increasing libidinal ties to the group members. In other words, the group must use libidinal ties (love, friendship, love of country) to inhibit a more basic hostility. However, the aggressive urges do not disappear. Since they cannot be directed against group members, they must be directed at those who are not members of the group. Hence there is an intimate relationship between love of one's own group and hostility toward others.

CONFLICT MODELS

Ethnocentrism may be "natural" because it is somehow biologically mandated, but there are other ways to think about the "naturalness" of such behavior. For example, some forms of behavior are efficient responses to the physical, social, and cultural ecologies we all inhabit, and are likely to be widely and independently discovered. In other words, outgroup hostility may be ubiquitous not because of common genetic heritage, but because of common discoveries of effective responses to common environmental demands.

Presumably, early humans lived in a world of physical danger, limited and unreliable food resources, and competition for sexual partners; group living may thus have been an efficient solution to many problems. In addition, sexual and affectional bonds as well as the demands of child rearing probably encouraged people to live in family units. Once people live in groups, it is not difficult to imagine why they might have strong preferences for members of their own groups. Similarity and familiarity both are important causes of interpersonal attraction (Berscheid & Reis, 1998). It is probable that people have more favorable and cooperative interactions with members of one's own group—another factor that would promote liking for fellow group members.

It is also not hard to explain why different groups might come into conflict. Although groups may be more efficient at finding and preparing food, building shelters, and protecting the young, there is still the insistent reality that groups as well as individuals must compete in times of scarce resources. Whereas ingroup competition may be muted, people from other groups may seem strange because of different language, customs, and dress, and there is no reason to dampen hostility toward them. Therefore, even without any strong assumptions about inherent aggressiveness or competitiveness in human nature, it still seems likely that people would come to prefer members of their own groups and to compete with or even aggress toward members of other groups.

SHERIF'S RESEARCH

Although social scientists have commented on intergroup conflict for generations, the area became a major part of social psychology with the research of Muzifer Sherif, who studied the development of groups and group conflict among boys attending camps during three summers in the late 1940s and early 1950s. The 1954 Robbers Cave experiment (Sherif, Harvey, White, Hood, & Sherif, 1961) was the best developed and is usually taken as prototypic. In this study, previously unacquainted

11-year-old boys came together at a summer camp. The boys played together and developed many friendships. Then they were divided arbitrarily into two groups, so that many of the boys now had close friends in the other group. Each group quickly achieved a high degree of group identity, achieving norms, leadership structures, and all the other qualities of groups; there was considerable pressure for boys to adhere to the norms of their respective groups. When the groups (now self-labeled as the "Rattlers" and the "Eagles") came together in a variety of games and competitive exercises, they not only competed fiercely; each group also began to derogate the other by name calling and the like. In due course, members of the two groups would hardly speak to one another, and there was an escalation of conflict. Some measure of order was restored to the camp when the experimenters had the two groups cooperate on solving a mutual problem (Sherif called these "superordinate goals").

In some ways, the Sherif research was a powerful demonstration of how hostility between groups could arise. Some might argue that "boys will be boys," and perhaps this is no more than a demonstration of some relatively mild *Lord of the Flies* scenario. But I doubt that anyone seriously believes that this is anything like a total explanation. We all—males and females, adults and children—have found ourselves being unfair to and discriminating against those from other groups, for no especially good reason other than the fact they have different group loyalties than we do. Students from one high school may criticize another for having "lower-class thugs" but another for having "upper-class snobs." Having gone to a rural high school in Indiana, where basketball rivalries are important, I can vividly remember our criticizing one neighboring school for being populated by "hillbillies and plowboys" and another for being too effete and not rural enough.[1] There is abundant evidence that ethnocentric attitudes are, if not quite universal across cultures, certainly ubiquitous (Brewer & Campbell, 1976; LeVine & Campbell, 1972), and that they increase during times of group conflict (e.g., Bar-Tal & Labin, 2001).

Identity Theories

SOCIAL IDENTITY THEORY

The most influential modern theory of ingroup bias was developed by Henri Tajfel (Tajfel, 1969, 1970, 1981a). In this theory, usually called "social identity theory" (SIT), Tajfel claimed that social groups are important sources of identity. Obviously, people can think about themselves in ways that do not involve explicit group membership (e.g., "I am smart," "I like opera"), but many of the answers to questions about who they are would involve references to explicit groups to which they belong. SIT also assumes that people generally want to feel positive about themselves, and that one (but not the only) way to accomplish this goal is for them to join groups that yield a positive identity or to increase the perceived worthiness of those groups to which they already belong. Strictly speaking, this model does not focus on hostility toward the outgroup, except as a by-product of the needs to see ingroups as positive. To the extent that people want to think highly of themselves, then, they will want to think highly of their groups. In particular, people will be motivated to see as much difference between ingroup and outgroup on dimensions that reflect positively on the ingroup (Tajfel & Turner, 1979). In addition to cognitive differentiation, people may also reinforce perceived differences behaviorally through adopting distinctive clothing styles or other emblems. Language, particularly slang, is often used as a means of differentiation (Giles & Johnson, 1987).

Chapter 3 has discussed Tajfel's ideas about categorization. He argued that the act of categorizing any set of objects tends to increase the perceived differences between categories and to make members of categories seem more alike. If we place ourselves and others into categories (groups) and are motivated to perceive our own groups as somehow better, it would also follow that we would be inclined to emphasize the ways in which other groups are different from us, especially along evaluative dimensions. Thus, although categorization and ingroup bias have independent cognitive bases, in everyday life they probably support one another to produce ethnocentrism.

SELF-CATEGORIZATION THEORY

John Turner (Oakes, Haslam, & Turner, 1994; Turner, Oakes, Haslam, & McGarty, 1994) has broadened SIT in what has been called "self-categorization theory" (SCT). This theory places more emphasis on the cognitive components of group-based identities. Generally, SCT emphasizes that the salience of group identities ebbs and flows, depending on a host of situational and cognitive variables. Sometimes you are placed in a situation where your group membership is made salient by virtue of contrasts with other groups. When you are in a situation that emphasizes one of your group memberships, it will play a larger role in your momentary identity (cf. Hogg & Turner, 1987). So a Texan in Paris may discover hidden feelings for fellow Texans. Or you may be more aware of your gender identity when you are in a minority in the group. Like SIT, SCT also predicts that self-categorization tends to accentuate interclass differences and to reduce perceived intracategory differences. When Caitlin thinks of herself as a lawyer, she will tend to see large differences between lawyers and doctors and tend to see lawyers as more alike than she might when her legal background is less salient. There is evidence that stereotypes of one's own group as well as others change, depending on what other groups are salient (Hopkins & Murdock, 1999; Hopkins, Regan, & Abell, 1997; Rutland & Cinnirella, 2000). It is also important to note that both SIT and SCT have a range of application that extends well beyond intergroup conflict (Brown, 2000). For example, both theories make strong predications about perceptions of status and inequality, as well as the importance of group loyalty, group cohesiveness, and social influence within groups.

The Nature of Groups

Given the importance of various groups in our everyday lives, it seems natural to categorize people in terms of their group memberships. We all belong to countless numbers of groups and categories, so one key question is why I think of myself as a member of some groups and not others. A corollary question is what the relevant outgroups are.

Group Identification

I belong to countless groups, and I identify with some of my groups more than others. The fact that I just renewed my Masterpiece I series subscription to the Houston

Symphony makes me a member of a group that actually meets nine times a year on Sunday afternoons. Yet, despite the fact that I recognize and even speak to several fellow Masterpiece I subscribers, I feel no particular identification with this group.[2] As a consequence, I have no special feelings about the subscribers to Masterpiece II or the full season, or nonsubscribers, or those who prefer season tickets to the ballet rather than the symphony. On the other hand, I do feel some identification with my college alumni group (although I draw the line at wearing silly hats and T-shirts), and consequently still catch myself feeling that students and alumni from the rival college are not quite fully human. I feel even more identification with my neighborhood group, taking both pride in the group and having some vague sense that other neighborhoods aren't quite as nice. At times I identify with my academic discipline, particularly when I represent psychology in a meeting of other social scientists. I become a fervent social scientist when I am in a group of physical scientists, a liberal arts kind of guy when I talk to engineers and business school people, and a complete academic when I am in a group of insurance sellers. Liberals and conservatives do battle in the U.S. Congress over foreign policy, but become part of a larger group of Americans when we are engaged in war.

When we identify with a group, we adopt group features as a part of our identity (Brewer, 1991). One implication is that we should be quicker and more facile in making judgments about ourselves when group and individual features agree—a prediction confirmed for both traits (Smith & Henry, 1996; E. R. Smith, Coats, & Walling, 1999) and attitudes (Coats, Smith, Claypool, & Banner, 2000).

NEED SATISFACTION

One obvious factor that determines group identification is how well the group satisfies basic needs. It should come as no surprise to discover that people identify with their business organizations more when they are making rapid promotion progress. Identification with an organization depends, in part, on how positively other people are perceived to value the organization and the extent to which the organization stereotypes are positive (Bergami & Bagozzi, 2000). As might be expected, people also tend to identify more with high-status than with low-status groups (Ellemers, Doosje, van Knippenberg, & Wilke, 1992; Ellemers, van Knippenberg, De Vries, & Wilke, 1988). Different people have different goals and agendas for their lives, and presumably value those groups that help them meet these goals. So I regard college alumni groups as being faintly silly, but others wear funny hats to alumni meetings and seem to take them quite seriously indeed.

OPTIMAL-DISTINCTIVENESS THEORY

Marilyn Brewer (1991) argues that social identities fulfill two somewhat incompatible goals. On the one hand, people want to be a part of groups—to feel similar to others as a means of self-validation. This is, of course, the linchpin of SCT, and ingroups generally satisfy this need. On the other hand, people want to feel unique and special, and this leads to intergroup comparison and sometimes to outgroup derogation. Thus I might identify with my particular university, being content to see myself as "at one" with my colleagues and students, but at the same time see myself as quite different from faculty members at a neighboring university.

According to Brewer (1991), people strive to identify with groups providing an optimal level of inclusiveness that satisfies both needs. However, what is optimal may vary from time to time and from context to context. I may come to feel cognitively smothered by being a generic faculty member at my university and derive little satisfaction from comparisons with those at other institutions. In that case, I may identify with my academic department and compare my plight with members of other academic departments at my university. Or I may feel cramped by being able to identify only with my institution, and may choose to identity with professors everywhere and see myself as distinctive from lawyers or physicians.

Generally, when assimilation needs are salient, people tend to perceive intragroup similarity as higher (Pickett & Brewer, 2001) and to prefer larger, more inclusive groups (Pickett, Silver, & Brewer, 2002). Alternatively when distinctiveness needs are more paramount, people see less ingroup similarity (Simon et al., 1997) and prefer smaller, more exclusive groups (Pickett et al., 2002).

IDENTIFICATION IS MULTIDIMENSIONAL

Obviously, identification with groups is multidimensional and complex and satisfies multiple needs (e.g., Deaux, 1993; Frable, 1997; Karasawa, 1991; Sanders Thompson, 2001; Sellers, Smith, Shelton, Rowley, & Chavous, 1998). One might identify with group goals, group achievements, the group as an entity, the other members, group prestige. One can take pride in a group or not, like its members or hate them, enjoy what the group does or not. Moreover, identifications wax and wane, depending on changing contexts and needs. Even something as important as ethnic identity depends on comparative and situational contexts (Verkuyten & de Wolf, 2002),

The most comprehensive attempt to examine the complexity of identification empirically (Jackson & Smith, 1999) showed that there are several aspects to identity: attraction to the group, interdependency (a sense that the group's fate is one's own), depersonalization (the sense that one is absorbed in the group so that members are more or less interchangeable), and intergroup context (a tendency to see one's own group identity in contrast to other groups). Jackson and Smith (1999) argue that those with secure group identification will be attracted to the group but will not have high levels of depersonalization and interdependency. Insecure attachment, by contrast, is based on high levels of attraction and both depersonalization and interdependency. Examination of relationships among several measures of identification supported this notion. Furthermore, those who were securely attached showed less ingroup bias than those who were insecurely attached.

What Constitutes an Outgroup?

To a certain extent, outgroups will change to reflect identifications with ingroups. But even when I identity with a particular group, I may or may not see alternative groups as relevant outgroups. For example, a conservative, fundamentalist Texas Baptist has a rich range of choices—nonconservative Baptists, liberal Christians, Methodists, Catholics, atheists, Jews, Muslims, humanists, social liberals, Eastern Republicans, and nonfundamentalists (and the list goes on).

CONTEXTS

Obviously, what counts as a relevant and salient outgroup varies from situation to situation. Haslam and Turner (1992) have argued that such distinctions depend in part on differences between the groups, as well as on frames of reference. For a constant difference between two groups on some trait, the two groups will be seen as closer together when the range of positions seen as relevant is larger. So a moderate conservative will see the moderate liberal as closer when a full range of political views is represented, from the ultraright to the radical liberal, than when only moderate points of view are represented. People are also more willing to stereotype others when they are seen as further away, and thus more as outgroupers. Turner's SCT emphasizes that group-based identity is very much a product of the context in which are groups are located.

THE RELEVANCE OF GROUPS

Lalonde and Gardner (1989) remind us that only those groups that are relevant will be seen as fit for stereotyping. I recognize that people who were born and live in Chicago constitute a group to which I do not belong, and now that I think about it, Chicagoans probably do have at least some characteristics in common. However, I have few if any definitive stereotypes about Chicagoans, living as I do in Texas. On the other hand, I do have stereotypes about people who live in Dallas—stereotypes that are probably not shared by most Midwesterners, who are blissfully ignorant of rivalries between various Texas cities. Because relevance is often confounded with knowledge and familiarity, there is an important lesson for those who claim that the answer to stereotyping is more contact with and knowledge about other groups. With greater familiarity and knowledge also comes relevance, so the net result may be that a group one knows well is seen in more stereotypic terms than a group less well known and hence less relevant. Several studies (e.g., Berry, 1970; Biernat & Crandall, 1994; Taft, 1959; Vinacke, 1956) confirm this somewhat counterintuitive idea.

INGROUP BIAS

Ingroup Favoritism

Questions of whether we give preferential treatment to, and evaluate more positively, those in our own groups has been a major theme for social psychology during the past two decades or more. This has been especially true for British and Australian social psychology, heavily influenced by the work of Henri Tajfel and John Turner.

The Tajfel Approach

Tajfel considered two closely related themes. The first, and theoretically more fundamental, was his concern with how categorization into groups affected our perceptions of self and others. Chapter 3 has discussed his theory that categorization of people into groups should increase intergroup differences and reduce intragroup differences, and I return to this theme later in this chapter. The second theme was his concern that people favor members from their own groups even when the basis of group membership is weak or arbitrary, and that is the focus of this chapter.

THE MINIMAL-GROUP SITUATION

Tajfel was clear that the effects he was discussing are cognitive, albeit with a strong motivational push. Ingroup bias is certain readily apparent among businesses, countries, racial groups, and athletic teams. One of the most extraordinary examples is the attachment people have to sports teams from their universities and cities. Many people seem to invest a great deal of emotion in whether "their" teams win or lose, even though those outcomes have little or no effect on them in other ways (Cialdini et al., 1976).

In everyday groups, it is hard to know how much of these effects are cognitive and how much are due to social pressure and other motivational factors. For example, is it any surprise that a member of a college fraternity believes that his group is superior to another fraternity? His fraternity competes with other fraternities in athletic, leadership, decorating, and (we can hope) academic endeavors. Surely his fraternity group has put a great deal of pressure on the young man to believe that his frat is superior in all the ways that count. Furthermore, he may have joined this fraternity because he likes the group goals and the other members. So there are many reasons why members of existing groups show favoritism toward their own.

Tajfel thought that "beneath" these effects is a more fundamental process, built on the idea that important parts of our identities are anchored in our groups. We want to differentiate our own groups from others, as well as to enhance ingroup worthiness, which helps to maintain self-esteem. With that in mind, Tajfel wanted to study these basic processes without the messiness of these social and motivational factors we have just been discussing. He began his research with what is now called the "minimal-group" paradigm. Subjects are arbitrarily divided into two groups (say, on the basis of personality patterns or even artistic preferences); the basis of division can be as arbitrary and devoid of psychological meaning as an investigator wishes, and generally the "group" members have not met each other. Then subjects are asked to assign points (sometimes representing money) to other people, who are identified only by their group membership; so a person who has been categorized as a member of A will be asked to assign points to a person identified as another member of A and to a person identified as a member of B. People do not themselves benefit directly from their assignment of points, although they may, of course, benefit from the assignments of others.

The distribution is done in terms of a defined matrix, and the matrix is set up so that a variety of reward structures are possible. To give a simplified example, imagine that the subjects must choose either to give 7 points to a member of their own group and only 1 point to the outgroup, or to give 19 to their own group and 25 to the outgroup. Now it is obvious that if individuals want to maximize the outcomes of their own group, they should pick the latter, and often people do. But they also often pick distributions such as the former, which provide the maximum ingroup differentiation, even if this means that members of their own group will get fewer total points. In general, subjects in this sort of situation show ingroup favoritism, despite the fact that the ingroup has been arbitrarily and recently created, and despite the absence of any meaningful contact with other group members or competition with the outgroup (Brewer, 1979; Mullen, Brown, & Smith, 1992).

The particular choices given to subjects in the Tajfel paradigm are somewhat complex to describe, but the effect can be replicated with much simpler ways of measuring ingroup favoritism, such as assignment of traits (Doise et al., 1972); it can even be shown with implicit measures of stereotyping (Ashburn-Nardo, Voils, & Monteith, 2001; Otten & Moskowitz, 2000; Otten & Wentura, 1999). The general pattern of ingroup favoritism or bias seems beyond dispute and does not depend fundamentally on a particular measurement strategy.

The effect itself is robust. Stimulated by Tajfel's initial research (Tajfel, Billig, Bundy, & Flament, 1971), ingroup bias has been demonstrated with people from several nationalities and with children as young as 6 (Bigler, Jones, & Lobliner, 1997; Nesdale & Flesser, 2001). It is also clear that it can be demonstrated with the most minimal of random group assignments (Locksley, Ortiz, & Hepburn, 1980).

POSITIVE–NEGATIVE ASYMMETRY

SIT makes it clear that the primary motive is enhancement of one's own group and only secondarily the derogation of outgroups. As SIT would predict, the ingroup bias effect is largely controlled by greater favoritism for the ingroup as opposed to hostility toward the outgroups (Brewer, 1979); this is sometimes called "positive–negative asymmetry." Furthermore, although this effect is generally found when individuals are distributing rewards, there is no strong ingroup bias effect when punishments or other negative outcomes are dispensed (e.g., Mummendey, 1995; Wenzel & Mummendey, 1996). However, when social identity is threatened, ingroup bias appears for both allocation of rewards and punishments (Otten, Mummendey, & Blanz, 1996). To some extent, this may be a function of normative expectations that it is better to reward than to punish differentially (Blanz, Mummendey, & Otten, 1997).

IS SOCIAL IDENTITY ALL THERE IS?

Although Tajfel's SIT has dominated thinking about ingroup bias for over two decades, others (e.g., Cadinu & Rothbart, 1996; Hong & Harrod, 1988; Horwitz & Rabbie, 1989; Rabbie, Schot, & Visser, 1989) have criticized the theory as a putatively complete explanation for the effects and have offered alternative explanations. For example, Lowell Gaertner and Chester Insko (2000) have raised the issue of whether the minimal-group paradigm is as minimal as the name implies. Recall that the logic behind this paradigm requires that the only factor operating is categorization. However, in most experimental tests people not only allocate to but also think they will receive rewards from other ingroup and outgroup members. In that case, they may give more rewards to ingroup members, becuase they hope and expect that their allocations will be reciprocated. Alternatively, they fear that they will be discriminated against by outgroup members, and therefore overallocate to their own group as a way of restoring some equality (see also Moy & Ng, 1996).

Other norms may also play a role; for example, those who construe the positive allocations as bonuses tend to show more ingroup bias than those who construe them as payments, because the latter are more strongly governed by norms of fairness (Gaertner & Insko, 2001). Needs to perceive oneself as fair (Singh, Choo, & Poh, 1998) tend to decrease ingroup bias, whereas group loyalty norms increase it (Hertel & Kerr, 2001). So even the minimal situation is not devoid of motives other than those surrounding seeking a positive identity. More generally, people can be selfish and egotistical without group support from self-definitions anchored in group identities (Gaertner, Sedikides, Vevea, & Iuzzini, 2002).

Factors Affecting Ingroup Bias

The minimal-group paradigm aids studying one of the most important motives for ingroup bias—one that may be hard to disentangle from other, more obvious motives in the complexities of everyday life. Furthermore, it does not require a great deal of cultural or psychological trappings to set off the ingroup bias. Seeking a positive social identity is a fundamental, baseline sort of motivation that can become a foundation for more extreme forms.

Still, though Tajfel has stressed an important reason for ingroup bias, the kinds of effects found in minimal groups do not necessarily underlie all or even most examples of ingroup favoritism in the real world. It seems highly unlikely, for example, that the ethnic conflicts we see in Bosnia or the Middle East can be entirely reduced to preferences for ingroup members based on minimal information (and Tajfel would have agreed wholeheartedly). The tendency for effects in the minimal-group situation to be localized in favoring the ingroup rather than derogating the outgroup also does not speak to the hatred that underlies so much group conflict in the world (Mummendey, 1995). The rather moderate preferences for ingroups must be enlivened by other prejudices or perceived group conflict (Struch & Schwartz, 1989) before we can arrive at a full explanation of wars and ethnic cleansing.

CONFLICT AND COMPETITION

The most obvious prediction from almost any theory is that conflict and competition should make ingroup bias stronger. SIT offers a straightforward explanation. When a group is threatened by an outgroup, identity and self-worth are also threatened. Derogation of the outgroup and enhancement of the ingroup promote a positive self-evaluation, which is presumably anchored in group identity. Conflict may also lead to stronger ingroup bias because group members are trying to impress fellow ingroup members or to solidify their standing in the group (Branscombe, Ellemers, Spears, & Doosje, 1999). On the other hand, when people feel secure in their attachment to and identification with the group, motivation to derogate the outgroup may be lessened even in times of conflict.

Research using samples of people during actual conflict suggests that negative stereotypes (presumably closely related to evaluative bias) are more prevalent during conflict. For example, negative stereotypes of outgroups are usually quite pronounced during wars and other national conflicts (Buchanan, 1951; Haslam, Turner, Oakes, McGarty, & Hayes, 1992; Meenes, 1943; Seago, 1947).

Although people are often threatened by the beliefs and behavior of members of outgroups, hostility toward outgroups may also increase because of the frustration arising from external threat or economic hard times (Chadwick-Jones, 1962). According to scapegoat theory, frustration is a major instigator of aggression, and when this cannot be directed at the direct cause it may be displaced onto a scapegoat (Dollard, Miller, Doob, Mowrer, & Sears, 1939). Scapegoating theory has fallen on hard times, in part because it was vague about such details as which outgroup would be chosen for the displaced aggression. However, economic hard times do tend to be correlated with violence, and more recent studies have shown that threat in the form of mortality salience increases ingroup bias as well as identification (Castano, Yzerbyt, Paladino, & Sacchi, 2002) although it may decrease identification with negative ingroups (Arndt, Greenberg, Schimel, Pyszczynski, & Solomon, 2002).

SUPERORDINATE GROUPS

Recall that in the original Sherif and colleagues (1961) research, once the competing groups discovered superordinate goals, intergroup competition and bias seemed to be inhibited. One possible reason suggested by Sherif is that cooperation simply makes people think of themselves as members of a larger, superordinate group. So hostility directed to former outgroup members may be reduced as people from competing groups are cognitively welcomed into the larger ingroup. Research by Gaertner, Mann, Murrell, and Dovidio (1989) showed that reclassifying former competing groups as one larger group reduced ingroup bias, because the former outgroup members were seen in more positive terms. Second, cooperation tends to make people from competing groups think of themselves partially in terms of superordinate group membership (S. L. Gaertner et al., 1999; Gaertner, Mann, Dovidio, Murrell, & Pomare, 1990).

There are, however, some downsides to this strategy. For one thing, having two formerly competing groups unite for the purposes of dealing with mutual external threat or superordinate outgroup may not reduce the amount of violence and discrimination, but merely redirect it (Kessler & Mummendey, 2001). Second, dissolving boundaries between rival groups can be quite threatening. Psychological boundaries and negative evaluations built up over decades or centuries and supported by strong religious and political ideologies cannot easily be erased. Bringing historic rivals or enemies together and emphasizing similarities may be threatening, and this ought to be especially strong when there is conflict, leading to even greater ingroup bias (Henderson-King, Henderson-King, Zhermer, Posokhova, & Chiker, 1997). SIT proposes that under these circumstances, maintaining the salience of preexisting subordinate categories as well as the new superordinate group may be crucial (Hornsey & Hogg, 2000b). People may be able to have their cake and eat it too when the subgroups have different levels of expertise that can be emphasized as supports for previous subordinate group identities (Dovidio, Gaertner, & Validzic, 1998).

Generally, however, encouraging people in different groups to think of themselves as part of one group seems to discourage ingroup bias. When superordinate goals encourage thinking of others in more individualistic terms, others become less "people from that other group" and more like "us" with all "our" glorious individuality (Neuberg & Fiske, 1987). Several studies (e.g., Dovidio, Gaertner, et al., 1997; Gaertner et al., 1989; Wilder, 1978) have shown that this strategy is effective; interestingly, it seems to occur primarily because the overly positive ratings of ingroup members are reduced (Gaertner et al., 1989).

IDENTIFICATION

Identification with the ingroup is an important mediator of ingroup bias. A person who is weakly identified with a group will probably not be especially motivated to differentiate this particular ingroup from various outgroups. I may belong to a book-reading group that meets four times a year, but since it forms a trivial part of my self-concept, I have little reason to elevate its standing, let alone to derogate other groups. When the group is threatened or criticized, I may find it easier to leave the group than to defend it. By contrast, those people who identify strongly with a group or who see themselves as prototypic group members (Jetten, Spears, & Manstead, 1997a) should be highly motivated to make it seem the best there is.

As might be expected, people who identity more strongly with a group tend to be more committed and attached to it, and have less desire to feel free to leave the group (Ellemers, Spears, & Doosje, 1997). They also perceive more ingroup homogeneity (Hortaçsu, 2000); conform more strongly to group norms (Jetten, Postmes, & McAuliffe, 2002); have more positive stereotypes of the ingroup (Haslam, Oakes, Reynolds, & Turner, 1999; Schmitt & Maes, 2002); see themselves as more typical group members, in what is usually called "self-stereotyping" (Tropp & Wright, 2001); and see deviant ingroup members as less typical (Castano, Paladino, Coull, & Yzerbyt, 2002).

So identification affects a variety of attitudes about the ingroup, but what of outgroup attitudes and behaviors? Although Turner (1999), one of the developers of the mature form of SIT, denies that the theory makes an explicit prediction that those who are more identified with the group will show more outgroup discrimination, the prediction is clearly consistent with the general model (Brown, 2000). Although early research was not strongly supportive (Hinkle & Brown, 1990), there are now several reports of significant relationships (e.g., Branscombe & Wann, 1994; Duckitt & Mphuthing, 1998; Guimond, 2000; Jetten, Spears, & Manstead, 1997b; Perreault & Bourhis, 1999; Verkuyten, Drabbles, & van den Nieuwenhuijzen, 1999). People who identity with a group but have rather peripheral status in it may be especially prone to urge outgroup derogation, especially when their evaluations are public, as a way of bolstering their perceived commitment to the group (Noel, Wann, & Branscombe, 1995).

SELF-STEREOTYPING

Self-stereotyping is the tendency to see oneself as similar to other group members or to endorse ingroup stereotypes, as indicated above. Although it is closely related to identification, some (e.g., Spears, Doosje, & Ellemers, 1997) have argued that it is the stronger causal player in ingroup bias. Self-stereotyping has been found to be the more powerful predictor of ingroup bias, especially under conditions in which group identity is threatened (Verkuyten & Nekuee, 1999). It is more common in smaller groups and for minority groups when they have higher status (Simon & Hamilton, 1994). Self-stereotyping also tends to be strong for those who identify strongly with the group when group identity is threatened on important issues (Burris & Jackson, 2000; Spears, Doosje, & Ellemers, 1999).

A dilemma is likely to arise when the ingroup is viewed negatively by others. In that case, one might argue that group identities are especially threatened and group members are thereby highly likely to self-stereotype. On the other hand, taking on the mantle of such a negative group means that members are endorsing a negative identity. To the extent that the norms and values of their group differ from those of the larger society, self-stereotyping can lead to acceptance by the minority ingroup but at the cost of rejection by the larger society. In one study (Biernat, Vescio, & Green, 1996), sorority and fraternity members resolved the dilemma by accepting the validity of the largely negative stereotypes of these groups in general, but accepting only the positive aspects and rejecting the negative as characteristic of their own fraternities and sororities. Another solution would be to devalue the dimensions on which one's low-status group is disadvantaged, and this occurs especially when the disadvantage is seen as illegitimate (Schmader, Major, Eccleston, & McCoy, 2001).

In some cases, ingroup pressures may be more important than those from the larger society. For example, Fordham and Ogbu (1986) suggest that black students with high academic aspirations and abilities may be accused by their classmates of selling out to white values and "acting white." Many will, of course, continue to do well academically, but others will be unwilling to make the sacrifice of cultural identity that this may entail. Such effects are not limited to ethnic minorities. The negative attitudes many women have toward math are caused in part by their identification with their gender and the perception that math is a male thing (Nosek, Banaji, & Greenwald, 2002b).

ENTITATIVITY

Entitativity (discussed in Chapter 3) may be closely related to the identification and/or self-stereotyping constructs we have just been considering. It is likely that more entitative groups satisfy the needs that lead people to join groups; therefore, people want to see their groups as more entitative and identify more strongly with those that they perceive to be so (Yzerbyt, Castano, Leyens, & Paladino, 2000). Gaertner and Schopler (1998) argue that ingroup bias is another consequence of perceived entitativity. They manipulated entitativity by the amount and quality of interaction group members had with one another. Those with the most interaction not only perceived themselves to belong to more entitative groups, but displayed more ingroup (but not outgroup) bias. Furthermore, the perceptions of entitativity largely mediated the effects of group interaction on ingroup bias.

CRISSCROSS CLASSIFICATION

Ingroup bias is typically reduced when classification becomes more complex by introducing new subgroups or group categorizations that crisscross (Bettencourt & Dorr, 1998; Brewer, Ho, Lee, & Miller, 1987; Brown & Turner, 1979; Commins & Lockwood, 1978; Deschamps & Doise, 1978; Hagendoorn & Henke, 1991; Marcus-Newhall, Miller, Holtz, & Brewer, 1993; Urban & Miller, 1998). It is worth stressing again that we are all members of many groups, and sometimes this messes up clean ingroup–outgroup discriminations. For example, how does a black female view a white female, who is a member of a racial outgroup but a gender ingroup?

Several patterns of response make sense. The most obvious is a kind of additive effect, where groups are rejected in proportion to their "outgroupness." Several studies have found exactly this pattern: People reject a double outgroup more than a double ingroup, with the mixed groups in between (Crisp & Hewstone, 1999a; Hewstone, Islam, & Judd, 1993; Migdal, Hewstone, & Mullen, 1998; Urban & Miller, 1998). Obviously, a lot depends on what the crisscrossed categories are, and especially on how important they are to a person. To take an extreme example, it is doubtful that a Palestinian would reject an Israeli Jew less after finding out that they share a hobby of raising tropical fish.

Other patterns have also been reported (Crisp & Hewstone, 1999a); the most common of these is social inclusion, where people equally like groups in which they have at least one membership. For instance, a black female would feel bonds not only with other black females but with black males and white females, rejecting only white males. Unfortunately, there are also reports of the opposite, where people are rejected if they are members of either outgroup or both. So, while emphasizing multiple group identities is sometimes useful in reducing ingroup bias, this is not inevitable.

SELF-ESTEEM

One prediction consistent with SIT is that self-esteem and group identification have a basic relationship, in the sense that one's self-esteem is partially dependent on evaluation of the groups to which one belongs. Although Turner (1999) has argued forcefully that SIT does not make such explicit claims, much research has been stimulated by Hogg and Abrams's (1990) extension along these lines. Two general predictions follow. The first is that derogating people in outgroups or elevating the positive features of ingroups raises self-esteem. The second is that people who have low self-esteem may be more inclined to show ingroup bias as a way of raising it. It seems reasonable that if I can improve the lot of my group psychologically through ingroup bias, my own positive self-worth would improve to the extent that it is dependent on group identification. Tests of these propositions have not been uniformly successful.

Does Ingroup Bias Raise Self-Esteem? Studies examining the first question—that is, whether the experience of showing ingroup bias actually raises self-esteem—have provided mixed support. However, reviews (e.g., Long & Spears, 1997; Rubin & Hewstone, 1998) of research in this area have concluded that identifying with one's own group and seeing it as better than relevant outgroups does generally contribute to high self-esteem.

Does Self-Esteem Affect Ingroup Bias? The second proposition—namely, that people with low self-esteem might be particularly prone to showing ingroup bias—has been supported in some studies (e.g., Fein & Spencer, 1997; Platow et al., 1997) but not in others (e.g., Brockner & Chen, 1996; Crocker, Thompson, McGraw, & Ingerman, 1987). On the one hand, it makes sense that people with low self-esteem would boost a fragile sense of worth by derogating others. But the opposite prediction—that people with high self-esteem have been able to maintain their self-worth by derogating others—also meets the common-sense test. So which is it? Are people with high or low self-esteem more prone to ingroup bias? A recent meta-analysis (Aberson, Healy, & Romero, 2000) found that it was the folks with high self-esteem, but only when they were making direct evaluative ratings.

Another complication is that self-esteem may encompass several distinct states, and self-esteem based on individual features differs in many ways from that based on group memberships (Abrams & Hogg, 1988; Bettencourt & Hume, 1999; L. Gaertner, Sedikides, & Graetz, 1999; Rubin & Hewstone, 1998). In fairness, predictions based on individual self-esteem are not especially relevant, because the sense of self anchored in group identification is what's crucial (Luhtanen & Crocker, 1992; Turner, 1999). Also, those with high individual self-esteem may be prone to positive ingroup evaluation, whereas those with low collective self-esteem may want to derogate the outgroup; both processes may lead to more positive evaluation of the ingroup (Verkuyten, 1997).

Status and Power. Other studies have manipulated self-esteem indirectly through manipulations of the status, power, or success of the groups, although there are legitimate concerns about their psychological equivalence (Abrams & Hogg, 1988). Most of the research in this area has examined the status of the groups. Some studies show more ingroup bias with relatively lower-status groups (e.g., Brauer, 2001), but others have found the opposite effect (e.g., Crocker & Luhtanen, 1990; Ellemers, Kortekaas, & Ouwerkirk, 1999; Guimond, Dif, & Aupy, 2002; Rudman, Feinberg, & Fairchild, 2002). Meta-analyses of relevant studies (Bettencourt, Charlton, Dorr, & Hume, 2001; Mullen et al., 1992) have found more ingroup bias for higher-status groups. Low-status groups discriminate more on dimensions unrelated to status (Reichl, 1997) and tend to devalue dimensions on which their low status is based (Major, Spencer, Schmader, Wolfe, & Crocker, 1998; Schmader & Major, 1999).

One problem is that members of a low-status group may be subjected to competing pressures. On the one hand, they want to buffer their own vulnerable self-esteem by seeing their group as especially positive. On the other hand, they are also cognizant of the higher status of the other group and its presumed better qualities. Jost and Banaji (1994) have called this "system justification"—the tendency of disadvantaged groups to internalize the beliefs and attitudes (including stereotypes) of the larger social system. For high-status groups, of course, both factors should contribute to ingroup bias. Research by Jost and Burgess (2000) did show that existing low-status groups displayed less ingroup bias than high-status groups, especially when the legitimacy of status differences was salient (and presumably system justification pressures were maximized).

Summary. Thus neither part of the self-esteem hypothesis receives strong and consistent support from the research literature. However, given that people with low or lowered self-esteem are more prone to derogate others (Fein & Spencer, 1997), and that self-esteem can be affected by group memberships and identifications, it is reasonable to expect that feelings of self-worth based on group memberships play a role in ingroup bias under at least some circumstances. Generally at the moment, there seems to be more support for the idea that intergroup discrimination raises self-esteem than for the idea that low self-esteem motivates discrimination (Rubin & Hewstone, 1998).

SALIENCE

Another strong prediction from SIT is that ingroup bias should be increased when one's own group becomes salient. One reason groups may become salient in everyday life is that they are small or otherwise in a minority, and several studies have shown that ingroup bias is increased when one's group becomes more salient by virtue of its small relative size (Mullen et al., 1992). Leonardelli and Brewer (2001) argue that smaller groups should be more appealing because they can more easily satisfy desires for both individuality and social identity, and that this greater satisfaction encourages a positive evaluation of the ingroup.

ATTRIBUTE RELEVANCE

Surely people do not think their own group is superior to others on every dimension. I may concede that your university excels in art and sculpture, but reserve claims of superiority for mine for the more important (at least to me) psychology or the social sciences. Mummendey and Schreiber (1983, 1984) have refered to this as the "different but better" strategy. The claim is that an ingroup will claim superiority on those dimensions most relevant to the ingroup and concede superiority on less relevant items. Despite the reasonableness of this idea and some supporting evidence (e.g., Mummendey & Simon, 1989; Schmader & Major, 1999), Mullen and colleagues' (1992) meta-analysis found that it is generally not true across studies. When an ingroup has relatively high status, this relationship is found, but the reverse seems to be true when the ingroup status is low.

Evaluating Individuals

I have been focusing on evaluations of ingroups and outgroups as undifferentiated collections of generic individuals. Yet everyday experience suggests that we often make sharp distinctions among people in both types of groups. I may think that professors at my university are generally superior to those at a neighboring institution, but still eagerly recognize superior talent there and deadwood here. Thus, in evaluations of specific ingroup and outgroup members, other motives may come into play.

THE BLACK-SHEEP EFFECT

Common experience suggests that often we are often more annoyed with people in our own groups than with others. I am much harder on a member of my academic department whom I consider to be intellectual deadwood or a poor teacher than I would be on a similar person at another university.

In what José Marques and his colleagues (Marques & Paez, 1994) have called the "black-sheep effect," unlikeable members of one's own group are evaluated more negatively than unlikeable members of an outgroup (Marques, 1990; Marques, Robalo, & Rocha, 1992; Marques & Yzerbyt, 1988; Marques, Yzerbyt, & Leyens, 1988). For example, when European American perceivers evaluate the performance of African American and European American targets, they tend to be especially hard on underachieving European Americans (Biernat, Vescio, & Billings, 1999). Marques also argues that ingroup members who perform especially well or who are quite likeable should be evaluated more positively than similar outgroup members. The net result is that evaluations of ingroup members should be polarized, relative to those of outgroup folks.

OUTGROUP POLARIZATION

The black-sheep effect applies to evaluations of ingroup members, but we may also differentiate sharply among members of outgroups. Although we may derogate outgroups generally, sometimes we evaluate members of outgroups especially positively. I'm sometimes struck by what I think is a tendency to overpraise athletes who do well in my classes, and I may evaluate their performance more highly than that of nonathletes who do as well. Unfortunately, it's also easy to dismiss the poor academic performance of athletes because "they're just dumb jocks," and give them even less credit than they deserve. Studies have demonstrated that evaluations of outgroup members are polarized: Those who perform well are seen as especially praiseworthy, and those who perform poorly are viewed as especially blameworthy (Hass, Katz, Rizzo, Bailey, & Eisenstadt, 1991; Linville, 1982; Linville & Jones, 1980).

There are several explanations for this effect. Attitude ambivalence theory (Katz, 1981) explains such effects in terms of the ambivalent attitudes that people often have toward members of outgroups (see Chapter 8 for a fuller description). For example, European Americans may genuinely like many African Americans, but also feel a sense of disgust or wariness about them. This ambivalence leads to feelings of discomfort. When they have positive experiences with African Americans, the positive part of their attitudes become more salient, and the reduction of the ambivalence-created discomfort may then amplify that positive reaction. Similar effects, *mutatis mutandis*, operate with negative experiences. Linville (1982) has advanced a more cognitive explanation, usually termed the "extremity–complexity model." She has argued that we generally have more complex representations of people and groups we know well; that ingroups are generally more familiar than outgroups; and that more extreme evaluations (both positive and negative) are likely to occur for less complex representations (such as those we hold for less familiar outgroups).

RECONCILIATION

The black-sheep hypothesis argues that evaluations of ingroup members should be polarized relative to those from the outgroup, whereas the extremity–complexity model argues that ratings of outgroup members should be more polarized. One can easily generate examples that seem to support both models, but obviously in a given situation both cannot be true (although, of course, each may yield successful predictions in different circumstances or situations). To complicate matters even more, expectancy violation theory (Jussim, Coleman, & Lerch, 1987) predicts that people who violate expectancies will be evaluated extremely. If we assume that most people have more negative expectations of outgroup than ingroup members, the theory predicts that with good performance the outgroup person will be evaluated more positively than the ingroup member, and with poor performance the ingroup member will be evaluated more negatively than the outgroup person. There are also data consistent with this hypothesis that evaluations are not affected by ingroup or outgroup status (e.g., Bettencourt, Dill, Greathouse, Charlton, & Mulholland, 1997; Coleman, Jussim, & Kelley, 1995; Kernahan, Bartholow, & Bettencourt, 2000). The predictions of the three models are provided in Table 7.1. Obviously, there are data supporting each model, and at the moment it is unclear which model works best in which circumstances

TABLE 7.1. Predictions of Various Theories for Evaluation of Ingroup and Outgroup Members

Theories	Groups and outcomes			
	Ingroup positive	Ingroup negative	Outgroup positive	Outgroup negative
Expectancy violation theory	Positive	Highly negative	Highly positive	Negative
Black-sheep effect	Highly positive	Highly negative	Positive	Negative
Extremity–complexity model	Positive	Negative	Highly positive	Highly negative

Cognitive Effects

Up to this point, I have focused on ingroup–outgroup bias, and in particular affective responses (such as evaluative ratings, reward allocations, and hostility). However, the primary focus of this book is on stereotypes. Let us now turn to how group assignment affects how traits and other dispositions are assigned to people as a function of group membership.

Traits and Dispositions

INGROUP–OUTGROUP RATINGS

Everyday experience suggests that people are particularly likely to ascribe stereotypic traits to members of outgroups. This has been found in several studies (e.g., Brigham, 1974; Jones, Wood, & Quattrone, 1981; Judd, Park, Ryan, Brauer, & Kraus, 1995; Park & Judd, 1990; Park & Rothbart, 1982; Park, Ryan, & Judd, 1992; Ryan & Bogart, 1997).

The tendency to assign stereotype traits to members of outgroups is affected by several factors. As might be expected from various theories, stereotype ratings of outgroup members are facilitated when the ingroup membership is made salient (Wilder & Shapiro, 1991). Stereotypic attributions are also affected by the range of outgroups considered. Although there are reports of assimilation effects (Haslam et al., 1992), most research supports a contrast effect, where stereotypes of a given outgroup become more positive when other negative outgroups are considered. Diab (1963b) found that Arab students' stereotypes of certain groups (French, Negroes, and Chinese) became more positive when these groups were judged in the context of negative groups (Jews and Turks) rather than a fuller range of groups. Diab (1963a) showed that stereotypes of Americans were more positive when Russia was also rated than when not, and that stereotypes of the French were more negative in the context of ratings of Algerians (a positive group for these subjects).

ATTRIBUTIONS

I have emphasized throughout this book that stereotypes are more than features attached to social categories. They also involve theories and explanations. One kind of explanation is causal attribution. Do people attribute the behavior of ingroup and outgroup members differently? Certainly there is abundant research supporting the proposition that attributions to self and others can be affected by wishes and desires; this is usually called "egocentric bias" or "ego bias" (Hewstone, 1990a). The most obvious prediction for group attributions, enunciated by Pettigrew (1979) in his description of what he called the "ultimate attribution error," is that negative behaviors by outgroup members will more often be seen as dispositional than will similar behaviors by members of one's own groups. "We" are bad because of the situation, luck, or other unstable and largely external factors, whereas "those other people" are bad because they are lazy, stupid, or just plain dispositionally bad. Conversely, good behaviors should be attributed more often to external or unstable forces for outgroups than for ingroups. Pettigrew also suggested that such biases should be greater for prejudiced people, in situations where group memberships are salient, and in cases where there is a history of intergroup conflict.

A review of attribution research by Hewstone (1990b) concludes that there is a general tendency for attributions to vary more for failure than for success situations, and that most studies find the predicted ingroup bias for ability ratings (i.e., ingroup failure is seen as due to lack of ability less often than outgroup failure is). However, predicted results are not as often found for attributions to effort, luck, and task difficulty (Hewstone, 1990b) and are not always found for all groups.

In a representative study using racial groups, Jackson, Sullivan, and Hodge (1993) had white subjects rate black and white targets who were described as having strong or weak academic records. Behavior that was inconsistent with the stereotype (i.e., poor records for the white students and strong ones for the blacks) tended to be seen as due to external (luck, task difficulty) or unstable (effort) reasons, especially for the black outgroup. The successful black students were seen as having about the same ability as the successful whites, but as having tried harder and been more lucky. Conversely, white students with weak credentials were viewed as not trying hard enough, but similar blacks were perceived as lacking ability. Thus ingroup success was seen less as due to effort and luck than was outgroup success, but ingroup failure was attributed more strongly to lack of effort than to ability; the reverse was true for outgroup members. Such ingroup-favoring evaluations can contribute to ingroup evaluative bias (Chatman & von Hippel, 2001).

There are other, more subtle attributional effects. For example, people tend to describe the positive behaviors of ingroup members and the negative behaviors of outgroup members in more abstract ways, which imply that the behaviors are caused by more stable, internal dispositions (Maass, 1999). Also, especially when people are threatened, they see the attitudes held by their group as being based more on rationality and less on emotion and external influence than the attitudes of outgroups (Kenworthy & Miller, 2001). Another subtle possibility is that people see members of ingroups as somehow more human than members of outgroups. Leyens and colleagues (2001) showed that secondary emotions (e.g., sorrow, contempt, conceit), which are found only in humans, are attributed less often to outgroups than to ingroups. Primary emotions (e.g., fear, surprise), which are found among many animal species and are thereby less human, are not differentially attributed to ingroups and outgroups. I consider attributional processing in more detail in Chapter 14.

Other Cognitive Effects

COMPLEXITY OF PROCESSING

Several people have suggested that information about ingroups is processed in more complex ways (e.g., Schaller, 1992a), in part because we typically have more information about our own groups (Linville & Fischer, 1993). It is also likely that we store memory for ingroups more in terms of exemplars and outgroups more in terms of prototypes (Coats & Smith, 1999; Jackson, Lewandowski, Ingram, & Hodge, 1997). Other research (Rothman & Hardin, 1997) has suggested that affect cues are more important in judging outgroups, whereas more informational cues are used for ingroups. Though not definitive, all these results point to our having a more cognitively differentiated view of ingroups, which facilitates more complex processing.

MEMORY

In the past four decades, cognitive psychologists have focused on cognitive biases associated with memory, so we might expect to find differential memory for ingroup and outgroup behaviors (e.g., Kanungo & Das, 1960; Schaller, 1991). For example, Howard and Rothbart (1980) found that subjects were better able to recognize negative items for the outgroup than for the ingroup. Stereotype-consistent behavior is recalled better for outgroups and stereotype-inconsistent behavior for ingroups (Koomen & Dijker, 1997). Subjects are also especially prone to recall negative behaviors that have dispositional explanations and positive behaviors that are situationally caused for outgroups (Ybarra, Stephan, & Schaberg, 2000).

Memory for other category information about people may also be important. For example, I may classify a person as a student, or in terms of major, year in college, postgraduate plans, and so forth. Another professor is seen in terms of departmental affiliation, gender, or seniority. On the other hand, I may be tempted to classify both the student and the other professor as part of the general Rice University community. Park and Rothbart (1982) found that superordinate membership should be equally well recalled for both ingroup and outgroup members, so that having encountered many people, I should remember which are part of the Rice community and which come from another university. On the other hand, subcategories for ingroup members ought to be especially useful, because we have a greater need to distinguish among the members of our own groups. So I should be more likely to remember the departmental affiliation of other faculty members than the majors of students. In an extension, Mackie and Worth (1989) showed that this superior recall of subcategory information for the ingroup was especially pronounced for comparatively rare subcategories, on the assumption that such categories provided more information.

PERCEPTIONS OF VALUES AND ATTITUDES

Generally, it is easy for people to assume that members of salient outgroups do not share their basic attitudes and values; as we will see in Chapter 8, this is a basic source of prejudice. In some cases, it may well be true. We would certainly expect that pro-life and pro-choice adherents, for example, would in fact differ in many important ways, as might Republicans and Democrats, atheists and conservative Christians. But we still have the right to ask whether these differences might not be exaggerated in ways that support group conflict.

Recent research has confirmed that people tend to see the attitudes of outgroups as more extreme than they are. This has been found for pro-choice and pro-life advocates, as well as political conservatives and liberals (Robinson, Keltner, Ward, & Ross, 1995). In one study (Keltner & Robinson, 1997), English professors who either were identified with traditional reading or wished to add more reading from minorities and women were asked to list books they thought the other group would pick for a freshman English course. The two groups agreed on half their choices, but both groups thought that the other group would pick more books representing their viewpoint than they did. Not only do people in other groups seem more extreme, but we also assume that their attitudes are based more on emotion and less on rationality than attitudes we share with ingroup members (Kenworthy & Miller, 2002).

Aside from the support these kinds of results provide for the idea that people try to differentiate themselves from outgroups, they are important if for no other reason than the interpersonal mischief they cause. It is hard for participants in a debate to remain reasonable when each thinks the other has extreme views, and the possibility that each debater thinks the other is defending a more extreme version than he or she is can lead to all manner of self-fulfilling prophecy effects, not to mention misunderstandings.

HOMOGENEITY EFFECTS

Clearly, we tend to stereotype members of outgroups more than members of ingroups, both in our assignment of traits and in more general attributions for behavior. However, there is a more subtle and potentially more important related effect: We tend to see members of outgroups as more similar to one another than we do members of our own groups. In effect, we say, "My own group is variable, but members of your group act, think, and look alike." This perception is usually referred to as "outgroup homogeneity."

Facial Recognition

Most of the research on outgroup homogeneity has dealt with traits, but a body of research on facial recognition also bears witness to this idea. Almost a century ago, Feingold (1914) argued that cross-race identification might be difficult because of people's lack of familiarity with members of other races. People in other racial groups "all look alike."

Basic Effects

The empirical fact of cross-race deficits in memory was first shown in a study by Malpass and Kravitz (1969) for whites rating blacks, but the general effect has since been confirmed for the reverse as well (e.g., Barkowitz & Brigham, 1982; Brigham & Barkowitz, 1978; Devine & Malpass, 1985; Teitelbaum & Geiselman,

1997). In general, both white and black people have more trouble recognizing members of the other race (Bothwell, Brigham, & Malpass, 1989), although the effect tends to be somewhat stronger for white subjects (Anthony, Copper, & Mullen, 1992; Cross, Cross, & Daly, 1971). The effects have also been demonstrated with other races and ethnic groups (Platz & Hosch, 1988; Teitelbaum & Geiselman, 1997).

Explanations

FACES MAY DIFFER

Unfortunately, we do not know why these deficits occur. Brigham and Malpass (1985) suggested four possibilities. One obvious explanation is that facial features actually are more homogeneous for some groups than for others. At present there is no evidence that black, Asian, and white faces are differentially homogeneous (Goldstein, 1979; Goldstein & Chance, 1978). At the same time, this explanation cannot be ruled out, given that selection of white and black faces for this kind of research is far from random.

PREJUDICE

Another possibility is that the relative inability to discriminate faces from another racial group is related to prejudice. However, most studies (e.g., Brigham & Barkowitz, 1978; Platz & Hosch, 1988; Slone, Brigham, & Meissner, 2000) find that the effect is not related to traditional measures of racial prejudice, and a meta-analysis finds no relationship generally (Meissner & Brigham, 2001). And even if there were such a relationship, we would still be no closer to uncovering the mechanisms underlying the effect.

CONTACT AND FAMILIARITY

The most obvious explanation is differential familiarity. Perhaps white people, for example, have more trouble recognizing individual blacks because they have not seen enough black faces to learn discriminable features, whereas blacks are generally exposed to more white faces because there are more whites in the general population of Western countries. The data for this hypothesis are mixed, with some studies finding small effects of familiarity (e.g., Brigham, Maass, Snyder, & Spaulding, 1982; Slone et al., 2000), but others finding no effects (e.g., Brigham & Barkowitz, 1978; Malpass & Kravitz, 1969). A meta-analytic summary finds reliable but small effects of contact (Meissner & Brigham, 2001).

On the assumption that contact may make a difference, we still need to know why. Anthony and colleagues (1992) argue that the effect results from differential cognition of large and small groups. In particular, smaller groups are more salient than larger groups, and consequently the smaller groups are processed in terms of prototype representations, whereas the larger groups are processed in terms of exemplars. According to this model (Mullen, 1991), prototypic representations, in which one exemplar stands for the whole, lead to perceptions of greater homogeneity than do exemplar representations. This model would predict that perceived homogeneity would be larger for the larger group (whites) perceiving the smaller (blacks); this is not always true, although generally effects are stronger for white subjects.

PROCESSING DIFFERENCES

A fourth line of attack has been to look for various cognitive mechanisms: Perhaps people process facial information from different races differently. At some level this has to be true, but we have not yet been able to uncover the whys in this case. One might argue that people simply pay less attention to faces from other races, but differential attention does not seem to mediate the effect (Devine & Malpass, 1985). Zebrowitz, Montepare, and Lee (1993) have shown that samples of European Americans, African Americans, and Koreans make similar trait attributions to faces of same and other races and use about the same cues in so doing. In fact, intraracial agreement on facial features was quite high. This suggests that people are capable of attending to the features of faces from other races and in discriminating one person from another, although it does not mean that they always do. Another possibility is that, especially for those with limited cross-race contact, the salience of skin color simply overwhelms other information. We know that blacks and whites find different aspects of faces salient. In one interesting study (Ellis, Deregowski, & Shepherd, 1975), white subjects tended to use hair color, hair texture, and eye color in describing pictures, whereas black subjects used tone of skin color, eye size, eyebrows, and ears. It may well be (although it was not shown in this study) that the latter cues are better for discriminating black faces and the former for white.

Practicalities

It is tempting to assume that this phenomenon is fairly unimportant. Yet a bit of reflection suggests the opposite. At the theoretical level, there are important unanswered questions about whether the cues used for facial recognition work better for some types of faces than for others, and whether this translates into judgments about people. At a practical level, failures to recognize people of other races can be seen as interpersonal slights and can contribute to interracial mischief. Even more importantly, such effects are bound to be important in criminal trials where eyewitness identification is crucial, and where the eyewitness and perpetrator are of different races (Shapiro & Penrod, 1986).

Trait Homogeneity

It is probable that the "they all look alike" phenomenon is limited to those groups for which group membership is largely based on physical appearance, although in fairness there have been no attempts to study whether people also think that doctors and lawyers, for example, have a homogeneous appearance (or at least have trouble discriminating them perceptually). Most of the research on outgroup homogeneity has concentrated on perceived trait homogeneity, but related work on memory confusions and the group attribution error (see Chapter 3) makes similar points.

Are Outgroups Perceived to Be More Homogeneous?

BASIC EFFECTS

The majority of published studies report ingroup versus outgroup effects, such that people in other groups are perceived in more stereotypic and less individual terms than people in one's own group (Linville, Salovey, & Fischer, 1986; Messick & Mackie, 1989; Mullen & Hu, 1989; Ostrom & Sedikides, 1992). Outgroup homogeneity effects tend to be fairly weak when present and are not found for all groups, but generally people from other groups are perceived as more similar or homogeneous than are people from ingroups. This is not a static effect; as SCT and Brewer's (1991) optimal-distinctiveness theory make clear, perceptions of other groups depend in part on whether social or individual identities are more salient, as well as on the comparison groups. Thus outgroup homogeneity is neither inevitable nor necessarily the most important form of homogeneity.

There are many individual demonstrations of outgroup homogeneity. For example, Jones and colleagues (1981) asked members of student clubs to rate members of their own and of other clubs. The range of ascribed traits across members was greater for own than for other clubs. White subjects have more complex views about whites than about blacks (Linville & Jones, 1980), and both black and white adults (but not college students) see the other group as more homogeneous (Judd et al., 1995). Similar effects have been found for age (Brewer & Lui, 1984; Linville, 1982; Linville, Fischer, & Salovey, 1989), nationalities (Linville et al., 1989), and college majors (Judd, Ryan, & Park, 1991; Park & Judd, 1990). Results for gender are mixed, with some studies (e.g., Park & Rothbart, 1982) finding the effects and others not (e.g., Linville et al., 1989).

SYMMETRY

In addition to some ambiguity of results, there are other issues with the studies just cited in terms of their implications for stereotyping. Since in many studies people from a single group rated those from another, one cannot be certain how much of a role actual experience and real group differences may have had. For example, in one study young people were shown to have less differentiated views of older than of younger people (Linville, 1982). Although the hypothesis of less complex perceptions of outgroups is reasonable and probable, it is also possible that older people really are less differentiated than younger people. If that were true, then everyone, young and old, would see older people as more homogeneous.

The obvious way around this problem is to have young and old people, men and women, and so forth rate one another. We would then expect to find that old people rate young people as less diverse than young people rate themselves, as well as the reverse. Several studies (Brauer, 2001; Judd et al., 1991; Linville et al., 1989; Park & Judd, 1990; Park & Rothbart, 1982) have shown that homogeneity effects are reasonably symmetrical, such that members of Group A rate members of Group B as more homogeneous, and vice versa.

TYPES OF VARIABILITY

When we stop and think about it, there are likely to be several kinds of variability in our perceptions of groups. Quattrone (1986) has suggested three types. The first is "dimensional variability": How much do we perceive people in a group to differ for a particular trait, attitude, or other characteristic? This is what most researchers in this area have had in mind when they considered variability.

Second, we might have "group variability" or "general variability": How much does the group differ across a wide range of dimensions? Kashima and Kashima (1993) point out that this is a part of stereotypes in its own right. For example, most Americans probably believe that the Japanese people are quite homogeneous as a group for most psychological features, because their culture encourages uniformity.[3]

Third, Quattrone (1986) points to what we might call "taxonomic variability," which refers to how various attributes are related. A colleague and I (Schneider & Blankmeyer, 1983) showed that one effect of stereotypes was to make features allegedly possessed by a group seem more closely related. In a sense, the stereotypes acted to cement feature relationships. Linville, Fischer, and Yoon (1996) further showed that traits were more highly intercorrelated for unfamiliar outgroups.

Taxonomic variability is potentially more important than it might seem at first glance. For example, politeness and intelligence might not be seen to be related for Americans (think of all the rude, arrogant, intelligent Americans out there), but might be seen to be highly positively related for Japanese. This has at least two important implications. Obviously, if traits are highly intercorrelated, we do not need as many trait subgroups—and, as we will see, the number of subgroups cognitively represented for groups turns out to be an important mediator of perceptions of homogeneity. A second and arguably more important implication is that if we see a group as generally homogeneous, knowing one trait about a person from that group gives us license to infer others (see Chapter 5).

MEASUREMENT OF HOMOGENEITY

Most research has focused on dimensional variability. This has been measured in several ways, and results are not always consistent from measure to measure. Therefore, we need to discuss the different measures.

Similarity Measures. One measure is simply a direct rating of similarity. Typically, this question is asked in terms of how similar to one another the members of the group are seen to be (e.g., Kraus, Ryan, Judd, Hastie, & Park, 1993; Park & Rothbart, 1982). A related measure has been the percentage of people who would endorse a particular stereotypic trait, attitude, or behavior, and (in some studies) the percentage of group members who would endorse counterstereotypic characteristics (Park & Hastie, 1987; Park & Rothbart, 1982; Quattrone & Jones, 1980).

Variability. Others have used more complex tasks that seem to capture the essence of the homogeneity concept by more directly examining variability. Perhaps the most straightforward measure of variability is the range. Subjects are asked to indicate the points on a scale that include the highest and lowest member of the group (Brown & Wooton-Millward, 1993; Jones et al., 1981; Simon & Brown, 1987).

Variability estimates can also be calculated from somewhat more sophisticated distribution tasks. Subjects can be asked to distribute percentages of people across the various scale points for some trait (Judd & Park, 1988; Linville et al., 1989; Park & Hastie, 1987). Or they can assign dots of different sizes to represent percentages of people in the group that fall at particular points along the dimension (Park & Judd,

1990). Imagine a subject rating groups on perceived intelligence. This subject might rate Groups A, B, and C as equally intelligent (say, 5 on a 7-point scale), but assign the distributions given in Table 7.2. Common sense suggests that although the groups are perceived as being alike in some important respects (namely, the mean rating), the perceiver still seems to have a more stereotyped view of Group A than of B or C. That is, the perceiver would be more confident that a person from Group A is really moderately intelligent than he or she would be for a member of Group B or Group C.

Given the distributions given in the example, there are at least two statistics of interest. One would be the common standard deviation (*SD*), which is related to the mean deviations from the mean.[4] Another measure suggested by Linville and her colleagues (1989) is usually called *PDIST*, which measures the extent to which two randomly chosen group members will be seen as different on the judged attribute.[5] This measure, while similar to the *SD* differs in that *PDIST* is maximized when the distribution is flat (equal numbers of people placed in each category), whereas *SD* is maximized with a bimodal distribution, with most scores being placed at the two endpoints of the distribution.

Relationships of Measures. The obvious question is how these measures are related to one another. If they are all highly correlated, we might as well use the simpler measures that subjects understand well and are easy to administer. If, on the other hand, they do not correlate highly with one another, we must ask which measure seems to be best. A careful study of these questions by Park and Judd (1990) suggests that, by and large, the measures do not correlate so highly that they are interchangeable. In fact, many of the correlations among these measures are remarkably low.

Which then is the best measure? Obviously, this is a difficult question to answer in the absence of a clear criterion for "best," but one approach would be to examine which measure best yields the expected ingroup–outgroup effect. By that criterion, Park and Judd (1990) found that the standard deviation from the dot task, the percentage estimates of the number of people in the group with the trait, and the rated range were the best measures. All measures showed differences in the predicted direction, but only these measures produced statistically significant differences between ingroups and outgroups.

In a latent-variable analysis, Park and Judd (1990) found two general factors. The first included measures of dispersion, and the second the extent to which people were seen as fitting the stereotype. The dispersion measures indicated how well members of the group clustered around the central tendency. The second factor was

TABLE 7.2. Hypothetical Distributions for Ratings of Intelligence

| | Unintelligent | | | Mid-point | Intelligent | | | *SD* | *PDIST* |
	Exceptionally	Highly	Moderately		Moderately	Highly	Exceptionally		
Group	(1)	(2)	(3)	(4)	(5)	(6)	(7)		
A				25	50	25		0.71	0.63
B			20	20	20	20	20	1.42	0.80
C			35	10	10	10	35	1.74	0.73

primarily defined by measures showing a difference between endorsement of stereotypic and counterstereotypic traits for a group. In other words, this measure reflected how many people in the group could be said to exemplify the stereotype.

Accuracy of Variability Judgments. Surely some groups really are more variable than others. For example, on a political liberal–conservative dimension, one might expect to find that a group of registered Democratic voters in Texas is probably more variable than a group of socialists along any number of political dimensions. Some religious groups seem to be less variable than others, if for no other reason than the fact that some religions impose a strong set of doctrinal beliefs on their members.

Is there any evidence that people's judgments of variability track these differences? Several studies show that such judgments are far from perfectly accurate, although people are sensitive to real differences in group variability (Judd et al., 1991; Nisbett, Krantz, Jepson, & Kunda, 1983; Nisbett & Kunda, 1985; Park & Hastie, 1987). Judd and colleagues (1991) have found that subjects typically overestimate the perceived standard deviation of group distributions (heterogeneity), but as one might expect, they do so more for ingroups than for outgroups. For range measures of variability, subjects typically underestimate variability, but more so for the outgroup than for the ingroup. Subjects also tend to be more accurate in judging dispersions for ingroups than for outgroups, particularly when using measures of the groups' stereotypicality. However, research by Ryan and Bogart (2001) finds that when people initially join a group they underestimate ingroup variability more than outgroup, but this gradually reverses over time. This latter result suggests that familiarity may play a role in accuracy (ingroups, presumably become more familiar over time).

Theories

Several theories have been postulated to account for outgroup homogeneity effects (see Linville & Fischer, 1998). Some of these are heavily cognitive, whereas others suggest that various motives may come into play. Even within the cognitive models, however, there are major differences in how such effects are produced.

EXEMPLAR MODELS

Linville and her colleagues (1989) have proposed an exemplar model, which, like other such models (see Chapter 3), requires that information be stored in terms of exemplars encountered. As we meet people, we remember things about them and store this information, along with information about their group memberships. Unlike many exemplar models, Linville and colleagues' does allow information to be stored at a more abstract level. So, for example, if I have previously made a judgment about the typical Rice student, I may have stored that judgment in memory. The next time I have to make such a judgment, I may reuse that summary judgment information as an exemplar, or I may bring forth additional individual exemplars to use. However, these abstract judgment exemplars have no special priority over more concrete instances and just serve as another kind of exemplar or instance. In a similar fashion, I may use as an exemplar secondhand accounts that are not based on firsthand experience (Linville & Fischer, 1993).

Implications. There are two major implications of this perspective. The first is that stereotype judgments are based on memories for behaviors and are not formed during the perception process. When I have to make a judgment about how lazy a group of people is, I bring forth exemplars (whether individual, previous-judgment, or secondhand) and calculate the judgment on the spot. The same is true for variability judgments. I retrieve several exemplars and try to estimate how variable they seem.

Second, Linville and her colleagues (1989) argue that exemplar representation in memory creates the outgroup homogeneity effect because of differential familiarity. As one meets more and more exemplars from a given group, not only the number but the variability of exemplars increases. There are statistical reasons for why large samples are generally more variable (see Linville & Fischer, 1993); thus more familiar ingroups containing more exemplars are likely to seem more variable. More recently, Linville and Fischer (1993) have argued that representations of unfamiliar outgroups may contain more secondhand representations. Since these exemplars could be expected to lie closer to the average for the group, they will reduce the perceived variability of outgroups if retrieved and used to generate variability judgments.

Empirical Support. Linville and her colleagues have done computer simulations that support the notion that exposure to more exemplars does lead to judgments of greater heterogeneity. In addition, greater familiarity with groups often does lead to greater perceived heterogeneity (Islam & Hewstone, 1993b; Linville & Fischer, 1993). For example, Linville and colleagues (1989) found that as students in an introductory psychology class got to know each other better over the course of a semester, perceptions of heterogeneity increased.

However, ratings of familiarity of groups do not seem to mediate outgroup homogeneity (Park et al., 1992). In addition, several studies have found outgroup homogeneity effects, at least under some circumstances, with minimal groups (Judd & Park, 1988; Mackie, Sherman, & Worth, 1993). In minimal groups, subjects would not have time to discover any real information about differential homogeneity even if it existed. Also, outgroup homogeneity effects have been found for well-acquainted groups where differential knowledge is also minimized (Boldry & Kashy, 1999; Park & Rothbart, 1982).

We must also be aware that while knowing more about a group may increase perceived variability on average, in individual cases we may gain information that either increases or decreases variability. Linville and her colleagues reasonably assume that generally groups are equally homogeneous, and that our learning of information about groups is relatively unbiased. But in everyday life, we might find out more information about the similarity of ingroups and differences among outgroups, and in such cases we might expect familiarity to lead to greater homogeneity for some groups (Kashima & Kashima, 1993). Differential familiarity with groups may and probably often does contribute to outgroup homogeneity effects, but it does not seem to be the primary cause of such effects.

DIFFERENTIAL PROCESSING

Tom Ostrom and his colleagues (Carpenter, 1993; Ostrom, Carpenter, Sedikides, & Li, 1993) have argued that at least part of the ingroup homogeneity effect arises from the way information is encoded and stored. When we initially form categories, we focus on how prospective exemplars are alike. If you wanted to know what a "xert" was, it would make perfect sense to think about all the ways prospective xerts fit the category and by implication are like other xerts. Even after you gain more information about a category, you may continue to emphasize the ways exemplars are similar. For categories to which we belong, however, there is often little reason to emphasize such similarities. For one thing, we are often aware of the fact that we are different from other people in our group, and sometimes we are motivated to differentiate ourselves from others in our groups, often in terms of subtypes (Brewer, 1993).

Thus information about outgroup members may be categorized in terms of attributes (i.e., in terms of dimensions of similarity), and information about ingroup people in terms of person. Ostrom and colleagues (1993) show that when information is presented about various people with various features, memory for outgroup information is clustered according to attribute, whereas ingroup information tends to be clustered according to person. Thus this model suggests that outgroup homogeneity is mediated in part by the possibility that we tend to think of outgroup people as exemplifying certain traits or attributes, which tend to emphasize the ways in which they are alike.

ONLINE ABSTRACTION

Park, Judd, and their colleagues (Judd & Park, 1988; Kraus et al., 1993; Park & Judd, 1990; Park, Judd, & Ryan, 1991) argue that abstractions are formed online during processing of new information. The Park–Judd model also allows for storing individual exemplars in addition to an abstract running summary of group characteristics.

Hastie and Park (1986) have argued that some judgments are formed continually online as we encounter new information (see Chapter 4). One important feature of these online judgments is that they are not based on memory for any particular bit of behavior. Each new bit of information (say, behaviors) contributes to the impression that is constantly updated, and we may not even be able to recall specific behaviors that helped create the impression. But, of course, we often do not have the time or interest to form impressions of people we meet, and when we have to generate an impression or evaluation of them, we are forced to rely on whatever memories of their behaviors we can dredge up.

Although there is some evidence that variability judgments can be memory-based (Mackie et al., 1993), the Park–Judd group has emphasized online judgments in its explanations for outgroup homogeneity effects. According to this model, when we process information about others online, we create abstract representations (impressions) that hold information about variability of a group (or individual over occasions) as well as the mean judgment. We also may store data on exemplars and subgroups as well as abstract information, especially about the ingroup.

In particular, we may also have a richly developed sense of various types of ingroup members, and thinking about these would probably emphasize differences among ingroup members. Park and colleagues (1992) expanded a suggestion by Park and Rothbart (1982) that ingroups may be more likely to be differentiated into subgroups of various kinds. After all, for a member of a particular group, it may not always be helpful simply to know that another person is a member of this group. For a Baptist woman, saying that another woman is also a Baptist may not tell her much about religious views, and she may want to further code this other woman in terms of which church she attends or where she falls on a dimension of fundamentalism. By contrast, knowing that someone is a Lutheran may be all the information she needs about that person.

Park and colleagues (1992) had business and engineering students rate one another. They did show that each group mentioned more subgroups with more distinguishing attributes for the ingroup than for the outgroup. More importantly, the tendency to subtype ingroups more was an important mediator of the relative outgroup homogeneity. When this tendency was statistically controlled for, the outgroup homogeneity effect was eliminated. In another experiment, research participants were encouraged to think about people in terms of their subtypes, and this produced judgments of greater variability compared to those who did not actively subtype. Thus one reason we perceive more variability among ingroups may well be that we can more readily think of them in terms of various subgroups differing from the generalized stereotype.

However, when we make judgments about an outgroup, we will be inclined to use only the abstract information, rather than exemplars and subtypes. Thus, according to this model, the stored information about ingroups and outgroups may be equal in variability, but at time of judgment additional information will affect the ingroup variability judgments. Estimates of group variability do not seem to be strongly mediated by what people can remember about group members (Judd & Park, 1988; Park & Hastie, 1987). This suggests that variability judgments are calculated online rather than from memory representations. Also, in studies where subjects are asked to talk aloud as they make these various judgments (e.g., Park & Judd, 1990), subjects tend to think about exemplars and subgroups more for ingroups than for outgroups.

Another reason for outgroup homogeneity may reflect the ways we generate frequency distributions online (Kraus et al., 1993). Instead of constantly updating an abstract variability estimate, we may place new exemplars we encounter on a scale. So as I meet a new person, I may code this person as moderately conservative, very kind, and moderately unattractive. I might then keep a tally of how many people I have met are highly conservative, moderately conservative, and the like. Thus for any given dimension (say, political position), I can, if need be, generate estimates of group variability by recalling approximate information about how many people are very conservative, slightly conservative, and so on.

However, these frequency dimensions can differ in terms of the number of scale points they represent. At this writing, when I think about French attitudes toward Americans as the United States has just gone to war in Iraq, I may be able to code these merely as pro-American versus anti-American (thus having only a 2-point scale). On the other hand, when I think about Americans' attitudes toward France, I recognize that a good many dimensions go into these attitudes; I therefore divide people into four, five or even more attitude categories. When I try to estimate the variability of French attitudes, I will probably see the variability as relatively low, since I have divided the scale into only two positions. However, I seem to recognize more degrees of difference for Americans, and hence may be inclined to see more variability for this sample. Kraus and colleagues argue that we generally use finer divisions for ingroup members, in part because we know more about them. This would then tend to produce the outgroup homogeneity effect.

There is some support for this model. Kraus and colleagues (1993) had subjects think aloud as they processed information about people who varied in some characteristic. When the information was numerical (SAT scores), subjects clearly did keep running tallies of how many people fell into various parts of the total dimension. Another experiment showed that for nonskewed distributions, when subjects used few rather than many discriminations along a dimension, their estimates of group variability were reduced.

SELF-CATEGORIZATION THEORY

SIT clearly makes a clear prediction that the mere act of categorization will lead to perceptions of intragroup homogeneity (a prediction not strongly confirmed—see Chapter 3), but it does not predict the general finding of differential homogeneity for ingroups and outgroups. However, both SIT and SCT, a close relative of SIT, emphasize that perceptions of group homogeneity are sensitive to many social and personal factors, and that ingroup versus outgroup status is generally not the most important.

Ingroup–Outgroup Differences. Nonetheless, SCT points to a number of factors that may lead to differential perceptions of ingroup and outgroup homogeneity (Voci, 2000). This theory emphasizes the proposition that sometimes one's identity is well grounded in group belongingness, whereas at other times personal identity is more important than one's social identity, leading to differentiation between oneself and one's groups. When people feel they are too submerged in their groups, they seek to show how they are different from others, but when they are feeling too different, they may emphasize ways in which they are like others (Brewer, 1993). People who see themselves as different from their groups are more likely to see those groups as diverse than are people who believe they are similar to other group members. Thus, when social identity is salient, the ingroup should actually be seen as especially homogeneous, although perceptions of the outgroup should be unaffected (Brewer, 1993). However, when personal or individual identity is emphasized, the ingroup should be seen as heterogeneous, as one emphasizes differences between oneself and relevant ingroup members. Indeed, thinking about oneself does affect perceptions of the ingroup more than of the outgroup (Park & Judd, 1990).

How does this help explain the ingroup–outgroup effect? One argument is that judgments of the two groups are made in different contexts. When I am asked to think about my ingroup, my personal identity is likely to be important, and hence ingroup homogeneity should be diminished. On the other hand, when I am judging the outgroup, the relevant context is the ingroup, and outgroup homogeneity should be enhanced (Haslam, Oakes, Turner, & McGarty, 1995).

Other Factors Affecting Perceptions of Homogeneity. SIT and especially SCT emphasize motivational reasons for outgroup homogeneity effects. In particular, different circumstances affect the motivations to see ingroups and outgroups differently. For example, when the ingroup comes under attack or threat, social identity is likely to be more important than personal identity; one will feel the need to see the group as maintaining a common front, promoting perceived ingroup homogeneity. My sense is that most of the time most Americans would regard Americans as a diverse group.

However, at times of war or threat (say, after 9/11), they probably emphasize their common features. Groups that are in a numerical minority should feel more threatened or at least take their group identifications more seriously. When a group is in a numerical minority, there is stronger ingroup identification (Simon & Brown, 1987), and ingroup homogeneity is known to be correlated with such greater group identification (Simon, Kulla, & Zobel, 1995; Simon & Pettigrew, 1990). Simon and Brown (1987) have also shown that numerical minorities tend to assume more homogeneity for ingroups than for outgroups, with the reverse being true for numerical majorities. After a review of several studies in this area, Mullen and Hu (1989) have concluded that as ingroups become relatively smaller, they are perceived as less variable and the outgroup is perceived as more heterogeneous.

The effects of status on perceptions of group homogeneity are likely to be complex. Possibly members of high-status groups are likely to perceive low-status groups as especially homogeneous (Lorenzi-Cioldi, 1998). There may be many reasons for this, including the possibility that such perceptions (especially for negative traits) help to maintain the higher-status group's power and sense of superiority, without the strain of having to think about individual differences. On the other hand, members of low-status groups may perceive themselves as especially heterogeneous, especially when the basis of status or comparison reflects negatively on them (Doosje, Spears, Ellemers, & Koomen, 1999). In part this results from the tendency of groups to see themselves as heterogeneous, but for negative features, this perception also promotes a sense that "we're not all bad." Of course, it is entirely possible that members of high-power groups have more freedom to behave in nonnormative ways, so that high-status/power groups may actually be more variable (Brauer, 2001; Guinote, Judd, & Brauer, 2002)

Additional evidence in support of this kind of model comes from studies in which salience of ingroup is correlated with relative ingroup homogeneity. For example, perceptions of ingroup homogeneity are also pronounced when judgments are made in the presence of the outgroup (Wilder, 1984). Finally, this model would suggest that ingroups would be seen as more homogeneous on characteristics central to the group than on those more peripheral (Brown & Wooton-Millward, 1993; Kelly, 1989; Simon & Brown, 1987; Wilder, 1984). As one example, we would expect that religious groups might see themselves as more homogeneous on doctrinal matters than on less relevant matters, such as which sports teams are best.

To summarize, then, SIT and SCT both emphasize that judgments of group features as well as homogeneity are not static, chiseled-in-stone judgments. They depend on the context of judgment, the types of identity that are salient, and desires to make the best case for one's positive qualities as possible. Although outgroups may sometimes (even often) be seen to be more homogeneous than ingroups, this is far from inevitable and not necessarily the most important factor in perceived homogeneity.

Implications of Group Variability

INDUCTION

The work here described would seem to fit one common observation: that "me and mine" are more variable than "you and yours." This has one important implication for the study of stereotyping? In Chapter 3 it was suggested that groups we perceive to be homogeneous provide for inductive potential. If we assume that members of a group (or any category) are pretty much alike, then we should be willing to infer group properties from the behavior or a very few individuals.

Several studies have confirmed that we are more likely to infer information about other group members from outgroups, in part because they are seen as more homogeneous than ingroups. For example, in a study by Quattrone and Jones (1980), students from two rival universities observed a person from either their university or the other performing three behaviors that varied in terms of stereotypicality. Weakly stereotypic behaviors affected judgments about the group as a whole, and more so for outgroup than for ingroups. However, this result was not strong for stereotypic behaviors; as one might expect, a single behavior by a single person is not likely to affect judgments about a group when one already has a strong sense (stereotype) of what the group is like. Additional research by Nisbett and colleagues (1983) has also shown that people are more willing to make judgments about an outgroup than an ingroup based on a single behavior.

EVALUATIONS

Although it now widely agreed that even arbitrary groupings can easily lead to ingroup preference and outgroup rejection, Linville and her colleagues have argued that the greater perceived differentiation of ingroups also plays a role in evaluation. They argue that more complex beliefs about groups (or individuals, for that matter) are likely to result in moderate evaluations. In the extreme case, if we know only that people from a group vary on ambition and intelligence, we can see them as being positive on both traits, on neither, or on only one, giving us three degrees of positiveness. On the other hand, if we know that people from the group vary also along dimensions of kindness, happiness, and politeness, there are five traits; any individual can have from five to no positive traits, providing for more degrees of positiveness.

In a study by Linville and Jones (1980), white subjects were shown to have less complex views of whites than blacks; for example, there were higher correlations among ratings of the blacks than of whites. The subjects were then asked to rate black and white candidates for law school. When an applicant's materials were quite good, the black applicant was rated higher, but the black applicant was also rated lower than the white when credentials were relatively poor. However, Hass and colleagues (1991) found no relationships between evaluation extremity and complexity.

In a subsequent set of studies, Linville (1982) was able to tie down these effects more closely. She showed that college students had less complex views of old people than of young people, and that there was a high correlation between these measures of complexity and evaluative extremity for an older stimulus person. Finally, she manipulated the complexity of thought about several cookies, and found that those who were induced to have more complex thoughts were less extreme in their ratings of the cookies.

These studies, taken collectively, suggest that we are more likely to infer from the individual to the group and the group to the individual for outgroups. We also tend to evaluate outgroup members in less complex ways, and this often leads to more extreme evaluations.

SUMMARY

We have stereotypes about most groups, including the many to which we belong, but the stereotypes for groups to which we do not belong (outgroups) often have a special vigor. Indeed, for thousands of years people have known that we are likely not only to stereotype outgroups but to be prejudiced against their members is often accompanied with behavioral hostility. At the same time, we often show decided positive bias toward ingroups to which we belong.

There are many reasons for this ingroup bias, but Henri Tajfel's early research suggests that the tendency is so basic it shows up even for minimal groups to which people have been arbitrarily assigned and which do not interact. Social identity theory (SIT) and the later self-categorization theory (SCT) argue that people want to feel positively about themselves, to have positive identities, and since they acquire important aspects of their identities from their group memberships, having the sense that ingroups are superior to outgroups support those feelings. Research generally supports this idea, but it is important to understand that most of the bias appears as preference for ingroups as opposed to hostility toward outgroups. Thus intergroup conflict and competition are also important causes of inner-group hostility. SIT and SCT have also stimulated considerable research on conditions that lead people to identify with their groups and the consequences of such identification for stereotyping of ingroups and outgroups as well as ingroup bias.

While people may generally prefer ingroup members to those from outgroups, the black-sheep effects suggests that we are especially prone to reject ingroup members who perform poorly or otherwise embarrass the group. Other theories have argued that outgroup members are evaluated especially extremely.

Chapter 3 argued that perceptions of group homogeneity are especially important parts of group stereotypes because if we assume a group is homogeneous then the behavior of one member can easily be generalized to all. Generally, research on cross-race facial identification as well as trait ascription to ingroups and outgroups suggests that outgroups are seen as more homogeneous than ingroups, although this is far from inevitable. This may result in part from unfamiliarity with outgroup members, but it is also likely that we process and store information about ingroups and outgroups differently.

Notes

1. It is a commentary of some sort that the former school now caters to the landed gentry outside Indianapolis, and the former is now a fairly typical urban high school (with all the problems that this implies).
2. However, the nice woman who called about renewal tried to make me feel that this was a special group: "Our renewals for Sunday afternoons are running a bit ahead of last year. Won't you join your fellow subscribers and help us meet our goal for Masterpiece I early?" Nice try. I did renew, but not because I have any positive feelings about this group. Honest.
3. And I suspect that most white Americans also think that Hispanics and blacks have more homogeneous attitudes than they, in fact, have. When I was a department chair, the department coordinator was a black woman, and we sometimes talked about race issues of one kind or another. I once asked her what black people thought about some issue of the

day, and without missing a beat (and with only a slight twinkle in her eye), she replied, "Whatever makes you think I would know what black *people* think about anything?" Gotcha! Obviously, I had assumed that black people thought alike about the issue.

4. To be perfectly, accurate the variance is directly proportional to the squared deviation of every score from every other score in a distribution—perhaps the most direct measure of intragroup similarity that one could imagine.

5. The exact formula is $P_d = 1 - \Sigma\, p_i^2$, where p is the proportion in each category i.

CHAPTER 8

Prejudice and Discrimination

As I have indicated in Chapter 1, studying stereotypes and stereotyping without considering their relationships to prejudice and discrimination is sterile and incomplete. Furthermore, it will simply not do to assume that stereotypes, prejudice, and discrimination form a neatly wrapped package. This chapter explores some of the complexities. It is not a complete review of the research on prejudice and discrimination; that would be a whole other book, and there are several excellent treatments available (e.g., Brown, 1995; Duckitt, 1992; J. M. Jones, 1997; M. Jones, 2002; Nelson, 2002). My aim is to provide an overview of recent thinking on prejudice and discrimination.

PREJUDICE

"Prejudice" is a kind of prejudgment, an affective or emotional response to a group of people or an individual from that group (see Chapter 1). Prejudice is an attitude, and like most attitudes, it is multifaceted, complex, and fairly labile. Traditionally, social psychologists have treated attitudes as more or less like possessions—things that are acquired with some effort and that, like carefully chosen furniture, sit in their assigned places in our mental homes undisturbed, subject to the occasional mental dusting. Some attitudes are like that. Although many of our political and religious attitudes remain fairly constant for a good many years and feel a bit like a cozy armchair, others are more changeable and less comfortable (Jonas, Broemer, & Diehl, 2000; MacDonald & Zanna, 1998). In many (perhaps most) cases, the attitudes we have toward classes of things change with moods, experiences, and the salience of goals, among other things. I have positive attitudes toward dogs when I play with mine, negative attitudes when the neighbor's dog barks at night, and so it goes. It is not that my attitudes change between playing at 8:00 P.M. and trying to sleep at midnight, but only that certain aspects of my attitudes are more salient at one time than another.

Furthermore, prejudice can encompass any number of feelings or emotions. It makes perfect sense to speak of positive prejudice, but prototypically prejudice is on intimate terms with hatred. It can also include other affective reactions, such as pity or envy. Susan Fiske and her colleagues (Fiske, Cuddy, Glick, & Xu, 2002) argue that prejudice as contempt is usually expressed toward groups that are assumed to be low in both competence and warmth (or, alternatively, in agentic and communal qualities). So poor people and homeless people are mostly viewed with contempt. Pity is mostly expressed toward people seen as warm but incompetent (e.g., elderly individuals, persons with mental retardation), envy toward people viewed as competent but cold (Jews, Asians), and admiration for people perceived to be both warm and clever. Although it is not necessarily a straight path from these emotions to the stronger feelings we think of as prejudice, we can be prejudiced on the basis of any and all of these emotions. And as if matters aren't complicated enough, some aspects of prejudice, as we will see later in this chapter, may be implicit and unavailable to ordinary consciousness.

Thus, right from the start, we ought to be suspicious of any attempt to reduce prejudice to a single thing—a number that presumably summarizes beliefs and feelings about a category of people. The geography of prejudice has hills and valleys, and it has layers. It cannot easily be captured through the two-dimensional cameras traditionally used by research psychologists.

Beliefs and Prejudice

There have, of course, been many attempts to relate stereotypes, prejudice, and discriminatory behaviors. Generally, there has been a strong implicit assumption that at least stereotypes and prejudices must be closely linked. In fact, Gordon Allport felt that this was so crucial that he embedded it in his definition of prejudice: "Ethnic prejudice is an antipathy based on a faulty and inflexible generalization" (Allport, 1954, p. 10).

Are Stereotypes and Prejudice Related?

What evidence do we have? Although there are reports of dissociations or low correlations between stereotypes and prejudices (e.g., Brigham, 1971b; Trafimow & Gannon, 1999), most studies find modest relationships between various measures of stereotypes (typically the favorability of traits attributed to groups or automatic activation of stereotypes) and attitudes about or prejudices toward that group (e.g., Biernat & Crandall, 1994; Bobo & Kluegel, 1997; Eagly, Mladinic, & Otto, 1994; Haddock, Zanna, & Esses, 1994a, 1994b; Katz & Braly, 1935; Kawakami, Dion, & Dovidio, 1998; Leach, Peng, & Volckens, 2000; Link & Oldendick, 1996; Locke, MacLeod, & Walker, 1994; Maio, Esses, & Bell, 1994; Stangor, Sullivan, & Ford, 1991; Stephan & Stephan, 1996; Stephan, Ybarra, & Bachman, 1999). In fact, given the links between cognitive and affective representations of groups (Stephan & Stephan, 1993), it would be quite surprising if the evaluative nature of stereotypes about a group had nothing to do with attitudes toward that group. At the same time, we should recognize that affective reactions to others may result from classical conditioning or other forms of association and have little or nothing to do with beliefs (Olson & Fazio, 2001).

However, when considering the effects of stereotypes on prejudice, we must examine at least three complicating issues. The first is whether the collective stereotypes waiting in the underbrush of our mental lives affect prejudice to the same degree that personal (and perhaps idiosyncratic) stereotypes do. Although this question has not received a great deal of research attention, available evidence suggests that personal stereotypes are more predictive of prejudice than are cultural stereotypes (Augoustinos, Ahrens, & Innes, 1994; Devine & Elliot, 1995; Stangor et al., 1991), especially when shared with a salient ingroup (Haslam & Wilson, 2000).

Second, we know that stereotypes and prejudice are related. It is easy to assume that the former causes the latter, but the causal direction may be reversed. It is not only possible but likely that we employ stereotypes to justify prejudices, as well as the reverse. This makes the prejudice story complex.

Third, stereotypes must be activated in a given situation to affect prejudice and discrimination (Bodenhausen, Macrae, & Garst, 1998), but as I have argued many times (Chapters 3 and 4), stereotypes of the same group of people may change from one situation or context to another. Furthermore, it is also important to recall that all people belong to multiple social categories and groups, and in a given situation one set of stereotypes may rule over others. We cannot predict how a person who has negative stereotypes about lawyers and positive ones about Asians will react to a particular law-degree-toting Chinese American. Stereotypes don't sit still, and neither do prejudices.

The Importance of Other Factors

SYMBOLIC BELIEFS AND AFFECT

What else, besides stereotypes, affects prejudice? Mark Zanna and his colleagues have explored this question in some detail (see Haddock & Zanna, 1999). Zanna (1993) argues that at least four somewhat independent factors predict prejudice. Two are types of beliefs—the first type being our old friend stereotypes, and the other type being beliefs about whether a group facilitates or blocks important value goals or symbolic beliefs. He also suggests that past experiences with a group may be important. Finally, affect or emotion, traditionally a central component of attitudes, should play an important and independent role.

A set of studies by Esses, Haddock, and Zanna (1993) can illustrate the general approach. Prejudice toward each of five groups (English Canadians, French Canadians, Native Canadians, homosexuals, and Pakistanis) was measured with a "feeling thermometer," in which people indicated on a scale from 0 to 100 degrees their general evaluation of typical members of the groups. As a measure of stereotypic beliefs, people listed features associated with each group, their evaluation of each feature, and the percentage of people in that group with the feature. The measure then was the mean product (across features) of the evaluation and the percentage (a kind of strength measure). Symbolic beliefs were measured in a similar way by asking subjects to list values they felt were facilitated or blocked by the group, their judgment as to how strongly the group blocked or facilitated these values (a kind of evaluative measure), and again the percentage of group members who did so. Affective responses were measured by asking subjects what emotions they experienced in response to typical group members, how positive or negative their reaction would be, and what percentage of people in the group elicited this emotion.

For each group, the correlation between the stereotype measure and the thermometer attitude measure was positive (ranging from .24 to .49). So far, so good. However, symbolic beliefs and affective or emotional responses also predicted attitudes and added to the final predictive power over and above that for stereotypes. Affect and symbolic beliefs were at least as important as, and for some groups more important than, stereotype beliefs in predicting attitudes. Additional research showed that reports of past contact and experiences with a group predicted prejudice independently of beliefs and affect (Haddock et al., 1994a).

Other studies have also shown that either affective/emotional reactions to groups (e.g., Jackson et al., 1996; Stangor et al., 1991) or assumed value incongruence (Schwartz & Struch, 1989) predicts somewhat better than do beliefs or cognitively based stereotypes, while other studies (e.g., Eagly et al., 1994) find the reverse. Affective reactions may be more important in the sense that they occur nonconsciously and more quickly than nonaffective ones (Stapel, Koomen, & Ruys, 2002). At this point it seems premature to say which is the more important, but in recent years many social psychologists have been inclined to stress affect over beliefs (Dovidio, Brigham, Johnson, & Gaertner, 1996; Fiske, 1998; Mackie & Smith, 1998; Pettigrew, 1997; E. R. Smith, 1993; Vanman & Miller, 1993). As I have stressed throughout this book, questions about which variables are the most important in affecting behavior and thought are almost always unanswerable in absolute terms. Much depends on the relative strengths of the variables and their interactions with situations and personalities.

INTERACTIONS WITH GROUPS AND SITUATIONS

Intuitively, one might expect these predictors of attitudes or prejudice to be different for different groups, perhaps in different situations, and for different perceivers. For example, my negative attitudes toward the National Rifle Association (NRA) are based (I think) almost entirely on my assessment that the NRA opposes important values I support. On the other hand, my attitudes toward different music groups, soloists, and composers seems to be based almost entirely on affective reactions. Although listening to Mozart piano concertos generally facilitates an important goal of being happy, and although I have some beliefs about Mozart the composer and the genius of his concertos, I think my love of them is almost entirely an emotional reaction, based on no relevant beliefs. My attitudes about psychology books I read seem, by contrast, to be based almost entirely on beliefs about how clear, accurate, informative, and well written the books are.

One might also imagine the relative importance of these factors to vary from situation to situation. Face to face with a member of a racist organization, I might be overwhelmed by my stereotypic beliefs about the traits this person exhibits and less about his or her retarding my goals. At other times and in other places, I am certainly capable of liking rascals whose catalogue of beliefs and traits is not exactly of Sunday School quality, if they are charming and make for a good time.

INDIVIDUAL DIFFERENCES

Individual differences also matter. Haddock, Zanna, and Esses (1993) found that authoritarianism was positively related to more negative attitudes, symbolic beliefs, stereotypes, and affective responses to homosexuals. Symbolic beliefs predicted attitudes more strongly for authoritarians than for nonauthoritarians—a finding that is consistent with the emphasis that conservatives generally and authoritarians in particular place on values, especially traditional ones. People also differ in whether they rely more on affect or beliefs for creating attitudes (Haddock & Zanna, 1998a). By extension, there are surely people whose attitudes toward various groups are based more on their emotional feelings and anxieties, and others whose attitudes are based more on an assessment of their stereotypic beliefs. For some of us in some situations for some stereotypes, affect drives belief more than the reverse. Here as elsewhere in the vexed area of prejudice, one size does not fit all, and one situation cannot stand for the whole.

THE SPECIAL CASE OF PRESUMED VALUE INCONGRUENCE

Recently many psychologists have emphasized the idea that at least part of white prejudice against members of other racial and ethnic groups is based on beliefs that such groups violate cherished values, especially those having to do with work ethics and morality (Biernat, Vescio, Theno, & Crandall, 1996; E. R. Smith, 1993). White students do see blacks and homosexuals as less supportive of their cherished values than they believe whites and heterosexuals are, and those who are relatively more prejudiced against these groups believe this to a larger extent (Biernat, Vescio, & Theno, 1996). Beliefs that outgroups are culturally different from ingroups (presumably in part because of perceived value differences) also produce negative attitudes toward outgroups (Leach et al., 2000). In particular, conservatives are willing to help groups (e.g., elderly persons) whose members they believe are disadvantaged but hold conventional values, but not blacks, whom they perceive as not conventional (Lambert & Chasteen, 1997).

BELIEF SIMILARITY

A related possibility is that people perceive those from other groups as having different attitudes, and given that perceived similarity is a powerful predictor of attraction, such perceptions of belief dissimilarity could be an important component of negative attitudes. Indeed, belief congruence theory (Rokeach, Smith, & Evans, 1960) explicitly states that perceived belief dissimilarity is an important factor in prejudice and discrimination. Several studies (e.g., Cox, Smith, & Insko, 1996; Insko, Nacoste, & Moe, 1983) have confirmed that both white and black subjects do reject those whose beliefs are different, and that belief dissimilarity effects are stronger than race effects in predicting social distance. However, race becomes increasingly important for more intimate social relationships, such as dating and joining one's family (e.g., Moe, Nacoste, & Insko, 1981; Stein, Hardyck, & Smith, 1965). It is all too easy to assume that prejudice is based on irrational fears and long histories of cultural indoctrination, and also easy to forget that perceptions of belief dissimilarity (often erroneous) play an important role in prejudice.

Is There a Prejudiced Personality?

Although prejudices vary over perceivers, targets, and situations, in practice we have yet to escape the legacy of the immediate post–World War II period, when prejudice seemed both more unitary and more of an aspect of personality (Fiske, 1998). It would have been much easier then than now to find people who generally rejected members of almost all minority groups, in all manner of ways, in all contexts and situations. It would not have been hard to find people who didn't want to work with black people, sit with them in movie theaters, have them vote in "their" elections, and have black children attend "their" schools. Although Jews did not face the same degree of legal discrimination, they too were largely avoided by most Gentiles. It is a legacy of the civil rights and women's movements that while overt discrimination and prejudice have diminished dramatically, we have also "broken apart" the integrity of classic prejudice. These days we are likely to encounter people who tolerate or even welcome people from some (but not all) racial and ethnic groups in parts of their lives, while resisting intrusions elsewhere. Nonetheless, discussions of prejudice among laypeople and social scientists continue to emphasize the importance of personality—in part, I suspect, because it allows easy pointing of fingers at others.

The authoritarian personality approach during the 1950s (see Chapter 1) made three major claims of relevance in the present context. First, prejudice was viewed as not merely an attitude but a way of thinking, and as such it was considered part and parcel of an entire personality structure. Prejudice was seen as intimately related to needs, drives, defenses, and anxiety, to name but four of the popular quasi-psychoanalytic notions the model used as a foundation. Second, because prejudice is home-brewed, it was thought to have relatively little to do with such external factors as conflict between groups, experiences with people from other groups, or other reality factors. By and large, prejudice was not seen as driven by reality. Third, it followed that prejudice would be perceived as widely broadcast; almost any and almost all outgroups were viewed as candidates for negative stereotypes, prejudice, and discrimination.

Two questions arise. The first is whether such people exist in sufficient numbers to be worthy of extended attention. Obviously there are virulent racists and extreme sexists, but it might be argued that such folks are a minor fringe of society—people who have to be watched, to be sure, but a fringe nonetheless.

Second, what mileage do we gain by studying such people? As I argue often throughout this book, strong racists probably do not provide good models for the kinds of prejudice most of us display. There are racists who would never work with or hire a person of color, but the discrimination experienced by most blacks and Hispanics is much more subtle and arguably nonconscious. It is possible, of course, to argue that studying racists is extremely important because they are our best laboratory specimens for studying racism: They are perfectly willing to discuss their prejudices, have little concern in presenting a politically correct image, and generally write in large bold letters what the rest of us write in invisible ink.

Generality of Prejudice

Is there evidence that supports the notion of a prejudiced personality? Gordon Allport strongly believed so: "One of the facts of which we are the most certain is that people who reject one outgroup will tend to reject other outgroups. If a person is anti-Jewish, he is likely to be anti-Catholic, anti-Negro, anti any outgroup" (Allport, 1954, p. 66). And several studies support this view. For example, Hartley (1946) reported high correlations among prejudice against several groups, including correlations above .90 between generalized prejudice and prejudice toward three fictional groups. *The Authoritarian Personality* (Adorno, Frenkel-Brunswik, Levinson, & Sanford, 1950) also reported very high correlations among various prejudices.

More recently, there have also been many reports of generalized rejection of outgroups, although typically with more modest correlations (Agnew, Thompson, & Gaines, 2000; Akrami, Ekehammar, & Araya, 2000; Baldwin, Day, & Hecht, 2000; Bierly, 1985; Crandall, 1994; Crandall & Biernat, 1990; Perez-Lopez, Lewis, & Cash, 2001). So, yes, prejudice tends to be general, but Allport joined this parade prematurely—prejudice is not nearly as general as he thought. This makes perfect sense in today's world, where nearly everyone has contact with other types of people in a variety of situations (via the media, if nowhere else). Surely different experiences with and knowledge about different groups should lead to at least some discrepant attitudes. Furthermore, different groups are likely to "push different buttons" for people. For example, although we might expect conservative values to predict attitudes toward homosexuals and blacks, there is no reason to expect the same for rejection of elderly people (Agnew et al., 2000; Lambert & Chasteen, 1997). Liberals might reject NRA members but feel warmly toward gays and lesbians.

Prejudice and Personality

THE F-SCALE

The original authoritarian personality research (Adorno et al., 1950) was built on the idea that personality should predict general prejudice, and not surprisingly the authors reported substantial correlations between prejudice and authoritarianism as measured by the California F-Scale. (Table 8.1 presents some sample items from this scale.) This basic finding has often been replicated both in the United States and various countries around the world, as well as for different target groups (see Brown, 1995, for a review). Chapters 11–13 cite many other studies that find such relationships.

CRITICISMS

However, there are a number of problems with accepting this relationship at face value. The first is that although such correlations support one basic idea of the authoritarian personality, there is limited and ambiguous support for the underlying theoretical structure of the syndrome, involving punitive parents and projection of

TABLE 8.1. Sample F-Scale Items

Obedience and respect for authority are the most important virtues children should learn.

Every person should have complete faith in some supernatural power whose decisions he obeys without question.

The businessman and the manufacturer are much more important to society than the artist and the professor.

The wild sex life of the old Greeks and Romans was tame compared to some of the goings-on in this country, even in places where people might least expect it.

Note. Items from Adorno et al. (1950).

aggression onto outgroups (see Chapter 9). Few social psychologists take the theoretical basis of prejudice proposed by Adorno and colleagues seriously these days.

A second problem is that the F-Scale has a number of unfortunate psychometric properties. One is that it is keyed such that agreement with every item yields a high score, and so it may be measuring tendencies to say yes or true; this is termed an "acquiescence bias" (Bass, 1955).

Third, as Milton Rokeach (1960) has pointed out, the form of authoritarianism tapped by the F-Scale is conservative. But as anyone old enough to have encountered a genuine Marxist (or, more recently, a strong devotee of political correctness) knows, left-wing ideologies are also havens for authoritarian types. Rokeach argued that the underlying personality characteristic is not authoritarianism per se, but dogmatism. Dogmatism and opinionation scales both correlate with outgroup rejection (see Brown, 1995, for a summary).

RIGHT-WING AUTHORITARIANISM

Bob Altemeyer (1981, 1988, 1996) has strongly defended the idea that some right-wing views are associated with prejudice, and has worked on the development and validation of a scale measuring right-wing authoritarianism (RWA). Whereas there were nine components of the original Adorno and colleagues (1950) conception of authoritarianism, Altemeyer finds that only three of those components hang together to form RWA. "Authoritarian submission" refers to a strong tendency to submit to established and legitimate authorities. "Authoritarian aggression" is hostility directed toward people when it is perceived to be sanctioned by legitimate authorities. "Conventionalism" is adherence to social and moral conventions in society. Altemeyer's RWA Scale is clearly similar to the F-scale, but is better psychometrically and in terms of general validation (Table 8.2 presents sample items.)

Correlates of the New Authoritarianism. As expected, the RWA Scale correlates moderately highly with measures of prejudice against various groups (Altemeyer, 1998), especially homosexuals (Whitley, 1999), and with scales measuring traditional sex role attitudes (Duncan, Peterson, & Winter, 1997). People who score high on the RWA Scale are more punitive against those they see as being immoral or lawbreakers, and they are more likely to report that people who lie outside conventional roles deserve

---

TABLE 8.2. Sample Items from the 1997 Right-Wing Authoritarianism (RWA) Scale

Our country will be destroyed someday if we do not smash the perversions eating away at our moral fiber and traditional beliefs.

God's laws about abortion, pornography, and marriage must be strictly followed before it is too late, and those who break them must be strongly punished.

There is no "ONE right way" to live life; everybody has to create their own way [reverse-scored].

What our country needs *most* is discipline, with everyone following our leaders in unity.

Gays and lesbians are just as healthy and moral as anybody else [reverse-scored].

The only way our country can get through the crisis ahead is to get back to our traditional values, put some tough leaders in power, and silence the troublemakers spreading bad ideas.

Note. Items from Altemeyer (1998).

whatever bad outcomes they get. So, for example, they are more likely to endorse punitive measures against people with AIDS and people who use drugs; to be more opposed to abortion; and to think that homeless individuals are lazy rather than unlucky (Peterson, Doty, & Winter, 1993). Although authoritarians may display generalized prejudice against many types of people, much of their antipathy toward various groups is based on the perception that people in those groups violate basic "American" values (Haddock & Zanna, 1998b). The scale is not highly correlated with political party preference, although conservatives tend to score higher. Generally authoritarians see the world as a dangerous place, and they have more limited experiences with the objects of their fear and prejudices, so that they have fewer opportunities to disconfirm their stereotypes and prejudices (Altemeyer, 1988). Authoritarians also tend to have less political knowledge than nonauthoritarians (Peterson, Duncan, & Pang, 2002).

The Special Case of Religion. It has long been known that various measures of religiosity correlate positively with prejudice (Batson & Burris, 1994; Gorsuch & Aleshire, 1974). At one level this makes no sense, given that one of the main messages of most religions is tolerance. Clearly something is amiss, and the culprit seems to be that there are different religious attitudes and ways of expressing those attitudes.

Altemeyer (1988) argues that RWA is not related to the content of most belief systems, but rather to the ways people support and defend their beliefs. Things are no different with religion. Although Protestants and Catholics tend to score higher on the RWA Scale than Jews, within each religion those who score highest are those whose religious beliefs are dogmatic—that is, those who are adamant that their religion is correct, and are sure that no evidence or arguments could sway them from their beliefs. Their beliefs are chiseled in stone. Not surprisingly, a measure of fundamentalism (a belief that some authority, such as the Bible, contains all truth), but not a measure of orthodox beliefs, correlates highly with the RWA Scale. Conversely, those who see religion as a quest for meaning tending to be less prejudiced than those who are more dogmatic (Altemeyer & Hunsberger, 1992; McFarland, 1989). It is not what people believe, but how they believe it.

SOCIAL DOMINANCE ORIENTATION

Jim Sidanius and Felicia Pratto (Pratto, 1999; Sidanius & Pratto, 1999) have argued for a somewhat different take on individual differences underlying prejudice and discrimination. They argue that all societies and cultures create status hierarchies and ideologies, and privilege values that legitimate and conserve the existing hierarchy. This may take the form of derogatory stereotypes of the less advantaged groups, beliefs about which abilities are most important in society, and overt or subtle discrimination. Usually these beliefs are widely (if implicitly) shared by the broader society, including members of the subdominant groups that are victimized by them. The result is that some groups in a society have more power than others, and that this power is used (often quite indirectly) to create beliefs and institutional structures that perpetrate this power differential.

Within a given society people differ in their adherence to this orientation, called "social dominance orientation" (SDO), and this has been measured by the SDO Scale (Pratto, Sidanius, Stallworth, & Malle, 1994). There are actually several versions of this scale, which have been validated in almost 50 samples employing almost 20,000 respondents in 11 nations (Sidanius & Pratto, 1999). Here, there is no particular need to distinguish among the various versions of the scale. Centrally for our purposes, scores on the SDO Scale constitute a strong predictor of prejudice (Pratto et al., 1994). They correlate with Modern Racism Scale scores (see below), sexism, and prejudice against relevant minorities in several countries, such as Canada, Taiwan, and Israel (Sidanius & Pratto, 1999).

It is important to know whether the SDO Scale is correlated with other variables that might explain its ability to predict prejudice. The SDO Scale does correlate with measures of political conservatism, the RWA Scale, support for various social policies (e.g., the death penalty and militaristic stances), and opposition to other social policies (e.g., affirmative action and social welfare) (Sidanius & Pratto, 1999). Given that SDO ideology appeals to conservatives, is it this political orientation that drives these correlations?

Apparently not. The correlations of SDO with prejudice and with conservative policy preferences remain significant even after RWA and conservative political philosophies are controlled for. By contrast, correlations between political conservatism and prejudice are reduced virtually to zero when controls for SDO are instituted, suggesting that the conservatism–prejudice link is caused by SDO. Moreover, opposition to programs designed to help subdominant groups is predicted by a range of political and ideological attitudes such as conservatism, adherence to the Protestant ethic, and racism, which themselves are intercorrelated and predicted by SDO (Sidanius & Pratto, 1999). Interestingly, people with more education tend to show these tendencies more strongly; that is, conservatism, racism, and SDO tend to predict opposition to affirmative action better for people with more education (Sidanius, Pratto, & Bobo, 1996). All these results would tend to suggest that more than sophisticated conservatism is really behind the correlations of racism with social policy preferences.

As might be expected people who have higher status tend to have higher SDO scores. This has been found across several cultures for males versus females, whites versus blacks and Hispanics, and straights versus gays and lesbians (Pratto, 1999). Moreover, SDO correlates with preferences for status- and dominance-enhancing positions (Sidanius, Pratto, Sinclair, & van Laar, 1996), and high-SDO people are also more likely to be attracted to and to be chosen for such positions (Pratto, Stallworth, Sidanius, & Siers, 1997). Not surprisingly, police officers score much higher on SDO than do those more oriented toward helping (Sidanius, Liu, Pratto, & Shaw, 1994). People high in SDO are more likely to reward people on the basis of merit, whereas those who are low on the scale are more influenced by how needy people are (Pratto, Tatar, & Conway-Lanz, 1999). High-SDO people support internal attributions (e.g., laziness, low ability) for income disparities between dominant and minority groups All of these relationships make perfect sense if we assume that those with power and status behave in ways designed to keep their dominant position.

Although SDO was conceived as a single dimension, Jost and Thompson (2000) argue that it actually consists of two kinds of items—support for group-based dominance, and general opposition to equality. A factor analysis does suggest two rather highly correlated factors of just those types. This would not be especially important, except that the factors correlate differentially with different variables for different groups. For example, opposition to equality is associated with higher self-esteem and greater ethnocentrism for whites, but the relationship is negative for blacks. Conservative social policy attitudes (such as dislike for affirmative action) are predicted more highly by opposition to equality than by group dominance, as are conservative political attitudes and a feeling thermometer measure of racial prejudice. The research of Jost and Thompson does not suggest that SDO need always be separated into the two components, since they are highly correlated, but it does suggest that under some circumstances a finer analysis may be appropriate.

RELATIONSHIPS BETWEEN RWA AND SDO

The RWA and SDO Scales are currently the most widely used instruments for measuring the personality and belief structure underlying prejudice. In some ways they are very much alike, and one might be forgiven for thinking they are really measuring the same thing. However, the two scales are positively but not strongly correlated (Altemeyer, 1998; Pratto et al., 1994). They predict prejudice independently, together accounting for over 40% of the variance (Altemeyer, 1998). The two scales also correlate differently with various variables (Altemeyer, 1998). For example, people high in SDO are not necessarily high in conformity, but those high in RWA are. There are gender differences for SDO but not for RWA. Those high in RWA are usually religious, but religious orientation is not correlated with SDO.

John Duckitt (2001) argues that the two scales measure two more or less independent and commonly found orientations toward social life. The RWA Scale relates to authoritarianism and social conservatism versus freedom and social liberalism, and the SDO Scale is oriented toward economic conservatism and power inequality versus social welfare and egalitarianism. Duckitt argues that high-RWA people tend to be conforming. Their worldview is that the world is dangerous and threatening, and because of this view they are motivated to achieve security and social control. Their prejudices will be largely directed toward those whom they see as threatening their own values. Those who score high on the SDO Scale, by contrast, tend to be rather tough-minded in their approach to the world. Because they see the world as a competitive jungle, their main motive is to gain power and dominance over others. Their prejudice should be directed toward lower-status people, particularly in competitive situations, as a way of justifying their superior status. Figure 8.1 illustrates Duckitt's model of the interconnections among all these variables. Large-scale tests of this model, using samples from around the world, have supported it in broad outline (Duckitt, Wagner, du Plessis, & Birum, 2002). In addition, experimental manipulations of relative deprivation and advantage both increase outgroup prejudice—the former presumably because of threat, and the latter because of more salient dominance concerns (Guimond & Dambrun, 2002).

Do Prejudiced People Have Reality-Testing Problems?

The original authoritarian personality work stressed the idea that authoritarians and prejudiced people assessed the world differently than their nonauthoritarian counterparts did. In particular, the former were thought to be inclined to let their internal needs rather than their experiences dictate their feelings about those from other groups. In addition, they were expected to be more rigid and dogmatic about defending their prejudices.

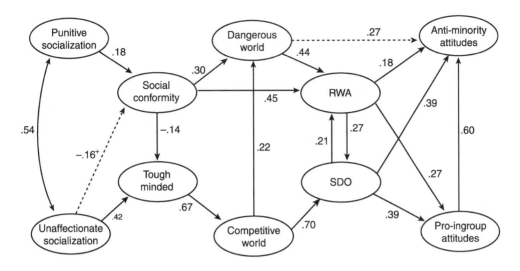

FIGURE 8.1. Paths for various attitudes related to right-wing authoritarianism (RWA) and social dominance orientation (SDO). The decimal fractions represent standardized maximum-likelihood coefficients from a European study ($n = 216$). From Duckitt (2001). Copyright 2001 by Elsevier. Adapted by permission.

There is little evidence on this one way or the other. Some early work by Rokeach (1948) and others (e.g., Koenig & King, 1964; MacDonald & Games, 1974) seemed to suggest that prejudiced people tended to be rigid in their thinking, but the overall evidence on this point is hardly compelling (Brown, 1995). Among the many problems in testing this sort of idea is that authoritarianism and prejudice tend to be negatively correlated with education and intelligence as well as socioeconomic status (all three of these also being intercorrelated), so it is hard to separate out specific intellectual styles from general intellectual abilities.

However, we ought not to dismiss this idea out of hand. For one thing, prejudice and stereotyping are positively related to needs for cognitive structure and closure (Neuberg & Newsom, 1993; Schaller, Boyd, Yohannes, & O'Brien, 1995; Stangor & Thompson, 2002). Although these variables are not the same thing as rigidity, they can produce such ways of thinking under appropriate circumstances. Also, anyone who has spent much time listening to racists quickly realizes that they have problems in their thinking. They make conceptual mountains out of empirical molehills in overgeneralizing from limited experiences, seem to be dogmatic in any number of areas, and treat their negative experiences with a kind of sacredness that most of us would avoid.

The Importance of Personality

COMPETITION WITH SITUATIONAL FORCES

Yes, there is some truth to the stereotype of the prejudiced personality. Such people do exist, and under certain circumstances their numbers can grow and exert the kinds of influence over public policy that they have from time to time throughout world history. But at present they constitute a minority of the population of most countries (see Pettigrew, 1998b, for the complexities in Western Europe), and their influence tends to be small.

That's the good news. The bad news is that the rest of us can be prejudiced in our thinking and discriminatory in our behaviors, at least from time to time. Individual differences among people are important, but so are political, cultural, and social forces (Blair, 2002). Almost 50 years ago, Tom Pettigrew (1958) showed that in both the Southern and Northern United States as well as South Africa, authoritarianism was related to prejudice; however, though these regions did not differ in overall levels of authoritarianism, they did in terms of overt racism. The norms that supported racist behavior in the U.S. South and in South Africa existed less strongly in the U.S. North, and levels of prejudice reflected this difference. More recently, Glaser and Gilens (1997) showed that people who lived in the U.S. South but moved to the North after age 16 became more liberal in their attitudes toward social programs designed to help minorities, and also less prejudiced. People who moved from the North to the South became more conservative and prejudiced. Furthermore, the amount of prejudice people report is dependent on context and the nature of the situation (Kleinpenning & Hagendoorn, 1991) and on the extent to which the object of the prejudice is prototypic of the category (Ramsey, Lord, Wallace, & Pugh, 1994). Sometimes situational and personality factors interact. For example, correlations between authoritarianism and prejudice tend to be stronger when people's individual rather than collective identities are salient (Reynolds, Turner, Haslam, & Ryan, 2001; Verkuyten & Hagendoorn, 1998).

CULTURAL AND SOCIAL FACTORS

So even people who are not conventionally prejudiced can be so under some circumstances. Chapter 7 has emphasized the fact that people generally prefer ingroups to outgroups and may exhibit active hostility to outgroups. Social identity theory argues that we derive some of our sense of self from identifications with various groups, and that we generally try to make these group identities as positive as possible. Values are important parts of group identities, and in that vein Eliot Smith (1993) argues that prejudice results from negative emotions created when we feel that members of another group violate the cherished ideals of our own groups. People who are highly identified with their groups tend to reject outgroup members more to the extent that they perceive realistic and symbolic threat from them, whereas those who are less group-identified rely more on their stereotypes (Bizman & Yinon, 2001).

Over and above identity issues that fuel outgroup derogation, often outgroups compete with ingroups or threaten them in some tangible way. We ought not to forget—in fact, we need to emphasize—that the most virulent forms of prejudice are often fueled by conflict between groups, as Sherif alerted us a half century ago (see Chapter 7). Walter Stephan and his colleagues (Stephan et al., 2002; C. W. Stephan, Stephan, Demitrakis, Yamada, & Clason, 2000; W. G. Stephan, Diaz-Loving, & Duran, 2000; Stephan & Stephan, 2000a; Stephan, Ybarra, Martinez, Schwarzwald, & Tur-Kaspa, 1998) have suggested that four types of threat may increase prejudice. First, other groups may compete with one's own group for resources, prestige, or other outcomes; this is called "realistic threat." "Symbolic threat" occurs because the perception of or existence of different norms, values, and beliefs in other groups threatens our own. "Intergroup anxiety" arises when interacting with others makes us uncomfortable because we think we may be ignored, rejected, or ridiculed by others. Finally, negative stereotyping can also lead to threat if the features of the stereotype suggest harmful outcomes. It is clear that these factors independently and in combination affect prejudice, sometimes against different groups in different circumstances (Stephan & Stephan, 2000a). Various indices of overt prejudice are higher when societal threat (as measured by such variables as lower national income, higher consumer price index, and higher prime interest rates) is high (Doty, Peterson, & Winter, 1991) or when people feel relatively and unjustly deprived (Grant & Brown, 1995; Guimond & Dambrun, 2002). In addition, according to terror management theory, threats in the form of reminders of our own mortality increase prejudice toward dissimilar others or outgroups whose beliefs challenge our defenses against such perceptions (Castano, Yzerbyt, Paladino, & Sacchi, 2002; Greenberg et al., 1990) and increase identification with our own groups (Arndt, Greenberg, Schimel, Pyszczynski, & Solomon, 2002). Just think of 9/11 and its aftermath (Pyszczynski, Solomon, & Greenberg, 2003) .

Prejudice in Disguise

Chapter 10 discusses the changes that have taken place in prejudice and discrimination over the past half century. But a preliminary summary is that there has been a seemingly sharp decline in overt prejudice over this period. However, there are many reasons to be suspicious of the reality of changes in prejudice. Given that it has become unfashionable to display overt prejudice, these changes may say more about changes in the normative structure of U.S. society than they do about any real and deep cultural change. Whatever its other virtues, the emphasis on political correctness may have driven prejudice underground.

There have been two general approaches to untangling "real" from presented prejudices. One basically accepts the validity and reality of people's expressions of nonprejudice, but claims that they have other values and attitudes that may lead to prejudicial responding under certain circumstances. The second has been to look for underlying, implicit aspects of prejudice

Prejudice and Competing Attitudes

Although many of our attitudes are evaluatively consistent and point us in the same direction, others may compete for our attention and control over behavior. Sing the chorus with me: Prejudice is no simple or unitary thing. This means that people can genuinely like, admire, and respect a particular group—say, African Americans[1]—but still evaluate some or many of their perceived behaviors negatively. In some situations conflict need not arise, because the situation and my goals emphasize the positive aspects. But in others I may find that my negative reactions fight with the positive, and I may look for opportunities to have my cake and eat it too.

SYMBOLIC AND MODERN RACISM

During the 1960s and early 1970s, legally sanctioned discrimination sharply declined. Public opinion polls consistently showed declines in negative stereotypes and support for racist attitudes and policies. Most social scientists would agree that this was a period of considerable progress in ongoing attempts to eliminate racism from society. By the early 1980s, however, there was a considerable backlash, with a hardening of attitudes against policies that seemed to favor racial minorities; the so-called "conservative revolution" of the 1980s was due in no small part to this backlash.[2]

Conceptual Underpinnings. In that context, social scientists wondered aloud whether the seeming changes in racial attitudes and stereotypes were anything other than evidence of people's realization that it was politically incorrect to display one's real racial prejudices in public. The notion of "symbolic racism" was developed by David Sears and his students (Kinder & Sears, 1981; Sears, 1993; Sears, Hensler, & Speer, 1979) as an explanation. According to the theory of symbolic racism, people's political attitudes are based on well-socialized and deeply held attachments to certain symbols, such as the value of hard work, individualism, and freedom from government control. Symbolic racism is based in part on many Americans' sense that blacks and members of other minority groups do not hold these same values strongly, and that their behavior routinely violates them. Modern racists are also prejudiced in the old-fashioned sense, but have hidden this, often from themselves. Thus symbolic racism is a blend of negative attitudes toward blacks and strong adherence to the Protestant ethic's values of hard work and individualism.

Political psychologist John McConahay (1986) has built on these ideas in the development of what he calls "modern racism." This is based on the notion that since formal discrimination has been abolished, some people believe that blacks and whites have equal opportunities to compete for jobs and other economic resources. Modern racists think that blacks have pushed for affirmative-action-type programs to give them unfair advantages, and that blacks have advantages they have not earned according to traditional criteria. Although there are differences in emphasis between the ideas of symbolic and modern racism, both models are built on the idea that old-fashioned racism—rejection of people based primarily on race or ethnicity—has been replaced by a more complex set of racial attitudes.

Because modern racists do not reject blacks out of hand or categorically, and because they are attuned to normative standards about expression of traditional racist views, they are most likely to display their racism where it cannot easily be detected. When race is salient in a public discrimination situation, people scoring high on McConahay's Modern Racism Scale (MRS; see Table 8.3 for sample items) do not discriminate. However, when racism is less salient and less easy to detect, they are likely to favor whites over blacks (McConahay, 1983). For example, higher scorers are

TABLE 8.3. Sample Items from the Modern Racism Scale

Over the past few years, the government and news media have shown more respect to blacks than they deserve.

It is easy to understand the anger of black people in America [reverse-scored].

Discrimination against blacks is no longer a problem in the United States.

Over the past few years, blacks have gotten more economically than they deserve.

Blacks have had more influence upon school desegregation plans than they ought to have.

Blacks are getting too demanding in their push for equal rights.

Blacks should not push themselves where they are not wanted.

Note. Items from McConahay (1986).

more likely to endorse discriminatory business practices, but only when these have the backing of legitimate authority (Brief, Dietz, Cohen, Pugh, & Vaslow, 2000).

Is the MRS Simply an Alternative Measure of Old-Fashioned Racism? The MRS is probably the most often used measure of prejudice these days, so it is important to be as clear as we can about what the scale is actually measuring. One justification for the MRS is that it is a sneaky measure of prejudice—that it allows prejudiced people to express attitudes that are normally not desirable. However, scores on this scale are clearly affected by social desirability concerns (Fazio, Jackson, Dunton, & Williams, 1995; Lambert, Cronen, Chasteen, & Lickel, 1996), so it's probably best not to take this particular justification to the bank. Some (e.g., Schuman, Steeh, & Bobo, 1985) have argued that modern racism is just a thin cover for old-fashioned racism. Does the MRS differ from more traditional measures of prejudice? Most studies (e.g., Akrami et al., 2000; Godfrey, Richman, & Withers, 2000; McConahay, 1986; Monteith, 1996b; Pedersen & Walker, 1997; Sears, van Laar, Carrillo, & Kosterman, 1997; Weigel & Howes, 1985) find correlations between modern and old-fashioned racism in the .30 to .60 range, suggesting that the two are related but do not measure the same thing.

Is the MRS Simply Measuring Political Conservatism in Disguise? Another claim is that modern racism is really nothing more than a kind of conservativism (Sniderman & Tetlock, 1986a, 1986b). Several studies find that various measures of conservatism correlate with the MRS, sometimes about as highly as do measures of traditional racism (Fazio et al., 1995; Pedersen & Walker, 1997). As one would expect, the MRS tends to be correlated with conservatives' favorite values, such as adherence to the Protestant ethic (hard work, emphasis on achievement), individualism, and egalitarianism (Monteith & Spicer, 2000; Sears, 1988; Sears et al., 1997; Swim, Aikin, Hall, & Hunter, 1995). Yet these correlations are not high enough to suggest that modern racism and political conservatism are the same thing.

Symbolic Racism 2000. The MRS has become a bit long in the tooth. The items have become somewhat old-fashioned, and there were some other statistical issues that needed to be cleared up. Henry and Sears (2002) have recently published what they call the Symbolic Racism 2000 Scale. This scale is based explicitly on four themes thought to characterize symbolic or modern racist views: (1) blacks have not progressed because they do not work hard enough; (2) blacks are demanding too much; (3) overt discrimination has largely disappeared; (4) blacks have an undeserved advantage. (See Table 8.4 for sample items from this scale.)

TABLE 8.4. Sample Items from the Symbolic Racism 2000 Scale

It's really a matter of some people not trying hard enough; if blacks would only try harder they could be just as well off as whites.

How much of the racial tension that exists in the United States today do you think blacks are responsible for creating?

How much discrimination against blacks do you feel there is in the United States today?

Over the past few years, blacks have gotten more economically than they deserve.

Note. Items from Henry and Sears (2002).

Scores on the scale are correlated with both political conservatism and old-fashioned racism, but this new version of racism seems to be a unique blend of the two. Symbolic Racism 2000 scores predict dislike of affirmative-action-type policies better than political conservatism does, and they contribute predictive power over and above conservatism. Certainly not all conservatives are racist, but as these things are parsed today, racists are almost always conservative. On the one hand, it is theoretically quite possible for a nonracist conservative to believe that blacks and whites are equal in the abilities and motives that count; that current disparities in outcomes for these two groups reflect a legacy of discrimination; but, nevertheless, that it is morally or pragmatically wrong for the government to attempt to be the equalizer and to correct past wrongs, for African Americans or any other minority group. Still, conservative values seem to be a large component of both symbolic and modern racism.

SUBTLE RACISM

Tom Pettigrew and Roel Meertens (Meertens & Pettigrew, 1997; Pettigrew & Meertens, 1995) have advanced a similar notion, which they call "subtle racism." According to their model, blatant or old-fashioned racism has been driven underground in both the United States and most Western European countries, only to be replaced by subtle racism. A scale designed to measure subtle racism has been used in several European countries (see Pettigrew & Meertens, 1995). Pettigrew and Meertens (1995) suggest that subtle racism is a sort of intermediate racism—not as virulent as blatant racism, but more prejudiced than egalitarianism.

AMBIVALENT RACISM

Irwin Katz and his colleagues (Katz, 1981; Katz, Wackenhut, & Hass, 1986) argue that many people have mixtures of positive and negative attitudes toward most stigmatized groups in society, especially racial minorities. In particular, whites both like and dislike blacks. This ambivalence has roots in a value conflict in U.S. society between values of egalitarianism and individualism, as noted by Myrdal (1944) and others. Most Americans genuinely believe that people should have equal opportunities for success, but also believe that victory should go to those who have superior ability, work hard, and save their money. Members of racial minorities are perceived to be less adherent to the latter set of values than to the former. This ambivalence can be resolved in favor or against blacks, depending on the situation. So a black woman who has sacrificed to make her way through college and land a challenging job will be highly respected, perhaps even more than a comparable white woman, but a black man who drops out of school and seems unwilling to work hard will encounter extreme disapproval.

This ambivalence leads white people to feel tense, anxious, and guilty when in the presence of blacks (Monteith, 1996b) or when exposed to controversial statements about blacks (Hass, Katz, Rizzo, Bailey, & Moore, 1992); these feelings in turn lead to efforts at threat reduction. Such efforts usually result in amplification of the positive or negative reactions that are predominant. In effect, whites say, "This black woman who has succeeded seems to share my values, so I view her quite positively. This black man who can't seem to get ahead deserves his fate, so I don't have to feel guilty about derogating him."

Experimental results do suggest that reactions to blacks are polarized relative to those for whites. A successful black is evaluated more positively than an equivalent white, but an unsuccessful black is evaluated more negatively than a white. People also tend to derogate black victims more than white, presumably as a means of justifying the harm, and again this tendency is stronger among those with ambivalent attitudes (Katz, Glass, & Cohen, 1973). On the positive side, people are also more willing to help a black than a white victim (Katz, Glass, Lucido, & Farber, 1979), and people are more willing to help a courteous black than a white (I. Katz, Cohen, & Glass, 1975).

AVERSIVE RACISM

Gaertner and Dovidio (1986, 2000) have argued for a somewhat different form of ambivalence as crucial in interracial encounters. On the one hand, whites have negative beliefs and stereotypes about blacks that they may be reluctant to admit even to themselves, let alone in public. These may result from individual experiences, but they are also a result of immersion in a culture that promotes such beliefs. These negative beliefs give rise to negative feelings—not necessarily hatred, more like anxiety or discomfort. On the other hand, aversive racists recognize that many blacks have been discriminated against, and because of their commitment to ideals of equality and fair play, they feel considerable sympathy with what they take to be the typical victim of racism. Both these positive and negative feelings can be amplified by guilt or societal pressures.

Aversive racists often avoid interracial encounters because of the unease they might feel. To the extent that they do interact with those from other races, they will be in a bit of a bind. When they are in the spotlight, they will usually move their egalitarian beliefs to center stage. For instance, in a situation in which a woman who is an aversive racist has to make a public choice between two more or less equally qualified other women, one black and one white, she may well choose the black woman (as if to prove to herself and others that she is not prejudiced). However, when a prejudicial choice can be defended on other grounds, the aversive racist may then discriminate or fail to help (Dovidio & Gaertner, 1998; Dovidio, Smith, Donnella, & Gaertner, 1997; Gaertner & Dovidio, 1977). These days, even highly prejudiced people are unlikely to discriminate against targets of their prejudice when their credentials otherwise are very strong or weak, but they do when they are more ambiguous (Hodson, Dovidio, & Gaertner, 2002). Another way to put this is that aversive racists tend not to discriminate in obvious ways, but use more indirect and hidden ways, sometimes quite unconsciously.

SEXISM

In the past 25 or so years, gender and race have been the focus of most public concern and social science research on discrimination and prejudice. Both groups have historically had lower power than their counterparts, and in many ways their struggles for equality have followed similar paths. In everyday language we are apt to lump them together as "minorities," and social scientists have often tended to see more similarities than differences between their situations.

Modern Racism and Sexism. Not surprisingly, psychologists have tried to measure prejudice against women (sexism) in parallel ways to racism. Swim and colleagues (1995) have developed a scale called the Modern Sexism Scale by building on conceptions of modern racism. As the MRS does for whites versus blacks, the scale measures perceptions that men and women have achieved equality, gender discrimination is not a major problem, and women push too hard for rights. The Modern Sexism Scale correlates with measures of old-fashioned sexism (items alleging the inferiority of women), and also negatively with support for humanitarian values and the Protestant work ethic—a pattern similar to that for MRS scores. As one might expect, men score higher on both old-fashioned and modern sexism. Tougas, Brown, Beaton, and Joly (1995) have developed a similar scale called the Neosexism Scale.

Differences between Race and Gender. Although prejudices against women and minority races may seem highly similar, it is likely that the two are quite different. The fact that women constitute roughly half the U.S. population and blacks about one-eighth produces a number of differences in the politics of discrimination, if not necessarily the substance. Consider further that whereas classical racism involves hatred toward people because of their race, it seems a bit odd to think of prejudice against women as having hatred at its core. In fact, the stereotypes of women (see Chapter 11) are quite positive, surely more so than those for racial minorities. There are, to be sure, some men (and perhaps a few women) who show the same sorts of hostile behaviors toward women that racists do towards blacks, but for the most part sexism seems a more subtle thing. Although arguably women were punished for their increasing power during the 16th and 17th centuries by being branded as witches (Barstow, 1994),[3] and until the early 20th century "uppity" women were occasionally sent to mental hospitals as a form of punishment, in modern times there have been few (if any) lynchings of women or pogroms directed toward them. Having said that, I must add that during times of war and civil unrest women are often sexually victimized, as recent events in the Balkans and Africa indicate. Women can also be subjugated in other ways, as conservative Muslims (and at different times, in different ways, Christians and Jews) make clear. However, generally even the most racist man usually expresses warm and tender feelings toward some women. Women may be seen as inferior in major ways that count, but are rarely disliked as a class (Jackman, 1994).

Another major difference has been that whereas the enforced status of racial minorities has been tolerated but heartily disliked by members of minority groups, until very recently many, perhaps most, women acquiesced in their lower-status roles. Indeed, it was (and still is in some circles) argued by women that they should be subservient and docile, not as a matter of pragmatics but as a moral duty. It would, in this day and age, be hard to find African Americans who would make the same argument about race. Stereotypes of women, but not racial minorities, tend to be prescriptive as well as putatively descriptive (see Chapter 11), and it may well be the prescriptive part that leads to most discrimination against women (Burgess & Borgida, 1999).

Men and women are intertwined in ways that members of different races are not. If all the Asian or Hispanic people in the United States suddenly left, there would be major economic disruptions, inconveniences, and emotional turmoil, but life would go on. If all the members of one gender disappeared, life would not go on for long, and much of the pleasure (and not just sexual) would be sucked out of the lives of those who remained. Men and women are dependent on each other for sex, for the sharing of child rearing and running a complex modern household, and for companionship. Partially because of this interdependence, there is usually more social interaction across gender than across racial lines; as a result, gender stereotypes tend to be more complex and to include more subtypes (Fiske & Stevens, 1993).

Relationships between men and women have always had a certain strain. Although we may presume that women in, say, 1400 were more accepting of their traditional roles than are women today, there surely were women long ago who saw other possibilities, if only dimly. The Bible, Greek drama, and Shakespeare (to name but a few of the classics) are filled with tensions between men and women not unlike those we see today. And each also presents examples of the kinds of selfless love and loyalty between genders that were as valuable then as now.

The strain arises, of course, from the traditional power imbalance that has existed between men and women. For a variety of physical, cultural, and historical reasons, men are generally more powerful than women—and since power is generally a nice thing to have and keep, men have an incentive to make sure that women are docile and obedient. Women, who have often been the victims of male dominance, have traditionally found it easy (or at least convenient) to adopt the docile and less powerful roles that are thrust upon them. Within this context of unequal power, warm feelings can, of course, still flourish.

Ambivalent Sexism. As we will see in Chapter 11, stereotypically men have qualities that connote strength and agency (what are usually called "agentic qualities"), whereas women specialize in interpersonal warmth and cooperation ("communal qualities"). Glick and Fiske (1999c) argue that these two dimensions underlie many other stereotypes and roles. Particularly in stable social systems, people who have relatively higher status will be seen as generally competent but not especially warm, whereas those in lower-status positions will tend to be characterized as warm but not especially competent. In our society, where men tend to have higher status overall, many men are inclined to see women as loveable but incompetent.

According to Glick and Fiske (2001), ambivalent sexism involves two distinct factors, which form subscales of the Ambivalent Sexism Inventory (see Table 8.5).[4] The Hostile Sexism subscale, based on men's greater perceived competence and power, assesses negative reactions to women who attempt to assert equality or gain power at the expense of men. The Benevolent Sexism subscale, based on the perceived communal qualities of females, measures beliefs that men are stronger so that women should be protected and nourished, and that women possess special qualities making them uniquely valuable. Although these two subscales are somewhat independent, a person who scores high on both would indeed have ambivalent feelings toward women.

Generally, the Hostile Sexism subscale is correlated with endorsement of negative stereotypes about women, and people who score high on the Benevolent Sexism subscale tend to have positive stereotypes about women (Glick & Fiske, 1996). In a cross-cultural study involving 15,000 people (Glick et al., 2000), these results were replicated, and the mean score on these subscales for nations predicts gender inequality across nations. Also, while men tend to score much higher than women on Hostile Sexism, in most countries the difference on Benevolent Sexism is much less, and in a few countries (Cuba, Botswana, Nigeria, and South Africa) women actually scored higher than men on this subscale. The more sexist countries, and more sexist

TABLE 8.5. Sample Items from the Ambivalent Sexism Inventory

Benevolent Sexism	Hostile Sexism
No matter how accomplished he is, a man is not truly complete as a person unless he has the love of a woman.	Most women interpret innocent remarks or acts as being sexist.
Women, compared to men, tend to have a superior moral sensibility.	Women exaggerate problems they have at work.
Women should be cherished and protected by men.	Women seek to gain power by getting control over men.
A good woman should be set on a pedestal by her man.	Once a woman gets a man to commit to her, she usually tries to put him on a tight leash.

Note. Items from Glick and Fiske (1996). Copyright 1996 by the authors. Reprinted by permission.

individuals within countries, show smaller positive correlations between the two subscales. More sexist men (those who score high on both subscales) tend to subtype women into more polarized types than do less sexist men. Furthermore, Hostile Sexism predicts evaluations of career women, whereas Benevolent Sexism predicts evaluations of homemakers (Glick, Diebold, Bailey-Werner, & Zhu, 1997).

Relationships among Sexism Measures. At least three measures of sexism have been developed in the last decade or so: the Ambivalent Sexism Inventory and the Neosexism and Modern Sexism Scales. Which is best? These scales have somewhat different patterns of correlations with other variables (Campbell, Schellenberg, & Senn, 1997; Masser & Abrams, 1999), and so the answer to that question depends on what one is trying to predict. Clearly the Neosexism Scale and the Modern Sexism Scale are similar in conception, although the latter tends to focus most on the belief that gender discrimination is no longer a problem, whereas the Neosexism Scale also includes more items related to beliefs that women are pushing too hard for their rights and that their recent gains are largely undeserved. In fact, there are positive correlations among all three scales, with the Hostile Sexism subscale tending to carry the burden for the Ambivalent Sexism Inventory (Campbell et al., 1997; Glick & Fiske, 1996; Masser & Abrams, 1999).

Implicit Prejudice

VARIOUS MEASURES

Most of the models just discussed involve conflicts between attitudes or values that are both relatively conscious, although they may not be equally salient in all situations. However, many attitudes may be buried deeply enough so they are not readily available. It is easy to imagine, for example, that a person who was raised in a racist home, but who later gets the religion of equality and fraternity, still retains some residues of the earlier lessons. Wilson, Lindsey, and Schooler (2000) argue that when attitudes change, the former attitude may persist as an implicit attitude. Thus people have dual attitudes toward many categories. In any event, it is easy to demonstrate the existence of implicit attitudes toward members of other races that may belie more explicit and easily available attitudes.

Implicit attitudes (Greenwald & Banaji, 1995) are all the rage in social psychology. Several cognitive measures have been used to get at such implicit attitudes, and these have been reviewed throughout the book (see also Banaji & Greenwald, 1994). Most rely on the idea that negative affect or stereotypic traits are associated with racial categories. Various latency measures (Brewer, Dull, & Lui, 1981; Diehl & Jonas, 1991) have shown that people can answer questions about whether groups have stereotypic traits more rapidly than they can about nonstereotypic traits. Other measures using priming of stereotypes or words related to group membership have shown that recognition of stereotype words is facilitated (Dovidio, Evans, & Tyler, 1986; Gaertner & McLaughlin, 1983; Wittenbrink, Judd, & Park, 1997). Fazio's bona fide pipeline (Fazio, 1995) rests on the assumption that for prejudiced people black faces will facilitate judgments about negative words and white faces about positive words.

The implicit association test (IAT), pioneered by Tony Greenwald (Greenwald, McGhee, & Schwartz, 1998) uses a more complex logic; it relies on the notion that same responses to two stimuli (say, punching the Enter key on a computer) are faster when the two are related than when they are not. In practice, prejudice is observed when black faces and negative traits mapped onto the same response are faster than when black faces and positive traits have the same response. This test has also been used to measure attitudes toward political candidates, age groups, and gender, as well as a variety of social and political issues (Nosek, Banaji, & Greenwald, 2002a). One potential caveat may be very important: The IAT measures associations between categories and affect, but associations between individual exemplars and affect may be quite different (De Houwer, 2001). In practice, this may mean that a person who has a negative implicit attitude toward black people generally may still have positive attitudes toward a given black individual. Another potential problem with the IAT is that for white perceivers white faces may be more familiar. However, experimental evidence suggests that familiarity is not a factor in such research (Banse, Seise, & Zerbes, 2001; Dasgupta, McGhee, Greenwald, & Banajii, 2000; Ottaway, Hayden, & Oakes, 2001).

Other measures, such as tendencies to use the linguistic intergroup bias (Chapters 7, 14)—the tendency to describe outgroup members using negative dispositional and positive nondispositional traits, with the reverse for ingroups—have also been used as implicit measures of prejudice (von Hippel, Sekaquaptewa, & Vargas, 1997). A number of physiological measures (arguably the ultimate implicit measures) of affect have been employed. For example, Vanman, Paul, Ito, and Miller (1997) found that although white subjects reported positive reactions to black targets, facial electromyographic activity told a different story of negative affect. Phelps and colleagues (2000) found that the IAT was correlated with patterns of amygdala activation, and Mendes, Blascovich, Lickel, and Hunter (2002) found that white subjects showed cardiovascular threat responses when interacting with blacks or lower-status people, even though these did not match their conscious reports.

RELATIONSHIP TO OTHER MEASURES OF PREJUDICE

As discussed in Chapter 2, implicit measures have many advantages over more direct and reactive ones. People often do not know that their attitudes toward groups are being assessed, and since such implicit attitudes are usually automatically invoked, they could do little about it even if they did. However, such measures are somewhat cumbersome to use, and probably would not be used if they were no better than the explicit measures. Are they?

We first need to know whether implicit measures are reliable and whether different types of implicit measures correlate with one another. The former is important because low reliability limits ability to correlate with other measures, and the latter because we need to know whether the world of implicit attitudes is as messy as the world of explicit ones. The reliability of various implicit measures based on priming is in the .50 range (Kawakami & Dovidio, 2001), just barely satisfactory. Reliability of the IAT is in the same ballpark (Greenwald et al., 2002), although some studies find higher estimates (Kühnen et al., 2001). The relationship between various implicit measures tends to be fairly low, in the range of what one usually finds with explicit measures (Brauer et al., 2000; Cunningham, Preacher, & Banaji, 2001; Rudman, Ashmore, & Gary, 2001).

Do implicit measures correlate highly enough with existing direct measures to tap into essentially the same attitudes or portions of attitude? If they do, why not use the more easily administered explicit measures? Although some research (Banse et al., 2001; Neumann & Seibt, 2001; Wittenbrink, Judd, & Park, 1997) reports respectable correlations between implicit and explicit measures, generally most research reports moderate to low positive relationships or some types of dissociations (Banaji & Greenwald, 1995; Banaji & Hardin, 1996; Bessenoff & Sherman, 2000; Brauer, Wasel, & Niedenthal, 2000; Cunningham et al., 2001; Devine, Plant, Amodio, Harmon-Jones, & Vance, 2002; Dovidio, Kawakami, Johnson, Johnson, & Howard, 1997; Fazio et al., 1995; Greenwald et al., 1998, 2002; Karpinski & Hilton, 2001; Kawakami & Dovidio, 2001; Lepore & Brown, 1997; Livingston, 2002; McConnell & Leibold, 2001; Monteith, Voils, & Ashburn-Nardo, 2001; Ottaway et al., 2001; Rudman, Greenwald, & McGhee, 2001; Skowronski & Lawrence, 2001; von Hippel et al., 1997). Conflicting results occur because different studies use different stimuli (e.g., faces vs. words) and types of tasks (evaluative vs. lexical); they also make different assumptions about whether cultural stereotypes, personal stereotypes, or affective responses are activated. At present we do not have enough research to sort all this out, but Lepore and Brown (1997) and Neumann and Seibt (2001) offer some suggestive leads.

As one example, Rudman, Greenwald, Mellott, and Schwartz (1999) examined IAT and explicit responses to a number of groups. They found that Jewish and Christian students each showed IAT responses more favorable to their own groups. For explicit measures, such as feeling thermometers and semantic differential scales (but not on an explicit measure of anti-Semitism), the two groups also differed. So both explicit and implicit measures showed that Christian students were less favorable to Jews than were Jewish students (and vice versa). However, the correlations between the IAT and the explicit measures were all quite low, the highest being .34. Similar results were shown when young people were tested for age stereotypes: Explicit and implicit measures both showed more positive reactions to young people, but the two types of measures were not highly correlated.

RELATIONSHIPS TO MEASURES OF DISCRIMINATION

There have actually been relatively few studies of the extent to which implicit measures of prejudice play out consistently in behavior. Implicit measures themselves may be more complex than appears on the surface. Brendl, Markman, and Messner

(2001) argue that the IAT has several components, which may differentially relate to various measures of prejudice and behavior.

However, we can still examine the relationship of the overall measure to discrimination. In one careful study (McConnell & Leibold, 2001), the IAT correlated modestly with various behavioral measures toward a black experimenter, and in this study explicit measures of prejudice did not correlate with these behavioral measures. The behavioral measures were basically nonverbal ones (e.g., seating distance, smiling), which can be, but usually are not, under conscious control. In another study involving attitudes toward types of fruit and candy bars, explicit measures predicted choices better than the IAT (Karpinski & Hilton, 2001). This raises the possibility that implicit measures may better predict automatically evoked prejudice and nondeliberate discrimination that are largely free of control due in part to desires to appear normative (Dovidio, Kawakami, et al., 1997; Fazio et al., 1995). Correspondingly, more explicit measures of prejudice may better predict deliberately chosen behaviors toward target groups, because both are controlled to some extent by desires to appear nonprejudiced (Dovidio, Kawakami, & Gaertner, 2002).

If control and deliberative processing are critical, we would expect that people's desires to control their prejudiced behaviors would play a major role. Dunton and Fazio (1997) have suggested that relationships between automatically activated and explicit measures of prejudice may be affected by how strongly a person wishes to control his or her prejudicial responses. Specifically, subjects in their study who were highly motivated to control prejudice reported little prejudice even if their implicit attitudes were negative, but for those with low motivation to control, the two measures were more consistent. In further support of the idea that motivation to engage in controlled processing is critical, low scorers on a measure of need for cognition (a tendency to use effortful processing) show positive relationships between the IAT and overt prejudice, whereas those who score high tend to display negative relationships (Florack, Scarabis, & Bless, 2001).

Will the Real Prejudice Please Stand Up?

Prejudice is at best a construct with many facets, and at worst an ill-defined mixture of notions masquerading under the same label. Where's the beef? What is real prejudice? There is a tendency to think that implicit prejudices are somehow more real or basic than explicit attitudes. In part, this is because Western culture assumes that attitudes, values, and behavior patterns learned early are more basic and important than those acquired later. However, this may not be true, at least generally. Although surely many of our experiences leave residues of one kind or another, it seems strange to assume that what I learned as a child cannot be overridden by my more extensive and mature experiences as an adult. Isn't that what education is all about?

Implicit in this bias is also the notion that since implicit attitudes seem less under direct control, they are somehow more basic. But this seems clearly perverse upon reflection. Is my repugnance at rotting food more basic than my acquired love of Belgian ales? Is my reflexively striking someone who is about to hit me more basic than my clearly intentional and loving behaviors toward my grandchildren? We might want to argue both sides of these questions, but it is not clear to me that those features of our personalities over which we have less control are any the more real or basic because of it.

It is certainly true that because the expression of our explicit attitudes can be controlled, this control will sometimes be exerted in the interests of creating a normative impression. Some people who appear nonprejudiced on explicit measures are clearly making public amends for their real attitudes. However, from this angle, explicit prejudice can probably be taken at face value. At the other end, some people who appear to be nonprejudiced are engaged in coverup activity, but others are not. Accordingly, explicitly expressed nonprejudiced attitudes may be nondiagnostic.

Keep in mind that it is also theoretically possible for explicit attitudes to be more prejudiced than implicit. It is easy to assume that the expression of explicit attitudes is controlled largely by self-presentational concerns, and often that is so. Those of us who work in university settings may find it easy to assume that praise and other social rewards shower down on those who express nonprejudiced views, but, of course, there are many situations in the outside world where a person with relatively low implicit prejudice might find it advantageous to express relatively prejudiced attitudes (and perhaps in that context take them as reflections of true beliefs).

It is also important to note that differences in public and private expression of explicit attitudes and stereotypes may be controlled by factors other than self-presentational concerns. Alan Lambert and his colleagues (2003) have shown that in public situations social anxiety and other forms of arousal may act as a kind of cognitive load that interferes with controls, which normally reduce prejudicial responding. Thus, under some circumstances people may be more rather than less prejudiced in public as opposed to private settings.

Implicit attitudes are usually assumed to be less controllable and thereby more trustworthy. However, implicit measures are affected by a host of motivational, cognitive, and situational factors (Blair, 2002). Although implicit attitudes are not easily faked (Kühnen et al., 2001), they can be changed (Karpinski & Hilton, 2001; Rudman, Ashmore, & Gary, 2001); they are also subject to several different social pressures (Lowery, Hardin, & Sinclair, 2001), situational conditions (Richeson & Ambady, 2001), and exposure to exemplars (Dasgupta & Greenwald, 2001). So we need to be even more wary of giving implicit attitudes pride of place on grounds of immutability.

It is important to note that we have focused our attention on race and, to a lesser extent, gender, and that statements about both categories are subject to public and private scrutiny and normative concerns. Thus we might expect a dissociation between implicit and explicit measures. However, for categories such as Islamic fundamentalism (at least in the West) that are not "normatively protected," intrinsic and extrinsic measures might be more closely related. A study done in Italy (Franco & Maass, 1999) found exactly that: The measures were positively correlated for Islamic fundamentalists targets but not for Jewish ones.

Implicit and unconscious attitudes are important, but they do not have privileged status. A better approach, I think, is to think of them as attitudes that are coexistent with or parallel to more consciously expressed attitudes (Guglielmi, 1999). The same might be said for the various measures of modern or symbolic racism. The main question then becomes this: What do each of these measures best predict? As a first approximation, it is likely that implicit measures best predict relatively subtle affective behaviors—how closely people of different races sit, as well as their eye contact, smiles, and gestures. And it is reasonable to believe that the more overt measures best predict planned and intentional behaviors.

DISCRIMINATION

Controversies surrounding discrimination dwarf those about prejudice. However, studying discrimination does have one potential advantage: Whereas prejudice is entirely mental and unseen, discrimination is behavioral and observable. Discrimination can be obvious, blatant, and declared, but as with most behaviors, the meanings depend on intentions that may not be so clearly displayed or even conscious. This, of course, gives rise to all manner of disagreement about whether decisions and behaviors are fair, and if not, whether they were intended to disadvantage people based on their category memberships. We must dig a little deeper, in two ways. The first, and in some respects easier, is to examine the many forms that individual discriminatory behavior can take. The second is to expand our treatment from the individual into the political, economic, and cultural realms.

Individual Discrimination

The prototype for discrimination involves consciously charted behaviors designed to reject or otherwise harm people from a particular group, simply on the basis of their group membership. Although there may be disagreements about whether a given instance of behavior qualifies as discrimination and how common such behavior is, nearly everyone from the political right to the political left and across all gender and racial groups agrees that blacks and whites, men and women, gays and straights have been treated differently, at least in the past—mostly to the detriment of the lower power group. People, of course, disagree about how prevalent such behavior is today.

Noncontroversial Discrimination

We all discriminate all the time, of course. Most of us would fight having a group home for convicted rapists placed next door to our home, no matter how "cleaned up" or "ex-" the rapists claimed to be. Most church groups do not invite homeless people to share their potluck dinners, and avid hunters probably prefer that people who weep at the sight of dead animals not accompany them on their forays into to the woods. Many women prefer their gynecologists to be female, and most males discriminate against males as their sexual partners. That's the kind of discrimination we all know and generally approve. So it is not the fact of discrimination that is controversial, but its application to specific groups.

Discrimination That Counts

Many forms of discrimination are not easily justified. Most Americans believe that people of different races and ethnicities, religions, and genders should be treated equally. Furthermore, since the Civil Rights Act of 1964 (Title VII), it is illegal to discriminate in employment and certain other situations on the basis of race, color, national origin, or religion—as well as features associated with these categories, such as hair color or type or even certain race-related illnesses such as sickle cell anemia (unless such an illness prevents a person from doing a job). Title VII also explicitly prohibits employment decisions that are based on racial stereotypes about abilities, traits, or performance. Segregation into specific positions, departments, or geographical locations is likewise generally prohibited, as is coding job applications by race. Race, national origin, religion, and gender are protected classes. The Age Discrimination in Employment Act of 1967 extended protection against job discrimination based on age to those over the age of 40, and the Americans with Disabilities Act of 1990 prohibits discrimination based on physical and mental disabilities. Although these laws are fairly clear, people still disagree about whether given behaviors constitute legal discrimination.

We get even more disagreement about discrimination based on nonprotected category status. Suppose a company selects only beautiful women (or men) for jobs as receptionists. Or, more commonly, what about a company that refuses to hire obese people, smokers, or gays and lesbians? Well, obviously these companies do discriminate, although in most cases it would not be illegal. The more important question is how we feel about this. Here I suspect we might get considerable division of opinion. Some of us might argue that since companies, like people, are judged on first impressions, having attractive (and well-mannered) people manning (or womanning) the front desk is a virtual necessity. A small company might refuse to hire obese persons because of fears that their added health costs will raise medical insurance premiums for everyone else. Ditto for smokers. And how do we feel about the argument that hiring a gay male to work closely with other males makes them uncomfortable? Don't straights have rights too?

There is not room here to discuss each of these and other problematic cases in detail, and I have not brought them up for the purposes of pushing one or another agenda. We are all likely to have our own resolutions, but the larger point is that reasonable people with different values and goals do disagree about such cases.

Straight-Line Discrimination

Many people believe that discrimination results from a straight psychological line between prejudice and behavior. That is, people who are prejudiced against members of minority groups deliberately and consciously exclude them from jobs and other opportunities. According to this model, discrimination must be based on negative attitudes and must involve more or less conscious decisions based on such attitudes. At least in the United States such straight-line discrimination does occur much less frequently now than a half century ago, and this has encouraged some people to suggest that discrimination is a thing of the past—that it only exists in the minds of thin-skinned people who don't have the abilities and motives to compete for the things they want.

Without dismissing such forms of discrimination, let me point to two major flaws in the straight-line discrimination model. First, discrimination need not be based on hatred for people from another group; simple preferences for members of one's own group also count. So a woman who feels comfortable around men but simply prefers to hire women discriminates just as much (although probably not as enthusiastically) as a person who dislikes men. Second, many forms of discrimination are quite subtle and can result from implicit prejudices, unconscious biases, social pressures, and just simply thoughtlessness. Behavior need not be consciously planned to be discriminatory.

Subtle Discrimination

As I have said, I suspect that many people take the prototypic case of straight-line discrimination as, well, prototypic. However, discrimination can take many forms, some of which are quite subtle and not even consciously articulated by the perceiver or perceived by the target (Crosby, Bromley, & Saxe, 1980). Discrimination may involve rejection, but it can also involve failures to help (Gaertner & Dovidio, 1977). It may involve cool nonverbal behaviors. It can be as subtle as the self-presentation of the perceiver to the target. For example, in one study (Kite & Deaux, 1986), subjects who thought they were interacting with a homosexual made fewer statements about artistic preferences and more positive statements about women than those who had no such expectation. In an experiment by Kleck, Ono, and Hastorf (1966), subjects interviewed by a physically disabled person downplayed their dating experiences and sports activities more than those interviewed by a nondisabled person. Introducing certain topics of conversation may disadvantage some people; couples who talk about their children at a dinner party may exclude (and bore) single people or couples without children.

In my experience, many people fail to recognize the importance of such indirect forms of discrimination. "Hell, people frown at me too. Those people are just too thin-skinned. I say they should get over it." This kind of reaction, however, ignores at least three salient points. First, more powerful, nonminority people can afford to be magnanimous toward the rude behavior of others, because it is likely to have little impact on them; the less powerful do not have this luxury. Second, as we have seen in Chapter 6, such forms of nonverbal behavior can lead to self-fulfilling prophecy spirals that result in seemingly justified rejection, and members of less powerful groups are probably more affected by such conditions. Third, indirect forms of discrimination are, for many members of minority groups, unremitting and a constant part of the social environment they inhabit. A black businessman may have trouble getting a cab to get him to a luncheon date, will get sidelong glances as he enters a fancy restaurant, has to cope with concealed but still noticeable surprise as his lunch companion (whom he has never met) finds out he is black, may deal with a waiter who seems slower to serve his table than those with white customers, and may find that he is offered neither dessert nor coffee. As recent lawsuits against the Denny's and Cracker Barrel restaurant chains testify, in some cases black people may not get served at all. For many members of minority groups (and females in a male world or gay people amidst straights), ordinary social encounters contain minefields and are accompanied with layers of meaning others do not need to confront.

As a result, members of minority groups may learn to behave defensively and cautiously. Consider the black male attorney who feels he has to dress more impeccably than his white colleagues, the professional woman who has to worry more than a man about exactly what clothes to wear in a business environment, the Hispanic man who avoids slipping into Spanish to distance himself from stereotypes about Hispanics, or the obese woman who thinks she has to behave energetically to combat the stereotype that fat people are lazy. Such behavioral strategies are not likely to be conducive to effortless interactions that most of us take for granted.

Stigmatized people have the additional burden of trying to interpret and deal with others' inconsistent and confusing behaviors. People may try (perhaps none too successfully) to hide discriminatory behavior, but more commonly their own ambivalence toward certain groups may lead to a mixture of positive and negative behaviors. Members of minority groups may also be "victims" of honest but ultimately condescending positive feedback, which is less nuanced and contingent on performance than that given to whites. For example, Harber (1998) showed that white evaluators may "go easy" on blacks by giving them higher evaluations than they deserve. Aside from whether this is fair, such noncontingent feedback inhibits the recipients' ability to calibrate their skills accurately against task demands. For these reasons and others, members of minority groups may feel that they cannot afford to fail—added performance pressure that majority people do not have. Such pressures and anxieties can lead to stereotype threat (Steele, 1997), resulting in performance decrements and stilted or awkward interpersonal behaviors (see Chapter 4).

Members of minority groups live in states of perpetual attributional ambiguity about the reasons for others' reactions to them ("Did he make that snide remark because he's an idiot, or because he's having a bad day, or because I'm Hispanic?"), and this ambiguity is surely not conducive to tension-free interactions (see later discussion). In performance situations this is a particular problem, because prejudice tends to play the largest role when nonracial factors are ambiguous (Dovidio & Gaertner, 2000)—precisely the set of circumstances where people need the most help calibrating their abilities and attributes.

Ability and Motivation to Discriminate

Social psychologists have long known that attitudes (such as prejudice) are far from perfect predictors of behaviors (such as discrimination). However, it would be surprising if attitudes did not predict some behavior some of the time, and more particularly if prejudice did not predict discriminatory behaviors. As a first step, let's focus on the common-sense notion that both ability and motivation affect performance of behavior.

ABILITY

To the extent that discrimination is a behavior designed to hurt someone, the actor must have the ability to do the hurt. To use an extreme example, a 12-year-old white girl living on a farm in Iowa may have decided prejudices against black people, but since she knows none, her prejudices will be utterly wasted. My strong prejudice (I am forced to confess) against eating cooked rats counts for little, since I live in a city with no restaurants (as far as I know) that serve this delicacy.

The ability component seems a fairly mundane aspect of the whole prejudice-and-discrimination equation. But at least two important features of ability require additional comment. In the first instance, we do not always have or exert the ability to control our behavior. Much of it is habitual and mindless. As we have seen in earlier chapters, much of our interpersonal behavior is on automatic pilot, and even when it can be controlled it usually is not.

Ability also enters in at the societal and cultural level. Obviously, some societies actively prohibit discriminatory behavior, whereas others encourage it. Strictly speaking, this is a part of the motivational component, but it often seems a lot like ability.

Several people have made the point that racism and sexism require institutional or personal power to do their dirty work (e.g, Jones, 1997, 1998). In recent years, Susan Fiske and her colleagues (e.g., Eberhardt & Fiske, 1996; Fiske, 1993; Glick & Fiske, 1999b) have emphasized the importance of power as a determinant of stereotyping, but it also affects discrimination (Operario & Fiske, 1998). Obviously, more powerful people can generally discriminate with less impunity than the less powerful. But power also affects discrimination more indirectly, because powerful people—those in charge—generally set the rules that determine who gets included and who excluded from particular positions and roles.

MOTIVATION

Motivation is a bit more complicated. We expect that prejudiced people would want to discriminate against people in the targeted category, all other things being equal. But they are not always equal. Some people's prejudices are relatively pastel and do not readily translate into behavior; mild avoidance is about the most we could expect from them under normal circumstances. Other people's prejudices involve strong elements of hatred, fear, and disgust—feelings that generally motivate people to more than passive avoidance. People with these emotions could be expected to look for opportunities to discriminate. Also, overt conflict between groups and perceived threat both increase prejudice and desires to translate it into behavior.

Psychologists have been most interested, however, in motivational factors that inhibit prejudiced responding, and the usual approach is to look for competing norms and values that mitigate against discrimination. I can be afraid of wild creatures (say, rattlesnakes), but can overcome my temptations to maim and kill because I also value ecological concerns, My frontal lobes recognize what my limbic system does not—namely, that such critters are not intrinsically harmful to me.

Prejudice with and without Compunction. Many (arguably most) people, even some who are prejudiced, do not want to act in prejudiced ways, and normally something on the order of a conscience may lead to pleasant and nondiscriminating behavior toward members of the target group. However, consciences are not always on high alert, and behavior sometimes has a mind of its own; thus even nonprejudiced people can find themselves behaving in prejudiced and discriminatory ways on occasion. Devine, Monteith, and their colleagues (e.g., Devine, Monteith, Zuwerink, & Elliot, 1991; Monteith, 1993; Monteith, Devine, & Zuwerink, 1993; Zuwerink, Devine, Monteith, & Cook, 1996) argue that when people become aware of such behavior and their standards are salient, they will feel guilty and attempt both to change that behavior and to monitor their behaviors more closely in the future. Cues associated with past discriminatory behavior may later serve as signals for controlling discriminatory behavior (Monteith, Ashburn-Nardo, Voils, & Czopp, 2002). People who report large discrepancies between what they should and would do in discrimination situations are more likely to feel guilty when clear evidence of negative racial attitudes is revealed to them (Monteith, Voils, & Ashburn-Nardo, 2001).

Nonprejudiced people report both that they are less likely to discriminate ("would not") and also that they ought not to ("should not") do so (Devine et al., 1991; Monteith et al., 1993). Prejudiced people are the most likely to report discriminating ("would") more than they think they should, although the prejudice–discrepancy link is far from perfect for both explicit (e.g., Monteith, 1996a) and implicit measures of prejudice (Monteith et al., 2001).

Of course, internal standards may not be the only sources of motivation to behave in a nondiscriminatory way. One can have negative feelings when one violates internal standards, but also when one fails to meet the expectations of others (Higgins, 1987). Even militant racists do not always go out of their way to discriminate against members of minority groups, and tolerant people sometimes participate in racist, sexist, or homophobic behavior unwittingly, or because of peer pressure or fear of labeling the behavior publicly for what it is.[5] Obviously, prejudiced people can try to be nonprejudiced when social norms or expectations from others promote such behavior. Several experimental studies show the power of social norms in affecting both prejudice and discrimination (e.g., Blanchard, Lilly, & Vaughn, 1991; Monteith, Deneen, & Tooman, 1996). Paradoxically, people who exhibit nondiscriminatory behavior in one situation may be more likely to discriminate in another—having paid their dues, as it were, to political correctness norms in the first situation (Monin & Miller, 2001). Furthermore, people who are primarily motivated by external pressures to inhibit expressions of prejudice resent the pressure and may demonstrate a backlash prejudice against minority groups (Plant & Devine, 2001).

Individual-Difference Scales. Dunton and Fazio (1997) have developed a measure of what they call "motivation to control prejudiced responses" (MCPR). In their initial research, whereas people with negative implicit attitudes toward blacks freely expressed their explicit prejudice in public when their MCPR was low, those who had strong MCPR reported positive explicit attitudes, even though their implicit attitudes continued to be negative. Furthermore, those high in MCPR were inclined to pay more attention to occupation than to race in judging the similarity of pictures and responded more slowly in making these judgments, suggesting a fairly controlled decision to weight race less (Fazio & Dunton, 1997). The MCPR scale is actually composed of two factors or types of items. The "concern with acting prejudiced" subscale measures a tendency to want to appear to be unprejudiced as well as more internally generated shame for prejudiced behavior. The "restraint to avoid dispute" items tap into motivation to avoid interracial conflict. When exposed to prejudiced stimuli, those who scored higher on the concern scale felt both more guilty and agitated, whereas those whose profile was higher on the restraint subscale were agitated but not guilty (Fazio & Hilden, 2001). Whereas the concern scale is strongly related to egalitarian values, the more externally driven avoidance of dispute seems to reflect lack of experience interacting with those from other races (Towles-Schwen & Fazio, 2001). Furthermore, white students who score high on the "restraint to avoid dispute" subscale tend to avoid interactions with black students (Towles-Schwen & Fazio, 2003), thus presumably exacerbating the problem.

Plant and Devine (1998) have also developed scales to measure what they call "internal and external motivation to avoid prejudice"; these scales are essentially independent of one another. When they behave in a prejudicial way, those high in internal motivation react with guilt, whereas those who are high in external motivation are more inclined to feel afraid or threatened. Moreover, people high in external motivation are more prejudiced when they respond in private (where external forces are mitigated) than in public, whereas those whose motivation is largely internal are nonprejudiced in both public and private. Those who are high in either internal or external motivation report less prejudice on overt measures than do those who are low, but on implicit measures those who are low in external but high in internal motivation show less prejudice than other combinations of motivation (Devine et al., 2002).

Despite the differing measures of the Devine and Fazio groups, both agree that people who are high in a desire to display nonprejudiced responses try to do just that. And as we might expect, those for whom this desire is fueled largely by concern for appearing normative are more subject to situational demands in their corrective behavior, whereas those whose standards are more internalized are less responsive to the situation.

Institutional Discrimination

Institutional discrimination occurs when overt prejudice becomes part of public or institutional policy, or when policies exist that restrict opportunities, access, or choices of people in targeted categories. (See Jones, 1997, for an extended discussion of institutional racism.) An example of the first type—deliberate or straight-line discrimination—would be the past, long-standing practice in the South of using all-white juries to try both black and white defendants (see Kennedy, 1997, for the history of this practice). An example of the second type would be the use of selection criteria for jobs or admission to college that incidentally favor one race or gender over another.

Most people would see straight-line discrimination as wrong, although it is likely to be defended by those in power as necessary for their well-being and perhaps that of the society as a whole. But generally most of us recognize (if admittedly belatedly) that refusing blacks the right to vote or to attend certain schools, refusing to admit women to state-supported colleges, or keeping businesswomen out of clubs where business deals are forged is wrong on the face of it, despite various defenses mounted in favor of such policies.

The second form of institutional discrimination—discrimination based on institutional criteria that disadvantage members of certain groups—is harder to get a firm handle on. Let us consider some cases. It seems reasonable that trash collectors be quite strong, even though that criterion might effectively eliminate most females. Similarly, not hiring convicted felons for most jobs seems reasonable (if not always charitable), even though blacks might be disproportionately rejected because of that decision.

There are plenty of clear cases. But then there are some that are less clear. Until fairly recently, many police departments required prospective recruits to pass a strength test that effectively eliminated most female candidates. Such a test seems reasonable enough on the face of it, because it is easy to understand why police departments would want to have strong officers. On the other hand, it can be argued that many older and effective policemen who were once strong enough to pass such tests no longer can because of too many trips to the donut shop—and, even more importantly, that strength is a weak predictor of successful job performance as a police officer. Yes, there are situations (although much fewer than people who like to watch cop shows realize) that require chasing and subduing suspects, but there are also situations where female officers might be more effective than males because of their better understanding of crimes against women, or their greater willingness to ask rather than order. Surely, then, although strength seems at first glance to be enormously important, it should be seen for what it is—a factor that correlates weakly (if at all) with performance, and that is far less important than a host of other factors.

Or consider a situation far more familiar to most readers of this book—the use of results on a standardized test (typically the SAT) as a major criterion for admitting students to college. It is no secret that African and Hispanic Americans typically score lower on such tests than European Americans (and Asian Americans score higher). But surely it is easy to defend the use of such tests. After all, college is all about learning and intellectual growth, and it makes good sense to educate those whose test scores suggest the highest ability, even though heavy reliance on ability tests will surely result in admitting lower percentages of students from various minorities. In support, we can cite data proving that SAT scores correlate at least a little and often reasonably highly with grades in college. So this is the paradigm case of institutional practice leading to relatively unfavorable outcomes for several racial minority groups, with seemingly no one really to blame.

The counterargument to this is twofold. The first is that most selective colleges use a range of criteria for admissions—and SAT scores constitute only one, and perhaps not even the most important one.[6] Besides, in selective colleges where children of alumni and rich donors, athletes, people who have interesting hobbies and accomplishments, and those from states far away are given preferences (as they are in almost all selective colleges), it is hard to justify SAT scores as being sacred and hard to ignore race and socioeconomic status as equally relevant factors.

A second, more important, but less obvious criticism is this. Yes, SAT scores correlate modestly with grades—but just as we did in the previous example of selecting police officers, let's take a hard look at the criterion. Are colleges in the business primarily of producing people with high grades? This would be hard to defend, it seems to me. Alternatively, it might be argued that colleges should try to enlarge the perspectives and effective intelligence of students they admit, and in that context people who play a mean jazz piano, are black,[7] have lived in foreign lands, can paint lovely portraits, and the like surely count as part of the broadening experience. I would even argue that colleges ought to add to the value of what their students bring from their own abilities. Although I do not see the primary mission of colleges as raising downtrodden individuals, it is worth considering that creating intellectual passion in a kid with modest abilities is more laudatory than adding a veneer of intellectual sophistication to a bright person who will probably be whatever he or she is going to be, with or without my help.

Similar problems occur in the world of hiring and firing. Madeline Heilman (1983) has argued that many women (and, by extension, people of other disadvantaged groups) are often not hired because of a perceived lack of fit to the job, and not because those making the decisions exert what I call straight-line discrimination ("I would never hire a female"). For example, male managers (who do, after all, usually get to set the rules about job requirements) tend to see men as having more agentic leadership qualities than females (Martell & DeSmet, 2001), and Eagly and Karau (2002) have argued that women are underrepresented in leadership roles because they are perceived to be relatively deficient in agentic (leadership) qualities. In addition, if they try to act in an agentic way, they are often criticized or evaluated more negatively than a male who behaves similarly (see Chapter 11 for further discussion, and S. T. Fiske, Bersoff, Borgida, Deaux, & Heilman, 1991, for a famous example). So a women may be denied a job as a coach because an athletic director thinks that women are not good enough motivators or recruiters. People also think that homosexuals are less suitable for jobs stereotypically associated with their gender than for those associated with the other gender (Griffith, 1999). Whether or not these perceptions are correct, the presumed lack of fit justifies discrimination, leaves victims confused about their reasons for their rejection, and makes perpetrators angry that their "perfectly good reasons" have been questioned.

Generally, we must be skeptical of claims made about the virtues of institutional practices and rites of passage that seem reasonable on the surface but that are also discriminatory. Some institutional practices are justified, even if they do discriminate against people from certain groups. But discriminatory practices are worthy of our attention and readiness to see excuses for what they are, and we should be wary of using selection devices of relatively low validity that also (and quite unintentionally) favor some groups over others.

This is controversial enough, but what about the use of group membership itself to make decisions? Perhaps the most controversial is racial profiling—the use of skin color as a cue for subsequent stopping and investigating. On my campus, a disproportionate number of nonstudents who commit crimes on campus are black, and many of the black students (who, like their white counterparts, can look a bit scruffy as they walk across campus late at night) feel that they are singled out for identification checks. This somehow seems wrong, but, in fact, skin color is a valid cue for crime proneness, at least in these parts.

In fact, we use group membership as a criterion for many decisions. Were I to try to get life insurance at this point in my life, I would have to pay several times more in annual premiums than my adult children, but it seems quite reasonable to use age as a decision criterion in this case. Young males pay greatly enhanced car insurance premiums, on the quite reasonable grounds that they are more likely to have accidents. Although young males (and their parents) may object, in fact this keeps me (I have never had an accident) from paying for the repairs and hospital bills of those who do. One could make an analogous argument that obese people and African Americans should pay higher health care insurance premiums because their health care costs are greater. But that seems unfair. My own position is that category information on race and gender should almost never be used in decisions of this kind. But my reasons are related to moral issues and not validity. Let's not confuse the two.

Cultural Discrimination

James M. Jones (1997) defines cultural racism as "the individual and institutional expression of the superiority of one race's cultural heritage over that of another race" (p. 14). Prototypic examples are not hard to find. The English professor who insists that no black writers are worthy to be taught in classes on modern American literature, or who disparages female authors, would be one example. The music critic who sees classical music as far superior to jazz ("a degenerate musical form") would be another. The problem in both cases is that certain values are privileged over others and then form the basis of comparative value.

But the notion of cultural racism goes far beyond that. Jones (1997) points to five domains of human experience on which black and white cultures are likely to differ; he calls this model TRIOS, for "time, rhythm, improvisation, oral expression, and spirituality." He notes, for example, that traditional African cultures valued patience and saw time as moving slowly. Time was a function of the position of the sun and the order of daily tasks. To the extent that this has been taken over by African American culture, it leads to an emphasis on the immediate, the present, with little emphasis on the future or on a sense of present activities leading to future rewards. European American culture, on the other hand, tends to be future-oriented and more controlled by the idea that present activities affect the future. Both are reasonable perspectives, although it is likely that the latter pays off more in European societies. To use just one other example, African cultures placed far more emphasis on oral expression, on creating collective understandings of events and history, whereas European culture is more oriented toward the abstract and written expression. So despite the fact as a spoken language black English is often much richer and expressive than standard versions, whites in America tend to denigrate black English.

The issues in this area seem to me immensely more complex than either liberals or conservatives make them out to be. I do not have space to discuss this more fully, and I doubt that I would have much wisdom to impart even if I did. I would only plead for open minds and for clear recognition of culturally conditioned value judgments, while recognizing that such a recommendation does not do much to solve the fundamental issues in this area.

Does Discrimination Exist?

Asking whether discrimination exists seems silly, in a way. Does anyone doubt that it does? Actually, quite a few people do. In particular, those who restrict discrimination to the straight-line version argue that discrimination has greatly diminished and is well on its way to being eliminated. They are surely correct in the former belief, if perhaps a bit optimistic in the latter. But there is an important debate, one with enormous policy implications, about the extent to which various groups of people continue to be treated unfairly.

There are basically four sources of data one might use to determine whether (or to what extent) discrimination occurs. The most obvious is simple self-reports of discrimination. Second, there are a great many experimental studies, some conducted in controlled laboratory settings and others in more realistic environments. Third, we can conduct what are called "job audits," where people of different races or genders with identical credentials apply for actual jobs. Fourth, we can examine statistics based on large-scale samples.

Self-Reported Discrimination

A number of studies have examined the extent to which people report they have experienced discrimination. Such surveys (e.g., Dion & Kawakami, 1996; Mellor, 2003), not surprisingly, consistently show that many members of minority groups report personal experiences of discrimination. In one 1997 Gallup Poll (Sidanius & Pratto, 1999), 23% of young black men reported that they had experienced discrimination at work within the last month. Such perceived discrimination is not restricted to the

United States; it appears in a number of countries, although of course the nature of the minority group varies from country to country (Sidanius & Pratto, 1999).

Moreover, far too many people with no particular axes to grind—for example, whites who "pass" as blacks (Griffin, 1960; Solomon, 1994), and observant members of dominant groups—report large amounts of blatant and subtle discrimination. Yes, surely some reports of bias are exaggerated or even manufactured, but reflexively dismissing such reports as due to inflated bias detectors is both socially and politically inept, and leads to more misunderstandings in an area that already has far too many.

BIASED REPORTING?

To some extent, our concerns here are generic. People may consciously lie about their experiences, or various nonconscious processes may interfere with accurate recall. Compounding the problem in this area is the fact that these behaviors are especially ambiguous. Most discrimination is not blatant, and most seemingly discriminatory behavior can have a number of underlying nondiscriminatory intentions. That means, of course, that all manner of personal biases as well as culturally and politically conditioned frameworks have fertile fields in which to work. Actual discrimination is often hidden by the mists of everyday interaction ambiguities; if it were clear and blatant, there would be little need for involving judges and juries in complex cases of alleged discrimination.

DO PEOPLE ACCURATELY PERCEIVE DISCRIMINATION?

Whether people accurately perceive discrimination is an important question, with an enormously high assertion-to-evidence ratio. Many people (typically from dominant groups) assert that minority group members are far too ready to perceive bias when it was neither intended nor present. Sometimes that assertion is accompanied with a loud sigh, suggesting that such people have been brainwashed with a victim mentality. In other cases the assertion is based on a less benign claim—namely, that minority people deliberately use charges of discrimination to further their political agendas and to paper over their relative incompetence. Members of minority groups may, in their turn, believe that members of majority groups are blind to discrimination that seems obvious to them. Unfortunately, much of the public's understanding of discrimination is based on telling stories. Whites tend to point to obvious cases of what they see as reverse discrimination or blatant political uses of discrimination charges; many members of minority communities rely on what they perceive to be clear cases of discrimination to bolster their sense that the white world is hostile to them and clueless about the effects.

We ought not to ignore such evidence, but at the end of the day such storytelling is a poor substitute for hard evidence and is a disastrous basis for public policy. What evidence do we have on whether people accurately perceive discrimination? Actually very little. Public opinion polls (e.g., Sigelman & Welch, 1994) and surveys tell us that members of black communities believe that discrimination is more prevalent than do members of majority white communities. Although interesting, such data do not, of course, tell us whether whites err in seeing too little or blacks in seeing too much discrimination (or both).

There have been several experimental studies of the abilities of people to detect discrimination or to label behavior as discriminatory. Not surprisingly, people report more discrimination when the labeling of questionnaires suggests that discrimination is being studied (Gomez & Trierweiler, 2001). Members of groups that have been traditional targets of discrimination are more prone to see discrimination against their own groups (Elkins, Phillips, & Konopaske, 2002; Elkins, Phillips, Konopaske, & Townsend, 2001). Also, women and members of ethnic minorities report more discrimination when responding privately or in the presence of fellow group members than when in the presence of nonmembers (Stangor, Swim, Van Allen, & Sechrist, 2002). When people are told that the reason they were rejected is their gender, they readily perceive discrimination—but, more interestingly, when they are rejected for a reason related to gender (such as body size), they are less ready to perceive it (Kappen & Branscombe, 2001).

It is clear that certain forms of differential outcomes are more likely to be perceived as biased than others. Rodin and her colleagues (Rodin & Harari, 1986; Rodin, Price, Bryson, & Sanchez, 1990; Rodin, Price, Sanchez, & McElligot, 1989) find empirical support for what they call the "asymmetry hypothesis"—namely, that discriminatory behavior by the strong toward the weak is more likely to be labeled as due to prejudice than the reverse. For a variety of cultural and political reasons, certain actions are seen to be more prototypic of prejudiced behaviors than others (Gomez & Trierweiler, 1999; Inman & Baron, 1996). For example, people (and especially members of minority groups) are more likely to label white actor–black target behaviors as discriminatory than other combinations, just because such behaviors are the ones most often discussed in the context of discrimination (Flournoy, Prentice-Dunn, & Klinger, 2002). Similarly, sexist behavior by males is seen as more sexist than that by females (Baron, Burgess, & Kao, 1991). Those who violate norms of social responsibility and who are in positions of power are also more likely to be perceived as prejudiced (Inman, Huerta, & Oh, 1998). People see race and gender as greater vehicles for discrimination than age or obesity, although the latter are detected when people are specifically primed to look for discrimination (Marti, Bobier, & Baron, 2000).

There are also likely to be individual differences in discrimination detection. For example, women who are high in stigma consciousness respond more negatively to men whom they believe to be sexist (Pinel, 2002). Those who identify strongly with their group or have a high level of group consciousness are also more likely to perceive discrimination (Major, Quinton, & McCoy, 2002). Situations also affect perceptions of discrimination. For example, people in good moods are less likely to report discrimination than those in bad moods (Sechrist, Swim, & Mark, 2003).

These studies have used examples of behaviors that are blatantly discriminatory, but often discrimination is hard to detect. Rarely do perpetrators announce that their behavior is due to beliefs about race, gender, or physical disability, and most of the time discriminatory behavior can seemingly be justified on other grounds. The only way to be sure that discrimination has occurred would be to look at many cases in the aggregate and try to partial out the justifications.[8] People are, in fact, better detectives when information is presented in aggregate form rather than case by case (Crosby, Clayton, Alksnis, & Hemker, 1986). Unfortunately, most of the time discrimination comes one case at a time, and the victims of discrimination are not likely to have aggregate data.

THE GROUP–PERSONAL DISCRIMINATION BIAS

We might expect individuals who are members of typically victimized groups to be most attuned to the cues that suggest bias, although it seems that observers and victims make use of the same sorts of decision rules given equivalent data (Inman, 2001). In his classic book, Allport (1954) suggested that members of minority groups are likely to be vigilant for signs of prejudice, and common sense as well as a great deal of political rhetoric suggests that members of historically victimized groups have quick trigger fingers in judging discrimination.

But common sense may not be correct, here as elsewhere. Faye Crosby (1984) discovered that in one company, women who clearly made less than their equivalently qualified male colleagues did not perceive any personal discrimination. A number of subsequent studies using both public opinion data and data gathered in controlled research settings have consistently found that members of various subdominant groups report having experienced less bias personally than they perceive for members of their group as a whole. What has come to be known as the "group–personal discrimination discrepancy" has been observed in groups as diverse as Haitian and South Asian immigrants to Canada, racial and ethnic minorities in Canada, working women, Anglophone and Francophone residents of Quebec, ethnic minorities in the Netherlands, inner-city African Americans, and people with visible stigmas (Dion & Kawakami, 1996; Perrott, Murray, Lowe, & Ruggiero, 2000; Taylor, Wright, Moghaddam, & Lalonde, 1990; Verkuyten, 1998a).

One concern is that comparing personal and group discrimination is a bit of an apples-and-oranges kind of thing. For example, group discrimination information is usually fairly abstract and aggregated, providing a not particularly useful criterion for evaluating individual outcomes that are experienced one at a time (Quinn, Roese, Pennington, & Olson, 1999). People may use different comparisons for the two judgments (Kessler, Mummendey, & Leisse, 2000; Postmes, Branscombe, Spears, & Young, 1999). For example, Sarah might compare her personal experiences against those of other ingroup members, whereas in making judgments of group-level discrimination she may compare her own group with others. It is, of course, quite reasonable for her to think that whereas people in her group have been treated badly compared to other groups, by contrast, she has not been treated as badly as others in her group.

Another possibility is that when people are asked about whether their group has been discriminated against, their social identities attached to that group become highly salient. According to self-categorization theory, this should lead to processing of information about the group and should make group-level discrimination highly salient. However, one's status as an individual member of that group would be minimized, and hence availability of individual experiences would be blunted (Foster & Matheson, 1999). A related result is that when people think about the differences between themselves and other group members, they report less individual discrimination than when similarities are more salient (Quinn & Olson, 2003). Yet another explanation is that people generally experience nonprototypic forms of discrimination that are common but not severe, and hence not prototypic of "real" discrimination. Thus, since they have not experienced what they consider to be prototypic discrimination, they tend to downplay that which they have experienced (Fuegen & Biernat, 2000).

Exaggerating Group Discrimination? Another set of possible explanations for this robust effect is that since a discrepancy is involved, people exaggerate the amount of discrimination faced by group members (Taylor et al., 1990). For example, members of victimized groups may report too much group discrimination, because they want to emphasize the discrimination that exists or to make a political point. Another possibility is that within minority communities such discrimination is widely discussed, and therefore instances of such discrimination become cognitively available, so it is actually easier to think of discrimination against others than against the self.

Minimizing Individual Discrimination?. The explanation that has been the focus of most recent research in this area suggests that the discrepancy results from minimizing individual discrimination. Why would people ever claim that they have not been victims of discrimination?

One possibility is that perceptions of discrimination are used to protect self-esteem. You might expect that seeing failures as due to discrimination might promote feelings of self-worth ("It's not my fault"). As I have discussed before, members of subdominant groups live in a world of attributional ambiguity, where their outcomes result from their own strengths and weaknesses as well as arbitrary or prejudiced evaluations from others (Major & Crocker, 1993). How does this affect self-esteem? Consider the situation of African Americans. Since they surely experience more negative outcomes in majority culture than European Americans, and negative outcomes lower self-esteem, we might expect African Americans to have lower self-esteem than European Americans. But they do not (Crocker & Quinn, 1998; Twenge & Crocker, 2002). Members of minority groups, like all people, have a variety of psychological mechanisms for dealing with failure (Crocker, 1999). They may increase group identification (Jetten, Branscomb, Schmitt, & Spears, 2001; Operario & Fiske, 2001; Schmitt, Branscomb, Kobrynowicz, & Owen, 2002), compare their outcomes only with people in their own group, devalue the importance of areas in which they do poorly, or claim that they are victims of prejudice (Crocker & Major, 1989). It might seem reasonable for people who wanted to protect their self-esteem to assign the causes of failures externally to biased evaluation and prejudice, especially when the bias is blatant and the outcome can easily be so attributed (Crocker, Voelkl, Testa, & Major, 1991; Kaiser & Miller, 2001a). This would suggest that victims of discrimination should be particularly prone to see discrimination against themselves individually.

Costs of Prejudice Attributions. However, there are costs attached to this strategy of attributing negative evaluations to prejudice. One is that people who claim to have experienced discrimination will be seen as whiners and complainers (Kaiser & Miller, 2001b). Understandably, then, members of disadvantaged groups do report less discrimination in public than in private (Stangor et al., 2002). Aside from self-presentational and social desirability concerns, people labeled as complainers are not likely to have their claims taken seriously by others and may fear, with some justification, that the perpetrators will retaliate against them.

Michael Schmitt and Nyla Branscombe (2002) argue that there are even stronger and more general costs of perceiving one's outcomes as due to prejudice, especially for members of low-status and disadvantaged groups. In the first place, such attributions are likely to be both stable and uncontrollable. To say that "I'm a victim today" implies that "I'll be a victim tomorrow, and that there isn't much I can do about it." In attributing negative outcomes to prejudice, one may gain a sense of competence at a given task or job, but at the expense of feeling generally less competent and hopeful. Furthermore, the theoretical advantages of external attributions to the prejudice of others are based on a dichotomy that is much too simple. In traditional attribution theory, there is a tradeoff between internal ("I'm at fault") and external ("They're at fault") attributions, and sometimes this means that blaming others reduces self-blame. But things are more complex for people in disadvantaged groups. As self-categorization theory reminds us, our important social identities are based on identification with groups. If I think that others dislike my group, this nominally external attribution also has important reverberations for the self and is therefore partially internal. So ascribing my failure to the prejudice of others may hurt my pride just as much as attributions to my own shortcomings, which at least I might remedy.

On the other hand, although perceiving prejudice against one's group certainly does have an "internal" component, it is surely not as internal as seeing failures as due entirely to one's own lacks of abilities and effort. There may well be circumstances when attributions to the prejudice of others does work to deflect self-blame (Major, Kaiser, & McCoy, 2003; Major, Quinton, & McCoy, 2002), especially when the victim identifies strongly with the stigmatized group (Crandall, Tsang, Harvey, & Britt, 2000).

Whether or not a negative evaluation "feels" directed at the self may reflect a number of factors. Major, Gramzow, and colleagues (2002) argue that support for the belief that advancement is open to members of all ethnic groups (individual mobility) is one such variable. In both survey results and laboratory experiments, they found that members of minority groups and women who endorsed beliefs in individual mobility were less likely to perceive discrimination than those who did not. By contrast, to the extent that members of dominant groups saw more discrimination, they endorsed such beliefs more strongly. Whether these effects are due to differing perceptions and labeling of experiences or represent a more defensive reaction to possible bias remains unclear.

There seems little point in coming down hard on one side or the other in this debate. Clearly, when members of disadvantaged groups fail at some task or in achieving some goal, they have available all the attributional resources that all of us have in such situations (e.g., "I was unlucky," "The task was unfair," "The evaluator was unfair") to help preserve self-esteem. It would be highly surprising if members of minority groups did not at least sometimes take advantage of the additional discrimination and prejudice attributions available to them. And, of course, in many situations this would not merely be an excuse, but an accurate perception. On the other hand, members of minority groups, like all of us, may find that such attributions, especially when chronically used, merely shift their problems to a new level and have costs in terms of diminished feedings of efficacy and well–being.

Laboratory Experimental Studies

If we define discrimination broadly (ranging from simple evaluative responses to actual differential behaviors), thousands of experimental studies have investigated it. These studies show mixed results. Generally most reviews (e.g., Huffcutt & Roth, 1998; Kraiger & Ford, 1985; Stone, Stone, & Dipboye, 1992) find slight to moderate discrimination effects for such categories as race, gender, and physical disability. However, a great many laboratory studies (e.g., Carver, Glass, Snyder, & Katz, 1977; Nordstrom, Huffaker, & Williams, 1998) show that blacks and whites, women and men, and persons with and without disabilities are evaluated equally highly or are seen as equally strong candidates for hiring. Sometimes members of traditional minority groups are actually evaluated more positively (Evans, Garcia, Garcia, & Baron, 2003).

Although I strongly believe in the value of laboratory experimental research, for present purposes there are at least four obvious problems with many of these studies. First, in many cases the research participants are college students with limited or no experience in making hiring and firing decisions. Second, it is reasonable to believe that many participants in these experiments are reacting to political correctness demands—a particular problem with fairly liberal college students. Third, the stimulus materials used in such studies are frequently fairly limited and only partially representative of the kinds of materials real job applicants present. Fourth, while such studies document the fact that people can or might discriminate, by their very nature they cannot show that discrimination does take place in a more complex environment. There's many a slip between lip and cup when it comes to moving from the lab to the real world. We can never be sure that the variables we so carefully manipulate in our experimental studies are salient in the actual world, or that they do not interact with other variables which affect their power or even reverse their effects under some conditions.

Experimental studies are important in helping us to identify important variables that do (or in some cases do not) affect discrimination, and often in the lab we can examine these variables in a purer fashion. Obviously, in experimental studies we are able to eliminate many of the nuisance factors that are often correlated with causal variables in the real world and that often render interpretation ambiguous. So such studies have their place in helping us understand *why* discrimination takes place, but they can never yield definitive evidence of *how much* of it there is in everyday life.

Job Audits

One way to get around these problems is to conduct field studies in which two people matched in all relevant qualifications, but differing in race or ethnicity, apply for the same job. In some cases the applications are based on paper credentials, but other studies also look at telephone and face-to-face interviews. These studies have used a number of different kinds of minority groups and have been conducted in both the United States and Canada, as well as several European countries. The net result, according to a review by Sidanius and Pratto (1999), is that there is a fair amount of discrimination: On average across studies, white applicants are 24% more likely to be hired than minority candidates.

Such studies thus reveal a disturbing amount of bias, but there are a few caveats. First, many of the studies reviewed by Sidanius and Pratto were done before the middle 1990s, and it might be argued that most companies have "cleaned up their acts" in the last decade or so. Moreover, many studies find that the great majority of decisions are nondiscriminatory. Second, in interviews that involve real people talking on the telephone with interviewers or actually being interviewed face to face, there are bound to be problems in assuring that the behavior of people from different racial or ethnic groups are the same. Obviously, the confederate applicants are well trained in how they should behave, and every effort is made to insure that their behavior is identical, but the training may not be entirely successful. Moreover, as I have pointed out earlier (Chapter 6), interviewers do not necessarily react in similar ways to blacks and whites, Hispanics and non-Hispanics, and this differential behavior may affect the behavior of the applicants differentially. For instance, some black applicants, well trained as they may be, may find it hard to keep irritation out of their voices as they sense a certain coolness on the part of interviewers. Finally, we have to be careful in assessing what the basis of the discrimination is. It may be that an interviewer is reacting more to speech patterns[9] or distinctive physical features than to race per se. For example, some personnel officers may believe (correctly or not) that people who do not speak "proper English" will make a bad impression on customers and may be irritating to coworkers. They claim that they are not rejecting blacks or recent immigrants from Asia because of their race, but because of a correlated feature that affects job performance. This is an example of the lack-of-fit notions addressed by Heilman (1983) (see above).

I hasten to point out that these latter two points concerning differential interview behavior and appearance are certainly more important to research psychologists than to those who are directly affected by discriminatory practices. If blacks and whites of equal qualifications are differentially hired, then there has been discrimination. I am not trying to excuse the behavior, but merely suggesting that this may result less from straight-line discrimination than from other cues associated with race that may seem quite diagnostic to interviewers. Those who study discrimination in the workplace need to understand as much as possible about the mechanics of the process; those who are directly affected by it may quite reasonably feel that this suggestion is a distinction without a difference.

Outcome Studies

At some level, the most powerful data are bound to be those that speak directly to differences between categories of people based in such important real-life outcomes as being employed, the kinds of jobs one holds, and income. Also important, but arguably of somewhat less concern, are data related to health care and welfare, criminality and criminal victimization, and the like. Governments in most industrialized countries collect vast amounts of statistical data on their citizens, so many of these questions can seemingly be answered quickly and definitively.

RACE, JOBS, AND INCOME

It comes as no surprise that there are substantial disparities between blacks[10] and whites on almost every income and job-related statistic.[11] For example, black Americans are over twice as likely to be unemployed (8.0 vs. 3.7% in 1999) as whites. This relative disparity exists at all levels of education. For example, the unemployment rate for black college graduates is 3.3%, and for similarly educated whites it is 1.7%. Of particular concern is that the unemployment rate among black males aged 16–19 is 27.9%, and for black males 20–24 years old it is 14.6%; comparable figures for whites are 12.0% and 6.3%, respectively. In 1998 white men earned 44% more than black men, and white women earned 7% more than black women (Sidanius & Pratto,

1999). In 1996 almost three times as many blacks (28%) as whites (11%) lived below the poverty line (Council of Economic Advisors, 1998).

Clearly, however, such general statistics do not tell the whole story, because blacks tend to be concentrated in lower-paying jobs and jobs that are more seasonable or in which layoffs are more likely. Although it is notoriously difficult to compare incomes for equivalent jobs, we can compare incomes for people with equivalent educations. Obviously people with more education make more money, but we want to know whether the race income disparities exist when we control for education. The answer is that for males the racial income differences exist at all levels of education, and white men gain more through additional education than do black men (Sidanius & Pratto, 1999). For high school graduates black men make 80% of what white men make, but for those with a doctorate the corresponding number is 65%. For women the picture is quite different. Women do earn less than men at every educational level, but there are only small differences between black and white women. Table 8.6 presents these data.

Such figures certainly support strong suspicions of discrimination. However, they do not tell us much about the source of the discrepancies or indicate whether they are justified in some sense. These data are too crude to tell the entire story, and finer analyses might show that the income differences can be accounted for by work-related variables (sometimes called "capital investments") other than race. For example, black men may have gone to less prestigious colleges than their white counterparts, or may have made worse grades or be otherwise less well prepared. Blacks may have majored in fields that are less well compensated than their white counterparts. Black males with advanced degrees may tend to get them in education, which tends to be underpaid compared to, say, law, business, or engineering—areas where black students tend to be dramatically underrepresented. One study (Abdul-Ghany & Sharpe, 1994) based on an extensive longitudinal cohort found that the black–white income disparity was largely due to differences in capital investments (e.g., education, type of job, job tenure, knowledge of the world of work), but that a substantial portion (as much as one-third in some analyses) was due to discrimination.

Some argue that income disparities are largely illusionary, in the sense that when one equates the races on capital investments and other seemingly relevant factors, the disparities are reduced or even disappear.[12] By contrast, liberals (a group that includes most social scientists) want to look beyond such figures and look for deeper explanations. Yes, black males are more likely to get advanced degrees that

TABLE 8.6. Mean Annual Earnings (2001) by Race and Education Level

	Less than 9th grade	Not high school graduate	High school graduate	College graduate	Doctorate
White male	18,834	23,268	31,672	51,923	76,029
Black male	16,452	20,758	25,339	41,650	49,581
White female	12,932	14,289	19,986	34,306	55,466
Black female	13,442	13,490	19,400	34,287	61,779

Note. Data from U.S. Census Bureau, PINC-03.

lead to lower-paying jobs (e.g., education, social work), but that leaves us wondering why they make these decisions. Conservative analysts such as Herrnstein and Murray (1994) would argue that choices of major and profession are related to background factors such as intelligence. Many of us argue that the differences reflect perceived opportunities and how welcoming various professions are to minorities. Many minority people may think that they will have a more even playing field in education or government work than in law or business. By contrast, engineering departments (leading to well-paying jobs) at most universities have a reputation, earned or not, for not welcoming minority students, and the perception of bias surely affects choice of major and subsequently profession.

There is a more subtle concern with partialing out capital investments. Capital investments are, to be sure, important predictors of who gets hired and well paid. However, they are not necessarily good predictors of who does well on the job. For example, it may seem reasonable to prefer hiring the graduate of an Ivy League university over someone from a third-tier state university. However, the more important issue is whether this distinction also predicts job performance. If it does not, then it is, of course, another example of using seemingly valid information correlated with race—in this instance, as a form of indirect discrimination (see above).

RACE, EDUCATION, AND HEALTH

Again, it is not surprising to discover that on almost every indicator of health, education, and well-being, minorities also lag behind members of the majority culture. For example, the infant mortality rate (often used as the main indicator of the health status of a society) is more than twice as great for black as for white families).[13] Life expectancy at birth for white men is 7 years longer than for black men, and for women the difference is over 5 years. Death rates by violence for people age 15–34 are 12 times greater for blacks than for whites (about eight times higher for all age groups), and the death rate from AIDS is over four times greater for blacks. Blacks are more likely to die of heart disease and stroke, diabetes, and most forms of cancer than are whites. Blacks are twice as likely to have no health insurance (thus probably reducing preventative care), and their children are less likely to have received the appropriate vaccinations. Controlling for income and socioeconomic status greatly reduces but does not eliminate race differences in health, and stress related to perceived discrimination is a predictor of such differences (Williams, Yu, Jackson, & Anderson, 1997).

There are also differences between the races in educational attainment (Council of Economic Advisors, 1998).[14] For adults 25 years and older blacks (74%) are slightly less likely than whites (86%) to have graduated from high school and are less likely to have completed 4 or more years of college (25% vs. 13%). Percentages of black and white students enrolled in college a year after high school graduation are virtually identical. Hispanics (45%)[15] and Native Americans (35%) are much less likely than either whites or blacks to have not graduated from high school or college. The good news is that the high school dropout rates for white and minority students are dropping, and the black–white difference is narrowing substantially.[16] Also, the enrollment of high school graduates in colleges is increasing, and the race difference is narrowing as well.

Aside from family, health, and jobs, nothing affects quality of life more than one's living arrangements. Blacks are less likely to own their own homes and more likely to live in homes with more than one person per room. Blacks report more problems of all sorts in their neighborhoods. They also live in more segregated neighborhoods than do whites and Asians. Blacks are discriminated against at various stages in attempting to rent or buy houses and are substantially less likely to be given loans to buy a house—a result that survives (8% less likely) even when almost 40 extraneous variables thought to influence granting of loans are partialed out (Sidanius & Pratto, 1999). There is also discrimination against minorities in a variety of other retail transactions. In an often-cited audit study (Ayers, 1995; Ayers & Siegelman, 1995), black men paid over $1,000 more for a new car than white men, even when other variables were controlled for.

RACE AND CRIME

Given that one of the strongest cultural stereotypes of blacks is that they are criminal and especially violent (see Chapter 11), it is important to assess the extent to which this is true and whether such stereotyping leads to discrimination in the criminal justice system (CJS). Here the going gets rough. Blacks and Hispanics have more than their share of involvement on the receiving end of the CJS. It is an article of faith among many that this results from past and present discrimination, and many people argue that this disparity results almost entirely from various biases in the ways people are arrested, tried, convicted, and sentenced in the United States. But faith is not evidence.

Again, we begin with the crudest statistics. Although there are many crimes for which black perpetrators are underrepresented (almost all so-called "white-collar" crimes, arguably far more damaging in the aggregate than violent crimes), blacks are overrepresented for those violent crimes people seem most to care about. Whereas they constitute slightly under 13% of the general U.S. population, over 50% of those arrested for murder, 40% of those arrested for rape, and 60% of those arrested for robbery are black. About 54% of felony convictions for violent crimes are black, as are 59% of those who are incarcerated for violent crimes (Council of Economic Advisors, 1998). Even more striking is the fact that although black males between the ages of 14 and 24 make up slightly more than 1% of the population, they represent 17% of murder victims[17] and 20% of homicide offenders. It is worth emphasizing that even if we consider only the rate of white murderers, the United States would still have a murder rate higher than those of most European countries (Zimring & Hawkins, 1997).

Whereas in the 1960s about twice as many whites as blacks were admitted to prison, in recent years those admitted have been almost equally divided between the races.[18] In 1996 over 3% of black adults were in prison, with almost 10% under correctional supervision (which includes parole and probation); the comparable figures for whites are 0.5% and a little over 2% (Council of Economic Advisors, 1998). Some analyses (e.g., Sidanius, Levin, & Pratto, 1998) suggest that as many as 40% of young black males will spend time in jail at some point in their lives. In selected cities (e.g., Washington, D.C.) and states (e.g., California), over 50% of black males will be arrested before their 30th birthday (Miller, 1996).

Crime Reporting. Just as with income statistics, we need to ask whether some or all of these striking disparities are due to direct, straight-line discrimination. As the figures above suggest, at each stage of the CJS, blacks constitute an increasing percentage of those involved. The opportunities for bias are legion. One of the biggest biases in the CJS is that many crimes are never reported. So it is possible that for some reason victims (say, whites) of black perpetrators are more likely to report crimes, but this seems unlikely to be a major factor, since the victims of black perpetrators are usually black themselves. In fact, given the greater mistrust of police by members of the black community, black-on-black crime may be more underreported than most other combinations.

Arrests. A second possible source of bias is that police may work more actively or effectively to catch black criminals. Although this is possible, a more likely bias is that police work less hard in black-on-black crime (the majority of crimes involving black perpetrators) because they fail to take the complaints of black victims as seriously as those of white victims. Several people, including the distinguished African American Harvard law professor Randall Kennedy (1997), argue forcefully that the real victims of race bias in the CJS are the black victims of crime, who tend to be ignored. Blacks are approximately eight times more likely than whites to be murder victims and are also at greater risk for other violent crimes. Blacks are just as likely as whites, if not more so, to be afraid of young black men as potential criminals. In a recent Gallup Poll, 59% of whites but only 33% of blacks reported being very satisfied with their safety from physical harm or violence (Saad & Newport, 2001).

Are police are more likely to arrest black than white perpetrators? Contrary to the reality portrayed on TV programs and the movies, police actually have a fair amount of discretion in whether to arrest someone they have caught committing a crime (Black, 1980), and they often do not do so if they suspect that victims will not testify against the criminal or think that the amounts of paperwork and court time required are not worth it. Arrests are also heavily affected by demeanor of the suspect, and blacks often are less respectful of arresting police officers (Black, 1980). There is less arrest discretion for the more serious violent crimes, rape being one notable exception. In fairness, definitive data in this area are difficult to collect—in part because we do not have a clean and clear criterion for whether someone should be arrested—but even many advocates (e.g., Tonry, 1995) of bias in the CJS do not see differential arrests as the main culprit.

Prosecution. Prosecutors may be more willing to prosecute black defendants. Again, there is little support for straight-line discrimination of this sort, but what about more indirect forms? In this regard, it is important to note that the vast majority (perhaps as many as 90%) of criminal cases are handled though plea bargaining. That this is a ripe area for all sorts of bias is beyond dispute. One possibility is that black perpetrators may be given more attractive plea bargains than whites, resulting in more of them being convicted. It seems unlikely to me that prosecutors would routinely offer lesser sentences to black defendants (thus making a guilty plea more attractive to them), unless one wants to argue (as I would) that prosecutors, like police, are less likely to see black-on-black crimes as serious than black-on-white or white-on-white (white-on-black crimes are comparatively rare). It is also possible that prosecutors who have enormous discretion in the severity of charges may charge black defendants with more serious crimes, which might increase the attractiveness of pleading guilty to a less costly charge. I also worry that black defendants may have less capable defense counsel than white defendants, and that such attorneys may be more likely to urge accepting a quick plea than bargaining further or going to trial. Public defenders are overburdened, and attorneys appointed by the court (and thus beholden to judges, who are usually ex-prosecutors, for subsequent appointments) are often paid on a case-by-case rather than an hourly basis—conditions making early settlement attractive to defense attorneys, if not their clients.[19] Moreover, black defendants who have less faith in the fairness of the CJS may be more eager to accept a "bird in the hand." Finally, black defendants may be less likely to be granted bail (Mann, 1993); thus they may be forced to serve jail time for crimes for which they have not been convicted, and may be less able to help with their defense.[20]

Conviction and Sentencing. It has long been a staple of racial politics that white judges and juries are more likely to convict black defendants. Although some laboratory experimental studies support racial bias in conviction and sentencing (Sweeney & Haney, 1992), the effects are small and may or may not generalize to real juries in real crimes.[21] There have been many studies of actual convictions, and the general result is that there are few crimes for which there is any evidence of differential conviction rates, given roughly equivalent crimes. On average, between 80% and 90% of the difference in incarceration rates for blacks and whites can be explained in terms of relevant background factors, such as seriousness of the crime and prior criminal history (e.g., Blumstein, 1993; Langan, 1985). The remaining 10%–20% probably reflects racial bias at least to some extent, and represents a large and salient number of people. For example, in 1982 over 32,000 black men were admitted to prison, and almost 4,800 of these were more than were expected from estimates of true black and white criminal activity, based on victimization surveys (Langan, 1985). Almost 5,000 people a year (and surely much higher today) does not strike me as a trivial figure.

There are three areas where race effects do show up quite clearly. First, until recently rape was a capital crime in many Southern states, and in cases where a black man raped a woman, the death sentence was given far more often than in other racial combinations of perpetrator and victim (Kennedy, 1997). The U.S. Supreme Court ruled in *Coker v. Georgia* (1976) that the death penalty for rape is unconstitutional, but avoided the race argument in doing so.

Second, blacks are more often convicted of drug crimes, and this occurs out of proportion to their use and/or involvement in dealing. In fact, the dramatic increases in prison populations over the past 20 years are largely due to drug-related convictions. In the 1990s, almost half of admissions to federal prisons and one-third to state prisons were for drug-related offenses (U.S. Department of Justice, 2000), and drug offenses account for a sizeable percentage of increases in the differential percentages of black and white incarceration. These differences result in part from the much greater penalties given for offenses involving crack cocaine (favored by blacks) as opposed to powder cocaine. However, even when types and amounts of drugs are held constant, there remain differential arrest and incarceration rates (Miller, 1996). All this is especially worrying, because there is no good evidence that imprisonment has been the least bit effective in the "war on drugs" (Tonry, 1995).

Third, murders in which the victim is white are far more likely (perhaps as much as 10 times more likely, 4 times more likely with relevant controls) to result in the death penalty. [22] In a famous study of Georgia murder cases, when a black killed a white, 21% were sentenced to death; when a white killed a white, 8% received the death penalty. However, when blacks were the victims, the comparable percentages were 1% and 3%, respectively (Thernstrom & Thernstrom, 1997). Between 1976 (when the death penalty was effectively reinstated by U.S. Supreme Court rulings) and 1991, 7 white men were executed for killing a black man, whereas 115 black killers of whites went to the execution chamber. Thus there were few differences between black and white killers, but a huge difference between those who killed whites and those who killed blacks. Even this may not represent racial bias per se. For example, juries may be harsher on murders committed during armed robberies (where uninvolved people such as guards are likely to be killed) than on disputes where victims are often unappealing and play a role in their own murder. And, in fact, 67% of black-on-white murders happen during armed robberies; only 7% of black-on-black murders involve robbery, but 73% happen during disputes (Thernstrom & Thernstrom, 1997).

Racial Bias Does Exist. I do not mean to say that there are no biases, racial or otherwise, in the CJS. I have heard white prison guards, police officers, probation officers, prosecutors, and even judges use racial epithets that, while no guarantee of discriminatory behavior, certainly alert one to the possibilities (to put it mildly). Bias does exist, but it does not flourish in the straight-line ways that many people seem to think. Understanding how racial bias works in the CJS requires that we abandon naive notions of discrimination and look for deeper causes.

Having said that, I must note some limitations in the kinds of data I have been presenting. First, I have relied heavily on data for murder and other serious crimes of violence. I have focused on violent crimes because we have more reliable data for them. Violent crimes, especially murder, are not dramatically underreported, and in nearly 75% of murders we actually know who the murderer was. Burglary, by contrast, is often not reported to the police, and a criminal is apprehended in fewer than 20% of the cases. That is not necessarily problematic, except that there is something approaching consensus among criminologists that racial biases are less prevalent for violent crimes such as murder than for property crimes and less serious violent ones (e.g., Miller, 1996; Tonry, 1995). Murder is the place where one is least likely to find racial bias.

Bias does enter into criminal decisions, but it is subtle and often camouflaged by other variables. One problem is that the general statistics on which I have heavily relied may conceal various competing biases. For example, if police, prosecutors, judges, and juries are biased against black victims (and thus more lenient on black perpetrators, who most often prey on other blacks) and also inclined to be tougher on black defendants because of prejudice, these two biases may well cancel one another out, leaving us with little opportunity to detect bias with our crude measures.

Racial bias shows up in subtle ways. For example, racial profiling by police contributes to the great mistrust by most urban blacks of the police, even if it does not dramatically affect arrest rates. Almost every black person, poor or middle-class, has stories to tell of being stopped and in some cases hassled by the police just because of skin color.[23] This not only is alarming on the moral face of things, but undercuts attempts to deal with crime problems, given that respect for police and their work is an important component of any solution. It is more likely for blacks to be physically and verbally abused by police and correctional officers (Mann, 1993). Although police brutality may be a relatively low-frequency event, it is ugly and highly salient to its victims and others who hear about it.

Even granted the fact that black Americans are more involved in crimes of violence (as well as many other types of crime) than whites, two additional points need to be stressed. First, we still must explain why this is so, and our search is likely to un-cover various types of discrimination in job opportunities and education that affect the choices young blacks have or think they have. A more subtle point is this: The high incarceration rate of young black males is due in part to their greater participa-tion in violent crime, but also to convictions for drug-related offenses. That point would merely be an important and unfortunate by-product of criminal statistics, were it not for the fact that imprisonment is not a good general solution for most prob-lems.[24] The United States has by far the highest rates of incarceration, the highest rates per crime, and the longest sentences of any Western country, and it is ex-tremely hard to find evidence that this approach is effective in reducing crime (Tonry, 1995). There is evidence that arrests reduce subsequent crime (Lott, 2000), but the data on whether imprisonment or long sentences also reduce crime rates are inconsistent, and even at their "best" indicate small effects. There are other punish-ments besides imprisonment (such as community-based rehabilitation, drug rehabili-tation, and education) that are at least as effective in improving crime rates; they are also cheaper per offender and disrupt fragile inner-city communities less. Prison teaches bad habits, and it is horribly expensive. Moreover, incarceration keeps peo-ple from learning relevant job and social skills, reduces their capacity to support fam-ilies, and creates major roadblocks in their abilities to gain meaningful employment once they are released; young black males are especially victimized by all this. Given the fact that community-based programs are likely to be at least as effective (if not more so) in rehabilitating criminals, our insistence that people must pay for their crimes with long prison sentences does great harm to the black community, with few or no compensating rewards by way of reducing crime (Tonry, 1995). The problem is even more insidious: When white Americans think of violent offenders, their exem-plars are usually black, and support for harsh penalties is associated with negative views of blacks. This suggests that "get tough on crime" attitudes are yet another manifestation of "acceptable," subtle, and potent racism (Peffley & Hurwitz, 2002). This is, of course, not discrimination in the classic sense, but it may do more harm to individuals and communities than more overtly expressed bias.

WOMEN, JOBS, AND INCOME

Discrimination against women in the workplace has been prevalent and remains so, even if in somewhat muted form. The figure cited most often in support of this is the so-called "earnings gap." In 1999 women who worked full-time made 72% of the in-come (on an annual basis) of men similarly employed full-time. Those paid on an hourly basis made 84% as much as comparable males (U.S. Department of Labor, 2000). The good news is that those figures have improved since the early 1980s, when the annual earnings gap was about 60%. The bad news is that the 1999 figures are slightly worse than 1997, when the gap was 74%.

Gender discrimination may be one obvious reason for this gap, but there are others. One is that women have traditionally been crowded into a relatively few fields that are not well compensated, either because the work is not highly valued or be-cause the labor supply in these areas is plentiful. Another is that working women may be less well educated than working men or may otherwise bring fewer capital invest-ments to their jobs. Women also tend to pick college majors from the humanities rather than from the sciences and economics; the latter typically lead to more lucrative jobs. Also, working women tend to be younger than working men, because those who have been working longer began their jobs at a time when relatively few women were in the labor force. All other things being equal, people who have worked more years make more money. The earnings gap narrows, but does not close, when college major, education, and work experience are taken into account.

Given that the Equal Employment Opportunity Commission, which adjudicates discrimination cases, has awarded at least $2 million in damages for gender discrimination each year for the past 10 years, it is apparent that individual discrimination remains an important problem. However, institutional discrimination also contributes. Why do we value college majors and jobs that have traditionally appealed to women less than we do male-oriented majors and jobs? Do we really think that the people who take care of our children in day care and schools are less important than computer programmers? Apparently so.

Another major factor is the greater responsibility for child care that women traditionally have had and continue to have. As a result, women may gravitate to relatively low-paying jobs such as teaching, which offer longer vacations and more flexible working conditions. In addition, women tend to take more time off during their careers; about 15% of women but only 2% of men do. The most obvious reason for this disparity is that women tend to have maternity leaves and to move to part-time or no work while their children are young. In any event, this reduces the seniority that women can accumulate, and (as noted above) seniority is a powerful predictor of income. When one compares younger men and women who do not have children, incomes are virtually identical (98% gap). The ultimate solution to this difference may not be to eliminate the "mommy track," but to have more men join it.

OTHER CATEGORIES AND DISCRIMINATION

I have focused the previous discussion on race and gender, partially because they are legally protected categories and partially because based on discrimination gender and race/ethnicity is highly salient. But let us not forget that many types of people are discriminated against every day and in many ways (see Chapters 11–13 for relevant examples). Older people have trouble getting jobs or being admitted to graduate or training programs. Obese persons arguably suffer the greatest amount of discrimination in Western society, in part because such discrimination is still sanctioned (Solovay, 2000). We do not need vast amounts of empirical research (although it certainly exists) to know that gay men and lesbians are less likely to be hired or given housing accommodations than are straights. Homosexual workers experience hostility from coworkers (Griffith & Hebl, 2002) and hate crimes against homosexuals, while relatively uncommon (although 25% of gay males and 20% of lesbians report being victims), have an impact on communities out of proportion to their incidence (Herek, Gillis, & Cogan, 1999). Jokes about gays, women, obese people, and members of racial minorities can still be heard in locker rooms and around the water cooler at work. People who are mentally ill, ugly, or physically disabled all experience both informal and formal discrimination. Various aspects of our tax codes favor those who are married over single people, and single mothers (and the relatively few single fathers) have enormous problems most of us can only begin to imagine. The fact that most of these forms of discrimination do not show up in our statistical analyses should not blind us to their reality or their impact on victims.

SUMMARY

Stereotypes are important for others only insofar as they result in public words or actions that affect others. Even private prejudice cannot do its dirty work unless translated into behavior. To paraphrase the old cliche, "Your words and deeds can do me harm, but your thoughts can never hurt me." Having said that, our thoughts and emotions usually do affect our behaviors, sometimes even when we least want them to and are unaware that they do.

It is easy to assume that stereotypes give rise to prejudices, which in turn create discriminatory behaviors, and that is one common enough scenario. Unfortunately, however, our beliefs (stereotypes), emotionally charged attitudes (prejudices), and behavior (discrimination) are related in many ways and often create a set of complex knots that are hard to untie.

While social scientists have tended to think of prejudice as a single kind of attitude, in fact it represents a complex set of attitudes. Our attitudes toward any category of people is likely to include both positive and negative elements, and even single attitudes usually contain both positive and negative features. Therefore, which set is operative at any given time reflects goals and needs as well as situational primes. People do differ in how much prejudice they have toward a given group, but whether this prejudice gets transformed in behavior depends on feelings of guilt and shame, self-presentational concerns, and whether the situational norms allow or encourage prejudice. Modern measures of right-wing authoritarianism and social dominance orientation measure constellations of attitudes that include prejudice.

Because expressing explicit prejudice has become relatively more unpopular over the past few decades, racist and sexist attitudes have been driven "underground" for many people. One manifestation of this is a kind of disguised prejudice where antipathy can be expressed in more conventionally approved ways. In particular, a constellation of attitudes, usually called modern or symbolic racism, is used to condemn members of minorities groups for their alleged lack of mainstream values and for taking advantage of unwarranted racial preferences. Prejudiced attitudes may be implicit as well, in the sense of being relatively nonconscious and often automatically invoked. Generally implicit, disguised, and explicit measures of prejudice are moderately related, but they seem to affect different forms of behavior. Disguised prejudices tend to affect attitudes toward policies designed to help non-mainstream people, implicit attitudes affect relatively noncontrollable aspects of behavior such as nonverbal behavior, and explicit attitudes affect more deliberately chosen behaviors. At this point in time it is misleading to think of one of these types of prejudice as being more basic; rather, they seem to be different facets of a constellation of attitudes, values, and feelings.

Discussions of discrimination have been handicapped by the assumption that the only kind that matters is the straight-line variety—discrimination that is overt and driven primarily by prejudice. But discrimination takes many forms and exists at institutional and cultural levels as well as individually. Members of minority groups do report experiencing a fair amount of discrimination, although less for themselves than for members of their category generally. Various experimental and statistical sources document discrimination. For example, blacks and whites and men and women do have different levels of income on average, and although this may appear to be straight-line discrimination, much of the differential results from other factors such as education are correlated with group status. Some discrimination results from our use of seemingly relevant but basically nondiagnostic information correlated with group status, for example, the use of tests that seem more valid than they are. The notion of straight-line discrimination not only fails to account for the complexities of discrimination but does not help in understanding the reasons why some groups are less well off than others. For example, the greater participation of members of minority groups on the receiving end of the criminal justice system can largely be explained in terms of their greater propensity to commit crimes. However, that only pushes the problem back one level, and we need to ask why different groups have different levels of crime participation. Likewise, racial and gender differences in income can be accounted for in part through different sorts of jobs held by different categories of people, but then we should ask why we value some jobs over others. As I have emphasized often throughout this book, we get more mileage from trying to understand the larger theoretical explanations for such effects.

Notes

1. Throughout this chapter, I adopt the convention of pretending that racism and prejudice are primarily directed at blacks and other minorities by whites. However, many members of racial minorities have corresponding prejudices about whites (Johnson & Lecci, 2003; Jones, 1997; Judd, Park, Ryan, Brauer, & Kraus, 1995; Stephan et al., 2002), or at least more favorable attitudes toward blacks than whites (Livingston, 2002). Much of the material in this section (and most of those that follow) probably applies equally well to the attitudes that blacks and Hispanics have about whites, although in fairness there is little relevant research. Clearly, members of minority groups have been much more victimized by racial prejudice than have whites. Still, it is preposterous to assume (implicitly or not) that only whites have prejudice, or for that matter that only whites discriminate (Shelton, 2000).

2. There is abundant evidence that the conservative revolution, begun by President Nixon in the 1968 election, deliberately tried to link race to various value-laden issues that came to the fore in the 1960s (Kinder & Sanders, 1996; Steinhorn & Diggs-Brown, 1999). Thus concerns about crime, drugs, welfare, and even abortion became covers, often in not subtle ways, for traditional antipathy to blacks. With this so-called "Southern strategy," President Nixon clearly used racial resentments held over from the 1960s to take votes away from the more overtly racist George Wallace (particularly in the South and among Northern blue-collar workers), but did so in ways that allowed whites to claim they were not being racist. President Nixon may have been the last American President to use the term "nigger" freely, and to state his belief openly (if only to subordinates and friends) that blacks were inferior. In subsequent elections, images of "welfare queens" and Willie Horton (see Chapter 9) became potent symbols linking racial prejudice to conservative ideology, whether this was overtly intended or not (Mendelberg, 2001).

3. The literature on the witchcraft craze that affected Europe (especially in Scotland and what is now Germany) from roughly 1550 to 1700 is large, with substantial disagreements about how many women were killed—ranging from 100,000 to several million (e.g., Barstow, 1994; Klaits, 1985). This literature should be better known to social psychologists than it is, because of the light it sheds on how stereotypes and preconceptions affect behavior (see Schneider, 1976, for an incomplete version) as well as on gender scapegoating.

4. Recently Glick and Fiske (1999a) have also developed an Ambivalence toward Men Inventory. It consists of Hostility toward Men items (e.g., "Men pay lip service to equality but

can't handle it") and Benevolence toward Men items (e.g., "Men are more willing to risk self to help others"). The two subscales are moderately correlated for both males and females. Benevolence toward Men is strongly correlated with Benevolent Sexism, which is expected, given that both measure attitudes toward traditional sexual differentiation. Hostility toward Men is correlated with both measures of sexism among women, but only with Benevolent Sexism among men.

5. Because of the extensive discussion of political correctness as a norm governing behavior, we have forgotten how enormously difficult it usually is to label publicly behavior or people as racist or sexist. It takes lots of practice and swallowing well-learned lessons about politeness to pull this off routinely. In one study where a male made three sexist remarks, fewer than 10% of the women participants confronted him on all three, but 45% did so for at least one of the remarks (Swim & Hyers, 1999). I wonder about the other 55%.

6. I am continually bemused by those people who argue that their white sons and daughters are denied admission to a selective college because "their place" was "taken" by a person of color. That kind of argument seems to assume that people should be lined up according to their SAT scores, and only those at the head of the line should get to register for classes. No college operates that way, and if colleges did, students would find themselves in a dull environment indeed. A second, somewhat more cynical point to be made is that if we did line up applicants in this way, the white offspring's place might well be taken by someone of Asian descent. I recently pointed this out to an enraged father of a white male applicant who did not get his first choice of an Ivy League university. He replied that he had no objection to that, because it would be a fair and objective decision. Forgive me, but I don't believe for a minute that he would be satisfied if his son had been "beaten out" by an Asian rather than a black student.

7. I am not suggesting that black students be admitted to colleges primarily to perform the service of being a learning experience for middle-class whites. They do perform that service, as do whites for blacks who have had limited experience with people from other races. But there is much more involved.

8. Those familiar with discrimination research and law will recognize this as what has come to be known as "disparate impact." In *Griggs v. Duke Power Company* (1971), the U.S. Supreme Court ruled that a pattern of racial disparity in hiring could be taken as evidence of discrimination, even in the absence of intent to discriminate. However, recent Court decisions (beginning with *Wards Cove Packing Company v. Atonio*, 1989) have backpedaled away from disparate impact as a criterion so that it has proved harder to prove legal discrimination. Arguably, *Wards Cove* was a case in which disparate impact was justified, given differences in education and other capital investments between the white and minority groups in the company; however, other, more recent cases have signaled the Court's mistrust of statistical arguments more generally. Apparently for conservative members of the Court as well as many others, discrimination is discrimination only when it is straight-line.

9. I recently spent a frustrating 3 hours with a computer tech support person who was, I am guessing from his accent, recently from (perhaps still in) India. I had difficulty in understanding him and was continually embarrassed by asking him to repeat suggestions or in some cases to spell words. I have no doubts that the young man was highly competent, and he was helpful and surprisingly tolerant of my ineptitude. Still, I did find myself wishing, and wishing often, that the computer company had hired someone who spoke my language with less of an accent.

10. Just to keep things simple, I will generally not discuss the data for Hispanics, Native Americans, or Asians. However, generally the data for Hispanics and blacks are quite similar, although Hispanics tend to be slightly more economically privileged than blacks and Native Americans slightly less so. The data for Asians resemble those for whites, but when differences are found, Asians tend to be better off economically. However, within the Asian group those of Japanese and Chinese descent are advantaged relative to whites, whereas

groups such as Cambodians and Vietnamese (with more recent immigration patterns) are disadvantaged.

11. These data, and those in the next several paragraphs, are readily available from various government publications and statistical abstracts. In this passage, data not otherwise attributed come from *Statistical Abstract of the United States 2000*, published by the U.S. Bureau of the Census. This is available through the Internet (http: //www.census.gov/statab/www/).

12. For those who believe that discrimination is a thing of the past, there are many convincing case studies—for example, the fairly recent case of blatant discrimination at Texaco (Roberts & White, 1998).

13. Again, the data here are from *Statistical Abstract of the United States 2000* (1997 data, in this context), unless otherwise noted.

14. We sometimes forget how far we have come in this area, even though we have not reached parity. In the 1930s, 1940s, and early 1950s, Southern states spent one-third to one-seventh as much on black schools as on white ones; many areas did not have high schools for blacks; and some teachers in black schools had not graduated from high school themselves. It was therefore no accident that in 1940 half of Southern blacks had completed less than 5 years of school, compared with 16% of whites (Thernstrom & Thernstrom, 1997). In his interesting autobiography, *Vernon Can Read* (Jordan, 2001), Vernon Jordan—a distinguished African American attorney, civil rights leader, and political figure—describes a summer job he held while he was a student at DePauw University in 1955. He worked as a chauffeur and butler in the home of a wealthy white man in Atlanta, and his duties allowed him free time to read in the home library. One day his employer discovered him reading. Later that evening, while Jordan was serving dinner, the employer told his family that he had an announcement. "Vernon can read," he told everyone, "and he goes to school with white children." The year 1955 is not so long ago for some of us.

15. The data for Hispanics are somewhat misleading, because a relatively large percentage of that group consists of recent immigrants to the United States, who tend to have been poorly educated in their home countries.

16. There are relatively trivial differences in the percentage of blacks and whites who have high school diplomas at age 25. However, if we examine graduation rates at age 18, the figures are much less appealing. At that point (which is when one "should" graduate), 78% of whites, 56% of blacks, and 54% of Hispanics have graduated (Greene, 2001). Some students, especially minority students, graduate late (mostly because of earlier academic difficulties) or get a general equivalency diploma (GED). A GED is arguably less satisfactory than a regular high school diploma.

17. Indeed, the leading cause of death among young black males is other black males.

18. Although arrest statistics are notoriously subject to biased reporting, victim surveys (subject, of course, to their own biases) provide comparable data, although they suggest a much greater prevalence of crime.

19. The sight of slovenly dressed court-appointed attorneys meeting for the first time with their clients 5 minutes before a hearing or a trial is a common one in Texas courthouse hallways, and I suspect elsewhere. There are well-publicized cases of court-appointed attorneys sleeping through most of the murder trials of their clients (see Cole, 1999, for these and other examples). In criminal trials, when attorneys have some say-so in jury selection, one can routinely observe attorneys (almost always prosecutors) excluding minority people on transparently specious grounds. The U.S. Supreme Court has generally held that racial exclusion from juries is unconstitutional, provided that race is the sole or main criterion for exclusion. However, their rulings have been inconsistent (as on so many other issues in recent years) and so riddled with exceptions that any competent prosecutor can find nonracial excuses for excluding blacks that meet the tests of the Court (Kennedy, 1997).

20. They may not be able to help in tracking down potential witnesses, for example. Also, defendants who are in jail at time of their trial are usually dressed in prison uniforms, and this surely affects juries (and arguably judges) adversely.

21. One recent study (Sommers & Ellsworth, 2000) found that white students playing the role of jurors did not take race into account in their decisions, but blacks were more lenient toward black defendants. However, white jurors were harsher on black defendants when race (and presumably political correctness norms) were less salient.

22. During the 1970s and 1980s, no issue divided the U.S. Supreme Court more than a series of death penalty cases, and this ideological split has reverberated throughout recent Court politics (see Lazarus, 1998, for an extended treatment). In *McCleskey v. Kemp* (1987), a black man accused of killing a white police officer appealed his death sentence on grounds of racial discrimination in terms of victims. The Court rejected his appeal by a 5–4 vote, with the reasoning that although discrimination might generally be present, McCleskey had not proved it had been a factor in his individual case. It did not help McCleskey that the Justices did not understand statistics, let alone statistically based arguments. In subsequent cases, the Court has so narrowed permissible evidence for individual discrimination that in practice it has proved almost impossible to prove discrimination in the CJS to the Court's satisfaction. The majority members of the Court were apparently worried that taking race into account in capital murder cases was the beginning of a slippery slope ultimately resulting in the effective abolishment of capital punishment, at least for blacks, and they were probably correct (for additional analyses, see Cole, 1999; Kennedy, 1997; Lazarus, 1998).

23. A prominent black person in Houston told me of having been stopped (while driving his expensive SUV) by a white policeman for running a stop sign, which he swears he did not do. One of the reasons that attempts at reining in racial profiling (stopping people merely because they are black) will not achieve easy success is that police officers can and do manufacture other reasons (such as alleged traffic violations) for stopping blacks (or, for that matter, whites) if they think individuals look suspicious. In *Whren v. United States* (1996), a unanimous Supreme Court ruled that stopping people was legal as long as police officers had observed a traffic violation, even if the officers had no intention of enforcing the violated regulation.

24. The only exceptions here would be the relatively few criminals who genuinely cannot be rehabilitated. I do not mean to suggest that criminals go unpunished or that prison is never appropriate, but rather that its advantages must be weighed against the very real costs (and not just monetary ones).

CHAPTER 9

The Development of Stereotypes

SOURCES OF OUR STEREOTYPES

There has been surprisingly little empirical work on the origins of our stereotypes. In part, that is because these seem so obvious. After all, stereotypes are a salient part of our culture. We see them exemplified on television and in the movies, and sometimes parents, teachers, and other socialization agents deliberately or inadvertently preach them under the guise of conveying the wisdom of age. They are part of the cultural air that we breathe.

The Two Approaches

Indeed, it has seemed so obvious that stereotypes are bound up with culture that many of the classic studies in this area (e.g., Katz & Braly, 1933) explicitly assumed not only that stereotypes are products of cultures, but that generalizations about groups of people can be stereotypes only if they are widely held. These two assumptions feed off one another. If stereotypes are a part of the general culture, it would be a bit strange if they were not generally believed. Cultural beliefs and values are, almost by definition, widely accepted. At the same time, if a large number of people hold the same beliefs, the easiest (but not, as we shall see, the only) explanation is that they have been subjected to the same cultural tuition.

Social Cognition

The more modern approach has been to forgo assumptions about the cultural heritage of stereotypes and to focus instead on how stereotypes affect how we process information about others. For much of the research discussed in this book, it matters little whether the stereotype being examined is held only by the subjects in the experiments or by nearly everyone. If I believe that violent career criminals are actually compassionate and caring people, then this will affect the ways I perceive, interpret,

321

and remember their behavior in much the same ways (although obviously with different outcomes) as nearly everyone else, whose stereotype is roughly the opposite.

The social cognition approach offers a number of mechanisms by which attitudes, prejudices, values, and beliefs can give rise to stereotypes. But these accounts turn out to be mostly unsatisfying. Do any of us seriously believe that most stereotypes, especially those that are most vicious, are merely due to the odd expectation or two biasing our experiences as well as our memories of them? This is not to deny that such effects occur, occur often, and are important when they occur. But it has the effect of leaving us in the middle of a lake teeming with fish without pole or bait. What seems to be so puzzling is how we acquired these very expectations, prejudices, values, and beliefs that cause so much cognitive mischief. The social cognition approach doesn't seem to scratch the particular itch of deeper origins.

And yet the social cognition approach does gingerly suggest one potentially important field from which our stereotypes may spring—our experiences with people from various groups. For instance, one reason Rosa may think that professors are intelligent, that doctors are compassionate, and that lawyers are interested in making a lot of money is that, in her experience, exactly those features have proved to be reasonable summaries of the behavior of such people. Of course, those working within the social cognition tradition would also be quick to point out that her experiences may have been parochial and biased. Nonetheless, we ought to keep our options open; maybe experiences do matter.

The Cultural Approach

THE PROMISE AND VAGUENESS OF CULTURAL EXPLANATION

It is easy enough to argue that culture generally provides the content of many of our stereotypes and encourages us to stereotype some groups and not others, precisely because many (perhaps most) of our stereotypes are in fact widely held and culturally sanctioned. We humans are profoundly both creators and creatures of our cultures. Unfortunately, culture often functions as an explanatory copout, because we are a long way from understanding how it does its dirty work. None of us, even children, absorb cultural lessons through some mental osmosis; nor are we little pails waiting to have culture poured into us (Milner, 1996). We lack precise models of how cultures enter our minds, and such haziness gives us licence to place far too many explanatory eggs in this basket. We all nod, shake our heads, and look grave: "Ah, yes, culture is at it again."

So, when all is said and done, we have two large and somewhat diffuse categories of explanations for why we develop certain stereotypes. They can be products of our cultures or subcultures, or they can be produced by our own experiences, corrupt or pure. Fortunately or not, these kinds of explanations are not mutually exclusive—far from it.

DOES CONSENSUS DEMAND CULTURAL EXPLANATION?

Before we can deal with the interplay between these explanations, we must devote some attention to an issue that affects both—whether most stereotypes are consensual. If we encounter a stereotype that is held by only a few people, we can virtually eliminate the larger culture as a major culprit. Admittedly, important subcultures, at odds with the larger culture, may still promote stereotypes. Certainly many stereo-types—say, on college campuses—are unique to local cultures, and people who are militantly prejudiced may find support in a group of like-minded racists. Still, if we were to find a person who holds deviant stereotypes about culturally salient groups, cultural explanations would probably be low on our menu of explanations.

However, even if we were to find that most people (or at least large groups of people) within a given culture hold a given stereotype, we cannot necessarily claim that these people have absorbed cultural lessons. There are at least three other possi-bilities. The most obvious is that the stereotype is actually accurate, and that people's beliefs reflect reality. The reason people have a consensual stereotype that men are stronger than women is that men are, in fact, stronger on average. In this analysis, culture is merely a reflection of many pooled individual experiences and is not a causal player.

Second, cultures may encourage some people to perform certain roles that in turn give rise to particular behaviors. So, as I have discussed earlier, women are often "assigned" to nurturing roles and men to roles that demand a more agentic ap-proach. Perceivers may well accurately see women as performing more nurturing be-haviors, but because they cannot separate the role from the person, they may con-clude that women are "naturally" more nurturing.

A third possibility is that people have common modes of processing information that give rise to consensual stereotypes. For example, the illusory-correlation ap-proach suggests that small or distinctive groups will be seen as having more of dis-tinctive (often negative) behaviors than larger groups. If most members of majority groups see minority group members performing a range of behaviors, according to this model they may all see the minority group as performing too many negative be-haviors, simply because of a common bias in the encoding and recall of information.

Are Stereotypes Consensual?

Is there, then, generally consensus on most stereotypes? The answer is that we really do not know. Here, as is often the case in the stereotype area, the assertion-to-evi-dence ratio is uncomfortably high. There has been considerable controversy over the issue of the importance of consensus as a feature of stereotypes (for a sampling of contrasting views, see Ashmore & Del Boca, 1981; Gardner, 1994; Haslam, Turner, Oakes, McGarty, & Reynolds, 1998). There is no disagreement that at least some ste-reotypes are widely accepted, and that often these are the ones most deeply rooted in culture and most harmful to others. Clearly, one of the main reasons we care about stereotypes is because they are consensual (Tajfel, 1981b).

What Evidence Do We Have?

There are several problems in this area. In the first place, most research has used measures that reflect mean strength of stereotypes rather than data on the percent-age of people who hold them, because measures of mean strength are more amena-ble to the kinds of statistical analyses preferred by social psychologists. Also, an over-whelming number of stereotype studies have been done with college students, who are probably not representative of the larger culture. Many public opinion polls ask questions related to race, but these tend to deal more with issues of public policy and social distance than with stereotype traits.

An additional problem is that although there are some reports of what percentages of people are willing to assign particular traits to particular group, in most cases these percentages do not rise above 50%. For example, in the classic replication of the original Katz–Braly research by Karlins, Coffman, and Walters (1969), only the following traits were endorsed by a majority of the subjects: "materialistic" for Americans, "loyal to family ties" for Chinese, "conservative" for English, and "industrious" for Germans and Japanese. Of course, 50% is an arbitrary cutoff, and other traits (such as "ambitious" for Americans, "reserved" for English, "efficient," and "extremely nationalistic" for Germans, "quick-tempered" for Irish, and "musical" for Negroes) would be added if the cutoff were lowered to 40%. I reemphasize that these percentages are for subjects who gave the traits as one of the five most characteristic; undoubtedly, consensus would have been higher if all the checked traits had been tallied.

How General Is the Consensus?

DO PEOPLE ENDORSE CULTURAL CONSENSUS?

However, if we can step back from our concerns with measurement issues, it is perfectly obvious that many stereotypes are widely believed, and widely believed to be widely believed even by those who do not fully endorse them. There are at least two other important issues with consensus. First, it is quite possible for a given stereotype to be part of the general cultural matrix without necessarily being held by a majority of the population. As Devine (1989) and others have argued, many of us might be aware of a general cultural stereotype without necessarily endorsing it personally. It is even possible (and likely, I suspect) that the majority of people believe that a majority of the people hold some cultural stereotypes that they actually do not. Only a minority of white Americans think that black Americans are intellectually less gifted than whites or are more violent, but it is probable that both whites and blacks think that such beliefs are widely held. However, even if a given person does not accept the validity of these stereotypes (at least consciously), the sneaky little devils may still, under certain circumstances, affect the ways he or she behaves (Devine, 1989). Having said all that, however, I suspect that a person's personal stereotypes are generally more important than cultural versions when the two disagree; there is evidence, for example, that personal stereotypes predict prejudice better than knowledge of cultural stereotypes does (Devine & Elliot, 1995; Haslam & Wilson, 2000).

WHAT IS THE REFERENCE GROUP FOR CONSENSUS?

A second and related issue is how we define the group that exhibits consensus. Implicitly, most people who have raised this issue assume that consensus is defined in terms of the culture or society as a whole. However, in many cases the relevant group may be much smaller. Does anyone seriously think that adolescent consensus views on particular rock stars are necessarily shared by the wider culture, or that the average teenager cares what the rest of us think? Similarly, a man with neo-Nazi sympathies may be perfectly aware that most people do not share his views about Jews, yet still anchor his views in the consensus that he shares with his reference group. If we mean to investigate the importance of consensus in forming, maintaining, and using stereotypes, we have to be alert to the strong possibility that different people look to different groups to define consensus for different stereotypes.

Creating Consensus

SELF-CATEGORIZATION THEORY

Throughout this book, I have argued that it is generally misleading to think of stereotypes as fixed entities—as dictionary-like attributes that we attach to groups, or as cognitive possessions. Although most stereotypes are not completely labile, what we think of people in other groups varies according to our moods, recent experiences, ingroup–outgroup status, and comparison groups, among other things. Self-categorization theory not only emphasizes the instability of stereotypes, but explains at least some of the consensus that exists for many stereotypes (Haslam, 1997; Haslam, Turner, Oakes, McGarty, & Reynolds, 1998).

There is an important implication of this perspective: Because what counts as an ingroup and an outgroup varies from situation to situation, so should both the content of stereotypes and their perceived consensus (Ellemers & van Knipperberg, 1997). A group of Asian Americans may have a particular view of European Americans in the United States, but when in Europe they may see Americans of European and Asian descent as more similar. Several experiments support this point of view. For example, when Australian students were asked to think of themselves in relationship to Americans, they were more likely to emphasize their Australian identity; they also had more consensus on traits they assigned to Australians when this identity was salient (Haslam, Turner, Oakes, Reynolds, et al., 1998). Other studies (Haslam, Oakes, Reynolds, & Turner, 1999) have also shown that when ingroup identity is important, there is more consensus on traits assigned to the ingroup, and the overall stereotype becomes more favorable.

This model also suggests that when social identity is salient, people tend to assume that other members of the salient ingroup share their opinions, producing perceived consensus. When such consensus is not obviously present, group members will exert social pressures on one another to achieve it. To the extent that group members have active stereotypes of outgroups (which they will tend to have when the ingroup is salient), they will have the sense that the stereotypes are widely shared and that everyone thinks they should be. Stereotypes are enhanced when an ingroup member supports them or an outgroup member disagrees with them (Haslam, Oakes, et al., 1996).

EVERYDAY DISCOURSE

North American experimental social psychologists have underemphasized one of the most profoundly social features of our lives—communication. Stereotypes, like other important beliefs, are forged in the crucible of everyday conversation and dialogue. The interplay between cultural forces and communication is complex and hard to capture experimentally, but communication and not direct tuition may be the most powerful vehicle for creating consensual meanings and cultural understandings (Hardin & Higgins, 1996; Lau, Chiu, & Lee, 2001).

In recent years there has been considerable interest in how people talk about race and what effects this might have on the development and strengthening of prejudice (e.g., Riley, 2002; van Dijk, 1984, 1993; Wetherell & Potter, 1992). People do communicate their prejudices and stereotypes both directly and indirectly by framing the behavior of others in ways that invite specific interpretations (Gamson, 1992).

There are several ways in which conversation helps to maintain prejudice, especially in situations where overt prejudice is frowned upon (Verkuyten, 1998b). People may emphasize the putative shortcomings of people from other groups, hold them to a stricter moral code, and see them as abnormal to the extent that they do not conform to ingroup norms and values (Verkuyten, 2001). "If only they would try to be more like us . . . " is the most blatant way of expressing this; there are more subtle and insidious conversational moves as well. As I have emphasized throughout this book, stereotypes involve theories about why people behave the ways they do. So in conversation people not only criticize the behavior of members of other groups, but offer explanations of a sort: "Of course, what can you expect, given the appalling conditions in which they bring up their children?"

Often people justify their own beliefs by suggesting that "everyone knows that . . . " or by relying on a personal but seemingly well-informed reality: "I don't care what some do-gooders say; when you work with them like I do, all you have to do is open your eyes and see that they are . . . " Another important conversation move is the employment of hedges. Most common is some version of "I'm not a racist, but . . . " Another, somewhat more insidious, is the disavowal of universality: "I'm sure there are plenty of hard-working Mexican men, but my Uncle Charlie . . . " Note that in both cases the speakers want to have it both ways, and because of the norms of dialogue get it. They have declared their generally honorable intentions, but have also managed to get in their stereotype licks. Whether listeners see through the attempt at camouflage is an open question, but at a minimum these sorts of conversational ploys tend to legitimize prejudicial statements and dialogue. If a self-declared nonracist says that blacks are violent, then it must be respectable enough. It is also hard to disagree with these sorts of statements, at least if one wants to seem polite. Most of us are not prepared to tell people who have just said they are not racists that they are, or to debate the precise percentages of hard-working and lazy Mexican men.

Often people tell stories to illustrate their points and to serve as explanations of sorts: "My Uncle Charlie had this Mexican man who worked for him, and he was always late for work. Uncle Charlie really wanted to give him a break, but he finally had to fire him because he couldn't get out of bed in the morning." One feature of such stories is that they are like sound bites on TV—they provide a quick summary of the behavior and then explain it in terms of individual responsibility. Left by the wayside are possible explanations of why this man couldn't get up or why people don't seem to try hard.

GROUP COMMUNICATION

Whereas the research described above emphasizes the processes involved in prejudice communication, Janet Ruscher (1998) initiated a program of research that emphasizes the consequences of communicating stereotypic information. When members of a group talk about members of an outgroup, they tend, at least under most circumstances, to emphasize their stereotypic qualities and the homogeneity of the outgroup. For example, in one experiment (Ruscher, Hammer, & Hammer, 1996), groups who were motivated to reach consensus tended to spend more time talking about the stereotype-consistent qualities of a person with alcoholism. An important bottom-line implication is that participants' perceptions of a target tend to become more stereotypic after such discussions (Ruscher & Hammer, 1994). In a typical serial reproduction paradigm where a story is repeated from person to person, stereotype-consistent material comes to predominate with successive reproductions (Kashima, 2000; Lyons & Kashima, 2001). This suggests that such communication increases the use of stereotypes, but stereotypes acquired secondhand tend to be more extreme and homogeneous than those taken from direct experience (Thompson, Judd, & Park, 2000).

People also tend to focus more on group features when they discuss outgroups, and negative comments about the outgroup especially tend to be about the group rather than individuals (Harasty, 1997). When conversations do focus on individuals, people tend to share negative information (Stewart, 1998). Furthermore, when describing members of an outgroup compared to members of the ingroup, people tend to use a more abstract language (see Chapter 14), especially when the outgroup's behavior is consistent with previously held stereotypes (Wigboldus, Semin, & Spears, 2000). As a result, recipients of these descriptions tend to form dispositional inferences for the behavior.

Of course, many different factors determine the content of group discussion; surely sometimes, at least, one person disrupts the conversational flow by drawing attention to stereotype-inconsistent qualities. One suggestive study (Brauer, Judd, & Jacquelin, 2001) found that when one person in a group had a great deal of nonstereotypic information about a group, group discussion focused more on such behaviors than it did when the same counterstereotypic information was dispersed among all members. Presumably an individual with discrepant information feels a special obligation to bring it up, whereas if each individual possesses only a piece or two, it may be overwhelmed by stereotype-consistent information. Another factor that might encourage the spread of nonstereotypic information is a desire to be accurate (Ruscher & Duval, 1998).

Still, except in special circumstances, discussion of groups and their members is likely to favor the promotion of stereotype-consistent information. Furthermore, more explicit group conformity pressures may facilitate stereotyping.

SOCIAL INFLUENCE PROCESSES

Social psychology has a long history of emphasizing the importance of social pressures in producing group consensus and social realities. Although people, even those who are strongly prejudiced, do not spend most of their time trying to convince others of the validity of stereotypes, conformity pressures surely do account for some of the stereotype consensus. Can an adolescent male who hears his comrades constantly telling jokes about "faggots" escape the feeling that something is basically wrong with gay males? When little boys declare that girls have "cooties," doesn't every boy learn that girls should be avoided? Can a black woman who grows up hearing her peers disparage whites avoid developing negative attitudes about them? Often it is not so much that people pressure one another to accept seemingly general stereotypes as that these stereotypes go unchallenged and hence become correct by default. When

Tom, Dick, and Harry make jokes about gays, and no one disagrees, Jim may well believe that everyone (or at least everyone in this particular group) agrees and start making jokes of his own (Burn, 2000). People feel freer to express their prejudices when they are socially approved (Crandall, Eshleman, & O'Brien, 2002).

Because stereotypes of outgroups are often so central to group identity, those who endorse stereotypes of outgroups may have particular influence on other ingroup members (Castelli, Vanzetto, Sherman, & Arcuri, 2001), and desires to impress others can affect the content of what one says about other groups and affect the resultant stereotypes held by the ingroup (Schaller & Conway, 1999). Countless experiments on conformity have shown that it is not necessary for people to actively pressure one another to get consensus; sometimes the appearance of consensus is sufficient to achieve it. Generally this can lead to a state of pluralistic ignorance, in which where people come to believe that stereotypes are more commonly held and normatively anchored than is the case (Prentice & Miller, 1996).

Does Consensus Matter?

I have chosen not to define stereotypes in terms of consensual agreement, for reasons described in Chapter 1. This does not mean that the fact that many stereotypes are consensual is a trivial add-on. There are at least three reasons why we might be deeply concerned about whether particular stereotypes are generally perceived to be true.

First, it seems likely that consensual stereotypes are more likely to be considered to be true, or at least more rarely questioned. "Everybody knows" is often a powerful argument in support of socially derived truths. As I have suggested, the appearance, if not the reality, of consensus validates stereotypes.

Second, consensually supported stereotypes may more readily form the basis of relevant action and inaction. Sechrist and Stangor (2001) have shown that when people think their stereotypes are supported by others, these stereotypes become more accessible and tend to guide behavior more. If members of a group are generally perceived to be lazy or stupid, it will be easy for politicians and other decision makers to justify poor educational and employment opportunities. For instance, knowledge that men in a certain job hold sexist attitudes may justify a personnel director's decision not to hire women, who "would feel uncomfortable in that environment."

Third, beliefs and attitudes bolstered by perceived consensus may play a more central role in our mental lives, and their becoming deeply anchored there may keep them from being easily changed. Devine (1989) has forcefully argued that cultural stereotypes are not only widely held but widely known, and hence tend to be activated automatically. That is not necessarily true (see Chapter 10 for an extended discussion), but it seems likely that many of the stereotypes we care most about (e.g., those dealing with race, gender, and sexual orientation) are deeply imprinted in at least some individuals and hold their place because of perceived cultural sanction. It is a reasonable hypothesis that culturally sanctioned stereotypes are easier for culturally uninitiated individuals to learn and harder for cultural pros to unlearn. Perceptions of universality do not provide many toeholds on the ladder to change, and discovering that others agree with one's stereotypes tends to harden them against any change (Stangor, Sechrist, & Jost, 2001).

ARE STEREOTYPES BASED ON EXPERIENCE?

The Mix of Experience and Culture

In obvious ways, stereotypes are direct reflections of our experiences. Many (perhaps most) of our important stereotypes are based on at least some contact, sometimes indirect, with relevant groups. Having said this, I quickly add that counterexamples leap to the fore. I could probably, if pushed, dredge up a stereotype or two about people who have lived their entire lives in Greenland, although to the best of my knowledge I have never met such a person. But even so, such stereotypes are hardly based on cultural lessons; so far as I know, I have never been told anything about Greenlanders, nor have I ever watched a movie or TV program that featured them. My stereotypes, such as they are, must be based on inferences from things I know about Greenland and other people who live in Northern climates. But, of course, in the final analysis my stereotypes about people from Greenland count for little. The first time I have the privilege of meeting a Greenlander, I am confident that whatever stereotypes I have will soon be overridden by my experiences. Or so I hope.

By contrast, all or nearly all of our important stereotypes are based on mixtures of what we have been taught and seen. We cannot separate cultural and experiential bases of our stereotypes—not because we lack the right modes of analyses or sophisticated computer programs, but rather because the two are integrally bound together. Trying to partial culture out of experience makes no more sense than trying to talk about a river without discussing its geography. Experiences are themselves products of culture. Does one seriously think that Japanese and American teenagers would understand TV programs such as *Friends* or *Everybody Loves Raymond* in the same way? How could they? Our different cultures provide us with different expectancies, labels, and explanations for behavior, and no one has ever had a naked experience, unclothed by culture.

The Manufacture of Experience

Usually we discuss "experience" as though we understood what we are talking about. Experiences are, of course, things that happen to us—but as I have stressed throughout this book, to some extent we manufacture our own experiences (Hardin & Higgins, 1996). Not only do we affect the behavior of others we are trying to understand, but we see the raw data before us through the lens of our own mental systems. Thus experience is no single or simple thing and cannot be easily objectified.

Obviously, some experiences seem to be more schema-driven and others more attuned to properties of environmental stimuli. We can all recognize differences between the man who meets another person with a relatively open mind and one whose whole cognitive demeanor seems to suggest that the encounter is designed to provide additional support for his favorite stereotypes. And each of us, if pressed just a little, could probably think of times when we have let our expectations bias our interpretations of someone else's behavior more than was appropriate.[1]

Not only are experiences filtered through cognitive schemas and stereotypes, but these mental theories are themselves partially products of culture and social forces. When Joe interprets male behavior as aggressive and female as merely assertive, he is making use of culturally conditioned categories and culturally sanctioned ways of interpreting behavior. He need not parse behavior along lines of biological gender; he need not make distinctions between aggressive and assertive behavior; and he need not label one behavior assertive and the other aggressive.

It is, however, important to distinguish between active and passive experiences. Sometimes we gain information about people through active interaction, and sometimes we gain information through relatively passive observation. A good deal of what I know about professors, chemists, and anthropologists has come from conversations and interactions with representatives of those categories. By contrast, almost everything I know about professional athletes, Native Americans, and people with drug addiction comes from watching television or movies or reading. At first blush, it might seem that direct experience provides less biased information. After all, we are all aware that the media (by which, these days, we usually mean TV) presents biased and unrepresentative views of groups of people. Surely it is better to "mix it up" with people, to search out information, to test our hypotheses about them actively. Many times it is. At the same time, one continuing theme of the present book (see Chapter 6) is that such active interactions often give rise to stereotype-driven processing. Although it can be trivially easy to point out all the many ways television biases our experiences for us, books, movies, and television programs can also provide a rich and detailed menu of information. Am I likely to find out more about Native Americans by meeting a few and discussing their lives, or by watching a good documentary that presents a wider range of people and experiences than I could encounter on my own? The answer is not obvious.

ARE STEREOTYPES ACCURATE?

The Traditional Assumption

A great deal rests on answers to the question of whether stereotypes are accurate. Both social scientists and ordinary people have tended to assume that stereotypes are by definition inaccurate, and this has retarded the study of the accuracy issue, as well as confusing many other conceptual issues (Fishman, 1956; Jussim, McCauley, & Lee, 1995; Schneider, 1996).

There are many reasons why we have tended to assume that stereotypes are inaccurate. The most obvious one is that some of them are in fact guilty as charged. Second, stereotypes are held (albeit not exclusively) by highly prejudiced individuals whose beliefs seem more dictated by their prejudices than the reverse. Such people give stereotypes a bad name. Third, many stereotypes seem to be based on relatively little direct experience, and it is easy to jump to the conclusion that such generalizations must be inaccurate. Fourth, most social scientists and laypeople do not like to believe that stereotypes, especially negative ones, may be accurate. Many of us are victims of stereotypes, and the fact that stereotypes have done so much dirty work for racists and other prejudiced people has made it seem incomprehensible that they could have even an element of truth. The putative accuracy of stereotypes may offend our liberal or at least humanitarian feelings (Mackie, 1973).

Researchers in social cognition have paid considerable recent attention to the whole notion of accuracy (Ambady, Bernieri, & Richeson, 2000; Funder, 1987, 1995;

Hastie & Rasinski, 1988; Jussim, 1991, 1993; Kruglanski, 1989b; Lee, Jussim, & McCauley, 1995; Ryan, Park, & Judd, 1996). There is now abundant evidence that people can be moderately accurate, at least, in their stereotypes about gender (e.g., Diekman, Eagly, & Kulesa, 2002; Hall & Carter, 1999; McCauley, 1995; McCauley & Thangavelu, 1991; Swim, 1994), nationality (Triandis & Vassiliou, 1967), physical attractiveness (Ashmore & Longo, 1995; Feingold, 1992b), race (McCauley & Stitt, 1978; Ryan, 1996), academic performance of ethnic groups (Ashton & Esses, 1999), college majors (Judd, Ryan, & Park, 1991; McCauley, 1995), members of campus residences (Brodt & Ross, 1998; Ryan & Bogart, 2001), and experimentally created groups (Biernat & Crandall, 1996). As I have discussed in Chapter 6, teachers, who are frequently accused of being the Typhoid Marys of stereotype transmission, are quite accurate in their assessments of student abilities. I am not even remotely claiming that our stereotypes are inevitably, or even usually, accurate—just that they can be. Determination of accuracy must be an empirical issue, rather than one decided through assumption and ideology.

Problems with Accuracy

Accuracy can mean different things to different people, because there are several ways of conceptualizing and measuring accuracy. At a more practical level, the seemingly simply question of whether stereotypes are accurate turns out to be exceedingly difficult to answer.

Situational Contingencies and Generality

As I have emphasized many times, our stereotypes are often heavily conditional on person, time, and place (see also Niemann & Secord, 1995). When Joe says that blacks are more violent than whites, he may mean, but not bother to say, that this stereotype applies only to unemployed and undereducated black males, and even then only to a minority under certain circumstances (say, black males of this description who are engaged in gang activity). In his own mind, he may be quite clear that he does not mean to say that black lawyers and truck drivers are more prone to violence than their white counterparts. It is important to recognize that people often overgeneralize; for example, they make statements about the superior athletic ability of blacks on the basis of observing "major" sports, without thinking about the possibility that blacks do not in fact excel in the majority of sports that are played. Nonetheless, we cannot fairly assess the accuracy of stereotypes without giving people a chance to discuss any qualifications they might place on the generality of their stereotypes

Criterion Measurement

Another important issue in accuracy is how we measure the criterion (Ashmore & Longo, 1995; McCauley, Jussim, & Lee, 1995; Ottati & Lee, 1995). What do we mean when we talk of athletic ability? Blacks have a lock on sports that require quickness; for example, their dominance in track sprint events is almost complete. For whatever reasons, whites dominate a variety of other sports—such as golf (Tiger Woods notwithstanding), tennis (again, despite the Williams sisters and the late Arthur Ashe), swimming, gymnastics, and figure skating. Is this because different skills are required in these sports, or is it because some sports require expensive facilities that may not be readily available to as many black youngsters? What do we mean by "athletic ability," anyway? Speed, endurance, quick reflexes?

I raise this point because athletic ability ought to be one of those things that is fairly objective and easy to measure. If we can't get a handle on the athletic stuff, what chance do we have for areas that are clearly less objective? When we speak of violence, do we mean only physical aggression toward strangers, or do we include aggression against family members and friends? Although today we would certainly include both, the latter would not have been as salient just a few years ago. Do we dare use official arrest statistics to measure violence, given that they are certainly biased in a number of ways? And if we do not use these statistics, how will we measure violence? Do we include yelling as well as hitting, stabbing, and shooting? When we consider the question of whether black males are more violent on average than whites, our answer will depend to some extent on what we mean by "violence." Having made that point, I must also note that for some stereotypic judgments—such as the percentage of males or females in particular occupations (McCauley & Thangavelu, 1991)—there are objective data that can be used as a criterion.

SELF-JUDGMENTS

Matters get even more complex when we consider traits such as laziness, happiness, or superstitiousness. To be sure we have well-validated psychological tests of many traits, but such measures usually depend heavily on self-reports. Can we trust people's judgments of their own traits? Suppose John takes a test of extroversion and scores highly. Yet his wife claims that he is deluded about the extent to which he performs many extroverted behaviors, and that he is really a closet introvert; she, who "knows him better than he knows himself," is quite sure about this. Is she inaccurate just because she disagrees with his own assessment? Who knows? John's wife does not observe him in all situations, and as we have known for decades, trait-related behavior is not generally consistent across all situations.

In the stereotype area, Group A's stereotype of Group B is often considered to be accurate if it agrees with Group B's "autostereotype" or stereotype of its own group (Ottati & Lee, 1995), and several studies show exactly this sort of convergence (e.g., Abate & Berrien, 1967; Bond, 1986; Brigham, 1974; Pennebaker, Rime, & Blankenship, 1996). There is no special reason to believe that this is flawed logic, but it is possible that people can be collectively deluded about their group's own qualities, just as individuals can about their individual features.

CONSENSUS JUDGMENTS

Often accuracy is defined in terms of consensus judgments. That is, a stereotype is considered accurate if a given judge matches the consensus of other judges, and there is some evidence that consensus estimates are especially good indices of personality (Kolar, Funder, & Colvin, 1996). One related tradition is to examine whether several perceiver groups (typically national or ethnic groups) agree in their stereotypes of a target group; people from different backgrounds often agree on the stereotypes of other groups (Hagendoorn & Linssen, 1994; McAndrew et al., 2000;

Triandis et al., 1982; Vinacke, 1949). This is often what laypeople mean when they say that Group A members have Feature X because "everyone knows they do." But, of course, in the stereotype arena this is highly problematic. A few generations ago, "everyone knew" that women were intellectually inferior and that black males were too lazy to play major sports.[2]

On the other hand, we should not dismiss this set of issues too quickly. If everyone knows that Group A has Feature X and people are in contact with cultural realities, then accuracy does provide an explanation of sorts for why people hold the stereotypes they do. They hold them because the culture they trust (or at least rarely question) has given them ample reason to believe these stereotypes to be true. This goes beyond merely saying that people hold stereotypes because they ingest them from the culture. It goes further in suggesting that people continue to hold stereotypes because they believe them to be accurate by virtue of cultural sanction. At a minimum, the cultural imprimatur discourages people from questioning the particular reality. And while we can all get on our high horses and suggest that people should question received truths, in practice most of us have neither the time nor energy to delve into more than a tiny sample of such social realities. The vast majority of things people believe to be true have no greater warrant than the fact that reference books, teachers, moral and religious leaders, and the culture at large say they are true. Knowledge about stereotypes should be no different.

A KERNEL OF TRUTH

It has sometimes been suggested (e.g., Campbell, 1967) that stereotypes are exaggerations of a kernel of truth—in other words, that people do have a fairly accurate sense of which groups tend to have which traits, but still exaggerate group differences. A careful review of past research relevant to this claim (McCauley, 1995) suggests that at least for the limited domains that have been studied, the exaggeration part is not generally true; if anything, people often underestimate real group differences. However, there is actually not much relevant research, and I suspect that while many people underestimate group differences, others (especially those who are prejudiced) may tend to exaggerate.

The Self-Categorization Perspective

Self-categorization theory (Oakes, Haslam, & Turner, 1994; Oakes & Reynolds, 1997; Turner, Oakes, Haslam, & McGarty, 1994) takes a quite different and more radical approach to the accuracy question. In the first place, it assumes that there is no privileged criterion of personality or other group features. In a situation where members of one group rate another, there is generally a comparative element; that is, people are motivated to differentiate their group from that of others, at least for some features. The resultant differentiation or accentuation is not an error just because it takes account of contextually appropriate representations—quite the contrary. Groups are usually seen in the context of other groups. It makes little sense to talk about men without implicitly contrasting them with women, or about obese people without skinny ones.

Because the features seen as most important will vary, depending on the relevant contrast, stereotypes have a relative quality. Seeing lawyers as greedy may make sense when they are contrasted with rabbis, but not when they are compared with stockbrokers. Since stereotypes are relative to context and comparison, it makes little sense to assess their general accuracy. This does not mean, however, that we must tolerate every stereotype as being equally valid. But whether stereotypes are accurate or not is a fairly meaningless question when phased in traditional terms.

Types of Accuracy

Because accuracy has been such a diffuse (and, some would argue, badly defined) concept, there have been many proposals for ways that we might think about types of accuracy. Accuracy is not any one thing; we can define it in terms of process and various kinds of criteria.

Circumscribed Accuracy

In an influential paper, William Swann (1984) argued that we can be accurate about what traits others possess, but that such information is also often relatively useless. Swann, as well as Kruglanski (1989b) and Baron (1995), has argued that in everyday life accuracy is often seen through the lens of pragmatic utility. When I interact with others, it may matter little to me whether women are in fact (by some criterion) less gifted mathematically than men, and men less gifted verbally. After all in ordinary social life math skills are relatively underutilized, and almost everyone I know has sufficient verbal skills to carry on a decent conversation and send the occasional e-mail. Do I really care that the women before me have slightly larger vocabularies than the men? Similarly, I have the luxury of living in a safe social milieu, where physical violence is such a rare occurrence that knowledge (accurate or not) about the relative violence rankings of people from different ethnic groups has almost no pragmatic value. As Fiske (1992) has commented, "The pragmatic perceiver does not necessarily maximize accuracy, efficiency, or adaptability; good-enough understanding, given his or her goals, is the rule" (p. 879).

Swann (1984) argues that what is more important is what he calls "circumscribed accuracy," the ability of people to predict the behavior of another in a fairly concrete situation. Generally I don't care whether a particular student is generally polite and nonviolent, as long as I can depend on the student to be so when he or she comes to my office hour. Or Mike, a statistics instructor, probably cares less about the notion that women are less gifted than men in mathematical areas than about observing their relative performance in his classes. His experience there may be that women outperform men, and he may care little whether this is because of biased sampling, the fact that women may be better in this one area of mathematics, his teaching style, or the fact that the women in the course more frequently request help from him during office hours.

But, as Swann recognized, there is a danger lurking behind all those qualifications. Consider Roy, a racist who employs a majority of black workers. Because he believes them to be lazy, he institutes a set of work practices that do in fact inhibit initiative, with the predictable result that his black workers appear to be lazy. He may even selectively use those practices with his black employees and treat his white employees in ways that enhance their work ethic. Now when Roy claims that he knows his black employees are lazier than his white ones, and can even produce empirical evidence that would satisfy an unbiased observer, can we be entirely happy with his brilliant defense of circumscribed accuracy?

Quantification of Stereotypes

We must also be aware of a methodological/measurement problem. When people pronounce their stereotypes, they generally do so in either global or comparative terms. People are prone to make such statements as "Men are better at math than women." If all that means is that on average males outperform females on standardized math tests and in advanced math classes, it is correct, at least for the present. On the other hand, we are not surprised to learn that the majority of accountants in many places are women, and that in many households women keep the family books. Similarly, a woman who claims that blacks are more violent than whites would be accurate if we examine arrest statistics for violent crimes, but would be inaccurate if she suggests that the most black men have committed violent crimes or that her black mailman is prone to assault the people to whom he delivers mail.

Before we can properly answer whether a stereotype is accurate, we must force the perceiver to translate a bald statement into something that we can quantify. How could we assess what Dorothy, a student, means when she claims that professors are kind? We might ask her to give a percentage estimate, and then we could, in principle (although with difficulty), compare her estimate with actual percentages of professors who are kind. Alternatively, she may mean something more basic, such as that professors are more kind than some relevant comparison group. So we must know whether she is explicitly or implicitly comparing professors to high school teachers, lawyers, her parents, people in general, students, or some other group.

When we ask whether stereotypes are accurate, we must also consider how leniently or stringently we define "accurate." Bob says that Asian American students are quiet. We probe and discover he means that 60% of Asian American students are quiet. Now suppose we have some measure of quietness, and we discover that in reality only 50% of Asian American students are quiet. Is Bob's stereotype inaccurate? Well, on the one hand he is only off by 10 percentage points, so he seems pretty accurate. But on the other hand, if 40% of all people could be described as quiet, Bob's estimate actually doubles the "true" difference between Asian and other Americans and seems less praiseworthy.

The point in not to get tied up in fairly arcane issues of measurement, but simply to make the point that few stereotype judgments will be absolutely accurate, and our judgments about their accuracy will depend in large part on how close we expect them to be. In practice, we often do an end run around the problem by using comparative judgments and having relaxed standards for exact judgments. We are often happy enough if people have some sense of the relative ranking of groups on some dimension, without requiring that they have precise knowledge about percentages and probabilities.

Four Types of Accuracy

It is natural to think of stereotype accuracy in terms of discrepancies between some criterion and the judgment. However, another way of thinking about stereotype accuracy is in terms of whether the perceiver has a precise sense of how much or little of

various traits or other features a group has. One way to assess this is through correlations across features between the criterion and the judgments; accuracy correlations
can be calculated for each perceiver and averaged over perceivers if necessary (see
Ryan, 1995, for a discussion). As with all correlations, this measure of accuracy is insensitive to discrepancies between criterion and judgment. It is possible for a given
perceiver to overestimate how much of a trait a group has by a huge amount, but still
to be accurate if he or she has the proper sense of relative standing on each trait.

Judd and his colleagues (Judd et al., 1991; Judd & Park, 1993; Ryan, 1995) have
also suggested that an important part of stereotypes is perceived dispersion within
groups. A person could err in seeing African Americans as more athletic on average
than they are, but also err in perceiving most African Americans to be athletic as opposed to seeing a wider dispersion of ability among this group. As I have earlier
shown (see Chapters 3 and 7), such dispersion judgments can have important consequences for stereotyping. And given measures of actual dispersion for one or more
traits, we can also calculate how accurate a given perceiver is in dispersion judgments
for a given trait, or how accurate the perceiver is across traits (again using a correlation measure).

Thus there are really four types of accuracy: discrepancy of mean judgment, discrepancy of dispersion judgment, correlations across features of mean judgments,
and similar correlations for dispersion judgments. Unfortunately for our ability to
summarize accuracy research, these measures do not always produce consistent results (Ryan, 1995)—although this is to be expected, given that these are quite different ways of measuring accuracy and presumably tap into different experiences and
judgmental processes. In one fairly comprehensive study, Ryan (1996) found no tendency for either whites or blacks to exaggerate stereotypes of the outgroup in terms
of mean measures. She also found that blacks underestimated dispersion of features
for both whites and blacks more than did whites, and that both groups tended to underestimate dispersion more for blacks than for whites. For sensitivity measures,
there was a different pattern: Blacks were more sensitive to the distribution of traits
than whites and were somewhat more accurate in judging whites (the outgroup) than
blacks. White subjects were not only less accurate in general, but were particularly so
in judging the outgroup. For sensitivity to dispersion, whites were more accurate
than blacks, and whites were judged more accurately than blacks. However, blacks
were about equal in judging the two groups (although slightly better when judging
black), but whites were much more accurate in judging their white ingroup. Interestingly, ratings of familiarity with outgroups did not significantly predict accuracy, although there was a tendency in that direction.

Accuracy of Metastereotypes

Although our focus is quite properly on whether a person or a group's stereotypes of
some target group are accurate, we must also realize that stereotypes rarely function
in a social vacuum. As an older white male, I have stereotypes of young black females
(as well as of older white males and all the other possible groups). Naturally, as I
interact with members of those groups, I will occasionally hint at a stereotype or two
and in some cases may blurt them out openly. At the same time, the people with
whom I interact may also be concerned about the stereotypes I have of them. I
should imagine that my students worry somewhat about professors' stereotypes of
students, and well they should. Do women have an accurate fix on the stereotypes

that men have of them? Do blacks have a clear conception of white stereotypes of blacks, and for that matter do whites understand what blacks think of them? These stereotypes about stereotypes are called "metastereotypes," and important as they may be in everyday interactions, they have not been systematically investigated (Vorauer, Main, & O'Connell, 1999).

Certainly at the individual level, there is some evidence that people have a fairly accurate view of how they are seen by others (Malloy & Albright, 1990). The situation is somewhat more complicated for group ratings. In one extensive study, Krueger (1996a) examined the stereotypes of blacks and white for each other and perceptions of those same stereotypes. Both blacks and whites underestimated the favorability of the other group's stereotypes of them. Sigelman and Tuch (1997) also found that blacks thought that whites were more negative toward them than they actually were. In another study, Tuohy and Wrennall (1995) found that Scottish police officers were fairly accurate in their perceptions of the public perceptions of attitudes toward the police, but thought that members of the public were more favorable in their stereotypes of police behavior than they were.

Conclusions: Are Stereotypes Accurate?

What can we conclude about the accuracy of stereotypes? Very little, actually. It is certainly clear from everyday experience and several lines of research that some people hold some inaccurate stereotypes of others. We also know that often stereotypes are accurate, although much depends on how they are measured and what criteria are used.

The major problem with stereotypes is not their putative accuracy, but how they are applied (Stangor, 1995). It may well be true that black males commit more than their share of violent crimes, but the great majority of black males do not commit such crimes. What is the unbiased observer to make of this? For most of us this is relatively useless information, since it does not tell us much about individual people, who are after all the bread and butter of our everyday behavior. As I have argued in Chapter 3, even stereotypes that are generally accurate can be misapplied to individuals. This is particularly likely for relatively low-frequency behaviors that may be differentially displayed by particular groups but still may be performed by relatively few of its members.

Finally, I mention somewhat in passing that there is a backhanded virtue to accurate stereotypes. If our stereotypes are accurate, it suggests (but does not prove) that they are based on experience. And if they are based on a legitimate reading of past experiences, the door is open to allow new experiences of a different flavor to change the stereotype.

None of this is meant to suggest that asking whether stereotypes are accurate is a meaningless question. But it is a vexed one, and we will be snake-bit unless we approach it with caution. The best we can do by way of general summary is to say that some stereotypes held by some people for some groups are sometimes accurate. This is not terribly compelling, perhaps. However, our main concern here is that accurate stereotypes tend to support the idea that stereotypes and the consensus that exists about some of them may be largely due to more or less veridical experiences. Even the fairly bland statement that sometimes stereotypes are accurate gives us enough wiggle room to assume that at least some stereotypes may be based on people's experiences.

ARE STEREOTYPES BASED ON CULTURAL TUITION?

Most of us feel vaguely uncomfortable with the notion than stereotypes may be accurate reflections of experience, and surely the most popular notion about the origins of stereotypes is that they result from cultural tuition of one kind or the other. It is easy to assume that they are deliberately taught. In some cases, teachers[3] or religious leaders[4] may explicitly state certain stereotypes as being indubitably true. There is no doubt that such direct teaching was common in an earlier day and still persists to some extent today. It is not clear, however, that it has ever been as effective as most socialization agents would hope. After all, many children who are reminded that swearing is bad and stealing is evil still manage to do a little of both. We should not be cynical about the power of lessons learned at home and school, but we must be skeptical of unexamined claims for the effectiveness of these.

Direct and Indirect Socialization

As I have argued elsewhere (Schneider, 1996), socialization can occur through both direct and indirect influence, and can affect the content of stereotypes as well as ways of thinking about people in general or specific groups. It is obvious that socialization agents sometimes tell us *what* to believe. It may be less salient that they also tell us *how* to think about certain issues. So, for example, Americans are likely to think about misdeeds in terms of individual responsibility and the failures of parents to instill moral values, whereas other cultures might place more emphasis on social constraints. Thus, when many Americans observe a member of a stereotyped group performing poorly at some task, it is easier to look for failures of the individual than failures of the larger social system.

Direct Effects

Parents' or teachers' explicitly telling children *what* to believe about members of specific groups is certainly the prototypic means of cultural transmission. Direct influences on processing (*how* to think) are also fairly commonplace. For example, religious communities tend to enforce particular ways of thinking about misdeeds; parents may remind their children that "those people" categorically are not to be trusted or have deviant values (or, conversely, that we should always try to think of people as individuals); and schools emphasize all manner of lessons about the importance of hard work in the classroom and on the playing fields, which can dramatically affect the ways we think about others. Generally, direct effects on both content and processing mode are salient enough to require no additional elaboration here.

Indirect Effects

TEACHING BY EXAMPLE

Sometimes socialization agents convey lessons about people, even though that was not their intention. Such indirect effects are especially salient when cultural agents provide readily available examples that illustrate culturally approved lessons. So if a little white girl only sees Asian children who are polite and docile, she will naturally assume that all such children are that way. Likewise, a little white boy who hears his parents explain the misdeeds of his black friends in terms of their parents' lack of good values will tend to adopt that same line of attack in his own explanations. The parents may not mention race in either case, but the connection is probably not lost on the children. I suspect that most parents spend relatively little time discussing philosophies of life, what groups have what features, or how to think about group differences. These lessons are taught through concrete example.

WHAT IS NOT TAUGHT

Indirect effects are important not only for what they include, but for what they exclude. A white father who talks openly about the failures of putative affirmative action hires down at his office not only teaches his children plenty about what he thinks of minority people without ever directly mentioning ethnicity, but also provides his children with a narrow and limited view of minority people. By stressing the putative incompetence of minority people, he fails to emphasize the incompetence of other workers and does not place incompetent behavior by any race in a useful context. Furthermore, he fails to emphasize the fact that most of these people also have children, husbands, and wives, and the same sorts of family problems he has. Seeing behavior exclusively in terms of moral categories does not encourage thinking about psychological and sociological causes. A child who is taught that sex is vaguely immoral does not need to be directly taught that homosexuality is wrong; the latter judgment comes along for the ride.

Throughout this chapter and the next, I stress the power of socialization agents to frame depictions of behavior in ways that privilege some interpretations over others. Often this is not deliberate, and is accomplished largely by presenting vivid examples and by emphasizing some interpretative frameworks over others. This may seem a precious kind of influence, but in the final analysis it may explain more about stereotyping and prejudice than more direct types of influence—which are probably far more rare, certainly in the media, than most social scientists seem to believe.

The Learning of Content

LEARNING CATEGORIES

There are at least four kinds of content that children can learn through a variety of cultural mechanisms. The first is the social categories that they should use. Not all categorizations are explicitly taught. Children come into the world ready to classify people into different types of groups (Hirschfeld, 1996), and as we have already seen (Chapter 3), they seem to learn race, gender, and age categories quite early. It is probable that children universally learn these categories without much help from the larger culture—which is not to say that socialization agents do not constantly reinforce use of these categories. Think, for example, how often we use gender-linked pronouns in our everyday conversation, and how often children are asked about their gender and the gender of friends, teachers, and others. Children are also often reminded of age when they are told they are not "big enough" to do certain things.

However, many categories are culturally specific and encouraged. For example, some occupational categories are available to some children that may not be to others; a rural child in Mexico may not understand the category of professors, but might have more finely articulated categories for farmers than an urban American child does. Americans use religious categories less than do citizens of many other countries, and they tend to use socioeconomic status less than race as a way of differentiating people. So there may be categories (such as gender) that children learn on their own, and others (such as relative prestige and status of people) that are almost entirely products of culture. In between, there are categories based on physical appearance, sexual orientation, religion, and occupation, which are present in most societies but tend to be differentially defined, explained, and salient from one culture to the next.

LEARNING FEATURES

Second, children must learn what features "go with" each of the social categories they acquire. As I have argued throughout this book, more is involved in this stereotype learning than simply acquiring a laundry list of features attached to some group node in memory. In most cases, children will also learn how widespread each feature is for the group.

LEARNING AFFECT

Third, children will probably learn to attach some affect or emotion to each of their categories. Initially this affect may be directly acquired through experience, as when a child has one or more bad experiences with members of a particular group. Certainly affect toward groups can be learned through classical conditioning and other modes of learning without the mediation of stereotypes (Olson & Fazio, 2001). In some cases, children may be directly taught to like or dislike certain groups by parents or other socialization agents. In time, their stereotypes may lay the foundation for affect; for example, a child who learns that a group has more negative than positive features is likely also to develop negative feelings toward that group.

LEARNING APPROPRIATE BEHAVIORS

Finally, children will learn a list of acceptable and unacceptable behaviors that are displayed toward members of this group, and as they get older they may learn a complex system of which behaviors are appropriate for which types of people under which circumstances. The children may simply learn that they should show hostility toward people from groups they do not like, and kindness toward people from favored groups. But they may learn that even though they do not like "those people," they do not act badly toward them (at least in public).

Learning How to Think about Others

THEORY LEARNING

I have emphasized throughout this book that stereotypes are more than group nodes with feature associations. People have theories about why features go with groups and how these features are related—theories based in part on what is culturally salient and encouraged as good explanations. Again, Americans tend to think of failures and successes as due to individual and dispositional sources such as motivation and ability, whereas other cultures place more emphasis on collective responsibility. Although such attributional preferences do not constitute a theory as such, any theory about why members of certain groups tend to be lazy or violent or shy will certainly be built around such basic notions. Parents and other socialization agents may convey that "they are all alike," or may preach the importance of looking beyond groups to the individual. We can learn to be threatened by the differences between ourselves and others, or to see such differences as opportunities for learning and personal growth. Some people learn to look for underlying similarities among people, others for ways that make people superficially different. In any event, among the important things children learn are theories about people, including what kinds of distinctions are important, what behavioral differences count, and why people behave as they do. Such general theories surely come to include subtheories about race, gender, and many of the other categories we have been considering.

THEORY LEARNING IS OFTEN SUBTLE AND UNSEEN

It is sometimes hard to get an intellectual grasp on such tuition, because it is ubiquitous, subtle, not well articulated, and nondeliberate. The cultural mists that surround us often obscure alternatives. Those of us who actively try to promote nonprejudiced thinking often find that it is easier to get people to accept new facts about other groups than it is to change ways of thinking that have been ingrained by a decade or two of what amounts to cultural indoctrination. It would be easier, I expect, to convince people that their estimate of the number of people in a group who exhibit a particular trait is wrong than to get them to internalize the complexities of the causal matrix that underlies behavior. Most of us like simple answers to seemingly straightforward questions, and the road to enlightenment on this particular issue is long and bumpy indeed.

The Agents of Socialization

Because the working assumption has generally been that stereotypes have been taught directly, psychologists have focused on cultural agents of such socialization. Several such agents have been identified. The most obvious (and seemingly most important) is the family, especially parents. Whereas many parents help their children avoid stereotypic and prejudicial thinking, others directly or indirectly promote it.

As most parents discover, when children enter school peers become an important part of their socialization experience. Although such factors become acute during adolescence—when teenagers are prone to form categories (and stereotypes) based on styles of dress, preferences in music, and behaviors that their parents may not fully comprehend—the peer influence process actually begins much earlier.

A third set of agents consists of institutions such as schools, religious groups, and other organizations (e.g., Scout troops) that are more or less explicitly assigned responsibility for certain sorts of moral and other instruction. Those of us who went to school in the 1950s got explicit lessons from teachers about evil Russians and other Communists.[5] In a brief (and unsuccessful) stint in the Boy Scouts, I learned about the (unspecified) dangers of spending too much time alone with other boys, and many churches explicitly taught the evils of sex and condemned those who violated sexual proprieties. My sense is that many teachers, ministers, and other socialization agents are much more tolerant and less prone to provide explicit instruction on such matters today than 40–50 years ago, but one would be naive to assume that shapers of the young do not have agendas that involve stereotypes.

Finally, some of our beliefs and attitudes are shaped by the mass media—especially, in this day and age, television and movies. Indeed, the media have become the scapegoats of politically incorrect socialization, being regularly blamed for all manner of ills in our society.

Parents

PARENTAL INFLUENCES ARE OFTEN HARD TO DOCUMENT

Historically in Western (and especially North American) cultures, parents tend to be viewed as responsible for everything—scientific achievement, athletic accomplishment, mental illness, childhood autism, criminality, business success, racism, and adult personality.[6] This is not merely a matter of ideological preference (and bias); every adult person can point to obvious positive and negative influences from parents, and most parents can point with pride (usually) to influences on their children.

Yet, it in most domains the actual empirical support for parental influence is often inconclusive, inconsistent, vague, weak, or nonexistent (Harris, 1998). It is not for want of trying, although Maccoby (2000) points out that the more recent studies employing better and more diverse methodologies have tended to find larger parental effects on children, at least for some traits. Thousands of research papers in developmental psychology in the last half century have attempted to document the seemingly obvious ways parents affect their children. And within this large literature, there are a great many reports of just that. Furthermore, large literatures on social learning and imitation as well as reinforcement-based learning give us the full arsenal of potential mechanisms we need to explain parental influence on their children. The problem is that the research findings often do not add up to a consistent picture, and even consistent findings are often weak.

IMPORTANT CONFOUNDS

There are several salient reasons why studying parental effects is difficult to pull off empirically and, when we get down to brass tacks, difficult to conceptualize cleanly. One is that many of the studies have used correlational methodologies that leave causality unclear. This is not just a methodological problem. Developmentalists now generally recognize that the relationships between parents and children are largely reciprocal. As every parent of a willful 2-year-old knows, children often have a great deal of control over parents. Stubborn refusals to move, temper tantrums, and loving embraces provide incentives for parents to alter their behavior to children, just as offers of candy and threats of "time out" affect the ways children behave.

Obviously, in the case of stereotypes it is more than mildly awkward to assume that children affect the content of their parents' beliefs, but parents do respond to their children's experiences. Parental explanations for the ways their sons and daughters are treated by members of other groups occur in the context of their children's outside experiences and may play a large role in the ways their children come to think of these other groups. For example, although parents may not look for opportunities to teach their white sons that girls are incompetent at math and sports or that blacks are dirty and dangerous, they may answer questions or explain situations in ways that contribute to prejudiced thinking.

Maccoby (2000) points out an additional important reason parental effects may fly under the radar of our empirical studies: There may be profound single episodes when children are willing to listen and parents to explain, often in response to especially emotional or salient experiences in the children's lives.[7] Such effects are not easily captured in traditional research paradigms, although Quackenbush and Barnett (2001) provide one interesting example.

There are other important variables that are deeply confounded with parental influence. One is genetics (see Rowe, 1994). Although an extended discussion is well beyond my present scope, it is not hard to manufacture relevant examples. It is possible, for instance, that propensities to dislike others may be related to temperament and other personality variables with a clear genetic basis. Children who inherit propensities that encourage prejudice may also have parents who directly encourage this as well.

Another important confounding variable is likely to be sibling influence within the family. Most children have highly charged relationships, both positive and negative and usually ambivalent, with their siblings. Older brothers and sisters can and do teach directly and indirectly important lessons about other groups, and, of course, older siblings may take seriously their obligations at developing attitude clones.[8] In some families parental influences may be mediated through older siblings or other family dynamics.

Peers

One response to the relative failure to document parental influences has been to suggest that peer influences are critical (Harris, 1995; Maccoby, 1998). At times such influences can be hard to disentangle from parental ones. After all, most parents seek schools that will support their families' values, and actively pick playmates for their children from other families with like-minded attitudes. When children are young, parents encourage them to participate in activities that, whether intended or not, produce selective peer interaction. Children who are encouraged to play the piano and take ballet lessons are likely to meet different children than those who are encouraged to play soccer. In high school, debaters tend to be a different group of students from athletes, and both may be isolated from those who have few school activities but a passion for cars or shopping for clothes. Even if parents pay relatively little attention to who their children's friends are, the children will still select peer groups nonrandomly, and the types of peer groups they pick may be confounded with what parents believe. More obviously, the facts of residential and school segregation by socioeconomic status and other factors mean that most American children grow up in relatively homogeneous environments, at least with regard to race and socioeconomic variables.

The Media

It has been a popular pastime among social scientists and laypeople alike to blame the media for the ills of modern society. Some hold television and movies responsible for undercutting traditional moral and political values, while others see media as promoting violence and licentious sexual behavior. The media have been blamed for spreading and perpetrating, or even creating, stereotypes of gender and race (among other important social categories).

THE POWER AND COMPLEXITY OF THE MEDIA

The media, of course, include magazines, newspapers, radio, movies, and even the Internet, as well as television. But when all is said and done, when social scientists speak of the media, they almost always mean television—and with good reason, since most people get most of their information from TV. Americans watch incredible amounts of television, and several decades of work on imitation and social learning have shown clearly that adults and especially children can and do learn important lessons from what they see and hear in the media (Bandura, 1994).

Still, there is many a step between lessons learned from watching TV and performance of those same lessons. Most children learn how to use guns and knives by watching TV, but few kill or even threaten others. And media lessons are nuanced and complex. To be sure, TV may show us that women are more likely to cook than men, but we may also learn that cooking is hardly the providence of females and that cooking may or may not be a rewarding activity. Children see black thugs, but they also see black athletes and businessmen; they see women who work, as well as women who stay home (and, increasingly, men who do the same). Thus TV teaches multiple lessons that interact in complex ways with realities provided by parents and peers.

One of the major advantages of televison is that it exposes us all to information we could not easily acquire on our own, and it does so in a vivid way. One could learn about Native Americans by reading books, but watching an hour-long documentary might convey the information in a way that is more interesting and memorable. Thus television has the capacity to broaden the scope of information children are exposed to, as many parents who wish to control such exposure find out. Children may learn more about sex and violence at an earlier age by watching TV than children did a couple of generations ago, but they also get exposed to roles, occupations, types of people, and alternative lifestyles that, for better or worse, they would probably never see directly. For example, children who probably never encounter a gay male in their daily commerce (or at least one who is openly out of the closet) may learn most of what they know about this category from watching TV. Children of working-class parents may see models of surgeons, lawyers, and business executives they would never meet, and the children of middle- or upper-class parents may learn about poverty mainly from television.

WAYS THAT THE MEDIA CREATE STEREOTYPES

TV, then, has the potential to teach children (and adults, for that matter) about alternatives and the complexity of social groups and roles. It is not inherently a vehicle for conveying negative and limiting stereotypes about groups. However, the media are powerful devices for communicating information, and there is little doubt that they do contribute to and even create stereotypes (see Gunter, 1995). As a rough guide, we may discuss four major ways in which the media might distort our perceptions of groups.

Underrepresentation. First, some groups of people have been and arguably still are absent from or underrepresented in media depictions. Women are well underrepresented in prime-time television (Durkin, 1985a), newspaper photographs (Luebke, 1989), music videos (Sommers-Flanagan, Sommers-Flanagan, & Davis, 1992), video games (Dietz, 1998), computer magazines (Ware & Stuck, 1985), children's cartoons (Klein, Shiffman, & Welka, 2000), and popular newspaper cartoons (Brabant & Mooney, 1997). Older women are particularly underrepresented in movies (Bazzini, McIntosh, Smith, Cook, & Harris, 1997).

Older people are underrepresented in a variety of media (Kovaric, 1993). Historically, members of various racial minorities have been seen less often in television than in everyday life (Graves, 1993; Greenberg & Brand, 1994; Kern-Foxworth, 1994). Despite the fear of television advertisers that greater representation of black people would alienate white viewers, there is little evidence for this; on the other hand, blacks are positively influenced by seeing blacks in advertisements (Kern-Foxworth, 1994). Although that situation improved for blacks during the 1980s and early 1990s, in recent years Asians and Hispanics have been underrepresented relative to both whites and blacks (Graves, 1993; Greenberg & Brand, 1994; Lin, 1998; Subervi-Vélaz & Colsant, 1993). We rarely see people who are physically disabled on television, and almost never in print advertisements (Greenberg & Brand, 1994). Obese women are underrepresented on TV and are often the targets of derogatory comments by males when they are present (Fouts & Burggraf, 2000). Other groups whose group membership is relatively invisible (e.g., persons with mild mental illness, homosexuals, etc.) are often underrepresented, for the simple reason that their group membership is not openly displayed.

Selective Presentation. Second, people may be selectively presented in certain roles or engaging in certain behaviors. It has been common for women to be presented more in home settings and men in work settings (Brabant & Mooney, 1997; Furnham & Schofield, 1986; Lovdal, 1989; McArthur & Resko, 1975). In college textbooks on marriage and the family, females are still presented mostly in traditional ways, although the situation has improved in the past two decades (Low & Sherard, 1999). In children's readers, men appear in a wider variety of occupations than do women (Purcell & Stewart, 1990) and are more often the main characters (Gooden & Gooden, 2001). Women are more often portrayed in passive roles (Furnham, Abramsky, & Gunter, 1997; Furnham & Thomson, 1999; Hurtz & Durkin, 1997), as consumers rather than givers of advice, and in subordinate work situations (Hawkins & Aber, 1992; McArthur & Resko, 1975). In commercials, women represent domestic products more often than do men (Lovdal, 1989); males are more likely to use reasoned arguments for product use (McArthur & Resko, 1975), to have more authority (Coltraine & Messineo, 2000), and to appear as the spokespersons for more expensive products (Mazzella, Durkin, Cerini, & Buralli, 1992). Even in computer clip art, men are presented as more active (Milburn, Carney, & Ramirez, 2001). In periodicals from several cultures and art work through the last six centuries, men have been depicted with more prominent faces than women (Nigro, Hill, Gelbein, & Clark, 1988), and blacks are also shown with less prominent faces than whites (Zuckerman & Kieffer, 1994). This may be important because facial prominence is positively related to perceived intelligence, among other traits (Archer, Iritani, Kimes, & Barrica, 1983).

Stereotypic Presentation. Third, people may be portrayed stereotypically in terms of behaviors, values, and attitudes. Generally television has presented men and women quite stereotypically (Durkin, 1985a; Livingston & Green, 1986), although the relative emphasis on particular stereotypes may vary throughout the day and even by day of the week as the gender composition of the viewing audience changes (Craig, 1992). In music videos men are presented as aggressive and women as sexually suggestive, provocatively clothed, subservient, and the targets of sexual advances (Sommers-Flanagan et al., 1992; Vincent, 1989). Advertisements also tend to emphasize women as sex objects more than men (Coltraine & Messineo, 2000; Lin, 1998), as do video games (Dietz, 1998). Women are often shown wearing revealing clothes and as averting their gaze or gazing away from the main scene—signs of submissiveness (Kang, 1997). Newspaper stories refer to the physical appearance and marital status of women more than men (Foreit et al., 1980), and articles about female athletes are more likely to emphasize attractiveness (Knight & Giuliano, 2001). On television women tend to be attractive and young (Davis, 1990), and in magazines to be blond (Rich & Cash, 1993). Women, more than men, are associated with commercials that preach the virtues of attractiveness (Downs & Harrison, 1985), and in movies physically attractive characters (both male and female) are presented more favorably (S. M. Smith, McIntosh, & Bazzini, 1999).

Lyrics in popular music tend to portray women in stereotypic ways—for example, as needing men, as attractive, and as sex objects (Cooper, 1985)—although men are probably presented even more stereotypically in this medium (Freudiger & Almquist, 1978). Women patients in medical advertisements tend to have pleasant expressions, whereas male patients are more serious (Leppard, Ogletree, & Wallen, 1993); this difference may contribute to the alleged tendency of physicians to take female complaints less seriously than males. Fictional characters in women's magazines are presented in quite stereotypic ways (Peirce, 1997). Teen magazines aimed at both boys and girls focus extreme attention on physical attractiveness and the opposite sex, and are quite stereotypic in content (Peirce, 1993; Schlenker, Caron, & Halteman, 1998; Willemsen, 1998). In Saturday morning cartoon shows, female characters are more likely to display happiness and sadness and less likely to appear angry (Klein et al., 2000). Although recent analyses of children's books have suggested less stereotyping than formerly, male characters are still described as more potent and active than are female characters (Evans & Davies, 2000; Turner-Bowker, 1996).

Media portrayals of the mentally ill (Matas, el-Guebaly, Harper, Green, & Perkin, 1986) and psychiatrists (Gabbard & Gabbard, 1992; Schneider, 1987) tend to be both stereotypic and negative. Psychiatrists in movies tend to be portrayed either as Olympian heroes or as easily duped buffoons or evil manipulators, and they mostly use talking cures (typically psychoanalytically oriented) rather than the more common medication or behavioral therapy approaches (Gabbard & Gabbard, 1999; Greenberg, 2000).

Blacks have traditionally been presented in advertisements in highly stereotypic ways—for instance, Aunt Jemima and Uncle Ben (Kern-Foxworth, 1994). Although blacks have increasingly been featured in advertisements and television programs, those in advertising tend disproportionately to have European features, although blacks (but probably not whites) actually respond more favorably to actors with more African features (Strutton & Lumpkin, 1993). Blacks also tend to occupy lower status occupations and are less often employed. Although blacks make up only 27% of truly poor Americans, 48% of news magazines articles concerning poor persons feature blacks (Clawson & Trice, 2000), and pictures featuring unemployed blacks are disproportionately used to illustrate poverty in economics textbooks (Clawson & Kegler, 2000). This means that among depictions of the poor, Asians and Hispanics are underrepresented, as are elderly persons and the 50% of poor Americans who hold full- or part-time jobs (Clawson & Trice, 2000). In advertisements, blacks are portrayed as less authoritative and, if male, are presented as more aggressive (Coltraine & Messineo, 2000). On local news programs, blacks are also portrayed as perpetrators of violent crime to a greater extent than is justified by actual crime statistics, and are presented in a higher proportion of crime than noncrime stories (Entman, 1994; Romer, Jamison, & de Coteau, 1998). Not surprisingly, blacks are featured much more prominently in sports programs (Campbell, 1995), but it may be relevant to wonder how much of that "extra" coverage is taken up with the antics of the likes of Dennis Rodman. Announcers of professional football are prone to praise black players for the physical abilities, but white players for their smart play (Rada, 1996).

Disabled people are often portrayed as monsters or evil (remember Dr. Strangelove?), as objects of pity (Makas, 1993), as resentful of nondisabled persons (Longmore, 1985), or as superheroes who have overcome great adversity (Balter, 1999). Although disabled individuals are often presented quite positively (Warzak, Majors, Hansell, & Allan, 1988), they are also presented as radically different from most people and as isolated from mainstream society (Norden, 1994). Elderly people are often the butt of jokes, especially in greeting cards (Demos & Jache, 1981).

Framing and Priming. We have been focusing on direct stereotypic portrayals of people, but sometimes the effects of media presentations can be quite subtle. Communication specialists often speak of the media in terms of agenda setting, priming, and framing (Iyengar, 1991; Iyengar & Kinder, 1987; Kinder, 1998). Some (e.g., Zaller, 1992) argue that most people have relatively undefined attitudes on even important issues, and that when they vote or answer public opinion surveys, they may respond in terms of the parts of the total attitude matrix that are currently salient—an argument consistent with the one made throughout this book that many stereotypes are complex, multifaceted, and labile.[9] It is not hard to imagine, for example, that a typical young woman who understands that many elderly people have health and financial problems, whereas others are healthy and vibrant, might shift her stereotype more toward the former when she sees a television program devoted to how many elderly people are not getting the health care they need.

Framing occurs when the media present complex issues within a particular framework, and there are abundant data supporting the idea that media framing does affect the way people and politicians interpret issues and political candidates (Domke, Shah, & Wackman, 1998; Iyengar, 1991; Schneider & Ingram, 1993; Shah, Domke, & Wackman, 1996). Support for social policies are especially affected by how issues are framed (Kinder & Sanders, 1990; Sears & Huddy, 1991). For example, support for bilingual education among non-Hispanics is more negative when it is presented as a strategy for preserving culture than when it is presented as a way to help children learn English (Sears & Huddy, 1991). Presentation of poverty as a general outcome encourages people to focus on societal and economic causes, whereas presentation in terms of individuals leads to assignment of individual responsibility (Iyengar, 1990). Affirmative action looks different through the lens of denying whites positions they have "earned" versus that of trying to level playing fields (Kinder & Sanders, 1996).

The O. J. Simpson trial provided one of the largest splits between races on attitudes in modern history. A CBS poll taken just after the verdict showed that 78% of blacks thought he was innocent and 75% of whites believed he was guilty (Hunt, 1999). Such huge differences cannot easily be explained in terms of the relative stupidity, ignorance, or bias of one race or the other. One reason for the profound disagreements between black and white Americans on the guilt of Simpson was the way the two groups framed the issues and images (Hunt, 1999). The mainstream media clearly framed the issues in terms of black stereotypes (Simpson as illiterate, stupid, violent, and sex-crazed) and emphasized evidence that pointed to his guilt. Not surprisingly, blacks tended to be put off by these presentations and to look for other realities.

A dramatic example of such priming occurred during the 1988 Presidential race between the elder George Bush and Michael Dukakis. In early October, the Bush campaign began emphasizing what came to be known as the "Willie Horton ad." Horton, a black man, was a convicted murderer who while on a Massachusetts furlough program had terrorized a white couple in Maryland. Dukakis, then governor of Massachusetts, defended the furlough program. Because pictures of Willie Horton featured prominently in the televised ad made it clear that he was black, it is probable that these ads primed anti-black attitudes. In any event, after the beginning of the ads, racial resentment became a much more powerful predictor of voting for Bush (Kinder & Sanders, 1996).

Iyengar (1991) suggests one stereotyping-relevant way in which the media frame issues. TV tends to focus attention on individual responsibility by presenting rather discrete, often striking, slices of reality; it generally does not present either historical or socioeconomic contexts. So when on our nightly news we see a parade of black men accused of violent crimes, we are typically not told anything about the circumstances of their crimes or the kinds of experiences these individuals had that produced their behavior. We see information about individuals, but not larger contexts. TV thus tends to reinforce theories of individual responsibility, without emphasizing alternative and more complex models of why people do the things they do.[10]

Here is the important point: The media can affect our attitudes and stereotypes not only by presenting activities, values, attitudes, and so forth allied with specific types of people, but also by providing easily comprehended contexts and few salient alternative explanatory frameworks for understanding the behaviors of people from different groups. These indirect socialization effects can be powerful.

ARE TIMES CHANGING?

Much of the research cited above comes from a decade or two ago, when both print and electronic media were less concerned about stereotypic representations. Is there evidence that stereotypes are diminishing? If we take the long view, we really do not need empirical studies. Those of us old enough to recall TV programs such as *I Love Lucy* and *Amos 'n Andy* know that things have changed.[11] Moreover, the news media have shown dramatic changes in the late 20th century in presentation of minority groups and their issues (Keever, Martindale, & Weston, 1997). For example, before the 1970s Southern newspapers routinely excluded black photos, always identified

blacks by race, refused to use courtesy titles such as Mr. or Mrs. for blacks, emphasized black-on-white crime, and ignored positive stories about black citizens; Northern newspapers were only marginally less overt in their racism (Martindale &
Dunlap, 1997).

For those more attuned to the past 30 or so years, several studies show that at
least gender stereotyping in the media has decreased, although not completely (e.g.,
Allan & Coltrane, 1996; Kortenhaus & Demarest, 1993; Thompson & Zerbinos,
1995). There tends to be less gender stereotyping during prime time, when there is a
fairly even balance of male and female viewers, and more on weekend afternoons
(where male viewers predominate) and weekdays (with more female viewers) (Craig,
1992). There is also some evidence that older people are currently being presented
in a much more positive light than formerly (Bell, 1992). Obviously blacks are presented in more, more varied, and more authoritative roles now than they were 30
years ago (Campbell, 1995; Entman, 1990; Gray, 1995).

PRACTICALITIES AND VALUES

Can we eliminate stereotypes from the media? One problem is that television simply
mirrors our world to some extent. Yes, women are seen more often than men in domestic situations—but, of course, that merely represents the way the world is at present. Would we really want to see a television world in which men performed domestic chores as often as women? The easy answer is "Yes, of course." Just as we want
young girls to grow up thinking that they have equal access to prestigious careers in
medicine, law, and business, boys need to get the message that they are equally responsible for home chores. Although some people might have value-based and ideological disagreements with the idea that domestic and work roles should be equally
divided, few social scientists (who have values and ideologies of their own) would disagree that this is a good thing.

Yet we might want to hesitate a bit before we declare the issue closed. To the extent that we are asking that the media deliberately misrepresent present realities, we
run the risk of letting values substitute for analysis, and we might want to think carefully before we give the media such putative control over the shaping of values and
realities. Value agendas can as easily work against us as for us in the future, as they
have in the past.

Furthermore, well-intentioned pressures may have untoward consequences. For
example, when the media present members of minority groups in authoritative and
positive ways, they may reinforce public opinions that there are no substantial issues
of discrimination in modern society (Coover & Godbold, 1998; Gray, 1989). In the
late 1980s and early 1990s, considerable controversy centered around *The Cosby
Show*, which presented a fairly ideal, middle-class black family whose lives seemed un-
tainted by financial or racial problems (Fuller, 1992; Gray, 1995; Jhally & Lewis,
1992). On the one hand, the program certainly presented a positive image of blacks
and made the Huxtables seem like regular people. On the other hand, the program
conveyed the message that for those who work hard and live right, there are no longer any fundamental issues of race and class for black Americans.

The Cosby Show strikes a deal with its white audience. It asks for an attitude that welcomes
a black family onto TV screens in white homes, and in return it provides white viewers

pleasure without culpability, with a picture of a comfortable, ordered world in which people (and the nation as a whole) are absolved of any responsibility for the position of black people. (Jhally & Lewis, 1992, p. 91)

Generally the media frame race in terms of assimilation to dominant white culture, and downplay the importance of racial differences (Campbell, 1995).

A second point has to do with decision processes and how people should be portrayed. I confess that I get a twinge of anxiety every time I see a black criminal on TV. Doesn't this contribute to the current stereotype of blacks as criminal and lawless? But what is the remedy? If I became a media czar, should my goal be never to present blacks as criminals? That seems fraudulent on the face of it. Well, I have a better idea. Let's have about 12% of the criminals be black, because about 12% of Americans are. That might work. But in our fit of reality matching, shouldn't we seek to represent about 50% of violent criminals as black—a proportion that approximates real life? And if we go with the latter idea as reflecting reality, we might want to parse reality a bit more. Almost all black victims of murder are killed by blacks, and most white victims are killed by whites. So let's make sure that we capture that bit of reality. We might go even further. Maybe we ought to check to see whether blacks commit more murders after arguments and whites more after drug deals. Where do we stop?

The issue is even more complicated, because our little thought experiment has assumed that we are striving for representation across all programs, but decisions are made one program at a time. We surely cannot demand that each and every program be perfectly representative, because they do not have enough characters and situations. Moreover, since our desire is to make sure that people generally watch a representative sample of black criminals, we ought to give some consideration to weighting the proportions on a given program by the popularity of the program, so we ensure that watchers see a more representative sample overall.

We might also wish to think about the extent to which drama (both high and low) is built on stereotypes. In some cases, the drama comes from explicit challenges to existing stereotypes—the often gradual realization that a main character is more than his or her stereotype would suggest. But just as often, the power of great drama comes from characters acting within the confines of stereotypes—consider Shakespeare's Richard III. Comedy is often built on stereotypic presentations; the novels of Charles Dickens are filled with such folks. And while we must recognize that much comedy uses stereotypes in cruel and demeaning ways, other versions manage what we might call an ironic view. Furthermore, all fiction and drama use stereotypes for dramatic contrast by tending to portray minor characters stereotypically. Think how many times fully drawn "good guys" develop their fullness by fighting stereotypic "bad guys," or how often people who are down and out are contrasted with stereotypic bad cops or politicians. No one wants to read detailed and individualized descriptions of minor characters in novels; stereotypes work just fine. In that way, stereotypes function for authors as they do for us—as shorthand depictions of reality. The point is not to defend the cardboard characterizations that infect so much popular culture, but simply to recognize that stereotypes are an integral part of high as well as low art and life.

A final and overwhelming practicality is that programming gurus and advertisers are interested in making money. Programs that move too far away from received realities may not make as much money as those that are more reflective. Let's try a thought experiment. Imagine that we are putting together an ad campaign for computers. Al has the idea of having one picture of a person in a wheelchair using the computer, and Matt suggests that we feature a dwarf in another. Susan says that she is tired of seeing svelte, beautiful women in ads, and she wants to see a plump, ugly woman using the computer. Now it is an open question whether these ads would increase sales (which is after all the only reason to have ads), but one imagines that the computer manufacturer would have decidedly muted enthusiasm for taking a chance on this approach.

None of this is meant to suggest that the media have complete freedom to present whomever in whatever ways they wish. Many social scientists (I among them) would prefer to see television depict people more often in ways that fit their ideals, but the reasons are often as much ideological as empirical. When we begin to dictate program and advertising content from explicit value agendas, questions arise that have no real answers.

DO THE MEDIA INFLUENCE STEREOTYPES?

There is no doubt that the media do present stereotypic images, although arguably not as strongly as many people suppose. There is a bottom line here. Is there any evidence that exposure to media affect people's stereotypes, attitudes, or behaviors? Somewhat surprisingly, there is relatively little definitive evidence one way or the other. The amount of television watched (especially of sex-stereotypic programs) does correlate with traditional views of gender roles (McGhee & Freuh, 1980; M. Morgan, 1987; Signorielli, 1989).

There are plenty of other examples. Those who watch a lot of entertainment TV (where blacks and whites tend to be portrayed as equal) tend to minimize black–white income differences, whereas the watching of news programs (which present more negative portrayals of blacks) is associated with perceptions of a greater income gap (Armstrong, Neuendorf, & Brentar, 1992). Men who watch a lot of TV are more prone to stereotype obese females (Harrison, 2000). In the Netherlands, exposure to certain newspapers that feature articles about ethnic crime correlates with negative ethnic attitudes (Vergeer, Lubbers, & Scheepers, 2000). Media stereotypes of the Innu (a group of Native Canadians) by Canadian media correlate reasonably well with college students' stereotypes (Claxton-Oldfield & Keefe, 1999). Well-publicized attacks on public figures by mentally ill persons increase desired social distance from and negative attitudes toward them (Angermeyer & Matschinger, 1995; Thornton & Wahl, 1996).

Unfortunately, of course, we cannot infer from such correlational data that TV watching affects stereotyping, and the correlational data are actually not all that strong and consistent in any case (Durkin, 1985b; Gunter & McAleer, 1990), although some would argue that the effects are stronger (Signorielli, 1993). A comprehensive study on gender (Morgan, 1982), which found mixed results, can serve as an example. In three different years, TV watching and gender stereotypes were measured for middle school boys and girls, although data were reported for only the second and third years. Generally, for both boys and girls, there was a modest relationship between TV watching and stereotypes in both years (the highest correlation was .34 for boys in the third year). However, these correlations were reduced substantially (and, except for boys in the third year, to nonsignificance) when age, grade, IQ, and mother's work status were controlled for. Furthermore, the correlations were significant only for medium-IQ boys and high-IQ girls. Across years there was a modest correlation (.14) for girls between TV watching in Year 2 and sexism scores in Year 3, but the equivalent correlation for boys was –.09. In looking at the possibility of reverse causality, Morgan reported that sexism in Year 2 did predict TV watching positively in Year 3 (r = .15) for boys, but negatively for girls (r = –.07). Although these findings do provide some support for the effects of TV watching on gender stereotypes, the effects are neither very consistent nor strong. Moreover, they provide some support for the idea that attitudes affect watching—an alternative explanation for the correlation between the two.

Most psychologists feel more comfortable with experiments than with correlational studies, and several experimental studies show that one-time exposure to stereotyped media affects stereotypes, behaviors, and attitudes in the short run (Ford, 1997; Ford, Wentzel, & Lorion, 2001; Gan, Zillman, & Mitrook, 1997; Garst & Bodenhausen, 1997; Hansen & Hansen, 1988; Lavine, Sweeny, & Wagner, 1999; MacKay & Covell, 1997; Power, Murphy, & Coover, 1996; S. M. Smith et al., 1999).

Recently there has been concern that the violent lyrics associated with rock music, especially black-oriented rap music, may affect the proclivities of young people for violent behavior. Johnson, Trawalter, and Dovidio (2000) performed an important experiment test in which they exposed white and black students to violent or nonviolent rap music, or in a control condition to no music at all. Then the participants read vignettes in which a black or white target was violent and were asked for attributional judgments. Both black and white subjects saw the black target's behavior as more dispositional when primed with violent rap music than with nonviolent rap music, but there were no music effects on the attributions for the white target's violent behavior. Also, when subjects read another vignette featuring intelligent behaviors, those who heard violent rap music lowered the ratings of intelligence for the black applicant but not for the white one. Note that in both cases exposure to violent music did not directly affect stereotypes, but did affect interpretations of the behavior of individuals; in many situations involving discrimination, this may be the more important effect. Of course, it must be said that experimental studies can only show that manipulated variables *can* affect behavior, and not that they necessarily do in everyday life.

CONCLUSIONS: MEDIA EFFECTS

So what can we conclude about the effects of the media on stereotyping and prejudice? Almost certainly, they play less of a direct role than many social scientists and laypeople assume. However, the indirect effects may be quite powerful. TV is a passive socialization device, and probably has its greatest effects in reinforcing rather than in challenging cultural truths. Children are not vessels into which cultural lessons are poured by parents and the media. Much of what children know they learn from their own experiences—heavily filtered, to be sure, by cultural lessons learned at home.

But these experiences are bound to be limited. Think of all the types of people an average white middle-class child may not be exposed to regularly and directly—

elderly people, Native Americans, lesbians, patients with cancer, female attorneys, male nurses, construction workers of any gender or race, hard-working (or lazy) Mexican American men and women, Asian gang members, and children being raised by fathers (and the list goes on). Of course, the child may come into contact with exemplars of these groups via television or even school books, but the portrayals there are likely to be one-dimensional and frankly stereotypic (although often in positive ways). The experiences of an impoverished Hispanic youngster may be even more limited.

Much of what they learn about people from these groups will come from the media (and education). This is the good news. The bad is that much of the information they get will be one-dimensional. A sensitive program might portray a gay male quite sympathetically, but fail to reveal that he has anxieties about meeting other people—a trait totally unrelated to his sexual orientation. Although a television series might make a stab at showing the humiliation a black woman has suffered to rise to a position of authority, they may not show the effects of this on her immediate family. Television is good at presenting slices of reality, but less successful at presenting full complexities. Unfortunately, the latter is what fighting stereotypes is all about. As I have emphasized throughout this book, stereotypes are, among other things, theories about people; while the media may change this or that group–feature relationship, they do little to change the explanations of and theories about group differences.

We can and should expect the media to do a better job than they have. But part of the solution should be to present alternatives to culturally condoned images and to show that the world is indeed more complex than our immediate environment suggests.

DEVELOPMENT OF RACE AND GENDER STEREOTYPES

The trajectory of children's stereotypes has been intensively studied, especially for gender and racial categories.[12] The development of racial stereotypes has been studied for well over half a century (Goodman, 1952; Horowitz, 1936; Lasker, 1929); the focus on how children acquire gender stereotypes is more recent. The most general summary we can provide is that children acquire these stereotypes quite early, well before they have firm concepts about these groups. As children get older, of course, they develop stereotypes about teachers, mommies, firefighters, physically disabled persons, and various types of TV characters, but there has been little attention paid to how these stereotypes develop—in part because these categories are more peripheral to our concerns about stereotypes, but also in part, I suspect, because it seems so obvious that such stereotypes are learned by contact with relevant exemplars. This assumption may, of course, be quite false.

Racial Stereotypes

The classic model articulated by Goodman (1952), among others, is that children first learn to categorize others by race, then learn evaluative responses (prejudice) to these labels, and finally learn to discriminate against those they do not like. However, matters turn out to be far more complex. For example, Aboud (1980) showed that children first acquire a preference for their own group, then notions of similarity with members of their own group, and finally ethnic labels—precisely the reverse of what the classic model might lead us to expect. They may acquire negative attitudes toward other ethnic groups well before they have supporting beliefs or stereotypes. Children do begin to learn racial categories very early, but, as with most things, it takes them a while to get these firmly in their grasp. Meanwhile, neither differential evaluation nor discriminative behaviors are content to wait their turn. They too begin to develop early, well before racial categories are completely or coherently formed.

Learning Racial Categories

Research (e.g., Davey, 1983) confirms that racial categories are salient to children in preschool and come to predominate as social categories by the early school years, although more so for prejudiced children (P. A. Katz, Sohn, & Zalk, 1975). This is not to suggest that race is inevitably the most important category. For example, under certain circumstances children may use hair color, facial expression, gender, or disability status to categorize other children (Brown, 1995; Richardson & Green, 1971; Verkuyten, Masson, & Elffers, 1995). In fact, young children sometimes divide the world into occupational categories with the same gusto they do for racial groups (Hirschfeld, 1995); this tends to "die out," in part because it does not receive the same cultural support as does racial and gender classification (Hirschfeld, 2001). The importance of ethnicity varies across situations, activities, and types of questions asked (Verkuyten & Kinket, 1999).

HOW CHILDREN MAKE RACE CATEGORIZATIONS

We should emphasize that children's racial categories are not necessarily the same as adults'. In fact, often children's categories are fairly incoherent by adult standards. For example, young European American children might group Chinese American and African American peers, in which case a distinction may be made those who are "a lot Chinese" and "a little Chinese" (Ramsey, 1987). Generally young children focus on observable, external, and fairly superficial features when describing others, and they may often use skin color, hair color, or any other observable feature unreliably from one situation to the next (e.g., Ramsey, 1987).

Obviously, the development of racial and ethnic categories is a gradual process and depends to some extent on maturing cognitive abilities (Clark, Hocevar, & Dembo, 1980). Children first learn that ethnic identity cannot be changed, and subsequently acquire the ability to label a person consistently, despite superficial changes in physical appearance such as clothing (Aboud, 1984). The latter may not be acquired until age 8 or so, significantly later than similar achievements for gender (see below). Indeed, children are not especially good even at identifying their own race until they are at least 4 or 5 years old (Aboud, 1989). However, white children tend to show adult-like categorization of children on racial grounds earlier than minority children, and also to see themselves as more similar to same-race models at an earlier age than do black children (Williams & Morland, 1976). Minority children often do not see themselves in racial terms until they are well into elementary school (Aboud, 1977; Semaj, 1980).

HOW IMPORTANT IS SKIN COLOR?

The standard assumption is that children learn racial categories because skin color is so perceptually salient. However, there is nothing privileged about skin color as a cue; sometimes children report, for example, that their race categories are based on teeth or type of hair (Aboud, 1977; Ramsey, 1987). More to the point, children do not always coordinate skin color and racial labels especially well.

Cognitive anthropologist Lawrence Hirschfeld (1996, 2001) prefers a different sort of explanation. He begins with the reasonably well-documented idea that children are biologically programmed to develop and use fairly specialized domains of competence. Language is the most obvious example, but there is now abundant evidence that mathematical reasoning and certain types of biological classification also represent specific domains of competences (Hirschfeld & Gelman, 1994). This does not mean that children are programmed at birth to count or solve algebraic equations, or that they are born with the ability to discriminate birds from fish. Rather, they are born with proclivities to pay attention to and develop theories about certain classes of things. For example, children at a very early age seem to discriminate animate from inanimate displays and to understand the difference between mechanical and animate motion. Children also easily learn differences between different types of animals and infer species features in the absence of direct tuition, often ignoring salient physical features to do so (Gelman, 2003). It is highly unlikely that these skills, involving subtle discriminations, are taught.

Hirschfeld proposes that children also have proclivities to classify people into meaningful groups. He does not mean to suggest that they are programmed to pay attention to skin color or to use racial designations; children discriminate people, not races. "It is therefore important to reiterate that I am not proposing the existence of a domain-specific competence for perceiving and reasoning about *race*. Instead, I am suggesting that racial thinking may be parasitic on a domain-specific competence for perceiving and reasoning about human kinds" (Hirschfeld, 1996, p. 72; emphasis in original). In a nutshell, Hirschfeld argues that children pay attention to skin color because they want to divide people into groups, rather than dividing people into groups because they pay attention to skin color.

The salience of skin color seems to vary according to task. In a series of experiments (Hirschfeld, 1994, 1995, 1996), children as young as age 3 were given a picture of a male or female adult who was either black or white, dressed in particular occupational clothes, and stout or skinny. Each adult picture was accompanied by child pictures that were similar to the adult in occupational dress, physique, or skin color. When the children were asked which child was most similar to the adult, their answers were fairly random; physique, race, and occupation were used equally often. In another study, when children were asked to recall lengthy narratives about people, race was mentioned less often than gender or occupation (Hirschfeld, 1993). So for these kinds of judgments, skin color is not an especially important way children divide up their social worlds.

However, skin color was important for other kinds of judgments (Hirschfeld, 1996). When children were given these pictures and asked which child was the child of the adult, race was preferentially used, and when they were asked which child was a picture of the adult when he or she was a child, race was again preferred as a basis of classification. These results suggest that even very young children have a sense that skin color is inherited more than is physique or occupation. Additional studies (Hirschfeld, 1994) confirmed that when children were told that infants were switched at birth (so that a black child was raised by white parents and vice versa), they recognized that each child maintained the same color over time. The latter result may seem fairly trivial until we remember that children are surely not explicitly told that skin color never changes, and so the development of race constancy at such an early age must reflect some strong inborn constraints on judgments.

Thus even young children seem to have deep commitments to the idea that people can be divided into kinds. They have theories of sorts about how and why these kinds differ, and they believe that different groups have different essences. What they are *not* committed to is the idea that skin color (or any other particular feature) defines the categories; indeed, they are relatively inarticulate about how blacks and whites are to be distinguished.

Stereotype Features

Assignment of features to ethnic groups also appears gradually. Children initially tend to overgeneralize about the features associated with stereotypes. For example, they may assume that because they see Chinese people eating in a Chinese restaurant, all Chinese people do so (Ramsey, 1987). Children eventually learn that people from different groups do not all share the same attributes, and that people from different groups may have the same attribute (Aboud, 1989; Katz, 1976). These abilities are almost entirely absent in preschool children, but develop gradually throughout the school years (Davey, 1983). By age 8 or 9, children regularly use internal, dispositional features to describe self, but they do not readily do so for members of ethnic groups (e.g., Aboud & Skerry, 1983). This too develops gradually over the years. By adolescence, what we think of as racial stereotypes are already in place for many. In one large survey of 8th, 10th, and 12th graders (Glock, Wuthnow, Piliavin, & Spencer, 1975), over 50% of the white students endorsed several (mostly negative) stereotypes of both blacks and Jews. However, stereotypes may tend to become less absolute over time as well. Although preschool children tend to assign positive features to their own racial or ethnic group and negative features to others, over time they show more flexibility in assigning both types of features to both in- and outgroups (Doyle, Beaudet, & Aboud, 1988).

Are Children Prejudiced?

INGROUP PREFERENCES AND OUTGROUP REJECTION

Preferences for their own racial group among white children appear as early as they can be reliably measured (Aboud, 1989). Naturally, children as young as 2 or 3 do not have well-developed racial attitudes. Major inconsistencies often appear, as when a child claims to dislike all members of a racial group but then names a member of that group as his or her best friend (Ramsey, 1987). Obviously, preference for one's own group does not necessarily imply active rejection of others, and children generally accept children of other races (Cameron, Alvarez, Ruble, & Fuligni, 2001).

Whether ingroup preference dictates outgroup rejection is an open question. Research by Phinney, Ferguson, and Tate (1997) suggests that identification with one's own ethnic group leads to more positive ingroup attitudes, which in turn predict positive attitudes toward outgroups. There are, however, other reports of a positive relationship between ingroup favoritism and outgroup rejection among children (Aboud, 1980; Doyle et al., 1988), suggesting that ingroup favoritism among children may not be benign.

Although children may show some preferences on tests for same-race others, most studies find that there is little racial animosity among elementary school children (Holmes, 1995), and that generally race plays a small role in playmate choices among preschoolers (Davey & Norburn, 1980; Verkuyten & Kinket, 1999). In playmate choice, gender (Holmes, 1995; Jarrett & Quay, 1984; Schofield, 1981) and disability status (Richardson & Emerson, 1970; Richardson & Royce, 1968) trump race hands down.[13] One way to think of this is that children show slight ingroup preferences from an early age, but do not develop active prejudice against children from other races until quite later, if at all (Davey, 1983).

DO BLACK CHILDREN REJECT THEIR RACE?

In this day and age, the notion that black children may reject their own race does not settle easily. Yet some of the earliest and certainly the most influential studies to be done in this domain, by Clark and Clark (1947),[14] seemed to demonstrate just that. The authors gave black children two dolls, one dark- and one light-complexioned, and they were asked to "give me the doll that looks bad" and "give me the nice doll." These black preschool children choose the dark doll over 60% of the time for the negative question, and the white doll over 70% of the time for the nice question. Older black children (in primary school) also showed a preference for the white dolls, but less strongly. These effects have been replicated in other countries (Gregor & McPherson, 1966; Madge, 1976; Milner, 1973; Vaughan, 1964).

In an elaboration of this methodology, John Williams and his colleagues have asked students a number of evaluative questions and asked them to pick whether a white or a black figure best fits the question. White students substantially evaluate the white figure more positively than the black one, and black children show the same tendency, albeit less strongly (Williams & Morland, 1976). Both Hispanic and white non-Hispanic children assign white non-Hispanic figures to positive stories and Hispanic figures to negative ones (Bernat & Balch, 1979). In some studies, both black and white children prefer white classmates on sociometric measures (Jarrett & Quay, 1984). More recently, in a study using children enrolled in Head Start, white children assigned more negative qualities to children with names common in the black community and positive qualities to children with "white names," but black children did not discriminate.

This research has been used to argue that black children grow up with a sense of racial self-hatred; indeed, these results were cited by the U.S. Supreme Court in the famous *Brown v. Board of Education* decision in 1954 that outlawed school segregation. Although several studies (e.g., Asher & Allen, 1969; Fox & Jordan, 1973; Greenwald & Oppenheim, 1968; Hraba & Grant, 1970) confirm that white children overwhelmingly prefer the white doll, there has been considerable controversy over whether black children still prefer the white over the black doll. Some studies find such preferences (e.g., Asher & Allen, 1969; Porter, 1971; Powell-Hopson & Hopson, 1992), but others find stronger identification of minority children with the black doll or photo (e.g., Epstein, Krupat, & Obuhdo, 1976; Greenwald & Oppenheim, 1968; Hraba & Grant, 1970). Generally, the tendency of black children to prefer the white doll seems to have lessened since the early 1970s (Milner, 1996).

Obviously, techniques in which children are forced to make choices have severe limitations, although methodological alternatives are few for young children. The problem arises for children who have no preference (e.g., who have no clue as to whether a black or a white figure is more likely to be, say, kind). In making such a choice, the child may simply be selecting the figure that looks more familiar, or may be selecting on the basis of the early-learned idea that white is a more positive color than is black (for further discussion, see Williams, Best, & Boswell, 1975; Williams & Morland, 1976). Thus, while the measure reveals something about relative preferences (although not necessarily for race as opposed to color), it cannot tell us whether attitudes toward either group are absolutely good or bad.

FACTORS THAT AFFECT DEVELOPMENT OF PREJUDICE

Several factors seem to affect the levels of prejudice that children display. Experiences count for something. Generally, children are less prejudiced in multiethnic schools (Aboud, 1989); as we will see in Chapter 10, however, mere contact with members of other groups is usually not sufficient to dispel prejudicial thinking (and may enhance it). It seems intuitively that those who have more positive experiences with members of other races should have less prejudice, and this has been found (Towles-Schwen & Fazio, 2001). High school students who make better grades and have higher academic aspirations are less prejudiced (Glock et al., 1975).

Parents' attitudes play some role, but not as much as one might think. Studies find moderate to low positive relationships (Bird, Monachisi, & Burdick, 1952; Carlson & Iovini, 1985; Gardner, Taylor, & Feenstra, 1970) or no relationships (Aboud & Doyle, 1996) between parentals' and children's attitudes. In fact, during the preschool years, children's attitudes toward other racial groups are sometimes negatively correlated with their parents' attitudes (Branch & Newcomb, 1980, 1986; Davey, 1983). Some studies find somewhat stronger relationships between attitudes and perceptions of parental attitudes (Epstein & Komorita, 1965, 1966a, 1966b), but a recent careful study of college students finds that even perceptions of parents' attitudes and measures of implicit prejudice are uncorrelated (Towles-Schwen & Fazio, 2001). Various psychodynamic theories, such as the authoritarian personality perspective (Adorno, Frenkel-Brunswik, Levinson, & Sanford, 1950), argue that highly punitive parents may force children to displace aggression outward toward minority group members. However, data suggest that moderate but not extreme levels of punitiveness are associated with prejudice (Epstein & Komorita, 1965), especially when parents are perceived to be highly prejudiced (Epstein & Komorita, 1966a). Parental effects in this area are probably mostly indirect, through parental selection of school and activities that affect both the quantity and quality of interracial contacts.

John Williams (see Williams & Morland, 1976) has argued that racial attitudes are generalizations of sorts from attitudes toward colors. In most Western cultures, the term "black" is associated with negative events, darkness, and dirt, whereas "white" is linked with purity and goodness. Certainly adults rate colors such as white and yellow more positively than black (Longshore, 1979). Children may learn evaluative associations to color terms through adults' use of language, or they may learn them on their own (as when frightening events happen in the dark). In either case, when African Americans are called "black" or children realize they have a dark color, they may generalize their previous attitudes toward black (or dark colors generally) to the category name.

Gender Stereotypes

The development of gender stereotypes has been intensively investigated. There are several processes involved (Hort, Leinbach, & Fagot, 1991; Ruble & Martin, 1998). Gender schemas, knowledge, identity, and stereotypes are individually complex cognitive achievements and are not related to each other in any crystallized way in adults, let alone children; nor do they show simple developmental patterns or relate the same ways to various socialization factors (Francis, 1999; Signorella, 1999; Spence & Hall, 1996; Turner & Gervai, 1995). At a minimum, we need to consider how children acquire knowledge about gender as a category, as well as actual gender stereotypes.

Stages of Gender Knowledge Acquisition

There are several steps or stages in the development of gender knowledge (Fagot & Leinbach, 1993; Huston, 1985; Martin, 1993). Children first learn to label gender; then develop the notion that it is stable over time; and finally grasp that it does not change, despite superficial changes in clothes and appearance (Intons-Peterson, 1988). The foundational achievements are learning that there are two genders and being able to reliably lable people as male and female. Long before they can speak, children can discriminate male and female faces and voices (Leinbach & Fagot, 1993; Miller, 1983). Typically within the second year, children learn that they are girls or boys, and gradually learn that they share this designation with one parent and with certain siblings and friends. There is no great mystery about how this learning takes place. Most parents explicitly refer to their children and to others as "little girls" or "little boys," and children are reminded of their gender often; the use of explicit gender pronouns such as "her" or "he" also reinforces this not-so-subtle message. Within the third year, children become much more accurate in designating people as male or female (Etaugh, Grinnell, & Etaugh, 1989), although the cues they use are likely to be surface appearance features (e.g., style of dress and length of hair) (Intons-Peterson, 1988). During this early stage, children are relatively unaware that gender is a permanent feature; they may say, for example, that changes in dress or length of hair also change one's gender. By age 4 ot 5, most children have acquired gender constancy (the notion that gender is a permanent attribute) and have learned that genital differences are important (Bem, 1989).

The Development of Stereotype Knowledge

Because gender itself is a multifaceted concept, it is not surprising that early learning of stereotypes is somewhat sporadic or at least not unified (e.g., Martin, Wood, & Little, 1990; Ruble & Martin, 1998). The earliest hint of gender stereotypes is that children show preferences for sex-appropriate toys and activities within the second year, well before they can label people by gender consistently or have acquired gender constancy (Martin, 1999; Serbin, Poulin-Dubois, Colburne, Sen, & Eichstedt, 2001). By age 3, children show a decided preference for playing with children of their own gender (Maccoby, 1998), and they also begin to develop an acute sense of which toys and activities are associated with which gender (Martin & Little, 1990). Within the third year, those children who catch on to gender labels tend to make more stereotypic judgments (Fagot, Leinbach, & O'Boyle, 1992; Martin, 1993).

As children acquire more knowledge about their social worlds, more and more domains are encompassed by gender (Martin, 1993). Children acquire different components of their stereotypes at different times; typically they learn first about activities and appearance, then about roles, with trait knowledge more or less bringing up the rear (Intons-Peterson, 1988; Martin, 1993) Certainly by age 6 they have learned that certain occupations "go with" each gender (G. D. Levy, Sadovsky, & Troseth, 2000), although this particular stereotype does tend to decline during the elementary school years (Miller & Budd, 1999). During the early school years, children begin to use traits generally, and also begin to associate traits differentially with boys and girls (Intons-Peterson, 1988; Stangor & Ruble, 1989a; Williams, Bennett, & Best, 1975).

Perhaps not surprisingly, children tend to learn stereotypes for their own gender before they learn stereotypes for the other (Martin, 1993; Martin et al., 1990), and male stereotypes are learned before female ones (Williams, Bennett, & Best, 1975). In the early years, girls are the stereotype experts; at age 3 girls know far more about female stereotypes than boys do, and know as much about the male stereotypes as do boys (O'Brien et al., 2000).

Prescriptiveness

Two other components of gender stereotypes need emphasis. First, these early stereotypes tend not only to be quite rigid but highly prescriptive (Golombok & Fivush, 1994). As my 4-year-old granddaughter used to remind me with a great show of exasperation, I cannot wear her shoes because they're girls' shoes, although if pushed she would sometimes add that they're too small for me. The mere suggestion that I might deck myself in a sparkly dress provoked gales of laughter. Children not only have well-developed notions of what toys and activities are appropriate for each gender by age 4 or so, but they are prone to criticize and reject their peers who fail to abide by these stereotypes (Carter & McCloskey, 1983–1984; Levy, Taylor, & Gelman, 1995). However, some research suggests that children may prefer children who behave in ways appropriate for the perceiver's sex, regardless of the sex of the actor (Zucker, Wilson-Smith, Kurita, & Stern, 1995); in other words, girls may prefer both boys and girls who exhibit feminine preferences.

As children gain knowledge about putative differences between males and females, this does not necessarily mean that the prescriptive nature of stereotypes also increases. With experience, children learn more about the complexity of gender scripts and roles and see exceptions to stereotypes; thus they may come to see gender as less rather than more prescriptive, as they simultaneously learn more about the actual content of stereotypes (Martin, 1999).

Flexibility

A related and important component of gender stereotypes is what is usually called "flexibility"—whether children think that an activity, job, role, or trait can be for both men and women. Although this measure shows a fairly steady increase during the early school years as children acquire more social and cultural information (Signorella, Bigler, & Liben, 1993), it increases dramatically when children enter middle or junior high school (perhaps because a new situation creates a need to be flexible), although there is a decline in flexibility after that point (Alfieri, Ruble, & Higgins, 1996). As children get older, they are also able to see stereotypes as only one (and not necessarily the most privileged) device for predicting behavior (Berndt & Heller, 1986; Martin, 1989). For example, Biernat (1991) found that young people from kindergarten through college age used gender as a cue for judgments, but that as they became older they increasingly also took account of individuating information about people.

Parental Effects

The research literature on gender socialization is voluminous. Many people have argued that gender stereotyping of children begins at birth. Some early research (Rubin, Provenzano, & Luria, 1974) did seem to suggest that parents' ascriptions of traits to a newborn are influenced by whether they believe the baby to be male or female, but a review of several subsequent studies (Stern & Karraker, 1989) suggests that such effects are weak and inconsistent, and probably weakening further over time (Karraker, Vogel, & Lake, 1995).

There are certainly bushels of studies documenting parental effects on gender socialization (see Katz, 1983, for one review) and correlations between parental beliefs about gender and various indices of gender stereotyping in their children (Fagot et al., 1992; Hoffman & Kloska, 1995; McHale, Crouter, & Tucker, 1999). However, the results tend to be correlational and the effects small and complex. For example, in one study that examined parental ideology (Weisner & Wilson-Mitchell, 1990), parents who were classified as avant-garde or countercultural in their orientation (the two types with the greatest commitment to gender equality) had daughters (but not sons) who were more likely to pick a traditionally male occupation, and their children were less likely to sex-stereotype objects. On the other hand, children from different types of families did not differ on perceived gender-related traits, tendency to play with gender-stereotyped toys, and preferences for a same-sex best friend.

Do parents react differently to sons and daughters? Common observation suggests that at least some parents promote conforming to gender stereotypes. Some parents may make occasional comments to their sons that "Boys play rough" or "If you play that way you'll be a sissy,"[15] but we do not know how general such direct tuition is. One review concludes that both fathers and mothers treat their sons and daughters much the same in terms of time spent with them, affection, responsiveness, and nurturance (Lytton & Romney, 1991). There are no consistent findings that parents encourage assertiveness more in their sons than in their daughters, or dependency more in daughters. There are, however, some differences. Mothers talk more to sons than to daughters (Leaper, Anderson, & Sanders, 1998), and parents may stimulate motor activity more in sons than in daughters. Both mothers and fathers (but especially the latter) encourage sex-typed activities (Fagot, 1978; Lytton & Rommey, 1991; Pomerleau, Bolduc, Malcuit, & Cossette, 1990),[16] and this may have some impact on the ways children learn to play with others (Leaper & Gleason, 1996) and on preferences for sports participation later in life (Giuliano, Popp, & Knight, 2000). Parents have different expectations for their sons' and daughters' math, social, and athletic abilities (Jacobs & Eccles, 1992), which can affect academic interests.

Such effects clearly can be important, but what seems most impressive about such studies is that parents do not seem to reinforce sex-typed behavior strongly and consistently in their children. Certainly, large effects can grow from small causes, but I suspect that whatever happens in the home needs amplification from the larger culture to produce the kinds of gender effects we see in adults. Children learn gender and racial stereotypes quite well on their own, despite the lack of parental pressure to adopt them, and sometimes in homes where parents have worked hard to make sure that children are immunized from them. They learn these stereotypes not from teachers or other socialization agents, but primarily through their own play with other children. A child would have to be completely unaware of everyday realities not to notice that boys do play rougher than girls and that girls are more likely to play with dolls than are boys. As I have been stressing with the notion of indirect effects, parents may have their largest impact in what they do *not* do—namely, not challenging existing gender stereotypes and providing their children with the sense that they can and should work to overcome limitations imposed by gender-related expectations. Parents are part of a larger matrix that includes the media, schools, children's own observations, and peer influences, and the impact they have on their children cannot easily be singled out.[17]

Peer Effects

An argument can and has been made (e.g., Harris, 1998; Maccoby, 1990, 1998) that a good deal of gender socialization takes place in peer groups. From an early age (say, 2 years), children prefer to play with same-sex peers, although they willingly play with children of the opposite sex if encouraged to do so; thus this is a preference rather than a rejection of others. By age 4 or 5, however, children do actively reject children of the other gender, and play (at least in public settings where peer pressure is most active) becomes almost exclusively with same-sex others. There is almost no direct evidence that parents or other socialization agents encourage this form of segregation, or that same-gender preferences are encoded genetically.

Eleanor Maccoby (1998) prefers a different sort of explanation. A simplified version is that within the first or second year of life, boys begin to play in more active and rough ways than girls. This may be partially due to parental encouragement, but there are fairly clear data suggesting that this gender difference may have a strong genetic component. Little girls do not relish such active play, and may even be frightened of its more robust forms; hence they form their own play groups. As early as 3 years of age, girls, especially those rated as more socially sensitive, prefer playing with other girls; although the effects are less strong for boys, those who are more active and socially disruptive tend to play more with other boys (Moller & Serbin, 1996). In time, boys' groups adopt rougher forms of play that feature competition. Girls' groups, by contrast, tend to emphasize a more collaborative style (Neppl & Murray, 1997). Boys demand and girls ask. At this point, boys get considerable peer reinforcement for what we have come to think of as a masculine style, and girls for a more feminine orientation. To some extent, this is due to simply imitation and practice at certain forms of play and interaction. If you practice being bossy, you get better at it. But to some extent there is also considerable conformity pressure for certain forms of activities, and this pressure tends to act more strongly on boys. Boys get teased if they play with girls and fall to the bottom of the boys' status hierarchy if they adopt girls' accommodating interpersonal style.

Maccoby's account rings true for anyone who has spent much time around preschool children. Even young children want to be like those whom they identify as being like them, and active peer pressure and imitative tendencies play an important role in gender-stereotypic behaviors and thereby indirectly in the stereotypes children develop about gender.

Gender Theories

Chapter 7 has raised the issue of what sorts of theories people have about gender differences, and it is important to ask what theories children have about such matters. Since children focus on surface, appearance features to diagnose gender and do not achieve gender constancy until age 5 or 6, one might hypothesize that for children gender is a social construct without much implication of biological destiny (Carey, 1985). However, Taylor (1996) suggests that younger children are not socialization theorists. She presented children with a story in which a boy or girl baby was raised entirely by members of the opposite sex, and then asked the subjects what the child would be like when he or she was 10. Until the subjects were 9 years old or so, they said that the boy would have stereotypically male features even when he had been raised by females, and that the girl would have stereotypically female ones even when raised by males. Taylor argues that, as with other natural-kind categories, children tend to think that gender has an essence—a set of qualities that will reveal themselves over time, with or without input from the environment. However, at least from age 6 or 7 through adolescence, there seems to be a gradual shift from an emphasis on biology to socialization (Smith & Russell, 1984).

THE FUNCTIONS OF STEREOTYPES

Because stereotypes seem to arrive from the outside, as it were, through experiences or some cultural/social mechanism, it is easy to forget that their acquisition and use may also be affected by internal states. No matter how well learned, stereotypes would not persist unless they performed some social or cognitive function for people. Surprisingly little attention has been paid to the functions of stereotypes, although there have been some recent attempts to discuss these (DeBono, 1987; Jost & Banaji, 1994; Samuels, 1973; Snyder & Miene, 1994a; Stangor & Schaller, 1996). Let us examine two major classes of stereotype functions: individual and social.

Individual Functions

There is a long tradition in the history of prejudice and stereotype research of seeing stereotypes as being part and parcel of prejudice and broader political attitudes. I have discussed such functions throughout the book. The general issue of how stereotypes relate to other beliefs, values, and goals is an important one, and it is convenient to divide individual functions into cognitive and affective or motivational components, although there may be many interactions between the two (Maass & Schaller, 1991).

Cognitive Functions

STEREOTYPES AS NECESSARY SIMPLIFICATION

As I have emphasized, stereotypes help to simplify the social world we inhabit, and they are essential to productive thought. I have neither the time nor desire to understand all the people I meet in terms of the complexities of their individuality. Obviously, there are times when it is both prudent and moral to do the extra work to get beyond category-based generalizations; just as obviously, there are many times when it is not necessary, possible, or even desirable. As one example, when I prepare lectures for my introductory psychology course, I consciously and willingly use my stereotypes of the average undergraduate to aid various decisions. I do not have the time to poll every student for his or her desires about coverage and presentation, and given the likely heterogeneity of the responses, it is not even clear that this would be of much help.

STEREOTYPES ENRICH

Yes, stereotypes simplify. But in some ways they also enrich our mental lives (Hirschfeld, 2001; Oakes & Turner, 1990). By being able to place a person in a particular group, we can draw on a rich mix of theoretical and empirically based knowledge about his behavior and why he does the things he does. We divide the social world into categories not because we lack cognitive capacity, but because we want to create meaningful partitions of this world—ones that will facilitate our behavior. I see you as a lawyer not because you are a complex stimulus I need to reduce to manageable proportions, but because I want to be able to draw on my knowledge base about how you're different from me and which of those differences I have to worry about.

STEREOTYPES AS PART OF A MENTAL MATRIX

Stereotypes are beliefs, and as such they are likely to have complex relationships with other important beliefs (Abelson, 1988). A white person who values freedom and fairness over material advantage probably has fewer negative stereotypes of blacks and Hispanics than someone who has the reverse values. None of us is completely consistent, of course, and we often find ourselves caught in the coils of our mental irregularities. Still, beliefs have a certain coherence, and there are abundant data showing that stereotypes are related to other political, religious, and cultural beliefs (see Chapters 11 and 12 for evidence pertaining to particular stereotypes).

There are two major implications. The first is that beliefs about groups of people are likely to be learned as a part of a cognitive package that includes beliefs about political, religious, and cultural matters. Second, it means that some stereotypes are going to be easier for people to learn (and probably harder to disavow), just because they have so many connections to everything else.

Belief structures are so complex that they have eluded our best efforts to understand them. However, if we take the time to listen to people, even people whose beliefs we abhor, we find that they generally have a fairly detailed and often sophisticated logic to their belief systems. Stereotypes, I hasten to emphasize again, are theories (Yzerbyt, Rocher, & Schradron, 1997). The man with neo-Nazi sympathies who claims that African Americans should all be killed or deported to Africa has strongly related beliefs about the behavior of African Americans, important values, U.S. history, and his place in the world. Surely many of his facts are wrong, assumptions faulty, and logic less than airtight, but the same might be said of some of my beliefs. Stupid and ignorant beliefs are not restricted to stupid and ignorant people. Obviously, I do not remotely mean to defend such views as legitimate—but I strongly suggest that we will never get a handle on this man's stereotypes and prejudices, and why they are so appealing to so many people, unless we look at how they function within a larger belief structure.

Affective Functions

Affect and emotion lie at the heart of the functional argument. Stereotypes encompass beliefs about the behavior of others that can affect us, and in that sense they facilitate prejudices. But just as clearly, people who are prejudiced develop supporting stereotypes. There is no doubt that one can find people whose deeply embedded prejudices and stereotypes are so interlocked that they play off one another in supportive ways (Allport, 1954). However, we also ought to be wary of taking racists, sexists, and other bigoted people as the models for how stereotypes function. Although most of our stereotypes (and certainly the ones we care most about) have deep ties to other beliefs, most of us have a more complex set of links among our beliefs that helps buffer the worst forms of prejudiced thinking.

EVOLUTIONARY BIASES

There is a long and not altogether honorable history of linking prejudices to some sense of naturalness. However, honorable or not, such arguments have a certain legitimacy. From the currently popular evolutionary perspective, given one important assumption, both quick categorization and resultant prejudices against those who are different are not only natural but essential. The assumption is that early humans were inclined to be antagonistic to one another—not necessarily because of some biologically determined aggression, but because of hedonistic and egoistic selfishness, a need to survive. Although such overriding self-interest does not necessarily entail antagonism between individuals and groups, in times of food scarcity and natural limitations on other resources it is hard to imagine that relations could be otherwise. Furthermore, abundant animal data support the notion that unrelated or distantly related groups often have it out with one another or develop mechanisms to promote territorial domains without overt fighting.[18]

Thus almost any reasonable evolutionary model is bound to see intergroup conflict as both natural and useful. Although several mechanisms could be involved, most models (Fishbein, 1996; Kurcz, 1995) would agree on something like the following. Individuals have as their primary biological imperative staying alive long enough to ensure that their genes get passed along. In nearly all higher mammals (and all primates), this has resulted in groups of relatively closely related individuals who work together in food gathering, infant rearing, and other maintenance tasks. Furthermore, when individuals in the group are related, the survival of the group perpetuates the genes of each individual even if that individual dies before his or her full reproductive potential has been realized, because others in the group share the individual's genes. In order for the group to survive, intragroup competition and fighting must be kept to a minimum, and various inhibitory mechanisms and cooperative strategies must evolve.

However, there is no reason for Adam from Tribe A to cooperate with, defend, or inhibit aggression against unrelated Cam from Tribe C. Quite the contrary. Since Cam may be competing for the same scarce food resources and perhaps trying to steal females from Tribe A, Adam has every reason to be highly suspicious of Cam, Calvin, and everyone else from Tribe C. Obviously things are reversed from Cam's perspective. Thus there is inevitable mistrust and antagonism between any two groups (assuming that the groups do not share many specific genes in common).

Although such antagonism does not require that Cam and Adam develop stereotypes about one another, it does strongly encourage them to learn to categorize fellow humans quickly into ingroup and outgroup members. And as Fishbein (1996) and others have argued, it is also likely to lead different groups to develop different modes of dress and behavioral customs (badges) so as to make group identification easier. It is a short skip and a jump from categorization to associated features—in short, to stereotypes (see Chapter 3).

IDENTITY CONCERNS

The influential tradition pioneered by Henri Tajfel (1981a) and continued by John Turner (1987) argues that stereotypes are one way in which we differentiate ourselves and our groups from other groups, and do so in a way that is flattering to ourselves. At least part of our sense of self-worth comes from our memberships in valued groups, and it follows that one way we have of maintaining self-esteem is to assign positive features to our ingroups and negative features to outgroups. Thus, from this perspective, it is natural both that we categorize people and that we assign groups evaluatively laden traits, or stereotypes. Such a process is universal and usually unconscious.

Group Images. A related and, in some ways, more detailed version of this model has been recently presented by Alexander, Brewer, and Herrmann (1999). Building on previous work in political psychology (e.g., Boulding, 1959; Herrmann, Voss, Schooler, & Ciarrochi, 1997), they argue that nations (and, by implication, other groups) develop specific kinds of images based on the specific relationships between the groups. For example, when two countries have essential equal status, similar power, and compatible goals, they should see each other as allies and develop stereotypes of each other as being peaceful, democratic, and intelligent. By contrast, countries or groups that have equal status and power but incompatible goals will see each other as enemies and develop stereotypes of each other as being hostile, untrustworthy, opportunistic, and the like. When the ingroup wishes to exploit a weaker and lower-status group, they will see the latter as incompetent and divided. And when the ingroup is actually weaker than the outgroup but has lower status, and the two have incompatible goals, the outgroup will be seen as barbarian (ruthless, evil, and irrational). Although this model has not been applied to less global domains, many psychologists (see below) have suggested that a proper accounting of prejudice and stereotyping requires an understanding of power and other relationships between groups.

Badges and Impression Management. I have suggested earlier that groups of ancient humans probably developed badges in the form of dress and behavioral customs to differentiate themselves from one another. Nothing has changed. Today many groups and members of groups actively promote public images of themselves that then give rise to stereotypes. We dress in certain ways, sometimes talk in ways designed to create impressions, display our possessions proudly, listen to and defend certain types of music as cues to who we are,[19] and the list goes on. It should come as no surprise that when young African Americans listen to rap music (often quite loudly) and defend its virtues, others will incorporate this information into their stereotypes of this group. People who drive pretentious cars or wear expensive jewelry surely want us to tap into stereotypes of wealthy or "with-it, cool" people. It is also no accident that dress and insignia play such an important role in youth gangs in urban areas.

Unfortunately from the standpoint of impression management, overt displays of musical preferences, clothing styles, and material possessions may also feed unintended stereotypes. The man who wears a Rolex watch to convey an image of wealth and status may also create an impression of pretentiousness or superficiality. Movie actresses who go to great efforts to display as much of their bodies as they can on public occasions can hardly complain that many of us then develop the stereotype that they lack, shall we say, a certain intellectual perspective. The larger point is, however, that whereas many stereotypes are more or less passively fashioned by perceivers, others are the result of deliberate attempts of targets to affect our perceptions of them and often to distinguish themselves from the rest of us.

THREAT

A number of theorists (e.g., Ehrlich, 1973; Stephan & Stephan, 2000b) have argued that when people are threatened, they will be more likely to engage in stereotypic thinking and exhibit their prejudices. One popular version of this theory is scapegoating (Allport, 1954; Zawadski, 1948). The argument is that people have trouble dealing with their conscious and unconscious anxiety about their shortcomings. As a way of dealing with the anxiety, these shortcomings are projected onto people in various outgroups. A less Freudian account is based on the venerable frustration–aggression hypothesis: Frustration leads to aggression, which may be displaced onto convenient (in the sense of relatively powerless) outgroups. There has never been much support for this perspective, although some studies suggest that when self-esteem (Fein & Spencer, 1997; Sinclair & Kunda, 2000; Spencer, Fein, Wolf, Fong, & Dunn, 1998) or values (Corneille, Yzerbyt, Rogier, & Buidin, 2001) are threatened, people are more likely to rely on negative stereotypes in evaluating outgroup members. Threat comes in a variety of forms, of course, and may affect cherished identities as well as self-esteem. Indeed, those Americans who have a stronger sense of an

"American identity" and what that means (e.g., belief in God, getting ahead on the basis of one's own efforts) tend to react more negatively to Hispanic and Asian immigrants as well as to oppose policies (e.g., bilingual education) designed to help them (Citrin, Reingold, & Green, 1990).

More recently, terror management theory (Solomon, Greenberg, & Pyszczynski, 1991) has been used to explain increased stereotyping. The theory suggests that people have culturally derived views of the world and their place in it—views that, among other things, protect them from their own fears of death and vulnerability to injury. People who are obviously different (outgroup members) tend to disagree with ingroup members on various important issues that may threaten the stability and perceived reality of the world view. Thus stereotypes and prejudice may develop as a means of explaining this disagreement and justifying ingroup members' dislike of those who seem to foster it. According to this view, then, stereotypes develop in concert with people's values, religious views, and attitudes about important political and cultural matters.

However, an important implication of the model is that when people's world views are threatened, and especially when their mortality is made salient, they should actively seek to bolster their worldview. Among the strategies they might use would be to use stereotypes about outgroups more actively, or more generally to derogate the outgroups (Dechesne, Jansen, & van Knippenberg, 2000). In one study (Schimel et al., 1999), for example, subjects were asked to write about their thoughts concerning their own death (mortality-salient) or about watching TV. Then they were asked for their stereotypes of Germans or Italians—groups that were important to them. As expected, there was more stereotyping of each group when mortality was salient than when it was not. In another experiment, mortality salience decreased liking for and desire to interact with a black who exhibited stereotypic features, compared to one who acted in a more "buttoned-down" manner.

Goals and Values

Generally speaking, people have positive reactions to other people who facilitate their goals and values, and negative reactions to those who hinder these. When one talks to people about their prejudices, they often provide reasons in terms of what they perceive as the tendency of outgroup members to violate cherished goals. This has been discussed extensively in Chapter 8, so I need not repeat the arguments in detail here. People's values and their beliefs about whether groups facilitate or inhibit these values are usually strong predictors of ethnic prejudice (Haddock, Zanna, & Esses, 1994a). More generally, motives may reverberate throughout the belief system and recruit stereotypes in their cause (Klein & Kunda, 1992).

Collective Functions

Several theorists (e.g., Augoustinos & Walker, 1998; Glick & Fiske, 1999c; Hoffman & Hurst, 1990; Jost & Banaji, 1994; Sidanius & Pratto, 1999; Stangor & Jost, 1997) have argued that in a social world in which people are divided along lines of status, prestige, and economic privilege, we need to explain, justify, and know why. At least in some cases, these perceived differences reflect actual differences in competence and motivation, but status is probably much more arbitrarily bestowed than most of us feel comfortable believing. We like to believe that high-status people have done something to earn their status. At the other end of the scale, Lerner's just-world theory (Lerner, 1980) suggests that we tend to believe that people who are less fortunate have deserved their fate. So it becomes particularly easy to see members of stigmatized groups as somehow deserving their fate, and stereotypes may function as vehicles for explaining status differences. Certainly people who do discriminate often activate supporting stereotypes of both ingroup and outgroup members as justification for their behavior (Rutland & Brown, 2001).

The Importance of Power

Arguably, the strongest and most pernicious stereotypes are reserved for those who have low power and status.[20] It has long been recognized (Allport, 1954; Sunar, 1978) that power is central to understanding stereotyping. As Operario and Fiske (1998) have pointed out, stereotypes of less powerful persons held by more powerful ones tend to create more mischief than the reverse, if for no other reason than that powerful people have greater ability to act on them as well as to make them part of the cultural consensus. There are three major ways in which power relationships affect stereotyping.

FAILURE TO INDIVIDUATE LESS POWERFUL PEOPLE

Susan Fiske and her colleagues (Dépret & Fiske, 1999; Fiske, 1993; Fiske & Morling, 1996; Operario, Goodwin, & Fiske, 1998; Stevens & Fiske, 2000) have integrated a consideration of power with the continuum model (see Chapter 4), which suggests that there is a continuum running from category-based processing through a more individualized approach. More powerful people have relatively little incentive to individuate the behavior of less powerful persons, particularly those who are subordinates, given that any given individual with less power is not likely to affect the more powerful people much. So long as subordinates perform their assigned responsibilities, a superior has little reason to be concerned with individual differences among them. Also, since a person with a superior role is likely to have several subordinates, individuating them may take considerable time and effort. A subordinate, on the other hand, typically has only one superior (or a very few) to worry about and may have a great deal of interest in knowing about his or her values, moods, typical behavior, traits, and the like. Thus it follows that generally a less powerful (or more dependent) person should pay more attention to the individual features of a more powerful person, whereas the more powerful person may rely more heavily on category-based inferences for the less powerful individual. Data indicate that power does affect attention in predicted ways (Fiske & Dépret, 1996).

EXPLAINING THE BEHAVIOR OF LESS POWERFUL PEOPLE IN DISPOSITIONAL WAYS

Powerful people can, and often do, constrain the behavior of less powerful individuals. Parents and teachers tell children what to do; bosses affect the behavior of their secretaries more than the reverse; and in most universities tenured members of the faculty can, to some extent, dictate the behavior of their untenured colleagues. A fair amount of informal and some experimental evidence (Sunar, 1978) suggests that more powerful people tend to see less powerful ones as being lazy or as basically having responded to the coercion of their superiors. In a way, the less powerful folks can't win. If they work hard and effectively, their superiors see external factors such as rules and supervision as responsible, and if they do not, then their own dispositional laziness is at fault.

Stereotypes tend to reinforce the status quo (from which the more powerful people benefit) as well as maintaining social identities of relative superiority. It follows that the more powerful persons should be especially attentive to information consistent with negative stereotypes of people from less powerful groups (Rodríguez-Bailón, Moya, & Yzerbyt, 2000). Also because of their superior status, the more powerful individuals may feel they are entitled, even obligated, to judge those with less status. Those who are more powerful do tend to pay particular attention to stereotype-consistent information (Fiske & Dépret, 1996; Goodwin, Gubin, Fiske, & Yzerbyt, 2000).

STEREOTYPIC BEHAVIOR BY LESS POWERFUL PEOPLE

Finally, especially in situations where powerful persons can reward or punish powerless ones, the latter may have enormous incentives to behave in a deferential and subordinate manner. Within living memory, many black Americans found it to their advantage to behave in accord with whites' stereotypes of them as being emotional, slow, and deferential. Some women married to domineering husbands will find it useful to play the role of the dependent woman, and may over time come to believe themselves to be this kind of person. In the process, they will provide their husbands and others with abundant evidence that they do lack agentic qualities. In an experimental demonstration, females in a job interview (perhaps the height of a power relationship) were more traditionally feminine in their behavior when interviewed by a male they thought held traditional views about women (von Baeyer, Sherk, & Zanna, 1981). Thus the expectations of powerful people may create stereotype-consistent behavior.[21]

Stereotypes Are Embedded in Cultures

Whatever else they provide, cultures give us a strong sense of reality (Hardin & Higgins, 1996). Augoustinos and Walker (1998) argue that stereotypes must be seen in terms of their deep embeddedness in our collective worlds. Stereotypes are not merely our cognitive take on what the culture preaches, but active attempts to provide explanations for deeply ingrained divisions. The individual perceiver makes use of various cultural representations, but applies them selectively and even creatively to explain the particulars of the social life he or she inhabits. Stereotypes are weapons in cultural wars (Reicher, Hopkins, & Condor, 1997). Thus stereotypes are somewhat fluid, as the perceiver draws on different aspects of the cultural stereotype to fit the needs of the moment (Oakes et al., 1994). For this approach, stereotypes are not merely (or even mostly) passive imprints of the culture on an individual mind. Each individual creates his or her own stereotypes in concert with and guided by the larger culture, and these may be negotiated in individual interactions. Thus stereotypes reflect justifications for existing social, political, and economic arrangements within a given society, but meanings forged in everyday interactions with others as a way of defining relative positions (Van Langenhove & Harre, 1994).

Beyond cultural targeting, cultures also affect our beliefs through well-known social influence processes. We continually join new groups as we move through life, and groups actively promote certain beliefs as the price of admission. We are not surprised to find that Catholics have beliefs somewhat different from Lutherans, or that members of Right to Life groups share values and attitudes beyond those on abortion. To the extent these beliefs are seen by group members as shared by group members, they may take on a kind of coercive quality as group beliefs (Bar-Tal, 1998). To the extent that I identify with my religious or political organizations, I will tend to internalize their relevant group beliefs and give them the force of social reality. In some cases, such beliefs may be important as ways one group is differentiated from another; in such cases, identification with an ingroup may lead to self-persuasion, rejection of attitude deviants, and enhanced acceptance of those who hew to the party line (see Chapter 7).

Clearly, not all stereotypes are created and maintained through such mechanisms. Many have a diffuse and free-floating quality and do not seem to be supported by deep cultural imprinting. Still, those stereotypes that seem to enjoy general support are particularly important, and there certainly is empirical evidence that consensual stereotypes do affect the acceptance of stereotypes by individuals (Maio, Esses, & Bell, 1994). In the rural Indiana of the 1950s where I grew up, there was no interpersonal mileage to be gained by sticking up for blacks against the frequent slurs of my classmates. Anyone who suggested that women could run a farm, let alone a major business, alone would have been ridiculed as having lost touch with reality. And in male locker rooms in high schools and country clubs still today, it is not only permissible but nearly obligatory to make fun of gay males. People whose knowledge about other groups comes largely from such informal peer discussions will have little reason to question the resulting stereotypes, and much to gain from supporting the existing social reality about them.

Earlier in the chapter, I have suggested that the traditional culprits we blame for stereotypes—education, parents, the mass media—may not be as culpable as we like to believe. It is highly unlikely that children would develop most of their stereotypes solely from watching TV if their families and the general culture disagreed. The media, peers, and parents probably have small effects by themselves, but in concert they are powerful indeed. Parents sometimes discover to their dismay how difficult it is to change their children's attitudes and behavior patterns when other cultural institutions and peer pressure provide dissonant lessons.

For a wide range of beliefs, values, and, yes, stereotypes, our religious and political institutions, the mass media, schools, and parents provide a consistent message. Take one influence away, and the rest tighten their coils more strongly. This is not a grand conspiracy; it's just the way cultures work. When all is said and done, the reason consensual stereotypes are so powerful is that there is little incentive for most of us to question their validity and to develop any theory about the reasons groups differ from one another, except the most superficial reasons provided by the culture. Whatever else they do, cultures typically do not encourage deep questions about their fundamental values, and perceptions of consensus further inhibit attempts to understand our experiences in any but culturally approved ways.

SUMMARY

When something has caused as much harm as stereotypes have, someone must be to blame. Culture is most seen as the culprit, and schools, religious institutions, parents, and the media most often appear on the docket. There is certainly a kernel of truth in these charges. It is not hard to find parents who pass along racist ideas, TV programs that perpetrate sexist stereotypes, and schools and churches that foster cultural wisdom about group differences and do little to help people question why they exist.

And yet, this chapter tries to suggest much of our thinking on these issues is far too simplistic. In the first place, some, perhaps many, of our stereotypes have a kernel of truth, which people may discover through their own experiences as well as being handed to us directly through cultural training. Cultural factors as well as our individual cognitive processes may, of course, exaggerate these stereotypes, make them more salient, or encourage us to ignore the many exceptions to most stereotypes.

Unfortunately, most culture-blaming arguments rest on a dichotomy between culture and individual experiences that is too neatly drawn. Cultures and their agents affect our thinking by providing stereotype content, but they also affect the ways we think about and explain group differences. Moreover, while such effects are often the result of direct tuition, they may also result from indirect effects as when certain perspectives are advanced by example or when such agents fail to suggest alternative ways of viewing such matters. Cultures, in short, channel our thinking even when they do not provide the water that flows.

Social scientists have debated for years whether generalizations about groups have to be collectively held to become stereotypes. On the one hand, even culturally deviant generalizations affect the ways we think about others, but on the other hand, stereotypes seem to acquire a particular power when they are widely held.

Research on the effects of parents on the development of stereotypes suggest that parents may not be the strong agents of stereotype indoctrination that many believe. Similarly, while the media present a continuous barrage of stereotypes, there is little evidence that they powerfully affect the stereotypes that children develop. I do not mean to suggest that socialization agents are not important in the development of stereotypes but only that their effects are more likely to be indirect and related to how we think rather than what we think about others. Another reason it may be hard to document the effects of particular agents is that it is hard to render apart what cultures have joined together—the media, schools, and parents tend to send the same, interlocking messages so that it is hard to separate out their individual effects.

Gender stereotypes appear quite early and do not seem to be closely related to parental behavior or attitudes. One theory is that such stereotypes are built on different play patterns of boys and girls and are subsequently reinforced by peer pressure. Racial stereotypes seem slower to develop. Children's initial theories about race categories and differences are fairly incoherent. Thus it is not until the early school years that children began to have notions of race that approximate adults', and stereotypes seem to develop gradually from that point on.

We must certainly continue to combat overt stereotyping where and when we find it and continue to educate each new generation about the problems it can cause. However, we should not be naive in assuming that stereotypes are caused by a single type of agent or that cultural and individual experience effects can be easily divorced.

Notes

1. I was recently visited during office hours by a young man in my introductory psychology course whose body shouted "football player." He told me that someone in the Athletics Department Academic Advising Office had told him to stop by, and this immediately confirmed him as an athlete. I asked him how he was doing in the course, and when he said, "Okay," I began to offer him advice about how to do better on the exams. He politely responded to my few questions, and after a few minutes I began to wrap up the conversation, convinced that this relatively passive young man was going to continue to do poorly. Before he left I asked whether he had any other questions, and he quietly told me that while he could always use advice about how to study better, he was in fact making an A in the course, and he had come to my office hour to chat about majoring in psychology and research opportunities. We reestablished a conversation along the lines he had desired. After he left, I was struck by the fact that based entirely on my stereotype of athletes, I had interpreted his fairly modest and polite behavior as evidence of low academic potential and perhaps a bit of training by an academic advisor. This was clearly a case where stereotypes dominated data.

2. Younger readers, who are used to seeing a mixture of black and white faces on athletic fields, may not fully realize how recent a phenomenon this is. As is well known, Jackie Robinson became the first black major league baseball player in 1947. The National Basketball Assocation (NBA) was integrated in the 1950–1951 season, but as late as 1959 the St. Louis Hawks were still all-white. The first black superstars in the NBA entered the league late in the 1950s (Bill Russell, 1957; Elgin Baylor, 1958; Wilt Chamberlain, 1959). Although professional football was slightly integrated from the 1920s on, there were few black players until the 1950s. The first black player to win the Heisman Trophy (in college football) was Ernie Davis in 1961, and many Southern colleges had no black players well into the 1960s. Ashe (1988) details all this and more in his massive treatment of black athletes in America.

3. I was reminded recently of my high school math teacher (it was a small school, so there was only one) who insisted publicly that my having a German last name endowed me with special math skills. She said again and again that Germans were especially gifted at science and math. If I turned in less than a perfect paper, she would say how disappointed she was in me because I had such a good German name. Actually, her faith in my lineage did motivate me to do well in her classes, but at the time it did not occur to me to wonder about the effects on those who were less linguistically endowed.

4. As a child of 12 or so, I had 2 years of Lutheran catechism classes. The minister who taught them was quite clear that Catholics were doomed to hell, and he wasn't willing to guarantee salvation for other Protestants. Fortunately, even at that tender age I recognized prejudice for what it was, even in the guise of revealed truth.

5. I vividly recall my fourth-grade teacher, a Mrs. Bush, who regularly told us that Communists were evil and that we should be alert to any signs of Communist sympathies among our parents and friends. My parents were decidedly unhappy with this indoctrination, especially the part about looking after our parents, and her message was toned down a bit after they had a friendly visit with the principal.

6. In the commentary on the 1999 shootings at Columbine High School in Littleton, Colorado, it was striking to me that many people tended to assume that the boys who committed the murders were products of poor parenting and the presumed failures of parents to transmit a strong moral code. Although this may have been a factor, one can just as easily look to the culture in the schools, violence in the media, and the easy availability of handguns as contributing factors.

7. I suspect that many of us could provide examples from our own childhoods. One I remember quite vividly occurred when I was about 5 and spending a week visiting a favorite

cousin who lived in a small town in a rural area of Indiana. We had spent the week making fun of a boy, a stranger in town (probably from a family of migrant workers), because he wore tattered overalls and had a dirty face. My cousin's house was at the top of a hill; one afternoon I mounted his tricycle, and before I knew it the thing was moving rapidly down the hill toward the center of town. I had no clue how to stop it, but I did know how to scream. As I reached the bottom of the hill and the major intersection in town, I had visions of being run over by a car (actually a realistic possibility). Just as I reached the intersection, the father of the boy we had targeted for abuse came out and stopped the trike, and as I dismounted I saw the "dirty" boy behind him. When I got back to my cousin's house, the story came out, and we mentioned that this boy and his father were hillbillies. My uncle (who was a man of few but pointed words) gave us both a stern lecture about not judging people by the way they were dressed, and at that point the lesson fell on very receptive ears. I think it taught me more about the evils of stereotyping than any other experience I ever had. When my uncle discovered that I had not thanked the man, I was required to seek him out and thank him. I was also told, as was my cousin, to find the boy and apologize. I did both and learned another important lesson about humility and civility. One-trial learning does occur and can be important.

8. The movie *American History X* presents a moving example of both effects.

9. Such effects are not new. For example, in a classic study, Charters and Newcomb (1958) showed that Catholics answered questions more in line with Catholic dogma when their religion was made salient. This so-called "reference group phenomenon" has direct relevance to the present topic, in that when the media present spokespersons for various political or religious groups who implicitly or explicitly promote certain stereotypes or group attitudes, they may encourage sympathetic viewers to think along the same lines. This may also be closely related to the well-known "interviewer effects," where people answer attitude items differently when interviewed by different types of people (Zaller & Feldman, 1992). The fact, for example, that blacks respond in a more "pro-black" manner to a black than to a white interviewer has typically been seen as driven by social influence or self-presentational concerns, but it might just as easily be thought of in terms of interviewers' making certain features of the constellation of racial attitudes more salient than others.

10. The same thing happens with evaluations of politicians and political leaders. Presidents get far more credit for economic good times and far more blame for bad ones than they deserve, based on their actual effects on the economy.

11. I recently watched a couple of episodes of *I Love Lucy*; I and my family watched the program religiously during the 1950s and found it incredibly funny (as did most Americans). Except for the occasional bit, it now seems juvenile and distinctly unfunny to me (but presumably not to others, since it can be found on various cable channels). Whatever its artistic virtues, it was certainly no advertisement for the competence of women.

12. There is an older literature on development of stereotypes of nationalities (Lambert & Klineberg, 1967; Zeligs, 1955), although such stereotypes develop later and may not follow the same developmental patterns as for gender (Rutland, 1999).

13. Language, which is often correlated with ethnicity, is also a predictor of interaction choices (Doyle, Rappard, & Connolly, 1980).

14. Earlier research by Horowitz (1939) and Clark and Clark (1939) with preschoolers found that black children picked a white drawing over a black when asked, "Which one is you?"

15. I recently witnessed a father roughhousing with his 4-year-old son. When the boy was hurt, the father mocked his whimpers by asking whether he was going to become a girl. Certainly such parents exist, but how common they are remains to be seen.

16. However, here, as elsewhere in this area, we have to be careful about jumping to conclusions about causality. As many parents who have religiously tried to get their sons to play with dolls and their daughters with trucks have discovered, children display marked and sometimes stubborn preferences for particular toys from an early age. It is quite possible

that by the time their children are 3 or 4, many parents have learned to "go with the flow" and encourage children to play with toys they already prefer. Thus we should not ignore the possibility that at any given point in life boys and girls may be treated differently because they *are* different, whether these differences are created by prior socialization or biology.

17. Obviously, parents are not the only important influence on acquisition of stereotype knowledge. Older siblings may have enormous impact, and although teachers are probably blamed too much for these and other evils, they do respond differently to boys and girls and their typical behaviors (Fagot, 1984, 1985; Meece, 1987).

18. However, Hirschfeld (2001) notes that existing data do not support the idea of intense competition among prehistoric groups. He agrees that the tendency to categorize people has strong evolutionary roots, but ties it more directly to needs to simplify and infer information about people who are not immediately recognized.

19. I do not spend much time looking at the personal Web pages of other people, but when I do I am struck by the attempts of many to define themselves to others in terms of pictures (family or vacation), links to other sites, and listings of favorite music and movies. The last of these strike me as especially interesting ways to manage impressions, although it's not clear to me how much in common I might have with people who share my musical tastes. This is an interesting question, actually.

20. Actually, this is not obviously true, and there are few if any data on relative strengths of various stereotypes. As counterexamples, I have reasonably powerful stereotypes of members of Congress, college presidents, and police officers—all of whom have a fair amount of power, and arguably more than I do. It is probably true that stereotypes of relatively powerless people are culturally more salient, but this could result from the tendencies of most social scientists to focus on society's treatment of minorities and those of lower status. It may also result from the tendency of less powerful individuals to complain more or at least more loudly about what they perceive to be negative stereotypes others have of them. Nonetheless, for theoretical reasons I am about to explain, the hypothesis that we actually have stronger and more negative stereotypes of relatively powerless persons makes good sense.

21. This should not be confused with self-fulfilling prophecies. In that case, expectations of perceivers affect their own behaviors, which in turn create consistent behavior in targets. An example would be a supervisor who, believing employees to be lazy, oversupervises them to the point where they do in fact cease to take much initiative. The mechanism being discussed here is more direct and only requires relatively powerless persons to think that more powerful people are prepared to issue rewards for expectation-consistent behavior.

CHAPTER 10

Change of Stereotypes
and Prejudice

A DIALOGUE

As in Chapter 1, I begin this chapter with an imaginary dialogue. Once again, OP is the Obnoxious Psychologist; in this dialogue, CS is a Concerned Student.

OP: I wonder if you could speculate about how we might change stereotypes. If you had unlimited resources and all the time in the world, how would you try to change the stereotypes that whites have about blacks?

CS: I'm pretty sure by this point that whatever I say will be wrong, but I'll give it a try. (*Pause*) I guess the most obvious thing to do would be to make sure that whites have more information about blacks.

OP: So it seems that your underlying assumption is that stereotypes result from ignorance. That whites think blacks are violent and unintelligent because they haven't had enough contact with them.

CS: Well, there certainly are some stupid and violent black people around, but I don't think they're representative. I think a lot of people get their stereotypes from watching TV and movies, and certainly you see lots of black people there who fit the stereotypes. But I think white people don't get a chance to know other types of black people. I have a friend, Andrew, who lives down the hall from me, and he's one of the nicest people you'd ever want to meet. And he's a computer genius; he sure isn't stupid.

OP: So if everyone could just meet Andrew, their stereotypes about blacks would become more positive?

CS: Well, it sure couldn't hurt.

OP: That's an interesting observation, actually. Are you sure it couldn't hurt?

CS: I don't see how.

OP: Let me suggest a possibility. Do you know any what I'll call hard-core racists?

CS: (*Long pause*). Nobody I know well. But there are a couple of guys in my home-town who are pretty extreme.

OP: Do you think if one of these guys met Andrew that his stereotypes about blacks would change?

CS: I think they might change a little. These guys have lived all their lives in this small town in east Texas, and they've never really had a chance to meet anyone like Andrew. So it might open their eyes a little. I'm not saying that they would change dramatically overnight or anything.

OP: Have you ever heard the expression "The exception proves the rule"?

CS: Sure. And I think I see what you're getting at. It might just confirm their view that most blacks aren't like Andrew. But I'd imagine that it might shake up their beliefs a little.

OP: And well it might, but my hunch is that nothing fundamental would change. And if you believe that most racists' prejudices are driven by feelings of inade-quacy, their stereotypes might even be strengthened as a way of bolstering their beliefs that have just been attacked.

CS: I suppose that's possible. You're the expert here. But that's not really a fair ex-ample.

OP: Why not?

CS: For one thing, these guys are really strong racists, but it's not like anyone takes them seriously or they have much effect on anyone but themselves. These guys are nut cases. I'm a lot more concerned with the other white people who live in my town and the ones who live in my dorm, who are more normal.

OP: And you think that contact with the Andrews of the world might affect them more?

CS: I do. And I've seen it happen.

OP: Really?

CS: Yeah, I've seen people in my dorm learn to see Andrew as a real person and not just as a black guy. And everyone really respects and likes him. He's funny, and he cares about other people. He's smart, too.

OP: Okay. I don't find it hard to believe that people don't have any problem liking a guy like this Andrew. He seems like a neat guy, whatever his race.

CS: Exactly. And I think if more white people could meet Andrew and the other peo-ple like him, they wouldn't have such negative stereotypes about blacks.

OP: But as I gather, what you're saying is that Andrew is a pretty special person?

CS: He certainly is.

OP: And maybe he's not representative of blacks in general. The way you describe him, he isn't even representative of whites in general. There just aren't that many funny, caring, smart people around.

CS: I never said he was a saint. He does have a temper, for example. But, yeah, he's a pretty exceptional person.

OP: Now I'm trying to imagine what the typical mildly racist white person who meets Andrew might think. Let's say Tammy meets him and likes him. But then I imagine that she'd say to herself something like "Andrew is great, but he certainly isn't like most of the black guys I know. I'll have to be more careful in the future about assuming that all black men are sullen and not all that bright. But my experiences speak for themselves, and I know a lot more black males who fit my stereotype of blacks than those like Andrew."

CS: I guess something like that could happen. And your point would be? . . .

OP: That it's hard for individual experiences to change general stereotypes. That people don't necessarily generalize their experiences in ways we might like.

CS: So I guess your point is that it's hard to change racial stereotypes.

OP: It's broader than that, actually. Let me change the frame of reference for a minute. Do you like apples?

CS: Sure.

OP: So you have a stereotype of sorts that apples taste good.

CS: Sure.

OP: Have you ever bit into an apple that looked okay but that was rotten or too sour?

CS: Hasn't everybody?

OP: I expect so. My question to you though is whether these bad experiences changed your stereotypes that apples taste good.

CS: I see what you're getting at. But apples are different from people. And you're talking about negative experiences changing positive stereotypes, and with racial stereotypes we're talking about the opposite.

OP: Points well taken. On the first, I would argue it's not a bit clear to me that when we're talking about change of our generalizations, people are all that much different from apples. I'm certainly willing to admit that people stereotypes might be harder to change than object ones. But you've just said that apple stereotypes don't change either, so what hope do we have for racial stereotypes if they're even harder to change?

CS: I guess none.

OP: And as for the fact that my example involved trying to change a positive stereotype, I could easily invent another example. Do you suppose that your stereotype that tigers are dangerous would be dramatically changed if I had you pet a tame and cuddly tiger?

CS: Probably not.

OP: And to return to your example of Andrew, we can't expect that merely meeting or talking to him is likely to be enough to change white people's stereotypes of blacks generally.

CS: I guess you're right, as usual. But now I'm really depressed, because from what you're saying, there doesn't seem to be any way we can change stereotypes.

OP: Well, certainly it isn't as easy as you and others imagine, but let's see.

POSSIBILITIES OF CHANGE

Change Is Not Easy

One way to think about the message of Chapter 9 is that stereotypes are easy to create. The experiences we digest and the cultural air we breathe provide all the ingredients we need, and the final baking requires little mental effort on our part. Stereotypes just happen. We might remind ourselves of the lessons from Chapter 3: Our very mental systems are programmed to categorize and to generalize about the qualities of those categories. No doubt we are also set up to be receptive to cultural lessons and not to question our experiences, biased as they are by all manner of societal roles and individual expectations. Even if we understood fully how we acquire stereotypes, we might not have much of a leg up on changing them. Although taking apart a physical object is generally the reverse of putting it together, our mental machinery doesn't work that way. This does not mean, of course, that we should regard stereotypic thinking as inevitable and surrender to the worst of it. But we need to understand that our job isn't going to be easy.

Cultural Change

Despite the obvious continued existence of stereotypes and prejudice, many cultural stereotypes have changed (and some quite dramatically) over the last half century or more (see Chapters 11–13). Of course, cultures can change without individuals' changing, as defenders of the old die and are replaced by the generations of the newly enlightened—but real change *has* taken place.

Problems in Assessing Cultural Change

THE LABORATORY AND THE REAL WORLD

We face a number of problems in trying to determine whether stereotypes have changed in the larger society. Much of the best research in this area has taken place in laboratory or classroom settings, but as we have known for some time (e.g., Hovland, 1959), research on attitude change in well-controlled situations may not readily generalize to the messy real world. Furthermore, even if we change stereotypes, we have no assurances that the change will "stick" and lots of reasons to believe that it will not. Often the best lab research can do is tell us what might work in an applied setting, and not necessarily what will work. This is a major step in the right direction, surely, but still . . .

WHAT CHANGES?

Relatively little research has tracked attitudes and beliefs of the same individuals over long periods of time. Longitudinal research is hard to do, but we can "cheat" (in a manner of speaking) by asking questions of different samples at various times.

Changes in Content. In assessing change in this way, we are often frustrated by the fact that questions are asked slightly differently at different times, and if they are asked the same way we run the risk of using items that are no longer applicable. We can shout "Hooray!" for the fact that most white Americans no longer think that black people are superstitious, but we should postpone any victory dances until we are sure that superstitiousness has not been replaced by even more negative traits (such as violence) that were not part of the earlier stereotype.

Potential Cohort Effects. In such studies, it is often hard to disentangle cohort effects from real change. Generally, younger and better-educated people show less evidence of stereotypes and negative attitudes (and age and education level are confounded). Therefore, if we find changes over time, we cannot be sure that these represent changes in individuals as opposed to replacement of older, more prejudiced people by younger and less prejudiced ones in the sample.

Evidence of Change

Having said all this, I reiterate that many stereotypes and prejudices have changed over time. For example, attitudes toward people with mental illness improved at least from the early 1950s through the early 1970s (see Chapter 12). Attitudes toward homosexuals have become more favorable over the past 15 years or so (Altemeyer, 2001). Gender stereotypes have probably lessened over time, although not dramatically (see Chapter 11). The most intensively studied area has been racial attitudes, and here there is considerable evidence of real change from the 1950s until at least the late 1980s, with suggestions of little further change or even backsliding in the 1990s. In terms of stereotype change, there is good and bad news. The news is that there has been continued stereotyping of blacks by whites from the early 1930s to the present, but the good news is that the stereotypes have largely become more positive (Dovidio, Brigham, Johnson, & Gaertner, 1996).

Even better news comes from large-scale surveys designed to measure white attitudes toward the position of blacks in the larger American society (Schuman, Steeh, Bobo, & Krysan, 1997). For example, the percentage of whites supporting integrated schools went from 32% in 1942 to 96% in 1995. In the early 1940s only 45% of white Americans thought that blacks should have equal opportunities to get any kind of job, but by 1972 97% supported this idea. The percentage of white people who agreed that whites should be able to keep blacks out of their neighborhoods declined from 60% in 1963 to 13% in 1996. In 1963 62% of whites supported laws against intermarriage, but in 1996 only 13% did, and whereas 73% disapproved of racial intermarriage in 1972, only 33% did in 1997. In 1958 only 37% said they would support a qualified black for President, but by 1996 that percentage had climbed to 95%. Various measures of social distance have also shown dramatic changes. For example, in 1958 45% said they might move or definitely would move if a black family moved next door, but that percentage was 2% in 1997. Fifty-two percent would not object if a family member invited a black guest for dinner in 1963, but that percentage had increased to 77% by 1985. The percentage of white people agreeing that blacks should not push themselves into situations where they are not wanted declined from 78% in 1963 to 42% in 1996. However, whites' average "feeling thermometer" rating of blacks—a measure that tends to be predictive of other attitudes—was 60 degrees in 1964 and 63 degrees in 1996, showing little change.

The changes in white perceptions of the causes of black disadvantage have been less dramatic. In 1977 41% said it was due to discrimination, but only 34% gave that answer in 1996. There has been a decline in perceptions that blacks have less ability (27% in 1977, 10% in 1996) and motivation (66% in 1977, 52% in 1996), although the percentage of white people agreeing that blacks should try harder increased from 69% in 1977 to 75% in 1996. Generally, white Americans have replaced traditional beliefs that blacks lack ability with beliefs that they lack adherence to middle-class values of hard work and dedication (Kinder & Sanders, 1996). This is actually a small improvement, because most people probably think that motives and values can change more easily than abilities, but it is surely small consolation to victims of discrimination.

White support for governmental policies designed to produce changes has generally declined over time. Support for federal intervention to desegregate schools declined from 42% in 1964 to 25% in 1994. School bussing has never been popular; it was supported by 13% in 1972 and only 6% in 1984. The percentage of people who think that the federal government spends too much money trying to improve the condition of blacks was 27% in 1973 and 26% in 1996. The percentage of people who disapprove of preferential consideration in hiring increased from 53% in 1985 to 66% in 1995.

We should remind ourselves that white Americans have probably moved further and faster in improving their perceptions of minority group members than any other society in history. Lest this seem a preposterous and perhaps insensitive statement, let's turn the clock back a half century or so—when the idea that black men could have jobs that required suits was laughable, as was the notion that black women could do more than wash and clean. In many areas of the country, blacks could not vote, attend public universities their tax dollars supported, or sit in public near whites. A black man and a white woman holding hands in public was grounds for the lynch mob in the South and the object of stares elsewhere. *Amos 'n' Andy* was replaced by *The Cosby Show*, surely a massive improvement even by the lights of those who have criticized *The Cosby Show* as a copout.

The changes in white attitudes toward blacks in the United States are, I think, genuine. At the same time, such attitudes are labile, abstract, and often ineffective in concrete situations. Although few white Americans report that blacks are intellectually inferior to whites, their behavior often belies these beliefs. This can be called hypocrisy, but in reality the same is true of most other human beliefs. People who are genuinely and deeply religious do not always act in concert with their values, and as we have seen in Chapter 8, those whose conscious attitudes are saintly may still exhibit deeper and less conscious prejudices.

More worrisome is the failure of white Americans to recognize the systematic nature of the problems that affect minority groups. Because they do not fully appreciate the differences between the experiences of black and white Americans, they fail to understand the need for changes in the larger society that may help to reduce those differences. Many have argued that this is a newer, more subtle, and perhaps more dangerous form of racism (Chapter 8). In the meantime, white Americans have every right to be proud of the changes they have made, so long as they also recognize the distance they have yet to travel.

THE CONTACT HYPOTHESIS

There was a day when social scientists as well as laypeople thought that stereotypes were basically aberrations of mental life. They were viewed as negative, ill considered, and rigid, and especially as based on prejudice rather than on high-quality experiences. Certainly a stronger case could be made then than now that most people's stereotypes were in fact based on limited exposure. As I have said earlier, before the middle 1950s many white Americans had never met a black person; many Protestants did not know any Catholics or Jews at all well; and women who did anything other than keep house or work at traditional nurturing jobs were rare indeed.

Changes during and immediately after World War II led to more contacts among various groups, and in the 1950s social scientists began to emphasize contact among members of different racial groups as an important tool, even a panacea, for eliminating prejudice (Pettigrew & Tropp, 2000). If the content of gender and race stereotypes came from cultural hearsay, radio and newspaper presentations, and other forms of indirect contact rather than direct experience, then such stereotypes were likely to be inaccurate and amenable to change with increased direct contact.

Basic Assumptions

There are three basic assumptions underlying this approach (Rothbart & John, 1985). First is the idea that stereotypes are basically false because of limited experiences. Second, the contact hypothesis assumes that experiences with individuals from stereotyped groups will provide clear evidence that disconfirms the stereotypes. And third, it assumes that people will recognize that their own stereotypes are fraudulent and be willing and able to change them. Ability is a nontrivial aspect of the process. It is much too easy to assume that people can change their beliefs about others if they only try, but this is almost always a naive assumption. For example, as we have seen in Chapter 9, individual stereotypes may be embedded in a matrix of other beliefs that preclude easy change.

We do not need loads of formal empirical data to see that in everyday life, one or more of these assumptions may easily be violated. And if one fails, the whole approach does as well. As an extreme and uncontroversial example, let's consider Katie, a person who is convinced that Princeton undergraduates are smart—not only smarter than the average person, but even smarter than the average college student. For obviously peculiar reasons that only a social scientist could endorse, we wish to disconfirm this stereotype by exposing Katie to several Princeton students. We would be likely to find that our little experiment would not work. In the first instance, the stereotype is not false, so it is not likely that Katie will be able to find evidence of gross stupidity among such students. This is not to say that stupid behaviors (in and out of the classroom) are unknown among this group, but Katie would have to have a very off day indeed to see a preponderance of them. And even if Katie did manage to find some seemingly stupid Princeton students, she might not be willing to change her opinion, for a variety of reasons.

I do not want to be taken as suggesting that all, or even most, stereotypes have a kernel (large or small) of truth in some broad sense. Some do; some don't. But most people think that their stereotypes are accurate, in part because the stereotypes themselves bias what they take to be confirming and disconfirming evidence. There are, to be sure, limits to a perceiver's abilities to ignore and distort, but in everyday life when it comes to judging the validity of stereotypes and their supporting data, the individual perceiver is both judge and jury. The contact hypothesis is about direct, individual, unpasteurized experiences, and not about truth as social scientists see it.

What Changes as a Result of Contact?

When we try to change people, we must always ask not only what changes but how extensive the change is. When Jim discovers that his Hispanic lab partner, José, is really a good guy despite his tough exterior and that they share many interests in common, we can certainly count that as a victory of sorts. But is there any general impact? Pettigrew (1998a) notes that we need to be concerned with at least three forms of generalization. First, do Jim's positive experiences with José in biology lab generalize to a changed view of him across situations? Before this, Jim has noticed that José seems to have an attitude problem, and we might hope that Jim considers the possibility that José has adopted this tough exterior to protect himself from what he thinks is a toxic environment. Can Jim form a fuller impression of José by generalizing across situations? Second, we would hope that Jim would use his experiences with José to reduce his prejudice against Hispanics in general, or at least to realize that his previous stereotyped image is not a "one size fits all." Third, we might wonder whether positive experiences encourage Jim to think about his racial stereotypes more broadly. Having discovered that Hispanic students are a diverse group and that many of them are okay, can he rethink his equally negative attitudes about African Americans?

There is a major problem with the notion of contact that will bedevil us throughout the remainder of this chapter. We will see it in a variety of flavors, but the essential problem is this: Can we expect people to generalize presumably positive experiences with a few people to their group as a whole? The contact hypothesis rests on the fundamental assumption that getting to know one or a few members of a group will provide sufficient information to change beliefs and attitudes about that group. Yet several decades of cognitive psychology should confirm our reluctance to adopt this assumption uncritically, and the red flags are waving.

Our human cognitive systems are set up precisely to encourage us to categorize and generalize—and, more to the point in the present context, to preserve those fruits of our cognitive labors. Would we want a cognitive system that reoriented itself completely every time we encountered something that didn't fit our previous ways of thinking? That boat would bob on rough seas indeed. Numerous cognitive mechanisms buffer the effects of individual experiences, and our perceptions of people and groups are no different in that regard from our perceptions of dogs, Brussels sprouts, and the effects of rain on plant growth. It may be that because our perceptions of people and the categories they inhabit are unusually complex and culturally conditioned, changing stereotypes of people is more tricky than changing stereotypes of dogs or Brussels sprouts. I examine the conditions that make this tricky process more likely to succeed throughout the chapter.

Empirical Evidence for Contact

Over the past half century and more, the contact hypothesis has been tested and retested. Much of the research in this area has studied real people in real groups in the real world who have, for one or another reason, been placed in situations where they had increased contact with members of other groups about which they had limited information. Settings have included the military in World War II and the Korean War, housing, schools, exchange programs, visits to foreign countries, jobs—indeed, almost any context in which people from different groups might meet.

This research has been reviewed many times (e.g., Amir, 1969; Hewstone & Brown, 1986; Pettigrew & Tropp, 2000), and every reviewer has come to the same basic conclusion: Contact generally does have positive effects on reducing prejudice and stereotyping, but (and this is an important "but") only under certain circumstances. As we will see in the next three chapters, a powerful predictor of positive attitudes and stereotypes toward a range of groups is knowing someone in a group, although in such correlational research it is possible (indeed, probable) that at least part of this correlation occurs because people who already have positive attitudes toward group members seek contact with them. An extensive analysis by Pettigrew and Tropp (2000) finds a general tendency of prejudice to affect contact, but a stronger tendency of contact to affect attitudes and prejudice.

Conditions That Favor Contact Effectiveness

That mere contact should, on average, have limited impact seems reasonable when we think about it. Suppose Jon, a white high school student, has come to believe that his black classmates are far more gifted at athletic endeavors than academic ones. At this point in his high school career, he is taking all honors classes, and he encounters few if any black students there. He is, however, the equipment manager for the football team; he thus has many encounters with black athletes and considers several of them to be his friends. Given those experiences, how would we possibly expect Jon to have experiences contradicting his stereotypes that black students are more athletic than academic? Or consider the situation in South Africa before the end of apartheid. Blacks and whites had little contact in purely social situations; most of the contact came at work, where whites enforced their enormous power and blacks tended to act out expected subservient roles as a means to keep their jobs (Foster & Finchilescu, 1986). This was not exactly the kind of contact we would design to counter white stereotypes of blacks.

These examples illustrate several points. First, many different types of contact are likely to reinforce rather than diminish stereotypes. We have to face the possibility that members of all stereotyped groups may on occasion act consistently with stereotypes, and more generally that some experiences with groups of people are bound to be negative as well as positive. Second, our contacts are likely to be selective. We see others only in certain types of situations and often fail to factor out situational forces in assessing people. Third, our experiences are never pure and unbiased. Whether or not there is a kernel of truth to a particular stereotype, any given perceiver can almost always find behavior that seems to confirm it and can reinterpret disconfirming behavior to fit.

So obviously contact in and of itself cannot remedy stereotypes. This is not a new insight. For at least 50 years, social psychologists have been saying—and saying loudly—that only some forms of contact in some circumstances will help reduce prejudice and stereotypes (Allport, 1954; Cook, 1962; Saenger, 1953; Williams, 1964). Moreover, there has been substantial agreement on the main conditions that ought to favor contact (Allport, 1954), although different authors have presented slightly different lists. Allport's summary statement is worth quoting:

> Prejudice (unless deeply rooted in the character structure of the individual) may be reduced by equal status contact between majority and minority groups in the pursuit of

common goals. The effect is greatly enhanced if this contact is sanctioned by institutional supports (i.e., by law, custom, or local atmosphere), and if it is of a sort that leads to the perception of common interests and common humanity between members of two groups. (Allport, 1954, p. 267)

Perception of Common Interests and Humanity

DEPTH OF CONTACT

There is contact, and then there is contact. My next-door neighbors may be black (as they are), but if my contact with them is limited to the occasional wave as we collect our morning newspapers or casual conversation in the driveway (as it is), there is little opportunity for gaining new information. Similarly, Joan may work in a racially diverse office, but limit her conversation with her Chinese American coworker to the occasional comment about the weather or parking problems.

Pettigrew (1998a) takes this a step further and argues that friendship between group members is essential. In their influential paper, Brewer and Miller (1984) similarly suggest that a key to effective contact is what they call "personalization," which involves finding common points of reference. Only as people begin to discuss their backgrounds, interests, values, and attitudes, as friends do, can they easily get beyond group boundaries. As people discover commonalities, perceptions of increased similarity will increase liking, which may help to reduce prejudice. In addition, depth of contact may facilitate ability and motivation to empathize and take the perspective of others, which also tend to reduce prejudice (Batson, Chang, Orr, & Rowland, 2002; Batson et al., 1997; Galinsky & Moskowitz, 2000).

A large survey study by Jackman and Crane (1986) showed that whites who reported having black friends and acquaintances were much less likely to stereotype blacks and have less prejudice toward them. For example, 60% of those with no black friends thought that blacks were less intelligent than whites; 51% of those who reported having a black friend but no acquaintances, or a black acquaintance but no friends, had the same view; but 39% of those who had both black friends and acquaintances agreed.[1] On a prejudice-like measure, 50% of those with no friends or acquaintances reported feeling warmer toward whites than blacks, whereas only 18% of those who had both friends and acquaintances reported the same. Prejudice and stereotypes were particularly low when a respondent both had black friends and acquaintances and also had a history of living in integrated neighborhoods; we might speculate that such conditions would favor generalization to the group from attitudes developed toward individuals, because neighborhood contact would be less likely to represent unequal status and to be based on limiting roles. Similarly, in studies of contact with ethnic groups in Europe, having friends among ethnic outgroups is especially important in reducing prejudice (Hamberger & Hewstone, 1997; Pettigrew, 1997).

Whether we go beyond superficial contact to friendship is affected by a number of ecological and personal variables. After all, I don't form deep friendships with most of my neighbors or coworkers, whatever their race, ethnicity, or gender. Beyond that, I may also actively avoid contact with people from various groups. Consider Jason, a young white businessman, who has never had any meaningful contact with people from other races or ethnic backgrounds. A black man moves into the apartment down the hall, and Jason thinks he really should get to know this guy, but feels awkward. What if this guy is hostile to white people, as Jason has heard many black men are? What would they talk about? Do they have anything in common? Hank, the black man, may be similarly shy about initiating contact, but for a different reason—because he has had one too many experiences of such overtures' being rejected. Such wariness is far more common, I think, than we believe. Such "intergroup anxiety," predicts intergroup bias and negative affect toward outgroups (Greenland & Brown, 1999; Islam & Hewstone, 1993a; Stephan & Stephan, 2000b; Wilder, 1993a) as well as intergroup contact (Plant & Devine, 2003; Towles-Schwen & Fazio, 2003). When the negative features of our stereotypes are primed, we tend to avoid people in those groups (Henderson-King & Nisbett, 1996). Most of us want to talk to and be friends with people we feel comfortable around, and differences in race, ethnicity, gender, sexual orientations, and/or religion may all be discomfort nurseries. The tragedy in all this, of course, is that the very people who could most benefit from more intimate contact are the very people who are most likely to avoid it.

BREADTH OF CONTACT

When we think about it, many of our contacts with people from other groups are limited to one or two situations. Children who attend integrated schools may live in neighborhoods that are almost completely segregated. The only contacts that young people have with elderly individuals may be with relatives at periodic family gatherings. The straight man who knows one or two gay men at the advertising agency he deals with may never encounter gay men (at least those out of the closet) on the golf course, at his church, or in his neighborhood. White students majoring in science or engineering and living in fraternities or sororities may see their black classmates only in passing or on the athletic fields. One theme of this book (and, indeed, all of modern social psychology) has been that what we take to be inherent qualities of people are often dictated by social situations. If my only real contact with black males consists of seeing them play football and hearing their relatively inarticulate answers in postgame interviews (a situation that does not invite intelligent answers), it would be easy to fall into the cultural stereotype that black males are violent, athletic, and dumb. To get a broader perspective, whites should see black males having gentle encounters with their wives and children, having the same problems raising children as they do, and talking clearly and complexly about their religious feelings—but those are precisely the kinds of events they are not likely to see when contacts are limited, superficial, and role-prescribed. Thus contact limited to particular situations is not a recipe for changing stereotypes and prejudices. There are several reports of people having positive experiences with members of another group in one situation (typically work), but maintaining negative attitudes overall (e.g., Gundlach, 1950; Minard, 1952; Saenger & Gilbert, 1950).

Type of Interaction

Obviously, if most of my contacts with members of other groups are contentious, such experiences are not likely to lead to warm and fuzzy stereotypes, let alone positive attitudes. Common sense and empirical research (Islam & Hewstone, 1993a) suggest that positive interaction should be a necessary if not sufficient condition for contact to be effective. Quality is surely more important than quantity of interaction (Pettigrew & Tropp, 2000; W. G. Stephan, Diaz-Loving, & Duran, 2000). Interaction quality has traditionally been broken into two categories: (1) seeking goals that unite rather than divide groups, and (2) cooperation.

SUPERORDINATE GOALS

Sherif's Robbers Cave study (Sherif & Sherif, 1953; Sherif, Harvey, White, Hood, & Sherif, 1961) emphasized developing goals that transcend the interests of particular groups which have conflicts about more specific goals. In this experiment, a group of boys at a camp were arbitrarily divided into competitive teams, and soon the competition led to real hostility between the groups (see Chapter 7). Sherif found that one effective mechanism for changing this hostility was to have members of the two teams work on mutual goals, which he called "superordinate goals." When the boys were encouraged to cooperate in this way, antagonism between the groups was lowered. As we will see later, this has strong echoes in the common-ingroup-identity model (Gaertner & Dovidio, 2000).

COOPERATION

Although recognition of commonalities may be useful in and of itself, if such recognition does not lead to cooperative behavior, little is likely to happen to change stereotypes and prejudice. This is one area where the research findings are strong and consistent. Working with others in cooperative groups leads to more positive attitudes toward other group members than working in competitive groups does (Johnson & Johnson, 2000). Cooperation probably has at least two major effects. First, it solidifies the idea that competing groups do have common interests, as well as a common fate in terms of outcomes. Second, cooperation that results in successful outcomes is likely to facilitate exchanges of personalizing information, which should reduce intergroup anxieties. Present research points to positive interaction as being more important than perception of a common fate (S. L. Gaertner et al., 1999).

Much of this research has been done in public schools, many of which have tried to create environments that foster racial integration. Cooperative learning techniques have been intensively studied and generally found to be quite effective, not only in creating more favorable intergroup attitudes but in improving academic performance (especially of minority group children). There are several different techniques that differ in superficial and important details, but I focus here on the technique that is most familiar to social psychologists—the "jigsaw classroom."

THE JIGSAW CLASSROOM

Originally developed by social psychologist Elliot Aronson to aid integration of schools in Austin, Texas, the jigsaw classroom has been used successfully in other schools and was partially responsible for stimulating additional forms of cooperative leaning that may even be more effective (Slavin, 1986). Aronson and his colleagues (Aronson, Blaney, Stephan, Sikes, & Snapp, 1978; Aronson & Patnoe, 1997) realized that just having students from different races and ethnic groups work together on school projects was not sufficient. In recently integrated schools, children from minority groups would be likely to have less complete academic skills and to be less confident in using the ones they had. The result would almost inevitably be groups in which the white students dominated the group discussion and took on most of the responsibility for producing the group project. This would be likely to strengthen stereotypes held by whites that minority group members are incompetent, and those held by minority students that whites are overbearing and insensitive.

Thus Aronson recognized that the key was to find a way of increasing the participation of minority youngsters in a way that would allow them to make meaningful contributions to the group effect. In a jigsaw classroom, students work in multiethnic groups on projects—say, producing a report on a country or person. The assignment is structured so that each child, majority or minority, is responsible for a particular piece; unless all the pieces are fitted together, the report will be inadequate. Under these circumstances the group members have incentives to help one another and to encourage those with fewer initial skills, rather than make fun of their inadequacies. Furthermore, each group member also participates in expert groups with other students who have the same "piece of the puzzle" in their groups, as an aid to developing expertise that can be taken back to the primary group. This technique results in better performance by minority children (Aronson & Gonzalez, 1988; Lucker, Rosenfield, Sikes, & Aronson, 1976). Cooperative learning enterprises also seem to facilitate cross-race friendships (Slavin, 1985; Warring, Johnson, Maruyama, & Johnson, 1985), although the extent to which they reduce prejudice is not well established.

The Importance of Status

Most social scientists have emphasized the importance of having people from different groups meet as equals. People who are used to having power use it and may not be shy about making sure others recognize that they have it. This tends to create withdrawal or hostility on the part of lower-status people, which then gets interpreted by the higher-status individuals as evidence of relative incompetence. To take this to an extreme, having white people interact primarily with black welfare recipients, even the whites are impoverished themselves, is not likely to create images of black competence. One striking demonstration of the importance of status comes from the earlier-discussed study by Jackman and Crane (1986), which showed that having friends and acquaintances who were black lowered prejudice and stereotyping markedly. Those effects were mediated by status, such that prejudice was lowest when white respondents had intimate contact with equal- or higher-status black people. For example, 58% of those who had no black friends or acquaintances thought that whites were more intelligent, and 47% said they felt more warmly toward whites. Those same percentages were 44% and 33% for those who had friends of the same socioeconomic status, and 29% and 5% for those who had a higher-status black friend.

It is worth remembering that institutions and environments convey status differentially and often somewhat arbitrarily. Furthermore, having power tends to promote stereotyping, at least of lower-status people by higher-status folks. When people are fully interdependent (in a sense a condition of equal status), they tend to pay attention to others as individuals, but when interdependence is not symmetrical, those with greater power tend to ignore individual and focus on categorical information (Fiske, 2000a).

Norms and Social Pressure

Sometimes it is alleged (usually on the basis of little evidence) that people's hearts and minds can't be changed through social pressure or legislation. This is simplistic to the point of being plain wrong. Apart from whether legal and social pressures, have positive or negative effects in and of themselves, they can provide support for other mechanisms. People who are encouraged, or even gently forced, to engage in constructive behavior toward others may, through processes of dissonance reduction or self-perception, come to internalize more positive attitudes. Unfortunately, although institutional support for change is widely assumed to be an important mediator of the effectiveness of contact (e.g., Taylor, 2000), there has been little empirical support for this idea—in part because it is hard to disentangle such support from other variables.

In the long run, external pressures may be important for another reason. People internalize norms that they learn from direct tuition from and observation of others. In modern industrialized societies, one such norm is that people should not be prejudiced. Individuals differ in how much they wish to control prejudicial behavior (Dunton & Fazio, 1997), and positive contact, especially during childhood years, is associated with motivation to control prejudiced reactions (Towles-Schwen & Fazio, 2001). In addition, people who have internalized such norms may feel guilty when they behave in prejudiced ways and try to learn ways to correct their behavior (Monteith, Zuwerink, & Devine, 1994).

Other Conditions

ACCUMULATING COMPLEXITY

Over the years, social psychologists have examined various additional conditions that mediate the effectiveness of contact. This list includes value similarity between groups (Cook, 1962), role relationships (Secord & Backman, 1964), positive outcomes of interactions (Blanchard, Adelman, & Cook, 1975), approximately equal number of people from the two groups (Amir, 1976), and values that promote a willingness to have contact (Sagiv & Schwartz, 1995).[2] By the middle 1980s, the list of important mediating variables had become perhaps 20 or so (see Stephan, 1987, for one extensive listing), and this led many social scientists (e.g., Rothbart & John, 1985) effectively to throw in the towel on the contact hypothesis. The problem was not merely that the list of important variables had become so uncomfortably long; most of us social scientists understand that reality refuses to honor our requests for the short and simple. Rather, the problem is we have the social policy equivalent of trying to herd cats; in designing effective contact situations, it proves hard to implement important variables successfully in concert.

It is also important to keep in mind the distinction between necessary and sufficient conditions. Probably no condition is sufficient to make contact effective, and arguably many of the classic as well as the more recently added ones are not necessary. While statements about the relative importance of one or another of these conditions are almost impossible to validate empirically, it is a reasonable guess that the only things that are absolutely necessary for contact to alleviate stereotyping and prejudice are favorable experiences. But, of course, pleasant experiences with members of other groups do not guarantee good feelings all around. What else is necessary or even facilitating depends on the groups involved, how ingrained previous prejudice is, and a host of other situational and contextual variables.

AFFECT AND COGNITION

As I have indicated, early conceptions of the contact hypothesis stressed the potential for contact to correct erroneous beliefs that were assumed to underlie and support prejudice. In recent years, more attention has been given to the importance of affect in contact effects. Affect may have two basic types of effects. First, and fundamentally, affect surely plays a role in how willing people are to have to contact with those who are different from them (Esses & Dovidio, 2002). Most of us pick our residences, schools for our children, and leisure activities to maximize contact with people more or less like us. Even for those of us who think we treasure diversity, trying to get to know homeless people, common criminals, and people whose political opinions differ radically from our own is not a high daily priority.

Second, emotion may mediate the effects of contact on prejudice and stereotypes. For example, Bill Ickes (1984), Walter Stephan (1999), and David Wilder (1993a, 1993b) have stressed the role of reducing the anxiety that may accompany intergroup encounters. There are several reasons for believing that affect may play a major role in mediating contact effects. The most obvious is that when a person has fairly neutral or even slightly negative feelings toward another group, especially when those have been based on minimal encounters, positive experiences with members of another group may readily generalize to the entire group. Obviously, we should not expect this to happen for racial antagonisms where affect is presumably based on multiple bad experiences and/or deep-seated beliefs and long-standing intergroup conflict. As noted in Chapter 3, when people are in a positive mood, they tend to see categories as broader and including more relatively atypical exemplars. If efforts are made to create superordinate categories for two formerly antagonistic groups, positive affect should facilitate abilities to see members of the two groups as similar (Dovidio, Gaertner, Isen, & Lowrance, 1995). Finally, anxiety as a particularly strong affective state tends to promote the use of stereotypes and lessens the impact of counterstereotypic and individuating information (Wilder, 1993a).

School Desegregation and Experiences as a Test Case

THE HOPE OF THE *BROWN* DECISION

As nearly every adult American knows, the U.S. Supreme Court unanimously ruled school desegregation unconstitutional in the famous *Brown v. Board of Education* (1954) decision, although it took considerable time for most schools to comply.[3] Ultimately there has been some degree of desegregation of schools in both the North and the South, although children still go to school predominantly with members of their own race. Social scientists (especially psychologists) contributed to the *Brown* decision through their opinions that segregated schools were detrimental to minority children.[4] In addition to the obvious fact that predominantly black schools received far fewer resources for education than did white schools (see Chapter 8), the psychologists argued that segregation undermined the self-concepts of black children. More to the point in the present context, they also argued that lack of contact with members of other races contributed to prejudice and negative stereotypes, especially of whites toward blacks. Although the *Brown* decision is important for its use of social science data, the decision rested fundamentally on moral issues of simple fairness and was surely the correct one, independently of whatever effects desegregation has had on reducing prejudice.

In any event, social scientists and others saw the ending of segregation as a way to reduce prejudice: Get children while they're young and before they have a chance to latch onto culturally created negative stereotypes. In effect, from 1954 to the present, U.S. schools have been engaged in a massive (if crude) test of the contact hypothesis.

EMPIRICAL STUDIES

And what have been the results? Not promising, unfortunately. For example, one comprehensive study (Gerard & Miller, 1975) of 1,800 children in a single school district in southern California found that, if anything, prejudice increased rather than decreased following integration. Walter Stephan's (1978) review of the early research literature suggested that 50% of the studies found decreases in prejudice among blacks toward whites, but 42% found increases. The results were even more grim for whites, with only 13% finding decreases of white prejudice against blacks and 53% finding increases. In addition, the notion that black self-esteem would improve in integrated schools was not supported; several studies found that desegregation was associated with lower self-esteem, and none that it was associated with higher self-esteem. Finally, the idea that desegregation would improve the academic performance of black students was found in some studies (29%) but not in others (68%). More recent meta-analyses have found small but significant achievement advantages for black students in integrated schools (e.g., Crain & Mahard, 1983; Wortman & Bryant, 1985). Unfortunately, most of these studies were not well controlled (an extremely difficult task in educational research), and few if any firm conclusions can be drawn about causal relationships. Still, it is striking that the remedy provided by *Brown*, as poorly administered as it surely was, did not have the effects almost all social scientists expected. Although some psychologists (e.g., Cook, 1979, 1988) have been less pessimistic, desegregation is certainly no poster child for the contact hypothesis.[5]

SHORT-TERM VERSUS LONG-TERM EFFECTS

However, before we conclude that desegregation has been a psychological failure, let's back up a moment. Perhaps most importantly, there is evidence that although the short-term effects of school desegregation have been unpromising, there may be positive longer-term effects. Most of the studies were based on effects within the first year of desegregation, and the political atmosphere surrounding most attempts at desegregation plus the abruptness of the change for many certainly provided a less than ideal context for positive change. Perhaps longer-term effects might be more positive, and some studies (see Schofield, 1989) have found exactly that. For example, whites who attend integrated schools are more likely as adults to live in integrated neighborhoods and to work in integrated environments, and blacks who have attended integrated schools are more likely to go to college and to attend formerly all-white colleges, as well as to work in integrated settings (Braddock, 1985; Stephan, 1999). Other studies show that whites who have more contact with blacks as children are less prejudiced as adults (Wood & Sonleitner, 1996). So desegregation may have longer-term and more subtle salutary effects.

IS DESEGREGATION A GOOD TEST OF THE CONTACT HYPOTHESIS?

To the extent that desegregation has failed to live up to its promise, it is not fair to see this as a failure of the contact hypothesis unless that hypothesis is taken in its crudest form. In the last few pages, I have stressed that increasing contact with members of other groups can reduce prejudice, increase it, or leave it unchanged. It all depends on, well, lots of things. But just for starters, let's consider the four traditional factors we have discussed. Gerard (1988) has argued that social scientists were naive to imagine that these conditions could be met in the typical school. He may be right, and yet to the extent that those conditions *can* be met, desegregation can be quite effective (Cook, 1985; Gaertner, Rust, Dovidio, Bachman, & Anastasio, 1994).

Breadth and Depth of Contact. The contact should be deep and broad. Is that likely to have happened in most school situations? No. Desegregation has not led to a large increase, if any, in cross-race friendships (Johnson, Johnson, & Maruyama, 1983; Schofield, 1981). In the first place, many (I suspect most) schools found legal ways to keep white and black children apart, tracking being the one most often used.[6] Even today, black and white children are often effectively segregated on the basis of the classes they take and activities they participate in (Schofield, 1986). Sports is one notable exception.[7] So contact between black and white children was unlikely to have been especially intimate, and it was also unlikely to have extended much outside the classroom—especially given that many of the children were bussed into schools not in their neighborhoods, reducing opportunities for after-school contact.

Type of Interaction. I have indicated earlier that cooperative behavior directed toward common goals facilitates reductions of prejudice. American schools are oriented more toward competition than cooperation, and unless schools actively implement cooperative learning experiences such as the jigsaw classroom, students are going to have little experience in schools of such experiences with members of other races. When schools try to create favorable conditions, in the form of cooperation, for the increased contact to work, they are likely to be more successful (Johnson et al., 1983; Schofield, 1979; Schofield & Sagar, 1977).

Equal Status. The contact should also ideally involve equal-status contact. Again, this is a condition likely to have been violated in most desegregation efforts—given the differing socioeconomic status that divided most black and white children, and given that many (probably most) of the black children entered the white schools with less strong academic credentials. After schools are integrated, students tend to resegregate along racial lines because of differences in academic achievement (Schofield, 1989). Obviously, stereotypes about blacks' being less intelligent are not going to be easily alleviated when minority children do worse in school and tend not to appear in advanced classes.

Norms and Social Pressures. Finally, I have noted that an important condition is that norms and social pressures must favor the contact. Again, this condition was certainly violated in the majority of school desegregation attempts. When most of the community (including some minority parents) felt that integration was being shoved down their throats, and when everyone knew that many schools had dragged their feet as long as possible to implement desegregation, children of any age were not likely to be enthusiastic about the possibilities of attending schools with people of a different race. Many of them were, I suspect, primed and willing to find as much stereotype-confirming evidence as they could. By contrast, a high school principals who are deeply committed to making integration work are more likely to be successful than ones who are only grudgingly committed (see Rich, Ari, Amir, & Eliassy, 1996, for one example).[8]

Some Theoretical Questions

In my experience, people—even some who are quite sophisticated—think that problems of prejudice and discrimination would be solved if "people would just get to know each other." We have seen that this model is both vague and naive, a dangerous combination. Though the issues are complex, two major theoretical questions underlie all of the research. The first is whether contact should seek to reduce categorization—to break down boundaries between groups. The second concerns the circumstances under which experiences with individuals generalize to the group as a whole.

Is Deemphasizing Categories a Good Thing?

The first question may seem silly. Is there any doubt in anyone's mind that humans' propensities to categorize, and then to assign features to these categories they use, are the root problems of stereotyping and prejudice? If people could just see past labels and group memberships and see other people as individuals, wouldn't they be well on our way to solving the prejudice-and-discrimination problem?

THE DECATEGORIZATION PERSPECTIVE

In Chapter 3 I have discussed what it might mean to deemphasize categories and noted that in some sense it may be impossible, because every feature I have points to some category or other. If you discover that in addition to being a professor I am also grouchy, you must still draw on your fund of information about the category of grouchy people to figure out what that means. Human thinking is categorical even when people individuate in terms of features.

Although that is true, the real issue before us is not how to get people to stop thinking in terms of categories, but rather how we can get them to stop using *particular* categories. And that is really a different matter. If you get to know me well, you will soon learn that although I am professorial in many ways, I deviate from the stereotypes in others. And as you get to know me and assemble a database of all the ways I am like and unlike prototypic professors (and, for that matter, opera lovers, grandfathers, liberals, and homeowners), the category of professors loses its usefulness.

Multiple Categories. Brewer's (1988) notions of personalization rest exactly on this idea. If I divide and subdivide primary categories into many parts, at some point the primary category loses its meaning. To use an extreme example, the category of living things has little utility for me, and I rarely use it. Even much more circumscribed categories, such as plants, are generally too broad to do much cognitive heavy lifting.

Trees and flowering plants are about my speed. By analogy, if through contact I learn to see various subtypes of women or professors or Asian persons as more informative than the larger categories, I may in time quit thinking in terms of the larger designations. Personalization involves making categories features of individuals rather than making people features of categories. One of the advantages of intimacy of contact—an important mediator of whether contact will be effective (see above)—is that it promotes exactly this kind of personalization.

Several authors, but most notably Brewer and Miller (1984, 1988), have argued that personalization is critical to the success of contact; unless contact results in a lowering of category boundaries, it will fail in its task of reducing stereotyping and prejudice. According to this model (Brewer, 1988, 1998), we first have to differentiate people within a given category—to see them as dissimilar in some ways. Then we personalize.

It also might be argued that decategorization destroys boundaries that tend to keep people from discovering important similarities. One of the best-established "laws" in social psychology is that similarity leads to attraction, and belief congruence theory (Rokeach, Smith, & Evans, 1960) specifically emphasizes perceptions of dissimilarity as promoting and supporting prejudice. So from this perspective, the idea that we are all alike "under the skin" has considerable appeal. However, despite the theoretical appeal of this idea, it is far from certain that the similarity–attraction relationship (which can be so powerful in interpersonal situations) works for intergroup relations (Johnston & Hewstone, 1990).

Crossing Categories. A related proposal is to encourage people to see others in terms of both ingroup and outgroup categories. I am a professional male, so professional females are an outgroup in terms of gender but an ingroup in terms of occupational status. Perhaps in interacting with people who are multiply categorized, I will ameliorate some of my outgroup reactions with more positive ingroup perceptions. At a minimum, this should promote personalization of such persons, because I will be forced to consider at least some of the ways they are similar to me. Recent reviews of the literature (see Chapters 3 and 7) suggest that negative bias is strongest toward people from double outgroups and weakest toward those from double ingroups.

Some Potential Problems. The hope of the personalization model is that after repeated contact and deeper interactions, categories and their associated stereotypes will become less relevant, and hence prejudices resulting from such stereotypes will disappear. However, note that this model does not work by changing stereotypes, but rather by decreasing the likelihood of their activation. This is not necessarily a flaw in the model; indeed, it is a virtue, because it stops mischief before it starts. Still, we need to remind ourselves that personalization (and the related individuation approach) are, strictly speaking, not models of stereotype change but of application.

A more major problem is that reducing salient group boundaries may be quite threatening to people. To be sure, I would willingly discard many of my group memberships for the greater good, but with others I may be less charitable. Often I am happy to forget being a Houstonian to make common cause with other Texans, and to forget being a Texan to be an American. But I might be less willing to forgo my professor identity in a group of architects, lawyers, and doctors representing their respective professional interests.

A more obvious problem with such models is that such strategies may not pro-mote generalization to the groups as a whole, but indeed may retard it (Miller & Har-rington, 1990). After all, before experiences with one individual can generalize to members of his or her category, the category must be salient (Ensari & Miller, 2002). Carried to an extreme, if Jared never thinks of Latoya as black, obviously he cannot generalize his positive attitudes about her to blacks in general. In one experimental test, Scarberry, Ratcliff, Lord, Lanicek, and Desforges (1997) found that supposedly gay targets who provided individuating information about themselves (and presum-ably personalized themselves to some extent) had less effect on changing general atti-tudes toward homosexuals than those who did not.

THE INTERDEPENDENCE PERSPECTIVE

Chapter 4 has discussed the impression continuum model of Fiske and Neuberg (1990). In the present context, their notion of interdependency is especially impor-tant. When one person is dependent on another, he or she is likely to want to dis-cover as much predictive information about the other as possible. Category informa-tion may be an important aid, but even more important would be information that is inconsistent with stereotypes related to categories. Thus, according to this model, de-pendency should facilitate going beyond superficial social stereotypes (Fiske, 2000a).

Unfortunately, interdependency does not grow on trees, and in many situations it may be hard to manufacture—not impossible, just hard. Dependencies are also of-ten asymmetrical, in the sense that one person has less power (is more dependent) than the other. Although almost all men and women have interdependent relation-ships with members of the other gender, many marriages and professional relation-ships have floundered on the shoals of attempts at power equalization. In schools, it is hard to create conditions of interdependency among children of different races and backgrounds. Work relationships often involve institutionally based power in-equalities that are not easily leveled. Still, this model does point to one important motivation for people to try to move beyond category-based information and stereo-types.

THE SOCIAL IDENTITY THEORY PERSPECTIVE

Social identity theory (SIT) presents a contrasting view. It specifically predicts that generalization from individual to group will generally be enhanced when categories are salient rather than deemphasized. Before discussing that hypothesis, I need to in-troduce an important distinction first made by Tajfel (1978) and amplified by Brown and Turner (1981): Behavior toward others can be "interpersonal" or "intergroup." In the former, one behaves to the other person with minimum or no reference to standard social categories. Such behavior can be intimate, but may not be especially intimate or revealing. When I stop to help a person who has fallen down, it is irrele-vant to me whether that person is a he or she, black or white, a baker or a candlestick maker. I pay for my purchases at a cash register, and I never think of the cashier as black or overweight—well, I may fleetingly note these things, but it's unlikely that my behavior is much affected by such thoughts.

Social categories can be nonsalient in many interpersonal interactions, but in more intimate friendship situations categories may also become irrelevant. When I get to know my student Kim well, I may quit treating her primarily as a student, and my behavior may be less and less affected by her gender. In a way, that's what it means to get to know someone and become her friend. It's not that I cease to notice all the categories that my friends belong to, but that they no longer matter—the lure of personalization.

Intergroup Behavior. However, we do not always behave toward others in an interpersonal way. Sometimes our category memberships are very central. Although I would like to have my students think I am nice, I have no desire to become their playmate. And I suspect that most of them don't want me for a special friend either—the thought of my participating in a 3:00 A.M. bull session in a dorm rather boggles the mind.[9] Both of us are perfectly content to base our interactions on well-defined role and category boundaries. This is what Tajfel called "intergroup behavior."

When behavior is largely intergroup, SIT makes a strong prediction about the effects of decategorization. Recall the theory's suggestion that our social identities are anchored in identifications with various groups. Knowing that we are similar to members of outgroups threatens not only our identities, but (indirectly) our sense of self-worth. To the extent that breaking down category boundaries leads to feelings of increased similarity with outgroup members (and that this is threatening), people in each group will be motivated to develop even stronger notions of distinctiveness with consequent devaluation of the other group. Thus SIT predicts that decategorization has the potential for increasing rather than decreasing prejudice.[10]

This model rests on a string of assumptions, none of which is obviously correct or unambiguously supported empirically. However, it does make one clear and important prediction that has received empirical support: When categories are salient, generalization from positive encounters with group members to the group as a whole are enhanced (Brown, Vivian, & Hewstone, 1999). Also, when intergroup categorization is strong, quality of contact is positively associated with lessened bias (Greenland & Brown, 1999).

The Challenge of Diversity. We should also note that, for better or worse, the idea of preserving group boundaries plays into attempts to deal with racial and other forms of diversity. Desegregation does not guarantee integration (Pettigrew, 1988), and there are important distinctions between assimilation and integration (Berry, 1984). In the former, attempts are made to reduce group differences, usually by requiring minority group members to adopt the features of the majority culture. The metaphor most often used for assimilation is the "melting pot." In integration, group differences are maintained, with some attempts made to increase understanding of these differences and to harmonize them at the behavioral level. Perhaps the relevant metaphor for integration ought to be a "stew" instead of a "melting pot," because a stew maintains the integrity of the ingredients while blending the best of their flavors.

Historically, the United States (and most other Western countries) has used an assimilation or melting pot model. Immigrants were expected to give up their native languages and dress, and generally to conform to mainstream American customs. Although one can, in selected cities, find pale reflections of differences between Italian and Portuguese Americans (to name just two groups), generally Americans have managed to erase such boundaries. Political conservatives largely still adopt the assimilation perspective ("Jews learned to behave like Americans; why can't those blacks or Cubans?"), while liberals are more inclined to lean on integration models. Although it is easy for some liberals to mock the assimilation model, it is far from clear that the model is an old-fashioned and outmoded recipe. After all, Americans have managed to avoid most of the ethnic conflict that infects so many countries today. The issues are more complex than either liberals or conservatives admit, in part because they involve a hodgepodge of values and empirical issues that are hard to sort out.

Though diversity programs vary considerably, those focused in the workplace and in universities typically preach the importance of getting people to respect the ways groups differ and to try to understand the basis for these differences. To be sure, in most programs a fair amount of emphasis is also placed on discovering commonalities, but the fact remains that members of minority groups often insist that those in the majority culture respect or at least respectfully tolerate the cultural heritage they bring to the situation. It seems that as many people have worked to break down racial categories, there has been a corresponding movement among some members of minority groups to assert their own racial identities and to be proud of features the majority culture frowns on.[11]

Most white Americans genuinely believe that they are unprejudiced and that they try to treat everyone fairly—that is, without regard to racial identity. Yet there is a price to be paid by minority group members. For example, Hispanics may be treated equitably so long as they speak English rather than Spanish, dress more or less like white middle-class Americans, and generally behave in ways that do not threaten middle-class values and sensibilities. But for many Hispanics this is a bad bargain, because they are forced not just to give up but to abrogate an important source of their identities. To the extent that this is true, it is no wonder, from an SIT perspective, that many members of this group respond by acting even more Hispanic than before. This is surely not limited to racial issues. At least some gay males and lesbians consciously act out stereotypic behaviors as a way of waving identity flags, and long-time foreigners in many countries often form groups that allow them to celebrate their home countries' customs and to speak their own languages. History provides many examples of contrasting clothing styles adopted by members of various religions in an effort to reinforce group distinctions, and for some religions that developed in the Middle East, male circumcision has also been a badge of identity.

Obviously, one important side effect of any approach that recognizes existing group boundaries is that stereotypes of people in the other group will be enhanced. Wolsko, Park, Judd, and Wittenbrink (2000) investigated this very possibility. After reading a statement that stressed racial "color-blindness" (an assertion that at the core, all people are alike) or multicultural ideology (a call for learning to respect racial differences), white subjects rated blacks. There was greater stereotyping in the multicultural condition, although it did produce lessened ingroup positivity compared to a control condition. Correlations between participants' ranking of values and the perceived ranking of blacks was higher in the color-blind than in the diversity condition, but subjects were also more accurate in judging the attributes of blacks in the diversity condition. Finally, subjects in the diversity condition tended to reply on their stereotypes more than those in the color-blind condition. When people focus attention on the features of an outgroup, especially those that may make the outgroup different from the ingroup, it is no surprise that they have a clearer and more accurate sense of what the outgroup is like, but also see the members of the outgroup as less like themselves and perhaps more homogeneous. Under some circumstances this might be good, but it is hard to argue for general success. On the other hand, in fairness, most diversity-based programs go well beyond emphasizing differences and try to change perceptions that these differences are necessarily negative, and this latter step was not tested in this study.

THE COMMON-INGROUP-IDENTITY MODEL

Sam Gaertner, Jack Dovidio, and their colleagues (Anastasio, Bachman, Gaertner, & Dovidio, 1997; Gaertner & Dovidio, 2000; Gaertner et al., 1994) have proposed the common-ingroup-identity (CII) model. This model has deep roots in the conflict model of Sherif (discussed in Chapter 7, and earlier in this chapter). Recall Sherif's argument that one solution to the all but inevitable intergroup conflict (and subsequent stereotyping and prejudice) that arises when people are placed into potentially competing groups is to create superordinate goals—goals that require joint participation rather than competition. The model also has strong affinities with the SIT and self-categorization theory (SCT) approaches.

The CII model suggests that one way to reduce ingroup bias is for members of different groups to see themselves as having a general superordinate identity that can include them both. In other words, people are recategorized rather than decategorized. This model is a familiar and comfortable one for most Americans, and has become a part of U.S. political rhetoric. Politicians often assert that "No matter what our political persuasion or race or religion, we are all Americans," and those who have seen service on the front lines of racial battles have also often tried to make common goals and identities salient.

There are two main reasons why emphasizing common identity ought to be effective (see Chapter 7). First, ingroup bias is largely based on positive bias toward the ingroup rather than hostility toward the outgroup, so that creating a new superordinate ingroup identity reaps psychological rewards with few costs. Second, members of ingroups frequently see themselves as having similar beliefs and values, and this too should enhance positive feelings for superordinate ingroup members, even if they were previously seen as part of an outgroup.

Several studies support the CII model in broad outline. Early research by Gaertner and his colleagues (Gaertner, Mann, Dovidio, Murrell, & Pomare, 1990; Gaertner, Mann, Murrell, & Dovidio, 1989) suggested that when people from different groups are encouraged to recategorize themselves into one superordinate group, bias toward the former other groups is reduced because of an increase in liking for former outgroup members. Creating a superordinate group also tends to increase intimacy of self-disclosure to outgroup members and to facilitate helping them (Dovidio, Gaertner, et al., 1997). In a study of a large multiethnic high school (Gaertner et al., 1994), students who felt that the students were part of a larger unit had less ingroup ethnic bias than those who did not. English-speaking Canadian military officers are less negative toward French speakers when their common identity as Canadian Forces officers is emphasized (Guimond, 2000).

The CII model does not suggest that recategorization is a panacea. The model agrees with SCT that if recategorization results in threats to previous ingroup identity, ingroup bias may be increased rather than decreased. Thus it is often helpful to keep ingroup identities salient at the same time as superordinate identities are also stressed (Hornsey & Hogg, 2000a, 2000b). It may also be helpful to stress different roles for members from the two groups (Deschamps & Brown, 1983) and to differentiate areas of expertise (Dovidio, Gaertner, & Validzic, 1998).

There are potential problems when groups of unequal status join together (Brewer, 2000). For example, members of low-status groups may resist recategorization if it means that they will have low status in the newly formed group (Seta, Seta, & Culver, 2000). Moreover, memberships in superordinate categories may be inherently less stable and salient than membership in smaller groups (Brewer, 2000). Although I may find common ground with members of the mechanical engineering department at my university when we pursue common goals, most of the time and for most things that concern me most directly, they will remain competitors for scare resources. More broadly, though I may often think of myself as a member of the faculty of Rice University, my identity as a member of the Psychology Department is likely to be more salient on a day-in-and-day-out basis.

PERSONALIZATION AND SOCIAL IDENTITY

There are important differences among the personalization, impression continuum, SIT, and CII approaches (e.g., Johnston & Hewstone, 1990), but I think the disagreements are, in practice, more apparent than real. For one thing, as I have explained it, the personalization and interdependency models seem to work best when behavior is largely interpersonal, whereas the SIT and CII predictions probably work best when interactions are based on group identities. Since these are assumed to be endpoints of a continuum, a given interaction can be either or some of both. It remains an open question which mode of behavior is most effective in reducing general stereotyping. Interpersonal behavior seems like a good bet, but we ought to be aware that such a mode may lead to changes that do not readily generalize (see above). On a day-to-day basis it may be quite important for Darnel and Joe to see each other as more than the result of their racial categories, but at the end of the day, when each thinks about larger racial groups, they will each have to think of the other in terms of race.

It is worth reemphasizing the point made by the CII model: One can have one's cake and eat it too, in the sense that it is possible to emphasize larger superordinate identities while not deemphasizing previous identities. In labor disputes, both labor unions and management can recognize their own well-honed interests while still finding common ground in the larger goal of keeping a company alive and flourishing (Haley, 2001). Some cities have allowed issues of racial identity to boil over into overt racial conflict, while others have managed to create a larger sense of identity without ignoring racial differences. This is not necessarily easy to achieve, and may require juggling rhetoric as well as real goals and outcomes. Still, when it works, it works well.

The Problem of Typicality

Contact between members of groups usually takes place one person at a time, and the kinds of interactions likely to produce the kinds of intimacy and friendship that are crucial for effective contact are dyadic. The house of tolerance is built one brick at a time. So far, so good.

THE TYPICALITY PARADOX

However, it has long been recognized that often contacts with individuals from an outgroup do not generalize to the group as a whole (see Hewstone, 1994; McClendon, 1974; Rothbart, 1996). In fact, it may be less common to show such generalization than not. The fly in this ointment is often typicality. The typicality paradox is that when a person holds a strong stereotype, an individual who disconfirms it may be seen as unrepresentative of the group and hence no stimulus for general change; the person perceived to be the typical member, on the other hand, may not disconfirm the stereotype. Atypical exemplars may well change perceptions of the dispersion of the group without affecting a feature's perceived central tendency (Garcia-Marques & Mackie, 1999). This is a victory of sorts, but not the one necessarily sought.

Suppose I have a stereotype that mathematicians are shy and unfriendly, and I now meet one who is the life of the party. We might hope that this will count as evidence disconfirming my stereotype, and that I will now think that mathematicians are quite friendly sorts, or at least that they are a diverse lot on this dimension. What could go wrong? Well, for starters, I could well decide that this person I have just met is an atypical mathematician. I may even bolster that with additional evidence that he works in an offbeat branch of the field, and that perhaps his scholarship is really not up to par for his area. Having now decided that he is atypical, I can place him in a category all to himself. I may even give it a name—"flaky math guys."

Rothbart and John (1985) pointed out that this may be one of the major stumbling blocks to the success of contact: People who don't fit the stereotype may be seen to be atypical of the category and hence provide few relevant data for stereotype disconfirmation. According to their model, disconfirming information may be effective only if it is associated with an otherwise typical member of the category. And in support, research by Rothbart and Lewis (1988) did show that disconfirming evidence associated with an otherwise typical category exemplar produces more change than evidence associated with an atypical exemplar. Moreover, information about typical group members is easier to retrieve than information about typical members (Rothbart, Sriram, & Davis-Stitt, 1996). Exposure to atypical exemplars does lower availability of stereotype information (Macrae, Bodenhausen, Milne, & Castelli, 1999), but this very lack of access may inhibit generalization.

Negotiating the typicality paradox may require a cognitive sleight of hand that does not hide reality from alert minds. When we meet Tom, a person who disconfirms the stereotype of his group, the tendency is to see him as atypical per se. Consequently, the more he disconfirms the stereotype of his group, the less likely he is to instigate change in perceivers. In one instructive study, Hewstone, Hopkins, and Routh (1992) examined attitudes toward police by students in England who had frequent contact with a nice and friendly school liaison officer. Perceptions of the individual officer were quite positive, but the liaison officer was seen as atypical of police in general, and attitudes toward the general police category were unmolested by this contact. Outgroup stereotypes are more easily modified when the outgroup member is seen as typical (Brown et al., 1999) and counterstereotypic behavior is seen as due to dispositional causes (Wilder, Simon, & Faith, 1996).

Another problem relates to our old friends assimilation and contrast (see Chapter 4). Recall that generally evaluations of stimuli are contrasted away from extremely discrepant standards of comparison and assimilated toward more compatible ones, especially when they are seen as part of the same category (Bless, Schwarz, Bodenhausen, & Thiel, 2001). The temptation is often to present an extreme exemplar, a model minority group member, or a person of vast accomplishment built on humble roots. This seems sensible enough. Yet there is obvious potential for contrast backfire, in which the group is "contrasted away" from the exemplar who serves as a standard of comparison. Research by Kunda and Oleson (1997) and Wänke, Bless, and Igou (2001) has found exactly that pattern of results. Research by Borg (1996) suggests that extreme exemplars may be effective only when they emphasize their continuities on other dimensions with the common folk. Clearly, this is tricky stuff.

TYPICALITY AND DISCONFIRMATION

We are not done with discouraging news. Change ought to be greatest when a typical member displays a disconfirming feature. Note, however, that while change may take place for that individual feature, the typical member, by definition, must confirm some (perhaps most) of the other stereotypic features.[12] Thus, according to this model, what contact giveth with one hand it taketh away with the other. When stereotypes are predominantly negative—the case where we are presumably most interested in change—the typical exemplar (who must, by definition, have many unpleasant features) comes with lots of undesirable baggage, and we run the risk of reinforcing the overall negative impression of the group while possibly changing one or two negative features.

As a concrete example, imagine Sarah, who thinks that gay males are effeminate, pretentious, and emotionally immature. If we expose her to a gay man who is none of these things, she will see him as atypical and uninformative about "real" gays. On the other hand, if she meets a man who is effeminate, pretentious, and mature, we might well get her to reconsider her stereotype that gays are immature—but at the considerable risk of reconfirming the rest of her stereotype. That may be a bad bargain indeed.

Mechanisms of Change

As every psychotherapist, teacher, parole office, clergy member, social worker, and parent knows, it is often difficult—indeed, seemingly impossible—to get people to change their fundamental attitudes, values, and ways of thinking about the world. Change ain't easy, and it comes with a hefty price tag of time, effort, and often traumatic inner struggle. When we are trying to change attitudes that have deep roots in culture, other beliefs, and personality dynamics, we are in for tough sledding. Moreover, as we have seen in Chapter 9, many stereotypes do have a kernel of truth, albeit often grossly exaggerated or more in the mind of the perceiver than the target group—so that when we try to change stereotypes and prejudice, we are also up against perceived reality.

What saves us is that for most people, many stereotypes and other bases of prejudice are fairly mild and superficially held. Although many social scientists tend to blur distinctions between people who are prejudiced and proud of it, and those of us whose prejudices are less overt and proudly held, by using one-label-fits-all designations such as "racist" and "sexist," we are on very thin ice psychologically when we implicitly or explicitly assume that the psychological processes creating and maintaining deep prejudices are the same for milder versions.

It might be helpful to imagine two paradigm cases. First, let's consider Buck, a poster child for virulent racism. He hates all minorities and thinks they ought to go back to Africa or wherever the hell they came from. He's convinced that they are, in conjunction with those awful Communist liberals, undercutting American society in ways that make it almost impossible for good people like him and his friends to raise decent families and keep their heads above water economically. Women are entirely out of bounds these days, and Buck gets red in the face when he thinks about all those faggots who are pushing their agendas on him. On it goes. Buck is the bigot we all have learned to hate.

Now let's consider Jennifer. She's a hard-working manager of a clothing store. She says she doesn't think of herself as prejudiced, but will admit that she doesn't really feel comfortable around people from minority groups, especially those who don't speak English well. And she suggests, perhaps a bit too readily, that almost all the shoplifters she has caught in the last several years have been black or Hispanic. She knows that these folks don't have much money, but she is running a business and not a welfare agency. She also says that she really doesn't know any Hispanics well, but she does know and like that lovely black family in her neighborhood who are just like white people. She likes to think she's pretty tolerant, but her religion demands her to draw the line at those homosexuals, although she doesn't know any and doesn't want to.

Now let's do a thought experiment and imagine how we might change their attitudes. Would we design the same campaign for the two of them? On the face, of it that seems fairly silly. What might we do to change Jennifer? Although there are hints in what she says that some of her attitudes and beliefs have deep roots, mostly they seem to be fairly superficial. She has a negative view of Hispanics, based on a few shoplifting incidents and perhaps on what she has read or seen in the media. Clearly, if we could just have Jennifer meet a few Hispanics—perhaps ones who share many of her values—she might change her mind. There is a hint that she might be amenable to that, because she seems to like a black family who fits that profile. But she doesn't seem to have generalized very much from her experiences with this one family. Though she doesn't say so directly, she seems to regard them as an exception to her stereotypes. In that case, we might want to expose Jennifer to a wider range of minority people, although we run the risk of having her confirm some of her stereotypes when she meets some people who are less likely to share her values and behavior patterns. The problem here is that she is using her own well-socialized values and behavior patterns to evaluate members of another group, and such value foundations are surely difficult to change. Her attitudes about gay men and lesbians also seem to have a large element of moral revulsion driving them. But again we might find that contact with a few exemplars might change her mind or at least increase her comfort level. The good news is that Jennifer seems mildly uncomfortable with her stereotypes and prejudices, and just might change them if we push the right buttons.

And what about Buck? Here we are tempted to say that we ought not even to waste our time or the taxpayers' money. He is proud of his prejudices. We imagine that every favorable comment we try to make about racial minorities, women, or homosexuals will be met with claims that we pointy-headed liberals don't live in the real world and see what he sees. And, you know, his daddy brought him up to be a God-fearing man and to respect American ideals, and all you have to do is look in your Bible to see why he abhors fags, and he can't imagine anything that is a greater affront to what he was taught than those minority people who are lazy, live off welfare, and take advantage of people like him. We suspect that no rational arguments, no data, are going to penetrate his mind—heavily armored as it is by a tempered combination of values, beliefs, and prejudices all designed to defend anxieties and fears, and supported by racist friends. And it is not that Buck's values or beliefs are totally corrupt; in fact, part of the problem is that they are in close enough touch with the realities he inhabits and the values of the larger culture that, with a nudge or two, his experiences lend constant support to his stereotypes. Furthermore, and this may be an even bigger problem, all his beliefs seem to hang together in a perverse sort of way. I suspect that if we were to try to change his beliefs about American ideals—perhaps by showing him that American history is more diverse than he thinks—he would retreat to a notion that American ideals are, after all, founded on values and morals that come straight out of the Bible. And with people like Buck, we can't argue with the Bible. If we could magically get him to change one of his stereotypes (say, that blacks are inherently lazy), that change would reverberate through his cognitive system and force changes elsewhere. And Buck's just happy with his beliefs the way they are, thank you, and scared to change. (See below for a real-life example of how one person like Buck *did* change, however.)

Heretofore we have not delved deeply into the cognitive processes that may underlie change. There are basically two kinds of information that we might present to people to encourage stereotype change. The dominant approach, which we have been discussing, has been to encourage contact with one or more exemplars; however, there are other possibilities, built around notions of rational argument, abstract information, and the like. Those approaches are considered in the next section. But first let's consider explicit models of how people respond to exemplars who disconfirm their stereotypes.

Classically, three general models have been proposed for how this change might take place, and in recent years a fourth model based on exemplar models has been used (Hilton & von Hippel, 1996). As we shall see, these models are quite different in many respects, but they all rely on a model of feature–group associations. Connectionist models of mental representation (Smith, 1996), which assume that features and groups are represented by patterns of activation, can model both stereotype learning (Smith & DeCoster, 1998) and change (Queller & Smith, 2002). More importantly for the present discussion, such models can account for the three primary mechanisms of change discussed in this chapter within the same general model. Unfortunately, here as elsewhere, the devil is in the details—and the details of connectionist models, particularly the distributed models favored by Eliot Smith, go beyond what I can discuss here (see Queller, 2002, for a lucid introduction to the implications of such models for change).

THE CONVERSION MODEL

The conversion model (Rothbart, 1981) suggests that change in the stereotype takes place in a relatively all-or-nothing fashion and relatively suddenly, because some piece of data or exemplar causes the whole belief structure to change. The analogy is, of course, to religious conversions in which some people (like the Biblical St. Paul) seem to find their religious feet in a dramatic way. Such conversions are relatively rare even in the religious realm, and may seem still more so in the area of stereotypes. Although, as Rothbart admits, it is a bit hard to specify the conditions that encourage conversion, it is a reasonable hypothesis that extreme disconfirmations by one or more exemplars would be one necessary condition. We do know that extreme exemplars have a strong effect on the development of stereotypes (Rothbart, Fulero, Jensen, Howard, & Birrell, 1978).

Yet examples of conversions do exist. Studs Terkel (1992) presents an interview with C. P. Ellis, a member of the Ku Klux Klan who publicly fought integration of schools in the North Carolina city where he lived—but then found himself cochairing a committee with Ann Atwater, a leader of the black people in the city. He discovered that both of their children had been rejected in school for their parents' positions, and he came to find that he and Ms. Atwater had a lot in common. He ended up supporting integration, running for the school board, and being elected as an officer of his predominantly black union. Obviously the changes in Mr. Ellis did not happen overnight, but as one reads the interview, one is struck by the radical changes that took place in his thinking over a relatively short time. The shifting of his mental gears is almost audible.

THE BOOKKEEPING MODEL

A second model described by Rothbart (1981) is the bookkeeping model. According to this model, each perceiver keeps a kind of mental scorecard on the number of behaviors that are consistent or inconsistent with the perceiver's stereotypes. When the disconfirming evidence for a stereotype begins to overpower the confirming, then the stereotype will change. Although Rothbart does not spell out the model in this way, it is possible that the strength of the stereotype would mirror the relative proportions of confirming and disconfirming evidence. This model makes a certain amount of sense, but it does depend on people's abilities to monitor fairly and accurately the information they have, and to code incoming information without substantial bias.

THE SUBTYPING MODEL

A third model, added by Weber and Crocker (1983), is the subtyping model. This is really a model of how change is resisted, and it addresses the typicality paradox directly. As incongruent information comes in, individuals who do not readily fit the stereotype will be placed in a distinct subtype of atypical group members. So a person of color who believes that white people are condescending and assertive, and who encounters a kind and meek white man, will recognize him as an exception to the stereotype rule and make a subtype of him: "He's one of the [few] good white guys."

As we have seen throughout this book, there is abundant evidence for the existence of subtypes. Generally subtyping ought to promote perceptions of the larger group's diversity, which in turn might have one of two contrasting effects. On the one hand, information gained from exposure to a person who disconfirms the stereotype might be lost, because the perceiver is used to seeing many people who disconfirm the larger stereotype, at least to a degree. On the other hand, when groups are heterogeneous, a person who strongly disconfirms the stereotype might be seen as fairly typical and information from his or her behavior might be readily incorporated into the stereotype, thus changing it.

The subtyping model does not demand that atypical persons be placed in one of the existing subtypes, but that they be placed in some group that fences them off cognitively from people considered to be more typical.[13] Experimental evidence does suggest that subtyping does protect stereotypes, but that focusing perceivers' attention on the variety of people in a group increases perceptions of group variability and tends to decrease stereotyping (Maurer, Park, & Rothbart, 1995; Park, Wolsko, & Judd, 2001).

EXEMPLAR AND PROTOTYPE MODELS

All of the models just discussed implicitly assume that stereotype information is represented in traditional associative networks. But, as I have previously argued, at least some parts of some stereotypes (and perhaps the majority) are represented in terms of exemplars. According to such models, a perceiver who uses a stereotype must access one or more relevant exemplars to form the basis of judgments. A person who thinks of Nobel Prize winner John Nash when thinking of persons with mental illness will have a quite different stereotype than the person who immediately thinks of an incoherent street person. It follows that changing stereotypes can be accomplished by adding exemplars or by affecting which exemplars come to mind (Hewstone & Lord, 1998).

When people encounter a prototypic member of a group, their attitudes toward the category predict behavior toward that individual better than when the person is not prototypic (Lord, Lepper, & Mackie, 1984; Ramsey, Lord, Wallace, & Pugh, 1994). Werth and Lord (1992) applied this kind of model directly to the issue of stereotype change. Subjects met a likeable person with AIDS. Those who had reported that they had an abstract notion of the typical person with AIDS changed their general attitudes more than did those who said they thought of a specific person with AIDS. Presumably, those with an exemplar representation saw the relatively atypical person as just another exemplar to add to the list, whereas those with the more abstract representation were forced to confront discrepant data in a more direct way.

Furthermore, those exemplars who present relatively personalized information about themselves (thus presumably inhibiting forming links between the person and the group) elicited less stereotype change than exemplars who present equivalent information in a relatively impersonal way (Scarberry et al., 1997). And exemplars who are explicitly chosen to represent their groups—a condition that ought to foster links to the group—also elicit more change (Desforges et al., 1997).

EXPERIMENTAL EVIDENCE

Which model best describes stereotype change? Generally, the conversion model predicts that having the disconfirming information concentrated in one individual should produce the strongest conversion effects, because such information is striking and vivid. The subtyping model suggests that when disconfirming evidence is concentrated in relatively few strongly disconfirming individuals who can be subtyped as exceptions to the rule, stereotype change should be retarded. Put another way, disconfirming evidence should have the most impact when spread across several individuals. The bookkeeping model doesn't care who has the disconfirming evidence, so long as there is a lot of it.

Research (e.g., Hewstone, Hassebrauck, Wirth, & Wänke, 2000; Johnston &

Hewstone, 1992; Johnston, Hewstone, Pendry, & Frankish, 1994; Weber & Crocker, 1983) consistently shows that change is greatest when disconfirming evidence is dispersed across several group members rather than concentrated in a few, although there is often some reduction in stereotyping even in the concentrated condition. Thus the subtyping model is generally most strongly supported. Further supporting this model is evidence that people pay more attention to atypical group members, especially when the group is fairly homogeneous (Verplanken, Jetten, & van Knippenberg, 1996). Moreover, when inconsistent information is concentrated in a few members, they are seen as atypical of the group and clearly placed in subtypes, as the subtyping model predicts (Hantzi, 1995; Johnston & Hewstone, 1992; Johnston et al., 1994). When information is presented in blocked form (all information about Person A, then all about Person B, etc.)—a condition that should foster subtyping—stereotyping is greater than when person information is more dispersed (Hewstone, Macrae, Griffiths, & Milne, 1994).

The subtyping process requires deliberation. Simply knowing that a homosexual male unstereotypically loves country music is not sufficient in and of itself to place him into a subtype. However, additional information, even if not particularly relevant, may aid the formation of subtypes. For example, if I were to discover that the a gay Waylon Jennings fan also grew up in Texas, then I could more easily relegate him to a subtype of Texas cowboy gay males. Kunda and Oleson (1995) showed that a category member who exhibited a single stereotype-inconsistent trait led to some change in the stereotype for that trait, but that if additional neutral information was also presented, consequent subtyping retarded change. Because subtyping requires reflection, it takes time and cognitive resources. Consequently, people who are distracted while processing stereotype-inconsistent information tend to change stereotypes more (Yzerbyt, Coull, & Rocher, 1999), presumably because they cannot subtype atypical exemplars.

One advantage of dispersing information across more group members is that they will be perceived as less deviant, but this makes each a less extreme version of the stereotyped group. It is hard to know whether the spread of information or perceptions of extremeness create the dispersion effects. Kunda and Oleson (1997) found that more moderate deviants not only led to more change of the general stereotype, but that extreme deviants could even lead to a boomerang effect and strengthen the stereotype (see above). This could occur because of contrast effects or because extreme deviance leads to active bolstering of the stereotype through attempts at recruiting stereotype-consistent information. In this regard, Kunda and Oleson note that extremity may very much be in the eye of the beholder. A gay male who is slightly masculine may seem more extremely deviant to a homophobic person who strongly believes that gay males are effeminate than to someone with a less extreme stereotype.

THE MEDIA, EDUCATION, AND PLANNED INTERVENTIONS

When social scientists discuss changing prejudice, they almost always emphasize some form of the contact hypothesis. However, even if contact were maximally effective, it would suffer from three major practical problems, one major theoretical limitation, and a rather strange conceptual issue. It is not the complete answer to our prayers and never can be.

Practical Problems

In a way, the extensive research on change has been held captive by somewhat naive views about the nature of intergroup contact. Contact is not always friendly or enlightening. To be sure, sometimes we can manage diversity in ways that increase its effectiveness, but often we cannot. There are three important resultant practical problems—selective interaction, accuracy, and realistic group conflict.

Highly Selective Contact in Everyday Life

We know little about the importance of voluntary versus involuntary contact, although it seems intuitively likely that the former is more likely to reduce prejudice. The fact of the matter is that most contact situations studied by social scientists have been more or less involuntary (the military, schools, etc.), and although we can force different sorts of people to rub shoulders, we cannot make them learn from one another. Even if we increasingly come into contact with people who are unlike us in various ways, there is no way to guarantee that we will develop the kinds of relationships with these others that would make contact effective. This is not a problem of avoidance, but of simple social pragmatics. I know very little about the vast majority of people I come into contact with every day. I socialize with some of my colleagues, but barely know the names of spouses of the others. The African American woman who empties my wastebasket every morning is pleasant enough, and we sometimes joke with one another—but now that I think about it, I don't have a clue as to whether she's married, has children, is religious, or is politically liberal.

Even so, despite recent attempts to provide more diverse work and educational environments, many of us have considerable discretion about whom we get to know well. Most of us work with, live near, go to religious services with, and spend our free time with people very much like us. And generally we prefer it that way, because it is safe and easy. We are often able to avoid people for whom we have negative stereotypes (Henderson-King & Nisbett, 1996), to interact with people who are different from us only in environments that level our differences, and even to selectively seek information that supports our stereotypes (Johnston, 1996).

The Accuracy Devil

The contact hypothesis was built largely around the idea that features are incorrectly ascribed to group members. But what if a stereotype is accurate? There is no doubt that for almost any stereotype we care about there is disconfirming evidence to be had, and it is important to remember that the accuracy of some stereotypes may be so low as to provide meaningless support for holding them tightly to the breast. Still, we should recognize that many stereotypes may be hard to change because they're perceived to be true (whether or not they are), and we are especially reluctant to change beliefs we think are based on reality. It's bound to take more than a few experiences to defeat perceived reality, which holds the high ground and is heavily armored. The good news is that if stereotypes are based on some version of reality, they are apt to change as groups of people change because their roles and situational constraints do. For example, people think gender differences are changing as a result of changing gender roles (Diekman & Eagly, 2000). However, in the short run, contact can reinforce stereotypes unless people are encouraged to understand the reasons for the features of group members.

Realistic Conflict

Many of our stereotypes, and especially those that seem most emotion-laden and important, operate in the service of supporting our own side in intergroup conflict. It is surely no accident that in time of war, negative stereotypes about the enemy proliferate. As I wrote the first draft of this chapter, U.S. forces were charging around Afghanistan trying to destroy what was left of the former rulers, the Taliban. And I (who think of myself as a tolerant kind of guy) and other Americans found ourselves dwelling on all the misdeeds of that group and what the media have portrayed as its medieval mentality. It's hard to imagine that it could be otherwise.

The problem is, of course, that when stereotypes are based even in small part on group conflict, they may be almost impossible to change. Religious, political, and business authorities may censor messages favorable to other groups, and people who seem even remotely accepting of counterstereotypic information will be seen as disloyal or unpatriotic. In our laboratories we often study stereotypes that are devoid of group conflict overtones, and so we may miss the important point that stereotypes that are so anchored may be almost impossible to change.

A Theoretical Concern

An even more fundamental issue has largely been overlooked by social scientists. By way of getting at this issue, let me once again pose a recurring question: What are we trying to change? Well, stereotypes and prejudices. But, as I have argued, stereotypes and prejudices are not simple things that change in one direction along one dimension. Each has several components, which surely are differentially responsive to different aspects of information. Saying that we want to change a stereotype is about as vague and useless as saying that we want to fix a car. We get points for good intentions, but unless we know what we're trying to fix, we're not likely to get the job done efficiently. The tools we use will depend on what we're trying to fix. There are at least five aspects of stereotypes we might want to change: category–feature relationships, affect, perceived homogeneity, theories, and behavioral consequences.

Category–Feature Relationships

MULTIPLE FEATURES

Most of the stereotypes we most care about have a large (perhaps uncountable) number of features, which tend to be locked together in complex ways. What are we to do with a male manager (other than fire him) who refuses to hire women because, in his view, they are numerically challenged, more concerned with their children than with work responsibilities, prone to emotional outbursts (especially at certain periods), and inclined to pass along disruptive gossip? We can find plenty of female workers who fail all or pass all of these tests, but it is also likely that some of the women he hires will disconfirm some of these stereotypic features while confirming others. Contact does not guarantee that all stereotypic features will be equally disconfirmed.

THE NATURE OF THE ASSOCIATION

I and nearly everyone else who has written about stereotypes assume that stereotypes are, among other things, relationships of features to categories. But what does that mean? When we want to change Megan's stereotype that lawyers are greedy, are we trying to get her to be slower to access "greedy" when she thinks of lawyers, get her to replace "greedy" with "not greedy" in her dictionary of associations, help her understand that lawyers are no more greedy than other people, lower her estimate of the percentage of lawyers who are greedy, and/or lower her percentage of greedy people who are lawyers? In many cases, we may not have the luxury of worrying about such matters; we'll take whatever change we can get. But presumably these different aspects of stereotypes play through our cognitive systems in different ways and may predict different forms of behavior. At some point, the "what" of change may become as important as the "how."

FEATURES ARE NOT EQUALLY DISCONFIRMABLE

Once we recognize that stereotype features are not alike, we must also face the strong possibility that some stereotypes features may be harder to change than others. To use an extreme example, it would surely be easier to change Kai's stereotype that Italians are emotional than that they speak Italian.

There are many reasons why some features are harder to change than others. As we will see in Chapter 14, there may be large differences in the essential disconfirmability of features. For example, abstract features tend to be more invulnerable to change. Maass, Montalcini, and Biciotti (1998) have shown that many negative features of outgroup stereotypes are cognitively represented in an abstract manner that makes them more difficult to change. Furthermore, those outgroups that are the oldest (and perhaps most strongly supported by the culture) tend to have the most abstract negative features. Arguably, then, for the groups we are most concerned with, the features we most want to change will present the most difficult challenge.

Chapters 4 and 5 have emphasized the importance of examining the structure of stereotypes—the glue that holds stereotypes together. Obviously, for example, if Victoria thinks that rudeness strongly implies violence, it may be hard to change one trait independently of the other. Queller and Smith (2002) have argued that such strong interfeature relationships can retard change of either feature. In particular, reductions of stereotypes that include sets of mutually supportive features should be strongest when the disconfirming information is dispersed across many exemplars (e.g., some rude but nonviolent and some violent but polite people). On the other hand, encountering people in the group who are neither rude nor violent (concentrated) may actually retard change, because it actually strengthens the perceived correlation between the two traits. Although Queller and Smith were concerned only with the patterns of feature and group relationships, I would add that stereotype features that are strongly embedded in a theory about stereotypes should also be harder to change.

As we have seen throughout this book, stereotypes are dynamic, and the salience of features changes from context to context. In particular, features that seem to discriminate two groups of interest tend to be played up in stereotypes (see Chapter 3), and such features are also the hardest to change (Wyer, Sadler, & Judd, 2002).

Affect

Some stereotypes are emotionally cool, and others are hot. I have little ego, affect, or emotion invested in my stereotypes about circus clowns, but I care a great deal more about my stereotypes about professors or political conservatives. We should not assume that interventions that change either affect or beliefs will necessarily work on the other (Asuncion & Mackie, 1996). In one instructive example, Trafimow and Gannon (1999) found that although Christian males rated Jews higher than Christians on various positive traits, they were not enthusiastic about having their daughters marry a Jew. Furthermore, indications of willingness to have their daughters marry a prospective male were positively correlated with trait ratings for Christian suitors but were not for Jewish swains.

Contact may well be the best way to change affective associations to groups. One supposes (although this has never been tested) that pleasant experiences with several members of a group may produce generally positive feelings about that group, even if specific stereotypes connected to the group are unmolested. Furthermore, hearing about or seeing the pain and hardships inflicted by one's own or others' discriminatory behavior may mitigate negative affect and lead to a deeper consideration of one's own stereotypes.

Tendencies toward Discrimination

As we have seen in Chapter 8, discrimination has lots of flavors: direct and indirect, deliberate and unintended, institutional and individual. People with impoverished stereotypes and hollow prejudices can still discriminate, and one goal of change attempts might simply be to get people to recognize the range of discriminatory behaviors they are apt to perform. A related goal might be to help people understand that their own behaviors may inadvertently discriminate, and that even seemingly innocuous behaviors may be perceived to be biased by those affected.

On the reverse side, people with active stereotypes and conscious prejudices need not discriminate, and may not if situational or personal factors inhibit such behavior or if they do not want to. Some people who are aware of their prejudices may feel guilty about discriminating, which they see as unjust. There are several measures of people's motivations to control their prejudices (e.g., Dunton & Fazio, 1997; Plant & Devine, 1998), which I have discussed in Chapter 8. Here I merely stress that changing both people's abilities to recognize the effects of their behaviors on others and their desires to act in accord with their values of fair play are potentially effective routes to reducing the behavioral effects of prejudice and stereotypes.

Diversity and Homogeneity

Reducing perceptions of group homogeneity is certainly an important aspect of stereotype reduction (Brewer & Miller, 1988; Hewstone & Hamberger, 2000). At first blush, it might seem that contact would be especially useful in conveying messages about diversity among groups. Yet further consideration suggests many reasons for caution. There are at least three major problems. The first is that perceptions of heterogeneity ideally require diversity of contact, and as I have already suggested, most of us are limited in how many different types of people with whom we have meaningful contact. I may know one or two black businesspeople or lawyers, but no black construction workers, ministers, athletes, welfare mothers, or fashion models.

Second, the very limitations of my contacts are likely to encourage subtyping. I may be well aware that my black physician does not fit the general stereotype of black males, but then fence him off from what I imagine as more prototypic blacks. Reinforcement of subtyping is not a good recipe for diminishing stereotypes.

Third, most interactions with others—especially those that cross important group lines—are heavily governed by situational norms and roles. Say I have lunch twice a week with Joan, whom I take to be a prototypic career woman; while I find her personable, helpful, and not at all aggressive (although she does make deliciously biting and witty observations about our coworkers), I discover little about her marriage, the two children she once casually mentioned having, or what she does with her spare time. Apparently Joan has learned an important lesson: Women who talk about their personal lives at work are perceived to be less than dedicated to their careers. All our interactions with most people we know are constrained by situational factors, but members of minority and other disadvantaged groups often experience the additional burden of "acting white" or adhering to situational norms especially slavishly.[14]

As I have stressed throughout the book, getting people to see that groups are heterogeneous has important practical consequences. For instance, we may not be able to convince Betty that black men are not violent because she knows as a matter of fact that they are, at least in comparison to whites. What we can hope to achieve is for her to recognize that the majority of black males have never committed major acts of violence and are as pacific as most whites. If we can make this a part of Betty's working knowledge, then we might affect her tendency to behave in cautious and unfriendly ways to black males, and even encourage her to give black males the same benefit of the doubt in the parking lot of a mall as she would a white male. Alternatively, we might get her to focus on cues for potential violence other than skin color—features that would alert her to potential problems with men of any color. Maybe we can get her to pay closer attention to situational cues. Or we might consider it a partial victory if we can get her to understand that there are strong cues for lack of violent tendencies. What we want to achieve in any case is a reduction in Betty's tendency to infer violence proneness from a stereotype that applies to black men but that fits only a minority of them.

Theory Change

Theory change is even more important. Theories about groups are always extremely important, but particularly when they are blessed with perceived truth. It is not so much that people have a secure hold on realities as that they hold on to those realities they have secured. For example, black men are comparatively violent, but the reasons for this are complex (and importantly so).[15] Understanding the interaction of personal, cultural, and situational causes of violence helps to humanize the violent person. But it also leads to a deeper understanding that can produce ways to distinguish the minority of violent blacks from the majority of nonviolent ones, and in that sense it produces a stable sense of group heterogeneity.

It is crucially important to assist people in understanding the reasons for group differences and the features associated with different groups. Theories promote stability of perceptions of features associated with groups as well as the diversity of group members, and changing theories helps to stabilize whatever changes in the content of stereotypes we might achieve.

For most of us, changing our theories about the world is difficult; they are the ocean liners of our mental life—relatively stable even in the rough seas of changing experience, but hard to steer in a different direction. Theories are well buffered from individual experience, and we usually do not want to change them. Our theories are personal and precious. More to the point in the present context, our theories about groups are not likely to be changed via direct contact with members. Trying to change a theory with a few experiences is like trying to steer an ocean liner with one finger. What we need is real muscle, and in this case that is likely to come in the form of abstract information.

A Conceptual Limitation

Some of the things we might want to change about stereotypes can be nudged one exemplar at a time. But changing perceived homogeneity and theories requires one thing that exemplar contact is not good at providing—namely, abstract information. As I have noted, exemplars are likely to come from too limited a set to be much help for these types of change.

Chapter 9 has discussed the problems television and other media have in providing representative exemplars, and this is the same problem in somewhat different garb. For instance, Hazel believes that mentally ill people are dangerous and unpredictable. We could, of course, expose her to kind and gentle persons with schizophrenia, but such limited exposure is not likely to give her much insight into the full range of diversity among people with mental illness. At best, it is likely to reinforce what she probably already knew—namely, that not all mentally ill people are dangerous. But how are we to expose her to the complexities of mental illness, exemplar by exemplar? She needs to know not only that most mentally ill people are not dangerous, but that many hold down jobs and have families; some are delusional, but others are not; medications are crucial mediators of their behavior; seemingly bizarre behavior is not always dangerous; some of these persons are hostile to family members but not friends; and different situations provoke hostility from different folks. Although contact can provide vivid examples of all these things and more, a few (which is all Hazel is likely to encounter) cannot give her a full sense of the lives of mentally ill people. Nor can they do much to give her a theory about mental illness and its relationships to hostility and other features.

Mechanisms

Sometimes we have to give people a boost in their attempts to understand other groups, and one traditional way to explore this is through well-documented social influence techniques. Broadly speaking, there are two routes by which social influence might change stereotypes. One is via campaigns that focus on information and emotion—the kinds of appeals that generally fall under the rubric of persuasion or attitude change. The second is through explicit or implicit social pressure. There are no hard and fast distinctions between the two. The attitude change literature tends to deal with fairly explicit attempts to get other people to change, whereas the social influence literature deals with less formal attempts.

Persuasion

TYPES OF PROCESSING

There is now general agreement that there are two basic routes to attitude change. Shelly Chaiken and her colleagues (e.g., Chaiken, Liberman, & Eagly, 1989) distinguish between "systematic" and "heuristic" processing, and Petty and Cacioppo (1986) distinguish between "central" and "peripheral" approaches. For present purposes these distinctions are identical, and I use the language of the former.

One way, called the systematic (or central) route, assumes that the target carefully considers new information in light of his or her old beliefs. That does not mean that the processing is rational, but at least it is careful and systematic. The target will be sensitive to the quality and number of arguments presented; because attention has been given to the information, it will be well remembered, and if change does take place it is likely to be fairly permanent. Heuristic (or peripheral) processing occurs when the person relies more on superficial cues that may have been associated with reliable information in the past. Such cues might include how attractive and prestigious the communicator is and whether the message is presented in a lively manner. Since relatively little attention is given to the message as such, its details are likely to be forgotten, and any change that occurs will be superficial and short-lived.

Obviously, it is generally desirable to try to achieve change through the systematic route, but that is not always possible. For this approach to be effective, the target has to be motivated to pay attention to the communication and must have the ability to process what may be quite complex information. Motivation does not come easily in the domain of concern here. Buck, our quintessential racist, is not going to be highly motivated to listen to a speech attacking his cherished views; even if we could get him to listen, he might lose interest or otherwise not be motivated to process the information deeply. Ability is also sometimes a difficult commodity. Unfortunately, understanding many of the arguments we would want to make about various stereotypes requires some intellectual sophistication.

MOTIVATIONAL AND AFFECTIVE FACTORS

The contact hypothesis has tended to incorporate the charming Platonic assumption that if only people knew the truth they would abide by it. Yet most modern psychologists agree that most of us generally do not change our beliefs unless we are motivated to do so. Some of our stereotypes may be deeply embedded in our cognitive systems and resistant to change because they are related to central values, goals, and fears (Lambert, Chasteen, Khan, & Manier, 1997). We may also have a high need for cognitive closure, which encourages us to seize upon any relevant explanation for events and people, and to freeze our beliefs around that explanation (Kruglanski, 1989a; Kruglanski & Webster, 1996). Time pressure may lead to such freezing, but a need to be accurate may help us unfreeze stereotypes (Kruglanski & Freund, 1983).

In Chapter 9 I have argued that stereotypic beliefs and prejudice may fulfill many cognitive functions. Attempts to change people may be most effective when the information speaks to the underlying reasons they hold a stereotype (Snyder & DeBono, 1987). Jake, whose stereotype about homosexuals relates to his strong religious views, may be motivated to change by different sorts of information than Marian, whose stereotypes are based more on what she considers to be realistic fears that her son will be molested by bands of roving gay pedophiles. Several studies (e.g.,

DeBono, 1987; Pryor, Reeder, & McManus, 1991) have shown that persuasion is more effective when the message is tailored to underlying functional support for attitudes.

Other factors may also motivate more systematic processing. For example, Maio, Bell, and Esses (1996) argue that many people have ambivalent attitudes about racial minorities, and that this ambivalence should both motivate people to process information about race systematically and give them the ability to deal with it more deeply. In support, they found that subjects who were more ambivalent were more responsive to a manipulation of argument strength—a variable that should be related to systematic processing.

CONSIDERING THE ALTERNATIVE

Another way to encourage systematic processing is to get people to elaborate the alternative perspective. The act of constructing reasons why the other position might be correct not only inhibits active counterarguing, but may induce the kinds of elaboration that encourage theory building. People develop theories to explain relationships among variables, and the development of such theories leads them to resist considering alternative points of view (Anderson, Lepper, & Ross, 1980). Having people consider different causal models for events lowers adherence to any one theory (Anderson, 1982; Lord, Lepper, & Preston, 1984). Although these studies have not explicitly dealt with stereotypes, they suggest that when stereotypes are supported by theories about groups people have learned or constructed, having people consider alternative models might be effective in creating more flexible explanatory models. Research along these lines that has dealt more directly with stereotyping also suggests that having people engage in counterstereotypic imagery can reduce implicit stereotypes and prejudice, usually considered to be impervious to easy change (Blair, Ma, & Lenton, 2001).

Direct and Indirect Social Influence

Under a wide variety of conditions, most of us will go with the social flow. There are no great mysteries about why this occurs. We are influenced by others because we want them to like or approve of us and because we think they have a superior handle on reality. Whereas attitude change typically requires presentation of some explicit communication, conformity processes may occur without any deliberate attempts at change. In some cases this social influence is fairly direct and the targets are perfectly aware that they are conforming, but in other cases the conformity may be quite unconscious.

DIRECT SOCIAL INFLUENCE

Conformity processes have been actively studied by social psychologists since at least the 1930s. The basic lesson is quite clear: People will do what others tell them, sometimes even when they are being asked to violate deeply held moral standards and convictions. This does not mean that they are mindless robots, because often such conformity occurs only after a fairly detailed processing of options. In any event, as noted in Chapter 9, stereotypes are affected by perceived social realities and consensus.

INDIRECT SOCIAL INFLUENCE

We do not lack for people in this world who exert all sorts of social pressure on others to get them to buy products, obey rules, perform assigned roles. Indeed, such people are central to the social world we inhabit. Still, most of the influence that occurs is not deliberately sought.

Many of our behaviors occur and thoughts pop into our heads from observing others and without much conscious consideration. Prejudicial thinking can be mindless in this way as well. People are less racist when they observe another responding in a nonracist fashion (Blanchard, Crandall, Brigham, & Vaughn, 1994; Blanchard, Lilly, & Vaughn, 1991) or are aware of nonprejudical norms in their groups (Crandall, Eshleman, & O'Brien, 2002); have more positive stereotypes when they see that their group endorses them (Tan et al., 2001); and respond less stereotypically upon finding out that others have less stereotypic views than they do themselves (Stangor, Sechrist, & Jost, 2001). Modeling of counterstereotypic behavior can be an effective change agent (Katz & Walsh, 1991). Even knowledge that a fellow member of an ingroup has a friend in the stereotyped group can promote tolerance (Liebkind & McAlister, 1999; Wright, Aron, McLaughlin-Volpe, & Ropp, 1997). Sometimes the exact opposite occurs, as when hearing or seeing blatant prejudicial behavior makes people less prejudiced, presumably because such behavior makes their own norms of nonprejudicial responding quite salient (Monteith, Deneen, & Tooman, 1996).

Of course, it may be quite pertinent to ask whether such effects represent internalized values or merely suppression of prejudicial responding. One reason why I am not a big fan of political correctness is that it often merely suppresses prejudice to a point where it cannot be confronted directly and (I would hope) changed more fundamentally, Also, overemphasis on political correctness often discourages the kind of open discussion that facilitates intergroup understanding. Nonetheless, we must take our victories where we find them; we can all recognize that social and normative pressures inhibiting overt expressions of prejudice and discrimination do help create an environment that encourages nonprejudicial thinking. In Chapter 9 I have argued that social influence from peers or even unacquainted others is one powerful ways stereotypes get reinforced. Here I suggest the obvious corollary—that either direct or indirect social influence represents an important device for changing both discriminatory behavior and prejudice.

Can the Media Help?

In today's world, television and the movies poke other types of people and cultures into our tidy lives. Even the most middle-class white male lawyer who lives and works in an all-white, mostly male-dominated world untroubled by overt homosexuality or unpleasant disabilities will encounter people of different races, language groups, education levels, sexual orientations, and all the rest if he watches TV or goes to the movies. As I have argued in Chapter 8 that indirect contact has the potential to broaden horizons as well as create stereotypes, and it does both.

Ideally, given the exposure of Americans to television programming, we would hope that the medium would be a major vehicle for disseminating the kinds of information that could substitute for favorable contact. Nonetheless, in Chapter 9 I have suggested several reasons why we cannot depend on the media to undo all the mischief that stereotypes create. The most important reason is that what social scientists wish people to see is less important than what advertisers are willing to support, and advertisers do not wish to move beyond established social realities. Second, such "contact" is likely to go past the very people we most want to change. It is unlikely that a homophobic father is going to encourage or even let his family watch programs with overt gay themes. And even if the family does watch a program that presents gay males in a sympathetic light, one does not need to be a playwright to imagine the dialogue that takes place among family members as the program whizzes by. Third, although television may be selectively able to present counterstereotypic exemplars, individual programs cannot generally present a full range of behaviors characteristic of a given group.

This does not mean that movies and TV cannot effect change. In fact, programs that have used television as a means of providing data for change have often been successful in ameliorating prejudice (Durkin, 1985c; Fishbein, 1996). Even short films with messages designed to reduce prejudice against various groups seem to be effective in lessening bias against racial minorities (Gorn, Goldberg, & Kanungo, 1976), homosexuality (Duncan, 1988), and physical disability (Westervelt & McKinney, 1980). However, these studies were done with school children, measuring short-term change, and we do not know how well such programs might work with adults. Furthermore, these programs almost always employ carefully crafted messages and speak directly to stereotypes in ways that commercial programs cannot easily do.

Are Educational Interventions Effective?

Among the most consistent and powerful correlates of unprejudiced and nonstereotypic thinking are education and information (e.g., Bobo & Kluegel, 1997; Coenders & Scheepers, 1998; Herek & Capitanio, 1996; Lottes & Kuriloff, 1994; Seltzer, 1992; Wagner & Schönbach, 1984; Williams, 1964). Of course, many other variables (e.g., intelligence and socioeconomic status) vary with education, so such correlations cannot be used to prove that education per se reduces prejudice. However, perhaps more in the spirit of faith than proof, it seems perfectly reasonable that education would produce more tolerant thinking, at least in some individuals.

There have been many reports of education and explicit attitude change programs, usually in existing classes at the college or secondary level, that do change attitudes (e.g., Aboud & Levy, 2000; Bigler & Liben, 1992; Gash & Morgan, 1993; Guo, Erber, & Szuchman, 1999; Henderson-King & Stewart, 1999; Irving, 2000; Katz, 1986; Liebkind & McAlister, 1999; Nelson & Krieger, 1997; Oskamp & Jones, 2000; Rudman, Ashmore, & Gary, 2001; Slone, Tarrasch, & Hallis, 2000; Stevenson, 1988; Thomsen, Basu, & Reinitz, 1995). There is little point in describing these interventions in detail, since the exact details of the intervention strategies vary according to group and educational context. However, I do want to highlight two quite different approaches that may be important. One may be effective with invisible stigmas. Many of us often encounter gays and lesbians, people with a history of mental illness, paroled convicts, and people with terminal illnesses without being aware that we have done so. Of course, many such people may choose to reveal their status, but an interesting question arises about what happens when a person who otherwise seems positive and "normal" reveals a stigma. Waldo and Kemp (1997) report that when an introductory psychology instructor revealed he was gay, attitudes toward homosexuality became more positive than in control classes with a nonrevealing instructor.

Second, given the emphasis of this book on stereotypes as theories, it is important to emphasize attempts to change such beasts. As suggested in Chapter 8, Americans (and arguably all Westerners) tend to assign individualistic causes to differences among people; important as these may be, however, there are also important structural causes. Lopez, Gurin, and Nagda (1998) demonstrated not only that a course emphasizing structural reasons for racial inequality resulted in students' greater acceptance of such explanations, but that these lessons generalized to theories about poverty. Changing theories requires a frontal assault; we cannot depend on wars of attrition through continuing exposure to exemplars to do the job.

Some Cautions

Most people, especially social scientists, are deeply committed to the idea that education is important—specifically, in this case, in changing stereotypes and prejudices. I have emphasized several justifications, conceptual and empirical, for that belief. And yet we must be cautious.

Interventions Often Fail

Our first step, as always, should be to examine the data. Although most published studies support the effectiveness of planned interventions, empirical studies often find that they have no or practically trivial effects (e.g., Cotten-Huston & Waite, 2000; Harris, Walters, & Waschull, 1991a; Shamai, 1994; Tuckman & Lorge, 1954), or that they even increase prejudice (Vrij & Smith, 1999). Surprisingly, there is little empirical evidence for the strategy that is most often advocated in school situations—the "Blue Eyes, Brown Eyes" exercise developed by Jane Elliott, a teacher (at the time in rural Iowa). In this exercise, students are divided into groups on the basis of eye color, and one group is given power, rewards, and praise while the other group is treated as inferior. This does produce a simulation of race relations in this country, and students respond to it powerfully. Perhaps because the exercise is so striking and so apparently effective, there have been few attempts to validate its successes empirically. One published attempt (Byrnes & Kiger, 1990) found that the exercise produced little prejudice reduction, even though the students found it highly meaningful.

The Effects Are Limited

Second, these effects are often limited to certain groups of subjects, to some aspects of the stereotype but not others, or to certain subcategories of the larger group. For example, students in one course on human sexuality became more accepting of lesbians, but there were minimal effects for prejudice against gay men (Stevenson & Gajarsky, 1991). A program designed to reduce anti-Semitic attitudes and stereotypes worked for Jewish participants but not for Protestants (Engel, O'Shea, Fischl, & Cummings, 1958). Attempts to change attitudes toward people with AIDS are effective for those who have positive attitudes toward homosexuals, but not for those who are prejudiced (Pryor et al., 1991).

Obviously, none of this is any surprise to those who know the literature on attitude change—an area that also shows remarkable interactions among various causal variables—but we should not lose sight of two important points. The first is that intervention strategies that work for one person may not work for the next one. It is also quite possible that some well-meaning intervention strategies may backfire, at least for some people. It does not strike me as obvious that an attempt to present a positive view of a gay sexual relationship would necessarily convince a moral conservative to be more tolerant of homosexuality; indeed, knowledge that there is widespread approval of such things might create even greater fears and prejudices, because it makes homosexuality seem more real and threatening. Similarly, attempts to demystify mental illness by stressing continuities with normality may only succeed in making normal people anxious about the possibility that they can become mentally ill (Nunnally, 1961).

Short-Term Change versus the Long Haul

A third problem is that almost all of these studies have examined short-term change, typically measuring postintervention attitudes shortly after the intervention. Not surprisingly, programs can produce short-term change that does not persist (Hill & Augoustinos, 2001). Given that stereotypes and prejudices are likely to be reinforced by a number of family, peer, and value pressures, one cannot be overly optimistic that changes effected in a classroom will persist long in the give and take of the real world. Can we really expect that a son of racist parents will suddenly change his attitudes as a result of a unit on tolerance in a social studies class or a speech by his principal? And what should we imagine the reaction of his parents will be when he comes home to show off his new and polished politically correct attitudes? Are we prepared to believe that what happens in the classroom is more important than what happens on the playground or in locker rooms after school?

Let Us Not Be Overly Pessimistic

On the other hand, let us not be too pessimistic about these techniques. In the first place, they are often the only viable strategies open to us; as such, we need to work harder at making them more effective rather than giving up hope. The message of the preceding paragraphs is not that interventions are doomed to failure, but rather that it is tricky to get them right and that the successful ones are likely to be tailored to particular types of individuals in particular situations. We are stuck with the message that people change one by one and often for quite idiosyncratic reasons. This does not mean that our task is impossible, just difficult.

CAN WE SUPPRESS CATEGORIZATION AND STEREOTYPING?

Pressures to Suppress

When we're honest with ourselves, we realize that we've all had those thoughts and feelings. The vague feeling of discomfort when sitting next to a person of a different race. The fleeting (or not so fleeting) thought that "She'd be so pretty if only she'd lose 70 pounds." The assumption that the slick-looking man talking with the woman he has just met is trying to get her into bed. The uncontrolled fear when meeting a dark-skinned man on the street late at night. The nagging suspicion that the Hispanic woman working the technical support desk won't be able to understand the problem. Not inviting an Asian friend for a late-night pizza run because he'll probably want to study. The guarded feeling that a black man may have when with a group of whites.

Yes, we all make stereotypic assumptions and unwittingly make discriminatory judgments. It happens with race. It happens with disability. It happens with occupation. It happens with gender, age, and physical appearance. And it happens just because that's the way it is: Our mental apparatus was designed to facilitate quick decisions based on category membership.

This does not, however, excuse us from the hurt we might cause our targets. Obviously, we should try to keep our errors to a minimum, our bias in its place, and our behavior honorable; some of us are more successful at doing so than others. There are tremendous individual differences in our stereotypes and prejudices, in our willingness to deploy them, and in the extent to which we work to eliminate them.

One of the really unfortunate consequences of race and gender politics in the past generation has been the assumption that large clumps of people are racist or sexist. When these terms are defined broadly, the assumption is true, and it is true of women, racial minorities, and other disadvantaged groups; members of those groups also can and do make stereotypic judgments of others. Yet, in the end, all this labeling is mostly unhelpful because it encourages the withering of hope and responsibility. Moreover, it ignores the changes that have occurred in society and in many individuals, and it fails to honor the hard work that has produced them.

Probably we will make more psychological, moral, and political progress, at least in the short run, by focusing our attention on those people who genuinely want to eliminate stereotypes from their mental lives and discrimination from their behavioral options. But what are such people to do when they discover, often to their horror, that they have unfairly judged another on the basis of group membership? In the long run, of course, they can attempt to rid themselves of this bias. But in the short run? Perhaps the only immediately effective strategy is to use some form of suppression. When one feels a twinge of anxiety or even disgust at learning that a fellow worker is a lesbian, then perhaps one will be motivated to work around these feelings. But is this as easy as it sounds?

Control of Categorization and Stereotyping

I have suggested earlier that some categorizations may be automatic in the sense of being hard, or even impossible, to control. Can we avoid seeing someone as Asian, old, or male? Put in more formal terms, the issue is whether some categorizations are cognitively automatic in the sense of using few cognitive resources, being uncontrollable (or at least unresponsive to intentions), and being largely unconscious. It has generally been assumed (often implicitly) that race, gender, and age categorizations are automatic and difficult if not impossible to control. A lot depends on what we mean by "categorization." If it means simply placing someone in a relevant race, age, or gender category—a kind of primitive identification—then my hunch is that such categorization is automatic. If, on the other hand, we take categorization to indicate placing someone in a meaningful category with some activation of associated features, then this process is likely to be much less automatic (Livingston & Brewer, 2002).

If we assume that category identification is more or less automatic, what about the second line of defense—control over the use of stereotypes associated with categories? Imagine that I have categorized you as a lesbian. Can I avoid assigning you the traits associated with my stereotype of lesbians? Although, to the best of my knowledge, no one has made the strong claim that we have little or no control over stereotyping (with some exceptions—e.g., Brewer, 1996; Fiske, 1989), it has been implicitly assumed that such control is difficult and perhaps impossible. At least the idea that well-ingrained cultural stereotypes are automatically activated has been a staple of modern stereotype research (Bargh, 1999). There are certainly demonstrations (e.g., Banaji & Hardin, 1996; Bessenoff & Sherman, 2000; Wittenbrink, Judd, & Park, 1997) that pictures and features associated with categories can prime stereotypes under conditions where control is effectively impossible.

The Devine Paradigm

AUTOMATIC AND CONTROLLED COMPONENTS

An influential paper by Patricia Devine (1989) argued that both automatic and controlled processes affect the use of stereotypes about black Americans. She assumed that categorization is fairly automatic; that is, we immediately and nonreflectively see a man as black, and we have little ability to control this categorization. Furthermore, because cultural stereotypes of blacks are well known even to people who do not agree with them, activation of the stereotype is also fairly automatic. Thus I cannot avoid seeing this man as black and at least initially thinking of him in terms of cultural stereotypes of blacks. That's the depressing news. The optimistic side is that some of us take control over our cognitive processes at that point and try to think in nonstereotypic terms. For some of us, presumably those who are relatively unprejudiced, our personal beliefs do not agree with the cultural stereotypes that we access automatically. And when we recognize stereotypic thoughts, we give ourselves a little mental spanking and try to mental amends.

INITIAL RESEARCH

In an initial study, Devine (1989) showed that high- and low-prejudice subjects (as measured by the Modern Racism Scale, or MRS; see Chapter 8) listed virtually the same traits when asked for the black stereotype, whether or not they agreed with these traits. Thus both high- and low-prejudiced subjects knew what the stereotype was.

In a second study, Devine made use of the fact that the most prominent part of the black stereotype consists of terms referring to hostility and aggression. In this study she used a priming paradigm by subliminally exposing subjects to words related to the black stereotype—words such as "Negro," "jazz," "Harlem," "ghetto," "slavery," "lazy," and "athletic." The data suggested that subjects were indeed unaware that they had read words related to the black stereotype. Following this priming, subjects read a paragraph about a person named Donald whose race was not specified; Donald's behaviors were relatively ambiguous with regard to hostility. Subjects then rated Donald on several traits related to hostility and others that were unrelated. Generally, those subjects who had been primed with the black stereotype traits rated Donald as more hostile than those who had not been so primed, and this was equally true for prejudiced and unprejudiced subjects. Devine interpreted these results as indicating that both prejudiced and unprejudiced subjects who had the black stereotype primed used this stereotype relatively automatically (because they were unaware of the primes) to judge Donald in more stereotypic (in this case, hostile) terms.

In a third study, high- and low-prejudice subjects were asked to list their personal thoughts about blacks and to provide as many labels as they could for the category of black Americans. The high- and low-prejudice subjects did not differ in their tendency to report pejorative labels for the category, so they were equally aware of cultural stereotypes or at least the labels used within a culture. However, the thoughts listed were different for the two groups. High-prejudice subjects listed more negative than positive thoughts, whereas the low-prejudice subjects did the reverse.

The three experiments taken together suggest the following. First, high- and low-prejudice individuals are equally knowledgeable about the stereotypes of blacks. Second, the two groups both use the stereotypes when they cannot control such use. Third, when given the opportunity to be more reflective, low-prejudice individuals consciously try to overcome stereotypes that presumably were automatically activated.

Criticisms

ADEQUACY OF PREJUDICE MEASURES

Because these studies have such important implications, they have been subjected to considerable scrutiny. There are, as it turns out, several problems. First, there have been several criticisms of the use of the MRS as a measure of prejudice. One problem is that it has been shown to be highly reactive to social desirability concerns (Fazio, Jackson, Dunton, & Williams, 1995), and this weakens the interpretation of the third set of results. If the MRS really measures tendencies to respond in socially desirable ways, then all that may have been shown is that subjects who were unwilling to admit to being racists in one situation (when they completed the MRS) were also unwilling to admit that they had negative thoughts about blacks in general. Thus the results may say more about self-presentation than about prejudice.

Also, if the MRS is a poor measure of prejudice, then the results showing that those scoring high and low on the scale did not differ in their knowledge and use of stereotypic information is largely irrelevant. Sometimes in such situations a *reductio ad absurdum* is useful. Suppose length of the ring finger was used as a measure of prejudice. Then the finding that people with long fingers (low-prejudice) had as much automatic activation of black stereotypes as those putatively higher in prejudice (short fingers) would be treated as a silly result. The MRS is clearly better at measuring prejudice than is length of ring fingers, but it is saturated with social desirability and political conservatism, and is at best a flawed measure of prejudice (see Chapter 8).

ASSUMPTIONS ABOUT PRIMING

Locke, MacLeod, and Walker (1994) have argued that the priming results in Devine's (1989) second study are also suspect. Recall that she presented words related to the black stereotype ("oppressed," "poor," "ghetto") and reasoned that such words activated the black stereotype—which, since it also includes hostility, led to interpretation of the ambiguous Donald materials as more hostile. That is certainly a strong possibility, but there is another. Suppose such words themselves directly prime hostility, so a person who sees words such as "poor" and "oppressed" may unconsciously think of hostility without using the unconscious intermediate step of activating the black stereotype. In other words, the race category may not have done the dirty work.

PROBLEMS WITH THE ASSUMPTION OF AUTOMATIC ACTIVATION

Devine (1989) made the strong assumption that at least in the United States, cultural stereotypes about blacks are so familiar that they should be automatically activated for everyone. There are four classic criteria for whether a cognitive process is automatic: It should (1) be nonconscious, (2) be impervious to intentional control, (3) require few or no cognitive resources, and (4) not interfere with other ongoing cognitive resources. But as John Bargh (1989, 1996, 1999) consistently reminds us, few if any studies have manipulated automaticity in ways that meet all four criteria. Furthermore (and even more importantly), there is no guarantee that these four criteria operate as a unit. For example, some processes can be relatively unconscious but still use cognitive resources, and the fact that a process is conscious does not imply that it is controllable (or vice versa).

So although the majority of studies in this area have manipulated automaticity by unconscious activation of stereotypes and have assumed that therefore this activation is not amenable to conscious control, this assumption may not be viable in all cases. It is therefore probably wise to assume that automaticity is multifaceted and graduated rather than all-or-nothing (Bargh, 1999; Devine & Monteith, 1999). Several lines of research have suggested that stereotype activation is not fully automatic, at least for all people.

Individual Differences in Automatic Stereotype Activation. Devine suggested that because cultural stereotypes about African Americans are so ingrained in U.S. culture, almost everyone should activate them automatically. However, several studies show that there are reliable individual differences in the extent to which racial stereotypes and prejudice are automatically activated (Fazio et al., 1995; Lepore & Brown, 1997; Locke et al., 1994; Moskowitz, Salomon, & Taylor, 2000).

As one example, Wittenbrink, Judd, and Park (1997) took advantage of a priming methodology pioneered in this domain by Gaertner and McLaughlin (1983) and Dovidio and colleagues (1986), which showed that people who were primed with black category labels could more quickly answer stereotype-related questions about blacks. Wittenbrink, Judd, and Park's subjects were subliminally primed with neutral primes or with the words "black" or "white." Then they were asked to indicate whether nonwords, neutral words, or words related to black and white stereotypes were or were not words. When the "black" prime was used, responses to black stereotype words that were negative were facilitated, and the "white" prime facilitated white positive words. Note that this methodology essentially precludes any conscious control over activation of stereotype information, so subjects in general were displaying automatic activation of negative stereotypes for blacks and positive stereotypes for whites. These results supported Devine's contention. However, these results were stronger for the more prejudiced subjects, and this must mean that stereotypes are differentially activated for different subjects.

Retraining. Stereotypes, even those that have become part of our cultural heritage, do not just happen. People have to learn them, and Devine's point was precisely that most of us have learned and relearned cultural stereotypes about African Americans. But what can be learned can also be unlearned. Can these associations be reversed through countertraining? Research by Kawakami, Dovidio, Moll, Hermsen, and Russin (2000) would seem to suggest that this might work. On a number of trials, subjects were exposed to pictures of stereotyped groups and asked to say the word "no" whenever a stereotype feature was paired with them. In subsequent tests of implicit stereotyping (where control was difficult if not impossible), people with this training were less stereotypic than those with no training. Obviously, in everyday life people are not likely to get such deliberate training, but it is certainly possible that those who routinely have positive and nonstereotypic experiences with people from stereotyped groups will replace a cultural stereotype with one that is more individual and generally less negative.

Importance of Cognitive Resources. Automatic processes theoretically require few if any cognitive resources. Therefore, automatically activated stereotypes should manifest themselves, whether or not the person is busy or distracted. Yet several studies show that activation of gender (e.g., Blair & Banaji, 1996) and racial (e.g., Spencer, Fein, Wolfe, Fong, & Dunn, 1998) stereotypes is sensitive to time and resource constraints.

In an important experiment, Gilbert and Hixon (1991) investigated the importance of cognitive resources in stereotype activation. They had research participants read word fragments presented by a female of European or Asian descent. The word fragments could either be completed by words related to the Asian stereotype (e.g., P_LI_ _ could be seen as "polite") or by unrelated words (e.g., "police"). Participants were also either cognitively busy or not busy as they watched the assistant present the fragments. Gilbert and Hixon argued that if stereotype activation was automatic (i.e., required few if any cognitive resources), the cognitively busy people would show as many stereotypic completions as those who were not busy, but that if activation was not automatic (i.e., required cognitive resources), the busy people would show less stereotypic responding than those not busy. Those facing the Asian target responded with more Asian-related words only when they had time to think, suggesting that activation of the Asian stereotype was not fully automatic.

In a second experiment, participants were kept busy during the viewing stage, during the completion stage, both, or neither. Word completion results replicated the first experiment. However, in this second study, people were also asked to explicitly rate the stimulus person on stereotype-relevant and irrelevant traits. In this case, one might argue that before the stereotype could be used, it would have to have been activated in the first phase; therefore, only those who had been not busy during the viewing stage could have an active stereotype to use. However, they might try to repress the use of the stereotype when they explicitly rated the assistant, and that suppression would require cognitive resources. Thus the most stereotyping should be shown by those people who had not been busy during the first phase (and who were able to activate their stereotype), but who were busy during the second phase (and could not suppress the stereotype). Results confirmed this reasoning (see Table 10.1).

These results then suggest that activation of stereotype-relevant material is not automatic when one sees someone of a different race. However, in that regard it is important to note that Devine's (1989) research was based on stereotypes of African Americans, whereas Gilbert and Hixon used Asian American stereotypes. It is quite possible that European American undergraduates have stronger stereotypes about African Americans than Asian Americans, or that the former are used more often and thus are more practiced and automatic (von Hippel, Sekaquaptewa, & Vargas, 1995).

Processing Goals and Motives. If stereotype activation is automatic, then it should not be affected by processing goals. An experiment by Macrae, Bodenhausen, Milne, Thorn, and Castelli (1997) found that gender stereotypes were less strongly activated (if at all) when subjects saw female faces and were asked to detect whether a dot appeared in the photograph than when they saw the same faces and were asked whether the photograph was of an animate or inanimate object. Other research by the same group (Macrae, Bodenhausen, & Milne, 1995) suggests that when racial categories are primed, gender stereotypes are inhibited, and vice versa—a result that should not occur if either stereotype or both are automatically activated.

There is also evidence that motivation can affect the activation of stereotypes (Kunda & Sinclair, 1999). For example, Sinclair and Kunda (1999) showed that people who had been criticized by a black doctor more rapidly identified black stereotype words in a lexical decision task than people who had not been criticized. In an experiment by Spencer and colleagues (1998), participants were subliminally primed with black or white faces and then given a word completion task similar to the one used by Gilbert and Hixon (1991). Those who were cognitively busy did not activate racial stereotypes (replicating the Gilbert–Hixon results) unless they had recently been given negative feedback on an intelligence-type test. Both sets of results suggest that strong motives can affect stereotype activation, which is normally thought to be fairly automatic.

TABLE 10.1. Asian Stereotype Completions and Ratings

	Stereotype completions in early phase	Stereotype ratings	
		Busy late	Not busy late
Busy early		*Not activated, can't inhibit*	*Not activated, can inhibit*
Asian	3.71	6.15	6.59
European	2.88	6.35	6.77
Not busy early		*Activated, can't inhibit*	*Activated, can inhibit*
Asian	3.09	7.30	6.36
European	3.18	6.07	6.42

Note. From Gilbert and Hixon (1991, Experiment 2). Copyright 1991 by the American Psychological Association. Reprinted by permission.

Of course, stereotypes can also be consciously applied or inhibited to particular people or groups, depending on individuals' motives. For example, people may be more or less unconsciously motivated to apply their stereotypes to groups as a means of reaffirming self-esteem or excusing failure (Fein & Spencer, 1997; Sinclair & Kunda, 2000). But it is also important to show that stereotype activation may also be under personal control, at least under some circumstances.

Intuitively, even a man who has fairly strong racial stereotypes might not activate them in the presence of a black or Hispanic neighbor whom he knows well, likes, and respects. It is possible, of course, that each time he encounters this person the stereotype is activated and he must continually push it to the background. But it also is quite possible that the stereotype is never even activated in this case.

SUMMARY

Devine's original set of hypotheses was bold and challenging, and her paper has been widely cited and has stimulated interesting and exciting research. The results of these subsequent studies are not perfectly consistent with one another, but they all suggest that Devine may have been hasty in assuming that because of their cultural currency, racial stereotypes are automatically activated for everyone. In fact, it now appears clear that there are individual differences in whether or how strongly the culturally provided race stereotypes are activated for people. People may also have personal stereotypes that they have acquired from their own experiences, which may or may not be consistent with cultural stereotypes and may or may not be activated in their place. Despite all this, however, it is still true that for many of us stereotypes are automatically activated, despite our intentions to the contrary.

Difficulties in Control of Stereotype Application

SELF-REGULATION OF ACTIVATION

Obviously, controlling the application of stereotypic thinking may be easier said than done, and may involve several distinct approaches (Devine & Monteith, 1999). Although activation of stereotypes may be relatively uncontrollable for most of us, the research reviewed in the last few pages suggests that this is not inevitable. Presumably, the same processes that give rise to undesirable stereotypes may also be employed to develop more positive ones or even no stereotypes at all. As we have seen in Chapter 9, some people are highly motivated to avoid prejudicial thinking, and when they catch themselves doing so try to fix matters for the future. No one is claiming that this form of control is easily achieved, and many of us lack the self-insight, attention to the effects of our behavior on others, or motivation to go far down this path. On the other hand, many people do have both the ability and motivation to work toward such control.

STEREOTYPE CORRECTION

Such self-regulation is obviously the strategy of choice, because it results in more or less permanent change in stereotypes and reduction of prejudice. But it can be painful and requires work and time. What is one to do in the meantime? Several strategies are more conscious and can be adapted to the situation; though arguably less effective in the long run, they may provide good service for the short haul. Let's take an example. I am quite aware that I have a stereotype that student athletes at my university are less intellectually capable than their nonathlete counterparts, and in this case the stereotype has more than a kernel of truth. I have no special desire to rid myself of this stereotype, precisely because it is true. Nonetheless, there are enough salient exceptions (two of the best students in my recent social psychology course were a male and a female basketball player) that I consciously guard against applying my stereotype indiscriminately to individual athletes. How can I pull this off?

Individuation. The most obvious possibility is that I should try to get to know as much as possible about individual athletes, so the fact that they are athletes recedes into the background and I can discover the many exceptions to my stereotype. This is, of course, the personalization approach. Thus when I talk to these students, I may spend a little time asking them about the sport they play and their role in it, because I actually do enjoy watching most college sports. But I also try to focus any conversation on the academic side of their dual lives. I often ask what other courses they are taking, what they are majoring in, what their career choices might be, and even (if the conversation heads in that direction) about their backgrounds and parents. In other words, I try to engage them in the same kinds of conversations I would have with almost any student.[16]

Making Category Information Irrelevant. Another strategy, and in some ways the exact opposite, is to make sure that category information cannot enter into important decisions that I make. This is easier in some situations than others. I can grade essay exams without knowing the identity of the student, or use multiple-choice exams (where instructor discretion does not enter in). A personnel director can hire people based on test results or highly structured interviews, where the race or gender of an applicant will make less difference than in a more subjective evaluation procedure. But, of course, in other cases this may be next to impossible. Admission of graduate students may depend heavily on letters of recommendation, which allow for stereotype bias on the part of both author and reader. Few companies pick executive-level personnel on the basis of objective tests. Many people claim that they never take gender or race into account when making decisions about hiring and promotion, but it is, of course, hard to know what to make of such claims. As I have argued in Chapter 8, the majority of dirty work stereotypes perform is not directly manifested in straight-line discrimination, but in more subtle interpretative and behavioral ways.

Correction Processes. People who are aware of their potential use of stereotypes or biases may, of course, make decisions and then attempt to correct for the bias. Suppose a male athlete in my class claims he has been unfairly graded. I am aware that I think he is probably less smart than the other students, and I am willing to admit to possible bias and try to make up for it. But how exactly am I supposed to do this? Add points to his final grade to reflect potential bias? If so, how many? We do not have clear answers to these questions, but we do know that cognitive compensation of this sort is generally hard to achieve (Wilson & Brekke, 1994) and may rest on theories about the source and effects of bias (Wegener & Petty, 1997).

Sometimes even when people are aware of their biases and are motivated to take account of them, they cannot. Nelson, Acker, and Manis (1996) asked research participants to judge whether several males and females, each identified by picture and a brief description indicating masculine or feminine interest patterns, were more likely to be enrolled in engineering or nursing programs. As expected, both gender and interest patterns predicted the choices. However, some of the subjects were told that equal numbers of males and females were enrolled in the two types of programs—information that should have reduced reliance on biological gender, but not reliance on interest patterns. Indeed, subjects were less likely to use gender to make their judgments when they had learned of the equal distribution, but gender remained a powerful basis of classification. A second study showed that these tendencies persisted even when subjects thought they were going to have to justify their decisions publicly. This study does not, of course, suggest that people can never be nonstereotypic in their thinking about jobs, but it does suggest that nonstereotypic thinking is a skill that perhaps does not come naturally.

STEREOTYPE SUPPRESSION

Perhaps the crudest, but conceivably most effective, method of dealing with pesky stereotypes is just to suppress them. But what happens when people deliberately try to suppress their stereotypes? Are they successful? A fair amount of research has been addressed to this question (Bodenhausen & Macrae, 1996, 1998), and the general answer is that they are successful at one level but not at another.

In the past several years, a large body of work on thought suppression and mental control (Wenzlaff & Wegner, 2000) has noted that the act of suppressing a thought often makes that thought highly accessible. In an experiment by Wegner, Schneider, Carter, and White (1987), subjects were asked not to think of a white bear, and they were partially able to suppress this thought. In a later phase, when they were allowed to express thoughts of white bears, they were more likely to do so than subjects who had not previously suppressed the thought. Wegner and his colleagues termed this a "rebound effect," and such an effect has reliably been produced in scores of studies (Wenzlaff & Wegner, 2000).

Rebound Effects. The leading explanation for such rebound effects was provided by Wegner (1994) in his theory of ironic mental control. He argued that the act of suppression requires two mental processes. The first, which is largely deliberative, is the suppression itself. Typically people try to suppress a thought by thinking of something in its stead (e.g., thinking of a red car instead of a white bear). However, a separate and largely automatic process operates in the background and outside of consciousness to monitor thoughts for the dreaded suppressed thought. This constant attention to unwanted thoughts makes them highly accessible or perhaps even primes them (Macrae, Bodenhausen, Milne, & Jetten, 1994). Thus, when the suppression is lifted, they flood back into consciousness. An alternative model has been presented by Liberman and Förster (2000). They argue that when people try to suppress a thought, they infer that they really wanted to express it, and this inference produces a need to express the thought.

In any event, this work of mental control has obvious relevance for the suppression of stereotypes. In the first published experiment on this topic, Macrae, Bodenhausen, and colleagues (1994) showed subjects a picture of a skinhead and then asked them to write an essay on a typical day for this person. Half the subjects were told to suppress their stereotypes as they wrote, and the other half were give no such instructions. As expected, the suppression group included less stereotypic material in their essays. This is the good news—suppression was effective. However, in a second part of the experiment, subjects were shown a second picture of a skinhead, and again were asked to write about his day. This time no instructions were given about suppression. Control subjects included about as much stereotypic material as they had in the first essay, but those who had suppressed their stereotypes in the first essay showed a dramatic increase in stereotypic material on the second essay; in fact, they were more stereotypic than the control group. These results are presented in Table 10.2. So suppression seems to work in the short run, but to produce a rebound of sorts in the long run. This is hardly the solution to stereotyping we would want.

These data were consciously produced and might have resulted from any number of conscious processes. For example, in writing the second essay suppression subjects might have reasoned that they were supposed to respond stereotypically since nothing more had been said about suppression. Or perhaps, in trying to suppress their stereotypes they felt that they had left out important information, and they used the second essay as an opportunity to impart it. Therefore, it is important to show that suppression has effects that go beyond highly reactive verbal reports. In a second study, Macrae, Bodenhausen, and colleagues (1994) repeated the suppression manipulation, and then took subjects to a room where they thought they would sit near a skinhead. Those who had suppressed during the first essay sat further away from the seat they thought he would occupy. And in a third study, after writing an essay under suppression or no-suppression conditions, subjects took part in a lexical decision task where they were asked to respond quickly to whether a string of letters was a word. Suppression and no-suppression subjects were equally fast in responding to non-stereotype-related words, but the suppression subjects responded faster to stereotype-related words, suggesting that stereotype material was especially accessible for them. Other research (e.g., Newman, Duff, Hedberg, & Blitzstein, 1996) also shows that suppressed material becomes highly salient after suppression.

Moreover, trying to forget stereotypic material only results in increased memory for the very material one is trying to forget (Macrae, Bodenhausen, Milne, & Ford, 1997; Sherman, Stroessner, Loftus, & Deguzman, 1997). Not only does suppression led to better memories for stereotypic material but to lessened memory for nonstereotypic, individuating material (Macrae, Bodenhausen, Milne, & Wheeler, 1996). Suppressing stereotypic thoughts about job applicants can result in more negative evaluations of them (Kulik, Perry, & Bourhis, 2000).

TABLE 10.2. Stereotype Material Included in Essays

	Suppress first	Control
First essay	5.54	6.95
Second essay	7.83	7.08

Note. From Macrae, Bodenhausen, Milne, and Jetten (1994, Table 1). Copyright 1994 by the American Psychological Association. Reprinted by permission.

One might argue that there is something a bit peculiar about having one person tell another to suppress stereotypes, and obviously this is the sort of motivation we would like to see internalized. However, research by Wyer, Sherman, and Stroessner (1998) suggests that the results generalize to conditions of self-generated suppression. In their studies they asked people to write about a typical day in the life of an African American. Suppression was induced either by directing subjects to suppress stereotypes, or by telling them that the study was sponsored by an African American group—a condition that presumably would lead subjects to want to suppress their stereotypes. Both the suppression groups indicated more stereotypic responding in a second phase than did a control group. In a conceptually related study by Macrae, Bodenhausen, and Milne (1998), subjects who were in a state of heightened self-awareness (typically manipulated by having subjects sit before a mirror or in front of a TV camera)—a state that is known to induce normative behavior—suppressed stereotypic responding more than those not in a state of self-awareness. Those who suppressed their stereotypes spontaneously showed the typical rebound effect.

Inevitable Suppression Effects? So merely trying to stop thinking about stereotypes may not always be successful, and may in fact lead to increases in the availability of stereotypes. However, this is not inevitable. Monteith, Sherman, and Devine (1998) suggest that sometimes stereotype suppression may be quite successful. They note that much of the research on suppression of stereotypes has used groups (e.g., skinheads, child molesters) for which there are few cultural and personal prohibitions against stereotyping. Thus subjects may not have been motivated to suppress their stereotypes effectively. Suppression does not seem to produce the rebound effect reliably with stereotypes of elderly people (Galinsky & Moskowitz, 2000), gays (Monteith, Spicer, & Tooman, 1998), or African Americans (Wyer, Sherman, & Stroessner, 2000). In addition, Monteith, Sherman, and Devine (1998) suggest that individual differences among people may be important, especially for more important categories such as race. For example, elderly people have more trouble inhibiting information, including stereotypes, despite having a greater desire to do so (von Hippel, Silver, & Lynch, 2000). Generally people who are motivated to control their prejudiced reactions (Dunton & Fazio, 1997), or who differ in the extent to which prejudiced reactions are automatically activated for race categories (Fazio et al., 1995), may be more successful not only in suppressing stereotypes but also in controlling their application to specific people. They may be more successful in suppression because they are more practiced at it or because they have a more readily available set of distractors to help suppression, among other reasons. In any event, rebound effects seem to be more likely among highly prejudiced people (Monteith, Spicer, & Tooman, 1998). We have already seen that even when stereotypic thoughts spring to mind, people who are low in prejudice are better able to monitor and control application to groups and individuals. We have much more to learn about the intricacies of controlling stereotypic thinking, but it seems likely that some people are able to do this more effectively than others. Unfortunately, those people who are most responsive to rebound effects are probably the very people (highly prejudiced) who cause more than their share of mischief by using their stereotypes, and whose stereotypes we would most like to see suppressed.

SUMMARY

Changing stereotypes and reducing prejudice is a more complex process than many people seem to assume. The strategy that has been most vigorously investigated is bringing people from different groups together "to get to know each other better." This"contact hypothesis" rests on three basic assumptions. First, the content of most stereotypes is false. Second, contact with people from groups who are targets of stereotypes will thus provide experiences that disconfirm the stereotypes. Third, given such disconfirming evidence, people will change their stereotypes and reduce their prejudices. Yet, common sense reflection and empirical data suggest that none of these assumptions is necessarily or inevitably correct. Some stereotypes are accurate, at least in general terms, contact with people from other groups may or may lead to experiences that disconfirm the stereotype, and because stereotypes are linked to a host of other beliefs and values, some deeply entrenched, they will not necessarily change even if manifestly wrong.

Generally, contact has been shown to be an effective way to change stereotypes, provided people from the different groups have mutually positive experiences from their interaction, have approximately equal status, and have contact within a context that has institutional support for change. In practice these conditions are sometimes hard to achieve. Also, contact is often quite selective and not intimate enough to lead to personalization, another factor that can aid in changing stereotypes.

Stereotypes can change because of experiences with one or more members of other groups. Although rare, that change can occur through a kind of conversion experience where a single, powerful experience forces change in stereotypes and often in connected values and beliefs. Most empirical evidence supports what has come to be called the subtyping model. When people who are exceptions to the stereotypes of their categories can be seen as exceptional subtypes and cognitively fenced away from the larger groups, stereotype change tends to be retarded. Accordingly, exemplars need to be seen as typical enough members of the group such that they do not get subtyped.

This illustrates an insistent problem with contact, which I have termed the typicality paradox. If a person is typical of her stereotyped group, she may not provide enough disconfirming evidence for the stereotype to change. If, on the other hand, she is seen as atypical, she may easily be subtyped as an exception and provide no incentive for change.

Another problem with the contact hypothesis is that even if effective it may only work at the surface of stereotypes by changing the associations between categories and features. While that is certainly desirable, more fundamental change is likely to occur when people's theories about why groups have particular features also change. However, experiences with relatively few exemplars of a group are not likely to lead to this kind of deeper change. Theory change may best be promoted through various kinds of educational efforts. These are often quite effective, although not inevitably so.

In the past decade there have been many investigations of whether stereotype activation is inevitable or can be controlled cognitively. For many of us activation of stereotypes when meeting a person from a target group does occur fairly automatically, but this is not inevitable. Some relatively unprejudiced people seem to be relatively immune from such automatic activation, and others can correct stereotype activation with more controlled processing. However, trying to suppress stereotypes can be somewhat dangerous. Clearly people can suppress their stereotypes, but in many cases the suppressed stereotype content will be better remembered and more accessible once the suppression is removed.

It is possible to change people's beliefs and attitudes about other groups of people. But such change, especially for important groups such as race and gender, cannot be taken to the bank and counted on as inevitable.

Notes

1. It is a little unclear what to make of the finding that cross-racial friendship alone does not reduce prejudice and stereotyping. Jackman and Crane (1986) argue that in such cases the black person is probably a token friend. I might add that when contact with members of other races are limited to one or two others, generalization to the entire group is likely to be modest.

2. It's interesting that in the vast literature on the contact hypothesis, little attention has been given to motivation and willingness to change. Social psychologists in this instance have fallen prey to the rather odd Platonic assumption that those who know the truth will, of necessity, act in accordance with it.

3. In a 1955 follow-up judgment (usually called "*Brown* II"), the Court urged "all deliberate speed" in desegregating schools. However, Southern school districts emphasized "deliberate" over "speed," and when there was little evidence of desegregation by the late 1960s, the Court pushed for effective policies—which generally meant school bussing. This policy was extremely unpopular in the white community and supported by only a bare majority of blacks. Bussing has done little to reduce prejudice or improve schools, and it arguably has encouraged many white parents to take their children out of public schools (Thernstrom & Thernstrom, 1997).

4. These opinions came in a variety of forms. Leading psychologists testified in trials that took place in lower courts, and several submitted an *amicus curiae* brief when the case was heard by the U.S. Supreme Court. While the *Brown* decision specifically dealt with segregated schools in Topeka, Kansas, several other lower-court cases were also dealt with in the *Brown* decision. Stephan (1978) provides an excellent discussion of the role of social scientists in this decision.

5. Quite understandably, most research related to the contact hypothesis in schools has dealt with race. There has also been a movement, usually called "mainstreaming," to integrate students with mild mental retardation, other mental disabilities, or physical disabilities into regular classrooms. These programs have been more successful in terms of changing prejudice and discrimination among the other students (Fishbein, 1996).

6. I do not mean to suggest that keeping black and white children apart was the primary or even deliberate goal of tracking, although in some cases I suspect it was. Probably in the majority of cases, white parents were worried that the infusion of several relatively low-performing children would hurt their children's performance. Even so, surely this basic fear was exaggerated by racial concerns. Keep in mind that many of these schools were in the South, with a strong legacy of overt racism.

7. Although there are a great many problems with the emphasis placed on sports among black teenagers, there is little doubt that white and black participation on the same teams can reduce and frequently has reduced the prejudices of both groups (see Slavin & Madden, 1979, for one example of positive effects on whites). The emphasis on team play, and the intimacies encouraged by locker room banter and long trips to away games, can (but do not always) break down comfort barriers and lead to greater intimacy.

8. I did a fair amount of consulting work in high schools during the 1960s and 1970s, and my informal observation was that desegregation did "work" in some schools in the North (I had no experience of Southern schools). And in each school where it did work, it was because the school board and especially the principal moved the faculty and students beyond the "this is being shoved down our throats" mentality. I spent time in one school that seemed to be well integrated behaviorally (in terms of clearly friendly relationships among at least some black and white students, and no overt hostility). I questioned some teachers about this, since the atmosphere contrasted so vividly with other schools I had visited. They all pointed to the principal, who had made it clear that desegregation was an opportunity rather than a constraint, and that they were going to make it work. He also had moved quickly to set up in-house teacher workshops to prepare the teachers for the increased demands he was placing on them.

9. I feel the need to point out that although I am sometimes awake and working at 3:00 A.M. and have nothing against bull sessions, this particular combination is unappealing.

10. I still vividly remember my first major foray into the world of race relations. During the early 1970s, Boston was in the throes of a school bussing controversy, and many whites were resisting what they saw as the intrusion of black students into "their" schools. I joined several social scientists in the Boston area who thought they could apply their expertise to defusing the situation. The first time I met with a very angry group of black men and women from Roxbury and whites from South Boston (a largely Irish American enclave), I began the meeting with some pious statements and concluded by saying that we were all brothers under the skin. This was greeted by hostile silence, until one black woman said something along the lines of "Mister, you can talk all the talk you want, but you ain't no brother of mine." And things went downhill from there. Although I'm sure that in calmer times I could have appealed to the commonalities among the people there (e.g., everyone genuinely wanted a good education for their children), what was on the table was not commonality of interests—but, rather, legitimate conflicts of interests in what amounted to a short-term zero-sum game. Given the situation at the time, for every black child who was allowed to attend a better school, a white child was going to have to attend a lesser one. That reality was recognized by all. In retrospect, I think I might have been more effective (I could not have been less so) by acknowledging real differences between the strong Irish American and African American cultures. It is not clear to me in hindsight that blurring these boundaries would have accomplished anything, even had I been more effective at it.

11. Fordham and Ogbu (1986) and Cross (1995), among others, have developed the idea of oppositional identity. The argument is that many young black people build their identities around acting as "nonwhite" as possible. However, empirical data (e.g., Arroyo & Zigler, 1995; Oyserman, Gant, & Ager, 1995) suggest a more complex set of relationships between identity and achievement (see Chapter 7).

12. It is an open, important, and interesting question why some people are seen as more typical of their categories than others—a judgment that may also be highly dependent on context. One possibility is that typicality of category membership for many social categories may be heavily determined by physical appearance. Certain stylistic behaviors may also be crucial (e.g., femininity for women and gay males). If typicality is indeed heavily affected by easily perceived features, then an exemplar might be typical in appearance but still exhibit a wide range of stereotype-disconfirming behaviors, and such a person might be an ideal vehicle for change.

13. Alert readers may note that whereas the model discussed here suggests that subtyping retards stereotype change, Brewer's model of decategorization and personalization (discussed earlier in the chapter) suggests that subtyping is an important aid in reducing stereotyping. There are at least two differences between these approaches. First, Brewer's model focuses on perceptions of individuals, whereas the subtyping model is oriented to-

ward change of general stereotypes. Second, it is likely that the cognitive consequences of trying to see a person in as many ways as possible differ from those of attempts to preserve the stereotype. It is important to maintain the distinction between subtyping and subgrouping (Maurer, Park, & Rothbart, 1995), but its exact nature is still awaiting a program of empirical research (Richards & Hewstone, 2001).

14. I have had many conversations with a black student whose background is clearly upper-middle-class, and whose behavior and manner of speaking are indistinguishable from those of his white classmates. Yet one day he commented that when he is with his black friends, he acts quite differently than with me; his way of putting it was that "I speak two languages." This particular man does not seem to feel uncomfortable with this moving into and out of roles (and, indeed, all of us do this to some extent), but others might. The point is, however, that I have no experience of this side of his life. He shows me what he wants me to see. For my part, there are also large ranges of my experience and background that he will never discover. This is not merely a fact of race; professors are more professional around students than around their families, and my students know little about my family life (or my family about my students). For that matter, men and women behave differently in single-sex than in integrated settings.

15. It must be said that being in possession of the "truth" does not convey a responsibility to announce it loudly on every possible occasion. Although I do believe that black males are more violent as a group than white males, I do not think that this is a particularly important feature of race. There are times when this is relevant, but most of the time it is not, and both common sense and common courtesy suggest that I keep quiet about it when it is not. Some people who fret endlessly about the environment of political correctness on college campuses fail to grasp that distinction. These same people are often obsessed with what they see as the decline of public civility. Go figure.

16. Several years ago, one of our star athletes failed the first exam in my social psychology course. As I do in such cases, I notified the Athletics Department Academic Advising Office, and the young man was in my office almost immediately. We talked a bit about the team he played on, but quickly moved to his difficulties in my course, the causes of which we managed to illuminate fairly quickly: Although he was far from a rocket scientist, he also hadn't been studying enough. I asked him about his academic aspirations, and we talked a little about his family. We talked for an hour or so, and when he left I said something along the lines of "You're too smart to be doing as poorly as you are in my course." As we shook hands, I noticed that he was beginning to get a bit teary, and I asked him what the problem was. He said (and this is a near-exact quote), "This is the first time anyone on this campus has ever taken me seriously as anything other than a jock." He ended up doing well in my course, graduated on time, and now has a responsible job in banking.

CHAPTER 11

Content of Stereotypes:
Gender, Race, and Age

Up to this point, I have followed contemporary practice and focused attention on general principles of how stereotypes affect processing of information about individuals and groups. Yet most people imagine that we social psychologists are in the business of documenting the content of various stereotypes. When I tell nonpsychologists that I study stereotyping, after the obligatory comment about how interesting that must be, they often ask me a question about some particular stereotype—for instance, "You know, I've often wondered why people think that lawyers are so mercenary." Or perhaps they will say something about how only prejudiced people have stereotypes. Or they may question me gingerly about some favorite stereotype of theirs being true: "I don't know why Mexicans get so angry when we say they are inclined to commit crimes. All you have to do is watch TV and see for yourself how many crimes they commit."

THE IMPORTANCE OF CONTENT

So far we have had little to say about the specific content of stereotypes. What do people think differentiates men from women? What is the stereotype of persons with mental illness? Are obese individuals seen to be lazy, and if so, why? If these questions seem appropriate, even interesting, why have we waited for 10 chapters to get to them?

The Social Cognition Approach

Modern social cognition, the area that has most influenced current research on stereotyping, focuses on processing concerns and pays little attention to the content that comes along for the ride (Schneider, 1991, 1996). After all, memory processes must work pretty much the same, whether we are trying to recall the names of high school classmates or people seen at a party last week. Does anyone seriously believe that the process of learning information about animal groups is much different than for plants or groups of people? Is there any reason to believe that our cognitive systems care much about whether they are forming an illusory correlation between one minority group and one trait or another group and another trait? Process is process, and content is superfluous.

Some Important Content Questions

The Origins of Stereotypes

And yet there are some things left out when we focus so exclusively on processing concerns and avoid discussion of content. First, though many of the processing models make important points about how stereotypes are maintained and how they affect our perceptions of people, most have little to say about the origins of stereotypes. Why are Jews seen as clannish and blacks as crime-prone, and not the reverse? To be sure, in many cases the source of stereotype content seems obvious enough. Culture and experience seem to provide a kernel of truth, which our cognitive and motivational processes then amplify. As we have seen, this is at best only a partial answer— but once we take content seriously, then we must poke at accuracy issues.

Stereotype Uniformity

Why is there more consensus that some groups have some traits than for other combinations? For example, why is there more general agreement that Asian Americans are hard-working than that Jews are mercenary? Does this uniformity make any difference in the ways we use these stereotypes?

Are Some Groups Magnets for Stereotypes?

An even more basic concern is why we seem to stereotype some groups and not others. Why do we have stereotypes about redheads and blonds, and not about people with mousey brown hair? Why do we seem to stereotype obese and not skinny people? Why are we more likely to have stereotypes of Roman Catholics than of Methodists? We will have to know something about content to answer these and other questions.

Content Affects Behavior

Our cognitive machinery may not care about the content of our stereotypes, but other people do, and they will be annoyed when we make mistakes—sometimes even when we're accurate. The "bottom line" is also important: The content of stereotypes has enormous impact on how we behave toward other people. For example, seeing Anthony as lazy and hostile is likely to lead to different sorts of interactions (or lack thereof) than seeing him as smart and hard-working. At a minimum, we want to know whether stereotypes of a given group are predominantly positive or negative. In Chapter 6 I have argued that stereotypes can be confirmed through social interaction, and here I discuss more generally the persistence of certain forms of stereotypes.

Features Are Not Created Equal

Traits and other features themselves are not interchangeable. Intuitively, once I have decided that my student Jessica is intelligent, it is hard for her to shed her smarts before my eyes. On the other hand, I may be happy to give up my attribution that she is fundamentally lazy when she proves that sometimes does work hard. In other words, some traits seem more ingrained than others. But traits are not created equal in other ways as well. Most stereotypes are mixtures of positive and negative qualities, but why then do the negative ones seem to predominate? Is this due to some ingroup–outgroup dynamic, in that we frequently stereotype people from disliked outgroups negatively? Or is there something more basic at work? Again, we will have to know something about the content of various stereotypes, as well as the social and cultural geography of the groups to which they are attached, to answer those sorts of questions.

GROUPS AND CATEGORIES

We are not at a loss for information about the content of stereotypes for a great many groups. Obviously, you don't have to be culturally cool to have a handle on stereotypes about culturally salient groups based on gender, race, age, and various stigmas. But when you think about it, we also have stereotypes about people who own one kind of car versus another (for that matter, people who drive bright red cars), people who live in one part of town versus another, and even people who prefer veggie burgers to Big Macs. These stereotypes have not been systematically studied, perhaps for good reason.

Cautions

In this chapter and the next two, I review what is known regarding the content of stereotypes about several groups. There are a few points to keep in mind, however. The first is that many of these stereotypes are ephemeral and fleeting. Advertisers may go to great lengths to create stereotypes about the users of their products, and what advertising giveth advertising often taketh away. It is doubtful that anyone much cares these days much about the effectively created stereotypes of people who drove Studebakers or smoked Chesterfields.

Second, some more important group stereotypes may be quite dated. For areas such as race and gender, for example, where we have data for 50 years or more, it is easy to take the stereotypes of a generation or two ago as still existing today—especially when there are political agendas lurking in the background. However, stereotypes of many groups have become less well defined and more positive over the past couple of decades, although, to be sure, there is always the lingering suspicion that this has more to do with "political correctness" norms than real beliefs. Whenever possible, I present data on traditional as well as contemporary stereotypes and discuss changes.

Finally, much of the research I am presenting did not carefully distinguish between attitudes toward and beliefs about various groups. This is particularly true of public opinion data—important data from our point of view, because they were not collected on limited samples such as college students. Again, I sometimes present data on the favorability of attitudes and do not make sharp distinctions between prejudice and stereotypes. There is no point in being overly pedantic about the distinctions at this point.

The Big Three

This chapter considers stereotypes of what we might think of as the "big three": gender, race, and, age. I call them the "big three" not because they are important, although they certainly are, or because we happen to have abundant data on them, which we do. Rather, there seems to be something special about race, gender, and age categories (Levin & Levin, 1982). The "big three" are the prototypic stereotype magnets. In the first place, they are categories people do not choose. Second (and related), they are categories that have at least a small and, for certain features, a large genetic component. Third, these categories are culturally salient—probably in almost all cultures, but certainly in our Western version. Fourth, they are not optional cognitive categories. I may forget the occupation of the man I talked to for 2 hours at a party, but I will not forget his race, age, or gender. Fifth, membership in these categories is ordinarily easily determined through the senses. There will always be marginal or ambiguous cases, but usually we do not have any trouble determining whether someone is female, black, or a teenager. Sixth, Sidanius and Pratto (1999) argue that all societies have power and status hierarchies based on age and gender—and, in more highly developed societies, based on arbitrary set categories. In U.S. society race and ethnicity are such categories, whereas religion, caste, or occupation may be more important in other societies.

Chapter 12 discusses stereotypes of various stigmatized categories, and Chapter 13 features stereotypes based primarily on physical appearance, language use, and roles such as occupations. Chapter 14 turns to a consideration of traits and other features.

GENDER

In the past quarter century, more research on stereotyping has been directed to gender than to any other category. Although there was some early work on gender stereotyping (Fernberger, 1948; Sherriffs & Jarrett, 1953; Sherriffs & McKee, 1957; Smith, 1939), the major research stimulus to modern research in this area was a paper by Rosenkrantz, Vogel, Bee, Broverman, and Broverman (1968). These authors simply had subjects rate the extent to which males and females exhibited 122 traits. The 41 items that at least 75% of men and 75% of women agreed "belonged" more to one gender than the other were designated as sex-stereotypic traits. There were 12 feminine traits (e.g., being talkative, religious, quiet; expressing tender feelings) and 29 masculine traits (e.g., being aggressive, objective, logical, self-confident, active). Male and female subjects showed high agreement as to which traits were masculine and which feminine, and self-ratings were also consistent with the stereotype ratings.

More male than female traits were perceived as socially desirable, but the mean ratings of male and female traits were similar. It is hard to know what to make of this. It is possible that the subjects genuinely thought males have more of the positive traits. Alternatively, the investigators may have inadvertently given the subjects more of the socially desirable traits likely to be chosen for males. There are actually more positive traits that are female than male, generally (Sankis, Corbitt, & Widiger, 1999).

Content

There was and remains broad consensus on what traits "belong" to men and to women; however, as we will see, there has been less agreement on what all this means. Nearly everyone in Western society (including even social psychologists) knows, in general terms, what gender stereotypes are. Not only do people infer traits from gender, but they are willing to infer which gender "goes with" particular constellations of traits (Cowan & Stewart, 1977). Table 11.1 shows some traits that have commonly been perceived to be gender-linked.

Despite clear differences in the kinds of traits that are ascribed to males and females, most researchers (e.g., De Lisi & Soundranayagam, 1990; Helgeson, 1994) in this area have found that gender stereotypes are only loosely and weakly held. Few people assume that males and females are from different planets (popular books notwithstanding), or that the traits traditionally associated with one gender are proscribed for the other. Popular assumptions to the contrary, having masculine traits does not preclude having feminine ones (Deaux & Lewis, 1984; Foushee, Helmreich, & Spence, 1979), and at the level of self-reports they tend to be independent (Spence, 1999), or even positively correlated (Spence, Helmreich, & Stapp, 1975).

Agentic and Communal Features

Although gender stereotypes are multifaceted and complex (Deaux & Kite, 1993), following the lead of Spence and Helmreich (1978), several authors have suggested that these gender-linked traits fall into broad categories. One way to summarize this is that men are perceived to have traits that have qualities of action and instrumental-

TABLE 11.1. Female and Male Stereotypic Traits

Female traits	Male traits
Affectionate	Adventuresome
Dependent	Achievement-oriented
Emotional	Active
Friendly	Ambitious
Kind	Coarse
Mild	Independent
Pleasant	Loud
Prudish	Robust
Sensitive	Self-confident
Sentimental	Stable
Warm	Tough
Whiny	Unemotional

Note. Items from De Lisi and Soundranayagam (1990) and Williams and Bennett (1975).

ity (i.e., what are sometimes called "agentic" qualities), and by contrast women are perceived to be more emotionally expressive and more concerned with relationships (i.e., to have what is sometimes called a "communal" orientation) (Eagly, 1987). Generally, men perceive agentic values such as freedom, accomplishment, and self-respect as relatively more important than do women, who value communal values such as friendship, equality, and happiness more (Di Dio, Saragovi, Koestner, & Aubé, 1996). Best, Williams, and Briggs (1980) found that on semantic differential scales male traits were rated as more active and strong or potent—a result that is found in many cultures (Williams & Best, 1990).

Susan Fiske and her colleagues (Fiske, Cuddy, Glick, & Xu, 2002) have argued that competence (agentic) and warmth (communal) dimensions characterize most stereotypes, not just those of gender. Groups with higher status are typically seen as higher in competence-related traits, and groups such as females that are seen as relatively more warm than competent are treated in a paternalistic way. Thus features get associated with gender because of more general status and power relationships (see also Sidanius & Pratto, 1999, and related arguments by Eagly presented below), rather than cultural conditioning.

Traits and Other Features

Throughout this book, I have emphasized the idea that stereotypes are broad and consist of more than just traits; gender seems to encompass an unusually wide variety of features (Deaux & LaFrance, 1998; Twenge, 1999). In fact, perceived gender differences are so pervasive that we even think of plants, animals, nonrepresentational paintings, and household objects such as tables and chairs as either masculine or feminine (Fagot, Leinbach, Hort, & Strayer, 1997)—a fact of potential importance when we consider how children learn cultural lessons about stereotypes.

Let's think about the features that most of us would agree differentiate the genders. Prominent among these are physical features. Males are generally larger, stronger, and faster (Nakdimen, 1984), and certainly we perceive them to be that way. We expect men to be more interested in sports and women more interested in the arts, especially dance and ballet. Children (Pellett, 1994) and their parents (Pellett & Ignico, 1994) have stereotyped views of which physical activities boys and girls are likely to enjoy. Adult men and women are sharply differentiated in terms of amount of sports participation and the sports they participate in (Csizma, Wittig, & Schurr, 1988; Engel, 1994); other leisure activities, such as alcoholic drinking behavior, also show tremendous gender differences (Ricciardelli & Williams, 1995). I suspect that men are more likely to prefer action movies, and I'm told that a species of movies called "chick flicks" appeals mostly to females.

Science and math are still seen as masculine disciplines, while arts and the humanities are seen as more feminine (Andre, Whigham, Henderickson, & Chambers, 1999; Whitehead, 1996). Occupations remain gender-stereotyped (see Chapter 13); even in these days of increasing gender equality, we are not likely to encounter male secretaries or female construction workers. The cultural stereotype is that men will make more money than women, and that women will be more involved with household and especially child-rearing responsibilities. Even the perfumes that people wear are gender-stereotyped (Sczesny & Stahlberg, 2002).

Men are seen to be more argumentative and verbally aggressive, in part because they are (Nicotera & Rancer, 1994). We perceive females to use nonverbal cues differently than males (Briton & Hall, 1995), to display and express more emotions (Fabes & Martin, 1991; Plant, Hyde, Keltner, & Devine, 2000), and to display different emotions in different situations than do males (Hess et al., 2000; Robinson & Johnson, 1997). Women and men have somewhat different language styles (again, see Chapter 13).

Given the importance of physical sex in relationships between men and women, we might also expect to find sexual characteristics in gender stereotypes as well, although this issue is underinvestigated (Ashmore, Del Boca, & Wohlers, 1986; Clements-Schreiber & Rempel, 1995; Deaux & Kite, 1987; Holland & Davidson, 1983). There is evidence (e.g., Abbey, 1982; Edmondson & Conger, 1995; Kowalski, 1993; Regan, 1997) that males are more prone to perceive both males and females as interested in and available for sex than are females, and to perceive females as more seductive and flirtatious than females see themselves as being (Shotland & Craig, 1988). Men and women have somewhat different conceptions of sexual self-identities (Andersen, Cyranowski, & Espindle, 1999).

So there is a wide range of real and perceived sex differences, and gender stereotypes track measured differences between males and females respectably well. Although several widely cited studies (e.g., Allen, 1995; Lunneborg, 1970; Martin, 1987) have shown that people exaggerate gender differences, summaries of such studies (Eagly, 1995; Swim, 1994) suggest that, if anything, people underestimate such differences..

When we stop and think about it, our stereotypes for males and females cover a lot of territory—appearance, interests, behaviors, traits, skills, and abilities. Research by Deaux and Lewis (1984) shows that people perceive moderate correlations among relative femininity and masculinity across a number of these areas. A male who likes ballet is usually also expected to have a more feminine job, to be more interested in children, and to have a well-developed emotional side to his nature. Alternatively, males who are sports addicts and Sunday couch potatoes may be seen to have more "guy" traits, interests, and values. Interestingly, in the Deaux and Lewis study, subjects drew inferences from physical appearance cues more readily than from any other kind of gender-related feature (such as roles or traits), although Freeman (1987) found that traits were stronger predictors than physical appearance.

Contexts

TRAIT AUGMENTATION

The kinds of traits we assign to males and females may also vary a good deal by particular context. Imagine, if you will, the traits you might associate with a male kindergarten teacher, José, as opposed to a female teacher, Maria. To be sure, both would be seen as nurturing, but might you be inclined to see José as even more kind and loving than Maria? After all, *she* might be a teacher either because teaching small children is generally seen as a female job or because of a preference based on preexisting traits, but the only reason *he* would want such an atypical job is because he has the requisite traits. In attribution language, this is called "augmentation." In a study of what they called the "talking platypus" phenomenon,[1] Abramson, Goldberg, Greenberg, and Abramson (1978) showed that women attorneys were seen as more competent than their male counterparts, presumably because they had to overcome gender roadblocks to get where they were. In a related study, women entrepreneurs were judged to be more competent than males (Baron, Markman, & Hirsa, 2001). And because females smile more than males, unsmiling females are seen as less happy than their male counterparts (Deutsch, Lebaron, & Fryer, 1987).

ROLE INTERACTIONS

We are male or female, but we also have different gender-related roles that affect stereotypes (Ganong, Coleman, & Mapes, 1990). Both married men and women are evaluated more positively than unmarried ones (Etaugh & Stern, 1984), unless they are teenagers (Stacy & Richman, 1997). Married women are seen to have better interpersonal skills than divorced women, and employed mothers with small children are rated as especially competent (Etaugh & Study, 1989), but lose some of their communal traits (Bridges & Orza, 1993). Stepmothers, divorced mothers, and unwed mothers are generally evaluated negatively (Ganong & Coleman, 1995).

Evaluation

It has often been suggested (e.g., Broverman, Vogel, Broverman, Clarkson, & Rosenkrantz, 1972; McKee & Sherriffs, 1957; Rosenkrantz et al., 1968; Wolff & Taylor, 1979) that male traits are seen as more positive than female traits—that while it is good to be instrumental and assertive as well as nurturant and emotional, generally the male (instrumental) traits are perceived to be more positive than the female (expressive) ones. However, like many depictions of real and perceived sex differences, this one turns out to be basically incorrect. Most recent studies find either no essential relationship between social desirability and gender-linked traits (Ashmore & Tumia, 1980; Williams & Best, 1977) or the reverse—namely, that female traits are more positive (e.g., Bergen & Williams, 1991; Eagly & Mladinic, 1989; Eagly, Mladinic, & Otto, 1991; Feingold, 1998; Langford & Mackinnon, 2000; Sankis et al., 1999). Recent studies have found that females are evaluated more positively than males by both male and female subjects (Beauvais & Spence, 1987; Eagly, Mladinic, & Otto, 1991; Haddock & Zanna, 1994). Much of this difference is accounted for by the much greater advantage of women relative to men on the positive female traits; this advantage is greater than the male advantage on positive male traits (Eagly & Mladinic, 1994). Generally, the relationship between masculinity–femininity and favorability is weak at best (Del Boca, Ashmore, & McManus, 1986), but stereotypes are probably more favorable for females at this time.

However, before we close this particular case file, there may be additional complexities. In particular, though women may be liked more than men, they are not respected as much. Respect ratings, which are not highly correlated with either male or female stereotypes, may just reflect socialization processes or cultural biases. In any event, differential respect may play a major role in discrimination against women (Jackson, Esses, & Burris, 2001).

Evaluation Is Situational

Traits, like the behaviors they summarize, have different "payoffs" in different situations, and few would want to argue that the female (communal) traits, are always more positive than the male (agentic) ones. In fact, to the extent that people tend to associate females with "warm and fuzzy" traits, they may well be evaluated less positively than men in situations (e.g., work) where communal traits arguably have less payoff (Eagly & Mladinic, 1994).

Eagly and Karau (2002) argue that women are disadvantaged in leadership situations in two ways. First, they are seen to lack the agentic traits supposed required for such positions. Males are described as closer to successful managers than females are (Heilman, Block, Martell, & Simon, 1989; Schein, 1973, 1975), although more strongly by men (Deal & Stevenson, 1998; Dodge, Gilroy, & Fenzel, 1995; Schein, Mueller, & Jacobson, 1989). Men are described as more competent and potent than women are, except when both are also described as successful (Heilman, Block, & Martell, 1995), and even then some differences are not entirely erased (Martell, Parker, Emrich, & Crawford, 1998). However, women are seen as having more communal-type leadership traits (Martell & DeSmet, 2001)—a possible advantage to women as our ideas of successful leadership evolve.

Second, Eagly and Karau (2002) suggest that females sometimes pay a price for agentic behaviors. Task-oriented female leaders are seen as more effective but less congenial, at least by subjects who have conservative sex role attitudes (Forsyth, Heiney, & Wright, 1997). Agentic women are rated low on interpersonal skills and are penalized when applying for jobs that seem to require them (Rudman & Glick, 1999, 2001). Furthermore, Rudman (1998) found that, given the norm that women should be meek and modest, women who used self-promotion tactics—something encouraged and valued in men—were often rated negatively (especially by other females). Thus women in job situations may be caught in a double bind: To the extent that they try to perform the agentic behaviors expected in the job, they will be seen as less warm—a negative perception that may outweigh the gains from being agentic.

So male traits are likely to be preferred in what we have traditionally thought of as male jobs, those that emphasize agentic qualities. Men's stereotypic lack of communal traits is likely to be devalued in situations (teaching, caring for small children) that would seem to call for these traits. Indeed, male homemakers are perceived more negatively than females in the same role (Rosenwasser, Gonzales, & Adams, 1985). As Eagly (1987) and others have argued, the real issue is not whether we value some traits more than others, but the extent to which certain traits are seen to have "payoff" for certain roles and in certain situations. A major culprit, then, is that Western culture prizes work over home and agentic roles over communal ones.

Androgyny

Of course, both males and females can (and sometimes do) have both stereotypic masculine and feminine features. This is generally an advantage. For example, people actually like others who are androgynous (i.e., those who possess both masculine and feminine traits) more than those who are strongly sex-typed (Green & Kenrick, 1994; Jackson, 1983; Jackson & Cash, 1985; Major, Carnevale, & Deaux, 1981; Street, Kimmel, & Kromrey, 1995). It would thus appear that, as many have argued, this is one area where we can have our cake and eat it too.

However, things may be more complex, especially for romantic relationships. Both males and females prefer feminine (expressive) to masculine (instrumental) traits in romantic partners (Green & Kenrick, 1994), but men seem to have a stronger preference for feminine women than females do for masculine men (Orlofsky, 1982; Scher, 1984). Men also like masculine men more than androgynous ones

(Street et al., 1995). So preferences for masculine males and feminine females are not exactly extinct, though they are perhaps somewhat more limited than many believe.

Is the Male Stereotype Clinically Healthier?

Contrary to the assumption of many social scientists, then, male traits are not generally more positive than female ones. A related finding—that masculine traits are seen to be clinically healthier—has been cited so often as to become part of the folklore on gender evaluation, but it is also misleading. Broverman, Broverman, Clarkson, Rosenkrantz, and Vogel (1970) asked mental health professionals to describe a mentally healthy male, female, and adult, and the descriptions of the mentally healthy male were more similar to the mentally healthy adult than were the descriptions of the mentally healthy female. This has led to the claim that standards of what is mentally healthy may favor a male definition. However, Widiger and Settle (1987) showed that this result was an artifact of the greater number of positive stereotype traits favoring men that were used in the study. In any event, other research (e.g., Kravetz, 1976; Phillips & Gilroy, 1985; Poole & Tapley, 1988) shows little or no bias toward the male norm in conceptions of mental health. This is not to say that therapists react the same to male and female patients; indeed, several studies suggest that males and females seeking therapy are evaluated differently and are seen as having different causes and prognoses for their problems (Hansen & Reekie, 1990; Heesacker et al., 1999; Teri, 1982).

Gender Roles Are Prescriptive

One of the important ways that gender differs from many other social and cultural categories is that gender stereotypes tend to be prescriptive as well as descriptive (Burgess & Borgida, 1999; Eagly, 1987; Fiske & Stevens, 1993). For example, people may well think that blacks are more athletic than whites and whites have more academic skills, but in this day and age few would want to argue that young black males ought to play basketball rather than do well in school. On the other hand, many people think that females are not only more nurturant than males but that it is their job to be so, and that males not only are but should be competitive and emotionally "strong."

Who suffers more from such norms? Obviously, in the context of historic discrimination against women, it is natural to assume that women are more stereotyped than are men and that they are held more strongly to their stereotypes. As we have seen from research on categorization, men tend to be the "default" category (i.e., to have the traits that we associate more with being normal humans), and so the traits that women are presumed to possess are departures from normality and hence possibly more stereotypic.

However, as is often the case, things look different when approached from a different perspective, because sometimes women are granted more freedom to depart from their stereotypic roles than are men. Being a tomboy is a permissible and even positive role for girls, but being a sissy and having traditionally feminine interests are less permissible for boys (Martin, 1990). Whereas tomboys are seen as highly similar to boys, and even more positively on traits such as likeability, adaptability, and conceit, sissies are seen more negatively than girls on traits such as aggression, likeability, independence, self-reliance, and warmth (Martin, 1990). Of course, grown women may not have the same freedoms as do children.

Women have entered traditional male occupations and roles, and gradually are becoming more successful in those roles. However, there has not been a corresponding movement by males toward traditionally female occupations, perhaps because traditionally female occupations are not as prestigious or financially lucrative. In any event, despite continued discrimination against women in certain occupations, women may feel they have more choices of careers than males do. Whereas earlier studies tended to suggest that girls "chose" careers from a more limited menu than did boys, more recent research has suggested the opposite (Helwig, 1998).

There are really two quite separable questions here, and they have often been confused. The first is whether stereotypes of males are stronger than those for females. The second is whether there is a sense that men and women ought to behave in line with stereotypes, and if so, whether women are punished more for deviations than men.

ARE MALES OR FEMALES MORE STRONGLY STEREOTYPED?

In Chapter 1 I have complained that we do not have good measures of how strong the stereotypes for different groups are, and so we really do not have good evidence on which gender is more strongly stereotyped. The evidence we have is mixed. Research by Hort, Fagot, and Leinbach (1990) suggested that both males and females (but especially females) see a larger difference between male and female traits for males than for females. In other words, males are perceived to be more stereotyped than females. Perceptions may be a bit more nuanced today. However, subjects generally think of males in terms of more numerous and more diverse subtypes (Carpenter, 1994), which might suggest less stereotyping of the general category of males. Also, people are more categorical (using "all" or "none") in rating females than in rating males (Jackman & Senter, 1980), which would indicate that females are more stereotyped. The evidence therefore is too fragile to support a definitive conclusion.

ARE MALES OR FEMALES MORE STRONGLY DISAPPROVED FOR CROSS-GENDERED BEHAVIOR?

There has been considerable research on the question of whether men and women are disapproved for behavior seen as appropriate to the opposite sex. Many studies find that both males and females are disapproved for cross-gendered behavior (Costrich, Feinstein, Kidder, Marecek, & Pascale, 1975; Fagot, 1978; Lindsey & Zakahi, 1996; Rojahn & Willemsen, 1994). However, although there are some exceptions (e.g., Malchon & Penner, 1981; Yoder & Schleicher, 1996), studies that find a difference generally show that males are disapproved more for female behavior than the reverse (e.g., Berndt & Heller, 1986; Carter & McCloskey, 1983–1984; Fagot, 1977; Lobel, Bempechat, Gewirtz, Shoken-Topaz, & Bashe, 1993; Tilby & Kalin, 1980). One possible major exception is that stereotypes of feminists, who might be thought of as women who are actively seeking to cross or blur traditional gender boundaries, are generally quite negative (Haddock & Zanna, 1994; Twenge & Zucker, 1999); this finding suggests disapproval for female cross-gendered behavior. In addition to negative evaluations for cross-sexed behavior, people are seen as more likely to be homosexual when they display cross-gendered styles (Kite & Deaux, 1987; Storms, Stivers, Lambers, & Hill, 1981).

Differences in Gender Stereotypes

Surely not everyone holds exactly the same gender stereotypes. Do they vary from culture to culture, person to person? Unfortunately, such questions usually produce a glass half-full, half-empty answer. There are differences, but there are also commonalities.

CULTURAL DIFFERENCES

Obviously there will be some differences across cultures (e.g., Belk, Snell, Holtzman, Hernandez-Sanchez, & Garcia-Falconi, 1989), but there is surprisingly good agreement from culture to culture on which traits characterize males and females—even for self-descriptions (Costa, Terracciano, & McCrae, 2001). In the extensive cross-cultural studies conducted by Williams and Best (1982, 1990), gender stereotypes in a U.S. sample are correlated quite highly with those from Australian, English, Canadian, and New Zealand samples, but less highly with Pakistani, Japanese, Italian, and French samples. There is more agreement across cultures on stereotypes for males than for females, except for traits relating to agreeableness (Williams, Satterwhite, & Best, 1999). Table 11.2 gives some examples of some national differences in gender stereotypes. Keep in mind that this table lists only some traits on which there was wide cultural disagreement. However, people in the different countries agreed on many more traits, such as that males are more rational, obnoxious, opinionated, and ambitious, and that females are more dependent, appreciative, sexy, sentimental, and sensitive (again, among other traits).

TABLE 11.2. Percentages of People in Various Countries Who Think Men Have More of Various Traits

Trait	Brazil	France	Italy	Japan	Nigeria	Pakistan	United States
Blustery	76	93	97	88	43	8	44
Cheerful	25	47	51	31	20	68	9
Conscientious	60	29	57	49	65	43	31
Effeminate	35	61	82	39	9	8	38
Excitable	47	42	59	42	12	86	9
Friendly	36	75	53	73	28	53	28
Loyal	47	86	81	83	24	18	47
Nagging	72	81	52	34	17	73	2
Pessimistic	42	46	57	31	25	62	75
Poised	76	67	62	39	47	50	16
Prejudiced	39	29	46	34	23	64	77
Snobbish	36	58	77	63	22	91	18

Note. Large numbers represent male traits and low numbers female. Data from Williams and Best (1990).

FEMALE–MALE DIFFERENCES

What about differences in stereotypes held by males and females? Surely, given all the discussions of gender politics in recent years, they must disagree. Interestingly enough, most studies find that males and females have surprisingly similar views on the content of gender stereotypes (e.g., Der-Karabetian & Smith, 1977; Jackman, 1994; Rosenkrantz et al., 1968; Williams & Best, 1977); this agreement also occurs across cultures (Williams et al., 1979). Implicit measures of gender stereotyping (e.g., Rudman, Greenwald, & McGhee, 2001) also support male and female similarities in gender stereotypes. To the extent that differences occur, males of all ages have stronger stereotypes of females than the reverse (Belk & Snell, 1986; Huston, 1985; Lewin & Tragos, 1987) and see more traits as gender-related (Der-Karabetian & Smith, 1977).

Not surprisingly, each gender tends to evaluate itself more positively than the other gender does (e.g., Etaugh, Levine, & Mannella, 1984). Furthermore, on a variety of attitudinal measures about traditional sex roles, egalitarianism, and the like, women are more positive toward freedom and equality for women than are men (Gibbons, Stiles, & Shkodriana, 1991; Haworth, Povey, & Clift, 1986; Jackson, Hodge, & Ingram, 1994; King & King, 1985, 1990).

ATTITUDE, VALUE, AND PERSONALITY CORRELATES

There is a substantial menu of personality correlates of gender stereotypes. The Right-Wing Authoritarianism Scale (see Chapter 8) predicts measures of traditional attitudes toward women (Duncan, Peterson, & Winter, 1997) as well as both negativity of stereotypes and attitudes toward feminist women but not women in general (Haddock & Zanna, 1994). The Hostile Sexism subscale of the Ambivalent Sexism Inventory (again, see Chapter 8), but not the Benevolent Sexism subscale, predicts negative stereotyping of women (Glick & Fiske, 1996).

Bem's (1981, 1985) gender schema theory suggests that people who are strongly sex-typed (i.e., strongly masculine males and feminine females) should be prone to process information about others in terms of gender. However, research using the Bem Sex Role Inventory (a scale developed to measure sex-typing) has yielded equivocal results with regard to predictions about the effects of this on stereotyping and differential evaluation of males and females (Deaux & Kite, 1993; Spence, 1993).

Other studies have found relationships between measures of traditional gender ideology and gender stereotyping (Cota, Reid, & Dion, 1991; Eagly & Mladinic, 1989; Innes, Dormer, & Lukins, 1993; Spence et al., 1975; Tilby & Kalin, 1980), especially on instrumental traits (Spence & Buckner, 2000). More religious people tend to have stronger gender stereotypes, as well as more traditional attitudes about appropriate roles for women (Larsen & Long, 1988; M. Y. Morgan, 1987). Lower-socioeconomic-status and less well-educated people have more traditional gender attitudes (Hoffman & Kloska, 1995).

DIFFERENCES OVER TIME

The research cited in this chapter spans a period from the late 1940s through the present, and we must be wary of assuming that results from earlier studies are still pertinent, given the considerable changes in norms, experiences, and education. Available data do suggest that younger people have weaker gender stereotypes than older ones (Dambrot, Papp, & Whitmore, 1984), and that gender stereotypes and attitudes have diminished somewhat over the past several years, with evidence of strongest change during the 1970s (Harris & Firestone, 1998; Helmreich, Spence, & Gibson, 1982; McBroom, 1987; Simon & Landis, 1989; Zuo, 1997). Generally the changes have not been dramatic (Spence & Buckner, 2000; Werner & LaRussa, 1985), and probably exist mostly at the level of how strongly men and women are stereotyped as opposed to the content of the stereotypes. Although it is possible that these changes reflect changes in perceptions, it is also possible that they reflect real changes in male and especially female behaviors (Twenge, 1997).

Gender Subtypes

The categories of male and female are large and diverse—so much so that it may be difficult to imagine prototypes or exemplars. What is a typical male, anyway? Gender groups may be too broad to carry much weight in terms of stereotypes, and obviously for gender as well as other categories, most of us have a number of subtypes that arguably carry the burden of stereotyping. Almost all of us have considerable exposure to both genders—a process that should promote subtyping (Fiske & Stevens, 1993)— and certainly we have a rich variety of labels for males and females (Holland & Skinner, 1987). Furthermore, since it is clear that behavior varies from situation to situation, even "cultural idiots" will have plenty of exposure to a wide range of behaviors by both genders (Deaux & LaFrance, 1998; Deaux & Major, 1987). There certainly are distinctive stereotypes of different kinds of males and females; an important question is whether these subtypes come to stand for the whole. For instance, when we think of the traditional female stereotype, are we really accessing the stereotype of a mother or housewife? And do the male stereotypes presuppose a male working at a traditionally male job?

Eagly's Social Role Model

There have been two general arguments along these lines. In the more theoretically important of these, Eagly (1987) has argued that stereotypes are really stereotypes about roles and not genders. Specifically, she suggests that men and women do differ in their behaviors, on average, but that these differences reflect the differing roles men and women typically occupy in our society. For example, women are often seen as more nurturant and concerned with the care of babies and infants. Women probably do perform more nurturing behaviors than do men, but this is because women are more often placed in positions (teacher, nurse) and roles (motherhood) where these behaviors are expected. Conversely, men are generally more aggressive and domineering than women, and again this is because men are more likely to have jobs where such behavior is encouraged. Both men and women who have more dominant roles actually behave in more agentic ways than those in less dominant roles (Moskowitz, Suh, & Desaulniers, 1994). In this study, communal behaviors were not affected by work roles; females were more communal than males across roles. This finding may reflect the fact that the work roles did not differ in their "call" for communal behaviors, but a more intriguing possibility is that communal behaviors are less responsive to situational demands than agentic ones are. Higher-status positions are generally assumed to carry more power and influence, and because women are less likely to occupy such positions, they are seen as less powerful (Conway, Pizzamiglio, & Mount, 1996; Conway & Vartanian, 2000). When women have power and status equal to or greater than men's, they are perceived as being just as agentic as the men in those positions (Eagly & Wood, 1982; Eagly & Steffen, 1984; Geis, Brown, Jennings, & Corrado-Taylor, 1984; Gerber, 1988; Smoreda, 1995).

Eagly recognizes that more is involved than simple social pressures to behave in certain ways in certain roles. By virtue of being placed in different roles (often from childhood on), males and females may develop different skills and abilities, may come to have differing expectations for their own behavior and accomplishments, and may adopt differing beliefs about their own traits and what they should do in a given situation. Indeed, people who have internalized traditional gender roles tend to feel most comfortable in situations that emphasize those roles (Wood, Christensen, Hebl, & Rothgerber, 1997). When all is said and done, however, gender stereotypes are largely driven by role pressures.

STEREOTYPES MAY ACCURATELY REFLECT OBSERVATIONS

I want to emphasize four related implications of the Eagly analysis. First, stereotypes may be built in part, perhaps in large part, on accurate observations of how men and women differ (see Chapter 9 for further discussion)—differences that are based more on roles men and women occupy than on their biological heritage (Eagly & Wood, 1999).

THE ROLE–GENDER CONFOUND

Second, since these stereotypes are really about roles and not about people, it follows that either changes in the behaviors we expect from people in different roles or a change in the distribution of men and women in various roles ought to have a direct impact on our stereotypes of males and females. If, for example, we decided to create new and improved business managers who stressed interpersonal and caring skills, and males remained overrepresented in those roles, we would expect to find that men on average would become more communal and that in time stereotypes of men would reflect this change. Conversely, if we increased the percentage of men in professions such as nursery school teaching and nursing, and these professions continued to emphasize nurturing activities, we would also expect men to be seen as more nurturing. In support, there is evidence that women's assertiveness has risen in periods when their status has increased (1931–1945, 1968–1993), and that it decreased during the 1950s, when women had lower status (Twenge, 2001). Clearly, people do see gender roles as decreasing over time and consequently see gender stereotypes as diminishing, especially for women's agentic qualities (Diekman & Eagly, 2000). But let's not go too fast. Eagly and Steffen (1986) found that women who worked part-time lost some of their communal attributes but did not gain much in agency. Similarly, part-time male workers lost agency without a compensating gain in communal virtues. Rudman and Glick (1999) point to similar sorts of problems with perceived "tradeoffs" between communal and agentic qualities.

IMPLICATIONS FOR OTHER GROUPS

Third, the arguments about roles are not restricted to gender. Many salient social groups have different roles that affect their behaviors and thus the perceptions that others have of them. We might, for example, think about racial groups as other large groups of people that tend to be differentially assigned to roles. Blacks may, for example, be seen as less smart than whites because they are more often placed in positions that make little use of their native intelligence and that do not allow them to develop their self-confidence in displaying intelligence. See Chapters 3 and 5, and a later section of the present chapter, for further discussion.

SOME SUBTYPES STAND FOR THE WHOLE

Fourth, although at some level we recognize differences among types of women and men, we may let one subcategory stand for the whole when we are not on our cognitive guards. For example, Riedle (1991) showed that ratings of mothers as a category were indistinguishable from ratings of mothers not working outside the home, but were somewhat dissimilar from ratings of mothers who did work. This would suggest that when people think of mothers, they still think in terms of traditional mothers who do not have outside employment.

Actual Subtypes

A second approach has been to stress subtypes of males and females. There is no doubt that we *can* divide the world into smaller and smaller categories, but the important questions are when we do so and with what effects. Plainly, women can be effective housewives, strippers, cops, businesswomen, mothers, and athletes (and these are not mutually exclusive). And men sometimes work, accompany their families to religious services, treat women as sexual objects, coach Little League teams, do household chores, and watch Sunday afternoon football from a supine position on the couch (TV remote at the ready). The questions are whether these behaviors are naturally assigned to different subtypes and, if so, whether they inform our thinking about gender. Given the many differences between types of men and women, do we even use global gender categories that much?

ARE SUBTYPES ASSIGNED DIFFERENT TRAITS?

Several studies have directly examined gender subtypes. In a widely cited study, Clifton, McGrath, and Wick (1976) asked subjects to check traits that described "bunnies," housewives, club women, career women, and female athletes. Some traits were used to describe two or more of the subtypes (e.g., bunnies, club women, career women, and athletes were all described as aggressive), but the majority of the traits were seen as characteristic of only one of the subtypes. England (1988) asked subjects to rate behaviors of different kinds of women in different situations, and as expected, there were differences. For example, although there were only weak tendencies to see the different types of women as differentially maternal, professional women were seen as taking financial provider responsibilities more seriously and as being more assertive than housewives, bunnies, and women in general. Even mothers—who themselves constitute a subtype of women—can be divided into subtypes, with married mothers, stepmothers, divorced mothers, and never-married mothers differing on several traits (Ganong & Coleman, 1995). A meta-analysis suggests that both marital status and to a lesser extent parental status affect stereotypes of men and women (Ganong et al., 1990).

Turning to male subtypes, England (1992) showed that businessmen, macho males, family men, and men in general were rated somewhat differently across a number of personality traits. However, there was a high degree of similarity across these categories for some traits (assertiveness) and expected behaviors for some roles (family responsibilities), suggesting that subjects may not strongly differentiate males, at least for expected behaviors. These and other studies show that people do have stereotypes of various gender subtypes, but most of the studies suggest some commonality of trait assignment across subtypes, as well as other traits that differentiate the types.

ARE SUBTYPES SALIENT?

Are these subtypes meaningful to people? The fact that people can generate subtypes and associate different features with them does not guarantee that they are actively used. Some studies (e.g., Deaux, Winton, Crowley, & Lewis, 1985) suggest that gender subtypes may not be especially salient, but other research tends to suggest that they are. For example, Green and Ashmore (1998) asked people to describe the pictures in their heads when they thought about four male and four female subtypes. A content analysis revealed considerable consensus on the images—a result suggesting some degree of salience. Certainly descriptions of subtypes are affected by exposure to exemplars (Coats & Smith, 1999).

In a now classic study, Noseworthy and Lott (1984) gave subjects groups of traits differentially associated with sex objects, career women, housewives, female athletes, and women's libbers. When asked to recall these traits, the recall did tend to cluster around these subtypes. That is, subjects tended to recall career woman traits, followed by (say) female athlete traits, and so on. In the cognitive psychology literature, this is usually taken as evidence of category salience. However, we have to be careful about what this says about subtyping. The results show that at least in memory, traits such as being beautiful, having a good figure, being fashion-conscious, and being popular go together, and traits such as being tidy, maternal, devoted to family, and gentle cluster together. But, of course, there may be many reasons for this clustering other than gender links. We may note that beautiful people are more popular and fashion-conscious without activating the knowledge that such traits may be characteristic of a subtype of women. Everyone, including males, may also tend to exhibit such correlated features, so such results may say more about the structure of behavior and traits than that of gender categories.

EMPIRICALLY DERIVED SUBTYPES

Another research strategy is to have people generate their own subcategories, usually by asking them to sort different types of men and women into categories that seem to go together (Six & Eckes, 1991). For example, Holland and Skinner (1987) asked college-age subjects to sort gender labels; through multidimensional scaling, they were able to determine the basic dimensions underlying these sortings. When males rated females, the dimensions were as follows: prestige as a sexual possession, tendency to overdependency/engulfing, and sexiness. When women rated men, the dimensions were these: use of power or attractiveness for selfish ends, being ineffective and unbearable, and unusual sexual appetites.

For males, Edwards (1992) found that people generated a number of subtypes that could be grouped into businessman, loser, blue-collar worker, athlete, family man, and ladies' man. When asked to list traits for each subtype, the most salient (top 10) for each subtype showed almost no overlap. When subjects were asked to group the traits most clearly assigned to each subtype, a clustering analysis showed that the traits did tend to be grouped in ways that represented each of the subtypes. But again, we cannot be sure whether the traits were being grouped in terms of subtypes, linguistic meaning, or some other extraneous feature. Furthermore, the fact that a trait is highly characteristic of one subtype does not mean that it is uncharacteristic of another.

Eckes (1994b) asked people to list traits that corresponded to a large number of male and female subtypes. Female subtypes included career woman, chick, feminist, hippy, housewife, intellectual, punk, secretary, vamp, trendy, society woman, and women's libber. For men, some representative subtypes were bum, cad, career man, confident type, intellectual, macho, manager, radical rocker, trendy, and yuppie. Then each of the subtypes was rated on scales that differentiated among the subtypes. Interestingly, different types of features were associated with different subtypes (Eckes, 1994a). For example, physical features and overt behaviors were more important than traits and attitudes for the bum subtype, but the reverse was true for the social climber subtype. For females, the career woman subtype was high on traits and physical appearance features, and the hippy subtype on attitudes. Eckes (1996) has also shown that gender subtypes are associated with situations. Subjects were asked to indicate whether the various subtypes would feel comfortable in a range of situations, and clusters of gender types and situations were extracted. For example, a typical woman, a housewife, and a wallflower were all associated with family get-togethers and watching TV, whereas a typical man, a career man, and a jock were associated with sports. Interestingly, female subtypes were seen on average as more comfortable in a wider range of situations than were male subtypes, indirectly supporting the idea that women are less subject to stereotype pressures than are men (see above).

GENDER AND COMPOUND CATEGORIES

One of the many reasons gender is such an important social category is that it crosscuts nearly every other social category; the same is arguably true of race and age. No matter what other categories we place people into (occupation, roles, personality, etc.), they will still be male or female. Gender subtypes are really combinations of gender with other categories—what I have previously called "compound categories" (see Chapter 3). As I have reported throughout this chapter, stereotypes of men and women change as gender is combined with other categories, such as occupation and marital status.

What about compound categories based on combination of the "big three" of age, gender, and race? There is some reason to believe that race affects the ways we view gender categories. A black female is not merely a female who happens to be black, for example. Deaux and Kite (1985) found that whereas white subjects had similar stereotypes for black men and white men, black women were seen as having more masculine traits than white women and were viewed as being much closer to black men than white women were to white men. Similarly, Weitz and Gordon (1993) found relatively little overlap in the stereotypes of females in general (presumably assumed to be white) and black females. Traits most often applied to females in general included being intelligent, materialistic, sensitive, attractive, sophisticated, emotional, and ambitious; for black females, the most common traits were being loud, talkative, aggressive, intelligent, straightforward, argumentative, and stubborn. Similarly, stereotypes of older and younger females differ (Kite, Deaux, & Miele, 1991; Turner & Turner, 1994).

Naive Theories about Gender

We can and do argue about how accurate certain stereotypes are, and to the extent that stereotypes track real differences between groups, we may further ask why such differences occur. What theories do people have about such differences? Most people assume that their stereotypes are accurate in the sense of being based on real differences between groups. Their theories about why these differences occur are thus part and parcel of the stereotyping process. Gender is a particularly appealing focus for research on stereotyping, because it is obvious that both biological and cultural factors produce actual gender differences. What do people think accounts for the differences they perceive between males and females?

In a large national survey done in 1975, Jackman (1994) reported that 28% of men and 21% of women attributed sex differences to genetics, and that 43% of men and 52% of women ascribed gender differences to home upbringing. Smith and Russell (1984) asked children aged 7, 10, and 15 about the causes of gender differences. Although both boys and girls switched from predominantly biological to primarily socialization-based explanations over the ages studied here, at all ages boys employed biological explanations more than did girls. Among a sample of college-age subjects, socialization and cultural explanations were preferred more than biological ones, and the latter were related to additional beliefs that gender differences are hard to eliminate (Martin & Parker, 1995). However, beliefs in biological causation and socialization were uncorrelated, and both predicted perceived sex differences in appearance and personality, whereas socialization beliefs were related to perceived differences in occupation and biological beliefs to perceived differences in interests.

RACE AND ETHNICITY

Much of the classic research in the stereotype area has focused on stereotypes of minority groups (blacks, Hispanics, Jews, Asians, etc.). At this point, we do not need any elaborate explanation for why this should be; such stereotypes have justified subtle as well as quite overt discrimination.

The Reality of Race and Ethnicity

We think we know what ethnic and racial groups are, but definitions of such groups are heavily culturally conditioned, arguably to the point of arbitrariness. If we think of race as based on strongly differentiated genetic differences among groups, then we are in for some hard times intellectually and scientifically. It is true that some genetic traits differ somewhat from one racial group to another (although there is typically greater within-group than between-group variability), but physical appearance is not generally one of them. On average, members of the so-called "Negro" race are darker-skinned than those of the so-called "Caucasian," but people who live in India have been classified as "Caucasian" and yet are often much darker-skinned than many people of African descent. So-called "Negroid" features certainly appear in some African Americans, but far from all. These days we speak of African Americans to emphasize the African origins of some Americans, but Africa itself contains the widest variations of skin color, hair and eye color, height, and facial features of any continent (Kohn, 1995). Among indigenous Africans there are blonds and redheads, as well as those with black hair; some Africans have flattened noses, but others have chiseled features.[2]

Of course, it might be argued that many of those we call "African American" have both European and African ancestors. However, it is unclear what identification problem, if any, this solves. Imagine a man whose ancestry we know to be 75% European and 25% African and yet who looks more "black," versus a person whose percentages are reversed and who looks more "white."[3] And what about a dark-skinned black woman whose cultural background seems more white than black, versus a lighter-skinned woman whose whole demeanor is "black and proud of it?" Exactly how much of one kind of "blood" or another does one need to have to be classified one way or the other? Does cultural background matter at all? In addition to the issues raised by the examples just given, it is important to note that because of recent immigration, Africans with no slave ancestors are a nontrivial portion of the group we classify as African American. Also, although the majority of African Americans are descendants of American slaves, many also have ancestors who were slaves in various Caribbean islands—a quite different cultural legacy. At any rate, in the United States the historical legacy has been the "one-drop" rule (Davis, 1991). That is, anyone with any identifiable African ancestry has tended to be classified as black, both legally (mostly in Southern states) and informally.

Few physical features, and even fewer (if any) psychological features, are unique to one or another of the putative races (Corcos, 1997). Even for biological factors such as blood types and various enzymes, diversity within racial groups is 8–10 times higher than diversity between groups (Zuckerman, 1990).[4] Furthermore, classification on the basis of various biological and genetic markers often leads to classifications quite different from the ones we informally use. In some cases, blacks are actually quite close to whites (Jones, 1997). It is not clear that hair type or skin color is more important than these less obvious features.

Matters are even more complex when we think about ethnicity. Is a man named Michael Johnson, who grew up in his mother's Mexican American home, Hispanic? What about Maria Gonzalez, who has blond hair, never heard Spanish spoken as a child, and only recently has begun to think about her fifth-generation Mexican heritage? "Ethnicity" may refer to cultural differences, ethnic identity, or distinctive experiences associated with treatment by others (Phinney, 1996), and many people are not clear about distinctions among race, ethnicity, and culture (Betancourt & Lopez, 1993).

In fact, people historically made arbitrary distinctions about race almost any time they did not like another group. For example, not only German Nazis but Americans have often referred to Jews as a separate race; at the turn of the century in North America, Italians were frequently seen as a nonwhite race; and the English often talked of the Irish as being a distinct race (Hirschfeld, 1996). It will not do blithely to suggest that earlier generations were deluded and that we modern folks have finally got the distinctions right. Whether we deal with cultural differences, physical appearance, or intragroup marriage, it is hard to find a clear principle that distinguishes race from ethnicity or one race from another (Corcos, 1997; Davis, 1991; Hirschfeld, 1996; Kohn, 1995; Stephan & Stephan, 2000b; Yee, Fairchild, Weizmann, & Wyatt, 1993).[5] It is not clear, then, what "race" and "ethnicity" ought to mean, and many authors (e.g., Allen & Adams, 1992; Hirschfeld, 1996; Jones, 1983; Kohn, 1995) have deplored their vagueness when used by social scientists, let alone less well-informed folks. At a minimum, they are not coherent ways to classify people. They are social constructions (Banks & Eberhardt, 1998; Jones, 1997).

Despite the fact that the concepts of race and ethnicity are muddled, most Americans think they know what races and the racial stereotypes that go with them are.[6] Yet, despite the salience of such stereotypes in the U.S. national debate about race issues, there is comparatively little contemporary research on stereotypes about various ethnic groups. In part, this is because the emphasis in modern stereotype research has shifted to processing rather than content. But in larger part, I suspect, it reflects the fact that it is often extremely hard to get college students to admit to stereotypes about people from other racial or ethnic groups. The fact that they have such stereotypes is beyond dispute, as studies that have used indirect and subtle measures have shown (e.g., Devine, 1989; Fazio, Jackson, Dunton, & Williams, 1995; Greenwald, McGhee, & Schwartz, 1998; Sigall & Page, 1971).

Cues for Group Membership

As with gender and age, it seems vaguely pedantic to ask how we identify the racial membership of individuals. After all, don't people simply look African American or Asian American? Obviously skin color and facial features are major cues for racial identification, but as I have been arguing, they are far from perfect. Some first and last names are fairly diagnostic. Vocal qualities and accents often differentiate. However, except for the work on identification of Jews reviewed in Chapter 7, there have been no systematic studies done on how people determine racial or ethnic group membership—perhaps because it seems so obvious.

One interesting question, however, which has been raised before (see Chapter 3), is whether group membership is considered all-or-none or is graded—and, if the latter, what cues determine the degree of group membership. Can someone be very black or only somewhat black, a little or a lot Jewish? Is Abe Rosenstein, who "looks Jewish," seen as more Jewish than Jon Miller, who does not? Is the very dark-complexioned black woman named Latoya seen as more black than her lighter counterpart named Rosanne? We make such graded distinctions sometimes, but informal observation suggests that it is often made on the basis of whether people exhibit relevant

stereotypic traits. A woman who exhibits traits that are part of the Jewish mother stereotype may be seen as very Jewish, whereas the businessman who does not fit the
stereotype of the Jewish merchant may not be seen as very Jewish at all: "Well, he's
Jewish, but he's not really Jewish, if you know what I mean." Certainly within the
black community (and, I suspect, within the white one as well), some blacks are seen
to embrace their racial heritage more strongly than others and thus to be "more
black." Do physical features matter?

Little systematic research has addressed these questions. In early research by
Secord (1959; Secord, Bevan, & Katz, 1956), white subjects rated photos labeled as
"Negro" or "white" that varied in "Negroidness"; the appearance variable had no effect on the tendency to assign stereotype traits to the pictures, but the label did. This
would suggest that physical features do not affect tendencies to stereotype. However,
there is good evidence that skin color and tone affect evaluations of blacks among
other blacks in both the United States (Breland, 1998; Russell, Wilson, & Hall, 1992)
and the Dominican Republic (Sidanius, Pena, & Sawyer, 2001). Within the black
community, lighter skin has historically been seen as more prestigious, and lighter-
skinned blacks do have considerable advantages in the larger community.[7] Several
surveys have found that light-skinned blacks have higher socioeconomic status, although often skin tone makes a bigger difference for females than for males (Edwards, 1973; Freeman, Ross, Armor, & Pettigrew, 1966; Keith & Herring, 1991; Seltzer & Smith, 1991; Udry, Bauman, & Chase, 1971). Also, those with darker skin
report more discrimination (Klonoff & Landrine, 2000).

Both blacks and whites assign more stereotypic traits to dark-skinned blacks
(Maddox & Gray, 2002), and at least for white perceivers, black faces with more prototypic African features lead to stronger automatic activation of negative affect than
do less prototypic faces (Blair, Judd, Sadler, & Jenkins, 2002; Livingston & Brewer,
2002). Skin color clearly affects trait ratings of blacks by blacks (Anderson & Cromwell, 1977; Bayton & Muldrow, 1968; Marks, 1943), and some studies (e.g., Bond &
Cash, 1992; Marks, 1943), but not all (Coard, Breland, & Raskin, 2001; Hamm, Williams, & Dalhouse, 1973), find that blacks prefer lighter skin. There is also some evidence that whereas whites evaluate dark-skinned blacks more unfavorably, blacks actually evaluate them more favorably (Kennedy, 1993; Lawson, 2003), possibly
because of resentment over the privileges accorded lighter-skinned people.

Other appearance and behavioral cues may also matter. The gender research of
Deaux and Lewis (1984; see above) showed that behavior and appearance are part of
gender stereotypes, and surely the same is true for other groups. Thus we should be
more likely to apply the black stereotype to a young black male who listens to rap
music and wears numerous gold chains, or the Jewish stereotype to a Jewish male
who wears a yarmulke.

African American Stereotypes

The Princeton Trilogy

It might be well to start with the path-breaking research of Katz and Braly (1933), together with the follow-ups by Gilbert (1951) and Karlins, Coffman, and Walters
(1969). Table 11.3 gives the most frequently checked traits for Negroes in the three
samples.

TABLE 11.3. Ten Most Frequently Selected Traits (and Percentages of Subjects Listing These Traits) for Negroes in Three Studies

Trait	1933	1951	1969
Superstitious	84	41	13
Lazy	75	31	26
Happy-go-lucky	38	17	27
Ignorant	38	24	11
Musical	26	33	47
Ostentatious	26	11	25
Very religious	24	17	8
Stupid	22	10	4
Physically dirty	17	–	3
Naive	14	–	4
Slovenly	13	–	5
Unreliable	12	–	6
Pleasure-loving	–	19	29
Sensitive	–	–	17
Gregarious	–	–	17
Talkative	–	–	14
Imitative	–	–	13

Note. The 1933 data are from Katz and Braly (1933), the 1951 data from Gilbert (1951), and the 1969 data from Karlins, Coffman, and Walters (1969).

For those who are interested in issues of change, there is both good news and bad. On the bad side, even in 1967 sizeable percentages of people were willing to check certain traits as characteristic of blacks. Although the percentages generally went down from 1933 to 1951, they seem to have rebounded by 1967. On the other hand, there is some good news, because many of the newer traits were relatively more positive than the older ones. Traits such as being stupid, physically dirty, and unreliable were replaced by traits such as being sensitive, gregarious, and talkative. Being superstitious went way down, but being musical went up. Other studies that have assessed changes in stereotypes over time (e.g., Clark & Pearson, 1982; Gordon, 1986; Hartsough & Fontana, 1970; Madon, Guyll, et al., 2001) have generally concluded that there has been a decline in negative stereotypes for blacks over time, with perhaps a bit of leveling off or increase in the 1980s.

More Recent Data

Devine and Elliot (1995) have been critical of the Princeton trilogy for several reasons. In the first place, people were asked to provide traits they thought went with various groups, but a better measure might have been to ask which traits subjects thought were part of the general stereotype. As Devine (1989) has shown, subjects may have good knowledge of cultural stereotypes without necessarily agreeing with them personally. Another criticism is that the three studies used the same traits for comparability reasons, despite the obvious possibility that current racial stereotypes may include features (e.g., being violent) that were not given to the earlier subjects.

In a more recent study at the University of Wisconsin, Devine and Elliot (1995) did find that while many of the original Katz–Braly traits (such as being superstitious, happy-go-lucky, ostentatious, naive, and materialistic) had essentially disappeared from whites' stereotypes of blacks, other traits (such as being athletic, rhythmic, low in intelligence, poor, criminal, and loud) were endorsed by at least a third of the subjects. These newer traits hardly give rise to optimism about the nature of whites' stereotypes of blacks. On the other hand, Jackson and colleagues (1996) found a general absence of character traits, positive or negative; their subjects tended to report traits such as being angry and noisy, which reflected a perception that blacks are disaffected from American society. In free descriptions of blacks, there is a mixture of positive and negative features (Jackson, Lewandowski, Ingram, & Hodge, 1997); for example, black males were described as being athletic, fun, easy to talk to, and charming, as well as violent, angry, and resentful.

Niemann, Jennings, Rozelle, Baxter, and Sullivan (1994) asked students at a large urban university to list features that they thought went with various groups. Unlike many previous researchers, they asked for these traits to be given separately for males and females in these groups. Also, they used a free-response format (i.e., subjects were asked to list traits rather than to select traits from an experimenter-provided list). Rankings for African American males and females are given in Table 11.4. As will be readily apparent, a number of features listed are physical characteristics, and those that might be termed psychological include a mixture of the positive and negative.

Other studies have also shown a mixed picture on stereotypes of blacks. Plous and Williams (1995) report data from a public opinion survey showing that whites were seen as superior in artistic ability and abstract thinking, whereas blacks were seen as superior in athletic ability and rhythmic ability. Almost half of the respondents felt that there was at least one difference between blacks and whites in terms of

TABLE 11.4. Ranking of Traits Given for African American Males and Females by 259 College Students

	Males	Females
Athletic	1	4
Antagonistic	2	3
Dark skin	3	2
Muscular	4	–
Criminal	5	–
Speak loudly	6	1
Tall	7	–
Intelligent	8	8
Unmannerly	9	6
Pleasant	10	5
Lower-class	11	10
Ambitionless	12	12
Non-college	13	–
Racist	14	–
Sociable	15	7
Attractive	–	9
Egotistical	–	11
Caring	–	13
Humorous	–	14
Honest	–	15

Note. Data from Niemann, Jennings, Rozelle, Baxter, and Sullivan (1994).

physical features; 31% believed white skin to be thinner than black, 14% viewed whites as more sensitive to physical pain, and 24% thought that blacks have longer arms than whites. Interestingly enough, these differences were more strongly endorsed in a black than in a white sample. In national survey data presented by Bobo and Kluegel (1997), over 50% thought that blacks were prone to violence, about 30% thought they were unintelligent, fewer than 20% endorsed "hard-working" as a characteristic feature, and over half said that blacks preferred to live off welfare. In another study (Weitz & Gordon, 1993), black women were seen as being loud, talkative, aggressive, intelligent, straightforward, argumentative, stubborn, quick-tempered, and bitchy, and as having too many children, by at least 10% of a sample of college students (predominantly white); by comparison, traits such as being intelligent, materialistic, sensitive, attractive, sophisticated, emotional, and ambitious were identified for white female stimulus persons.

Although stereotypes held by whites about blacks are presently somewhat more positive than formerly, and certainly have a mixture of both positive and negative features, the overall picture is not one that suggests a fast track to economic success. Indeed, ratings of successful business managers match ratings of whites much more closely than ratings of blacks (Tomkiewicz, Brenner, & Adeyemi-Bello, 1998). To be sure, some negative features (e.g., shiftless, lazy, and stupid) have dropped off the primary list, but other traits (e.g., loud, violence-prone, and unmannerly) that have replaced them may not be great improvements, at least as features conducive to getting high-paying jobs.

Subtypes for African Americans

Given the interest in gender subtypes, it is surprisingly that there has been relatively little interest in assessing the subtypes of various ethnic groups. Identifying racial subtypes is also important, given the diversity of visible black exemplars such as Bill Cosby, Oprah Winfrey, O. J. Simpson, and Dennis Rodman. Whereas black males may be identified with crime, there are also highly visible black athletes, a much more positive type (Sailes, 1998). Stereotypes based on these images are likely to be quite different. The most complete study for race subtyping was reported by Devine and Baker (1991). They asked subjects to list features for the following groups: blacks in general, black athletes, black businessmen, ghetto blacks, militant blacks, "Oreo cookies," streetwise blacks, "Uncle Toms," and welfare blacks. The features varied along three major dimensions: good–bad (e.g., hostile and poor vs. intelligent and ambitious), athletic (athletic and ostentatious vs. upward and jobless), and unique features. On the first (evaluative) dimension, athletes and businessmen were distinguished from all other groups, and on the second (athletic), athletes and blacks in general were different from the other groups. Generally, then, subjects did not distinguish among streetwise, ghetto, and welfare blacks; they were all seen as being hostile, poor, and unintelligent, and as having negative personality traits. Black athletes were seen as unintelligent, athletic and ambitious, and black businessmen as well-dressed, successful, ambitious, and upward. What about blacks in general? To some extent, they shared the features of streetwise blacks and athletes. Like the former, they were seen as hostile, poor, unintelligent, and jobless, but like the latter, they were seen as athletic. Blacks in general were quite distinct from the positive stereotype of black businessmen.

Black Stereotypes of Blacks and Whites

The majority of studies in this area have employed white subjects rating members of minority groups (Shelton, 2000). This results from the implicit stereotype of blacks as victims—a view that is somewhat condescending and certainly limiting. Moreover, even though whites generally have more power than blacks, progress toward racial harmony will require understanding the perspective of blacks as well as whites. However, two immediate questions occur. First, do members of minority groups share the stereotypes assigned to them by white subjects? Second, what sorts of stereotypes do members of minority groups (and whites) have about white people? James Bayton and his colleagues initiated research on these questions. Using samples from the 1930s and 1940s, they reported that blacks and whites had highly similar stereotypes of blacks (Bayton, 1941; Bayton & Byoune, 1947). For example, black and white subjects[8] selected traits such as being musical, very religious, superstitious, happy-go-lucky, and loud to describe blacks. On the other hand, traits such as being ignorant, stupid, naive, slovenly, physically dirty, and ostentatious, which were part of the white stereotype of blacks, were not prominent in blacks' stereotypes of blacks, and blacks assigned positive traits such as being progressive and ambitious to themselves that whites did not. Other older studies (e.g., Maykovich, 1972; Meenes, 1943) also confirmed that blacks and whites tended to have similar stereotypes of blacks.

It is not uncommon for members of majority and minority groups to share the same stereotypes of the minority group (Sidanius & Pratto, 1999). For example, Australian Aboriginal people have as negative a stereotype of their own group as do Australians of European descent (Majoribanks & Jordan, 1986). Hispanic and white non-Hispanic Americans generally agree on the traits ascribed to each group, although in both cases self-stereotypes are more positive than the stereotypes of the other group (Triandis et al., 1982). Sarnoff (1951) and Engel, O'Shea, Fischl, and Cummins (1958) reported that Jews and non-Jews share many of the same stereotypes of Jews. One must be careful, however, in assuming that stereotypes of one group by two other groups are identical because the same terms are used (Stephan & Rosenfield, 1982). For example, in the Bayton data, blacks saw both whites and blacks as intelligent, but in their stereotypes of whites this was combined with being sly and deceitful—which gave intelligence a more sinister cast in the white stereotype.

Blacks and whites also have stereotypes of whites, and the Bayton data again suggest that both groups shared common stereotypes. Whites were seen as industrious, progressive, and sportsmanlike by both whites and blacks, but whites also described themselves as aggressive and straightforward, while blacks described whites as conceited and sophisticated (Bayton, 1941; Bayton & Byoune, 1947).

These pioneering studies were conducted many years ago; needless to say, there may be less racial consensus today. In fact, more recent studies in this area suggest more striking differences, and generally each group (but especially blacks) rates positive traits as more characteristic of its own group (e.g., Brigham, 1974; Clark, 1985; Clark & Pearson, 1982; Hudson & Hines-Hudson, 1999; Jackman, 1994). For example, Allen (1996) found that whereas traits such as being corrupt, independent, funny, friendly, and poor were used by both whites and blacks to describe blacks, the black sample was much more likely to use traits such as being smart, strong, oppressed, beautiful, and intelligent to describe their own group, whereas the white sample was more likely to describe blacks as athletic, humorous, loud, mean, moody, obnoxious, and arrogant. As is apparent from this listing that blacks had a more positive stereotype of blacks than did the whites. In considering stereotypes of whites, both groups depicted whites as incentive, smart, greedy, educated, and rich, but whites also described themselves as competitive, lazy, intelligent, independent, arrogant, and friendly, whereas blacks were more inclined to describe them as prejudiced, corrupt, mean, and selfish. Again, ingroup stereotypes were the more positive.

Other data have suggested stronger consensus. In a content analysis of essays, Monteith and Spicer (2000) found that whites and blacks used similar positive terms to describe blacks, but that the two groups differed in the nature of negative information. Whites used themes related to modern racism, whereas black respondents discussed black reactions to racism. Judd, Park, Ryan, Brauer, and Kraus (1995) found that both white[9] and black subjects reported more positive stereotypes of blacks than of whites, although this was true to a larger extent for the black subjects. In a particularly careful study, Ryan (1996) had blacks and whites rate the percentage of each group that had various stereotype features. These estimates could be compared with the actual percentages of each group that claimed to have the relevant features. Generally, both groups overestimated the percentage of respondents who possessed various features, and this was true to a larger extent for black subjects. Blacks overestimated the prevalence of features in their own groups as much as they did for the white group.

Krueger (1996a) also reported substantial agreement among the stereotypes of blacks held by white and black subjects. Among the traits assigned by both groups to blacks were being athletic, family-oriented, hard-working, and musical. Blacks saw blacks as more aggressive, ambitious, friendly, intelligent, prone to violence, and practical (among other traits), whereas whites saw blacks as more self-confident. There was greater disagreement on stereotypes of whites, with blacks seeing whites as more aggressive, arrogant, intelligent, and self-confident than whites saw themselves.

Can Blacks Predict Whites' Stereotypes of Them?

One interesting and potentially important question is whether blacks and whites each have a clear understanding of the stereotypes the other group has of them. Sigelman and Tuch (1997) provide data from a large national sample on blacks' perceptions of whites' beliefs. Over 60% of the black sample agreed that whites thought that blacks are more likely to commit violent crimes, are better athletes, are less intelligent, would rather live off welfare than work, have low moral standards, are more likely to abuse drugs and alcohol, are always whining about racism, are lazy, have no self-discipline, and are religious. Substantial percentages of whites do in fact endorse many of these statements. For example, 59% of whites said that blacks prefer to live off welfare, 54% that they are violent, 47% that they ae lazy, and 31% that they are unintelligent.

Krueger (1996a) asked black and white subjects to report their personal stereotypes, their estimates of cultural stereotypes, and their estimates of the responses of the other racial group. White subjects had high correlations between their personal stereotypes about blacks and their estimates of what blacks would rate, suggesting that they were projecting their own beliefs onto the outgroup. However, the corresponding correlation for black subjects between personal stereotypes and estimates of what whites would rate for whites was near 0. Both whites and blacks underestimated the favorability of the other group's stereotypes of them, and both groups also thought that the cultural stereotype was more negative than it actually was.

Jewish Stereotypes

Although much of the work on stereotypes of minority groups has naturally focused on African Americans, there are also data on stereotypes of other minority groups. The most intensively studied is the Jewish American group. Three large clusters of traits are part of the Jewish stereotype (Wuthnow, 1982). First, Jews are seen as being powerful and manipulative. Second, they are accused of dividing their loyalties between the United States and Israel. A third set of traits concerns Jewish materialistic values, aggressiveness, and clannishness. In an early study, Jews were seen to differ from other Americans in being more clannish, money-loving, dishonest, aggressive, individualistic, radical, and good businessmen (Cahalan & Trager, 1949). Ehrlich (1962) found that over 50% endorsed stereotypes of Jews as sticking together in business; preventing others from having a fair chance; being overaggressive; never being content; trying to get the best jobs; preferring luxurious, extravagant, sensual ways of living; having a high regard for property; and so on. In a large study of junior high and high school students, Glock, Wuthnow, Piliavin, and Spencer (1975) found that at least 50% of the students endorsed the following traits as characteristic of Jews: being intelligent, good citizens, greedy, "civil rightist," and religious, with substantial numbers also endorsing such traits as being conceited, vain, selfish, and bossy. Although only small minorities of people currently endorse these traits (Rosenfield, 1982; Wuthnow, 1982), they are part of the cultural landscape. Anti-Semitism and Jewish stereotypes have declined over the past few years, although it is unclear how much of this represents real change and how much cohort effects.

There are also questions about how positive the Jewish stereotype is. Whereas many of the traditional features of the stereotype are clearly negative (e.g., being clannish, materialistic, and overly ambitious), others are quite positive (e.g., being intelligent, family-oriented, generous, and ambitious). There has generally been more agreement for the positive than for the negative stereotypes (Wuthnow, 1982; Wilson, 1996b), but this finding may be less favorable than it seems. Wilson (1996b) argues that the underlying psychology of the benign stereotypes is subtly anti-Semitic. For example, in a large national sample those subjects who endorsed malevolent stereotypes about Jews were, not surprisingly, more likely to endorse negative stereotypes about blacks, but those who endorsed the positive stereotypes of Jews were also more likely to report black stereotypes. In addition, those who held benign stereotypes were not less likely to endorse negative ones. This suggests that there is a general tendency to hold stereotypes, and that positive stereotypes of Jews are as much a part of this tendency as negative ones are.

Hispanic Stereotypes

The Hispanic (or Latino) community in the United States is actually quite diverse, although it is unlikely that most Americans have distinct stereotypes for each group. Historically, the largest group, concentrated in the Southwest, has consisted of people with origins in Mexico.[10] In Eastern cities, Puerto Ricans are more common; in

TABLE 11.5. Rankings of Traits Reported for Mexican American Males and Females

	Males	Females
Lower-class	1	
Hard worker	2	
Antagonistic	3	15
Dark skin	4	4
Non-college	5	11
Pleasant	6	3
Dark hair	7	1
Ambitionless	8	12
Family-oriented	9	7
Short	10	14
Criminal	11	
Poorly groomed	12	
Unmannerly	13	
Intelligent	14	9
Alcohol user	15	
Attractive		2
Overweight		5
Baby makers		6
Caring		8
Sociable		10
Passive		13

Note. Data from Niemann et al. (1994).

the Southeast, those of Cuban ancestry are predominant. In recent years, emigrants from other areas of Central and South America as well as the Caribbean islands have diversified the Spanish-speaking community in the United States even more.

Most studies have focused on Mexican Americans. Niemann and colleagues (1994) found the traits listed in Table 11.5 most commonly reported for male and female Mexican Americans.

Asian Americans

Again, Asian Americans constitute a group of considerable genetic and especially cultural diversity. For example, Japanese and Chinese cultures are quite different; in fact, the two home countries have a long history of mutual antagonism. Lumping Chinese Americans and Japanese Americans into one group makes about as much sense as grouping African Americans and Mexican Americans. In more recent years, immigrants from Korea, Vietnam, Cambodia, and Laos (to name just four countries) have diversified Asian American culture even more. Nonetheless, because it is likely that most non-Asian Americans cannot discriminate these groups visually, let alone behaviorally and culturally, most research has simply used the term "Asian American." Although Asian Americans are often called the model minority, European Americans have ambivalent attitudes toward them, seeing them as intelligent and hard-working but also as unassimilated and financially aggressive (Ho & Jackson, 2001), not unlike the classic Jewish stereotype. Research by Niemann and colleagues (1994) provides a fairly recent listing of commonly ascribed Asian American traits (see Table 11.6).

TABLE 11.6. Rankings of Traits Assigned to Asian American Males and Females

Trait	Males	Females
Intelligent	1	1
Short	2	4
Achievement-oriented	3	7
Speak softly	4	2
Hard worker	5	12
Pleasant	6	3
Dark hair	7	10
Good student	8	14
Small build	9	6
Caring	10	8
Slender	11	11
Family-oriented	12	
Upper-class	13	
Shy	14	9
Speak with accent	15	
Attractive		5
Passive		13
Well-mannered		15

Note. Data from Niemann et al. (1994).

Change over Time

A fair amount of social science research has been devoted to documenting changes in prejudice (and, to some extent, stereotypes) over time. Most studies (e.g., Bobo & Kluegel, 1997; Firebaugh & Davis, 1988; Ransford & Palisi, 1992; Schuman, Steeh, Bobo, & Krysan, 1997; T. W. Smith, 1993) find that prejudice and stereotypic beliefs have declined rather steadily over the last 40 or 50 years; however, as we have seen in Chapter 8, there has also been a decline in support for public policies designed to eradicate racism and to assist historic victims of it.

There has been some debate about the nature of those changes. One possibility is that people (or at least some people) change their racial attitudes over time, and there is some evidence that this has occurred (Firebaugh & Davis, 1988; Schuman et al., 1997). Stereotypes of blacks became more favorable between 1972 and 1988, but most of that improvement was attributed to middle-aged subjects suggesting that they had changed over time (Dowden & Robinson, 1993). Most social scientists have focused on cohort effects. Younger adults are generally better educated and less prejudiced, so that the general reduction in prejudice can also be explained through replacement of older, prejudiced people by younger, less prejudiced ones. Cohort effects are also found (e.g., Firebaugh & Davis, 1988; Schuman et al., 1997), although there is also some evidence that members of the most recent cohort (those born between 1961 and 1972) are not less prejudiced than the immediately preceding cohort (Wilson, 1996a). A third possibility (discussed in Chapter 8) is that changes are "skin-deep" and really reflect recent norms about the inappropriateness of expressing stereotypes and prejudiced attitudes even to public opinion pollsters.

Some stereotypes have also declined. For example, ratings of African, Hispanic, Asian, and Jewish Americans as unintelligent, violent, lazy, welfare-dependent, and unpatriotic are generally less strong for groups born after World War II than for those born before, although for those who live outside the South there has actually been a slight increase for the most recent cohort studied—those born between 1960 and 1972 (Wilson, 1996a). So there has been change, at least in self-reported attitudes, but it has come in fits and starts and has progressed more slowly in recent years.

Individual Differences

What kinds of people are most likely to have stereotypes about and prejudice toward members of other ethnic and racial groups? Perhaps the most important point (made in Chapter 8) is that despite real differences among minority groups, people who tend to stereotype one group also stereotype others. And generally the predictors of prejudice do not differ from group to groups, so we can discuss the predictors without distinguishing the targets.

There are no surprises, given the review of individual difference predictors in Chapter 8. White people with less education (Bobo & Kluegel, 1997; Hughes, 1997; Link & Oldendick, 1996; Schuman et al., 1997; Sigelman, 1995; Vrij & Smith, 1999; Wilson, 1996b)[11] and lower-prestige occupations (D'Alessio & Stolzenberg, 1991; Wilson, 1996b) tend to exhibit more prejudice. Males (D'Alessio & Stolzenberg, 1991; Sigelman, 1995), especially those who are older (Link & Oldendick, 1996; Schuman et al., 1997) and who live in the South (Hughes, 1997; Link & Oldendick, 1996; Schuman et al., 1997; Sigelman, 1995), all tend to have stronger stereotypes and more negative racial attitudes. Political conservatives and people who claim more pride in their country are also more likely to be prejudiced (Altemeyer, 1988; Vrij & Smith, 1999). Obviously, the standard measures of racism—the Symbolic Racism 2000, Modern Racism, Right-Wing Authoritarianism, and Social Dominance Orientation Scales—all predict various measures of prejudice and racial stereotyping (see Chapter 8).

Of course, prejudice is not restricted to whites, although there has been little research on prejudice between people of various minority groups. Blacks are neither more nor less likely to stereotype Hispanics than are whites (Sigelman, Shockey, & Sigelman, 1993), but one consistent finding is that blacks are much more anti-Semitic than are whites (e.g., Martire & Clark, 1982; Sigelman et al., 1993). Other studies (Madon, Guyll, et al., 2001) find some differences between stereotypes of various groups by white and minority college students.

Assumed Characteristics

Obviously, race and ethnicity are associated with many other variables. For example, Jews are better educated than non-Jews; blacks tend to have both less education and income than whites; and Hispanics are more likely to be Roman Catholics than are Asian Americans. Those who subscribe to what is called the assumed-characteristics perspective (Coleman, Jussim, & Kelley, 1995) argue that stereotypes of various minority groups are really stereotypes of other features of these groups, such as socioeconomic status. Thus when white people think of black people they tend to imagine relatively lower-status persons, whereas when Gentiles rate Jews they imagine persons who are better educated. A similar kind of argument has been made by Eagly (1987) with regard to gender: Stereotypes of women are really stereotypes of housewives and women who occupy traditional roles (see above).

According to this logic, we might expect to find that stereotypes of blacks and whites become erased or at least more similar when socioeconomic status is equated, and this is exactly what has been found (Bayton, McAlister, & Hamer, 1956; Feldman, 1972; Smedley & Bayton, 1978). A similar study with Hispanic targets found that both race and socioeconomic status make a difference for employee ratings, but although differences between white non-Hispanic and Hispanic targets were smaller for the higher-status conditions, the interaction was not significant (Jones, 1991). In a somewhat different approach, Niemann, Pollak, Rogers, and O'Connor (1998) found that both dress and location (near a crime scene or in a scholarly environment) affected whether Hispanic traits were assigned to a young man.

Thus, for race as for gender, putative stereotypes of these categories may say more about the roles and occupations we assume people occupy than about race or gender per se. Stereotypically, race is linked to socioeconomic variables, and inferences are likely to be somewhat symmetrical. For example, it is likely that most people think of blacks when they think of people who use drugs or mothers on welfare.[12] If that is true, racial stereotypes may also "leak" into stereotypes of other groups. For example, given that dangerousness is part of the stereotype of blacks, it is interesting that ratings of the dangerousness of homeless people is predicted by estimates of the percentage of homeless people who are black (Whaley & Link, 1998).[13]

There is plenty to be concerned about in this picture. On the other hand, there is a bright side. As we have seen throughout this book, most people's stereotypes are not fixed in time or consistent across situation. Blacks and Hispanics (to name two groups) who fulfill the prototype roles will be seen to fit the stereotype, but those who do not will have a good chance to be seen in other ways. In one classic study (Jussim, Coleman, & Lerch, 1987), subjects rated black and white job applicants who were either impoverished or middle-class in appearance and who spoke standard English or nongrammatical English. As expected, subjects rated the person dressed in middle-class clothes and speaking standard English higher. These variables also had a much larger effect on the perceptions of the black than of the white applicant. When the candidate generally appeared impoverished and spoke poorly, there were few differences between the black and white applicants. However, when the speech and dress were more closely aligned with middle-class values, the black applicants were actually seen in a more favorable light than the white. Other studies (e.g., Branscombe & Smith, 1990) also find that blacks are evaluated especially positively when they are perceived to have characteristics stereotypically associated with whites.

So the good news is that white people may try to bend over backwards in evaluating members of minority groups that seem to share their values, attitudes, and behavior patterns quite positively. The bad news is that such a price of admissions may be too steep for many and serves to keep otherwise qualified members of such groups out of the mainstream.

Explanations for Differences

Ethnic groups do differ from one another. Obviously, Asian, Jewish, and African Americans celebrate different holidays, speak with different accents and vocabularies, and have different cultural customs. Most professional sports have higher percentages of African American than of Chinese American participants, and there are undoubtedly higher percentages of Asian Americans majoring in math and science than African Americans. Income, family size, religious preferences, and a host of other more or less important variables vary with race and ethnicity. How do most Americans explain such differences?

A number of national surveys have addressed that question over the years, and they have focused on black–white differences. Generally, there are three distinct types of explanations for race differences (Kluegel, 1990; Kluegel & Bobo, 1993). A relatively small minority endorse genetic or supernatural explanations for race differences, and such people tend to exhibit relatively high levels of traditional prejudice. Fortunately, acceptance of such explanations has tended to decline sharply over time. In 1972 31% of whites agreed that blacks come from a less able race, but this had declined to 14% by 1986 (Kluegel & Bobo, 1993).

A second class of explanations is generally called "individualistic," and it focuses on perceived lack of hard work, being on welfare, and lack of parental teaching of hard-work ethics. Such beliefs are not associated with traditional, overt prejudice, but rather with more indirect, symbolic racism (see Chapter 8). In 1972 67% of whites agreed that income differences between races existed because some people did not try hard enough, and in 1986 54% still agreed (Kluegel & Bobo, 1993).

Finally, some people accept what are usually called "structural" explanations. In 1972 72% of white Americans said that slavery and discrimination had created conditions making it hard for blacks to work their way out of poverty, but that number had declined to 61% in 1986 (Kluegel & Bobo, 1993). In a different survey in 1988–1989 (Kluegel, 1990), 21% said that income differences were due to innate ability, 44% to lack of motivation, and 30% to discrimination. In a study with college students, Martin and Parker (1995) reported that while some subjects accepted biological explanations for race differences, most preferred explanations based on socialization and opportunities.

One potentially important aspect of stereotypes concerns perceptions of how well various groups are integrated into the general society. In that regard whites perceive blacks to be generally disaffected (poor, rebellious, noisy, and angry), and to be less concerned than whites with national security and more concerned with reducing discrimination (Jackson et al., 1996). The reality is that blacks and whites have remarkably similar attitudes as groups on most issues, especially when socioeconomic status is controlled for (Smith & Seltzer, 1992). The one major exception is that blacks perceive more discrimination against blacks than do whites, have different explanations for its causes, and endorse different solutions (Sigelman & Welch, 1994). Although this is not necessarily an explanation for black stereotypes, it does fit with the research reviewed in the preceding paragraph suggesting that blacks are seen as outside the mainstream.

AGE

Age is, along with gender and race, one of the primary ways we categorize people. Think of how closely certain ages (e.g., 16, 18, 21, and 65) are associated with various milestones in life. Age affects friendship patterns, careers, parental status, interests, and attitudes—and the list goes on. Thus it should come as no surprise that we do have stereotypes of age groups in our society. We have strong stereotypes of adolescents, 30-somethings, yuppies, and even people in their 20s, although there has been comparatively little research on stereotypes of younger groups (but see Buchanan & Holmbeck, 1998; Hummert, 1990; Matheson, Collins, & Kuehne, 2000). However, since at least the early 1950s, there has been a steady stream of research concentrating on stereotypes of older people (Branco & Williamson, 1982; Montepare & Zebrowitz, 1998).

Unlike race and gender, age is a continuous category.[14] Thus to the extent that we want to categorize people by age, we have to decide where to draw boundaries. When does someone leave infancy behind and become a child? Does adolescence begin at age 13, at the point when sexual maturation starts, or when certain attitudes and behaviors manifest themselves? Is adulthood a matter of chronological age, culturally defined responsibilities, or psychological maturity? Is middle age a matter of chronology or attitude? Does one become old when one reaches a certain age, retires, acquires grey hair and wrinkles, or begins to decline physically? Most of these questions have not been addressed by empirical research, although a few studies have examined where people draw boundaries for different age categories. For example, Aaronson (1966) found that people are especially likely to delineate the age groupings of 5–15, 25–55, and 65–85.

Cues for Age

Like race and gender classification, age classification in our culture is essentially unproblematic. Abundant evidence (Montepare & Zebrowitz, 1998) suggests that adults reliably use facial cues (Henss, 1991; Mark et al., 1980; Muscarella & Cunningham, 1996), voice cues (Hummert, Mazloff, & Henry, 1999), and movement and gait (Montepare & Zebrowitz-McArthur, 1988) in judging age. Children also can classify people by age within the first year of life (Fagan, 1972; Lasky, Klein, & Martinez, 1974) and can make crudely accurate age judgments by age 2 or so (Brooks-Gunn & Lewis, 1979; Pope Edwards, 1984). In addition, as we will see in Chapter 13 when we discuss stereotypes based on physical features, people who carry young-looking features into adulthood are perceived differently than are those whose faces become more mature.

Are Elderly Stereotypes Positive or Negative?

Much of this research has been fueled by a continuing debate about whether stereotypes of elderly persons are more negative than stereotypes of younger people. The earliest studies in this area conducted by Tuckman and Lorge (1952, 1953) found that subjects had fairly negative beliefs about older people (e.g., "They are afraid of death," "They never take a bath," "They worry about unimportant things") and thought that younger people were happier than old people (Tuckman & Lorge, 1956).

Mixed Results

However, these studies used items that were predominantly negative in tone, so a well-documented agreement bias on the part of subjects could have led to this kind of result. More recent studies have found mixed results, with some showing that the elderly persons are seen more negatively and others finding that they are seen more positively. A meta-analysis of published studies (Kite & Johnson, 1988) shows that generally old people are seen in more negative terms. In addition, implicit measures based on memory (Hense, Penner, & Nelson, 1995; Snyder & Miene, 1994b), the implicit association test (IAT) (Rudman, Greenwald, Mellott, & Schwartz, 1999), and priming (Perdue & Gurtman, 1990) confirm that elderly stereotypes are more negative. In addition, the responses of several thousand people using the IAT suggest not only that stereotypes of elderly people are negative, but that they are more strongly so than race and gender stereotypes (Nosek, Banaji, & Greenwald, 2002a).

Obviously, as has been recognized for some time (e.g., Golde & Kogan, 1959), young people are seen more positively for some features and older people for others. Older persons tend to be rated relatively lower than younger ones on physical but not on cognitive and personality attributes (Slotterback & Saarnio, 1996). Generally, elderly individuals are seen as less potent, active, decisive, instrumental, and autonomous (Naus, 1973; Sherman & Gold, 1978–1979). On the other hand, they tend to be seen as more positive on social warmth traits such as nurturance (Harris, 1975; Labouvie-Vief & Baltes, 1976). This should not be surprising from a social role perspective on stereotypes. Some physical and mental capacities do decline with age (although generally not as sharply as people assume), but as people get older, they may have more time to devote to interpersonal activities and nurturing roles.

Generally, negative stereotypes are most apparent when people rate only labels (e.g., "elderly person") and weaker when other information is provided about the stimulus person (see also Crockett & Hummert, 1987). Traits assigned to elderly people vary by context. When older stimulus persons are presented as competent and active or in positive contexts, they are often rated the same as younger people (Braithwaite, 1986; Drevenstedt, 1981; Kite, 1996) or even more positively (Crockett, Press, & Osterkamp, 1979; Jackson & Sullivan, 1988; Krueger, Heckhausen, & Hundertmark, 1995; Sherman, Gold, & Sherman, 1978). As we have seen before, stereotypes often function as a basis for a kind of default judgment, but are easily overridden by other data. We may assume that older people are fragile, forgetful, and cranky, but we readily accept the fact that powerful, intellectually competent, happy older people exist, and that a particular individual before us is one of them.

Age Differences

Not surprisingly, younger subjects are often more inclined to rate elderly persons more negatively than older subjects rate themselves (e.g., Canetto, Kaminski, & Felicio, 1995; Collette-Pratt, 1976; Kite, Deaux, & Miele, 1991; Luszcz & Fitzgerald, 1986; Rothbaum, 1983). Young respondents are inclined to see elderly stereotypic terms (Hummert, Garstka, Shaner, & Strahm, 1995) and negative exemplars (Chasteen, 2000) as more typical of older people. In addition, older subjects tend to use fewer stereotypes and to have more complex representations of older people than younger subjects do (Brewer & Lui, 1984), although there is considerable agreement among age groups on the features that characterize aging (Hummert, Garstka, Shaner, & Strahm, 1994). Older subjects also have a more complex view of changes, tending to see them as spread more evenly over the life span (Heckhausen, Dixon, & Baltes, 1989).

Effects of Age Stereotypes on Elderly People

In recent years we have increasingly realized that the stereotypic mental and physical deterioration of people as they age is neither inevitable nor an accurate portrayal for all. To some extent, elderly persons may become relatively incompetent because younger people treat them as such, especially by using patronizing language (e.g., Giles, Fox, & Smith, 1993; Williams & Giles, 1996).

Becca Levy has conducted several studies suggesting that stereotypes of elderly persons may affect them directly. In a now classic study, Levy (1996) subliminally primed older people with the word "senility" or "wisdom" and then tested them on memory tasks. Those primed with "wisdom" performed better, suggesting that elderly persons may live in a world where they are constantly reminded of their cognitive deficits. In a subsequent study (Hausdorff, Levy, & Wei, 1999) elderly subjects were primed with either positive or negative stereotypes of aging. Those with the positive primes not only walked faster but were more spry when they were observed subsequently. Older people primed with negative stereotypes are more likely to display handwriting judged to be more stereotypic of older people (Levy, 2000), to show cardiovascular stress reactions (B. Levy, Hausdorff, Hencke, & Wei, 2000), and to reject life-prolonging medical treatments in hypothetical situations (B. Levy, Ashman, & Dror, 2000).

Given that stereotypes of elderly people differ some from culture to culture, we might expect also to find differences in performance and behavior. Levy and Langer (1994) have found that elderly persons in China have better memories than those in the United States, although other studies have found fewer differences (Yoon, Hasher, Feinberg, Rahhal, & Winocur, 2000). There could, of course, be many reasons for this, including real physical differences in the ways people age in different cultures; however, another strong possibility is that the more negative stereotypes of elderly persons in the United States contribute to memory decrements.

Subtypes of Elderly Persons

Two other points are worth making in this context, both of which should be obvious. The first is that terms such as "old" and "elderly" may mean different things to different people. Young people may be inclined to think that people in their early 60s are old, whereas older samples may be inclined to draw the line in the 70s (Drevenstedt, 1976). Although only 10 years separate these two ages, they actually vary a good deal in general lifestyle. People in their 60s are generally still working and may be at a point where energy, income, and wisdom are at a peak. People in their 70s are much more likely to be retired and to suffer from physical problems. So we might expect to find more explicit stereotypes with the older age groups. People do have a sense of the extent to which various traits change over the life span, with perceived positive changes outnumbering negative ones until approximately age 80 (Heckhausen et al., 1989). Moreover, it is clear that the most negative stereotypes of older people tend to be seen as more characteristic of very old (over 80) than of younger elderly people (Hummert, 1990).

Second, not everyone ages in the same way. Furthermore, as a social role perspective suggests, people often move into different sorts of roles and role demands as they move through the final stages of careers and into retirement. Therefore, as we have seen with other social categories, it is surely simplistic to assume that there is a single stereotype of older people. One would expect a widowed woman who has lived in the same apartment for 40 years in a deteriorating neighborhood to be a different sort of person from a happily retired businesswoman living in an exclusive retirement center or a doting grandfather living with his extended family.

Content of Subtypes

Are there different types of elderly stereotypes, as there are for women, men, and many other categories? Yes, there are. Brewer, Dull, and Lui (1981) asked subjects to perform a picture-sorting task from which three meaningful clusters emerged. The "grandmother" photos were rated as high in traits such as accepting, being helpful, serving, and being calm, cheerful, and old-fashioned. The "elder statesman" cluster was seen as aggressive, intelligent, conservative, dignified, neat, and authoritarian. Finally, a "senior citizen" was viewed as lonely, old-fashioned, and traditional.

Schmidt and Boland (1986) asked subjects to sort traits that could be used to describe older people. Several different subtypes emerged (e.g., shrew, curmudgeon, sage, bag lady/vagrant, John Wayne conservative, perfect grandparent), and as one might expect, these subtypes were rated quite differently on semantic differential scales. Subsequent studies by Hummert and her colleagues (e.g., Hummert, 1990; Hummert et al., 1994) have found evidence for several positive and negative subtypes. Examples of the resultant subtypes are given in Table 11.7.

These subtypes have different "flavors" to them, but they also affect how people think about elderly individuals (Hummert, 1990). In other research, Hummert, Garstka, and Shaner (1995) found that both in terms of language and conversational competence, both young and old subjects perceived more decline with age for an el-

TABLE 11.7. Traits Given for Positive and Negative Subtypes of Older People by College-Age Subjects

Positive subtypes	Negative subtypes	
Golden ager	*Shrew/curmudgeon*	*Severely impaired*
Active	Snobbish	Hopeless
Sexual	Demanding	Senile
Independent	Inflexible	Inarticulate
Interesting	Complaining	Feeble
Perfect grandparent	*Despondent*	*Recluse*
Intelligent	Fragile	Quiet
Loving	Sad	Timid
Generous	Neglected	Dependent
Trustworthy	Lonely	Forgetful
John Wayne conservative	*Vulnerable*	
Patriotic	Afraid	
Conservative	Bored	
Old-fashioned	Sedentary	
Mellow	Miserly	

Note. Data from Hummert et al. (1994).

derly person labeled as despondent, a shrew, or a curmudgeon than for one labeled as a golden ager or a John Wayne conservative.

Does Age Dominate Other Categories?

There are old and young men and women, blacks and whites, saints and sinners. How does age combine with other social categories? In a Canadian study, Bassili and Reil (1981) found that ratings of young people were more differentiated across other categories than ratings of old people were. For example, "conservative" tended to appear in ratings of old males, old females, old Native Canadians, and "traditional" appeared for old males, old females, old former bus drivers, old Native Canadians, and old Canadians of European descent. When young people were rated, there was much less redundancy of trait usage. In a sense, then, old people were assigned about the same traits regardless of what else they were, whereas the other designations were far more important for younger stimulus persons.

There has been special interest in how age combines with gender, because it has been frequently alleged that in a society placing particular emphasis on the attractiveness of females, the aging process should lead to more attractiveness devaluation for females than for males. Several studies (Henss, 1991; Mathes, Brennan, Haugen, & Rice, 1985) do find that women take a greater attractiveness "hit" as they age, especially among younger raters (Deutsch, Zalenski, & Clark, 1986). On the other hand, in the most comprehensive study thus far done, Zebrowitz, Olson, and Hoffman (1993) found no differences in attractiveness decline between men and women. Thus we do not have consistent support for the stereotype that women age less gracefully than men, at least in the eyes of younger persons.

One popular sort of notion is that both males and females become more communal and less agentic as they age—in other words, that both men and women become more feminine as Western culture defines these things. In one study (Deutsch et al., 1986), ratings of femininity for women declined with age, but ratings of masculinity for the male photos showed no age effects. The younger subjects rated the males as stronger, more competent, more successful, more active, and more independent than the females, but the older raters did not discriminate between the sexes in such ratings.

In another study (Kite et al., 1991) college-age and older subjects were asked to describe a 35-year-old man, a 35-year-old woman, a 65-year-old man, and a 65-year-old woman. The descriptions were far more similar within age categories than within gender. That is, the older woman was seen to resemble the older man more than the younger woman. The ratings of the descriptions showed complex effects. Generally, the college students rated the older stimulus persons as lower on masculine traits than the younger stimulus persons, but the older subjects did not discriminate between the ages. For male targets, ratings of masculine traits were about the same for both young and older targets, but for females, the older targets were rated as lower on femininity than the younger targets. Other studies (e.g., Canetto et al., 1995; O'Connell & Rotter, 1979) have also found that women lose their traditional stereotypic qualities more with age than do men. In any event, these results suggest that females lose their femininity with age without gaining in masculinity, whereas males do not lose their masculinity. Generally, then, these data, though not definitive, do suggest that age has a certain priority at least over gender.

Notes

1. The idea is that "it matters little what the platypus says, the wonder is that it can say anything at all" (Abramson et al., 1978, p. 123).

2. Recently DNA testing has supported the claims of the Lemba people in Southern Africa that they are descendants of Israeli Jews, even though they seem to be indistinguishable from other black Africans on the basis of casual appearance.

3. And let us not even get into issues of people whose heritage includes mixtures of three or more racial groups. For example, Hispanics, traditionally considered an ethnic group, have ancestors classified as African, European, Asian, and Native American, as well as various mixtures of these.

4. Some argue that "races" should be abandoned in favor of "breeding populations." Yes, there generally is far more breeding within than between putative races, but interbreeding also varies by geography and a host of other factors, so that meaningful breeding populations may be much smaller than racial groups. If we allow interbreeding to be a criterion for race, then we may have to admit Jews and Mexican Americans (to name just two groups) as races, given the considerable intramarriage among those groups. Of course, Jews may marry within their group less often than blacks, but that only raises the unanswerable question of how much intragroup breeding must take place for a group to be counted as a race. National groups such as Icelanders, and religious groups such as American and Canadian Hutterites, have extremely high rates of intermarriage, yet we do not consider them separate races (Kohn, 1995). Furthermore, at a point when evolution was supposedly differentiating the races, breeding populations in Africa were quite small.

5. When I once presented this material to adult students, an older man chuckled and said something along the lines that I must be letting my political correctness do my perceiving for me, because he sure could distinguish blacks from whites. Well, I can too, but I responded that I am also adept at distinguishing Mexican Americans in the Southwest, those of Nordic descent in the upper Midwest, and Vietnamese from Japanese Americans in the West (all with admittedly frequent errors)—although none of these distinctions involves a race by any conventional definition.

6. Americans are not uniquely confused about such matters, of course. However, one difference between victims of prejudice in the United States and Western Europe is that minority groups in the latter tend to be defined on the basis of nationality (e.g, Turks in Germany and the Netherlands; West Indians and Pakistanis in England; North Africans in France). If anything, prejudice against these groups is even stronger than that exhibited by European Americans toward African Americans (Pettigrew, 1998b).

7. Both American Hispanics and Chileans also have more implicit negative attitudes toward darker-skinned people (Uhlmann, Dasgupta, Elgueta, Greenwald, & Swanson, 2002).

8. The data for white subjects came from Katz and Braly (1933).

9. However, these studies were done with college students. More representative national surveys clearly show that whites have more negative stereotypes of blacks than of whites (Bobo & Kluegel, 1997).

10. Mexicans themselves are a diverse group. Some are pure descendants of various Native American groups (ultimately from Asia), while others also have African, Spanish, other European, and Asian ancestors.

11. In fairness, it must be said that there is a debate about how to interpret education effects. Mary Jackman (1978; Jackman & Muha, 1984), among others, has argued that education effects are actually quite weak, and that what seem to be less prejudiced responses by more highly educated people can be attributed to responses biases or to the desire and ability of better-educated persons to disguise antiblack attitudes and feelings. One intriguing finding is that measures of social dominance orientation (Federico & Sidanius, 2002)

and symbolic racism (Sears, van Laar, Carrillo, & Kosterman, 1997) predict reactions to race-related public policies better as educational levels rise.

12. These pictures in our heads may be hard to change. I was somewhat chagrined to discover recently that although the group of physicians I have consulted over the last 20 years includes three Jewish males, one African American male, one Italian American male, one African American female, two Hispanic American females, and two Asian American females—all much younger than I, and none even remotely white Anglo-Saxon Protestants (WASPs)—when I think of a doctor I still conjure up an image of a vaguely WASPish, grey-haired male.

13. I occasionally participate in conservatively oriented Internet discussion groups and recently was embroiled in a controversy over health care. It became clear that when the other participants discussed poor people and their putative failures, their image was of a lazy, black, drug-addicted welfare mother. Although I provided data showing that the majority of people on welfare, below the poverty line, and addicted to drugs were white, and that a large percentage (about 35%) of people who do not have health insurance are employed, facts took a distinct back seat to these "pictures in their heads."

14. It also differs markedly from race and gender, in that while we are stuck with our race and gender, we will (if we are lucky and live right) become members of the various age categories.

CHAPTER 12

Content of Stereotypes: Stigmas

Chapter 11 has considered stereotypes about three of the most important, and certainly most salient, social categories—race, gender, and age. This chapter considers several other categories, based on conditions that people strongly reject—stigmas.

GENERAL ISSUES

The Nature of Stigmas

Although we certainly have stereotypes of groups that are positive (e.g., novelists, scientists), we seem to reserve our strongest stereotypes for groups we do not like. Perhaps this occurs for the most obvious of reasons: When we dislike certain groups, we are motivated to stereotype them in ways that give our negative affect a cognitive foundation or rationalization. We can dislike almost any group, but we have a cultural warrant for selecting certain groups as especially deserving of our disdain. Such groups are called "stigmatized" groups. A "stigma" can be defined as "an attribute or characteristic that conveys a social identity that is devalued in a particular context" (Crocker, Major, & Steele, 1998, p. 505). Note that this definition is quite broad and would include such conditions as cancer, AIDS, homelessness, mental illness, facial scarring, blindness, use of a wheelchair, obesity, or even tattoos and facial piercing (at least in some situations). Moreover, the devaluation or negative reaction presumably has to be shared by a large group of people or a culture, although this is not part of the formal definition. It seems a bit odd to elevate my dislike, say, of tall people to stigma status unless I can recruit others who agree.

In his brilliant book *Stigma*, Erving Goffman (1963) noted that if we take stigma to be any negatively evaluated condition, almost any feature could be stigmatizing in certain circumstances. For example, I imagine that the virtues of a star football quarterback might be somewhat muted at a meeting of the college chess club; indeed, I suspect that he might be stigmatized in such a group. Gay people sometimes look on straight people with disdain, and members of some disability pride groups may refer

474

to people who are not disabled with derogatory language. Whereas a black person may feel stigmatized in a group of whites, whites may also sometimes feel the same in groups of blacks.[1] Furthermore, to the extent that being stigmatized rests on possessing a salient negative feature, almost all of us will feel stigmatized from time to time.[2]

Who Is Stigmatized?

Stigma is a broad designation, but our stereotypes, attitudes, and behaviors toward various stigmatized groups differ considerably. Thus considerable research has been addressed to questions of how stigmas are perceived to vary, in the hope that a typology of stigmas might aid us in understanding the different reactions that members of stigmatized groups face.

How Do Stigmas Differ?

Several social scientists have proposed fundamental dimensions that underlie stigmas (e.g., Elliott, Ziegler, Altman, & Scott, 1982; Frable, 1993b; Towler & Schneider, in press; Weiner, Perry, & Magnusson, 1988). I follow the lead of Jones and colleagues (1984), who identify six major dimensions along which stigmas may vary. (I add a seventh one later.)

CONCEALABILITY

Perhaps the most important of these is concealability. Some conditions, such as inability to walk, facial disfigurement, and speech impediments, are usually readily apparent to anyone who interacts with the stigmatized target. On the other hand, conditions such as a history of mental illness, a prison record, or homosexuality can be readily concealed. Mild mental retardation and many physical illnesses are potentially observable, but only after some inspection of or knowledge about the target persons.

Concealability is important, because immediately available cues allow for ready categorization and often affect how much information we have about stigmatized individuals. If we avoid people we can easily identify as stigmatized, then we will not to get to know them as individuals, and our stereotypes are likely to remain intact. By contrast, we may learn a fair amount about a given person before we discover that he or she has a hidden stigma, and knowledge of the stigma at that point may make little difference in our impressions of the person.

TIME COURSE

Some conditions (such as terminal illnesses) may worsen over time, whereas others (such as skin diseases or illiteracy) may improve, and still others (e.g., blindness) once acquired do not change. Stigmas can appear suddenly (e.g., paraplegia because of an accident) or, like many illnesses, can appear gradually. People are born with some stigmatizing conditions (such as mental retardation), but acquire others later in life (e.g., prison record, not graduating from high school). Some conditions can be ameliorated through drugs, surgery, or therapy (e.g., cleft palate, depression, epilepsy), whereas others are not treatable (e.g., amputated limbs).

AESTHETIC VALUE

Some stigmas render people physically unattractive as their culture measures such things. Obesity, facial scars, and bodily disfigurement all lead to dramatic diminution of attractiveness. As we will see in Chapter 13, being physically unattractive is itself a kind of stigma, and at a minimum people prefer to associate with beautiful rather than ugly people.

STIGMA ORIGINS

It is likely that the perceived origins of stigmas play a major role in how we react to people so labeled. Perhaps the most important element is whether the person is seen as responsible for the stigma. Some conditions (such as obesity, a criminal record, or homosexuality) are generally seen, fairly or not, as matters of choice, and people who suffer from other conditions (such as mental illness) are seen as at least partially responsible for their condition. By contrast, accidental dismemberment and many medical conditions (e.g., cancer) are perceived to be outside the control of the afflicted individual.

    We are particularly likely to devalue those whom we think have some responsibility for or control over their condition. Several studies confirm that we are seem more inclined to blame or devalue people with conditions that we believe somehow caused or could control (Bordieri & Drehmer, 1986; Crandall & Moriarty, 1995; Esses & Beaufoy, 1994; Frable, 1993b; Menec & Perry, 1998; Rush, 1998; Towler & Schneider, in press; Weiner et al., 1988).

PERIL OR DANGER

Many stigmatizing conditions are also seen as sources of peril or danger. Many of us would be anxious having a conversation with a convicted murderer, and even conversations with persons who are terminally ill or people with highly salient facial scars can be quite tense.

Why Are Stigmatized People Threatening? Some stigmatized people are in fact a source of physical threat. Violent criminals, for example, scare us for good reason. As we will see, mentally ill persons are widely thought to be dangerous because their behavior seems unpredictable, and some people fear that openly homosexual males try to recruit children into a gay lifestyle. People with contagious diseases represent obvious dangers. Still, when all is said and done, we may be forgiven for the suspicion that the putative threat of stigmatized people is often less real than imagined. Murderers may kill the odd person or two but probably not us, and the vast majority of gay males have no interest in our children.

    To some extent, the perceived threat is based on our fear of the unknown and perhaps on ambiguity about how to respond to someone with an obviously stigmatizing condition. Do I mention the condition or not? Do I offer sympathy, and if so, how can I avoid seeming to be patronizing? How can I employ normal eye contact when a facial scar keeps attracting my attention?

    Another form of perceived peril is that contact with some kinds of people may force us to realize, "There for the grace of God go I." One reason why we often shun those with cancer and other terminal diseases is that such diseases seem to strike randomly and leave us feeling vulnerable.

Courtesy Stigmas. Some people may fear a kind of guilt by association when they associate with some stigmatized individuals. Some conditions, mostly diseases, can contaminate those around them. People with dangerous and highly communicable diseases are often isolated from nondiseased individuals for just that reason, but as the recent AIDS epidemic (and earlier reactions to leprosy) has made clear, people's fears of contamination may be out of all proportion to the actual dangers. We also tend to segregate people with mental or developmental disabilities, and many people think that criminals should live in prisons and homosexuals should stay in the closet.

Goffman (1963) coined the term "courtesy stigma" to refer to the possibility that people who associate with stigmatized individuals may take on some of their stigma. This is easy to understand with some groups. For example, a person with a close friend who is a convicted murderer will probably be assumed to share the friend's presumed low moral standards. And one could make a case that those with mentally ill relatives may themselves have psychological problems due to common genetic or environmental influences. Men who are homosexuals are probably more likely to have homosexual friends than are straight men, and so it might be inferred that a straight male friend of a homosexual man may himself have homosexual tendencies. On the other hand, a case for psychological or physical contamination is hard to make for some other groups, such as patients with cancer, Alzheimer's disease, or amputations.

Several studies (e.g., Goldstein & Johnson, 1997; Mehta & Farina, 1988) have shown that friends or relatives of stigmatized people are devalued, but this could result from perceived choices or genetic influences, as just discussed. For example, a man who chooses to room with a gay male is also seen as having stereotypic male homosexual traits (Sigelman, Howell, Cornell, Cutright, & Dewey, 1991). Straight women who are strongly prejudiced against lesbians make clear their disagreements with views (unrelated to sexual orientation) expressed by lesbians, presumably in an effort to avoid stigma by association (Swim, Ferguson, & Hyers, 1999).

Although these studies do not directly show that a stigma itself "rubs off" on associated nonstigmatized people, two studies make a stronger case. Neuberg, Smith, Hofman, and Russell (1994) found that people who were seen talking to a homosexual were rated more negatively than those who talked to a heterosexual. The best evidence for courtesy stigmas comes from a study by Hebl and Mannix (2003). They found that job interviewees who were friends with an obese woman were given lower ratings. More strikingly, even those who were merely waiting with an obese woman and who had no relationships to her were also rated more negatively. Thus, while evidence for "ruboff" in courtesy stigmas is not abundant, these results do suggest that associations with stigmatized persons can be damaging to the perceptions of nonstigmatized people.

DISRUPTIVENESS

According to Jones and colleagues (1984), stigmas vary in their disruptiveness. Perhaps the most disruptive are various mental disorders such as mental illness. Severe facial scars and use of a wheelchair also tend to make interactions awkward. On the other hand, such stigmas such as obesity or facial tics may be much less disruptive. Obviously, concealable stigmas tend to be less disruptive to the extent that they are actually concealed.

Sources of Disruptiveness. Although many students of stigmas have noted the potential of stigmas to mess up interactions, it is not perfectly clear why this should be so. One obvious possibility is that many stigmatized people are thought to be unpredictable or non-normative in their behavior. The flow of ordinary interaction depends heavily on perceptions that each person can trust the other to do the normative thing. Furthermore, the perceived potential dangerousness associated with some forms of stigma may keep nonstigmatized persons "on their toes" and disrupt easy interaction.

Many people find interacting with stigmatized individuals awkward because they are not quite sure what to say or do. What should they do when persons with a severe stutter struggle to get a word out? Say it for them, look away, try to appear empathetic or perhaps disinterested? Should they extend help to disabled persons, fearing that not offering help will be seen as insensitive, but that offering it will be seen as condescending? If mentally ill persons say something strange, should others comment on it? Do nondisabled people get embarrassed when they inadvertently ask a blind person, "Do you see the point of my argument?" or request a hearing-impaired person to "hear me out"? Whether or not nonstigmatized persons can avoid such *faux pas*, trying to guard against saying the wrong thing may paradoxically make it more likely (Wegner, 1994).

The nonstigmatized persons may be curious about the causes of the stigma, but may be unwilling to ask lest they seem intrusive and rude. They may simply be unclear as to whether mentioning the stigma is appropriate. If that is the case, the stigmatized persons can "break the ice" by mentioning the stigma, even when it is obvious. Hastorf, Wildfogel, and Cassman (1979) found that when a man in a wheelchair talked openly about his visible stigma (use of the wheelchair), he was liked more than when he did not. One possible reason for this is that such acknowledgment reduces some uncertainty about how to interact with the person. Another possibility is that people who openly mention their condition are perceived to be less troubled by it. Acknowledging a stigma is especially important for those with controllable stigmas (Hebl & Kleck, 2002).

Finally, many visible stigmas create obvious visual focal points (a facial scar, a wheelchair, a missing limb), and people may have to combat a tendency to stare when they know they shouldn't. If a condition is highly visible, a nonstigmatized person may try to avoid looking at it, thus making interaction more effortful than it usually is (Langer, Fiske, Taylor, & Chanowitz, 1976). Stigmatized people do invite scrutiny. Langer and Imber (1980) showed that subjects were far more attentive to the features of someone they thought was a former mental patient, a homosexual, a divorced person, a millionaire, a divorced person, or a patient with cancer than someone not so labeled.

Interaction Problems. Strained interactions with stigmatized individuals can produce a deadly mixture of conflicting and ambiguous verbal and nonverbal cues. Not surprisingly, other people avoid such individuals whenever possible (e.g., Houston & Bull,

1994; Snyder, Kleck, Strenta, & Mentzer, 1979). And those who are highly conscious of being stigmatized may avoid interactions with "normal" people, thus reducing opportunities to ameliorate stereotypes (Pinel, 1999). Generally, people report discomfort in interacting with those who are disabled (Blascovich, Mendes, Hunter, Lickel, & Kowai-Bell, 2001; Kleck, Ono, & Hastorf, 1966), and physiological indices confirm that such interactions are physiologically arousing (Kleck et al., 1966). Even seeing disfigured faces is physiologically arousing (Kleck & Strenta, 1985). There is also abundant evidence that people behave differently toward those with and without visible stigmas, often in quite subtle ways (Kleck, 1968; Kleck et al., 1968; Rumsey, Bull, & Gahagan, 1982).

Those who are stigmatized may contribute their own "dis-ease" to interactions with nonstigmatized others. Some stigmatized people seem to define themselves in terms of their condition and to become defensive or thin-skinned, even hostile. Nonstigmatized individuals may want to avoid the hassles of dealing with people they assume will be interpersonally difficult.

Several studies suggest that even if stigmatized people are not especially hostile, they do worry about how they will be perceived. In one important demonstration, Kleck and Strenta (1980) had two subjects interact. Person A was led to believe that Person B thought A was physically deviant; in fact, B had no such knowledge. Subjects in the A position who thought they were stigmatized rated their partners (the people in the B position) as liking them less, as being more tense, and as seeing them as less attractive. Entering a conversation thinking that others do not like you is not the best recipe for easy flow. Stigmatized people may have learned to monitor the behavior of interaction partners carefully for signs of pity or disdain, sometimes with the motive of helping the conversation along. Experiments suggest that stigmatized people may be particularly attentive to the behavior of others (Strenta & Kleck, 1984), and to try to take their partners' point of view and consequently recall more information about the interaction (Frable, Blackstone, & Scherbaum, 1990). This is often a virtue, but such hypervigilance may also paradoxically make the conversation more stilted and awkward. In addition, those who try to conceal a non-visible stigma may become preoccupied with thoughts about it (Smart & Wegner, 1999), also potentially reducing attention to the cues necessary for having a smooth interaction. Even worse, they may adopt a paranoid attributional style about the behavior of their partners, becoming suspicious and forming negative attributions for partners' behaviors (Santuzzi & Ruscher, 2002). This can lead to classic self-fulfilling prophecy effects, in which their suspicions elicit negative behavior from others (Pinel, 2002).

MENTAL VERSUS PHYSICAL STIGMAS

Although the distinction between mental and physical stigmas is not a dimension proposed by Jones and colleagues (1984), several studies have found that people readily distinguish between the two types, and generally those stigmas that are seen to be mental in origin tend to be viewed in more negative terms (Esses & Beaufoy, 1994; Frable, 1993b; Furnham & Pendred, 1983; Weiner et al., 1988) and lead to more discrimination (Bordieri & Drehmer, 1986; Stone & Sawatzki, 1980). Mental stigmas include such things as mental illness and retardation, homosexuality, substance abuse, and criminality, whereas physical stigmas include most physical illnesses, physical disabilites, and obesity. The mental–physical distinction is closely related to many of the dimensions already discussed, so perhaps it is best to think of it as a composite dimension. For example, mental stigmas tend to be more concealable and less aesthetically displeasing than physical ones. People are probably seen as more responsible for having caused mental stigmas. Finally another reason for the greater rejection of mental disabilities is that whereas physical disabilities merely disrupt normal social interactions, mental stigmas are seen to represent real threat and danger to others (Towler & Schneider, in press). After all, most physical disabilities and diseases actually inhibit physical (but not verbal) threat, whereas many mental stigmas lead to unpredictable and even physically threatening behavior, or so most people assume. Because people with mental stigmas are much more likely to be rejected by others, I focus in the remainder of this chapter on two such stigmas: mental illness and homosexuality.[3]

Identification and Labeling

As indicated above, many stigmatized conditions are immediately obvious, but others are not. This chapter considers two that are normally concealable, although not necessarily for long. Moreover, whereas appearance is a cue for many important categories (including the three covered in Chapter 11), both "mental illness" and "homosexuality" are labels for categories based on behavior. This raises two important questions. The first is what cues lead to someone's being seen as mentally ill or homosexual. Obviously, in some cases this identification is based on self-designation, group membership (e.g., Gay Alliance), or location (e.g., mental hospital, gay bar), but in many cases categorization must rely on cues with unknown and probably low feature-to-category probabilities.

The second question is whether labels themselves lead to stereotyping or whether behaviors are also important. A mentally ill person can behave quite normally in some situations or while medicated, and while some lesbians behave in stereotypic "butch" ways, the behavior of others is indistinguishable from that of straight women. Does a woman have to behave in a "lesbian" way to be stereotyped?

Effects on Stigmatized Persons

Although the focus throughout this chapter is on how other people view stigmatized individuals, these reactions multiplied over thousands of occasions will also affect how stigmatized persons view themselves. Obviously, most members of stigmatized groups know that others look down on them, and they learn this fairly early (Crocker et al., 1998), although people differ in stigma consciousness (Pinel, 1999). Do they simply internalize the negative views others have of them?

Fortunately, human self-esteem is usually not entirely dependent on others' evaluations. Crocker (1999; Crocker & Wolfe, 2001) argues that the self-concept, particularly self-esteem, is dependent on shared meanings constructed in situations and so changes from situation to situation. Rich people do not necessarily have high self-esteem because of their high status, and members of stigmatized groups often do not have the lowered self-esteem that one might expect from a history of rejection by others, because they have many strategies for dealing with such rejection (Crocker et al., 1998; Twenge & Crocker, 2002).

DEVALUING STIGMATIZED FEATURES

One obvious possibility is to devalue characteristics that lead to rejection by others (Major, Spencer, Schmader, Wolfe, & Crocker, 1998; Schmader & Major, 1999). For instance, a deaf woman may recognize her limitations in some areas but see these as relatively trivial compared to her other abilities and virtues, just as I downplay my relatively poor tennis-playing abilities in favor of my more intellectual pursuits.

VIEWING REJECTION AS PREJUDICE

Frequently, stigmatized people attribute criticism for both stigma-related and other behavior to ignorance or prejudice. Crocker and her colleagues (e.g., Crocker, Cornwell, & Major, 1993; Crocker, Voelkl, Testa, & Major, 1991) have found that people in stigmatized groups are prone to attribute negative reactions from others to their prejudices, although (as we have seen in Chapter 8) this strategy has the potential cost of creating a victim mentality, which implies stable and continuing negative evaluations.

SEEKING SUPPORT

Another possibility is to seek validation and support from similarly affected others through increased identification with the stigmatized group (Bat-Chava, 1994).[4] However, one problem with many hidden or concealable stigmas is that people do not reveal them to others, and hence finding similar others may be difficult, especially in new environments. Major and Gramzow (1999) have shown that women who have had abortions tend to keep this a secret from family and friends, and that such secrecy promotes suppressing abortion-related thoughts, which in turn led to increased levels of psychological distress. If people with concealable stigmas do in fact conceal them and hence have reduced opportunities to find support from similar others, they should feel more odd or unusual (Frable, 1993a)—a state that is not always a psychological advantage. Furthermore, because they lack opportunities to seek support from accepting others, they may have relatively low self-esteem (Frable, Platt, & Hoey, 1998). Because of its very anonymity, the Internet provides an opportunity for marginalized people to seek support, and McKenna and Bargh (1998) found that members of newsgroups dealing with concealable stigmas had higher self-acceptance as a function of their participation.

SELECTIVE COMPARISONS

Finally, stigmatized people may draw their psychological wagons into a circle by restricting relevant comparisons to similar others. People who feel discriminated against may more strongly identify with their stigmatized group, and may seek to compare their outcomes only with those of fellow group members (see Chapter 8). For hearing-impaired individuals to compare their accomplishments with those whose hearing is normal can highlight the limitations imposed by their condition, but they have a more even playing field when comparing themselves with others who have the same problems and issues.

Pointing out such coping mechanisms is not meant to minimize the problems that many members of stigmatized groups may have. Being denied opportunities for friendships and jobs is hurtful. Being stared at and ridiculed by others smarts as well. However, the point is that stigmatized persons employ the same psychological mechanisms that we all do to blunt the effects of such disapproval.

PARTICULAR STIGMAS

Mental Illness

Persons with mental illness[5] have arguably been the most stigmatized and stereotyped group of people in history. Until comparatively recently, they have been treated with the kinds of disdain and hostility that can only be understood if we assume that they have been regarded as less than fully human. There is a substantial body of research on attitudes toward mentally ill people (Rabkin, 1972). Both older and more recent studies (Lyons & Hayes, 1993; Shears & Jensema, 1969; Skinner, Berry, Griffith, & Byers, 1995; Tringo, 1970) consistently show that attitudes toward this group are among the most negative for any stigmatized group, including persons with alcoholism, mental retardation, physical disabilities, or prison records. Fortunately, attitudes toward mentally ill persons have improved since the early 1950s (Rabkin, 1974; Segal, 1978).

Stereotypes

There have been several attempts over the years to assess the structure of attitudes toward persons with mental illness (e.g., Brockington, Hall, Levings, & Murphy, 1993; Cohen & Struening, 1962; Nunnally, 1961; Wolff, Pathare, Craig, & Leff, 1996a). Unfortunately, despite the powerful and general rejection of this group, attitudes toward and stereotypes of it are unusually complex or perhaps incoherent. For example, Nunnally (1961) gave a large sample of subjects 240 statements about mental illness to rate. A factor analysis of these ratings yielded 10 major factors, which Nunnally labeled (1) look and act different; (2) will power is key to mental health; (3) women more prone; (4) avoidance of morbid thought as the basis of mental health; (5) guidance and support are important; (6) mental illness is hopeless; (7) mental health is dependent on the immediate environment; (8) emotional problems are nonserious; (9) emotional problems get worse with age; and (10) mental illness is due to organic causes. However, these 10 factors accounted for less than 25% of the variance; at a minimum, one would conclude that the subjects did not have well-defined and articulated attitudes. Other studies (e.g., Brockington et al., 1993; Wolff et al., 1996a) have found different patterns of attitudes, but generally attitudes toward mentally ill people have at least three major components: fear of them, the perceived need to control and discriminate against them, and a kind of benevolence (sometimes with condescending overtones).

THE MENTALLY ILL PERSONS AS DANGEROUS AND UNPREDICTABLE

Not surprisingly, a particular constellation of attributes is associated with mentally ill persons. Generally, they are described as withdrawn, depressed, tense, unpredictable, dangerous, and aggressive (Green, McCormick, Walkey, & Taylor, 1987; Green,

Walkey, Taylor, & McCormick, 1987; O'Mahony, 1979; Wolff et al., 1996a). This has led some authors (e.g., Cumming & Cumming, 1957; Nunnally, 1961) to argue that at the core of the mental illness stereotype are perceptions of dangerousness and unpredictability. It is important to recognize that unpredictable people are not necessarily dangerous or vice versa, and either could lead to negative attitudes. There could be many reasons other than attributions of dangerousness for why putatively unpredictable, mentally ill people would be negatively evaluated. For example, those in the immediate environment may not be sure how to respond to behavior that seems to be out of kilter or is unresponsive to well-established norms. So negative reactions to unpredictability may not be based on perceptions of dangerousness. Nor is danger necessarily related to unpredictability. Violent behavior is not necessarily unpredictable; violence-prone people (e.g., those who abuse their spouses) may be quite predictable in being "set off" by a known pattern of events.

Nonetheless, for better or worse, most people seem to see a high correlation between unpredictability and dangerousness in the persons with mental illness (e.g., Fracchia, Canale, Cambria, Ruest, & Sheppard, 1976), and to see them as more dangerous than those who are not mentally ill (Appleby & Wessely, 1988; Phelan, Link, Moore, & Stueve, 1997). The media often play up mental illness as a factor in violent crime, and negative attitudes toward mentally ill people are primed by well-publicized crimes committed by a few such people (Angermeyer & Matschinger, 1995; Thornton & Wahl, 1996).

Recent research strongly suggests a kernel of truth in the popular perception: Mentally ill persons are, in fact, more dangerous than "normal" people (Monahan, 1992; Steadman, 1981).[6] For example, those who have been in a mental hospital are subsequently about three times more likely to be arrested for violent crimes than those with no history of mental illness. However, there is a major qualification of this finding: Ex-mental patients with no prior arrests are no more likely than "normal" people to be arrested. Thus the differential dangerousness of ex-patients is due almost entirely to extremely high arrest rates of a few who were violent before and again after hospitalization (Monahan et al., 2001).

A diagnosis of schizophrenia (arguably the prototypic mental illness) is associated with lower, not higher, rates of violence, although command hallucinations and suspicious attitudes toward others do predict higher violence. Substance abuse among former mental patients is strongly related to violence, but the same is true among those who are not mentally ill (Monahan et al., 2001).

Finally, the base rate of violence even among patients who have repeated contact with mental health facilities is low. For example, Link, Andrews, and Cullen (1992) found that for what they termed "repeat-contact" patients, 12% had been arrested for crimes (6% for violent crimes), 15% reported hitting someone in the last year, 29% reported fighting with someone in the past 5 years, and 12% reported hurting someone badly in their lifetime. Although these rates were two to three times the rates for the comparison sample with no mental illness, the base rates of violent behavior among present or former patients were still comparatively low. Indeed, probably fewer than 5% of all violent crimes are associated with mental illness (Levey & Howells, 1994). Because both mental illness and violence have extremely low base rates, the assumed correlation between them may be an illusory correlation based on the distinctiveness of statistical minorities and low-prevalence behaviors. In any event, the common stereotype of mentally ill individuals as violent is exaggerated.

PERCEIVED CAUSES OF MENTAL ILLNESS

A number of studies have examined laypeople's assumptions about the causes of mental illness. Generally, laypeople see a number of quite different causes at work, and the constellation of causes perceived by the lay public does not readily match any particular psychological theory of mental illness (Furnham & Bower, 1992), although professionals and laypeople seem to agree to some extent on the causes of depression (Kuyken, Brewin, Power, & Furnham, 1992).

Several studies have examined lay ideas about causes. Furnham and Rees (1988) found five factors of causes for schizophrenia, which they labeled (1) stress and pressure; (2) biological (viruses, disturbed pregnancies, excessive use of alcohol or drugs); (3) genetic; (4) backwardness (low birth weight, low intelligence); and (5) brain damage (serious accident, sexual or physical abuse). These causes were related to stereotypes of those with schizophrenia. For example, those who viewed biological causes as important also tended to believe that persons with schizophrenia are egocentric (can't concentrate, commit outrageous acts in public), and that the illness is associated with socioeconomic status, race, and gender. Those who saw schizophrenia as a result of backwardness endorsed those perceptions plus the idea that persons with the illness are dangerous and amoral (commit sex crimes, do not believe in God, easy to identify, cannot work because cannot be trusted). Brain damage explanations and genetic explanations did not correlate with any of the perceptions of people with schizophrenia, and the stress and pressure explanation only predicted ratings of amorality.

Obviously, even laypeople recognize the behavioral differences associated with, say, schizophrenia and obsessive–compulsive disorder. Barry (1994) makes the quite reasonable point that people probably see different types of causes for different types of mental illness. For example, depression is seen as due more to interpersonal problems and stress, whereas schizophrenia is seen to be caused more by heredity and less by stress. Childhood problems are seen as more important for phobias than are social problems, but the reverse is true for depression (Barry & Greene, 1992).

Individual Differences

Several personality and demographic variables correlate with both attitudes toward and stereotypes about mentally ill persons. Younger people (Brockington et al., 1993; Whatley, 1958–1959; Wolff et al., 1996a) and those with better education (Cohen & Struening, 1962; Ojanen, 1992) tend to have more favorable attitudes and stereotypes, but typically these are not strong predictors. Some evidence suggests that women are more accepting of mentally ill people than are men (Farina, 1981; Morrison, de Man, & Drumheller, 1994).

With many negatively evaluated groups, attitudes and stereotypes generally become more positive with more contact; as expected, attitudes toward persons with mental illness are more favorable among those who have had more contact with them (Angermeyer & Matschinger, 1997; Farina, 1982; Kolodziej & Johnson, 1996; Trute, Tefft, & Segall, 1989), although some studies (Reda, 1996) show that superficial contact does not mitigate negative attitudes. Knowledge about mental illness is also associated with less negative attitudes toward the group (Wolff, Pathare, Craig, & Leff, 1996b) and lessened perceptions that such persons are dangerous (Ogedengbe, 1993; Penn et al., 1994).

The Importance of the "Mental Illness" Label

THE LABELING THEORY PERSPECTIVE

There have been fierce debates within and without the mental health professions about the reality of mental illness. On the one side have been those, chiefly sociologists and anthropologists, who have argued that mental illness is primarily a social and cultural creation. One version, known as "labeling theory" (e.g., Scheff, 1966, 1974), suggests that mental illness and various associated labels are given to those who behave in socially deviant ways, and that at least some of the pathologies associated with mental illness are due to the tendency of those so labeled to be stigmatized and to play out their assigned roles. Contrary to the caricature of labeling theory that many psychologists love to hate, such theories do not generally deny the possibility that there are underlying physiological and developmental reasons for the deviant behavior, but they do emphasize the "multiplier effect" of labels in creating real problems for those who behave in socially unacceptable ways (for whatever reasons). Such models naturally see the label of "mental illness" (or "ex-mental patient") as being stigmatizing in its own right.

A contemporary version of labeling theory has been offered by Hope Landrine (1987, 1992), who argues that people who occupy dominant roles in society (e.g., white middle-class males) come to define what is "normal." Other people are assigned to subdominant roles, which differ from dominant roles in power, privilege, and prestige. People whose characteristics fit them for one of the subdominant roles will be rewarded for portraying the expected behaviors, but there are also pathologies associated with extreme role fulfillment. For example, the traditional role of a young adult middle-class housewife is to be dependent, somewhat childish, suggestible, vain, nonanalytical, and so on. Landrine argues that extreme versions of these behaviors are the very behaviors that lead to a diagnosis of hysterical (or, more recently, histrionic) personality disorder. Similarly, according to this argument, lower-status people are socialized to perform boring, repetitive work, which leads to a lack of self-definition and to social isolation. In extreme forms, these behaviors characterize schizophrenia. Trained clinicians rated stereotypic descriptions of socioeconomic status and roles in line with associated forms of mental illness (e.g., describing a person described as lower-income as having schizophrenia). Although these data are suggestive, they do not, of course, prove that mental illness categories are caused in some sense by role enactment.

Opponents of labeling theory (e.g., Gove & Fain, 1973) argue that there are distinct constellations of symptoms and dysfunctional behaviors associated with each form of mental illness—in other words, that there is a reality to mental illness over and above labels. Clearly, many of the symptoms of mental illness occur across diverse cultures and are universally recognized as symptoms of mental illness, although the labels given to such behaviors vary widely (Murphy, 1976). For example, although many traditional African cultures recognize mental illness, they often place more emphasis than Western cultures on behavioral rather than cognitive problems, usually do not label neurotic problems as mental illness, and see spiritual causes as important (Patel, 1995). Some cultures place emphasis on the concept of an "evil soul" (Alzubaidi, Baluch, & Moafi, 1995).

Still, there are substantial cross-cultural agreements on the recognition of more serious forms of mental illness, and certainly it is now clear that many forms of mental illness do have articulated biological and chemical correlates, strongly suggesting a biological and universal foundation for various symptoms. Thus the extreme versions of labeling theory cannot be correct—but this does not mean that labels are never important in affecting the behavior and perceptions of those with mental illness.

This debate about whether various mental illness labels are cultural creations or accurate summaries of behavior has important echoes for research concerning perceptions of mentally ill persons. Labeling theory suggests that labels are important cues for our perceptions, and that the label of "mental illness" affects our reactions to people so labeled, independently of their actual behaviors. Others argue that our reactions to these persons are affected more by the behaviors they perform than by how they are labeled. Are they rejected, stereotyped, and stigmatized because of how they are labeled or because of their behaviors?

DO PEOPLE RECOGNIZE MENTAL ILLNESS?

Obviously, before individuals can be victimized by a group stereotype, they must first be seen as members of that group. Do people accurately recognize those whose behavior would lead them to be strong candidates for "mental illness" labels? Evidence on this is mixed. Much of the research on this topic has been conducted with variations of several brief scenarios first presented in an unpublished paper by Star (1955).[7] Subjects were given brief behavioral descriptions of persons with alcoholism, anxiety neurosis, compulsive phobia, childhood behavior disorder, somewhat violent paranoid schizophrenia, and simple schizophrenia. Star found that a majority of respondents did not label any of the people as mentally ill, with the exception of the person with paranoid schizophrenis. Rabkin (1979) gave subjects 15 possible indicators of mental illness and found that only four items (currently in a mental hospital, currently in a psychiatric ward of a general hospital, having shock treatments, and having previously attempted suicide) garnered majority endorsements as indicating mental illness. Smaller percentages saw a previous stay in a mental hospital (10%), regularly taking psychiatric medications (31%), and missing work regularly (44%) as good indicators of mental illness.

However, other studies have shown that a high percentage of people are willing to say that the targets displaying deviant behavior are mentally ill (e.g., Blizard, 1968; Crocetti, Spiro, & Siassi, 1974; Rootman & Lafave, 1969). Generally, more people are likely to identify the milder forms of mental illness as mental illness now than formerly (Segal, 1978). In a recent study using Star-type vignettes for schizophrenia, major depression, cocaine addiction, and alcohol dependence, a majority of people recognized the first two as mental illness. When asked directly whether the person was experiencing the more precise diagnosis (e.g., schizophrenia), the vast majority identified the condition (Link, Phelan, Bresnahan, Stueve, & Pescosolido, 1999).

Although it is certainly possible that some behaviors are so extreme and incomprehensible that the person exhibiting them would be immediately seen as mentally ill,[8] generally recognition of mental illness is a gradual process, "not so much by particular signs and symptoms as by the accumulation of many inexplicable actions and statements" (Clausen & Huffine, 1975, p. 411). Several researchers (Sampson, Messinger, & Towne, 1962; Schwartz, 1957; Yarrow, Clausen, & Robbins, 1955) who have studied the family dynamics of mental illness have provided illuminating discussions of how family members (typically spouses) define and recognize incipient mental illness. Often the bizarre behavior is initially tolerated by the family, and the decision to hospitalize is made when the behaviors can no longer be tolerated. Thus intolerance for behaviors rather than an explicit recognition of mental illness drives the commitment decision (Sampson et al., 1962).

ARE MENTALLY ILL PERSONS REJECTED BECAUSE OF BEHAVIORS OR LABELS?

This issue is part of a larger theoretical debate. Some would argue that because mental illness is so frightening, people try to ward it off by denying that critically dysfunctional behaviors are in fact evidence of mental disorder.[9] From this perspective, the label of "mental illness" is a highly negative one and must be avoided (at least for family and close friends) at all costs. This would suggest that recognition of mental illness and rejection of a person should be positively related—as they are, although only weakly (Phillips, 1967). However, other would argue that people recognize mental illness but do not reject people so labeled until they perform disagreeable behaviors (e.g., Crocetti et al., 1974).

Predictably, the evidence on whether labels are important and whether labels or actual behaviors are more important is mixed. This is a close cousin to our earlier discussion (Chapter 4) of whether stereotypes or individuating information is more important in forming impressions; as I have argued there, a lot depends on how strongly labels and behaviors are manipulated and how diagnostic each is. So there can be no general answer to the question of which is more important. As I have suggested before for this type of issue, a thought experiment might be useful. A man labeled as a "homicidal madman" would probably be rejected no matter how many saintly behaviors he performed. Similarly, a man who murdered small children and ate them would surely be universally rejected, whether or not he was explicitly labeled as "mentally ill."

Labels Are Important. It is clear that labels do make a difference, at least in some contexts (Farina, 1981; Farina, Fisher, & Fischer, 1992; Link, 1987; Link, Cullen, Mirotznik, & Streuning, 1992; Phillips, 1966; Sibicky & Dovidio, 1986). There is also overt and covert discrimination in hiring ex-mental patients (Farina, Felner, & Boudreau, 1973; Farina, Murray, & Groh, 1978; Wansbrough & Cooper, 1980).

Whether a person has sought help for psychological problems can also affect perceptions. Langer and Abelson (1974) had clinicians evaluate a man being interviewed. Half were told that he was a job applicant and half that he was a patient ("mental patient" was not explicitly specified). Whereas behavioral therapists interpreted his behavior as reasonably well adjusted regardless of label, the more traditional, analytically inclined therapists saw him as more disturbed when he was a patient. People who seek counseling for psychological problems are rated differently than are those who have no problems or who have problems but do not seek help (Dovidio, Fishbane, & Sibicky, 1985); generally those without problems are seen to be sociable and to be more secure, but those who seek help are rated as especially high on competence and character. In an interpersonal situation, subjects behave more negatively toward someone they think is seeking counseling (Sibicky & Dovidio, 1986).

Obviously, evaluations depend to some extent on the type of label used. Research studies have used labels such as "mentally ill," "hospitalized mental patient," and "ex-mental patient," as well as specific diagnostic categories such as "paranoid schizophrenic." Generally, labels such as "insane" or "crazy" lead to more negative reactions than "mental patient" or "ex-mental patient" (Walkey, Green, & Taylor, 1981; Weiss, 1986, 1994). As one might expect, rejection of those who are mentally ill also varies by type of mental illness. Blizard (1970) found that subjects rejected a person with paranoid schizophrenia more than one with simple schizophrenia, followed by those with alcoholism, neurosis, and no mental illness in order. With a German sample, Angermeyer and Matschinger (1997) found that a person with alcoholism was rejected most, followed by those with schizophrenia, narcissistic personality, depression, and panic disorder.

Whether or not labels do make a difference, patients and others think they do. In a longitudinal study of ex-mental patients and their families (Clausen, 1981), patients reported little discrimination unless they had continuing behavioral problems, but both patients and families said they were embarrassed to tell others and were apprehensive about the reactions they would get from others. Link, Cullen, Struening, Shrout, and Dohrenwend (1989) found that 75% of a community sample thought that employers would discriminate against ex-mental patients, 71% thought they would be seen as less trustworthy, and so on. A sample of current and former patients generally agreed with these assessments. Moreover, those ex-patients who expected to be devalued and rejected were more demoralized and had a worse posthospital work history and social support network (Link, 1987; Link et al., 1989), and perceptions of discrimination were also related to lowered self-esteem (Link, Struening, Neese-Todd, Asmussen, & Phelan, 2001).

Interpersonal Effects of Labels. People who are labeled as "mentally ill" can be rejected outright because of their behavior or the label, but there may also be more subtle effects. Not only are they treated more harshly than "normal" people, but "normal" people have various expectations about their performance and ability.

Obviously, these expectations may be communicated to the people being labeled and may thus affect their behavior (see Chapter 6). If I think you think I am mentally ill, my behavior around you is likely to be affected. In an experimental demonstration, Farina, Allen, and Saul (1968) had pairs of subjects describe themselves in a written statement and then interact and perform a joint task. One of the subjects (A) was privately told to describe himself as mentally ill or homosexual, but his partner (B) actually received information indicating that he was fairly normal. The A subjects (those who thought they were stigmatized, but were not) were spoken to less by their B partners than those who thought that the B partners perceived them to be normal; obviously the "stigmatized" and "normal" subjects must have behaved in different ways, which led to their partners' perceiving them differently. Actual ex-mental patients feel they are less appreciated by their partners, perform more poorly, and are perceived to be more tense and less well adjusted when they think their partner knows their mental status (Farina, Gliha, Boudreau, Allen, & Sherman, 1971).

Behaviors Are Important. Is behavior important? Obviously, it is. Mentally ill people do sometimes behave in seemingly weird ways that make others uncomfortable, so they might be rejected even if people did not explicitly label them as "mentally ill." Several studies (e.g., Arkar & Eker, 1994; Aubry, Tefft, & Currie, 1995; Lehmann, Joy, Kriesman, & Simmens, 1976; Phillips, 1963, 1964; Socall & Holtgraves, 1992;

Thurman, Lam, & Rossi, 1988) find that behavior is as important as, or more important than, labels in judgments of people who might be seen as mentally ill.

Summary: Mental Illness

There is little to celebrate here for those who are mentally ill. Stereotypes about them are almost entirely negative; they are especially seen to be unpredictable and dangerous—surely traits that would lead to interpersonal wariness and rejection as well as overt discrimination. The only bright spot (and it is dim enough) is that people are fairly confused about the realities of mental illness; this confusion creates a possible window of opportunity for change. Not surprisingly, mentally ill persons are negatively evaluated—in part because the label of "mental illness" (and its many cousins) is stigmatizing, but also because such persons often do behave in ways that seem odd and incomprehensible to others.

Homosexuality

Everyday experience suggests that homosexuals are among the most stereotyped groups in modern life. Certainly it is fairly common to hear generalizations about both gay males and lesbians from people who otherwise seem to be cautious about expressing stereotypes of racial and gender groups. Homosexuality is widely condemned in U.S. society, and this condemnation creates a rich mixture of attitudes, beliefs, and stereotypes. There is abundant evidence for strong and fairly general rejection of homosexuality.[10] A number of surveys have found that relatively high percentages (and often majorities) of Americans think that homosexuality is immoral, and that homosexuals are dangerous and sick or mentally ill. For example, in a large national survey on sexual attitudes. Levitt and Klassen (1974) found that over 70% of respondents said that homosexual relations were always wrong, 84% said that homosexuality is obscene and vulgar, and almost 50% said that homosexuality can cause the downfall of a civilization. Over 70% thought that homosexuals were dangerous in jobs involving children or government security, and almost 40% thought that they tended to corrupt their fellow workers. A 1998 Gallup Poll (Gallup, 1998a) found that 59% of Americans thought that homosexuality is morally wrong, but a more recent Gallup Poll (Newport, 2001) found that 54% of Americans thought that homosexual relations among adults should be legal, 85% supported equal job rights, and 52% said that homosexuality is an acceptable lifestyle. So although prejudice against homosexuals may be decreasing, gay men and lesbians suffer verbal abuse and sometimes physical threat (Herek, 1993; Herek, Gillis, & Cogan, 1999) and are discriminated against in everyday situations (Hebl, Foster, Mannix, & Dovidio, 2002; Walters & Curran, 1996).

Stereotypes and Beliefs

Many studies find that attitudes toward homosexuals consists of a large evaluative factor (Bouton et al., 1989; Herek, 1984a; Kite & Deaux, 1986; Kurdek, 1988). Given that result, it is not surprising to discover that most homosexual stereotype traits are negative, although some studies find that these stereotypes include some positive features (Haddock, Zanna, & Esses, 1993; Staats, 1978).

STEREOTYPES AND INVERSION THEORY

Most research suggests that such stereotypes largely reflect what is usually called "inversion theory"—the idea that gay men are feminine and lesbians are masculine. Data on whether homosexuals do have more features of the opposite sex are mixed. A review by Pillard (1991) suggests that gay men do not differ from straight men in their masculinity scores, but have higher average femininity scores. Lesbians do not differ from their heterosexual counterparts in femininity scores, but do tend to have higher masculinity scores. Bailey and Zucker (1995) conclude that feminine boys and masculine girls have a greater likelihood of later being homosexual than those whose gender and behavior are more culturally consistent. Homosexuals differ markedly from heterosexuals in terms of occupational interests and self-defined masculinity and femininity (Lippa, 2000). Having said all that, I must add that feminine and masculine behaviors among gay males and lesbians vary tremendously, as they do among straights. Anyone who has spent time in a gay environment can easily see that the behavior of gay males ranges from quite feminine to hypermasculine.

In any event, popular stereotypes are built on inversion notions. This is apparent not only for trait ratings (Gross, Green, Storck, & Vanyur, 1980; Gurwitz & Marcus, 1978; Kite & Deaux, 1987; Page & Yee, 1986), but for free descriptions (Jackson, Lewandowski, Ingram, & Hodge, 1997) as well as ratings of physical attributes, gender roles, and occupations (Kite & Deaux, 1987). Madon (1997) did a careful study of stereotypes of gay males among college students, using subject-generated features as well as ones provided by the experimenter, and physical features and behaviors as well as traits. A sample of the features is given in Table 12.1. Note that some of the gay traits are positive, although one might argue that such

TABLE 12.1. Traits Listed by At Least 60% of People for Gay Male Stereotypes

Very or somewhat characteristic		Very or somewhat uncharacteristic
Engage in anal sex	Soft voice	Tough
Gay activist	Understanding	Masculine
Feminine	Different	Unemotional
Sensitive	Artistic	Close-minded
Transvestites	Soft-hearted	Act macho
Open-minded	Fashionable	Pick fights
Emotional	Touchy-feely	Hurt animals
Liberal	Hairdressers	Mean
Open about feelings	Lot of female friends	Cruel
Gentle	Sentimental	Prejudiced
Walk like girls	Melodramatic	Old-fashioned
In touch with themselves	Limp-wristed	Hard-hearted
Dainty		Traditional
Affectionate		Deep voice
Compassionate		Sloppy-looking

Note. Data from Madon (1997).

traits as being compassionate are less positive when applied to males than to females.

VIEWS OF CAUSES AND CURES

There is surprisingly little research on lay conceptions of the causes and possible "cures" for homosexuality. A recent Gallup Poll (Gallup, 2001) found that 40% thought that people are "born" homosexual, whereas 39% saw "upbringing" as the cause; corresponding figures in 1977 were 13% and 56% (Newport, 1998). The most extensive study (Furnham & Taylor, 1990) asked people to respond to a series of items about causes of and attitudes toward male homosexuality, as well as possible cures. A factor analysis of responses indicated six factors for causes: (1) early childhood experiences (e.g., "having one's first sexual experience with another male," "having early sexual relations with females that prove dissatisfying"); (2) genetic factors ("existence of hormonal imbalances in the fetus"); (3) father problems ("having a strong, dominant mother and a weak, ineffective father," "having a traumatic relationship with one's father"); (4) fear of women ("having a fear of the opposite sex"); (5) mental illness ("coming from a weird family"); and (6) early sexual abuse ("being sexually abused by a male during childhood"). There were five factors for attitudes toward homosexuality: (1) general intolerance; (2) homosexuals are effeminate; (3) homosexuality should not be open and overt; (4) homosexuals are easily identified; and (5) homosexuals are promiscuous. There were also five factors for possible cures: (1) learning and unlearning of homosexual behaviors; (2) different forms of formal therapy; (3) hormone and other biological treatments; (4) radical biological interventions (e.g., brain surgery, castration); and (5) exposure to members of opposite sex.

Most relationships among the factors were positive, although none of the correlations was above .50. As one might expect, those who believed that homosexuality is affected by early experiences, father problems, or unsatisfying sexual experiences with women were more inclined to endorse cures based on unlearning, formal therapy, and better exposure to members of the opposite sex. Belief in the efficacy of hormonal treatment was related to belief in genetic factors and mental illness as causes. Interestingly, there were relatively few strong relationships between beliefs in causes and attitudes. Generally, the belief that gay males are effeminate was weakly related to most of the putative causes, and the belief that homosexuality is a form of mental illness was weakly related to most of the attitudes.

Many people believe that homosexuality is basically learned, and these beliefs are correlated with negative attitudes toward homosexuality.[11] Put differently, beliefs that homosexuality is biological rather than learned predict positive attitudes toward homosexuals, as do beliefs that there are fundamental psychological differences between homosexual and heterosexual people (Hegarty & Pratto, 2001b). Those who see homosexuality as a choice also tend to avoid lesbians more (King, 2001). Despite the almost total lack of evidence to suggest that children of gay and lesbian couples have any greater sexual identity issues or personality problems than children from conventional heterosexual families (Patterson, 1992), people do believe that gay male couples will produce children with more sexual identity problems, largely because they believe that gay fathers are more effeminate than heterosexual fathers (McLeod, Crawford, & Zechmeister, 1999).

The Functions of Attitudes and Beliefs about Homosexuals

Both empirically and theoretically, it is difficult to separate the strong affective reactions to homosexuality from the more specific beliefs and stereotypes associated with this group. Here as in other areas, negative stereotypes may create prejudice, but attitudes derived from, say, religious philosophies may also create stereotypes. Our attitudes—those toward people, as well as those toward cars, schools, political institutions, and dogs—fulfill several distinct functions, and these functional foundations are especially strong for homosexual attitudes and stereotypes. In the case of homosexuality, three major functions have been identified by Herek (1984b): symbolic, defensive, and experiential. I add a fourth, instrumental.

SYMBOLIC FUNCTIONS

Attitudes have symbolic functions when they support a person's value system and abstract ideologies; in addition, many attitudes contribute to self-definitions and how people are perceived by various kinds of other people. One important symbolic basis for many attitudes is religion, and given the traditional hostility of most religions to homosexuality, it is no accident that negative attitudes toward and stereotypes of homosexuality are correlated with various measures of conservative religious beliefs and behaviors (Agnew, Thompson, Smith, Gramzow, & Currey, 1993; Cotten-Huston & Waite, 2000; Estrada & Weiss, 1999; Fisher, Derison, Polley, Cadman, & Johnston, 1994; Herek, 1987, 1988; Johnson, Brems, & Alford-Keating, 1997; Kurdek, 1988; Seltzer, 1992).

Attitudes toward homosexuality play a central role in the debate over family values. For many people, homosexuality threatens the foundations of a stable society by undercutting traditional sexual standards, sex roles, and family values. Not surprisingly, then, many studies also find that negative attitudes toward homosexuality are correlated with beliefs in traditional sex role attitudes (e.g., Buckner, 1991; Cotten-Huston & Waite, 2000; Kurdek, 1988; Whitley, 1987), with measures of sexism (Masser & Abrams, 1999; Morrison, Parriag, & Morrison, 1999); and with conservative sexual attitudes (MacDonald, Huggins, Young, & Swanson, 1973; Simon, 1995).

In Chapter 8 I have discussed the fact that people who are prejudiced against one group are often biased against others as well, and that many prejudices are correlated with conservative, dominance-oriented, and authoritarian beliefs. This is especially true for attitudes toward homosexuality, with right-wing authoritarianism (RWA) being the best predictor (Whitley & Lee, 2000). People who are perceived to have a choice in their sexual orientation are held more responsible and condemned more strongly by those in a condemning frame of mind. Homosexuals are more rejected by people who see the causes of homosexuality as learned (King & Black, 1999; Matchinsky & Iverson, 1996) or attribute the causes to controllable factors (Whitley, 1990). More positive attitudes are associated with a belief in biological causes (Matchinsky & Iverson, 1996).

These symbolic functions are more important for some people than for others. Two people might each value traditional sexual morality, but one see this as centrally important to his or her ways of thinking about the world, and the other may have more of a "live and let live" attitude. Haddock and Zanna (1998b) review a research program suggesting not only that those who score high on the RWA Scale (Altemeyer, 1996; see Chapter 8) have more negative attitudes toward gay people, but that their attitudes are more strongly predicted by the extent to which they think that gays violate their values. For those with lower RWA scores, symbolic beliefs are not predictive, but stereotypic beliefs are. High scorers, compared to low scorers, also tend to perceive greater value disparities between themselves and homosexuals, and this value disparity predicts their attitudes better.

EGO-DEFENSIVE FUNCTIONS

Attitudes may also serve what is usually called an "ego-defensive" or simply "defensive" function. At least some attitudes are developed and elaborated to make people feel good about themselves, often by denying threatening and unacceptable feelings or rejecting other people who seem different. Clearly, sexual identity is important to most people, and attitudes toward homosexuals may reflect perceived threats to people's sense of their own sexual identity. Some (e.g., Kantor, 1998) have speculated that homophobia stems from defenses against one's own latent homosexual urges. However, we do not have to "buy into" a kind of psychoanalytic model to recognize that in a culture where sexuality is strongly constrained by morality and where people's sense of self-worth is, to some extent, tied up with their abilities to perform expected and approved sexual roles, some people will feel threatened by those who disagree.

Probably these burdens fall more heavily on males than on females in U.S. society. Not only is sexuality a more central part of the identity of most males, but males in general are given less flexibility in deviating from established sex roles (see Chapter 11), especially those that seem to involve manifest behaviors of the opposite sex. If that were the case, we would expect to find that males would have the strongest negative reactions to homosexuals, especially gay males. In fact, a meta-analysis of several studies (Kite & Whitley, 1996) does suggest that males generally do reject homosexuals more than females, and that males are especially harsh toward gay males; similar results are found with the implicit association test (Banse, Seise, & Zerbes, 2001). Other meta-analyses (Oliver & Hyde, 1993; Whitley & Kite, 1995), however, suggest that the gender difference is found only for younger samples.

EXPERIENTIAL FUNCTIONS

Many attitudes are simply reflections of reality and serve to guide behavior in a complex world. I have negative attitudes toward guns, which I associate with violent crime. Obviously, people with different experiences—say, hunters—have different experiences and associations and generally different attitudes than I. Likewise, we would expect that people's experiences (or lack thereof) may affect their attitudes toward homosexuals. One problem is that many people have little or only highly selective exposure to homosexuals, because sexual orientation is often deliberately hidden and usually not immediately obvious.

Causal or media contact can reinforce traditional stereotypes. Whereas many homosexuals think of themselves as like everyone else except in sexual orientation and downplay their differences from their straight neighbors and friends, others sometimes deliberately act out one of a number of homosexual scripts in efforts to celebrate their orientation or to differentiate themselves from straights. The media, in turn, may give more attention to homosexuals who act in stereotypic ways than to those who act in ways considered more appropriate to their gender.[12] Thus many people have little or no direct contact with people they can identify as homosexual, and the "pictures in their heads" may be based more on cultural transmission of one-sided behaviors than on their own experiences.[13]

If this reasoning is correct, we should expect that people who have more contact with homosexuals should have more positive attitudes (assuming their experiences are largely positive) or at least more differentiated stereotypes. As expected, people who have homosexual friends or who report knowing homosexuals tend to have more positive attitudes toward the group (Cotten-Huston & Waite, 2000; Estrada & Weiss, 1999; Haddock et al., 1993; Herek & Capitanio, 1996; Herek & Glunt, 1993a; Simon, 1995; Wills & Crawford, 2000). I restate the obvious about such correlational findings: Contact could produce more positive attitudes, but positive attitudes could also induce more contact. These possibilities are not mutually exclusive, and I assume that both happen. Attitudes toward homosexuals are also correlated with perceptions of friends' attitudes (Larsen, Reed, & Hoffman, 1980), suggesting that such attitudes may have an element of social influence. Educated people are less prejudiced against homosexuals, perhaps they are more likely to have gay friends who are out of the closet, or because they are better informed about the complexities of sexual orientation (Irwin & Thompson, 1987; Lottes & Kuriloff, 1994; Seltzer, 1992).

INSTRUMENTAL FUNCTIONS

Instrumental attitudes are based on the perception that a person or category hinders or helps important goals. For example, a person who believes that homosexuals are likely to prey sexually on children or to constitute a major security risk will surely have a negative attitude toward them. Haddock and colleagues (1993) found that perceptions that homosexuals blocked important goals did contribute to negative attitudes about them. As one example, those people who feel that having gay men in the military would create problems of AIDS, undermining morale and discipline, and unwelcome sexual advances are more likely to favor continuing the ban on having openly gay men in the armed services (Wyman & Snyder, 1997). Obviously, beliefs that gay men would make advances to other servicemen or undermine morale may themselves be biased by a more general rejection of homosexuality for other reasons. Attitudes toward having gays in the military are also strongly predicted by general perceptions that homosexuality is morally wrong and that lifting the ban would be condoning homosexuality. Nonetheless, people who genuinely believe that gay men in service would create problems certainly have some justification for their belief that gays should be banned from the military.

Behaviors versus Stereotypes

Here is the labeling question again. Are perceptions of homosexuals driven more by their sexual preferences per se or by the behaviors they supposedly exhibit? Generally it has been assumed that homosexuals are rejected for who they are and not for how they behave, but there is an alternative view. Could male homosexuals be rejected because they are assumed to behave in an effeminate way? If this were true, than perhaps gay males who behaved in a more masculine manner might not be disliked as much (MacDonald & Games, 1974). On the other hand, we could argue the reverse; perhaps gay males who are quite masculine in appearance and behavior (as many in fact are) would be especially threatening to those who have somewhat traditional views of how people are supposed to behave and what correlates with what in the world.[14] The issue is whether people prefer other people's behavior to be consistent with stereotypes of their biological gender or with stereotypes of their sexual orientation.

Thus we need to look at behavior and sexual orientation separately. Those studies that have done so have tended to find that both sexual orientation and behavior are sources of evaluative bias (Abrams, Carter, & Hogg, 1989; Buckner, 1991; Laner & Laner, 1979, 1980; Storms, 1978). On the other hand, there are also hints of relevant interactions that would signal preferences for homosexuals who act stereotypically like homosexuals (Golebiowska, 2000; Millham & Weinberger, 1977; Storms, 1978). However, results supporting the other perspective (preferences for people whose behavior is consistent with gender rather than sexual orientation) have also been reported (Buckner, 1991; Corley & Pollack, 1996; Laner & Laner, 1979). Again, we need to remind ourselves that the question of whether labels or behaviors are more important is generally unanswerable. It all depends on how extreme the behaviors are, the situation in which they are exhibited, and how salient the label is.

Identification of Homosexuality

Finally, there is the important and interesting issue concerning whether sexual orientation can be detected by observing behavior. We have seen that people do assign certain traits to homosexuality, and the question is now whether these same traits also lead to ascriptions of homosexuality. Recall that $p(\text{Group}/\text{Trait})$ is generally not the same as $p(\text{Trait}/\text{Group})$; however, often people do treat these probabilities are reasonably symmetrical. For example, masculine-appearing/behaving women and feminine-appearing/behaving men are often assumed to be homosexual (Deaux & Lewis, 1984; Dunkle & Francis, 1990; Storms, Stivers, Lambers, & Hill, 1981). Male body builders are seen as less likely to be homosexual than those with less attachment to muscles, whereas among females the body builders are seen as more likely to be lesbian (Freeman, 1988). Male athletes who participate in more "feminine" sports (e.g., figure skating) and females who are involved with more masculine sports (e.g., softball) are seen as more likely to be homosexual (McKinney & McAndrew, 2000). Males and females in cross-gendered occupations are more likely to be seen as homosexual (Wong, McCreary, Carpenter, Engle, & Korchynsky, 1999). The rule, then, seems to be that behavior not conforming to conventional sex role standards is grist for the gay mill.

Are people accurate in their identifications? People are able to identify homosexuals from both 1-second and 10-second video clips. Supporting the stereotype that "it takes one to know one," homosexual subjects were more accurate than heterosexuals for the shorter, but not the longer, clips (Ambady, Hallahan, & Conner, 1999). There have, however, been no systematic investigations of what cues people use for "diagnosing" homosexuality.

AIDs and Homosexuality

THE LINK TO HOMOSEXUALITY

An issue closely related to stereotyping of homosexuals is reactions to people with AIDS (PWAs). Although HIV/AIDS is a stigma itself, there is no doubt that it is associated with homosexuality in most people's minds. The Centers for Disease Control estimate that approximately 60% of new HIV/AIDS cases in the United States are caused by gay sexual practices, although heterosexual sex is a far more common vehicle worldwide (National Institute of Allergy and Infectious Diseases, 2002). Given various well-publicized cases, it will come as no surprise to discover that people generally reject those who have AIDS (Crawford, 1996; Fish & Rye, 1991; Page, 1999; Pryor, Reeder, Vinacco, & Kott, 1989), especially when the disease has been associated with homosexuality (Fish & Rye, 1991; St. Lawrence, Husfeldt, Kelly, Hood, & Smith, 1990) or has been contracted through sexual activity or drug use (Bailey, Reynolds, & Carrico, 1989; D'Angelo, McGuire, Abbott, & Sheridan, 1998; Dowell, Presto, & Sherman, 1991).

Several studies have shown that people who fear or have negative attitudes toward AIDS also have negative attitudes toward homosexuality (e.g., D'Angelo et al., 1998; Herek & Glunt, 1993b; Young, Gallaher, Belasco, Barr, & Webber, 1991). Is fear of AIDS, then, merely a cover for strong homophobia? Perhaps. In 1987, 27% of people in a poll agreed that "AIDS is a punishment God has given homosexuals for the way they live" (Herek & Glunt, 1988). In a more recent Gallup Poll (Gallup, 1997), 40% of the sample thought that AIDS was a person's own fault, 31% thought that it was a punishment for a decline in moral standards, and 7% said that people with AIDS should be isolated from the rest of society.

FUNCTIONS OF ATTITUDES TOWARD AIDS

Pryor, Reeder, and McManus (1991) have noted that attitudes toward PWAs, like most other attitudes, can serve at least two basic functions. First, these attitudes might be based on a sense of the rewards and costs of interacting with the attitude object (instrumental attitudes). In this case, people might think that they are more likely to catch AIDS by interacting with a PWA, or they might think they would find the interactions socially awkward; alternatively, they might also imagine positive consequences from (such interactions such as opportunities to show compassion, to become better educated, etc.). Second, people hold certain attitudes as a way of telling the world (and themselves) about their values. So people might reject PWAs as a way of making clear their disgust with homosexuality.

Several lines of research support the importance of the instrumental function. For example, Bishop, Alva, Cantu, and Rittiman (1991) argue that fear of AIDS is more closely related to fears of contagion—a factor known to predict people's desires not to interact with diseased others.[15] They asked their subjects to respond to a person with a fictitious disease that was either contagious or not and associated with homosexuals or not. Contagion was a better predictor of desire to interact with the person than was homosexuality; in fact, there was a nonsignificant tendency to want to interact more with the homosexual with the contagious disease than the heterosexual with the same disease. They also showed that people with negative attitudes toward homosexuality resisted contact with people with all manner of diseases and cancer conditions in addition to PWAs; this suggested that the relationships between attitudes toward AIDS and homosexuality may be somewhat spurious. Along the same lines, Crandall, Glor, and Britt (1997) showed that perceptions of disease severity rather than the association with homosexuality was the most powerful predictor of attitudes toward PWAs, and that attitudes toward homosexuality actually correlated somewhat higher with desired social distance toward accident victims than with PWAs. These studies, then, cast doubt on the widely held view that people's attitudes toward attitudes are nothing more than veils for rejections of homosexuality, although they do not rule out the idea that such attitudes are relevant pushes.

Of course, these functions are not mutually exclusive, and one might even generate a plausible theory for why people who reject homosexuals might also be likely to fear catching AIDS. For example, Magruder, Whitbeck, and Ishii-Kuntz (1993) provide data suggesting that attitudes toward homosexuality affect what information is read about the condition. In other words, those with negative attitudes may read more information that raises fears about the contagiousness of AIDS. Alternatively, people with less education are known to have more negative attitudes toward homosexuals (see above), and less educated people are probably also less well informed about the contagiousness of the disease.

Several studies have shown that both kids of attitudes predict reactions to PWAs. Pryor and colleagues (1989) found that subjects (including parents) who were reluctant to have their child attend school with another child who had AIDS did so in part because of various instrumental attitudes about what that contact would mean, even though a child is extremely unlikely to "catch" AIDS through such school contact; however, those people who had negative attitudes toward homosexuality also rejected such contact, suggesting instrumental attitudes are not the whole story. Both negative attitudes about homosexuality and fear of AIDS also predict negative reactions to a neighborhood residential AIDS treatment center (Colon & Marston, 1999).

In a large survey study, Herek and Capitanio (1998) found that subjects whose attitudes toward PWAs were fueled primarily by a fear of contracting the disease rejected and stigmatized PWAs to the extent that they felt causal contact with them was a risk factor. However, for those males whose attitudes were primarily expressive (based on political or religious values), stigmatization of PWAs was also predicted by attitudes toward homosexuality.

STEREOTYPES OF PWAS

Apart from general affective reactions, PWAs are also seen to have a number of distinct features. This has potentially important consequences if those features are used as ways to identify potential sexual partners. Informally, gay men often report that they were willing to have unprotected sex with someone who looked or acted as if he was HIV–. Gold and Skinner (1996) found that homosexual men thought that potential partners who were physically attractive, intelligent, and healthy-looking were less likely to be HIV+. In a subsequent study (Gold, Skinner, & Hinchy, 1999), homosexual men thought that other men who hung out in saunas, sex clubs, or public toilets (as opposed to bars and discos), who preferred anal receptive sex (as opposed to insertive anal sex), who dressed in leather or denim, whose access to gay venues was high, whose occupations were commercial (as opposed to medical), and whose sexual orientation was straight or bisexual (as opposed to exclusively gay) were more likely to be infected. Whether or not these stereotypes are accurate, they are not accurate enough to be used as cues for unprotected sexual contact.

Notes

1. I recently attended a play performed by a local black theater group and found myself at intermission a lone white among many blacks. I was a bit amused by feeling vaguely uncomfortable at the sidelong glances I received, and at the overly effusive welcomes I received from a few people. *Par pari refero.*

2. One of Goffman's useful intellectual tricks was to use analyses of particular groups as mirrors for reflection on our own situations. In the present case, after analysis of the problems of people from clearly stigmatized groups (mostly persons with mental illness, criminal records, and physical disfigurements or disabilities), Goffman commented: "For example, in an important sense there is only one complete unblushing male in America: a young, married, white, urban, northern, heterosexual Protestant father of college education, fully employed, of good complexion, weight, and height, and a recent record in sports" (1963, p. 128). I fail several of those tests, but I'm not saying which.

3. Obviously, other groups (such as those with physical disability, obesity, or chronic illness) are often rejected and may in addition encounter real physical impediments to their living unimpaired lives. I do not mean to diminish such concerns by not considering them more fully in this book. However, I would prefer to discuss two stigmas in more detail than try to cover every nuance related to differences among stigmas. Furthermore, there are probably more extensive research literatures on mental illness and homosexuality than on other stigmas, and these literatures raise somewhat more interesting theoretical issues. Obesity, which is another important stigmatizing condition, is discussed in Chapter 13.

4. It is important to remember that while members of some stigmatized groups (e.g, people who use wheelchairs) spend most of their time with "normal" people, members of other stigmatized groups (e.g., racial minorities) spend more time with members of their own groups, thus providing continuing and available support. This is potentially important, because members of stigmatized groups may feel devalued primarily when having consequential interactions with nonstigmatized people (Brown, 1998; Postmes & Branscombe, 2002).

5. I greatly dislike the term "mental illness," but more accurate terms (such as "people suffering from emotional, cognitive, or behavioral problems") are too comprehensive and a mouthful to boot. Therefore I continue to use the term "mental illness."

6. It must be said that good research in this area is hard to do. Picking a representative sample of mentally ill persons is not a trivial exercise, given different diagnoses and symptoms. It is hard to find an appropriate control sample of putatively "normal" people, and since persons with and without mental illness differ in many ways, it is often hard to know what variables should be controlled. For example, controlling for socioeconomic status often reduces differences in violence between the two groups; this is an appropriate control if socioeconomic status causes both mental illness and violence, but a case could be made that mental illness lowers socioeconomic status, rendering this control problematic. Measuring violence and dangerousness is itself difficult. Monahan (1992) provides an excellent discussion of these and other methodological issues.

7. This paper was never published (and I have not read it), but the vignettes have been widely reproduced.

8. It seems as if nearly every time there is a brutal murder in Houston, I get a call from various members of the news media asking me whether it isn't highly likely that the murderer is mentally ill. Many well-educated people have suggested to me that killers must be mentally ill, because "I can't imagine killing someone like that."

9. Cumming and Cumming (1957) cite the case of a woman who had accepted and lived more or less successfully with her mentally ill sister for many years. When this woman was gone for a period of time, the sister was briefly hospitalized. The woman subsequently rejected her sister because she must be mentally ill now that she had spent time in a mental hospital. In the same vein, Schwartz (1957) has an interesting discussion of how wives cope with a diagnosis of mental illness for their husbands. A substantial number think that their husbands' illness is not prototypic, and that therefore they are not fully mentally ill.

10. Like mental illness, homosexuality is not a fixed quality with clear boundaries, so it is virtually impossible to give precise estimates of the percentage of the U. S. population that is homosexual. Estimates depend heavily on what questions are asked. In one fairly recent comprehensive survey (Michael, Gagnon, Laumann, & Kolata, 1994), 6% of men reported being attracted to other men, 2% had sex with another man in the last year, 9% had sex with another man since puberty, 5% had sex with another man since age 18, and about 3% identified themselves as homosexual. There is obvious overlap among these measures, but they do not yield a perfect scale. For example, one might take self-identification as the key, but many men have sex with other men without identifying themselves as gay. In his study of men who had fleeting homosexual encounters in public restrooms, Humphreys (1970) reported that many were married and did not define themselves as homosexual or even bisexual. If we take the broadest possible definition and include men who gave homosexually oriented answers to one or more of the Michael and colleagues (1994) questions, 10% could be construed as gay. However, about 2.5% could be considered gay if we define it as narrowly as possible and require that a man identify himself as homosexual, have had at least one sexual encounter with another man, and report current attraction to other men. The percentages for lesbians are similar but lower

11. Recently the Rice University football coach (a man I like and respect) said that he had never had a football player "come out" to him (strongly implying that he had never had any gay players), and furthermore that if one did, he would have to ask why he had changed since he had been recruited and would have to think hard about whether to kick the fellow off the team. The university president made it clear to the coach that although he was entitled to his views, he could not discriminate on the basis of sexual orientation. Interestingly, as a result, male and female athletes on other teams did publicly admit to their homosexual orientation. Unfortunate as the episode was, it proved educational for students.

12. I live in a city with a large gay male and lesbian population, and I am often struck by the television attention given to underdressed and flamboyant homosexuals during gay pride parades and the lack of attention given to quiet gay male and lesbian couples such as those living in my neighborhood. I want to make it clear (and see Chapter 9 for a more extended discussion) that I do not believe this is a plot by the media to bias our perceptions. Television is a visual medium, and gay males behaving in stereotypic ways make better "copy" than ones engaging in nonstereotypic behavior. A case can be (and often is) made that in the long run, acceptance of homosexuality depends on people's getting used to (if not actively embracing) such "deviant" behaviors. The jury is still out on that idea. In any event, the only point I want to make here is that people's stereotypes of gay males and lesbians are reinforced by what they see on television.

13. I recently ran a study on stereotypes of homosexuals. One of the student subjects commented as he handed in his data sheet that it had been an interesting experience to try to

produce stereotypes for gay men, because he didn't know any. Another student standing nearby said, "Oh, yes, you do. You just don't know it."

14. I once made a comment in a class containing a large number of athletes that a number of gay males work out regularly with weights. During my next office hour, I was visited by two or three muscular football players who assured me that they worked out regularly and certainly had never seen any homosexuals in their gym. This led to a conversation about identification of homosexuality, but what struck me most at the time was how threatening my initial observation had been to these hypermasculine (and, incidentally, quite nice) young men.

15. Such fears can be quite powerful. Rozin, Nemeroff, and Markwith (1992) found that subjects lowered their ratings of a sweater that had been owned or worn once by a PWA. Although there may have been many irrational factors at work here, certainly fear of contagion may have been one.

CHAPTER 13

Content of Stereotypes: Other Categories

This chapter considers a range of other social categories that give rise to stereotypes. The collection may seem a potpourri, and in some respects it is. However, there are some commonalities. It is assumed that people more or less deliberately "join" most of the groups in these categories. For example, my occupation, hair style, and use of a nickname may have little in common, except that others may reasonably assume that each results from choices that reveal something about me. As always, behavior that is assumed to reflect conscious choice says a lot about a person—or so we believe.

Also, for the most part, the stereotypes of these groups—with some notable exceptions—are fairly uncontroversial. No one seems to mind much if I express stereotypes of doctors as caring, professors as naive about finances, or women who dress in business suits as ambitious. Of course, in each case there will be exceptions, and there are always voices telling us that not all members of a group are alike. But often people display the cues that give rise to the stereotypes precisely because they want to create a particular impression. They adorn their bodies, homes, and offices in ways designed to create impressions based on stereotypes.

PHYSICAL FEATURES

We have many ways of learning about new people, but for most of us the most salient way is through direct face-to-face contact—where we will immediately have access to cues about race, gender, and age, and, if the person speaks, possibly cues to ethnicity, socioeconomic status, and degree of education. Face-to-face contact also provides a wealth of additional cues that are bases for stereotypes (Zebrowitz, 1996). We may notice hair color and facial complexion, as well as the person's body type, height, and weight. We may notice whether a woman is wearing cosmetics, or whether a man's hair is properly groomed. We judge both on the basis of the suitability of the clothes they are wearing, and whether these seem stylish or vulgar.

Many of our stereotypes are based on physical appearance. One of the earliest lines of research on stereotyping looked at judgments of intelligence based on photographs (Anderson, 1921; Gaskill, Fenton, & Porter, 1927; Pintner, 1918). Contemporary research confirms that people agree at better than chance levels on what faces "go with" various occupations (Hassin & Trope, 2000; Klatzky, Martin, & Kane, 1982; Yarmey, 1993), gender subtypes (Green & Ashmore, 1998) crimes (Bull & Green, 1980; Goldstein, Chance, & Gilbert, 1984; Thornton, 1939; Yarmey, 1993), and other forms of deviance (Shoemaker, South, & Lowe, 1973).[1] Of course, consensus does not guarantee accuracy (Hassin & Trope, 2000).

Body Shape

Although it may well be true that we are pretty much stuck with the bodies Mother Nature gave us, we often assume that the appearance of bodies provides important cues about the people who inhabit them. Obese persons, no less than highly muscular individuals, are seen as having made deliberate choices about how to present their bodies to the world.

Body Type

One of the most salient features that we may notice about a person is whether he or she has a shapely body or is unusually fat or thin. Most research in this areas has identified stereotypes associated with the three major components of body-typing identified by Sheldon, Stevens, and Tucker (1940). Those who are muscular are called "mesomorphs," those who are high in fat tissue are "endomorphs," and those who are thin are "ectomorphs." As is well known, Sheldon and colleagues (1940) thought that people with different body types also differed in personality. However, a review by Montemayor (1978) finds few differences in measured personality among body types, although there are some differences for self-ratings, social behavior, and delinquency. Research generally shows that mesomorphs are stereotypically assigned positive traits,[2] endomorphs are assigned largely negative traits, and ectomorphs lie somewhere in between (Butler, Ryckman, Thornton, & Bouchard, 1993; Gacsaly & Borges, 1979; Sleet, 1969; Wells & Siegel, 1961).

Fat, muscular, and skinny people do, of course, get assigned specific traits. For example, in one recent study (Ryckman et al., 1991), mesomorphs were seen as having more friends; as working harder; and as being more attractive, healthy, brave, competitive, and adventuresome. Endomorphs were seen mostly as the opposite: sloppy, uncompetitive, lazy, unhealthy, unattractive, and unadventuresome. Ectomorphs were viewed as intelligent, neat, afraid, tense, and likely to be homosexual. Table 13.1 lists some of the stereotype traits. Naturally, there were some gender differences (Ryckman, Robbins, Kaczor, & Gold, 1989); for example, while women were generally seen as neater and cleaner than men, male endomorphs were seen as especially sloppy and dirty. Male mesomorphs were especially advantaged in perceptions of being popular and in being good-looking. For judgments of intelligence, body type was not much of a factor for women, but male ectomorphs were especially likely to be seen as smart and those popular, muscular mesomorphs as stupid.

TABLE 13.1. Stereotypes of Body Types

Mesomorphs (muscular)	Endomorphs (fat)	Ectomorphs (thin)
More friends	Sloppy	Intelligent
Hard work	Lazy	Neat
Attractive	Unattractive	Afraid
Healthy	Unhealthy	Tense
Adventuresome	Unadventuresome	Likely homosexual
Competitive	Uncompetitive	
Brave		
Unpredictable temper		
Unintelligent		
Intolerant		

Note. Data from Ryckman et al. (1991).

SUBTYPES OF BODY TYPES

As we have seen often throughout this book, there are often powerful subtypes of what we might think of as primary social categories, and body type is no exception. Ryckman, Butler, Thornton, and Lindner (1997) have found not only that people distinguish between various subtypes of the three main body types, but that each has a distinct stereotype. For example, among endomorphs, both male and female couch potatoes are rated negatively; however, clowns, Santa Claus types, and mothers are more positive subtypes. For ectomorphs, "wimps" are seen as more negative than "brains," and steroid users are rated more negatively than jocks among male mesomorphs.

OBESITY

Although we have definite stereotypes about muscular and thin people, we are particularly prone to stereotype endomorphs—those who are fat. Several studies have confirmed that people, including young children, have definite and largely negative stereotypes of obese individuals (Brylinsky & Moore, 1994; DeJong & Kleck, 1986; Goldfield & Chrisler, 1995; Harris, Harris, & Bochner, 1982; Harris & Smith, 1983; Lerner, 1969; Ryckman et al., 1989, 1991; Stager & Burke, 1982; Staffieri, 1967). In particular, fat people are believed to be lazy, sloppy, unattractive, unhappy, unenergetic, and unpowerful (Harris, 1983; Harris, Walters, & Waschull, 1991b). They are also seen as having low self-esteem, to be less involved in dating, and to rate lower on various love scales (Harris, 1990). Obese women are seen to be less sexually attractive and interested in sex (Regan, 1996). Overweight children are usually ranked last or near to last in preferences for physically deviant children by other children (Goodman, Richardson, Dornbush, & Hastorf, 1963; Richardson, Hastorf, Goodman, & Dornbush, 1961) and by adults (Maddox, Back, & Liederman, 1968).

Cultural Differences. There are some cultural differences in attitudes toward and stereotypes of obese persons. Generally, in economically developed countries people of higher socioeconomic status are thinner, but the reverse is true in underdeveloped countries (Furnham & Baguma, 1994). In countries where food is hard come by, being overweight may be a sign of financial security and high socioeconomic status, since obviously many poor people cannot afford enough calorie-rich food to become fat. Not surprisingly, people from underdeveloped countries evaluate overweight people more positively and skinny people less positively than do people in more Westernized countries (Cogan, Bhalla, Sefa-Dedeh, & Rothblum, 1996; Furnham & Alibhai, 1983; Furnham & Baguma, 1994).[3] In the United States, black people also have preferences for larger women than whites do (Collins, 1991; Cunningham, Roberts, Barbee, Druen, & Wu, 1995; Jackson & McGill, 1996), and older black women who are obese are more satisfied with their weight than their white counterparts (Stevens, Kumanyika, & Keil, 1994). In addition, white women rate obese women as lower on attractiveness, happiness, popularity, intelligence, job success, and relationship success than nonobese women, but these negative stereotypes were not present when black women rated other obese black women (Hebl & Heatherton, 1998).

Discrimination. In general, overweight people not only are assigned negative qualities by others, but are also discriminated against in everyday interactions, job situations, and college admissions (Solovay, 2000). The research does not show a perfectly consistent pattern. Whereas some studies find that obese people, especially men, are not disadvantaged on the job (McLean & Moon, 1980), other studies strongly suggest that overweight people, especially women, do have problems. One study found that very obese women report more types of job discrimination, although they do not receive lower salaries (Rothblum, Brand, Miller, & Oetjen, 1990). Although it is possible that obese people magnify the amount of discrimination they face, or that employers discriminate in ways that do not show up in paychecks, the obese subjects in this study reported that they had to work harder than the nonobese subjects to overcome negative stereotypes.

However, other research suggests more discrimination. Sargent and Blanchflower (1994) found that women (but not men) who were fat at age 16 earned less money at age 23 than those who were not. Several studies (see Sobal & Stunkard, 1989, for a review) find that people with lower socioeconomic status are more overweight than those with higher socioeconomic status. Though causality in such cases is obviously indeterminate and complex (Sobal, 1991), the fact that those who seem "downwardly mobile" are fatter than those who appear more "upwardly mobile" might indicate that obesity lowers ability to get well-paying jobs (Sobal & Stunkard, 1989). Alternatively, since there is evidence that obese women have lower social skills than their nonobese peers (Miller, Rothblum, Barbour, Brand, & Felicio, 1990), it is possible that what seems to be discrimination based on body type reflects personality features. To complicate matters further, obese women tend to assume that their social failures are due to discrimination and fail to use the social skills they have to compensate for problems (Miller, Rothblum, Felicio, & Brand, 1995).

There have been claims that obese people are less likely either to go to college or to be admitted to high-prestige colleges. Canning and Mayer (1966) found that obese women were less in evidence at high-prestige colleges and universities than in high schools, despite the fact that the two groups had equivalent academic aspirations and credentials. Other studies (e.g., Crandall, 1995) also find that there are proportionally fewer fat women (but not men) in college than in the general population for the relevant age ranges. This might result from discrimination in the admissions process, but there are, of course, several alternative explanations. For example,

Crandall (1991, 1995) has shown that obese college women are less likely to receive financial support from their parents, and (although this was not tested) they may also get less emotional support and encouragement generally from parents and peers for their college choices. Alternatively, given that overweight people generally have lowered self-esteem (Miller & Downey, 1999), young women who are overweight may fear rejection and lack the self-confidence to apply to high-prestige colleges or to college in general.

Why Do We Derogate Obese Persons? There can be no doubt that Western cultural ideals strongly frown on obesity, especially for women—a fact that accounts in part for the much greater rate of eating disorders among women (Tiggemann & Rothblum, 1988). In Western culture, physical attractiveness is closely linked to body type, and women are especially valued for their physical attributes. Therefore women bear the brunt of largely negative stereotypes about obesity.

However, the reactions of people to obesity go beyond adherence to a cultural ideal. After all, Western culture also values physical attractiveness, but we don't make as much fun of ugly people as we do of fat people. We consider it desirable to be intelligent, but most of us would see mocking mentally retarded people as vulgar, insensitive, or even immoral. Yet fat people are routinely the butt of jokes and snickers. Why is obesity so much a matter of scorn in Western society? One reason may be that obesity is seen to be a controllable condition in ways that ugliness and mental retardation are not. Several studies (Allison, Basile, & Yuker, 1991; DeJong, 1980; Tiggemann & Anesbury, 2000) have shown that negative attitudes toward obese people were predicted by beliefs that they could control their weight, and this also been found in six countries (Crandall et al., 2001).

Perhaps obese persons are seen as indulging their bodies—something that is frowned upon in puritanical U.S. society in particular. Indeed, anti-fat attitudes are associated with a range of other attitudes, such as racism, political conservatism, authoritarianism, belief in a just world, a tendency to blame the poor for their poverty, and rejection of homosexuals and disabled persons (Crandall, 1994; Crandall & Biernat, 1990; Crandall & Martinez, 1996). Thus anti-fat attitudes are related to an emphasis on individualism and cultural conservatism, as well as a rejection of those who are different and who may require special attention.

Height

It is interesting that we seem to have few stereotypes about height, another obvious feature of our physical presence. This may be related to the perception that we have less control over our height than our weight. However, there is some evidence that tall people are seen as more imposing and potent than short people (Elman, 1977; Roberts & Herman, 1986), and they are in fact more assertive (Collins & Zebrowitz, 1995). Tallness is associated with both perceived and real status and competence (Cann, 1991; Egolf, 1991; Jackson & Ervin, 1992; Lindeman & Sundvik, 1994), even at an early age (Eisenberg, Roth, Bryniarski, & Murray, 1984).

Does height affect the bottom line? Sargent and Blanchflower (1994) report that tall boys at age 16 earn more at age 23 than do short boys, and other research (Collins & Zebrowitz, 1995) supports this relationship between height and earning power. However, height effects tend to be small. In a study (Mazur, Mazur, &

Keating, 1984) of West Point graduates from 1950, those who were taller had achieved slightly higher military rank 30 years later, but the effects of height were tiny compared to effects of athletic participation at West Point. One review of the literature (Hensley & Cooper, 1987) concludes that height may offer slight initial advantages in getting hired for jobs, but has no effect on subsequent performance or ratings.

Facial Features

There is a long history, extending back at least as far as Aristotle, of assuming that character and personality can be "read" from the face (Liggett, 1974). To some extent, this is based on transient cues such as smiling and frowning; the person who never seems to smile will surely be seen as different from the one who seems to smile all the time. But mostly we are interested in more or less permanent features of faces—noses, eyes, hair color and style, and wrinkles, just to name several cues.

Facial Cues

Research on stereotypes about people with various facial features extends back a half century or more (Secord, 1958). The research has been relatively successful in documenting the fact that perceivers agree on what traits should be assigned to particular photographs (e.g., Secord & Bevan, 1956; Secord, Bevan, & Dukes, 1953; Secord, Dukes, & Bevan, 1954; Secord & Muthard, 1955) and on what faces fit particular personality descriptions (Secord, 1958), but it has been less successful in documenting which particular facial features act as cues for these trait attributions. Still, there are some relationships. For example, Secord and colleagues (1954) found that mouth curvature was positively correlated with traits such as sense of humor and easygoing nature, and negatively related to perceived hostility. Other research (Keating, 1985) has shown that for male targets, small eyes and thin lips lead to perceptions of dominance. Lowered brows and nonsmiling faces are seen as dominant (Keating et al., 1981). Perceptions of honesty are associated with relatively large eye size (Berry & Zebrowitz-McArthur, 1986; Zebrowitz-McArthur & Apatow, 1983–1984; Zebrowitz, Voinescu, & Collins, 1996) and with facial symmetry and positivity of facial expression (Zebrowitz et al., 1996).

Baby-Faceness

STEREOTYPES

More recently, Leslie Zebrowitz and her students have explored perceptions of facial immaturity ("baby-faceness") and its consequences for other trait ratings (see Berry & Zebrowitz-McArthur, 1986, and Montepare & Zebrowitz, 1998, for reviews). This research has shown that adult faces that are closer to the physiognomy of infant faces (large forehead and short chin, fuller cheeks, larger eyes, smaller and wider nose, etc.) are perceived as being more baby-faced—not in itself a surprising finding. What is more interesting, however, is that baby-faced adults are often assigned traits such as warmth, honesty, naiveté, and kindness that tend to be stereotypically characteristic of children (Berry, 1991; Berry & Zebrowitz-McArthur, 1985; Zebrowitz-McArthur

& Apatow, 1983–1984). Baby-faced and more mature-looking people also differ on some measures of actual personality (Berry & Brownlow, 1989). Ratings of vocal babyishness affect how people are perceived in much the same way (Berry, 1990b; Montepare & Zebrowitz-McArthur, 1987). These effects seem to be quite general. Korean students respond to the same features of faces as do American students in perceiving baby-faceness, and they draw the same trait conclusions (Zebrowitz-McArthur & Berry, 1987).

REASONS FOR STEREOTYPES

This could be a simple metaphorical cognitive leap: Babies are immature, and therefore anyone who looks like a baby must also be immature. Obviously, such an inference is likely to be largely nonconscious, as most people would probably be aware of the uncertain validity of such a generalization. Zebrowitz and her colleagues (e.g., Berry & Zebrowitz-McArthur, 1986) have preferred a somewhat different explanation, however. They argue that babies and infants are dependent on adults for their survival, and that therefore their particular facial (and other) features probably elicit caretaking activities on the part of adults as a part of an inherited disposition. In other words, people are programmed to pay close attention to physical features that are found in babies, and they are programmed to respond with particular perceptions and behaviors—which are not easily "turned off" when dealing with an adult stimulus person.

CONSEQUENCES

Whatever the correct explanation may be, there are important consequences. For males more mature faces indicate dominance and attractiveness, whereas for females a corresponding increase in perceptions of dominance due to facial maturity is accompanied by ratings of lower attractiveness (Keating, 1985). Friedman and Zebrowitz (1992) argue that since baby-faced features are generally part of the female stereotype, and females tend to be more baby-faced than males, at least part of the stereotype of females may be due to their unconsciously perceived immaturity. They showed that when baby-faceness was equated for males and females, gender stereotypes were strongly reduced or eliminated.

Obviously, we have different standards of behavior for young and mature people and assign them different moral capacities. Typically we assume that the young are naive, fairly honest, and not especially likely to be naughty (Zebrowitz, Kendall-Tackett, & Fafel, 1991). In a simulated trial, Berry and Zebrowitz-McArthur (1988) found that baby-faced defendants were more often found guilty of an offense resulting from negligence (drawing on the stereotype of their relative naiveté), and less often found guilty of crimes involving intentional wrongdoing (because they are perceived to be more honest). Since baby-faced boys are expected to be better behaved than more mature-appearing boys, they are likely to receive more negative outcomes from their misdeeds (Zebrowitz & Lee, 1999). Part of the baby-faced stereotype is intellectual immaturity, and so males who are baby-faced may compensate for stereotypes of goodness and intellectual immaturity by excelling academically or by misbehaving. Both results have been reported (Zebrowitz, Andreoletti, Collins, Lee, & Blumenthal, 1998).

Other Physical Features

Thus far we have considered body shape and facial features. But as any reader of *Gentleman's Quarterly* or *Cosmopolitan* quickly learns, there is more—much more—to how we present our bodies to others. We get rid of some parts of our bodies (e.g., leg hair for women), pick the color of our hair, change the color of our faces and bodies through cosmetics and tans, and camouflage our natural body smells. Whole industries arise from our desires to mold and change our bodies.

Controllable Features

Some physical features are more controllable than others. We can do little to alter our height, and (short of cosmetic surgery) cannot affect the facial features with which we were endowed. By contrast, it is trivially easy to use readily available products to affect the color of our hair, how much hair we display on various parts of the body, how we smell (or even taste, for those who are inclined to sample the products of sexual boutiques), and how much of our bodies are covered with what kinds of apparel.

HAIR

Hair has an enormous amount of ideological significance (Synnott, 1987). Not only do the amount, color, and style of our hair make a fashion statement, but hair proclaims our gender and sometimes our political position. Generally men cut their hair and women wear it longer, but men revel in and reveal body hair, whereas women pretend they have none. Those who wear their countercultural tendencies on their sleeves worry a lot about their hair. Some have argued that women should cut their hair short and let their body hair have its way, and male radicals tend to have long scalp hair (or sometimes none at all). Scalp and body hair tend to be major issues for gay males. Even today, when it's harder to find good old-fashioned male radicals, long hair and ponytails tend to declare a certain antiestablishment bias.

Hair Style and Color. If one has scalp hair, its length can be controlled. Several studies (Pancer & Meindl, 1978; Peterson & Curran, 1976; Roll & Verinis, 1971) have shown that hair length and style do affect impressions of people. Obviously, our inferences about hair length are heavily culturally conditioned, so it is far from clear that these differences would be apparent today.[4] Hair color is also important. Those who doubt this need only visit their local drugstore to see the extensive array of products designed to alter hair color. In a study by Roll and Verinis (1971), blond males were positively evaluated, and those with black hair were seen as high on potency and activity scales, whereas redheads were lowest on all three dimensions. Other studies confirm obvious stereotypes based on hair color (Lawson, 1971a); surely there are stereotypes of people who dye their hair bright red or in a rainbow array.

Facial and Body Hair. Baldness, facial hair, and chest and arm hair on males also affect how they are rated on a variety of traits. For example, chest and arm hair is associated with virility (Addison, 1989; Hellström & Tekle, 1994; Verinis & Roll, 1970). Bearded men are seen as relatively high on such traits as potency, masculinity, and strength (Roll & Verinis, 1971). Bald men are seen as less attractive and older (Cash, 1990; Muscarella & Cunningham, 1996), but as relatively potent (Roll & Verinis, 1971) and intelligent (Wogalter & Hoise, 1991). Although I know of no research on how women are perceived as a function of whether they shave or do not shave their bodies, it seems likely that women with hairy legs are perceived differently from those who shave them. Classically, women have sought to minimize body hair (perhaps to differentiate themselves from males), and in many cultures women's scalp hair is seen as sexually arousing (Etcoff, 1999).

COSMETICS AND CLOTHES

Cosmetics affect ratings of females (Cash, Dawson, Davis, Bowen, & Galumbeck, 1989; Cox & Glick, 1986; Kyle & Mahler, 1996), and we also draw inferences about people from the clothes they wear (Bardack & McAndrew, 1985; Forsythe, 1990; Forsythe, Drake, & Cox, 1985; Johnson & Roach-Higgins, 1987; Kaiser, 1985; Scherbaum & Shepherd, 1987). There seems little point in discussing such stereotypes in detail, because they are so heavily dependent on cultural norms and contexts. The obvious rule of thumb is that culturally approved use of cosmetics and clothes is associated with positive stereotypes (Graham & Jouhar, 1980). It is interesting to speculate about the reasons for this. Is it because those who dress appropriately are assumed to be plugged into what's new and trendy, to have important social knowledge, or to being making an effort to meet the expectations of others? Should we care? Most of the time probably not, but we might want to consider that stereotypes of those who are culturally "cool" are probably quite different from those of people who aim to please.

EYEGLASSES

One of the most intensively studied of what we might call artifactual variables is the wearing of eyeglasses. In early stereotype studies (Thornton, 1943, 1944), people who wore glasses were seen as being more intelligent. Most recent research agrees that the wearing of glasses leads to perceptions of mental competence and intelligence (Harris, 1991; Hellström & Tekle, 1994; Terry & Krantz, 1993) as well as authority (Bartolini et al., 1988), although some studies find that the wearing of glasses leads to diminished ratings of social competence and forcefulness (Elman, 1977; Terry & Krantz, 1993). For those who need a self-esteem injection, people rate themselves as more intellectually competent when wearing glasses than when not (Kellerman & Laird, 1982). Many studies find that the wearing of glasses diminishes ratings of physical attractiveness, especially for females (Harris et al., 1982; Terry, 1989; Terry & Hall, 1989).

Movement

The way our faces move can affect ratings of femininity, age, and power (Berry, 1990c), and the ways we walk can affect age judgments (Montepare & Zebrowitz-McArthur, 1988). These perceptions are based in part on real behavioral differences. We need minimal information to identify gender, amount of physical effort, and identity of friends on the basis of movement (Berry, 1990a; Runeson, 1985). Even handwriting, a result of movement, leads to stereotypes (Jarrett & Loewenthal, 1991; Vine, 1974).

Physical Attractiveness

Surely we do not have to prove that we have stereotypes about attractive and unattractive people. Huge fashion, cosmetics, and body-training enterprises exist primarily to make us more physically attractive, so that we can take advantage of stereotypes of the beautiful, well-toned folks. When was the last time any of us saw an ugly leading lady, or a man with a large nose and a receding chin, in a shampoo or deodorant advertisement? It is unlikely that most of us go to the trouble to make ourselves as attractive as possible merely for aesthetic reasons. As many psychologists have shown in what amounts to a gold mine for research, attractive people are generally liked and approved in a variety of ways (Etcoff, 1999; Hatfield & Sprecher, 1986; Jackson, 1992; Langlois et al., 2000).

Specific Stereotypes Based on Physical Attractiveness

But over and above this global approval for attractive people, there are more specific stereotypes associated with physical attractiveness. Let's think about it for a moment. Who seems more intellectual—the beautiful young woman whose every crease and cosmetic are properly in place, or the more dowdy, frumpy woman whose glasses are perched precariously on her nose and who is fighting back unkempt hair? Is it possible that the slight young man who has yet to recover from a bad case of adolescent acne could be as extroverted as the man who is wearing designer clothes and whose body bespeaks many hours in the gym? Whether accurate or not, such stereotypes are reinforced through advertisements and other cultural mechanisms.

GENERAL TRAITS

Several research studies do support the idea that physical attractiveness is important, not only for general evaluation but for the traits we attribute to others (Adams, 1982; Dion, 1986; Eagly, Ashmore, Makhijani, & Longo, 1991; Feingold, 1992b; Langlois et al., 2000). Stereotypes based on attractiveness occur for both genders (Langlois et al., 2000), show up even in preschoolers (Dion, 1973), and are found in non-Western cultures (Shaffer, Crepaz, & Sun, 2000).

Stereotypes in this area are stronger for traits having to do with social competence and adjustment than for traits connotating altruistic concern for others (Feingold, 1992b). Beyond traits, there is also considerable evidence that physically attractive people are advantaged in decisions about hiring (Dipboye, Arvey, & Terpstra, 1977; Dipboye, Fromkin, & Wiback, 1975; Stone, Stone, & Dipboye, 1992) and salaries (Frieze, Olson, & Russell, 1991; Umberson & Hughes, 1987). If we take media representations as a sign of a cultural consensus, in American movies physically attractive characters are portrayed more favorably (Smith, McIntosh, & Bazzini, 1999). Physically attractive political candidates are evaluated more positively than less attractive ones (Budesheim & DePaola, 1994). No one is surprised to learn that beautiful and handsome people are more desirable as romantic partners (e.g., Green, Buchanan, & Heuer, 1984). Even having an attractive companion raises one's status

(Kernis & Wheeler, 1981; Meiners & Sheposh, 1977; Sigall & Landy, 1973), although there is some empirical evidence that women do not like other women who are attractive (Jackson, 1992).

SUBTYPES

There are different forms of attractiveness—subtypes of attractiveness, as it were. Ashmore, Solomon, and Longo (1996) studied how male and female subjects categorized and rated pictures of female models. For female subjects, there were three basic categories: (1) cute and natural associated with ratings as sociable, moral, interesting, and not challenging); (2) sexy good looks associated with ratings as not moral, not interesting, and not well-adjusted); and (3) trendy (which did not have clear stereotypes for the features measured). The categories for male perceivers were a bit different: (1) girl next door (social, interesting, well-adjusted); (2) sexually attractive (no clear stereotype); (3) trendy (no clear stereotype); and (4) intelligent/elegant (strong, intelligent). To the best of my knowledge, there has been no documentation of different types of physical attractiveness for males, but a quick mental run-through of various ads and movies suggests that such subtypes must exist. Are we not likely to have quite different stereotypes of the equally attractive androgynous Calvin Klein model and a more rugged he-man type? If not, then why do advertisers so carefully choose their models?

PHYSICAL ATTRACTIVENESS, ROMANCE, AND EVOLUTION

Popularity, especially with the opposite sex, is moderately correlated with physical attractiveness, and the emphasis on beauty seems to reach its zenith in the context of sex and romance. However, males and females probably approach this somewhat differently, or at least those who work from an evolutionary perspective (e.g., Buss & Schmitt, 1993; Kenrick & Trost, 1993) so argue. Modern evolutionary psychology is built on the assumption that people want to ensure that as many copies of their genes as possible are carried over to the next generation.

Male Preferences. According to such accounts, men can best maximize gene transmission by producing as many healthy children as possible. As long as they can have multiple sexual partners, they can produce thousands of children. Males should therefore prefer multiple sexual partners who appear to be able to produce and raise lots and lots of children. That should lead men to prefer attractive women, because physical attractiveness in women is presumed to be a significant correlate of youth and physical health—both indicators of reproductive potential.

However, this hypothesis is far from definitively established. Physical attractiveness (and features such as facial symmetry, which contribute to attractiveness) may be a reliable, albeit weak, cue for health (Shackelford & Larsen, 1999), although some do not find a relationship (e.g., Kalick, Zebrowitz, Langlois, & Johnson, 1998; Rhodes et al., 2001) or find that the relationships differ for males and females (Hume & Montgomerie, 2001). A high hip-to-waist ratio, a substantial predictor of female attractiveness, is related to successful birthing (Singh, 1993b). In fairness, however, evidence based on modern people with access to good health care may conceal relationships that existed a few hundred thousand years ago, when presumably all this was set in stone (or fixed in the genes). It is, however, also important to point out that even weak relationships can, over many generations, have important evolutionary significance.

Female Preferences. Theoretically, because women can produce far fewer children, they best maximize inheritance of their genes by caring for the relatively small number of children they produce, and they will seek partners who can help in this endeavor. Therefore, women should prefer more selective sexual encounters—ideally, with mates who will stick around for the long haul and can provide both protection from physical harm and also material benefits such as food (and, in modern days, wealth). Thus women should prefer men who appear to be sexually mature, rich, dominant, and able to hold their own in fights with foe and beast. Women should not be as swayed by physical attractiveness as men, but more by appearance cues and behavioral symbols of status (Townsend & Levy, 1990). To the extent that they are swayed by attractiveness, they should prefer men who have mature features, such as a prominent chin.

Environmental Contingencies. However, environmental conditions may alter these strategies. For example, in an environment where disease is rampant, women might prefer male partners who look healthy rather than those who look like good providers, so the importance of attractiveness should be higher when disease is an important threat. Attractiveness is, in fact, relatively more important for mate selection in cultures where disease is a major problem (Gangestad & Buss, 1993).

Finally, it is important to note that culture and learning experiences play an important role—surely a more important one than our genes—in what we value for potential mates. One of the reasons we have cultures is to protect us from our genetic heritage and to direct genetic pushes and pulls toward prosocial ends. Some of us learn that personal compatibility, value similarity, and compassion, among other virtues, count for something in our relationships (Li, Bailey, Kenrick, & Linsenmeier, 2002).

Evidence. Whether or not the evolutionary argument is correct, there is abundant evidence that men emphasize physical attractiveness in their choice of mates, whereas women are more concerned with social status and earning potential. Buss (1989) found that in a study of 37 cultures from around the world, males valued physical attractiveness more highly than females did. Other studies in American culture have confirmed that men are more concerned with physical attractiveness and women with status and earning potential (Feingold, 1990, 1992a; Kenrick, Groth, Trost, & Sadalla, 1993; Sprecher, Sullivan, & Hatfield, 1994). Attractive females are more likely to marry higher-status men (Elder, 1969), and very unattractive young women are 10 times more likely to be unmarried than their very attractive counterparts (Udry & Eckland, 1984). Analyses of personal ads consistently find that physical attractiveness is the most often mentioned desirable feature by men but is less important for women (Feingold, 1992a; Smith, Waldorf, & Trembath, 1990). Not only do men desire stress physical attributes more, but women tend to offer them; moreover, males tend to stress their financial security, which is exactly what women tend to emphasize wanting (Thiessen, Young, & Burroughs, 1993; Wiederman, 1993).

Deviancy and Physical Unattractiveness

In addition to less romantic success, physical unattractiveness is associated with various kinds of deviancy. Adolescents who are unattractive are more likely than their unattractive peers to be involved in crimes and to be in trouble in school (Agnew, 1984; Cavior, Hayes, & Cavior, 1974; Cavior & Howard, 1973), and correctable facial abnormalities are much more common among criminals than the general population (Masters & Greaves, 1967). Unattractive adolescents are more maladjusted than their attractive peers and, if female, have lower self-esteem (O'Grady, 1982). Hospitalized mental patients are less attractive than controls without mental illness (Napoleon, Chassin, & Young, 1980), and more attractive patients have a better prognosis after release (Farina, Burns, Austad, Bugglin, & Fischer, 1986; Farina et al., 1977), although such effects tend to weaken when socioeconomic status is taken into account (Archer & Cash, 1985; Sussman & Mueser, 1983). It is, of course, impossible to tell what causes what in such research. Physically unattractive people may engage in deviant behavior because of rejection by others, or perhaps those who are so engaged take less care of their bodies or are less concerned with buying and using grooming and beauty aids.

Most of these studies have compared the attractiveness of known stigmatized groups. But what about the reverse? Are unattractive people seen as having psychological problems? For starters, people rate attractive females as less psychologically disturbed than unattractive ones (Cash, Kehr, Polyson, & Freeman, 1977; Jones, Hannson, & Phillips, 1978). Also, when people were asked to reconstruct a face from a photograph, they constructed one that was independently judged to be less attractive and intelligent when they thought the photograph was of a murderer rather than a laborer (Shepherd, Ellis, McMurran, & Davies, 1978). Unattractive persons are seen as more politically radical (Unger, Hilderbrand, & Madar, 1982). Attractive people are more likely to be gender-stereotyped, and those who are physically unattractive are more likely to be seen as being homosexual (Dunkle & Francis, 1996; Unger et al., 1982).

Cues for Attractiveness

ARE CUES CULTURALLY UNIVERSAL?

A most interesting and important question is what predicts attractiveness. To some extent this is surely a cultural matter (Fallon, 1990), but contrary to widespread assumptions, empirical data suggest a universality of features associated with physical attractiveness (Etcoff, 1999; Langlois et al., 2000). For example, Martin (1964) found that black and white subjects produced the same basic attractiveness ratings of black female faces. Asians, Hispanics, and white Americans all rate black, white, Asian, and Hispanic pictures similarly in terms of attractiveness (Chen, Shaffer, & Wu, 1997; Cunningham, Roberts, Barbee, Druen, & Wu, 1995; Wheeler & Kim, 1997). People assess beauty quickly; trait ratings favoring attractive persons occur with brief exposures (100 milliseconds) to faces (Locher, Unger, Sociedade, & Wahl, 1993). And they discover beauty early; children as young as 2–3 months of age look longer at attractive than at unattractive adult faces, suggesting that such preferences are not merely a matter of cultural tuition (Langlois, 1986; Langlois et al., 1987).

SPECIFIC CUES

Overall attractiveness is affected by both facial and bodily attractiveness (Brown, Cash, & Noles, 1986), with the eyes and mouth carrying much of the burden (Alley & Hildebrandt, 1988). Langlois and her colleagues (Langlois & Roggman, 1990; Langlois, Roggman, & Musselman, 1994) have argued that attractive faces are those that are average for their gender. In support, they found that composite pictures (created roughly by taking the average of all features) were generally rated higher in attractiveness than the average rating of the pictures making up the composite (especially as more pictures were entered into the composite). However, even in this research some individual faces were rated higher than the composite, and a composite based on the most attractive faces from a group was rated more positively than the composite of the whole group in another study (Perrett, May, & Yoshikawa, 1994). Moreover, when composite faces exaggerated the features that empirically discriminate attractive from unattractive faces, these were rated most positively of all.

There has been some debate about possible confounds in this research. Composite faces are more symmetrical and have idiosyncratic features (e.g., facial blemishes) "averaged out." Symmetrical faces are more attractive (Hume & Montgomerie, 2001; Rhodes, Profitt, Grady, & Sumich, 1998). However, more recent research (Rhodes, Sumich, & Byatt, 1999) has found that averageness does increase attractiveness even when these potentially confounding factors have been taken into account.

Although average faces seem to be particularly attractive, from an evolutionary standpoint there are reasons to believe that for some features extremeness may be a virtue (Alley & Cunningham, 1991). For example, if clear skin is a sign of good health, then one ought to seek mates with the clearest skin. Since most theorists assume that males seek female mates who are young (because they can have more children), extreme signs of immaturity for some facial features may be favored in females, and females may prefer males with the exaggerated features associated with maturity.

Specific Facial Cues. Facial features that define attractiveness differ for men and women, obviously. Cunningham (1986) had white male subjects rate pictures of women, including white, black, and Asian beauty pageant contestants. Those who were judged to be most attractive had neonate features of large eyes, small nose, small chin, and widely spaced eyes; the mature features of wide cheekbones and narrow cheeks; and expressive features of highly set eyebrows, wide pupils, and a large smile. These features were present in both the white and nonwhite beauty contestants. Women who have features associated with maturity, such as a prominent chin and jaws, are considered unattractive; furthermore, in several cultures features associated with youth (e.g., large eyes, small nose, large lips) are associated with attractiveness in women (Jones, 1995).

Cunningham, Barbee, and Pike (1990) and Cunningham and colleagues (1995) found that attractive males tended to have neonate features of large eyes and small noses; the mature features of prominent cheekbones and a large chin; and the expressive feature of a large smile. Research by Johnston, Hagel, Franklin, Fink, and Grammer (2001) showed that women preferred male faces with longer, broader, and lower jaws, along with more pronounced brow ridges and cheekbones—all features that are generally perceived to be more masculine, and that are in fact associated with higher levels of testosterone. Interestingly, these preferences were strongest when the women were ovulating.

Body Cues. Women who have a relatively low waist-to-hip ratio (i.e., narrow waist and broad hips) are judged more attractive by both men and women in the United States (Singh, 1993a; Singh & Young, 1995) and other cultures (Singh & Luis, 1995). Other research has shown that generally men prefer women with moderately large breasts, moderately small buttocks, and moderately large legs (Wiggins, Wiggins, & Conger, 1968). So *Playboy* has it right—men prefer hourglass figures in women (Furnham, Hester, & Weir, 1990). For their part, women prefer men who have moderately large chests and small buttocks (Beck, Ward-Hull, & McLear, 1976).

As common experience suggests, there are substantial individual differences in preferences for various body types (Wiggins & Wiggins, 1969). The traditionally masculine V-shape is preferred by traditionally feminine women more than less traditional types (Lavrakas, 1975). People living in more traditional cultures (e.g., Portugal) have stronger preferences for V-shaped male forms and hourglass-shaped female forms than do people in less traditional cultures (e.g., Denmark) (Furnham & Nordling, 1998).

LANGUAGE

The language we use often provides powerful cues for the types of persons we are. Speaking styles and accents provide information about where we grew up and perhaps how educated we are. Whether we prefer to be called Miss or Ms., Mr. or just plain John, Dr. or Professor may provide cues about status and pretensions.

Names

Among of the first pieces of information others gain about us are our names. First and last names may, of course, provide information about nationality, ethnicity, and even socioeconomic status. However, there is no evidence to suggest that our reactions to last names are any different from what would be predicted by knowing our reactions to the gender, nationality, and ethnicity to which names point. In other words, we probably do not have stereotypes about last names per se, but rather use them to identify membership in groups about which we have stereotypes. Matters are different with first names.

Social Desirability

It has long been known that some first names are seen as more attractive and desirable than others (Joubert, 1993). A recent survey found that names such as Jennifer, Ashley, Michelle, Lisa, Michael, David, Brian, and Mark were seen as more attractive than names such as Bertha, Gertrude, Martha, Jane, George, Fred, Eugene, and Ralph (Willis & Henderson, 1994). One would not have deep insights into American culture to know that a child named Reginald is going to be teased by his classmates more than one named Kevin. It is probably no accident that we have few movie stars named Bertha, Pearl, Ruby, Faith, and Hortense. Male actors have names such as

Clint, Jack, and Tom rather than Elmer. It would be fascinating to study the "traits" of TV and movie characters as a function of their names. This might offer telling insights into popular stereotypes because presumably characters' names are chosen deliberately to match the behaviors and traits they display.

Names that are more desirable are also more common (Allen, Brown, Dickinson, & Pratt, 1941; Mehrabian, 1992)—not the most surprising result. However, the social desirability (and popularity) of names does change over time, and people who have names that were more popular a generation or so ago than now (e.g., Frank, Norman, Walter, Edith, Norma, Shirley) are evaluated less positively than those with more up-to-date names (e.g., Brian, Mark, Ronald, Deborah, Jennifer, Lisa); in particular, people with old-fashioned names are seen as less intelligent and popular, and are ranked less highly in a simulated job hiring (Young, Kennedy, Newhouse, Browne, & Thiessen, 1993).

Name Stereotypes

Names vary in more than social desirability, of course. People assign different traits to different names (Mehrabian, 1992; Schoenfeld, 1942). Semantic differential ratings of traits also show that some names are rated higher in potency and activity, as well as evaluated more positively, than others (Buchanan & Bruning, 1971; Darden & Robinson, 1976; Lawson, 1971b, 1973, 1974, 1980; Lawson & Roeder, 1986). Table 13.2 provides ratings for a sample of names. Unconventional male names are seen as less masculine, but unconventional female names are seen as more masculine

TABLE 13.2. Ratings (High Numbers Indicate More) of Male and Female Names on Six Traits

	Success	Morality	Health	Warmth	Cheerfulness	Masculinity
Brad	90	45	91	49	65	79
Bud	1	23	46	30	49	79
Dave	64	38	68	50	68	76
David	92	54	85	72	73	81
Davy	34	44	43	54	71	65
Mitch	60	46	78	47	59	75
Richard	74	55	80	59	66	79
Dick	67	49	65	59	64	76
Ross	99	56	88	66	82	80
Tab	27	27	52	28	58	64
Walter	82	77	29	69	36	64
Barbie	22	25	73	59	74	12
Caroline	70	60	58	54	56	28
Dana	55	23	73	49	65	34
Caitlin	61	50	71	62	62	28
Flora	10	40	31	33	28	35
Doris	36	65	40	79	40	27
Joan	75	56	52	52	33	35
Jennifer	63	49	84	82	87	28
Kristen	63	55	69	63	76	29
Lois	65	61	34	52	46	43
Sadie	12	26	52	73	63	33

Note. Data from Mehrabian (1992).

(Mehrabian & Piercy, 1993c). Longer names for males suggest higher social position, and short names for both males and females are seen as warmer (Mehrabian & Piercy, 1993a). Male names are rated as more powerful (Duffy & Ridinger, 1981) and more positive (Dion, 1985) than female names. Kasof (1993) has argued that psychologists who have investigated gender discrimination have often chosen male names that have stronger connotations of competence and attractiveness than the female names that were used. Possibly studies showing women are seen as less competent may have more to do with the names that were used than with gender per se.

Nicknames

Although we are more or less stuck with the names we are assigned at birth, many of us use nicknames associated with our more formal given names. Davids can be Daves or even Davys. Williams can be Bills or Wills, and Susans can be Sues or Susies. Generally people who use the more formal names (William) are seen as less extroverted, and more conscientious, stable, and cultured, than people who use informal (Bill) and adolescent (Billy) names (Leirer, Hamilton, & Carpenter, 1982). Compared to more formal names, nicknames are rated as less successful and moral, but more popular and cheerful (Mehrabian & Piercy, 1993b). There are surely exceptions, but these results suggest that more formal names are associated with power and competence, whereas nicknames seem to connote a more social orientation. This is presumably why they are used.

There are important differences between male and female nicknames. Female nicknames more often end in "ie" or "y" and are rated as more positive but less powerful (Phillips, 1990). Female nicknames are more often coined in the home and are more likely to be affectionate and childish, whereas male nicknames tend to be given by peers and are more often based on personal attributes (e.g., Fatboy, Bat Breath) (De Klerk & Bosch, 1996; Phillips, 1990). Although nicknames are often weapons of derision, among some groups of children and adolescents being given a nickname (even an offensive one) is considered a sign of acceptance (Morgan, O'Neill, & Harré, 1979).

Do Name Stereotypes Have Any Effects?

Though it may not be entirely fair that some children get stuck with names that lead to a certain amount of teasing and perhaps initial dislike, perhaps such names have trivial practical effects. Is there any evidence that the power of names goes beyond a simple and fleeting affective reaction?

EFFECTS ON EVALUATION AND ACHIEVEMENT

The research evidence is mixed, but most seems to suggest that the power of names is weak indeed. In one widely cited study, Harari and McDavid (1973) found that essays supposedly authored by children with popular names were judged better than the same essays supposedly written by children with less popular names. However, the data were actually quite weak; essays authored by David (popular) were rated higher than those by Michael (popular), Elmer, and Hubert (both unpopular), but for girls' names Lisa (popular) and Adelle (unpopular) led to higher ratings than did Karen (popular) or Bertha (unpopular). Some subsequent studies have found that names affect evaluations (Erwin & Calev, 1984; Infante, Pierce, Rancer, & Osborne, 1980), but others have not (Tompkins & Boor, 1980).

Other studies have shown attractiveness of names to be associated with better school achievement (Busse & Seraydarian, 1978b; Garwood, 1976); higher pay, at least among journalists (Infante et al., 1980); and more popularity among school children (Busse & Seraydarian, 1979; McDavid & Harari, 1966). Other studies, however, find essentially no relationship between names and actual (Crisp, Apostal, & Luessenheide, 1984; Zweigenhaft, 1977) or perceived (Tompkins & Boor, 1980) success.

EFFECTS ON PERSONAL ADJUSTMENT

There are reports that people with relatively uncommon names have disturbed or neurotic personalities (Ellis & Beechley, 1954; Savage & Wells, 1948), are more likely to be in a psychiatric hospital (Anderson & Schmitt, 1990), have a higher incidence of psychosis (Hartman, Nicolay, & Hurley, 1968), and are more likely to be lonely (Bell, 1984). Personal adjustment and self-esteem are related to how well people like their own names (Joubert, 1991; Strunk, 1958), but are less highly related to social desirability ratings by others (Twenge & Manis, 1998).

However, the effects of names on personal adjustment and self-esteem are often quite weak and limited to one gender or the other. It is also far from clear why such effects occur. It is tempting to conclude that people with uncommon names have a tougher time socially, which leads over time to mental health problems, but it is also possible that families who give their children relatively uncommon names differ from other parents in ways that might produce later problems. Although there is no direct support for the latter possibility, socioeconomic status and race do have slight effects on tendencies to use uncommon names (Levine & Willis, 1994; Willis, Willis, & Grier, 1982; Zweigenhaft, 1977), especially for females (Lieberson & Bell, 1992). Effects of name desirability on intellectual and social competence tend to wash out when race is controlled for; blacks tend to give children more uncommon names, and also to have children with more academic and social difficulties (Ford, Miura, & Masters, 1984).

Two things seem clear: We do have name stereotypes, but it is likely that names are not terribly important in our social lives. We can all think of people whose names seem to fit their successful personalities, and others who have made their unconventional names into badges of identification. Being named Jennifer or Chris is far from a key to success, although some parents struggle with naming newborns as if this matters a great deal; their belief results from cultural stereotypes, no doubt.

Forms of Address

Does it make a difference whether I am called Dr., Mr., Professor, or just Dave? Should women care whether they are addressed as Ms., Miss, or Mrs.? It seems obvious that this would make a difference, but there are surprisingly few data on these issues. Because choice is involved, we would expect that there are stereotypes associated with forms of address. Are there? Several studies suggest that for women the use of Ms. leads to higher ratings on agentic traits. Dion (1987) found that a person with the Ms. title was rated as more achievement-oriented and socially assertive, but as less interpersonally warm, than a person designated as Mrs. or Miss (or, interestingly enough, Mr.). In a follow-up study, Dion and Schuller (1990) showed that women who preferred to be called Ms. were rated as having traits closer to the requisite traits of a successful middle manager than women who preferred Miss or Mrs. Also, women who keep their own last names at marriage or hyphenate them with their husbands' are seen as more agentic and less communal than those who adopt their husbands' last names (Etaugh, Bridges, Cummings-Hill, & Cohen, 1999).

Gender-Related Pronouns

In recent years there has been some controversy over the use of masculine terms as generic terms. Many people have objected to the use of masculine pronouns such as "he" and "his" to refer to humans in general as opposed to males. Others have argued that in context it is usually clear when masculine pronouns refer to men specifically or people generally, and that little harm is done by using masculine terms as generics.

   Is there evidence on this controversy? Actually, there is quite a bit, and for once it all points in the same direction: When masculine pronouns are used, people usually assume that the generic person involved is male (Fisk, 1985; Hyde, 1984; MacKay, 1980; Moulton, Robinson, & Elias, 1978; Schneider & Hacker, 1973; Switzer, 1990; Todd-Mancillas, 1981). For example, when subjects were asked to describe any mental images associated with reading sentences, they more often "saw" males when the sentence used "he" than when it used "they" or "he/she"; males were less affected by these variations than females, especially because they tended to see the "he/she" as a "he" (Gastil, 1990). Other studies that involve more subtle dependent measures (Ng, 1990; Wilson & Ng, 1988) have also shown that the masculine terms are generally interpreted as masculine rather than as inclusive of both genders. McConnell and Fazio (1996) found that the use of masculine suffixes for titles (e.g., "chairman") increased ratings of masculinity, whereas use of neutral suffixes (e.g., "chairperson") decreased them, compared to a no-suffix control (e.g., "chair"). Such effects were stronger for subjects who endorsed traditional gender ideology. Additional research by Banaji and Hardin (1996) shows that words such as "chairman" prime male pronouns, whereas feminized terms such as "chairwoman" prime female pronouns.

Ethnic Labels

Preferred Labels

As I have argued throughout this book, stereotypes and attitudes toward groups are not fixed or stable. For many groups we draw on a rich array of features, and a number of factors affect how which ones come to the fore—recent experiences, priming, prominent exemplars, and the like. One factor that might affect our perceptions of groups is how they are labeled. Are our stereotypes of "blacks," "Negroes," and "African Americans" different? Does it matter whether someone is called "Hispanic," "Latino," "Chicano," or "Mexican American"? Are "Asians" and "Orientals" the same?

   Some data suggests that labels do make a difference. For example, Fairchild and Cozens (1981) found that "Chicanos" were rated as more ignorant and cruel and less faithful than "Mexican Americans" or "Hispanics," and "Hispanics" were rated most talkative and tradition-loving. Marín (1984) showed that "Mexican Americans" were rated more highly on semantic differential scales than were "Chicanos." In the 1970s, the then-recent term "black" was rated as more potent and active than "Negro" or "colored" (Lessing & Zagorin, 1972). Fairchild (1985) found that "Afro-American" had a less negative stereotype than did "Negro" or "black." On the other hand, using a Canadian sample, Donakowski and Esses (1997) found no stereotype differences for terms such as "Native Indians," "First Natives," "Native people," and "aboriginals," although such terms did affect attitudes to some extent.

Ethnophaulisms

"Ethnophaulisms" are the nicknames or labels, usually derogatory, given to members of ethnic groups. There are literally thousands of such terms in English alone; terms such as "wop," "nigger," "spic," "kike," and "honky" are familiar enough examples. Because such terms are largely derogatory, they are often used to make fun of people of another group,[5] or to reinforce status and power relationships. They are, in short, overt and real verbal expressions of discrimination and racism. Palmore (1962) showed that the number of ethnophaulisms available for use against a given group is strongly related to prejudice against that group. For example, in American society we have many more ethnophaulisms to refer to blacks than to Jews or Germans, and we also have more prejudice against the former.

In further research, Allen (1983) found more ethnophaulisms for larger than for smaller minority groups, and this result held even when prejudice was partialed out. Although there may be many explanations for this, Allen favored the idea that larger minority groups are more likely to come into more contact with members of the majority culture, and that this greater contact gives rise to more opportunities for conflict and prejudice.

Mullen and Johnson (1993) argue that such terms index an additional feature of group relationships. Mullen (1991) suggests that we usually have exemplar representations of large and cognitively diverse groups, but that we are more likely to employ prototype representations of smaller groups. Mullen and Johnson and Mullen, Rozell, and Johnson (2001) showed that ethnophaulisms for larger ethnic groups in the United States tend to be spread across several different types. For example, for Italians (a fairly large group) Americans have no terms that refer to physical traits, but several terms that refer to food ("grape stomper") as well as to cultural differences ("dago," "wop"). For other groups (such as Turks), there are relatively few terms, and those few come from a restricted domain ("Arab," "Abdul"). In any event, ethnophaulisms for the larger groups are not only more numerous but span more types and therefore reflect more complex representations.

The worst effect of such labels is that because of their emotional power, they reduce people so described to only their category membership. The very term "African American" seems to connote historical participation in at least two cultures and a complexity of cultural orientation that allows for individuation. On the other hand, "nigger" gives rise to no such connotations. Not only is the term extremely negative and offensive, but it is ordinarily used only when one means to convey a message that someone is nothing more than a particular kind of person. Such terms are the most succinct and, in some ways, most powerful means we have of communicating prejudice and hatred.

Language Styles

Although just looking at someone provides many cues for group membership and hence provides a basis for stereotyping, verbal cues generated in conversations may also form the basis of stereotypes. When we stop and think about it, our speech provides a good many cues that help others categorize us. At the most basic level, the language we speak—English, French, Mandarin, Swahili—often tells others about our country of origin, and in multilingual cultures may say something about our preferences for a national or ethnic identity. In most countries there are pronounced regional variations in speech, and these may be associated with inferences about socioeconomic status. In addition to regional accents, there may be accents associated with particular ethnic groups or socioeconomic variations. Even written language may provide cues for education, socioeconomic status, and national identity.

Regional and Ethnic Accents

There is a long tradition of studying regional and ethnic accents as the basis for stereotyping, and a number of national, ethnic, and regional accents affect all manner of inferences (Anisfeld, Bogo, & Lambert, 1962; Bond, 1985; Cheyne, 1970; Foon, 1986; Lambert, Hodgson, Gardner, & Fillenbaum, 1960; Nesdale & Rooney, 1996; Sachdev & Wright, 1996). Of particular concern in the current American context, research on speech styles associated with race show that whereas "substandard" English is negatively evaluated by whites when used by both blacks and whites, blacks speaking "standard" English are evaluated especially positively (Jussim, Coleman, & Lerch, 1987; Jussim, Fleming, Coleman, & Kohberger, 1996; Larimer, Beatty, & Broadus, 1988). Generally, this research can be summarized by saying that whites have positive stereotypes of people who speak as they do—a clear case of ingroup bias. Furthermore, speech accommodation theory (Giles, Mulac, Bradac, & Johnson, 1987) predicts that we all like people who try to accommodate their speech style to ours[6]; however, there is also evidence of negative stereotypes for those who are overaccommodative and who appear to be patronizing (e.g., Giles, Fox, & Smith, 1993; Giles & Williams, 1994).

There are, of course, distinct stereotypes associated with particular speech styles, but this reflects little more than the fact the idea that language styles are cues for membership in socioeconomic, educational, national, and ethnic categories that are themselves vehicles for stereotypes. On the other hand, there are hints from both the literature on racial accents and speech accommodation theory that people in the mainstream have especially positive stereotypes of those who make an effort to speak in what might be described as mainstream ways.[7]

Gender-Related Styles

Although the effects of language and accent are obvious, considerable attention has also been given to gender differences in speech. Do men and women talk differently? Obviously, at some level, the higher-pitched voices of women are cues for gender itself. At a more subtle level, Tannen (1990) and others have argued that women and men structure their ways of speaking differently. Lakoff (1975) in particular has argued that women speak differently from men in at least seven ways. First, women have a richer and more precise vocabulary for certain domains, such as colors. Second, women use particular adjectives, such as "sweet," "lovely," and "charming," more than men; such adjectives connate empathy rather than power. Third, women swear less and use weaker expletives. Fourth, women use more hedges (i.e., they begin more sentences with phrases such as "I believe" or "It seems to me that. . . . ") Fifth, women use the term "so" rather than very more than men as an intensifier—men say, "It was very warm," but women are more inclined to say, "It was so warm." Sixth, women use polite forms such as compound questions, as opposed to commands—"Would you mind waiting a minute?" instead of "Wait up." Seventh, women use tag questions as a part of statements—"That was a moving performance, wasn't it?"

The actual research literature shows mixed support for Lakoff's specific conjectures about how men and women actually talk (Ng & Bradac, 1993), but there is no doubt that there are general masculine and feminine styles (Haas, 1979). For example, people can identify with great accuracy whether anonymous authors of e-mail messages are male or female (Thomson & Murachver, 2001). To the extent that women use these more indirect and polite forms, this may reflect the fact that they are often placed in roles where they are expected to be polite (Rasmussen & Moely, 1986); in this case, speech style—like so many other gender-linked behaviors—may have more to say about roles than about sex differences.

The more central issue before us here, however, is how people are evaluated who speak in the alleged feminine versus masculine style. Generally, research does suggest that people (usually regardless of biological gender) who use the more indirect and feminine style are seen as less competent and domineering, but as warmer and more polite (Crosby & Nyquist, 1977; Newcombe & Arnkoff, 1979; Quina, Wingard, & Bates, 1987; Rasmussen & Moely, 1986; Wiley & Eskilson, 1985). Men who speak in the feminine style are seen as being more homosexual than those who use the traditional masculine style (Rasmussen & Moely, 1986). So speaking style, like other behaviors we associate with gender, affects the gender-related stereotypes we apply to others.

OCCUPATIONS AND SOCIOECONOMIC STATUS

Job Stereotypes

Perhaps the epitome of the inoffensive stereotype is one based on an occupation. Though lawyers may be upset by the stereotype that they are immoral and greedy ambulance chasers, and doctors by the idea that they are more interested in their stock portfolios than their patients, for the most part occupational stereotypes seem to excite relatively few people; my guess would be that most of us assume that most occupational stereotypes have at least a kernel of truth. Surely most of them do.

Occupational Stereotypes Have a Kernel of Truth

One reason for this is that people in different occupations must have differing patterns of abilities and motives. One would not expect computer scientists to have the same intellectual strengths and weaknesses as literary critics, and one can only hope that divorce attorneys and nursery school teachers have different values and approaches to their work. There is no mystery about this. In fact, people in various occupations often do have personalities that resemble the occupational stereotypes (McLean & Kalin, 1994), and people select their occupations partially on the basis of largely accurate stereotypes of the kinds of persons who occupy them (Holland, 1985). To be sure, occupational choices are not always based on well-considered plans, and individuals do not always end up in the jobs they most want or are best suited for.

Occupational Stereotypes Exist

Several studies demonstrate that stereotypes of people in different jobs do exist (e.g., Levy, Kaler, & Schall, 1988; McLean & Kalin, 1994; Triandis, 1959; Westbrook & Molla, 1976), and that particular constellations of traits are deemed more suitable for some jobs than for others (Arkkelin & O'Connor, 1992; Jackson, Peacock, & Smith, 1980). In this regard, we may need reminding that although certain jobs do require certain skills, there are also strong cultural expectations about jobs as well. For example, Japanese and American students describe a good manager quite differently (Powell & Kido, 1994). Presumably a manager or secretary in a Japanese firm requires different abilities and behavioral patterns than in the United States—or so we have been led to believe.

Interactions of Gender and Occupation

In recent years, interest has shifted from documenting stereotypes of people in occupations to discussions of how gender interacts with occupation. Are some jobs perceived to be "for women" and others "for men"?

Some Occupations Are Gender-Stereotyped

Clearly, people do see some jobs as masculine and others as feminine (Beggs & Doolittle, 1993; Cejka & Eagly, 1999; Gatton, DuBois, & Faley, 1999; Glick, 1991). Males and females also differ in the kinds of jobs they like, with males having a relative preference for jobs involving things and females for those dealing more with people (Lippa, 1998; Lupaschuk & Yewchuk, 1998). Although there is a certain amount of informal evidence that parents and teachers selectively push young people toward gender-congruent jobs, respondents to a recent national poll (Gallup, 1998b) were asked what careers they would recommend for young people; with the exception of military careers and nursing, the lists were remarkably similar for boys and girls.

Causes of Gender Stereotyping of Occupations

EMPIRICAL OBSERVATION

The stereotype that jobs (like many other roles) are sex-typed might, of course, have resulted from empirical observation; it doesn't take an observational genius to note that more doctors are male than female and more nurses are female than male, for example. People are actually quite accurate in judging the sex ratios of jobs (Cejka & Eagly, 1999; McCauley & Thangavelu, 1991). To the extent inaccuracies occur, people tend to underestimate the extent to which jobs are dominated by one sex or the other—in other words, to see them as less sex-typed than they are (McCauley & Thangavelu, 1991). Even children as young as 2½ years of age hold stereotypes about the gender-linked nature of jobs (Blaske, 1984; Cann & Garnett, 1984; Cann & Haight, 1983; Franken, 1983) and prefer jobs that are traditionally appropriate for their gender (Nemerowicz, 1979; Trice & Rush, 1995). Although children may have some rudimentary knowledge about the traits of men and women and their suitability for various jobs, it seems far more likely that children simply create occupational stereotypes based on what they see. As one might expect, children's (Reid, 1995) and adults' (Sastre, Fouquereau, Igier, Salvatore, & Mullet, 2000) ratings of the femininity or masculinity of a job are highly correlated with the actual gender breakdown of people who hold that job.

SOME JOBS MAY SEEM TO REQUIRE GENDER-RELATED TRAITS

So one reason people assume that some jobs are male jobs is that, for whatever reason, males are actually more likely to occupy them. Another possibility is that people see jobs as masculine because they believe that the job calls for those traits typically possessed by males (Cejka & Eagly, 1999; Mellon, Crano, & Schmitt, 1982; Shinar, 1975). And, indeed, people do expect that males will be better at masculine jobs and females at the feminine ones (Croxton, Van Rensselaer, Dutton, & Ellis, 1989). If one believes, for example, that police officers should be strong and assertive, then it would make sense to assume that more males should hold this job than females, to the extent that one has traditional beliefs about the traits men and women possess.

However, as Yount (1986) and Eagly (1987) have suggested (see also Chapter 3), this argument may have the causality backwards. Jobs and roles may attract people of a particular personality type, but they may also mold personality. So if male jobs require more intelligence than female ones, and the female jobs require more nurturance, social and role pressure (rather than self-selection into jobs) may at least partially account for the differential personalities of people across jobs.

GENDER AND JOB STATUS

A striking feature of occupations is that those dominated by males usually have higher prestige than those that include a higher percentage of females. Is it an accident that doctors (masculine) are given higher status than nurses (feminine), or that bosses are more often male than their secretaries? Even within professions, specialties dominated by males usually have higher status. Within medicine, for instance, surgery (heavily male) is a higher-prestige specialty than pediatrics (more female); within psychology, neuropsychology (more heavily male) has historically had higher status than developmental and social psychology (both more heavily female). Research confirms that jobs considered masculine do have higher prestige than those considered feminine (Bose & Rossi, 1978; Jacobs & Powell, 1985), and that "masculine" jobs command better salaries as well (Glick, 1991). Glick, Wilk, and Perreault (1995) found that prestige and gender-relatedness were two independent ways that jobs differed. However, ratings of whether the job required masculine traits loaded on both the gender and prestige dimensions, and most of the highest-prestige jobs were masculine.

Differential Attraction to Jobs. There could, of course be any number of reasons for this correlation. One among many possibilities is that historically females, because of home responsibilities, were more attracted to jobs that required less job devotion. Or perhaps men are more concerned with prestige when they pick careers. However, in the stereotyping context, a more interesting possibility is that jobs are devalued precisely because they are frequently held by women. If the latter were true, then whether a job is described as typically male or female might affect its status; alternatively, a female in a particular job might be devalued relative to a male in the same job, and this has been found (Jacobs & Powell, 1985; Kanekar, Kolsawalla, & Nazareth, 1989; Nilson, 1976). Not surprisingly, given evidence of greater role constriction for males than for females, the evaluation "hit" for males in inconsistent jobs may be greater than for females (Nilson, 1976).

Changes in Prestige and Gender Composition. Another approach to this issue is to study changes in occupation prestige as a function of gender composition. If a job has high prestige because (in part) it has a high percentage of males, then that prestige should be lowered with an influx of females. Touhey (1974b) showed that when subjects expected the percentage of females in a particular job to rise, they rated the prestige of the job lower than when they expected a maintenance of the status quo ratio. In a related study, Touhey (1974a) found that raising the ratio of males in traditional female occupations raised the prestige of the job. These findings have been widely cited (and decried), but there are many failures to replicate them (e.g., Hawkins & Pingree, 1978; Johnson, 1986; Shaffer, Gresham, Clary, & Thielman, 1986; Suchner, 1979), so perhaps it is best not to get our collective knickers in a twist.

Socioeconomic Status

Occupations are obviously not the same as socioeconomic status, but the prestige and financial rewards of work are among the main determinants of this status. Although Americans may (stereotypically) be less concerned with socioeconomic differences than people from many other countries, research by Coleman and Rainwater (1978) suggests that Americans do recognize and utilize seven distinct socioeconomic groupings (old rich, new rich, professional, middle Americans with comfortable finances, middle Americans just getting by, working poor, and nonworking/welfare).

There are distinct stereotypes of unemployed or working-class and middle- to upper-class people (Morris & Williamson, 1982). For example, people at all levels see upper-class persons as more intelligent and selfish. Middle-class people see themselves as more thrifty and less lazy than poor people, but these stereotypes are not as prevalent among poorer respondents (Jackman, 1994). In general, ratings of positive agentic qualities increase with income levels, and ratings of communal qualities decrease slightly (Johannesen-Schmidt & Eagly, 2002).

Most of the relevant data come from public opinion polls and deal with perceived causes of one's economic fortune. A fairly consistent result, both in the United States and in other Western countries, is that poverty is seen to result from internal or individualistic factors (motives, abilities, traits) rather than structural ones (discrimination, poor education, etc.). For example, in a relatively early study, Centers (1948) found that the most popular reasons for explaining poverty were poor management, laziness, lack of ambition, lack of ability, lack of thrift, and lack of opportunity. In a more recent study (Feagin, 1975), the most important reasons given were lack of thrift and proper money management (88% saying that these factors were very or somewhat important), lack of effort (88%), lack of ability (85%), sickness and physical disabilities (85%), loose morals and drunkenness (79%), low wages in some industries (77%), prejudice and discrimination (70%), failure of industry to provide enough jobs (63%), failure of society to provide good schools (61%), being taken advantage of by rich people (48%), and bad luck (35%). Similar results have been found in more recent surveys (Lopez, Gurin, & Nagda, 1998), and in other countries such as Australia (Campbell, Carr, & MacLachlan, 2001; Feather, 1974) and England (Furnham, 1982), although typically Americans emphasize individual reasons more than people in other countries do. Generally, there are weak tendencies for richer people to emphasize individualistic explanations more strongly, as do Protestants and older people (Morris & Williamson, 1982). Political conservatives find individualistic explanations more appealing (Furnham, 1982). Recall (see Chapter 11) that conservatives are also attached to individualistic explanations for the lower socioeconomic status of minority group members.

Such stereotypes probably do have a bare kernel of truth: Some people are poor precisely because they are lazy, have substance abuse problems, or lack abilities. However, most (but not all)[8] social scientists would argue that there are also important structural reasons for poverty. Some people are poor because they went to poor schools, had limited models of achievement as children, or have been actively discriminated against. More to the point, there are surely important interactions among various factors. The lad who finds himself doing poorly in school because of bad teaching, poor school facilities, or lack of parental encouragement may in time lose interest in school and give every appearance of being lazy. Teachers may then give him even less attention, resulting in further lack of interest; it would thus not be surprising that he would drop out of school before finishing or would not seek education beyond high school. If he then lacks important skills needed to make more money, he may become resentful and adopt further behaviors (e.g., surliness, substance abuse), which hurt his chances to advance or even hold a job. To be sure, he has made choices that have affected his present status, but those choices were also dictated to some extent by his environment.

The stereotypes we have about poor people (and rich people) have an impact on the social policies we support (see Chapter 9). Those of us who believe that rich people have arrived at their condition through hard work and ability are probably much less likely to support high income taxes for rich folks than those of us who believe that being rich is largely a matter of luck and connections. Similarly, the popularity of individualistic explanations for poverty have had tremendous impact on various social policies, such as welfare and support for helping homeless persons. This is one place where stereotypes probably do make a major difference.

NATIONAL GROUPS

Most people will admit to having one kind of stereotypes: those for national groups. Germans are efficient and authoritarian, the English are reserved, and Americans are friendly or perhaps a bit brash. And, not surprisingly, many studies (especially from the early days of stereotype research) confirm the existence of stereotypes of national groups by other groups.

The extensive literature often seems naive to modern eyes. We may note with mild amusement that 40 years ago students at Patna University in India saw American Negroes as backward, easily satisfied, and faithful (Sinha & Upadhyaya, 1960). How could these students have made any sort of informed statement about American Negroes in the late 1950s? However, when we step back from such data, we may see that one of the reasons why the study of national stereotypes is interesting is precisely that many of them exemplify the old and common assumption that stereotypes are inaccurate because they are based on little information. In our modern global information state, most people around the world who have access to televisions will at least see media portrayals (accurate or inaccurate) of people from various cultures, and such information will be incorporated into their stereotypes (Lambert & Klineberg, 1967). However, in the 1930s, 1940s, and 1950s, when many of these studies were done, most people knew precious little about people from other cultures at first hand. Even today most American college students are likely to have limited direct exposure to French, Algerian, and (East) Indian people. So research on national stereotypes is a sort of museum of the prototypic stereotypes that the early workers in this area featured.

Accuracy

This is not to say, however, that all national stereotypes are necessarily inaccurate. If different countries have somewhat different cultures, and cultures affect people, then it should not be surprising to discover that people from both the national ingroup and outgroups would have a rough handle on differences between countries. People from different countries often agree with one another on stereotypes of particular target countries, and stereotypes of one's own country generally agree with the stereotypes held by people from other countries (Bond, 1986; Hagendoorn & Linssen, 1994; Koomen & Bähler, 1996; Krueger, 1996b; Peabody, 1985; Prothro, 1954a, 1954b; Rath & Das, 1958; Vinacke, 1949).

Ingroup and Outgroup Effects

There is a second reason why the study of national stereotypes can be important. Most of us feel that we belong to a single national group and identify fairly strongly with our nationalities. This means that the study of national stereotypes is a natural laboratory for the study of ingroup and outgroup stereotypes. Not surprisingly (see Chapter 7), stereotypes of one's own national ingroup tend to be more positive than others' stereotypes for the group as an outgroup (e.g., Driedger & Clifton, 1984; Koomen & Bähler, 1996; McAndrew, 1990; Salazar & Marin, 1977).

National stereotypes also provide a nice test of a hypothesis derived from self-categorization theory—that stereotypes of one's own country should emphasize salient differences between that country and other countries as outgroups. So Americans emphasize their efficiency when comparing themselves with China, but are more likely to emphasize sense of humor when comparing themselves with Germans (Hopkins & Murdock, 1999; Hopkins, Regan, & Abell, 1997). Smaller countries probably have more difficulty establishing an identity, given the hegemony of most larger countries, and if identity concerns tend to create conditions for stereotypes, we might expect them to show greater differences in evaluations of ingroups and outgroups; they do (van Oudenhoven, Askevis-Leherpeux, Hannover, Jaarsma, & Dardenne, 2002).

A related reason for this interest has been that relationships between countries change, sometimes quite quickly. There are degrees of "outgroupness," and shifts in alliances among countries, threatened and actual wars, and the like may well change the stereotypes of outgroups despite little or no change in actual experiences. Not surprisingly, stereotypes of people from other countries are affected by wars, conflicts, and economic conditions (e.g., Conover, Mingst, & Sigelman, 1980; Diab, 1962; Dudycha, 1942; Meenes, 1943; Phalet & Poppe, 1997; Poppe, 2001). In cases of extreme conflict, people in two countries may view each other in the same way (e.g., aggressive, dictatorial, deluded, etc.); this is often called a "mirror image" (Bronfenbrenner, 1961). However, interesting asymmetries may appear. For example, in one study (Stephan et al., 1993), Russians and Americans generally agreed on the stereotypes of Americans but not on those of Russians. In addition, Americans had a more complex stereotype of Russians than of Americans, which belies the conventional wisdom (see Chapter 7) that stereotypes of ingroups are somewhat more complex than those of outgroups.

Perhaps the most extensive study of national stereotypes in recent years was conducted by Peabody (1985). He had people in several European countries rate Americans and people from other European countries. Generally, there was considerable agreement across national samples (including the country being judged) as to the characteristics possessed by people in each national group. Furthermore, with a few exceptions, the traits assigned to people from different countries agreed quite well with various earlier analyses of cultural and social scientists about national character. Although it is, of course, possible that people from different cultures are all subject to the same "brainwashing" from the media and other sources of false stereotypes, Peabody argues that such impressive agreement suggests that people really do differ in their modal traits. Table 13.3 gives some representative results.

Features Associated with National Stereotypes

Despite the rather extensive research literature documenting national stereotypes, there have been few attempts to determine why such stereotypes arise. Eagly and Kite (1987) have shown that stereotypes of countries differ along the two fundamental dimensions of how communal and agentic the traits are that characterize each country. It is not accidental that these are also categories of traits associated with females and males (see Chapter 11); it is also not accidental that the ratings of a country are generally more closely related to ratings of males than of females from that country, presumably because males are more salient exemplars.[9] The countries that most closely match the male stereotype are also seen to be less likely to promote gender equality, less democratic, and more militaristic, among other features.

TABLE 13.3. Traits Assigned to People from Different Countries

Traits	English	Germans	French	Italians	Russians	Americans
Thrifty–extravagant	0.9	1.1	−0.8	−0.8	1.2	−1.3
Stingy–generous	−0.4	−0.3	0.7	0.7	0	1.3
Self-controlled–impulsive	1.8	0.6	−1	−1.7	0.5	−0.3
Inhibited–spontaneous	−0.2	0	1.4	1.5	−0.2	1.4
Cautious–rash	1.4	0.9	−0.2	−0.6	1.3	−0.6
Timid–bold	0.4	1	0.6	0.5	0.7	1.2
Calm–agitated	1.6	0.4	−0.8	−1.6	0.7	−0.3
Inactive–active	0.8	1.4	1.3	1	1	1.6
Peaceful–aggressive	1.2	−0.6	−0.3	−0.6	−0.2	−0.3
Passive–forceful	0.6	1.6	0.5	0.2	1.1	1.3
Modest–conceited	−0.4	−0.9	−1.2	−0.8	0.4	−1.4
Unassured–confident	1.4	1.4	1.3	0.8	1	1.8
Cooperative–uncooperative	0.4	0.5	0.2	0.2	0.1	0.9
Conforming–independent	0.1	−0.1	0.7	−0.3	−0.9	0.8
Practical–impractical	1.2	1.3	0.2	−0.2	0.9	1.1
Opportunistic–idealistic	0.1	0.1	0.5	0.3	0.6	−0.2

Note. Positive numbers indicate that the countries are seen to possess the trait on the right, negative numbers that they possess the trait on the left. Data from Peabody (1985).

Poppe and Linssen (1999) argue that four features of nations help to determine their stereotypes. First, countries that are highly industrialized should be perceived as high on traits reflecting competence, and a study of perceptions by students in several European countries confirmed that. Second, they argue that perceived morality (considered broadly to encompass such traits as warmth and kindness) should be affected by relative size of the country. As expected, the European students rated smaller countries as higher in morality. Third, Poppe and Linssen argue that relationships among states should affect stereotypes; as expected, variables such as perceived nationalism and perceived conflicts lowered morality ratings of one country by students in another country.

Finally, geography is often important. Poppe and Linssen (1999) found that in Europe, countries in the west were generally perceived to be more competent than those in the east (mostly former Communist bloc countries), although geographical status was also highly correlated with economic development. A common stereotype is that people who live further from the equator are more efficient and agentic, while those living nearer (in the Northern Hemisphere, those further south) are typically seen as more emotional and perhaps as more empathetic (Peabody, 1985).[10] For example, the data presented in Table 13.3 portray the French and Italians as more extravagant, impulsive, and agitated than the English, Russians, or Germans. Pennebaker, Rime, and Blankenship (1996) found that within a large sample of Northern Hemisphere countries southerners were seen as more emotional than northerners, but there was no difference for the Southern Hemisphere countries. This was further confirmed in a study of European stereotypes by Linssen and Hagendoorn (1994). These authors also showed that the stereotypes for efficiency were partially determined by perceptions of economic advancement. However, the stereotypes of emotionality for more southern countries are not based on objective differences between north and south. Of course, to the extent that regional stereotypes are based on some version of reality, this still leaves unexplained why regional differences occur.

MISCELLANEOUS BASES OF STEREOTYPES

As I have argued consistently throughout this book, almost any social category or feature, especially those assumed to be chosen, can serve as the basis of a stereotype. An important reminder is that there is no principled distinction between categories and features. We might have the stereotype that gay males are effeminate, but also that effeminate men are gay. Thus, although most of the research on stereotypes has used generally recognized social categories, there is no reason to restrict ourselves to that convention. Having now broadened the relevant bases of stereotypes beyond comprehension, I do not offer a lengthy summary of this additional research on stereotyping; to do so would take dozens of pages, and in many cases to little effect. It is nonetheless impressive to see the extensive kinds of features that have associated stereotypes. I'll present a sample.

Possessions and Acquisitions

One of the most important, but least examined, bases of our stereotypes is what we choose to buy and display. To be sure, we acquire some material possessions because we need them. People who live in rural areas, for example, may prefer trucks to sports cars for good reasons, and we may eat some food because it tastes better to culturally conditioned palates. In such cases, possessions convey little information about people. However, sometimes possessions are bought and displayed to make a point. Obviously, some people drive expensive cars to make statements about who they are, and some urban residents drive trucks to proclaim their identification with rural values. Thus the things we buy and the possessions we choose to display are certainly meant in part to convey information about wealth, taste, and other proclivities, and they do so (Csikszentmihalyi & Rochberg-Halton, 1981; Dittmar, 1992, 1994). In some respects, one's home or room is the ultimate expression of choices, often designed to impress others. People do form distinct impressions of others on the basis of seeing their rooms, and often these impressions are quite accurate (Gosling, Ko, Mannarelli, & Morris, 2002).

I personally think that whether a person owns a gun tells me a lot about that person, and I could even be right; certainly the possession of handguns affects perceptions of people, especially females (Branscombe & Owen, 1991). The kinds of food that one buys (Orpen & Chase, 1976) and eats (Stein & Nemeroff, 1995) lead to assignment of stereotype traits. Think about it: Doesn't the person who eats steak every night seem different from the person who is a strict vegetarian? Although I know of no relevant research, surely we view people who buy trashy novels differently from those who buy mostly computer-oriented books, or people who have classical records differently from people who have mostly jazz or rock. The list of potential stereotypes based on possessions seems endless.

Location

Locations can also affect stereotypes. We have stereotypes of people who attend particular colleges (Fink & Cantril, 1937). Few would object to stereotypes that the average student at an Ivy League college is smarter than the random person encountered at a gym, or that the latter is more likely to have an attractive body. Most of us would expect to meet different kinds of people at a rodeo and a poetry reading, a university library and a biker bar, a wealthy suburb and a deteriorating inner-city neighborhood. Indeed, many people worry about being seen at the right places and with the right people—a sure sign that there are distinct stereotypes about such matters. Research does support the idea that physical surroundings do affect how people and the behavior within the situation are perceived (e.g., Cherulnik & Bayless, 1987; Leather & Lawrence, 1995; Sadalla, Vershure, & Burroughs, 1987; Vershure, Magel, & Sadalla, 1977). There is no mystery about how these stereotypes arise. People make choices about where to park their bodies, and these choices are often perfectly reasonable cues to personality.

Activities and Choice of Groups

Because we assume that deliberate choices are especially revealing about our traits and values, the activities that we choose are likely to give rise to stereotypes. For instance, adolescents have stereotypes of people who smoke, and those whose stereotypes are relatively close to their self-images are more likely to initiate smoking (Aloise-Young, Hennigan, & Graham, 1996). Research shows that people have stereotypes of those who use steroids and cocaine (Schwerin & Corcoran, 1996).

There are stereotypes of people who exercise (Martin, Sinden, & Fleming, 2000), of male and female college athletes (Die & Holt, 1989; McMartin & Klay, 1983; Sailes, 1993, 1998; Vickers, Lashuk, & Taerum, 1980), and of people who prefer different sports (Sadalla, Linder, & Jenkins, 1988). There are surely stereotypes on every college campus about people who live in different dorms[11] or sororities, who belong to different clubs, who have different academic majors. We have stereotypes about people who belong to different religions (Biela, McKeachie, Lin, & Lingoes, 1993). Even such trivial features as whether we are nocturnal in our lifestyle affect impressions (McCutcheon, 1998). I have stereotypes about people who jog, barbecue regularly, take their families to Disney World, like opera, or are fans of Elvis Presley—and the list goes on.

Are Such Stereotypes Important?

One might think that these types of stereotypes are parochial and trivial—mildly interesting, to be sure, but in the end socially inconsequential. Does anyone, even my wife, care what my stereotypes are of people who jog by my house at 6:00 A.M.? My stereotype of boat owners does little good or harm in the world, since I rarely encounter such people. And, frankly, I'm little concerned about impressions others may have of me when I don my Birkenstocks; I really do have more important concerns.

Surely most of this material can be safely ignored as basically irrelevant? Well, let's not be hasty here. For starters, let's consider that I tend to avoid people I know who are fans of Elvis; I seek out fellow opera fans instead. I generally don't encounter boat owners, but when I'm with my boat-owning brother-in-law, I'm ever vigilant for suggestions that involve water skis, my excuses at the ready. A good deal of my behavior (and yours) is dictated or at least channeled by what amount to stereotypes based on various behaviors, activities, and possessions of others.

There is one group of people who specialize in making hay from such stereotypes–advertisers. Would you advertise the same products in *Opera News* as in *Seventeen* or *People*? You wouldn't be in the advertising business for long if you did. Advertisers target audiences based on all sorts of demographic and other variables in television advertising. Many restaurants try to create images that appeal to a particular clientele, and cars of approximately equal cost and performance are marketed to different types of people. Perhaps we ought not to dismiss the importance of such seemingly mundane stereotypes quite so readily. This is real bottom-line stuff.

Stereotypes based on possessions and activities tend to be perceived as accurate, are noncontroversial, and typically don't result in much discrimination. And because we have not built elaborate models of stereotypes for these categories, they may seem less theoretically interesting. But they may be more important in our everyday lives than those stereotypes we seem to care most about. It is an interesting and open question whether we think we learn more about people by knowing what magazines they read or cars they own than their occupation or even race or gender.

Notes

1. I confess that when I pass a car with a particularly unappealing bumper sticker, I am always satisfied when the driver appears to have a fierce demeanor and the slack jaw I associate with gross stupidity. My world would be far more satisfactory if the people I consider political idiots could be readily identified through physical appearance. We need more research on reverse stereotyping in this area–how traits and behaviors affect our expectations for appearance (Hassin & Trope, 2000).
2. On the other hand, Ryckman, Dill, Dyer, Sanborn, and Gold (1992) found that both male and female body builders (extreme mesomorphs) were seen as having less desirable traits than people who were not body builders, perhaps because they were seen as being too involved with their bodies. However, males who are body builders are seen as more masculine and less likely to be homosexual than those who are not (Freeman, 1988).
3. It may or may not be relevant to note that ideals in feminine beauty in the United States became more Rubenesque as we moved from the affluent 1920s into the economically depressed 1930s (Fallon, 1990).
4. Indeed, my own stereotype, based on extremely casual observation, is that long hair is now more likely to be found on macho types. In considering cultural changes, I am reminded of a personal incident. In 1971 my family and I were traveling across the country, and we stopped for breakfast early one morning in a cafe in a small town in Utah. At the time I had shoulder-length hair, and as we sat having our breakfast, my wife and I became aware that the men sitting at the counter 20 or so feet away were nudging one another, pointing in our direction, and laughing. After checking for all the obvious possibilities of semidress, we concluded that my hair was the object of their (by this time, not remotely concealed) amusement. My sense is that this is the very type of men who would now be wearing long hair in ponytails and sporting mustaches and beards, whereas my own hair has become shorter (as well as thinner and greyer) during the same period.
5. However, in some cases they may be incorporated in ironical ways by the group itself– "nigger" used by African Americans is one example (Kennedy, 2002).
6. There is a large research literature on the tendencies of people to speak differently to different classes of people. For example, people often speak in condescending ways to mentally and physically disabled individuals (Fox & Giles, 1996) and to elderly persons (Caporael, 1981; Giles, Fox, & Smith, 1993; Ryan, Hummert, & Boich, 1995). We often accommodate our speech patterns to those of our conversational partners (Giles et al., 1987;

Willemyns, Gallois, Callan, & Pittman, 1997), although sometimes we exaggerate our cultural patterns as a way of reaffirming our cultural identities (Giles & Johnson, 1987).

7. As I have suggested from time to time, it is often useful to look at impression management strategies when we are trying to get a handle on stereotypes, because people presumably present themselves in ways they think will feed the positive stereotypes of others. I lived for nearly 15 years in San Antonio, a city with a majority Hispanic population. As might be expected, there were a number of Hispanic anchors and reporters on the local TV stations. What was amazing was that not one of them spoke with any identifiable Spanish accent. And in Houston (where I now live), if I close my eyes I cannot tell the black, white, Hispanic, and Asian reporters and anchors apart by voice alone.

8. Most conservative social scientists would disagree, and indeed a relative preference for individual versus structural explanations for social problems is a main difference between conservatives and liberals generally.

9. One exception may be the United States (Kosmitzki, Cheng, & Chik, 1994).

10. This also works within countries. Peabody (1985) found that northern Europeans (and within Italy, northern Italians) were seen as more controlled than their southern counterparts. Although I know of no relevant data, surely stereotypes of Americans who live in the South are more "laid back" than those who live in the North.

11. Rice University has a system of residential colleges where students live and eat during their undergraduate years. Despite the fact that assignment to the colleges is random, many of them have distinct personalities, and there are well-established and consensually accepted stereotypes of many of them.

CHAPTER 14

Stereotype Content and Features

A DIALOGUE ABOUT LAZINESS

Let's imagine a conversation between the Obnoxious Psychologist (OP) and a man named John, who is a supervisor in a small manufacturing plant. John has just decided to fire one of his employees, Claire, because of a poor work record that he attributes to laziness. OP has just asked John why he thinks Claire is lazy.

JOHN: Well, she just is. It's not hard to see.

OP: Oh, I don't doubt what you say. I'm just trying to be a psychologist here. Your assessment just seems like a vague generalization to me. Do you mean to say that Claire is always lazy?

JOHN: No, of course not. Sometimes she works hard just like my other employees.

OP: Would you say that more than half her behaviors are lazy?

JOHN: (*Thinks for a moment*) No, I guess not. Probably less than half.

OP: A lot less?

JOHN: I guess so. But I really don't want to be pinned down here. It's not like she's lazy all the time, you know. She has her good days and her bad days. But she certainly doesn't perform up to standards like the other people do.

OP: So when you say she is lazy, you are really comparing her to other people. You seem to be saying that she is more lazy than other workers.

JOHN: That's exactly what I'm saying.

OP: Could you give me some examples of how Claire is lazier than most?

JOHN: Sure. It's not hard. We have to document that sort of thing these days, you know. Well, for starters, she simply doesn't produce as much as most of the other workers. I admit that there are a couple who produce even less than she does, but one has only been working for a couple of weeks, and the other is somewhat retarded. We took him on as a kind of experiment, and it's still too early to tell how it will work out. But he works hard. Anyway, it's not hard to figure out why Claire has problems. She frequently shows up for work late, sometimes an hour or more, and she almost always is at least 10 minutes late. Look, I'm not oriented toward the time clock, and I'm always willing to cut my people some slack when they're a few minutes late on occasion. We all have emergencies at home, and many of my workers have special problems because they're single mothers. Hell, sometimes I'm a few minutes late. But I do expect them to make up the time at the end of the day, or some other time. And most of them appreciate my attitude and are happy to cooperate. But Claire acts like it isn't even a problem. I've talked to her about it a lot, and she never has any real reason for being late. She'll say stuff like she forgot to set her alarm, or she wasn't feeling good, or she had to stop at the store on the way. And she never volunteers to make up the time, so we have to dock her pay, and that really makes her mad.

OP: So you seem to be saying that she has a bad attitude—she's lazy because her attitude is poor?

JOHN: Well, that's certainly part of it. But there's more. Even when Claire works a full day, she is often the first to leave for lunch and the last to come back. We give our people 45 minutes, and I tend to look the other way if they take an hour, but Claire often leaves at 11:45 and doesn't show up again until after 1. I think she runs errands during lunch. She also goes to the bathroom a lot, and she tends to be gone a long time when she goes. And when she's at her bench, she tends to daydream a lot.

OP: How do you know she's daydreaming?

JOHN: I guess I really don't. But she sorta stares off into space and neglects her work. She also tries to talk to the other employees, and while that's allowed, it does tend to disrupt work. Some of the other people resent her because they think she interferes with their ability to get their work done. I'd have to say, though, that when she applies herself, she does good work. She's sometimes careless, but her product control statistics aren't bad. I actually think she could be one of our best workers if she'd apply herself.

OP: Have you talked to her about this?

JOHN: Until I'm blue in the face. I even offered to put her on an incentive plan where her pay would be based partially on product control and output, but she just laughed.

OP: So you're saying that Claire is lazy because she just doesn't put in as much time as others do.

JOHN: That's exactly what I'm saying. You don't have to be a rocket scientist to make these judgments.

OP: But you also seem to be saying that part of her laziness is related to her attitude.

JOHN: She certainly does have a bad attitude. Just talk to her, and you'll see. She seems to hate the work and hate me. I could live with that if she got the work done, but she just doesn't seem to care.

OP: If she did the same sorts of things—showing up late, daydreaming, and so forth—and didn't have the attitude problem, would you still call her lazy?

JOHN: (*After a moment*) It's hard to say, actually. If I thought she wanted to do better, and something was stopping her, I might feel different.

OP: Suppose she had a drug or drinking problem? Have you thought about that?

JOHN: We don't do drug testing here, and I hope we never do. We have had some problems in the past, and I think I recognize the symptoms. Claire has never shown up drunk as far as I can tell, and she doesn't act like she has a hangover or anything.

OP: But suppose Claire has a drug problem that affects her work. Would you still call her lazy?

JOHN: That's a tough one. But if I'm honest, I suppose I wouldn't. We'd still fire her, of course, because of her work record, but I guess I wouldn't call her lazy.

OP: In that case, would you say she is lazy because she has a drug problem?

JOHN: I suppose you could, but that's really not the way I think about laziness.

OP: Well, how do you explain laziness? Let's start with Claire.

JOHN: Glad you asked. I've thought a lot about her, actually. You see, Claire comes from the kind of background where hard work isn't valued. Her parents aren't exactly cherished citizens of the community. Her problem is that no one ever taught her how to get ahead, and at the rate she's going, she's never going to amount to anything. I'm going to fire her, and I feel badly about it. It isn't entirely her fault that she is so lazy, but I have a business to run.

OP: So you don't think that Claire is motivated to be lazy or wants to be?

JOHN: Who knows? It's hard to say. I don't think people want to be lazy—they just don't know any better. They don't want to work, but they don't want to be lazy, if you can connect with that distinction.

OP: I think I can. Rather interesting, actually. So some traits such as being lazy are really the absence of something, whereas other traits such as being conscientious are used to describe things people want to do.

JOHN: If you say so. You're the psychologist.

OP: One would hope that counts for something, but let's move on. Do you think Claire can change?

JOHN: I doubt it. But she's smart enough, and maybe she could.

OP: Let's try a little thought experiment here. I want you to imagine that Claire suddenly gets the religion of capitalism. She wants to turn her life around. She asks you to give her another chance, and she vows to mend her ways.

JOHN: (*Smiling*) It ain't gonna happen. Trust me.

OP: Thought experiment. Okay? I just want you to imagine that happening. Now my question to you is this: What would Claire have to do to convince you that she was no longer lazy?

JOHN: Well, she'd have to start showing up on time and working a full day, for starters.

OP: Fair enough. About how many days would she have to show up on time before you started to change you mind? A couple? A week? A month?

JOHN: At least a month. Maybe longer. I just wouldn't trust her over the short haul. It's too easy to fake.

OP: So you imagine that Claire might be more interested in trying to convince you that she's not lazy than in actually changing her basic attitudes?

JOHN: Those kinds of basic attitudes are hard to change. She's had 20 or so years of living with that family of hers. I just don't think she could turn it around that quickly.

OP: So you're saying that once a person is lazy, she's always lazy?

JOHN: That sounds a little harsh. I guess I wouldn't go that far. But I know that she could change her behaviors in the short run, but I'd have to see a lot of change over a long period of time before I'd believe that she wasn't lazy any more.

THE FEATURES OF STEREOTYPES

I have used laziness as an example trait, in part because this trait appears often in lists of stereotypes, and in part because it clearly illustrates some of the problems we might have in assigning traits to others. There are four points worth emphasizing. First, for John (and I suspect for the rest of us), traits such as being lazy are not merely summaries of behavior. John assumes that underlying Claire's lazy behavior is a set of motives and attitudes that dictates her behavior. Second, while John seems to think that Claire's laziness is obvious, he still has inferred this trait from her behavior. Third, we note that John has a theory of sorts, correct or incorrect, about why Claire is lazy. We think we know why people have the traits they have. Fourth, John more or less confesses that he thinks Claire's laziness is a far from superficial part of her personality. It seems to be a central part of her personality, and he thinks she cannot change her lazy disposition quickly or easily.

As we will see, other traits vary on these and other dimensions. And just to make matters more complex, we may need to remind ourselves that stereotypes include many features besides traits. Stereotypes are beliefs that we have about the characteristics of other people. As such, the content of stereotypes can include information about appearance, likely or unlikely behaviors, medical and psychological conditions, mannerisms, goals, motivations, desires, assigned roles, and nearly everything else of psychological interest.

Furthermore, as we have seen in Chapter 5, people readily infer traits from physical descriptions and indications of status, as well as the reverse (Deaux & Lewis, 1984; Freeman, 1987; Jackson & Cash, 1985). If I tell you that a woman is sexually promiscuous, you are likely to infer various other traits about her, as well as her appearance, age, occupation, and how she spends her Sunday mornings. Conversely, women who dress provocatively or who work in certain occupations (say, as waitresses in a topless bar) are likely to be seen as sexually available. I might easily assume that a guy who wears an open silk shirt and lots of neck chains probably has fairly sexist attitudes and is more likely to be a cellular phone salesman than a professor. I also imagine that such men are more likely to prefer going to bars than to symphonies on Saturday night. And speaking of the symphony, my stereotype of symphony subscribers includes information about other musical tastes, relative wealth, level of education, favorite restaurants, and so on. However, let us now turn to traits—a topic about which we have abundant information.

TRAITS

The Status of Traits

We might ask a number of questions about traits. As the chapter moves forward, we will wonder about how traits are inferred, as well as the many ways traits differ and what this means for stereotyping. Initially, however, we need to pose a series of questions about the status of traits: How important are they in our representations of others, and how easily can we infer them?

How Important Are Traits?

ARE TRAITS USED IN DESCRIPTIONS OF OTHERS?

It is not altogether obvious that traits should be the coin of the realm in social cognition. After all, we do not observe traits directly, although of course we may acquire trait information through reading and conversations with others. And given that we seem to have virtually unlimited memory capacity for recalling specific behaviors that others have performed, there seems to be no special cognitive imperative for engaging in the risky enterprise of summarizing behavioral information in terms of traits. However, research consistently shows that mainstream Americans do employ a fair amount of trait language in free descriptions (Fiske & Cox, 1979; Hampson, 1983; Park, 1986). Not all cultures are as fixated on dispositional description. Generalized dispositions seem to be less prominent in collectivist cultures, such as the Japanese (Cousins, 1989), (East) Indian (Miller, 1984), Chinese (Morris, Menon, & Ames, 2001), and Mexican American (Trafimow & Finlay, 2001) cultures. Furthermore, traits are inferred spontaneously (see below for further discussion) by white non-Hispanic Americans but not by Mexican Americans (Zárate, Uleman, & Voils, 2001). Finally, even in mainstream Western cultures there are individual differences; those who hold the view that traits are fairly stable and permanent (see below) tend to use trait terms more (Levy, Stroessner, & Dweck, 1998).

CONDITIONS THAT FAVOR USE OF TRAITS

Because we can use traits or not as circumstances dictate, a more fruitful question might be what conditions favor the use of a trait language. We are more inclined to use traits when we need to predict (Berscheid, Graziano, Monson, & Dermer, 1976; Newman, 1996) and explain (Budesheim & Bonnelle, 1998) the behavior of others, or when we are explicitly trying to form an impression (Bassili & Smith, 1986). Since traits are summary statements, and often we want to be fairly succinct in our conversations with others, communication often facilitates the use of more abstract categories (Fiedler, Semin, & Bolten, 1989). Traits conceal complexities, but they're easy to use, and they get us where we need to get cognitively and socially.

However, Mimi Rodin has suggested that traits do not in fact convey as much information as we might suppose. Rodin (1972) showed that trait descriptors were not as helpful as behavioral descriptions in identifying people, and in another study (Rodin, 1975), subjects were not very accurate in picking which behaviors went with particular traits. Mischel, Jeffrey, and Patterson (1974) also showed that in making behavioral predictions, subjects preferred information about behavior in a similar situation to trait information, but preferred trait information to behavior in a dissimilar situation.

TRAITS ARE REPRESENTED IN MEMORY

It is clear that people store both behavioral and trait information about others (Klein & Loftus, 1990; Petzold & Edeler, 1995; Wyer & Lambert, 1994; Wyer & Srull, 1989), although the exact relationships between their representations are hard to determine. When people are asked to form an impression based on behaviors, memory recall tends to cluster around traits (Hamilton, Katz, & Leier, 1980); such clustering is usually taken as evidence for the existence of a more abstract representation (in this case, traits). Other research (e.g., Gordon & Wyer, 1987; Wyer & Gordon, 1982) also suggests that behavioral information is encoded in terms of traits when people have a goal to form an impression, and that these inferred traits can serve as cues in recall of behavior. In research to be reviewed later, Uleman, Newman, and Moskowitz (1996) have shown that traits are sometimes inferred spontaneously and without conscious effort from behaviors, again suggesting that traits have some pride of place in memory representations.

Klein and Loftus (1993) summarize a program of research that further supports trait representations, at least for the self. In one set of experiments (Klein, Loftus, & Burton, 1989), subjects made various kinds of judgments about the self. Sometimes they judged whether a trait described them (I call this the "trait condition"), and sometimes they were asked to remember an incident in which they displayed the trait (the "behavior condition"). The times needed to make these judgments were recorded. The trait judgments were made more rapidly than the behavioral judgments, and once subjects had made one of these judgments it was made more rapidly a second time. For instance, once subjects judged whether they were timid, this judgment was substantially facilitated subsequently. The interesting comparisons occurred when the behavioral task preceded the trait task or vice versa. If making a trait judgment involves first gaining access to relevant behavioral episodes, a trait judgment should have facilitated making a later behavioral judgment, because a subject had already implicitly made a behavioral judgment before. However, the results provided little evidence of such facilitation. Thus, according to the logic of the Klein–Loftus model, self-judgments are made directly without accessing behavioral information; traits must be accessed directly.

However, when people make judgments about another person (say, Mother), prior trait judgments do facilitate subsequent behavioral judgments (Klein, Loftus, Trafton, & Fuhrman, 1992). By the logic of this paradigm, then, in making judgments about Mother, a person does use previous behavior to calculate traits "on the fly." Subsequent analyses suggest that the relevant difference between these two domains (self and Mother) is amount of experience. When people make trait judgments that are well practiced, they seem to gain direct access to trait information. However, for less familiar domains, they may access behavioral information to make trait judgments. Additional research by Hampson (1983) suggests that traits are more often used in descriptions of well-known others, and that trait judgments for such people are made especially rapidly. It is also interesting to note that people use more inconsistent traits (suggesting a more complex representation) for themselves and those they know well than for those they know less well (Hampson, 1997; Sande, Goethals, & Radloff, 1988).

Traits Must Be Inferred

One advantage that most nontrait features have over traits is that they are readily observable and easily measured. Women who dress provocatively either do or do not have more active sex lives than those who dress demurely, but we could determine which. People at symphony concerts either do or do not make more money than those who prefer country and Western music (these days symphony subscription staffs have access to this kind of information), and we can easily make a reasonably accurate judgment about what percentage of them are dressed in particular ways at a given symphony concert.

Traits, on the other hand, must be inferred. Whereas some traits are merely summaries of behavior and hence fairly objective, most imply internal features such as motives, attitudes, values, and beliefs, which cannot be directly observed. To be sure, most traits can, in principle, be measured by personality tests, but there always remains the nagging question of how real these constructs are. That does not mean that we need to fold up our tents when it comes to thinking about traits. But it does mean that we have to recognize that inferential processes are likely to be far more important in studying how we arrive at trait judgments than about most other features. It seems ludicrous to ask how we determine whether someone stays at home or works in an office, is a lawyer or a doctor, is rich or poor. That is not to suggest that judgments about whether people have such features enter our minds mysteriously and capriciously. There are cues we use to determine all of these things, and we recognize that there may be marginal cases: Is someone who makes $500,000 a year really rich or merely comfortable? Is a movie star really handsome? But for the most part, there are no great mysteries involved in how these decisions are made once the relevant information becomes available.

Traits are quite different. Two people can see the same target person behave and argue about whether the target is kind or not, lazy or hard-working. A person who shows up for work late because of an alcohol problem might not be seen as lazy, and a salesperson who behaves nicely to others is not necessarily kind. Moreover, one person might interpret a given bit of behavior as aggressive or hostile, whereas another is more inclined to call it assertive or self-protective. These debates are not, for the most part, about how much of a behavior a target person needs to exhibit to possess the relevant trait (as would be the case with features such as obesity and promiscuity). Rather, they are disagreements about what the target intended and what his or her general proclivities are.

Two Ways We Know Traits

SECONDHAND KNOWLEDGE

Basically, we ascribe traits to others in two ways. First, we may simply learn about a person's traits through secondhand information. Someone tells us that Joan is a happy, or kind, or insincere person. The circumstances under which we readily accept these secondhand reports are not well documented. I suspect that much of the time, we simply accept them for what they are—observations of unknown validity.

INFERRING TRAITS FROM BEHAVIORS

Second, we may infer traits from observations of behavior. The study of how we infer traits from behaviors has largely been the province of attribution theorists such as Fritz Heider (1958), who have tended to argue that dispositions (including traits) help us both understand past behavior and predict the future. The thrust of this kind of argument is that traits must be fairly available cognitive constructs and hence are probably inferred fairly effortlessly. Certainly traits are readily and accurately inferred on the basis of tiny amounts of behavioral information (Ambady, Bernieri, & Richeson, 2000). Also, people tend to infer traits from behavior more readily than behavior from traits (Maass, Colombo, Colombo, & Sherman, 2001), and still other data suggest that trait inferences are sometimes quite spontaneous.

Spontaneous Trait Attributions

James Uleman and his colleagues (see Uleman, Newman, & Moskowitz, 1996, for a summary) have shown that trait inferences are fairly spontaneous if not fully automatic. The Uleman paradigm makes use of a standard memory principle called "encoding specificity"; according to this principle, information that is present when material is encoded into memory will serve as a good retrieval cue for later recall of the material.

In research using the Uleman cued-recall paradigm (Winter & Uleman, 1984; Winter, Uleman, & Cunniff, 1985), subjects read sentences that are known to imply certain traits. For example, a subject might read, "The plumber slips an extra $50 into his wife's purse," which implies the trait "generous." According to the logic of encoding specificity if subjects spontaneously inferred that the plumber is generous when they read this sentence, then "generous" would be a good cue for recalling information in the sentence. In fact, when subjects were asked to recall the sentences, giving them the trait cue was better than no cue at all and even superior to providing a semantic cue (e.g., "pipes"). Moreover, subjects reported that they were unaware of having inferred the traits when they read the behavioral sentences.

Are Trait Inferences Automatic?

Although it initially appeared that such trait inferences are automatic, it is now clear that they are not fully so (Uleman, Newman, & Moskowitz, 1996). As I have suggested many times (see Chapter 4), there are many aspects to automaticity of cognitive processes, and they are not always unified. In the research just described, there was clear evidence that subjects performed such inferences without conscious guidance or intention. They reported that they were unaware of forming trait inferences, and there is no evidence that they usually did. On the other hand, such spontaneous inferences do require at least some attention to the meaning of the stimuli, because when subjects read the behavioral sentences searching for particular letters, the effect did not occur (Uleman & Moskowitz, 1994). Furthermore, although spontaneous trait inferences do appear under a wide variety of encoding conditions and goals, such goals do affect the strength of the phenomenon. For example, trait-cued recall is better under impression set than rote memory (Bassili & Smith, 1986; Uleman & Moskowitz, 1994). Also, since such inferences are reduced under conditions of heavy cognitive load, spontaneous trait inferences seem to require some cognitive capacity (Uleman, Newman, & Winter, 1992). More relevant to the concerns of this chapter, spontaneous trait attributions are stronger for stereotype-consistent behaviors than for stereotype-inconsistent behaviors (Wigboldus, Dijksterhuis, & Knippenberg, 2003).

A Problem with Interpretation of Results

There are several potential problems with interpretation of this research (D'Agostino & Beegle, 1996). One important criticism is that traits may be effective cues not because they are directly linked to the actor or the behavior, but because they facilitate more effective searches for information, which in turn acts as a cue (Wyer & Srull, 1989). The subjects who read that the plumber gave his wife $50 may not have spontaneously inferred that he is generous (Uleman's interpretation); rather, when given "generous" as a retrieval cue, they may have thought about generous behaviors and then stumbled onto the act of giving money to the wife. However, other methodologies that are not subject to this criticism produce equivalent results (Bassili & Smith, 1986; Carlston & Skowronski, 1994; Carlston, Skowronski, & Sparks, 1995; Uleman, Hon, Roman, & Moskowitz, 1996; Whitney, Waring, & Zingmark, 1992). It is also unclear whether the traits that are presumably inferred are merely summary descriptions of the behavior or dispositions assigned to the actor, since conflicting results with different experimental paradigms have been reported (Brown & Bassili, 2002; Todorov & Uleman, 2002; Van Overwalle, Drenth, & Marsman, 1999).

Thin Slices of Behavior

There is another paradigm that bears on this question. For many years Robert Rosenthal and his students have explored the extent to which people can accurately infer traits from minimal amounts of information, often called "thin slices of behavior." This work has recently been summarized by Ambady and colleagues (2000). There are three essential lessons from this work. The first is that people are often remarkably accurate in inferring all manner of traits and other dispositions from rather small samples of behavior. For example, observers can do a good job of detecting teachers' biases with 10-second samples of behavior, and Ambady and Rosenthal (1993) found that ratings of teacher effectiveness based on 10-second slices correlated highly both with other measures of teaching effectiveness and with the amount students learned. People can judge with better than chance accuracy whether someone is homosexual from a 1-second sample of behavior (Ambady, Hallahan, & Conner, 1999).

Second, although people can be accurate with thin slices of behavior, they tend to be more accurate when traits are associated with highly observable behaviors. Third, it is far from clear how people make these sorts of judgments; however, they seem to be fairly automatic in the sense that their accuracy is invulnerable to effort and training, not readily available to consciousness, and not linked with other variables that are typically associated with more controlled processing (Ambady et al.,

2000). This research also suggests that judgments about people are made quickly, if perhaps not quite spontaneously.

The Attribution Paradigm

Despite the fact that traits seem to be central to the ways we think about people, there has been surprisingly little research devoted to the question of how we infer traits from behavior. Attribution research[1] has been dominated by the question of whether behavior is perceived to be controlled by generic psychological states such as motives and abilities, and even more generically by internal or external qualities, rather than by the more interesting question of how we infer specific dispositions. In the arena of stereotypes, the dominant but largely implicit assumption has been that the content of our stereotypes is provided by culture. If we assume that culture rather than experience provides the trait information in stereotypes, then there is no need to consider deeply the issue of how we turn behavioral information into trait ascriptions.

Internal Attributions and Traits

There is, of course, a voluminous literature on attributions (Hewstone, 1990a; Smith, 1994), but the bulk of this research deals with the broad issue of internal versus external causality. Heider (1958) argued that the causes of human behavior can generally be assigned either to personal dispositions, abilities, and motives, or to situational or external causes. Clearly, traits can be one kind of disposition. After all, when we say that a person is hostile, we are basically saying that the person is disposed to behave hostilely (at least under some circumstances).

Unfortunately, the internal–external distinction maps onto trait attributions clumsily at the conceptual level, and at the empirical level measures of internality and trait attribution often produce quite different results (Reeder & Fulks, 1980; Trafimow & Schneider, 1994). It's reasonable to suppose that a decision that a behavior is caused by some internal disposition is a necessary, albeit not sufficient, condition for a trait attribution. But, upon reflection, this cannot be generally true. As we have just seen, the behavior-to-trait link may be fairly automatic and require little time; it is implausible that this is mediated by a second decision about internality. More directly, an experiment by Smith and Miller (1983) strongly suggests the implausibility of the two-stage model. They asked subjects to read behavioral sentences and then asked them to make various judgments. A judgment about whether the person who performed the behavior had a particular trait was just as fast as a judgment about whether the person had intended the behavior. Since, according to the two-stage model, the trait judgment includes a judgment about internal causality, it is logically impossible for a trait judgment that requires two steps to be equal to one of the component steps (the intentionality judgment).

The Two Attribution Questions

Most of the trait ascriptions we make about others are presumably based on our own observations. We infer traits from observed behaviors and other cues. There are really two major questions we need to address. The first is which family of traits I use to summarize your behavior; let's call this the "horizontal" attribution issue. Is your behavior kind, warm, or merely polite?

The second question is how deeply I wish to go in interpreting behavior; let's call this the "vertical" question. I observe you sitting and behaving in a somewhat agitated way. Are you restless or anxious? It may make a difference. Restless people may be calm tomorrow, but anxiety tends to stick around for the long haul. Similarly, "diffident" is less dispositional than "shy" or "introverted," and "timid" seems to convey less about a person than "cowardly."

HORIZONTAL ATTRIBUTION

I observe Tom yelling at a salesclerk, but unfortunately that does not help me very much in deciding which of many dispositions I might pick to explain the behavior. Is Tom angry, hostile, aggressive, assertive, ill-tempered, thin-skinned, sexist, cruel? The decision that something about Tom caused his yelling fit doesn't help me very much in determining which of several dozen motives, goals, abilities, and traits might have caused the dirty deed.

Why This Is Important. Well, you say, it really doesn't make all that much difference. After all, aren't we splitting hairs just a little worrying about whether Tom is hostile, angry, aggressive, or assertive, since those terms mean much the same thing? You would be correct in the sense that it often doesn't make much difference, but then sometimes it does. Would Tom rather be thought of as assertive or hostile? Beyond matters of social desirability lie additional questions of meaning. Although it certainly is true that many of the same behaviors can be coded alternatively as assertive or hostile, others cannot. I can be hostile by refusing to be assertive, and many people manage to be assertive without a hint of raised blood pressure or feelings of anger.

This leads to a second reason. We generally have quite different behavioral expectations for a hostile and an assertive person. We might, for example, expect an assertive person to be better at getting a problem resolved and a hostile one to be better at making other people go away. We might expect that different situational cues produce hostile and assertive behaviors.

David Dunning and his colleagues have argued that we often shift the behavioral domain for traits, depending on whether we think we have the trait. Dunning and McElwee (1995) asked subjects who described themselves as dominant or nondominant to rate whether various behaviors exemplified dominance. Those who described themselves as dominant tended to see the more positive behaviors (e.g., displayed courage in an emergency, settled a dispute among group members) as better exemplars, whereas the nondominant subjects thought that negative behaviors (e.g., monopolized conversations, directed the conversation around to him- or herself) were more prototypic. Even the same trait can have different behavioral referents, depending on person and situation (see Chapter 4).

Identifying the Behavior. How do we determine whether someone is being hostile or assertive? One important factor is surely the behavior itself. Behaviors themselves carry a vast amount of information (Baron & Misovich, 1993), and hostile behavior may well be accompanied by voice tones, facial expressions, and redness of face that differentiate it from garden-variety assertiveness. Quite simply, assertive yelling just looks different from hostile yelling. Hard-working behavior isn't often confused with lazy behavior, and athletic behaviors speak for themselves.

Certain cultural understandings inform our interpretation of behaviors. In almost any culture, hitting another person hard in the face is not liable to be interpreted as loving behavior, no matter what the situational context (the claims of abusing husbands to the contrary). Similarly, caressing another is generally going to give rise to attributions about loving and caring rather than hostility, although one could imagine situations to the contrary (e.g., a caress as a signal for a planned murder). Second, as we have seen in prior discussions of priming (see Chapter 4; see also Wyer & Lambert, 1994), certain categories may be primed because of recent or frequent experience, or momentary goals.

Third, as Trope (1986) emphasizes, situational cues may affect interpretation of behavioral cues (as well as the reverse). An arm around the shoulder can be seen as sexual harassment in an office context, but as a form of sympathy at a funeral. A man who is yelling at a cowering child will have his behavior labeled differently than one who is yelling at a smirking adult. And so it goes.

Situational cues affect the availability of trait labels. One would not normally think of creativity as a label to describe the behavior of a worker on the assembly line, and one would not easily come up with laziness to describe the work of a chief executive officer (CEO) of a major cooperation. This is not to suggest that line workers can never be creative or CEOs lazy, but the situations in which we find such people do not encourage such labels. By the same token, "lazy" may be a term waiting to be applied in certain situations. We are used to the notion that our stereotypes of certain types of people may predispose us to seeing them as lazy, hard-working, or hostile, but stereotypes (of a sort) about situations may also lead to easy activation of particular trait and behavior labels. This may in turn indirectly affect how we label people, because certain sorts of people are typically found in certain sorts of situations.

Moreover, behaviors are affected by situations, and traits are more easily seen in some situations than in others (Kenrick, McCreath, Govern, King, & Bordin, 1990; Wright & Mischel, 1988). Suppose you wanted to see aggressive behavior. Would you not be more successful in your observations at a honky-tonk bar than in a university library on a Saturday evening? Wouldn't you see more extroverted behavior at a party than at a lecture?

Fourth, Trope (1986) notes that our previous knowledge of an actor may affect how we interpret the actor's behavior. In an office situation, a person known to be ambitious will have a compliment to the boss interpreted differently than a person who is thought to be kind and considerate will. Obviously, many of our everyday interactions occur with people we know relatively well, and in such cases our expectations play a major role in how we interpret behavior. But we may have expectations even for people we have never met if they belong to a recognized social category—stereotypes ride again. The black man who is trying to be assertive runs the risk of being seen as hostile by those who believe black males are hostile and angry (Chapter 4). Thus information about actors can also affect how their behavior is seen.

VERTICAL ATTRIBUTION

Although we often talk of traits as if they are a single kind of thing, in fact traits vary in a good many ways. One way is that they differ in how abstract or "interior" they seem to be. Newman and Uleman (1993) distinguish at least five different ways that trait terms are used, and these really refer to how abstract the trait is. The first is simply to describe behavior ("That was a hostile remark"). Second, traits can be used to describe a person at a particular time ("Tom was hostile today"). Third, we might want to refer to behavioral regularities we observe in a person without necessarily making any reference to causes ("Tom certainly does behave in a hostile way"). Fourth, we can use terms such as "hostile" to refer to regularities in Tom ("Tom certainly is hostile") without necessarily referring to reasons for Tom's behavior. Fifth, traits may be used to assign dispositional causes ("Tom behaves in a hostile way because he is truly a hostile person"). I discuss the nature of trait abstractness in a later section.

Moreover, some traits lend themselves to extensive regression in terms of deeper and deeper qualities. Tom yelled at the clerk because he is hostile, and he is hostile because he's insecure, and he's insecure because he has low self-esteem, and he has low self-esteem because of his father's overbearing behavior. Obviously, we do not usually engage in this sort of explanatory chain, but we can—and when we do, we affect the meanings and evaluations of behavior. Tom's hostility may mean something different when it is seen as due to insecurity rather than as a part of a macho personality or as a deliberate strategy for getting his way.

This sort of thing is likely to be especially important when we employ stereotype knowledge and theories. When people say that black men are hostile, they may be using a different kind of theory than when they say that lawyers are hostile. We have seen in Chapter 4 that behaviors may be interpreted differently in different stereotype contexts, and here we extend that model to dispositions themselves.

Attributing Traits

BEHAVIOR-TO-TRAIT LINKS

Getting from behaviors to traits is not always easy. In an influential paper, Trope (1986) noted that often the same trait terms can be used to describe behavior and the dispositional causes of that behavior. So a person can exhibit friendly behavior or be described as a friendly person; however, not all friendly behaviors stem from a friendly disposition. Car salespeople are usually friendly enough while on the job, but they may be actual curmudgeons once they leave the sales floor. Furthermore, most dispositions give rise to a wide range of behaviors that could also be "caused" by other traits. Criticizing another person could be a manifestation of hostility, but also of genuine concern and even love.

What then determines whether we move from a characterization of a behavior to an underlying disposition or trait? One possibility is that there are direct links to dispositions from some behaviors (Baron & Misovich, 1993). Just as some behaviors are easily labeled, many may also carry their own interpretations. When one watches, say, Michael Jordan or Sammy Sosa do his thing, there is no doubt that one is watching superior talent. Grace, agility, and efficiency of movement carry their own messages. Similarly, some aggressive behaviors appear to be so vicious that one does not need elaborate processing to know that the person exhibiting them has the corresponding disposition.

A more general answer to the question of how we negotiate the behavior–trait inference process requires that we distinguish among various kinds of traits, and unfortunately there are enough typologies of traits and dispositions to fill a chapter. In this chapter I distinguish among five types of traits: frequency-based, goal-oriented, attitude-based, morality-based, and competence- or ability-based. This is not meant to be a rigid distinction, nor are these categories necessarily exhaustive or mutually exclusive. The reason I make this distinction is that each of these trait categories seems to have somewhat different rules for how traits are inferred from behaviors.

Frequency-Based Traits. It has long been recognized (Buss & Craik, 1983) that many traits simply refer to regularities of behavior and seem to describe how frequently someone does something. When we say that person is restless or depressed, we may mean to say nothing more than that the person behaves in certain ways more often than most people do. In this sense, sometimes a trait is just a convenient summary label. There is no great mystery about how we infer frequency-based traits: People who exhibit large amounts of relevant behavior will "have" the trait (Borkenau & Müller, 1992). It is also probable that such traits are also assigned when people display relevant behaviors across different types of situations or display a behavior in situations that do not seem to call for it. For example, Felix may be seen as neat not only because he exhibits more neat behavior in a given day than most people, but because his proclivities display themselves in his person, his desk, his home, and his car. He may also be seen as neat if he cleans his living room in the middle of the night, especially if the room already seems neat enough to the untrained eye.

Goal-Based Traits. Many traits are associated with intentions and goals. The aggressive person intends to hurt, and the kind person intends to help. Note that such traits are often indistinguishable from frequency-based traits; an aggressive person may intend to hurt, but also tends to exhibit more aggressive behaviors than average. However, I make this distinction for two reasons. First, there are frequency-based traits (e.g., being restless) for which we may be hard pressed to specify relevant goals or intentions. Second, though frequency of behavior may enter into inferences of goal-based traits, we suspect that there are additional factors at work.

Specifically, for goal-based traits, some behaviors may be perceived to be particularly diagnostic of a given trait or a more prototypic exemplar. Punching someone to the ground is surely seen as more likely to result from an aggressive disposition than is raising one's voice to a surly salesclerk. People generally agree as to which behaviors are most prototypic of a given trait (Borkenau, 1990; Buss & Craik, 1983; Hampson, 1982), and such prototypic behaviors lead more readily to inferences about traits than do less prototypic behaviors (Borkenau, 1990; Fleeson, Zirkel, & Smith, 1995; Hampson, 1982; Riemann & Angleitner, 1993).

What determines whether a behavior is prototypic of a trait? As noted in Chapter 3, Barsalou (1985) argues that for categories defined in terms of goals (what I have earlier called "ad hoc categories"), prototypicality is determined by how well an exemplar advances the defining goal. So a gun is a more prototypic murder weapon than a shoe, because the former can kill others more quickly and efficiently. An aggressive person intends to hurt other people, and the most prototypic aggressive behaviors may be those that most efficiently advance this cause. Following this line of reasoning, how well acts are seen to achieve goals predicts how prototypic of the trait they are (Borkenau, 1990; Read, Jones, & Miller, 1990). Generally, more extreme behaviors are better at fulfilling goals; as this would suggest, the prototypicality of behaviors is generally more closely related to their rated extremity than to their general similarity to other behaviors that might exemplify the trait (Fleeson et al., 1995).

Attitude-Based Traits. I use the term "attitude" here quite broadly to refer both to evaluative reactions to people and things, and also to beliefs and other related mental states. We all have multiple beliefs and attitudes about almost anything we encounter, and we often assume that these beliefs have an underlying integrity. So terms such as "conservative" and "liberal" may be used to provide a kind of cultural and political framework for beliefs that are otherwise somewhat disconnected. According to Reeder, Pryor, and Wojciszke (1992) we often infer attitude-based traits as ways of simplifying mental states and the relationships between behaviors and those states. Inferring such traits is probably based on cultural conventions and understandings. A liberal is a person who expresses beliefs that most people would call liberal, and a religious person is one who holds beliefs most people would call religious.

Morality-Based Traits. In an influential paper, Reeder and Brewer (1979) argued that some traits have closer ties to some behaviors than to others. In particular, for some trait dimensions, behaviors are more diagnostic of one end than the other. Consider traits that have strong moral overtones. As an example, dishonest people may behave honestly or dishonestly as the mood or situational demands strike them, but the truly honest person is expected to be honest almost all the time. Therefore, it follows that honest behaviors can be performed by both honest and dishonest people and are therefore not especially diagnostic. Dishonest behaviors, by contrast, are more diagnostic because they are generally performed only by dishonest people. Reeder and Spores (1983) showed that people tended to see a person who committed an immoral behavior as immoral, regardless of whether situational forces encouraged this behavior; on the other hand, attributions based on moral behavior were heavily influenced by the situation. Moreover, it takes fewer behaviors to disconfirm morality-based traits than other types of traits (Trafimow & Trafimow, 1999), and moral people are expected to be more consistently moral than immoral people are to be immoral (Skowronski & Carlston, 1987). This is exactly what we would expect if immoral behavior is more diagnostic than moral.

Competence- and Ability-Based Traits. Traits that connote abilities also have diagnostic and nondiagnostic behaviors associated with them (Reeder & Brewer, 1979); in particular, high-ability behaviors are more diagnostic than low-ability ones (Skowronski & Carlston, 1987). Consider a basketball player who hits 10 shots in a row from beyond the 3-point line. Is she a gifted basketball player (or at least a good shot)? I think I would claim she is. I would grant her 1 or even 2 shots in a row from luck, but ordinary players do not drill 10 in a row. However, if I observe a player miss 4 in a row, I am not as tempted to assume that he is a poor shot. He could be having an off day or may just not be trying.[2] Similarly, everyone can screw up a simple math problem (through carelessness or stupidity), but only gifted people can solve really difficult problems. Generally, attributions following high-ability behavior are less affected by situational demands than are attributions following low-ability behavior (Reeder, 1979, 1997; Reeder & Fulks, 1980; Reeder, Messick, & Van Avermaet, 1977).

ATTRIBUTION MODELS

We have been considering the possibility that features of behaviors themselves may lead directly to trait inferences, but most behaviors can be due to any number of situationally and dispositionally determined factors. Classic attribution models are useful in helping to explain how we get through this tangle. Generally, when situational forces are strong, attributions to dispositional factors should be relatively weak; in other words, we should discount dispositions as the cause of behavior when the situation could have also produced it.

The Trope–Gilbert Model. Trope (Trope, 1986; Trope & Liberman, 1993) argues that people actively integrate situational and behavioral information to form such judgments. In Trope's model, situational forces play a complex role. Situations are often important cues for the interpretation of behavior, especially when that behavior is ambiguous (Trope, 1986; Trope, Cohen, & Alfieri, 1991). Accordingly, an initial step in the attribution process is the characterization of behavior in trait-like terms. Sally's behavior must be identified as aggressive before Sally herself can be seen as aggressive. Daniel Gilbert (Gilbert, McNulty, Giuliano, & Benson, 1992; Gilbert, Pelham, & Krull, 1988) has argued that there are two additional stages beyond that of behavior identification. In the first, the perceiver must actually make an inference that the person is characterized by the same trait that was used to characterize the behavior. This stage is assumed to be fairly automatic, in the sense of not being under conscious control and not requiring much by way of cognitive resources. However, people realize that most behaviors can have situational as well as dispositional causes, and so a third stage often occurs in which the perceiver tries to determine what role, if any, situational forces might have exerted in the behavior. So when you enter your local Ford dealer to look at new cars, and Hank rushes out to greet you with a warm smile, a firm handshake, and questions about how your family is getting along, you will initially see him as a friendly guy—but subsequently realize that his friendly behavior is due to his desire to sell you a car rather than any intrinsic friendliness on his part.

If for some reason you fail to make the correction, you may find yourself stuck with the notion that Hank is really a friendly guy (as he may well be, of course). When you are not motivated or do not have the cognitive resources to make these corrections, you will be more inclined to infer dispositions from behavior than when you have the opportunity to perform corrective action. Indeed, when people are cognitively busy (Gilbert et al., 1988) or when identification of the behavior itself uses up valuable cognitive resources (Gilbert et al., 1992), they fail to take situational forces into account and are highly prone to infer a correspondent disposition.[3] This has been called "correspondence bias" (Gilbert & Malone, 1995; Jones, 1990).

Correspondence Bias. One of the most widely replicated effects in the psychological literature is the tendency for people to assume that the behavior of others is caused by their dispositions, even when there are strong situational reasons for the behavior. In other words, perceivers often fail to discount dispositional causes when they should. For instance, we assume that people who perform aggressive behaviors are aggressive, even when we know that they had ample justification for their behavior. There may be many reasons for these tendencies to pay insufficient attention to situational influences on behavior (Gilbert & Malone, 1995), but correspondence biases are likely to be extremely important in stereotype-driven perceptions. For example, Kristin thinks that black men tend to be violent. This will surely lead her to code ambiguous behaviors by black males as violent, and if she fails to take into account all the background and situational factors that may lead such a person to behave in an aggressive way, she may conclude that he is in fact quite violent. Indeed, she may fail to take such additional possible causes into effect precisely because of her stereotype. That is, whereas a person who does not have a stereotype that black men are violent or who actively tries to get beyond stereotypic thinking will correct initial characterizations of such a person as violent by taking account of situational forces, Kristin will not be as motivated to perform this sort of correction. Similarly, those of us who expect males to perform better than females on a male-oriented task may be prone to see female success as due to unstable causes such as effort or luck, and male success as due to more stable ability (Swim & Sanna, 1996).

Generally, stereotype-consistent information tends to be attributed internally (Ben-Ari, Schwarzwald, & Horiner-Levi, 1994; Bodenhausen, 1988), and this may support essentialist assumptions about categories (Yzerbyt, Rocher, & Schadron, 1997). Moreover, there is a pervasive bias to attribute negative behaviors more dispositionally than positive (Ybarra, 2002) and to recall better negative dispositional and positive situational behaviors (Ybarra & Stephan, 1996). People who predisposed to use dispositional attributions are also more inclined to predict negative behavior for others (Ybarra & Stephan, 1999).

Although Gilbert and his colleagues have emphasized the role of cognitive resources in correction processes, they also recognize that sometimes people simply don't go to the bother of engaging in fairly effortful correction. If a given person's behavior appears to be about what others expect, it may not even occur to them to worry about other causes. Thus Kristin, who already thinks that blacks are violent and observes behavior that she readily codes as such, may have no inclination to imagine other reasons for the behavior. All is right with her cognitive world; why rock the boat? Even if she does try to suppress her dispositional explanations, she may engender a rebound effect (see Chapter 10) and use them even more in the future (Yzerbyt, Corneille, Dumont, & Hahn, 2001).

Correspondence bias also occurs in perceptions of groups, especially when those groups are seen as high in entitativity (see Chapters 3 and 7). Yzerbyt, Rogier, and Fiske (1998) had groups of subjects answer questions put to them by other groups of subjects. Observers judged that the performance was more due to abilities when the groups were presented as coherent entities.

Traits Are Not All Alike

As the previous discussion has indicated, traits vary in how closely tied they are to situations and how easily they are inferred, but they vary in other ways as well. In the subsequent discussion, I emphasize three basic ways that traits differ: evaluative, dispositional, and linguistic.

Evaluative Differences

Perhaps the most obvious way that traits differ is in their evaluative nature; everyone is aware that some traits are socially desirable, whereas others are more negative. And as nearly a half century's work on the semantic differential (Osgood, Suci, &

Tannenbaum, 1957) indicates, traits also vary according to how active versus passive or strong versus weak they are.

THE SOURCE OF TRAIT POSITIVENESS

Why are some traits positive whereas others are negative? As it turns out, there are many reasons (Brendl & Higgins, 1996). Part of the answer is surely that negative traits summarize behaviors that are harmful to others, and positive traits summarize behaviors that are more prosocial. So, for example, hostile behaviors generally hurt others, and warm behaviors are generally helpful to others and make them feel good. Having said that, however, some would be prepared to argue that there is hardly anything very objective about this state of affairs. After all, one could easily imagine that my hostility toward my student Anita might motivate her to work harder and achieve more (thus having positive results of sorts), and that my warm behavior toward Steve might help him to feel good at the expense of his figuring out solutions to his problems (thus leading to negative outcomes).

Furthermore, there is more than a whiff of cultural perfume in the air. To be sure, harming others physically is almost always bad in almost all cultures, and, all things being equal, kindness and warmth are probably universally better than the reverse. On the other hand, it is easy to imagine a culture—just look around—in which warm and kind people are taken advantage of and hostile people get more than their share of prestige and money. Ambition may well be important in U.S. society, at least for those who want to be self-sufficient and who lack family wealth, but in less complex societies it is far from clear that ambition has nearly as high a payoff. Some extroverted behaviors seen as friendly and positive in America might be seen as intrusive and negative in England or Japan.

Traits such as being cultured, confident, vulgar, humorous, informal, optimistic, extroverted, prudish, sensitive, and hurried seem to be defined as positive or negative almost entirely in terms of cultural values. In saying this, I do not mean to suggest that such values are arbitrary—that cultures simply randomly select some traits as valued and others as less so. What I mean is that evaluative judgments are a central part of the cultural matrix and cannot be seen independently of other cultural products.

Another factor that affects the positiveness of traits is their extremity. Generally, extreme behaviors and traits are evaluated less positively than their more moderate versions—a fact that Aristotle discussed in his notion of the "golden mean." Peabody (1967, 1970) noted that many trait dimensions have different terms for extreme and moderate forms of the same behaviors. For example, "stingy" is generally a more extreme version of "thrifty," and "spendthrift" is a more extreme form of "generous." A wealthy man who gives large amounts of money to charity would generally be seen in a positive light, whereas the man who gives all his money to charity might be seen as foolish. A devoutly religious woman crosses some evaluative line when she becomes a religious fanatic. So from the Peabody perspective, many (but not all) negative behaviors are simply too much of a good thing.

Situations as well as cultures can affect the meanings of traits. The charms of a happy-go-lucky person would be in full flower during a party, but considerably muted during a study session for an important exam. Staring into space can be seen as a positive, creative act in a book-lined office, and as dangerous behavior by a worker on the assembly line. Assertiveness can be viewed as good in a business context and as bad in a social context.

CONSEQUENCES OF TRAIT EVALUATION

Should we care about the evaluative nature of traits and behaviors? There are at least two reasons why we should. The more obvious is simply that applying positive or negative labels to people and their behavior has enormous interpersonal consequences.

A more subtle reason for our interest is related to the central concerns of this chapter—inferring traits and dispositions from behaviors. Are positive and negative behaviors differentially diagnostic? More generally, negative behaviors are more likely to lead to attributional processing (Bohner, Bless, Schwarz, & Strack, 1988). Negative behaviors usually lead to more correspondent attributions than positive behaviors, regardless of the causes (Vonk, 1998), and negative behaviors are usually seen as more salient and diagnostic than positive ones (Kanouse & Hanson, 1972; Rowe, 1989; Skowronski & Carlston, 1989). There may be many reasons for this. One we have already discussed is that negative traits (and their corresponding behaviors) tend to be more extreme. Extreme behaviors may be seen as more diagnostic in their own right, or they may be less common and thus provide more information.

Dispositional Differences

Traits vary in their evaluative linguistic meaning, and these meanings change from context to context, situation to situation, stereotype to stereotype. But traits differ in other ways as well. A large body of literature suggests that traits vary in their importance, abstractness, scope, centrality, and the like (Gidron, Koehler, & Tversky, 1993; Hampson, 1982; Hampson, John, & Goldberg, 1986; John, Hampson, & Goldberg, 1991; Kirby & Gardner, 1972; Semin & Fiedler, 1988).

TRAIT RATINGS

In an early paper, I (Schneider, 1971) argued that traits vary in dispositionality and that dispositionality has several aspects. In particular, more dispositional traits (1) should be more stable over time and situation, (2) should be more likely to motivate behavior or otherwise have a seeming causal agency, and (3) should be seen as more central to personality and more informative about a person. Several studies have shown that traits do differ in these ways (e.g., Gifford, 1975; Schneider, 1971; Schneider & Fazio, 1998).

Another important dimension of traits is how behaviorally obvious or simply visible they are. Some traits (such as being restless, lazy, shy, and extroverted) are readily apparent in behavior, but other traits (such as being ambitious, mature, and open to experience) may not be so easily judged. It is clear that some traits are in fact judged more easily than others (Gifford, 1994). Much of this research has been conducted with the so-called Big Five personality dimensions (Extroversion, Conscientiousness, Agreeableness, Emotional Stability, and Culture). When perceivers who were previously unacquainted with targets see even a brief sample of target behaviors, they tend to agree on their ratings of Extroversion and Conscientiousness, arguably the most observable of these five dimensions (Albright, Kenny, & Malloy, 1988;

Kenny, Albright, Malloy, & Kashy, 1994; Kenny, Horner, Kashy, & Chu, 1992; Levesque, 1997). Traits that have easily observed behaviors also yield greater accuracy (Blackman & Funder, 1998; Funder & Colvin, 1988; Hayes & Dunning, 1997; John & Robins, 1993), so it is quite likely that trait dimensions such as Extroversion are more accurately judged, because relevant behaviors are more easily observed and relate more closely to the trait in question.

IMPLICIT THEORIES ABOUT TRAITS

Not only do traits themselves vary in their perceived dispositionality, but people differ in how dispositional they see traits as being. Carol Dweck and her colleagues (Dweck, Chiu, & Hong, 1995; Dweck, Hong, & Chiu, 1993) have pioneered a line of research based on the fact that some people (referred to as "entity theorists") see personality and people's qualities as fairly fixed and unchanging, whereas others (called "incremental theorists") see them as more labile. Entity theorists not only make dispositional judgments more readily (and often base them on more minimal evidence) than incremental theorists do, but they also are more prone to use the dispositions they have assigned to targets to make further judgments about them (Levy & Dweck, 1998). Entity theorists tend to make stronger predictions from behaviors (Chiu, Hong, & Dweck, 1997) and to be more responsive to the evaluative features of behavioral information (Hong, Chiu, Dweck, & Sacks, 1997). At least among children, entity theorists are less willing to change negative impressions when the target behaves in a positive way (Erdley & Dweck, 1993) and are more likely to apply a group stereotype to an individual member of that group (Levy & Dweck, 1999).

   In one set of studies relevant to stereotyping, Levy and colleagues (1998) found that entity and incremental theorists generated the same number and quality of traits for various ethnic groups, but that the entity theorists rated these stereotypic traits as more likely to be true than did the incremental theorists. In a subsequent experiment, entity theorists not only reported more agreement with stereotypes of African Americans, but also rated the stereotypic traits as more due to innate factors. When describing a group described by various behaviors, the entity theorists listed more traits and made more extreme judgments on relevant trait dimensions. In another relevant stereotype experiment, Eberhardt, Dasgupta, and Banaszynski (2003) found that entity theorists were especially prone to perceive an ambiguous face as African American rather than European American, arguably because they see race as a more categorical, fixed category. These data, then, suggest that entity theorists are more prone to stereotyping.

Linguistic Differences

TYPES OF VERBS

It has long been known (Abelson & Kanouse, 1966; Garvey & Caramazza, 1974; McArthur, 1972) that different kinds of actions (and the verbs that describe them) tend to elicit different kinds of causal attributions. Roger Brown (Brown & Fish, 1983; Brown & Van Kleeck, 1989; Van Kleeck, Hillger, & Brown, 1988) noted that certain verbs (termed "interpersonal action verbs" or just "action verbs" by Brown) imply actions, whereas others (called "state verbs") are more attuned to mental states. Examples of the former are "hit," "help," and "hinder," and of the latter are "like," "astonish," and "hate."

Distinguishing Action and State Verbs. There are no perfect ways to distinguish action and state verbs, but there are differences. Brown and Fish (1983) noted that action verbs are defined in terms of "to do something," whereas state verbs are defined in terms of "to feel" or "to experience." Action verbs also tend to imply voluntary behavior of the large muscles, whereas state verbs are mental; as a consequence, action verbs describe observable behaviors, whereas state verbs describe states that are unobservable. Linguistically, action verbs tend to have derived adjectives that describe the *actor* ("help–helper," "cheat–cheater," "murder–murderer"), but comparable adjectives describing the *object* of the action are rare ("help–helpee?," "cheat–cheatee?," "murder–murderee?"). On the other hand, state verbs tend to have adjectives that describe the stimulus rather than the experiencer ("astonish"–"astonishing" but not "astonishable," "like"–"likeable" but not "liking"). Action verbs can readily be used in the imperative mode ("don't hit me," "please help me"), but state verbs sound odd as imperatives ("please amaze me"). Action verbs are more likely to take progressive tenses ("he is hitting her"), but such forms seem strange for state verbs ("he is fearing her"). Semin and Marsman (1994) have also suggested that whereas action verbs have a defined temporal course (e.g., we can usually point to the beginning and ending of hitting and helping episodes), state verbs are temporally indistinct (e.g., when did I begin to love or hate someone?).

Implicit Causality of Action and State Verbs. According to the initial Brown analyses, action verbs lead people to assume that the causal agent (typically the subject of the sentence) rather than the recipient (sometimes called the patient) has caused the action. So if you read that "Jane hit Michael," you would be inclined to assume that Jane is the causal agent rather than Michael. State verbs refer to more emotional reactions where the experiencer is placed in some state because of a reaction to a stimulus, and consequently the stimulus is seen as the cause. Linguistically, state verbs can be used in two ways. "Stimulus–experiencer" sentences have the stimulus as the grammatical subject and the experiencer as the object (e.g., "John astonishes James," "John shocks Mary"); the reverse is true for "experiencer–stimulus" sentences (e.g., "Mary dislikes John," "Sandy admires John"). In each case it is the stimulus that is seen as most potent (John in each of the cases above). This distinction seems fairly universal across language communities, for both adults and children, and for active- and passive-voice sentences (Rudolph & Försterling, 1997).

Subsequent research has confirmed that state verbs are well behaved in the sense that in most cases the stimulus is seen as the cause. However, while most action verbs show biases toward actor or agent causality, there are many exceptions (e.g., Au, 1986; Semin & Fiedler, 1988). This has led to several proposals for further refinement. Au (1986) and Rudolph (1997), among others, have suggested that there are two kinds of action verbs. Many, perhaps most, action verbs (e.g., "hit," "help," "seduce," "control," "manipulate," "encourage") suggest that the actor has initiated some action, but others (e.g., "answer," "praise," "accuse," "flee") imply that the agent or actor is reacting in some way to previous behavior by the patient. Such verbs, called "agent–evocator" verbs by Rudolph, tend to imply patient causality. This distinction between types of action verbs produces more predictable results. Table 14.1 provides a summary of the various kinds of verbs.

TABLE 14.1. Features of Verb Types

	State verbs		Action verbs	
Criteria	Relatively involuntary mental states		Relatively voluntary behaviors	
Observable?	No		Yes	
Imperative mode?	No		Yes	
Progressive tense?	No		Yes	
Subtypes	Experiencer-stimulus	Stimulus-experiencer	Agent–patient	Agent–evocator
Criteria	State in sentence subject	State in sentence object	Agent initiates action	Object initiates action
Examples	"John admires Mary" "John likes Mary"	"Mary astonishes John" "Mary disappoints John"	"John cheats Mary" "John helps Mary"	"John praises Mary" "John comforts Mary"
Attribution	Stimulus (Mary)	Stimulus (Mary)	Agent (John)	Object (Mary)

Note. From Rudolph (1997). Copyright 1997 by Sage Publications. Reprinted by permission.

Other Implicit Causality Factors. However, no one claims that such implicit causality effects are too powerful to be overridden. One standard criticism of this area of research is that subjects are given quite impoverished sentences as stimuli (e.g., "Mary astonishes John"), and effects might be quite different with more extensive information (Edwards & Potter, 1993). For example, though "Mary astonishes John" usually leads subjects to think that something about Mary rather than John caused this reaction, this could easily be reversed by stating that "Mary astonishes John, who is a rather gullible person."

More generally, other linguistic expectations play a major role in implicit causality. Roberta Corrigan (2001, 2002) has shown that implicit causality is affected by evaluative agreement between verb and subject as well as between verb and object. When verb, subject, and object agree, then the typical effects described in the last paragraphs are obtained. However, when there are disagreements, causality is assigned to the subject or object that agrees with the verb. So when the subject is positive and the object negative (or vice versa), good actions are assigned to the positive one, and negative actions are assigned to the negative one. When bad John does something bad to good Harry (e.g., selfish John hurts warm Harry), John is seen as the cause, and when bad John does something good to good Harry (e.g., selfish John helps nice Harry), Harry is seen as the cause. Potency of subjects, objects, and verbs also affect assignment of causality. Potent verbs (e.g., "protect") produce stronger attributions of causality than do less potent verbs (e.g., "telephone"), and potent subjects and objects are also assigned stronger causality than less potent ones. This may explain why female agents are given less causal power than male agents (Lafrance, Brownell, & Hahn, 1997). So when Mary helps John, she is seen as less causally important than when John helps Mary.

Lest these various results seem esoteric, we might consider that members of outgroups and stereotyped groups are often seen as less positive (and probably less potent) than members of ingroups. Thus when Jason, a member of your group (and thereby likely to be positive), does something negative to Darnel, a member of a negative outgroup, these results suggest that you will see Darnel as having gotten what he deserves. Conversely, when Darnel does something positive to Jason, Jason will get the credit. In other words, members of outgroups get credit for negative things, and ingroup folks receive credit for positive ones. Ingroup biases are not surprising (Chapter 7), and now I am suggesting that this may be due to language biases as well as our desires to see outgroup members as less positive than ingroup members.

Explanations. Several explanations have been offered for this phenomenon. Brown and Fish (1983) argued that causal potency is a matter of differential information. In considering action verbs, we see that more people can be recipients than agents of actions. For example, it doesn't take much skill or motivation to be helped, but because the act of helping requires some minimal planning, ability, and motivation, fewer people help than are helped. Put another way, we learn more about Mary by knowing she helped than by knowing she was helped. In the case of experiencer-stimulus and stimulus–experiencer verbs, more people can experience emotions than can be stimuli for them. It is easy to like someone or to be astonished, but relatively harder to be a likeable person or one who astonishes. Hence we assign causality to the less common factor.

A similar sort of argument about causal schemas has been made by Fiedler and Semin (1988). They argue that different kinds of sentences imply different sorts of contexts. Specifically, action verbs (the agent–patient schema) imply a previous agent state and a consequent patient state. For example, when one knows that John helps Mary, one might reasonably assume that John likes Mary and that Mary will thank John. Conversely, with state verbs, people are more likely to assume a preceding stimulus person behavior and a consequent experiencer behavior. When we know that John likes Mary, we assume that Mary has done something nice for John and that subsequently John will do something nice for Mary. Thus judgments that John helps because he is a helpful person, and that Mary is liked because she is a likeable person, really reflect a whole set of implicit assumptions about what causes the behavior.

Gilovich and Regan (1986) argue that we assign causality to the agent because we assume that agents have more volitional control than patients; a person has to try to help, but not necessarily to be helped. Similarly, we assume that a person has more control over being likeable or astonishing than the person who experiences these emotions. Along these same lines, Greene and McKoon (1995) and McKoon, Greene, and Ratcliff (1993) argue that the causality goes with the person who initiates the action. Semin and Marsman (1994) have provided evidence that action verbs imply subject initiation of action and state verbs imply object initiation. Thus we are not at a loss for explanations of implicit causality effects.

THE LINGUISTIC CATEGORY MODEL

The work on implicit causality of verbs has been elaborated and expanded upon by Semin and Fiedler (1991, 1992) and their colleagues. They have arranged verbs on a continuum of abstractness. Descriptive action verbs (DAVs) are concrete behaviors with a clear beginning and end; they are generally not strongly positive or negative in themselves, and both their interpretation and evaluation depend heavily on the situational context. Examples would be "hit," "yell," "tell," "push," "talk," "pull," and "walk." At a more abstract level, we have interpretative action verbs (IAVs); though these have a clear beginning and end, they do not refer to any particular behavior. So one can help another through a variety of ways. IAVs are usually strongly positive or negative. Examples would be (in addition to "help") "save," "imitate," "hurt," "hinder," "care for." State verbs (SVs) refer to mental and emotional states: "believe," "hate," "love," "respect." Fourth, state action verbs (SAVs) also refer to mental or emotional states, but the emotional state exists in the object of the verb. These should not be confused with SVs, where the subject of the action has the mental state. So when Joshua hates (SV) Rachel, it is Joshua who experiences the state, but when Joshua surprises (SAV) Rachel, it is Rachel who has the experience. Originally, the linguistic category model postulated a fifth level of abstractness—namely, adjectives or traits (ADJ)—but more recent versions (e.g., Semin & Fiedler, 1992) have suggested that each of the four types of verbs may have a corresponding trait or adjective. Someone who talks (DAV) a lot is talkative, someone who helps (IAV) often is helpful, someone who loves (SV) is loving, and a person who bores (SAV) others is boring. Not every verb has a corresponding adjective or trait (e.g., "hit"); adjectives derived from the highly concrete DAVs are comparatively rare in English, German, and Italian (Semin & Fiedler, 1991). Other verbs have traits that change the verb meaning (e.g., the fact that John amazes Sue does not make him amazing). Furthermore, a great many other traits do not have clear verb referents ("extroverted," "cold," "warm").

What difference does all this make for stereotyping? I have argued earlier in this chapter that the vertical dimension of attributions is crucial, and the Semin–Fiedler model is one way to make sense of it. Think about the implications of assigning a more abstract or dispositional trait versus a more concrete one to another person. Would you rather be seen as anxious or restless? Depressed or unhappy? Angry or hostile? The more abstract traits imply that a general and stable quality of the person caused the behavior, whereas more concrete traits imply less stable and more transitory causes. More particularly, the more abstract qualities are more informative, less easily verified, less confirmable (or disconfirmable), more likely to generate interpersonal disagreement, and less informative about situations, as well as having a longer temporal duration (Semin & Fiedler, 1988, 1992). More abstract traits stick with you.

Linguistic Intergroup Bias. One of the most important implications for stereotyping of this line of research rests on a phenomenon first labeled the "ultimate attribution error" by Pettigrew (1979, 1981). This is the tendency to describe outgroups less favorably than ingroups by assuming that negative behaviors of outgroups are due to more dispositional reasons than negative behaviors of ingroups, whereas their positive behaviors are seen as more situationally caused than positive behaviors of ingroups. Several experiments discussed in Chapter 7 support this idea.

In terms of the language model we have been discussing, we might expect that outgroups would be described with abstract negative qualities and rather concrete positive ones. The ultimate insult to someone is to brand the person with a negative trait that is part and parcel of personality—one that won't go away. There are several demonstrations of exactly that phenomenon, usually called the "linguistic intergroup bias." Maass, Salvi, Arcuri, and Semin (1989) used a naturally occurring example of intergroup conflict to test the hypothesis. They picked members of Italian towns and cities that identified with competing horse-racing teams and asked them to respond to cartoons describing behaviors of people from their own and a competing team. These subjects picked more abstract terms in describing positive ingroup and negative outgroup behaviors, but were more concrete when describing positive outgroup and negative ingroup behaviors. Schmid (1999) found that in professional wrestling, the "good guys" were described with more abstract positive than negative features, while the reverse was true for "bad guys." This kind of linguistic intergroup bias has also been found for gender (Fiedler, Semin, & Finkenauer, 1993; Guerin, 1994) and for competing schools, teams, and nations (Arcuri, Maass, & Portelli, 1993; Maass, Montalcini, & Biciotti, 1998). Moreover in communication situations people tend to describe stereotype-consistent behavior in more abstract terms, and recipients of these messages therefore attribute the stereotypic behavior more to dispositional factors (Wigboldus, Semin, & Spears, 2000). von Hippel, Sekaquaptewa, and Vargas (1997) have argued that the linguistic intergroup bias can even be used as a somewhat disguised measure of prejudice; a measure of the bias was related to tendencies to interpret the behavior of a black man as threatening. People who are more prejudiced describe African American stereotypic behavior in more abstract terms than do less prejudiced sorts (Schnake & Ruscher, 1998).

There are at least two reasonable explanations for this kind of linguistic bias effect (Maass & Arcuri, 1992). One possibility, which could be derived from social identity theory (see Chapter 7), is that people dislike outgroups more than ingroups and use language in a way that is particularly harmful to the outgroups (highly stable and hard-to-change negative qualities, and more concrete and fleeting positive qualities). Maass, Montalcini, and Biciotti (1998) found that negative aspects of outgroup stereotypes required little evidence to be seen as true, but a great deal to be refuted. Furthermore, when subjects' group identities are threatened (e.g., by reading a hostile statement written by a member of the outgroup), people display the linguistic intergroup bias to a larger extent (Maass, Ceccarelli, & Rudin, 1996).

The other alternative is a more cognitive, attributional one. We generally expect people we like and admire to perform more positive than negative behaviors; hence negative behaviors by ingroup members, as well as positive behaviors by outgroup members, will be fairly unexpected and will be seen as more situationally determined (following well-recognized attribution rules). Conversely, positive behaviors by the ingroup as well as negative behaviors by the outgroup will be seen as expected, even normal, and ascribed to stable dispositional terms. There is in fact evidence (Karpinski & von Hippel, 1996; Maass, Milesi, Zabbini, & Stahlberg, 1995; Rubini & Semin, 1994) that stereotype-inconsistent events are described more concretely than more expected ones. Also, people are more likely to show the linguistic intergroup bias when they have a high need for cognitive closure (Webster, Kruglanski, & Pattison, 1997).

Questioning and Seeking Information. The kinds of verbs and dispositions we use to describe others have another potentially important implication. Semin, Rubini, and Fiedler (1995) argued that when one person questions another, the verb used may bias the response. When the question was phrased with a state verb ("Why do you like *Titanic*?"), answers tended to implicate the object (e.g., "The movie had good special effects"). However, questions that were asked with an action verb ("Why did you see *Titanic*?") elicited answers that implicated the actor ("Because I like romantic tragedies").

Does this have any implications for stereotyping? One possibility is that people may (probably inadvertently) phrase questions that elicit more abstract or dispositional answers for the negative behaviors of stereotyped groups. So a white non-Hispanic individual may find it relatively easy to ask why an Hispanic teenager participates in gang violence (predisposing an answer in terms of actor dispositions), whereas the mother of that same teenager may be more apt to ask why he likes such behavior (predisposing an answer in terms of the activity). In a study by Semin and de Poot (1997b), subjects who were more suspicious of a person's trustworthiness were more inclined to phrase questions in ways that implied fault. Also, individual differences may be important. For example, a high need for cognitive closure also predisposes people to use action verbs as opposed to state verbs in their questions (Rubini & Kruglanski, 1997), and we may have a high need for closure in explaining outgroup behavior.

DISCONFIRMING TRAITS

I have argued that the more abstract terms are seen as more dispositional and hence tend to say more about a person and his or her group. In fact, the abstract terms in the Maass and colleagues (1989) study were rated as more informative about the person and as more likely to describe behavior that would be repeated. There is a related implication—namely, that because the more abstract terms are more general and stable, they may also be harder to change. If I describe you as a helpful (concrete) person, I may be quite prepared to see this as situationally controlled and as something that comes and goes. Hence it may be fairly easy for me to decide that you are really not as helpful as I thought if I see you behaving in nonhelpful ways in other circumstances. On the other hand, if I have decided that you are a kind (relatively abstract) person, it may take a good many instances of unkind behavior for me to change my mind about you.

Chapter 10's discussion of stereotype and prejudice change has focused on groups and perceivers, but it is highly likely that for any group some traits can get "lost" more easily than others. As I have just suggested, more abstract traits, especially negative ones (precisely the ones that tend to be part of outgroup stereotypes), should be especially Teflon-coated.

Also, it should be relatively hard to change traits that have high-ability or low-morality implications (see above). In particular, it would be hard to change a judgment that someone has high ability, because it is so easy to assume that low-ability behaviors are due to low effort or carelessness. Similarly, a person who is labeled as having a low moral character would have trouble behaving in a way that would change others' minds, precisely because people with a bad moral character can so easily fake moral behavior. Moral people who behave immorally have their morality revised more than the reverse (Reeder & Coovert, 1986).

A colleague and I (Trafimow & Schneider, 1994) manipulated whether a person was described as having a trait and whether he or she performed a behavior consistent or inconsistent with the trait under situational pressure or not. So, for example, the question was whether a friendly person who performed a friendly or unfriendly behavior under pressures to be friendly or not would be seen as friendly. Obviously, the trait description and performance of behavior both affected trait attributions. However, the behavior manipulation was stronger for ability- and morality-based traits. Moreover, situational information and prior trait information had less effect for these traits. In other words, ability and morality attributions were affected less by prior knowledge about ability and morality and by whether the situation called for moral or high-ability behavior. Traits such as being friendly, which do not have such strong moral or ability overtones, were relatively more affected by situational and prior impression information. The implications for stereotyping are these: If stereotypes lead us to believe that a person has low ability, behavioral outcomes can easily change that attribution. However, a person who is seen as immoral can do little behaviorally to change that attribution.

Rothbart and Park (1986) measured this directly. They simply asked subjects to indicate how easily they could imagine behaviors that confirmed or disconfirmed a trait, and how many behaviors would be needed before the trait would be confirmed or disconfirmed. They found that negative traits in general were fairly easy to acquire (in the sense that few consistent behaviors were necessary for confirmation), and that negative traits were also hard to disconfirm (in the sense that many inconsistent behaviors would be required to disconfirm an already attributed trait). Positive traits were fairly hard to get and easy to lose, whereas the reverse was true for negative qualities. Funder and Dobroth (1987) found similar results, although the correlations were much weaker. In unpublished data, a colleague and I (Schneider & Fazio, 1998) confirmed that positive traits are harder to acquire in the sense of requiring more confirming instances than negative traits, but we also found that positive traits required more instances to disconfirm. We also showed that traits that required more confirming instances were also seen as more stable over time and situation, and were seen as more deep-seated and pervasive in personality—in other words, as more dispositional. Furthermore, Arcuri and Cadinu (1992) have argued that other linguistic factors mediate the effects. In particular, they argue that negative traits are typically narrower in focus and encompass a smaller range of behaviors that may account for the effects. Nonetheless, there is clear evidence that some traits are harder to change than others, even though the precise mediators of this are still unknown.

TRAIT COMMUNICABILITY

Mark Schaller and his colleagues (2002) have argued that traits vary in how likely they are to be the subject of conversation and other communication. They found that subjects could reliably rate how likely they were to discuss trait perceptions of particular people with others. Traits that were highly communicable were a bit more frequent in the language and were also behaviorally frequent and easy to judge. More to the point, the traits that were communicable were also more prevalent in stereotypes of Canadian ethnic groups and were likely to have persisted over time in the stereotypes of ethnic and nationality groups reported in the three Princeton University studies from the early 1930s through the middle 1960s (see Chapter 11). At present, we do not know exactly why some traits are more communicable than others. Perhaps they describe culturally more important or interesting behavior; alternatively, perhaps they are more "sticky" in the sense that they are easier for people to think about and remember. But whatever the underlying reasons, this research reminds us of a major theme of this chapter, namely that just as some groups appear to be magnets for stereotypes, so some traits appear to be easier to attach to groups and harder to get rid of than others.

SUMMARY

Most stereotype research focuses on groups and categories, and with good reason. However, we ought not forget that traits and other features (the content of stereotypes) are not merely passive players in the whole stereotyping process. We are all aware that some traits are more positive than others, and that this has enormous consequences for how we evaluate groups and behave toward them.

That much is obvious. What may not be as obvious is that other features of traits may also play a large role in stereotyping and its effects on thoughts, emotions, and behaviors. It seems clear that at least people from Western countries readily infer traits and other underlying dispositions from observations of behavior. More broadly, they seem to have a decided proclivity for fairly abstract representations of other people and the groups they represent, and they tend not to take enough account of situational influences on behavior. But traits themselves vary in how abstract they are. Moreover, some actions more easily implicate actors, whereas others orient us more toward targets of behavior. In addition, some traits seem easy to confirm in the sense that we need few behaviors to attribute them to people and these may also be traits that are hard to disconfirm. One reason this is enormously important is that we tend to attribute more abstract negative traits and less abstract positive traits to people from other groups than to our own groups. That would suggest that our stereotypes of other groups may consist of negative traits that are hard to change and positive ones that are easy to change.

Notes

1. Although attribution models have dominated in this area of research, there are certainly other viable and largely unexplored approaches including Bayesian models (Ajzen & Fishbein, 1975; Trope & Liberman, 1993), general probability models (Morris & Larrick, 1995), connectionist models (Read & Miller, 1993), and models based on text comprehension (e.g., Read, Druian, & Miller, 1989).
2. On the other hand, even good players miss a few shots and poor players occasionally get lucky, so judgments of ability in this area may also be partially frequency-based (Trafimow, 1997)
3. However, in Asian cultures which rely more on communal and situational explanations, cognitive busyness does not affect tendencies toward dispositional explanations, presumably because people are more practiced in making these corrections (Knowles, Morris, Chiu, & Hong, 2001). However, Asians are just as prone to correspondence bias when situations are not salient (Norenzayan, Choi, & Nisbett, 2002) or when behavior is reasonably diagnostic of dispositions (Miyamoto & Kitayama, 2002). Generally, because their theories about human behavior are more holistic and complex, Asians consider more information before making a final attribution (Choi, Dalal, Kim-Prieto, 7 Park, 2003).

CHAPTER 15

Summary

Social scientists have been obsessed with stereotypes for well over half a century. Have we learned anything in those 70-plus years? Yes, we have. Quite a bit, actually, and it is probably fair to say that modern conceptions of stereotypes would hardly be recognized by early investigators in this area. I conclude this lengthy book with a brief discussion of what has changed, in part because it is always good to document progress in the social sciences, but also because so many people, including some social scientists, have not fully grasped the "new look" in stereotypes.

STEREOTYPES ARE NOT ROGUE GENERALIZATIONS

In the early days, there was essentially universal agreement that stereotypes were rotten generalizations that smelled up the mental household. They were inaccurate, largely produced by prejudiced minds or shoveled into ignorant minds by prejudiced culture. They were negative, rigidly held, and impervious to disconfirming evidence. Unfortunately, most of this is wrong. Some stereotypes are like that, but most are not, not usually, not inevitably.

The first assumption was that stereotypes were inaccurate generalizations, maintained through ignorance, prejudice, and cultural realities. Today few social psychologists would endorse this as a general description, racist stereotypes notwithstanding. We now recognize that stereotypes cannot easily be divorced from more "normal" ways of thinking about people. As a cognitive process, stereotyping seems pretty much like business as usual. Stereotypes are simply generalizations about groups of people, and as such they are similar to generalizations about dogs, computers, Anne Rice novels, city buses, or Beethoven piano sonatas. We have them because they are useful. I use stereotypes about students when I prepare my lectures (and, for that matter, stereotypes about prospective readers of this book while I write it); my physician uses them when he categorizes me as a guy with sinus problems; movie producers use them when they decide how to cast movies; politicians eagerly embrace

562

them when they campaign for votes; and anyone with any sense uses them when deciding where to take a car for repair or whether to open the door to a stranger late at night. We all use them all the time. To deny ourselves the use of generalizations about people would result in intellectual and social chaos.

Stereotypes are also not always negative. The belief that Asian students are good at math is just as much a stereotype as the belief that fat people are lazy. Of course, we may be more concerned about the latter, negative generalization, and we'd probably be more inclined to denounce it by calling it a stereotype. But unless we take racist stereotypes as prototypic, positive and negative generalizations seem to have the same underlying psychologies.

Furthermore, there's no reason to believe that stereotypes are any more rigid and impervious to disconfirmation than any other generalization. Certainly, we may be reluctant to give up our stereotypes in the face of disconfirming evidence, but that's normal. Stereotypes, like all generalizations, resist change. An efficient and effective mental system couldn't have it any other way. Of course, stereotypes, like all generalizations, make for errors. Some Asian students are bad at math and good at poetry, gentle-looking dogs bite, tasty-looking grapes turn out to be sour; and a stranger who looks like a friendly sort totes a gun and a thieving disposition. Yes, stereotypes are often inaccurate (see below), but it's far from clear that they are any less accurate in principle than generalizations about much of anything else.

So up to a point, stereotypes share the same advantages and disadvantages as other generalizations. But I expect most readers share my uneasy feeling that saying black men are violent, gay men are effeminate, Texans are crass, and religious people are kind isn't quite the same thing as saying red, ripe apples taste good and Honda makes reliable cars.

There are, I think, at least four related ways in which stereotypes differ from other sorts of generalizations. First, people are much more likely to complain about being stereotyped than are apples or Hondas. That's fair enough, and it is a political and social difference of some considerable consequence. To some extent, it is created by political correctness norms doing their thing, but the difference goes deeper.

Second, on average people are more complex than apples, dogs, or even computers, and stereotypes seem to violate this sense of complexity. One way people are more complex is that they are less consistent in behavior over time and situation than are most objects and animals. Most features for most objects sit tight. Apples never taste rotten on Tuesday and then good on Wednesday. My computer has its good and bad days, but it's absurdly reliable about transforming particular keystrokes into appropriate letters on the screen, and it never does the laundry, reads novels, or breaks into song, whereas I sometimes do those things, usually unpredictably. My students seem to have the stereotype that professors are nice, and so I am, most of the time. But sometimes I have a bad day, and I'm certainly much less nice when I am negotiating the freeways of Houston than when I am in my faculty office.

Third, not only are people less predictable than objects, but most people categories have more important features than most object ones. The size and taste of apples are the only features of apples I really care about, and reliability, comfort, fuel efficiency, number of cup holders, and safety just about exhaust my interest in cars. However, with people, there's lots to consider; when I single out one or even a couple of features as the focus of my stereotype, people may rightfully object that they are much more than a feature or two. So when I say that Asians are good at math, not only do I run the risk of seeing Lui as better at statistics than she turns out to be, but, even if I am correct, I have highlighted only one of the many things that go into her identity and make her the person she is. Apples are indifferent to whether taste or color is paramount.

Fourth, generalizations about people tend to be more deeply embedded in our mental lives and cultures than other generalizations. Our theories about computers, dogs, and particular makes of cars tend not to be especially elaborate; nor do they have many links with our other ideas or concepts. Person categories are more likely to have strong and complex links to other beliefs, attitudes, and values. Perhaps this is just another way of saying that people are more important to most of us than dogs and computers, but for whatever reason, people generalizations seem to be especially rich.

My strong intuition is that stereotypes are also more strongly embedded in cultures than most object generalizations. Culture affects how we think about almost everything, but its role in our beliefs about people are likely to be particularly strong, in large part I suspect, because human behavior is inherently more ambiguous than that of most plants, animals, and objects. Therefore, consensual stereotypes often have a sense of legitimacy that individually developed stereotypes ordinarily do not have.

These are important differences, but they are differences in degree, not in kind. Stereotypes usually look and act like other generalizations. They are not so much rogue generalizations as they are generalizations with deep resonances in our mental lives and profound consequences for our social behavior. They may differ from object generalizations in their complexity, but at their heart they are still generalizations.

THE CULTURE WARS

Stereotypes have also been accused of being bad because they are created or at least supported by cultures that are prejudiced and discriminatory. There is something to be said for this argument, but not in the simple accusatory form that is usually advanced. Many people still seem to think that in adopting and using stereotypes, people let their cultures do their thinking for them. But as I have suggested many times, this is hardly a bad thing per se. Certainly many, probably most, of our generalizations are basically products of what we have read, seen on TV, or learned in school without direct supporting experiences; such cultural wisdom is often valuable, or even essential to our survival. I am grateful for books that can tell me what brands of cars are most likely to suit my purposes, what wild critters I should avoid, and what wines are likely to taste the best. I am likely to rely on secondhand stereotypes about people who live in parts of cities before I buy a house, and stereotypes based on uniforms when I want help in a computer store or pay for my meal in a restaurant.

Are stereotypes cultural products? Of course, but so are most of our generalizations, even those that seem entirely based on individual experience. There are no raw experiences. The categories I use, my articulated schemas and theories, the ways I explain, are all joint products of past experience and cultural realities. In what amounts to a huge bootstrapping operation, culture affects experience; culturally conditioned experiences combine with culture to affect new experiences; and on it goes.

This is not to say, of course, that culture gets a clean bill of health when it comes to looking at the mischief stereotypes cause. Just because "everybody knows" that gay males are likely to seduce boys and that out-of-work Hispanic males are lazy doesn't make these things true. Cultural wisdom can be wrong, but just because it is trivially easy to show that cultural stereotypes (as well as other culturally sponsored generalizations) are often not right, we ought not to commit the opposite error of assuming that they are always wrong. Cultures provide plenty of accurate generalizations, and some really faulty ones as well. But stereotypes based on individual experience can also be inaccurate, distorted by prejudice, or based on parochial experiences. There is no inherent accuracy advantage to what I know as opposed to what we know.

THE ACCURACY ISSUE

In some ways, the classic assumption that stereotypes must be inaccurate nourished most of the others. There was a kind of implicit and naive notion that the negative stereotypes about others could not possibly be true, and could not be based on any sort of reasonable set of experiences with people from those groups. However, the fact of the matter is that some stereotypes are accurate and some are not.

There are several senses in which accuracy of stereotypes is a misguided issue. First, accuracy is more or less indeterminate for most stereotypes. What does it mean to say that fat people are lazy? That they move slowly, participate in active sports less often, show up for work late, produce less in a given amount of time, or make lower grades in school? And what about black people being musical? Do they sing more or better, compose more, know all about Beethoven, dominate jazz combos or symphony orchestras, or buy more CDs? The important point isn't so much that terms such as "musical" and "lazy" are vague (although they surely are), but that any reasonable person can manufacture evidence in support of or against stereotypes involving these terms just by expanding or restricting the relevant behavioral domain. This makes it fairly meaningless to suggest that the obese-people-are-lazy stereotype is accurate, but, by the same token, it is just as meaningless to argue that it is false. Generally, questions that don't have meaningful answers ought be left to suffer alone and in peace.

More importantly, even for features that are potentially verifiable, our minds and behavior create a fair amount of wiggle room for verification. I can make the obese-people-are-lazy stereotype accurate by selectively paying attention to their behavior and treating them in ways that would make anyone act in a lazy manner. Our stereotypes bias what we pay attention to, how we interpret the behavior of others, what we will remember, and what inferences we think we can legitimately draw. Beyond the tricks our minds play, at the interpersonal level our stereotypes may affect our behavior in ways that affect the behavior of other people, often in ways that confirm stereotypes. Our behavior and our minds make truth as much as they uncover it.

A third bug in the accuracy program is that people respond to situations in ways that objects and animals do not. Many times when we are accurate in our judgments about others, it is because we have a handle on the situation, not the person. In the Indiana of my youth, it was a well-known "fact" that blacks were not good athletes because they never seemed to appear on high school or college championship basketball teams. Now it is easy to see that people cannot excel at sports they are not en-couraged to play (or, in many cases, were kept from playing). Generally, even accurate stereotypes depend on situations and are more accurate in some contexts than in others. Taking this point seriously would force us to think more deeply than we generally do about why people behave the way they do in a given situation, and whether context might be more important than group in our explanations.

So arguments about whether stereotypes are accurate usually boil down to relay-ing experiences, telling stories, or presenting this or that kind of statistical data in support. But the former cannot speak to general realities, but only parochial realties, and even "objective" statistics do not speak to the ultimate truths we desire. Statistics are generalizations about behavior and typically not about the underlying reasons for those behaviors, arguably the more important level.

STEREOTYPES AND PREJUDICE ARE COMPLEX

Stereotypes are complex sets of beliefs, sometimes held together by cultural glue or prejudice, but more often through theories that reflect some combination of experi-ence and culture. Most stereotypes have both positive and negative features, and these may vary in terms of how tenaciously they are held and how likely they are to be deployed for a given target. Different parts of the stereotype are likely to be salient in different contexts. Stereotypes come and go, purr and roar. As I have argued, preju-dice and discrimination are also not simple, unidimensional constructs. The same person can be positive toward Juan and negative toward Latoya today, and can re-verse those feelings tomorrow. This is not a unique feature of prejudice—it's just the way attitudes work.

Arguably the most important discovery in this area in the past couple of decades has been that stereotypes and prejudice exist at several levels of consciousness. There are two somewhat independent issues facing us. The first is what to make of implicit processes and how they are related to more explicit ones. What we think we believe does not always capture all we do believe. It is, of course, vitally important to docu-ment implicit beliefs and attitudes, and to make people aware that they may not be fully conscious of their stereotypes, their prejudices, and the ways they discriminate. At a theoretical level, we need to understand when and how these implicit processes affect our behavior.

Related is the issue of how easily we can control our stereotypes and prejudices. Most social psychologists would not claim that such control is impossible, but they would see it as hard. A program based on "Just say no to stereotypes" is not only laughably simplistic but likely to be ineffective. Although we certainly have consider-able control over the expression of our stereotypes and prejudices, backlash may be the product of vigorous attempts at suppression, and the more implicit our beliefs and attitudes, the harder they are to control, especially when people deny that they have them.

Likewise, behaviors related to stereotypes and prejudice are not as one-dimen-sional as most people seem to assume. Discrimination can be subtle as well as direct, and can reflect situational and institutional pressures as well as being caused in a straight-line fashion by prejudice. Those who claim that discrimination is caused by racist people doing their thing also tend to claim that discrimination is yielding to a more merit-based as opposed to category-based approach to jobs and access to other social rewards and costs. But this is a truncated view of discrimination at best; other, more subtle and less consciously controlled, forms of discrimination may be just as pernicious in their results if less overt in their behaviors.

ARE STEREOTYPES ACCEPTABLE?

Some readers may think I am making apologies for stereotypes and, by implication, for prejudice and discrimination. Nothing could be further from my intentions. I do think that before we can make progress in this area, we have to bring stereotypes out of the musty rooms they have inhabited and give them a good airing out. Not only have stereotypes been treated simplistically, but they have been used in lazy ways to explain far too much social mischief. Not all the problems with race, gender, and other categories are due to stereotyping, and even those that are have complex underlying causes. Like most readers of this book, I abhor the harm that stereotypes can cause, but I think that our stereotypes about stereotypes have impeded rather than helped in our search for remedies.

If we assume I am correct that stereotypes are simply generalizations about people, does this mean that stereotyping is inevitable and that therefore nothing can be done? Well, the short answers are "yes" and "no." At one level, stereotyping is inevitable. We can no more stop generalizing about people than about cars or animals.

What is not inevitable, however, is that such generalizations have the force in our interpersonal lives that they presently do. To disarm stereotypes, we need to do at least three things. First, we need to emphasize and reemphasize that people in almost all groups are diverse with regard to nearly all features. Almost no stereotypes apply to all, or in most cases to even a majority of, the people in the relevant category. Not all apples taste good; not all Hondas will go for 100,000 miles; not all professors are smart; and not all Asians are good at math. One size does not fit all, and many people just don't squeeze into their groups' stereotypes the way they're supposed to.

The generalizations that should be important in our lives are not just the ones that discriminate one group from another, but rather those that have a high probability of applying to a given person. I happen to believe that dogs are far more likely to bite than most animals I encounter—cats, gerbils, cockroaches, birds, and the occasional pig, goat, horse, or cow. But this seems to play no role in my behavior toward dogs, because I give them the benefit of the doubt on biting until growls or owner warnings tell me otherwise. Yes, black males are more likely to be violent than white males, but so what? The vast majority of black males I (and most of you) are likely to encounter are no more violent than white males. If I want to avoid being punched, stabbed, or shot, I can improve my odds much better by using generalizations about time of day, location, and situation than race or even gender. Saying that people in groups differ is more than celebrating a cliche. Generally speaking, we ought to use our stereotypes (or any other generalizations) gingerly unless they have a relatively high probability of applying to a given individual. Many of the stereotypes that are culturally salient may be statistically accurate, but provide little guidance in our everyday dealings with real and complex individuals.

Second, we need to reinforce a search for deeper explanations for group differences that give rise to stereotypes. I have emphasized throughout this book that stereotypes are more than feature lists—they are also theories we have about people and why they behave the way they do. Unfortunately, many people, and not just overt racist and sexists, tend to have impoverished, muddled, and even wrong theories about people. We need to continually remind ourselves and educate others that human behavior is complex, and that group membership is generally a poor explanation for most behavior.

Third, and finally, we need to be more aware than most of us are about the complexity of our own attitudes and behaviors and their effects on others. We have all seen people who swear they "don't have a prejudiced bone in their bodies" behave in ways that prove they do. Hypocrisy and self-delusion aside, all of us, some of the time, behave in ways that belie our best conscious intentions. Before we can learn to behave in ways that honor our values, we need to be aware of our behaviors that do not. To be sure, it is counterproductive for others to remind us of our every misdeed, and political correctness norms often do more harm than good in inhibiting much-needed dialogue about issues related to stereotypes. Still, it's hard to imagine that we can make much progress in eliminating prejudice and discrimination so long as people maintain righteous beliefs about the purity of their hearts and their inability to behave in discriminatory ways.

So my hope is not that we eliminate stereotypes (a Sisyphean task if ever there was one), but that we all work toward a better understanding of their complexity, their subtlety, and the many ways they affect our behavior. Then perhaps we can use that knowledge to treat our fellow human beings with the dignity they deserve. This is a major goal indeed, one that requires work and dedication, but also one that we can achieve. As we see now in so many parts of the world, failures to make progress toward this goal create misery and cost lives. As I hope this book has demonstrated, we now know enough to make progress, but whether we have the will is quite another story.

References

Aaronson, B. W. (1966). Personality stereotypes of aging. *Journal of Gerontology, 21,* 458–462.

Abate, M., & Berrien, F. K. (1967). Validation of stereotypes: Japanese versus American students. *Journal of Personality and Social Psychology, 7,* 435–438.

Abbey, A. (1982). Sex differences in attributions for friendly behavior: Do males misperceive females' friendliness? *Journal of Personality and Social Psychology, 42,* 830–838.

Abdel-Ghany, M., & Sharpe, D. L. (1994). Racial wage differentials among young adults: Evidence from the 1990s. *Journal of Family and Economic Issues, 15,* 279–294.

Abele, A. E., & Gendolla, G. H. E. (1999). Satisfaction judgments in positive and negative moods: Effects of concurrent assimilation and contrast producing processes. *Personality and Social Psychology Bulletin, 25,* 883–895.

Abele, A. E., Gendolla, G. H. E., & Petzold, P. (1998). Positive mood and in-group–out-group differentiation in a minimal group setting. *Personality and Social Psychology Bulletin, 24,* 1343–1357.

Abelson, R. P. (1988). Conviction. *American Psychologist, 43,* 267–275.

Abelson, R. P., & Kanouse, D. E. (1966). Subjective acceptance of verbal generalizations. In S. Feldman (Ed.), *Cognitive consistency: Motivational antecedents and behavioral consequents* (pp. 171–197). New York: Academic Press.

Aberson, C. L., Healy, M., & Romero, V. (2000). Ingroup bias and self-esteem: A meta-analysis. *Personality and Social Psychology Review, 4,* 157–173.

Aboud, F. E. (1977). Interest in ethnic information: A cross-cultural developmental study. *Canadian Journal of Behavioural Science, 9,* 134–146.

Aboud, F. E. (1980). A test of ethnocentrism with young children. *Canadian Journal of Behavioural Science, 12,* 195–209.

Aboud, F. E. (1984). Social and cognitive bases of ethnic identity constancy. *Journal of Genetic Psychology, 145,* 217–230.

Aboud, F. E. (1989). *Children and prejudice.* Oxford: Blackwell.

Aboud, F. E., & Doyle, A. B. (1996). Parental and peer influences on children's racial attitudes. *International Journal of Intercultural Relations, 20,* 371–383.

Aboud, F. E., & Levy, S. R. (2000). Interventions to reduce prejudice and discrimination in children and adolescents. In S. Oskamp (Ed.), *Reducing prejudice and discrimination* (pp. 269–293). Mahwah, NJ: Erlbaum.

Aboud, F. E., & Skerry, S. A. (1983). Self and ethnic concepts in relation to ethnic constancy. *Canadian Journal of Behavioural Science, 15,* 14–26.

Abrams, D., Carter, J., & Hogg, M. A. (1989). Perceptions of male homosexuality: An application of social identity theory. *Social Behaviour, 4,* 253–264.

Abrams, D., & Hogg, M. A. (1988). Comments on the motivational stratus of self-esteem in social identity and intergroup discrimination. *European Journal of Social Psychology, 18,* 317–334.

Abramson, P. E., Goldberg, P. A., Greenberg, J. H., & Abramson, U. M. (1978). The talking platypus phenomenon: Competency ratings as a function of sex and professional status. *Psychology of Women Quarterly, 2,* 114–124.

Acorn, D. A., Hamilton, D. L., & Sherman, S. J. (1988). Generalization of biased perceptions of groups based on illusory correlation. *Social Cognition, 6,* 345–372.

Adams, G. R. (1982). Physical attractiveness. In A. G. Miller (Ed.), *In the eye of the beholder: Contemporary issues in stereotyping* (pp. 253–304). New York: Praeger.

Addison, W. E. (1989). Beardedness as a factor in perceived masculinity. *Perceptual and Motor Skills, 68,* 921–922.

Adorno, T. W., Frenkel-Brunswik, E., Levinson, D. J., & Sanford, R. N. (1950). *The athoritarian personality.* New York: Harper & Row.

Agnew, C. R., Thompson, V. D., & Gaines, S. O., Jr. (2000). Incorporating proximal and distal influences on prejudice: Testing a general model across outgroups. *Personality and Social Psychology Bulletin, 26,* 403–418.

Agnew, C. R., Thompson, V. D., Smith, V. A., Gramzow, R. H., & Currey, D. P. (1993). Proximal and distal predictors of homophobia: Framing the multivariate roots of outgroup rejection. *Journal of Applied Social Psychology, 23,* 2013–2042.

Agnew, R. (1984). Appearance and deliquency. *Criminology: An Interdisciplinary Journal, 22,* 421–440.

Ahn, W. (1998). Why are different features central for natural kinds and artifacts?: The role of causal status in determining feature centrality. *Cognition, 69,* 135–178.

Ahn, W. (1999). Effect of causal structure on category construction. *Memory and Cognition, 27,* 1008–1023.

Ahn, W., Kalish, C., Gelman, S. A., Medin, D. L., Luhlman, C., Atran, S., Coley, J. D., & Shafto, P. (2001). Why essences are essential in the psychology of concepts. *Cognition, 82,* 59–69.

Ahn, W., Kim, N. S., Lassaline, M. E., & Dennis, M. J. (2000). Causal status as a determinant of feature centrality. *Cognitive Psychology, 41,* 361–416.

Ajzen, I., & Fishbein, M. (1975). A Bayesian analysis of attribution processes. *Psychological Bulletin, 82,* 261–277.

Ajzen, I., & Fishbein, M. (2000). Attitudes and the attitude-behavior relation: Reasoned and automatic processes. In W. Stroebe & M. Hewstone (Eds.), *European review of social psychology* (Vol. 11, pp. 1–33). Chichester, UK: Wiley.

Akrami, N., Ekehammar, B., & Araya, T. (2000). Classical and modern racial prejudice: A study of attitudes toward immigrants in Sweden. *European Journal of Social Psychology, 30,* 521–532.

Alba, J. W., & Hasher, L. (1983). Is memory schematic? *Psychological Bulletin, 93,* 203–231.

Albright, L., Kenny, D. A., & Malloy, T. E. (1988). Consensus in personality judgments at zero acquaintance. *Journal of Personality and Social Psychology, 55,* 387–395.

Alexander, M. G., Brewer, M. B., & Herrmann, R. K. (1999). Images and affect: A functional analysis of out-group stereotypes. *Journal of Personality and Social Psychology, 77,* 78–93.

Alexander, V., & Thoits, P. (1985). Token achievement: An examination of proportional representation and performance outcomes. *Social Forces, 64,* 332–340.

Alfieri, T., Ruble, D. N., & Higgins, E. T. (1996). Gender stereotypes during adolescence: Developmental changes and the transition to junior high school. *Developmental Psychology, 32,* 1129–1137.

Allan, K., & Coltrane, S. (1996). Gender displaying television commercials: A comparative study of television commercials in the 1950s and 1980s. *Sex Roles, 35,* 185–203.

Allen, B. P. (1995). Gender stereotypes are not accurate: A replication of Martin (1987) using diagnostic vs. self-report and behavioral criteria. *Sex Roles, 32,* 583–600.

Allen, B. P. (1996). African Americans' and European Americans' mutual attributions: Adjective generation technique (AGT) stereotyping. *Journal of Applied Social Psychology, 26,* 884–912.

Allen, B. P., & Adams, J. Q. (1992). The concept "race": Let's go back to the beginning. *Journal of Social Behavior and Personality, 7,* 163–168.

Allen, I. L. (1983). *The language of ethnic conflict: Social organization and lexical culture.* New York: Columbia University Press.

Allen, L., Brown, V., Dickinson, L., & Pratt, K. (1941). The relation of first name preferences to their frequency in the culture. *Journal of Social Psychology, 14,* 279–293.

Alley, T. R., & Cunningham, M. R. (1991). Averaged faces are attractive but very attractive faces are not average. *Psychological Science, 2,* 123–125.

Alley, T. R., & Hildebrandt, K. A. (1988). Determinants and consequences of facial asthetics. In T. R. Alley (Ed.), *Social and applied aspects of perceiving faces* (pp. 101–140). Hillsdale, NJ: Erlbaum.

Allison, D. B., Basile, V. C., & Yuker, H. E. (1991). The measurement of attitudes toward and beliefs about obese persons. *International Journal of Eating Disorders, 5,* 599–607.

Allison, S. T., Beggan, J. K., Midgley, E. H., & Wallace, K. A. (1995). Dispositional and behavioral inferences about inherently democratic and unanimous groups. *Social Cognition, 13,* 105–125.

Allison, S. T., Mackie, D. M., & Messick, D. M. (1996). Outcome biases in social perception: Implications for dispositional inference, attitude change, stereotyping and social behavior. In M. P. Zanna (Ed.), *Advances in experimental social psychology* (Vol. 28, pp. 53–93). San Diego, CA: Academic Press.

Allison, S. T., & Messick, D. M. (1985). The group attribution error. *Journal of Experimental Social Psychology, 21,* 563–579.

Allison, S. T., Worth, L. T., & King, M. W. C. (1990). Group decisions as social inference heuristics. *Journal of Personality and Social Psychology, 58,* 801–811.

Alloy, L. B., & Tabachnik, N. (1984). Assessment of covariation by humans and animals: The joint influence of prior expectations and current situational information. *Psychological Review, 91,* 112–149.

Allport, G. W. (1954). *The nature of prejudice.* Garden City, NY: Doubleday/Anchor.

Allport, G. W., & Kramer, B. M. (1946). Some roots of prejudice. *Journal of Psychology, 22,* 9–39.

Aloise-Young, P. A., Hennigan, K. M., & Graham, J. W. (1996). Role of the self-image and smoker stereotype in smoking onset during early adolescence: A longitudinal study. *Health Psychology, 15,* 494–497.

Altemeyer, B. (1981). *Right-wing authoritarianism.* Winnipeg: University of Manitoba Press.

Altemeyer, B. (1988). *Enemies of freedom: Understanding right-wing authoritarianism.* San Francisco: Jossey-Bass.

Altemeyer, B. (1996). *The authoritarian specter.* Cambridge, MA: Harvard University Press.

Altemeyer, B. (1998). The other "authoritarian personality." In M. P. Zanna (Ed.), *Advances in Experimental Social Psychology* (Vol. 30, pp. 47–92). San Diego, CA: Academic Press.

Altemeyer, B., & Hunsberger, B. (1992). Authoritarianism, religious fundamentalism, quest, and prejudice. *International Journal for the Psychology of Religion, 2,* 113–133.

Alzubaidi, A., Baluch, B., & Moafi, A. (1995). Attitudes toward the mentally disabled in a non-Western society. *Journal of Social Behavior and Personality, 10,* 933–938.

Ambady, N., Bernieri, F. J., & Richeson, J. A. (2000). Toward a histology of social behavior: Judgmental accuracy from thin slices of the behavioral stream. In M. P. Zanna (Ed.), *Advances in experimental social psychology* (Vol. 32, pp. 201–271). San Diego, CA: Academic Press.

Ambady, N., Hallahan, M., & Conner, B. (1999). Accuracy of judgments of sexual orientation from thin slices of behavior. *Journal of Personality and Social Psychology, 77,* 538–547.

Ambady, N., & Rosenthal, R. (1993). Half a minute: Predicting teacher evaluations from thin slices of nonverbal behavior and physical attractiveness. *Journal of Personality and Social Psychology, 64,* 431–441.

Amir, Y. (1969). Contact hypothesis in ethnic relations. *Psychological Bulletin, 71,* 319–342.

Amir, Y. (1976). The role of intergroup contact in change of prejudice and ethnic relations. In P. Katz (Ed.), *Towards the elimination of racism* (pp. 245–308). New York: Pergamon Press.

Anastasio, P., Bachman, B., Gaertner, S., & Dovidio, J. (1997). Categorization, recategorization and common group identity. In R. Spears, P. J. Oakes, N. Ellemers, & S. A. Haslam (Eds.), *The social psychology of stereotyping and group life* (pp. 236–256). Oxford: Blackwell.

Andersen, B. L., Cyranowski, J. M., & Espindle, D. (1999). Men's sexual self-schema. *Journal of Personality and Social Psychology, 76*, 645–661.

Andersen, S. M., & Baum, A. (1994). Transferences in interpersonal relations: Inferences and affect based on significant-other representations. *Journal of Personality, 62*, 459–498.

Andersen, S. M., & Cole, S. W. (1990). "Do I know you?": The role of significant others in general social perception. *Journal of Personality and Social Psychology, 59*, 384–399.

Andersen, S. M., Glassman, N. S., Chen, S., & Cole, S. W. (1995). Transference in social perception: The role of chronic accessibility in significant-other representations. *Journal of Personality and Social Psychology, 69*, 41–57.

Andersen, S. M., & Klatzky, R. L. (1987). Traits and social stereotypes: Levels of categorization in person perception. *Journal of Personality and Social Psychology, 53*, 235–246.

Andersen, S. M., Klatzky, R. L., & Murray, J. (1990). Traits and social stereotypes: Efficiency differences in social information processing. *Journal of Personality and Social Psychology, 59*, 192–201.

Anderson, C., & Cromwell, R. L. (1977). "Black is beautiful" and the color preferences of Afro-American youth. *Journal of Negro Education, 46, 76–88.*

Anderson, C. A. (1982). Inoculation and counterexplanation: Debiasing techniques in the perseveration of social theories. *Social Cognition, 1*, 126–139.

Anderson, C. A. (1995). Implicit personality theories and empirical data: Biased assimilation, belief perseverance and chance, and covariation detection sensitivity. *Social Cognition, 13*, 25–48.

Anderson, C. A., Lepper, M. R., & Ross, L. (1980). Perseveration of social theories: The role of explanation in the persistence of discredited information. *Journal of Personality and Social Psychology, 39*, 1037–1049.

Anderson, C. A., & Sedikides, C. (1991). Thinking about people: Contributions of a typological alternative to associationistic and dimensional models of person perception. *Journal of Personality and Social Psychology, 60*, 203–217.

Anderson, J. R. (1991). The adaptive nature of human categorization. *Psychological Review, 98*, 409–429.

Anderson, J. R., & Fincham, J. M. (1996). Categorization and sensitivity to correlation. *Journal of Experimental Psychology: Learning, Memory, and Cognition, 22*, 259–277.

Anderson, L. D. (1921). Estimating intelligence by means of printed photographs. *Journal of Applied Psychology, 5*, 152–155.

Anderson, R. C., & Pichert, J. W. (1978). Recall of previously unrecallable information following a shift in perspective. *Journal of Verbal Learning and Verbal Behavior, 17*, 1–12.

Anderson, T., & Schmitt, R. R. (1990). Unique first names in male and female psychiatric in-patients. *Journal of Social Psychology, 130*, 835–837.

Andre, T., Whigham, M., Hendrickson, A., & Chambers, S. (1999). Competency beliefs, positive affect, and gender stereotypes of elementary students and their parents about science versus other school subjects. *Journal of Research in Science Teaching, 36*, 719–747.

Angermeyer, M. C., & Matschinger, H. (1995). Violent attacks on public figures by persons suffering from psychiatric disorders: Their effect on the social distance towards the mentally ill. *European Archives of Psychiatry and Clinical Neuroscience, 245*, 159–164.

Angermeyer, M. C., & Matschinger, H. (1997). Social distance toward the mentally ill: Results of representative surveys in the Federal Republic of Germany. *Psychological Medicine, 27*, 131–141.

Anisfeld, M., Bogo, N., & Lambert, W. E. (1962). Evaluative reactions to accented English speech. *Journal of Abnormal and Social Psychology, 65*, 223–231.

Anthony, T., Copper, C., & Mullen, B. (1992). Cross-racial facial identification: A social cognitive integration. *Personality and Social Psychology Bulletin, 18*, 296–301.

Appleby, L., & Wessely, S. (1988). Public attitudes to mental illness: The influence of the Hungerford massacre. *Medicine, Science, and the Law, 28*, 291–295.

Archer, D., Iritani, B., Kimes, D. D., & Barrica, M. (1983). Face-ism: Five studies of sex differences in facial prominence. *Journal of Personality and Social Psychology, 45*, 725–735.

Archer, R. P., & Cash, T. F. (1985). Physical attractiveness and maladjustment among psychiatric patients. *Journal of Social and Clinical Psychology, 3*, 170–180.

Arcuri, L. (1982). Three patterns of social categorization in attribution memory. *European Journal of Social Psychology, 12*, 271–282.

Arcuri, L., & Cadinu, M. R. (1992). Asymmetries in the attributional processes: The role of linguistic mediators. In L. Arcuri & C. Serino (Eds.), *Asymmetry Phenomena in interpersonal comparison: Cognitive and social issues* (pp. 87–100). Naples, Italy: Liguori.

Arcuri, L., Maass, A., & Portelli, G. (1993). Linguistic intergroup bias and implicit attributions. *British Journal of Social Psychology, 32,* 277–285.

Arkar, H., & Eker, D. (1994). Effect of psychiatric labels on attitudes toward mental illness in a Turkish sample. *International Journal of Social Psychiatry, 40,* 205–213.

Arkkelin, D., & O'Connor, R., Jr. (1992). The "good" professional: Effects of trait-profile gender type, androgyny, and likeableness on impressions of incumbents of sex-typed occupations. *Sex Roles, 26,* 517–532.

Armstrong, G. B., Neuendorf, K. A., & Brentar, J. E. (1992). TV entertainment, news and racial perceptions of college students. *Journal of Communication, 42,* 153–175.

Armstrong, S. L., Gleitman, L. R., & Gleitman, H. (1983). What some concepts might not be. *Cognition, 13,* 263–308.

Arndt, J., Greenberg, J., Schimel, J., Pyszczynski, T., & Solomon, S. (2002). To belong or not to belong, that is the question: Terror management and identification with gender and ethnicity. *Journal of Personality and Social Psychology, 83,* 26–43.

Aronson, E., Blaney, N., Stephan, C., Sikes, J., & Snapp, M. (1978). *The jigsaw classroom.* Beverly Hills, CA: Sage.

Aronson, E., & Gonzalez, A. (1988). Desegregation, jigsaw, and the Mexican-American experience. In P. A. Katz & D. A. Taylor (Eds.), *Eliminating Racism: Profiles in Controversy* (pp. 301–314). New York: Plenum Press.

Aronson, E., & Patnoe, S. (1997). *The Jigsaw Classroom* (2nd ed.). New York: Longman.

Aronson, J., Lustina, M. J., Good, C., Keough, K., Steele, C. M., & Brown, J. (1999). When white men can't do math: Necessary and sufficient factors in stereotype threat. *Journal of Experimental Social Psychology, 35,* 29–46.

Arroyo, C. G., & Zigler, E. (1995). Racial identity, academic achievement, and the psychological well-being of economically disadvantaged adolescents. *Journal of Personality and Social Psychology, 69,* 903–914.

Ashburn-Nardo, L., Voils, C. I., & Monteith, M. J. (2001). Implicit associations as the seeds of intergroup bias: How easily do they take root? *Journal of Personality and Social Psychology, 81,* 789–799.

Ashe, A. R., Jr. (1988). *A hard road to glory: A history of the African-American athlete.* New York: Warner Books.

Asher, S. R., & Allen, V. (1969). Racial preference and social comparison processes. *Journal of Social Issues, 25,* 157–166.

Ashmore, R. D. (1981). Sex stereotypes and implicit personality theory. In D.L. Hamilton (Ed.), *Cognitive processes in stereotyping and intergroup behavior* (pp. 37–81). Hillsdale, NJ: Erlbaum.

Ashmore, R. D., & Del Boca, F. K. (1979). Sex stereotypes and implicit personality theory: Toward a cognitive–social psychological conceptualization. *Sex Roles, 5,* 219–248.

Ashmore, R. D., & Del Boca, F. K. (1981). Conceptual approaches to stereotypes and stereotyping. In D. L. Hamilton (Ed.), *Cognitive processes in stereotyping and intergroup behavior* (pp. 1–35). Hillsdale, NJ: Erlbaum.

Ashmore, R. D., Del Boca, F. K., & Wohlers, A. J. (1986). Gender stereotypes. In R. D. Ashmore & F. K. Del Boca (Eds.), *The social psychology of female–male relations: A critical analysis of central concepts* (pp. 69–119). Orlando, FL: Academic Press.

Ashmore, R. D., & Longo, L. C. (1995). Accuracy of stereotypes: What research on physical attractiveness can teach us. In Y.-T. Lee, L. J. Jussim, & C. R. McCauley (Eds.), *Stereotype accuracy: Toward appreciating group differences* (pp. 63–86). Washington, DC: American Psychological Association.

Ashmore, R. D., Solomon, M. R., & Longo, L. C. (1996). Thinking about fashion models' looks: A multidimensional approach to the structure of perceived physical attractiveness. *Personality and Social Psychology Bulletin, 22,* 1083–1104.

Ashmore, R. D., & Tumia, M. (1980). Sex stereotypes and implicit personality theory: I. A personality description approach to the assessment of sex stereotypes. *Sex Roles, 6,* 501–518.

Ashton, M. C., & Esses, V. M. (1999). Stereotype accuracy: Estimating the academic performance of ethnic groups. *Personality and Social Psychology Bulletin, 25,* 225-236.

Asuncion, A. G., & Mackie, D. M. (1996). Undermining social stereotypes: Impact of affect-relevant and behavior-relevant information. *Basic and Applied Social Psychology, 18,* 367-386.

Au, T. K.-F. (1986). A verb is worth a thousand words: The causes and consequences of interpersonal events implicit in language. *Journal of Memory and Language, 25,* 104-122.

Aubry, T. D., Tefft, B., & Currie, R. F. (1995). Public attitudes and intentions regarding tenants of community mental health residences who are neighbours. *Community Mental Health Journal, 31,* 39-52.

Augoustinos, M., Ahrens, C., & Innes, J. M. (1994). Stereotypes and prejudice: The Australian experience. *British Journal of Social Psychology, 33,* 125-141.

Augoustinos, M., & Walker, I. (1998). The construction of stereotypes within social psychology: From social cognition to ideology. *Theory and Psychology, 8,* 629-652.

Ayers, I. (1995). Further evidence of discrimination in new car negotiations and estimates of its cause. *Michigan Law Review, 94,* 109-147.

Ayers, I., & Siegelman, P. (1995). Race and gender discrimination in bargaining for a new car. *American Economic Review, 85,* 304-322.

Babad, E. Y., Inbar, J., & Rosenthal, R. (1982). Pygmalion, Galatea, and the Golem: Investigations of biased and unbiased teachers. *Journal of Educational Psychology, 74,* 459-474.

Babey, S. H., Queller, S., & Klein, S. B. (1998). The role of expectancy violating behaviors in the representation of trait knowledge: A summary-plus-exception model of social memory. *Social Cognition, 16,* 287-339.

Bailenson, J. N., Shum, M. S., Atran, S., Medin, D. L., & Coley, J. (2002). A bird's eye view: Biological categorization and reasoning within and across cultures. *Cognition, 84,* 1-53.

Bailey, R. C., Reynolds, F., & Carrico, M. (1989). College students' perceptions of AIDS victims. *Social Behavior and Personality, 17,* 199-204.

Bailey, J. M., & Zucker, K. J. (1995). Childhood sex-typed behavior and sexual orientation: A conceptual analysis and quantitative review. *Developmental Psychology, 31,* 43-55.

Baldwin, J. R., Day, L. E., & Hecht, M. L. (2000). The structure(s) of racial attitudes among white college students. *International Journal of Intercultural Relations, 24,* 553-577.

Balter, R. (1999). From stigmatization to patronization: The media's distorted portrayal of physical disability. In L.L. Schwartz (Ed.), *Psychology and the media: A second look* (pp. 147-171). Washington, DC: American Psychological Association.

Banaji, M. R., & Greenwald, A. G. (1994). Implicit stereotyping and prejudice. In M. P. Zanna & J. M. OLson (Eds.), *The Ontario Symposium: Vol. 7. The psychology of prejudice* (pp. 55-76). Hillsdale, NJ: Erlbaum.

Banaji, M. R., & Greenwald, A. G. (1995). Implicit gender stereotyping in judgments of fame. *Journal of Personality and Social Psychology, 68,* 181-198.

Banaji, M. R., & Hardin, C. D. (1996). Automatic stereotyping. *Psychological Science, 7,* 136-141.

Bandura, A. (1994). Social cognitive theory of mass communication. In J. Bryant & D. Zillmann (Eds.), *Media effects: Advances in theory and research* (pp. 61-90). Hillsdale, NJ: Erlbaum.

Banks, R. R., & Eberhardt, J. L. (1998). Social psychological processes and the legal bases of racial categorization. In J. L. Eberhardt & S. T. Fiske (Eds.), *Confronting racism: The problem and the response* (pp. 54-75). Thousand Oaks, CA: Sage.

Banse, R., Seise, J., & Zerbes, N. (2001). Implicit attitudes towards homosexuality: Reliability, validity, and controllability of the IAT. *Zeitschrift für Experimentelle Psychologie, 48,* 145-160.

Bardack, N. R., & McAndrew, F. T. (1985). The influence of physical attractiveness and manner of dress on success in a simulated personnel decision. *Journal of Social Psychology, 125,* 777-778.

Bargh, J. A. (1989). Conditional automaticity: Varieties of automatic influence in social perception and cognition. In J. S. Uleman & J. A. Bargh (Eds.), *Unintended thought* (pp. 3-51). New York: Guilford Press.

Bargh, J. A. (1996). Automaticity in social psychology. In E. T. Higgins & A. W. Kruglanski (Eds.), *Social psychology: Handbook of basic principles* (pp. 169-183). New York: Guilford Press.

Bargh, J. A. (1999). The cognitive monster: The case against the controllability of automatic stereotype effects. In S. Chaiken & Y. Trope (Eds.), *Dual-process theories in social psychology* (pp. 361–382). New York: Guilford Press.

Bargh, J. A., Bond, R. N., Lombardi, W. J., & Tota, M. E. (1986). The additive nature of chronic and temporary sources of construct accessibility. *Journal of Personality and Social Psychology, 50,* 869–878.

Bargh, J. A., Chen, M., & Burrows, L. (1996). Automaticity of social behavior: Direct effects of trait construct and stereotype activation on action. *Journal of Personality and Social Psychology, 71,* 230–244.

Bargh, J. A., & Thein, R. D. (1985). Individual construct accessibility, person memory, and the recall-judgment link: The case of information overload. *Journal of Personality and Social Psychology, 49,* 1129–1146.

Bar-Hillel, M. (1984). Representativenss and fallacies of probability. *Acta Psychologica, 55,* 91–107.

Bar-Hillel, M., & Fischhoff, B. (1981). When do base rates affect predictions? *Journal of Personality and Social Psychology, 41,* 671–680.

Barkowitz, P., & Brigham, J.C. (1982). Recognition of faces: Own-race bias, incentive, and time delay. *Journal of Applied Social Psychology, 12,* 255–268.

Baron, R. A., Markman, G. D., & Hirsa, A. (2001). Perceptions of women and men as entrepreneurs: Evidence for differential effects of attributional augmenting. *Journal of Applied Psychology, 86,* 923–929.

Baron, R. M. (1995). An ecological view of stereotype accuracy. In Y.-T. Lee, L. J. Jussim, & C. R. McCauley (Eds.), *Stereotype accuracy: Toward appreciating group differences* (pp. 115–140). Washington, DC: American Psychological Association.

Baron, R. M., & Misovich, S. J. (1993). Dispositional knowing from an ecological perspective. *Personality and Social Psychology Bulletin, 19,* 541–552.

Baron, R. S., Burgess, M. L., & Kao, C. F. (1991). Detecting and labeling prejudice: Do female perpetrators go undetected? *Personality and Social Psychology Bulletin, 17,* 115–123.

Barry, M. M. (1994). Community perceptions of mental disorder: An Irish perspective. *Irish Journal of Psychology, 15,* 418–447.

Barry, M. M., & Greene, S. M. (1992). Implicit models of mental disorder: A qualitative approach to the delineation of public attitudes. *Irish Journal of Psychology, 13,* 141–160.

Barsalou, L. W. (1983). Ad hoc categories. *Memory and Cognition, 11,* 211–227.

Barsalou, L. W. (1985). Ideals, central tendency, and frequency of instantiation as determinants of graded structure in categories. *Journal of Experimental Psychology: Learning, Memory, and Cognition, 11,* 629–649.

Barsalou, L. W. (1987). The instability of graded structure: Implications for the nature of concepts. In U. Neisser (Ed.), *Concepts and conceptual development ecological and intellectual factors in categorization* (pp. 101–140). Cambridge, UK: Cambridge University Press.

Barsalou, L. W. (1989). Intraconcept similarity and its implications for interconcept similarity. In S. Vosniadou & A. Ortony (Eds.), *Similarity and analogical reasoning* (pp. 76–121). Cambridge, UK: Cambridge University Press.

Barstow, A. L. (1994). *Witchcraft: A new history of the European witch hunts.* New York: Harper-Collins.

Bartlett, F. F. (1932). *Remembering.* Cambridge, UK: Cambridge University Press.

Bar-Tal, D. (1998). Group beliefs as an expression of social identity. In S. Worchel, J.F. Morales, D. Páez, & J.-C. Deschamps (Eds.), *Social identity: International perspectives* (pp. 93–113). London: Sage.

Bar-Tal, D., & Labin, D. (2001). The effect of a major event on stereotyping: Terrorist attacks in Israel and Israeli adolescents' perceptions of Palestinians, Jordanians and Arabs. *European Journal of Social Psychology, 31,* 265–280.

Bartolini, T., Kresge, J., McLennan, M. M., Windham, B., Buhr, T. A., & Pryor, B. (1988). Perceptions of personal characteristics of men and women under three conditions of eyewear. *Perceptual and Motor Skills, 67,* 779–782.

Bass, B. M. (1955). Authoritarianism or acqiescence? *Journal of Abnormal and Social Psychology, 51,* 616–623.

Bassili, J. N., & Reil, R. (1981). On the dominance of the old-age stereotype. *Journal of Gerontology,* *36,* 682–688.

Bassili, J. N., & Smith, M. C. (1986). On the spontaneity of trait attributions: Converging evidence for the role of cognitive strategy. *Journal of Personality and Social Psychology, 50,* 239–245.

Bassok, M., & Trope, Y. (1983–1984). People's strategies for testing hypotheses about another's personality: Confirmatory or diagnostic? *Social Cognition, 2,* 199–216.

Bat-Chava, Y. (1994). Group identification and self-esteem of deaf adults. *Personality and Social Psychology Bulletin, 20,* 494–502.

Batson, C. D., & Burris, C. T. (1994). Personal religion: Depressant or stimulant of prejudice and discrimination? In M. P. Zanna & J. M. Olson (Eds.), *The Ontario Symposium: Vol. 7. The psychology of predice* (pp. 149–169). Hillsdale, NJ: Erlbaum.

Batson, C. D., Chang, J., Orr, R., & Rowland, J. (2002). Empathy, attitudes and action: Can feeling for a member of a stigmatized group motivate one to help the group? *Personality and Social Psychology Bulletin, 28,* 1656–1666.

Batson, C. D., Polycarpou, M. P., Harmon-Jones, E., Imhoff, H. J., Mitchener, E. C., Bednar, L. L., Klein, T. R., & Highberger, L. (1997). Empathy and attitudes: Can feeling for a member of a stigmatized group improve feelings toward the group? *Journal of Personality and Social Psychology, 72,* 105–118.

Bayton, J. A. (1941). The racial stereotypes of Negro college students. *Journal of Abnormal and Social Psychology, 36,* 97–102.

Bayton, J. A., & Byoune, E. (1947). Racio-national stereotypes held by Negroes. *Journal of Negro Education, 16,* 49–56.

Bayton, J. A., McAlister, L. B., & Hamer, J. R. (1956). Race–class stereotypes. *Journal of Negro Education, 25,* 75–78.

Bayton, J. A., & Muldrow, J. W. (1968). Interacting variables in the perception of racial personality traits. *Journal of Experimental Research in Personality, 3,* 39–44.

Bazzini, D. G., McIntosh, W. D., Smith, S. M., Cook, S., & Harris, C. (1997). The aging woman in popular film: Underrepresented, unattractive, unfriendly, and unintelligent. *Sex Roles, 36,* 531–543.

Beauvais, C., & Spence, J. T. (1987). Gender, prejudice, and categorization. *Sex Roles, 16,* 89–100.

Beck, L., McCauley, C., Segal, M., & Hershey, L. (1988). Individual differences in prototypicality judgments about trait categories. *Journal of Personality and Social Psychology, 55,* 286–192.

Beck, S. B., Ward-Hull, C. I., & McLear, P. M. (1976). Variables related to women's somatic preferences of the male and female body. *Journal of Personality and Social Psychology, 34,* 1200–1210.

Beckett, N. E., & Park, B. (1995). Use of category versus individuating information: Making base rates salient. *Personality and Social Psychology Bulletin, 21,* 21–31.

Beggs, J. M., & Doolittle, D. C. (1993). Perceptions now and then of occupational sex typing: A replication of Shinar's 1975 study. *Journal of Applied Social Psychology, 23,* 1435–1453.

Belk, S. S., & Snell, W. E., Jr. (1986). Beliefs about women: Components and correlates. *Personality and Social Psychology Bulletin, 12,* 403–413.

Belk, S. S., Snell, W. E., Jr., Holtzman, W. H., Jr., Hernandez-Sanchez, J., & Garcia-Falconi, R. (1989). The impact of ethnicity, nationality, counseling orientation, and mental health standards on stereotypic beliefs about women: A pilot study. *Sex Roles, 21,* 671–695.

Bell, J. (1992). In search of a discourse on aging: The elderly on television. *Gerontologist, 32,* 305–311.

Bell, R. A. (1984). Relationship of loneliness to desirability and uniqueness of first names. *Psychological Reports, 55,* 950.

Bem, S. L. (1981). Gender schema theory: A cognitive account of sex typing. *Psychological Review, 88,* 354–364.

Bem, S. L. (1985). Androgyny and gender schema theory: A conceptual and empirical integration. In T. B. Sonderegger (Ed.), *Nebraska Symposium on Motivation* (Vol. 32, pp. 179–226). Lincoln: University of Nebraska Press.

Bem, S. L. (1989). Genital knowledge and gender constancy in preschool children. *Child Development, 60,* 649–662.

Ben-Ari, R., Schwarzwald, J., & Horiner-Levi, E. (1994). The effects of prevalent social stereotypes on intergroup attribution. *Journal of Cross-Cultural Psychology, 25*, 489–500.

Bergami, M., & Bagozzi, R. P. (2000). Self-categorization, affective commitment and group self-esteem as distinct aspects of social identity in the organization. *British Journal of Social Psychology, 39*, 555–577.

Bergen, D. J., & Williams, J. E. (1991). Sex stereotypes in the United States revisited: 1972–1988. *Sex Roles, 24*, 413–423.

Berman, J. S., & Kenny, D. A. (1976). Correlational bias in observer ratings. *Journal of Personality and Social Psychology, 34*, 263–273.

Bernat, G., & Balch, P. (1979). The Chicano Racial Attitude Measure (CRAM): Results of an initial investigation. *American Journal of Community Psychology, 7*, 137–146.

Berndsen, M., Spears, R., McGarty, C., & van der Pligt, J. (1998). Dynamics of differentiation: Similarity as the precursor and product of stereotype formation. *Journal of Personality and Social Psychology, 74*, 1451–1463.

Berndsen, M., Spears, R., & van der Pligt, J. (1996). Illusory correlation and attitude-based vested interest. *European Journal of Social Psychology, 26*, 247–264.

Berndt, T. J., & Heller, K. A. (1986). Gender stereotypes and social inferences: A developmental study. *Journal of Personality and Social Psychology, 50*, 889–898.

Berninger, V. W., & DeSoto, C. (1985). Cognitive representation of personal stereotypes. *European Journal of Social Psychology, 15*, 189–211.

Berry, D. S. (1990a). The perceiver as naive scientist or the scientist as naive perceiver?: An ecological view of social knowledge acquisition. *Contemporary Social Psychology, 14*, 145–153.

Berry, D. S. (1990b). Vocal attractiveness and vocal babyishness: Effects on stranger, self- and friend impressions. *Journal of Nonverbal Behavior, 14*, 141–153.

Berry, D. S. (1990c). What can a moving face tell us? *Journal of Personality and Social Psychology, 58*, 1004–1014.

Berry, D. S. (1991). Attractive faces are not all created equal: Joint effects of facial babyishness and attractiveness on social perception. *Personality and Social Psychology Bulletin, 17*, 523–531.

Berry, D. S., & Brownlow, S. (1989). Were the physiognomists right?: Personality correlates of facial babyishness. *Personality and Social Psychology Bulletin, 15*, 266–279.

Berry, D. S., & Zebrowitz-McArthur, L. Z. (1985). Some components and consequences of a babyface. *Journal of Personality and Social Psychology, 48*, 312–323.

Berry, D. S., & Zebrowitz-McArthur, L. Z. (1986). Perceiving character in faces: The impact of age-related craniofacial changes on social perception. *Psychological Bulletin, 100*, 3–18.

Berry, D. S., & Zebrowitz-McArthur, L. (1988). What's in a face?: Facial maturity and the attribution of legal responsibility. *Personality and Social Psychology Bulletin, 14*, 23–33.

Berry, J. W. (1970). A functional approach to the relationship between stereotypes and familarity. *Australian Journal of Psychology, 22*, 29–33.

Berry, J. W. (1984). Cultural relations in a plural society: Alternatives to segregation and their sociopsychological implication. In N. Miller & M. B. Brewer (Eds.), *Groups in contact: The psychology of desegregation* (pp. 11–27). Orlando, FL: Academic Press.

Berscheid, E., Graziano, W., Monson, T., & Dermer, M. (1976). Outcome dependency: Attention, attribution, and attraction. *Journal of Personality and Social Psychology, 34*, 978–789.

Berscheid, E., & Reis, H. T. (1998). Attraction and close relationships. In D. T. Gilbert, S. T. Fiske, & G. Lindzey (Eds.), *The handbook of social psychology* (4th ed., Vol. 2, pp. 193–282). Boston: McGraw-Hill.

Bessenoff, G. R., & Sherman, J. W. (2000). Automatic and controlled components of prejudice toward fat people: Evaluation versus stereotype activation. *Social Cognition, 18*, 329–353.

Best, D. L., Williams, J. E., & Briggs, S. R. (1980). A further analysis of the affective meanings associated with male and female sex-trait stereotypes. *Sex Roles, 6*, 735–746.

Betancourt, H., & Lopez, S. (1993). The study of culture, ethnicity, and race in American psychology. *American Psychologist, 48*, 629–637.

Bettencourt, B. A., Charlton, K., Dorr, N., & Hume, D. L. (2001). Status differences and in-group bias: A meta-analytic examination of the effects of status stability, status legitimacy, and group permeability. *Psychological Bulletin, 127*, 520–542.

Bettencourt, B. A., Dill, K. E., Greathouse, S. A., Charlton, K., & Mulholland, A. (1997). Evaluations of ingroup and outgroup members: The role of category-based expectancy violation. *Journal of Experimental Social Psychology, 33,* 244–275.

Bettencourt, B. A., & Dorr, N. (1998). Cooperative interaction and intergroup bias: Effects of numerical representation and cross-cut role assignment. *Personality and Social Psychology Bulletin, 24,* 1276–1293.

Bettencourt, B. A., & Hume, D. (1999). The cognitive contents of social-group identity: Values, emotions, and relationships. *European Journal of Social Psychology, 29,* 113–121.

Biela, A., McKeachie, W. J., Lin, Y.-G., & Lingoes, J. (1993). Judgment of in-groups and out-groups by members of three denominations in the United States and Poland. *Journal of Psychology and Christianity, 12,* 225–235.

Bierly, M. M. (1985). Prejudice toward contemporary outgroups as a generalized attitude. *Journal of Applied Social Psychology, 15,* 189–199.

Biernat, M. (1990). Stereotypes on campus: How contact and liking influence perceptions of group distinctiveness. *Journal of Applied Social Psychology, 20,* 1485–1513.

Biernat, M. (1991). Gender stereotypes and the relationship between masculinity and femininity: A developmental analysis. *Journal of Personality and Social Psychology, 61,* 351–365.

Biernat, M., & Crandall, C. S. (1994). Stereotyping and contact with social groups: Measurement and conceptual issues. *European Journal of Social Psychology, 24,* 659–677.

Biernat, M., & Crandall, C. S. (1996). Creating stereotypes and capturing their content. *European Journal of Social Psychology, 26,* 867–898.

Biernat, M., Crandall, C. S., Young, L. V., Kobrynowicz, D., & Halpin, S. M. (1998). All that you can be: Stereotyping of self and others in a military context. *Journal of Personality and Social Psychology, 75,* 301–317.

Biernat, M., & Kobrynowicz, D. (1997). Gender- and race-based standards of competence: Lower minimum standards but higher ability standards for devalued groups. *Journal of Personality and Social Psychology, 72,* 544–557.

Biernat, M., & Manis, M. (1994). Shifting standards and stereotype-based judgments. *Journal of Personality and Social Psychology, 66,* 5–20.

Biernat, M., Manis, M., & Nelson, T. E. (1991). Stereotypes and standards of judgment. *Journal of Personality and Social Psychology, 60,* 485–499.

Biernat, M., & Thompson, E. R. (2002). Shifting standards and contextual variation in stereotyping. In W. Stroebe & M. Hewstone (Eds.), *European Review of Social Psychology* (Vol. 12, pp. 103–137). Chichester, UK: Wiley.

Biernat, M., & Vescio, T. K. (1993). Categorization and stereotyping: Effects of group context on memory and social judgment. *Journal of Experimental Social Psychology, 29,* 166–202.

Biernat, M., & Vescio, T. K. (2002). She swings, she hits, she's great, she's benched: Implications of gender-based shifting standards for judgment and behavior. *Personality and Social Psychology Bulletin, 28,* 66–77.

Biernat, M., Vescio, T. K., & Billings, L. S. (1999). Black sheep and expectancy violation: Integrating two models of social judgment. *European Journal of Social Psychology, 29,* 523–542.

Biernat, M., Vescio, T. K., & Green, M. L. (1996). Selective self-stereotyping. *Journal of Personality and Social Psychology, 71,* 1194–1209.

Biernat, M., Vescio, T. K., & Manis, M. (1998). Judging and behaving toward members of stereotyped groups: A shifting standards perspective. In C. Sedikides, J. Schopler, & C. A. Insko (Eds.), *Intergroup cognition and intergroup behavior* (pp. 151–175). Mahwah, NJ: Erlbaum.

Biernat, M., Vescio, T. K., & Theno, S. A. (1996). Violating American values: A "value congruence" approach to understanding outgroup attitudes. *Journal of Experimental Social Psychology, 32,* 387–410.

Biernat, M., Vescio, T. K., Theno, S. A., & Crandall, C. S. (1996). Values and prejudice: Toward understanding the impact of American values on outgroup attitudes. In C. Seligman & M. P. Zanna (Eds.), *The Ontario Symposium: Vol. 8. The psychology of values* (pp. 153–189). Mahwah, NJ: Erlbaum.

Biesanz, J. C., Neuberg, S. L., Smith, D. M., Asher, T., & Judice, T. N. (2001). When accuracy-motivated perceivers fail: Limited attentional resources and the reemerging self-fulfilling prophecy. *Personality and Social Psychology Bulletin, 27,* 621–629.

Bigler, R. S., Jones, L. C., & Lobliner, D. B. (1997). Social categorization and the formation of intergroup attitudes in children. *Child Development, 68,* 530–543.

Bigler, R. S., & Liben, L. S. (1992). Cognitive mechanisms in children's gender stereotyping: Theoretical and educational implications of a cognitive-based intervention. *Child Development, 63,* 1351–1363.

Bird, C., Monachesi, E. O., & Burdick, H. (1952). Infiltration and the attitudes of white and Negro parents and children. *Journal of Abnormal and Social Psychology, 47,* 688–699.

Bishop, G. D., Alva, A. L., Cantu, L., & Rittiman, T. K. (1991). Responses to persons with AIDS: Fear of contagion or stigma? *Journal of Applied Social Psychology, 21,* 1877–1888.

Bizman, A., & Yinon, Y. (2001). Intergroup and interpersonal threats as determinants of prejudice: The moderating role of in-group identification. *Basic and Applied Social Psychology, 23,* 191–196.

Black, D. (1980). *The Manners and Customs of the Police.* New York: Academic Press.

Blackman, M. C., & Funder, D. C. (1998). The effect of infrmation on consensus and accuracy in personality judgment. *Journal of Experimental Social Psychology, 34,* 164–181.

Blair, I. V. (2002). The malleability of automatic stereotypes and prejudice. *Personality and Social Psychology Review, 6,* 242–261.

Blair, I. V., & Banaji, M. R. (1996). Automatic and controlled processes in stereotype priming. *Journal of Personality and Social Psychology, 70,* 1142–1163.

Blair, I. V., Judd, C. M., Sadler, M. S., & Jenkins, C. (2002). The role of Afrocentric features in person perception: Judging by features and categories. *Journal of Personality and Social Psychology, 83,* 5–25.

Blair, I. V., Ma, J. E., & Lenton, A. P. (2001). Imagining stereotypes away: The moderation of implicit stereotypes through mental imagery. *Journal of Personality and Social Psychology, 81,* 828–841.

Blanchard, F. A., Adelman, L., & Cook, S. W. (1975). Effect of group success and failure upon interpersonal attraction in cooperating interracial groups. *Journal of Personality and Social Psychology, 31,* 1020–1030.

Blanchard, F. A., Crandall, C. S., Brigham, J. C., & Vaughn, L. A. (1994). Condemning and condoning racism: A socal context approach to interracial settings. *Journal of Applied Psychology, 79,* 993–997.

Blanchard, F. A., Lilly, T., & Vaughn, L. A. (1991). Reducing the expression of racial prejudice. *Psychological Science, 2,* 101–105.

Blanz, M. (1999). Accessibility and fit as determinants of the salience of social categorizations. *European Journal of Social Psychology, 29,* 43–74.

Blanz, M., & Aufderheide, B. (1999). Social categorization and category attribution: The effects of comparative and normative fit on memory and social judgment. *British Journal of Social Psychology, 38,* 157–179.

Blanz, M., Mummendey, A., & Otten, S. (1997). Normative evaluations and frequency expectations regarding positive versus negative outcome allocations between groups. *European Journal of Social Psychology, 27,* 165–176.

Blascovich, J., Mendes, W. B., Hunter, S. B., Lickel, B., & Kowai-Bell, N. (2001). Perceiver threat in social interactions with stigmatized others. *Journal of Personality and Social Psychology, 80,* 253–267.

Blascovich, J., Spencer, S. J., Quinn, D., & Steele, C. (2001). African Americans and high blood pressure: The role of stereotype threat. *Psychological Science, 12,* 225–229.

Blascovich, J., Wyer, N. A., Swart, L. A., & Kibler, J. L. (1997). Racism and racial categorization. *Journal of Personality and Social Psychology, 72,* 1364–1372.

Blaske, D. M. (1984). Occupational sex-typing by kindergarten and fourth-grade children. *Psychological Reports, 54,* 795–801.

Bless, H., Clore, G. L., Schwarz, N., Golisano, V., Rabe., C., & Wölk, M. (1996). Mood and the use of scripts: Does a happy mood really lead to mindlessness? *Journal of Personality and Social Psychology, 71,* 665–679.

Bless, H., Schwarz, N., Bodenhausen, G. V., & Thiel, L. (2001). Personalized versus generalized benefits of stereotype disconfirmation: Trade-offs in the evaluation of atypical exemplars and their social groups. *Journal of Experimental Social Psychology, 37,* 386–397.

Bless, H., Schwarz, M., & Kemmelmeier, M. (1996). Mood and stereotyping: Affective states and the use of general knowledge structures. In W. Stroebe & M. Hewstone (Eds.), *European review of social psychology* (Vol. 7, pp. 63–93). Chichester, UK: Wiley.

Blizard, P. J. (1968). Public images of the mentally ill in New Zealand. *New Zealand Medical Journal, 68,* 297–303.

Blizard, P. J. (1970). The social rejection of the alcoholic and the mentally ill in New Zealand. *Social Science and Medicine, 4,* 513–526.

Bloom, P. (1996). Intention, history, and artifact concepts. *Cognition, 60,* 1–29.

Bloom, P., & Veres, C. (1999). The perceived intentionality of groups. *Cognition, 71,* B1–B9.

Blumstein, A. (1993). Racial disproportionality of U.S. prison populations revisited. *University of Colorado Law Review, 64,* 743–760.

Bobo, L., & Kluegel, J. R. (1997). Status, ideology, and dimensions of whites' racial beliefs and attitudes: Progress and stagnation. In S. A. Tuch & J. K. Martin (Eds.), *Racial attitudes in the 1990s: Continuity and change* (pp. 93–120). Westport, CT: Praeger.

Bodenhausen, G. V. (1988). Stereotypic biases in social decision making and memory: Testing process models of stereotype use. *Journal of Personality and Social Psychology, 55,* 726–737.

Bodenhausen, G. V. (1990). Stereotypes as judgmental heuristics: Evidence of circadian variations in discrimination. *Psychological Science, 1,* 319–322.

Bodenhausen, G. V., Kramer, G. P., & Süsser, K. (1994). Happiness and stereotypic thinking in social judgment. *Journal of Personality and Social Psychology, 66,* 621–632.

Bodenhausen, G. V., & Lichtenstein, M. (1987). Social stereotypes and information-processing strategies: The impact of task complexity. *Journal of Personality and Social Psychology, 52,* 871– 880.

Bodenhausen, G. V., & Macrae, C. N. (1996). The self-regulation of intergroup perception: Mechanisms and consequences of stereotype suppression. In C. N. Macrae, C. Stangor, & M. Hewstone (Eds.), *Stereotypes and stereotyping* (pp. 227–253). New York: Guilford Press.

Bodenhausen, G. V., & Macrae, C. N. (1998). Stereotype activation and inhibition. In R. S. Wyer, Jr. (Ed.), *Advances in social cognition: Vol. 11. Stereotype activation and inhibition* (pp. 1–52). Mahwah, NJ: Erlbaum.

Bodenhausen, G. V., Macrae, C. N., & Garst, J. (1998). Stereotypes in thought and deed: Social-cognitive origins of intergroup discrimination. In C. Sedikides, J. Schopler, & C. A. Insko (Eds.), *Intergroup cognition and intergroup behavior* (pp. 311–335). Mahwah, NJ: Erlbaum.

Bodenhausen, G. V., Macrae, C. N., & Sherman, J. W. (1999). On the dialectics of discrimination: Dual processes in social stereotyping. In S. Chaiken & Y. Trope (Eds.), *Dual-process theories in social psychology* (pp. 271–290). New York: Guilford Press.

Bodenhausen, G. V., Sheppard, L. A., & Kramer, G. P. (1994). Negative affect and social judgment: The differential impact of anger and sadness. *European Journal of Social Psychology, 24,* 45–62.

Bodenhausen, G. V., & Wyer, R. S., Jr. (1985). Effects of stereotypes on decision making and information-processing strategies. *Journal of Personality and Social Psychology, 48,* 267–282.

Bohner, G., Bless, H., Schwarz, N., & Strack, F. (1988). When do events trigger attributions?: The impact of valence and subjective probability. *European Journal of Social Psychology, 18,* 335–345.

Boldry, J. G., & Kashy, D. A. (1999). Intergroup perception in naturally occurring groups of differential status: A social relations perspective. *Journal of Personality and Social Psychology, 77* 1200–1212.

Bond, M. H. (1972). Effect of impression set on subsequent behavior. *Journal of Personality and Social Psychology, 24,* 301–305.

Bond, M. H. (1985). Language as a carrier of ethnic stereotypes in Hong Kong. *Journal of Social Psychology, 125,* 53–62.

Bond, M. H. (1986). Mutual stereotypes and the facilitation of interaction across cultural lines. *International Journal of Intercultural Relations, 10,* 259–276.

Bond, S., & Cash, T. F. (1992). Black beauty: Skin color and body images among African-American college women. *Journal of Applied Social Psychology, 22,* 874–888.

Bordieri, J. E., & Drehmer, D. E. (1986). Hiring decisions for disabled workers: Looking at the cause. *Journal of Applied Social Psychology, 16,* 197–208.

Borg, M. R. (1996). *The role of career model prototypicality and age on children's occupational gender stereotypes and career interest.* Unpublished doctoral dissertation, Rice University.

Borgida, E., & Brekke, N. (1981). The base rate fallacy in attribution and prediction. In J. H. Harvey, W. Ickes, & R. F. Kidd (Eds.), *New directions in attribution research* (Vol. 3, pp. 63–95). Hillsdale, NJ: Erlbaum.

Borgida, E., Rudman, L. A., & Manteufel, L. L. (1995). On the courtroom use and misuse of gender stereotyping research. *Journal of Social Issues, 51,* 181–192.

Borkenau, P. (1990). Traits as ideal-based and goal-directed social categories. *Journal of Personality and Social Psychology, 58,* 381–396.

Borkenau, P., & Müller, B. (1992). Inferring act frequencies and traits from behavior observations. *Journal of Personality, 60,* 553–573.

Borkenau, P., & Ostendorf, F. (1987). Fact and fiction in implicit personality theory. *Journal of Personality, 55,* 415–443.

Bose, C. E., & Rossi, P. H. (1978). Gender and jobs: Prestige standings of occupations as affected by gender. *American Sociological Review, 48,* 316–330.

Bothwell, R. K., Brigham, J. C., & Malpass, R. S. (1989). Cross-racial identification. *Personality and Social Psychology Bulletin, 15,* 19–25.

Boulding, K. (1959). National images and international systems. *Journal of Conflict Resolution, 3,* 120–131.

Bouton, R. A., Gallaher, R. E., Garlinghouse, R. A., Leal, T., Rosenstein, L. D., & Young, R. K. (1989). Demographic variables associated with fear of AIDS and homophobia. *Journal of Applied Social Psychology, 19,* 885–901.

Bower, G. H. (1981). Mood and memory. *American Psychologist, 36,* 129–148.

Bower, G. H. (1991). Mood congruity of social judgments. In J. P. Forgas (Ed.), *Emotion and social judgments* (pp. 31–53). New York: Pergamon Press.

Bower, G. H., Black, J. B., & Turner, T. J. (1979). Scripts in memory for text. *Cognitive Psychology, 11,* 177–220.

Brabant, S., & Mooney, L. A. (1997). Sex role stereotyping in the Sunday comics: A twenty year update. *Sex Roles, 37,* 269–281.

Braddock, J. H., II. (1985). School desegregation and black assimilation. *Journal of Social Issues, 41*(3), 9–23.

Braithwaite, V. A. (1986). Old age stereotypes: reconciling contradictions. *Journal of Gerontology, 41,* 353–360.

Branch, C. W., & Newcomb, N. (1980). Racial attitudes of black preschoolers as related to parental civil rights activism. *Merrill–Palmer Quarterly, 26,* 425–428.

Branch, C. W., & Newcomb, N. (1986). Racial attitude development among young black children as a function of parental attitudes: A longitudinal and cross-sectional study. *Child Development, 57,* 712–721.

Branco, K. J., & Williamson, J. B. (1982). Stereotyping and the life cycle: Views of aging and the aged. In A. G. Miller (Ed.), *In the eye of the beholder: Contemporary issues in stereotyping* (pp. 364–410). New York: Praeger.

Branscombe, N. R., Deaux, K., & Lerner, M. S. (1985). Individual differences and the influence of context on categorization and prejudice. *Representative Research in Social Psychology, 15,* 25–35.

Branscombe, N. R., Ellemers, N., Spears, R., & Doosje, B. (1999). The context and content of social identity threat. In N. Ellemers, R. Spears, & B. Doosje (Eds.), *Social identity: Context, commitment, content* (pp. 35–58). Oxford: Blackwell.

Branscombe, N. R., & Owen, S. (1991). Influence of gun ownership on social inferences abour women and men. *Journal of Applied Social Psychology, 21,* 1567–1589.

Branscombe, N. R., & Smith, E. R. (1990). Gender and racial stereotypes in impression formation and social decision-making processes. *Sex Roles, 22,* 627–647.

Branscombe, N. R., & Wann, D. L. (1994). Collective self-esteem consequences of outgroup derogation when a valued social identity is on trial. *European Journal of Social Psychology, 24,* 641–657.

Brauer, M. (2001). Intergroup perception in the social context: The effects of social status and group membership on perceived out-group homogeneity and ethnocentrism. *Journal of Experimental Social Psychology, 37,* 15–31.

Brauer, M., Judd, C. M., & Jacquelin, V. (2001). The communication of social stereotypes: The effects of group discussion and information distribution on stereotypic appraisals. *Journal of Personality and Social Psychology, 81*, 463–475.

Brauer, M., Wasel, W., & Niedenthal, P. (2000). Implicit and explicit components of prejudice. *Review of General Psychology, 4*, 79–101.

Breland, A. M. (1998). A model for differential perceptions of competence based on skin tone among African Americans. *Journal of Multicultural Counseling and Development, 26*, 294–311.

Brendl, C. M., & Higgins, E. T. (1996). Principles of judging valence: What makes events positive or negative? In M. P. Zanna (Ed.), *Advances in experimental social psychology* (Vol. 28, pp. 95–160). San Diego, CA: Academic Press.

Brendl, C. M., Markman, A. B., & Messner, C. (2001). How do indirect measures of evaluation work?: Evaluating the inference of prejudice in the implicit association test. *Journal of Personality and Social Psychology, 81*, 760–773.

Brewer, M. B. (1979). In-group bias in the minimal intergroup situation: A cognitive-motivational analysis. *Psychological Bulletin, 86*, 307–324.

Brewer, M. B. (1988). A dual process model of impression formation. In T. K. Srull & R. S. Wyer, Jr. (Eds.), *Advances in social cognition* (Vol. 1, pp. 1–36). Hillsdale, NJ: Erlbaum.

Brewer, M. B. (1991). The social self: On being the same and different at the same time. *Personality and Social Psychology Bulletin, 17*, 475–482.

Brewer, M. B. (1993). Social identity, distinctiveness, and in-group homogeneity. *Social Cognition, 11*, 150–164.

Brewer, M. B. (1996). When stereotypes lead to stereotyping: The use of stereotypes in person perception. In C. N. Macrae, C. Stangor, & M. Hewstone (Eds.), *Stereotypes and stereotyping* (pp. 254–275). New York: Guilford Press.

Brewer, M. B. (1998). Category-based vs. person-based perception in intergroup contexts. In W. Stroebe & M. Hewstone (Eds.), *European review of social psychology* (Vol. 9, pp. 77–106). Chichester, UK: Wiley.

Brewer, M. B. (2000). Reducing prejudice through cross-classification: Effects of multiple social identities. In S. Oskamp (Ed.), *Reducing prejudice and discrimination* (pp. 165–183). Mahwah, NJ: Erlbaum.

Brewer, M. B., & Campbell, D. T. (1976). *Ethnocentrism and intergroup attitudes: East African evidence.* New York: Halsted Press.

Brewer, M. B., Dull, V., & Lui, L. (1981). Perceptions of the elderly: Stereotypes as prototypes. *Journal of Personality and Social Psychology, 41*, 656–670.

Brewer, M. B., & Harasty, A. S. (1996). Seeing groups as entities: The role of perceiver motivation. In R. M. Sorrentino & E. T. Higgins (Eds.), *Handbook of motivation and cognition: Vol. 3. The interpersonal context* (pp. 347–370). New York: Guilford Press.

Brewer, M. B., & Feinstein, A. S. H. (1999). Dual processes in the cognitive representation of persons and social categories. In S. Chaiken & Y. Trope (Eds.), *Dual-process theories in social psychology* (pp. 255–270). New York: Guilford Press.

Brewer, M. B., Ho, H., Lee, J., & Miller, M. (1987). Social identity and social distance among Hong Kong school children. *Personality and Social Psychology Bulletin, 13*, 156–165.

Brewer, M. B., & Lui, L. N. (1984). Categorization of the elderly by the elderly: Effects of perceiver's category membership. *Personality and Social Psychology Bulletin, 10*, 585–595.

Brewer, M. B., & Lui, L. N. (1989). The primacy of age and sex in the structure of person categories. *Social Cognition, 7*, 262–274.

Brewer, M. B., & Miller, N. (1984). Beyond the contact hypothesis: Theoretical perspectives on desegregation. In N. Miller & M.B. Brewer (Eds.), *Groups in Contact: The psychology of desegregation* (pp. 281–302). Orlando, FL: Academic Press.

Brewer, M. B., & Miller, N. (1988). Contact and cooperation: When do they work? In P. Katz & D. Taylor (Eds.), *Eliminating racism: Profiles in controversy* (pp. 315–326). New York: Plenum Press.

Brewer, M. B., Weber, J. G., & Carini, B. (1995). Person memory in intergroup contexts: Categorization versus individuation. *Journal of Personality and Social Psychology, 69*, 29–40.

Bridges, J. S., & Orza, A. M. (1993). Effects of maternal employment-childrearing pattern on college students' perceptions of a mother and her child. *Psychology of Women Quarterly, 17*, 103–117.

Brief, A. P., Dietz, J., Cohen, R. R., Pugh, S. D., & Vaslow, J. B. (2000). Just doing business: Modern racism and obedience to authority as explanations for employment discrimination. *Organizational Behvaior and Human Decision Processes, 81,* 72–97.

Brigham, J. C. (1971a). Ethnic stereotypes. *Psychological Bulletin, 76,* 15–33.

Brigham, J. C. (1971b). Racial stereotypes, attitudes, and evaluations of and behavioral intentions toward Negroes and whites. *Sociometry, 34,* 360–380.

Brigham, J. C. (1972). Racial stereotypes: Measurement variables and the stereotype-attitude relationship. *Journal of Applied Social Psychology, 2,* 63–76.

Brigham, J. C. (1973). Ethnic stereotypes and attitudes: A different mode of analysis. *Journal of Personality, 41,* 206–233.

Brigham, J. C. (1974). Views of black and white children concerning the distribution of personality characteristics. *Journal of Personality, 42,* 144–158.

Brigham, J. C., & Barkowitz, P. (1978). Do "they all look alike"?: The effect of race, sex, experience, and attitudes on the ability to recognize faces. *Journal of Applied Social Psychology, 8,* 306–318.

Brigham, J. C., Bloom, L. M., Gunn, S. P., & Torok, T. (1974). Attitude measurement via the bogus pipeline: A dry well? *Representative Research in Social Psychology, 5,* 97–114.

Brigham, J. C., Maass, A., Snyder, L. D., & Spaulding, K. (1982). Accuracy of eyewitness identification in a field setting. *Journal of Personality and Social Psychology, 42,* 673–681.

Brigham, J. C., & Malpass, R. S. (1985). The role of experience and contact in the recognition of faces of own- and other-race persons. *Journal of Social Issues, 41,* 139–156.

Briton, N. J., & Hall, J. A. (1995). Beliefs about female and male nonverbal communication. *Sex Roles, 32,* 79–90.

Brockington, I. F., Hall, P., Levings, J., & Murphy, C. (1993). The community's tolerance of the mentally ill. *British Journal of Psychiatry, 162,* 93–99.

Brockner, J., & Chen, Y. (1996). The moderating roles of self-esteem and self-construal in reaction to athreat to the self: Evidence from the People's Republic of China and the United States. *Journal of Personality and Social Psychology, 71,* 603–615.

Brodt, S. E., & Ross, L. D. (1998). The role of stereotyping in overconfident social prediction. *Social Cognition, 16,* 225–252.

Bronfenbrenner, U. (1961). The mirror image in Soviet-American relations: A social psychologist's report. *Journal of Social Issues, 17*(3), 45–56.

Brooks, J., & Lewis, M. (1976). Infants' responses to strangers: Midget, adult, and child. *Child Development, 47,* 323–332.

Brooks-Gunn, J., & Lewis, M. (1979). Why mama and papa?: The development of social labels. *Child Development, 50,* 1203–1206.

Broverman, I. K., Broverman, D. M., Clarkson, F. E., Rosenkrantz, P. S., & Vogel, S. R. (1970). Sex-role stereotypes and clinical judgments of mental health. *Journal of Consulting and Clinical Psychology, 34,* 1–7.

Broverman, I. K., Vogel, S. R., Broverman, D. M., Clarkson, F. E., & Rosenkrantz, P. S. (1972). Sex-role stereotypes: A current appraisal. *Journal of Social Issues, 28*(2), 59–78.

Brown v. Board of Education, 347 U.S. 483 (1954).

Brown, L. M. (1998). Ethnic stigma as a contextual experience: A possible selves perspective. *Personality and Social Psychology Bulletin, 24,* 163–172.

Brown, Roger. (1965). *Social psychology.* New York: Free Press.

Brown, Roger, & Fish, D. (1983). The psychological causality implicit in language. *Cognition, 14,* 237–273.

Brown, Roger, & Van Kleeck, M. H. (1989). Enough said: Three principles of explanation. *Journal of Personality and Social Psychology, 57,* 590–604.

Brown, Rupert. (1995). *Prejudice: Its social psychology.* Oxford: Blackwell.

Brown, Rupert. (2000). Social identity theory: Past achievements, current problems and future challenges. *European Journal of Social Psychology, 30,* 745–778.

Brown, Rupert, Vivian, J., & Hewstone, M. (1999). Changing attitudes through intergroup contact: The effects of group membership salience. *European Journal of Social Psychology, 29,* 741–764.

Brown, Rupert, & Wootton-Millward, L. (1993). Perceptions of group homogeneity during group formation and change. *Social Cognition, 11,* 126–149.

Brown, R. D., & Bassili, J. N. (2002). Spontaneous trait associations and the case of the superstitious banana. *Journal of Experimental Social Psychology, 38*, 87–92.

Brown, R. J., & Turner, J. C. (1979). The criss-cross categorization effect in intergroup discrimination. *British Journal of Social and Clinical Psychology, 18*, 371–383.

Brown, R. J., & Turner, J. C. (1981). Interpersonal and intergroup behaviour. In J. Turner & H. Giles (Eds.), *Intergroup behaviour* (pp. 33–65). Oxford: Blackwell.

Brown, R. P., & Josephs, R. A. (1999). A burden of proof: Stereotype relevance and gender differences in math performance. *Journal of Personality and Social Psychology, 76*, 246–257.

Brown, T. A., Cash, T. F., & Noles, S. W. (1986). Perceptions of physical attractiveness among college students: Selected determinants and methodological matters. *Journal of Social Psychology, 126*, 305–316.

Bruner, J. S. (1957). On perceptual readiness. *Psychological Review, 64*, 123–151.

Bruner, J. S., & Taguiri, R. (1954). Person perception. In G. Lindzey (Ed.), *Handbook of social psychology* (Vol. 2, pp. 634–654). Reading, MA: Addison-Wesley.

Brylinsky, J. A., & Moore, J. C. (1994). The identification of body build stereotypes in young children. *Journal of Research in Personality, 28*, 170–181.

Buchanan, B. A., & Bruning, J. L. (1971). Connotative meanings of first names and nicknames on three dimensions. *Journal of Social Psychology, 85*, 143–144.

Buchanan, C. M., & Holmbeck, G. N. (1998). Measuring beliefs about adolescent personality and behavior. *Journal of Youth and Adolescence, 27*, 607–627.

Buchanan, W. (1951). Stereotypes and tensions as revealed by the UNESCO international poll. *International Social Science Bulletin, 3*, 515–528.

Buckner, C. E. (1991). *The effects of sexual orientation and sex role behavior on attitudes toward homosexuals*. Unpublished senior project, Rice University.

Budesheim, T. L., & Bonnelle, K. (1998). The use of abstract trait knowledge and behavioral exemplars in causal explanations of behavior. *Personality and Social Psychology Bulletin, 24*, 575–587.

Budesheim, T. L., & DePaola, S. J. (1994). Beauty or the beast?: The effects of appearance, personality, and issue information on evaluations of political candidates. *Personality and Social Psychology Bulletin, 20*, 339–348.

Bull, R. H. C., & Green, J. (1980). The relationship between physical appearance and criminality. *Medical Science Law, 20*, 79–83.

Burgess, D., & Borgida, E. (1999). Who women are, who women should be: Descriptive and prescriptive gender stereotyping in sex discrimination. *Psychology, Public Policy, and Law, 5*, 665–692.

Burn, S. M. (2000). Heterosexuals' use of "fag" and "queer" to deride one another: A contributor to heterosexism and stigma. *Journal of Homosexuality, 40*, 1–11.

Burris, C. T., & Jackson, L. M. (2000). Social identity and the true believer: Responses to threatened self-stereotypes among the intrinsically religious. *British Journal of Social Psychology, 39*, 257–278.

Buss, D. M. (1989). Sex differences in human mate preferences: Evolutionary hypothesis tested in 37 cultures. *Behavioral and Brain Sciences, 12*, 1–14.

Buss, D. M. (1999). *Evolutionary psychology: The new science of the mind*. Boston: Allyn & Bacon.

Buss, D. M., & Craik, K. H. (1983). The act frequency approach to personality. *Psychological Review, 90*, 105–126.

Buss, D. M., & Schmitt, D. P. (1993). Sexual strategies theory: An evolutionary perspective on human mating. *Psychological Review, 100*, 204–232.

Busse, T. V., & Seraydarian, L. (1978). The relationships between first name desirability and school readiness, IQ, and school achievement. *Psychology in the Schools, 15*, 297–302.

Busse, T. V., & Seraydarian, L. (1979). First names and popularity in grade school children. *Psychology in the Schools, 16*, 149–153.

Butler, J. C., Ryckman, R. M., Thornton, B., & Bouchard, R. L. (1993). Assessment of the full content of physique stereotypes with a free-response format. *Journal of Social Psychology, 133*, 147–162.

Byrnes, D. A., & Kiger, G. (1990). The effect of a prejudice-reduction simulation on attitude change. *Journal of Applied Social Psychology, 20*, 341–356.

Cadinu, M. R., & Rothbart, M. (1996). Self-anchoring and differentiation processes in the minimal group setting. *Journal of Personality and Social Psychology, 70*, 661–677.

Cahalan, D., & Trager, F. (1949). Free answer stereotypes and anti-Semitism. *Public Opinion Quarterly, 13*, 93–104.

Cameron, J. A., Alvarez, J. M., Ruble, D. N., & Fuligni, A. J. (2001). Children's lay theories about ingroups and outgroups: Reconceptualizing research on prejudice. *Personality and Social Psychology Review, 5*, 118–128.

Campbell, B., Schellenberg, E. G., & Senn, C. Y. (1997). Evaluating measures of contemporary sexism. *Psychology of Women Quarterly, 21*, 89–102.

Campbell, C. P. (1995). *Race, myth, and the news.* Thousand Oaks, CA: Sage.

Campbell, D., Carr, S. C., & MacLachlan, M. (2001). Attributing "third world poverty" in Australia and Malawi: A case of donor bias? *Journal of Applied Social Psychology, 31*, 409–430.

Campbell, D. T. (1956). Enhancement of contrast as a composite habit. *Journal of Abnormal and Social Psychology, 53*, 350–355.

Campbell, D. T. (1958). Common fate, similarity and other indices of the status of aggregate persons as social entities. *Behavioral Science, 3*, 14–25.

Campbell, D. T. (1967). Stereotypes and the perception of group differences. *American Psychologist, 22*, 817–829.

Canetto, S. S., Kaminski, P. L., & Felicio, D. M. (1995). Typical and optimal aging in women and men: Is there a double standard? *International Journal of Aging and Human Development, 40*, 187–207.

Cann, A. (1991). Stereotypes about physical and social characteristics based on social and professional competence information. *Journal of Social Psychology, 131*, 225–231.

Cann, A., & Garnett, A. K. (1984). Sex stereotype impacts on competence ratings by children. *Sex Roles, 11*, 333–343.

Cann, A., & Haight, J. M. (1983). Children's perceptions of relative competence in sex-typed occupations. *Sex Roles, 9*, 767–773.

Canning, H., & Mayer, J. (1966). Obesity: Its possible effect on college acceptance. *New England Journal of Medicine, 275*, 1172–1174.

Cantor, N., & Mischel, W. (1979a). Prototypes in person perception. In L. Berkowitz (Ed.), *Advances in experimental social psychology* (pp. 3–52). New York: Academic Press.

Cantor, N., & Mischel, W. (1979b). Prototypicality and personality: Effects on free recall and personality impressions. *Journal of Research in Personality, 13*, 187–205.

Caporael, L. (1981). The paralanguage of caretaking: Baby talk to the institutionalized aged. *Journal of Personality and Social Psychology, 40*, 876–884.

Capozza, D., Dazzi, C., & Minto, B. (1996). Ingroup overinclusion: A confirmation of the effect. *International Review of Social Psychology, 9*, 7–18.

Carey, S. (1985). *Conceptual changes in childhood.* Cambridge, MA: Bradford Books.

Carlson, J. M., & Iovini, J. (1985). The transmission of racial attitudes from fathers to sons: A study of blacks and whites. *Adolescence, 20*, 233–237.

Carlston, D. E., & Skowronski, J. J. (1994). Savings in the relearning of trait information as evidence for spontaneous inference generation. *Journal of Personality and Social Psychology, 66*, 840–856.

Carlston, D. E., Skowronski, J. J., & Sparks, C. (1995). Savings in relearning: II. On the formation of behavior-based trait associations and inferences. *Journal of Personality and Social Psychology, 69*, 420–436.

Carlston, D. E., & Smith, E. R. (1996). Principles of mental representation. In E. T. Higgins & A. W. Kruglanski (Eds.), *Social psychology: Handbook of basic principles* (pp. 184–210). New York: Guilford Press.

Carpenter, S. (1993). Organization of in-group and out-group information: The influence of gender-role orientation. *Social Cognition, 11*, 70–91.

Carpenter, S. (1994). Gender categorization: Cognitive effects of personality and situations. *Journal of Social Behavior and Personality, 9*, 119–128.

Carter, D. B., & McCloskey, L. A. (1983–1984). Peers and the maintenance of sex-typed behavior: The development of children's conceptions of cross-gender behavior in their peers. *Social Cognition, 2*, 294–314.

Carver, C. S., Glass, D. C., Snyder, M. L., & Katz, I. (1977). Favorable evaluations of stigmatized others. *Personality and Social Psychology Bulletin, 3*, 232–235.

Cash, T. F. (1990). Losing hair, losing points?: The effects of male pattern baldness on social impression formation. *Journal of Applied Social Psychology, 20*, 154–167.

Cash, T. F., Dawson, K., Davis, P., Bowen, M., & Galumbeck, C. (1989). The effects of cosmetics use on the physical attractiveness and body image of college women. *Journal of Social Psychology, 129*, 349–356.

Cash, T. F., Kehr, J. A., Polyson, J., & Freeman, V. (1977). Role of physical attractiveness in peer attribution of psychological disturbance. *Journal of Consulting and Clinical Psychology, 45*, 987–993.

Castano, E., Paladino, M.-P., Coull, A., & Yzerbyt, V. Y. (2002). Protecting the ingroup stereotype: Ingroup identification and the management of deviant ingroup members. *British Journal of Social Psychology, 41*, 365–385.

Castano, E., Yzerbyt, V., Bourguignon, D., & Seron, E. (2002). Who may enter?: The impact of ingroup identification on in-group/out-group categorization. *Journal of Experimental Social Psychology, 38*, 315–322.

Castano, E., Yzerbyt, V., Paladino, M.-P., & Sacchi, S. (2002). I belong, therefore, I exist: Ingroup identification, ingroup entitativity, and ingroup bias. *Personality and Social Psychology Bulletin, 28*, 135–143.

Castelli, L., Vanzetto, K., Sherman, S. J., & Arcuri, L. (2001). The explicit and implicit perception of in-group members who use stereotypes: Blatant rejection but subtle conformity. *Journal of Experimental Social Psychology, 37*, 419–426.

Cavior, H., Hayes, S., & Cavior, N. (1974). Physical attractiveness of female offenders. *Criminal Justice and Behavior, 1*, 321–331.

Cavior, N., & Howard, L. (1973). Facial attractivenss and juvenile deliquency among black and white offenders. *Journal of Abnormal Child Psychology, 1*, 202–213.

Cejka, M. A., & Eagly, A. H. (1999). Gender-stereotypic images of occupations correspond to the sex segregation of employment. *Personality and Social Psychology Bulletin, 25*, 413–423.

Centers, R. (1948). Attitude and belief in relation to occupational stratification. *Journal of Social Psychology, 27*, 159–185.

Centers, R. (1951). An effective classroom demonstration of stereotypes. *Journal of Social Psychology, 34*, 41–46.

Chadwick-Jones, J. K. (1962). Intergroup attitudes: A stage in attitude formation. *British Journal of Sociology, 13*, 57–63.

Chaiken, S., Liberman, A., & Eagly, A. H. (1989). Heuristic and systematic information processing within and beyond the persuasion context. In J. S. Uleman & J. A. Bargh (Eds.), *Unintended thought* (pp. 212–252). New York: Guilford Press.

Chapman, L. J. (1967). Illusory correlation in observational report. *Journal of Verbal Learning and Verbal Behavior, 6*, 151–155.

Chapman, L. J., & Chapman, J. P. (1967). Genesis of popular but erronous psycho-diagnostic observations. *Journal of Abnormal Psychology, 72*, 193–204.

Chapman, L. J., & Chapman, J. P. (1969). Illusory correlation as an obstacle to the use of valid psychodiagnostiv signs. *Journal of Abnormal Psychology, 74*, 271–280.

Charters, W. W., Jr. & Newcomb, T. M. (1958). Some attitudinal effects of experimentally increased salience of a membership group. In E. E. Maccoby, T. M. Newcomb, & E. L. Hartley (Eds.), *Readings in social psychology* (3rd ed., pp. 276–281). New York: Holt.

Chartrand, T. L., & Bargh, J. A. (1999). The chameleon effect: The perception–behavior link and social interaction. *Journal of Personality and Social Psychology, 76*, 893–910.

Chasteen, A. L. (2000). The role of age and age-related attitudes in perceptions of elderly individuals. *Basic and Applied Social Psychology, 22*, 147–156.

Chatman, C. M., & von Hippel, W. (2001). Attributional mediation of in-group bias. *Journal of Experimental Social Psychology, 37*, 267–272.

Chen, N. Y., Shaffer, D. R., & Wu, C. (1997). On physical attractiveness stereotyping in Taiwan: A revised sociocultural perspective. *Journal of Social Psychology, 137*, 117–124.

Chen, S., Andersen, S. M., & Hinkley, K. (1999). Triggering transference: Examining the role of applicability in the activation and use of significant-other representations in social perception. *Social Cognition, 17*, 332–365.

Cherulnik, P. D., & Bayless, J. K. (1986). Person perception in environmental context: The influence of residential settings on impressions of their occupants. *Journal of Social Psychology, 126,* 667–673.

Cheryan, S., & Bodenhausen, G. V. (2000). When positive stereotypes threaten intellectual performance: The psychological hazards of "model minority" status. *Psychological Science, 11,* 399–402.

Cheyne, W. M. (1970). Stereotyped reactions to speakers with Scottish and English regional accents. *British Journal of Social and Clinical Psychology, 9,* 77–79.

Chiu, C.-Y., Hong, Y.-Y., & Dweck, C. S. (1997). Lay dispositionism and implicit theories of personality. *Journal of Personality and Social Psychology, 73,* 19–30.

Choi, I., Dalal, R., Kim-Prieto, C., & Park, H. (2003). Culture and judgment of causal relevance. *Journal of Personality and Social Psychology, 84,* 46–59.

Cialdini, R. B., Borden, R. J., Thorne, A., Walker, M. R., Freeman, S., & Sloan, L. R. (1976). Basking in reflected glory: Three (football) field studies. *Journal of Personality and Social Psychology, 34,* 366–375.

Citrin, J., Reingold, B., & Green, D. P. (1990). American identity and the politics of ethnic change. *Journal of Politics, 52,* 1124–1154.

Claire, T., & Fiske, S. T. (1998). A systematic view of behavioral confirmation: Counterpoint to the individualis view. In C. Sedikides, J. Schopler, & C. A. Insko (Eds.), *Intergroup cognition and intergroup behavior* (pp. 205–231). Mahwah, NJ: Erlbaum.

Clark, A., Hocevar, D., & Dembo, M. (1980). The role of cognitive development in children's explanations and preferences for skin color. *Developmental Psychology, 16,* 332–339.

Clark, K. B., & Clark, Y. K. (1939). The development of consciousness of self and the emergence of racial identification in Negro preschool children. *Journal of Social Psychology, 10,* 591–599.

Clark, K. B., & Clark, M. P. (1958). Racial identification and preference in Negro children. In T. M. Newcomb & E. L. Hartley (Eds.), *Readings in social psychology* (pp. 602–611). New York: Holt. (Original work published 1947)

Clark, M. L. (1985). Social stereotypes and self-concept in black and white college students. *Journal of Social Psychology, 125,* 753–760.

Clark, M. L., & Pearson, W. (1982). Racial stereotyping revisited. *International Journal of Intercultural Relations, 6,* 381–393.

Clausen, J. (1981). Stigma and mental disorder: Phenomenology and terminology. *Psychiatry, 44,* 287–296.

Clausen, J. A., & Huffine, C. L. (1975). Sociocultural and social-psychological factors affecting social responses to mental disorder. *Journal of Health and Social Behavior, 16,* 405–420.

Clawson, R. A., & Kegler, E. R. (2000). The "race coding" of poverty in American government college textbooks. *Howard Journal of Communications, 11,* 179–188.

Clawson, R. A., & Trice, R. (2000). Poverty as we know it: Media portrayals of the poor. *Public Opinion Quarterly, 64,* 53–64.

Claxton-Oldfield, S., & Keefe, S. M. (1999). Assessing stereotypes about the Innu of Davis Inlet, Labrador. *Canadian Journal of Behavioural Science, 31,* 86–91.

Clements-Schreiber, M. E., & Rempel, J. K. (1995). Women's acceptance of stereotypes about male sexuality: Correlations with strategies to influence reluctant partners. *Canadian Journal of Human Sexuality, 4,* 223–234.

Clifton, A. K., McGrath, D. & Wick, B. (1976). Stereotypes of women: A single category? *Sex Roles, 2,* 135–148.

Clore, G. L., & Parrott, G. (1991). Moods and their vicissitudes: Thoughts and feelings as information. In J. P. Forgas (Ed.), *Emotion and social judgments* (pp. 107–123). Oxford: Pergamon Press.

Coard, S. I., Breland, A. M., & Raskin, P. (2001). Perceptions of and preferences for skin color, black racial identity, and self-esteem among African Americans. *Journal of Applied Social Psychology, 31,* 2256–2274.

Coats, S., & Smith, E. R. (1999). Perceptions of gender subtypes: Sensitivity to recent exemplar activation and in-group/out-group differences. *Personality and Social Psychology Bulletin, 25,* 515–526.

Coats, S., Smith, E. R., Claypool, H. M., & Banner, M. (2000). Overlapping mental representations of self and in-group: Reaction time evidence and its relationship with explicit measures of group indentification. *Journal of Experimental Social Psychology, 36,* 304–315.

Coenders, M., & Scheepers, P. (1998). Support for ethnic discrimination in the Netherlands 1979–1993: Effects of period, cohort, and individual characteristics. *European Sociological Review, 14,* 405–422.

Cogan, J. C., Bhalla, S. K., Sefa-Dedeh, A., & Rothblum, E. D. (1996). A comparison study of United States and African students on perceptions of obesity and thinness. *Journal of Cross-Cultural Psychology, 27,* 98–113.

Cohen, B., & Murphy, G. L. (1984). Models of concepts. *Cognitive Science, 8,* 27–58.

Cohen, C. E. (1981). Person categories and social perception: Testing some boundaries of the processing effects of prior knowledge. *Journal of Personality and Social Psychology, 40,* 441–452.

Cohen, J., & Struening, E. L. (1962). Opinions about mental illness in the personnel of two large mental hospitals. *Journal of Abnormal and Social Psychology, 64,* 349–360.

Cohen, L. L., & Swim, J. K. (1995). The differential impact of gender ratios on women and men: Tokenism, self-confidence, and expectations. *Personality and Social Psychology Bulletin, 21,* 876–884.

Coker v. Georgia, 433 U.S. 584, 97 S.Ct. 2861 (1976).

Cole, D. (1999). *No equal justice: Race and class in the American criminal justice system.* New York: New Press.

Coleman, L. M., Jussim, L., & Kelley, S. H. (1995). A study of stereotyping: Testing three models with a sample of blacks. *Journal of Black Psychology, 21,* 322–356.

Coleman, R. P., & Rainwater, L. (1978). *Social standing in America: New dimensions of class.* New York: Basic Books.

Coley, J. D., Medin, D. L., & Atran, S. (1997). Does rank have its privilege?: Inductive inferences within folk biological taxonomies. *Cognition, 63,* 73–112.

Collette-Pratt, C. (1976). Attitudinal predictors of devaluation of old age in a multigenerational sample. *Journal of Gerontology, 31,* 193–196.

Collins, M. A., & Zebrowitz, L. A. (1995). The contribution of appearance to occupational outcomes in civilian and military settings. *Journal of Applied Social Psychology, 25,* 129–163.

Collins, M. E. (1991). Body figure perceptions and preferences among preadolescent children. *International Journal of Eating Disorders, 10,* 199–208.

Colon, I., & Marston, B. (1999). Resistance to a residential AIDS home: An empirical test of NIMBY. *Journal of Homosexuality, 37,* 135–145.

Coltraine, S., & Messineo, M. (2000). The perpetuation of subtle prejudice: Race and gender imagery in 1990s television advertising. *Sex Roles, 42,* 363–389.

Commins, B., & Lockwood, J. (1978). The effects of intergroup relations of mixing Roman Catholics and Protestants: An experimental investigation. *European Journal of Social Psychology, 8,* 383–386.

Conover, P., Mingst, K., & Sigelman, L. (1980). Mirror images in Americans' perception of nations and leaders during the Iranian hostage crisis. *Journal of Peace Research, 17,* 325–337.

Conway, M., Pizzamiglio, T., & Mount, L. (1996). Status, communality, and agency: Implication for stereotypes of gender and other groups. *Journal of Personality and Social Psychology, 71,* 25–38.

Conway, M., & Ross, M. (1984). Getting what you want by revising what you had. *Journal of Personality and Social Psychology, 47,* 738–748.

Conway, M., & Vartanian, L. R. (2000). A status account of gender stereotypes: Beyond communality and agency. *Sex Roles, 43,* 181–199.

Cook, S. W. (1962). The systematic analysis of socially significant events: A strategy for social research. *Journal of Social Issues, 18,* 66–84.

Cook, S. W. (1979). Social science and school desegregation: Did we mislead the Supreme Court? *Personality and Social Psychology Bulletin, 5,* 420–437.

Cook, S. W. (1985). Experimenting on social issues: The case of school desegregation. *American Psychologist, 40,* 452–460.

Cook, S. W. (1988). The 1954 social science statement and school desegregation: A reply to Gerard. In P. A. Katz & D. A. Taylor (Eds.), *Eliminating racism: Profiles in controversy* (pp. 237–256). New York: Plenum Press.

Cooper, V. W. (1985). Women in popular music: A quantitative analysis of feminine images over time. *Sex Roles, 13,* 499–506.

Coover, G. E., & Godbold, L. C. (1998). Convergence between racial and political identities: Boundary erasure or aversive racism? *Communication Research, 25,* 669–688.

Copeland, J. T. (1994). Prophecies of power: Motivational implications of social power for behavioral confirmation. *Journal of Personality and Social Psychology, 67,* 264–277.

Copeland, J. T., & Snyder, M. (1995). When counselors confirm: A functional analysis. *Personality and Social Psychology Bulletin, 21,* 1210–1220.

Corcos, A. F. (1997). *The Myth of Human Races.* East Lansing: Michigan State University Press.

Corley, T. J., & Pollack, R. H. (1996). Do changes in the stereotypic depiction of a lesbian couple affect heterosexuals' attitudes toward lesbianism? *Journal of Homosexuality, 32*(2), 1–17.

Corneille, O., & Judd, C. M. (1999). Accentuation and sensitization effects in the categorization of multifaceted stimuli. *Journal of Personality and Social Psychology, 77,* 927–941.

Corneille, O., Yzerbyt, V. Y., Rogier, A., & Buidin, G. (2001). Threat and the group attribution error: When threat elicits judgments of extremity and homogeneity. *Personality and Social Psychology Bulletin, 27,* 437–446.

Correll, J., Park, B., Judd, C. M., & Wittenbrink, B. (2002). The police officer's dilemma: Using ethnicity to disambiguate potentially threatening individuals. *Journal of Personality and Social Psychology, 83,* 1314–1329.

Corrigan, R. (2001). Implicit causality: Event participants and their interactions. *Journal of Language and Social Psychology, 20,* 285–320.

Corrigan, R. (2002). The influence of evaluation and potency on perceivers' casual attributions. *European Journal of Social Psychology, 32,* 363–382.

Corter, J. E., & Gluck, M. A. (1992). Explaining basic categories: Feature predictability and information. *Psychological Bulletin, 111,* 291–303.

Costa, P., Jr., Terracciano, A., & McCrae, R. R. (2001). Gender differences in personality traits across cultures: Robust and surprising findings. *Journal of Personality and Social Psychology, 81,* 322–331.

Costrich, N., Feinstein, J., Kidder, L., Marecek, J., & Pascale, L. (1975). When stereotypes hurt: Three studies of penalties for sex-role reversals. *Journal of Experimental Social Psychology, 11,* 520–530.

Cota, A. A., Reid, A., & Dion, K. L. (1991). Construct validity of a diagnostic ratio measure of gender stereotypes. *Sex Roles, 25,* 225–235.

Cotten-Huston, A. L., & Waite, B. M. (2000). Anti-homosexual attitudes in college students: Predictors and classroom interventions. *Journal of Homosexuality, 38,* 117–133.

Council of Economic Advisors for the President's Initiative on Race. (1998). *Changing America: Indicators of social and economic well-being by race and Hispanic origin.* Washington, DC: U.S. Government Printing Office.

Cousins, S. D. (1989). Culture and self-perception in Japan and the U.S. *Journal of Personality and Social Psychology, 56,* 124–131.

Cowan, M. L., & Stewart, B. J. (1977). A methodological study of sex stereotypes. *Sex Roles, 3,* 205–216.

Cox, C. L., & Glick, W. H. (1986). Resume evaluations and cosmetic use: When more is not better. *Sex Roles, 14,* 51–58.

Cox, C. L., Smith, S. L., & Insko, C. A. (1996). Categorical race versus individuating belief as determinants of discrimination: A study of Southern adolescents in 1966, 1979, and 1993. *Journal of Experimental Social Psychology, 32,* 39–70.

Craig, R. S. (1992). The effect of television day part on gender portrayals in televison commercials: A content analysis. *Sex Roles, 26,* 197–211.

Crain, R. L., & Mahard, R. E. (1983). The effect of research methodology on desegregation achievement: A meta-analysis. *American Journal of Sociology, 88,* 839–854.

Crandall, C. S. (1991). Do heavy-weight students have more difficulty paying for college? *Personality and Social Psychology Bulletin, 17,* 606–611.

Crandall, C. S. (1994). Prejudice against fat people: Ideology and self-interest. *Journal of Personality and Social Psychology, 66,* 882–894.

Crandall, C. S. (1995). Do parents discriminate against their heavyweight daughters? *Personality and Social Psychology Bulletin, 29,* 724–735.

Crandall, C. S., & Biernat, M. (1990). The ideology of anti-fat attitudes. *Journal of Applied Social Psychology, 20,* 227–243.

Crandall, C. S., D'Anello, S., Sakalli, N., Lazarus, E., Wieczorkowska, G., & Feather, N. T. (2001). An attribution–value model of prejudice: Anti-fat attitudes in six nations. *Personality and Social Psychology Bulletin, 27,* 30–37.

Crandall, C. S., Eshleman, A., & O'Brien, L. (2002). Social norms and the expression and suppression of prejudice: The struggle for internalization. *Journal of Personality and Social Psychology, 82,* 359–378.

Crandall, C. S., Glor, J., & Britt, T. W. (1997). AIDs related stigmatization: Instrumental and symbolic attitudes. *Journal of Applied Social Psychology, 27,* 95–123.

Crandall, C. S., & Martinez, R. (1996). Culture, ideology, and antifat attitudes. *Personality and Social Psychology Bulletin, 22,* 1165–1176.

Crandall, C. S., & Moriarty, D. (1995). Physical illness stigma and social rejection. *British Journal of Social Psychology, 34,* 67–83.

Crandall, C. S., Tsang, J.-A., Harvey, R. D., & Britt, T. W. (2000). Group identity-based self-protective strategies: The stigma of race, gender, and garlic. *European Journal of Social Psychology, 30,* 355–381.

Crawford, A. M. (1996). Stigma associated with AIDS: A meta-analysis. *Journal of Applied Social Psychology, 26,* 398–416.

Crawford, M. T., Sherman, S. J., & Hamilton, D. L. (2002). Perceived entitativity, stereotype formation, and the interchangeability of group members. *Journal of Personality and Social Psychology, 83,* 1076–1094.

Crisp, D. R., Apostal, R. A., & Luessenheide, H. D. (1984). The relationship of frequency and social desirability of first names with academic and sex role variables. *Journal of Social Psychology, 123,* 143–144.

Crisp, R. J., & Hewstone, M. (1999a). Differential evaluation of crossed category groups: Patterns, processes, and reducing intergroup bias. *Group Processes and Intergroup Relations, 2,* 1–27.

Crisp, R. J., & Hewstone, M. (1999b). Subcategorization of physical stimuli: Category differentiation and decategorization processes. *European Journal of Social Psychology, 29,* 665–671.

Crisp, R. J., Hewstone, M., & Cairns, E. (2001). Multiple identities in Northern Ireland: Hierarchical ordering in the representation of group membership. *British Journal of Social Psychology, 40,* 501–514.

Crocetti, G. M., Spiro, H. R., & Siassi, I. (1974). *Contemporary Attitudes toward Mental Illness.* Pittsburgh, PA: University of Pittsburgh Press.

Crocker, J. (1981). Judgment of covariation by social perceivers. *Psychological Bulletin, 90,* 272–292.

Crocker, J. (1999). Social stigma and self-esteem: Situational construction of self-worth. *Journal of Experimental Social Psychology, 35,* 89–107.

Crocker, J., Cornwell, B., & Major, B. (1993). The stigma of overweight: Affective consequences of attributional ambiguity. *Journal of Personality and Social Psychology, 64,* 60–70.

Crocker, J., & Luhtanen, R. (1990). Collective self-esteem amd ingroup bias. *Journal of Personality and Social Psychology, 58,* 60–67.

Crocker, J., & Major, B. (1989). Social stigma and self-esteem: The self-protective properties of stigma. *Psychological Review, 96,* 608–630.

Crocker, J., Major, B., & Steele, C. (1998). Social stigma. In D. Gilbert, S. T. Fiske, & G. Lindzey (Eds.), *The handbook of social psychology* (4th ed., Vol. 2, pp. 504–553). Boston: McGraw-Hill.

Crocker, J., & Quinn, D. (1998). Racism and self-esteem. In J. L. Eberhardt & S. T. Fiske (Eds.), *Confronting racism: The problem and the response* (pp. 169–201). Thousand Oaks, CA: Sage.

Crocker, J., Thompson, L. J., McGraw, K. M., & Ingerman, C. (1987). Downward comparison, prejudice, and evaluation of others: Effects of self-esteem and threat. *Journal of Personality and Social Psychology, 52,* 907–916.

Crocker, J., Voelkl, K., Testa, M., & Major, B. (1991). Social stigma: The affective consequences of attributional ambiguity. *Journal of Personality and Social Psychology, 60,* 218–228.

Crocker, J., & Wolfe, C. T. (2001). Contingencies of self-worth. *Psychological Review, 108,* 593–623.

Crockett, W. H., & Hummert, M. (1987). Perceptions of aging and the elderly. *Annual Review of Gerontology and Geriatrics, 7,* 217–241.

Crockett, W. H., Press, A. N., & Osterkamp, M. (1979). The effect of deviations from stereotyped expectations upon attitudes toward older persons. *Journal of Gerontology, 34,* 368–374.

Croizet, J.-C., & Claire, T. (1998). Extending the concept of stereotype and threat to social class: The intellectural underperformance of students from low socioeconomic backgrounds. *Personality and Social Psychology Bulletin, 24,* 588–594.

Crosby, F. (1984). The denial of personal discrimination. *American Behavioral Scientist, 27,* 371–386.

Crosby, F., Bromley, S., & Saxe, L. (1980). Recent unobtrusive studies of black and white discrimination and prejudice: A literature review. *Psychological Bulletin, 87,* 546–563.

Crosby, F., Clayton, S., Alksnis, O., & Hemker, K. (1986). Cognitive biases in the perception of discrimination: The importance of format. *Sex Roles, 14,* 637–646.

Crosby, F., & Nyquist, L. (1977). The female register: An empirical study of Lakoff's hypotheses. *Language in Society, 6,* 313–322.

Cross, J. F., Cross, J., & Daly, J. (1971). Sex, race, age, and beauty as factors in the recognition of faces. *Perception and Psychophysics, 10,* 393–396.

Cross, W. E., Jr. (1995). Oppositional identity and African-American youth: Issues and prospects. In W. D. Hawley & A. W. Jackson (Eds.), *Toward a common destiny* (pp. 185–204). San Francisco: Jossey-Bass.

Crott, H. W., Giesel, M., & Hoffmann, C. (1998). The process of inductive inference in groups: The use of positive and negative hypothesis and target testing in sequential rule-discovery tasks. *Journal of Personality and Social Psychology, 75,* 938–952.

Croxton, J. S., Van Rensselaer, B., Dutton, D. L., & Ellis, J. W. (1989). Mediating effect of prestige on occupational stereotypes. *Psychological Reports, 64,* 723–732.

Csikszentmihalyi, M., & Rochberg-Halton, E. (1981). *The meaning of things: Domestic symbols and the self.* Cambridge, UK: Cambridge University Press.

Csizma, K. A., Wittig, A. F., & Schurr, K. T. (1988). Sport stereotypes and gender. *Journal of Sport and Exercise Psychology, 10,* 62–74.

Cumming, J., & Cumming, E. (1957). *Closed ranks: An experiment in mental health education.* Cambridge, MA: Harvard University Press.

Cunningham, M. R. (1986). Measuring the physical in physical attractiveness: Quasi-experiments on the sociobiology of female facial beauty. *Journal of Personality and Social Psychology, 50,* 925–935.

Cunningham, M. R., Barbee, A. P., & Pike, C. L. (1990). What do women want?: Facialmetric assessment of multiple motives in the perception of male facial physical attractiveness. *Journal of Personality and Social Psychology, 59,* 61–72.

Cunningham, M. R., Roberts, A. R., Barbee, A. P., Druen, P. B., & Wu, C.-H. (1995). "Their ideas of beauty are, on the whole, the same as ours": Consistency and variability in the cross-cultural perception of female physical attractiveness. *Journal of Personality and Social Psychology, 68,* 261–279.

Cunningham, W. A., Preacher, K. J., & Banaji, M. R. (2001). Implicit attitude measures: Consistency, stability, and convergent validity. *Psychological Science, 12,* 163–170.

D'Agostino, P. R., & Beegle, W. (1996). Reevaluation of the evidence for spontaneous trait inferences. *Journal of Experimental Social Psychology, 32,* 153–164.

Dahlgren, K. (1986). The cognitive structure of social categories. *Cognitive Science, 9,* 379–398.

D'Alessio, S. J., & Stolzenberg, L. (1991). Anti-semitism in America: The dynamics of prejudice. *Sociological Inquiry, 61,* 359–364.

Dambrot, F. H., Papp, M. E., & Whitmore, C. (1984). The sex-role attitudes of three generations of women. *Personality and Social Psychology Bulletin, 10,* 469–473.

D'Andrade, R. G. (1965). Trait psychology and componential analysis. *American Anthropologist, 67,* 215–228.

D'Angelo, R. J., McGuire, J. M., Abbott, D. W., & Sheridan, K. (1998). Homophobia and perceptions of people with AIDS. *Journal of Applied Social Psychology, 28,* 157–170.

Darden, D. K., & Robinson, I. E. (1976). Multidimensional scaling of men's first names: A sociolinguistic approach. *Sociometry*, *39*, 422–431.

Darley, J. M., & Fazio, R. H. (1980). Expectancy confirmation processes arising in the social interaction sequence. *American Psychologist*, *35*, 867–881.

Darley, J. M., & Gross, P. H. (1983). A hypothesis-confirming bias in labeling effects. *Journal of Personality and Social Psychology*, *44*, 20–33.

Dasgupta, N., Banaji, M. R., & Abelson, R. P. (1999). Group entitativity and group perception: Associations between physical features and psychological judgment. *Journal of Personality and Social Psychology*, *77*, 991–1003.

Dasgupta, N., & Greenwald, A. G. (2001). On the malleability of automatic attitudes: Combating automatic prejudice with images of admired and disliked individuals. *Journal of Personality and Social Psychology*, *81*, 800–814.

Dasgupta, N., McGhee, D. E., Greenwald, A. G., & Banaji, M. R. (2000). Automatic preference for white Americans: Eliminating the familiarity explanation. *Journal of Experimental Social Psychology*, *36*, 316–328.

Davey, A. (1983). *Learning to be prejudiced: Growing up in multi-ethnic Britain*. London: Arnold.

Davey, A., & Norburn, M. (1980). Ethnic awareness and ethnic differentiation amongst primary school children. *New Community*, *8*, 51–60.

Davidson, O. B., & Eden, D. (2000). Remedial self-fulfilling prophecy: Two field experiments to prevent Golem effects among disadvantaged women. *Journal of Applied Psychology*, *85*, 386–398.

Davies, P. G., Spencer, S. J., Quinn, D. M., & Gerhardstein, R. (2002). Consuming images: How television commercials that elicit stereotype threat can restrain women academically and professionally. *Personality and Social Psychology Bulletin*, *28*, 1615–1628.

Davis, D. M. (1990). Portrayals of women in prime-time network television: Some demographic characteristics. *Sex Roles*, *23*, 325–332.

Davis, F. J. (1991). *Who is black: One nation's definition*. University Park: Pennsylvania State University Press.

Dawes, R. M., Mirels, H. L., Gold, E., & Donahue, E. (1993). Equating inverse probabilities in implicit personality judgments. *Psychological Science*, *4*, 396–400.

Deal, J. J., & Stevenson, M. A. (1998). Perceptions of female and male managers in the 1990s: Plus ça change. . . . *Sex Roles*, *38*, 287–300.

Deaux, K. (1984). From individual differences to social categories: Analysis of a decade's research on gender. *American Psychologist*, *39*, 105–116.

Deaux, K. (1993). Reconstructing social identity. *Personality and Social Psychology Bulletin*, *19*, 4–12.

Deaux, K., & Emswiller, T. (1974). Explanations of successful performance on sex-linked tasks: What is skill for the male is luck for the female. *Journal of Personality and Social Psychology*, *29*, 80–85.

Deaux, K., & Kite, M. (1985). Gender stereotypes: Some thoughts on the cognitive organization of gender-related information. *Academic Psychology Bulletin*, *7*, 123–144.

Deaux, K., & Kite, M. E. (1987). Thinking about gender. In B. Hess & M. M. Ferree (Eds.), *Analyzing gender: A handbook of social science research* (pp. 92–117). Newbury Park, CA: Sage.

Deaux, K., & Kite, M. E. (1993). Gender stereotypes. In F. Denmark & M. Paludi (Eds.), *Psychology of women: A handbook of issues and theories* (pp. 107–139). New York: Greenwood Press.

Deaux, K., & LaFrance, M. (1998). Gender. In D. T. Gilbert, S. T. Fiske, & G. Lindzey (Eds.), *The handbook of social psychology* (4th ed., Vol. 1, pp. 788–827). Boston: McGraw-Hill.

Deaux, K., & Lewis, L. L. (1984). Structure of gender stereotypes: Interrelationships among components and gender label. *Journal of Personality and Social Psychology*, *46*, 991–1004.

Deaux, K., & Major, B. (1987). Putting gender into context: An interactive model of gender-related behavior. *Psychological Review*, *94*, 369–389.

Deaux, K., Winton, W., Crowley, M, & Lewis, L. L. (1985). Level of categorization and content of gender stereotypes. *Social Cognition*, *3*, 145–167.

DeBono, K. G. (1987). Investigating the social adjustive and value expressive functions of attitudes: Implications for persuasion processes. *Journal of Personality and Social Psychology*, *52*, 279–287.

Dechesne, M., Janssen, J., & van Knippenberg, A. (2000). Derogation and distancing as terror management strategies: The moderating role of need for closure and permeability of group boundaries. *Journal of Personality and Social Psychology*, *79*, 923–932.

DeDreu, C. K. W., Yzerbyt, V. Y., & Leyens, J.-P. (1995). Dilution of stereotype-based cooperation in mixed-motive interdependence. *Journal of Experimental Social Psychology, 31,* 575–593.

De Houwer, J. (2001). A structural and process analysis of the implicit association test. *Journal of Experimental Social Psychology, 37,* 443–451.

DeJong, W. (1980). The stigma of obesity: The consequences of naive assumptions concerning the causes of physical deviance. *Journal of Health and Social Behavior, 81,* 75–87.

DeJong, W., & Kleck, R. E. (1986). The social psychological effects of overweight. In C. P. Herman, M. P. Zanna, & E. T. Higgins (Eds.), *The Ontario Symposium: Vol. 3. Physical appearance, stigma, and social behavior* (pp. 65–87). Hillsdale, NJ: Erlbaum.

De Klerk, V., & Bosch, B. (1996). Nicknames as sex-role stereotypes. *Sex Roles, 35,* 525–541.

Del Boca, F. K., & Ashmore, R. D. (1980). Sex stereotypes and implicit personality theory: II. A trait-inference approach to the assessment of sex stereotypes. *Sex Roles, 6,* 519–535.

Del Boca, F. K., Ashmore, R. D., & McManus, M. A. (1986). Gender-related attitudes. In R. D. Ashmore & F. K. Del Boca (Eds.), *The social psychology of female–male relations: A critical analysis of central concepts* (pp. 121–163). Orlando, FL: Academic Press.

De Lisi, R., & Soundranayagam, L. (1990). The conceptual structure of sex role stereotypes in college students. *Sex Roles, 23,* 593–611.

Demos, V., & Jache, A. (1981). When you care enough: An analysis of attitudes toward aging in humorous birthday cards. *Gerontologist, 21,* 209–215.

Denhaerinck, P., Leyens, J.-P., & Yzerbyt, Y (1989). The dilution effect and group membership: An instance of the persuasive impact of out-group homogeneity. *European Journal of Social Psychology, 19,* 243–250.

Dépret, E., & Fiske, S. T. (1999). Perceiving the powerful: Intriguing individuals versus threatening groups. *Journal of Experimental Social Psychology, 35,* 461–480.

Der-Karabetian, A., & Smith, A.J. (1977). Sex-role stereotyping in the United States. Is it changing? *Sex Roles, 3,* 193–198.

Deschamps, J. C., & Brown, R. J. (1983). Superordinate goals and intergroup conflict. *British Journal of Social Psychology, 22,* 189–195.

Deschamps, J. C., & Doise, W. (1978). Crossed-category membership in intergroup relations. In H. Tajfel (Ed.), *Differentiation between social groups* (pp. 141–158). London: Academic Press.

Desforges, D. M., Lord, C. G., Pugh, M. A., Sia, T. L., Scarberry, N. C., & Ratcliff, C.D. (1997). Role of group representativeness in the generalization part of the contact hypothesis. *Basic and Applied Social Psychology, 19,* 183–204.

Deutsch, F. M., Lebaron, D., & Fryer, M. M. (1987). What is in a smile? *Psychology of Women Quarterly, 11,* 341–352.

Deutsch, F. M., Zalenski, C. M., & Clark, M. E. (1986). Is there a double standard of aging? *Journal of Applied Social Psychology, 16,* 771–785.

Devine, P. G. (1989). Stereotypes and prejudice; Their automatic and controlled components. *Journal of Personality and Social Psychology, 56,* 5–18.

Devine, P. G., & Baker, M. (1991). Measurement of racial stereotype subtyping. *Personality and Social Psychology Bulletin, 17,* 44–50.

Devine, P. G., & Elliot, A. J. (1995). Are racial stereotypes really fading?: The Princeton trilogy revisited. *Personality and Social Psychology Bulletin, 21,* 1139–1150.

Devine, P. G., Hirt, E. R., & Gehrke, E. M. (1990). Diagnostic and confirmation strategies in trait hypothesis testing. *Journal of Personality and Social Psychology, 58,* 952–963.

Devine, P. G., & Malpass, R. S. (1985). Orienting strategies in differential face recognition. *Personality and Social Psychology Bulletin, 11,* 33–40.

Devine, P. G., & Monteith, M. J. (1999). Automaticity and control in stereotyping. In S. Chaiken & Y. Trope (Eds.), *Dual-process theories in social psychology* (pp. 339–360). New York: Guilford Press.

Devine, P. G., Monteith, M. J., Zuwerink, J. R., & Elliot, A. J. (1991). Prejudice with and without compunction. *Journal of Personality and Social Psychology, 60,* 817–830.

Devine, P. G., Plant, E. A., Amodio, D. M., Harmon-Jones, E., & Vance, S. L. (2002). The regulation of explicit and implicit race bias: The role of motivations to respond without prejudice. *Journal of Personality and Social Psychology, 82,* 835–848.

Diab, L. N. (1962). National stereotypes and the "reference group" concept. *Journal of Social Psychology, 57*, 339–351.

Diab, L. N. (1963a). Factors affecting studies of national stereotypes. *Journal of Social Psychology, 59*, 29–40.

Diab, L. N. (1963b). Factors determining group stereotypes. *Journal of Social Psychology, 61*, 3–10.

Di Dio, L., Saragovi, C., Koestner, R., & Aube, J. (1996). Linking personal values to gender. *Sex Roles, 34*, 621–636.

Die, A. H., & Holt, V. R. (1989). Perceptions of the typical female, male, female athlete, and male athlete. *International Journal of Sport Psychology, 20*, 135–146.

Diehl, M., & Jonas, K. (1991). Measures of national stereotypes as predictors of the latencies of inductive versus deductive stereotypic judgements. *European Journal of Social Psychology, 21*, 317–330.

Diekman, A. B., & Eagly, A. H. (2000). Stereotypes as dynamic constructs: Women and men of the past, present, and future. *Personality and Social Psychology Bulletin, 26*, 1171–1188.

Diekman, A. B., Eagly, A. H., & Kulesa, P. (2002). Accuracy and bias in stereotypes about the social and political attitudes of women and men. *Journal of Experimental Social Psychology, 38*, 268–282.

Dietz, T. L. (1998). An examination of violence and gender role portrayals in video games: Implications for gender socialization and aggressive behavior. *Sex Roles, 38*, 425–442.

Dijksterhuis, A., Aarts, H., Bargh, J. A., & van Knippenberg, A. (2000). On the relation between associative strength and automatic behavior. *Journal of Experimental Social Psychology, 36*, 531–544.

Dijksterhuis, A., & Bargh, J. A. (2001). The perception–behavior expressway: Automatic effects of social perception on social behavior. In M. P. Zanna (Ed.), *Advances in experimental social psychology* (Vol. 33, pp. 1–40). San Diego, CA: Academic Press.

Dijksterhuis, A., Spears, R., & Lépinasse, V. (2001). Reflecting and deflecting stereotypes: Assimilation and contrast in impression formation and automatic behavior. *Journal of Experimental Social Psychology, 37*, 286–299.

Dijksterhuis, A., Spears, R., Postmes, T., Stapel, D., Koomen, W., van Knippenberg, A., & Scheepers, D. (1998). Seeing one thing and doing another: Contrast effects in automatic behavior. *Journal of Personality and Social Psychology, 75*, 862–871.

Dijksterhuis, A., & van Knippenberg, A. (1995). Memory for stereotype-consistent and stereotype-inconsistent information as a function of processing pace. *European Journal of Social Psychology, 25*, 689–694.

Dijksterhuis, A., & van Knippenberg, A. (1996). The knife that cuts both ways: Facilitated and inhibited access to traits as a result of stereotype activation. *Journal of Experimental Social Psychology, 32*, 271–288.

Dijksterhuis, A., & van Knippenberg, A. (1998). The relation between perception and behavior, or how to win a game of Trivial Pursuit. *Journal of Personality and Social Psychology, 74*, 865–877.

Dijksterhuis, A., & van Knippenberg, A. (1999). On the parameters of associative strength: Central tendency and variability as determinants of stereotype accessibility. *Personality and Social Psychology Bulletin, 25*, 527–536.

Dion, K. K. (1973). Young children's stereotyping of facial attractiveness. *Developmental Psychology, 9*, 183–188.

Dion, K. K. (1986). Stereotyping based on physical attractiveness: Issues and conceptual perspectives. In C. P. Herman, M. P. Zanna, & E. T. Higgins (Eds.), *The Ontario Symposium: Vol. 3. Physical appearance, stigma, and social behavior* (pp. 7–21). Hillsdale, NJ: Erlbaum.

Dion, K. L. (1985). Sex differences in desirability of first names: Another nonconscious sexist bias. *Academic Psychology Bulletin, 7*, 287–298.

Dion, K. L. (1987). What's in a title?: The Ms. stereotype and images of women's titles of address. *Psychology of Women Quarterly, 11*, 21–36.

Dion, K. L., & Kawakami, K. (1996). Ethnicity and perceived discrimination in Toronto: Another look at the personal/group discrimination discrepency. *Canadian Journal of Behavioural Science, 28*, 203–213.

Dion, K. L., & Schuller, R. A. (1990). Ms. and the manager: A tale of two stereotypes. *Sex Roles*, *22*, 569–577.

Dipboye, R. L. (1982). Self-fulfilling prophecies in the selection–recruitment interview. *Academy of Management Review*, *7*, 579–586.

Dipboye, R. L. (1985). Some neglected variables in research on discrimination in appraisals. *Academy of Management Journal*, *10*, 116–127.

Dipboye, R. L. (1992). *Selection interviews: Process perspectives.* Cincinnati, OH: South-Western.

Dipboye, R. L., Arvey, R. D., & Terpstra, D. E. (1977). Sex and physical attractiveness of raters and applicants as determinants of resume evaluations. *Journal of Applied Psychology*, *62*, 288–294.

Dipboye, R. L., Fromkin, H. L., & Wiback, K. (1975). Relative importance of applicant sex, attractiveness, and scholastic standing in evaluation of job applicant resumes. *Journal of Applied Psychology*, *60*, 39–43.

Dipboye, R. L., & Wiley, J. W. (1978). Reactions of male raters to interviewee self-presentation style and sex: Extensions of previous research. *Journal of Vocational Behavior*, *13*, 192–203.

Dittmar, H. (1992). Perceived material wealth and first impressions. *British Journal of Social Psychology*, *31*, 379–391.

Dittmar, H. (1994). Material possessions as stereotypes: Material images of different socio- economic groups. *Journal of Economic Psychology*, *15*, 561–585.

Dodge, K. A., Gilroy, F. D., & Fenzel, L. M. (1995). Requisite management characteristics revisited: Two decades later. *Journal of Social Behavior and Personality*, *10*, 253–264.

Doise, W., Csepeli, G., Dann, H. D., Gouge, C., Larsen, K., & Ostell, A. (1972). An experimental investigation into the formation of intergroup representations. *European Journal of Social Psychology*, *2*, 202–204.

Doise, W., Deschamps, J.-C., & Meyer, G. (1978). The accentuation of intra-category similarities. In H. Tajfel (Ed.), *Differentiation between social groups* (pp. 159–168). London: Academic Press.

Dollard, J., Miller, N., Doob, L. W., Mowrer, O. H., & Sears, R. R. (1939). *Frustration and aggression.* New Haven, CT: Yale University Press.

Domke, D., Shah, D. V., & Wackman, D. (1998). Media priming effects: Accessibility, association, and activism. *International Journal of Public Opinion Research*, *1*, 51–74.

Donakowski, D. W., & Esses, V. M. (1997). Native Canadians, First Nations, or Aboriginals: The effect of labels on attitudes toward native peoples. *Canadian Journal of Behavioural Science*, *28*, 86–91.

Dooling, D. J., & Lachman, R. (1971). Effects of comprehension on retention of prose. *Journal of Experimental Psychology*, *88*, 216–222.

Doosje, B., Spears, R., Ellemers, N., & Koomen, W. (1999). Perceived group variability in intergroup relations: The distinctive role of social identity. In W. Strobe & M. Hewstone (Eds.), *European review of social psychology* (Vol. 10, pp. 41–73). Chichester, UK: Wiley.

Doty, R., Peterson, B., & Winter, D. (1991). Threat and authoritarianism in the United States, 1978–1987. *Journal of Personality and Social Psychology*, *61*, 629–640.

Dovidio, J. F., Brigham, J. C., Johnson, B. T., & Gaertner, S. L. (1996). Stereotyping, prejudice, and discrimination: Another look. In C. N. Macrae, C. Stangor, & M. Hewstone (Eds.), *Stereotypes and stereotyping* (pp. 276–319). New York: Guilford Press.

Dovidio, J. F., Evans, N., & Tyler, R. B. (1986). Racial stereotypes: The contents of their cognitive representations. *Journal of Experimental Social Psychology*, *22*, 22–37.

Dovidio, J. F., Fishbane, R., & Sibicky, M. (1985). Perceptions of people with psychological problems: Effects of seeking counseling. *Psychological Reports*, *57*, 1263–1270.

Dovidio, J. F., & Gaertner, S. L. (1998). On the nature of contemporary prejudice. In J. L. Eberhardt & S. T. Fiske (Eds.), *Confronting racism: The problem and the response* (pp. 3–32). Thousand Oaks, CA: Sage.

Dovidio, J. F., & Gaertner, S. L. (2000). Aversive racism and selection decisions: 1989 and 1999. *Psychological Science*, *11*, 315–319.

Dovidio, J. F., Gaertner, S. L., Isen, A. M., & Lowrance, R. (1995). Group representations and intergroup bias: Positive affect, similarity, and group size. *Personality and Social Psychology Bulletin*, *21*, 856–865.

Dovidio, J. F., Gaertner, S. L., & Validzic, A. (1998). Intergroup bias: Status, differentiation, and a common in-group identity. *Journal of Personality and Social Psychology, 75,* 109–120.

Dovidio, J. F., Gaertner, S. L., Validzic, A., Matoka, K., Johnson, B., & Frazier, S. (1997). Extending the benefits of recategorization: Evaluations, self-disclosure, and helping. *Journal of Experimental Social Psychology, 33,* 401–420.

Dovidio, J. F., Kawakami, K., & Gaertner, S. L. (2002). Implicit and explicit prejudice and interracial interaction. *Journal of Personality and Social Psychology, 82,* 62–68.

Dovidio, J. F., Kawakami, K., Johnson, C., Johnson, B., & Howard, A. (1997). On the nature of prejudice: Automatic and controlled processes. *Journal of Experimental Social Psychology, 33,* 510–540.

Dovidio, J. F., Smith, J. K., Donnella, A. G., & Gaertner, S. L. (1997). Racial attitudes and the death penalty. *Journal of Applied Social Psychology, 37,* 1468–1487.

Dowden, S., & Robinson, J. P. (1993). Age and cohort differences in American racial attitudes: The generational hypothesis revisited. In P. M. Sniderman, P. E. Tetlock, & E. G. Carmines (Eds.), *Prejudice, politics, and the American dilemma* (pp. 86–103). Stanford, CA: Stanford University Press.

Dowell, K. A., Presto, C. T., & Sherman, M. F. (1991). When are AIDS patients to blame for their disease?: Effects of patients' sexual orientation and mode of transmission. *Psychological Reports, 69,* 211–219.

Downs, A. C., & Harrison, S. K. (1985). Embarrassing age spots or just plain ugly?: Physical attractiveness stereotyping as an instrument of sexism on American telivision commercials. *Sex Roles, 13,* 9–19.

Doyle, A., Rappard, P., & Connolly, J. (1980). Two solitudes in the preschool classroom. *Canadian Journal of Behavioural Science, 12,* 221–232.

Doyle, A. B., Beaudet, J., & Aboud, F. E. (1988). Developmental patterns in the flexibility of children's ethnic attitudes. *Journal of Cross-Cultural Psychology, 19,* 3–18.

Dreidger, L., & Clifton, R. A. (1984). Ethnic stereotypes: Images of ethnocentrism, reciprocity, or dissimilaarity? *Canadian Review of Sociology and Anthropology, 21,* 287–301.

Drevenstedt, J. (1976). Perceptions of onsets of young adulthood, middle age and old age. *Journal of Gerontology, 31,* 53–57.

Drevenstedt, J. (1981). Age bias in evaluation of achievment: What determines? *Journal of Gerontology, 36,* 453–454.

Duckitt, J. (1992). *The social psychology of prejudice.* New York: Praeger.

Duckitt, J. (2001). A dual-process cognitive-motivational theory of ideology and prejudice. In M. P. Zanna (Ed.), *Advances in experimental social psychology* (Vol. 33, pp. 41–113). San Diego, CA: Academic Press.

Duckitt, J., & Mphuthing, T. (1998). Group identification and intergroup attitudes: A longitudinal analysis in South Africa. *Journal of Personality and Social Psychology, 74,* 80–85.

Duckitt, J., Wagner, C., du Plessis, I., & Birum, I. (2002). The psychological bases of ideology and prejudice: Testing a dual process model. *Journal of Personality and Social Psychology, 83,* 75–93.

Dudycha, G. J. (1942). The attitudes of college students toward war and the Germans before and during the Second World War. *Journal of Social Psychology, 15,* 317–324.

Duffy, J. C., & Ridinger, B. (1981). Stereotyped connotations of masculine and feminine names. *Sex Roles, 7,* 25–33.

Duncan, B. L. (1976). Differential social perception and attribution of intergroup violence: Testing the lower limits of stereotyping of blacks. *Journal of Personality and Social Psychology, 34,* 590–598.

Duncan, D. F. (1988). Effects on homophobia of viewing a gay-themed film. *Psychological Reports, 63,* 46.

Duncan, L. E., Peterson, B. E., & Winter, D. G. (1997). Authoritarianism and gender roles: Toward a psychological analysis of hegemonic relationships. *Personality and Social Psychology Bulletin, 23,* 41–49.

Dunkle, J. H., & Francis, P. L. (1990). The role of facial masculinity/femininity in the attribution of homosexuality. *Sex Roles, 23,* 157–167.

Dunkle, J. H., & Francis, P. L. (1996). "Physical atractiveness stereotype" and the attribution of homosexuality revisited. *Journal of Homosexuality, 30,* 13–29.

Dunning, D., & McElwee, R. O. (1995). Idiosyncratic trait definitions: Implications for self-descriptions and social judgment. *Journal of Personality and Social Psychology, 68,* 936–946.

Dunning, D., & Sherman, D. A. (1997). Stereotypes and tacit inference. *Journal of Personality and Social Psychology, 73,* 459–471.

Dunton, B. C., & Fazio, R. H. (1997). An individual difference measure of motivation to control prejudiced reactions. *Personality and Social Psychology Bulletin, 23,* 316–326.

Dupré, J. (1981). Biological taxa as natural kinds. *Philosophical Review, 90,* 66–90.

Durkin, K. (1985a). Television and sex-role acquisition: 1. Content. *British Journal of Social Psychology, 24,* 101–113.

Durkin, K. (1985b). Television and sex-role acquisition: 2. Effects. *British Journal of Social Psychology, 24,* 191–210.

Durkin, K. (1985c). Television and sex-role acquisition: 3. Counter-stereotyping. *British Journal of Social Psychology, 24,* 211–222.

Dutton, S. E., Singer, J. A., & Devlin, A. S. (1998). Racial identity of children in integrated, predominantly white, and black schools. *Journal of Social Psychology, 138,* 41–53.

Dweck, C. S., Chiu, C., & Hong, Y. (1995). Implicit theories and their role in judgments and reactions: A world from two perspectives. *Psychological Inquiry, 6,* 267–285.

Dweck, C. S., Hong, Y-Y., & Chiu, C-Y. (1993). Implicit theories: Individual differences in the likelihood and meaning of dispositional inference. *Personality and Social Psychology Bulletin, 19,* 644–656.

Eagly, A. H. (1987). *Sex differences in social behavior: A social-role interpretation.* Hillsdale, NJ: Erlbaum.

Eagly, A. H. (1995). The science and politics of comparing women and men. *American Psychologist, 50,* 145–158.

Eagly, A. H., Ashmore, R. D., Makhijani, M. G., & Longo, L. C. (1991). What is beautiful is good, but . . . : A meta-analytic review of research on the physical attractiveness stereotype. *Psychological Bulletin, 110,* 109–128.

Eagly, A. H., & Karau, S. J. (2002). Role congruity theory of prejudice toward female leaders. *Psychological Review, 109,* 573–598.

Eagly, A. H., & Kite, M. E. (1987). Are stereotypes of nationalities applied to both women and men? *Journal of Personality and Social Psychology, 53,* 451–462.

Eagly, A. H., & Mladinic, A. (1989). Gender stereotypes and attitudes toward women and men. *Personality and Social Psychology Bulletin, 15,* 543–558.

Eagly, A. H., & Mladinic, A. (1994). Are people prejudiced against women?: Some answers from research on attitudes, gender stereotypes, and judgments of competence. In W. Stroebe & M. Hewstone (Eds.), *European review of social psychology* (Vol. 5, pp. 1–35). Chichester, UK: Wiley.

Eagly, A. H., Mladinic, A., & Otto, S. (1991). Are women evaluated more favorably than men?: An analysis of attitudes, beliefs, and emotions. *Psychology of Women Quarterly, 15,* 203–216.

Eagly, A. H., Mladinic, A., & Otto, S. (1994). Cognitive and affective bases of attitudes toward social groups and social policies. *Journal of Experimental Social Psychology, 30,* 113–137.

Eagly, A. H., & Steffen, V. J. (1984). Gender stereotypes stem from the distribution of women and men into social roles. *Journal of Personality and Social Psychology, 46,* 735–754.

Eagly, A. H., & Steffen, V. J. (1986). Gender stereotypes, occupational roles, and beliefs about part-time employees. *Psychology of Women Quarterly, 10,* 252–262.

Eagly, A. H., & Steffen, V. J. (1988). A note on assessing stereotypes. *Personality and Social Psychology Bulletin, 14,* 676–680.

Eagly, A. H., & Wood, W. (1982). Inferred sex differences in status as a determinant of gender stereotypes about social influence. *Journal of Personality and Social Psychology, 43,* 915–928.

Eagly, A. H., & Wood, W. (1999). The origins of sex differences in human behavior: Evolved dispositions versus social roles. *American Psychologist, 54,* 408–423.

Eberhardt, J. L., Dasgupta, N., & Banaszynski, T. L. (2003). Believing is seeing: The effects of racial labels and implicit beliefs on face perception. *Personality and Social Psychology Bulletin, 29,* 360–370.

Eberhardt, J. L., & Fiske, S. T. (1996). Motivating individuals to change: What is a target to do? In C. N. Macrae, C. Stangor, & M. Hewstone (Eds.), *Stereotypes and stereotyping* (pp. 369–415). New York: Guilford Press.

Eckes, T. (1994a). Explorations in gender cognition: Content and structure of female and male subtypes. *Social Cognition, 12,* 37–60.

Eckes, T. (1994b). Features of men, features of women: Assessing stereotypic beliefs about gender subtypes. *British Journal of Social Psychology, 33,* 107–123.

Eckes, T. (1996). Linking female and male subtypes to situations: A range-of-situation-fit effect. *Sex Roles, 35,* 401–426.

Eddy, D. M. (1982). Probabilistic reasoning in clinical medicine: Problems and opportunities. In D. Kahneman, P. Slovic, & A. Tversky (Eds.), *Judgment under uncertainty: Heuristics and biases* (pp. 249–267). Cambridge, UK: Cambridge University Press.

Edmondson, C. B., & Conger, J. C. (1995). The impact of mode of presentation on gender differences in social perception. *Sex Roles, 32,* 169–183.

Edwards, A. L. (1940). Studies of stereotypes: I. The directionality and uniformity of responses to stereotypes. *Journal of Social Psychology, 12,* 357–366.

Edwards, D., & Potter, J. (1993). Language and causation: A discursive action model of description and attribution. *Psychological Review, 100,* 23–41.

Edwards, G. H. (1992). The structure and content of the male gender role stereotype: An exploration of subtypes. *Sex Roles, 26,* 533–551.

Edwards, J. A., & Weary, G. (1993). Depression and the impression-formation continuum: Piecemeal processing despite the availability of category information. *Journal of Personality and Social Psychology, 64,* 636–645.

Edwards, O. L. (1973). Skin color as a variable in racial attitudes of black urbanites. *Journal of Black Studies, 3,* 433–454.

Egolf, D. B. (1991). Height differences of low and high job status, female and male corporate employees. *Sex Roles, 24,* 365–373.

Ehrlich, H. J. (1962). Stereotyping and Negro–Jewish stereotypes. *Social Forces, 41,* 171–176.

Ehrlich, H. J. (1973). *The social psychology of prejudice.* New York: Wiley.

Ehrlich, H. J., & Rinehart, J. W. (1965). A brief report on the methodology of stereotype research. *Social Forces, 43,* 564–575.

Eisenberg, N., Roth, K., Bryniarski, K. A., & Murray, E. (1984). Sex differences in the relationship of height to children's actual and attributed social and cognitive competencies. *Sex Roles, 11,* 719–734.

Eiser, J. R. (1990). *Social judgment.* Pacific Grove, CA: Brooks/Cole.

Eiser, J. R., Martijn, C., & van Schie, E. (1991). Categorization and interclass assimilation in social judgment. *European Journal of Social Psychology, 21,* 493–505.

Elashoff, J. D., & Snow, R. E. (1971). *Pygmalion reconsidered.* Worthington, OH: Jones.

Elder, G. H. (1969). Appearance and education in marriage mobility. *American Sociological Review, 34,* 519–533.

Elkins, T. J., Phillips, J. S., & Konopaske, R. (2002). Gender-related biases in evaluations of sex discrimination allegations: Is perceived threat the key? *Journal of Applied Psychology, 87,* 280–292.

Elkins, T. J., Phillips, J. S., Konopaske, R., & Townsend, J. (2001). Evaluating gender discrimination claims: Is there a gender similarity bias? *Sex Roles, 44,* 1–15.

Ellemers, N., Doosje, B., van Knippenberg, A., & Wilke, H. (1992). Status protection in high status minority groups. *European Journal of Social Psychology, 22,* 123–140.

Ellemers, N., Kortekaas, P., & Ouwerkerk, J. W. (1999). Self-categorisation, commitment to the group and group self-esteem as related but distinct aspects of social identity. *European Journal of Social Psychology, 29,* 371–389.

Ellemers, N., Spears, R., & Doosje, B. (1997). Sticking together or falling apart: In-group identification as a psychological determinant of group commitment versus individual mobility. *Journal of Personality and Social Psychology, 72,* 617–626.

Ellemers, N., & van Knippenberg, A. (1997). Stereotyping in social context. In R. Spears, P. J. Oakes, N. Ellemers, & S. A. Haslam (Eds.), *The social psychology of stereotyping and group life* (pp. 208–235). Oxford: Blackwell.

Ellemers, N., van Knippenberg, A., De Vries, N., & Wilke, H. (1988). Social identification and the permeability of group boundaries. *European Journal of Social Psychology, 18,* 497–513.

Elliott, D. N., & Wittenberg, B. H. (1955). Accuracy of identification of Jewish and non-Jewish photographs. *Journal of Abnormal and Social Psychology, 51,* 339–341.

Elliott, G. C., Ziegler, H. L., Altman, B. M., & Scott, D. R. (1982). Understanding stigma: Dimensions of deviance and coping. *Deviant Behavior, 3,* 275–300.

Elliott, T. R., MacNair, R. R., Herrick, S. M., Yoder, B., & Byrne, C. A. (1991). Interpersonal reactions to depression and physical disability in dyadic interactions. *Journal of Applied Social Psychology, 21,* 1293–1302.

Ellis, A., & Beechley, R. M. (1954). Emotional disturbance in children with peculiar given names. *Journal of Genetic Psychology, 85,* 337–339.

Ellis, H. D., Deregowski, J. B., & Shepherd, J. W. (1975). Description of white and black faces by white and black subjects. *International Journal of Psychology, 10,* 119–123.

Elman, D. (1977). Physical characteristics and the perception of masculine traits. *Journal of Social Psychology, 103,* 157–158.

Engel, A. (1994). Sex roles and gender stereotyping in young women's participation in sport. *Feminism and Psychology, 4,* 439–448.

Engel, G., O'Shea, H. E., Fischl, M. A., & Cummings, G. M. (1958). An investigation of anti-Semitic deelings in two groups of college students: Jewish and non-Jewish. *Journal of Social Psychology, 48,* 75–82.

England, E. M. (1988). College student stereotypes of female behavior: Maternal professional women and assertive housewives. *Sex Roles, 19,* 365–385.

England, E. M. (1992). College student gender stereotypes: Expectations about the behavior of male subcategory members. *Sex Roles, 26,* 699–716.

Ensari, N., & Miller, N. (2002). The out-group must not be so bad after all: The effects of disclosure, typicality, and salience on intergroup bias. *Journal of Personality and Social Psychology, 83,* 313–329.

Entman, R. M. (1990). Modern racism and the images of blacks in local television news. *Critical Studies in Mass Communication, 7,* 332–345.

Entman, R. M. (1994). Representation and reality in the portrayal of blacks on network television news. *Journalism Quarterly, 71,* 509–520.

Epstein, R., & Komorita, S. S. (1965). Parental discipline, stimulus characteristics of out-groups, and social distance in children. *Journal of Personality and Social Psychology, 2,* 416–420.

Epstein, R., & Komorita, S. S. (1966a). Childhood prejudice as a function of parental ethnocentrism, punitiveness, and outgroup characteristics. *Journal of Personality and Social Psychology, 3,* 259–264.

Epstein, R., & Komorita, S. S. (1966b). Prejudice among Negro children as related to parental ethnocentrism and punitiveness. *Journal of Personality and Social Psychology, 4,* 643–647.

Epstein, Y. M., Krupat, E., & Obudho, C. (1976). Clean is beautiful: Identification and preference as a function of race and classification. *Journal of Social Issues, 32,* 109–118.

Erber, R., & Fiske, S. T. (1984). Outcome dependency and attention to inconsistent information. *Journal of Personality and Social Psychology, 47,* 709–726.

Erdley, C. A., & Dweck, C. S. (1993). Children's implicit personality theories as predictors of their social judgments. *Child Development, 64,* 863–878.

Erwin, P. G., & Calev, A. (1984). The influence of Christian name stereotypes on the marking of children's essays. *British Journal of Educational Psychology, 54,* 223–227.

Esses, V. M., & Beaufoy, S. L. (1994). Determinants of attitudes toward people with disabilities. *Journal of Social Behavior and Personality, 9,* 43–64.

Esses, V. M., & Dovidio, J. F. (2002). The role of emotions in determining willingness to engage in intergroup contact. *Personality and Social Psychology Bulletin, 28,* 1202–1214.

Esses, V. M., Haddock, G., & Zanna, M. P. (1993). Values, stereotypes, and emotions as determinants of intergroup attitudes. In D. M. Mackie & D. L. Hamilton (Eds.), *Affect, cognition, and stereotyping: Interactive processes in group perception* (pp. 137–166). San Diego, CA: Academic Press.

Esses, V. M., Haddock, G., & Zanna, M. P. (1994). The role of mood in the expression of intergroup stereotypes. In M. P. Zanna & J. M. Olson (Eds.), *The Ontario Symposium: Vol. 7. The psychology of prejudice* (pp. 77–101). Hillsdale, NJ: Erlbaum.

Esses, V. M., & Maio, G. R. (2002). Expanding the assessment of attitude components and strucutre:

The benefits of open-ended measures. In W. Stroebe & M. Hewstone (Eds.), *European review of social psychology* (Vol. 12). Chichester, UK: Wiley.

Esses, V. M., & Zanna, M. P. (1995). Mood and the expression of ethnic stereotypes. *Journal of Personality and Social Psychology, 69,* 1052–1968.

Estrada, A. X., & Weiss, D. J. (1999). Attitudes of military personnel toward homosexuals. *Journal of Homosexuality, 37,* 83–97.

Etaugh, C. E., Bridges, J. S., Cummings-Hill, M., & Cohen, J. (1999). Names can never hurt me: The effects of surname use on perceptions of married women. *Psychology of Women Quarterly, 23,* 819–823

Etaugh, C., Grinnell, K., & Etaugh, A. (1989). Development of gender labeling: Effect of age of pictured children. *Sex Roles, 21,* 769–773.

Etaugh, C., Levine, D., & Mennella, A. (1984). Development of sex biases in children: 40 years later. *Sex Roles, 10,* 913–924.

Etaugh, C., & Stern, J. (1984). Person-perception: Effects of sex, marital status, and sex-typing occupation. *Sex Roles, 11,* 413–424.

Etaugh, C., & Study, G. G. (1989). Perceptions of mothers: Effects of employment status, marital status, and age of child. *Sex Roles, 20,* 59–70.

Etcoff, N. (1999). *Survival of the prettiest: The science of beauty.* New York: Doubleday.

Evans, D. C., Garcia, D. G., Garcia, D. M., & Baron, R. S. (2003). In the privacy of their own homes: Using the Internet to assess racial bias. *Personality and Social Psychology Bulletin, 29,* 273–284.

Evans, L., & Davies, K. (2000). No sissy boys here: A content analysis of the representation of masculinity in elementary school reading textbooks. *Sex Roles, 42,* 255–270.

Eysenck, H. J., & Crown, S. (1948). National stereotypes: An experimental and methodological study. *Journal of Opinion and Attitude Research, 2,* 26–39.

Fabes, R. A., & Martin, L. (1991). Gender and age stereotypes of emotionality. *Personality and Social Psychology Bulletin, 17,* 532–540.

Fagan, F. F. (1972). Infants' recognition memory for faces. *Journal of Experimental Child Psychology, 14,* 453–476.

Fagot, B. I. (1977). Consequences of moderate cross gender behavior in preschool children. *Child Development, 48,* 902–907.

Fagot, B. I. (1978). The influence of sex of child on parental reaction to toddler children. *Child Development, 49,* 459–465.

Fagot, B. I. (1984). Teacher and peer reactions to boys' and girls' play styles. *Sex Roles, 11,* 691–702.

Fagot, B. I. (1985). Beyond the reinforcement principle: Another step toward understanding sex role development. *Developmental Psychology, 21,* 1097–1104.

Fagot, B. I., & Leinbach, M. D. (1993). Gender-role development in young children: From discrimination to labeling. *Developmental Review, 13,* 205–224.

Fagot, B. I., Leinbach, M. D., Hort, B. E., & Strayer, J. (1997). Qualities underlying the definitions of gender. *Sex Roles, 37,* 1–18.

Fagot, B. I., Leinbach, M. D., & O'Boyle, C. (1992). Gender labeling, gender stereotyping, and parenting behaviors. *Developmental Psychology, 28,* 225–230.

Fairchild, H. H. (1985). Black, Negro, or Afro-American?: The differences are crucial. *Journal of Black Studies, 16,* 47–55.

Fairchild, H. H., & Cozens, J. A. (1981). Chicano, Hispanic, or Mexican-American: What's in a name? *Hispanic Journal of Behavioral Sciences, 3,* 191–198.

Fallon, A. (1990). Culture in the mirror: Sociocultural determinants of body image. In T. F. Cash & T. Pruzinsky (Eds.), *Body images: Development, deviance, and change* (pp. 80–109). New York: Guilford Press.

Falwell thinks Tinky Winky is gay. (1999, February 10). *Houston Chronicle,* Section A, p. 9.

Farina, A. (1981). Are women nicer people than men?: Sex and the stigma of mental disorder. *Clinical Psychology Review, 1,* 223–243.

Farina, A. (1982). The stigma of mental disorders. In A. G. Miller (Ed.), *In the eye of the beholder: Contemporary issues in stereotyping* (pp. 305–363). New York: Praeger.

Farina, A., Allen, J. G., & Saul, B. B. (1968). The role of the stigmatized person in affecting social relationships. *Journal of Personality, 36,* 169–182.

Farina, A., Burns, G. L., Austad, C., Bugglin, C., & Fischer, E. H. (1986). The role of physical attractiveness in the readjustment of discharged psychiatric patients. *Journal of Abnormal Psychology*, *95*, 139–143.

Farina, A., Felner, R. D., & Boudreau, L. A. (1973). Reactions of workers to male and female mental patient job applicants. *Journal of Consulting and Clinical Psychology*, *41*, 363–372.

Farina, A., Fischer, E. H., Sherman, S., Smith, W. T., Groh, T., & Mermin, P. (1977). Physical attractiveness and mental illness. *Journal of Abnormal Psychology*, *86*, 510–517.

Farina, A., Fisher, J. D., & Fischer, E. H. (1992). Societal factors in the problems faced by deinstitutionalized psychiatric patients. In P. J. Fink & A. Tasman (Eds.), *Stigma and mental illness* (pp.167–184). Washington, DC: American Psychiatric Press.

Farina, A., Gliha, D., Boudreau, L. A., Allen, J. G., & Sherman, M. (1971). Mental illness and the impact of believing others know about it. *Journal of Abnormal Psychology*, *77*, 1–5.

Farina, A., Murray, P. J., & Groh, T. (1978). Sex and worker acceptance of a former mental patient. *Journal of Consulting and Clinical Psychology*, *46*, 887–891.

Fazio, R. H. (1995). Attitudes as object–evaluation associations: Determinants, consequences, and correlates of attitude accessibility. In R. E. Petty & J. A. Krosnick (Eds.), *Attitude strength: Antecedents and consequences* (pp. 247–282). Mahwah, NJ: Erlbaum.

Fazio, R. H., & Dunton, B. C. (1997). Categorization by race: The impact of automatic and controlled components of racial prejudice. *Journal of Experimental Social Psychology*, *33*, 451–470.

Fazio, R. H., & Hilden, L. E. (2001). Emotional reactions to a seemingly prejudiced response: The role of automatically activated racial attitudes and motivation to control prejudiced reactions. *Personality and Social Psychology Bulletin*, *27*, 538–549.

Fazio, R. H., Jackson, J. R., Dunton, B. C., & Williams, C. J. (1995). Variability in automatic activation as an unobtrusive measure of racial attitudes: A bona fide pipeline. *Journal of Personality and Social Psychology*, *69*, 1013–1027.

Feagin, J. R. (1975). *Subordinating the poor: Welfare and American beliefs*. Englewood Cliffs, NJ: Prentice-Hall.

Feather, N. T. (1974). Explanations of poverty in Australian and American samples: The person, society, or fate? *Australian Journal of Psychology*, *26*, 99–216.

Federico, C. M., & Sidanius, J. (2002). Racism, ideology, and affirmative action revisited: The antecedents and consequences of "principled objections" to affirmative action. *Journal of Personality and Social Psychology*, *82*, 488–502.

Fein, S., & Spencer, S. J. (1997). Prejudice as self-image maintenance: Affirming the self through derogating others. *Journal of Personality and Social Psychology*, *73*, 31–44.

Feingold, A. (1990). Gender differences in effects of physical attractiveness on romantic attraction: Comparison across five research domains. *Journal of Personality and Social Psychology*, *59*, 981–993.

Feingold, A. (1992a). Gender differences in mate selection preferences: A test of the parental investment model. *Psychological Bulletin*, *112*, 125–139.

Feingold, A. (1992b). Good-looking people are not what we think. *Psychological Bulletin*, *111*, 304–341.

Feingold, A. (1998). Gender stereotyping for sociability, dominance, character, and mental health: A meta-analysis of findings from the bogus stranger paradigm. *Genetic, Social, and General Psychology Monographs*, *124*, 253–270.

Feingold, C. A. (1914). The influence of environment on identification of persons and things. *Journal of Criminal Law and Police Science*, *5*, 39–51.

Feldman, J. (1988). Objects in categories and objects as categories. In T. K. Srull & R. S. Wyer, Jr. (Eds.), *Advances in social cognition* (Vol. 1, pp. 53–64). Hillsdale, NJ: Erlbaum.

Feldman, J. M. (1972). Stimulus characteristics and subject prejudice as determinants of stereotype attribution. *Journal of Personality and Social Psychology*, *21*, 333–340.

Feldman, J. M., & Hilterman, R. J. (1975). Stereotype attribution revisited: The role of stimulus characteristics, racial attitude, and cognitive differentiation. *Journal of Personality and Social Psychology*, *31*, 1177–1188.

Fernberger, S. W. (1948). Persistence of stereotypes concerning sex differences. *Journal of Abnormal and Social Psychology*, *43*, 97–101.

Fiedler, K. (1991). The tricky nature of skewed freqeunce tables: An information loss account of distinctiveness-based illusory correlation. *Journal of Personality and Social Psychology, 60,* 24–36.

Fiedler, K. (1996). Explaining and simulating judgment biases as an aggregation phenomenon in probabilistic, multiple-cue enviorments. *Psychological Review, 103,* 193–214.

Fielder, K. (2000). Illusory correlations: A simple associative algorithm provides a convergent account of seemingly divergent paradigms. *Review of General Psychology, 4,* 25–58.

Fiedler, K., & Armbruster, T. (1994). Two halfs may be better than one whole: Category-split effects on frequency illusions. *Journal of Personality and Social Psychology, 66,* 633–645.

Fiedler, K., Russer, S., & Gramm, K. (1993). Illusory correlations and memory performance. *Journal of Experimental Social Psychology, 29,* 111–136.

Fiedler, K., & Semin, G. R. (1988). On the causal information conveyed by different interpersonal verbs: The role of implicit sentence context. *Social Cognition, 6,* 21–39.

Fiedler, K., Semin, G. R., & Bolten, S. (1989). Language use and reification of social information: Top-down and bottom-up processing in person cognition. *European Journal of Social Psychology, 19,* 271–295.

Fiedler, K., Semin, G. R., & Finkenauer, C. (1993). The battle of words between gender groups: A language-based approach to intergroup processes. *Human Communication Research, 19,* 409–441.

Fink, K., & Cantril, H. (1937). The collegiate stereotype as a frame of reference. *Journal of Abnormal and Social Psychology, 32,* 352–356.

Firebaugh, G., & Davis, K. E. (1988). Trends in antiblack prejudice, 1972–1984: Region and cohort effects. *American Journal of Sociology, 94,* 251–272.

Fischhoff, B., & Beyth-Marom, R. (1983). Hypothesis evaluation from a Bayesian perspective. *Psychological Review, 90,* 239–260.

Fish, T. A., & Rye, B. J. (1991). Attitudes toward a homosexual or heterosexual person with AIDS. *Journal of Applied Social Psychology, 21,* 651–667.

Fishbein, H. D. (1996). *Peer prejudice and discrimination: Evolutionary, cultural, and developmental dynamics.* Boulder, CO: Westview Press.

Fisher, R. D., Derison, D., Polley, C. F., III, Cadman, J., & Johnston, D. (1994). Religiousness, religious orientation, and attitudes toward gays and lesbians. *Journal of Applied Social Psychology, 24,* 614–630.

Fishman, J. A. (1956). An examination of the process and function of social stereotyping. *Journal of Social Psychology, 43,* 27–64.

Fisk, W. R. (1985). Responses to "neutral" pronoun presentations and the development of sex-biased responding. *Developmental Psychology, 21,* 481–485.

Fiske, A. P., Haslam, N., & Fiske, S. T. (1991). Confusing one person with another: What errors reveal about the elementary forms of social relations. *Journal of Personality and Social Psychology, 60,* 656–674.

Fiske, S. T. (1988). Compare and contrast: Brewer's dual process model and Fiske et al.'s continuum model. In T. K. Srull & R. S. Wyer, Jr. (Eds.), *Advances in social cognition* (Vol. 1, pp. 65–76). Hillsdale, NJ: Erlbaum.

Fiske, S. T. (1989). Examining the role of intent: Toward understanding its role in stereotyping and prejudice. In J. S. Uleman & J. A. Bargh (Eds.), *Unintended thought* (pp. 253–283). New York: Guilford Press.

Fiske, S. T. (1992). Thinking is doing: Portraits of social cognition from daguerreotype to laserphoto. *Journal of Personality and Social Psychology, 63,* 877–889.

Fiske, S. T. (1993). Controlling other people: The impact of power on stereotyping. *American Psychologist, 48,* 621–628.

Fiske, S. T. (1998). Stereotyping, prejudice, and discrimination. In D. T. Gilbert, S. T. Fiske, & G. Lindzey (Eds.), *The handbook of social psychology* (4th ed., Vol. 2, pp. 357–411). Boston: McGraw-Hill.

Fiske, S. T. (2000a). Interdependence and the reduction of prejudice. In S. Oskamp (Eds.), *Reducing prejudice and discrimination* (pp. 115–135). Mahwah, NJ: Erlbaum.

Fiske, S. T. (2000b). Stereotyping, prejudice, and discrimination at the seam between the centuries: Evolution, culture, mind, and brain. *European Journal of Social Psychology, 30,* 299–322.

Fiske, S. T., Bersoff, D. N., Borgida, E., Deaux, K., & Heilman, M. E. (1991). Social science research on trial: Use of sex stereotyping research in *Price Waterhouse v Hopkins*. *American Psychologist, 46*, 1049–1060.

Fiske, S. T., & Cox, M. G. (1979). Person concepts: The effect of target familarity and descriptive purpose on the process of describing others. *Journal of Personality, 47*, 136–161.

Fiske, S. T., Cuddy, A. J. C., Glick, P., & Xu, J. (2002). A model of (often mixed) stereotype content: Competence and warmth respectively follow from perceived status and competition. *Journal of Personality and Social Psychology, 82*, 878–902.

Fiske, S. T., & Dépret, E. (1996). Control, independence, and power: Understanding social cognition in its social context. In W. Strobe & M. Hewstone (Eds.), *European review of social psychology* (Vol. 7, pp. 31–61). Chichester, UK: Wiley.

Fiske, S. T., Kenny, D. A., & Taylor, S. E. (1982). Structural models for the mediation of salience effects on attribution. *Journal of Experimental Social Psychology, 18*, 105–127.

Fiske, S. T., Lin, M., & Neuberg, S. L. (1999). The continuum model: Ten years later. In S. Chaiken & Y. Trope (Eds.), *Dual-process theories in social psychology* (pp. 231–245). New York: Guilford Press.

Fiske, S. T., & Morling, B. (1996). Stereotyping as a function of personal control motives and capacity constraints: The odd couple of power and anxiety. In R. M. Sorrentino & E. T. Higgins (Eds.), *Handbook of motivation and cognition: Vol. 3. The interpersonal context* (pp. 322–346). New York: Guilford Press.

Fiske, S. T., Morling, B., & Stevens, L. E. (1996). Controlling self and others: A theory of anxiety, mental control, and social control. *Personality and Social Psychology Bulletin, 22*, 115–123.

Fiske, S. T., & Neuberg, S. L. (1989). Category-based and individuating processes as a function of information and motivation: Evidence from our laboratory. In D. Bar-Tal, C. F. Graumann, A. W. Kruglanski, & W. Stroebe (Eds.), *Stereotyping and prejudice: Changing conceptions* (pp. 83–103). New York: Springer-Verlag.

Fiske, S. T., & Neuberg, S. L. (1990). A continuum of impression formation, from category-based to individuating processes: Influences of information and motivation on attention and interpretation. In M. P. Zanna (Ed.), *Advances in experimental social psychology* (Vol. 23, pp. 1–74). San Diego, CA: Academic Press.

Fiske, S. T., Neuberg, S. L., Beattie, A. E., & Milberg, S. J. (1987). Category-based and attribute-based reactions to others: Some informational conditions of stereotyping and individuating processes. *Journal of Experimental Social Psychology, 23*, 399–427.

Fiske, S. T., & Pavelchak, M. A. (1986). Category-based versus piecemeal-based affective responses: Developments in schema-triggered affect. In R. M. Sorrentino & E. T. Higgins (Eds.), *Handbook of Motivation and cognition: Vol. 1. Foundations of social behavior* (pp. 167–203). New York: Guilford Press.

Fiske, S. T., & Stevens, L. E. (1993). What's so special about sex?: Gender stereotyping and discrimination. In S. Oskamp & M. Costanzo (Eds.), *Gender issues in contemporary society* (pp. 173–196). Newbury Park, CA: Sage.

Fiske, S. T., & Taylor, S. E. (1991). *Social cognition* (2nd ed.). New York: McGraw-Hill.

Fiske, S. T., & von Hendy, H. M. (1992). Personality feedback and situational norms can control stereotyping processes. *Journal of Personality and Social Psychology, 62*, 577–596.

Fleeson, W., Zirkel, S., & Smith, E. E. (1995). Mental representations of trait categories and their influences on person perception. *Social Cognition, 13*, 365–397.

Floge, L., & Merrill, D. M. (1986). Tokenism reconsidered: Male nurses and female physicians in a hospital setting. *Social Forces, 64*, 925–947.

Florack, A., Scarabis, M., & Bless, H. (2001). When do associations matter?: The use of automatic associations toward ethnic groups in person judgements. *Journal of Experimental Social Psychology, 37*, 518–524.

Flournoy, J. M., Jr., Prentice-Dunn, S., & Klinger, M. R. (2002). The role of prototypical situations in the perceptions of prejudice of African Americans. *Journal of Applied Social Psychology, 32*, 406–423.

Foon, A. E. (1986). A social structural approach to speech evaluation. *Journal of Social Psychology, 126*, 521–530.

Ford, M. E., Miura, I., & Masters, J. C. (1984). Effects of social stimulus value on academic achievement and social competence: A reconsideration of children's first name characteristics. *Journal of Educational Psychology, 76,* 1149–1158.

Ford, T. E. (1997). Effects of stereotypical television portrayals of African-Americans on person perception. *Social Psychology Quarterly, 60,* 266–275.

Ford, T. E. (2000). Effects of sexist humor on tolerance of sexist events. *Personality and Social Psychology Bulletin, 26,* 1094–1107.

Ford, T. E., & Kruglanski, A. W. (1995). Effects of epistemic motivations on the use of accessible constructs in social judgment. *Personality and Social Psychology Bulletin, 21,* 950–962.

Ford, T. E., & Stangor, C. (1992). The role of diagnosticity in stereotype formation: Perceiving group means and variances. *Journal of Personality and Social Psychology, 63,* 356–367.

Ford, T. E., & Thompson, E. P. (2000). Preconscious and postconscious processes underlying construct accessibility effects: An extended search model. *Personality and Social Psychology Review, 4,* 317–336.

Ford, T. E., Wentzel, E. R., & Lorion, J. (2001). Effects of exposure to sexist humor on perceptions of normative tolerance of sexism. *European Journal of Social Psychology, 31,* 677–691.

Fordham, S., & Ogbu, J. (1986). Black students' school success: Coping with the burden of acting white. The *Urban Review, 18*(3), 176–206.

Foreit, K. G., Agor, T., Byers, J., Larue, J., Lokey, H., Palazzini, M., Patterson, M., & Smith, L. (1980). Sex bias in the newspaper treatment of male-centered and female-centered news stories. *Sex Roles, 6,* 475–480.

Forgas, J. P. (1995). Mood and judgment: The Affect Infusion Model (AIM). *Psychological Bulletin, 117,* 39–66.

Forgas, J. P., & Fiedler, K. (1996). Us and them: Mood effects on intergroup discrimination. *Journal of Personality and Social Psychology, 70,* 28–40.

Forgas, J. P., & Moylan, S. (1991). Affective influences on stereotypic judgments. *Cognition and Emotion, 5,* 379–395.

Förster, J., Higgins, E. T., & Strack, F. (2000). When stereotype disconfirmation is a personal threat: How prejudice and prevention focus moderate incongruency effects. *Social Cognition, 18,* 178–197.

Forsyth, D. R., Heiney, M. M., & Wright, S. S. (1997). Biases in appraisals of women leaders. *Group Dynamics, 1,* 98–103.

Forsythe, S. (1990). Effect of applicant's clothing on interviewer's decision to hire. *Journal of Applied Social Psychology, 20,* 1579–1595.

Forsythe, S., Drake, M. F., & Cox, C. E. (1985). Influence of applicant's dress on interviewer's selection decisions. *Journal of Applied Psychology, 70,* 374–378.

Foschi, M., & Foddy, M. (1988). Standards, performances, and the formation of self–other expectations. In M. Webster, Jr. & M. Foschi (Eds.), *Status generalization: New theory and research.* Stanford, CA: Stanford University Press.

Foster, D., & Finchilescu, G. (1986). Contact in a "non-contact" society: The case of South Africa. In M. Hewstone & R. Brown (Eds.), *Contact and conflict in intergroup encounters* (pp. 119–136). Oxford: Blackwell.

Foster, M. D., & Matheson, K. (1999). Perceiving and responding to the personal/group discrimination discrepancy. *Personality and Social Psychology Bulletin, 25,* 1319–1329.

Foushee, H. C., Helmreich, R. L., & Spence, J. T. (1979). Implicit theories of masculinity and femininity: Dualistic or bipolar? *Psychology of Women Quarterly, 3,* 259–269.

Fouts, G., & Burggraf, K. (2000). Television situation comedies: Female weight, male negative comments, and audience reactions. *Sex Roles, 42,* 925–932.

Fox, D. J., & Jordan, V. B. (1973). Racial preferences and identification of black, American Chinese, and white children. *Genetic Psychology Monographs, 88,* 229–286.

Fox, S. A., & Giles, H. (1996). Interability communication: Evaluating patronizing encounters. *Journal of Language and Social Psychology, 15,* 265–290.

Frable, D. E. S. (1993a). Being and feeling unique: Statistical deviance and psychological marginality. *Journal of Personality, 61,* 85–110.

Frable, D. E. S. (1993b). Dimensions of marginality: Distinctions among those who are different. *Personality and Social Psychology Bulletin, 19,* 370–380.

Frable, D. E. S. (1997). Gender, racial, ethnic, sexual, and class identities. *Annual Review of Psychology*, *48*, 139–162.

Frable, D. E. S., Blackstone, T., & Scherbaum, C. (1990). Marginal and mindful: Deviants in social interaction. *Journal of Personality and Social Psychology*, *59*, 140–149.

Frable, D. E. S., Platt, L., & Hoey, S. (1998). Concealable stigmas and positive self-perceptions: Feeling better around similar others. *Journal of Personality and Social Psychology*, *74*, 909–922.

Fracchia, J., Canale, D., Cambria, E., Ruest, E., & Sheppard, C. (1976). Public views of ex-mental patients: A note on perceived dangereousness and unpredictability. *Psychological Reports*, *38*, 495–498.

Francis, B. (1999). An investigation of the discourses children draw on their constructions of gender. *Journal of Applied Social Psychology*, *29*, 300–316.

Franco, F. M., & Maass, A. (1999). Intentional control over prejudice: When the choice of the measure matters. *European Journal of Social Psychology*, *29*, 469–477.

Franken, M. W. (1983). Sex role expectations in children's vocational aspirations and perceptions of occupations. *Psychology of Women Quarterly*, *8*, 59–68.

Freeman, H. E., Ross, M. J., Armor, D., & Pettigrew, T. F. (1966). Color gradation and attitudes among middle-income Negroes. *American Sociological Review*, *31*, 365–374.

Freeman, H. R. (1987). Structure and content of gender stereotypes: Effects of somatic appearance and trait information. *Psychology of Women Quarterly*, *11*, 59–68.

Freeman, H. R. (1988). Social perception of body builders. *Journal of Sport and Exercise Psychology*, *10*, 281–293.

Freud, S. (1930). *Civilization and its discontents* (J. Riviere, Trans.). London: Hogarth Press.

Freudiger, P., & Almquist, E. M. (1978). Male and female roles in the lyrics of three genres of contemporary music. *Sex Roles*, *4*, 51–65.

Friedman, A. (1979). Framing pictures: The role of knowledge in automatized encoding and memory. *Journal of Experimental Psychology: General*, *108*, 316–355.

Friedman, H., & Zebrowitz, L. A. (1992). The contribution of typical sex differences in facial maturity to sex role stereotypes. *Personality and Social Psychology Bulletin*, *18*, 430–438.

Frieze, I. H., Olson, J. E., & Russell, J. (1991). Attractiveness and income for men and women in management. *Journal of Applied Social Psychology*, *21*, 1039–1057.

Fuegen, K., & Biernat, M. (2000). Defining discrimination in the personal/group discrimination discrepancy. *Sex Roles*, *43*, 285–310.

Fuegen, K., & Biernat, M. (2002). Reexamining the effects of solo status for women and men. *Personality and Social Psychology Bulletin*, *28*, 913–925.

Fuller, L. K. (1992). *The Cosby Show: Audiences, impact, and implications*. Westport, CT: Greenwood Press.

Funder, D. C. (1987). Errors and mistakes: Evaluating the accuracy of social judgment. *Psychological Bulletin*, *101*, 75–90.

Funder, D. C. (1995). On the accuracy of personality judgment: A realistic approach. *Psychological Review*, *102*, 652–670.

Funder, D. C., & Colvin, C. R. (1988). Friends and strangers: Acquaintanceship, agreement, and the accuracy of personality judgment. *Journal of Personality and Social Psychology*, *55*, 149–158.

Funder, D. C., & Dobroth, K. M. (1987). Differences between traits: properties associated with intrajudge agreement. *Journal of Personality and Social Psychology*, *52*, 409–418.

Funk, S. G., Horowitz, A. D., Lipshitz, R., & Young, F. W. (1976). The perceived structure of American ethnic groups: The use of multidimensional scaling in stereotype research. *Sociometry*, *39*, 116–130.

Furnham, A. (1982). Why are the poor always with us?: Explanations for poverty in Britain. *British Journal of Social Psychology*, *21*, 311–322.

Furnham, A. (1988). *Lay theories: Everyday understanding of problems in the social sciences*. Oxford, UK: Pergamon Press.

Furnham, A., Abramsky, S., & Gunter, B. (1997). A cross-cultural content analysis of children's television advertisements. *Sex Roles*, *27*, 91–99.

Furnham, A., & Alibhai, N. (1983). Cross-cultural differences in the perception of female body shapes. *Psychological Medicine*, *13*, 829–837.

Furnham, A., & Baguma, P. (1994). Cross-cultural differences in the evaluation of male and female body shapes. *International Journal of Eating Disorders, 15*, 81–89.

Furnham, A., & Bower, P. (1992). A comparison of academic and lay theories of schizophrenia. *British Journal of Psychiatry, 161*, 201–210.

Furnham, A., Hester, C., & Weir, C. (1990). Sex differences in preferences for specific female body shapes. *Sex Roles, 22*, 743–754.

Furnham, A., & Nordling, R. (1998). Cross-cultural differences in preferences for specific male and female body shapes. *Personality and Individual Differences, 25*, 635–648.

Furnham, A., & Pendred, J. (1983). Attitudes towards the mentally and physically disabled. *British Journal of Medical Psychology, 56*, 179–187.

Furnham, A., & Rees, J. (1988). Lay theories of schizophrenia. *International Journal of Social Psychiatry, 34*, 212–220.

Furnham, A., & Schofield, S. (1986). Sex-role stereotyping in British radio advertisements. *British Journal of Social Psychology, 25*, 165–171.

Furnham, A., & Taylor, L. (1990). Lay theories of homosexuality: Aetiology, behaviours and "cures." *British Journal of Social Psychology, 29*, 135–147.

Furnham, A., & Thomson, L. (1999). Gender role stereotyping in advertisements on two British radio stations. *Sex Roles, 40*, 153–165.

Fyock, J., & Stangor, C. (1994). The role of memory biases in stereotype maintenance. *British Journal of Social Psychology, 33*, 331–343.

Gabbard, G. O., & Gabbard, K. (1992). Cinematic stereotypes contributing to the stigmatization of psychiatrists. In P. J. Fink & A. Tasman (Eds.), *Stigma and mental illness* (pp. 113–126). Washington, DC: American Psychiatric Press.

Gabbard, K., & Gabbard, G. O. (1999). *Psychiatry and the cinema* (2nd ed.). Washington, DC: American Psychiatric Press.

Gacsaly, S. A., & Borges, C. A. (1979). The male physique and behavioral expectations. *Journal of Psychology, 101*, 97–102.

Gaertner, L., & Insko, C. A. (2000). Intergroup discrimination in the minimal group paradigm: Categorization, reciprocation, or fear? *Journal of Personality and Social Psychology, 79*, 77–94.

Gaertner, L., & Insko, C. A. (2001). On the measurement of social orientations in the minimal group paradigm: Norms as moderators of the expression of intergroup bias. *European Journal of Social Psychology, 31*, 143–154.

Gaertner, L., & Schopler, J. (1998). Perceived ingroup entitativity and intergroup bias: An interconnection of self and others. *European Journal of Social Psychology, 28*, 963–980.

Gaertner, L., Sedikides, C., & Graetz, K. (1999). In search of self-definition: Motivational primacy of the individual self, motivational primacy of the collective self, or contextual primacy? *Journal of Personality and Social Psychology, 76*, 5–18.

Gaertner, L., Sedikides, C., Vevea, J. L., & Iuzzini, J. (2002). The "I," the "we," and the "when": A meta-analysis of motivational primacy in self-definition. *Journal of Personality and Social Psychology, 83*, 574–591.

Gaertner, S. L., & Dovidio, J. F. (1977). The subtlety of white racism, arousal, and helping behavior. *Journal of Personality and Social Psychology, 35*, 691–707.

Gaertner, S. L., & Dovidio, J. F. (1986). The aversive form of racism. In J. F. Dovidio & S. L. Gaertner (Eds.), *Prejudice, discrimination, and racism* (pp. 61–89). Orlando, FL: Academic Press.

Gaertner, S. L., & Dovidio, J. F. (2000). *Reducing intergroup bias: The Common Ingroup Identity Model.* London: Taylor & Francis.

Gaertner, S. L., Dovidio, J. F., Rust, M. C., Nier, J. A., Banker, B. S., Ward, C. M., Mottola, G. R., & Houlette, M. (1999). Reducing intergroup bias: Elements of intergroup cooperation. *Journal of Personality and Social Psychology, 76*, 388–402.

Gaertner, S. L., Mann, J., Murrell, A., & Dovidio, J. F. (1989). Reducing intergroup bias: The benefits of recategorization. *Journal of Personality and Social Psychology, 57*, 239–249.

Gaertner, S. L., Mann, J. A., Dovidio, J. F., Murrell, A. J., & Pomare, M. (1990). How does cooperation reduce intergroup bias? *Journal of Personality and Social Psychology, 59*, 692–704.

Gaertner, S. L., & McLaughlin, J. P. (1983). Racial stereotypes: Associations and ascriptions of positive and negative characteristics. *Social Psychology Quarterly, 46*, 23–30.

Gaertner, S. L., Rust, M. C., Dovidio, J. F., Bachman, B. A., & Anastasio, P. A. (1994). The contact hypothesis: The role of common ingroup identity on reducing intergroup bias. *Small Group Research, 25,* 244–249.

Gahagan, L. (1933). Judgments of occupations from printed photographs. *Journal of Social Psychology, 4,* 128–134.

Galinsky, A. D., & Moskowitz, G. B. (2000). Perspective-taking: Decreasing stereotype expression, stereotype accessibility, and in-group favoritism. *Journal of Personality and Social Psychology, 78,* 708–724.

Gallup, G. (1997). Gallup poll, Oct 17, 1997. *The Gallup Poll,* pp. 164–169.

Gallup, G. (1998a). Gallup poll of July 25, 1998. *The Gallup Poll,* pp. 89–91.

Gallup, G. (1998b). Gallup poll Nov 20–22, 1998. *The Gallup Poll,* pp. 238–239.

Gallup, G. (2001). Gallup poll of May 10–14, 2001. *The Gallup Poll,* pp. 133–134.

Gamson, W. (1992). *Talking Politics.* Cambridge, UK: Cambridge University Press.

Gan, S. L., Zillmann, D., & Mitrook, M. (1997). Stereotyping effect of black women's sexual rap on white audiences. *Basic and Applied Social Psychology, 19,* 381–399.

Gangestad, S. W., & Buss, D. M. (1993). Pathogen prevalence and human mate preferences. *Ethology and Sociobiology, 14,* 89–96.

Ganong, L. H., & Coleman, M. (1995). The content of mother stereotypes. *Sex Roles, 32,* 495–512.

Ganong, L. H., Coleman, M., & Mapes, D. (1990). A meta-analytic review of family structure stereotypes. *Journal of Marriage and the Family, 52,* 287–297.

Gara, M. A., & Rosenberg, S. (1981). Linguistic factors in implicit personality theory. *Journal of Personality and Social Psychology, 41,* 450–457.

Garcia-Marques, L., & Hamilton, D. L. (1996). Resolving the apparent discrepency between the incongruity effect and the expectancy-based illusory correlation effect: The TRAP model. *Journal of Personality and Social Psychology, 71,* 845–860.

Garcia-Marques, L., Hamilton, D. L., & Maddox, K. B. (2002). Exhaustive and heuristic retrieval processes in person cognition: Further tests of the TRAP model. *Journal of Personality and Social Psychology, 82,* 193–207.

Garcia-Marques, L., & Mackie, D. M. (1999). The impact of stereotype-incongruent information on perceived group variability and stereotype change. *Journal of Personality and Social Psychology, 77,* 979–990.

Gardner, R. C. (1973). Ethnic stereotypes: The traditional approach, a new look. *Canadian Psychologist, 14,* 133–148.

Gardner, R. C. (1994). Stereotypes as consensual beliefs. In M. P. Zanna & J. M. Olson (Eds.), *The Ontario Symposium: Vol. 7. The psychology of prejudice* (pp. 1–31). Hillsdale, NJ: Erlbaum.

Gardner, R. C., Kirby, D. M., & Finlay, J. C. (1973). Ethnic stereotypes: The significance of consensus. *Canadian Journal of Behavioural Science, 5,* 4–12.

Gardner, R. C., Kirby, D. M., Gorospe, F. H., & Villamin, A. C. (1972). Ethnic stereotypes: An alternative assessment technique, the stereotype differential. *Journal of Social Psychology, 87,* 259–267.

Gardner, R. C., Lalonde, R. N., Nero, A. M., & Young, M. Y. (1988). Ethnic stereotypes: Implications of measurement strategy. *Social Cognition, 6,* 40–60.

Gardner, R. C., MacIntyre, P. D., & Lalonde, R. N. (1995). The effects of multiple social categories on stereotyping. *Canadian Journal of Behavioural Science, 27,* 466–483.

Gardner, R. C., Taylor, D. M., & Feenstra, H. J. (1970). Ethnic stereotypes: Attitudes or beliefs? *Canadian Journal of Psychology, 24,* 321–334.

Garst, J., & Bodenhausen, G. V. (1997). Advertising's effects on men's gender role attitudes. *Sex Roles, 36,* 551–572.

Garvey, C., & Caramazza, A. (1974). Implicit causality in verbs. *Linguistic Inquiry, 5,* 459–464.

Garwood, S. G. (1976). First-name stereotypes as a factor in self-concept and school achievement. *Journal of Educational Psychology, 68,* 482–487.

Gash, H., & Morgan, M. (1993). School-based modifications of children's gender-related beliefs. *Journal of Applied Developmental Psychology, 14,* 277–287.

Gaskill, P. C., Fenton, N., & Porter, J. P. (1927). Judging the intelligence of boys from their photographs. *Journal of Applied Psychology, 11,* 394–403.

Gastil, J. (1990). Generic pronouns and sexist language: The oxymoronic character of masculine generics. *Sex Roles, 23,* 629–643.

Gatton, D. S., DuBois, C. L. Z., & Faley, R. H. (1999). The effects of organizational context on occupational gender-stereotyping. *Sex Roles, 40,* 567–582.

Gavanski, I., & Hui, C. (1992). Natural sample spaces and uncertain belief. *Journal of Personality and Social Psychology, 63,* 766–780.

Geis, F. L., Brown, V., Jennings, J. W., & Corrado-Taylor, D. (1984). Sex vs. status in sex-associated stereotypes. *Sex Roles, 11,* 771–786.

Gelman, S. A. (2000). The role of essentialism in children's concepts. *Advances in Child Development and Behavior, 27,* 55–98.

Gelman, S. A. (2003). *The essential child: Origins of essentialism in everyday life.* New York: Oxford University Press.

Gelman, S. A., Coley, J. D., & Gottfried, G. M. (1994). Essentialist beliefs in children: The acquisition of concepts and theories. In L. A. Hirschfeld & S. A. Gelman (Eds.), *Mapping the mind: Domain specificity in cognition and culture* (pp. 341–365). New York: Cambridge University Press.

Gelman, S. A., & Gottfried, G. M. (1996). Children's causal explanations of animate and inanimate motion. *Child Development, 67,* 1970–1987.

Gelman, S. A., & Hirschfeld, L. A. (1999). How biological is essentialism? In D. L. Medin & S. Atran (Eds.), *Folkbiology* (pp. 403–446). Cambridge, MA: MIT Press.

Gelman, S. A., & Markman, E. M. (1986). Categories and induction in young children. *Cognition, 23,* 183–208.

Gelman, S. A., & Medin, D. L. (1993). What's so essential about essentialism?: A different perspective on the interaction of perception, language, and conceptual knowledge. *Cognitive Development, 8,* 157–167.

Gelman, S. A., & Wellman, H. M. (1991). Insides and essences: Early understanding of the non-obvious. *Cognition, 38,* 213–244.

Gerard, H. B. (1988). School desegregation: The social science role. In P. A. Katz & D. A. Taylor (Eds.), *Eliminating racism: Profiles in controversy* (pp. 225–236). New York: Plenum Press.

Gerard, H. B., & Miller, N. (1975). *School desegregation: A long-term study.* New York: Plenum Press.

Gerber, G. L. (1988). Leadership roles and the gender stereotype traits. *Sex Roles, 18,* 649–668.

Gibbons, J. L., Stiles, D. A., & Shkodriani, G. M. (1991). Adolescents' attitudes toward family and gender roles: An international comparison. *Sex Roles, 25,* 625–643.

Gidron, D., Koehler, D. J., & Tversky, A. (1993). Implicit qualification of personality traits. *Personality and Social Psychology Bulletin, 19,* 594–604.

Gifford, R. (1994). A lens-mapping framework for understanding the encoding and decoding of interpersonal dispositions in nonverbal behavior. *Journal of Personality and Social Psychology, 66,* 398–412.

Gifford, R. K. (1975). Information properties of descriptive words. *Journal of Personality and Social Psychology, 31,* 727–734.

Gilbert, D. T. (1991). How mental systems believe. *American Psychologist, 46,* 107–119.

Gilbert, D. T., & Hixon, J. G. (1991). The trouble of thinking: Activation and application of stereotypic beliefs. *Journal of Personality and Social Psychology, 60,* 509–517.

Gilbert, D. T., & Malone, P. S. (1995). The correspondence bias. *Psychological Bulletin, 117,* 21–38.

Gilbert, D. T., McNulty, S. E., Giuliano, T. A., & Benson, J. E. (1992). Blurry words and fuzzy deeds: The attribution of obscure behavior. *Journal of Personality and Social Psychology, 62,* 18–25.

Gilbert, D. T., Pelham, B. W., & Krull, D. S. (1988). On cognitive busyness: When person perceivers meet persons perceived. *Journal of Personality and Social Psychology, 54,* 733–740.

Gilbert, G. M. (1951). Stereotype persistence and change among college students. *Journal of Abnormal and Social Psychology, 46,* 245–254.

Giles, H., Fox, S. A., & Smith, E. (1993). Patronizing the elderly: Intergenerational evaluations. *Research in Language and Social Interaction, 26,* 129–150.

Giles, H., & Johnson, P. (1987). Ethnolinguistic identity theory: A social, psychological approach to language maintenance. *International Journal of the Sociology of Language, 68,* 69–99.

Giles, H., Mulac, A., Bradac, J., & Johnson, P. (1987). Speech accomodation theory: The first decade and beyond. *Communication Yearbook, 10,* 13–48.

Giles, H., & Williams, A. (1994). Patronizing the young: Forms and evaluations. *International Journal of Aging and Human Development, 39,* 33–53.

Gilovich, T. (1981). Seeing the past in the present: The effect of association to familiar events on judgments and decisions. *Journal of Personality and Social Psychology, 40,* 797–808.

Gilovich, T., & Regan, D. (1986). The actor and the epxeriencer: Divergent patterns of causal attribution. *Social Cognition, 4,* 342–352.

Giner-Sorolla, R., & Chaiken, S. (1994). The causes of hostile media judgments. *Journal of Experimental Social Psychology, 30,* 165–180.

Giuliano, T. A., Popp, K. E., & Knight, J. L. (2000). Footballs versus barbies: Childhood play activities as predictors of sport participation by women. *Sex Roles, 42,* 159–181.

Glaser, J., & Banaji, M. R. (1999). When fair is foul and foul is fair: Reverse priming in automatic evaluation. *Journal of Personality and Social Psychology, 77,* 669–687.

Glaser, J. M., & Gilens, M. (1997). Interregional migration and political resocialization: A study of racial attitudes under pressure. *Public Opinion Quarterly, 61,* 72–86.

Glick, P. (1991). Trait-based and sex-based discrimination in occupational prestige, occupational salary, and hiring. *Sex Roles, 25,* 351–378.

Glick, P., Diebold, J., Bailey-Werner, B., & Zhu, L. (1997). The two faces of Adam: Ambivalent sexism and polarized attitudes toward women. *Personality and Social Psychology Bulletin, 23,* 1323–1334.

Glick, P., & Fiske, S. T. (1996). The Ambivalent Sexism Inventory: Differentiating hostile and benevolent sexism. *Journal of Personality and Social Psychology, 70,* 491–512.

Glick, P., & Fiske, S. T. (1999a). The Ambivalence toward Men Inventory: Differentiating hostile and benevolent beliefs about men. *Psychology of Women Quarterly, 23,* 519–536.

Glick, P., & Fiske, S. T. (1999b). Gender, power dynamics, and social interaction. In M. Feree, J. Lorker, & B. B. Hess (Eds.), *Revisioning gender* (pp. 365–398). Thousand Oaks, CA: Sage.

Glick, P., & Fiske, S. T. (1999c). Sexism and other "isms": Interdependence, status, and the ambivalent content of stereotypes. In W. B. Swann, Jr., J. H. Langlois, & L. A. Gilbert (Eds.), *Sexism and stereotypes: The gender science of Janet Taylor Spence* (pp. 193–211). Washington, DC: American Psychological Association.

Glick, P., & Fiske, S. T. (2001). Ambivalent sexism. In M. P. Zanna (Ed.), *Advances in experimental social psychology* (Vol. 33, pp. 115–188). San Diego, CA: Academic Press.

Glick, P., Fiske, S. T., Mladinic, A., Saiz, J. L., Abrams, D., & Masser, B. (2000). Beyond prejudice as simple antipathy: Hostile and benevolent sexism across cultures. *Journal of Personality and Social Psychology, 79,* 763–775.

Glick, P., Wilk, K., & Perreault, M. (1995). Images of occupations: Components of gender and status in occupational stereotypes. *Sex Roles, 32,* 565–582.

Glick, P., Zion, C., & Nelson, C. (1988). What mediates sex discrimination in hiring decisions? *Journal of Personality and Social Psychology, 55,* 178–186.

Glock, C. Y., Wuthnow, R., Piliavin, J. A., & Spencer, M. (1975). *Adolescent prejudice.* New York: Harper & Row.

Godfrey, S., Richman, C. L., & Withers, T. N. (2000). Reliability and validity of a new scale to measure prejudice: The GRISMS. *Current Psychology: Developmental, Learning, Personality, Social, 19,* 3–20.

Goffman, E. (1963). *Stigma: Notes on the management of spoiled identity.* Englewood Cliffs, NJ: Prentice-Hall.

Gold, R. S., & Skinner, M. J. (1996). Judging a book by its cover: Gay men's use of perceptible characteristics to infer antibody status. *International Journal of STD and AIDS, 7,* 39–43.

Gold, R. S., Skinner, M. J., & Hinchy, J. (1999). Gay men's stereotypes about who is HIV infected: A further study. *International Journal of STD and AIDS, 10,* 600–605.

Goldberg, P., (1968). Are women prejudiced against women? *Trans-Action, 5,* 28–30.

Golde, P., & Kogan, N. A. (1959). A sentence completion procedure for assessing attitudes toward old people. *Journal of Gerontology, 14,* 355–363.

Goldfield, A., & Chrisler, J. C. (1995). Body stereotyping and stigmatization of obese persons by first graders. *Perceptual and Motor Skills, 81,* 909–910.

Goldstein, A. G. (1979). Race-related variation of facial features: Anthropomorphic data I. *Bulletin of the Psychonomic Society, 13,* 187–190.

Goldstein, A. G., & Chance, J. (1978). Judging face similarity in own and other races. *Journal of Psychology, 98,* 185–193.

Goldstein, A. G., Chance, J. E., & Gilbert, B. (1984). Facial stereotypes of good guys and bad guys: A replication and extension. *Bulletin of the Psychonomic Society, 22,* 549–552.

Goldstein, S. B., & Johnson, V. A. (1997). Stigma by association: Perceptions of the dating partners of college students with physical disabilities. *Basic and Applied Social Psychology, 19,* 495–504.

Golebiowska, E. A. (2000). The etiology of individual-targeted intolerance: Group stereotypes and judgments of individual group members. *Political Psychology, 21,* 443–464.

Golombok, S., & Fivush, R. (1994). *Gender development.* Cambridge, UK: Cambridge University Press.

Gomez, J. P., & Trierweiler, S. J. (1999). Exploring cross-group discrimination: Measuring the dimensions of inferiorization. *Journal of Applied Social Psychology, 29,* 1900–1926.

Gomez, J. P., & Trierweiler, S. J. (2001). Does discrimination terminology create response bias in questionnaire studies of discrimination? *Personality and Social Psychology Bulletin, 27,* 630–638.

Gonzales, P. M., Blanton, H., & Williams, K. J. (2002). The effects of stereotype threat and double-minority status on the test performance of Latino women. *Personality and Social Psychology Bulletin, 28,* 659–670.

Gooden, A. M., & Gooden, M. A. (2001). Gender representation in notable children's picture books: 1995–1999. *Sex Roles, 45,* 89–101.

Goodman, M. E. (1952). *Race awareness in young children.* Cambridge, MA: Addison-Wesley.

Goodman, N., Richardson, A., Dornbush, S. M., & Hastorf, A. H. (1963). Variant reactions to physical disabilities. *American Sociological Review, 28,* 429–435.

Goodwin, S. A., Gubin, A., Fiske, S. T., & Yzerbyt, V. Y. (2000). Power can bias impression processes: Stereotyping subordinates by default and by design. *Group Processes and Intergroup Relations, 3,* 227–256.

Gordon, L. (1986). College student stereotypes of blacks and Jews on two campuses: Four studies spanning 50 years. *Sociology and Social Research, 70,* 200–201.

Gordon, R. (1962). *Stereotypy of imagery and belief as an ego defense.* London: Cambridge University Press.

Gordon, R. A. (1990). Attributions for blue-collar and white-collar crime: The effects of subject and defendant race on simulated juror decisions. *Journal of Applied Social Psychology, 20,* 971–983.

Gordon, R. A., & Anderson, K. S. (1995). Perceptions of race-stereotypic and race-nonstereotypic crimes: The impact of response-time instructions on attributions and judgments. *Basic and Applied Social Psychology, 16,* 455–470.

Gordon, S. E., & Wyer, R. S., Jr. (1987). Person memory: Category-set-size effects on the recall of a person's behaviors. *Journal of Personality and Social Psychology, 53,* 648–662.

Gorn, G. L., Goldberg, M. E., & Kanung, R. N. (1976). The role of educational television in changing intergroup attitudes of children. *Child Development, 47,* 277–280.

Gorsuch, R., & Aleshire, D. (1974). Christian faith and ethnic prejudice: A review and interpretation of results. *Journal for the Scientific Study of Religion, 13,* 281–307.

Gosling, S. D., Ko, S. J., Mannarelli, T., & Morris, M. E. (2002). A room with a cue: Personality judgments based on offices and bedrooms. *Journal of Personality and Social Psychology, 82,* 379–398.

Gove, W., & Fain, T. (1973). The stigma of mental hospitalization: An attempt to evaluate its consequences. *Archives of General Psychiatry, 29,* 494–500.

Graesser, A., Woll, S., Kowalski, D., & Smith, D. (1980). Memory for typical and atypical actions in scripted activities. *Journal of Experimental Psychology: Human Learning and Memory, 6,* 503–515.

Graham, J. A., & Jouhar, A. J. (1980). Cosmetics considered in the context of physical attractiveness: A review. *International Journal of Cosmetics Science, 2,* 77–101.

Grant, R. P., & Brown, R. (1995). From ethnocentrism to collective protest: Responses to relative deprivation and threats to social identity. *Social Psychology Quarterly, 58,* 195–211.

Graves, S. B. (1993). Television, the portrayal of African Americans, and the development of children's attitudes. In G. L. Berry & J. K. Asamen (Eds.), *Children and television: Images in a changing sociocultural world* (pp. 179–190). Newbury Park, CA: Sage.

Gray, H. (1989). Television, black Americans, and the American dream. *Critical Studies in Mass Communication, 6,* 376–386.

Gray, H. (1995). *Watching race: Television and the struggle for the sign of blackness.* Minneapolis: University of Minnesota Press.

Green, B. L., & Kenrick, D. T. (1994). The attractiveness of gender-typed traits at different relationship levels: Androgynous characteristics may be desirable after all. *Personality and Social Psychology Bulletin, 20,* 244–253.

Green, D. E., McCormick, I. A., Walkey, F. H., & Taylor, A. J. (1987). Community attitudes to mental illness in New Zealand twenty-two years on. *Social Science and Medicine, 24,* 417–422.

Green, D. E., Walkey, F. H., Taylor, A. J., & McCormick, I. A. (1987). New Zealand attitudes to mental health. *New Zealand Journal of Psychology, 16,* 37–41.

Green, R. J., & Ashmore, R. D. (1998). Taking and developing pictures in the head: Assessing the physical stereotypes of eight gender types. *Journal of Applied Social Psychology, 28,* 1609–1636.

Green, S., Buchanan, D. R., & Heuer, S. K. (1984). Winners, losers, and choosers: A field investigation of dating initiation. *Personality and Social Psychology Bulletin, 10,* 502–511.

Greenberg, B. S., & Brand, J. E. (1994). Minorities and the mass media: 1970s to 1990s. In J. Bryant & D. Zillmann (Eds.), *Media effects: Advances in theory and research* (pp. 273–314). Hillsdale, NJ: Erlbaum.

Greenberg, H. R. (2000). A field guide to cinetherapy: On celluloid psychoanalysis and its practitioners. *American Journal of Psychoanalysis, 60,* 329–339.

Greenberg, J., & Pyszczynski, T. (1985). The effects of an overheard ethnic slur on evaluations of the target: How to spread a social disease. *Journal of Experimental Social Psychology, 21,* 61–72.

Greenberg, J., Pyszczynski, T., Solomon, S., Rosenblatt, A., Veeder, M., Kirkland, S., & Lyon, D. (1990). Evidence for terror management theory: II. The effects of mortality salience on reactions to those who threaten or bolster the cultural worldview. *Journal of Personality and SocialPsychology, 58,* 308–318.

Greene, J. P. (2001, November). *High school graduate rates in the United States.* New York: Black Alliance for Educational Options.

Greene, S. B., & McKoon, G. (1995). Telling something we can't know: Experimental approaches to verbs exhibiting implicit causality. *Psychological Science, 6,* 262–270.

Greenland, K., & Brown, R. (1999). Categorization and intergroup anxiety in contact between British and Japanese nationals. *European Journal of Social Psychology, 29,* 503–521.

Greenwald, A. G., & Banaji, M. R. (1995). Implicit social cognition: Attitudes, self-esteem, and stereotypes. *Psychological Review, 102,* 4–27.

Greenwald, A. G., Banaji, M. R., Rudman, L. A., Farnham, S. D., Nosek, B. A., & Mellott, D. S. (2002). A unified theory of implicit attitudes, stereotypes, self-esteem, and self-concept. *Psychological Review, 109,* 3–25.

Greenwald, A. G., McGhee, D. E., & Schwartz, J. L. K. (1998). Measuring individual differences in implicit cognition: The implicit association test. *Journal of Personality and Social Psychology, 74,* 1464–1480.

Greenwald, H. J., & Oppenheim, D. B. (1968). Reported magnitude of self-misidentification among Negro children—artifact? *Journal of Personality and Social Psychology, 8,* 49–52.

Gregor, A. J., & McPherson, D. A. (1966). Racial preference and ego identity among white and Bantu children in the Republic of South Africa. *Genetic Psychology Monographs, 73,* 217–254.

Grier, S. A., & McGill, A. L. (2000). How we explain depends on whom we explain: The impact of social category on the selection of causal comparisons and causal explanations. *Journal of Experimental Social Psychology, 36,* 545–566.

Griffin, J. H. (1960). *Black like me.* New York: New American Library.

Griffith, K. H. (1999). *Sexual orientation, gender roles, and occupation: Bias during the selection process.* Unpublished master's thesis, Rice University.

Griffith, K. H., & Hebl, M. R. (2002). The disclosure dilemma for gay men and lesbians: "Coming out" at work. *Journal of Applied Psychology, 87,* 1191–1199.

Griggs v. Duke Power Comany, 401 U.S. 424 (1971).

Gross, A. E., Green, S. K., Storck, J. T., & Vanyur, J. M. (1980). Disclosure of sexual orientation and impressions of male and female homosexuals. *Personality and Social Psychology Bulletin, 6,* 307–314.

Guerin, B. (1994). Gender bias in the abstractness of verbs and adjectives. *Journal of Social Psychology, 134,* 421–428.

Guglielmi, R. S. (1999). Psychophysiological assessment of prejudice: Past research, current status, and future directions. *Personality and Social Psychology Review, 3,* 123–157.

Guimond, S. (2000). Group socialization and prejudice: The social transmission of intergroup attitudes and beliefs. *European Journal of Social Psychology, 30,* 335–354.

Guimond, S., & Dambrun, M. (2002). When prosperity breeds intergroup hostility: The effects of relative deprivation and relative gratification on prejudice. *Personality and Social Psychology Bulletin, 28,* 900–912.

Guimond, S., Dif, S., & Aupy, A. (2002). Social identity, relative group status and intergroup attitudes: When favorable outcomes change intergroup relations . . . for the worse. *European Journal of Social Psychology, 32,* 739–760.

Guinote, A., Judd, C. M., & Brauer, M. (2002). Effects of power on perceived and objective group variability: Evidence that more powerful groups are more variable. *Journal of Personality and Social Psychology, 82,* 708–721.

Gundlach, R. H. (1950). The effect of on-the-job experience with Negroes upon social attitudes of white workers in union shops. *American Psychologist, 5,* 300.

Gunter, B. (1995). *Television and gender representation.* London: Libbey.

Gunter, B., & McAleer, J. J. (1990). *Children and television: The one eyed monster.* London: Routledge.

Guo, X., Erber, J. T., & Szuchman, L. T. (1999). Age and forgetfulness: Can stereotypes be modified? *Educational Gerontology, 25,* 457–466.

Gurwitz, S. B., & Marcus, M. (1978). Effects of anticipated interaction, sex and homosexual stereotypes on first impressions. *Journal of Applied Social Psychology, 8,* 47–56.

Haas, A. (1979). Male and female spoken language differences: Stereotypes and evidence. *Psychological Bulletin, 86,* 616–626.

Haddock, G., & Zanna, M. P. (1994). Preferring "housewives" to "feminists": Categorization and the favorability of attitudes toward women. *Psychology of Women Quarterly, 18,* 25–52.

Haddock, G., & Zanna, M. P. (1998a). Assessing the impact of affective and cognitive information in predicting attitudes toward capital punishment. *Law and Human Behavior, 22,* 325–339.

Haddock, G., & Zanna, M. P. (1998b). Authoritarianism, values, and the favorability and structure of antigay attitudes. In G. M. Herek (Ed.), *Stigma and sexual orientation: Understanding prejudice against lesbians, gay men, and bisexuals* (pp. 82–107). Thousand Oaks, CA: Sage.

Haddock, G., & Zanna, M. P. (1998c). On the use of open-ended measures to assess attitudinal components. *British Journal of Social Psychology, 37,* 129–149.

Haddock, G., & Zanna, M. P. (1999). Cognition, affect, and the prediction of social attitudes. In W. Strobe & M. Hewstone (Eds.), *European review of social psychology* (Vol. 10, pp. 75–99). Chichester, UK: Wiley.

Haddock, G., Zanna, M. P., & Esses, V. M. (1993). Assessing the structure of prejudicial attitudes: The case of attitudes toward homosexuals. *Journal of Personality and Social Psychology, 65,* 1105–1118.

Haddock, G., Zanna, M. P., & Esses, V. M. (1994a). The (limited) role of trait-laden stereotypes in predicting attitudes toward Native peoples. *British Journal of Social Psychology, 33,* 83–106.

Haddock, G., Zanna, M. P., & Esses, V. M. (1994b). Mood and the expression of intergroup attitudes: The moderating effect of affect intensity. *European Journal of Social Psychology, 24,* 189–205.

Hadjimarcou, J., & Hu, M. Y. (1999). Global product stereotypes and heuristic processing: The impact of ambient task complexity. *Psychology and Marketing, 16,* 583–612.

Hagendoorn, L., & Henke, R. (1991). The effect of multiple category membership on intergroup evaluations in a north Indian context: Class, caste, and religion. *British Journal of Social Psychology, 30,* 247–260.

Hagendoorn, L., & Kleinpenning, G. (1991). The contribution of domain-specific stereotypes to ethnic social distance. *British Journal of Social Psychology, 30,* 63–78.

Hagendoorn, L., & Linssen, H. (1994). National characteristics and national stereotypes: A seven-nation comparative study. In R. Farnen (Ed.), *Cross-national perspectives in nationality, identity, and ethnicity* (pp. 103–126). New Brunswick, NJ: Transaction.

Haley, E. A. (2001). *Effects of work attitudes on reactions to a pending corporate acquisition: A qualitative and quantitative investigation.* Unpublished doctoral dissertation, Rice University.

Hall, J. A., & Carter, J. D. (1999). Gender-stereotype accuracy as an individual difference. *Journal of Personality and Social Psychology, 77,* 350–359.

Hamberger, J., & Hewstone, M. (1997). Inter-ethnic contact as a predictor of blatent and subtle prejudice: Tests of a model in four West European nations. *British Journal of Social Psychology, 36,* 173–190.

Hamilton, D. L. (1979). A cognitive-attributional analysis of stereotyping. In L. Berkowitz (Ed.), *Advances in experimental social psychology* (Vol. 12, pp. 53–84). New York: Academic Press.

Hamilton, D. L. (Ed.). (1981a). *Cognitive processes in stereotyping and intergroup behavior.* Hillsdale, NJ: Erlbaum.

Hamilton, D. L. (1981b). Illusory correlation as a basis for stereotyping. In D. L. Hamilton (Ed.), *Cognitive processes in stereotyping and intergroup behavior* (pp. 115–144). Hillsdale, NJ: Erlbaum.

Hamilton, D. L., Driscoll, D. M., & Worth, L. T. (1989). Cognitive organization of impressions: Effects of incongruity in complex representations. *Journal of Personality and Social Psychology, 58,* 1–14.

Hamilton, D. L., Dugan, P. M., & Trolier, T. K. (1985). The formation of stereotypic beliefs: Further evidence for distinctiveness-based illusory correlations. *Journal of Personality and Social Psychology, 48,* 5–17.

Hamilton, D. L., & Gifford, R. K. (1976). Illusory correlation in interpersonal perception: A cognitive basis of stereotypic judgments. *Journal of Experimental Social Psychology, 12,* 392–407.

Hamilton, D. L., Katz, L. B., & Leier, V. O. (1980). Organizational processes in impression formation. In R. Hastie, T. M. Ostrom, E. B. Ebbesen, R. S. Wyer, Jr., D. L. Hamilton, & D. Carlston (Eds.), *Person memory: The cognitive basis of social perception* (pp. 121–153). Hillsdale, NJ: Elrbaum.

Hamilton, D. L., & Rose, T. (1980). Illusory correlation and the maintenance of stereotypic beliefs. *Journal of Personality and Social Psychology, 39,* 832–845.

Hamilton, D. L., & Sherman, S. J. (1989). Illusory correlations: Implications for stereotype theory and research. In D. Bar-Tal, C. F. Graumann, A. W. Kruglanski, & W. Stroebe (Eds.), *Stereotyping and prejudice: Changing conceptions* (pp. 59–82). New York: Springer-Verlag.

Hamilton, D. L., & Sherman, J. W. (1994). Stereotypes. In R. S. Wyer, Jr., & T. K. Srull (Eds.), *Handbook of Social Cognition* (2nd ed., pp. 59–82). Hillsdale, NJ: Erlbaum.

Hamilton, D. L., & Sherman, S. J. (1996). Perceiving persons and groups. *Psychological Review, 103,* 336–355.

Hamilton, D. L., Sherman, S. J., & Castelli, L. (2002). A group by any other name: The role of entitativity in group perception. In W. Stroebe & M. Hewstone (Eds.), *European review of social psychology* (Vol. 12, pp. 139–165). Chichester, UK: Wiley.

Hamilton, D. L., Sherman, S. J., & Lickel, B. (1998). Perceiving social groups: The importance of the entitativity contimuum. In C. Sedikides, J. Schopler, & C. A. Insko (Eds.), *Intergroup cognition and intergroup behavior* (pp. 47–74). Mahwah, NJ: Erlbaum.

Hamilton, D. L., Sherman, S. J., & Maddox, K. B. (1999). Dualities and continua: Implications for understanding perceptions of persons and groups. In S. Chaiken & Y. Trope (Eds.), *Dual-process theories in social psychology* (pp. 606–626). New York: Guilford Press.

Hamilton, D. L., Sherman, S. J., & Ruvolo, C. M. (1990). Stereotype-based expectancies: Effects of information processing and social behavior. *Journal of Social Issues, 46*(2), 35–60.

Hamilton, D. L., Stroessner, S. J., & Driscoll, D. M. (1994). Social cognition and the study of stereotyping. In P. G. Devine, D. L. Hamilton, & T. M. Ostrom (Eds.), *Social cognition: Impact on social psychology* (pp. 291–321). San Diego, CA: Academic Press.

Hamilton, D. L., & Trolier, T. K. (1986). Stereotypes and stereotyping. In J. Dovidio & S. L. Gaertner (Eds.), *Prejudice, discrimination, and racism: Theory and research* (pp. 127–163). Orlando, FL: Academic Press.

Hamm, N. H., Williams, D. O., & Dalhouse, A. D. (1973). Preferences for black skin among Negro adults. *Psychological Reports, 32,* 1171–1175.

Hampson, S. E. (1982). Person memory: A semantic category model of personality traits. *British Journal of Psychology, 73,* 1–11.

Hampson, S. E. (1983). Trait ascription and depth of acquaintance: The preference for traits in personality descriptions and its relation to target familarity. *Journal of Research in Personality, 17,* 398–411.

Hampson, S. E. (1997). Determinants of inconsistent personality descriptions: Trait and target effects. *Journal of Personality, 65,* 249–290.

Hampson, S. E., John, O. P., & Goldberg, L. R. (1986). Category breadth and hierarchical structure in personality: Studies of asymmetries in judgments of trait implications. *Journal of Personality and Social Psychology, 51,* 37–54.

Hampton, J. A. (1987). Inheritance of attributes in natural concept conjunctions. *Memory and Cognition, 15,* 55–71.

Hampton, J. A. (1997). Emergent attributes in combined categories. In T. B. Ward, S. M. Smith, & J. Vaid (Eds.), *Creative thought: An investigation of conceptual structures and processes* (pp. 83–110). Washington, DC: American Psychological Association.

Hanita, M., Gavanski, I., & Fazio, R. H. (1997). Influencing probability judgments by manipulating the accessibility of sample spaces. *Personality and Social Psychology Bulletin, 23,* 801–813.

Hannah, M. E., & Midlarsky, E. (1987). Differential impact of labels and behavioral descriptions on attitudes toward people with disabilities. *Rehabilitation Psychology, 32,* 227–238.

Hanno, M. S., & Jones, L. E. (1973). Effects of a change in reference person on the multidimensional structure and evaluation of trait adjectives. *Journal of Personality and Social Psychology, 28,* 368–375.

Hansen, C. H., & Hansen, R. D. (1988). How rock music videos can change what is seen when boy meets girl: Priming stereotypic appraisal of social interactions. *Sex Roles, 19,* 287–316.

Hansen, F. J., & Reekie, L.-J. (1990). Sex differences in clinical judgments of male and female therapists. *Sex Roles, 23,* 51–64.

Hantzi, A. (1995). Change in stereotypic perceptions of familiar and unfamiliar groups: The pervasiveness of the subtyping model. *British Journal of Social Psychology, 34,* 463–477.

Harari, H., & McDavid, J. W. (1973). Name stereotypes and teachers' expectations. *Journal of Educational Psychology, 65,* 222–225.

Harasty, A. S. (1997). The interpersonal nature of social stereotypes: Differential discussion patterns about in-groups and out-groups. *Personality and Social Psychology Bulletin, 23,* 270–284.

Harber, K. D. (1998). Feedback to minorities: Evidence of a positive bias. *Journal of Personality and Social Psychology, 74,* 622–628.

Hardin, C. D., & Higgins, E. T. (1996). Shared reality: How social verification makes the subjective objective. In R. M. Sorrentino & E. T. Higgins (Eds.), *Handbook of motivation and cognition: Vol. 3. The interpersonal context* (pp. 28–84). New York: Guilford Press.

Harding, J., Proshansky, H., Kutner, B., & Chein, I. (1969). Prejudice and ethnic relations. In G. Lindzey & E. Aronson (Eds.), *The handbook of social psychology* (2nd ed., Vol. 5, pp. 1–76). Reading, MA: Addison-Wesley.

Harris, J. R. (1995). Where is the child's environment?: A group socialization theory of development. *Psychological Review, 102,* 458–489.

Harris, J. R. (1998). *The nurture assumption: Why children turn out the way they do.* New York: Free Press.

Harris, L. (1975). *The myth and reality of aging in America.* Washington, DC: National Council on Aging.

Harris, M. B. (1983). Eating habits, restraint, knowledge, and attitudes toward obesity. *International Journal of Obesity, 7,* 271–276.

Harris, M. B. (1990). Is love seen as different for the obese? *Journal of Applied Social Psychology, 20,* 1209–1224.

Harris, M. B. (1991). Sex differences in stereotypes of spectacles. *Journal of Applied Social Psychology, 21,* 1659–1680.

Harris, M. B., Harris, R. J., & Bochner, S. (1982). Fat, four-eyed, and female: Stereotypes of obesity, glasses, and gender. *Journal of Applied Social Psychology, 12,* 503–516.

Harris, M. B., & Smith, S. D. (1983). The relationships of age, sex, ethnicity, and weight to stereotypes of obesity and self-perception. *International Journal of Obesity, 7,* 361–371.

Harris, M. B., Walters, L. C., & Waschull, S. (1991a). Altering attitudes and knowledge about obesity. *Journal of Social Psychology, 131,* 881–884.

Harris, M. B., Walters, L. C., & Waschull, S. (1991b). Gender and ethnic differences in obesity-related behaviors and attitudes in a college sample. *Journal of Applied Social Psychology, 21,* 1545–1566.

Harris, M. J., Milich, R., Corbitt, E., Hoover, D. W., & Brady, M. (1992). Self-fulfilling effects of stigmatizing information on children's social interactions. *Journal of Personality and Social Psychology*, *63*, 41–50.

Harris, M. J., Milich, R., Johnston, E. M., & Hoover, D. W. (1990). Effects of expectancies on children's social interactions. *Journal of Experimental Social Psychology*, *26*, 1–12.

Harris, M. J., & Rosenthal, R. (1985). Mediation of interpersonal expectancy effects: 31 meta-analyses. *Psychological Bulletin*, *97*, 363–386.

Harris, R. J., & Firestone, J. M. (1998). Changes in predictors of gender role ideologies among women: A multivariate analysis. *Sex Roles*, *38*, 239–252.

Harrison, K. (2000). Television viewing, fat stereotyping, body shape standards, and eating disorder symptomatology in grade school children. *Communication Research*, *27*, 617–640.

Hartley, E. (1946). *Problems in prejudice*. New York: King's Crown Press.

Hartman, A. A., Nicolay, R. C., & Hurley, J. (1968). Unique personal names as a social adjustment factor. *Journal of Social Psychology*, *75*, 107–110.

Hartsough, W. R., & Fontana, A. F. (1970). Persistence of ethnic stereotypes and the relative importance of positive and negative stereotyping for association preferences. *Psychological Reports*, *27*, 723–731.

Haslam, N., Rothschild, L., & Ernst, D. (2000). Essentialist beliefs about social categories. *British Journal of Social Psychology*, *39*, 113–127.

Haslam, N., Rothschild, L., & Ernst, D. (2002). Are essentialist beliefs associated with prejudice? *British Journal of Social Psychology*, *41*, 87–100.

Haslam, S. A. (1997). Stereotyping and social influence: Foundations of stereotype consensus. In R. Spears, P. J. Oakes, N. Ellemers, & S. A. Haslam (Eds.), *The social psychology of stereotyping and group life* (pp. 119–143). Oxford, UK: Blackwell.

Haslam, S. A., McGarty, C., & Brown, P. M. (1996). The search for differentiated meaning is a precursor to illusory correlation. *Personality and Social Psychology Bulletin*, *22*, 611–619.

Haslam, S. A., McGarty, C., Oakes, P. J., & Turner, J. C. (1993). Social comparative context and illusory correlation: Testing between ingroup bias and social identity models of stereotype formation. *Australian Journal of Psychology*, *45*, 97–101.

Haslam, S. A., Oakes, P. J., McGarty, C., Turner, J. C., Reynolds, K. J., & Eggins, R. A. (1996). Stereotyping and social influence: The mediation of stereotype appplicability and sharedness by the views of in-group and out-group members. *British Journal of Social Psychology*, *35*, 369–397.

Haslam, S. A., Oakes, P. J., Reynolds, K. J., & Turner, J. C. (1999). Social identity salience and the emergence of stereotype consensus. *Personality and Social Psychology Bulletin*, *25*, 809–818.

Haslam, S. A., Oakes, P. J., Turner, J. C., & McGarty, C. (1995). Social categorization and group homogeneity: Changes in the perceived applicability of stereotype content as a function of comparative context and trait favorableness. *British Journal of Social Psychology*, *34*, 139–160.

Haslam, S. A., & Turner, J. C. (1992). Context-dependent variation in social stereotyping: 2. The relationship between frame of reference, self-categorization and accentation. *European Journal of Social Psychology*, *22*, 251–277.

Haslam, S. A., Turner, J. C., Oakes, P. J., McGarty, C., & Hayes, B. K. (1992). Context-dependent variation in social stereotyping: 1. The effects of intergroup relations as mediated by social change and frame of reference. *European Journal of Social Psychology*, *22*, 3–20.

Haslam, S. A., Turner, J. C., Oakes, P. J., McGarty, C., & Reynolds, K. J. (1998). The group as a basis for emergent stereotype consensus. In W. Stroebe & M. Hewstone (Eds.), *European review of social psychology* (Vol. 8, pp. 203–239). Chichester, UK: Wiley.

Haslam, S. A., Turner, J. C., Oakes, P. J., Reynolds, K. J., Eggins, R. A., Nolan, M., & Tweedie, J. (1998). When do stereotypes become really consensual?: Investigating the group-based dynamics of the consensualization process. *European Journal of Social Psychology*, *28*, 755–776.

Haslam, S. A., & Wilson, A. (2000). In what sense are prejudicial beliefs personal?: The importance of an in-group's shared stereotypes. *British Journal of Social Psychology*, *39*, 45–63.

Hass, R. G., Katz, I., Rizzo, N., Bailey, J., & Eisenstadt, D. (1991). Cross-racial appraisal as related to attitude ambivalence and cognitive complexity. *Personality and Social Psychology Bulletin*, *17*, 83–92.

Hass, R. G., Katz, I., Rizzo, N., Bailey, J., & Moore, L. (1992). When racial ambivalence evokes negative affect, using a disguised measure of mood. *Personality and Social Psychology Bulletin, 18,* 786–797.

Hassin, R., & Trope, Y. (2000). Facing faces: Studies on the cognitive aspects of physiognomy. *Journal of Personality and Social Psychology, 78,* 837–852.

Hastie, R. (1980). Memory for behavioral information that confirms or contradicts a personality impression. In R. Hastie, T. M. Ostrom, E. B. Ebbesen, R. S. Wyer, Jr., D. L. Hamilton, & D. Carlston (Eds.), *Person memory: The cognitive basis of social perception* (pp. 155–157). Hillsdale, NJ: Erlbaum.

Hastie, R., & Kumar, P. (1979). Person memory: Personality traits as organizing principles in memory for behaviors. *Journal of Personality and Social Psychology, 37,* 25–38.

Hastie, R., & Park, B. (1986). The relationship between memory and judgment depends on whether the judgment task is memory-based or on-line. *Psychological Review, 93,* 258–268.

Hastie, R., & Rasinski, K. A. (1988). The concept of accuracy in social judgment. In D. Bar-Tal & A. W. Kruglanski (Eds.), *The social psychology of knowledge* (pp. 193–208). Cambridge, UK: Cambridge University Press.

Hastie, R., Schroeder, C., & Weber, R. (1990). Creating complex social conjunction categories from simple categories. *Bulletin of the Psychonomic Society, 28,* 242–247.

Hastorf, A. H., Wildfogel, I., & Cassman, T. (1979). Acknowledgement of handicap as a tactic in social interaction. *Journal of Personality and Social Psychology, 37,* 1790–1797.

Hatfield, E., & Sprecher, S. (1986). *Mirror, mirror: The importance of looks in everyday life.* Albany: State University of New York Press.

Hattrup, K., & Ford, J. K. (1995). The roles of information characteristics and accountability in moderating stereotype-driven processes during social decision making. *Organizational Behavior and Human Decision Processes, 63,* 73–86.

Hausdorff, J. M., Levy, B. R., & Wei, J. Y. (1999). The power of ageism on physical function of older persons: Reversibility of age-related gait changes. *Journal of the American Geriatrics Society, 47,* 1346–1349.

Hawkins, J. W., & Aber, C. S. (1992). Women in advertisements in medical journals. *Sex Roles, 26,* 233–242.

Hawkins, R. P., & Pingree, S. (1978). Effects of changing proportions of the sexes on ratings of occupational prestige. *Psychology of Women Quarterly, 2,* 314–321.

Haworth, G., Povey, R., & Clift, S. (1986). The Attitudes towards Women Scale (AWS-B): A comparison of women in engineering and traditional occupations with male engineers. *British Journal of Social Psychology, 25,* 329–334.

Hayes, A. F., & Dunning, D. (1997). Construal processes and trait ambiguity: Implications for self-peer agreement in personality judgments. *Journal of Personality and Social Psychology, 72,* 664–667.

Hebl, M. R., Foster, J. B., Mannix, L. M., & Dovidio, J. F. (2002). Formal and interpersonal discrimination: A field study of bias toward homosexual applicants. *Personality and Social Psychology Bulletin, 28,* 815–825.

Hebl, M. R., & Heatherton, T. F. (1998). The stigma of obesity in women: The difference is black and white. *Personality and Social Psychology Bulletin, 24,* 417–426.

Hebl, M. R., & Kleck, R. E. (2002). Acknowledging one's stigma in the interview setting: Effective strategy or liability? *Journal of Applied Social Psychology, 32,* 223–249.

Hebl, M. R., & Mannix, L. M. (2003). The weight of obesity in evaluating others: A mere proximity effect. *Personality and Social Psychology Bulletin, 29,* 28–38.

Heckhausen, J., Dixon, A., & Baltes, P. B. (1989). Gains and losses in development throughout adulthood as perceived by different age groups. *Developmental Psychology, 25,* 109–121.

Heesacker, M., Wester, S. R., Vogel, D. L., Wentzel, J. T., Mejia-Millan, C. M., & Goodholm, C. R., Jr. (1999). Gender-based emotional stereotyping. *Journal of Counseling Psychology, 46,* 483–495.

Hegarty, P., & Pratto, F. (2001a). The effects of social category norms and stereotypes on explanations for intergroup differences. *Journal of Personality and Social Psychology, 80,* 723–735.

Hegarty, P., & Pratto, F. (2001b). Sexual orientation beliefs: Their relationship to anti-gay attitudes and biological determinist arguments. *Journal of Homosexuality, 41,* 121–135.

Heider, F. (1958). *The psychology of interpersonal relations.* New York: Wiley.

Heilman, M. E. (1980). The impact of situational factors on personnel decisions concerning women: Varying the sex composition of the applicant pool. *Organizational Behavior and Human Performance, 26,* 386–395.

Heilman, M. E. (1983). Sex bias in work settings: The lack of fit model. In B. M. Staw & L. L. Cummings (Eds.), *Research in organizational behavior* (Vol. 5, pp. 269–298). Greenwich, CT: JAI Press.

Heilman, M. E., Block, C. J., & Martell, R. F. (1995). Sex stereotypes: Do they influence perceptions of managers? *Journal of Social Behavior and Personality, 10,* 237–252.

Heilman, M. E., Block, C. J., Martell, R. F., & Simon, M. C. (1989). Has anything changed?: Current characterizations of men, women, and managers. *Journal of Applied Psychology, 74,* 935–942.

Heilman, M. E., Martell, R. F., & Simon, M. C. (1988). The vagaries of sex bias: Conditions regulating the undervaluation, equivaluation, and overvaluation of female job applicants. *Organizational Behavior and Human Decision Processes, 41,* 98–110.

Heit, E., & Hahn, U. (2001). Diversity-based reasoning in children. *Cognitive Psychology, 43,* 243–273.

Helgeson, V. S. (1994). Prototypes and dimensions of masculinity and femininity. *Sex Roles, 30,* 653–682.

Hellström, A., & Tekle, J. (1994). Person perception through facial photographs: Effects of glasses, hair, and beard on judgments of occupation and personal qualities. *European Journal of Social Psychology, 24,* 693–705.

Helmreich, R. L., Spence, J. T., & Gibson, R. H. (1982). Sex role attitudes 1972–1982. *Personality and Social Psychology Bulletin, 8,* 656–663.

Helwig, A. A. (1998). Gender-role stereotyping: Testing theory with a longitudinal sample. *Sex Roles, 38,* 403–423.

Henderson-King, D., & Stewart, A. J. (1999). Educational experiences and shifts in group consciousness: Studying women. *Personality and Social Psychology Bulletin, 25,* 390–399.

Henderson-King, E., Henderson-King, D., Zhermer, N., Posokhova, S., & Chiker, V. (1997). In-group favoritism and perceived similarity: A look at Russians' perceptions in the post-Soviet era. *Personality and Social Psychology Bulletin, 23,* 1013–1021.

Henderson-King, E. I., & Nisbett, R. E. (1996). Anti-black prejudice as a function of exposure to the negative behavior of a single black person. *Journal of Personality and Social Psychology, 71,* 654–664.

Henry, P. J., & Sears, D. O. (2002). The Symbolic Racism 2000 Scale. *Political Psychology, 23,* 253–283.

Hensley, W. E., & Cooper, R. (1987). Height and occupational success: A review and critique. *Psychological Reports, 60,* 843–849.

Henss, R. (1991). Perceiving age and attractiveness in facial photographs. *Journal of Applied Social Psychology, 21,* 933–946.

Herek, G. M. (1984a). Attitudes toward lesbians and gay men: A factor-analytic study. *Journal of Homosexuality, 10,* 39–51.

Herek, G. M. (1984b). Beyond "homophobia": A social psychological perspective on attitudes toward lesbians and gay men. *Journal of Homosexuality, 10,* 1–21.

Herek, G. M. (1987). Religious orientation and prejudice: A comparison of racial and sexual attitudes. *Personality and Social Psychology Bulletin, 13,* 34–44.

Herek, G. M. (1988). Heterosexuals' attitudes toward lesbians and gay men: Correlates and gender differences. *Journal of Sex Research, 25,* 451–477.

Herek, G. M. (1993). Documenting prejudice against lesbians and gay men on campus: The Yale sexual orientation survey. *Journal of Homosexuality, 25,* 15–29.

Herek, G. M., & Capitanio, J. P. (1996). "Some of my best friends": Intergroup contact, concealable stigma, and heterosexuals' attitudes toward gay men and lesbians. *Personality and Social Psychology Bulletin, 22,* 412–424.

Herek, G. M., & Capitanio, J. P. (1998). Symbolic prejudice or fear of infection?: A functional analysis of AIDS-related stigma among heterosexual adults. *Basic and Applied Social Psychology, 20,* 230–241.

Herek, G. M., Gillis, J. R., & Cogan, J. C. (1999). Psychological sequelae of hate-crime victimization among lesbian, gay, and bisexual adults. *Journal of Consulting and Clinical Psychology, 67,* 945–951.

Herek, G. M., & Glunt, E. K. (1988). An epidemic of stigma: Public reactions to AIDS. *American Psychologist, 43,* 886–891.

Herek, G. M., & Glunt, E. K. (1993a). Interpersonal contact and heterosexuals' attitudes toward gay men: Results from a national survey. *Journal of Sex Research, 30,* 239–244.

Herek, G. M., & Glunt, E. K. (1993b). Public attitudes toward AIDS-related issues in the United States. In J.B. Pryor & G.D. Reeder (Eds.), *The social psychology of HIV infection* (pp. 229–261). Hillsdale, NJ: Erlbaum.

Herr, P. M. (1986). Consequences of priming: Judgment and behavior. *Journal of Personality and Social Psychology, 51,* 1106–1115.

Herr, P. M., Sherman, S. J., & Fazio, R. H. (1983). On the consequences of priming: Assimilation and contrast effects. *Journal of Experimental Social Psychology, 19,* 323–340.

Herrmann, R. K., Voss, J., Schooler, T., & Ciarrochi, J. (1997). Images in international relations: An experimental test of cognitive schemata. *International Studies Quarterly, 41,* 403–433.

Herrnstein, R. E., & Murray, C. A. (1994). *The bell curve.* New York: Free Press.

Hertel, G., & Kerr, N. L. (2001). Priming in-group favoritism: The impact of normative scripts in the minimal group paradigm. *Journal of Experimental Social Psychology, 37,* 316–324.

Hess, U., Senécal, S., Kirouac, G., Herrera, P., Philippot, P., & Kleck, R.E. (2000). Emotional expressivity in men and women: Stereotypes and self-perceptions. *Cognition and Emotion, 14,* 609–642.

Hewstone, M. (1990a). *Causal attribution: From cognitive processes to collective beliefs.* Oxford, UK: Blackwell.

Hewstone, M. (1990b). The "ultimate attribution error"?: A review of the literature on intergroup causal attribution. *European Journal of Social Psychology, 20,* 311–335.

Hewstone, M. (1994). Revision and change of stereotypic beliefs: In search of the elusive subtyping model. In W. Stroebe & M. Hewstone (Eds.), *European review of social psychology* (Vol. 5, pp. 69–109). Chichester, UK: Wiley.

Hewstone, M., & Brown, R. J. (1986). Contact is not enough: An intergroup perspective on the "contact hypothesis." In M. Hewstone & R. J. Brown (Eds.), *Contact and conflict in intergroup encounters* (pp. 1–44). Oxford, UK: Blackwell.

Hewstone, M., & Hamberger, J. (2000). Perceived variability and stereotype change. *Journal of Experimental Social Psychology, 36,* 103–124.

Hewstone, M., Hantzi, A., & Johnston, L. (1991). Social categorization and person memory: The pervasiveness of race as an organizing principle. *European Journal of Social Psychology, 21,* 517–528.

Hewstone, M., Hassebrauck, M., Wirth, A., & Wänke, M. (2000). Pattern of disconfirming information and processing instructions as determinants of stereotype change. *British Journal of Social Psychology, 39,* 399–411.

Hewstone, M., Hopkins, N., & Routh, D. A. (1992). Cognitive models of stereotype change: 1. Generalization and subtyping in young people's views of the police. *European Journal of Social Psychology, 22,* 219–234.

Hewstone, M., Islam, M. R., & Judd, C. M. (1993). Models of crossed categorization and intergroup relations. *Journal of Personality and Social Psychology, 64,* 779–793.

Hewstone, M., Johnston, L., & Aird, P. (1992). Cognitive models of stereotype change: 2. Perceptions of homogeneous and hetereogeneous groups. *European Journal of Social Psychology, 22,* 235–249.

Hewstone, M., & Lord, C. G. (1998). Changing intergroup cognitions and intergroup behavior: The role of typicality. In C. Sedikides, J. Schopler, & C. A. Insko (Eds.), *Intergroup cognition and intergroup behavior* (pp. 367–392). Mahwah, NJ: Erlbaum.

Hewstone, M., Macrae, C. N., Griffiths, R., & Milne, A. B. (1994). Cognitive models of stereotype change: 5. Measurement, development, and consequences of subtyping. *Journal of Experimental Social Psychology, 30,* 505–526.

Higgins, E. T. (1987). Self-discrepency theory: A theory relating self and affect. *Psychological Review, 94*, 319–340.

Higgins, E. T. (1996). Knowledge activation: Accessibility, applicability, and salience. In E. T. Higgins & A. W. Kruglanski (Eds.), *Social psychology: Handbook of basic principles* (pp. 133–168). New York: Guilford Press.

Higgins, E. T., King, G. A., & Mavin, G. H. (1982). Individual construct accessibility and subjective impressions and recall. *Journal of Personality and Social Psychology, 43*, 35–47.

Higgins, E. T., & McCann, C. D. (1984). Social encoding and subsequent attitudes, impressions, and memory: "Context-driven" and motivational aspects of processing. *Journal of Personality and Social Psychology, 47*, 26–39.

Higgins, E. T., Rholes, W. S., & Jones, C. R. (1977). Category accessibility and impression formation. *Journal of Experimental Social Psychology, 13*, 141–154.

Hill, M. E., & Augoustinos, M. (2001). Stereotype change and prejudice reduction: Short- and long-term evaluation of a cross-cultural awareness programme. *Journal of Community and Applied Social Psychology, 11*, 243–262.

Hilton, J. L., & Darley, J. M. (1985). Construing other persons: A limit on the effect. *Journal of Experimental Social Psycholgoy, 21*, 1–18.

Hilton, J. L., & Fein, S. (1989). The role of typical diagnosticity in stereotype-based judgments. *Journal of Personality and Social Psychology, 57*, 201–211.

Hilton, J. L., Klein, J. G., & von Hippel, W. (1991). Attention allocation and impression formation. *Personality and Social Psychology Bulletin, 17*, 548–559.

Hilton, J. L., & von Hippel, W. (1990). The role of consistency in the judgment of stereotype-relevant behaviors. *Personality and Social Psychology Bulletin, 16*, 430–448.

Hilton, J. L., & von Hippel, W. (1996). Stereotypes. *Annual Review of Psychology, 47*, 237–271.

Himmelfarb, S. (1966). Studies in the perception of ethnic group members: I. Accuracy, response bias, and anti-Semitism. *Journal of Personality and Social Psychology, 4*, 347–355.

Hinkle, S., & Brown, R. (1990). Intergroup comparisons and social identity: Some links and lacunae. In D. Abrams & M. Hogg (Eds.), *Social identity theory: Constructive and critical advances* (pp. 48–70). New York: Springer-Verlag.

Hintzman, D. L. (1986). "Schema abstraction" in a multiple-trace memory model. *Psychological Review, 93*, 411–428.

Hirschfeld, L. A. (1988). On acquiring social categories; Cognitive development and anthropological wisdom. *Man, 23*, 611–638.

Hirschfeld, L. A. (1993). Discovering social difference: The role of appearance in the development of racial awareness. *Cognitive Psychology, 25*, 317–350.

Hirschfeld, L. A. (1994). The child's representation of human groups. In D. Medin (Ed.), *The psychology of learning and motivation: Advances in research and theory* (Vol. 31, pp. 133–185). San Diego, CA: Academic Press.

Hirschfeld, L. A. (1995). Do children have a theory of race? *Cognition, 54*, 209–252.

Hirschfeld, L. A. (1996). *Race in the making: Cognition, culture, and the child's construction of human kinds*. Cambridge, MA: MIT Press.

Hirschfeld, L. A. (2001). On a folk theory of society: Children, evolution, and mental representations of social groups. *Personality and Social Psychology Review, 5*, 107–117.

Hirschfeld, L. A., & Gelman, S. A. (Eds.). (1994). *Mapping the mind: Domain specificity in cognition and culture*. New York: Cambridge University Press.

Hirt, E. R. (1990). Do I see only what I expect?: Evidence for an expectancy-guided retrieval model. *Journal of Personality and Social Psychology, 58*, 937–951.

Hirt, E. R., Erickson, G. A., & McDonald, H. E. (1993). Role of expectancy timing and outcome consistency in expectancy guided retrieval. *Journal of Personality and Social Psychology, 65*, 640–656.

Ho, C., & Jackson, J. W. (2001). Attitudes toward Asian Americans: Theory and measurement. *Journal of Applied Social Psychology, 31*, 1553–1581.

Ho, E. A., Sanbonmatsu, D. M., & Akimoto, S. A. (2002). The effects of comparative status on social stereotypes: How the perceived success of some persons affects the stereotypes of others. *Social Cognition, 20*, 36–57.

Hodson, G., Dovidio, J. F., & Gaertner, S. L. (2002). Processes in racial discrimination: Differential weighting of conflicting information. *Personality and Social Psychology Bulletin, 28,* 460–471.

Hoffman, C., & Hurst, N. (1990). Gender stereotypes: Perception or rationalization. *Journal of Personality and Social Psychology, 58,* 197–208.

Hoffman, L. W., & Kloska, D. D. (1995). Parents' gender-based attitudes toward marital roles and child rearing: Development and validation of new measures. *Sex Roles, 32,* 273–295.

Hogg, M. A., & Abrams, D. (1990). Social motivation, self-esteem, and social identity. In D. Abrams & M. A. Hogg (Eds.), *Social identity and social cognition* (pp. 28–47). Oxford, UK: Blackwell.

Hogg, M. A., & Turner, J. C. (1987). Intergroup behaviour, self-stereotyping and the salience of social categories. *British Journal of Social Psychology, 26,* 325–340.

Holland, D., & Davidson, D. (1983). Themes in American folk models of gender. *Social Science News Letter, 68,* 49–60.

Holland, D., & Skinner, D. (1987). Prestige and intimacy: The cultural models behing Americans' talk about gender types. In D. Holland & N. Quinn (Eds.), *Cultural models in language and thought* (pp. 78–111). Cambridge, UK: Cambridge University Press.

Holland, J. H., Holyoak, K. J., Nisbett, R. E., & Thagard, P. R. (1986). *Induction: Processes of inference, learning, and discovery.* Cambridge, MA: MIT Press.

Holland, J. L. (1985). *Making vocational choices.* Englewood Cliffs, NJ: Prentice-Hall.

Holmes, R. M. (1995). *How young children perceive race.* Thousand Oaks, CA: Sage.

Hong, O. P., & Harrod, W. J. (1988). The role of reasons in the ingroup bias phenomenon. *European Journal of Social Psychology, 18,* 537–545.

Hong, Y. Y., Chiu, C. Y., Dweck, C. S., & Sacks, R. (1997). Implicit theories and evaluative processes in person cognition. *Journal of Experimental Social Psychology, 33,* 296–323.

Hopkins, N., & Murdoch, N. (1999). The role of the 'other' in national identity: Exploring the context dependence of the national ingroup stereotype. *Journal of Community and Applied Social Psychology, 9,* 321–338.

Hopkins, N., Regan, M., & Abell, J. (1997). On the context dependence of national stereotypes: Some Scottish data. *British Journal of Social Psychology, 36,* 553–563.

Hornsey, M. J., & Hogg, M. A. (2000a). Intergroup similarity and subgroup relations: Some implications for assimilation. *Personality and Social Psychology Bulletin, 26,* 948–958.

Hornsey, M. J., & Hogg, M. A. (2000b). Subgroup relations: A comparison of mutual intergroup differentiation and common ingroup identity models of prejudice reduction. *Personality and Social Psychology Bulletin, 26,* 242–256.

Horowitz, E. L. (1936). The development of attitude toward the Negro. *Archives of Psychology,* No. 194, 1–48.

Horowitz, R. E. (1939). Racial aspects of self-identification in nursery school children. *Journal of Psychology, 7,* 91–99.

Hort, B. E., Fagot, B. I., & Leinbach, M. D. (1990). Are people's notions of maleness more stereotypically framed than their notions of femaleness? *Sex Roles, 23,* 197–212.

Hort, B. E., Leinbach, M. D., & Fagot, B. I. (1991). Is there coherence among the cognitive components of gender acquisition? *Sex Roles, 24,* 195–207.

Hortaçsu, N. (2000). Intergroup relations in a changing political context: The case of veiled and unveiled university students in Turkey. *European Journal of Social Psychology, 30,* 733–744.

Horwitz, M., & Rabbie, J. M. (1989). Stereotypes of groups, group members, and individuals in categories: A differential analysis. In D. Bar-Tal, C. F. Graumann, A. W. Kruglanski, & W. Stroebe (Eds.), *Stereotyping and prejudice: Changing conceptions* (pp. 105–129). New York: Springer-Verlag.

Houghton, G., & Tipper, S. P. (1994). A model of inhibitory mechanisms in selective attention. In D. Dagenbach & T. H. Carr (Eds.), *Inhibitory processes in attention, memory, and language* (pp. 53–112). San Diego, CA: Academic Press.

Houston, V., & Bull, R. (1994). Do people avoid sitting next to someone who is facially disfigured? *European Journal of Social Psychology, 24,* 279–284.

Hovland, C. I. (1959). Reconciling conflicting results derived from experiments and survey studies of attitude change. *American Psychologist, 14,* 8–17.

Howard, J. W., & Rothbart, M. (1980). Social categorization and memory for in-group and out-group behavior. *Journal of Personality and Social Psychology, 38*, 301–310.

Hraba, J., & Grant, G. (1970). Black is beautiful: A reexamination of racial preference and identification. *Journal of Personality and Social Psychology, 16*, 398–402.

Hudson, J. B., & Hines-Hudson, B. M. (1999). A study of the contemporary racial attitudes of Whites and African Americans. *Western Journal of Black Studies, 23*, 22–34.

Huffcutt, A. L., & Roth, P. L. (1998). Racial group differences in employment interview evaluations. *Journal of Applied Psychology, 83*, 179–189.

Hughes, M. (1997). Symbolic racism, old-fashioned racism, and whites' oppostion to affirmative action. In S. A. Tuch & J. K. Martin (Eds.), *Racial attitudes in the 1990s: Continuity and change* (pp. 45–75). Westport, CT: Praeger.

Hume, D. K., & Montgomerie, R. (2001). Facial attractiveness signals different aspects of "quality" in women and men. *Evolution and Human Behavior, 22*, 93–112.

Hummert, M. L. (1990). Multiple stereotypes of elderly and young adults: A comparison of structure and evaluations. *Psychology and Aging, 5*, 182–193.

Hummert, M. L., Garstka, T. A., & Shaner, J. L. (1995). Beliefs about language performance: Adults' perceptions about self and elderly targets. *Journal of Language and Social Psychology, 14*, 235–259.

Hummert, M. L., Garstka, T. A., Shaner, J. L., & Strahm, S. (1994). Stereotypes of the elderly held by young, middle-aged, and elderly adults. *Journal of Gerontology, 49*, P240–P249.

Hummert, M. L., Garstka, T. A., Shaner, J. L., & Strahm, S. (1995). Judgments about stereotypes of the elderly: Attitudes, age associations, and typicality ratings of young, middle-aged, and elderly adults. *Research on Aging, 17*, 168–189.

Hummert, M. L., Mazloff, D., & Henry, C. (1999). Vocal characteristics of older adults and stereotyping. *Journal of Nonverbal Behavior, 23*, 111–132.

Humphreys, L. (1970). *Tearoom trade: Impersonal sex in public restrooms.* Chicago: Aldine.

Hunt, D. M. (1999). *O.J. Simpson facts and fictions: News rituals in the construction of reality.* Cambridge, UK: Cambridge University Press.

Hurtig, M.-C., & Pichevin, M.-F. (1990). Salience of the sex category system in person perception: Contextual variations. *Sex Roles, 22*, 369–395.

Hurtz, W., & Durkin, K. (1997). Gender role stereotyping in Australian radio commercials. *Sex Roles, 36*, 103–114.

Huston, A. (1985). The development of sex-typing: Themes from recent research. *Developmental Review, 5*, 1–17.

Hyde, J. S. (1984). Children's understanding of sexist language. *Developmental Psychology, 20*, 697–706.

Ickes, W. (1984). Compositions in black and white: Determinants of interaction in interracial dyads. *Journal of Personality and Social Psychology, 47*, 330–341.

Ickes, W., Patterson, M. L., Rajecki, D. W., & Tanford, S. (1982). Behavioral and cognitive consequences of reciprocal versus compensatory responses to preinteraction expectancies. *Social Cognition, 1*, 160–190.

Infante, D. A., Pierce, L. L., Rancer, A. S., & Osborne, W. J. (1980). Effects of physical attractiveness and likeableness of first name on impressions formed of journalists. *Journal of Applied Communication Research, 8*, 1–9.

Inman, M. L. (2001). Do you see what I see?: Similarities and differences in victims' and observers' perceptions of discrimination. *Social Cognition, 19*, 521–546.

Inman, M. L., & Baron, R. S. (1996). Influence of prototypes on perceptions of prejudice. *Journal of Personality and Social Psychology, 70*, 717–739.

Inman, M. L., Huerta, J., & Oh, S. (1998). Perceiving discrimination: The role of prototypes and norm violation. *Social Cognition, 16*, 418–450.

Innes, J. M., Dormer, S., & Lukins, J. (1993). Knowledge of gender stereotypes and attitudes towards women: A preliminary report. *Psychological Reports, 73*, 1005–1006.

Insko, C. A., Nacoste, R. W., & Moe, J. L. (1983). Belief congruence and racial discrimination: Review of the evidence and critical evaluation. *European Journal of Social Psychology, 13*, 153–174.

Intons-Peterson, M. J. (1988). *Children's concepts of gender.* Norwood, NJ: Ablex.

Inzlicht, M., & Ben-Zeev, T. (2000). A threatening intellectual environment: Why females are susceptible to experiencing problem-solving deficits in the presence of males. *Psychological Science, 11,* 365–371.

Irving, L. M. (2000). Promoting size acceptance in elementary school children: The EDAP puppet program. *Eating Disorders: The Journal of Treatment and Prevention, 8,* 221–232.

Irwin, P., & Thompson, N. (1987). Acceptance of the rights of homosexuals. *Journal of Homosexuality, 3,* 107–121.

Isen, A. M., & Daubman, K. A. (1984). The influence of affect on categorization. *Journal of Personality and Social Psychology, 47,* 1206–1217.

Isen, A. M., Niedenthal, P. M., & Cantor, N. (1992). An influence of positive affect of social categorization. *Motivation and Emotion, 16,* 65–78.

Islam, M. R., & Hewstone, M. (1993a). Dimensions of contact as predictors of intergroup anxiety, perceived out-group variability, and out-group attitude: An integrative model. *Personality and Social Psychology Bulletin, 19,* 700–710.

Islam, M. R., & Hewstone, M. (1993b). Intergroup attributions and affective consequences in majority and minority groups. *Journal of Personality and Social Psychology, 64,* 936–950.

Iyengar, S. (1990). Framing responsibility for political issues: The case of poverty. *Political Behavior, 12,* 19–40.

Iyengar, S. (1991). *Is anyone responsible?: How television frames political issues.* Chicago: University of Chicago Press.

Iyengar, S., & Kinder, D. R. (1987). *News that matters.* Chicago: University of Chicago Press.

Jackman, M. R. (1978). General and applied tolerance: Does education increase commitment to racial integration? *American Journal of Political Science, 22,* 302–324.

Jackman, M. R. (1994). *The velvet glove: Paternalism and conflict in gender, class, and race relations.* Berkeley: University of California Press.

Jackman, M. R., & Crane, M. (1986). "Some of my best friends are black" . . . : Interracial friendship and whites' racial attitudes. *Public Opinion Quarterly, 50,* 459–486.

Jackman, M. R., & Muha, M. J. (1984). Education and intergroup attitudes: Moral enlightenment, superficial democratic commitment, or ideological refinement. *American Sociological Review, 49,* 751–769.

Jackman, M. R., & Senter, M. S. (1980). Images of social groups: Categorical or qualified? *Public Opinion Quarterly, 44,* 341–362.

Jackson, D. N., Peacock, A. C., & Smith, J. P. (1980). Impressions of personality in the employment interview. *Journal of Personality and Social Psychology, 39,* 294–298.

Jackson, J. W., & Smith, E. R. (1999). Conceptualizing social identity: A new framework and evidence for the impact of different dimensions. *Personality and Social Psychology Bulletin, 25,* 120–135.

Jackson, L. A. (1983a). The perception of androgyny and physical attractiveness: Two is better than one. *Personality and Social Psychology Bulletin, 9,* 405–413.

Jackson, L. A. (1992a). *Physical appearance and gender: Sociobiological and sociocultural perspectives.* Albany: State University of New York Press.

Jackson, L. A., & Cash, T. F. (1985). Components of gender stereotypes: Their implications for inferences on stereotypic and nonstereotypic dimensions. *Personality and Social Psychology Bulletin, 11,* 326–344.

Jackson, L. A., & Ervin, K. S. (1992). Height stereotypes of women and men: The liabilities of shortness for both sexes. *Journal of Social Psychology, 132,* 433–445.

Jackson, L. A., Hodge, C. N., Gerard, D. A., Ingram, J. M., Ervin, K. S., & Sheppard, L. A. (1996). Cognition, affect, and behavior in the prediction of group attitudes. *Personality and Social Psychology Bulletin, 22,* 306–316.

Jackson, L. A., Hodge, C. N., & Ingram, J. M. (1994). Gender and self-concept: A reexamination of stereotypic differences and the role of gender attitudes. *Sex Roles, 30,* 615–630.

Jackson, L. A., Lewandowski, D. A., Ingram, J. M., & Hodge, C. N. (1997). Group stereotypes: Content, gender specificity, and affect associated with typical group members. *Journal of Social Behavior and Personality, 12,* 381–396.

Jackson, L. A., & McGill, O. D. (1996). Body type preferences and body characteristics associated with attractive and unattractive bodies by African Americans and Anglo Americans. *Sex Roles*, *35*, 295–307.

Jackson, L. A., & Sullivan, L. A. (1988). Age stereotype disconfirming information and evaluations of old people. *Journal of Social Psychology*, *128*, 721–729.

Jackson, L. A., Sullivan, L. A., & Hodge, C. N. (1993). Stereotype effects on attributions, predictions, and evaluations: No two social judgments are quite alike. *Journal of Personality and Social Psychology*, *65*, 69–84.

Jackson, L. M., Esses, V. M., & Burris, C. T. (2001). Contemporary sexism and discrimination: The importance of respect for men and women. *Personality and Social Psychology Bulletin*, *27*, 48–61.

Jacobs, J. A., & Powell, B. (1985). Occupational prestige: A sex-neutral concept? *Sex Roles*, *12*, 1061–1071.

Jacobs, J. E., & Eccles, J. S. (1992). The impact of mothers' gender-role stereotypic beliefs on mothers' and children's ability perceptions. *Journal of Personality and Social Psychology*, *63*, 932–944.

Jacoby, L. L., & Brooks, L. R. (1984). Nonanalytic cognition: Memory, perception, and concept learning. In G. H. Bower (Ed.), *The psychology of learning and motivation: Advances in research and theory* (Vol. 18, pp. 1–47). Orlando, FL: Academic Press.

Jacoby, L. L., Kelley, C. M., Brown, J., & Jasechko, J. (1989). Becoming famous overnight: Limits on the ability to control unconscious influences of the past. *Journal of Personality and Social Psychology*, *56*, 326–338.

Jarrett, A., & Loewenthal, K. (1991). Employers' social judgments based on handwriting and typewriting. *Journal of Social Psychology*, *131*, 747–748.

Jarrett, O. S., & Quay, L. C. (1984). Crossracial acceptance and best friend choice. *Urban Education*, *19*, 215–225.

Jetten, J., Branscombe, N. R., Schmitt, M. T., & Spears, R. (2001). Rebels with a cause: Group identification as a response to perceived discrimination from the mainstream. *Personality and Social Psychology Bulletin*, *27*, 1204–1213.

Jetten, J., Postmes, T., & McAuliffe, B. J. (2002). "We're all individuals": Group norms of individualism and collectivism, levels of identification and identity threat. *European Journal of Social Psychology*, *32*, 189–207.

Jetten, J., Spears, R., & Manstead, A. S. R. (1997a). Distinctiveness threat and prototypicality: Combined effects on intergroup discrimination and collective self-esteem. *European Journal of Social Psychology*, *27*, 635–657.

Jetten, J., Spears, R., & Manstead, A. S. R. (1997b). Strength of identification and intergroup differentiation: the influence of group norms. *European Journal of Social Psychology*, *27*, 603–609.

Jhally, S., & Lewis, J. (1992). *Enlightened racism: The Cosby Show, audiences, and the myth of the American dream*. Boulder, CO: Westview Press.

Johannesen-Schmidt, M. C., & Eagly, A. H. (2002). Diminishing returns: The effects of income on the content stereotypes of wage earners. *Personality and Social Psychology Bulletin*, *28*, 1538–1545.

John, O. P., Hampson, S. E., & Goldberg, L. R. (1991). The basic level in personality-trait hierarchies: Studies of trait use and accessibility in different contexts. *Journal of Personality and Social Psychology*, *60*, 348–361.

John, O. P., & Robins, R. W. (1993). Determinants of interjudge agreement on personality traits: The Big Five domains, observability, evaluativeness, and the unique perspective of the self. *Journal of Personality*, *61*, 521–551.

Johnson, C., & Mullen, B. (1994). Evidence for the accessibility of paired distinctiveness in distinctiveness-based illusory correlation in stereotyping. *Personality and Social Psychology Bulletin*, *20*, 65–70.

Johnson, C., Mullen, B., Carlson, D., & Southwick, S. (2001). The affective and memorial components of distinctiveness-based illusory correlations. *British Journal of Social Psychology*, *40*, 337–358.

Johnson, D. L., Hallinan, C. J., & Westerfield, R. C. (1999). Picturing success: Photographs and stereotyping in men's collegiate basketball. *Journal of Sport Behavior*, *22*, 45–53.

Johnson, D. W., & Johnson, R. T. (2000). The three Cs of reducing prejudice and discrimination. In S. Oskamp (Ed.), *Reducing prejudice and discrimination* (pp. 239–268). Mahwah, NJ: Erlbaum.

Johnson, D. W., Johnson, R., & Maruyama, G. (1983). Interdependence and interpersonal attraction among heterogeneous and homogeneous individuals: A theoretical formulation and a meta-analysis of the research. *Review of Educational Research, 53,* 5–54.

Johnson, J. D., & Lecci, L. (2003). Assessing anti-white attitudes and predicting perceived racism: The Johnson–Lecci scale. *Personality and Social Psychology Bulletin, 29,* 299–312.

Johnson, J. D., Trawalter, S., & Dovidio, J. F. (2000). Converging interracial consequences of exposure to violent rap music on stereotypical attributions of blacks. *Journal of Experimental Social Psychology, 36,* 233–251.

Johnson, K. K. P., & Roach-Higgins, M. E. (1987). The influence of physical attractiveness and dress on campus recruiters' impressions of female job applicants. *Home Economics Research Journal, 16,* 87–95.

Johnson, M. E., Brems, C., & Alford-Keating, P. (1997). Personality correlates of homophobia. *Journal of Homosexuality, 34, 57–69.*

Johnson, R. D. (1986). The influence of gender composition on evaluation of professions. *Journal of Social Psychology, 126,* 161–167.

Johnston, L. (1996). Resisting change: Information-seeking and stereotype change. *European Journal of Social Psychology, 26,* 799–825.

Johnston, L., & Hewstone, M. (1990). Intergroup contact: Social identity and social cognition. In D. Abrams & M. A. Hogg (Eds.), *Social identity theory: Constructive and critical advances* (pp. 185–210). New York: Springer-Verlag.

Johnston, L., & Hewstone, M. (1992). Cognitive models of stereotype change: 3. Subtyping and the perceived typicality of disconfirming group members. *Journal of Experimental Social Psychology, 28,* 360–386.

Johnston, L., Hewstone, M., Pendry, L., & Frankish, C. (1994). Cognitive models of stereotype change: 4. Motivational and cognitive influences. *European Journal of Social Psychology, 24,* 237–265.

Johnston, V. S., Hagel, R., Franklin, M., Fink, B., & Grammer, K. (2001). Male facial attractiveness; Evidence for hormone-mediated adaptive design. *Evolution and Human Behavior, 22,* 251–267.

Jonas, K., Broemer, P., & Diehl, M. (2000). Attitudinal ambivalence. In W. Stroebe & M. Hewstone (Eds.), *European review of social psychology* (Vol. 11, pp. 35–74). Chichester, UK: Wiley.

Jones, D. (1995). Sexual selection, physical attractiveness, and facial neoteNew York: Cross-cultural evidence and implications. *Current Anthropology, 36,* 723–748.

Jones, E. E. (1990). *Interpersonal perception.* New York: Freeman.

Jones, E. E., Farina, A., Hastorf, A. H., Markus, H., Miller, D. T. & Scott, R. A. (1984). *Social stigma: The psychology of marked relationships.* New York: Freeman.

Jones, E. E., & McGillis, D. (1976). Correspondent inferences and the attribution cube: A comparative reappraisal. In J. H. Harvey, W. J. Ickes, & R. F. Kidd (Eds.), *New directions in attribution research* (Vol. 1, pp. 389–420). Hillsdale, NJ: Erlbaum.

Jones, E. E., & Sigall, H. (1971). The bogus pipeline: A new paradigm for measuring affect and attitude. *Psychological Bulletin, 76,* 349–364.

Jones, E. E., Wood, G. C., & Quattrone, G. A. (1981). Perceived variability of personal characteristics in in-groups and out-groups: The role of knowledge and evaluation. *Personality and Social Psychology Bulletin, 7,* 523–528.

Jones, J. M. (1983). The concept of race in social psychology: From color to culture. In L. Wheeler & P. Shaver (Eds.), *Review of personality and social psychology* (Vol. 4, pp. 117–150). Beverly Hills, CA: Sage.

Jones, J. M. (1997). *Prejudice and racism* (2nd ed.). New York: McGraw-Hill.

Jones, J. M. (1998). The essential power of racism: Commentary and conclusion? In J. L. Eberhardt & S. T. Fiske (Eds.), *Confronting racism: The problem and the response* (pp. 280–294). Thousand Oaks, CA: Sage.

Jones, M. (1991). Stereotyping Hispanics and whites: Perceived differences in social roles as a determinant of ethnic stereotypes. *Journal of Social Psychology, 131,* 469–476.

Jones, M. (2002). *Social psychology of prejudice.* Upper Saddle River, NJ: Prentice-Hall.

Jones, R. A. (1977). *Self-fulfilling prophecies: Social, psychological, and physiological effects of expectancies.* Hillsdale, NJ: Erlbaum.

Jones, R. A. (1982). Perceiving other people: Stereotyping as a process of social cognition. In A. G. Miller (Ed.), *In the eye of the beholder: Contemporary issues in stereotyping* (pp. 41–91). New York: Praeger.

Jones, R. A., & Ashmore, R. D. (1973). The structure of intergroup perception: Categories and dimensions in views of ethnic groups and adjectives used in stereotype research. *Journal of Personality and Social Psychology, 25,* 428–438.

Jones, W. H., Hannson, R. C., & Phillips, A. L. (1978). Physical attractiveness and judgments of psychopathology. *Journal of Social Psychology, 105,* 79–84.

Jordan, V. E., Jr. (2001). *Vernon can read: A memoir.* New York: Public Affairs.

Jost, J. T., & Banaji, M. R. (1994). The role of stereotyping in system-justification and the production of false consciousness. *British Journal of Social Psychology, 33,* 1–27.

Jost, J. T., & Burgess, D. (2000). Attitudinal ambivalence and the conflict between group and system justification motives in low status groups. *Personality and Social Psychology Bulletin, 26,* 293–305.

Jost, J. T., & Thompson, E. P. (2000). Group-based dominance and opposition to equality as independent predictors of self-esteem, ethnocentrism, and social policy attitudes among African Americans and European Americans. *Journal of Experimental Social Psychology, 36,* 209–232.

Joubert, C. E. (1991). Relationship of liking of one's given names to self-esteem and social desirability. *Psychological Reports, 69,* 821–822.

Joubert, C. E. (1993). Personal names as a psychological variable. *Psychological Reports, 73,* 1123–1145.

Judd, C. M., & Park, B. (1988). Out-group homogeneity: Judgments of variability at the individual and group levels. *Journal of Personality and Social Psychology, 54,* 778–788.

Judd, C. M., & Park, B. (1993). Definition and assessment of accuracy in social stereotypes. *Psychological Review, 100,* 109–128.

Judd, C. M., Park, B., Ryan, C. S., Brauer, M., & Kraus, S. (1995). Stereotypes and ethnocentrism: Diverging interethnic perceptions of African American and white American youth. *Journal of Personality and Social Psychology, 69,* 460–481.

Judd, C. M., Ryan, C. S., & Park, B. (1991). Accuracy in the judgment of in-group and out-group variability. *Journal of Personality and Social Psychology, 61,* 366–379.

Judice, T. N., & Neuberg, S. L. (1998). When interviewers desire to confirm negative expectations: Self- fulfilling prophecies and inflated applicant self-perceptions. *Basic and Applied Social Psychology, 20,* 175–190.

Jussim, L. J. (1986). Self-fulfilling prophecies: A theoretical and integrative review. *Psychological Review, 93,* 429–445.

Jussim, L. J. (1989). Teacher expectations: Self-fulfilling prophecies, perceptual biases, and accuracy. *Journal of Personality and Social Psychology, 57,* 469–480.

Jussim, L. J. (1991). Social perception and social reality: A reflection–construction model. *Psychological Review, 98,* 54–73.

Jussim, L. J. (1993). Accuracy in interpersonal expectations: A reflection–construction analysis of current and classic research. *Journal of Personality, 61,* 637–668.

Jussim, L. J., Coleman, L. M., & Lerch, L. (1987). The nature of stereotypes: A comparison and integration of three theories. *Journal of Personality and Social Psychology, 52,* 536–546.

Jussim, L. J., & Eccles, J. S. (1992). Teacher expectations: II. Construction and reflection of student achievement. *Journal of Personality and Social Psychology, 63,* 947–961.

Jussim, L. J., & Eccles, J. (1995). Are teacher expectations biased by students' gender, social class, or ethnicity? In Y.-T. Lee, L. J. Jussim, & C. R. McCauley (Eds.), *Stereotype accuracy: Toward appreciating group differences* (pp. 245–271). Washington, DC: American Psychological Association.

Jussim, L. J., Eccles, J., & Madon, S. (1996). Social perception, social stereotypes, and teacher expectations: Accuracy and the quest for the powerful self-fulfilling prophecy. In M. P. Zanna (Ed.), *Advances in experimental social psychology* (Vol. 28, pp. 281–388). San Diego, CA: Academic Press.

Jussim, L. J., & Fleming, C. (1996). Self-fulfilling prophecies and the maintenance of social stereotypes: The role of dyadic interactions and social forces. In C. N. Macrae, C. Stangor, & M. Hewstone (Eds.), *Stereotypes and stereotyping* (pp. 161–192). New York: Guilford Press.

Jussim, L. J., Fleming, C. J., Coleman, L., & Kohberger, C. (1996). The nature of stereotypes: II. A multiple-process model of evaluations. *Journal of Applied Social Psychology, 26,* 283–312.

Jussim, L. J., McCauley, C. R., & Lee, Y.-T. (1995). Why study stereotype accuracy and inaccuracy? In Y.-T. Lee, L. J. Jussim, & C. R. McCauley (Eds.), *Stereotype accuracy: Toward appreciating group differences* (pp. 3–25). Washington, DC: American Psychological Association.

Jussim, L. J., Nelson, T. E., Manis, M., & Soffin, S. (1995). Prejudice, stereotypes, and labeling effects: Sources of bias in person perception. *Journal of Personality and Social Psychology, 68,* 228–246.

Kahneman, D., & Miller, D. T. (1986). Norm theory: Comparing reality to its alternatives. *Psychological Review, 93,* 136–153.

Kaiser, C. R., & Miller, C. T. (2001a). Reacting to impending discrimination: Compensation for prejudice and attributions to discrimination. *Personality and Social Psychology Bulletin, 27,* 1357–1367.

Kaiser, C. R., & Miller, C. T. (2001b). Stop complaining!: The social costs of making attributions to discrimination. *Personality and Social Psychology Bulletin, 27,* 254–263.

Kaiser, S. B. (1985). *Social psychology of clothing and personal adornment.* New York: Macmillan.

Kalick, S. M., Zebrowitz, L. A., Langlois, J. H., & Johnson, R. M. (1998). Does human facial attractiveness honestly advertise health?: Longitudinal data on an evolutionary question. *Psychological Science, 9,* 8–13.

Kameda, T. (1985). Stereotype-based expectancy and academic evaluation: The joint influence of prior expectancy and the diagnosticity of current information. *Japanese Psychological Research, 27,* 27–33.

Kanekar, S., Kolsawalla, M. B., & Nazareth, T. (1989). Occupational prestige as a function of occupant's gender. *Journal of Applied Social Psychology, 19,* 681–688.

Kang, M. E. (1997). The portrayal of women's images in magazine advertisements: Goffman's gender analysis revisited. *Sex Roles, 37,* 979–996.

Kanouse, D. E., & Hanson, L. R. (1972). Negativity in evaluations. In E. E. Jones, D. E. Kanouse, H. H. Kelley, R. E. Nisbett, S. Valins, & B. Weiner (Eds.), *Attribution: Perceiving the causes of behavior* (pp. 47–62). Morristown, NJ: General Learning Press.

Kanter, R. M. (1977a). *Men and women of the corporation.* New York: Basic Books.

Kanter, R. M. (1977b). Some effects of proportions on group life: Skewed sex ratios and responses to token women. *American Journal of Sociology, 82,* 965–990.

Kantor, M. (1998). *Homophobia: Description, development, and dynamics of gay bashing.* Westport, CT: Praeger.

Kanungo, R., & Das, J. P. (1960). Differential learning and forgetting as a function of the social frame of reference. *Journal of Abnormal and Social Psychology, 61,* 82–86.

Kappen, D. M., & Branscombe, N. R. (2001). The effects of reasons given for ineligibility on perceived gender discrimination and feelings of injustice. *British Journal of Social Psychology, 40,* 295–313.

Karasawa, M. (1991). Toward an assessment of social identity: The structure of group identification and its effects on in-group evaluations. *British Journal of Social Psychology, 30,* 293–307.

Karasawa, M. (1998). Eliminating national stereotypes: Direct versus indirect disconfirmation of beliefs in covariation. *Japanese Psychological Research, 40,* 61–73.

Karlins, M., Coffman, T. L., & Walters, G. (1969). On the fading of social stereotypes: Studies in three generations of college students. *Journal of Personality and Social Psychology, 13,* 1–16.

Karpinski, A., & Hilton, J. L. (2001). Attitudes and the implicit association test. *Journal of Personality and Social Psychology, 81,* 774–788.

Karpinski, A., & von Hippel, W. (1996). The role of the linguistic intergroup bias in expectancy maintenance. *Social Cognition, 14,* 141–163.

Karraker, K. H., Vogel, D. A., & Lake, M. A. (1995). Parents' gender-stereotyped perceptions of newborns: The eye of the beholder revisited. *Sex Roles, 33,* 687–701.

Karylowski, J. J., Konarzewski, K., & Motes, M. A. (2000). Recruitment of exemplars as reference points in social judgments. *Journal of Experimental Social Psychology, 36,* 275–303.

Kashima, E. S., & Kashima, Y. (1993). Perceptions of general variability of social groups. *Social Cognition, 11,* 1–21.

Kashima, Y. (2000). Maintaining cultural stereotypes in the serial reproduction of narratives. *Personality and Social Psychology Bulletin, 26,* 594–604.

Kasof, J. (1993). Sex bias in the naming of stimulus persons. *Psychological Bulletin, 113,* 140–163.

Katz, D., & Braly, K. (1933). Racial stereotypes in one hundred college students. *Journal of Abnormal and Social Psychology, 28,* 280–290.

Katz, D., & Braly, K. (1935). Racial prejudice and racial stereotypes. *Journal of Abnormal and Social Psychology, 30,* 175–193.

Katz, I. (1981). *Stigma: A social psychological analysis.* Hillsdale, NJ: Erlbaum.

Katz, I., Cohen, S., & Glass, D. (1975). Some determinants of cross-racial helping behavior. *Journal of Personality and Social Psychology, 32,* 964–970.

Katz, I., Glass, D. C., & Cohen, S. (1973). Ambivalence, guilt, and the scapegoating of minority group victims. *Journal of Experimental Social Psychology, 9,* 423–436.

Katz, I., Glass, D. C., Lucido, D. J., & Farber, J. (1979). Harm-doing and victim's racial or orthopedic stigma as determinants of helping behavior. *Journal of Personality, 47,* 340–364.

Katz, I., Wackenhut, J., & Hass, R. G. (1986). Racial ambivalence, value duality, and behavior. In J. F. Dovidio & S. L. Gaertner (Eds.), *Prejudice, discrimination, and racism* (pp. 35–59). Orlando, FL: Academic Press.

Katz, P. A. (1976). The acquisition of racial attitudes in children. In P. A. Katz (Ed.), *Towards the elimination of racism* (pp. 125–154). New York: Pergamon.

Katz, P. A. (1983). Developmental foundations of gender and racial attitudes. In R. L. Leahy (Ed.), *The child's construction of social inequality* (pp. 41–78). New York: Academic Press.

Katz, P. A. (1986). Modification of children's gender-stereotyped behavior: General issues and research considerations. *Sex Roles, 14,* 591–602.

Katz, P. A., Sohn, M., & Zalk, S. (1975). Perceptual concomitants of racial attitudes in urban grade-school children. *Developmental Psychology, 11,* 135–144.

Katz, P. A., & Walsh, P. V. (1991). Modification of children's gender-stereotyped behavior. *Child Development, 62,* 338–351.

Kawakami, K., Dion, K. L., & Dovidio, J. F. (1998). Racial prejudice and stereotype activation. *Personality and Social Psychology Bulletin, 24,* 407–416.

Kawakami, K., & Dovidio, J. F. (2001). The reliability of implicit stereotyping. *Personality and Social Psychology Bulletin, 27,* 212–225.

Kawakami, K., Dovidio, J. F., Moll, J., Hermsen, S., & Russin, A. (2000). Just say no (to stereotyping): Effects of training in the negation of stereotypic associations on stereotype activation. *Journal of Personality and Social Psychology, 78,* 871–888.

Kawakami, K., Young, H., & Dovidio, J. F. (2002). Automatic stereotyping: Category, trait, and behavioral activations. *Personality and Social Psychology Bulletin, 28,* 3–15.

Keating, C. F. (1985). Gender and the physiognomy of dominance and attractiveness. *Social Psychology Quarterly, 48,* 61–70.

Keating, C. F., Mazur, A., Segall, M. H., Cysneiros, P., Divale, W. T., Kilbride, J. E., Komin, S., Leahy, P., Thurman, B., & Wirsing, R. (1981). Culture and the perception of social dominance from facial expression. *Journal of Personality and Social Psychology, 40,* 615–626.

Keever, B. A. D., Martindale, C., & Weston, M. A. (Eds.). (1997). *U.S. news coverage of racial minorities: A sourcebook, 1934–1996.* Westport, CT: Greenwood Press.

Keil, F. C. (1989). *Concepts, kinds, and cognitive development.* Cambridge, MA: MIT Press.

Keinan, G., Friedland, N., & Even-Haim, G. (2000). The effect of stress and self-esteem on social stereotyping. *Journal of Social and Clinical Psychology, 19,* 206–219.

Keith, A. (1931). *The place of prejudice in modern civilization.* London: Williams & Norgate.

Keith, V. M., & Herring, C. (1991). Skin tone and stratification in the black community. *American Journal of Sociology, 97,* 760–778.

Kellerman, J. M., & Laird, J. D. (1982). The effect of appearance on self-perceptions. *Journal of Personality, 50,* 296–315.

Kelly, C. (1989). Political identity and perceived intragroup homogeneity. *British Journal of Social Psychology, 28,* 239–250.

Keltner, D., & Robinson, R. J. (1997). Defending the status quo: Power and bias in social conflict. *Personality and Social Psychology Bulletin, 23,* 1066–1077.

Kennedy, A. H. (1993). *"The darker the berry . . . ": An investigation of skin color effects on perceptions of job suitability.* Unpublished master's thesis, Rice University.

Kennedy, R. (1997). *Race, crime, and the law.* New York: Vintage.

Kennedy, R. (2002). *Nigger: The strange career of a troublesome word.* New York: Random House.

Kennelly, I. (1999). "That single-mother element": How white employers typify black women. *Gender and Society, 13,* 168–192.

Kenny, D. A., Albright, L., Malloy, T. E., & Kashy, D. A. (1994). Consensus in interpersonal perception: Acquaintance and the Big Five. *Psychological Bulletin, 116,* 245–258.

Kenny, D. A., Horner, C., Kashy, D. A., & Chu, L.-C. (1992). Consensus at zero acquaintance: Replication, behavioral cues, and stability. *Journal of Personality and Social Psychology, 62,* 88–97.

Kenrick, D. T., Groth, G. E., Trost, M. R., & Sadalla, E. K. (1993). Integrating evolutionary and social exchange perspectives on relationships: Effects of gender, self-appraisal, and involvement on mate selection criteria. *Journal of Personality and Social Psychology, 64,* 951–961.

Kenrick, D. T., McCreath, H. E., Govern, J., King, R., & Bordin, J. (1990). Person–environment intersections: Everyday settings and common trait dimensions. *Journal of Personality and Social Psychology, 58,* 685–698.

Kenrick, D. T., & Trost, M. R. (1993). The evolutionary perspective. In A. E. Beall & R. J. Sternberg (Eds.), *The psychology of gender* (pp. 148–172). New York: Guilford Press.

Kenworthy, J. B., & Miller, N. (2001). Perceptual asymmetry in consensus estimates of majority and minority members. *Journal of Personality and Social Psychology, 80,* 597–612.

Kenworthy, J. B., & Miller, N. (2002). Attributional biases about the origins of attitudes: Externality, emotionality and rationality. *Journal of Personality and Social Psychology, 8,* 693–707

Kern-Foxworth, M. (1994). *Aunt Jemima, Uncle Ben, and Rastus: Blacks in advertising, yesterday, today, and tomorrow.* Westport, CT: Greenwood Press.

Kernahan, C., Bartholow, B. D., & Bettencourt, B. A. (2000). Effects of category-based expectancy violation on affect-relate evaluations: Toward a comprehensive model. *Basic and Applied Social Psychology, 22,* 85–100.

Kernis, M., & Wheeler, L. (1981). Beautiful friends and ugly strangers: Radiation and contrast effects in perception of same-sex pairs. *Personality and Social Psychology Bulletin, 7,* 617–620.

Kessler, T., & Mummendey, A. (2001). Is there any scapegoat around?: Determinants of intergroup conflicts at different categorization levels. *Journal of Personality and Social Psychology, 81,* 1090–1102.

Kessler, T., Mummendey, A., & Leisse, U.-K. (2000). The personal–group discrepancy: Is there a common information basis for personal and group judgment? *Journal of Personality and Social Psychology, 79,* 95–109.

Kim, H., & Baron, R. S. (1988). Exercise and the illusory correlation: Does arousal heighten stereotypic processing. *Journal of Experimental Social Psychology, 24,* 366–380.

Kinder, D. R. (1998). Communication and opinion. *Annual Review of Political Science, 1,* 167–197.

Kinder, D. R., & Sanders, L. M. (1990). Mimicking political debate with survey questions: The case of white opinion on affirmative action. *Social Cognition, 8,* 73–103.

Kinder, D. R., & Sanders, L. M. (1996). *Divided by color: Racial politics and democratic ideals.* Chicago: University of Chicago Press.

Kinder, D. R., & Sears, D. O. (1981). Prejudice and politics: Symbolic racism versus racial threats to the good life. *Journal of Personality and Social Psychology, 40,* 414–431.

King, B. R. (2001). Ranking of stigmatization toward lesbians and their children and the influence of perceptions of controllability of homosexuality. *Journal of Homosexuality, 41,* 77–97.

King, B. R., & Black, K. N. (1999). Extent of relational stigmatization of lesbians and their children by heterosexual college students. *Journal of Homosexuality, 37,* 65–81.

King, L. A., & King, D. W. (1985). Sex-role egalitarianism: Biographical and personality correlates. *Psychological Reports, 57,* 787–792.

King, L. A., & King, D. W. (1990). Abbreviated measures of sex role egalitarian attitudes. *Sex Roles, 23,* 659–673.

Kirby, D. M., & Gardner, R. C. (1972). Ethnic stereotypes: Norms on 208 words typically used in their assessment. *Canadian Journal of Psychology, 26,* 140–154.

Kirkland, S. L., Greenberg, J., & Pyszczynski, T. (1987). Further evidence of the deleterious effects of overheard derogatory ethnic labels: Derogation beyond the target. *Personality and Social Psychology Bulletin, 13,* 216–227.

Kite, M. E. (1996). Age, gender, and occupational label: A test of social role theory. *Psychology of Women Quarterly, 20,* 361–374.

Kite, M. E., & Deaux, K. (1986). Attitudes toward homosexuality: Assessment and behavioral consequences. *Basic and Applied Social Psychology, 7,* 137–162.

Kite, M. E., & Deaux, K. (1987). Gender belief systems: Homosexuality and the implicit inversion theory. *Psychology of Women Quarterly, 11,* 83–96.

Kite, M. E., Deaux, K., & Miele, M. (1991). Stereotypes of young and old: Does age outweigh gender? *Psychology and Aging, 6,* 19–27.

Kite, M. E., & Johnson, B. T. (1988). Attitudes toward the elderly: A meta-analysis. *Psychology and Aging, 3,* 233–244.

Kite, M. E., & Whitley, B. E., Jr. (1996). Sex differences in attitudes toward homosexual persons, behaviors, and civil rights: A meta-analysis. *Personality and Social Psychology Bulletin, 22,* 336–353.

Klaits, J. (1985). *Servants of Satan: The age of the witch hunts.* Bloomington: Indiana University Press.

Klatzky, R. A., Martin, G. L., & Kane, R. A. (1982). Semantic interpretation effects on memory for faces. *Memory and Cognition, 10,* 195–206.

Klauer, K. C., & Meiser, T. (2000). A source-monitoring analysis of illusory correlations. *Personality and Social Psychology Bulletin, 26,* 1074–1093.

Klayman, J. (1995). Varieties of confirmation bias. In J. Busemeyer, D. L. Medin, & R. Hastie (Eds.), *The psychology of learning and motivation* (Vol. 32, pp. 385–418). San Diego, CA: Academic Press.

Klayman, J., & Ha, Y.-W. (1987). Confirmation, disconfirmation, and information in hypothesis testing. *Psychological Review, 94,* 211–228.

Kleck, R. E. (1968). Physical stigma and nonverbal cues emitted in face-to-face interaction. *Human Relations, 21,* 19–28.

Kleck, R. E., Buck, P. L., Goller, W. L., London, R. S., Pfeiffer, J. R., & Vucker, D. P. (1968). Effects of stigmatizing conditions on the use of personal space. *Psychological Reports, 23,* 111–118.

Kleck, R. E., Ono, H., & Hastorf, A. H. (1966). The effects of physical deviance upon face-to-face interaction. *Human Relations, 19,* 425–426.

Kleck, R. E., & Strenta, A. C. (1980). Perceptions of the impact of negatively valued physical characteristics on social interaction. *Journal of Personality and Social Psychology, 39,* 861–873.

Kleck, R. E., & Strenta, A. C. (1985). Gender and responses to disfigurement in self and others. *Journal of Social and Clinical Psychology, 3,* 257–267.

Klein, H., Shiffman, K. S., & Welka, D. A. (2000). Gender-related content of animated cartoons, 1930 to the present. In V. Demos & M. T. Segal (Eds.), *Advances in gender research* (Vol. 4, pp. 291–317). Stamford, CT: JAI Press.

Klein, S. B., & Loftus, J. (1990). Rethinking the role of organization in person memory: An indepedent trace storage model. *Journal of Personality and Social Psychology, 59,* 400–410.

Klein, S. B., & Loftus, J. (1993). The mental representation of trait and autobiographical knowledge about the self. In T. K. Srull & R. S. Wyer, Jr. (Eds.), *Advances in social cognition: Vol. 5. The mental representation of trait and autobiographical knowledge about the self* (pp. 1–49). Hillsdale, NJ: Erlbaum.

Klein, S. B., Loftus, J., & Burton, H. A. (1989). Two self-reference effects: The importance of distinguishing between self-descriptiveness judgments and autobiographical retrieval in self-referent encoding. *Journal of Personality and Social Psychology, 56,* 853–865.

Klein, S. B., Loftus, J., Trafton, J. G., & Fuhrman, R. W. (1992). Use of exemplars and abstractions in trait judgments: A model of trait knowledge about the self and others. *Journal of Personality and Social Psychology, 63,* 739–753.

Klein, W. M., & Kunda, Z. (1992). Motivated person perception: Constructing justifications for desired beliefs. *Journal of Experimental Social Psychology, 28,* 145–168.

Kleinpenning, G., & Hagendoorn, L. (1991). Contextual aspects of ethnic stereotypes and interethnic evaluations. *European Journal of Social Psychology, 21,* 331–348.

Kleiter, G. D., Krebs, M. Doherty, M. E., Garavan, H., Chadwick, R., & Brake, G. (1997). Do subjects understand base rates? *Organization Behavior and Human Decision Processes, 72,* 25–61.

Klonoff, E., & Landrine, H. (2000). Is skin color a marker for racial discrimination: Explaining the skin color–hypertension relationship. *Journal of Behavioral Medicine, 23,* 329–338.

Kluegel, J. R. (1990). Trends in whites' explanations of the black–white gap in socioeconomic status, 1977–1989. *American Sociological Review, 55,* 512–525.

Kluegel, J. R., & Bobo, L. (1993). Dimensions of whites' beliefs about the black–white socioeconomic gap. In P. M. Sniderman, P. E. Tetlock, & E. G. Carmines (Eds.), *Prejudice, politics, and the American dilemma* (pp. 127–147). Stanford, CA: Stanford University Press.

Knight, J. L., & Giuliano, T. A. (2001). He's a Laker; she's a "looker": The consequences of gender-stereotypical portrayals of male and female athletes by the print media. *Sex Roles, 45,* 217–229.

Knowles, E. D., Morris, M. W., Chiu, C.-Y., & Hong, Y.-Y. (2001). Culture and the process of person perception: Evidence for automaticity among East Asians in correcting for situational influences on behavior. *Personality and Social Psychology Bulletin, 27,* 1344–1356.

Kobrynowicz, D., & Biernat, M. (1997). Decoding subjective evaluations: How stereotypes provide shifting standards. *Journal of Experimental Social Psychology, 33,* 579–601.

Koehler, J. J. (1993). The influence of prior beliefs on scientific judgments of evidence quality. *Organizational Behavior and Human Decision Processes, 56,* 28–55.

Koehler, J. J. (1996). The base rate fallacy reconsidered: Descriptive, normative, and methodological challenges. *Behavioral and Brain Sciences, 19,* 1–53.

Koenig, F. W., & King, M. B. (1964). Cognitive simplicity and out-group stereotyping. *Social Forces, 42,* 324–327.

Kohn, M. (1995). *The race gallery: The return of racial science.* London: Cape.

Kolar, D. W., Funder, D. C., & Colvin, C. R. (1996). Comparing the accuracy of personality judgments by the self and knowledgeable others. *Journal of Personality, 64,* 311–337.

Kolodziej, M. E., & Johnson, B. T. (1996). Interpersonal contact and acceptance of persons with psychiatric disorders: A research synthesis. *Journal of Consulting and Clinical Psychology, 64,* 1387–1396.

Koltuv, B. B. (1962). Some characteristics of intrajudge trait intercorrelations. *Psychological Monographs, 76*(33, Whole No. 552).

Komatsu, L. K. (1992). Recent views of conceptual structure. *Psychological Bulletin, 112,* 500–526.

Koomen, W., & Bähler, M. (1996). National stereotypes: Common representations and ingroup favoritism. *European Journal of Social Psychology, 26,* 325–331.

Koomen, W., & Dijker, A. J. (1997). Ingroup and outgroup stereotypes and selective processing. *European Journal of Social Psychology, 27,* 589–601.

Kortenhaus, C. M., & Demarest, J. (1993). Gender role stereotyping in children's literature: An update. *Sex Roles, 28,* 219–232.

Kosmitzki, C., Cheng, J. Y., & Chik, S. W. K. (1994). Do national stereotypes apply equally to individual members of social minority and majority groups? *Journal of Social Psychology, 134,* 395–397.

Kovaric, P. M. (1993). Television, the portrayal of the elderly, and children's attitudes. In G. L. Berry & J. K. Asamen (Eds.), *Children and television: Images in a changing sociocultural world* (pp. 243–254). Newbury Park, CA: Sage.

Kowalski, R. M. (1993). Inferring sexual interest from behavioral cues: Effects of gender and sexually relevant attitudes. *Sex Roles, 29,* 13–36.

Kraiger, K., & Ford, J. K. (1985). A meta-analysis of ratee race effects in performance ratings. *Journal of Applied Psychology, 70,* 56–65.

Kraus, S., Ryan, C. S., Judd, C. M., Hastie, R., & Park, B. (1993). Use of mental frequency distributions to represent variability among members of social categories. *Social Cognition, 11,* 22–43.

Krauth-Gruber, S., & Ric, F. (2000). Affect and stereotypic thinking: A test of the mood-and-general-knowledge model. *Personality and Social Psychology Bulletin, 26,* 1587–1597.

Kravetz, D. F. (1976). Sex role concepts of women. *Journal of Consulting and Clinical Psychology, 44,* 437–443.

Kray, L. J., Galinsky, A. D., & Thompson, L. (2002). Reversing the gender gap in negotiations: An exploration of stereotype regeneration. *Organizationl Behavior and Human Decision Processes, 87,* 386–409.

Kray, L. J., Thompson, L., & Galinsky, A. (2001). Battle of the sexes: Gender stereotype confirmation and reactance in negotiations. *Journal of Personality and Social Psychology, 80,* 942–958.

Krueger, J. (1992). On the overestimation of between-group differences. In W. Stroebe & M. Hewstone (Eds.), *European review of social psychology* (Vol. 3, pp. 31–56). Chichester, UK: Wiley.

Krueger, J. (1996a). Personal beliefs and cultural stereotypes about racial characteristics. *Journal of Personality and Social Psychology, 71*, 536–548.

Krueger, J. (1996b). Probabilistic national stereotypes. *European Journal of Social Psychology, 26*, 961–980.

Krueger, J., & Clement, R. W. (1994). Memory-based judgments about multiple categories: A revision and extension of Tajfel's accentuation theory. *Journal of Personality and Social Psychology, 67*, 35–47.

Krueger, J., Heckhausen, J., & Hundertmark, J. (1995). Perceiving middle-aged adults: Effects of stereotype-congruent and incongruent information. *Journal of Gerontology, 50B, P82–P93*.

Krueger, J., & Rothbart, M. (1988). Use of categorical and individuating information in making inferences about personality. *Journal of Personality and Social Psychology, 55*, 187–195.

Krueger, J., & Rothbart, M. (1990). Contrast and accentuation effects in category learning. *Journal of Personality and Social Psychology, 59*, 651–663.

Krueger, J., Rothbart, M., & Sriram, N. (1989). Category learning and change: Differences in sensitivity to information that enhances or reduces intercategory distinctions. *Journal of Personality and Social Psychology, 56*, 866–875.

Krueger, J. I., Hasman, J. F., Acevedo, M., & Villano, P. (2003). Perceptions of trait typicality in gender stereotypes: Examining the role of attribution and categorization processes. *Personality and Social Psychology Bulletin, 29*, 108–116.

Kruglanski, A. W. (1989a). *Lay epistemics and human knowledge: Cognitive and motivational biases*. New York: Plenum Press.

Kruglanski, A. W. (1989b). The psychology of being "right": The problem of accuracy in social perception and cognition. *Psychological Bulletin, 106*, 395–409.

Kruglanski, A. W., & Freund, T. (1983). The freezing and unfreezing of lay-inferences: Effects on impression primacy, ethnic stereotyping, and numerical anchoring. *Journal of Experimental Social Psychology, 19*, 448–468.

Kruglanski, A. W., & Mayseless, O. (1988). Contextual effects in hypothesis testing: The role of competing alternatives and epistemic motivations. *Social Cognition, 6*, 1–20.

Kruglanski, A. W., & Webster, D. M. (1996). Motivated closing of the mind: "Seizing" and "freezing." *Psychological Review, 103*, 263–283.

Kühnen, U., Schiessl, M., Bauer, N., Paulig, N., Pöhlmann, C., & Schmidthals, K. (2001). How robust is the IAT?: Measuring and manipulating implicit attitudes of East- and West-Germans. *Zeitschrift für Experimentelle Psychologie, 48*, 135–144.

Kulik, C. T., Perry, E. L., & Bourhis, A. C. (2000). Ironic evaluation processes: Effects of thought suppression on evaluations of older job applicants. *Journal of Organizational Behavior, 21*, 689–711.

Kulik, J. A. (1983). Confirmatory attribution and the perpetration of social beliefs. *Journal of Personality and Social Psychology, 44*, 1171–1181.

Kunda, Z., Davies, P. G., Adams, B. D., & Spencer, S. J. (2002). The dynamic time course of stereotype activation: Activation, dissipation, and resurrection. *Journal of Personality and Social Psychology, 82*, 283–299.

Kunda, Z., Miller, D. T., & Claire, T. (1990). Combining social concepts: The role of causal reasoning. *Cognitive Science, 14*, 551–577.

Kunda, Z., & Oleson, K. C. (1995). Maintaining stereotypes in the face of discrimination: Constructing grounds for subtyping deviants. *Journal of Personality and Social Psychology, 68*, 565–579.

Kunda, Z., & Oleson, K. C. (1997). When exceptions prove the rule: How extremity of deviance determines the impact of deviant examples on stereotypes. *Journal of Personality and Social Psychology, 72*, 965–979.

Kunda, Z., & Sherman-Williams, B. (1993). Stereotypes and the construal of individuating information. *Personality and Social Psychology Bulletin, 19*, 90–99.

Kunda, Z., & Sinclair, L. (1999). Motivated reasoning with stereotypes: Activation, application, and inhibition. *Psychological Inquiry, 10*, 12–22.

Kunda, Z., Sinclair, L., & Griffin, D. (1997). Equal ratings but separate meanings: Stereotypes and the construal of traits. *Journal of Personality and Social Psychology, 72*, 720–734.

Kunda, Z., & Thagard, P. (1996). Forming impressions from stereotypes, traits, and behaviors: A parallel-constraint-satisfaction theory. *Psychological Review, 103,* 284–308.

Kurcz, I. (1995). Inevitability and changeability of stereotypes: A review of theories. *Polish Psychological Bulletin, 26,* 113–128.

Kurdek, L. A. (1988). Correlates of negative attitudes toward homosexuality in heterosexual college students. *Sex Roles, 11,* 727–738.

Kurzban, R., & Leary, M. R. (2001). Evolutionary origins of stigmatization: The functions of social exclusion. *Psychological Bulletin, 127,* 187–208.

Kuyken, W., Brewin, C. R., Power, M. J., & Furnham, A. (1992). Causal beliefs about depression in depressed patients, clinical psychologists and lay persons. *British Journal of Medical Psychology, 65,* 257–268.

Kyle, D. J., & Mahler, H. I. M. (1996). The effects of hair color and cosmetic use on perceptions of a female's ability. *Psychology of Women Quarterly, 20,* 447–455.

Labouvie-Vief, G., & Baltes, P. (1976). Reduction of adolescent misperceptions of the aged. *Journal of Gerontology, 31,* 68–71.

Lafrance, M., Brownell, H., & Hahn, E. (1997). Interpersonal verbs, gender, and implicit causality. *Social Psychology Quarterly, 60,* 138–152.

Lakoff, R. (1975). *Language and women's place.* New York: Harper & Row.

Lalonde, R. N., & Gardner, R. C. (1989). An intergroup perspective on stereotype organization and processing. *British Journal of Social Psychology, 28,* 289–303.

Lambert, A. J., & Chasteen, A. L. (1997). Perceptions of disadvantage versus conventionality: Political values and attitudes toward the elderly versus blacks. *Personality and Social Psychology Bulletin, 23,* 469–481.

Lambert, A. J., Chasteen, A. L., Khan, S., & Manier, J. (1998). Rethinking some assumptions about stereotype inhibition: Do we need to correct our theories about correction? In R. S. Wyer, Jr. (Ed.), *Advances in social cognition: Vol. 11. Stereotype activation and inhibition* (pp. 127–144). Mahwah, NJ: Erlbaum.

Lambert, A. J., Cronen, S., Chasteen, A. L., & Lickel, B. (1996). Private vs. public expressions of racial projudice. *Journal of Experimental Social Psychology, 32,* 437–459.

Lambert, A. J., Khan, S. R., Lickel, B. A., & Fricke, K. (1997). Mood and the correction of positive versus negative stereotypes. *Journal of Personality and Social Psychology, 72,* 1002–1016.

Lambert, A. J., Payne, B. K., Jacoby, L. L., Shaffer, L. M., Chasteen, A. L., & Khan, S. R. (2003). Stereotypes as dominant responses: On the "social facilitation" of prejudice in anticipated public contexts. *Journal of Personality and Social Psychology, 84,* 277–295.

Lambert, W. E., Hodgson, R. C., Gardner, R. C., & Fillenbaum, S. (1960). Evaluative reactions to spoken languages. *Journal of Abnormal and Social Psychology, 60,* 44–51.

Lambert, W. E., & Klineberg, O. (1967). *Children's views of foreign peoples.* New York: Appleton-Century-Crofts.

Landis, C., & Phelps, L. W. (1928). The prediction from photographs of success and vocational aptitude. *Journal of Experimental Psychology, 11,* 313–324.

Landrine, H. (1987). On the politics of madness: A preliminary analysis of the relationships between social roles and psychotherapy. *Genetic, Social, and General Psychology Monographs, 113,* 341–406.

Landrine, H. (1992). *The politics of madness.* New York: Lang.

Laner, M. R., & Laner, R. H. (1979). Personal style or sexual preference?: Why gay men are disliked. *International Review of Modern Sociology, 9,* 215–228.

Laner, M. R., & Laner, R. H. (1980). Sexual preference or personal style?: Why lesbians are disliked. *Journal of Homosexuality, 5,* 339–356.

Langan, P. A. (1985). Racism on trial: New evidence to explain the racial composition of prisons in the United States. *Journal of Criminal law and Criminology, 76,* 666–683.

Langer, E. J., & Abelson, R. P. (1974). A patient by any other name . . . : Clinician group differences in labeling bias. *Journal of Consulting and Clinical Psychology, 42,* 4–9.

Langer, E. J., & Imber, L. (1980). Role of mindlessness in the perception of deviance. *Journal of Personality and Social Psychology, 39,* 360–367.

Langer, E. J., Fiske, S., Taylor, S. E., & Chanowitz, B. (1976). Stigma, staring, and discomfort: A novel-stimulus hypothesis. *Journal of Experimental Social Psychology*, *12*, 451–463.

Langford, T., & Mackinnon, N. J. (2000). The affective bases for the gendering of traits: Comparing the United States and Canada. *Social Psychology Quarterly*, *63*, 34–48.

Langlois, J. H. (1986). From the eye of the beholder to behavioral reality: Development of social behaviors and social relations as a function of physical attractivness. In C. P. Herman, M. P. Zanna, & E. T. Higgins (Eds.), *The Ontario Symposium: Vol 3. Physical appearance, stigma, and social behavior* (pp. 23–52). Hillsdale, NJ: Erlbaum.

Langlois, J. H., Kalakanis, L., Rubenstein, A. J., Larson, A., Hallam, M., & Smoot, M. (2000). Maxims or myths of beauty?: A meta-analytic and theoretical review. *Psychological Bulletin*, *126*, 390–423.

Langlois, J. H., & Roggman, L. A. (1990). Attractive faces are only average. *Psychological Sciences*, *1*, 115–121.

Langlois, J. H., Roggman, L. A., Casey, R. J., Ritter, J. M., Rieser-Danner, L. A., & Jenkins, V. Y. (1987). Infant preferences for attractive faces: Rudiments of a stereotype? *Developmental Psychology*, *32*, 363–369.

Langlois, J. H., Roggman, L. A., & Musselman, L. (1994). What is average and what is not average about attractive faces? *Psychological Sciences*, *5*, 214–220.

LaPiere, R. T. (1936). Type-rationalizations of group antipathy. *Social Forces*, *15*, 232–237.

Larimer, G. S., Beatty, E. D., & Broadus, A. C. (1988). Indirect assessment of interracial prejudices. *Journal of Black Psychology*, *14*, 47–56.

Larsen, K., & Long, E. (1988). Attitudes toward sex roles: Traditional or egalitarian. *Sex Roles*, *19*, 1–12.

Larsen, K., Reed, M., & Hoffman, S. (1980). Attitudes of hetereosexuals toward homosexuality: A Likert-type scale and construct validity. *Journal of Sex Research*, *16*, 245–257.

Lasker, B. (1929). *Race attitudes in children*. New York: Holt.

Lasky, R. E., Klein, R. E., & Martinez, S. (1974). Age and age-discrimination in five- and six-month old infants. *Journal of Psychology*, *88*, 317–324.

Lau, I.Y.-M., Chiu, C.-Y., & Lee, S.-L. (2001). Communication and shared reality: Implications for the psychological foundations of culture. *Social Cognition*, *19*, 350–371.

Lavine, H., Sweeney, D., & Wagner, S. H. (1999). Depicting women as sex objects in television advertising: Effects on body dissatisfaction. *Personality and Social Psychology Bulletin*, *25*, 1049–1058.

Lavrakas, P. J. (1975). Female preferences for male physiques. *Journal of Research in Personality*, *9*, 324–334.

Lawson, E. D. (1971a). Hair color, personality, and the observer. *Psychological Reports*, *28*, 311–322.

Lawson, E. D. (1971b). Semantic differential analysis of men's first names. *Journal of Psychology*, *78*, 229–240.

Lawson, E. D. (1973). Men's first names, nicknames, and short names: A semantic differential analysis. *Names*, *21*, 22–27.

Lawson, E. D. (1974). Women's first names: A semantic differential analysis. *Names*, *22*, 52–58.

Lawson, E. D. (1980). First names on the campus: A semantic differential analysis. *Names*, *28*, 69–83.

Lawson, E. D., & Roeder, L. (1986). Women's full first names, short names, and affectionate names: A semantic differential analysis. *Names*, *34*, 175–184.

Lawson, K. (2003). *Processing categorical variables on a continuum*. Unpublished paper, Rice University.

Lay, C. H., & Jackson, D. N. (1969). Analysis of the generality of trait-inferential relationships. *Journal of Personality and Social Psychology*, *12*, 12–21.

Lazarus, E. (1998). *Closed chambers: The rise, fall, and future of the modern Supreme Court*. New York: Vintage.

Leach, C. W., Peng, T. R., & Volckens, J. (2000). Is racism dead?: Comparing (expressive) means and (structural equation) models. *British Journal of Social Psychology*, *39*, 449–465.

Leaper, C., Anderson, K. J., & Sanders, P. (1998). Moderators of gender effects on parents' talk to their children: A meta-analysis. *Developmental Psychology*, *34*, 3–27.

Leaper, C., & Gleason, J. B. (1996). The relationship of play activity and gender to parent and child sex-typed communication. *International Journal of Behavioural Development, 19,* 689–703.

Leather, P., & Lawrence, C. (1995). Perceiving pub violence: The symbolic influence of social and environmental factors. *British Journal of Social Psychology, 34,* 395–407.

Lee, Y.-T, Jussim, L. J., & McCauley, C. (Eds.). (1995). *Stereotype accuracy: Toward appreciating group differences.* Washington, DC: American Psychological Association.

Lehmann, S., Joy, V., Kriesman, D., & Simmens, S. (1976). Responses to viewing symptomatic behaviors and labelling of prior mental illness. *Journal of Community Psychology, 4,* 327–334.

Leinbach, M. D., & Fagot, B. I. (1993). Categorical habituation to male and female faces: Gender schematic processing in infancy. *Infant Behavior and Development, 16,* 317–332.

Leirer, V. O., Hamilton, D. L., & Carpenter, S. (1982). Common first names as cues for inferenes about personality. *Personality and Social Psychology Bulletin, 8,* 712–718.

Lenton, A. P., Blair, I. V., & Hastie, R. (2001). Illusions of gender: Stereotypes evoke false memories. *Journal of Experimental Social Psychology, 37,* 3–14.

Leonardelli, G. J., & Brewer, M. B. (2001). Minority and majority discrimination: When and why. *Journal of Experimental Social Psychology, 37,* 468–485.

Lepore, L., & Brown, R. (1997). Category and stereotype activation: Is prejudice inevitable? *Journal of Personality and Social Psychology, 72,* 275–287.

Lepore, L., & Brown, R. (2002). The role of awareness: Divergent automatic stereotype activation and implicit judgment correction. *Social Cognition, 20,* 321–351.

Leppard, W., Ogletree, S. M., & Wallen, E. (1993). Gender stereotyping in medical advertising: Much ado about something? *Sex Roles, 29,* 829–838.

Lerner, M. (1980). *The belief in a just world: A fundamental delusion.* New York: Plenum Press.

Lerner, R. M. (1969). The development of stereotyped expectancies of body–behavior relations. *Child Development, 40,* 137–141.

Lessing, E. E., & Zagorin, S. W. (1972). Black power ideology and college students' attitudes toward their own and other racial groups. *Journal of Personality and Social Psychology, 21,* 61–73.

Levesque, M. J. (1997). Meta-accuracy among acquainted individuals: A social relations analysis of interpersonal perception and metaperception. *Journal of Personality and Social Psychology, 72,* 66–74.

Levey, S., & Howells, K. (1994). Accounting for the fear of schizophrenia. *Journal of Comunity and Applied Social Psychology, 4,* 313–328.

Levin, J., & Levin, W. (1982). *The functions of discrimination and prejudice.* New York: Harper & Row.

Levine, M. B., & Willis, F. N. (1994). Public reactions to unusual names. *Journal of Social Psychology, 134,* 561–568.

LeVine, R. A., & Campbell, D. T. (1972). *Ethnocentrism: Theories of conflict, ethnic attitudes, and group behavior.* New York: Wiley.

Levitt, E. E., & Klassen, A. D. (1974). Public attitudes toward homosexuality: Part of the 1970 national survey by the Institute for Sex Research. *Journal of Homosexuality, 1,* 29–43.

Levy, B. (1996). Improving memory in old age through implicit self-stereotyping. *Journal of Personality and Social Psychology, 71,* 1092–1107.

Levy, B. (2000). Handwriting as a reflection of aging self-stereotypes. *Journal of Geriatric Psychiatry, 33,* 81–94.

Levy, B., Ashman, O., & Dror, I. (2000). To be or not to be: The effects of aging stereotypes on the will to live. *Omega: A Journal of Death and Dying, 40,* 409–420.

Levy, B., & Langer, E. (1994). Aging free from negative stereotypes: Successful memory in China and among the American deaf. *Journal of Personality and Social Psychology, 66,* 989–997.

Levy, D. A., Kaler, S. R., & Schall, M. (1988). An empirical investigation of role schemata: Occupations and personality characteristics. *Psychological Reports, 63,* 3–14.

Levy, G. D., Sadovsky, A. L., & Troseth, G. L. (2000). Aspects of young children's perceptions of gender-typed occupations. *Sex Roles, 42,* 993–1006.

Levy, G. D., Taylor, M. G., & Gelman, S. A. (1995). Traditional and evaluative aspects of flexibility in gender roles, social conventions, moral rules, and physical laws. *Child Development, 66,* 515–531.

Levy, S. R., & Dweck, C. S. (1998). Trait- versus process-focused social judgment. *Social Cognition, 16,* 151–172.

Levy, S. R., & Dweck, C. S. (1999). The impact of children's static versus dynamic conceptions of people on stereotype formation. *Child Development, 70,* 1163–1180.

Levy, S. R., Stroessner, S. J., & Dweck, C. S. (1998). Stereotype formation and endorsement: The role of implicit theories. *Journal of Personality and Social Psychology, 74,* 1421–1436.

Lewicki, P. (1985). Nonconscious biasing effects of single instances on subsequent judgments. *Journal of Personality and Social Psychology, 48,* 563–574.

Lewin, M., & Tragos, L. M. (1987). Has the feminist movement influenced adolescent sex role attitudes?: A reassessment after a quarter century. *Sex Roles, 16,* 125–135.

Leyens, J.-P., Dardenne, B., Yzerbyt, V., Scaillet, N., & Snyder, M. (1999). Confirmation and disconfirmation: Their social advantages. In W. Strobe & M. Hewstone (Eds.), *European review of social psychology* (Vol. 10, pp. 199–230). Chichester, UK: Wiley.

Leyens, J.-P., Desert, M., Croizet, J.-C., & Darcis, C. (2000). Stereotype threat: Are lower status and history of stigmatization preconditions of stereotype threat? *Personality and Social Psychology Bulletin, 26,* 1189–1199.

Leyens, J.-P., Rodriguez-Perez, A., Rodriguez-Torres, R., Gaunt, R., Paladino, M.-P., Vaes, J., & Demoulin, S. (2001). Psychological essentialism and the differential attribution of uniquely human emotions to ingroups and outgroups. *European Journal of Social Psychology, 31,* 395–411.

Leyens, J.-P., & Yzerbyt, V. Y. (1992). The ingroup overexclusion effect: Impact of valence and conformation on stereotypic information search. *European Journal of Social Psychology, 22,* 549–569.

Leyens, J.-P., Yzerbyt, V. Y., & Schadron, G. (1992). The social judgeability approach to stereotypes. In W. Strobe & M. Hewstone (Eds.), *European review of social psychology* (Vol. 3, pp. 91–120). Chichester, UK: Wiley.

Li, N. P., Bailey, J. M., Kenrick, D. T., & Linsenmeier, J. A. W. (2002). The necessities and luxuries of mate preferences: Testing the tradeoffs. *Journal of Personality and Social Psychology, 82,* 947–955.

Liberman, N., & Förster, J. (2000). Expression after suppression: A motivational explanation of postsuppressional rebound. *Journal of Personality and Social Psychology, 79,* 190–203.

Lickel, B., Hamilton, D. L., & Sherman, S. J. (2001). Elements of a lay theory of groups: Types of groups, relationship styles, and the perception of group entitavity. *Personality and Social Psychology Review, 5,* 129–140.

Lickel, B., Hamilton, D. L., Wieczorkowska, G., Lewis, A., Sherman, S. J., & Uhles, A. N. (2000). Varieties of groups and the perception of group entitativity. *Journal of Personality and Social Psychology, 78,* 223–246.

Lickel, B., Schmader, T., & Hamilton, D. L. (2003). A case of collective responsibility: Who else was to blame for the Columbine High School shootings? *Personality and Social Psychology Bulletin, 29,* 194–204.

Lieberson, S., & Bell, E. O. (1992). Children's first names: An empirical study of social taste. *American Journal of Sociology, 98,* 511–554.

Liebkind, K., & McAlister, A. L. (1999). Extended contact through peer modelling to promote tolerance in Finland. *European Journal of Social Psychology, 29,* 765–780.

Liggett, J. (1974). *The human face.* New York: Stein & Day.

Light, L. L., Kayra-Stuart, F., & Hollander, S. (1979). Recognition memory for typical and unusual faces. *Journal of Experimental Psychology: Human Learning and Memory, 5,* 212–228.

Lin, C. A. (1998). Uses of sex appeals in prime-time television commercials. *Sex Roles, 38,* 461–475.

Lindeman, M., & Sundvik, L. (1994). Impact of height on assessments of Finnish job applicants' managerial abilities. *Journal of Social Psychology, 134,* 169–174.

Lindsey, A. E., & Zakahi, W. R. (1996). Women who tell and men who ask: Perceptions of men and women departing from gender stereotypes during initial interaction. *Sex Roles, 34,* 767–786.

Lindzey, G., & Rogolsky, S. (1950). Prejudice and identification of minority group membership. *Journal of Abnormal and Social Psychology, 45,* 37–53.

Lingle, J. H., Altom, M. W., & Medin, D. L. (1984). Of cabbages and kings: Assessing the extendability of natural concept models to social things. In R. Wyer, Jr. & T. K. Srull (Eds.), *Handbook of social cognition* (Vol. 1, pp. 71–117). Hillsdale, NJ: Erlbaum.

Link, B. G. (1987). Understanding labeling effects in the area of mental disorders: An assessment of the effects of expectations of rejection. *American Sociological Review, 52,* 96–112.

Link, B. G., Andrews, H., & Cullen, F. T. (1992). The violent and illegal behavior of mental patients reconsidered. *American Sociological Review, 57,* 275–292.

Link, B. G., & Cullen, F. T. (1983). Reconsidering the social rejection of ex-mental patients: Understanding why labels matter. *American Journal of Community Psychology, 11,* 261–273.

Link, B. G., Cullen, F. T., Mirotznik, J., & Struening, E. (1992). The consequences of stigma for persons with mental illness: Evidence from the social sciences. In P. J. Fink & A. Tasman (Eds.), *Stigma and mental illness* (pp. 87–96). Washington, DC: American Psychiatric Press.

Link, B. G., Cullen, F. T., Struening, E., Shrout, P. E., & Dohrenwend, B. P. (1989). A modified labeling theory approach to mental disorders: An empirical assessment. *American Sociological Review, 54,* 400–423.

Link, B. G., Phelan, J. C., Bresnahan, M., Stueve, A., & Pescosolido, B. A. (1999). Public conceptions of mental illness: Labels, causes, dangerousness, and social distance. *American Journal of Public Health, 89,* 1328–1333.

Link, B. G., Struening, E. L., Neese-Todd, S., Asmussen, S., & Phelan, J. C. (2001). Stigma as a barrier to recovery: The consequences of stigma for the self-esteem of people with mental illness. *Psychiatric Services, 52,* 1621–1626.

Link, M. W., & Oldendick, R. W. (1996). Social construction and white attitudes toward equal opportunity and multiculturalism. *Journal of Politics, 58,* 149–168.

Linssen, H., & Hagendoorn, L. (1994). Social and geographical factors in the explanation of the content of European nationality stereotypes. *British Journal of Social Psychology, 33,* 165–182.

Linville, P. W. (1982). The complexity–extremity effect and age-based stereotyping. *Journal of Personality and Social Psychology, 42,* 193–211.

Linville, P. W., & Fischer, G. W. (1993). Exemplar and abstraction models of perceived group variability and stereotypicality. *Social Cognition, 11,* 92–125.

Linville, P. W., & Fischer, G. W. (1998). Group variability and covariation: Effects on intergroup judgment and behavior. In C. Sedikides, J. Schopler, & C. A. Insko (Eds.), *Intergroup cognition and intergroup behavior* (pp. 123–150). Mahwah, NJ: Erlbaum.

Linville, P. W., Fischer, G. W., & Salovey, P. (1989). Perceived distributions of the characteristics of in-group and out-group members: Empirical evidence and a computer simulation. *Journal of Personality and Social Psychology, 57,* 165–188.

Linville, P. W., Fischer, G. W., & Yoon, C. (1996). Perceived covariation among the features of ingroup and outgroup members: The outgroup covariation effect. *Journal of Personality and Social Psychology, 70,* 421–436.

Linville, P. W., & Jones, E. E. (1980). Polarized appraisals of outgroup members. *Journal of Personality and Social Psychology, 38,* 689–703.

Linville, P. W., Salovey, P., & Fischer, G. W. (1986). Stereotyping and perceived distributions of social characteristics: An application to ingroup–outgroup perception. In J. Dovidio & S. L. Gaertner (Eds.), *Prejudice, discrimination, and racism: Theory and research* (pp. 165–208). Orlando, FL: Academic Press.

Lippa, R. A. (1998). Gender-related individual differences and the structure of vocational interests: The importance of the "people–things" dimension. *Journal of Personality and Social Psychology, 74,* 996–1009.

Lippa, R. A. (2000). Gender-related traits in gay men, lesbian women, and heterosexual men and women: The virtual identity of homosexual–heterosexual diagnosticity and gender diagnosticity. *Journal of Personality, 68,* 899–926.

Lippmann, W. (1922). *Public opinion.* New York: Harcourt, Brace.

Litterer, O. F. (1933). Stereotypes. *Journal of Social Psychology, 4,* 56–69.

Livingston, R. W. (2001). What you see is what you get: Systematic variability in perceptual-based social judgment. *Personality and Social Psychology Bulletin, 27,* 1086–1096.

Livingston, R. W. (2002). The role of perceived negativity in the moderation of African Americans' implicit and explicit racial attitudes. *Journal of Experimental Social Psychology, 38,* 405–413.

Livingston, R. W., & Brewer, M. B. (2002). What are we really priming?: Cue-based versus category-based processing of facial stimuli. *Journal of Personality and Social Psychology, 82,* 5–18.

Livingston, S., & Green, G. (1986). Television advertisements and the portrayal of gender. *British Journal of Social Psychology*, 25, 149–154.

Lobel, T. E., Bempechat, J., Gewirtz, J. C., Shoken-Topaz, T., & Bashe, E. (1993). The role of gender-related information and self-endorsement of traits in preadolescents' inferences and judgments. *Child Development*, 64, 1285–1294.

Locher, P., Unger, R. K., Sociedade, P. W., & Wahl, J. (1993). At first glance: Accessibility of the physical attractiveness stereotype. *Sex Roles*, 28, 729–743.

Locke, V., MacLeod, C., & Walker, I. (1994). Automatic and controlled activation of stereotypes: Individual differences associated with prejudice. *British Journal of Social Psychology*, 33, 29–46.

Locksley, A., Borgida, E., Brekke, N., & Hepburn, C. (1980). Sex stereotypes and social judgment. *Journal of Personality and Social Psychology*, 39, 821–831.

Locksley, A., Hepburn, C., & Ortiz, V. (1982). Social stereotypes and judgments of individuals: An instance of the base-rate fallacy. *Journal of Experimental Social Psychology*, 18, 23–42.

Locksley, A., Ortiz, V., & Hepburn, C. (1980). Social categorization and discriminatory behavior: Extinguishing the minimal intergroup discrimination effect. *Journal of Personality and Social Psychology*, 39, 773–783.

Lombardi, W. J., Higgins, E. T., & Bargh, J. A. (1987). The role of consciousness in priming effects on categorization: Assimilation versus contrast as a function of awareness of the priming task. *Personality and Social Psychology Bulletin*, 13, 411–429.

Long, K., & Spears, R. (1997). The self-esteem hypothesis revisited: Differentiation and the disaffected. In R. Spears, P. J. Oakes, N. Ellemers, & S. A. Haslam (Eds.), *The social psychology of stereotyping and group life* (pp. 296–317). Oxford: Blackwell.

Longmore, P. K. (1985). Screening stereotypes: Images of disabled people. *Social Policy*, 16, 31–37.

Longshore, D. (1979). Color connotations and racial attitudes. *Journal of Black Studies*, 10, 183–197.

López, A., Atran, S., Coley, J. D., Medin, D. L., & Smith, E. E. (1997). The tree of life: Universal and cultural features of folkbiological taxonomies and inductions. *Cognitive Psychology*, 32, 251–295.

Lopez, G. E., Gurin, P., & Nagda, B. A. (1998). Education and understanding structural causes of group inequalities. *Political Psychology*, 19, 305–329.

Lord, C. G., Desforges, D. M., Fein, S., Pugh, M. A., & Lepper, M. R. (1994). Typicality effects in attitudes toward social policies: A concept-mapping approach. *Journal of Personality and Social Psychology*, 66, 658–673.

Lord, C. G., Desforges, D. M., Ramsey, S. L., Trezza, G. R., & Lepper, M. R. (1991). Typicality effects in attitude–behavior consistency: Effects of category discrimination and category knowledge. *Journal of Experimental Social Psychology*, 27, 550–575.

Lord, C. G., Lepper, M. R., & Mackie, D. (1984). Attitude prototypes as determinants of attitude-behavior consistency. *Journal of Personality and Social Psychology*, 46, 1254–1266.

Lord, C. G., Lepper, M. R., & Preston, E. (1984). Considering the opposite: A corrective strategy for social judgment. *Journal of Personality and Social Psychology*, 47, 1231–1243.

Lord, C. G., Ross, L., & Lepper, M. R. (1979). Biased assimilation and attitude polarization: The effects of prior theories on subsequently considered evidence. *Journal of Personality and Social Psychology*, 37, 2098–2109.

Lord, C. G., & Saenz, D. S. (1985). Memory deficits and memory surfeits: Differential cognitive consequences on tokenism for tokens and observers. *Journal of Personality and Social Psychology*, 49, 918–926.

Lord, C. G., Saenz, D. S., & Godfrey, D. K. (1987). Effects of perceived scrutiny on participant memory for social interactions. *Journal of Experimental Social Psychology*, 23, 498–517.

Lorenzi-Cioldi, F. (1993). They all look alike, but so do we . . . sometimes: Perceptions on in-group and out-group homogeneity as a function of sex and context. *British Journal of Social Psychology*, 32, 111–124.

Lorenzi-Cioldi, F. (1998). Group status and perceptions of homogeneity. In W. Stroebe & M. Hewstone (Eds.), *European review of social psychology* (Vol. 9, pp. 31–75). Chichester, UK: Wiley.

Lott, J. R., Jr. (2000). *More guns, less crime: Understanding crime and gun control laws*. Chicago: University of Chicago Press.

Lottes, I. L., & Kuriloff, P. J. (1994). The impact of college experience on political and social attitudes. *Sex Roles*, 31, 31–54.

Lovdal, L. T. (1989). Sex role messages in television commercials: An update. *Sex Roles, 21,* 715–724.

Low, J., & Sherrard, P. (1999). Portrayal of women in sexuality and marriage and family textbooks: A content analysis of photographs from the 1970s to the 1990s. *Sex Roles, 40,* 309–318.

Lowery, B. S., Hardin, C. D., & Sinclair, S. (2001). Social influence effects on automatic racial prejudice. *Journal of Personality and Social Psychology, 81,* 842–855.

Lucker, G. W., Rosenfield, D., Sikes, J., & Aronson, E. (1976). Performance in the interdependent classroom: A field study. *American Education Research Journal, 13,* 115–123.

Luebke, B. F. (1989). Out of focus: Images of women and men in newspaper photographs. *Sex Roles, 20,* 121–133.

Luhtanen, R., & Crocker, J. (1992). A collective self-esteem scale: Self-evaluation of one's social identity. *Personality and Social Psychology Bulletin, 18,* 302–318.

Lui, L., & Brewer, M. B. (1983). Recognition accuracy as evidence of category-consistency effects in person memory. *Social Cognition, 2,* 89–107.

Lunneborg, P. W. (1970). Stereotypic aspect in masculinity–femininity measurement. *Journal of Consulting and Clinical Psychology, 34,* 113–118.

Lupaschuk, D., & Yewchuk, C. (1998). Student perceptions of gender roles: Implications for counsellors. *International Journal for the Advancement of Counselling, 20,* 301–318.

Luszcz, M. A., & Fitzgerald, K. M. (1986). Understanding cohort differences in cross-generational self and peer perceptions. *Journal of Gerontology, 41,* 234–240.

Lyons, A., & Kashima, Y. (2001). The reproduction of culture: Communication processes tend to maintain cultural stereotypes. *Social Cognition, 19,* 372–394.

Lyons, M., & Hayes, R. (1993). Student perceptions of persons with psychiatric and other disorders. *American Journal of Occupational Therapy, 47,* 541–548.

Lytton, H., & Romney, D. M. (1991). Parents' differential socialization of boys and girls: A meta-analysis. *Psychological Bulletin, 109,* 267–296.

Maass, A. (1999). Linguistic intergroup bias: Stereotype perpetration through language. In M. P. Zanna (Ed.), *Advances in experimental social psychology* (Vol. 31, pp. 79–121). San Diego, CA: Academic Press.

Maass, A., & Arcuri, L. (1992). The role of language in the persistence of stereotypes. In G. R. Semin & K. Fiedler (Eds.), *Language, interaction and social cognition* (pp. 129–143). London: Sage.

Maass, A., Ceccarelli, R., & Rudin, S. (1996). Linguistic intergroup bias: Evidence for in-group-protective motivation. *Journal of Personality and Social Psychology, 71,* 512–526.

Maass, A., Colombo, A., Colombo, A., & Sherman, S. J. (2001). Inferring traits from behaviors versus behaviors from traits: The induction–deduction asymmetry. *Journal of Personality and Social Psychology, 81,* 391–404.

Maass, A., Milesi, A., Zabbini, S., & Stahlberg, D. (1995). Linguistic intergroup bias: Differential expectancies or in-group protection. *Journal of Personality and Social Psychology, 68,* 116–126.

Maass, A., Montalcini, F., & Biciotti, E. (1998). On the (dis-)confirmability of stereotypic attributes. *European Journal of Social Psychology, 28,* 383–402.

Maass, A., Salvi, D., Arcuri, L., & Semin, G. (1989). Language use in intergroup contexts: The linguistic intergroup bias. *Journal of Personality and Social Psychology, 57,* 981–993.

Maass, A., & Schaller, M. (1991). Intergroup biases and the cognitive dynamics of stereotype formation. In W. Stroebe & M. Hewstone (Eds.), *European Review of Social Psychology* (Vol. 2, pp. 189–209). Chichester, UK: Wiley.

Macan, T. H., & Dipboye, R. L. (1988). The effects of interviewers' initial impression on information gathering. *Organizational Behavior and Human Decision Processes, 42,* 364–387.

Maccoby, E. E. (1990). Gender and relationships: A developmental account. *American Psychologist, 45,* 513–520.

Maccoby, E. E. (1998). *The two sexes: Growing up apart, coming together.* Cambridge, MA: Harvard University Press.

Maccoby, E. E. (2000). Parenting and its effects on children: On reading and misreading behavior genetics. *Annual Review of Psychology, 51,* 1–27.

MacDonald, A. P., & Games, R. G. (1974). Some characteristics of those who hold positive and negative attitudes toward homosexuals. *Journal of Homosexuality, 1,* 9–27.

MacDonald, A. P., Huggins, J., Young, S., & Swanson, R. A. (1973). Attitudes toward homosexuality: Preservation of sex morality or the double standard. *Journal of Consulting and Clinical Psychology, 40,* 161.

MacDonald, T. K., & Zanna, M. P. (1998). Cross-dimension ambivalence toward social groups: Can ambivalence affect intentions to hire feminists? *Personality and Social Psychology Bulletin, 24,* 427–441.

MacKay, D. G. (1980). Psychology, prescriptive grammar and the pronoun problem. *American Psychologist, 35,* 444–449.

MacKay, N. J., & Covell, K. (1997). The impact of women in advertisements on attitudes toward women. *Sex Roles, 36,* 573–583.

Mackie, D. M., Ahn, M. N., Asuncion, A. G., & Allison, S. T. (2001). The impact of perceiver attitudes on outcome-biased dispositional inferences. *Social Cognition, 19,* 71–93.

Mackie, D. M., Allison, S. T., Worth, L. T., & Asuncion, A. G. (1992a). The generalization of outcome-biased counter-stereotypic inferences. *Journal of Experimental Social Psychology, 28,* 43–64.

Mackie, D. M., Allison, S. T., Worth, L. T., & Asuncion, A. G. (1992b). The impact of outcome biases on counterstereotypic inferences about groups. *Personality and Social Psychology Bulletin, 18,* 44–51.

Mackie, D. M., Sherman, J. W., & Worth, L. T. (1993). On-line and memory-based processes in group variability judgments. *Social Cognition, 11,* 44–69.

Mackie, D. M., & Smith, E. R. (1998). Intergroup cognition and intergroup behavior: Crossing the boundaries. In C. Sedikides, J. Schopler, & C. A. Insko (Eds.), *Intergroup cognition and intergroup behavior* (pp. 423–450). Mahwah, NJ: Erlbaum.

Mackie, D. M., & Worth, L. T. (1989). Differential recall of subcategory information about in-group and out-group members. *Personality and Social Psychology Bulletin, 15,* 401–413.

Mackie, M. (1973). Arriving at "truth" by definition: The case of stereotype inaccuracy. *Social Problems, 20,* 431–447.

Macrae, C. N., & Bodenhausen, G. V. (2000). Social cognition: Thinking categorically about others. *Annual Review of Psychology, 51,* 93–120.

Macrae, C. N., Bodenhausen, G. V., & Milne, A. B. (1995). The dissection of selection in person perception: Inhibitory processes in social stereotyping. *Journal of Personality and Social Psychology, 69,* 397–407.

Macrae, C. N., Bodenhausen, G. V., & Milne, A. B. (1998). Saying no to unwanted thoughts: Self-focus and the regulation of mental life. *Journal of Personality and Social Psychology, 74,* 578–589.

Macrae, C. N., Bodenhausen, G. V., Milne, A. B., & Castelli, L. (1999). On disregarding deviants: Exemplar typicality and person perception. *Current Psychology: Developmental, Learning, Personality, Social, 18,* 47–70.

Macrae, C. N., Bodenhausen, G. V., Milne, A. B., Castelli, L., Schloerscheidt, A. M., & Greco, S. (1998). On activating exemplars. *Journal of Experimental Social Psychology, 34,* 330–354.

Macrae, C. N., Bodenhausen, G. V., Milne, A. B., & Ford, R. L. (1997). On the regulation of recollection: The intentional forgetting of stereotypical memories. *Journal of Personality and Social Psychology, 72,* 709–719.

Macrae, C. N., Bodenhausen, G. V., Milne, A. B., & Jetten, J. (1994). Out of mind but back in sight: Stereotypes on the rebound. *Journal of Personality and Social Psychology, 67,* 808–817.

Macrae, C. N., Bodenhausen, G. V., Milne, A. B., Thorn, T. M. J., & Castelli, L. (1997). On the activation of social stereotypes: The moderating role of processing objectives. *Journal of Experimental Social Psychology, 33,* 471–489.

Macrae, C. N., Bodenhausen, G. V., Milne, A. B., & Wheeler, V. (1996). On resisting the temptation for simplification: Counterintentional effects of stereotype suppression on social memory. *Social Cognition, 14,* 1–20.

Macrae, C. N., Hewstone, M., & Griffiths, R. J. (1993). Processing load and memory for stereotype-based information. *European Journal of Social Psychology, 23,* 77–87.

Macrae, C. N., Milne, A. B., & Bodenhausen, G. V. (1994). Stereotypes as energy-saving devices: A peek inside the cognitive toolbox. *Journal of Personality and Social Psychology, 66,* 37–47.

Macrae, C. N., Mitchell, J. P., & Pendry, L. (2002). What's in a forename?: Cue familiarity and stereotypical thinking. *Journal of Experimental Social Psychology, 38,* 186–193.

Macrae, C. N., & Shepherd, J. W. (1989a). Do criminal stereotypes mediate juridic judgments? *British Journal of Social Psychology*, *28*, 189–191.

Macrae, C. N., & Shepherd, J. W. (1989b). Stereotypes and social judgments. *British Journal of Social Psychology*, *28*, 319–325.

Macrae, C. N., Shepherd, J. W., & Milne, A. B. (1992). The effects of source credibility on the dilution of stereotype-based judgments. *Personality and Social Psychology Bulletin*, *18*, 765–775.

Macrae, C. N., Stangor, C., & Milne, A. B. (1994). Activating stereotypes: A functional analysis. *Journal of Experimental Social Psychology*, *30*, 370–389.

Maddox, G. L., Back, K., & Liederman, V. (1968). Overweight as social deviance and disability. *Journal of Health and Social Behavior*, *9*, 287–298.

Maddox, K. B., & Gray, S. A. (2002). Cognitive representations of black Americans: Reexploring the role of skin tone. *Personality and Social Psychology Bulletin*, *28*, 250–259.

Madey, S. F., & Ondrus, S. A. (1999). Illusory correlations in perceptions of obese and hypertensive patients' noncooperative behaviors. *Journal of Applied Social Psychology*, *29*, 1200–1217.

Madge, N. J. H. (1976). Context and the expressed ethnic preferences of infant school children. *Journal of Child Psychology and Psychiatry*, *17*, 337–344.

Madon, S. (1997). What do people believe about gay males?: A study of stereotype content and strength. *Sex Roles*, *37*, 663–685.

Madon, S., Guyll, M., Aboufadel, K., Montiel, E., Smith, A., Palumbo, P., & Jussim, L. (2001). Ethnic and national stereotypes: The Princeton trilogy revisited and revised. *Personality and Social Psychology Bulletin*, *37*, 996–1010.

Madon, S., Jussim, L., & Eccles, J. (1997). In search of the powerful self-fulfilling prophecy. *Journal of Personality and Social Psychology*, *72*, 791–809.

Madon, S., Jussim, L., Keiper, S., Eccles, J., Smith, A., & Palumbo, P. (1998). The accuracy and power of sex, social class, and ethnic stereotypes: A naturalistic study in person perception. *Personality and Social Psychology Bulletin*, *24*, 1304–1318.

Madon, S., Smith, A., Jussim, L., Russell, D. W., Eccles, J., Palumbo, P., & Walkiewicz, M. (2001). Am I as you see me or do you see me as I am?: Self-fulfilling prophecies and self-verification. *Personality and Social Psychology Bulletin*, *27*, 1214–1224.

Magruder, B., Whitbeck, L. B., & Ishii-Kuntz, M. (1993). The relationship between AIDS-related information sources and homophobic attitudes: A comparison of two models. *Journal of Homosexuality*, *25(4)*, 47–68.

Maio, G. R., Bell, D. W., & Esses, V. M. (1996). Ambivalence and persuasion: The processing of information about immigrant groups. *Journal of Experimental Social Psychology*, *32*, 513–536.

Maio, G. R., Esses, V. M., & Bell, D. W. (1994). The formation of attitudes toward new immigrant groups. *Journal of Applied Social Psychology*, *24*, 1762–1776.

Maio, G. R., Olson, J. M., & Bush, J. E. (1997). Telling jokes that disparage social groups: Effects on the joke teller's stereotypes. *Journal of Applied Social Psychology*, *27*, 1986–2000.

Major, B., Carnevale, P. J. P., & Deaux, K. (1981). A different perspective on androgyNew York: Evaluations of masculine and feminine personality characteristics. *Journal of Personality and Social Psychology*, *41*, 1033–1043.

Major, B., & Crocker, J. (1993). Social stigma: The consequences of attributional ambiguity. In D. M. Mackie & D. L. Hamilton (Eds.), *Affect, cognition, and stereotyping: Interactive processes in group perception* (pp. 345–370). San Diego, CA: Academic Press.

Major, B., & Gramzow, R. H. (1999). Abortion as stigma: Cognitive and emotional implications of concealment. *Journal of Personality and Social Psychology*, *77*, 735–745.

Major, B., Gramzow, R. H., McCoy, S. K., Levin, S., Schmader, T., & Sidanius, J. (2002). Perceiving personal discrimination: The role of group status and legitimizing ideology. *Journal of Personality and Social Psychology*, *82*, 269–282.

Major, B., Kaiser, C. R., & McCoy, S. K. (2003). It's not my fault: When and why attributions to prejudice protect self-esteem. *Personality and Social Psychology Bulletin*, *29*, 772–781.

Major, B., Quinton, W. J., & McCoy, S. K. (2002). Antecedents and consequences of attributions to discrimination: Theoretical and empirical advances. In M. P. Zanna (Ed.), *Advances in experimental social psychology* (Vol. 34, pp. 251–330). San Diego, CA: Academic Press.

Major, B., Spencer, S., Schmader, T., Wolfe, C., & Crocker, J. (1998). Coping with negative stereotypes about intellectual performance: The role of psychological disengagement. *Personality and Social Psychology Bulletin, 24,* 34–50.

Majoribanks, K., & Jordan, D. (1986). Stereotyping among Aborignal and Ango-Australians. *Journal of Cross-Cultural Psychology, 17,* 17–28.

Makas, E. (1993). Changing channels: The portrayal of people with disabilities on television. In G.L. Berry & J.K. Asamen (Eds.), *Children and television: Images in a changing sociocultural world* (pp. 255–268). Newbury Park, CA: Sage.

Malchon, M. J., & Penner, L. A. (1981). The effects of sex and sex-role identity on the attribution of maladjustment. *Sex Roles, 1,* 363–378.

Malloy, T. E., & Albright, L. (1990). Interpersonal perception in a social context. *Journal of Personality and Social Psychology, 58,* 419–428.

Malpass, R., & Kravitz, L. (1969). Recognition for faces of own and other race. *Journal of Personality and Social Psychology, 13,* 330–334.

Malt, B. C. (1994). Water is not H-sub-2O. *Cognitive Psychology, 27,* 41–70.

Manis, M., Nelson, T. E., & Shedler, J. (1988). Stereotypes and social judgment: Extremity, assimilation, and contrast. *Journal of Personality and Social Psychology, 55,* 28–36.

Manis, M., & Paskewitz, J. R. (1984). Judging pathology: Expectation and contrast. *Journal of Experimental Social Psychology, 20,* 363–381.

Manis, M., Paskewitz, J., & Cotler, S. (1986). Stereotypes and social judgment. *Journal of Personality and Social Psychology, 50,* 461–473.

Mann, C. R. (1993). *Unequal justice: A question of color.* Bloomington: Indiana University Press.

Mann, J. W. (1967). Inconsistent thinking about group and individual. *Journal of Social Psychology, 71,* 235–245.

Marcus-Newhall, A., Miller, N., Holtz, R., & Brewer, M. G. (1993). Cross-cutting category membership with role assignment: A means of reducing intergroup bias. *British Journal of Social Psychology, 32,* 125–146.

Marín, G. (1984). Stereotyping Hispanics: The differential impact of research method, label, and degree of contact. *International Journal of Intercultural Relations, 8,* 17–27.

Mark, L. S., Pittenger, J. B., Hines, H., Carello, C., Shaw, R. E., & Todd, J. T. (1980). Wrinkling and head shape as coordinated sources of age-level information. *Perception and Psychophysics, 27,* 117–124.

Marks, E. (1943). Skin color judgments of Negro college students. *Journal of Abnormal and Social Psychology, 38,* 370–376.

Marques, J. M. (1990). The black-sheep effect: Out-groups homogeneity in social comparison settings. In D. Abrams & M. A. Hogg (Eds.), *Social identity theory: Constructive and critical advances* (pp. 131–151). New York: Springer-Verlag.

Marques, J. M., & Paez, D. (1994). The "black sheep effect": Social categorization, rejection of ingroup deviates and perception of group variability. In W. Stroebe & M. Hewstone (Eds.), *European review of social psychology* (Vol. 5, pp. 37–68). Chichester, UK: Wiley.

Marques, J. M., Robalo, E. M., & Rocha, S. A. (1992). Ingroup bias and the "black sheep" effect: Assessing the impact of social identification and perceived variability on group judgements. *European Journal of Social Psychology, 22,* 331–352.

Marques, J. M., & Yzerbyt, V. Y. (1988). The black sheep effect: Judgment extremity towards ingroup members in inter- and intra-group situations. *European Journal of Social Psychology, 18,* 287–292.

Marques, J. M., Yzerbyt, V. Y., Leyens, J.-P. (1988). The "black sheep effect": Extremity of judgments towards ingroup members as a function of group identification. *European Journal of Social Psychology, 18,* 1–16.

Martell, R. F. (1991). Sex bias at work: The effects of attentional and memory demands on performance ratings of men and women. *Journal of Applied Social Psychology, 21,* 1939–1960.

Martell, R. F., & DeSmet, A. L. (2001). A diagnostic-ratio approach to measuring beliefs about the leadership abilities of male and female managers. *Journal of Applied Psychology, 86,* 1223–1231.

Martell, R. F., Lane, D. M., & Emrich, C. E. (1996). Male–female differences: A computer simulation. *American Psychologist, 51,* 157–158.

Martell, R. F., Parker, C., Emrich, C. G., & Crawford, M. S. (1998). Sex stereotyping in the executive suite: "Much ado about something." *Journal of Social Behavior and Personality, 13,* 127–138.

Marti, M. W., Bobier, D. M., & Baron, R. S. (2000). Right before our eyes: The failure to recognize non-prototypical forms of prejudice. *Group Processes and Intergroup Relations, 3*, 403–418.

Martin, C. L. (1987). A ratio measure of sex stereotyping. *Journal of Personality and Social Psychology, 52*, 489–499.

Martin, C. L. (1989). Children's use of gender-related information in making social judgments. *Developmental Psychology, 25*, 80–88.

Martin, C. L. (1990). Attitudes and expectations about children with nontraditional and traditional gender roles. *Sex Roles, 22*, 151–165.

Martin, C. L. (1993). New directions for investigating children's gender knowledge. *Developmental Review, 13*, 184–204.

Martin, C. L. (1999). A developmental perspective on gender effects and gender concepts. In W. B. Swann, Jr., J. H. Langlois, & L. A. Gilbert (Eds.), *Sexism and stereotypes: The gender science of Janet Taylor Spence* (pp. 45–73). Washington, DC: American Psychological Association.

Martin, C. L., & Little, J. K. (1990). The relation of gender understanding to children's sex-typed preferences and gender stereotypes. *Child Development, 61*, 1427–1439.

Martin, C. L., & Parker, S. (1995). Folk theories about sex and race differences. *Personality and Social Psychology Bulletin, 21*, 45–57.

Martin, C. L., Wood, C. H., & Little, J. K. (1990). The development of gender stereotype components. *Child Development, 61*, 1891–1904.

Martin, J. G. (1964). Racial ethnocentrism and judgment of beauty. *Journal of Social Psychology, 63*, 59–63.

Martin, K. A., Sinden, A. R., & Fleming, J. C. (2000). Inactivity may be hazardous to your image: The effects of exercise participation on impression formation. *Journal of Sport and Exercise Psychology, 22*, 283–291.

Martin, L. L. (1986). Set/reset: Use and disuse of concepts in impression formation. *Journal of Personality and Social Psychology, 51*, 493–504.

Martin, L. L., & Achee, J. W. (1992). Beyond accessibility: The role of processing objectives in judgment. In L. Martin & A. Tesser (Eds.), *The construction of social judgment* (pp. 195–216). Hillsdale, NJ: Erlbaum.

Martin, L. L., Ward, D. W., Achee, J. W., & Wyer, R. S. (1993). Mood as input: People have to interpret the motivational implications of their moods. *Journal of Personality and Social Psychology, 64*, 317–326.

Martindale, C., & Dunlap, L. R. (1997). The African Americans. In B. A. D. Keever, C. Martindale, & M. A. Weston (Eds.), *U.S. news coverage of racial minorities: A sourcebook, 1934–1996* (pp. 63–145). Westport, CT: Greenwood Press.

Martire, G., & Clark, R. (1982). *Anti-semitism in the United States*. New York: Praeger.

Marx, D. M., & Roman, J. S. (2002). Female role models: Protecting women's math test performance. *Personality and Social Psychology Bulletin, 28*, 1183–1193.

Masser, B., & Abrams, D. (1999). Contemporary sexism: The relationships among hostility, benevolence, and neosexism. *Psychology of Women Quarterly, 23*, 503–517.

Masters, F. W., & Greaves, D. C. (1967). The Quasimodo complex. *British Journal of Plastic Surgery, 20*, 204–210.

Matas, M., el-Guebaly, N., Harper, D., Green, M., & Perkin, A. (1986). Mental illness and the media: II. Content analysis of press coverage of mental health topics. *Canadian Journal of Psychiatry, 31*, 431–433.

Matchinsky, D. J., & Iverson, T. G. (1996). Homophobia in heterosexual female undergraduates. *Journal of Homosexuality, 31*, 123–128.

Mathes, E. W., Brennan, S. M., Haugen, P. M., & Rice, H. B. (1985). Ratings of physical attractiveness as a function of age. *Journal of Social Psychology, 125*, 157–168.

Matheson, D. H., Collins, C. L., & Kuehne, V. S. (2000). Older adults' multiple stereotypes of young adults. *International Journal of Aging and Human Development, 51*, 245–257.

Maurer, K. L., Park, B., & Rothbart, M. (1995). Subtyping versus subgrouping processes in stereotype representation. *Journal of Personality and Social Psychology, 69*, 812–824.

Maykovich, M. (1972). Reciprocity in racial stereotypes: White, black, and yellow. *American Journal of Sociology, 77*, 876–897.

Mazur, A., Mazur, J., & Keating, C. F. (1984). Military rank attainment of a West Point class: Effects of cadets' physical features. *American Journal of Sociology, 90,* 125–150.

Mazzella, C., Durkin, K., Cerini, E., & Buralli, P. (1992). Sex role stereotyping in Australian television advertisements. *Sex Roles, 26,* 243–259.

McAndrew, F. T. (1990). Auto- and heterostereotyping in Pakistani, French, and American college samples. *Journal of Social Psychology, 130,* 341–351.

McAndrew, F. T., Akande, A., Bridgstock, R., Mealey, L., Gordon, S. C., Scheib, J. E., Akande-Adetoun, B. E., Odewale, F., Morakinyo, A., Nyahete, P., & Mubvakure, G. (2000). A multicultural study of stereotyping in English-speaking countries. *Journal of Social Psychology, 140,* 487–502.

McArthur, L. Z. (1972). The how and what of why: Some determinants and consequences of causal attribution. *Journal of Personality and Social Psychology, 22,* 171–193.

McArthur, L. Z., & Ginsberg, E. (1981). Causal attribution to salient stimuli: An investigation of visual fixation mediators. *Personality and Social Psychology Bulletin, 7,* 547–553.

McArthur, L. Z., & Post, D. L. (1977). Figural emphasis and person perception. *Journal of Experimental Social Psychology, 13,* 520–535.

McArthur, L. Z., & Resko, B. G. (1975). The portrayal of men and women in American television commercials. *Journal of Social Psychology, 97,* 209–220.

McBroom, W. H. (1987). Longitudinal changes in sex role orientations: Differences between men and women. *Sex Roles, 16,* 439–451.

McCauley, C. (1995). Are stereotypes exaggerated?: A sampling of racial, gender, academic, occupational, and political stereotypes. In Y.-T. Lee, L. J. Jussim, & C. R. McCauley (Eds.), *Stereotype accuracy: Toward appreciating group differences* (pp. 215–243). Washington, DC: American Psychological Association.

McCauley, C., Jussim, L. J., & Lee, Y.-T. (1995). Stereotype accuracy: Toward appreciating group differences. In Y.-T. Lee, L. J. Jussim, & C. R. McCauley (Eds.), *Stereotype accuracy: Toward appreciating group differences* (pp. 293–312). Washington, DC: American Psychological Association.

McCauley, C., & Stitt, C. L. (1978). An individual and quantitative measure of stereotypes. *Journal of Personality and Social Psychology, 36,* 929–940.

McCauley, C., Stitt, C. L., & Segal, M. (1980). Stereotyping: From prejudice to prediction. *Psychological Bulletin, 87,* 195–208.

McCauley, C., & Thangavelu, K. (1991). Individual differences in sex stereotyping of occupations and personality traits. *Social Psychology Quarterly, 54,* 267–279.

McClendon, M. J. (1974). Interracial contact and the reduction of prejudice. *Sociological Focus, 7,* 47–65.

McCleskey v. Kemp, 481 U.S. 279 (1987).

McConahay, J. B. (1983). Modern racism and modern discrimination: The effects of race, racial attitudes, and context on simulated hiring decisions. *Personality and Social Psychology Bulletin, 9,* 551–558.

McConahay, J. B. (1986). Modern racism, ambivalence, and the Modern Racism Scale. In J. F. Dovidio, & S. L. Gaertner (Eds.), *Prejudice, discrimination, and racism* (pp. 91–125). Orlando, FL: Academic Press.

McConnell, A. R., & Fazio, R. H. (1996). Women as men and people: Effects of gender-marked language. *Personality and Social Psychology Bulletin, 22,* 1004–1013.

McConnell, A. R., & Leibold, J. M. (2001). Relations among the implicit association test, discriminatory behavior, and explicit measures of racial attitudes. *Journal of Experimental Social Psychology, 37,* 435–442.

McConnell, A. R., Leibold, J. M., & Sherman, S. J. (1997). Within-target illusory correlations and the formation of context-dependent attitudes. *Journal of Personality and Social Psychology, 73,* 675–686.

McConnell, A. R., Sherman, S. J., & Hamilton, D. L. (1994a). Illusory correlation in the perception of groups: An extension of the distinctiveness-based account. *Journal of Peronality and Social Psychology, 67,* 414–429.

McConnell, A. R., Sherman, S. J., & Hamilton, D. L. (1994b). On-line and memory-based aspects of individual and group target judgments. *Journal of Personality and Social Psychology, 67,* 173–185.

McConnell, A. R., Sherman, S. J., & Hamilton, D. L. (1997). Target entitativity: Implications for information processing about individual and group targets. *Journal of Personality and Social Psychology, 72*, 750–762.

McCutcheon, L. E. (1998). Stereotyping the nocturnal person: Findings with some alarming implications. *Journal of Social Psychology, 138*, 411–413.

McDavid, J. W., & Harari, H. (1966). Stereotyping of names and popularity in grade school children. *Child Development, 37*, 453–459.

McFarland, S. G. (1989). Religious orientations and the targets of discrimination. *Journal for the Scientific Study of Religion, 28*, 324–336.

McGarty, C., & de la Haye, A.-M. (1997). Stereotype formation: Beyond illusory correlation. In R. Spears, P. J. Oakes, N. Ellemers, & S. A. Haslam (Eds.), *The social psychology of stereotyping and group life* (pp. 144–170). Oxford, UK: Blackwell.

McGarty, C., Haslam, S. A., Turner, J. C., & Oakes, P. J. (1993). Illusory correlation as accentuation of actual intercategory difference: Evidence for the effect with minimal stimulus information. *European Journal of Social Psychology, 23*, 391–410.

McGarty, C., & Penny, R. E. C. (1988). Categorization, accentuation, and social judgment. *British Journal of Social Psychology, 27*, 147–157.

McGarty, C., & Turner, J. C. (1992). The effects of categorization on social judgment. *British Journal of Social Psychology, 31*, 253–268.

McGarty, C., Yzerbyt, V. Y., & Spears, R. (Eds.). (2002). *Stereotypes as explanations*. Cambridge, UK: Cambridge University Press.

McGhee, P. E., & Frueh, T. (1980). Television viewing and the learning of sex-role stereotypes. *Sex Roles, 6*, 179–188.

McGuire, W. J., McGuire, C. V., Child, P., & Fujioka, T. (1978). Salience of ethnicity in the spontaneous self-concept as a function of one's ethnic distinctiveness in the social environment. *Journal of Personality and Social Psychology, 36*, 511–520.

McHale, S. M., Crouter, A. C., & Tucker, C. J. (1999). Family context and gender role socialization in middle childhood: Comparing girls to boys and sisters to brothers. *Child Development, 70*, 990–1004.

McHoskey, J. W., & Miller, A. G. (1994). Effects of constraint identification, processing, mode, expectancies, and intragroup variability on attributions toward group members. *Personality and Social Psychology Bulletin, 20*, 266–276.

McIntyre, R. B., Paulson, R. M., & Lord, C. G. (2003). Alleviating women's mathematics stereotype threat through salience of group achievements. *Journal of Experimental Social Psychology, 39*, 83–90.

McKee, J. P., & Sherriffs, A. C. (1957). The differential evaluation of males and females. *Journal of Personality, 25*, 356–371.

McKenna, K. Y. A., & Bargh, J. A. (1998). Coming out in the age of the Internet: Identity "demarginalization" through virtual group participation. *Journal of Personality and Social Psychology, 75*, 681–694.

McKenzie-Mohr, D., & Zanna, M. P. (1990). Treating women as sexual objects: Look to the (gender schematic) male who has viewed pornography. *Personality and Social Psychology Bulletin, 16*, 296–308.

McKinney, B. A., & McAndrew, F. T. (2000). Sexuality, gender, and sport: Does playing have a price? *Psi Chi Journal of Undergraduate Research, 5*, 152–158.

McKoon, G., Greene, S. B., & Ratcliff, R. (1993). Discourse models, pronoun resolution, and the impliict causality of verbs. *Journal of Experimental Psychology: Learning, Memory, and Cognition, 19*, 1040–1052.

McLean, H. M., & Kalin, R. (1994). Congruence between self-image and occupational stereotypes in students entering gender-dominated occupations. *Canadian Journal of Behavioural Science, 26*, 142–162.

McLean, R. A., & Moon, M. (1980). Health, obesity, and earnings. *American Journal of Public Health, 70*, 1006–1009.

McLeod, A. C., Crawford, I., & Zechmeister, J. (1999). Heterosexual undergraduates' attitudes toward gay fathers and their children. *Journal of Psychology and Human Sexuality, 11*, 43–62.

McMartin, J., & Klay, J. (1983). Some perceptions of the student athlete. *Perceptual and Motor Skills*, *57*, 687–690.

McMullen, M. N., Fazio, R. H., & Gavanski, I. (1997). Motivation, attention, and judgment: A natural sample spaces account. *Social Cognition*, *15*, 77–90.

McNatt, D. B. (2000). Ancient Pygmalion joins contemporary management: A meta-analysis of the result. *Journal of Applied Psychology*, *85*, 314–322.

Medin, D. L. (1988). Social categorization: Structures, processes, and purposes. In T. K. Srull & R. S. Wyer, Jr. (Eds.), *Advances in social cognition* (Vol. 1, pp. 119–126). Hillsdale, NJ: Erlbaum.

Medin, D. L. (1989). Concepts and conceptual structure. *American Psychologist*, *44*, 1469–1481.

Medin, D. L., Altom, M. W., & Murphy, T. D. (1984). Given versus induced category representations: Use of prototype and exemplar information in classification. *Journal of Experimental Psychology: Learning, Memory, and Cognition*, *10*, 333–352.

Medin, D. L., Goldstone, R. L., & Gentner, D. (1993). Respects for similarity. *Psychological Review*, *100*, 254–278.

Medin, D. L., Lynch, E. B., Coley, J. D., & Altran, S. (1997). Categorization and reasoning among tree experts: Do all roads lead to Rome? *Cognitive Psychology*, *32*, 49–96.

Medin, D. L., Lynch, E. B., & Solomon, K. O. (2000). Are there kinds of concepts? *Annual Review of Psychology*, *51*, 121–147.

Medin, D., & Ortony, A. (1989). Psychological essentialism. In S. Vosniadou & A. Ortony (Eds.), *Similarity and analogical reasoning* (pp. 179–195). Cambridge, UK: Cambridge University Press.

Meece, J. L. (1987). The influence of school experiences on the development of gender schemata. In L. S. Liben & M. L. Signorella (Eds.), *Children's gender schemata* (pp. 57–73). San Francisco: Jossey-Bass.

Meehan, A. M., & Janik, L. M. (1990). Illusory correlation and the maintenance of sex role stereotypes in children. *Sex Roles*, *22*, 83–95.

Meenes, M. A. (1943). A comparison of racial stereotypes of 1935 and 1942. *Journal of Social Psychology*, *17*, 327–336.

Meertens, R. W., & Pettigrew, T. F. (1997). Is subtle prejudice really prejudice? *Public Opinion Quarterly*, *61*, 54–71.

Mehrabian, A. (1992). *The name game: A decision that lasts a lifetime*. New York: Signet Books.

Mehrabian, A., & Piercy, M. (1993a). Affective and personality characteristics inferred from length of first names. *Personality and Social Psychology Bulletin*, *19*, 755–758.

Mehrabian, A., & Piercy, M. (1993b). Differences in positive and negative connotations of nicknames and given names. *Journal of Social Psychology*, *133*, 737–739.

Mehrabian, A., & Piercy, M. (1993c). Positive or negative connotations of unconventionally and conventionally spelled names. *Journal of Social Psychology*, *133*, 445–451.

Mehta, S., & Farina, A. (1988). Associative stigma: Perceptions of the difficulties of college-aged children of stigmatized fathers. *Journal of Social and Clinical Psychology*, *7*, 192–202.

Meichenbaum, D. H., Bowers, K. S., & Ross, R. P. (1969). A behavioral analysis of teacher expectancy effects. *Journal of Personality and Social Psychology*, *13*, 306–316.

Meiners, M. L., & Sheposh, J. P. (1977). Beauty or brains: Which image for your mate? *Personality and Social Psychology Bulletin*, *3*, 262–265.

Meiser, T., & Hewstone, M. (2001). Crossed categorization effects on the formation of illusory correlations. *European Journal of Social Psychology*, *31*, 443–466.

Meissner, C. A., & Brigham, J. C. (2001). Thirty years of investigating the own-race bias in memory for faces: A meta-analytic review. *Psychology, Public Policy, and Law*, *7*, 3–35.

Mellon, P. M., Crano, W. D., & Schmitt, N. (1982). An analysis of the role and trait components of sex-biased occupational beliefs. *Sex Roles*, *8*, 533–541.

Mellor, D. (2003). Contemporary racism in Australia: The experiences of Aborigines. *Personality and Social Psychology Bulletin*, *29*, 474–486.

Melotti, U. (1987). In-group/out-group relations and the issue of group selection. In V. Reynolds, V. Falger, & I. Vine (Eds.), *The sociobiology of ethnocentrism: Evolutionary dimensions of xenophobia, discrimination, racism, and nationalism* (pp. 94–111). London: Croom Helm.

Mendelberg, T. (2001). *The race card: Campaign strategy, implicit messages, and the norm of equality*. Princeton, NJ: Princeton University Press.

Mendes, W. B., Blascovich, J., Lickel, B., & Hunter, S. (2002). Challenge and threat during social interaction with white and black men. *Personality and Social Psychology Bulletin, 28*, 939–952.

Menec, V. H., & Perry, R. P. (1998). Reactions to stigmas among Canadian students: Testing an attribution–affect–help judgment model. *Journal of Social Psychology, 138*, 443–453.

Merton, R. K. (1948). The self-fulfilling prophecy. *Antioch Review, 8*, 193–210.

Merton, R. K. (1957). *Social theory and social structure.* Glencoe, IL: Free Press.

Messick, D. M., & Mackie, D. M. (1989). Intergroup relations. *Annual Review of Psychology, 40*, 45–81.

Mettrick, J., & Cowan, G. (1996). Individuating information, gender, and the 1995 America's Cup. *Journal of Social Behavior and Personality, 11*, 399–410.

Michael, R. T., Gagnon, J. H., Laumann, E. O., & Kolata, G. (1994). *Sex in America: A definitive survey.* Boston: Little, Brown.

Migdal, M. J., Hewstone, M., & Mullen, B. (1998). The effects of crossed categorization on intergroup evaluations: A meta-analysis. *British Journal of Social Psychology, 37*, 303–324.

Milburn, S. S., Carney, D. R., & Ramirez, A. M. (2001). Even in modern media, the picture is still the same: A content analysis of clipart images. *Sex Roles, 44*, 277–294.

Miller, A. G. (1982). Historical and contemporary perspectives on stereotyping. In A. G. Miller (Ed.), *In the eye of the beholder: Contemporary issues in stereotyping* (pp. 1–40). New York: Praeger.

Miller, A. G., McHoskey, J. W., Bane, C. M., & Dowd, T. G. (1993). The attitude polarization phenomenon: Role of response measure, attitude exremity, and behavioral consequences of reported attitude change. *Journal of Personality and Social Psychology, 64*, 561–574.

Miller, C. L. (1983). Developmental changes in male–female voice classifications by infants. *Infant Behavior and Development, 6*, 313–330.

Miller, C. T. (1986). Categorization and stereotypes about men and women. *Personality and Social Psychology Bulletin, 12*, 502–512.

Miller, C. T. (1988). Categorization and the physical attractiveness stereotype. *Social Cognition, 6*, 231–251.

Miller, C. T., & Downey, K. T. (1999). A meta-analysis of heavyweight and self-esteem. *Personality and Social Psychology Review, 3*, 68–84.

Miller, C. T., Rothblum, E. D., Barbour, L., Brand, P. A., & Felicio, D. (1990). Social interactions of obese and nonobese women. *Journal of Personality, 58*, 365–380.

Miller, C. T., Rothblum, E. D., Felicio, D., & Brand, P. (1995). Compensating for stigma: Obese and nonobese women's reactions to being visible. *Personality and Social Psychology Bulletin, 21*, 1093–1106.

Miller, D. T., Taylor, B., & Buck, M. L. (1991). Gender gaps: Who needs to be explained? *Journal of Personality and Social Psychology, 61*, 5–12.

Miller, D. T., & Turnbull, W. (1986). Expectations and interpersonal processes. *Annual Review of Psychology, 37*, 233–256.

Miller, J. G. (1984). Culture and development of everyday social explanation. *Journal of Personality and Social Psychology, 46*, 961–978.

Miller, J. G. (1996). *Search and destroy: African-American males in the criminal justice system.* Cambridge, UK: Cambridge University Press.

Miller, L., & Budd, J. (1999). The development of occupational sex-role stereotypes, occupational preferences and academic subject preferences in children at ages 8, 12 and 16. *Educational Psychology, 19*, 17–35.

Miller, N., & Harrington, H. J. (1990). A model of social category salience for intergroup relations: Empirical tests of relevant variables. In P. Drenth, J. Sergeant, & R. Takens (Eds.), *European perspectives in psychology* (Vol. 3, pp. 205–220). Chichester, UK: Wiley.

Millham, J., & Weinberger, L. E. (1977). Sexual preference, sex role appropriateness, and restriction of social access. *Journal of Homosexuality, 2*, 343–357.

Mills, C. J., & Tyrrell, D. J. (1983). Sex-stereotypic encoding and release from proactive interference. *Journal of Personality and Social Psychology, 45*, 772–781.

Milner, D. (1973). Racial identification and preference in black British school children. *European Journal of Social Psychology, 3*, 281–295.

Milner, D. (1996). Children and racism: Beyond the value of the dolls. In W. P. Robinson (Ed.),

Social groups and identities: Developing the legacy of Henri Tajfel (pp. 249–268). Oxford, UK: Butterworth-Heinemann.

Minard, R. D. (1952). Race relations in the Pocahontas coal field. *Journal of Social Issues, 8,* 29–44.

Mischel, W., Jeffery, K. M., & Patterson, C. J. (1974). The layman's use of trait and behavioral information to predict behavior. *Journal of Research in Personality, 8,* 231–242.

Miyamoto, Y., & Kitayama, S. (2002). Cultural variation in correspondence bias: The critical role of attitude diagnosticity of socially constrained behavior. *Journal of Personality and Social Psychology, 83,* 1239–1248.

Moe, J. L., Nacoste, R. W., & Insko, C. A. (1981). Belief versus race as determinants of discrimination: A study of Southern adolescents in 1966 and 1979. *Journal of Personality and Social Psychology, 41,* 1031–1050.

Moller, L. C., & Serbin, L. A. (1996). Antecedents of toddler gender segregation: Cognitive consonance, gender-typed toy preferences and behavioral compatibility. *Sex Roles, 35,* 445–460.

Monahan, J. (1992). Mental disorder and violent behavior: Perceptions and evidence. *American Psychologist, 47,* 511–521.

Monahan, J., Steadman, H., Silver, E., Appelbaum, P., Robbins, P., Mulvey, E., Rothm, L., Grisso, T., & Banks, S. (2001). *Rethinking risk assessment: The McArthur study of mental disorder and violence.* New York: Oxford University Press.

Monin, B., & Miller, D. T. (2001). Moral credentials and the expression of prejudice. *Journal of Personality and Social Psychology, 81,* 33–43.

Monteith, M. J. (1993). Self-regulation of prejudiced responses: Implications for progress in prejudice-reduction efforts. *Journal of Personality and Social Psychology, 65,* 469–485.

Monteith, M. J. (1996a). Affective reactions to prejudice-related discrepant responses: The impact of standard salience. *Personality and Social Psychology Bulletin, 22,* 48–59.

Monteith, M. J. (1996b). Contemporary forms of prejudice-related conflict: In search of a nutshell. *Personality and Social Psychology Bulletin, 22,* 461–473.

Monteith, M. J., Ashburn-Nardo, L., Voils, C. I., & Czopp, A. M. (2002). Putting the brakes on prejudice: On the development and operation of cues for control. *Journal of Personality and Social Psychology, 83,* 1029–1050.

Monteith, M. J., Deneen, N. E., & Tooman, G. D. (1996). The effect of social norm activation on the expression of options concerning gay men and blacks. *Basic and Applied Social Psychology, 18,* 267–288.

Monteith, M. J., Devine, P. G., & Zuwerink, J. R. (1993). Self-directed versus other-directed affect as a consequence of prejudice-related discrepancies. *Journal of Personality and Social Psychology, 64,* 198–210.

Monteith, M. J., Sherman, J. W., & Devine, P. G. (1998). Suppression as a stereotype control strategy. *Personality and Social Psychology Review, 1,* 63–82.

Monteith, M. J., & Spicer, C. V. (2000). Contents and correlates of whites' and blacks' racial attitudes. *Journal of Experimental Social Psychology, 36,* 125–154.

Monteith, M. J., Spicer, C. V., & Tooman, G. D. (1998). Consequences of stereotype suppression: Stereotypes on AND not on the rebound. *Journal of Experimental Social Psychology, 34,* 355–377.

Monteith, M. J., Voils, C. I., & Ashburn-Nardo, L. (2001). Taking a look underground: Detecting, interpreting, and reacting to implicit racial biases. *Social Cognition, 19,* 395–417.

Monteith, M. J., Zuwerink, J. R., & Devine, P. G. (1994). Prejudice and prejudice reduction: Classic challenges, contemporary approaches. In P. G. Devine, D. L. Hamilton, & T. M. Ostrom (Eds.), *Social cognition: Impact on social psychology* (pp. 323–346). San Diego, CA: Academic Press.

Montemayor, R. (1978). Men and their bodies: The relationship between body type and behavior. *Journal of Social Issues, 34*(1), 48–64.

Montepare, J. M., & Zebrowitz-McArthur, L. (1987). Perceptions of adults with childlike voices in two cultures. *Journal of Experimental Social Psychology, 23,* 331–349.

Montepare, J. M., & Zebrowitz-McArthur, L. (1988). Impressions of people created by age-related qualities of their gaits. *Journal of Personality and Social Psychology, 55,* 547–556.

Montepare, J. M., & Zebrowitz, L. A. (1998). Person perception comes of age: The salience and significance of age in social judgments. In M. P. Zanna (Ed.), *Advances in experimental social psychology* (Vol. 30, pp. 93–161). San Diego, CA: Academic Press.

Morgan, J., O'Neill, C., & Harré, R. (1979). *Nicknames: Their origins and social consequences*. London: Routledge & Kegan Paul.

Morgan, M. (1982). Television and adolescents' sex role stereotypes: A longitudinal study. *Journal of Personality and Social Psychology, 43*, 947–955.

Morgan, M. (1987). Television, sex-role attitudes, and sex-role behavior. *Journal of Early Adolescence, 7*, 269–282.

Morgan, M. Y. (1987). The impact of religion on gender-role attitudes. *Psychology of Women Quarterly, 11*, 301–310.

Morier, D., & Seroy, C. (1994). The effect of interpersonal expectancies on men's self-presentation of gender role attitudes to women. *Sex Roles, 30*, 493–504.

Morris, M., & Williamson, J. B. (1982). Stereotypes and social class: A focus on poverty. In A. G. Miller (Ed.), *In the eye of the beholder: Contemporary issues in stereotyping* (pp. 411–465). New York: Praeger.

Morris, M. W., & Larrick, R. P. (1995). When one cause casts doubt on another: A normative analysis of discounting in causal attribution. *Psychological Review, 102*, 331–355.

Morris, M. W., Menon, T., & Ames, D. R. (2001). Culturally conferred conceptions of agency: A key to social perception of persons, groups, and other actors. *Personality and Social Psychology Review, 5*, 169–182.

Morrison, M., de Man, A. F., & Drumheller, A. (1994). Multidimensional locus of control and attitudes toward mental illness. *Perceptual and Motor Skills, 78*, 1281–1282.

Morrison, T. G., Parriag, A. V., & Morrison, M. A. (1999). The psychometric properties of the Homonegativity Scale. *Journal of Homosexuality, 37*, 111–126.

Moskowitz, G. B., Salomon, A. R., & Taylor, C. M. (2000). Preconsciously controlling stereotyping: Implicitly activated egalitarian goals prevent the activation of stereotypes. *Social Cognition, 18*, 151–177.

Moskowitz, D. S., Suh, E. J., & Desaulniers, J. (1994). Situational influences on gender differences in agency and communion. *Journal of Personality and Social Psychology, 66*, 753–761.

Moulton, J., Robinson, G. M., & Elias, C. (1978). Sex bias in language use: "Neutral" pronouns that aren't. *American Psychologist, 33*, 1032–1036.

Moy, J., & Ng, S. H. (1996). Expectation of outgroup behaviour: Can you trust the outgroup? *European Journal of Social Psychology, 26*, 333–340.

Mullen, B. (1991). Group composition, salience, and cognitive representations: The phenomenology of being in a group. *Journal of Experimental Social Psychology, 27*, 1–27.

Mullen, B., Brown, R., & Smith, C. (1992). Ingroup bias as a function of salience, relevance, and status: An integration. *European Journal of Social Psychology, 22*, 103–122.

Mullen, B., & Hu, L. (1989). Perceptions of ingroup and outgroup variability: A meta-analytic integration. *Basic and Applied Social Psychology, 10*, 233–252.

Mullen, B., & Johnson, C. (1990). Distinctiveness-based illusory correlations and stereotyping: A meta- analytic integration. *British Journal of Social Psychology, 29*, 11–28.

Mullen, B., & Johnson, C. (1993). Cognitive representation in ethnophaulisms as a function of group size: The phenomenology of being in a group. *Personality and Social Psychology Bulletin, 19*, 296–304.

Mullen, B., Migdal, M. J., & Hewstone, M. (2001). Crossed categorization versus simple categorization and intergroup evaluations: A meta-analysis. *European Journal of Social Psychology, 31*, 721–736.

Mullen, B., Rozell, D., & Johnson, C. (2001). Ethnophaulisms for ethnic immigrant groups: The contributions of group size and familiarity. *European Journal of Social Psychology, 31*, 231–246.

Mummendey, A. (1995). Positive distinctiveness and social discrimination: An old couple living in divorce. *European Journal of Social Psychology, 25*, 657–670.

Mummendey, A., & Schreiber, H.-J. (1983). Better or just different?: Positive social identity by discrimination against, or by differentiation from outgroups. *European Journal of Social Psychology, 13*, 389–397.

Mummendey, A., & Schreiber, H.-J. (1984). "Different" just means "better": Some obvious and some hidden pathways to in-group favoritism. *British Journal of Social Psychology, 23*, 363–368.

Mummendey, A., & Simon, B. (1989). Better or different?: III. The impact of importance of comparison dimension and relative in-group size upon intergroup discrimination. *British Journal of Social Psychology, 28,* 1–16.

Munro, G. D., & Ditto, P. H. (1997). Biased assimilation, attitude polarization, and affect in reactions to stereotype-relevant scientific infomation. *Personality and Social Psychology Bulletin, 23,* 636–653.

Murphy, G. L. (1990). Noun phrase interpretation and conceptual combination. *Journal of Memory and Language, 29,* 259–288.

Murphy, G. L. (1993a). A rational theory of concepts. In G. V. Nakamura, D. L. Medin, & R. Taraban (Eds.), *The psychology of learning and motivation* (Vol. 29, pp. 327–359). San Diego, CA: Academic Press.

Murphy, G. L. (1993b). Theory and concept formation. In I. Van Mechelen, J. Hampton, R. Michalski, & P. Theuns (Eds.), *Categories and concepts: Theoretical views and inductive data analysis* (pp. 173–200). London: Academic Press.

Murphy, G. L., & Allopenna, P. D. (1994). The locus of knowledge effects in concept learning. *Journal of Experimental Psychology: Learning, Memory, and Cognition, 20,* 904–919.

Murphy, G. L., & Medin, D. L. (1985). The role of theories in conceptual coherence. *Psychological Review, 92,* 289–316.

Murphy, J. M. (1976). Psychiatric labeling in cross-cultural perspective. *Science, 191,* 1019–1028.

Murray, N., Sujan, H., Hirt, E. R., & Sujan, M. (1990). The influence of mood on categorization: A cognitive flexibility interpretation. *Journal of Personality and Social Psychology, 59,* 411–425.

Muscarella, F., & Cunningham, M. R. (1996). The evolutionary significance and social perception of male pattern baldness and facial hair. *Ethology and Sociobiology, 17,* 99–117.

Myrdal, G. (1944). *An American dilemma: The negro problem and modern democracy.* New York: Harper.

Nakdimen, K. A. (1984). The physiognomic basis of sexual stereotyping. *American Journal of Psychiatry, 141,* 499–503.

Napoleon, T., Chassin, L., & Young, R. D. (1980). A replication and extension of "Physical attractiveness and mental illness." *Journal of Abnormal Psychology, 89,* 250–253.

National Institute of Allergy and Infectious Diseases. (2002). *Fact sheet* [Online]. Available: http://www.niaid.nih.gov/factsheet/aidsstat.htm

Naus, P. J. (1973). Some correlates of attitudes toward old people. *International Journal of Aging and Human Development, 4,* 229–243.

Nelson, E. S., & Krieger, S. L. (1997). Changes in attitudes toward homosexuality in college students: Implementation of a gay men and lesbian peer panel. *Journal of Homosexuality, 33,* 63–81.

Nelson, T. D. (2002). *The psychology of prejudice.* Boston: Allyn & Bacon.

Nelson, T. E., Acker, M., & Manis, M. (1996). Irrepressible stereotypes. *Journal of Experimental Social Psychology, 32,* 13–38.

Nelson, T. E., Biernat, M. R., & Manis, M. (1990). Everyday base rates (sex stereotypes): Potent and resilient. *Journal of Personality and Social Psychology, 59,* 664–675.

Nemerowicz, G. M. (1979). *Children's perceptions of gender and work roles.* New York: Praeger.

Neppl, T. K., & Murray, A. D. (1997). Social dominance and play patterns among preschoolers: Gender comparisons. *Sex Roles, 36,* 381–393.

Nesdale, D., & Flesser, D. (2001). Social identity and the development of children's group attitudes. *Child Development, 72,* 506–517.

Nesdale, D., & Rooney, R. (1996). Evaluations and stereotyping of accented speakers by pre-adolescent children. *Journal of Language and Social Psychology, 15,* 101–132.

Neuberg, S. L. (1989). The goal of forming accurate impressions during social interactions: Attenuating the impact of negative expectancies. *Journal of Personality and Social Psychology, 56,* 374–386.

Neuberg, S. L. (1996). Social motives and expectancy-tinged social interactions. In R. M. Sorrentino & E. T. Higgins (Eds.), *Handbook of motivation and cognition: Vol. 3. The interpersonal context* (pp. 225–261). New York: Guilford Press.

Neuberg, S. L., & Fiske, S. T. (1987). Motivational influences on impression formation: Outcome dependency, accuracy-driven attention, and individuating processes. *Journal of Personality and Social Psychology, 53*, 431–444.

Neuberg, S. L., Judice, T. N., Virdin, L. M., & Carrillo, M. A. (1993). Perceiver self-presentational goals as moderators of expectancy influences: Ingratiation and the disconfirmation of negative expectancies. *Journal of Personality and Social Psychology, 64*, 409–420.

Neuberg, S. L., & Newsom, J. T. (1993). Personal need for structure: Individual differences in the desire for simple structure. *Journal of Personality and Social Psychology, 65*, 113–131.

Neuberg, S. L., Smith, D. M., Hofman, J. C., & Russell, F. J. (1994). When we observe stigmatized and "normal" individuals interacting: Stigma by association. *Personality and Social Psychology Bulletin, 20*, 196–209.

Neumann, R., & Seibt, B. (2001). The structure of prejudice: Associative strength as a determinant of stereotype endorsement. *European Journal of Social Psychology, 31*, 609–620.

Newcomb, T. M. (1947). Austistic hostility and social reality. *Human Relations, 1*, 69–86.

Newcombe, N., & Arnkoff, D. B. (1979). Effects of speech style and sex of speaker on person perception. *Journal of Personality and Social Psychology, 37*, 1293–1303.

Newman, L. S. (1996). Trait impressions as heuristics for predicting future behavior. *Personality and Social Psychology Bulletin, 22*, 395–411.

Newman, L. S., Duff, K. J., Hedberg, D. A., & Blitzstein, J. (1996). Rebound effects in impression formation: Assimilation and contrast effects following thought supression. *Journal of Experimental Social Psychology, 32*, 460–483.

Newman, L. S., & Uleman, J. S. (1990). Assimilation and contrast effects in spontaneous trait inference. *Personality and Social Psychology Bulletin, 16*, 224–240.

Newman, L. S., & Uleman, J. S. (1993). When are you what you did?: Behavior identification and dispositional inference in person memory, attribution, and social judgment. *Personality and Social Psychology Bulletin, 19*, 513–525.

Newport, F. (1998, July). Americans remain more likely to believe sexual orientation due to environment, not genetics. *The Gallup Poll Monthly*, pp. 14–16.

Newport, F. (2001). American attitudes toward homosexuality continue to becom more tolerant. *The Gallup Poll Monthly, 429*, 5–9.

Ng, S. H. (1990). The androcentric coding of *man and his* in memory by language users. *Journal of Experimental Social Psychology, 26*, 455–464.

Ng, S. H., & Bradac, J. J. (1993). *Power in language: Verbal communication and social influence.* Newbury Park, CA: Sage.

Nicotera, A. M., & Rancer, A. S. (1994). The influence of sex on self-perceptions and social stereotyping of aggressive communication predispositions. *Western Journal of Communication, 58*, 283–307.

Niemann, Y. F., Jennings, L., Rozelle, R. M., Baxter, J. C., & Sullivan, E. (1994). Use of free responses and cluster analysis to determine stereotypes of eight groups. *Personality and Social Psychology Bulletin, 20*, 379–390.

Niemann, Y. F., Pollak, K. I., Rogers, S., & O'Connor, E. (1998). Effects of physical context on stereotyping of Mexican American males. *Hispanic Journal of Behavioral Sciences, 20*, 349–362.

Niemann, Y. F., & Secord, P. F. (1995). Social ecology of stereotyping. *Journal for the Theory of Social Behavior, 25*, 1–14.

Nier, J. A., Mottola, G. R., & Gaertner, S. L. (2000). The O. J. Simpson criminal verdict as a racially symbolic event: A longitudinal analysis of racial attitude change. *Personality and Social Psychology Bulletin, 26*, 507–516.

Nigro, G. N., Hill, D. E., Gelbein, M. E., & Clark, C. L. (1988). Changes in the facial prominence of women and men over the last decade. *Psychology of Women Quarterly, 12*, 225–235.

Nilson, L. B. (1976). The occupational and sex-related components of social standing. *Sociology and Social Research, 60*, 328–336.

Nisbett, R. E., Krantz, D. H., Jepson, C., & Kunda, Z. (1983). The use of statistical heuristics in everyday reasoning. *Psychological Review, 339–363.*

Nisbett, R. E., & Kunda, Z. (1985). Perception of social distributions. *Journal of Personality and Social Psychology, 48*, 297–311.

Nisbett, R. E., Peng, K., Choi, I., & Norenzayan, A. (2001). Culture and systems of thought: Holistic versus analytic cognition. *Psychological Review, 108*, 291–310.

Nisbett, R. E., & Wilson, T. D. (1977). The halo effect: Evidence for unconscious alteration of judgments. *Journal of Personality and Social Psychology, 35*, 250–256.

Nisbett, R. E., Zukier, H., & Lemley, R. E. (1981). The dilution effect: Nondiagnostic information weakens the implications of diagnostic information. *Cognitive Psychology, 13*, 248–177.

Noel, J. G., Wann, D. L., & Branscombe, N. R. (1995). Peripheral ingroup membership status and public negativity toward outgroups. *Journal of Personality and Social Psychology, 68*, 127–137.

Norden, M. (1994). *The cinema of isolation: A history of physical disability in the movies.* New Brunswick, NJ: Rutgers University Press.

Nordstrom, C. R., Huffaker, B. J., & Williams, K. B. (1998). When physical disabilities are not liabilities: The role of applicant and interviewer characteristics on employment interview outcomes. *Journal of Applied Social Psychology, 28*, 283–306.

Norenzayan, A., Choi, I., & Nisbett, R. E. (2002). Cultural similarities and differences in social inference: Evidence from behavioral predictions and lay theories of behavior. *Personality and Social Psychology Bulletin, 28*, 109–120.

Nosek, B. A., & Banaji, M. R. (2001). The go/no go association test. *Social Cognition, 19*, 625–666.

Nosek, B. A., Banaji, M. R., & Greenwald, A. G. (2002a). Harvesting implicit group attitudes and beliefs from a demonstration Web site. *Group Dynamics: Theory, Research, and Practice, 6*, 101–115.

Nosek, B. A., Banaji, M. R., & Greenwald, A. G. (2002b). Math = male, me = female, therefore math not = me. *Journal of Personality and Social Psychology, 83*, 44–59.

Noseworthy, C. M., & Lott, A. J. (1984). The cognitive organization of gender-stereotypic categories. *Personality and Social Psychology Bulletin, 10*, 474–481.

Nunnally, J. C., Jr. (1961). *Popular conceptions of mental health.* New York: Holt, Rinehart & Winston.

Oakes, P. J. (1987). The salience of social categories. In J. C. Turner, *Rediscovering the social group: A self-categorization theory* (pp. 117–141). Oxford: Blackwell.

Oakes, P. J., Haslam, S. A., & Turner, J. C. (1994). *Stereotyping and social reality.* Oxford, UK: Blackwell.

Oakes, P. J., & Reynolds, K. J. (1997). Asking the accuracy question: Is measurement the answer. In R. Spears, P. J. Oakes, N. Ellemers, & S. A. Haslam (Eds.), *The social psychology of stereotyping and group life* (pp. 51–71). Oxford, UK: Blackwell.

Oakes, P. J., & Turner, J. C. (1986). Distinctiveness and the salience of social category memberships: Is there an automatic perceptual bias towards novelty. *European Journal of Social Psychology, 16*, 325–344.

Oakes, P. J., & Turner, J. C. (1990). Is limited information processing capacity the cause of social stereotyping. In W. Stroebe & M. Hewstone (Eds.), *European review of social psychology* (Vol. 1, pp. 111–135). Chichester, UK: Wiley.

Oakes, P. J., Turner, J. C., & Haslam, S. A. (1991). Perceiving people as group members: The role of fit in the salience of social categorizations. *British Journal of Social Psychology, 31*, 125–144.

O'Brien, L. T., & Crandall, C. S. (2003). Stereotype threat and arousal: Effects on women's math performance. *Personality and Social Psychology Bulletin, 29*, 782–789.

O'Brien, M., Peyton, V., Mistry, R., Hruda, L., Jacobs, A., Caldera, Y., Huston, A., & Roy, C. (2000). Gender-role cognition in three-year-old boys and girls. *Sex Roles, 42*, 1007–1025.

O'Connell, A. N., & Rotter, N. G. (1979). The influence of stimulus age and sex on person perception. *Journal of Gerontology, 34*, 220–228.

Ogedengbe, R. O. (1993). Prior contacts and perceptions of previously mentally disturbed patients. *International Journal of Nursing Studies, 30*, 247–259.

O'Grady, K. E. (1982). Sex, physical attractiveness and perceived risk of mental illness. *Journal of Personality and Social Psychology, 43*, 1064–1071.

Ojanen, M. (1992). Attitudes toward mental patients. *International Journal of Social Psychiatry, 38*, 120–130.

O'Laughlin, M. J., & Malle, B. F. (2002). How people explain actions performed by groups and individuals. *Journal of Personality and Social Psychology, 82*, 33–48.

Oliver, M. B., & Hyde, J. S. (1993). Gender differences in sexuality: A meta-analysis. *Psychological Bulletin, 114,* 29–51.

Olson, J. M., Maio, G. R., & Hobden, K. L. (1999). The (null) effects of exposure to disparagement humor on stereotypes and attitudes. *International Journal of Humor Research, 12,* 195–219.

Olson, J. M., Roese, N. J., & Zanna, M. P. (1996). Expectancies. In E. T. Higgins & A. W. Kruglanski (Eds.), *Social psychology: Handbook of basic principles* (pp. 211–238). New York: Guilford Press.

Olson, M. A., & Fazio, R. H. (2001). Implicit attitude formation through classical conditioning. *Psychological Science, 12,* 413–417.

O'Mahony, P. D. (1979). Attitudes to the mentally ill: A trait attribution approach. *Social Psychiatry, 14,* 95–105.

Operario, D., & Fiske, S. T. (1998). Racism equals power plus prejudice: A social psychological equation for racial oppression. In J. L. Eberhardt & S. T. Fiske (Eds.), *Confronting racism: The problem and the response* (pp. 33–53). Thousand Oaks, CA: Sage.

Operario, D., & Fiske, S. T. (2001). Ethnic identity moderates perceptions of prejudice: Judgments of personal versus group discrimination and subtle versus blatant bias. *Personality and Social Psychology Bulletin, 27,* 550–561.

Operario, D., Goodwin, S. A., & Fiske, S. T. (1998). Power is everywhere: Social control and personal control both operate at stereotype activation, interpretation, and response. In R. S. Wyer, Jr. (Ed.), *Advances in social cognition: Vol. 11. Stereotype activation and inhibition* (pp. 163–175). Mahwah, NJ: Erlbaum.

Orlofsky, J. L. (1982). Psychological androgyny, sex-typing, and sex-role ideology as predictors of male–female interpersonal attraction. *Sex Roles, 8,* 1057–1073.

Orpen, C., & Chase, A. (1976). A shopping list experiment of the images of prepared and non-prepared foods. *Journal of Social Psychology, 98,* 145–146.

Osborne, J. W. (2001). Testing stereotype threat: Does anxiety explain race and sex differences in achievement? *Contemporary Educational Psychology, 26,* 291–310.

Osgood, C., Suci, G. J., & Tannenbaum, P. H. (1957). *The measurement of meaning.* Urbana: University of Illinois Press.

Osherson, D. N., Smith, E. E., Wilkie, O., Lopez, A., & Shafir, E. (1990). Category-based induction. *Psychological Review, 97,* 185–200.

Oskamp, S., & Jones, J. M. (2000). Promising practices in reducing prejudice: A report from the President's initiative on race. In S. Oskamp (Ed.), *Reducing prejudice and discrimination* (pp. 319–304). Mahwah, NJ: Erlbaum.

Ostrom, T. M. (1973). The bogus pipeline: A new ignis fatuus? *Psychological Bulletin, 79,* 252–259

Ostrom, T. M. (1984). The sovereignity of social cognition. In R. S. Wyer, Jr., & T. Srull (Eds.), *Handbook of social cognition* (Vol. 1, pp. 1–38). Hillsdale, NJ: Erlbaum.

Ostrom, T. M., Carpenter, S. L., Sedikides, C., & Li, F. (1993). Differential processing of in-group and out-group information. *Journal of Personality and Social Psychology, 64,* 21–34.

Ostrom, T. M., Pryor, J. B., & Simpson, D. D. (1981). The organization of social information. In E. T. Higgins, C. P. Herman, & M. P. Zanna (Eds.), *The Ontario Symposium: Vol. 1. Social cognition* (pp. 3–38). Hillsdale, NJ: Erlbaum.

Ostrom, T. M., & Sedikides, C. (1992). Out-group homogeneity effects in natural and minimal groups. *Psychological Bulletin, 112,* 536–552.

Ott, E. M. (1989). Effects of the male–female ratio at work: Policewomen and male nurses. *Psychology of Women Quarterly, 13,* 41–57.

Ottati, V., & Lee, Y.-T. (1995). Accuracy: A neglected component of stereotype research. In Y.-T. Lee, L. J. Jussim, & C. R. McCauley (Eds.), *Stereotype accuracy: Toward appreciating group differences* (pp. 29–59). Washington, DC: American Psychological Association.

Ottaway, S. A., Hayden, D. C., & Oakes, M. A. (2001). Implicit attitudes and racism: Effects of word familiarity and frequency on the implicit association test. *Social Cognition, 19,* 97–144.

Otten, S., & Moskowitz, G. B. (2000). Evidence for implicit evaluative in-group bias: Affect-biased spontaneous trait inference in a minimal group paradigm. *Journal of Experimental Social Psychology, 36,* 77–89.

Otten, S., Mummendey, A., & Blanz, M. (1996). Intergroup discrimination in positive and negative outcome allocations: Impact of stimulus valence, relative group status, and relative group size. *Personality and Social Psychology Bulletin, 22,* 568–581.

Otten, S., & Wentura, D. (1999). About the impact of automaticity in the minimal group paradigm: Evidence from affective priming tasks. *European Journal of Social Psychology, 29,* 1049–1071.

Overbeck, J. R., & Park, B. (2001). When power does not corrupt: Superior individuation processes among powerful perceivers. *Journal of Personality and Social Psychology, 81,* 549–565.

Oyserman, D., Gant, L., & Ager, J. (1995). A socially contextualized model of African American identity: Possible selves and school persistence. *Journal of Personality and Social Psychology, 69,* 1216–1232.

Page, S. (1999). Accommodating persons with AIDS: Acceptance and rejection in rental situations. *Journal of Applied Social Psychology, 29,* 261–270.

Page, S., & Yee, M. (1986). Conception of male and female homosexual stereotypes among university undergraduates. *Journal of Homosexuality, 12,* 109–118.

Palmore, E. B. (1962). Ethnophaulisms and ethnocentrism. *American Journal of Sociology, 67,* 442–445.

Pancer, S. M., & Meindl, J. R. (1978). Length of hair and beardedness as determinants of personality impressions. *Perceptual and Motor Skills, 46,* 1328–1330.

Park, B. (1986). A method for studying the development of impressions of real people. *Journal of Personality and Social Psychology, 51,* 907–917.

Park, B., & Hastie, R. (1987). Perception of variability in category development: Instance- versus abstraction-based stereotypes. *Journal of Personality and Social Psychology, 53,* 621–635.

Park, B., & Judd, C. M. (1990). Measures and models of perceived group variability. *Journal of Personality and Social Psychology, 59,* 173–191.

Park, B., Judd, C. M., & Ryan, C. S. (1991). Social categorization and the representation of variability information. In W. Strobe & M. Hewstone (Eds.), *European review of social psychology* (Vol. 2, pp. 211–245). Chichester, UK: Wiley.

Park, B., & Rothbart, M. (1982). Perception of out-group homogeneity and levels of social categorization: Memory for the subordinate attributes of in-group and out-group members. *Journal of Personality and Social Psychology, 42,* 1051–1068.

Park, B., Ryan, C. S., & Judd, C. M. (1992). Role of meaningful subgroups in explaining differences in perceived variability for in-groups and out-groups. *Journal of Personality and Social Psychology, 63,* 553–567.

Park, B., Wolsko, C., & Judd, C. M. (2001). Measurement of subtyping in stereotype change. *Journal of Experimental Social Psychology, 37,* 325–332.

Park, J., & Banaji, M. R. (2000). Mood and heuristics: The influence of happy and sad states on sensitivity and bias in stereotyping. *Journal of Personality and Social Psychology, 78,* 1005–1023.

Patel, V. (1995). Explanatory models of mental illness in sub-Saharan Africa. *Social Science and Medicine, 40,* 1291–1298.

Patterson, C. J. (1992). Children of lesbian and gay parents. *Child Development, 63,* 1025–1042.

Paulhus, D. L., Martin, C. L., & Murphy, G. K. (1992). Some effects of arousal on sex stereotyping. *Personality and Social Psychology Bulletin, 18,* 325–330.

Pavelchak, M. A. (1989). Piecemeal and category-based evaluation: An idiographic analysis. *Journal of Personality and Social Psychology, 56,* 354–363.

Payne, B. K. (2001). Prejudice and perception: The role of automatic and controlled processes in misperceiving a weapon. *Journal of Personality and Social Psychology, 81,* 181–192.

Payne, B. K., Lambert, A. J., & Jacoby, L. L. (2002). Best laid plans: Effects of goals on accessibility bias and cognitive control in race-based misperceptions of weapons. *Journal of Experimental Social Psychology, 38,* 384–396.

Peabody, D. (1967). Trait inferences: Evaluative and descriptive aspects. *Journal of Personality and Social Psychology Monograph, 7*(No. 4), 1–18.

Peabody, D. (1970). Evaluative and descriptive aspects in personality perception: A reappraisal. *Journal of Personality and Social Psychology, 16,* 639–646.

Peabody, D. (1985). *National characteristics.* New York: Cambridge University Press.

Pedersen, A., & Walker, I. (1997). Prejudice against Australian Aborigines: Old-fashioned and modern forms. *European Journal of Social Psychology, 27,* 561–587.

Peffley, M., & Hurwitz, J. (2002). The racial components of "race-neutral" crime policy attitudes. *Political Psychology*, *23*, 59–75.

Peirce, K. (1993). Socialization of teenage girls through teen-magazine fiction: The making of a new woman or an old lady? *Sex Roles*, *29*, 59–68.

Peirce, K. (1997). Women's magazine fiction: A content analysis of the roles, attributes, and occupations of main characters. *Sex Roles*, *37*, 581–593.

Pellett, T. L. (1994). Children's stereotypical perceptions of physical activities: A K–12 analysis. *Perceptual and Motor Skills*, *79*, 1128–1130.

Pellett, T. L., & Ignica, A. A. (1994). Relationship between children's and parents' stereotyping of physical activities. *Perceptual and Motor Skills*, *77*, 1283–1289.

Pendry, L. F. (1998). When the mind is otherwise engaged: Resource depletion and social stereotyping. *European Journal of Social Psychology*, *28*, 293–299.

Pendry, L. F., & Macrae, C. N. (1994). Stereotypes and mental life: The case of the motivated but twarted tactician. *Journal of Experimental Social Psychology*, *30*, 303–325.

Pendry, L. F., & Macrae, C. N. (1996). What the disinterested perceiver overlooks: Goal-directed social categorization. *Personality and Social Psychology Bulletin*, *22*, 249–256.

Pendry, L. F., & Macrae, C. N. (1999). Cognitive load and person memory: The role of perceived group variability. *European Journal of Social Psychology*, *29*, 925–942.

Penn, D. L., Guynan, K., Dailey, T., Spaulding, W. D., Garbin, C. P., & Sullivan, M. (1994). Dispelling the stigma of schizophrenia: What sort of information is best? *Schizophrenia Bulletin*, *20*, 567–578.

Pennebaker, J. W., Rime, B., & Blankenship, V. E. (1996). Stereotypes of emotional expressiveness of Northerners and Southerners: A cross-cultural test of Montesquieu's hypothesis. *Journal of Personality and Social Psychology*, *70*, 372–380.

Perdue, C. W., Dovidio, J. F., Gurtman, M. B., & Tyler, R. B. (1990). Us and them: Social categorization and the process of intergroup bias. *Journal of Personality and Social Psychology*, *59*, 475–486.

Perdue, C. W., & Gurtman, M. B. (1990). Evidence for the automaticity of ageism. *Journal of Experimental Social Psychology*, *26*, 199–216.

Perez-Lopez, M. S., Lewis, R. J., & Cash, T. F. (2001). The relationship of antifat attitudes to other prejudicial and gender-related attitudes. *Journal of Applied Social Psychology*, *31*, 683–697.

Perreault, S., & Bourhis, R. Y. (1999). Ethnocentrism, social identification, and discrimination. *Personality and Social Psychology Bulletin*, *25*, 92–103.

Perrett, D. I., May, K. A., & Yoshikawa, S. (1994). Facial shape and judgments of female attractiveness. *Nature*, *368*, 239–242.

Perrott, S. B., Murray, A. H., Lowe, J., & Ruggiero, K. M. (2000). The personal-group discrimination discrepancy in persons living with psoriasis. *Basic and Applied Social Psychology*, *22*, 57–67.

Peterson, B. E., Doty, R., & Winter, D. (1993). Authoritarianism and attitudes toward contemporary social issues. *Personality and Social Psychology Bulletin*, *19*, 174–184.

Peterson, B. E., Duncan, L. E., & Pang, J. S. (2002). Authoritarianism and political impoverishment: Deficits in knowledge and civic disinterest. *Political Psychology*, *23*, 97–112.

Peterson, K., & Curran, J. P. (1976). Trait attribution as a function of hair length and correlates of subjects' preferences for hair style. *Journal of Psychology*, *93*, 331–339.

Pettigrew, T. F. (1979). The ultimate attribution error: Extending Allport's cognitive analysis of prejudice. *Personality and Social Psychology Bulletin*, *5*, 461–476.

Pettigrew, T. F. (1981). Extending the stereotype concept. In D. L. Hamilton (Ed.), *Cognitive processes in stereotyping and intergroup behavior* (pp. 303–331). Hillsdale, NJ: Erlbaum.

Pettigrew, T. F. (1988). Integration and pluralism. In P.A. Katz & D.A. Taylor (Eds.), *Eliminating racism: Profiles in controversy* (pp. 19–30). New York: Plenum Press.

Pettigrew, T. F. (1997). The affective component of prejudice: Empirical support for the new view. In S. A. Tuch & J. K. Martin (Eds.), *Racial attitudes in the 1990s: Continuity and change* (pp. 76–90). Westport, CT: Praeger.

Pettigrew, T. F. (1998a). Intergroup contact theory. *Annual Review of Psychology*, *49*, 65–85.

Pettigrew, T. F. (1998b). Reactions to the new minorities of Western Europe. *Annual Review of Sociology*, *24*, 771–803.

Pettigrew, T. F., & Meertens, R. W. (1995). Subtle and blatant prejudice in Western Europe. *European Journal of Social Psychology*, *25*, 57–75.

Pettigrew, T. F., & Tropp, L. R. (2000). Does intergroup contact reduce prejudice?: Recent meta-ana-lytic findings. In S. Oskamp (Ed.), *Reducing prejudice and discrimination* (pp. 93–114). Mahwah, NJ: Erlbaum.

Pettigrew, T. W. (1958). Personality and sociocultural factors in intergroup attitudes: A cross-national perspective. *Journal of Conflict Resolution, 2,* 29–42.

Petty, R. E., & Cacioppo, J. T. (1986). The elaboration likelihood model of persuasion. In L. Berkowitz (Ed.), *Advances in experimental social psychology* (Vol. 19, pp. 123–205). Orlando, FL: Academic Press.

Petzold, P., & Edeler, B. (1995). Organization of person memory and retrieval processes in recognition. *European Journal of Social Psychology, 25,* 249–267.

Pezdek, K., Whetstone, T., Reynolds, K., Askari, N., & Dougherty, T. (1989). Memory for real-world scenes: The role of consistency with schema expectation. *Journal of Experimental Psychology: Learning, Memory, and Cognition, 15,* 587–595.

Phalet, K., & Poppe, E. (1997). Competence and morality dimensions of national and ethnic stereotypes: A study in six Eastern-European countries. *European Journal of Social Psychology, 27,* 703–723.

Phelan, J., Link, B. G., Moore, R. E., & Stueve, A. (1997). The stigma of homelessness: The impact of the label "homeless" on attitudes toward poor persons. *Social Psychology Quarterly, 60,* 323–337.

Phelps, E. A., O'Connor, K. J., Cunningham, W. A., Gatenby, J. C., Funayama, E. S., Gore, J. C., & Banaji, M. R. (2000). Amygdala activation predicts performance on indirect tests of racial bias. *Journal of Cognitive Neuroscience, 12,* 729–738.

Pheterson, G. I., Kiesler, S. B., & Goldberg, P. A. (1971). Evaluation of the performance of women as a function of their sex, achievement, and personal history. *Journal of Personality and Social Psychology, 19,* 114–118.

Phillips, A., & Dipboye, R. L. (1989). Correlational tests of predictions from a process model of the interview. *Journal of Applied Psychology, 74,* 41–52.

Phillips, B. S. (1990). Nicknames and sex role stereotypes. *Sex Roles, 23,* 281–289.

Phillips, D. L. (1963). Rejection: A possible consequence of seeking help for mental disorders. *American Sociological Review, 28,* 963–972.

Phillips, D. L. (1964). Rejection of the mentally ill: The influence of behavior and sex. *American Sociological Review, 29,* 679–687.

Phillips, D. L. (1966). Public identification and acceptance of the mentally ill. *American Journal of Public Health, 56,* 755–763.

Phillips, D. L. (1967). Identification of mental illness: Its consequences for rejection. *Community Mental Health Journal, 3,* 262–266.

Phillips, R. D., & Gilroy, F. D. (1985). Sex-role stereotypes and clinical judgemnts of mental health: The Brovermans' findings reexamined. *Sex Roles, 12,* 179–193.

Phinney, J. S. (1996). When we talk about American ethnic groups, what do we mean? *American Psychologist, 51,* 918–927.

Phinney, J. S., Ferguson, D. L., & Tate, J. D. (1997). Intergroup attitudes among ethnic minority adolescents: A causal model. *Child Development, 68,* 955–969.

Pichevin, M. F., & Hurtig, M. C. (1996). Describing men, desibing women: Sex membership salience and numberical distinctiveness. *European Journal of Social Psychology, 26,* 513–522.

Pickett, C. L. (2001). The effects of entitativity beliefs on implicit comparisons between group members. *Personality and Social Psychology Bulletin, 27,* 515–525.

Pickett, C. L., & Brewer, M. B. (2001). Assimilation and differentiation needs as motivational determinants of perceived in-group and out-group homogeneity. *Journal of Experimental Social Psychology, 37,* 341–348.

Pickett, C. L., Silver, M. D., & Brewer, M. B. (2002). The impact of assimilation and differentiation needs on perceived group importance and judgments of ingroup size. *Personality and Social Psychology Bulletin, 28,* 546–558.

Pillard, R. C. (1991). Masculinity and femininity in homosexuality: "Inversion" revisited. In J. C. Gonsiorek & J. D. Weinrich (Eds.), *Homosexuality: Research implications for public policy* (pp. 32–43). Newbury Park, CA: Sage.

Pinel, E. C. (1999). Stigma consciousness: The psychological legacy of social stereotypes. *Journal of Personality and Social Psychology, 76,* 114–128.

Pinel, E. C. (2002). Stigma consciousness in intergroup contexts: The power of conviction. *Journal of Experimental Social Psychology, 38,* 178–185.

Pintner, R. (1918). Intelligence as estimated from photographs. *Psychological Review, 25,* 286–196.

Pittinsky, T. L., Shih, M., & Ambady, N. (2000). Will a category cue affect you?: Category cues, positive stereotypes and reviewer recall for applicants. *Social Psychology of Education, 4,* 53–65.

Plant, E. A., & Devine, P. G. (1998). Internal and external motivation to respond without prejudice. *Journal of Personality and Social Psychology, 75,* 811–832.

Plant, E. A., & Devine, P. G. (2001). Responses to other-imposed pro-black pressure: Acceptance or backlash? *Journal of Experimental Social Psychology, 37,* 486–501.

Plant, E. A., & Devine, P. G. (2003). The antecedents and implications of interracial anxiety. *Personality and Social Psychology Bulletin, 29,* 790–801.

Plant, E. A., Hyde, J. S., Keltner, D., & Devine, P. G. (2000). The gender stereotyping of emotions. *Psychology of Women Quarterly, 24,* 81–92.

Platow, M. J., Harley, K., Hunter, J. A., Hanning, P., Shave, R., & O'Connell, A. (1997). Interpreting in-group-favouring allocations in the minimal group paradigm. *British Journal of Social Psychology, 36,* 107–117.

Platz, S. J., & Hosch, H. M. (1988). Cross-racial/ethnic eyewitness identification: A field study. *Journal of Applied Social Psychology, 18,* 972–984.

Plessner, H., Freytag, P., & Fiedler, K. (2000). Expectancy-effects without expectancies: Illusory correlations based on cue-overlap. *European Journal of Social Psychology, 30,* 837–851.

Plous, S., & Williams, T. (1995). Racial stereotypes from the days of American slavery: A continuing legacy. *Journal of Applied Social Psychology, 25,* 795–817.

Pollak, K. I., & Niemann, Y. F. (1998). Black and white tokens in academia: A difference of chronic versus acute distinctiveness. *Journal of Applied Social Psychology, 28,* 954–972.

Pomerleau, A., Bolduc, D., Malcuit, G., & Cossette, L. (1990). Pink or blue: Enviromental gender stereotypes in the first two years of life. *Sex Roles, 22,* 359–367.

Poole, D. A., & Tapley, A. E. (1988). Sex roles, social roles, and clinical judgments of mental health. *Sex Roles, 19,* 265–272.

Pope Edwards, C. (1984). The age group labels and categories of preschool children. *Child Development, 55,* 440–452.

Poppe, E. (2001). Effects of changes in GNP and perceived group characteristics on national and ethnic stereotypes in Central and Eastern Europe. *Journal of Applied Social Psychology, 31,* 1689–1708.

Poppe, E., & Linssen, H. (1999). In-group favouritism and the reflection of realistic dimensions of difference between national states in Central and Eastern European nationality stereotypes. *British Journal of Social Psychology, 38,* 85–102.

Porter, J. D. R. (1971). *Black child, white child.* Cambridge, MA: Harvard University Press.

Postmes, T., & Branscombe, N. R. (2002). Influence of long-term racial environmental composition on subjective well- being in African Americans. *Journal of Personality and Social Psychology, 83,* 735–751.

Postmes, T., Branscombe, N. R., Spears, R., & Young, H. (1999). Comparative processes in personal and group judgments: Resolving the discrepancy. *Journal of Personality and Social Psychology, 76,* 320–338.

Powell, G. N., & Kido, Y. (1994). Managerial stereotypes in a global economy: A comparative study of Japanese and American business students' perspectives. *Psychological Reports, 74,* 219–226.

Powell-Hopson, D., & Hopson, D. (1992). Implications of doll color preferences among black preschool children and white preschool children. In A. Burlew, W. C. Banks, H. McAdoo, & D. Azibo (Eds.), *African American psychology* (pp. 183–198). Newbury Park, CA: Sage.

Power, J. G., Murphy, S. T., & Coover, G. (1996). Priming prejudice: How stereotypes and counter-stereotypes influence attribution of responsibility and credibility among ingroups and outgroups. *Human Communication Research, 23,* 36–58.

Pratto, F. (1999). The puzzle of continuing group inequality: Piecing together psychological, social, and cultural forces in social dominance theory. In M. P. Zanna (Ed.), *Advances in experimental social psychology* (Vol. 31, pp. 191–263). San Diego, CA: Academic Press.

Pratto, F., & Bargh, J. A. (1991). Stereotyping based on apparently individuating information: Trait and global components of sex stereotypes under attention overload. *Journal of Experimental Social Psychology, 27,* 26–47.

Pratto, F., Sidanius, J., Stallworth, L. M., & Malle, B. F. (1994). Social dominance orientation: A personality variable predicting social and political attitudes. *Journal of Personality and Social Psychology, 67,* 741–763.

Pratto, F., Stallworth, L. M., Sidanius, J., & Siers, B. (1997). The gender gap in occupational role attainment: A social dominance approach. *Journal of Personality and Social Psychology, 72,* 37–53.

Pratto, F., Tatar, D., & Conway-Lanz, S. (1999). Who gets what and why?: Determinants of social allocations. *Political Psychology, 20,* 127–150.

Prentice, D. A., & Miller, D. T. (1996). Pluralistic ignorance and the perpetration of social norms by unwitting actors. In M. P. Zanna (Ed.), *Advances in experimental social psychology* (Vol. 28, pp. 161–209). San Diego, CA: Academic Press.

Proffitt, J. B., Coley, J. D., & Medin, D. L. (2000). Expertise and category-based induction. *Journal of Experimental Psychology: Learning, Memory, and Cognition, 26,* 811–828.

Prothro, E. T. (1954a). Cross-cultural patterns of national stereotypes. *Journal of Social Psychology, 40,* 53–59.

Prothro, E. T. (1954b). Studies in stereotypes: IV. Lebanese business men. *Journal of Social Psychology, 40,* 275–280.

Pryor, J. B., Reeder, G. D., & McManus, J. A. (1991). Fear and loathing in the workplace: Reactions to AIDS-infected co-workers. *Personality and Social Psychology Bulletin, 17,* 133–139.

Pryor, J. B., Reeder, G. D., Vinacco, R., Jr., & Kott, T. L. (1989). The instrumental and symbolic functions of attitudes toward persons with AIDS. *Journal of Applied Social Psychology, 19,* 377–404.

Purcell, P., & Stewart, L. (1990). Dick and Jane in 1989. *Sex Roles, 22,* 177–185.

Putnam, H. (1975). The meaning of meaning. In H. Putnam (Ed.), *Mind, language, and reality* (Vol. 2, pp. 139–152). Cambridge, UK: Cambridge University Press. (Original work published 1970)

Pyszczynski, T., Solomon, S., & Greenberg, J. (2003). *In the wake of 9/11: The psychology of terror.* Washington, DC: American Psychological Association.

Quackenbush, S. W., & Barnett, M. A. (2001). Recollection and evaluation of critical experiences in moral development: A cross-sectional examination. *Basic and Applied Social Psychology, 23,* 55–64.

Quattrone, G. A. (1986). On the perception of a group's variability. In S. Worchel & W. G. Austin (Eds.), *Psychology of intergroup relations* (2nd ed., pp. 25–48). Chicago: Nelson-Hall.

Quattrone, G. A., & Jones, E. E. (1980). The perception of variability within ingroups and outgroups: Implications for the law of small numbers. *Journal of Personality and Social Psychology, 38,* 141–152.

Queller, S. (2002). Stereotype change in a recurrent network. *Personality and Social Psychology Review, 6,* 295–303.

Queller, S., Mackie, D. M., & Stroessner, S. J. (1996). Ameliorating some negative effects of positive mood: Encouraging happy people to perceive intragroup variability. *Journal of Experimental Social Psychology, 32,* 361–386.

Queller, S., & Smith, E. R. (2002). Subtyping versus bookkeeping in stereotype learning and change: Connectionist simulations and empirical findings. *Journal of Personality and Social Psychology, 82,* 300–313.

Quina, K., Wingard, J. A., & Bates, H. G. (1987). Language style and gender stereotypes in person perception. *Psychology of Women Quarterly, 11,* 111–122.

Quine, W. V. (1977). Natural kinds. In S. P. Schwartz (Ed.), *Naming, necessity, and natural kinds* (pp. 155–175). Ithaca, NY: Cornell University Press.

Quinn, D. M., & Spencer, S. J. (2001). The interference of stereotype threat with women's generation of mathematical problem-solving strategies. *Journal of Social Issues, 57,* 55–71.

Quinn, K. A., & Olson, J. M. (2003). Framing social judgement: Self-ingroup comparison and perceived discrimination. *Personality and Social Psychology Bulletin, 29,* 228–236.

Quinn, K. A., Roese, N. J., Pennington, G. L., & Olson, J. M. (1999). The personal/group discrimination discrepancy: The role of informational complexity. *Personality and Social Psychology Bulletin, 25,* 1430–1440.

Rabbie, J., Schot, J. C., & Visser, L. (1989). Social identity theory: A conceptual and empirical critique from the perspective of a behavioural interaction model. *European Journal of Social Psychology, 19,* 171–202.

Rabkin, J. G. (1972). Opinions about mental illness: A review of the literature. *Psychological Bulletin, 77, 153–171.*

Rabkin, J. G. (1974, Fall). Public attitudes toward mental illness: A review of the literature. *Schizophrenia Bulletin,* pp. 9–33.

Rabkin, J. G. (1979). Who is called mentally ill: Public and professional views. *Journal of Community Psychiatry, 7,* 254–258.

Rada, J. A. (1996). Color blind-sided: Racial bias in network's television coverage of professional football games. *Howard Journal of Communications, 7,* 234–236.

Ramsey, P. G. (1987). Young children's thinking about ethnic differences. In J. S. Phinney & M. J. Rotheram (Eds.), *Children's ethnic socialization* (pp. 56–72). Beverly Hills, CA: Sage.

Ramsey, S. L., Lord, C. G., Wallace, D. S., & Pugh, M. A. (1994). The role of subtypes in attitudes towards superordinate social categories. *British Journal of Social Psychology, 33,* 387–403.

Ransford, H. E., & Palisi, B. J. (1992). Has there been a resurgence of racist attitudes in the general population. *Sociological Spectrum, 12,* 231–255.

Rasinski, K. A., Crocker, J., & Hastie, R. (1985). Another look at sex stereotypes and social judgments: An analysis of the social perceiver's use of subjective probabilities. *Journal of Personality and Social Psychology, 49,* 317–326.

Rasmussen, J. L., & Moely, B. E. (1986). Impression formation as a function of the sex role appropriateness of linguistic behavior. *Sex Roles, 14,* 149–161.

Rath, R., & Das, J. P. (1958). Study in stereotypes of college freshmen and service holders in Orissa, India, towards themselves and four other foreign nationalities. *Journal of Social Psychology, 47,* 373–385.

Read, S. J. (1987). Similarity and causality in the use of social analogies. *Journal of Experimental Social Psychology, 23,* 189–207.

Read, S. J., Druian, P. R., & Miller, L. C. (1989). The role of causal sequence in the meaning of actions. *British Journal of Social Psychology, 28,* 341–351.

Read, S. J., Jones, D. K., & Miller, L. C. (1990). Traits as goal-based categories: The importance of goals in the coherence of dispositional categories. *Journal of Personality and Social Psychology, 58,* 1048–1061.

Read, S. J., & Miller, L. C. (1993). Rapist or "regular guy": Explanatory coherence in the construction of mental models of others. *Personality and Social Psychology Bulletin, 19,* 526–541.

Reda, S. (1996). Public perceptions of former psychiatric patients in England. *Psychiatric Services, 47,* 1253–1255.

Reeder, G. D. (1979). Context effects for attributions of ability. *Personality and Social Psychology Bulletin, 5,* 65–68.

Reeder, G. D. (1997). Dispositional inferences of ability: Content and process. *Journal of Experimental Social Psychology, 33,* 171–189.

Reeder, G. D., & Brewer, M. B. (1979). A schematic model of dispositional attribution in interpersonal perception. *Psychological Review, 86,* 61–79.

Reeder, G. D., & Coovert, M. D. (1986). Revising an impression of morality. *Social Cognition, 4,* 1–17.

Reeder, G. D., & Fulks, J. L. (1980). When actions speak louder than words: Implicational schemata and the attribution of ability. *Journal of Experimental Social Psychology, 16,* 33–46.

Reeder, G. D., Messick, D. M., & Van Avermaet, E. (1977). Dimensional asymmetry in attributional inference. *Journal of Experimental Social Psychology, 13,* 46–57.

Reeder, G. D., Pryor, J. B., & Wojciszke, B. (1992). Trait–behavior relations in social information processing. In G. R. Semin & K. Fiedler (Eds.), *Language, interaction and social cognition* (pp. 37–57). London: Sage.

Reeder, G. D., & Spores, J. M. (1983). The attribution of morality. *Journal of Personality and Social Psychology, 44,* 736–745.

Regan, P. C. (1996). Sexual outcasts: The perceived impact of body weight and gender on sexuality. *Journal of Applied Social Psychology, 26,* 1803–1815.

Regan, P. C. (1997). The impact of male sexual request style on perceptions of sexual interactions:

The mediational role of beliefs about female sexual desire. *Basic and Applied Social Psychology*, *19*, 519–532.

Reicher, S., Hopkins, N., & Condor, S. (1997). Stereotype construction as a strategy of influence. In R. Spears, P. J. Oakes, N. Ellemers, & S. A. Haslam (Eds.), *The social psychology of stereotyping and group life* (pp. 94–118). Oxford, UK: Blackwell.

Reichl, A. J. (1997). Ingroup favouritism and outgroup favouritism in low status minimal groups: Differential responses to status-related and status-unrelated measures. *European Journal of Social Psychology*, *27*, 617–633.

Reid, G. M. (1995). Children's occupational sex-role stereotyping in 1994. *Psychological Reports*, *76*, 1155–1165.

Reynolds, K. J., & Oakes, P. J. (2000). Variability in impression formation: Investigating the role of motivation, capacity, and the categorization process. *Personality and Social Psychology Bulletin*, *26*, 355–373.

Reynolds, K. J., Turner, J. C., Haslam, S. A., & Ryan, M. K. (2001). The role of personality and group factors in explaining prejudice. *Journal of Experimental Social Psychology*, *37*, 427–434.

Rhodes, G., Proffitt, F., Grady, J. M., & Sumich, A. (1998). Facial symmetry and the perceptions of beauty. *Psychonomic Bulletin and Review*, *5*, 659–669.

Rhodes, G., Sumich, A., & Byatt, G. (1999). Are average face configurations attractive only because of their symmetry? *Psycholgical Science*, *10*, 53–59.

Rhodes, G., Zebrowitz, L. A., Clark, A., Kalick, S. M., Hightower, A., & McKay, R. (2001). Do facial averageness and symmetry signal health? *Evolution and Human Behavior*, *22*, 31–46.

Ric, F. (1997). Effects of control deprivation on subsequent use of stereotype. *Journal of Social Psychology*, *137*, 333–342.

Ricciardelli, L. A., & Williams, R. J. (1995). Desirable and undesirable gender traits in three behavioral domains. *Sex Roles*, *33*, 637–655.

Rice, S. A. (1926). "Stereotypes": A source of error in judging human character. *Journal of Personnel Research*, *5*, 267–276.

Rice, S. A. (1928). *Quantitative methods in politics*. New York: Knopf.

Rich, M. K., & Cash, T. F. (1993). The American image of beauty: Media representations of hair color for four decades. *Sex Roles*, *29*, 113–124.

Rich, Y., Ari, R. B., Amir, Y., & Eliassy, L. (1996). Effectiveness of schools with a mixed student body of natives and immigrants. *International Journal of Intercultural Relations*, *20*, 323–339.

Richards, Z., & Hewstone, M. (2001). Subtyping and subgrouping: Processes for the prevention and promotion of stereotype change. *Personality and Social Psychology Review*, *5*, 52–73.

Richardson, S. A., & Emerson, P. (1970). Race and physical handicap in children's preference for other children. *Human Relations*, *23*, 31–36.

Richardson, S. A., & Green, A. (1971). When is black beautiful?: Colored and white children's reactions to skin color. *British Journal of Educational Psychology*, *41*, 62–69.

Richardson, S. A., Hastorf, A. H., Goodman, N., & Dornbush, S. M. (1961). Cultural uniformity in reaction to physical disabilities. *American Sociological Review*, *26*, 241–247.

Richardson, S. A., & Royce, J. (1968). Race and physical handicap in children's preferences for other children. *Child Development*, *39*, 467–480.

Richeson, J. A., & Ambady, N. I (2001). Who's in charge?: Effects of situational roles on automatic gender bias. *Sex Roles*, *44*, 493–512.

Riedle, J. E. (1991). Exploring the subcategories of stereotypes: Not all mothers are the same. *Sex Roles*, *24*, 711–723.

Riemann, R., & Angleitner, A. (1993). Inferring interpersonal traits from behavior: Act prototypicality versus conceptual similarity of trait concepts. *Journal of Personality and Social Psychology*, *64*, 356–364.

Riley, S. C. E. (2002). Constructions of equality and discrimination in professional men's talk. *British Journal of Social Psychology*, *41*, 443–461.

Rips, L. J. (1975). Inductive judgments about natural categories. *Journal of Verbal Learning and Verbal Behavior*, *14*, 665–681.

Rips, L. J. (1989). Similarity, typicality, and categorization. In S. Vosniadou & A. Ortony (Eds.), *Similarity and analogical reasoning* (pp. 21–59). Cambridge, UK: Cambridge University Press.

Rips, L. J. (2001). Necessity and natural categories. *Psychological Bulletin, 127*, 827–852.

Rips, L. J., & Collins, A. (1993). Categories and resemblance. *Journal of Experimental Psychology: General, 122*, 468–486.

Roberts, B.-E., & White, J. E. (1998). *Roberts vs. Texaco.* New York: Avon.

Roberts, J. V., & Herman, C. P. (1986). The psychology of height: An empirical review. In C. P. Herman, M. P. Zanna, & E. T. Higgins (Eds.), *The Ontario Symposium: Vol. 3. Physical appearance, stigma, and social behavior* (pp. 113–140). Hillsdale, NJ: Erlbaum.

Robinson, M. D., & Johnson, J. T. (1997). Is it emotion or is it stress?: Gender stereotypes and the perception of subjective experience. *Sex Roles, 36*, 235–258.

Robinson, R. J., & Keltner, D. (1996). Much ado about nothing?: Revisionists and traditionalists choose an English syllabus. *Psychological Science, 7*, 18–24.

Robinson, R. J., Keltner, D., Ward, A., & Ross, L. (1995). Actual versus assumed differences in construal: "Naive realism" in intergroup perception and conflict. *Journal of Personality and Social Psychology, 68*, 404–417.

Rodin, M. J. (1972). The informativeness of trait descriptions. *Journal of Personality and Social Psychology, 21*, 341–344.

Rodin, M. J. (1975). The trait encoding of behavior. *Bulletin of the Psychonomic Society, 6*, 638–640.

Rodin, M. J. (1987). Who is memorable to whom: A study of cognitive disregard. *Social Cognition, 5*, 144–165.

Rodin, M. J., & Harari, H. (1986). Fact, belief, and the attribution of prejudice. *Social Cognition, 4*, 437–445.

Rodin, M. J., Price, J. M., Bryson, J. B., & Sanchez, F. J. (1990). Asymmetry in prejudice attribution. *Journal of Experimental Social Psychology, 26*, 481–504.

Rodin, M. J., Price, J., Sanchez, F., & McElligot, S. (1989). Derogation, exclusion, and unfair treatment of persons with social flaws: Controlability of stigma and the atttribution of prejudice. *Personality and Social Psychology Bulletin, 15*, 439–451.

Rodríguez-Bailón, R., Moya, M., & Yzerbyt, V. (2000). Why do superiors attend to negative stereotypic information about their subordinates?: Effects of power legitimacy on social perception. *European Journal of Social Psychology, 30*, 651–671.

Rogier, A., & Yzerbyt, V. Y. (1999). Social attribution: The role of homogeneity in subjective essentialism. *Swiss Journal of Psychology, 54*, 233–240.

Rojahn, K., & Pettigrew, T. F. (1992). Memory for schema-relevant information: A meta-analytic resolution. *British Journal of Social Psychology, 31*, 81–109.

Rojahn, K., & Willemsen, T. M. (1994). The evaluation of effectiveness and likability of gender-role congruent and gender-role incongruent leaders. *Sex Roles, 30*, 109–119.

Rokeach, M. (1948). Generalized mental rigidity as a factor in ethnocentrism. *Journal of Abnormal and Social Psychology, 43*, 259–278.

Rokeach, M. (1960). *The open and closed mind.* New York: Basic Books.

Rokeach, M., Smith, P. W., & Evans, R. I. (1960). Two kinds of prejudice or one? In M. Rokeach, *The open and closed mind* (pp. 132–168). New York: Basic Books.

Roll, S., & Verinis, J. S. (1971). Stereotypes of scalp and facial hair as measured by the semantic differential. *Psychological Reports, 28*, 975–980.

Romer, D., Jamieson, K. H., & de Coteau, N. (1998). The treatment of persons of color in local television news: Ethnic blame discourse or realistic group conflict. *Communication Research, 25*, 286–305.

Rootman, I., & Lafave, H. (1969). Are popular attitudes toward the mentally ill changing? *American Journal of Psychiatry, 126*, 261–265.

Rosch, E. (1978). Principles of categorization. In E. Rosch & B. B. Lloyd (Eds.), *Cognition and categorization* (pp. 27–48). Hillsdale, NJ: Erlbaum.

Rosch, E., Mervis, C. B., Gray, W. D., Johnson, D. M., & Boyes-Braem, P. (1976). Basic objects in natural categories. *Cognitive Psychology, 8*, 382–439.

Rosenberg, S., Nelson, C., & Vivekananthan, P. S. (1968). A multidimensional approach to the structure of personality impressions. *Journal of Personality and Social Psychology, 9*, 283–294.

Rosenberg, S., & Sedlak, A. (1972). Structural representations of implicit personality theory. In L.

Berkowitz (Ed.), *Advances in experimental social psychology* (Vol. 6, pp. 235–297). New York: Academic Press.

Rosenfield, G. (1982). The polls: Attitudes toward American Jews. *Public Opinion Quarterly, 46*, 431–443.

Rosenkrantz, P., Vogel, S. R., Bee, H., Broverman, I. K., & Broverman, D. M. (1968). Sex-role stereotypes and self-concepts in college students. *Journal of Consulting and Clinical Psychology, 32*, 287–295.

Rosenthal, R., & Jacobson, L. (1968). *Pygmalion in the classroom.* New York: Holt, Rinehart & Winston.

Rosenwasser, S. M., Gonzales, M. H., & Adams, V. (1985). Perception of a housespouse: The effects of sex, economic productivity, and subject background variables. *Psychology of Women Quarterly, 9*, 258–264.

Roskos-Ewoldsen, D. R., & Fazio, R. H. (1992). On the orienting value of attitudes: Attitude accessibility as a determinant of an object's attraction of visual attention. *Journal of Personality and Social Psychology, 63*, 198–211.

Ross, B. H., & Murphy, G. L. (1996). Category-based predictions: Influence of uncertainty and feature associations. *Journal of Experimental Psychology: Learning, Memory, and Cognition, 22*, 736–753.

Ross, M. (1989). Relation of implicit theories to the construction of personal histories. *Psychological Review, 96*, 341–357.

Ross, M., McFarland, C., & Fletcher, G. J. O. (1981). The effect of atitude on recall of past histories. *Journal of Personality and Social Psychology, 40*, 627–634.

Roth, E. M., & Shoben, E. J. (1983). The effect of context on the structure of categories. *Cognitive Psychology, 15*, 346–378.

Rothbart, M. (1981). Memory processes and social beliefs. In D. L. Hamilton (Ed.), *Cognitive processes in stereotyping and intergroup behavior* (pp. 145–181). Hillsdale, NJ: Erlbaum.

Rothbart, M. (1996). Category-exemplar dynamics and stereotype change. *International Journal of Intercultural Relations, 20*, 305–321.

Rothbart, M., Davis-Stitt, C., & Hill, J. (1997). Effects of arbitrarily placed category boundaries on similarity judgments. *Journal of Experimental Social Psychology, 33*, 122–145.

Rothbart, M., Evans, M., & Fulero, S. (1979). Recall for confirming events: Memory processes and the maintenance of social stereotypes. *Journal of Experimental Social Psychology, 15*, 343–355.

Rothbart, M., Fulero, S., Jensen, C., Howard, J., & Birrell, P. (1978). From individual to group impressions: Availability heuristics in stereotype formation. *Journal of Experimental Social Psychology, 14*, 237–255.

Rothbart, M., & John, O. P. (1985). Social categorization and behavioral episodes: A cognitive analysis of the effects of intergroup contact. *Journal of Social Issues, 41*, 81–104.

Rothbart, M., & Lewis, S. (1988). Inferring category attributes from exemplar attributes: Geometric shapes and social categories. *Journal of Personality and Social Psychology, 55*, 861–872.

Rothbart, M., & Park, B. (1986). On the confirmability and disconfirmability of trait concepts. *Journal of Personality and Social Psychology, 50*, 131–142.

Rothbart, M., Sriram, N., & Davis-Stitt, C. (1996). The retrieval of typical and atypical category members. *Journal of Experimental Social Psychology, 32*, 309–336.

Rothbart, M., & Taylor, M. (1992). Category labels and social reality: Do we view social categories as natural kinds? In G. R. Semin & K. Fiedler (Eds.), *Language, interaction and social cognition* (pp. 11–36). London: Sage.

Rothbaum, F. (1983). Aging and age stereotypes. *Social Cognition, 2*, 171–184.

Rothblum, E. D., Brand, P. A., Miller, C. T., & Oetjen, H. A. (1990). The relationship between obesity, employment discrimination, and employment- related victimization. *Journal of Vocational Behavior, 37*, 251–266.

Rothman, A. J., & Hardin, C. D. (1997). Differential use of the availability heuristic in social judgment. *Personality and Social Psychology Bulletin, 23*, 123–138.

Rowe, D. C. (1994). *The limits of family influence: Genes, experience, and behavior.* New York: Guilford Press.

Rowe, P. M. (1989). Unfavorable information and interview decisions. In R. W. Eder & G. R. Ferris (Eds.), *The employment interview: Theory, research, and practice* (pp. 77–89). Newbury Park, CA: Sage.

Rozendal, K. (1995). *What are you?: Social categorization and the nature of dominant identities.* Unpublished Ford Honors paper, Rice University.

Rozin, P., Nemeroff, C., & Markwith, M. (1992). Magical contagion beliefs and fear of AIDS. *Journal of Applied Social Psychology, 22,* 1081–1092.

Rubin, J. Z., Provenzano, F. J., & Luria, Z. (1974). The eye of the beholder: Parents' views on the sex of their newborns. *American Journal of Orthopsychiatry, 44,* 512–519.

Rubin, M., & Hewstone, M. (1998). Social identity theory's self-esteem hypothesis: A review and some suggestions for clarification. *Personality and Social Psychology Review, 1,* 40–62.

Rubini, M., & Kruglanski, A. W. (1997). Brief encounters ending in estrangement: Motivated language use and interpersonal rapport in the question-answer paradigm. *Journal of Personality and Social Psychology, 72,* 1047–1060.

Rubini, M., & Semin, G. R. (1994). Language use in the context of congruent and incongruent ingroup behaviors. *British Journal of Social Psychology, 33,* 355–362.

Ruble, D. N., & Martin, C. L. (1998). Gender development. In W. Damon (Series Ed.) & J. H. Flavell & E. Markman (Vol. Eds.), *Handbook of child psychology: Vol. 3. Social, emotional, and personality development* (5th ed., pp. 933–1016). New York: Wiley.

Rudman, L. A. (1998). Self-promotion as a risk factor for women: The costs and benefits of counterstereotypical impression management. *Journal of Personality and Social Psychology, 74,* 629–645.

Rudman, L. A., Ashmore, R. D., & Gary, M. L. (2001). "Unlearning" automatic biases: The malleability of implicit prejudice and stereotypes. *Journal of Personality and Social Psychology, 81,* 856–868.

Rudman, L. A., & Borgida, E. (1995). The afterglow of construct accessibility: The cognitive and behavioral consequences of priming men to view women as sexual objects. *Journal of Experimental Social Psychology, 31,* 493–517.

Rudman, L. A., Feinberg, J., & Fairchild, K. (2002). Minority members' implicit attitudes: Automatic ingroup bias as a function of group status. *Social Cognition, 20,* 294–320.

Rudman, L. A., & Glick, P. (1999). Feminized management and backlash toward agentic women: The hidden costs to women of a kinder, gentler image of middle managers. *Journal of Personality and Social Psychology, 77,* 1004–1010.

Rudman, L. A., & Glick, P. (2001). Prescriptive gender stereotypes and backlash toward agentic women. *Journal of Social Issues, 57,* 743–762.

Rudman, L. A., Greenwald, A. G., & McGhee, D. E. (2001). Implicit self-concept and evaluative implicit gender stereotypes: Self and ingroup share desirable traits. *Personality and Social Psychology Bulletin, 27,* 1164–1178.

Rudman, L. A., Greenwald, A. G., Mellott, D. S., & Schwartz, J. L. K. (1999). Measuring the automatic components of prejudice: Flexibility and generality of the implicit association test. *Social Cognition, 17,* 437–465.

Rudmin, F. W. (1989). The pleasure of serendipity in historical research: On finding "stereotype" in Morier's (1924) Hajji Baba. *Cross-Cultural Psychology Bulletin, 23,* 8–11.

Rudolph, U. (1997). Implicit verb causality: Verbal schemas and covariation information. *Journal of Language and Social Psychology, 16,* 132–158.

Rudolph, U., & Försterling, F. (1997). The psychological causality implicit in verbs: A review. *Psychological Bulletin, 121,* 192–218.

Rumsey, N., Bull, R., & Gahagan, D. (1982). The effect of facial disfigurement on the proxemic behavior of the general public. *Journal of Applied Social Psychology, 12,* 137–150.

Runeson, S. (1985). Perceiving people through their movements. In B. D. Kirkcaldy (Ed.), *Individual differences in movement* (pp. 43–66). Lancaster, UK: MTP Press.

Ruscher, J. B. (1998). Prejudice and stereotyping in everyday communication. In M. P. Zanna (Ed.), *Advances in experimental social psychology* (Vol. 30, pp. 241–307). San Diego, CA: Academic Press.

Ruscher, J. B., & Duval, L. L. (1998). Multiple communicators with unique target information transmit less stereotypicalimpressions. *Journal of Personality and Social Psychology*, *74*, 329–344.

Ruscher, J. B., & Fiske, S. T. (1990). Interpersonal competition can cause individuating processes. *Journal of Personality and Social Psychology*, *58*, 832–843.

Ruscher, J. B., Fiske, S. T., Miki, H., & van Manen, S. (1991). Individuating processes in competition: Interpersonal versus intergroup. *Personality and Social Psychology Bulletin*, *17*, 595–605.

Ruscher, J. B., & Hammer, E. D. (1994). Revising disrupted impressions through conversation. *Journal of Personality and Social Psychology*, *66*, 530–541.

Ruscher, J. B., & Hammer, E. D. (1996). Choosing to sever or maintain association induces biased impression formation. *Journal of Personality and Social Psychology*, *70*, 710–712.

Ruscher, J. B., Hammer, E. Y., & Hammer, E. D. (1996). Forming shared impressions through conversation: An adaptation of the continuum model. *Personality and Social Psychology Bulletin*, *22*, 705–720.

Rush, L. L. (1998). Affective reactions to multiple social stigmas. *Journal of Social Psychology*, *138*, 421–430.

Russell, K., Wilson, M., & Hall, R. (1992). *The color complex: The politics of skin color among African Americans*. New York: Harcourt Brace Jovanovich.

Rutland, A. (1999). The development of national prejudice, in-group favouritism and self-stereotypes in British children. *British Journal of Social Psychology*, *38*, 55–70.

Rutland, A., & Brown, R. (2001). Stereotypes as justifications for prior intergroup discrimination: Studies of Scottish national stereotyping. *European Journal of Social Psychology*, *31*, 127–141.

Rutland, A., & Cinnirella, M. (2000). Context effects on Scottish national and European self-categorization: The importance of category accessibility, fragility and relations. *British Journal of Social Psychology*, *39*, 495–519.

Ryan, C. S. (1995). Motivations and the perceiver's group membership: Consequences for stereotype accuracy. In Y.-T. Lee, L. J. Jussim, & C. R. McCauley (Eds.), *Stereotype accuracy: Toward appreciating group differences* (pp. 189–214). Washington, DC: American Psychological Association.

Ryan, C. S. (1996). Accuracy of black and white college students' in-group and out-group stereotypes. *Personality and Social Psychology Bulletin*, *22*, 1114–1127.

Ryan, C. S., & Bogart, L. M. (1997). Development of new group members' in-group and out-group stereotypes: Changes in perceived variability and ethnocentrism. *Journal of Personality and Social Psychology*, *73*, 719–732.

Ryan, C. S., & Bogart, L. M. (2001). Longitudinal changes in the accuracy of new group members' in-group and out-group stereotypes. *Journal of Experimental Social Psychology*, *37*, 118–133.

Ryan, C. S., Judd, C. M., & Park, B. (1996). Effects of racial stereotypes on judgments of individuals: The moderating role of perceived group variability. *Journal of Experimental Social Psychology*, *32*, 71–103.

Ryan, C. S., Park, B., & Judd, C. M. (1996). Assessing stereotype accuracy: Implications for understanding the stereotyping process. In C. N. Macrae, C. Stangor, & M. Hewstone (Eds.), *Stereotypes and stereotyping* (pp. 121–157). New York: Guilford Press.

Ryan, E. B., Hummert, M. L., & Boich, L. H. (1995). Communication predicaments of aging: Patronizing behavior toward older adults. *Journal of Language and Social Psychology*, *14*, 144–166.

Ryckman, R. M., Butler, J. C., Thornton, B., & Lindner, M. A. (1997). Assessment of physique subtype stereotypes. *Genetic, Social, and General Psychology Monographs*, *123*, 101–128.

Ryckman, R. M., Dill, D. A., Dyer, N. L., Sanborn, J. W., & Gold, J. A. (1992). Social perceptions of male and female extreme mesomorphs. *Journal of Social Psychology*, *132*, 615–627.

Ryckman, R. M., Robbins, A., Kaczor, L. M., & Gold, J. A. (1989). Male and female raters' stereotyping of male female physiques. *Personality and Social Psychology Bulletin*, *15*, 244–251.

Ryckman, R. M., Robbins, M. A., Thornton, B., Kaczor, L. M., Gayton, S. L., & Anderson, C. V. (1991). Public self-consciousness and physique stereotyping. *Personality and Social Psychology Bulletin*, *17*, 400–405.

Saad, L., & Newport, F. (2001, July). Blacks and whites differ about treament of blacks in America today. *The Gallup Poll Monthly*, pp. 58–63.

Sachdev, I., & Wright, A. (1996). Social influence and language learning: An experimental study. *Journal of Language and Social Psychology, 15,* 230–245.

Sadalla, E. K., Linder, D. E., & Jenkins, B. A. (1988). Sport preference: A self-presentational analysis. *Journal of Sport and Exercise Psychology, 10,* 214–222.

Sadalla, E. K., Vershure, B., & Burroughs, J. (1987). Identity symbolism in housing. *Environment and Behavior, 19,* 569–587.

Saenger, G. (1953). *The social psychology of prejudice.* New York: Harper.

Saenger, G., & Gilbert, E. (1950). Customer reactions to the integration of Negro sales personnel. *International Journal of Opinion and Attitude Research, 4,* 57–76.

Saenz, D. S. (1994). Token status and problem-solving deficits: Detrimental effects of distinctiveness and performance monitoring. *Social Cognition, 12,* 61–74.

Saenz, D. S., & Lord, C. G. (1989). Reversing roles: A cognitive strategy for undoing memory deficits associated with token status. *Journal of Personality and Social Psychology, 56,* 698–708.

Sagar, H. A., & Schofield, J. W. (1980). Racial and behavioral cues in black and white children's perceptions of ambiguously aggressive acts. *Journal of Personality and Social Psychology, 39,* 590–598.

Sagiv, L., & Schwartz, S. H. (1995). Value priorities and readiness for out-group social contact. *Journal of Personality and Social Psychology, 69,* 437–448.

Sailes, G. A. (1993). An investigation of campus typecasts: The myth of black athletic superiority and the dumb jock stereotype. *Sport Sociology Journal, 10,* 88–97.

Sailes, G. A. (1998). The African American athlete: Social myths and stereotypes. In G. A. Sailes (Ed.), *African Americans in sport* (pp. 183–198). New Brunswick, NJ: Transaction.

Salazar, J. M., & Marin, G. (1977). National stereotypes as a function of conflict and territorial proximity: A test of the mirror image hypothesis. *Journal of Social Psychology, 101,* 13–19.

Sampson, H., Messinger, S., & Towne, R. (1962). Family processes and becoming a mental patient. *American Journal of Sociology, 68,* 88–96.

Samuels, F. (1973). *Group images: Racial, ethnic, and religious stereotyping.* New Haven, CT: College & University Press.

Sanbonmatsu, D. M., Shavitt, S., & Gibson, B. D. (1994). Salience, set size, and illusory correlation: Making moderate assumptions about extreme targets. *Journal of Personality and Social Psychology, 66,* 1020–1033.

Sanbonmatsu, D. M., Shavitt, S., & Sherman, S. J. (1991). The role of personal relevance in the formation of distinctiveness-based illusory corrleations. *Personality and Social Psychology Bulletin, 17,* 124–132.

Sanbonmatsu, D. M., Sherman, S. J., & Hamilton, D. L. (1987). Illusory correlation in the perception of individuals and groups. *Social Cognition, 5,* 1–25.

Sande, G. N., Goethals, G. R., & Radloff, C. E. (1988). Perceiving one's own traits and others': The multifaceted self. *Journal of Personality and Social Psychology, 54,* 13–20.

Sanders Thompson, V. L (2001). The complexity of African American racial identification. *Journal of Black Studies, 32,* 155–165.

Sanitioso, R., Freud, K., & Lee, J. (1996). The influence of self-related goals on the use of stereotypical and individuating information. *European Journal of Social Psychology, 26,* 751–761.

Sankis, L. M., Corbitt, E. M., & Widiger, T. A. (1999). Gender bias in the English language? *Journal of Personality and Social Psychology, 77,* 1289–1295.

Santuzzi, A. M., & Ruscher, J. B. (2002). Stigma salience and paranoid social cognition: Understanding variability in metaperceptions among individuals with recently-acquired stigma. *Social Cognition, 20,* 171–197.

Sargent, J. D., & Blanchflower, D. G. (1994). Obesity and stature in adolesence and earning in young adulthood. *Archives of Pediatrics and Adolescent Medicine, 148,* 681–687.

Sarnoff, I. (1951). Identification with the aggressor: Some personality correlates of anti-Semitism among Jews. *Journal of Personality, 20,* 199–218.

Sastre, M. T. M., Fouquereau, E., Igier, V., Salvatore, N., & Mullet, E. (2000). Perception of occupational gender typing: A replication on European samples of Shinar's (1975) and Beggs and Doolittle's (1993) studies. *Journal of Applied Social Psychology, 30,* 430–441.

Savage, B. M., & Wells, F. L. (1948). A note on the singularity of given names. *Journal of Social* Psychology, *27*, 271-272.

Scarberry, N. C., Ratcliff, C. D., Lord, C. G., Lanicek, D. L., & Desforges, D. M. (1997). Effects of individuating information on the generalization part of Allport's contact hypothesis. *Personality and Social Psychology Bulletin, 23*, 1291-1299.

Schaller, M. (1991). Social categorization and the formation of group stereotypes: Further evidence for biased information processing in the perception of group–behavior correlations. *European Journal of Social Psychology, 21*, 25-35.

Schaller, M. (1992). In-group favoritism and statistical reasoning in social inference: Implications for formation and maintance of group stereotypes. *Journal of Personality and Social Psychology, 63*, 61-74.

Schaller, M. (1994). The role of statistical reasoning in the formation, preservation and prevention of group stereotypes. *British Journal of Social Psychology, 33*, 47-61.

Schaller, M., Asp, C. H., Rosell, M. C., & Heim, S. J. (1996). Training in statistical reasoning inhibits the formation of erroneous group stereotypes. *Personality and Social Psychology Bulletin, 22*, 829-844.

Schaller, M., Boyd, C., Yohannes, J., & O'Brien, M. (1995). The prejudiced personality revisited: Personal need for structure and formation of erroneous group stereotypes. *Journal of Personality and Social Psychology, 68*, 544-555.

Schaller, M., & Conway, L. G., III. (1999). Influence of impression-management goals on the emerging contents of group stereotypes: Support for a social-evolutionary process. *Personality and Social Psychology Bulletin, 25*, 819-833.

Schaller, M., Conway, L. G., III, & Tanchuk, T. L. (2002). Selective pressures on the once and future contents of ethnic stereotypes: Effects of the communicability of traits. *Journal of Personality and Social Psychology, 82*, 861-877.

Schaller, M., & Maass, A. (1989). Illusory correlation and social categorization: Toward an integration of motivational and cognitive factors in stereotype formation. *Journal of Personality and Social Psychology, 56*, 709-721.

Schaller, M., & O'Brien, M. (1992). "Intuitive analysis of covariance" and group stereotype formation. *Personality and Social Psychology Bulletin, 18*, 776-785.

Scheff, T. J. (1966). *Being mentally ill: A sociological theory.* Chicago: Aldine.

Scheff, T. J. (1974). The labelling theory of mental illness. *American Sociological Review, 39*, 444-452.

Schein, V. E. (1973). The relationship between sex role stereotypes and requisite management characteristics. *Journal of Applied Psychology, 57*, 95-100.

Schein, V. E. (1975). Relationships between sex role stereotypes and requisite management characteristics among female managers. *Journal of Applied Psychology, 60*, 340-344.

Schein, V. E., Mueller, R., & Jacobson, C. (1989). The relationship between sex role stereotypes and requisite management characteristics among college students. *Sex Roles, 20*, 103-110.

Scher, D. (1984). Sex-role contradictions: Self-perceptions and ideal perceptions. *Sex Roles, 10*, 651-656.

Scherbaum, C. J., & Shepherd, D. H. (1987). Dressing for success: Effects of color and layering on perceptions of women in business. *Sex Roles, 16*, 391-399.

Schimel, J., Simon, L., Greenberg, J., Pyszczynski, T., Solomon, S., Waxmonsky, J., & Arndt, J. (1999). Stereotypes and terror management: Evidence that mortality salience enhances stereotypic thinking and preferences. *Journal of Personality and Social Psychology, 77*, 905-926.

Schlenker, J. A., Caron, S. L., & Halteman, W. A. (1998). A feminist analysis of *Seventeen* magazine: Content analysis from 1945 to 1995. *Sex Roles, 38*, 135-149.

Schmader, T. (2002). Gender identification moderates stereotype threat effects on women's math performance. *Journal of Experimental Social Psychology, 38*, 194-201.

Schmader, T., & Major, B. (1999). The impact of ingroup vs. outgroup performance on personal values. *Journal of Experimental Social Psychology, 35*, 47-67.

Schmader, T., Major, B., Eccleston, C. P., & McCoy, S. K. (2001). Devaluing domains in response to threatening intergroup comparisons: Perceived legitimacy and the status value asymmetry. *Journal of Personality and Social Psychology, 80*, 782-796.

Schmid, J. (1999). Pinning down attributions: The linguistic category model applied to wrestling reports. *European Journal of Social Psychology, 29*, 895–907.

Schmidt, D. F., & Boland, S. M. (1986). Structure of perceptions of older adults: Evidence for multiple stereotypes. *Psychology and Aging, 1*, 255–260.

Schmitt, M., & Maes, J. (2002). Stereotypic ingroup bias as self-defense against relative deprivation: Evidence from a longitudinal study of the German unification process. *European Journal of Social Psychology, 32*, 309–326.

Schmitt, M. T., & Branscombe, N. R. (2002). The meaning and consequences of perceived discrimination in disadvantaged and privileged social groups. In W. Stroebe & M. Hewstone (Eds.), *European review of social psychology* (Vol. 12, pp. 167–199). Chichester, UK: Wiley.

Schmitt, M. T., Branscombe, N. R., Kobrynowicz, D., & Owen, S. (2002). Perceiving discrimination against one's gender group has different implications for well-being in women and men. *Personality and Social Psychology Bulletin, 28*, 197–210.

Schnake, S. B., & Ruscher, J. B. (1998). Modern racism as a predictor of the linguistic intergroup bias. *Journal of Language and Behavior, 17*, 484–491.

Schneider, A., & Ingram, H. (1993). Social construction of target populations: Implications for politics and policy. *American Political Science Review, 87*, 334–347.

Schneider, D. J. (1971, August). *Extra-linguistic aspects of trait implications.* Paper presented at the annual convention of the American Psychological Association, Washington, DC.

Schneider, D. J. (1973). Implicit personality theory: A review. *Psychological Bulletin, 79*, 294–309.

Schneider, D. J. (1976). *Social psychology.* Reading, MA: Addison-Wesley.

Schneider, D. J. (1988). *Introduction to social psychology.* San Diego, CA: Harcourt Brace Jovanovich.

Schneider, D. J. (1991). Social cognition. *Annual Review of Psychology, 42*, 527–561.

Schneider, D. J. (1992). Red apples, liberal college professors, and farmers who like Bach. *Psychological Inquiry, 2*, 190–193.

Schneider, D. J. (1996). Modern stereotype research: Unfinished business. In C. N. Macrae, C. Stangor, & M. Hewstone (Eds.), *Stereotypes and stereotyping* (pp. 419–453). New York: Guilford Press.

Schneider, D. J., & Blankmeyer, B. L. (1983). Prototype salience and implicit personality theories. *Journal of Personality and Social Psychology, 44*, 712–722.

Schneider, D. J., & Fazio, R. (1998). [The dispositional nature of traits]. Unpublished raw data.

Schneider, D. J., Haley, B., & Towler, A. (2002). *Social categories are not all the same: Essentialism, entitativity, and stereotype proneness.* Unpublished manuscript.

Schneider, D. J., Hastorf, A. H., & Ellsworth, P. C. (1979). *Person perception* (2nd ed.). Reading, MA: Addison-Wesley.

Schneider, I. (1987). The theory and practice of movie psychiatry. *American Journal of Psychiatry, 144*, 996–1002.

Schneider, J. W., & Hacker, S. L. (1973). Sex role imagery and use of the generic "man" in introductory texts: A case in the sociology of sociology. *American Sociologist, 8*, 12–18.

Schoenfeld, N. (1942). An experimental study of some problems relating to stereotypes. *Archives of Psychology, 38*(Monograph No. 270).

Schofield, J. W. (1979). The impact of positively structured contact on intergroup behavior. *Social Psychology Quarterly, 42*, 280–284.

Schofield, J. W. (1981). Complimentary and conflicting identities: Images of interaction in an interracial school. In S. A. Asher & J. M. Gottman (Eds.), *The development of children's friendships* (pp. 53–90). New York: Cambridge University Press.

Schofield, J. W. (1986). Black–white contact in desegrated schools. In M. Hewstone & R. Brown (Eds.), *Contact and conflict in intergroup encounters* (pp. 79–92). Oxford, UK: Blackwell.

Schofield, J. W. (1989). *Black and white in school: Trust, tension, or tolerance.* New York: Teachers College Press.

Schofield, J. W., & Sagar, H. A. (1977). Peer interaction patterns in an integrated middle school. *Sociometry, 40*, 130–138.

Schroeder, S. R. (1970). Usage of stereotypy as a descriptive term. *Psychological Record, 20*, 337–342.

Schuman, H., Steeh, C., & Bobo, L. (1985). *Racial attitudes in America: Trends and interpretations.* Cambridge, MA: Harvard University Press.

Schuman, H., Steeh, C., Bobo, L., & Krysan, M. (1997). *Racial attitudes in America: Trends and interpretations* (rev. ed.). Cambridge, MA: Harvard University Press.

Schwartz, C. G. (1957). Perspectives on deviance—wives' definitions of their husbands' mental illness. *Psychiatry, 20,* 275–291.

Schwartz, S. H., & Struch, N. (1989). Values, stereotypes, and intergroup antagonism. In D. Bar-Tal, C. F. Graumann, A. W. Kruglanski, & W. Stroebe (Eds.), *Stereotyping and prejudice: Changing conceptions* (pp. 151–167). New York: Springer-Verlag.

Schwartz, S. P. (1979). Natural kind terms. *Cognition, 7,* 301–315.

Schwartz, S. P. (1980). Natural kinds and nominal kinds. *Mind, 89,* 182–195.

Schwarz, N. (1990). Feelings as information: Informational and motivational functions of affective states. In E. T. Higgins & R. M. Sorrentino (Eds.), *Handbook of motivation and cognition: Vol. 2. Foundations of social behavior* (pp. 527–561). New York: Guilford Press.

Schwarz, N., & Bless, H. (1991). Happy and mindless, but sad and smart?: The impact of affective states on analytic reasoning. In J. P. Forgas (Ed.), *Emotion and social judgment* (pp. 55–71). Oxford, UK: Pergamon Press.

Schwarz, N., & Bless, H. (1992). Constructing reality and its alternatives: An inclusion/exclusion model of assimilation and contrast effects in social judgment. In L. L. Martin & A. Tesser (Eds.), *The construction of social judgments* (pp. 217–245). Hillsdale, NJ: Erlbaum.

Schwarz, N., & Clore, G. L. (1983). Mood, misattribution, and judgments of well-being: Informative and directive functions of affective states. *Journal of Personality and Social Psychology, 45,* 513–523.

Schwarz, N., & Clore, G. L. (1988). How do I feel about it?: Informative functions of affective states. In K. Fiedler & J. Forgas (Eds.), *Affect, cognition, and social behavior* (pp. 44–62). Toronto: Hogrefe.

Schwerin, M. J., & Corcoran, K. J. (1996). A multimethod examination of the male anabolic steroid user. *Journal of Applied Social Psychology, 26,* 211–217.

Scodel, A., & Austrin, H. (1957). The perception of Jewish photographs by non-Jews and Jews. *Journal of Abnormal and Social Psychology, 54,* 278–280.

Sczesny, S., & Stahlberg, D. (2002). The influence of gender-stereotyped perfumes on leadership attribution. *European Journal of Social Psychology, 32,* 815–828.

Seago, D. W. (1947). Stereotypes: Before Pearl Harbor and after. *Journal of Psychology, 23,* 55–63.

Sears, D. O. (1988). Symbolic racism. In P. Katz & D. Taylor (Eds.), *Towards the elimination of racism: Profiles in controversy* (pp. 53–84). New York: Plenum Press.

Sears, D. O. (1993). Symbolic politics: A socio-psychological theory. In S. Iyengar & W. J. McGuire (Eds.), *Explorations in political psychology* (pp. 113–149). Durham, NC: Duke University Press.

Sears, D. O., Hensler, C. P., & Speer, L. K. (1979). Whites' opposition to "busing": Self interest or symbolic racism? *American Political Science Review, 73,* 369–384.

Sears, D. O., & Huddy, L. (1991). The symbolic politics of oposition to bilingual education. In J. Simpson, & S. Worchel (Eds.), *Conflict between people and peoples* (pp. 145–169). Hillsdale, NJ: Erlbaum.

Sears, D. O., van Laar, C., Carrillo, M., & Kosterman, R. (1997). Is it really racism?: The origins of white Americans' opposition to race-targeted policies. *Public Opinion Quarterly, 61,* 16–53.

Sechrist, G. B., & Stangor, C. (2001). Perceived consensus influences intergroup behavior and stereotype accessibility. *Journal of Personality and Social Psychology, 80,* 645–654.

Sechrist, G. B., Swim, J. K., & Mark, M. M. (2003). Mood as information in making attributions to discrimination. *Personality and Social Psychology Bulletin, 29,* 524–531.

Secord, P. F. (1958). Facial features and inference processes in interpersonal perception. In R. Taguiri & L. Petrullo (Eds.), *Person perception and interpersonal behavior* (pp. 300–315). Stanford, CA: Stanford University Press.

Secord, P. F. (1959). Stereotyping and favorableness in the perception of Negro faces. *Journal of Abnormal and Social Psychology, 59,* 309–315.

Secord, P. F., & Backman, C. W. (1964). *Social psychology.* New York: McGraw-Hill.

Secord, P. F., & Berscheid, E. S. (1963). Stereotyping and the generality of implicit personality theory. *Journal of Personality, 31,* 65–78.

Secord, P. F., & Bevan, W. (1956). Personality in faces: III. A cross-cultural comparison of impressions of physiognomy and personality in faces. *Journal of Social Psychology, 43,* 282–286.

Secord, P. F., Bevan, W., Jr., & Dukes, W. F. (1953). Occupational and physiognomic stereotypes in the perception of photographs. *Journal of Social Psychology, 37,* 261–270.

Secord, P. F., Bevan, W., Jr., & Katz, B. (1956). The Negro stereotype and perceptual accentuation. *Journal of Abnormal and Social Psychology, 53,* 78–83.

Secord, P. F., Dukes, W. F., & Bevan, W. (1954). Personality in faces: I. An experiment in social perceiving. *Genetic Psychology Monographs, 49,* 231–279.

Secord, P. F., & Muthard, J. E. (1955). Personality in faces: IV. A descriptive analysis of the perception of women's faces and the identification of some physiognomic determinants. *Journal of Psychology, 39,* 269–178.

Sedikides, C. (1990). Effects of fortuitously activated constructs versus activated communication goals on person impressions. *Journal of Personality and Social Psychology, 58,* 397–408.

Sedikides, C., & Anderson, C. A. (1994). Causal perceptions of intertrait relations: The glue that holds person types together. *Personality and Social Psychology Bulletin, 20,* 294–302.

Sedikides, C., Olsen, N., & Reis, H. T. (1993). Relationships as natural categories. *Journal of Personality and Social Psychology, 6,* 71–82.

Segal, S. (1978). Attitudes toward the mentally ill: A review. *Social Work, 23,* 211–217.

Sekaquaptewa, D., & Thompson, M. (2002). The differential effects of solo status on members of high- and low-status groups. *Personality and Social Psychology Bulletin, 28,* 694–707.

Sekaquaptewa, D., & Thompson, M. (2003). Solo status, stereotype threat, and performance expectancies: Their effects on women's performance. *Journal of Experimental Social Psychology, 39,* 68–74.

Sellers, R. M., Smith, M. A., Shelton, J. N., Rowley, A. A. J., & Chavous, T. M. (1998). Multidimensional model of racial identity: A reconceptualization of African Amercian racial identity. *Personality and Social Psychology Review, 1,* 18–39.

Seltzer, R. (1992). The social location of those holding antihomosexual attitudes. *Sex Roles, 26,* 391–398.

Seltzer, R., & Smith, R. C. (1991). Color differnces in the Afro-American community and the differences they make. *Journal of Black Studies, 21,* 279–286.

Semaj, L. (1980). The development of racial evaluation and preference. *Journal of Black Psychology, 6,* 59–79.

Semin, G., & De Poot, C. J. (1997a). Bringing partiality to light: Question wording and choice as indicators of bias. *Social Cognition, 15,* 91–106.

Semin, G. R., & De Poot, C. J. (1997b). The question–answer paradigm: You might regret not noticing how a question is worded. *Journal of Personality and Social Psychology, 73,* 472–480.

Semin, G. R., & Fiedler, K. (1988). The cognitive functions of linguistic categories in describing persons: Social cognition and language. *Journal of Personality and Social Psychology, 54,* 558–568.

Semin, G. R., & Fiedler, K. (1991). The linguistic category model, its bases, applications, and range. In W. Stroebe & M. Hewstone (Eds.), *European review of social psychology* (Vol. 2, pp. 1–50). Chichester, UK: Wiley.

Semin, G. R., & Fiedler, K. (1992). The inferential properties of interpersonal verbs. In G. R. Semin & K. Fiedler (Eds.), *Language, interaction and social cognition* (pp. 58–78). London: Sage.

Semin, G., & Marsman, J. G. (1994). Multiple inference-inviting properties of interpersonal verbs: Event instigation, dispositional inference, and implicit causality. *Journal of Personality and Social Psychology, 67,* 836–849.

Semin, G., Rubini, M., & Fiedler, K. (1995). The answer is in the question: The effect of verb causality on locus of explanation. *Personality and Social Psychology Bulletin, 21,* 834–841.

Serbin, L. A., Poulin-Dubois, D., Colburne, K. A., Sen, M. G., & Eichstedt, J. A. (2001). Gender stereotyping in infancy: Visual preferences for and knowledge of gender-stereotyped toys in the second year. *International Journal of Behavioural Development, 25,* 7–15.

Seta, C. E., Hayes, N. S., & Seta, J. J. (1994). Mood, memory, and vigilance: The influence of distraction on recall and impression formation. *Personality and Social Psychology Bulletin, 20,* 170–177.

Seta, C. E., Seta, J. J., & Culver, J. (2000). Recategorization as a method for promoting intergroup cooperation: Group status matters. *Social Cognition, 18,* 354–376.

Shackelford, T. K., & Larsen, R. J. (1999). Facial attractiveness and physical health. *Evolution and Human Behavior, 20,* 71–76.

Shaffer, D. R., Crepaz, N., & Sun, C.-R. (2000). Physical attractiveness stereotyping in cross-cultural perspective: Similarities and differences between Americans and Taiwanese. *Journal of Cross-Cultural Psychology, 31,* 557–582.

Shaffer, D. R., Gresham, A., Clary, E. G., & Thielman, T. J. (1986). Sex-ratios as a basis for occupational evaluations: A contemporary view. *Social Behavior and Personality, 14,* 77–83.

Shah, D. V., Domke, D., & Wackman, D. (1996). "To thine own self be true": Values, framing, and voter decision making strategies. *Communication Research, 23,* 509–560.

Shakespeare, W. (1974). The merchant of Venice. In G. B. Evans (Ed.), *The Riverside Shakespeare* (pp. 250–285). Boston: Houghton Mifflin. (Original work composed ca. 1596)

Shamai, S. (1994). Possibilities and limitations of a gender stereotypes intervention program. *Adolescence, 29,* 665–680.

Shapiro, P., & Penrod, S. (1986). Meta-analysis of facial identification. *Psychological Bulletin, 100,* 139–156.

Shears, L. M., & Jensema, C. J. (1969). Social acceptability of anomalous persons. *Exceptional Children, 36,* 91–96.

Sheldon, W. H., Stevens, S. S., & Tucker, S. (1940). *The varieties of temperament: An introduction to constitutional psychology.* New York: Harper & Row.

Shelton, J. N. (2000). A reconceptualization of how we study issues of racial prejudice. *Personality and Social Psychology Review, 4,* 374–390.

Shepherd, J. W., Ellis, H. D., McMurran, M., & Davies, G. M. (1978). Effect of character attribution on photofit construction of a face. *European Journal of Social Psychology, 8,* 263–268.

Sherif, M., Harvey, O. J., White, B. J., Hood, W. R., & Sherif, C. W. (1961). *Intergroup conflict and cooperation: The Robbers Cave experiment.* Norman: University of Oklahoma Book Exchange.

Sherif, M., & Sherif, C. W. (1953). *Groups in harmony and tension: An integration of studies on intergroup relations.* New York: Harper & Row.

Sherman, J. W. (1996). Development and mental representation of stereotypes. *Journal of Personality and Social Psychology, 70,* 1126–1141.

Sherman, J. W., & Bessenoff, G. R. (1999). Stereotypes as source-monitoring cues: On the interaction between episodic and semantic memory. *Psychological Science, 10,* 106–110.

Sherman, J. W., & Klein, S. B. (1994). Development and representation of personality impressions. *Journal of Personality and Social Psychology, 67,*.

Sherman, J. W., Lee, A. Y., Bessenoff, G. R., & Frost, L. A. (1998). Stereotype efficiency reconsidered: Encoding flexibility under cognitive load. *Journal of Personality and Social Psychology, 75,* 589–606.

Sherman, J. W., Macrae, C. N., & Bodenhausen, G. V. (2000). Attention and stereotyping: Cognitive constraints on the construction of meaningful social impressions. In W. Stroebe & M. Hewstone (Eds.), *European review of social psychology* (Vol. 11, pp. 145–175). Chichester, UK: Wiley.

Sherman, J. W., Stroessner, S. J., Loftus, S. T., & Deguzman, G. (1997). Stereotype suppression and recognition memory for stereotypical and nonstereotypical information. *Social Cognition, 15,* 205–215.

Sherman, N. C., & Gold, J. A. (1978–1979). Perceptions of ideal and typical middle and old age. *International Journal of Aging and Human Development, 9,* 67–73.

Sherman, N. C., Gold, J. A., & Sherman, M. F. (1978). Attribution theory and evaluations of older men among college students, their parents, and grandparents. *Personality and Social Psychology Bulletin, 4,* 440–442.

Sherman, S. J., Castelli, L., & Hamilton, D. L. (2002). The spontaneous use of a group typology as an organizing principle in memory. *Journal of Personality and Social Psychology, 82,* 328–342.

Sherman, S. J., Hamilton, D. L., & Roskos-Ewoldsen, D. R. (1989). Attenuation of illusory correlation. *Personality and Social Psychology Bulletin, 15,* 559–571.

Sherman, S. J., McMullen, M. N., & Gavanski, I. (1992). Natural sample spaces and the inversion of conditional judgments. *Journal of Experimental Social Psychology, 28,* 401–421.

Sherriffs, A. C., & Jarrett, R. F. (1953). Sex differences in attitudes about sex differences. *Journal of Psychology, 35,* 161–168.

Sherriffs, A. C., & McKee, J. P. (1957). Qualitative aspects of beliefs about men and women. *Journal of Personality, 25,* 451–464.

Shih, M., Ambady, N., Richeson, J. A., Fujita, K., & Gray, H. M. (2002). Stereotype performance boosts: The impact of self-relevance and the manner of stereotype activation. *Journal of Personality and Social Psychology, 83,* 638–647.

Shih, M., Pittinsky, T. L., & Ambady, N. (2000). Stereotype susceptibility: Identity salience and shifts in quantitative performance. *Psychological Science, 10,* 80–83.

Shinar, E. H. (1975). Sexual stereotypes of occupations. *Journal of Vocational Behavior, 7,* 99–111.

Shipley, E. F. (1993). Categories, hierarchies, and induction. In D. L. Medin (Ed.), *The psychology of learning and motivation* (Vol. 30, pp. 265–301). San Diego, CA: Academic Press.

Shoemaker, D. J., South, D. R., & Lowe, J. (1973). Facial stereotypes of deviants and judgments of guilt or innocence. *Social Forces, 51,* 427–433.

Shotland, R. L., & Craig, J. M. (1988). Can men and women differentiate between friendly and sexually interested behavior? *Social Psychology Quarterly, 51,* 66–73.

Shweder, R. A. (1977). Likeness and likelihood in everyday thought: Magical thinking in judgments about personality. *Current Anthropology, 18,* 637–658.

Shweder, R. A. (1982). Fact and artifact in trait perception: The systematic distortion hypothesis. In B. A. Maher & W. B. Maher (Eds.), *Progress in experimental personality research* (Vol. 11, pp. 65–100). New York: Academic Press.

Shweder, R. A., & D'Andrade, R. G. (1980). The systematic distortion hypothesis. In R. A. Shweder (Ed.), *Falliable judgment in behavioral research.* San Francisco: Jossey-Bass.

Sia, T. L., Lord, C. G., Blessum, K. A., Ratcliff, C. D., & Lepper, M. R. (1997). Is a rose always a rose?: The role of social category exemplar change in attitude stability and attitude–behavior consistency. *Journal of Personality and Social Psychology, 72,* 501–514.

Sibicky, M., & Dovidio, J. F. (1986). Stigma of psychological therapy: Stereotypes, interpersonal reactions, and the self-fulfilling prophecy. *Journal of Counseling Psychology, 33,* 148–154.

Sidanius, J. M., Levin, S., & Pratto, F. (1998). Hierarchical group relations, institutional terror, and the dynamics of the criminal justice system. In J. L. Eberhardt & S. T. Fiske (Eds.), *Confronting racism: The problem and the response* (pp. 136–165). Thousand Oaks, CA: Sage.

Sidanius, J., Liu, J., Pratto, F., & Shaw, J. (1994). Social dominance orientation, hierarchy attenuators and hierarchy enhancers: Social dominance theory and the criminal justice system. *Journal of Applied Social Psychology, 24,* 338–366.

Sidanius, J., Pena, Y., & Sawyer, M. (2001). Inclusionary discrimination: Pigmentocracy and patriotism in the Dominican Republic. *Political Psychology, 22,* 827–851.

Sidanius, J., & Pratto, F. (1999). *Social dominance: An intergroup theory of hierarchy and oppression.* New York: Cambridge University Press.

Sidanius, J., Pratto, F., & Bobo, L. (1996). Racism, conservatism, affirmative action, and intellectual sophistication: A matter of principled conservatism or group dominance? *Journal of Personality and Social Psychology, 70,* 476–490.

Sidanius, J., Pratto, F., Sinclair, S., & van Laar, C. (1996). Mother Teresa meets Genghis Khan: The dialectics of hierarchy-enhancing and hierarchy-attenuating career choices. *Social Justice Research, 9,* 145–170.

Sigall, H., & Landy, D. (1973). Radiating beauty: The effects of having a physically attractive partner on person perception. *Journal of Personality and Social Psychology, 28,* 218–224.

Sigall, H., & Page, R. (1971). Current stereotypes: A little fading, a little faking. *Journal of Personality and Social Psychology, 18,* 247–255.

Sigelman, C. K., Howell, J. L., Cornell, D. P., Cutright, J. D., & Dewey, J. C. (1991). Courtesy stigma: The social implications of associating with a gay person. *Journal of Social Psychology, 131,* 45–56.

Sigelman, L. (1995). Blacks, whites and anti-Semitism. *Sociological Quarterly, 36,* 649–656.

Sigelman, L. Shockley, J. W., & Sigelman, C. K. (1993). Ethnic stereotyping: A black–white comparison. In P. M. Sniderman, P. E. Tetlock, & E. G. Carmines (Eds.), *Prejudice, politics, and the American dilemma* (pp. 104–126). Stanford, CA: Stanford University Press.

Sigelman, L., & Tuch, S. A. (1997). Metastereotypes: Blacks' perceptions of whites' stereotypes of blacks. *Public Opinion Quarterly, 61,* 87–101.

Sigelman, L., & Welch, S. (1994). *Black Americans' views of racial inequality: The dream deferred.* New York: Cambridge University Press.

Signorella, M. L. (1999). Multidimensionality of gender schemas: Implications for the development of gender-related characteristics. In W. B. Swann, Jr., J. H. Langlois, & L. A. Gilbert (Eds.), *Sexism and stereotypes: The gender science of Janet Taylor Spence* (pp. 107–127). Washington, DC: American Psychological Association.

Signorella, M. L., Bigler, R. S., & Liben, L. (1993). Development differences in children's gender schemata about others: A meta-analytic review. *Developmental Review, 13,* 106–126.

Signorella, M. L., & Liben, L. S. (1984). Recall and reconstruction of gender-related pictures: Effects of attitude, task difficulty, and age. *Child Development, 55,* 393–405.

Signorielli, N. (1989). Television and conceptions about sex roles: Maintaining conventionality and the status quo. *Sex Roles, 21,* 341–360.

Signorielli, N. (1993). Television, the portrayal of women, and children's attitudes. In G. L. Berry & J. K. Asamen (Eds.), *Children and television: Images in a changing sociocultural world* (pp. 229–242). Newbury Park, CA: Sage.

Simon, A. (1995). Some correlates of individuals' attitudes toward lesbians. *Journal of Homosexuality, 29,* 89–103.

Simon, B., & Brown, R. (1987). Perceived intragroup homogeneity in minority–majority contexts. *Journal of Personality and Social Psychology, 53,* 703–711.

Simon, B., & Hamilton, D. L. (1994). Self-stereotyping and social context: The effects of relative in-group size and in-group status. *Journal of Personality and Social Psychology, 66,* 699–711.

Simon, B., Kulla, C., & Zobel, M. (1995). On being more than just a part of the whole: Regional identity and social distinctiveness. *European Journal of Social Psychology, 25,* 325–340.

Simon, B., & Pettigrew, T. F. (1990). Social identity and perceived group homogeneity: Evidence for the in-group homogeneity effect. *European Journal of Social Psychology, 20,* 269–286.

Simon, L., & Greenberg, J. (1996). Further progress in understanding the effects of derogatory ethnic labels: The role of preexisting attitudes toward the targeted group. *Personality and Social Psychology Bulletin, 22,* 1195–1204.

Simon, L., Greenberg, J., Arndt, J., Pyszczynski, T., Clement, R., & Solomon, S. (1997). Perceived consensus, uniqueness, and terror management: Compensatory responses to threats to inclusion and distinctiveness following mortality salience. *Personality and Social Psychology Bulletin, 23,* 1055–1065.

Simon, R. J., & Landis, J. M. (1989). Women's and men's attitudes about a woman's place and role. *Public Opinion Quarterly, 53,* 265–276.

Sinclair, L., & Kunda, Z. (1999). Reactions to a black professional: Motivated inhibition and activation of conflicting stereotypes. *Journal of Personality and Social Psychology, 77,* 885–904.

Sinclair, L., & Kunda, Z. (2000). Motivated stereotyping of women: She's fine if she praised me but incompetent if she criticized me. *Personality and Social Psychology Bulletin, 26,* 1329–1342.

Singh, D. (1993a). Adaptive significance of female physical attractiveness: Role of waist-to-hip ratio. *Journal of Personality and Social Psychology, 59,* 1192–1201.

Singh, D. (1993b). Body shape and woman's attractiveness: The critical role of waist-to-hip ratio. *Human Nature, 4,* 297–321.

Singh, D., & Luis, S. (1995). Ethnic and gender consensus for the effect of waist-to-hip ratio on judgments of women's attractiveness. *Human Nature, 6,* 51–65.

Singh, D., & Young, R. K. (1995). Body weight, waist-to-hip ratio, breasts and hips: Role in judgments of female attractiveness and desirability in relationships. *Ethology and Human Biology, 16,* 483–507.

Singh, R., Choo, W. M., & Poh, L. L. (1998). In-group bias and fair-mindedness as strategies of self-presentation in intergroup perception. *Personality and Social Psychology Bulletin, 24,* 147–162.

Sinha, A. K. P., & Upadhyaya, O. P. (1960). Change and persistence in the stereotypes of university students toward different ethnic groups during Sino-Indian border dispute. *Journal of Social Psychology, 52,* 31–39.

Six, B., & Eckes, T. (1991). A closer look at the complex structure of gender stereotypes. *Sex Roles, 24,* 57–71.

Skinner, L. J., Berry, K. K., Griffith, S. E., & Byers, B. (1995). Generalizability and specificity of the stigma associated with the mental illness label: A reconsideration twenty-five years later. *Journal of Community Psychology, 23,* 3–17.

Skov, R. B., & Sherman, S. J. (1986). Information-gathering processes: Diagnosticity, hypothesis-confirmatory strategies, and perceived hypothesis conformation. *Journal of Experimental Social Psychology, 22,* 93–121.

Skowronski, J. J., & Carlston, D. E. (1987). Social judgment and social memory: The role of cue diagnosticity in negativity, positivity, and extremity biases. *Journal of Personality and Social Psychology, 52,* 689–699.

Skowronski, J. J., & Carlston, D. E. (1989). Negativity and extremity biases in impression formation: A review of explanations. *Psychological Bulletin, 105,* 131–142.

Skowronski, J. J., Carlston, D. E., & Isham, J. T. (1993). Implicit versus explicit impression formation: The differing effects of overt labeling and covert priming on memory and impressions. *Journal of Experimental Social Psychology, 29,* 17–41.

Skowronski, J. J., & Lawrence, M. A. (2001). A comparative study of the implicit and explicit gender attitudes of children and college students. *Psychology of Women Quarterly, 25,* 155–165.

Skrypnek, B. J., & Snyder, M. (1982). On the self-perpetrating nature of stereotypes about men and women. *Journal of Experimental Social Psychology, 18,* 277–291.

Slavin, R. E. (1985). Cooperative learning: Applying contact theory in desegregated schools. *Journal of Social Issues, 41,* 45–62.

Slavin, R. E. (1986). Cooperative learning: Engineering social psychology in the classroom. In R. S. Feldman (Ed.), *The social psychology of education: Current research and theory* (pp. 153–171). Cambridge, UK: Cambridge University Press.

Slavin, R. E., & Madden, N. A. (1979). School practices that improve race relations. *American Educational Research Journal, 16,* 169–180.

Sleet, D. A. (1969). Physique and social image. *Perceptual and Motor Skills, 28,* 295–299.

Sloman, S. A. (1993). Feature-based induction. *Cognitive Psychology, 25,* 231–280.

Sloman, S. A. (1996). The empirical case for two systems of reasoning. *Psychological Bulletin, 119,* 3–22.

Slone, A. E., Brigham, J. C., & Meissner, C. A. (2000). Social and cognitive factors affecting the own-race bias in whites. *Basic and Applied Social Psychology, 22,* 71–84.

Slone, M., Tarrasch, R., & Hallis, D. (2000). Ethnic stereotypic attitudes among Israeli children: Two intervention programs. *Merrill–Palmer Quarterly, 46,* 370–389.

Slotterback, C. S., & Saarnio, D. A. (1996). Attitudes toward older adults reported by young adults: Variation based on attitudinal task and attribute categories. *Psychology and Aging, 11,* 563–571.

Slusher, M. P., & Anderson, C. A. (1987). When reality monitoring fails: The role of imagination in stereotype maintenance. *Journal of Personality and Social Psychology, 52,* 653–662.

Smart, L., & Wegner, D. M. (1999). Covering up what can't be seen: Concealable stigma and mental control. *Journal of Personality and Social Psychology, 77,* 474–486.

Smedley, J. W., & Bayton, J. A. (1978). Evaluative race-class stereotypes by race and perceived class of subjects. *Journal of Personality and Social Psychology, 36,* 530–535.

Smith, A. E., Jussim, L., & Eccles, J. (1999). Do self-fulfilling prophecies accumulate, dissipate, or remain stable over time? *Journal of Personality and Social Psychology, 77,* 548–565.

Smith, A. E., Jussim, L., Eccles, J., VanNoy, M., Madon, S., & Palumbo, P. (1998). Self-fulfilling prophecies, perceptual biases, and accuracy at the individual and group levels. *Journal of Experimental Social Psychology, 34,* 530–561.

Smith, E. E., & Medin, D. L. (1981). *Categories and Concepts.* Cambridge, MA: Harvard University Press.

Smith, E. R. (1990). Content and process specificity in the effects of prior experiences. In T. K. Srull & R. S. Wyer, Jr. (Eds.), *Advances in social cognition* (Vol. 3, pp. 1–59). Hillsdale, NJ: Erlbaum.

Smith, E. R. (1991). Illusory correlation in a simulated exemplar-based memory. *Journal of Experimental Social Psychology, 27,* 107–123.

Smith, E. R. (1993). Social identity and social emotions: Toward new conceptualizations of prejudice. In D. M. Mackie & D. L. Hamilton (Eds.), *Affect, cognition, and stereotyping: Interactive processes in group perception* (pp. 297–315). San Diego, CA: Academic Press.

Smith, E. R. (1994). Social cognition contributions to attribution theory and research. In P. G. Devine, D. L. Hamilton, & T. M. Ostrom (Eds.), *Social cognition: Impact on social psychology* (pp. 77–108). San Diego, CA: Academic Press.

Smith, E. R. (1996). What do connectionism and social psychology offer each other? *Journal of Personality and Social Psychology, 70,* 893–912.

Smith, E. R., Coats, S., & Walling, D. (1999). Overlapping mental representations of self, in-group, and partner: Further response time evidence and a connectionist model. *Personality and Social Psychology Bulletin, 25,* 873–882.

Smith, E. R., & DeCoster, J. (1998). Knowledge acquisition, accessibility, and use in person perception and stereotyping: Simulation with a recurrent connectionist network. *Journal of Personality and Social Psychology, 74,* 21–35.

Smith, E. R., & DeCoster, J. (2002). Dual-process models in social and cognitive psychology. Conceptual integration and links to underlying memory systems. *Personality and Social Psychology Review, 4,* 108–131.

Smith, E. R., Fazio, R. H., & Cejka, M. A. (1996). Accessible attitudes influence categorization of multiply categorizable objects. *Journal of Personality and Social Psychology, 71,* 888–198.

Smith, E. R., & Henry, S. (1996). An in-group becomes part of the self: Response time evidence. *Personality and Social Psychology Bulletin, 22,* 635–642.

Smith, E. R., & Miller, F. D. (1983). Mediation among attributional inferences and comprehension processes: Initial findings and a general method. *Journal of Personality and Social Psychology, 44,* 492–505.

Smith, E. R., & Zárate, M. A. (1990). Exemplar and prototype use in social categorization. *Social Cognition, 8,* 243–262.

Smith, E. R., & Zárate, M. A. (1992). Exemplar-based model of social judgment. *Psychological Review, 99,* 3–21.

Smith, J., & Russell, G. (1984). Why do males and females differ?: Children's beliefs about sex differences. *Sex Roles, 11,* 1111–1120.

Smith, J. E., Waldorf, V. A., & Trembath, D. L. (1990). "Single white male looking for thin, very attractive. . . . " *Sex Roles, 23,* 675–685.

Smith, R. C., & Seltzer, R. (1992). *Race, class, and culture: A study in Afro-American mass opinion.* Albany: State University of New York Press.

Smith, S. (1939). Age and sex differences in children's opinion concerning sex differences. *Journal of Genetic Psychology, 54,* 17–25.

Smith, S. M., McIntosh, W. D., & Bazzini, D. G. (1999). Are the beautiful good in Hollywood?: An investigation of the beauty-and-goodness stereotype on film. *Basic and Applied Social Psychology, 21,* 69–80.

Smith, T. W. (1993). Actual trends or measurement artifacts?: A review of three studies of anti-Semitism. *Public Opinion Quarterly, 57,* 380–393.

Smoreda, Z. (1995). Power, gender stereotypes, and perceptions of heterosexual couples. *British Journal of Social Psychology, 34,* 421–435.

Sniderman, P. M., & Tetlock, P. E. (1986a). Reflections on American racism. *Journal of Social Issues, 42,* 173–187.

Sniderman, P. M., & Tetlock, P. E. (1986b). Symbolic racism: Problems of motive attribution in political analysis. *Journal of Social Issues, 42,* 129–150.

Snyder, M. (1981). Seek and ye shall find: Testing hypotheses about other people. In E. T. Higgins, C. P. Herman, & M. P. Zanna (Eds.), *The Ontario Symposium: Vol. 1. Social cognition* (pp. 277–303). Hillsdale, NJ: Erlbaum.

Snyder, M. (1984). When belief creates reality. In L. Berkowitz (Ed.), *Advances in experimental social psychology* (Vol. 18, pp. 247–305). Orlando, FL: Academic Press.

Snyder, M. (1992). Motivational foundations of behavioral confirmation. In M. Zanna (Ed.), *Advances in experimental social psychology* (Vol. 25, pp. 67–114). San Diego, CA: Academic Press.

Snyder, M., Campbell, B. H., & Preston, E. (1982). Testing hypotheses about human nature: Assessing the accuracy of social stereotypes. *Social Cognition, 1,* 256–272.

Snyder, M., & DeBono, K. G. (1987). A functional approach to attitudes and persuasion. In M. P. Zanna, J. M. Olson, & C. P. Herman (Eds.), *The Ontario Symposium: Vol. 5. Social influence* (pp. 107–125). Hillsdale, NJ: Erlbaum.

Snyder, M., & Haugen, J. A. (1994). Why does behavioral confirmation occur?: A functional perspective on the role of the perceiver. *Journal of Experimental Social Psychology, 30,* 218–246.

Snyder, M., & Haugen, J. A. (1995). Why does behavioral confirmation occur?: A functional perspective on the role of the target. *Personality and Social Psychology Bulletin, 21,* 963–974.

Snyder, M., Kleck, R. E., Strenta, A., & Mentzer, S. (1979). Avoidance of the handicapped: An attributional ambiguity analysis. *Journal of Personality and Social Psychology, 37,* 2297–2306.

Snyder, M., & Miene, P. K. (1994a). On the functions of stereotypes and prejudice. In M. P. Zanna & J. M. Olson (Eds.), *The Ontario Symposium: Vol. 7. The psychology of prejudice* (pp. 33–54). Hillsdale, NJ: Erlbaum.

Snyder, M., & Miene, P. K. (1994b). Stereotyping of the elderly: A functional approach. *British Journal of Social Psychology, 33,* 63–82.

Snyder, M., & Swann, W. B., Jr. (1978a). Behavioral confirmation in social interaction: From social perception to social reality. *Journal of Experimental Social Psychology, 14,* 148–162.

Snyder, M., & Swann, W. B., Jr. (1978b). Hypothesis-testing processes in social interaction. *Journal of Personality and Social Psychology, 36,* 1202–1212.

Snyder, M., Tanke, E. D., & Berscheid, E. (1977). Social perception and interpersonal behavior: On the self-fulfilling nature of social stereotypes. *Journal of Personality and Social Psychology, 35,* 656–666.

Sobal, J. (1991). Obesity and socioeconomic status: A framework for examining relationships between physical and social variables. *Medical Anthropology: Cross-Cultural Studies in Health and Illness, 13,* 231–248.

Sobal, J., & Stunkard, A. J. (1989). Socioeconomic status and obesity: A review of the literature. *Psychological Bulletin, 105,* 260–275.

Socall, D. W., & Holtgraves, T. (1992). Attitudes toward the mentally ill: The effects of label and beliefs. *Sociological Quarterly, 33,* 435–445.

Solomon, J. (1994, October 30). Skin deep: Reliving *Black like Me*; My own journey into the heart of race-conscious America. *Washington Post,* pp. C1.

Solomon, S., Greenberg, J., & Pyszczynski, T. (1991). A terror management theory of social behavior: The psychological functions of self-esteem and cultural world-views. In M. P. Zanna (Ed.), *Advances in experimental social psychology* (Vol. 24, pp. 91–159). San Diego, CA: Academic Press.

Solovay, S. (2000). *Tipping the scales of justice: Fighting weight-based discrimination.* Amherst, NY: Prometheus Books.

Sommers, S. R., & Ellsworth, P. C. (2000). Race in the courtoom: Perceptions of guilt and dispositional attributions. *Personality and Social Psychology Bulletin, 26,* 1367–1379.

Sommers-Flanagan, R., Sommers-Flanagan, J., & Davis, B. (1992). What's happening on music television?: A gender role content analysis. *Sex Roles, 26,* 745–753.

Spalding, T. L., & Murphy, G. L. (1996). Effects of background knowledge on category construction. *Journal of Experimental Psychology: Learning, Memory, and Cognition, 22,* 525–538.

Spangler, E., Gordon, M. A., & Pipkin, R. M. (1978). Token women: An empirical test of Kanter's hypothesis. *American Journal of Sociology, 84,* 160–170.

Spears, R., Doosje, B., & Ellemers, N. (1997). Self-stereotyping in the face of threats to group status and distinctiveness: The role of group identification. *Personality and Social Psychology Bulletin, 23,* 538–553.

Spears, R., Doosje, B., & Ellemers, N. (1999). Commitment and the context of social perception. In N. Ellemers, R. Spears, & B. Doosje (Eds.), *Social identity: Context, commitment, content* (pp. 59–83). Oxford, UK: Blackwell.

Spears, R., Oakes, P. J., Ellemers, N., & Haslam, S. A. (1997). Introduction: The social psychology of stereotyping and group life. In R. Spears, P. J. Oakes, N. Ellemers, & S. A. Haslam (Eds.), *The social psychology of stereotyping and group life* (pp. 1–19). Oxford, UK: Blackwell.

Spears, R., van der Pligt, J. & Eiser, J. R. (1985). Illusory correlation in the perception of group attitudes. *Journal of Personality and Social Psychology, 48,* 863–875.

Spears, R., van der Pligt, J., & Eiser, J. R. (1986). Generalizing the illusory correlation effect. *Journal of Personality and Social Psychology, 51,* 1127–1134.

Spence, J. T. (1993). Gender-related traits and gender ideology: Evidence for a multifactorial theory. *Journal of Personality and Social Psychology, 64,* 624–635.

Spence, J. T. (1999). Thirty years of gender research: A personal chronicle. In W. B. Swann, Jr., J. H.

Langlois, & L. A. Gilbert (Eds.), *Sexism and stereotypes: The gender science of Janet Taylor Spence* (pp. 255–289). Washington, DC: American Psychological Association.

Spence, J. T., & Buckner, C. E. (2000). Instrumental and expressive traits, trait stereotypes, and sexist attitudes. *Psychology of Women Quarterly, 24,* 55–62.

Spence, J. T., & Hall, S. K. (1996). Children's gender-related self-perceptions, activity preferences, and occupational stereotypes: A test of three models of gender constructs. *Sex Roles, 35,* 659–691.

Spence, J. T., & Helmreich, R. L. (1978). *Masculinity and femininity: Their psychological dimensions, correlates and antecedents.* Austin: University of Texas Press.

Spence, J. T., Helmreich, R., & Stapp, J. (1975). Ratings of self and peers on sex role attributes and their relation to self-esteem and conceptions of masculinity and femininity. *Journal of Personality and Social Psychology, 32,* 29–39.

Spencer, S. J., Fein, S., Wolfe, C. T., Fong, C., & Dunn, M. A. (1998). Automatic activation of stereotypes: The role of self-image threat. *Personality and Social Psychology Bulletin., 24,* 1139–1152.

Spencer, S. J., Steele, C. M., & Quinn, D. M. (1999). Stereotype threat and women's math performance. *Journal of Experimental Social Psychology, 35,* 4–28.

Spencer, W. (1892–1893). *The principles of ethics* (2 vols.). New York: Appleton.

Sprecher, S., Sullivan, Q., & Hatfield, E. (1994). Mate selection preferences: Gender differences examined in a national sample. *Journal of Personality and Social Psychology, 66,* 1074–1080.

Srull, T. K. (1981). Person memory: Some tests of associative storage and retrieval models. *Journal of Experimental Psychology: Human Learning and Memory, 7,* 440–463.

St. Lawrence, J. S., Husfeldt, B. A., Kelly, J. A., Hood, H. V., & Smith, S. (1990). The stigma of AIDS: Fear of disease and prejudice against gay men. *Journal of Homosexuality, 19,* 85–101.

Staats, G. R. (1978). Stereotype content and social distance: Changing views of homosexuality. *Journal of Homosexuality, 3,* 15–27.

Stacy, N. L., & Richman, C. L. (1998). Activating stereotypes undermines task performance expectations. *Journal of Personality and Social Psychology, 75,* 1191–1197.

Staffieri, J. F. (1967). A study of social stereotype of body image in children. *Journal of Personality and Social Psychology, 7,* 101–104.

Stager, S. F., & Burke, P. J. (1982). A reexamination of body build stereotypes. *Journal of Research in Personality, 16,* 435–446.

Stangor, C. (1988). Stereotype accessibility and information processing. *Personality and Social Psychology Bulletin, 14,* 694–708.

Stangor, C. (1995). Content and application inaccuracy in social stereotyping. In Y.-T. Lee, L. J. Jussim, & C. R. McCauley (Eds.), *Stereotype accuracy: Toward appreciating group differences* (pp. 275–292). Washington, DC: American Psychological Association.

Stangor, C., Carr, C., & Kiang, L. (1998). Activating stereotypes undermines task performance expectations. *Journal of Personality and Social Psychology, 75,* 1191–1197.

Stangor, C., & Duan, C. (1991). Effects of multiple task demands upon memory for information about social groups. *Journal of Experimental Social Psychology, 27,* 357–378.

Stangor, C., & Jost, J. T. (1997). Commentary: Individual, group and system levels of analysis and their relevance for stereotyping and intergroup relations. In R. Spears, P. J. Oakes, N. Ellemers, & S. A. Haslam (Eds.), *The social psychology of stereotyping and group life* (pp. 336–358). Oxford, UK: Blackwell.

Stangor, C., & Lange, J. E. (1994). Mental representations of social groups: Advances in understanding stereotypes and stereotyping. In M. P. Zanna (Ed.), *Advances in experimental social psychology* (Vol. 26, pp. 357–416). San Diego, CA: Academic Press.

Stangor, C., Lynch, L., Duan, C., & Glass, B. (1992). Categorization of individuals on the basis of multiple social features. *Journal of Personality and Social Psychology, 62,* 207–218.

Stangor, C., & McMillan, D. (1992). Memory for expectancy-congruent and expectancy-incongruent information: A review of the social and social developmental literatures. *Psychological Bulletin, 111,* 42–61.

Stangor, C., & Ruble, D. N. (1989a). Differential influences of gender schemata and gender constancy on children's information processing and behavior. *Social Cognition, 7,* 353–372.

Stangor, C., & Ruble, D. N. (1989b). Strength of expectancies and memory for social information:

What we remember depends on how much we know. *Journal of Experimental Social Psychology*, *25*, 18–35.

Stangor, C., & Schaller, M. (1996). Stereotypes as individual and collective representations. In C. N. Macrae, C. Stangor, & M. Hewstone (Eds.), *Stereotypes and stereotyping* (pp. 3–37). New York: Guilford Press.

Stangor, C., Sechrist, G. B., & Jost, J. T. (2001). Changing racial beliefs by providing consensus information. *Personality and Social Psychology Bulletin*, *27*, 486–496.

Stangor, C., Sullivan, L. A., & Ford, T. E. (1991). Affective and cognitive determinants of prejudice. *Social Cognition*, *9*, 359–380.

Stangor, C., Swim, J. K., Van Allen, K. L., & Sechrist, G. B. (2002). Reporting discrimination in public and private contexts. *Journal of Personality and Social Psychology*, *82*, 69–74.

Stangor, C., & Thompson, E. P. (2002). Needs for cognitive economy and self-enhancement as unique predictors of intergroup attitudes. *European Journal of Social Psychology*, *32*, 563–575.

Stapel, D. A., & Koomen, W. (1997). Using primed exemplars during impression formation: Interpretation or comparison. *European Journal of Social Psychology*, *27*, 357–367.

Stapel, D. A., & Koomen, W. (2000). How far do we go beyond the information given?: The impact of knowledg activation on interpretation and inference. *Journal of Personality and Social Psychology*, *78*, 19–37.

Stapel, D. A., Koomen, W., & Ruys, K. I. (2002). The effects of diffuse and distinct affect. *Journal of Personality and Social Psychology*, *83*, 60–74.

Stapel, D. A., Koomen, W., & Zeelenberg, M. (1998). The impact of accuracy motivation on interpretation, comparison, and correction processes: Accuracy × knowledge accessibility effects. *Journal of Personality and Social Psychology*, *74*, 878–893.

Stapel, D. A., & Schwarz, N. (1998). Similarities and differences between the impact of traits and expectancies: What matters is whether the target stimulus is ambiguous or mixed. *Journal of Experimental Social Psychology*, *34*, 227–245.

Star, S. (1955). *The public's ideas about mental illness.* Chicago: National Opinion Research Center.

Steadman, H. J. (1981). Critically reassessing the accuracy of public perceptions of the dangerousness of the mentally ill. *Journal of Health and Social Behavior*, *22*, 310–316.

Steele, C. M. (1997). A threat in the air: How stereotypes shape intellectual identity and performance. *American Psychologist*, *52*, 613–629.

Steele, C. M., & Aronson, J. (1995). Stereotype threat and the intellectual test performance of African Americans. *Journal of Personality and Social Psychology*, *69*, 797–811.

Steele, C. M., Spencer, S. J., & Aronson, J. (2002). Contending with group image: The psychology of stereotype and social identity threat. In M. P. Zanna (Ed.), *Advances in experimental social psychology* (Vol. 34, pp. 379–440). San Diego, CA: Academic Press.

Stein, D. D., Hardyck, J. A., & Smith, M. B. (1965). Race and belief: An open and shut case. *Journal of Personality and Social Psychology*, *1*, 281–289.

Stein, R. I., & Nemeroff, C. J. (1995). Moral overtones of food: Judgments of others based on what they eat. *Personality and Social Psychology Bulletin*, *21*, 480–490.

Steinhorn, L., & Diggs-Brown, B. (1999). *By the color of our skin: The illusion of integration and the reality of race.* New York: Dutton.

Stephan, C. W., Stephan, W. G., Demitrakis, K. M., Yamada, A. M., & Clason, D. L. (2000). Women's attitudes toward men: An integrated threat theory approach. *Psychology of Women Quarterly*, *24*, 63–73.

Stephan, W. G. (1978). School desegregation: An evaluation of predictions made in *Brown v. Board of Education.* *Psychological Bulletin*, *85*, 217–238.

Stephan, W. G. (1985). Intergroup relations. In G. Lindzey & E. Aronson (Eds.), *Handbook of social psychology* (3rd ed., Vol. 2, pp. 599–658). New York: Random House.

Stephan, W. G. (1987). The contact hypothesis in intergroup relations. In C. Hendrick (Ed.), *Group processes and intergroup relations* (pp. 13–40). Newbury Park, CA: Sage.

Stephan, W. G. (1989). A cognitive approach to stereotyping. In D. Bar-Tal, C. F. Graumann, A. W. Kruglanski, & W. Stroebe (Eds.), *Stereotyping and prejudice: Changing conceptions* (pp. 37–57). New York: Springer-Verlag.

Stephan, W. G. (1999). *Reducing prejudice and stereotyping in schools.* New York: Teachers College Press.

Stephan, W. G., Ageyev, V., Stephan, C. W., Abalakina, M., Stefanenko, T., & Coates-Shrider, L. (1993). Measuring stereotypes: A comparison of methods using Russian and American samples. *Social Psychology Quarterly*, *56*, 54–64.

Stephan, W. G., Boniecki, K. A., Ybarra, O., Bettencourt, A., Ervin, K. S., Jackson, L. A., McNatt, P. S., & Renfro, C. L. (2002). The role of threats in the racial attitudes of blacks and whites. *Personality and Social Psychology Bulletin*, *28*, 1242–1254.

Stephan, W. G., Diaz-Loving, R., & Duran, A. (2000). Integrated threat theory and intercultural attitudes: Mexico and the United States. *Journal of Cross-Cultural Psychology*, *31*, 240–249.

Stephan, W. G., & Rosenfield, D. (1982). Racial and ethnic stereotypes. In A. G. Miller (Ed.), *In the eye of the beholder: Contemporary issues in stereotyping* (pp. 92–136). New York: Praeger.

Stephan, W. G., & Stephan, C. W. (1993). Cognition and affect in stereotyping: Parallel interactive networks. In D. M. Mackie & D. L. Hamilton (Eds.), *Affect, cognition, and stereotyping: Interactive processes in group perception* (pp. 111–136). San Diego, CA: Academic Press.

Stephan, W. G., & Stephan, C. W. (1996). Predicting prejudice. *International Journal of Intercultural Relations*, *20*, 409–426.

Stephan, W. G., & Stephan, C. W. (2000a). An integrated theory of prejudice. In S. Oskamp (Ed.), *Reducing prejudice and discrimination* (pp. 23–45). Mahwah, NJ: Erlbaum.

Stephan, C. W., & Stephan, W. G. (2000b). The measurement of racial and ethnic identity. *International Journal of Intercultural Relations*, *24*, 541–552.

Stephan, W. G., Ybarra, O., & Bachman, G. (1999). Prejudice toward immigrants. *Journal of Applied Social Psychology*, *29*, 2221–2237.

Stephan, W. G., Ybarra, O., Martinez, C. M., Schwarzwald, J., & Tur-Kaspa, M. (1998). Prejudice toward immigrants to Spain and Israel: An integrated threat theory analysis. *Journal of Cross-Cultural Psychology*, *29*, 559–576.

Stern, L. D., Marrs, S., Millar, M. G., & Cole, E. (1984). Processing time and the recall of inconsistent and consistent behaviors of individuals and groups. *Journal of Personality and Social Psychology*, *47*, 253–262.

Stern, M., & Karraker, K. H. (1989). Sex stereotyping of infants: A review of gender labeling studies. *Sex Roles*, *20*, 501–522.

Stevens, J., Kumanyika, S. K., & Keil, J. E. (1994). Attitudes toward body and dieting: Differences between elderly black and white women. *American Journal of Public Health*, *84*, 1322–1325.

Stevens, L. E., & Fiske, S. T. (2000). Motivated impressions of a powerholder: Accuracy under task dependency and misperception under evaluation dependency. *Personality and Social Psychology Bulletin*, *26*, 907–922.

Stevens, M. (2000). The essentialist aspect of naive theories. *Cognition*, *74*, 149–175.

Stevenson, M. R. (1988). Promoting tolerance for homosexuality: An evaluation of intervention strategies. *Journal of Sex Research*, *25*, 500–511.

Stevenson, M. R., & Gajarsky, W. M. (1991). Issues of gender in promoting tolerance for homosexuality. *Journal of Psychology and Human Sexuality*, *3*, 155–163.

Stewart, D. D. (1998). Stereotypes, negativity bias, and the discussion of unshared information in decision-making groups. *Small Group Research*, *29*, 643–668.

Stewart, T. L., Doan, K. A., Gingrich, B. E., & Smith, E. R. (1998). The actor as context for social judgments: Effects of prior impressions and stereotypes. *Journal of Personality and Social Psychology*, *75*, 1132–1154.

Stillwell, A. M., & Baumeister, R. F. (1997). The construction of victim and perpetrator memories: Accuracy and distortion in role-based accounts. *Personality and Social Psychology Bulletin*, *23*, 1157–1172.

Stone, C. I., & Sawatzki, B. (1980). Hiring bias and the disabled interviewee: Effects of manipulating work history and disability information of the disabled job applicant. *Journal of Vocational Behavior*, *16*, 96–104.

Stone, E. F., Stone, D. L., & Dipboye, R. L. (1992). Stigmas in organizations: Race, handicaps, and physical unattractiveness. In K. Kelley (Ed.), *Issues, theory, and research in industrial/organizational psychology* (pp. 385–457). Amsterdam: Elsevier.

Stone, J., Lynch, C. I., Sjomeling, M., & Darley, J. M. (1999). Stereotype threat effects on black and white athletic performance. *Journal of Personality and Social Psychology*, *77*, 1213–1227.

Stone, J., Perry, Z. W., & Darley, J. M. (1997). "White men can't jump": Evidence for the perceptual confirmation of racial stereotypes following a basketball game. *Basic and Applied Social Psychology, 19,* 291–306.

Storms, M. D. (1978). Attitudes toward homosexuality and femininity in men. *Journal of Homosexuality, 3,* 257–263.

Storms, M. D., Stivers, M. L., Lambers, S. M., & Hill, C. A. (1981). Sexual scripts for women. *Sex Roles, 7,* 699–707.

Street, S., Kimmel, E. B., & Kromrey, J. D. (1995). Revisiting university student gender role perceptions. *Sex Roles, 33,* 183–201.

Strenta, A. C., & Kleck, R. E. (1984). Physical disability and the perception of social interaction: It's not what you look at but how you look at it. *Personality and Social Psychology Bulletin, 10,* 279–288.

Stroessner, S. J. (1996). Social categorization by race or sex: Effects of perceived non-normalcy on response times. *Social Cognition, 14,* 247–276.

Stroessner, S. J., Hamilton, D. L., & Mackie, D. M. (1992). Affect and stereeotyping: The effect of induced mood on distinctiveness-based illusory correlations. *Journal of Personality and Social Psychology, 62,* 564–576.

Stroessner, S. J., & Mackie, D. M. (1992). The impact of induced affect on the perception of variability in social groups. *Personality and Social Psychology Bulletin, 18,* 546–554.

Stroessner, S. J., & Mackie, D. M. (1993). Affect and perceived group variability: Implications for stereotyping an prejudice. In D. M. Mackie & D. L. Hamilton (Eds.), *Affect, cognition, and stereotyping: Interactive processes in group perception* (pp. 63–86). San Diego, CA: Academic Press.

Struch, N., & Schwartz, S. H. (1989). Intergroup aggression: Its predictors and distinctness from ingroup bias. *Journal of Personality and Social Psychology, 56,* 364–373.

Strunk, O. (1958). Attitudes toward one's name and one's self. *Journal of Individual Psychology, 14,* 64–67.

Strutton, D., & Lumpkin, J. R. (1993). Stereotypes of black in-group attractiveness in advertising: On possible psychological effects. *Psychological Reports, 73,* 507–511.

Subervi-Velez, F. A., & Colsant, S. (1993). The television worlds of Latino children. In G. L. Berry & J. K. Asamen (Eds.), *Children and television: Images in a changing sociocultural world* (pp. 215–228). Newbury Park, CA: Sage.

Suchner, R. W. (1979). Sex ratios and occupational prestige: Three failures to replicate a sexist bias. *Personality and Social Psychology Bulletin, 5,* 236–239.

Sumner, W. G. (1907). *Folkways.* Boston: Ginn.

Sunar, D. (1978). Stereotypes of the powerless: A social psychological analysis. *Psychological Reports, 43,* 511–528.

Susskind, J., Maurer, K., Thakkar, V., Hamilton, D. L., & Sherman, J. W. (1999). Perceiving individuals and groups: Expectancies, dispositional inferences, and causal attributions. *Journal of Personality and Social Psychology, 76,* 181–191.

Sussman, S., & Mueser, K. T. (1983). Age, socioeconomic status, severity of mental disorder, and chronicity as predictors of physical attractiveness. *Journal of Abnormal Psychology, 92,* 255–258.

Swan, S., & Wyer, R. S., Jr. (1997). Gender stereotypes and social identity: How being in the minority affects judgment of self and others. *Personality and Social Psychology Bulletin, 23,* 1265–1276.

Swann, W. B., Jr. (1984). Quest for accuracy in person perception: A matter for pragmatics. *Psychological Review, 91,* 457–477.

Swann, W. B., Jr. (1996). *Self-traps: The elusive quest for higher self-esteem.* New York: Freeman.

Swann, W. B., Jr., & Giuliano, T. (1987). Confirmatory search strategies in social interaction: How, when, why, and with what consequences. *Journal of Social and Clinical Psychology, 5,* 511–524.

Swann, W. B., Jr., & Snyder, M. (1980). On translating beliefs into action: Theories of ability and their application in an instructional setting. *Journal of Personality and Social Psychology, 38,* 879–888.

Sweeney, L. T., & Haney, C. (1992). The influence of race on sentencing: A meta-analytic review of experimental studies. *Behavioral Sciences and the Law, 10,* 179–195.

Swim, J. K. (1993). In search of gender bias in evaluations and trait inferences: The role of diagnosticity and gender stereotypicality of behavioral information. *Sex Roles, 29,* 213–237.

Swim, J. K. (1994). Perceived versus meta-analytic effect sizes: An assessment of the accuracy of gender stereotypes. *Journal of Personality and Social Psychology, 66,* 21–36.

Swim, J. K., Aikin, K. J., Hall, W. S., & Hunter, B. A. (1995). Sexism and racism: Old-fashioned and modern prejudices. *Journal of Personality and Social Psychology, 68*, 199–214.

Swim, J., Borgida, E., Maruyama, G., & Myers, D. G. (1989). Joan McKay versus John McKay: Do gender stereotypes bias evaluations? *Psychological Bulletin, 105*, 409–429.

Swim, J. K., Ferguson, M. J., & Hyers, L. L. (1999). Avoiding stigma by association: Subtle prejudice against lesbians in the form of social distancing. *Basic and Applied Social Psychology, 21*, 61–68.

Swim, J. K., & Hyers, L. L. (1999). Excuse me—What did you just say?!: Women's public and private responses to sexist remarks. *Journal of Experimental Social Psychology, 35*, 68–88.

Swim, J. K., & Sanna, L. J. (1996). He's skilled, she's lucky: A meta-analysis of observers' attributions for women's and men's successes and failures. *Personality and Social Psychology Bulletin, 22*, 507–519.

Switzer, J. Y. (1990). The impact of generic word choices: An empirical investigation of age- and sex-related differences. *Sex Roles, 22*, 69–82.

Synnott, A. (1987). Shame and glory: A sociology of hair. *British Journal of Sociology, 38*, 381–413.

Taft, R. (1959). Ethnic stereotypes, attitudes, and familiarity: Australia. *Journal of Social Psychology, 49*, 177–186.

Tajfel, H. (1959). Quantitative judgement in social perception. *British Journal of Psychology, 50*, 16–29.

Tajfel, H. (1969). Cognitive aspects of prejudice. *Journal of Social Issues, 25*, 79–97.

Tajfel, H. (1970). Experiments in intergroup discrimination. *Scientific American, 223*, 96–102.

Tajfel, H. (1978). Interindividual behaviour and intergroup behaviour. In H. Tajfel (Ed.), *Differentiation between social groups: Studies in the social psychology of intergroup relations* (pp. 27–60). London: Academic Press.

Tajfel, H. (1981a). *Human groups and social categories.* New York: Cambridge University Press.

Tajfel, H. (1981b). Social stereotypes and social groups. In J. Turner & H. Giles (Eds.), *Intergroup behaviour* (pp. 144–167). Oxford, UK: Blackwell.

Tajfel, H., Billig, M. G., Bundy, R. P. & Flament, C. (1971). Social categorization and intergroup behavior. *European Journal of Social Psychology, 1*, 149–178.

Tajfel, H., & Forgas, J. P. (1981). Social categorization: Cognitions, values, and groups. In J. P. Forgas (Ed.), *Social cognition: Perspectives on everyday understanding* (pp. 113–140). New York: Academic Press.

Tajfel, H., & Turner, J. C. (1979). An integrative theory of intergroup conflict. In W. Austin & S. Worchel (Eds.), *The social psychology of intergroup conflict* (pp. 33–47). Monterey, CA: Brooks/Cole.

Tajfel, H., & Wilkes, A. L. (1963). Classification and quantitative judgment. *British Journal of Psychology, 54*, 101–114.

Tan, A., Tan, G., Avdeyeva, T., Crandall, H., Fukushi, Y., Nyandwi, A., Chin, H.-Y., & Wu, C.-G. (2001). Changing negative racial stereotypes: The influence of normative peer information. *Howard Journal of Communications, 12*, 171–180.

Tannen, D. (1990). *You just don't understand: Women and men in conversation.* New York: Morrow.

Taylor, D. M., Wright, C., Moghaddam, F. M., & Lalonde, R. N. (1990). The personal/group discrimination discrepency: Perceiving my group, but not myself, to be a target for discrimination. *Personality and Social Psychology Bulletin, 16*, 254–262.

Taylor, M. C. (2000). Social contextual strategies for reducing racial discrimination. In S. Oskamp (Ed.), *Reducing prejudice and discrimination* (pp. 71–89). Mahwah, NJ: Erlbaum.

Taylor, M. G. (1996). The development of children's beliefs about social and biological aspects of gender differenes. *Child Development, 67*, 1555–1571.

Taylor, S. E. (1981). A categorizing approach to stereotyping. In D. L. Hamilton (Ed.), *Cognitive processes in stereotyping and intergroup behavior* (pp. 83–114). Hillsdale, NJ: Erlbaum.

Taylor, S. E., & Crocker, J. (1981). Schematic bases of social information processing. In E. T. Higgins, C. P. Herman, & M. P. Zanna (Eds.), *The Ontario Symposium: Vol. 1. Social cognition* (pp. 89–134). Hillsdale, NJ: Erlbaum.

Taylor, S. E., Crocker, J., Fiske, S. T., Sprinzen, M., & Winkler, J. D. (1979). The generalizabilty of salience effects. *Journal of Personality and Social Psychology, 37*, 357–368.

Taylor, S. E., & Falcone, H. (1982). Cognitive basis of stereotyping: The relationship between categorization and prejudice. *Personality and Social Psychology Bulletin, 8*, 426–432.

Taylor, S. E., & Fiske, S. T. (1975). Point of view and perceptions of causality. *Journal of Personality and Social Psychology, 32*, 439–445.

Taylor, S. E., Fiske, S. T., Etcoff, N. & Ruderman, A. (1978). The categorical and contextual bases of person memory and stereotyping. *Journal of Personality and Social Psychology, 36*, 778–793.

Teitelbaum, S., & Geiselman, R. E. (1997). Observer mood and cross-racial recognition of faces. *Journal of Cross Cultural Psychology, 28*, 93–106.

Teri, L. (1982). Effects of sex and sex-role style on clinical judgment. *Sex Roles, 8*, 639–649.

Terkel, S. (1992). *Race: How blacks and whites think and feel about the American obsession.* New York: Anchor Books.

Terry, R. L. (1989). Eyeglasses and gender stereotypes. *Optometry and Vision Science, 66*, 694–697.

Terry, R. L., & Hall, C. A. (1989). Affective responses to eyeglasses: Evidence of a sex difference. *Journal of the American Optometric Association, 60*, 609–611.

Terry, R. L., & Krantz, J. H. (1993). Dimensions of trait attributions associated with eyeglasses, men's facial hair, and women's hair length. *Journal of Applied Social Psychology, 23*, 1757–1769.

Thernstrom, S., & Thernstrom, A. (1997). *America in black and white: One nation indivisible.* New York: Simon & Schuster.

Thiessen, D., Young, R. K., & Burroughs, R. (1993). Lonely hearts advertisements reflect sexually dimorphic mating strategies. *Ethology and Sociobiology, 14*, 209–229.

Thompson, E. P., Roman, R. J., Moskowitz, G. B., Chaiken, S., & Bargh, J. A. (1994). Accuracy motivation attenuates covert priming: The systematic reprocessing of social information. *Journal of Personality and Social Psychology, 66*, 474–489.

Thompson, M. S., Judd, C. M., & Park, B. (2000). The consequences of communicating social stereotypes. *Journal of Experimental Social Psychology, 36*, 567–599.

Thompson, T. L., & Zerbinos, E. (1995). Gender roles in animated cartoons: Has the picture changed in 20 years? *Sex Roles, 32*, 651–673.

Thomsen, C. J., Basu, A. M., & Reinitz, M. T. (1995). Effects of women's studies courses on gender-related attitudes of women and men. *Psychology of Women Quarterly, 19*, 419–426.

Thomson, R., & Murachver, T. (2001). Predicting gender from electronic discourse. *British Journal of Social Psychology, 40*, 193–208.

Thorndike, E. L. (1920). A constant error in psychological ratings. *Journal of Applied Psychology, 4*, 25–29.

Thornton, G. R. (1939). The ability to judge crimes from photographs of criminals: A contribution to technique. *Journal of Abnormal and Social Psychology, 34*, 378–383.

Thornton, G. R. (1943). The effect upon judgments of personality traits of varying a single factor in a photograph. *Journal of Social Psychology, 18*, 127–148.

Thornton, G. R. (1944). The effect of wearing glasses upon judgments of personality traits of persons seen briefly. *Journal of Applied Psychology, 28*, 203–207.

Thornton, J. A., & Wahl, O. F. (1996). Impact of a newspaper article on attitudes toward mental illness. *Journal of Community Psychology, 24*, 17–25.

Thurman, Q. C., Lam, J. A., & Rossi, P. H. (1988). Sorting out the cuckoo's nest: A factorial survey approach to the study of popular conceptions of mental illness. *Sociological Quarterly, 29*, 565–588.

Tiggemann, M., & Anesbury, T. (2000). Negative stereotyping of obesity in children: The role of controllability beliefs. *Journal of Applied Social Psychology, 30*, 1977–1993.

Tiggemann, M., & Rothblum, E. D. (1988). Gender differences in social consequences of perceived overweight in the United States and Australia. *Sex Roles, 18*, 75–86.

Tilby, P. J., & Kalin, R. (1980). Effects of sex-role deviant lifestyles in otherwise normal persons on the perception of maladjustment. *Sex Roles, 6*, 581–592.

Todd-Mancillas, W. (1981). Masculine generics = sexist language: A review of the literature and implications for speech communication professionals. *Communication Quarterly, 29*, 107–115.

Todorov, A., & Uleman, J. S. (2002). Spontaneous trait inferences are bound to actors' faces: Evidence from a false recognition paradigm. *Journal of Personality and Social Psychology, 83*, 1051–1065.

Tomkiewicz, J., Brenner, O. C., & Adeyemi-Bello, T. (1998). The impact of perceptions and stereotypes on the managerial mobility of African Americans. *Journal of Social Psychology, 138*, 88–92.

Tompkins, R. C., & Boor, M. (1980). Effects of students' physical attractiveness and name popularity on student teachers' perceptions of social and academic attributes. *Journal of Psychology, 106,* 37–42.

Tonry, M. (1995). *Malign neglect: Race, crime, and punishment in America.* New York: Oxford University Press.

Tougas, F., Brown, R., Beaton, A. M., & Joly, S. (1995). Neosexism: Plus ça change, plus c'est pareil. *Personality and Social Psychology Bulletin, 21,* 842–849.

Touhey, J. C. (1974a). Effects of additional men on prestige and desirability of occupations typically performed by women. *Journal of Applied Social Psychology, 4,* 330–335.

Touhey, J. C. (1974b). Effects of additional women professionals on ratings of occupational prestige and desirability. *Journal of Personality and Social Psychology, 29,* 86–89.

Towler, A. J., & Schneider, D. J. (in press). Identities and distinctions among stigmatized groups. *Journal of Applied Social Psychology.*

Towles-Schwen, T., & Fazio, R. H. (2001). On the origins of racial attitudes: Correlates of childhood experiences. *Personality and Social Psychology Bulletin, 27,* 162–175.

Towles-Schewn, T., & Fazio, R. H. (2003). Choosing social situations: The relation between automatically activated racial attitudes and anticipated comfort interacting with African Americans. *Personality and Social Psychology Bulletin, 29,* 170–182.

Townsend, J. M., & Levy, G. D. (1990). Effects of potential partner's physical attractiveness and socioeconomic status on sexuality and partner selection. *Archives of Sexual Behavior, 371,* 149–164.

Trafimow, D. (1997). The implications of success for hierarchically and partially restrictive ability dimensions. *Social Cognition, 15,* 312–326.

Trafimow, D., & Finlay, K. A. (2001). An investigation of three models of multitrait representations. *Personality and Social Psychology Bulletin, 27,* 226–241.

Trafimow, D., & Gannon, T. (1999). What if your daughter married a Jew?: The dissociation of stereotypic trait judgments from prejudicial attitudes. *Social Science Journal, 36,* 299–311.

Trafimow, D., & Radhakrishnan, P. (1995). The cognitive organization of sex and occupation stereotypes. *British Journal of Social Psychology, 34,* 189–197.

Trafimow, D., & Schneider, D. J. (1994). The effects of behavioral, situational, and person information on different attribution judgments. *Journal of Experimental Social Psychology, 30,* 351–369.

Trafimow, D., & Trafimow, S. (1999). Mapping perfect and imperfect duties onto hierarchically and partially restrictive trait dimensions. *Personality and Social Psychology Bulletin, 25,* 686–695.

Triandis, H. C. (1959). Differential perception of certain jobs and people by managers, clerks, and workers in industry. *Journal of Applied Psychology, 43,* 221–225.

Triandis, H. C., Lisansky, J., Setiadi, B., Chang, B., Marin, G., & Betancourt, H. (1982). Stereotyping among Hispanics and Anglos: The uniformity, intensisty, direction, and quality of auto- and heterostereotypes. *Journal of Cross-Cultural Psychology, 13,* 409–426.

Triandis, H. C., & Vassiliou, V. (1967). Frequency of contact and stereotyping. *Journal of Personality and Social Psychology, 7,* 316–328.

Trice, A. D., & Rush, K. (1995). Sex-stereotyping in four-year-olds' occupational aspirations. *Perceptual and Motor Skills, 81,* 701–702.

Tringo, J. (1970). The hierarchy of preference toward disability groups. *Journal of Special Education, 4,* 295–306.

Trolier, T. K., & Hamilton, D. L. (1986). Variables influencing judgments of correlational relations. *Journal of Personality and Social Psychology, 50,* 879–888.

Trope, Y. (1986). Identification and inferential processes in dispositional attribution. *Psychological Review, 93,* 239–257.

Trope, Y., & Bassok, M. (1982). Confirmatory and diagnosing strategies in social information gathering. *Journal of Personality and Social Psychology, 43,* 22–34.

Trope, Y., & Bassok, M. (1983). Information-gathering strategies in hypothesis testing. *Journal of Experimental Social Psychology, 19,* 560–576.

Trope, Y., Bassok, M., & Alon, E. (1984). The questions lay interviewers ask. *Journal of Personality, 52,* 90–106.

Trope, Y., Cohen, O., & Alfieri, T. (1991). Behavior identification as a mediator of dispositional inference. *Journal of Personality and Social Psychology, 61,* 873–883.

Trope, Y., & Liberman, A. (1993). The use of trait conceptions to identify other people's behavior and to draw inferences about their personalities. *Personality and Social Psychology Bulletin, 19,* 553–562.

Trope, Y., & Liberman, A. (1996). Social hypothesis testing: Cognitive and motivational mechanisms. In E. T. Higgins & A. W. Kruglanski (Eds.), *Social psychology: Handbook of basic principles* (pp. 239–270). New York: Guilford Press.

Trope, Y., & Mackie, D. M. (1987). Sensitivity to alternatives in social hypothesis-testing. *Journal of Experimental Social Psychology, 23,* 445–459.

Trope, Y., & Thompson, E. P. (1997). Looking for truth in all the wrong places?: Asymmetrical search of individuating information about stereotyped group members. *Journal of Personality and Social Psychology, 73,* 229–241.

Tropp, L. R., & Wright, S. C. (2001). Ingroup identification as the inclusion of ingroup in the self. *Personality and Social Psychology Bulletin, 27,* 585–600.

Trouilloud, D. O., Sarrrazin, P. G., Martinek, T. J., & Guillet, E. (2002). The influence of teacher expectations on student achievement in physical education classes: Pygmalion revisited. *European Journal of Social Psychology, 32,* 591–607.

Trute, B., Tefft, B., & Segall, A. (1989). Social rejection of the mentally ill: A replication study of public attitude. *Social Psychiatry and Psychiatric Epidemology, 24,* 69–76.

Tuckman, J., & Lorge, I. (1952). The best years of life: A study in ranking. *Journal of Psychology, 34,* 137–149.

Tuckman, J., & Lorge, I. (1953). Attitudes toward old people. *Journal of Social Psychology, 37,* 249–260.

Tuckman, J., & Lorge, I. (1954). The influence of changed directions on stereotypes about aging; before and after instruction. *Educational and Psychological Measurement, 14,* 128–132.

Tuckman, J., & Lorge, I. (1956). Perceptual stereotypes about life and adjustments. *Journal of Social Psychology, 43,* 239–245.

Tuohy, A. P., & Wrennall, M. J. (1995). Seeing themselves as others see them: Scottish police officers' metaperceptions of public opinion. *Journal of Community and Applied Social Psychology, 5,* 311–326.

Turner, B. F., & Turner, C. B. (1994). Social cognition and gender stereotypes for women varying in age and race. In B. F. Turner & L. E. Troll (Eds.), *Women growing older: Psychological perspectives* (pp. 94–139). Thousand Oaks, CA: Sage.

Turner, J. C. (1987). *Rediscovering the social group: A self-categorization theory.* Oxford, UK: Blackwell.

Turner, J. C. (1991). *Social influence.* Pacific Grove, CA: Brooks/Cole.

Turner, J. C. (1999). Some current issues in research on social identity and self-categorization theories. In N. Ellemers, R. Spears, & B. Doosje (Eds.), *Social identity: Context, commitment, content* (pp. 6–34). Oxford, UK: Blackwell.

Turner, J. C., Oakes, P. J., Haslam, S. A., & McGarty, C. (1994). Self and collective: Cognition and social context. *Personality and Social Psychology Bulletin, 20,* 454–463.

Turner, P. J., & Gervai, J. (1995). A multidimensional study of gender typing in preschool children and their parents: Personality, attitudes, preferences, behavior, and cultural differences. *Developmental Psychology, 31,* 759–779.

Turner-Bowker, D. M. (1996). Gender stereotyped descriptors in children's picture books: Does "Curious Jane" exist in the literature. *Sex Roles, 35,* 461–488.

Twenge, J. M. (1997). Changes in masculine and feminine traits over time: A meta-analysis. *Sex Roles, 36,* 305–325.

Twenge, J. M. (1999). Mapping gender: The multifactorial approach and the organization of gender-related attributes. *Psychology of Women Quarterly, 23,* 485–502.

Twenge, J. M. (2001). Changes in women's assertiveness in response to status and roles: A cross-temporal meta-analysis, 1931–1993. *Journal of Personality and Social Psychology, 81,* 133–145.

Twenge, J. M., & Crocker, J. (2002). Race and self-esteem: Meta-analyses comparing whites, blacks, Hispanics, Asians, and American Indians and comment on Gray-Little and Hafdahl (2000). *Psychological Bulletin, 128,* 371–408.

Twenge, J. M., & Manis, M. (1998). First-name desirability and adjustment: Self-satisfaction, others' ratings, and family background. *Journal of Applied Social Psychology, 28,* 41–51.

Twenge, J. M., & Zucker, A. N. (1999). What is a feminist?: Evaluations and stereotypes in closed- and open-ended responses. *Psychology of Women Quarterly, 23,* 591–605.

Udry, J. R., Bauman, K. E., & Chase, C. (1971). Skin color, status and mate selection. *American Journal of Sociology, 76,* 722–733.

Udry, J. R., & Eckland, B. K. (1984). Benefits of being attractive: Differential payoffs for men and women. *Psychological Reports, 54,* 47–56.

Uhlmann, E., Dasgupta, N., Elgueta, A., Greenwald, A. G., & Swanson, J. (2002). Subgroup prejudice based on skin color among Hispanics in the United States and Latin America. *Social Cognition, 20,* 198–226.

Uleman, J. S., Hon, A., Roman, R. J., & Moskowitz, G. B. (1996). On-line evidence for spontaneous trait inferences at encoding. *Personality and Social Psychology Bulletin, 22,* 377–394.

Uleman, J. S., & Moskowitz, G. B. (1994). Unintended effects of goals on unintended inferences. *Journal of Personality and Social Psychology, 66,* 490–501.

Uleman, J. S., Newman, L. S., & Moskowitz, G. B. (1996). People as flexible interpreters: Evidence and issues from spontaneous trait inference. In M. P. Zanna (Ed.), *Advances in experimental social psychology* (Vol. 28, pp. 211–279). San Diego, CA: Academic Press.

Uleman, J. S., Newman, L., & Winter, L. (1992). Can personality traits be inferred automatically?: Spontaneous inferences require cognitive capacity at encoding. *Consciousness and Cognition, 1,* 77–90.

Umberson, D., & Hughes, M. (1987). The impact of physical attractiveness on achivement and psychological well-being. *Social Psychology Quarterly, 50,* 227–236.

Unger, R. K., Hilderbrand, M., & Madar, T. (1982). Physical attractiveness and assumptions about social deviance: Some sex-by-sex comparisons. *Personality and Social Psychology Bulletin, 8,* 293–301.

Urban, L. M., & Miller, N. (1998). A theoretical analysis of crossed categorization effects: A meta-analysis. *Journal of Personality and Social Psychology, 74,* 894–908.

U.S. Bureau of the Census. (2000). *Statistical abstract of the United States 2000* [Online]. Available: http://www.census.gov/statab/www/

U.S. Department of Justice. (2000). *Correctional populations in the United States, 1997.* Washington, DC: U.S. Government Printing Office.

U.S. Department of Labor. (2000). *Earnings differences between women and men* [Online]. Washington, DC: U.S. Government Printing Office. Available: http://www.dol.gov/dol/wb/public/wb_pubs/wagegap2000.htm

Vallone, R. P., Ross, L., & Lepper, M. P. (1985). The hostile media phenomenon: Biased perception and perceptions of media bias in coverage of the Beruit massacre. *Journal of Personality and Social Psychology, 49,* 577–585.

Van Avermaet, E. (1988). Testing hypotheses about other people: Confirmatory and disagnostic strategies. *Communication and Cognition, 21,* 179–189.

van Dijk, T. A. (1984). *Prejudice and discourse: An analysis of ethnic prejudice in cognition and conversation.* Amsterdam: Benjamins.

van Dijk, T. A. (1993). *Elite discourse and racism.* Newbury Park, CA: Sage.

Van Kleeck, M., Hillger, L., & Brown, R. (1988). Pitting verbal schemas against information variables in attribution. *Social Cognition, 6,* 89–106.

van Knippenberg, A., & Dijksterhuis, A. (1996). A posteriori stereotype activation: The preservation of stereotypes through memory distortion. *Social Cognition, 14,* 21–53.

van Knippenberg, A., Dijksterhuis, A., & Vermeulen, D. (1999). Judgement and memory of a criminal act: The effects of stereotypes and cognitive load. *European Journal of Social Psychology, 29,* 191–201.

van Knippenberg, D., & van Knippenberg, A. (1994). Social categorization, focus of attention and judgements of group opinions. *British Journal of Social Psychology, 33,* 477–489.

van Knippenberg, A., van Twuyver, M., & Pepels, J. (1994). Factors affecting social categorization processes in memory. *British Journal of Social Psychology, 33,* 419–431.

Van Langenhove, L., & Harre, R. (1994). Cultural stereotypes and positioning theory. *Journal for the Theory of Social Behaviour, 24,* 359–372.

Vanman, E. J., & Miller, N. (1993). Applications of emotion theory and research to stereotyping and intergroup relations. In D. M. Mackie & D. L. Hamilton (Eds.), *Affect, cognition, and stereotyping: Interactive processes in group perception* (pp. 213–238). San Diego, CA: Academic Press.

Vanman, E. J., Paul, B. Y., Ito, T. A., & Miller, N. (1997). The modern face of prejudice and structural features that moderate the effect of cooperation on affect. *Journal of Personality and Social Psychology, 73*, 941–959.

van Oudenhoven, J. P., Askevis-Leherpeux, F., Hannover, B., Jaarsma, R., & Dardenne, B. (2002). Asymmetrical international attitudes. *European Journal of Social Psychology, 32*, 275–289.

Van Overwalle, F., Drenth, T., & Marsman, G. (1999). Spontaneous trait interferences: Are they linked to the actor or to the action? *Personality and Social Psychology Bulletin, 25*, 450–462.

Van Rijswijk, W., & Ellemers, N. (2002). Context effects on the application of stereotype content to multiple categorizable targets. *Personality and Social Psychology Bulletin, 28*, 90–101.

van Twuyver, M., & van Knippenberg, A. (1995). Social categorization as a function of priming. *European Journal of Social Psychology, 25*, 695–701.

Vaughan, G. M. (1964). The development of ethnic attitudes in New Zealand school children. *Genetic Psychology Monographs, 70*, 135–175.

Veness, T. (1969). Trait assessment intercorrelation and occupational stereotyping. *British Journal of Social and Clinical Psychology, 8*, 227–234.

Vergeer, M., Lubbers, M., & Scheepers, P. (2000). Exposure to newspapers and attitudes toward ethnic minorities: A longitudinal analysis. *Howard Journal of Communications, 11*, 127–143.

Verinis, J. S., & Roll, S. (1970). Primary and secondary male characteristics: The hairiness and large penis stereotypes. *Psychological Reports, 26*, 123–126.

Verkuyten, M. (1997). Intergroup evaluation and self-esteem motivations: Self-enhancement and self-protection. *European Journal of Social Psychology, 27*, 115–119.

Verkuyten, M. (1998a). Perceived discrimination and self-esteem among ethnic minority adolescents. *Journal of Social Psychology, 138*, 479–493.

Verkuyten, M. (1998b). Personhood and accounting for racism in conversation. *Journal for the Theory of Social Behavior, 28*, 147–167, 215–216.

Verkuyten, M. (2001). "Abnormalization" of ethnic minorities in conversation. *British Journal of Social Psychology, 40*, 257–278.

Verkuyten, M., & de Wolf, A. (2002). Ethnic minority identity and group context: Self-descriptions, acculturation attitudes and group evaluations in an intra- and intergroup situation. *European Journal of Social Psychology, 32*, 781–800.

Verkuyten, M., Drabbles, M., & van den Nieuwenhuijzen, K. (1999). Self-categorisation and emotional reactions to ethnic minorities. *European Journal of Social Psychology, 29*, 605–619.

Verkuyten, M., & Hagendoorn, L. (1998). Prejudice and self-categorization: The variable role of authoritarianism and in-group stereotypes. *Personality and Social Psychology Bulletin, 24*, 99–100

Verkuyten, M., & Kinket, B. (1999). The relative importance of ethnicity: Ethnic categorization among older children. *International Journal of Psychology, 34*, 107–118.

Verkuyten, M., Masson, K., & Elffers, H. (1995). Racial categorization and preference among older children in the Netherlands. *European Journal of Social Psychology, 25*, 637–656.

Verkuyten, M., & Nekuee, S. (1999). Ingroup bias: The effect of self-stereotyping, identification and group threat. *European Journal of Social Psychology, 29*, 411–418.

Verplanken, B., Jetten, J., & van Knippenberg, A. (1996). Effects of stereotypicality and perceived group variability on the use of attitudinal information in impression formation. *Personality and Social Psychology Bulletin, 22*, 960–971.

Vershure, B., Magel, S., & Sadalla, E. K. (1977). House form and social identity. In P. Suedfeld, J. A. Russel, L. M. Ward, & G. Davis (Eds.), *The behavioral basis of design* (pp. 273–278). Stroudsberg, PA: Douden, Hutchinson, & Ross.

Vickers, J., Lashuk, M., & Taerum, T. (1980). Differences in attitude toward the concepts of "male," "female," "male athlete," and "female athlete." *Research Quarterly for Exercise and Sport, 51*, 407–461.

Vinacke, W. E. (1949). Stereotyping among national–racial groups in Hawaii: A study in ethnocentrism. *Journal of Social Psychology, 30*, 265–291.

Vinacke, W. E. (1956). Explorations in the dynamic processes of stereotyping. *Journal of Social Psychology, 43*, 105–132.

Vinacke, W. E. (1957). Stereotypes as social concepts. *Journal of Social Psychology, 46,* 229–243.

Vincent, R. C. (1989). Clio's consciousness raised?: Portrayal of women in rock videos re-examined. *Journalism Quarterly, 66,* 155–160.

Vine, I. (1974). Stereotypes in the judgement of personality from handwriting. *British Journal of Social and Clinical Psychology, 13,* 61–64.

Voci, A. (2000). Perceived group variability and the salience of personal and social identity. In W. Stroebe & M. Hewstone (Eds.), *European review of social psychology* (Vol. 11, pp. 177–221). Chichester, UK: Wiley.

von Baeyer, C. L., Sherk, D. L., & Zanna, M. P. (1981). Impression management in the job interview: When the female applicant meets the male (chauvinist) interviewer. *Personality and Social Psychology Bulletin, 7,* 45–51.

von Hippel, W., Sekaquaptewa, D., & Vargas, P. (1995). On the role of encoding processes in stereotype maintenance. In M. P. Zanna (Ed.), *Advances in experimental social psychology* (Vol. 27, pp. 177–254). San Diego, CA: Academic Press.

von Hippel, W., Sekaquaptewa, D., & Vargas, P. (1997). The linguistic ingroup bias as an implicit indicator of prejudice. *Journal of Experimental Social Psychology, 33,* 490–509.

von Hippel, W., Silver, L. A., & Lynch, M. E. (2000). Stereotyping against your will: The role of inhibitory ability in stereotyping and prejudice among the elderly. *Personality and Social Psychology Bulletin, 26,* 523–532.

Vonk, R. (1994). Trait inferences, impression formation, and person memory: Strategies in processing inconsistent information about persons. In W. Stroebe & M. Hewstone (Eds.), *European review of social psychology* (Vol. 5, pp. 111–149). Chichester, UK: Wiley.

Vonk, R. (1998). Effects of behavioral causes and consequences on person judgments. *Personality and Social Psychology Bulletin, 24,* 1065–1074.

Vorauer, J. D., Hunter, A. J., Main, K. J., & Roy, S. A. (2000). Meta-stereotype activation: Evidence from indirect measures for specificevaluative concerns experienced by members of dominant groups in intergroup interaction. *Journal of Personality and Social Psychology, 78,* 690–707.

Vorauer, J. D., Main, K. J., & O'Connell, G. B. (1998). How do individuals expect to be viewed by members of lower status groups? Content and implications of meta-stereotypes. *Journal of Personality and Social Psychology, 75,* 917–937.

Vrij, A., & Smith, B. J. (1999). Reducing ethnic prejudice by public campaigns: An evaluation of a present and a new campaign. *Journal of Community and Applied Social Psychology, 9,* 195–216.

Vrugt, A. J., & Schabracq, M. (1996). Stereotypes with respect to elderly employees: The contribution of attribute information and representativeness. *Journal of Community and Applied Social Psychology, 6,* 287–292.

Wagner, U., & Schönbach, P. (1984). Links between educational status and prejudice: Ethnic attitudes in West Germany. In N. Miller & M. B. Brewer (Eds.), *Groups in contact: The psychology of desegregation* (pp. 29–52). Orlando, FL: Academic Press.

Waldo, C. R., & Kemp, J. L. (1997). Should I come out to my students?: An empirical investigation. *Journal of Homosexuality, 34,* 79–94.

Walker, P., & Antaki, C. (1986). Sexual orientation as a basis for categorization in recall. *British Journal of Social Psychology, 25,* 337–339.

Walkey, F. H., Green, D. E., & Taylor, A. J. W. (1981). Community attitudes to mental health: A comparative study. *Social Science and Medicine, 15,* 139–144.

Walters, A. S., & Curran, M.-C. (1996). "Excuse me, sir? May I help you and your boyfriend?": Salespersons' differential treatment of homosexual and straight customers. *Journal of Homosexuality, 31,* 135–152.

Wanke, M., Bless, H., & Igou, E. R. (2001). Next to a star: Paling, shining, or both? Turning interexemplar contrast into interexemplar assimilation. *Personality and Social Psychology Bulletin, 27,* 14–29.

Wansbrough, N., & Cooper, P. (1980). *Open employment after mental illness.* London: Tavistock.

Wards Cove Packing Company v. Atonio, 490 U.S. 642 (1989).

Ware, M. C., & Stuck, M. F. (1985). Sex-role messages vis-a-vis microcomputer use: A look at the pictures. *Sex Roles, 13,* 205–214.

Warring, D., Johnson, D. W., Maruyama, G., & Johnson, R. (1985). Impact of different types of coopertive learning on cross-ethnic and cross- sex relationships. *Journal of Educational Psychology, 77*, 53–59.

Warzak, W., Majors, C., Hansell, A., & Allan, T. (1988). An analysis of televised presentations of disability. *Rehabilitiation Psychology, 33*, 106–112.

Wattenmaker, W. D. (1991). Learning modes, feature correlations, and memory-based categorization. *Journal of Experimental Psychology: Learning, Memory, and Cognition, 17*, 908–923.

Wattenmaker, W. D. (1995). Knowledge structures and linear separability: Integrating information in object and social categorization. *Cognitive Psychology, 28*, 274–328.

Weary, G., Jacobson, J. A., Edwards, J. A., & Tobin, S. J. (2001). Chronic and temporarily activated causal uncertainty beliefs and stereotype usage. *Journal of Personality and Social Psychology, 81*, 206–219.

Weber, R., & Crocker, J. (1983). Cognitive processes in the revision of stereotypic beliefs. *Journal of Personality and Social Psychology, 45*, 961–977.

Webster, D. M., Kruglanski, A. W., & Pattison, D. A. (1997). Motivated language use in intergroup contexts: Need-for-closure effects on the linguistic intergroup bias. *Journal of Personality and Social Psychology, 72*, 1122–1131.

Wegener, D. T., & Petty, R. E. (1997). The flexible correction model: The role of naive theories of bias in bias correction. In M. P. Zanna (Ed.), *Advances in experimental social psychology* (Vol. 29, pp. 141–208). San Diego, CA: Academic Press.

Wegner, D. M. (1994). Ironic processes of thought control. *Psychological Review, 101*, 34–52.

Wegner, D. M., Schneider, D. J., Carter, S., III, & White, L. (1987). Paradoxical consequences of thought suppression. *Journal of Personality and Social Psychology, 53*, 1–9.

Weigel, R. H., & Howes, P. W. (1985). Conceptions of racial prejudice: Symbolic racism reconsidered. *Journal of Social Issues, 41*, 117–139.

Weiner, B., Perry, R. P., & Magnusson, J. (1988). An attributional analysis of reactions to stigmas. *Journal of Personality and Social Psychology, 55*, 738–748.

Weisner, T. S., & Wilson-Mitchell, J. E. (1990). Nonconventional family life-styles and sex typing in six-year-olds. *Child Development, 61*, 1915–1933.

Weiss, M. F. (1986). Children's attitudes toward the mentally ill: A developmental analysis. *Psychological Reports, 58*, 11–20.

Weiss, M. F. (1994). Children's attitudes toward the mentally ill: An eight-year longitudinal follow-up. *Psychological Reports, 74*, 51–56.

Weisz, C., & Jones, E. E. (1993). Expectancy disconfirmation and dispositional inference: Latent strength of target-based and category-based expecatancies. *Personality and Social Psychology Bulletin, 19*, 563–573.

Weitz, R., & Gordon, L. (1993). Images of black women among Anglo college students. *Sex Roles, 28*, 19–34.

Welbourne, J. L. (1999). The impact of perceived entitivity on inconsistency resolution for groups and individuals. *Journal of Experimental Social Psychology, 35*, 481–508.

Wells, W. D., & Siegel, B. (1961). Stereotyped somatotypes. *Psychological Record, 8*, 77–78.

Wenzel, M., & Mummendey, A. (1996). Positive–negative asymmetry of social discrimination: A normative analysis of differential evaluations of in-group and out-group on positive and negative attributes. *British Journal of Social Psychology, 35*, 493–507.

Wenzlaff, R. M., & Wegner, D. M. (2000). Thought suppression. *Annual Review of Psychology, 51*, 59–91.

Werner, P. D., & LaRussa, G. W. (1985). Persistence and change in sex-role stereotypes. *Sex Roles, 12*, 1089–1100.

Werth, J. L., & Lord, C. G. (1992). Previous conceptions of the typical group member and the contact hypothesis. *Basic and Applied Social Psychology, 13*, 351–369.

Westbrook, F. D., & Molla, D. M. (1976). Unique stereotypes for Holland's personality types, testing the traits attributed to men and women in Holland's typology. *Journal of Vocational Behavior, 9*, 21–30.

Westervelt, V. D., & McKinney, J. D. (1980). Effects of a film on nonhandicapped children's attitudes toward handicapped children. *Exceptional Children, 46*, 294–296.

Wetherell, M., & Potter, J. (1992). *Mapping the language of racism: Discourse and the legitimation of exploitation.* New York: Columbia University Press.

Whaley, A. L., & Link, B. G. (1998). Racial categorization and stereotype-based judgments about homeless people. *Journal of Applied Social Psychology, 28,* 189–205.

Whatley, C. (1958–1959). Social atttitudes toward discharged patients. *Social Problems, 6,* 313–320.

Wheeler, L., & Kim, Y. (1997). What is beautiful is culturally good: The physical attractiveness stereotype has different content in collectivist cultures. *Personality and Social Psychology Bulletin, 23,* 795–800.

Wheeler, S. C., Jarvis, W. B. G, & Petty, R. E. (2001). Think unto others: The self-destructive impact of negative racial stereotypes. *Journal of Experimental Social Psychology, 37,* 173–180.

Wheeler, S. C., & Petty, R. E. (2001). The effects of stereotype activation on behavior: A review of possible mechanisms. *Psychological Bulletin, 127,* 797–826.

White, J. D., & Carlston, D. E. (1983). Consequences of schemata for attention, impressions, and recall in complex social interactions. *Journal of Personality and Social Psychology, 45,* 538–549.

Whitehead, J. M. (1996). Sex stereotypes, gender identity and subject choice at A-level. *Educational Research, 38,* 147–160.

Whitley, B. E., Jr. (1987). The relationship of sex-role orientation to hetereosexuals' attitudes toward homosexuals. *Sex Roles, 17,* 103–113.

Whitley, B. E., Jr. (1990). The relationship of heterosexuals' attributions for the causes of homosexuality to attitudes toward lesbians and gays. *Personality and Social Psychology Bulletin, 16,* 369–277.

Whitley, B. E., Jr. (1999). Right-wing authoritarianism, social dominance orientation, and prejudice. *Journal of Personality and Social Psychology, 77,* 126–134.

Whitley, B. E., Jr., & Kite, M. E. (1995). Sex differences in attitudes toward homosexuality: A comment on Oliver and Hyde (1993). *Psychological Bulletin, 117,* 146–154.

Whitley, B. E., Jr., & Lee, S. E. (2000). The relationship of authoritarianism and related constructs to attitudes toward homosexuality. *Journal of Applied Social Psychology, 30,* 144–170.

Whitney, P., Waring, D. A., & Zingmark, B. (1992). Task effects on the spontaneous activation of trait concepts. *Social Cognition, 10,* 377–396.

Whren v. United States, 517 U.S. 806 (1996).

Widiger, T. A., & Settle, S. A. (1987). Broverman et al. revisited: An artifactual sex bias. *Journal of Personality and Social Psychology, 53,* 463–469.

Wiederman, M. W. (1993). Evolved gender differences in mate preferences: Evidence from personal advertisements. *Ethology and Sociobiology, 14,* 331–352.

Wigboldus, D. H. J., Dijksterhuis, A., & Van Knippenberg, A. (2003). When stereotypes get in the way: Stereotypes obstruct stereotype-inconsistent trait inferences. *Journal of Personality and Social Psychology, 84,* 470–484.

Wigboldus, D. H. J., Semin, G. R., & Spears, R. (2000). How do we communicate stereotypes?: Linguistic bases and inferential consequences. *Journal of Personality and Social Psychology, 78,* 5–18.

Wiggins, J. S., Wiggins, N., & Conger, J. C. (1968). Correlates of heterosexual somatic preferences. *Journal of Personality and Social Psychology, 10,* 82–90.

Wiggins, N., & Wiggins, J. S. (1969). A typological analysis of male preferences for female body types. *Multivariate Behavioral Research, 4,* 89–102.

Wilder, D. A. (1978). Perceiving persons as a group: Effects on attributions of causality and beliefs. *Social Psychology, 1,* 13–23.

Wilder, D. A. (1984). Predictions of belief homogeneity and similarity following special categorization. *British Journal of Social Psychology, 54,* 323–333.

Wilder, D. A. (1986). Social categorization: Implications for creation and reduction of intergroup bias. In L. Berkowitz (Ed.), *Advances in experimental social psychology* (Vol. 19, pp. 291–355). Orlando, FL: Academic Press.

Wilder, D. A. (1993a). Freezing intergroup evaluations: Anxiety fosters resistence to counter-stereotypic information. In M. A. Hogg & D. Abrams (Eds.), *Group motivation: Social psychological perspectives* (pp. 68–86). New York: Harvester Wheatsheaf.

Wilder, D. A. (1993b). The role of anxiety in facilitating stereotypic judgments of outgroup behavior. In D. M. Mackie & D. L. Hamilton (Eds.), *Affect, cognition, and stereotyping: Interactive processes in group perception* (pp. 87–109). San Diego, CA: Academic Press.

Wilder, D. A., & Shapiro, P. (1989a). Effects of anxiety on impression formation in a group context: An anxiety–assimilation hypothesis. *Journal of Experimental Social Psychology, 25,* 481–499.

Wilder, D. A., & Shapiro, P. (1989b). Role of competition-induced anxiety in limiting the beneficial impact of positive behavior by an outgroup member. *Journal of Personality and Social Psychology*, *56*, 60–69.

Wilder, D. A., & Shapiro, P. (1991). Facilitation of outgroup stereotypes by enhanced ingroup identity. *Journal of Experimental Social Psychology*, *27*, 431–452.

Wilder, D. A., Simon, A. F., & Faith, M. (1996). Enhancing the impact of counterstereotypic information: Dispositional attributions for deviance. *Journal of Personality and Social Psychology*, *71*, 276–287.

Wiley, M. G., & Eskilson, A. (1985). Speech style, gender stereotypes, and corporate success: What if women talk more like men? *Sex Roles*, *12*, 993–1007.

Willemsen, T. M. (1998). Widening the gender gap: Teenage magazines for girls and boys. *Sex Roles*, *38*, 851–861.

Willemyns, M., Gallois, C., Callan, V. J., & Pittman, J. (1997). Accent accommodation in the job interview: Impact of interviewer accent and gender. *Journal of Language and Social Psychology*, *16*, 3–22.

Williams, A., & Giles, H. (1996). Intergenerational conversations: Young adults' retrospective accounts. *Human Communication Research*, *23*, 220–250.

Williams, C. L. (1992). The glass escalator: Hidden advantages for men in the "female" professions. *Social Problems*, *39*, 253–267.

Williams, D. R., Yu, Y, Jackson, J., & Anderson, N. (1997). Racial differences in physical and mental health: Socioeconomic status, stress, and discrimination. *Journal of Health Psychology*, *2*, 335–351.

Williams, J. E., & Bennett, S. M. (1975). The definition of sex stereotypes via the Adjective Check List. *Sex Roles*, *1*, 327–337.

Williams, J. E., Bennett, S. M., & Best, D. L. (1975). Awareness and expression of sex stereotypes in young children. *Developmental Psychology*, *11*, 635–642.

Williams, J. E., & Best, D. L. (1977). Sex stereotypes and trait favorability on the Adjective Check List. *Educational and Psychological Measurement*, *37*, 101–110.

Williams, J. E., & Best, D. L. (1982). *Measuring sex stereotypes: A thirty-nation study*. Beverly Hills, CA: Sage.

Williams, J. E., & Best, D. L. (1990). *Sex and psyche: Gender and self viewed cross-culturally*. Newbury Park, CA: Sage.

Williams, J. E., Best, D. L., & Boswell, D. A. (1975). The measurement of children's racial attitudes in the early school years. *Child Development*, *46*, 494–500.

Williams, J. E., Daws, J. T., Best, D. L., Tilquin, C., Wesley, F., & Bjerke, T. (1979). Sex-trait stereotypes in France, Germany, and Norway. *Journal of Cross-Cultural Psychology*, *10*, 133–156.

Williams, J. E., & Morland, J. K. (1976). *Race, color, and the young vhild*. Chapel Hill: University of North Carolina Press.

Williams, J. E., Satterwhite, R. C., & Best, D. L. (1999). Pancultural gender stereotypes revisited: The five factor model. *Sex Roles*, *40*, 513–525.

Williams, R. M. (1964). *Strangers next door*. Englewood Cliffs, NJ: Prentice Hall.

Willis, F. N., & Henderson, M. (1994). Names associated with attractiveness. *Psychological Reports*, *74*, 1275–1279.

Willis, F. N., Willis, L. A., & Grier, J. A. (1982). Given names, social class, and professional achievement. *Psychological Reports*, *51*, 543–549.

Wills, G., & Crawford, R. (2000). Attitudes toward homosexuality in Shreveport–Bossier City, Louisiana. *Journal of Homosexuality*, *38*, 97–116.

Wilson, E., & Ng, S. H. (1988). Sex bias in visual images evoked by generics: A New Zealand study. *Sex Roles*, *18*, 159–169.

Wilson, T. C. (1996a). Cohort and prejudice: Whites' attitudes toward blacks, Hispanics, Jews and Asians. *Public Opinion Quarterly*, *60*, 253–274.

Wilson, T. C. (1996b). Compliments will get you nowhere: Benign stereotypes, prejudice and anti-Semitism. *Sociological Quarterly*, *37*, 465–479.

Wilson, T. D., & Brekke, N. (1994). Mental contamination and mental correction: Unwanted influences on judgments and evaluations. *Psychological Bulletin*, *116*, 117–142.

Wilson, T. D., Lindsey, S., & Schooler, T. Y. (2000). A model of dual attitudes. *Psychological Review, 107,* 101–126.

Winter, L., & Uleman, J. S. (1984). When are social judgments made?: Evidence for the spontaneousness of trait inferences. *Journal of Personality and Social Psychology, 47,* 237–252.

Winter, L., Uleman, J. S., & Cunniff, C. (1985). How automatic are social judgments? *Journal of Personality and Social Psychology, 49,* 904–917.

Wisniewski, E. (1995). Prior knowledge and functionally relevant features in concept learning. *Journal of Experimental Psychology: Learning, Memory, and Cognition, 21,* 449–468.

Wittenbrink, B., Gist, P. L., & Hilton, J. L. (1997). Structural properties of stereotypic knowledge and their influences on the construal of social situations. *Journal of Personality and Social Psychology, 72,* 526–543.

Wittenbrink, B., & Henly, J. R. (1996). Creating social reality: Informational social influence and the content of stereotypic beliefs. *Personality and Social Psychology Bulletin, 22,* 598–610.

Wittenbrink, B., Hilton, J. L., & Gist, P. L. (1998). In search of similarity: Stereotypes as naive theories in social categorization. *Social Cognition, 16,* 31–55.

Wittenbrink, B., Judd, C. M., & Park, B. (1997). Evidence for racial prejudice at the implicit level and its relationship with questionnaire measures. *Journal of Personality and Social Psychology, 72,* 262–274

Wittenbrink, B., Park, B., & Judd, C. M. (1998). The role of stereotypic knowledge in the construal of person models. In C. Sedikides, J. Schopler, & C. A. Insko (Eds.), *Intergroup cognition and intergroup behavior* (pp. 177–202). Mahwah, NJ: Erlbaum.

Wittgenstein, L. (1953). *Philosophical investigations.* New York: Macmillan.

Wogalter, M. S., & Hoise, J. A. (1991). Effects of cranial and facial hair on perceptions of age and person. *Journal of Social Psychology, 131,* 589–591.

Wolff, G., Pathare, S., Craig, T., & Leff, J. (1996a). Community attitudes to mental illness. *British Journal of Psychiatry, 168,* 183–190.

Wolff, G., Pathare, S., Craig, T., & Leff, J. (1996b). Community knowledge of and reaction to mentally ill people. *British Journal of Psychiatry, 168,* 191–198.

Wolff, L., & Taylor, S. E. (1979). Sex, sex-role identification, and awareness of sex-role stereotypes. *Journal of Personality, 47,* 177–184.

Woll, S., & Graesser, A. (1982). Memory discrimination for information typical or atypical of person schemata. *Social Cognition, 1,* 287–310.

Wolman, C., & Frank, H. (1975). The solo woman in a professional peer group. *American Journal of Orthopsychiatry, 45,* 164–171.

Wolsko, C., Park, B., Judd, C. M., & Wittenbrink, B. (2000). Framing interethnic ideology: Effects of multicultural and color-blind perspectives on judgments of groups and individuals. *Journal of Personality and Social Psychology, 78,* 635–654.

Wong, F. Y., McCreary, D. R., Carpenter, K. M., Engle, A., & Korchynsky, R. (1999). Gender-related factors influencing perceptions of homosexuality. *Journal of Homosexuality, 37,* 19–31.

Wood, P. B., & Sonleitner, N. (1996). The effect of childhood interracial contact on adult antiblack prejudice. *International Journal of Intercultural Relations, 20,* 1–17.

Wood, W., Christensen, P. N., Hebl, M. R., & Rothgerber, H. (1997). Conformity to sex-typed norms, affect, and the self-concept. *Journal of Personality and Social Psychology, 73,* 523–535.

Word, C. O., Zanna, M. P., & Cooper, J. (1974). The nonverbal mediation of self-fulfilling prophecies in interracial interaction. *Journal of Experimental Social Psychology, 10,* 109–120.

Worth, L. T., Allison, S. T., & Messick, D. M. (1987). Impact of a group decision on perceptions of own and others' attitudes. *Journal of Personality and Social Psychology, 53,* 673–683.

Wortman, P. M., & Bryant, F. B. (1985). School desegregation and black achievement: An integrative review. *Sociological Methods and Research, 13,* 289–324.

Wrangman, R., & Peterson, D. (1996). *Demonic males: Apes and the origins of human violence.* Boston: Houghton Mifflin.

Wright, J. C., & Mischel, W. (1988). Conditional hedges and the intuitive psychology of traits. *Journal of Personality and Social Psychology, 55,* 454–469.

Wright, S. C., Aron, A., McLaughlin-Volpe, T., & Ropp, S. A. (1997). The extended contact effect: Knowledge of cross-group friendships and prejudice. *Journal of Personality and Social Psychology, 73,* 73–90.

Wuthnow, R. (1982). Anti-Semitism and stereotyping. In A. G. Miller (Ed.), *In the eye of the beholder: Contemporary issues in stereotyping* (pp. 137–187). New York: Praeger.

Wyer, N. A., Sadler, M. S., & Judd, C. M. (2002). Contrast effects in stereotype formation and change: The role of comparative context. *Journal of Experimental Social Psychology, 38*, 443–458.

Wyer, N. A., Sherman, J. W., & Stroessner, S. J. (1998). The spontaneous suppression of racial stereotypes. *Social Cognition, 16*, 340–352.

Wyer, N. A., Sherman, J. W., & Stroessner, S. J. (2000). The roles of motivation and ability in controlling the consequences of stereotype suppression. *Personality and Social Psychology Bulletin, 26*, 13–25.

Wyer, R. S., Jr. (1977). The role of logical and nonlogical factors in making inferences about category membership. *Journal of Experimental Social Psychology, 13*, 577–595.

Wyer, R. S., Jr., Clore, G. L., & Isbell, L. M. (1999). Affect and information processing. In M. P. Zanna (Ed.), *Advances in experimental social psychology* (Vol. 31, pp. 1–77). San Diego, CA: Academic Press.

Wyer, R. S., Jr., & Gordon, S. E. (1982). The recall of information about persons and groups. *Journal of Experimental Social Psychology, 18*, 128–164.

Wyer, R. S., Jr., & Lambert, A. J. (1994). The role of trait constructs in person perception: A historical perspective. In P. G. Devine, D. L. Hamilton, & T. M. Ostrom (Eds.), *Social cognition: Impact on social psychology* (pp. 109–142). San Diego, CA: Academic Press.

Wyer, R. S., & Srull, T. K. (1989). *Memory and social cognition in its social context.* Hillsdale, NJ: Erlbaum.

Wyman, M., & Snyder, M. (1997). Attitudes toward "gays in the military": A functional perspective. *Journal of Applied Social Psychology, 27*, 306–329.

Yarmey, A. D. (1993). Stereotypes and recognition memory for faces and voices of good guys and bad guys. *Applied Cognitive Psychology, 7*, 419–431.

Yarrow, M., Clausen, J., & Robbins, P. (1955). The social meaning of mental illness. *Journal of Social Issues, 11*, 33–48.

Ybarra, O. (1999). Misanthropic person memory when the need to self-enhance is absent. *Personality and Social Psychology Bulletin, 25*, 261–269.

Ybarra, O. (2002). Naive causal understanding of valenced behaviors and its implications for social information processing. *Psychological Bulletin, 128*, 421–441.

Ybarra, O., Schaberg, L., & Keiper, S. (1999). Favorable and unfavorable target expectancies and social information processing. *Journal of Personality and Social Psychology, 77*, 698–709.

Ybarra, O., & Stephan, W. G. (1996). Misanthropic person memory. *Journal of Personality and Social Psychology, 70*, 691–700.

Ybarra, O., & Stephan, W. G. (1999). Attributional orientations and the prediction of behavior: The attribution- prediction bias. *Journal of Personality and Social Psychology, 76*, 718–727.

Ybarra, O., Stephan, W. G., & Schaberg, L. (2000). Misanthropic memory for the behavior of group members. *Personality and Social Psychology Bulletin, 26*, 1515–1525.

Yee, A. H., Fairchild, H. H., Weizmann, F., & Wyatt, G. E. (1993). Addressing psychology's problems with race. *American Psychologist, 48*, 1132–1140.

Yoder, J. D. (1991). Rethinking tokenism: Looking beyond numbers. *Gender and Society, 5*, 178–192.

Yoder, J. D. (1994). Looking beyond numbers: The effects of gender status, job prestige, and occupational gender-typing on tokenism outcomes. *Social Psychology Quarterly, 57*, 150–159.

Yoder, J. D. (2002). 2001 Division 35 presidential address: Context matters: Understanding tokenism processes and their impact on women's work. *Psychology of Women Quarterly, 26*, 1–8.

Yoder, J. D., Adams, J., & Prince, H. T. (1983). The price of a token. *Journal of Political and Military Sociology, 11*, 325–337.

Yoder, J. D., & Berendsen, L. L (2001). "Outsider within" the firehouse: African American and white women firefighters. *Psychology of Women Quarterly, 25*, 27–36.

Yoder, J. D., & Schleicher, T. L. (1996). Undergraduates regard deviation from occupational gender stereotypes as costly for women. *Sex Roles, 34*, 171–188.

Yoon, C., Hasher, L., Feinberg, F., Rahhal, T.A., & Winocur, G. (2000). Cross-cultural differences in memory: The role of culture-based stereotypes about aging. *Psychology and Aging, 15*, 694–704.

Young, R. K., Gallaher, P., Belasco, J., Barr, A., & Webber, A. W. (1991). Changes in fear of AIDS and homophobia in a university population. *Journal of Applied Social Psychology, 21*, 1848–1858.

Young, R. K., Kennedy, A., Newhouse, A., Browne, P., & Thiessen, D. (1993). The effects of names on perceptions of intelligence, popularity, and competence. *Journal of Applied Social Psychology*, *23*, 1770–1788.

Yount, K. (1986). A theory of productive activity: The relationships among self-concept, gender, sex-role stereotypes, and work-emergent traits. *Psychology of Women Quarterly*, *10*, 63–88.

Yzerbyt, V., Castano, E., Leyens, J.-P., & Paladino, M.-P. (2000). The primacy of the in-group: The interplay of entitativity and identification. In W. Stroebe & M. Hewstone (Eds.), *European review of social psychology* (Vol. 11, pp. 257–295). Chichester, UK: Wiley.

Yzerbyt, V. Y., Corneille, O., Dumont, M., & Hahn, K. (2001). The dispositional inference strikes back: Situational focus and dispositional suppression in causal attribution. *Journal of Personality and Social Psychology*, *81*, 365–376.

Yzerbyt, V., Corneille, O., & Estrada, C. (2001). The interplay of subjective essentialism and entitativity in the formation of stereotypes. *Personality and Social Psychology Review*, *5*, 141–155.

Yzerbyt, V. Y., Coull, A., & Rocher, S. J. (1999). Fencing off the deviant: The role of cognitive resources in the maintenance of stereotypes. *Journal of Personality and Social Psychology*, *77*, 449–462.

Yzerbyt, V. Y., Leyens, J.-P., & Bellour, F. (1995). The ingroup overexclusion effect: Identity concerns in decisions about group membership. *European Journal of Social Psychology*, *25*, 1–16.

Yzerbyt, V. Y., Leyens, J.-P., & Schadron, G. (1997). Social judgeability and the dilution of stereotypes: The impact of the nature and sequence of information. *Personality and Social Psychology Bulletin*, *23*, 1312–1322.

Yzerbyt, V., Rocher, S., & Schadron, G. (1997). Stereotypes as explanations: A subjective essentialist view of group perception. In R. Spears, P. J. Oakes, N. Ellemers, & S. A. Haslam (Eds.), *The social psychology of stereotyping and group life* (pp. 20–50). Oxford, UK: Blackwell.

Yzerbyt, V. Y., Rogier, A., & Fiske, S. T. (1998). Group entitativity and social attribution: On translating situational constraints into stereotypes. *Personality and Social Psychology Bulletin*, *24*, 1089–1103.

Zaller, J. R. (1992). *The nature and origins of mass opinion*. Cambridge, UK: Cambridge University Press.

Zaller, J. R., & Feldman, S. (1992). A simple theory of the survey response: Answering questions versus revealing preferences. *American Journal of Political Science*, *36*, 579–616.

Zanna, M. P. (1994). On the nature of prejudice. *Canadian Psychology*, *35*, 11–23.

Zanna, M. P., & Pack, S. J. (1975). On the self-fulfilling nature of apparent sex differences in behavior. *Journal of Experimental Social Psychology*, *11*, 583–591.

Zanna, M. P., Sheras, P. L., Cooper, J., & Shaw, C. (1975). Pygmalion and Galatea: The interactive effects of teacher and student expectancies. *Journal of Experimental Social Psychology*, *11*, 279–287.

Zárate, M. A., & Sanders, J. D. (1999). Face categorization, graded priming, and the mediating influences of similarity. *Social Cognition*, *17*, 367–389.

Zárate, M. A., & Sandoval, P. (1995). The effects of contextual cues on making occupational and gender categorizations. *British Journal of Social Psychology*, *34*, 353–362.

Zárate, M. A., & Smith, E. R. (1990). Person categorization and stereotyping. *Social Cognition*, *8*, 161–185.

Zárate, M. A., Uleman, J. S., & Voils, C. I. (2001). Effects of culture and processing goals on the activation and binding of trait concepts. *Social Cognition*, *19*, 295–323.

Zawadski, B. (1948). Limitations of the scapegoat theory of prejudice. *Journal of Abnormal and Social Psychology*, *43*, 127–141.

Zebrowitz, L. A. (1996). Physical appearance as a basis of stereotyping. In C. N. Macrae, C. Stangor, & M. Hewstone (Eds.), *Stereotypes and stereotyping* (pp. 79–120). New York: Guilford Press.

Zebrowitz, L. A., Andreoletti, C., Collins, M. A., Lee, S. Y., & Blumenthal, J. (1998). Bright, bad, babyfaced boys: Appearance stereotypes do not always yield self-fulfilling prophecy effects. *Journal of Personality and Social Psychology*, *75*, 1300–1320.

Zebrowitz, L. A., Kendall-Tackett, K., & Fafel, J. (1991). The influence of children's facial maturity on parental expectations and punishments. *Journal of Experimental Child Psychology*, *52*, 221–238.

Zebrowitz, L. A., & Lee, S. Y. (1999). Appearance, stereotype-incongruent behavior, and social relationships. *Personality and Social Psychology Bulletin*, *25*, 569–584.

Zebrowitz, L. A., Montepare, J. M., & Lee, H. K. (1993). They don't all look alike: Individuated impressions of other racial groups. *Journal of Personality and Social Psychology, 65*, 85–101.

Zebrowitz, L. A., Olson, K., & Hoffman, K. (1993). Stability of babyfaceness and attractiveness across the life span. *Journal of Personality and Social Psychology, 64*, 453–466.

Zebrowitz, L. A., Voinescu, L., & Collins, M. A. (1996). "Wide-eyed" and "crooked-faced": Determinants of perceived and real honesty across the life span. *Personality and Social Psychology Bulletin, 22*, 1258–1269.

Zebrowitz-McArthur, L., & Apatow, K. (1983–1984). Impressions of baby-faced adults. *Social Cognition, 2*, 315–342.

Zebrowitz-McArthur, L., & Berry, D. S. (1987). Cross-cultural agreement in perceptions of baby-faced adults. *Journal of Cross-Cultural Psychology, 18*, 165–192.

Zeligs, R. (1955). Children's concepts and stereotypes of American, Greek, English, German, and Japanese. *Journal of Educational Sociology, 28*, 360–268.

Zimring, F. E., & Hawkins, G. (1997). *Crime is not the problem: Lethal violence in America.* New York: Oxford University Press.

Zucker, K. J., Wilson-Smith, D. N., Kurita, J. A., & Stern, A. (1995). Children's appraisals of sex-typed behavior in their peers. *Sex Roles, 33*, 703–725.

Zuckerman, M. (1990). Some dubious premises in research and theory on racial differences: Scientific, social, and ethical issues. *American Psychologist, 45*, 1297–1303.

Zuckerman, M., & Kieffer, S. C. (1994). Race differences in face-ism: Does facial prominence imply dominance? *Journal of Personality and Social Psychology, 66*, 86–92.

Zuo, J. P. (1997). The effect of men's breadwinner status on their changing gender beliefs. *Sex Roles, 37*, 799–816.

Zuwerink, J. R., Devine, P. G., Monteith, M. J., & Cook, D. A. (1996). Prejudice toward blacks: With and without compunction? *Basic and Applied Social Psychology, 18*, 131–150.

Zweigenhaft, R. L. (1977). The other side of unusual first names. *Journal of Social Psychology, 103*, 291–302.

Index